MyManagementLab®: Improves Student Engagement Before, During, and After Class

Prep and Engagement

- **NEW! VIDEO LIBRARY –** Robust video library with over 100 new book-specific videos that include easy-to-assign assessments, the ability for instructors to add YouTube or other sources, the ability for students to upload video submissions, and the ability for polling and teamwork.

- **Decision-making simulations – NEW and improved feedback for students.** Place your students in the role of a key decision-maker! Simulations branch based on the decisions students make, providing a variation of scenario paths. Upon completion students receive a grade, as well as a detailed report of the choices and the associated consequences of those decisions.

- **Video exercises – UPDATED with new exercises.** Engaging videos that bring business concepts to life and explore business topics related to the theory students are learning in class. Quizzes then assess students' comprehension of the concepts covered in each video.

- **Learning Catalytics –** A "bring your own device" student engagement, assessment, and classroom intelligence system helps instructors analyze students' critical-thinking skills during lecture.

- **Dynamic Study Modules (DSMs) – UPDATED with additional questions.** Through adaptive learning, students get personalized guidance where and when they need it most, creating greater engagement, improving knowledge retention, and supporting subject-matter mastery. Also available on mobile devices.

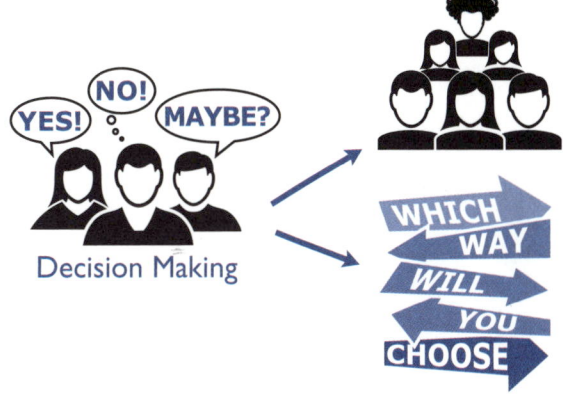

Decision Making

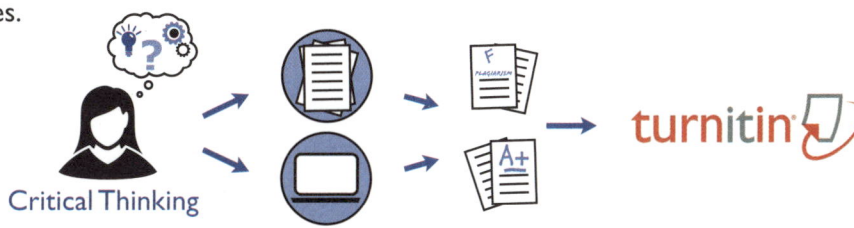

Critical Thinking

turnitin

- **Writing Space – UPDATED with new commenting tabs, new prompts, and a new tool for students called Pearson Writer.** A single location to develop and assess concept mastery and critical thinking, the Writing Space offers automatic graded, assisted graded, and create your own writing assignments, allowing you to exchange personalized feedback with students quickly and easily.

  Writing Space can also check students' work for improper citation or plagiarism by comparing it against the world's most accurate text comparison database available from **Turnitin**.

- **Additional Features** – Included with the MyLab are a powerful homework and test manager, robust gradebook tracking, Reporting Dashboard, comprehensive online course content, and easily scalable and shareable content.

http://www.pearsonmylabandmastering.com

PEARSON

STRATEGIC MANAGEMENT
Concepts and Cases

A COMPETITIVE ADVANTAGE APPROACH

STRATEGIC MANAGEMENT
Concepts and Cases

SIXTEENTH EDITION

A COMPETITIVE ADVANTAGE APPROACH

Fred R. David

Francis Marion University
Florence, South Carolina

Forest R. David

Strategic Planning Consultant

Boston   Columbus   Indianapolis   New York   San Francisco   Amsterdam
Cape Town   Dubai   London   Madrid   Milan   Munich   Paris   Montréal   Toronto   Delhi
Mexico City   São Paulo   Sydney   Hong Kong   Seoul   Singapore   Taipei   Tokyo

Vice President, Business Publishing: Donna Battista
Editor-in-Chief: Stephanie Wall
Acquisitions Editor: Daniel Tylman
Editorial Assistant: Linda Albelli
Vice President, Product Marketing: Maggie Moylan
Director of Marketing, Digital Services and Products: Jeanette Koskinas
Field Marketing Manager: Lenny Ann Raper
Product Marketing Assistant: Jessica Quazza
Team Lead, Program Management: Ashley Santora
Program Manager: Claudia Fernandes
Team Lead, Project Management: Jeff Holcomb
Project Manager: Ann Pulido
Operations Specialist: Carol Melville
Creative Director: Blair Brown
Art Director: Janet Slowik
Vice President, Director of Digital Strategy & Assessment: Paul Gentile
Manager of Learning Applications: Paul Deluca
Digital Editor: Brian Surette
Director, Digital Studio: Sacha Laustsen
Digital Studio Manager: Diane Lombardo
Digital Studio Project Manager: Robin Lazrus
Digital Studio Project Manager: Alana Coles
Digital Studio Project Manager: Monique Lawrence
Full-Service Project Management and Composition: Integra
Interior Designer: Integra
Cover Designer: Integra
Cover Image: Francesco Pezzotta
Printer/Binder: LSC Communications/Kendallville
Cover Printer: LSC Communications

Library of Congress Cataloging-in-Publication Data
David, Fred R.
    Strategic management: concepts and cases—a competitive advantage approach / Fred R. David, Francis Marion University, Florence, South Carolina, Forest R. David, Strategic Planning Consultant.—Sixteenth Edition.
       pages cm
    ISBN 978-0-13-416784-8 (alk. paper) — ISBN 0-13-416784-8 (alk. paper)
    1. Strategic planning.   2. Strategic planning—Case studies.   I. David, Forest R.   II. Title.
HD30.28.D3785 2015
658.4'012—dc23
                                                                                    2015021210

7   18

ISBN 10:   0-13-416784-8
ISBN 13: 978-0-13-416784-8

**Thank you to the following companies
that graciously provided the substance of the Cohesion Cases
over a 30-year span of 16 editions of this book.**

- 1st edition, 1987: Ponderosa
- 2nd edition, 1989: Ponderosa
- 3rd edition, 1991: Hershey Company
- 4th edition, 1993: Hershey Company
- 5th edition, 1995: Hershey Company
- 6th edition, 1997: Hershey Company
- 7th edition, 1999: Hershey Company
- 8th edition, 2001: America Online (AOL)
- 9th edition, 2003: American Airlines
- 10th edition, 2005: Krispy Kreme Doughnuts, Inc.
- 11th edition, 2007: Google Inc.
- 12th edition, 2009: The Walt Disney Company
- 13th edition, 2011: Apple, Inc.
- 14th edition, 2013: McDonald's Corporation
- 15th edition, 2015: PepsiCo, Inc.
- 16th edition, 2017: Hershey Company

Brief Contents

Contents

Cases

Preface

Why Adopt This Text?

This textbook is trusted across five continents to provide managers the latest skills and concepts needed to effectively formulate and efficiently implement a strategic plan—a game plan, if you will—that can lead to sustainable competitive advantage for any type of business. The Association to Advance Collegiate Schools of Business (AACSB) International increasingly advocates a more skills-oriented, practical approach in business books, which this text provides, rather than a theory-based approach. *Strategic Management Concepts and Cases: A Competitive Advantage Approach* meets all AACSB International guidelines for the strategic-management course at both the graduate and undergraduate levels, and previous editions have been used at more than 500 colleges and universities globally. We believe you will find this sixteenth edition to be the best textbook available for communicating both the excitement and value of strategic management. Concise and exceptionally well organized, this text is now available in English, Chinese, Spanish, Thai, German, Japanese, Farsi, Indonesian, Indian, Vietnamese, and Arabic. A version in Russian is being negotiated. In addition to universities, hundreds of companies, organizations, and governmental bodies use this text as a management guide.

An MBA student using this text recently wrote the following:

Dear Dr. David: I am in the midst of my MBA at Adams State University here in Colorado. I'm 7 of 12 classes in with a 4.0 average. As a result, I've been through about 14 textbooks (not to mention the 60 or so I went through for my BBA at the University of California (UC)-Berkeley. This is the first time I've written to the author of a textbook. Why? Because the David book is by far the best textbook I have ever used. It's clear. It's accurate. It's not full of opinion masquerading as fact! You, sir, are to be commended. Usually when I spend an insane amount of money on a text, I'm broke. But your text is worth every cent, and I'll keep it forever. Well done sir! Respectively, Eric Seiden, MBA Student in Littleton, Colorado (August 10, 2015)

Eric N. Sims, a professor who has used this text for his classes at Sonoma State University in California, says:

I have read many strategy books. I am going to use the David book. What I like—to steal a line from Alabama coach Nick Saban—is your book teaches "a process." I believe at the end of your book, you can actually help a company do strategic planning. In contrast, other books teach a number of near and far concepts related to strategy.

A recent reviewer of this textbook shares his opinion:

One thing I admire most about the David text is that it follows the fundamental sequence of strategy formulation, implementation, and evaluation. There is a basic flow from vision/mission to internal/external environmental scanning, to strategy development, selection, implementation, and evaluation. This has been, and continues to be, a hallmark of the David text. Many other strategy texts are more disjointed in their presentation, and thus confusing to the student, especially at the undergraduate level.

New to This Edition

1. This 16th edition is 40 percent new and improved from the prior edition.
2. A brand new **COHESION CASE** on The Hershey Company (2015) is provided. Hershey is one of the most successful, well-known, and best-managed global companies in the world. Students apply strategy concepts to Hershey at the end of each chapter through new, innovative Assurance of Learning Exercises.

3. Brand-new one-page **MINI-CASES** appear at the end of each chapter, complete with questions designed to apply chapter concepts. Provided for the first time ever in this text, the mini-cases focus on the following companies:

    Chapter 1: Kroger Company
    Chapter 2: Walt Disney Company
    Chapter 3: Coach
    Chapter 4: Buffalo Wild Wings
    Chapter 5: LinkedIn
    Chapter 6: Starbucks
    Chapter 7: Hilton Worldwide
    Chapter 8: Alibaba
    Chapter 9: TJX Companies
    Chapter 10: Avon Products
    Chapter 11: Domino's Pizza

4. Original, half-page **ACADEMIC RESEARCH CAPSULES** are presented in each chapter to showcase how new strategic-management research is impacting business practice. Two capsules per chapter are provided—for the first time ever in this text.

5. At the end of each chapter are new sections titled **IMPLICATIONS FOR STRATEGISTS** and **IMPLICATIONS FOR STUDENTS** that highlight how companies can best gain and sustain competitive advantages.

6. Brand new **EXEMPLARY COMPANY CAPSULES** appear at the beginning of each chapter and showcase a company that is employing strategic management exceptionally well. The capsules focus on the following companies:

    Chapter 1: Apple
    Chapter 2: H&R Block
    Chapter 3: Chipotle Mexican Grill
    Chapter 4: Netflix
    Chapter 5: Signet Jewelers Limited
    Chapter 6: Smith & Wesson Holding Corp.
    Chapter 7: Papa John's International
    Chapter 8: Foot Locker
    Chapter 9: Nike
    Chapter 10: Chick-fil-A
    Chapter 11: Alcoa

7. Chapter 2, The Business Vision and Mission, is 60 percent new, due to current research and practice that reveals the need for "these statements to be more customer-oriented."

8. Chapter 11, Global and International Issues, is shortened by 30 percent but provides new coverage of cultural and conceptual strategic-management differences across countries. Doing business globally has become a necessity in most industries.

9. Chapter 10, Business Ethics, Social Responsibility, and Environmental Sustainability, provides extensive new coverage of ethics, workplace romance, flirting, hiring away rival firms' employees, wildlife welfare, and sustainability. "Good ethics is good business." Unique to strategic-management texts, the sustainability discussion is strengthened in this edition to promote and encourage firms to conduct operations with respect for the environment—an important concern for consumers, companies, society, and AACSB International.

10. Sixty-four unique **ASSURANCE OF LEARNING EXERCISES** appear at the end of chapters to apply chapter concepts. The exercises prepare students for strategic-management case analysis. An additional excellent exercise for each chapter is provided in the *Chapter Instructor's Resource Manual*.

11. More than 200 new **EXAMPLES** bring the chapters to life.

12. At the end of chapters are 78 new (459 total) **REVIEW QUESTIONS** related to chapter content.

13. All the Current Readings at the end of the chapters are new, and up-to-date research and theories of seminal thinkers are included. However, practical aspects of strategic management are center stage and the trademark of this text.

14. Every sentence and paragraph has been scrutinized, modified, clarified, streamlined, updated, and improved to enhance the content and caliber of presentation.

15. An enhanced, continually updated **AUTHOR WEBSITE** (www.strategyclub.com) provides new author videos, case and chapter updates, sample case analyses, and the popular, FREE EXCEL STUDENT TEMPLATE. The template enables students to more easily develop strategic-planning matrices, tables, and analyses needed for case analysis.

New Case Features

1. All 30 cases have a 2015 time setting, offering students up-to-date issues to evaluate.
2. All 30 cases focus on exciting, well-known companies, effective for students to apply strategy concepts.
3. All 30 cases are undisguised, featuring real organizations in real industries using real names (nothing is fictitious in any case).
4. All 30 cases feature an organization and industry undergoing strategic change.
5. All 30 cases provide ample, excellent quantitative information, so students can prepare a defensible strategic plan.
6. All 30 cases are written in a lively, concise writing style that captures the reader's interest.
7. All 30 cases are "comprehensive," focusing on multiple business functions, rather than a single problem or issue.
8. All 30 cases include current financial statements for the firm, so students can show the impact of a proposed strategic plan.
9. All 30 cases provide an organizational chart and a vision and mission statement— important strategy concepts.
10. All 30 cases are supported by an excellent teacher's note, provided to professors in a new *Case Instructor's Resource Manual*.
11. All 30 cases are available for inclusion in a customized tailored text to meet the special needs of some professors.
12. All 30 cases facilitate coverage of all strategy concepts, but as revealed in the new Concepts by Cases Matrix, some cases especially exemplify some concepts, enabling professors to effectively use an assortment of cases with various chapters in the text.
13. All 30 cases have been class-tested to ensure that they are interesting, challenging, and effective for illustrating strategy concepts.
14. All 30 cases appear in no other textbooks, thus offering a truly fresh, new, up-to-date learning platform.
15. The 30 cases represent an excellent mix of firms performing really well and some performing very poorly, including 14 U.S. service-based organizations, 10 U.S. manufacturing-based firms, and 2 nonprofit organizations (World Relief and World Wildlife Fund for Nature). Also included are 4 outside-U.S. headquartered firms (Michael Kors Holdings Ltd., SABMiller plc, Gruma SAB de CV, and Restaurant Brands International).
16. All 30 case companies have excellent websites in English that provide detailed financial information, history, sustainability statements, ethics statements, and press releases, so students can easily access current information to apply strategy concepts.

Time-Tested Features

1. This text meets all AACSB International guidelines that support a practitioner orientation rather than a theory/research approach. It offers a skills-oriented process for developing a vision and mission statement; performing an external audit; conducting an internal assessment; and formulating, implementing, and evaluating strategies.
2. The author's writing style is concise, conversational, interesting, logical, lively, and supported by numerous current examples.
3. A simple, integrative strategic-management model appears in all chapters and on the inside back cover. The model is widely used by strategic-planning consultants and companies worldwide.
4. An exciting, new Cohesion Case on Hershey Company follows Chapter 1 and is revisited at the end of each chapter, allowing students to apply strategic-management concepts and techniques to a real company as the text develops, thus preparing students for case analysis as the course evolves.

5. End-of-chapter Assurance of Learning Exercises apply chapter concepts and techniques in a challenging, meaningful, and enjoyable manner. Eighteen exercises apply text material to the Cohesion Case; 11 exercises apply textual material to a college or university; another 9 exercises send students into the business world to explore important strategy topics.

6. There is excellent pedagogy, including Learning Objectives opening each chapter as well as Key Terms, Current Readings, Discussion Questions, and Assurance of Learning Exercises ending each chapter.

7. The various strategy-formulation issues are outstanding, covering topics such as business ethics, global versus domestic operations, vision and mission, matrix analysis, partnering, joint venturing, competitive analysis, value chain analysis, governance, and matrices for assimilating and evaluating information.

8. Strategy-implementation issues are covered thoroughly and include items such as corporate culture, organizational structure, outsourcing, marketing concepts, financial analysis, business ethics, whistleblowing, bribery, pay and performance linkages, and workplace romance.

9. A systematic, analytical "process" is presented that includes nine matrices: IFEM, EFEM, CPM, SWOT, BCG, IE, GRAND, SPACE, and QSPM.

10. Both the chapter material and case material is published in color.

11. Chapters-only and e-book versions of the text are available.

12. Custom-case publishing is available whereby an instructor can combine chapters from this text with cases from a variety of sources or select any number of the 30 cases provided.

13. For the chapter material, an outstanding ancillary package includes a comprehensive *Chapter Instructor's Resource Manual, Case Instructor's Resource Manual,* Test Bank, TestGen, and Chapter PowerPoints, and vastly improved Chapter MyLab and Case MyLab products to promote assurance of learning.

Why Is This Text Different/Better Than Other Strategic-Management Texts?

Strategic Management Concepts and Cases: A Competitive Advantage Approach is by far the most practical, skills-oriented strategic management textbook on the market. This text is designed to enable students to learn "how to do strategic planning," rather than simply memorize seminal theories in strategy. Students using this text follow an integrative model that appears in every chapter as the "process" unfolds. Students learn how to construct strategic planning matrices, such as the Strengths, Weaknesses, Opportunities, and Threats (SWOT) and the Boston Consulting Group (BCG) matrices. Readers also learn how to perform strategic-planning analyses, such as earnings-per-share/earnings-before-interest-and-taxes (EPS/EBIT) and corporate valuation. The focus throughout this text is on "learning by doing." This overarching, differentiating aspect has been improved with every edition and has led to this text becoming perhaps the leading strategic-management text globally, now available in 10 languages. The practical, skills-oriented approach is manifested through eight specific features:

1. A Cohesion Case that appears after Chapter 1 with 64 end-of-chapter assurance of learning exercises, many that apply concepts to the Cohesion Case, thus allowing students to gain practice doing strategic planning by performing analysis. No other strategic-management textbook provides a Cohesion Case or an array of end-of-chapter exercises.

2. A strategy formulation analytical framework in Chapter 6 integrates nine widely used planning matrices (IFEM, EFEM, CPM, SWOT, BCG, IE, SPACE, GRAND, and QSPM) into three stages (Input, Matching, and Decision), which guide the strategic-planning process in all companies. Firms gather strategic information (Input), array key external with internal factors (Matching), and then make strategic decisions (Decision).

3. A far wider coverage of strategy topics than any other strategic-management textbook, for two primary reasons: (a) As firms formulate and implement strategies, a wide variety of functional business topics arise and (b) as the capstone, integrative course in nearly all Schools of Business, strategic management entails students applying functional business skills to case companies.

4. This text provides 30 comprehensive, exciting, exceptionally up-to-date cases designed to apply chapter concepts as students develop a strategic plan for the case companies. For example, every case includes (a) the company's vision/mission statements (if the firm has one); (b) the company's by-segment revenue breakdown (since allocating resources divisions is perhaps the key strategy decision made by firms); (c) the company's organizational chart (since structure is a key strategy topic); and (d) the company's financial statements so students can show the impact of a proposed strategic plan on a firm's financial statements. Thus, the cases take a total-firm, multifunctional approach, which by definition is the nature of strategic management. In addition, this text offers end-of-chapter mini-cases to further apply chapter concepts.

5. More coverage of business ethics, social responsibility, and sustainability is provided in this text than in any other strategic-management textbook, including topics such as bribery, workplace romance, devising codes of ethics, taking a position (or not) on social issues, and wildlife welfare—topics that other textbooks do not mention, even though companies continually face strategic decisions in these areas.

6. This text offers more coverage of global/international issues than any other strategic-management textbook, including topics such as how business culture and practice vary across countries, as well as how taxes, tariffs, political stability, and economic conditions vary across countries—all framed from a strategic planning perspective.

7. The conversational, concise writing style is supported by hundreds of current examples, all aimed at arousing and maintaining the reader's interest as the "process" unfolds from start to finish. The unique writing style is in stark contrast to some strategic-management books that seem to randomly present theory and research for the sake of discussion, rather than material being presented in a logical flow that emulates the actual practice of strategic planning among companies and organizations.

8. This text is supported by outstanding ancillaries, including author-developed manuals, and an author website at **www.strategyclub.com** that offers practical author-developed videos, templates, sample case analyses, special resources, and even a Facebook page for the text. Pearson Education also offers outstanding support materials for instructors and students. For more information, visit **www.pearsonhighered.com**.

Instructor Resources

At the Instructor Resource Center, **www.pearsonhighered.com/irc**, instructors can easily register to gain access to a variety of instructor resources available with this text in downloadable format. If assistance is needed, our dedicated technical support team is ready to help with the media supplements that accompany this text. Visit **http://247.pearsoned.com** for answers to frequently asked questions and toll-free user support phone numbers.

The following supplements are available with this text:

- *Case Instructor's Resource Manual*
- *Chapter Instructor's Resource Manual*
- **Test Bank**
- **TestGen® Computerized Test Bank**
- **PowerPoint Presentation**

Sample of Universities Recently Using This Textbook

Abraham Baldwin Agricultural College

Adelphi University

Akron Institute

Albany State University

Albertus Magnus College

Albright College

Alcorn State University

Alvernia University

Ambassador College

Amberton University

American Intercontinental University—Weston

American International College

American International Continental (AIU) University—Houston

American International University

American University

Anderson University

Angelo State University

Aquinas College

Arizona State University—Polytechnic Campus

Art Institute of California

Averett University

Avila University

Azusa Pacific University

Baker College—Flint

Baldwin Wallace College

Barry University

Belhaven University—Jackson

Bellevue University

Belmont Abbey College

Benedictine University

Black Hills State University

Bloomsburg University

Briar Cliff University

Brooklyn College

Broward College—Central

Broward College—North

Broward College—South

Bryant & Stratton—Orchard Park

Buena Vista University—Storm Lake

Caldwell College

California Polytechnic State University

California State University—Sacramento

California State University—San Bernadino

California University of PA

Calumet College

Capella University

Carlow University

Carson-Newman College

Catawba College

Catholic University of America

Cedar Crest College

Central Connecticut State University

Central Michigan University

Central New Mexico Community College

Central Washington University

Chatham University

Chestnut Hill College

Chicago State University

Christian Brothers University

Claflin University

Clarion University of Pennsylvania

Clarkson College

Clatsop Community College

Cleveland State University

College of William & Mary

Colorado State University—Pueblo

Columbia College

Columbia Southern University—Online

Concordia University

Concordia University Wisconsin

Curry College

Cuyahoga Community College

Daniel Webster College

Davis & Elkins College

Delaware State University

Delaware Technology & Community College—Dover

Delaware Technology & Community College—Wilmington

DePaul University—Loop Campus

East Stroudsburg University

Eastern Michigan University

Eastern Oregon University

Eastern Washington University

ECPI College of Technology—Charleston

ECPI Computer Institute

Elmhurst College

Embry-Riddle Aero University—Prescott

Ferrum College

Florida Agricultural & Mechanical University

Florida Southern College

Florida State University

Florida Technical College—Deland

Florida Technical College—Kissimmee

Florida Technical College—Orlando

Fort Valley State College

Francis Marion University

Fresno Pacific University

Frostburg State University

George Fox University

Georgetown College

Georgia Southern University

Georgia Southwestern State University

Hampton University

Harding University

Harris Stowe State University

Herzing College—Madison

Herzing College—New Orleans

Herzing College—Winter Park

Herzing University—Atlanta

High Point University

Highline Community College

Hofstra University

Hood College

Hope International University

Houghton College

Huntingdon College

Indiana University Bloomington

Indiana Wesleyan CAPS

Iona College

Iowa Lakes Community College—
  Emmetsburg

Jackson Community College

Jackson State University

John Brown University

Johnson & Wales—Charlotte

Johnson & Wales—Colorado

Johnson & Wales—Miami

Johnson & Wales—Rhode Island

Johnson C. Smith University

Kalamazoo College

Kansas State University

Keene State College

Kellogg Community College

La Salle University

Lake Michigan College

Lebanon Valley College

Lee University

Lehman College of CUNY

Liberty University

Limestone College—Gaffney

Lincoln Memorial University

Loyola College Business Center

Loyola College—Chennai

Loyola University—Maryland

Lyndon State College

Madonna University

Manhattan College

Manhattanville College

Marian University—Indiana

Marshall University

Marshall University Graduate College

Marymount University—Arlington

Medgar Evers College

Medical Careers Institute/Newport News

Mercer University—Atlanta

Mercer University—Macon

Miami-Dade College—Homestead

Miami-Dade College—Kendal

Miami-Dade College—North

Miami-Dade College—Wolfson

Michigan State University

Mid-America Christian

Millersville University

Mississippi University for Women

Morgan State University

Morrison College of Reno

Mount Marty College—South Dakota

Mount Mercy University

Mount Wachusett Community College

Mt. Hood Community College

Mt. Vernon Nazarene

MTI Western Business College

Muhlenberg College

Murray State University

New England College

New Mexico State University

New York University

North Carolina Wesleyan College

North Central College

North Central State College

Northwest Arkansas Community College

Northwestern College

Northwood University—Cedar Hill

Notre Dame of Maryland University

Nyack College

Oakland University

Ohio Dominican University

Oklahoma Christian University

Oklahoma State University

Olivet College

Oral Roberts University

Pace University—Pleasantville

Park University

Penn State University—Abington

Penn State University—Hazleton

Pensacola State College

Philadelphia University

Point Park University

Prince George's Community College

Queens College of CUNY

Richard Stockton University

Rider University

Roger Williams University

Saint Edwards University

Saint Leo University

Saint Mary's College

Saint Mary's College—Indiana

Saint Xavier University

San Antonio College

Santa Fe College

Savannah State University

Shippensburg University

Siena Heights University

Southern Nazarene University

Southern New Hampshire University

Southern Oregon University

Southern University—Baton Rouge

Southern Wesleyan University

Southwest Baptist University

Southwest University

St. Bonaventure University

St. Francis University

St. Louis University

St. Martins University

Sterling College

Stevenson University

Strayer University—DC

Texas A&M University—Commerce

Texas A&M University—Texarkana

Texas A&M—San Antonio

Texas Tech University

The College of St. Rose

The Masters College

Tri-County Technical College

Trinity Christian College

Troy State University

Troy University—Dothan

Troy University—Main Campus

Troy University—Montgomery

University of Alabama—Birmingham

University of Arkansas—Fayetteville

University of Findlay

University of Houston—Clearlake

University of Louisiana at Monroe

University of Maine at Augusta

University of Maine—Fort Kent

University of Maryland

University of Maryland—College Park

University of Massachusetts—Boston Harbor

University of Massachusetts—Dartmouth

University of Miami

University of Michigan—Flint

University of Minnesota—Crookston

University of Mobile

University of Montevallo

University of Nebraska—Omaha

University of Nevada Las Vegas

University of New Orleans

University of North Texas

University of North Texas—Dallas

University of Pikeville

University of Sioux Falls

University of South Florida

University of St. Joseph

University of Tampa

University of Texas—Pan American

University of The Incarnate Word

University of Toledo

Upper Iowa University

Valley City State University

Virginia Community College System

Virginia State University

Virginia Tech

Wagner College

Wake Forest University

Washington University

Webber International University

Webster University

West Chester University

West Liberty University

West Valley College

West Virginia Wesleyan College

Western Connecticut State University

Western Kentucky University

Western Michigan University

Western Washington University

William Jewell College

Williams Baptist College

Winona State University

Winston-Salem State University

WSU Vancouver

Sample of Countries Outside the United States Where This Textbook Is Widely Used

Mexico, China, Japan, Australia, Singapore, Canada, Indonesia, Pakistan, Iran, Kenya, Congo, Hong Kong, India, England, Argentina, Equador, Zambia, Guam, Italy, Cyprus, Colombia, Philippines, South Africa, Peru, Turkey, Malaysia, and Egypt

The Case Rationale

Case analysis remains the primary learning vehicle used in most strategic-management classes, for five important reasons:

1. Analyzing cases gives students the opportunity to work in teams to evaluate the internal operations and external issues facing various organizations and to craft strategies that can lead these firms to success. Working in teams gives students practical experience in solving problems as part of a group. In the business world, important decisions are generally made within groups; strategic-management students learn to deal with overly aggressive group members as well as timid, noncontributing group members. This experience is valuable because strategic-management students are near graduation and soon enter the working world full time.

2. Analyzing cases enables students to improve their oral and written communication skills as well as their analytical and interpersonal skills by proposing and defending particular courses of action for the case companies.

3. Analyzing cases allows students to view a company, its competitors, and its industry concurrently, thus simulating the complex business world. Through case analysis, students learn how to apply concepts, evaluate situations, formulate strategies, and resolve implementation problems.

4. Analyzing cases allows students to apply concepts learned in many business courses. Students gain experience dealing with a wide range of organizational problems that impact all the business functions.

5. Analyzing cases gives students practice in applying concepts, evaluating situations, formulating a "game plan," and resolving implementation problems in a variety of business and industry settings.

The Case MyLab Testing Feature

As revealed in the Concepts by Cases matrix, student learning of 30 key strategic-management concepts can easily be tested by using the 30 cases. The new Case MyLab Testing feature assures that the cases are excellent for testing student learning of the key strategic-management concepts, thus serving as a great mechanism for professors to achieve AACSB's Assurance of Learning Objectives. This new testing feature simplifies grading for professors in both traditional and online class settings.

The Case MyLab testing feature includes 25 multiple-choice questions for each case, comprised of 10 *Basic* questions that simply test whether the student read the case before class, and 15 *Applied* questions that test the student's ability to apply various strategic-management concepts. In addition, there are 2 *Discussion* questions per case. This testing feature enables professors to determine, before class if desired, whether students (1) read the case in *Basic* terms, and/or (2) are able to *Apply* strategy concepts to resolve issues in the case. For example, the MyLab case *Basic* question may be: In what country is SABMiller headquartered? Whereas a MyLab case *Applied* question may be: What are three aspects of the organizational chart given in the SABMiller case that violate strategic-management guidelines?

The New Concepts by Cases Matrix

All 30 cases facilitate coverage of all strategy concepts, but as revealed by purple cells, some cases especially exemplify some key strategy concepts. The purple cells reveal which concepts are tested with multiple-choice questions in the MyLab. The Concepts by Cases matrix enables professors to effectively utilize different cases to assure student learning of various chapter concepts. Note from the purple boxes that two, three, or four cases are used to test each strategic-management concept. This new, innovative ancillary promises to elevate the case learning method to new heights in teaching strategic management.

Case Number	USA Headquartered	Key Strategic-Management Concepts	Strategy Model/Process	Vision/Mission Statements	Competitive Profile Matrix	Porter's Five Forces	EFE Matrix	Resource Based View	Financial Ratios & Breakeven	Value Chain Analysis	IFE Matrix	Strategy Types	Porter's Five Generic Strategies
			3	3	3	5	4	3	4	2	4	3	4
USA-Based Service Companies													
Case 1	Dunkin' Brands Group, Inc.				■								
Case 2	Krispy Kreme Doughnuts, Inc.									■			
Case 3	Marriott International, Inc.		■			■							
Case 4	Wynn Resorts Limited					■							■
Case 5	Cinemark Holdings, Inc.			■							■		
Case 6	Facebook, Inc.												
Case 7	Zynga, Inc.						■						
Case 8	The Priceline Group, Inc.												
Case 9	The TJX Companies, Inc.												
Case 10	Tiffany & Company												■
Case 11	Citigroup Inc.												
Case 12	JetBlue Airways Corporation				■			■					
Case 13	FedEx Corporation												
USA-Based Manufacturing Companies													
Case 14	Tyson Foods, Inc.									■	■	■	
Case 15	Constellation Brands Inc.			■									
Case 16	GoPro, Inc.										■		
Case 17	Artic Cat, Inc.						■				■		
Case 18	Tesla Motors, Inc.		■						■		■		
Case 19	Ford Motor Company							■	■				
Case 20	Harely-Davidson, Inc.								■				■
Case 21	Apple Inc.				■							■	
Case 22	International Business Machines Corp.												
Case 23	Taser International, Inc.					■							
Case 24	Revlon, Inc.		■										
Case 25	World Relief						■						
	Outside-USA Headquartered													
Case 26	World Wildlife Fund										■		
Case 27	Michael Kors Holdings Limited												
Case 28	SABMiller plc					■							■
Case 29	Gruma, S.A.B. de C.V.							■					
Case 30	Restaurant Brands International, Inc.						■		■				

First Mover Advantages	Outsourcing	SWOT Matrix	SPACE Matrix	BCG & IE Matrices	Grand Strategy & QSPM	Organizational Structure	Organizational Culture	Product Positioning	EPS-EBIT Analysis	Projected Financial Statements	Company Valuation	Balanced Scorecard	Business Ethics	Environmental Sustainability	Foreign Business Culture
3	1	4	4	4	3	4	1	3	4	3	4	2	2	2	1

The Case Synopses

USA-Headquartered Service Firms

RESTAURANTS

1. Dunkin' Brands Group, Inc. (DNKN) — Headquartered in Canton, Massachusetts, Dunkin' Brands owns, operates, and franchises quick-service restaurants under the Dunkin' Donuts and Baskin-Robbins brands worldwide.

2. Krispy Kreme Doughnuts, Inc. (KKD) — Headquartered in Winston-Salem, North Carolina, KKD operates about 750 doughnut locations, of which about 650 are franchise owned. Most KKD locations (515) are outside the United States. The company plans to reach 900 stores internationally by 2017. Most restaurants "produce" their own doughnuts.

LODGING AND MOVIES

3. Marriott International, Inc. (MAR) — Headquartered in Bethesda, Maryland, and having 127,000 employees worldwide, Marriott owns and manages a broad range of hotels and lodging facilities. Marriott's CEO, Anne Sorenson, is leading the firm's expansion throughout Africa. The Ritz-Carlton is a subsidiary of Marriott.

4. Wynn Resorts Limited (WYNN) — Headquartered in Paradise, Nevada, Wynn Resorts is a global developer and operator of high-end casinos and hotels, especially in Las Vegas and Macau. Wynn Cotai opened in Macau in 2014 amidst overall Macau gambling revenues declining.

5. Cinemark Holdings, Inc. (CNK) — Headquartered in Plano, Texas, Cinemark is a chain of movie theaters operating in North and South America and Taiwan. Cinemark has over 300 theaters in the United States, is the largest movie theater firm in Brazil, the fourth largest in Mexico, and the second largest globally.

INTERNET BASED

6. Facebook, Inc. (FB) — Headquartered in Menlo Park, California, Facebook is the largest online social networking website with over 1.3 billion users (but reportedly more than 10 percent are fake). Facebook charges for placing advertisements; its vision is "to connect the world."

7. Zynga, Inc. (ZNGA) — Headquartered in San Francisco, California, Zynga develops, markets, and operates online social media games primarily under the FarmVille, Words With Friends, and Zynga Poker franchises. Founded in 2007, Zynga's games are accessible on Facebook and Zynga.com.

8. The Priceline Group, Inc. (PCLN) — Headquartered in Norwalk, Connecticut, Priceline is an online travel, car rental, and hotel reservation company with products that include Booking.com and, in Asia, Agoda.com.

STORES AND BANKS

9. The TJX Companies, Inc. (TJX) — Headquartered in Framingham, Massachusetts, TJX operates off-price apparel and home fashion retail stores in the United States and globally under the names T. J. Maxx, Marshalls, HomeGoods, Winners, HomeSense, and Sierra Trading Post.

10. Tiffany & Company (TIF) — Headquartered in New York City, Tiffany designs, produces, and sells jewelry, as well as watches, china, crystal, stationery, and fragrances worldwide. The company owns and operates 275 stores in 24 countries.

11. Citigroup Inc. (C) — Headquartered in New York City, Citigroup is one of the world's largest bank holding companies with more than 16,000 offices and 255,000 employees worldwide. Citi operates through two segments: Citicorp (primarily banking) and City Holdings (primarily brokerage).

AIRLINES AND AIRFREIGHT

12. JetBlue Airways Corporation (JBLU) — Headquartered in Long Island City, New York, JetBlue is a passenger airline company that serves the United States, the Caribbean, and Latin America.

13. FedEx Corporation (FDX) — Headquartered in Memphis, Tennessee, FedEx is a global delivery services company with over 300,000 employees competing daily with UPS, DHL, USPS, and online emailing.

USA-Headquartered Manufacturing Firms

FOOD

14. Tyson Foods, Inc. (TSN) — Headquartered in Springdale, Arkansas, Tyson Foods is the world's second-largest processor and marketer of chicken, beef, and pork. With 115,000 employees, Tyson is the largest meat producer in the world.

15. Constellation Brands Inc. (STZ) — Headquartered in Victor, New York, Constellation Brands is the largest wine producer in the world and has more than 100 wine, beer, and spirits brands, including Robert Mondavi, Corona, Paul Masson, and Black Velvet Canadian Whisky.

LEISURE SPORTS

16. GoPro, Inc. (GPRO) — Headquartered in San Mateo, California, GoPro develops and produces sportswear, sports cameras, and accessories widely used by surfers, divers, and sports enthusiasts. The company has about 700 employees.

17. Arctic Cat Inc. (ACAT) — Headquartered in Plymouth, Minnesota, Arctic Cat designs, produces, and, through independent dealers, markets snowmobiles and all-terrain vehicles (ATVs), and accessory parts, including lights, racks, snow plows, wheels, and a full garment portfolio.

AUTOMOBILES AND MOTORCYCLES

18. Tesla Motors, Inc. (TSLA) — Headquartered in Palo Alto, California, Tesla designs, manufactures, and markets all-electric cars and lithium batteries. After 10 years being in business, Tesla turned its first profit ever in Q1 2013. Tesla's sports car, the Roadster, and its Model S are especially popular.

19. Ford Motor Company (F) — Headquartered in Dearborn, Michigan, Ford develops, produces, and markets automobiles, trucks, and accessories globally. The company also has a large financial services segment.

20. Harley-Davidson, Inc. (HOG) — Headquartered in Milwaukee, Wisconsin, Harley develops, produces, and markets motorcycles and related parts and accessories through independent dealers globally. The company also has a large financial services segment.

COMPUTERS/SOFTWARE

21. Apple Inc. (AAPL) — Headquartered in Cupertino, California, Apple designs, produces, and markets laptop computers, tablets, smartphones, watches, portable digital music players, and accessories globally.

22. International Business Machines Corporation (IBM) — Headquartered in Armonk, New York, IBM is a large technology and consulting company with about 100,000 employees in the United States and more than 330,000 outside the United States. The IBM's chairman, president, and CEO is Ginni Rometty.

PERSONAL PRODUCTS

23. TASER International, Inc. (TASR) — Headquartered in Scottsdale, Arizona, TASER develops, produces, and markets conducted electrical weapons (CEWs) for use in law enforcement, federal, military, security, and personal defense markets globally. The company also offers AXON body cameras.

24. Revlon, Inc. (REV) — Headquartered in New York City, Revlon develops, manufactures, and markets cosmetics, fragrances, and personal care products globally. Revlon competes with L'Oreal, Avon, Estee Lauder, and Mary Kay Cosmetics.

Nonprofit Organizations

25. World Relief — Headquartered in Baltimore, Maryland, World Relief is a nonprofit, international relief and development agency that offers assistance globally to victims of poverty, disease, hunger, war, disasters, and persecution. With over 100,000 volunteers, World Relief serves over four million vulnerable people annually.

26. World Wildlife Fund for Nature (WWF) — Headquartered in Gland, Vaud, Switzerland, WWF is the world's largest nonprofit conservation organization working on more than 1,300 wildlife projects. Its mission is "to stop the degradation of the planet's natural environment and to build a future in which humans live in harmony with nature."

Outside-USA Headquartered Firms

27. Michael Kors Holdings Ltd. (KORS) — Headquartered in Hong Kong, Michael Kors designs, produces, and markets luxury apparel and accessories for men and women, through about 250 stores in North America and 80 stores in Europe and Japan. The firm also licenses its trademarks and products to third parties globally.

28. SABMiller plc (SAB) — Headquartered in London, SABMiller is the world's second-largest beer brewer behind Anheuser-Busch InBev. With operations in over 75 countries, some popular SABMiller brands include Miller, Fosters, Castle, Eagle, and Pilsner. SAB is short for South African Brewery.

29. Gruma, S.A.B. de C.V. (GMK) — Headquartered in Monterrey, Mexico, Gruma is the world's largest producer of corn flour and tortillas. Brand names include Mission, Meseca, and Guerrero. The company's USA headquarters is in Irving, Texas.

30. Restaurant Brands International, Inc. (QSR) — Headquartered in Oakville, Ontario, outside of Toronto, Canada, QSR consists of Burger King and Tim Hortons. Burger King is the world's second-largest hamburger chain (behind McDonald's), with 13,000+ restaurants in the United States and 85 other countries. Burger King acquired the Canadian donut company Tim Hortons in December 2014 as an inversion, moving their headquarters from Miami.

Acknowledgments

Many persons have contributed time, energy, ideas, and suggestions for improving this text over many editions. The strength of this text is largely attributed to the collective wisdom, work, and experiences of strategic-management professors, researchers, students, and practitioners. Names of particular individuals whose published research is referenced in this edition are listed alphabetically in the Name Index. To all individuals involved in making this text so popular and successful, we are indebted and thankful.

Many special persons and reviewers contributed valuable material and suggestions for this edition. We would like to thank our colleagues and friends at Auburn University, Mississippi State University, East Carolina University, the University of South Carolina, Campbell University, the University of North Carolina at Pembroke, and Francis Marion University. We have taught strategic management at all these universities. Scores of students and professors at these schools helped shape the development of this text.

We thank the following guest writers who contributed a case(s) to this sixteenth edition:

Meredith E. David, Baylor University

Mark L. Frigo, DePaul University

Debora J. Gilliard, Metropolitan State University of Denver

David Lynn Hoffman, Metropolitan State University of Denver

Edward Moore, Liberty University

Alvaro Polanco, Baylor University

Lori Radulovich, Baldwin Wallace University

Raj Selladurai, Indiana University Northwest

Diana Tsaw, California Lutheran University

John D. Varlaro, Johnson & Wales University

Jason Willoughby, Elizabethtown Community College

We thank you, the reader, for investing the time and effort to read and study this text. It will help you formulate, implement, and evaluate strategies for any organization with which you become associated. We hope you come to share our enthusiasm for the rich subject area of strategic management and for the systematic learning approach taken in this text. We welcome and invite your suggestions, ideas, thoughts, comments, and questions regarding any part of this text or the ancillary materials. Please contact Dr. Fred R. David at the following e-mail: freddavid9@gmail.com, or write him at the School of Business, Francis Marion University, Florence, SC 29501. We sincerely appreciate and need your input to continually improve this text in future editions. Your willingness to draw our attention to specific errors or deficiencies in coverage or exposition will especially be appreciated.

Thank you for using this text.

Fred R. David and Forest R. David

About the Authors

Fred R. and Forest R. David, a father–son team, have published more than 50 articles in journals such as *Academy of Management Review, Academy of Management Executive, Journal of Applied Psychology, Long Range Planning, International Journal of Management, Journal of Business Strategy,* and *Advanced Management Journal.* Fred and Forest's recent article titled "Mission Statement Theory and Practice: A Content Analysis and New Direction," published in the *International Journal of Business, Marketing, and Decision Sciences,* is changing the way organizations devise and use vision and mission statements.

Fred R. David

Fred and Forest are coauthors of *Strategic Management: Concepts and Cases—A Competitive Advantage Approach* that has been on a two-year revision cycle since 1987, when the first edition was published. This text has been a leader in the field of strategic management for almost three decades, providing an applications, practitioner-approach to the discipline. More than 500 colleges and universities have used this textbook over the years. For seven editions of this book, Forest has been sole author of the *Case Instructor's Resource Manual,* having developed extensive teachers' notes (solutions) for all the cases. Forest is author of the Case MyLab and Chapter MyLab ancillaries, as well as the free Excel Student Template found on the author website (**www.strategyclub.com**).

The authors actively assist businesses globally in doing strategic planning. They have written and published more than 100 strategic-management cases. They were keynote speakers in September 2015 in Monterrey, Mexico, at the "XXII Congreso Industrial," the largest Congress of Industrial Engineering in Latin America. They were also invited keynote speakers at the Pearson International Forum in Monterrey, Mexico, delivering a one-hour presentation to 80 Spanish-speaking management professors.

Forest R. David

With a Ph.D. in Management from the University of South Carolina, Fred is the TranSouth Professor of Strategic Planning at Francis Marion University in Florence, South Carolina. Forest has taught strategic-management courses at Mississippi State University, Campbell University, and Francis Marion University.

STRATEGIC
MANAGEMENT
Concepts and Cases

## PART 1

OVERVIEW OF STRATEGIC MANAGEMENT

1

Source: Odua Images/Fotolia

The Nature of Strategic Management

LEARNING OBJECTIVES

After studying this chapter, you should be able to do the following:

1-1. Describe the strategic-management process.

1-2. Discuss the three stages of strategy formulation, implementation, and evaluation activities.

1-3. Explain the need for integrating analysis and intuition in strategic management.

1-4. Define and give examples of key terms in strategic management.

1-5. Illustrate the comprehensive strategic-management model.

1-6. Describe the benefits of engaging in strategic management.

1-7. Explain why some firms do no strategic planning.

1-8. Describe the pitfalls in actually doing strategic planning.

1-9. Discuss the connection between business and military strategy.

ASSURANCE OF LEARNING EXERCISES

The following exercises are found at the end of this chapter:

When CEOs from the big three U.S. automakers—Ford, General Motors (GM), and Chrysler—showed up several years ago without a clear strategic plan to ask congressional leaders for bailout monies, they were sent home with instructions to develop a clear strategic plan for the future. Austan Goolsbee, one of President Barack Obama's top economic advisers, said, "Asking for a bailout without a convincing business plan was crazy." Goolsbee also said, "If the three auto CEOs need a bridge, it's got to be a bridge to somewhere, not a bridge to nowhere."[1] This text gives the instructions on how to develop a clear strategic plan—a bridge to somewhere rather than nowhere.

The chapter provides an overview of strategic management. It introduces a practical, integrative model of the strategic-management process, and it defines basic activities and terms in strategic management.

At the beginning of each chapter, a different company is showcased doing an exemplary job applying strategic-planning concepts, tools, and techniques. The first company featured for excellent strategic management practices is Apple, Inc., one of the best-managed companies ever, and currently led by one of the best strategists in the world, Mr. Tim Cook, who followed a legendary strategist, Mr. Steve Jobs. At the end of each chapter, a new, one-page, mini-case on a company is provided with respective questions that examine various concepts, tools, and techniques presented.

What Is Strategic Management?

Once there were two company presidents who competed in the same industry. These two presidents decided to go on a camping trip to discuss a possible merger. They hiked deep into the woods. Suddenly, they came upon a grizzly bear that rose up on its hind legs and snarled. Instantly, the first president took off his knapsack and got out a pair of jogging shoes. The second president said, "Hey, you can't outrun that bear." The first president responded, "Maybe I can't

Apple, Inc. (AAPL)

Headquartered in Cupertino, California, Apple, Inc. designs, produces, and markets smartphones, watches, personal computers, digital music players, and much more worldwide. Apple is arguably the most successful company in modern times. The company was founded in 1977 by a great strategist, an American legend, the late Mr. Steve Jobs. According to *Financial Times*, the best corporate strategist in 2014 was Apple CEO Tim Cook, who led Apple to a record $700 billion market capitalization, with booming iPhone and personal computer sales, and handed billions of dollars back to shareholders. *Financial Times* named CEO Cook as "Person of the Year" for Apple's huge achievements as well as Cook's courage. Cook came forward as the Fortune 500's first openly gay CEO when he published an essay in October 2014 in *Bloomberg Businessweek* saying he was "proud to be gay." Cook was courageous in other ways too. For example, at an Apple's shareholder meeting, when someone questioned the profitability of Apple's environmental initiatives, Cook responded, "We do things for other reasons than a profit motive; we do things because they are right and just. If that's a hard line for you...then you should get out of the stock."

Amidst tremendous fanfare, Apple recently released its iWatch and is poised to introduce iTV, along with an electric car. Apple and IBM have released the first apps to emerge from their collaboration—a collection that CEO Cook says is "the most enterprising apps ever." Also, Apple recently entered the e-book business as well as the banking business with its Apple Pay system, whereby customers use their iPhone to pay for merchandise at hundreds of retail checkout counters. In addition, Apple recently acquired Metaio, a company that makes augmented-reality (AR) technologies, a concept that allows developers to overlay digital information on top of the real world. A number of companies are working on AR, including Microsoft and Google with their HoloLens and Magic Leap projects, respectively. Many scientists expect AR and virtual reality (VR) to be the next major computing platform after mobile devices such as smartphones and tablets. For the eighth year in a row, *Fortune* recently named Apple the world's most admired company.

Source: Company documents and a variety of sources.

outrun that bear, but I surely can outrun you!" This story captures the notion of strategic management, which is to gain and sustain competitive advantage.

What Is a Cohesion Case?

A distinguishing, popular feature of this text is the Cohesion Case, named so because a written case on a company appears at the end of this chapter, and then all other chapters feature end-of-chapter Assurance of Learning Exercises to apply strategic-planning concepts, tools, and techniques to the Cohesion Case company. The Hershey Company is featured as the new Cohesion Case in this edition, because Hershey is a well-known, well-managed global firm undergoing strategic change. By working through the Hershey-related exercises at the end of each chapter, students become well prepared to develop an effective strategic plan for any company assigned to them (or their team) to perform a strategic-management case analysis. Case analysis is a core part of almost every strategic-management course globally.

Defining Strategic Management

Strategic management is the art and science of formulating, implementing, and evaluating cross-functional decisions that enable an organization to achieve its objectives. As this definition implies, strategic management focuses on integrating management, marketing, finance and accounting, production and operations, research and development (R&D), and information systems to achieve organizational success. The term *strategic management* in this text is used synonymously with the term **strategic planning**. The latter term is more often used in the business world, whereas the former is often used in academia. Sometimes the term *strategic management* is used to refer to strategy formulation, implementation, and evaluation, with *strategic planning* referring only to strategy formulation. The purpose of strategic management is to exploit and create new and different opportunities for tomorrow; **long-range planning**, in contrast, tries to optimize for tomorrow the trends of today.

The term *strategic planning* originated in the 1950s and was popular between the mid-1960s and the mid-1970s. During these years, strategic planning was widely believed to be the answer for all problems. At the time, much of corporate America was "obsessed" with strategic planning. Following that boom, however, strategic planning was cast aside during the 1980s as various planning models did not yield higher returns. The 1990s, however, brought the revival of strategic planning, and the process is widely practiced today in the business world. Many companies today have a *chief strategy officer (CSO)*. McDonald's hired a new CSO in October 2015.

A strategic plan is, in essence, a company's game plan. Just as a football team needs a good game plan to have a chance for success, a company must have a good strategic plan to compete successfully. Profit margins among firms in most industries are so slim that there is little room for error in the overall strategic plan. A strategic plan results from tough managerial choices among numerous good alternatives, and it signals commitment to specific markets, policies, procedures, and operations in lieu of other, "less desirable" courses of action.

The term *strategic management* is used at many colleges and universities as the title for the capstone course in business administration. This course integrates material from all business courses, and, in addition, introduces new strategic-management concepts and techniques being widely used by firms in strategic planning.

Stages of Strategic Management

The **strategic-management process** consists of three stages: strategy formulation, strategy implementation, and strategy evaluation. **Strategy formulation** includes developing a vision and a mission, identifying an organization's external opportunities and threats, determining internal strengths and weaknesses, establishing long-term objectives, generating alternative strategies, and choosing particular strategies to pursue. Strategy-formulation issues include deciding what new businesses to enter, what businesses to abandon, whether to expand operations or diversify, whether to enter international markets, whether to merge or form a joint venture, and how to avoid a hostile takeover.

Because no organization has unlimited resources, strategists must decide which alternative strategies will benefit the firm most. Strategy-formulation decisions commit an organization to specific products, markets, resources, and technologies over an extended period of time. Strategies determine long-term competitive advantages. For better or worse, strategic decisions have major multifunctional consequences and enduring effects on an organization. Top managers have the best perspective to understand fully the ramifications of strategy-formulation decisions; they have the authority to commit the resources necessary for implementation.

Strategy implementation requires a firm to establish annual objectives, devise policies, motivate employees, and allocate resources so that formulated strategies can be executed. Strategy implementation includes developing a strategy-supportive culture, creating an effective organizational structure, redirecting marketing efforts, preparing budgets, developing and using information systems, and linking employee compensation to organizational performance.

Strategy implementation often is called the "action stage" of strategic management. Implementing strategy means mobilizing employees and managers to put formulated strategies into action. Often considered to be the most difficult stage in strategic management, strategy implementation requires personal discipline, commitment, and sacrifice. Successful strategy implementation hinges on managers' ability to motivate employees, which is more an art than a science. Strategies formulated but not implemented serve no useful purpose.

Interpersonal skills are especially critical for successful strategy implementation. Strategy-implementation activities affect all employees and managers in an organization. Every division and department must decide on answers to questions such as "What must we do to implement our part of the organization's strategy?" and "How best can we get the job done?" The challenge of implementation is to stimulate managers and employees throughout an organization to work with pride and enthusiasm toward achieving stated objectives.

Strategy evaluation is the final stage in strategic management. Managers desperately need to know when particular strategies are not working well; strategy evaluation is the primary means for obtaining this information. All strategies are subject to future modification because external and internal factors constantly change. Three fundamental strategy-evaluation activities are (1) reviewing external and internal factors that are the bases for current strategies, (2) measuring performance, and (3) taking corrective actions. Strategy evaluation is needed because success today is no guarantee of success tomorrow! Success always creates new and different problems; complacent organizations experience demise.

Formulation, implementation, and evaluation of strategy activities occur at three hierarchical levels in a large organization: corporate, divisional or strategic business unit, and functional. By fostering communication and interaction among managers and employees across hierarchical levels, strategic management helps a firm function as a competitive team. Most small businesses and some large businesses do not have divisions or strategic business units; they have only the corporate and functional levels. Nevertheless, managers and employees at these two levels should be actively involved in strategic-management activities.

Peter Drucker says the prime task of strategic management is thinking through the overall mission of a business—

> that is, of asking the question, "What is our business?" This leads to the setting of objectives, the development of strategies, and the making of today's decisions for tomorrow's results. This clearly must be done by a part of the organization that can see the entire business; that can balance objectives and the needs of today against the needs of tomorrow; and that can allocate resources of men and money to key results.[2]

Integrating Intuition and Analysis

Edward Deming once said, "In God we trust. All others bring data." The strategic-management process can be described as an objective, logical, systematic approach for making major decisions in an organization. It attempts to organize qualitative and quantitative information in a way that allows effective decisions to be made under conditions of uncertainty. Yet strategic management is not a pure science that lends itself to a nice, neat, one-two-three approach.

Based on past experiences, judgment, and feelings, most people recognize that **intuition** is essential to making good strategic decisions. Intuition is particularly useful for making decisions in situations of great uncertainty or little precedent. It is also helpful when highly interrelated variables exist or when it is necessary to choose from several plausible alternatives. Some managers and owners of businesses profess to have extraordinary abilities for using intuition alone in devising brilliant strategies. For example, Will Durant, who organized GM, was described by Alfred Sloan as "a man who would proceed on a course of action guided solely, as far as I could tell, by some intuitive flash of brilliance. He never felt obliged to make an engineering hunt for the facts. Yet at times, he was astoundingly correct in his judgment."[3] Albert Einstein acknowledged the importance of intuition when he said, "I believe in intuition and inspiration. At times I feel certain that I am right while not knowing the reason. Imagination is more important than knowledge, because knowledge is limited, whereas imagination embraces the entire world."[4]

Although some organizations today may survive and prosper because they have intuitive geniuses managing them, many are not so fortunate. Most organizations can benefit from strategic management, which is based on integrating intuition and analysis in decision making. Choosing an intuitive or analytic approach to decision making is not an either-or proposition. Managers at all levels in an organization inject their intuition and judgment into strategic-management analyses. Analytical thinking and intuitive thinking complement each other.

Operating from the I've-already-made-up-my-mind-don't-bother-me-with-the-facts mode is not management by intuition; it is management by ignorance.[5] Drucker says, "I believe in intuition only if you discipline it. 'Hunch' artists, who make a diagnosis but don't check it out with the facts, are the ones in medicine who kill people, and in management kill businesses."[6] As Henderson notes:

> The accelerating rate of change today is producing a business world in which customary managerial habits in organizations are increasingly inadequate. Experience alone was an adequate guide when changes could be made in small increments. But intuitive and experience-based management philosophies are grossly inadequate when decisions are strategic and have major, irreversible consequences.[7]

In a sense, the strategic-management process is an attempt to duplicate what goes on in the mind of a brilliant, intuitive person who knows the business and assimilates and integrates that knowledge using analysis to formulate effective strategies.

Adapting to Change

The strategic-management process is based on the belief that organizations should continually monitor internal and external events and trends so that timely changes can be made as needed. The rate and magnitude of changes that affect organizations are increasing dramatically, as evidenced by how the drop in oil prices caught so many firms by surprise. Firms, like organisms, must be "adept at adapting" or they will not survive. To survive, all organizations must astutely identify and adapt to change. The strategic-management process is aimed at allowing organizations to adapt effectively to change over the long run. Waterman noted:

> In today's business environment, more than in any preceding era, the only constant is change. Successful organizations effectively manage change, continuously adapting their bureaucracies, strategies, systems, products, and cultures to survive the shocks and prosper from the forces that decimate the competition.[8]

On a political map, the boundaries between countries may be clear, but on a competitive map showing the real flow of financial and industrial activity, the boundaries have largely disappeared. The speedy flow of information has eaten away at national boundaries so that people worldwide readily see for themselves how other people live and work. We have become a borderless world with global citizens, global competitors, global customers, global suppliers, and global distributors! Many firms headquartered in the United States are challenged by outside-U.S.–based companies in many industries. For example, Toyota, Honda, Yamaha, Suzuki, Volkswagen, Samsung, and Kia have huge market shares in the United States.

The need to adapt to change leads organizations to key strategic-management questions, such as "What kind of business should we become?" "Are we in the right field(s)?" "Should we reshape our business?" "What new competitors are entering our industry?" "What strategies should we pursue?" "How are our customers changing?" "Are new technologies being developed that could put us out of business?"

The Internet promotes endless comparison shopping, enabling consumers worldwide to band together to demand discounts. The Internet has transferred power from businesses to individuals. Buyers used to face big obstacles when attempting to get the best price and service, such as limited time and data to compare, but now consumers can quickly scan hundreds of vendor offerings. Both the number of people shopping online and the average amount they spend is increasing dramatically. Digital communication has become the name of the game in marketing. Consumers today are flocking to blogs, sending tweets, watching and posting videos on YouTube, and spending hours on Tumbler, Facebook, Reddit, Instagram, and LinkedIn, instead of watching television, listening to the radio, or reading newspapers and magazines. Facebook recently unveiled features that further marry these social sites to the wider Internet. Facebook users can now log onto various business shopping sites from their social site, so their friends can see what items they have purchased from what companies. Facebook wants their members to use their identities to manage *all* their online identities. Most traditional retailers boost in-store sales using their websites to promote in-store promotions.

Key Terms in Strategic Management

Before we further discuss strategic management, we should define nine key terms: *competitive advantage, strategists, vision and mission statements, external opportunities and threats, internal strengths and weaknesses, long-term objectives, strategies, annual objectives,* and *policies.*

Competitive Advantage

Strategic management is all about gaining and maintaining **competitive advantage**. This term can be defined as any activity a firm does especially well compared to activities done by rival firms, or any resource a firm possesses that rival firms desire.

Having fewer fixed assets than rival firms can provide major competitive advantages. For example, Apple has virtually no manufacturing facilities of its own, and rival Sony has 57 electronics factories. Apple relies almost entirely on contract manufacturers for production of all its products, whereas Sony owns its own plants. Having fewer fixed assets has enabled Apple to remain financially lean.

According to CEO Paco Underhill of Envirosell, "Where it used to be a polite war, it's now a 21st-century bar fight, where everybody is competing with everyone else for the customers' money." Shoppers are "trading down: Nordstrom is taking customers from Neiman Marcus and Saks Fifth Avenue, T.J. Maxx and Marshalls are taking customers from most other stores in the mall, and Family Dollar is taking revenues from Walmart.[9] Getting and keeping competitive advantage is essential for long-term success in an organization. In mass retailing, big-box companies, such as Walmart, Best Buy, and Sears, are losing competitive advantage to smaller stores, reflecting the dramatic shift in mass retailing to becoming smaller. As customers shift more to online purchases, less brick and mortar is definitely better for sustaining competitive advantage in retailing. Walmart Express stores of less than 40,000 square feet each, rather than its 185,000-square-foot Supercenters, and Office Depot's new 5,000-square-foot stores are examples of smaller is better.

Normally, a firm can sustain a competitive advantage for only a certain period because of rival firms imitating and undermining that advantage. Thus, it is not adequate simply to obtain competitive advantage. A firm must strive to achieve **sustained competitive advantage** by (1) continually adapting to changes in external trends and events and internal capabilities, competencies, and resources; and (2) effectively formulating, implementing, and evaluating strategies that capitalize on those factors.

Strategists

Strategists are the individuals most responsible for the success or failure of an organization. They have various job titles, such as *chief executive officer, president, owner, chair of the board, executive director, chancellor, dean,* and *entrepreneur.* Jay Conger, professor of organizational behavior at the London Business School and author of *Building Leaders*, says, "All strategists have to be chief learning officers. We are in an extended period of change. If our leaders aren't highly adaptive and great models during this period, then our companies won't adapt either, because ultimately leadership is about being a role model."

Strategists help an organization gather, analyze, and organize information. They track industry and competitive trends, develop forecasting models and scenario analyses, evaluate corporate and divisional performance, spot emerging market opportunities, identify business threats, and develop creative action plans. Strategic planners usually serve in a support or staff role. Usually found in higher levels of management, they typically have considerable authority for decision making in the firm. The CEO is the most visible and critical strategic manager. Any manager who has responsibility for a unit or division, responsibility for profit and loss outcomes, or direct authority over a major piece of the business is a strategic manager (strategist).

In the last few years, the position of CSO has become common in many organizations, including Sun Microsystems, Network Associates, Clarus, Lante, Marimba, Sapient, Commerce One, BBDO, Cadbury Schweppes, General Motors, Ellie Mae, Cendant, Charles Schwab, Tyco, Campbell Soup, Morgan Stanley, and Reed-Elsevier. This corporate officer title represents recognition of the growing importance of strategic planning in business. Franz Koch, the CSO of German sportswear company Puma AG, was recently promoted to CEO of Puma. When asked about his plans for the company, Koch said on a conference call, "I plan to just focus on the long-term strategic plan." Academic Research Capsule 1-1 reveals when CSOs are most often hired.

Strategists differ as much as organizations do, and these differences must be considered in the formulation, implementation, and evaluation of strategies. Strategists differ in their attitudes, values, ethics, willingness to take risks, concern for social responsibility, concern for profitability, concern for short-run versus long-run aims, and management style—some will not even consider various types of strategies because of their personal philosophies.. The founder of Hershey, Milton Hershey, built the company so that he could afford to manage an orphanage. From corporate profits, Hershey today cares for about 900 boys and 1,000 girls in its boarding school for pre-K through grade 12.

Athletic coaches are also strategists. Football, basketball, baseball, soccer, and in fact most athletic contests are often won or lost based a team's game plan. For example, a basketball coach may plan to fast break and play up-tempo, rather than play more half court, if the players are smaller and faster, or if the team has more depth than the opposing team. A few great college basketball coaches today are Mike Krzyzewski at Duke, John Calipari at Kentucky, Jim Boeheim at Syracuse, and Tom Izzo at Michigan State. Great college basketball coaches years ago included John Wooden, Jim Valvano, Dean Smith, and Bobby Knight. Another great coach of yesteryear was Nolan Richardson, who developed excellent game plans and, in 1994, as the first black head coach at a major university in the South, led the Arkansas Razorbacks men's basketball team to

ACADEMIC RESEARCH CAPSULE 1-1

When Are Chief Strategy Officers (CSOs) Hired/Appointed?

An increasing number of firms are employing a chief strategy officer (CSO). In an article published in 2014, Menz and Sheef examined 200 S&P 500 firms over a 5-year period to examine what factors contribute to firms hiring a CSO and what factors contribute to a CSO affecting a firm's financial performance. Of the sampled firms, on average, during the study, 42 percent employed a CSO. Although many factors may lead to a firm's decision to appoint a CSO, the authors focused on five key areas that prior research suggests as most important and most likely to lead to a CSO appointment:

1) As the business portfolio increases (e.g., the firm becomes more diversified)

2) As acquisition activity expands

3) As alliance activity increases

4) As a firm's size grows

5) As top management team interdependence increases

Results of the Menz and Sheef study reveal that an increase in management interdependence and growth in acquisition activity were most commonly associated with hiring a new CSO.

Source: Based on Markus Menz and Christine Sheef, "Chief Strategy Officers: Contingency Analysis of Their Presence in Top Management Teams," *Strategic Management Journal* 35, no. 3 (March 2014): 461–471.

TABLE 1-1 Ten Famous, Strategic-Planning–Relevant Quotes from NFL Coaches

1. "Perfection is not attainable. But if we chase perfection, we can catch excellence." —*Vince Lombardi, Head Coach Green Bay Packers (1959–67)*

2. "Leadership is a matter of having people look at you and gain confidence…. If you're in control, they're in control." —*Tom Landry, Head Coach Dallas Cowboys (1960–88)*

3. "On a team, it's not the strength of the individual players, but it is the strength of the unit and how they all function together." —*Bill Belichick, Head Coach New England Patriots (2000– Present), New York Jets (1999), Cleveland Browns (1991–95)*

4. "If you want to win, do the ordinary things better than anyone else does them day in and day out." —*Chuck Noll, Head Coach Pittsburgh Steelers (1969–91)*

5. "Leaders are made, they are not born. They are made by hard effort, which is the price which all of us must pay to achieve any goal that is worthwhile." —*Vince Lombardi, Head Coach Green Bay Packers (1959–67)*

6. "Try not to do too many things at once. Know what you want, the number one thing today and tomorrow. Persevere and get it done." —*George Allen, Head Coach Los Angeles Rams (1957, 1966–70), Chicago Bears (1958–65), Washington Redskins (1971–77)*

7. "You fail all the time, but you aren't a failure until you start blaming someone else." —*Bum Phillips, Head Coach Houston Oilers (1975–80), New Orleans Saints (1981–85)*

8. "Success demands singleness of purpose." —*Vince Lombardi, Head Coach Green Bay Packers (1959–67)*

9. "Stay focused. Your start does not determine how you're going to finish." —*Herm Edwards, Head Coach New York Jets (2001–05), Kansas City Chiefs (2006–08)*

10. "Nobody who ever gave his best regretted it." —*George S. Halas, Head Coach Chicago Bears (1933–42, 1946–55, 1958–67)*

Source: A variety of sources.

win the NCAA college basketball national championship versus Duke.[10] Switching to football, some inspirational, strategic-planning–related quotes from legendary National Football League (NFL) coaches are provided in Table 1-1.

Vision and Mission Statements

Many organizations today develop a **vision statement** that answers the question "What do we want to become?" Developing a vision statement is often considered the first step in strategic planning, preceding even development of a mission statement. Many vision statements are a single sentence. For example, the vision statement of Stokes Eye Clinic in Florence, South Carolina, is "Our vision is to take care of your vision."

Mission statements are "enduring statements of purpose that distinguish one business from other similar firms. A mission statement identifies the scope of a firm's operations in product and market terms."[11] It addresses the basic question that faces all strategists: "What is our business?" A clear mission statement describes the values and priorities of an organization. Developing a mission statement compels strategists to think about the nature and scope of present operations and to assess the potential attractiveness of future markets and activities. A mission statement not only broadly charts the future direction of an organization but it also serves as a constant reminder to its employees of why the organization exists and what the founders envisioned when they put their fame and fortune (and names) at risk to breathe life into their dreams.

External Opportunities and Threats

External opportunities and **external threats** refer to economic, social, cultural, demographic, environmental, political, legal, governmental, technological, and competitive trends and events that could significantly benefit or harm an organization in the future. Opportunities and threats are largely beyond the control of a single organization—thus the word *external*. Some general categories of opportunities and threats are listed in Table 1-2, but be mindful that dollars, numbers, percentages, ratios, and quantification are essential, so strategists can assess the magnitude

TABLE 1-2 Some General Categories of Opportunities and Threats

- Availability of capital can no longer be taken for granted.
- Consumers expect green operations and products.
- Marketing is moving rapidly to the Internet.
- Commodity food prices are increasing.
- An oversupply of oil is driving oil and gas prices down.
- Computer hacker problems are increasing.
- Intense price competition is plaguing most firms.
- Unemployment and underemployment rates remain high globally.
- Interest rates are low but rising.
- Product life cycles are becoming shorter.
- State and local governments are financially weak.
- Drug cartel–related violence is increasing in Mexico.
- Winters are colder and summers are hotter than usual.
- Birth rates are declining in most countries.
- Global markets offer the highest growth in revenues.
- New laws are passed.
- Competitors introduce new products.
- National catastrophes occur.
- The value of the Euro is rebounding.
- The separation between the rich and poor is growing.
- Social media networking is greatly expanding.
- The Russian ruble has dropped 60 percent in value.

of opportunities and threats and take appropriate actions. For example, in Table 1-2, rather than saying "Marketing is moving rapidly to the Internet," strategists who take the time to do research would find, for example, that "spending on online advertisements globally rose about 25 percent in 2014, according to eMarketer, and represented about 39 percent of total advertising spending in the USA.[12] Strategies must be formulated and implemented based on specific factual information to the extent possible—because so much is at stake in having a good game plan.

External trends and events are creating a different type of consumer and consequently a need for different types of products, services, and strategies. Many companies in many industries face the severe threat of online sales eroding brick-and-mortar sales. A competitor's strength could be a threat, or a rival firm's weakness could be an opportunity.

A basic tenet of strategic management is that firms need to formulate strategies to take advantage of external opportunities and avoid or reduce the impact of external threats. For this reason, identifying, monitoring, and evaluating external opportunities and threats are essential for success. This process of conducting research and gathering and assimilating external information is sometimes called **environmental scanning** or *industry analysis*. Lobbying is one activity that some organizations use to influence external opportunities and threats.

Internal Strengths and Weaknesses

Internal strengths and **internal weaknesses** are an organization's controllable activities that are performed especially well or poorly. They arise in the management, marketing, finance/accounting, production/operations, research and development, and management information systems (MIS) activities of a business. Identifying and evaluating organizational strengths and weaknesses in the functional areas of a business is an essential strategic-management activity. Organizations strive to pursue strategies that capitalize on internal strengths and eliminate internal weaknesses.

Strengths and weaknesses are determined relative to competitors. *Relative deficiency or superiority is important information.* Also, strengths and weaknesses can be determined by elements of *being* rather than *performance.* For example, a strength may involve ownership of natural resources or a historic reputation for quality. Strengths and weaknesses may be determined relative to a firm's own objectives. For instance, high levels of inventory turnover may not be a strength for a firm that seeks never to stock-out.

In performing a strategic-management case analysis, it is important to be as divisional as possible when determining and stating internal strengths and weaknesses. In other words, for a company such as Walmart saying, "Sam Club's revenues grew 11 percent in the recent quarter," is much better than Walmart couching all of its internal factors in terms of the firm as a *whole*. "Being divisional" will enable strategies to be more effectively formulated because in strategic planning, firms must allocate resources among divisions (segments) of the firm (that is, by product, region, customer, or whatever the various units of the firm are), such as Walmart's Sam's Club versus Walmart's Supercenters, or Walmart's Mexico segment versus Walmart's Europe segment.

Both internal and external factors should be stated as specifically as possible, using numbers, percentages, dollars, and ratios, as well as comparisons over time to rival firms. *Specificity is important because strategies will be formulated and resources allocated based on this information.* The more specific the underlying external and internal factors, the more effectively strategies can be formulated and resources allocated. Determining the numbers takes more time, but survival of the firm often is at stake, so doing some research and incorporating numbers associated with key factors is essential.

Internal factors can be determined in a number of ways, including computing ratios, measuring performance, and comparing to past periods and industry averages. Various types of surveys also can be developed and administered to examine internal factors, such as employee morale, production efficiency, advertising effectiveness, and customer loyalty.

Long-Term Objectives

Objectives can be defined as specific results that an organization seeks to achieve in pursuing its basic mission. Long-term means more than one year. Objectives are essential for organizational success because they provide direction; aid in evaluation; create synergy; reveal priorities; focus coordination; and provide a basis for effective planning, organizing, motivating, and controlling activities. Objectives should be challenging, measurable, consistent, reasonable, and clear. In a multidimensional firm, objectives are needed both for the overall company and each division.

Strategies

Strategies are the means by which **long-term objectives** will be achieved. Business strategies may include geographic expansion, diversification, acquisition, product development, market penetration, retrenchment, divestiture, liquidation, and joint ventures. Strategies currently being pursued by some companies are described in Table 1-3.

Strategies are potential actions that require top-management decisions and large amounts of the firm's resources. They affect an organization's long-term prosperity, typically for at least five years, and thus are future-oriented. Strategies also have multifunctional and multidivisional consequences and require consideration of both the external and internal factors facing the firm.

Annual Objectives

Annual objectives are short-term milestones that organizations must achieve to reach long-term objectives. Like long-term objectives, annual objectives should be measurable, quantitative, challenging, realistic, consistent, and prioritized. They must also be established at the corporate, divisional, and functional levels in a large organization. Annual objectives should be stated in terms of management, marketing, finance/accounting, production/operations, R&D, and MIS accomplishments. A set of annual objectives is needed for each long-term objective. These objectives are especially important in strategy implementation, whereas long-term objectives are particularly important in strategy formulation. Annual objectives provide the basis for allocating resources.

TABLE 1-3 Sample Strategies in Action in 2015

General Electric Company (GE)

General Electric Company recently sold its appliance business to Sweden-based Electrolux AB for $3.3 billion, leaving GE focused almost entirely on finance and big-ticket industrial equipment, such as power turbines, locomotives, and aircraft engines. GE's CEO Jeff Immelt, when asked "What is GE?," recently responded with the word *energy,* rather than *insurance, plastics, media, consumer finance,* or *appliances.* Founded by Thomas Edison in 1889 and originally named Edison General Electric Company, GE is returning to its roots as an energy company. The company has spent about $14 billion lately buying oil-and-gas service companies, while divesting dishwashers, radios, stoves, microwaves, and toasters.

Chuy's (CHUY)

Chuy's is a chain of 59 small Mexican restaurants scattered across the United States. It is not "fast casual," like Chipotle Mexican Grill; rather, it is a sit-down, table-service restaurant that is uniquely festive, including, for example, Elvis shrines and complimentary Happy Hour nacho bars served out of makeshift car trunks. The décor also includes walls that feature customer-submitted snapshots of their pet dogs. Chuy's uniqueness and strategies are working great, as revenue soared 20 percent to $64.1 million in its latest quarter. The company opened 11 more locations in the last 12 months. At the individual restaurant level, Chuy's reported a 3 percent improvement in comps, comprised of a 1.3 percent increase in customers and a 1.7 percent bump in the average check. Chuy's comparable restaurant sales have increased for 17 consecutive quarters. Unlike Chipotle, which recently increased prices, Chuy's has absorbed numerous commodity increases, keeping most of its menu items below $10.

Source: Company documents and a variety of sources.

Policies

Policies are the means by which annual objectives will be achieved. Policies include guidelines, rules, and procedures established to support efforts to achieve stated objectives. Policies are guides to decision making and address repetitive or recurring situations. Usually, policies are stated in terms of management, marketing, finance/accounting, production/ operations, R&D, and MIS activities. They may be established at the corporate level and apply to an entire organization, at the divisional level and apply to a single division, or they may be established at the functional level and apply to particular operational activities or departments.

Like annual objectives, policies are especially important in strategy implementation because they outline an organization's expectations of its employees and managers. Policies allow consistency and coordination within and between organizational departments. Policy change is sometimes difficult. For example, years ago, it was unquestioningly accepted that people could smoke in their offices, in restaurants, in hotels, and on airplanes. But as people and companies became educated about the harms of smoking—not only to smokers but also to nonsmokers —policy in businesses began to change. Even with the vast changes in smoking in public areas, smoking rates are still high. In the United States, Kentucky takes the lead in having more smokers than in any other state: 30.2 percent of residents, followed by West Virginia and Mississippi; Utah has the lowest rate (12.2%), followed by California and Minnesota.[13] In the United States overall, 20.5 percent of men smoke, compared to 15.8 percent of women. For a brief time, people thought the answer might be "tobacco-less" cigarettes, as electronic cigarettes hit the market. Unfortunately, however, the product still injects nicotine into the smoker's body.

Substantial research suggests that a healthier workforce can more effectively and efficiently implement strategies. Smoking has become a heavy burden for Europe's state-run social welfare systems, with smoking-related diseases costing more than $100 billion a year. Smoking also is a huge burden on companies worldwide, so firms are continually implementing policies to curtail smoking. Starbucks has banned smoking within 25 feet of its 7,000 stores not located inside another retail establishment.

The Strategic-Management Model

The strategic-management process can best be studied and applied using a model. Every model represents some kind of process. The framework illustrated in Figure 1-1 is a widely accepted, comprehensive model of the strategic-management process.[14] This model does not guarantee success, but it does represent a clear and practical approach for formulating, implementing, and evaluating strategies. Relationships among major components of the strategic-management process are shown in the model, which appears in all subsequent chapters with appropriate areas shaped to show the particular focus of each chapter. This text is organized around this model because the model reveals how organizations actually do strategic planning. Three important questions to answer in developing a strategic plan are as follows:

Where are we now?

Where do we want to go?

How are we going to get there?

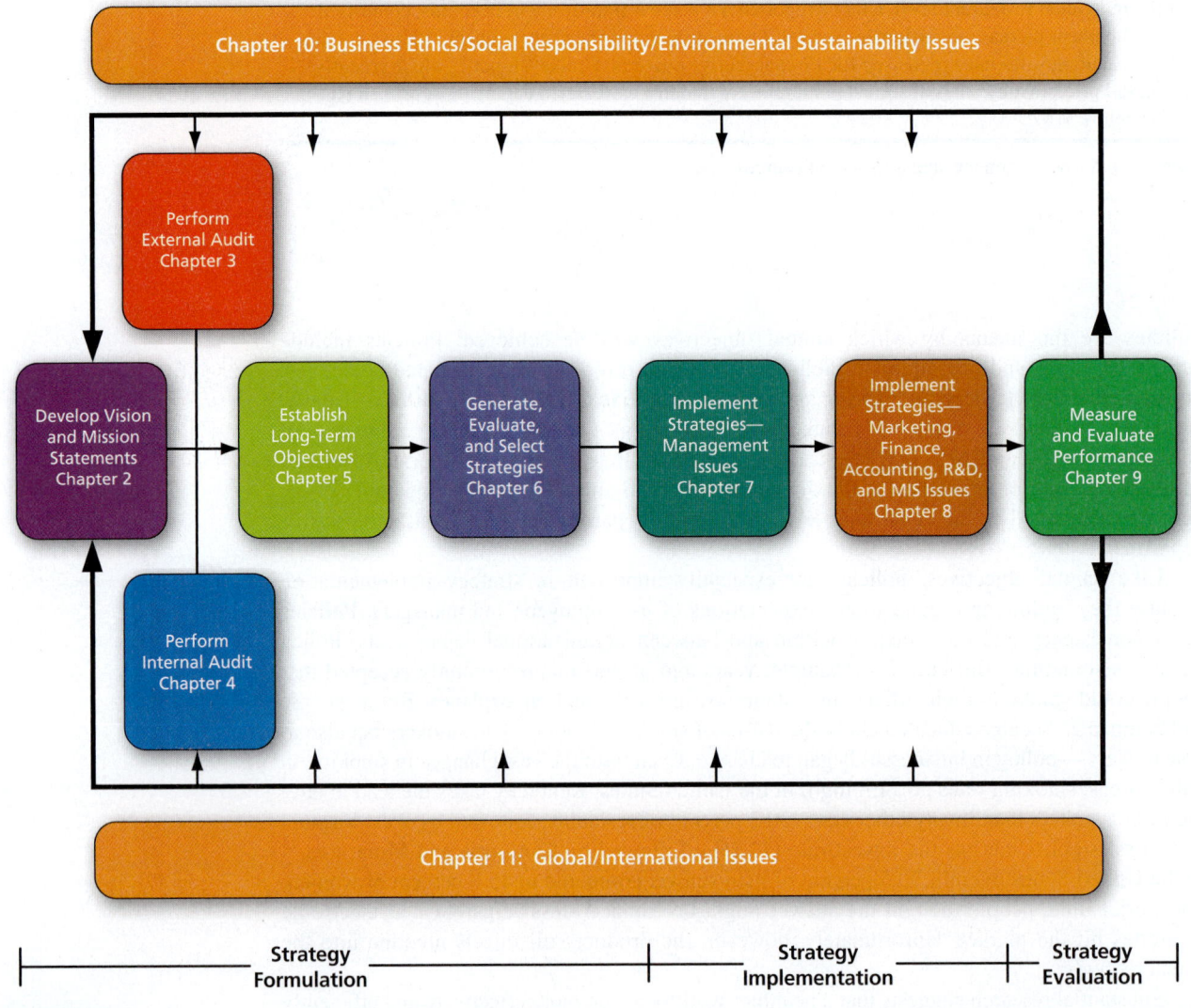

FIGURE 1-1

A Comprehensive Strategic-Management Model

Source: Fred R. David, "How Companies Define Their Mission," *Long Range Planning* 22, no. 3 (June 1988): 40. See also Anik Ratnaningsih, Nadjadji Anwar, Patdono Suwignjo, and Putu Artama Wiguna, "Balance Scorecard of David's Strategic Modeling at Industrial Business for National Construction Contractor of Indonesia," *Journal of Mathematics and Technology,* no. 4 (October 2010): 20.

Identifying an organization's existing vision, mission, objectives, and strategies is the logical starting point for strategic management because a firm's present situation and condition may preclude certain strategies and may even dictate a particular course of action. Every organization has a vision, mission, objectives, and strategy, even if these elements are not consciously designed, written, or communicated. The answer to where an organization is going can be determined largely by where the organization has been!

The strategic-management process is dynamic and continuous. A change in any one of the major components in the model can necessitate a change in any or all of the other components. For instance, African countries coming online could represent a major opportunity and require a change in long-term objectives and strategies; a failure to accomplish annual objectives might require a change in policy; or a major competitor's change in strategy might require a change in the firm's mission. Therefore, strategy formulation, implementation, and evaluation activities should be performed on a continual basis, not just at the end of the year or semiannually. The strategic-management process never really ends.

Note in the **strategic-management model** that business ethics, social responsibility, and environmental sustainability issues impact all activities in the model, as discussed in Chapter 10. Also, note in the model that global and international issues impact virtually all strategic decisions, as described in detail in Chapter 11.

The strategic-management process is not as cleanly divided and neatly performed in practice as the strategic-management model suggests. Strategists do not go through the process in lockstep fashion. Generally, there is give-and-take among hierarchical levels of an organization. Many organizations conduct formal meetings semiannually to discuss and update the firm's vision, mission, opportunities, threats, strengths, weaknesses, strategies, objectives, policies, and performance. These meetings are commonly held off-premises and are called **retreats**. The rationale for periodically conducting strategic-management meetings away from the work site is to encourage more creativity and candor from participants. Good communication and feedback are needed throughout the strategic-management process. The Academic Research Capsule 1-2 reveals what activity is most important in the strategic-management process.

Application of the strategic-management process is typically more formal in larger and well-established organizations. Formality refers to the extent that participants, responsibilities, authority, duties, and approach are specified. Smaller businesses tend to be less formal. Firms that compete in complex, rapidly changing environments, such as technology companies, tend to be more formal in strategic planning. Firms that have many divisions, products, markets, and technologies also tend to be more formal in applying strategic-management concepts. Greater formality in applying the strategic-management process is usually positively associated with organizational success.[15]

Benefits of Engaging in Strategic Management

Strategic management allows an organization to be more proactive than reactive in shaping its own future; it allows an organization to initiate and influence (rather than just respond to) activities—and thus to exert control over its own destiny. Small business owners, chief executive

ACADEMIC RESEARCH CAPSULE **1-2**

What Activity Is Most Important in the Strategic-Management Process?

Recent research has examined the strategic-management process and concluded that perhaps the most important "activity" is the feedback loop, because strategy must be thought of as a "verb rather than a noun." Rose and Cray contend that strategy is a "living, evolving conceptual entity," and as such must be engulfed in flexibility. "Flexibility" should also be reflected in the structures put in place to monitor and modify strategic plans. Flexibility safeguards should increasingly be known and practiced throughout the firm, especially at lower levels of the organization. The stages of strategic management (formulation, implementation, and evaluation) are so fluid as

to be virtually indistinguishable when one starts and the other ends. Thus, in the comprehensive model illustrated, the encompassing feedback loop is vitally important to enable firms to readily adapt to changing conditions. A significant change in any activity (box) in the model could necessitate change(s) in other activities.

Source: Based on Wade Rose and David Cray "The Role of Context in the Transformation of Planned Strategy into Implemented Strategy," *International Journal of Business Management and Economic Research* 4, no. 3 (2013): 721–737.

officers, presidents, and managers of many for-profit and nonprofit organizations have recognized and realized the benefits of strategic management.

Historically, the principal benefit of strategic management has been to help organizations formulate better strategies through the use of a more systematic, logical, and rational approach for decision making. In addition, the process, rather than the decision or document, is also a major benefit of engaging in strategic management. Through involvement in the process (i.e., dialogue and participation), managers and employees become committed to supporting the organization. *Communication is a key to successful strategic management.* Communication *may be the most important word in management.* Figure 1-2 illustrates this intrinsic benefit of a firm engaging in strategic planning. Note that all firms need all employees "on a mission" to help the firm succeed.

Dale McConkey said, "Plans are less important than planning." The manner in which strategic management is carried out is therefore exceptionally important. A major aim of the process is to achieve understanding and commitment from all managers and employees. Understanding may be the most important benefit of strategic management, followed by commitment. When managers and employees understand what the organization is doing and why, they often feel a part of the firm and become committed to assisting it. This is especially true when employees also understand links between their own compensation and organizational performance. Managers and employees become surprisingly creative and innovative when they understand and support the firm's mission, objectives, and strategies. A great benefit of strategic management, then, is the opportunity that the process provides to empower individuals. **Empowerment** is the act of strengthening employees' sense of effectiveness by encouraging them to participate in decision making and to exercise initiative and imagination, and rewarding them for doing so. William Fulmer said, "You want your people to run the business as it if were their own."

Strategic planning is a learning, helping, educating, and supporting process, not merely a paper-shuffling activity among top executives. Strategic-management dialogue is more important than a nicely bound strategic-management document. The worst thing strategists can do is develop strategic plans themselves and then present them to operating managers to execute. Through involvement in the process, line managers become "owners" of the strategy. Ownership of strategies by the people who have to execute them is a key to success!

Although making good strategic decisions is the major responsibility of an organization's owner or chief executive officer, both managers and employees must also be involved in strategy formulation, implementation, and evaluation activities. Participation is a key to gaining commitment for needed changes. An increasing number of corporations and institutions are using strategic management to make effective decisions. But strategic management is not a guarantee for success; it can be dysfunctional if conducted haphazardly.

Financial Benefits

Organizations that use strategic-management concepts are generally more profitable and successful than those that do not. Businesses using strategic-management concepts show significant improvement in sales, profitability, and productivity compared to firms without systematic

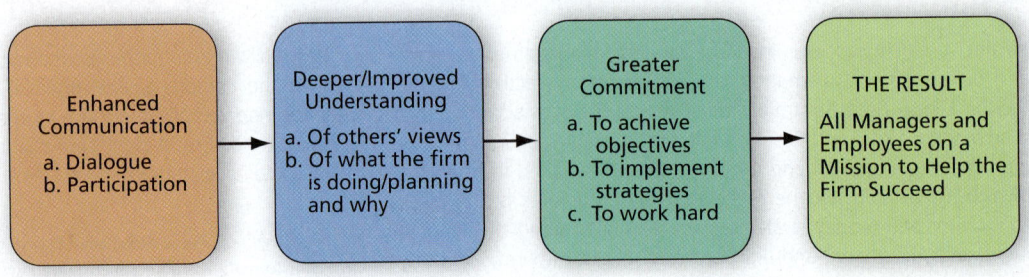

FIGURE 1-2

Benefits to a Firm That Does Strategic Planning

planning activities. High-performing firms tend to do systematic planning to prepare for future fluctuations in their external and internal environments. Firms with management systems that utilize strategic-planning concepts, tools, and techniques generally exhibit superior long-term financial performance relative to their industry.

High-performing firms seem to make more informed decisions with good anticipation of both short- and long-term consequences. In contrast, firms that perform poorly often engage in activities that are shortsighted and do not reflect good forecasting of future conditions. Strategists of low-performing organizations are often preoccupied with solving internal problems and meeting paperwork deadlines. They typically underestimate their competitors' strengths and overestimate their own firm's strengths. They often attribute weak performance to uncontrollable factors such as a poor economy, technological change, or foreign competition.

More than 100,000 businesses in the United States fail annually. Business failures include bankruptcies, foreclosures, liquidations, and court-mandated receiverships. Although many factors besides a lack of effective strategic management can lead to business failure, the planning concepts and tools described in this text can yield substantial financial benefits for any organization.

Nonfinancial Benefits

Besides helping firms avoid financial demise, strategic management offers other tangible benefits, such as enhanced awareness of external threats, improved understanding of competitors' strategies, increased employee productivity, reduced resistance to change, and a clearer understanding of performance–reward relationships. Strategic management enhances the problem-prevention capabilities of organizations because it promotes interaction among managers at all divisional and functional levels. Firms that have nurtured their managers and employees, shared organizational objectives with them, empowered them to help improve the product or service, and recognized their contributions can turn to them for help in a pinch because of this interaction.

In addition to empowering managers and employees, strategic management often brings order and discipline to an otherwise floundering firm. It can be the beginning of an efficient and effective managerial system. Strategic management may renew confidence in the current business strategy or point to the need for corrective actions. The strategic-management process provides a basis for identifying and rationalizing the need for change to all managers and employees of a firm; it helps them view change as an opportunity rather than as a threat. Some nonfinancial benefits of a firm utilizing strategic management, according to Greenley, are increased discipline, improved coordination, enhanced communication, reduced resistance to change, increased forward thinking, improved decision making, increased synergy, and more effective allocation of time and resources.[16]

Why Some Firms Do No Strategic Planning

Some firms do no strategic planning, and some firms do strategic planning but receive no support from managers and employees. Ten reasons (excuses) often given for poor or no strategic planning in a firm are as follows:

1. No formal training in strategic management
2. No understanding of or appreciation for the benefits of planning
3. No monetary rewards for doing planning
4. No punishment for not planning
5. Too busy "firefighting" (resolving internal crises) to plan ahead
6. View planning as a waste of time, since no product/service is made
7. Laziness; effective planning takes time and effort; time is money
8. Content with current success; failure to realize that success today is no guarantee for success tomorrow; even Apple Inc. is an example
9. Overconfident
10. Prior bad experience with strategic planning done sometime/somewhere

Pitfalls in Strategic Planning

Strategic planning is an involved, intricate, and complex process that takes an organization into uncharted territory. It does not provide a ready-to-use prescription for success; instead, it takes the organization through a journey and offers a framework for addressing questions and solving problems. Being aware of potential pitfalls and being prepared to address them is essential to success.

Here are some pitfalls to watch for and avoid in strategic planning:

- Using strategic planning to gain control over decisions and resources
- Doing strategic planning only to satisfy accreditation or regulatory requirements
- Too hastily moving from mission development to strategy formulation
- Failing to communicate the plan to employees, who continue working in the dark
- Top managers making many intuitive decisions that conflict with the formal plan
- Top managers not actively supporting the strategic-planning process
- Failing to use plans as a standard for measuring performance
- Delegating planning to a "planner" rather than involving all managers
- Failing to involve key employees in all phases of planning
- Failing to create a collaborative climate supportive of change
- Viewing planning as unnecessary or unimportant
- Becoming so engrossed in current problems that insufficient or no planning is done
- Being so formal in planning that flexibility and creativity are stifled[17]

Comparing Business and Military Strategy

A strong military heritage underlies the study of strategic management. Terms such as *objectives, mission, strengths,* and *weaknesses* were first formulated to address problems on the battlefield. According to *Webster's New World Dictionary, strategy* is "the science of planning and directing large-scale military operations, of maneuvering forces into the most advantageous position prior to actual engagement with the enemy."[18] The word *strategy* comes from the Greek *strategos,* which refers to a military general and combines *stratos* (the army) and *ago* (to lead). The history of strategic planning began in the military. A key aim of both business and military strategy is "to gain competitive advantage." In many respects, business strategy is like military strategy, and military strategists have learned much over the centuries that can benefit business strategists today.

Both business and military organizations try to use their own strengths to exploit competitors' weaknesses. If an organization's overall strategy is wrong (ineffective), then all the efficiency in the world may not be enough to allow success. Business or military success is generally not the happy result of accidental strategies. Rather, success is the product of both continuous attention to changing external and internal conditions and the formulation and implementation of insightful adaptations to those conditions. The element of surprise provides great competitive advantages in both military and business strategy; information systems that provide data on opponents' or competitors' strategies and resources are also vitally important.

A fundamental difference between military and business strategy is that business strategy is formulated, implemented, and evaluated with an assumption of *competition,* whereas military strategy is based on an assumption of *conflict.* Nonetheless, military conflict and business competition are so similar that many strategic-management techniques apply equally to both. Business strategists have access to valuable insights that military thinkers have refined over time. Superior strategy formulation and implementation can overcome an opponent's superiority in numbers and resources.

Born in Pella in 356 BCE, Alexander the Great was king of Macedon, a state in northern ancient Greece. Tutored by Aristotle until the age of 16, Alexander had created one of the largest empires of the ancient world by the age of 30, stretching from the Ionian Sea to the Himalayas. Alexander was undefeated in battle and is considered one of history's most successful commanders. He became the measure against which military leaders even today compare themselves, and military academies throughout the world still teach his strategies and tactics. Alexander the Great once said, "Greater is an army of sheep led by a lion, than an army of lions led by a sheep." This quote reveals the overwhelming importance of an excellent strategic plan for any organization to succeed. The legendary Alabama football coach Bear Bryant asserted, "I will defeat the opposing coach's team with my players, but if given a week's notice, I could defeat the opposing coach's team with his players and he take my players."

Both business and military organizations must adapt to change and constantly improve to be successful. Too often, firms do not change their strategies when their environment and competitive conditions dictate the need to change. Gluck offered a classic military example of this:

> When Napoleon won, it was because his opponents were committed to the strategy, tactics, and organization of earlier wars. When he lost—against Wellington, the Russians, and the Spaniards—it was because he, in turn, used tried-and-true strategies against enemies who thought afresh, who were developing the strategies not of the last war but of the next.[19]

Sun Tzu's *The Art of War* has been applied to many fields well outside of the military. Much of the text is about how to fight wars without actually having to do battle: It gives tips on how to outsmart one's opponent so that physical battle is not necessary. As such, the book has found application as a training guide for many competitive endeavors that do not involve actual combat, such as in devising courtroom trial strategy or acquiring a rival company. There are business books applying its lessons to office politics and corporate strategy. Many Japanese companies make the book required reading for their top executives. The book is a popular read among Western business managers who have turned to it for inspiration and advice on how to succeed in competitive business situations.

The Art of War has also been applied in the world of sports in preparing for athletic contests. NFL coach Bill Belichick is known to have read the book and used its lessons to gain insights in preparing for games. Australian cricket coaches, as well as Brazilian association football coaches Luis Felipe Scolari and Carolos Alberto Parreira, embraced the text. Scolari made the Brazilian World Cup squad of 2002 study the ancient work during their successful campaign.

Similarities can be construed from Sun Tzu's writings to the practice of formulating and implementing strategies among businesses today. Table 1-4 provides narrative excerpts from *The Art of War*. As you read through the table, consider which of the principles of war apply to business strategy as companies today compete aggressively to survive and grow.

TABLE 1-4 Excerpts from Sun Tzu's *The Art of War* Writings

- War is a matter of vital importance to the state: a matter of life or death, the road either to survival or ruin. Hence, it is imperative that it be studied thoroughly.

- Warfare is based on deception. When near the enemy, make it seem that you are far away; when far away, make it seem that you are near. Hold out baits to lure the enemy. Strike the enemy when he is in disorder. Avoid the enemy when he is stronger. If your opponent is of choleric temper, try to irritate him. If he is arrogant, try to encourage his egotism. If enemy troops are well prepared after reorganization, try to wear them down. If they are united, try to sow dissension among them. Attack the enemy where he is unprepared, and appear where you are not expected. These are the keys to victory for a strategist. It is not possible to formulate them in detail beforehand.

- A speedy victory is the main object in war. If this is long in coming, weapons are blunted and morale depressed. When the army engages in protracted campaigns, the resources of the state will fall short. Thus, while we have heard of stupid haste in war, we have not yet seen a clever operation that was prolonged.

- Generally, in war the best policy is to take a state intact; to ruin it is inferior to this. To capture the enemy's entire army is better than to destroy it; to take intact a regiment, a company, or a squad is better than to destroy it. For to win one hundred victories in one hundred battles is not the epitome of skill. To subdue the enemy without fighting is the supreme excellence. Those skilled in war subdue the enemy's army without battle.

- The art of using troops is this: When ten to the enemy's one, surround him. When five times his strength, attack him. If double his strength, divide him. If equally matched, you may engage him with some good plan. If weaker, be capable of withdrawing. And if in all respects unequal, be capable of eluding him.

- Know your enemy and know yourself, and in a hundred battles you will never be defeated. When you are ignorant of the enemy but know yourself, your chances of winning or losing are equal. If ignorant both of your enemy and of yourself, you are sure to be defeated in every battle.

- He who occupies the field of battle first and awaits his enemy is at ease, and he who comes later to the scene and rushes into the fight is weary. And therefore, those skilled in war bring the enemy to the field of battle and are not brought there by him. Thus, when the enemy is at ease, be able to tire him; when well fed, be able to starve him; when at rest, be able to make him move.

- Analyze the enemy's plans so that you will know his shortcomings as well as his strong points. Agitate him to ascertain the pattern of his movement. Lure him out to reveal his dispositions and to ascertain his position. Launch a probing attack to learn where his strength is abundant and where deficient. It is according to the situation that plans are laid for victory, but the multitude does not comprehend this.

- An army may be likened to water, for just as flowing water avoids the heights and hastens to the lowlands, so an army should avoid strength and strike weakness. And as water shapes its flow in accordance with the ground, so an army manages its victory in accordance with the situation of the enemy. And as water has no constant form, there are in warfare no constant conditions. Thus, one able to win the victory by modifying his tactics in accordance with the enemy situation may be said to be divine.

- If you decide to go into battle, do not announce your intentions or plans. Project "business as usual."

- Unskilled leaders work out their conflicts in courtrooms and battlefields. Brilliant strategists rarely go to battle or to court; they generally achieve their objectives through tactical positioning well in advance of any confrontation.

- When you do decide to challenge another company (or army), much calculating, estimating, analyzing, and positioning bring triumph. Little computation brings defeat.

- Skillful leaders do not let a strategy inhibit creative counter-movement. Nor should commands from those at a distance interfere with spontaneous maneuvering in the immediate situation.

- When a decisive advantage is gained over a rival, skillful leaders do not press on. They hold their position and give their rivals the opportunity to surrender or merge. They do not allow their forces to be damaged by those who have nothing to lose.

- Brilliant strategists forge ahead with illusion, obscuring the area(s) of major confrontation, so that opponents divide their forces in an attempt to defend many areas. Create the appearance of confusion, fear, or vulnerability so the opponent is helplessly drawn toward this illusion of advantage.

Note: Substitute the words *strategy* or *strategic planning* for *war* or *warfare*.

Source: Sun Tzu's The Art of War Writings, 1910, Lionel Giles.

IMPLICATIONS FOR STRATEGISTS

Figure 1-3 reveals that to gain and sustain competitive advantages, a firm must create and nurture a clear vision and mission, and then systematically formulate, implement, and evaluate strategies. Consistent business success rarely happens by chance; it most often results from careful planning followed by diligent, intelligent, hard work. If the process were easy, every business would be successful. Consistent success requires that strategists gather and assimilate relevant data, make tough trade-off decisions among various options that would benefit the firm, energize and reward employees, and continually adapt to change. To survive and prosper, a business must gain and sustain at least several major competitive advantages over rival firms.

The strategic-management process represents a systematic means for creating, maintaining, and strengthening a firm's competitive advantages. This text provides step-by-step guidance throughout the process to help strategists gain and sustain a firm's competitive advantages. As the eleven chapters unfold, more than 100 key elements of the process, ranging from developing portfolio matrices to managing workplace romance, are examined to help strategists lead the firm in delivering prosperity to shareholders, customers, and employees. The eleven chapters provide a clear, planned, journey through the strategic-management process, with numerous highlights accented along the way, so strategists can perform essential analyses and anticipate and resolve potential problems in leading their firm to success.

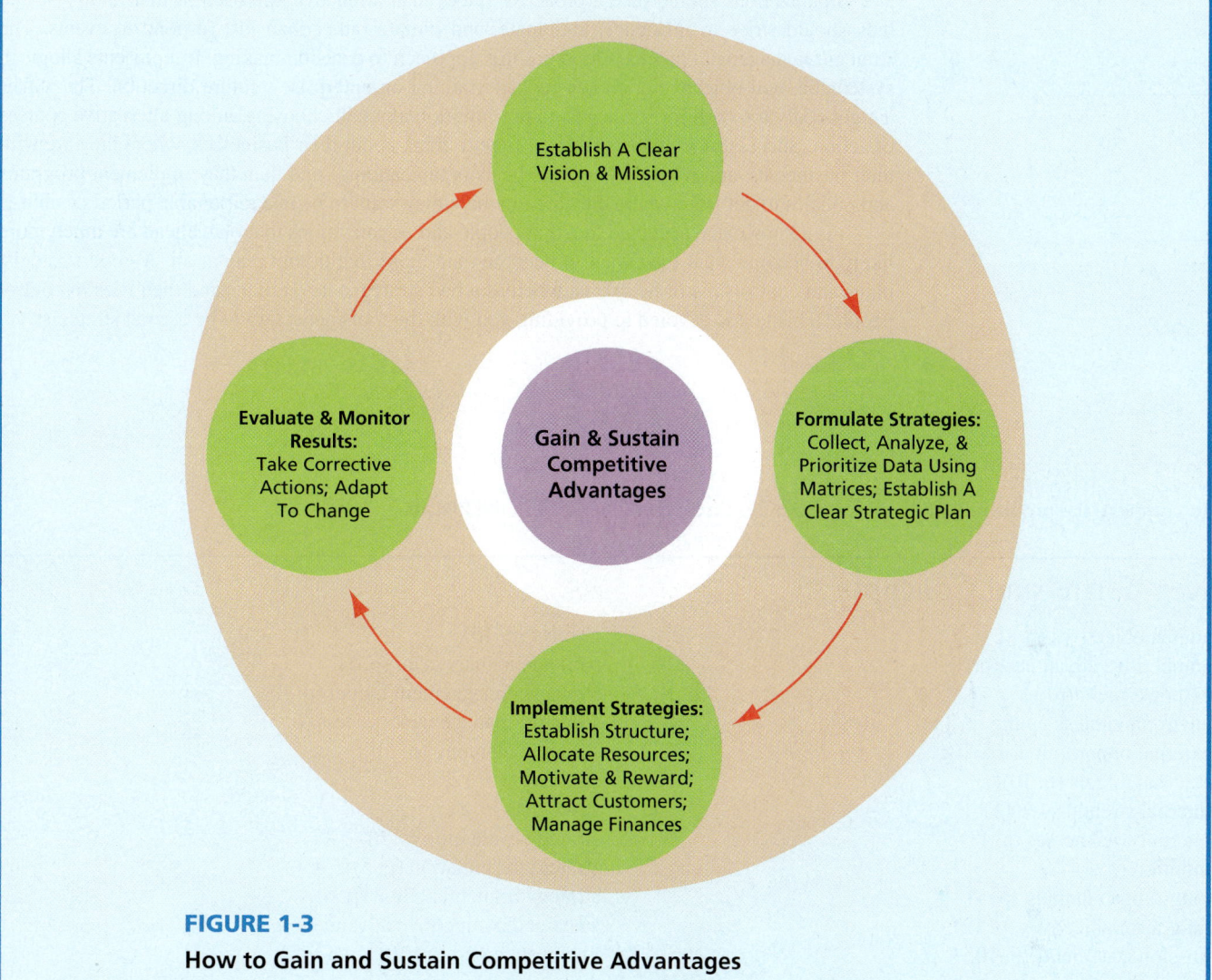

FIGURE 1-3

How to Gain and Sustain Competitive Advantages

IMPLICATIONS FOR STUDENTS

In performing strategic-management case analysis, emphasize throughout your project, beginning with the first page or slide, where your firm has competitive advantages and disadvantages. More importantly, emphasize throughout how you recommend the firm sustain and grow its competitive advantages and how you recommend the firm overcome its competitive disadvantages. Pave the way early and often in your presentation for what you ultimately recommend your firm should do over the next three years. The notion of competitive advantage should be integral to the discussion of every page or PowerPoint slide. Therefore, avoid being merely *descriptive* in your written or oral analysis; rather, be *prescriptive*, insightful, and forward-looking throughout your project.

Chapter Summary

All firms have a strategy, even if it is informal, unstructured, and sporadic. All organizations are heading somewhere, but unfortunately some organizations do not know where they are going. The old saying "If you do not know where you are going, then any road will lead you there!" accents the need for organizations to use strategic-management concepts and techniques. The strategic-management process is becoming more widely used by small firms, large companies, nonprofit institutions, governmental organizations, and multinational conglomerates alike. The process of empowering managers and employees has almost limitless benefits.

Organizations should take a proactive rather than a reactive approach in their industry, and they should strive to influence, anticipate, and initiate rather than just respond to events. The strategic-management process embodies this approach to decision making. It represents a logical, systematic, and objective approach for determining an enterprise's future direction. The stakes are generally too high for strategists to use intuition alone in choosing among alternative courses of action. Successful strategists take the time to think about their businesses, where they are with their businesses, and what they want to be as organizations—and then they implement programs and policies to get from where they are to where they want to be in a reasonable period of time.

It is a known and accepted fact that people and organizations that plan ahead are much more likely to become what they want to become than those that do not plan at all. A good strategist plans and controls his or her plans, whereas a bad strategist never plans and then tries to control people! This text is devoted to providing you with the tools necessary to be a good strategist.

MyManagementLab®

To complete the problems with the ★, go to EOC Discussion Questions in the MyLab.

Key Terms and Concepts

annual objectives (p. 12)
competitive advantage (p. 8)
empowerment (p. 16)
environmental scanning (p. 11)
external opportunities (p. 10)
external threats (p. 10)
internal strengths (p. 11)
internal weaknesses (p. 11)
intuition (p. 6)
long-range planning (p. 5)
long-term objectives (p. 12)
mission statements (p. 10)
policies (p. 13)

retreats (p. 15)
strategic management (p. 5)
strategic-management model (p. 15)
strategic-management process (p. 5)
strategic planning (p. 5)
strategies (p. 12)
strategists (p. 8)
strategy evaluation (p. 6)
strategy formulation (p. 5)
strategy implementation (p. 6)
sustained competitive advantage (p. 8)
vision statement (p. 10)

Issues for Review and Discussion

1-1. Diagram the comprehensive strategic-management model.

1-2. Develop a diagram to reveal the benefits to a firm for doing strategic planning. Include "improved understanding," "enhanced communication," "all managers and employees on a mission," and "greater commitment"—in the correct order.

1-3. How important do you believe "having an excellent game plan" is to winning a basketball or football game against your university's major rival? Discuss.

1-4. Are *strategic management* and *strategic planning* synonymous terms? Explain.

1-5. Why do many firms move too hastily from vision and mission development to devising alternative strategies?

1-6. Why are strategic-planning retreats often conducted away from the worksite? How often should firms have a retreat, and who should participate in them?

1-7. Distinguish between long-range planning and strategic planning.

1-8. Compare a company's strategic plan with a football team's game plan.

1-9. How important do you think "being adept at adapting" is for business firms? Explain.

1-10. As cited in the chapter, famous businessman Edward Deming once said, "In God we trust. All others bring data." What did Deming mean in terms of developing a strategic plan?

1-11. What strategies do you believe can save newspaper companies from extinction?

1-12. Distinguish between the concepts of *vision* and *mission*.

1-13. Your university has fierce competitors. List three external opportunities and three external threats that face your university.

1-14. List three internal strengths and three internal weaknesses that characterize your university.

1-15. List reasons why objectives are essential for organizational success.

1-16. Why are policies especially important in strategy implementation?

1-17. What is a "retreat," and why do firms take the time and spend the money to have these?

1-18. Discuss the notion of strategic planning being more formal versus informal in an organization. On a 1-to-10 scale from formal to informal, what number best represents your view of the most effective approach? Why?

1-19. List what you believe are the five most important lessons for business that can be garnered from *The Art of War* book.

1-20. What is the fundamental difference between business strategy and military strategy in terms of basic assumptions?

1-21. Explain why the strategic-management class is often called a "capstone course."

1-22. What aspect of strategy formulation do you think requires the most time? Why?

1-23. Why is strategy implementation often considered the most difficult stage in the strategic-management process?

1-24. Why is it so important to integrate intuition and analysis in strategic management?

1-25. Explain the importance of a vision and a mission statement.

1-26. Discuss relationships among objectives, strategies, and policies.

1-27. Why do you think some chief executive officers fail to use a strategic-management approach to decision making?

1-28. Discuss the importance of feedback in the strategic-management model.

1-29. How can strategists best ensure that strategies will be effectively implemented?

1-30. Give an example of a recent political development that changed the overall strategy of an organization.

1-31. Who are the major competitors of your college or university? What are their strengths and weaknesses? What are their strategies? How successful are these institutions compared to your college?

1-32. In your opinion, what is the single major benefit of using a strategic-management approach to decision making? Justify your answer.

1-33. Most students will never become a chief executive officer or even a top manager in a large company. So why is it important for all business majors to study strategic management?

1-34. Describe the content available at the Strategy Club website at www.strategyclub.com.

1-35. List four financial and four nonfinancial benefits of a firm engaging in strategic planning.

1-36. Why is it that a firm can normally sustain a competitive advantage for only a limited period of time?

1-37. Why it is not adequate simply to obtain competitive advantage?

1-38. How can a firm best achieve sustained competitive advantage?

1-39. In sequential order in the strategic-planning process, arrange the following appropriately: policies, objectives, vision, strategies, mission, strengths.

1-40. Label the following as an opportunity, a strategy, or a strength.

   a. XYZ Inc. is hiring 50 more salespersons.
   b. XYZ Inc. has 50 salespersons.
   c. XYZ Inc.'s rival firm has only 50 salespersons.

1-41. What two factors most often result in a CSO being hired or appointed by the firm?

1-42. Explain why internal strengths and weaknesses should be stated in divisional terms to the extent possible.

1-43. Explain why both internal and external factors should be stated in specific terms (that is, using numbers, percentages, money ratios, and comparisons over time) to the extent possible.

1-44. Identify the three activities that comprise strategy evaluation.

1-45. List six characteristics of annual objectives.

1-46. Would strategic-management concepts and techniques benefit foreign businesses as much as domestic firms? Justify your answer.

1-47. What do you believe are some potential pitfalls or risks in using a strategic-management approach to decision making?

1-48. What does recent research reveal to be the most important component/activity in the strategic-management process?

MyManagementLab®

Go to the Assignments section of your MyLab to complete these writing exercises.

1-49. Strengths and weaknesses should be determined relative to competitors, or by elements of being or relative to a firm's own objectives. Explain.

1-50. What are the three stages in strategic management? Which stage is more analytical? Which relies most on empowerment to be successful? Which relies most on statistics? Justify your answers.

MINI-CASE ON THE KROGER COMPANY (KR)

Source: ifoto/Fotolia

WHAT AMERICAN COMPANY DOES THE BEST JOB OF STRATEGIC PLANNING?

The answer to this question may be Kroger Company. Founded in 1883 and headquartered in Cincinnati, Ohio, Kroger is one of America's best companies for effectively formulating, implementing, and evaluating strategies. Kroger manufacturers, processes, and distributes food for sale in its supermarkets, drugstores, and convenience stores. The company not only owns and operates 325 jewelry stores—it also owns City Market, Dillons, Food 4 Less, Fred Meyer, Frys, Harris Teeter, Jay C. King Soopers, OFC, Ralphs, and Smiths. All total, Kroger operates nearly 2,700 supermarkets, and more than 1,300 of these have fuel centers. Kroger is recognized by *Forbes* as the most generous company in the United States because it actively supports hunger relief, breast cancer awareness, the military and their families, and more than 30,000 schools and grassroots organizations. The company also contributes food and funds equal to 200 million meals a year through more than 100 Feeding America food bank partners. And Kroger does all of this very profitably. In fact, Kroger dominates the supermarket industry as the largest and most profitable firm. Kroger purchased Harris Teeter Supermarkets in 2014.

Kroger tries every day to help consumers stretch their food budget in a variety of ways, including weekly promotions and fuel rewards. And Kroger continues to make natural and organic foods affordable and accessible to all customers, especially with Simple Truth. The company's brands (labels) represent about 27.3 percent of total units sold and 25.8 percent of sales dollars, excluding fuel and pharmacy. Kroger appears to be perfectly vertically integrated, owning substantial parts of its supplier, production, and distribution business network.

Even the most successful firms, however, are vulnerable strategically. Kroger is concerned that two of the world's largest supermarket chains are discussing a merger. Specifically, Dutch company Royal Ahold NV and Belgium-based Delhaize Group are talking about combining into one company. Ahold operates Giant Food Stores in Maryland, Virginia, and Washington, DC, where Kroger wants to build more Harris Teeter Supermarkets Inc. Ahold also owns Martin's Food Markets stores in Virginia. Delhaize operates Food Lion in the South, where Kroger is strong. Ahold owns Peapod, an online grocery ordering service that delivers products to customers' homes or lets them pick up orders at stores. Kroger is trying hard to enter the online grocery ordering and customer pickup service. Ahold also operates Stop & Shop in New England and the Northeast, where Kroger plans to build its first stores. Delhaize runs Hannaford stores in New England. If Ahold and Delhaize merge, that would create a company with 2,034 supermarkets in the United States, compared to Kroger's 2,625 in 34 states, and could result in a more price competitive grocery business.

Questions

1. Explain why Kroger is recognized by *Forbes* as one of the most generous companies in America. Is being generous consistent with (or inconsistent with) being a highly profitable? Discuss.
2. Which supermarket do you shop most often and why?
3. What are the three most important criteria that determine in which supermarket you shop? Does Kroger meet your criteria?
4. What response would be appropriate for Kroger if Ahold and Delhaize merge?
5. Go to the website www.finance.yahoo.com, put in KR as the stock symbol, and then click on Profile, Statistics, Competitors, and Headlines. Determine whether Kroger has continued its fantastic performance lately. Use this website, among others, throughout this course to gather research about companies.
6. Determine from the www.finance.com website who are Kroger's two primary competitors, and how is Kroger performing versus those rival companies?

Source: Company documents and a variety of sources.

Current Readings

Alber, Laura. "The CEO of Williams-Sonoma on Blending Instinct with Analysis." *Harvard Business Review* 92.9 (2014): 41–44. *Business Source Premier*. Web. 5 Sept. 2014.

Courtney, Hugh, Dan Lovallo, and Carmina Clarke. "Deciding How to Decide (Cover Story)." *Harvard Business Review* 91.11 (2013): 62–70. *Business Source Premier*. Web. 5 Sept. 2014.

Hon, Alice H. Y., Matt Bloom, and J. Michael Crant. "Overcoming Resistance to Change and Enhancing Creative Performance." *Journal of Management* 40.3 (2014): 919–941. *Business Abstracts with Full Text (H. W. Wilson)*. Web, 5 Sept. 2014.

Martin, Roger L. "The Big Lie of Strategic Planning." *Harvard Business Review* 92.1/2 (2014): 78–84. *Business Source Premier*. Web. 5 Sept. 2014.

Priem, Richard L., John E. Butler, and Sali Li. "Toward Reimagining Strategy Research: Retrospection and Prospection on the 2011 AMR Decade Award Article." *Academy of Management Review* 38.4 (2013): 471–489. *Business Source Premier*. Web. 5 Sept. 2014.

Rosenzweig, Phil. "What Makes Strategic Decisions Different (Cover Story)." *Harvard Business Review* 91.11 (2013): 88–93. *Business Source Premier*. Web. 5 Sept. 2014.

Weaver, Gary R., Scott J. Reynolds, and Michael E. Brown. "Moral Intuition: Connecting Current Knowledge to Future Organizational Research and Practice." *Journal of Management* 40.1 (2014): 100–129. *Business Abstracts with Full Text (H. W. Wilson)*. Web. 5 Sept. 2014.

Endnotes

1. Kathy Kiely, "Officials Say Auto CEOs Must Be Specific on Plans," *USA Today*, November 24, 2008, 3B.

2. Peter Drucker, *Management: Tasks, Responsibilities, and Practices* (New York: Harper & Row, 1974), 611.

3. Alfred Sloan, Jr., *Adventures of the White Collar Man* (New York: Doubleday, 1941), 104.

4. Quoted in Eugene Raudsepp, "Can You Trust Your Hunches?" *Management Review* 49, no. 4 (April 1960): 7.

5. Stephen Harper, "Intuition: What Separates Executives from Managers," *Business Horizons* 31, no. 5 (September–October 1988): 16.

6. Ron Nelson, "How to Be a Manager," *Success* (July–August 1985): 69.

7. Bruce Henderson, *Henderson on Corporate Strategy* (Boston: Abt Books, 1979), 6.

8. Robert Waterman, Jr., *The Renewal Factor: How the Best Get and Keep the Competitive Edge* (New York: Bantam, 1987). See also *BusinessWeek*, September 14, 1987, 100; and *Academy of Management Executive* 3, no. 2 (May 1989): 115.

9. Jayne O'Donnell, "Shoppers Flock to Discount Stores," *USA Today*, February 25, 2009, B1.

10. Richie Brand, "Nolan Richardson Scored a Championship Career," *Investor's Business Daily* (November 14, 2014): A3.

11. John Pearce, II, and Fred David, "The Bottom Line on Corporate Mission Statements," *Academy of Management Executive* 1, no. 2 (May 1987): 109.

12. Jack Marshall, "Online Ads Lure Cash, But Losses Still Mount," *Wall Street Journal* (August 18, 2014), B1.

13. Mike Esterl, Karishma Mehrotra, and Valerie Bauerlein, "America's Smokers: Still 40 Million Strong," *Wall Street Journal* (July 16, 2014), B1.

14. Fred R. David, "How Companies Define Their Mission," *Long Range Planning* 22, no. 1 (February 1989): 91.

15. G. L. Schwenk and K. Schrader, "Effects of Formal Strategic Planning in Financial Performance in Small Firms: A Meta-Analysis," *Entrepreneurship and Practice* 3, no. 17 (1993): 53–64. See also C. C. Miller and L. B. Cardinal, "Strategic Planning and Firm Performance: A Synthesis of More Than Two Decades of Research," *Academy of Management Journal* 6, no. 27 (1994): 1649–1665; Michael Peel and John Bridge, "How Planning and Capital Budgeting Improve SME Performance," *Long Range Planning* 31, no. 6 (October 1998): 848–856; Julia Smith, "Strategies for Start-Ups," *Long Range Planning* 31, no. 6 (October 1998): 857–872.

16. Gordon Greenley, "Does Strategic Planning Improve Company Performance?" *Long Range Planning* 19, no. 2 (April 1986): 106.

17. Adapted from www.des.calstate.edu/limitations.html and www.entarga.com/stratplan/purposes.html

18. Victoria Neufeldt, ed. *Webster's New World Dictionary*, 4th ed. (Hoboken, NJ: Pearson, 1998). Pearson purchased this dictionary from Simon & Schuster in 1998, but sold it to IDG Books in 1999.

19. Frederick Gluck, "Taking the Mystique Out of Planning," *Across the Board* (July–August 1985), 59.

THE COHESION CASE

The Hershey Company, 2015

BY FOREST R. DAVID AND MEREDITH E. DAVID

www.hersheys.com, HSY

Headquartered in Hershey, Pennsylvania, Hershey Company is the largest chocolate producer in North America and a confectionary leader worldwide, with over 80 brands, annual revenues over $7 billion, about 20,000 employees, and operations in about 80 countries. Hershey offers chocolates as well as other candies, mints, and chewing gum. Notable products include Hershey Kisses, Mr. Goodbar, Twizzlers, Jolly Ranchers, Ice Breakers, and, what may be the best-selling candy bar on the planet—Reese's, a Hershey brand that recently became an official sponsor of ESPN college football game day. Hershey is currently expanding globally with strategic emphasis on markets in China and Mexico, but the company still derives more than 85 percent of its revenue from the United States. In 2015, Hershey introduced the following new products: Kit Kat White Minis, Hershey's Caramels, Ice Breakers Cool Blast Chews, Reese's Spreads Snacksters, and Graham Dippers.

Hershey's net income for the first quarter (Q1) of 2015 declined 3.1 percent to $244 million from Q4 of 2014. Hershey's Q1 2015 revenues in China declined 47 percent. In response to this downturn, Hershey shifted its strategy in China to combat slower consumer spending by focusing on smaller rather than the largest cities, increasing its e-commerce offerings, and decreasing its reliance on hypermarkets. Also for Q1 of 2015, Hershey's advertising expenses increased 8 percent, but its selling and marketing expenses increased about 15 percent. Analysts have turned pessimistic about Hershey meeting its 20 percent sales growth guidance in China for calendar year 2015. The company's sales rose 3.5 percent to $1.94 billion for Q1 of 2015. Hershey has retail stores in New York City, Chicago, Niagara Falls, Shanghai, Dubai, Singapore, and Hershey (PA).

Copyright by Fred David Books LLC. (Written by Forest R. David and Meredith E. David)

History

In 1894, Milton Hershey of Lancaster, Pennsylvania, decided to coat his popular caramels with a sweet chocolate. This venture was actually Mr. Hershey's third attempt in the confectionary business. In a 1927 interview, Mr. Hershey shared some advice from his mother that he attributed to his success: "When you tackle a job, stick to it until you have won the battle." Mr. Hershey was never an advocate of heavy advertising, instead telling anyone who would listen that providing a quality product is the best advertising in the world. A personal motto in Mr. Hershey's office read "Business is a matter of human service."

By 1900, Hershey was producing chocolate not only for caramel coatings but also in bars and other shapes, including the world famous Hershey's Kiss in 1907. A defining feature of Hershey from early on was its assembly line systems that lowered the unit cost of chocolate to a level that most everyone could afford. The 1950s through 1980s saw great growth for Hershey from acquisitions. Most notably was the 1956 acquisition of Reese Candy Company, which produced the world-famous Reese Peanut Butter Cups that had always used Hershey's chocolate to coat its peanut butter cups. After formally changing its name to Hershey Foods Corporation in 1968, Hershey acquired marketing rights to the English firm Rowntree Mackintosh; Y&S Candies, famous for Twizzlers; and Peter Paul/Cadbury's USA confectionery operations. Peter Paul's most notable products include Almond Joy and Mounds Bars. In 2012, according to *Advertising Age* and Euromonitor International, the Hershey's Reese's brand was the No. 1-ranked candy in America, with annual sales of $2.6 billion. Globally, Reese's stood at No. 4.

Hershey's net sales for the fourth quarter of 2014 totaled $2.01 billion, but fell short of the $2.07 billion estimated by analysts. That was the sixth quarter over the past two years that Hershey's sales underperformed. However, the company's sales were higher than the prior year, partly due to Hershey acquiring the Shanghai Golden Monkey based in China. Acquiring the firm in China more than doubled Hershey's revenue derived from that country. On December 30, 2014, Hershey entered into an agreement to divest its Mauna Loa macadamia nut business, $68 million annually, to Hawaiian Host, Inc.

In early 2015, Hershey acquired KRAVE Pure Foods, Inc. for about $300 million. KRAVE is a maker of beef jerky and other high-protein snacks. Hershey made the move reportedly to tap rising interest in meat snacks, and to further the company's reach in making foods that consumers want to snack on. Hershey says the estimated $2.5 billion U.S. meat snacks category is growing at a double-digit pace. Founded in 2009, KRAVE generated about $35 million in sales in 2014. Hershey plans to operate KRAVE as a stand-alone business within its Hershey North America division; KRAVE's founder, Jon Sebastiani, continues to lead the business as President of KRAVE.

Internal Issues

Organizational Structure

Hershey has 10 top executives, as illustrated in the organizational chart given in Exhibit 1. Notice there are two segments: North America and International, with those executives reporting to the Chief Corporate Strategy and Administrative Officer. The North America segment includes only the USA and Canada. The Hershey Board of Directors is comprised of 11 members, each serving terms that expire annually.

EXHIBIT 1 **Hershey's Organizational Chart**

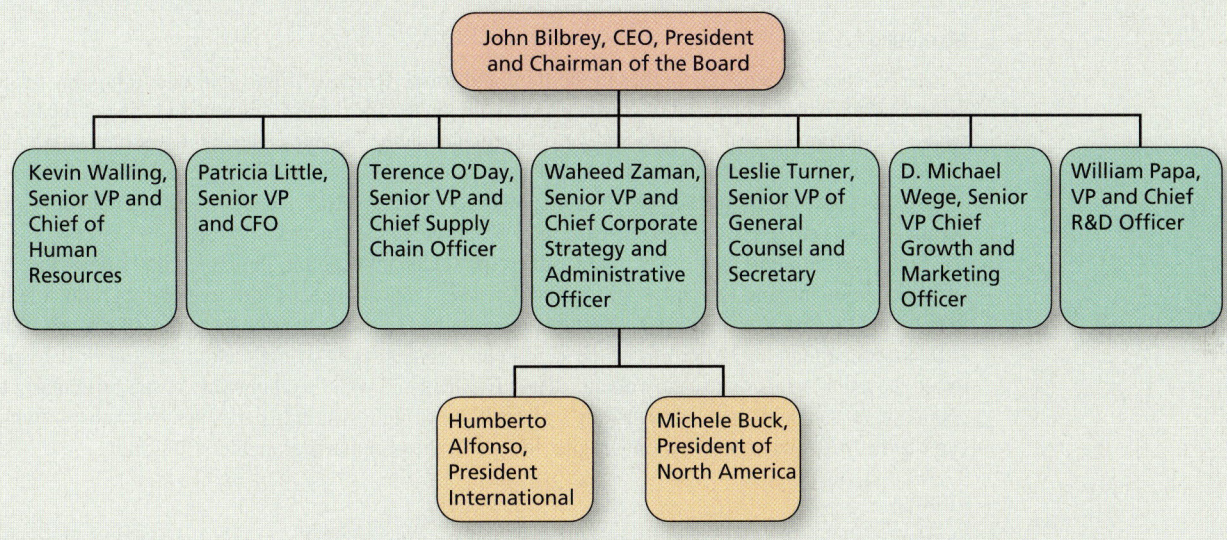

Vision/Mission

Hershey's vision statement reads: "We bring goodness to the world through great tasting snacks. One smile, one moment, and one person at a time." The company's mission statement reads as follows: "Bringing sweet moments of Hershey happiness to the world every day."

Social Responsibility

Hershey is one of the most socially responsible companies in the world and has won numerous accolades, including membership on the Dow Jones Sustainability Index and membership on The Civic 50. Hershey often ranks among the top corporations for improving the communities in which it operates. Hershey's website gives extensive narrative, numerous pictures, and many videos that substantiate the company's social responsibility efforts. For over 100 years, Hershey has been well known for owning and operating the Milton Hershey School, originally for orphan children. Today, the Milton Hershey School is the nation's largest and wealthiest boarding school for needy children, with $7.5 billion in assets for 1,900 students. Hershey spends about $110,000 a year per student, according to its nonprofit IRS tax filing—more than the nation's most expensive and elite prep schools.

In response to growing consumer demand for healthier, natural food and menu transparency, Hershey is replacing high-fructose corn syrup from its candy products as part of its efforts to use "ingredients that are simple and easy to understand." Rival Nestlé is removing all artificial flavors and FDA-certified colors from its chocolate candy, replacing them with ingredients from natural sources— a move that Nestlé says affects more than 250 products and 10 brands.

Hershey's latest Corporate Social Responsibility (CSR) Report (issued in early 2015) highlights advances the company made in 2014 on business ethics, environmental sustainability, ingredient transparency, and simple ingredients. In particular, the report revealed that in 2014, Hershey achieved 30 percent use of certified cocoa, putting Hershey ahead of schedule to hit its 2015 goal of 50 percent. Hershey has pledged to use 100 percent certified and sustainable cocoa in all chocolate products by 2020. Hershey also helped establish CocoaAction, a precompetitive industry collaboration seeking to align the cocoa sustainability efforts of the world's largest cocoa and chocolate companies to improve farmer productivity, address child labor challenges, make basic education available, and improve gender parity in cocoa production. In addition, the report stated that Hershey reduced its waste per pound of product by 1.4 percent and reduced packaging waste by a cumulative 1.75 million points through 26 companywide initiatives; reduced greenhouse gas emissions in United States distribution and logistics by 4.75 percent from 2013 baseline; and achieved zero-waste-to-landfill status at the El Salto, Mexico, facility, one of eleven Hershey facilities to achieve this milestone. In recognition of the company's many accomplishments, CEO J. P. Bilbrey was honored as a 2014 Responsible CEO of the Year by *CR Magazine*. Other 2014 notable honors for Hershey include:

Selected to Dow Jones Sustainability World and North America Index for second consecutive year
Obtained 100 percent on Corporate Equality Index
Recognized for environmental achievements by being named No.46 out of 400 in the Newsweek Green Rankings

Marketing

Hershey's sales are generally higher in the third and fourth quarters of the year, due to holiday-related sales patterns. About 25 percent of Hershey's sales are made to McLane Company, Inc., one of the largest wholesale distributors in the United States to convenience stores and mass merchandisers such as Walmart stores. Hershey has increased its overall candy, mint, and gum (CMG) market share in the United States in 2014 to 31.4 percent, an increase of 0.3 share points compared to 2013. Hershey's selling, marketing, and administrative (SM&A) expenses decreased $21.5 million, or 1.1 percent, in 2014.

Since consumption patterns of confectionery products are becoming more similar worldwide, one strategic option moving forward would be for Hershey to report financial information by product, rather than by region, and alter the firm's structure accordingly. Hershey accounts for about 44 percent of the U.S. chocolate market, 21 percent of the U.S. nonchocolate candy market, and 5 percent of the world chocolate and nonchocolate candy market share. Elevated and volatile commodity costs, particularly for cocoa, sugar, and dairy, may hurt Hershey's profitability going forward. In particular, dairy costs—which can't be hedged—have been trending higher in light of the prolonged drought in California.

Strategy

Hershey has recently embarked on a multiyear joint venture with 3D Systems, makers of 3-D printing technology, to start producing new confectionary products using this technology. 3D Systems currently produces two 3-D printers capable of making chocolate. The firm's ChefJet is priced around $5,000 and prints single-colored candy much like a plain Hershey candy bar. The ChefJet Pro, priced at around $10,000, can produce multicolored candies. Both printers are capable of printing complex candy designs at a rate of one inch per hour and sizes up to 8 inches by 10 inches by 14 inches. Some analysts, however, do not believe 3-D printing is an option for confectionaries until 2020 due to slow production and high cost factors. The technology will be affordable enough to produce specialized candies for Valentine's Day and other holidays around that time but still not affordable enough for mainstream production.

Recently, Hershey purchased Brookside-branded candy, famous for its dark-chocolate–covered candies with fruit-juice centers such as pomegranate and blueberry. Hershey purchased Shanghai Golden Monkey Food in 2014. In that year, Hershey began distribution of acquired confectionery and protein-based bean curd snacks into the China modern trade. For all of 2014, Hershey's chocolate sales in various countries grew, including China (12% vs. 7% prior year), Mexico (2% vs. 7% prior year), and Brazil (1% vs. 5% prior year).

With the KRAVE acquisition in 2015, and with the company's vision statement, Hershey's strategy is to broaden its product line more by adding healthful snacks to complement its numerous types of chocolate and nonchocolate candies. Since protein snacks are growing rapidly in popularity globally, the KRAVE acquisition may be the first of many for Hershey in that line of business. The acquisition represents one of the first times Hershey has taken a big step outside confectionery.

Hershey's 2014 international net sales increased nearly 15 percent, including a net sales contribution of approximately 7 percent, or $54 million, from Shanghai Golden Monkey Food Joint Stock Co., Ltd. (SGM). Excluding SGM and the unfavorable foreign currency exchange impact, Hershey's international net sales increased approximately 10 percent in 2014.

Segments

Hershey's primary operations and markets are in the United States. The percentage of total Hershey net sales outside of the U.S. was 17.5 percent for 2014, 16.6 percent for 2013, and 16.2 percent for 2012. The percentage of total consolidated assets outside of the U.S. was 35.4 percent as of December 31,

2014, and 19.4 percent as of December 31, 2013. Although Hershey does not report sales and income by product category, the company keeps internal records by three product segments: Chocolate, Sweets and Refreshments, and Snacks and Adjacencies. The Chocolate category consists of fancier options such as acquired Cadbury, traditional products such as Mr. Goodbar and Hershey's Kisses, and Dagoba organic chocolates. Twizzlers, Jolly Rancher, PayDay, and others are included under the Confectionary Products umbrella. Breath Savors, Bubble Yum, and Icebreakers fall under Sweets and Refreshments, and Hershey's baking chocolates and syrups are included under Snacks and Adjacencies. Hershey also offers a full line of sugar-free products. Many Hershey products are naturally gluten free and kosher in nature.

Hershey's sales and income by geographic region are given in Exhibit 2. North America accounted for 85.6, 86.8, and 87.5 percent of the company's sales in 2014, 2013, and 2012, respectively. Note in Exhibit 2 that Hershey's income from outside North America has declined steadily. All sales and income from Hershey stores are included in the International and Other segment.

EXHIBIT 2 Hershey's Net Sales and Income (in millions)

	2014	2013	2014
Sales			
North America	$6,352.7	$6,200.1	$5,812.7
International and Other	1,069.1	946.0	831.6
Total	7,421.8	7,146.1	6,644.3
Income			
North America	1,916.2	1,862.6	1,656.1
International and Other	40.0	44.6	51.4
Total	$1,956.2	$1,907.2	$1,707.5

Source: Based on Hershey's 2014 *Form 10K*, p. 25.

Finance

Hershey reported a 3.9 percent increase in revenues in 2014 to $7.42 billion, whereas company earnings increased about 7 percent overall from the prior year. The company's international net sales increased nearly 15 percent, including the negative impact of foreign currency exchange rates and positive contribution of about $54 million from Hershey's acquisition of Shanghai Golden Monkey in China.

Hershey has gained market share in every measured channel three years running, even after raising prices on many items 10 percent over the same period. In fact, Hershey has produced higher earnings every year but two since 2000. With a 34 percent market share in North America, Hershey instituted an 8 percent price hike in late 2014 on most of its chocolate products, partly in response to higher cocoa prices. The company's most recent income statements and balance sheets are provided in Exhibits 3 and 4, respectively. Note the steady increases in both revenues and net income.

EXHIBIT 3 Hershey's Income Statements (in thousands, except per share amounts)

	2014	2013	2012
Sales	$7,421,768	$7,146,079	$6,644,252
Costs and expenses			
Cost of sales	4,085,602	3,865,231	3,784,370
Selling, marketing, and administrative	1,900,970	1,922,508	1,703,796
Business realignment and impairment	45,621	18,665	44,938
Total costs and expenses	6,032,193	5,806,404	5,533,104
Income before interest and taxes	1,389,575	1,339,675	1,111,148
Interest expense	83,532	88,356	95,569
Income before taxes	1,306,043	1,251,319	1,015,579
Income taxes	459,131	430,849	354,648
Net Income	846,912	820,470	660,931
Net income per share	3.91	3.76	3.01
Dividends paid per share	2.04	1.81	1.56

Source: Based on Hershey's 2014 *Form 10K*, p. 45.

EXHIBIT 4 Hershey's Balance Sheets (in thousands)

	2014	2013
Assets		
Cash and Cash Equivalents	$ 374,854	$ 1,118,508
Short-Term Investments	97,131	—
Accounts Receivable—Trade (Net)	596,940	477,912
Inventories	801,036	659,541
Deferred Income Taxes	100,515	52,511
Prepaid Expenses and Other	276,571	178,862
Total Current Assets	2,247,047	2,487,334
Net Property, Plant, and Equipment	2,151,901	1,805,345
Goodwill	792,955	576,561
Other Intangibles	294,841	195,244
Other Assets	142,772	293,004
Total Assets	**$ 5,629,516**	**$ 5,357,488**
Liabilities and Stockholders' Equity		
Short-Term Borrowings	$ 635,501	$ 166,875
Accounts Payable	482,017	461,514
Accrued Liabilities	813,513	699,722
Accrued Income Taxes	4,616	79,911
Total Current Liabilities	1,935,647	1,408,022
Long-Term Debt	1,548,963	1,795,142
Other Long-Term Liabilities	526,003	434,068
Deferred Income Taxes	99,373	104,204
Total Liabilities	**$ 4,109,986**	**$ 3,741,436**
Stockholders' Equity		
Preferred stock shares issued: none in 2014 and 2013		
Common stock, shares issued: 299,281,967 in 2014 and 299,281,527 in 2013		
Class B common stock, shares issued: 60,619,777 in 2014 and 60,620,527 in 2013		
Additional paid-in capital	754,186	664,944
Retained earnings	5,860,784	5,454,286
Treasury stock: 138,856,786 in 2014 and 136,007,023 in 2013	(5,161,236)	(4,707,730)
Accumulated other comprehensive loss	(358,573)	(166,567)
Stockholders' equity	1,455,062	1,604,834
Noncontrolling interests in subsidiaries	64,468	11,218
Total stockholders' equity	1,519,530	1,616,052
Total liabilities and stockholders' equity	**$ 5,629,516**	**$ 5,357,488**

Source: Hershey's 2014 *Form 10K*, p. 47.

Competitors

The chocolate industry is dominated by five companies: (1) Hershey, (2) Nestlé, (3) Mars, (4) Lindt & Sprungli AG, and (5) Tootsie Roll Industries. Europe, the United States, and South America account for 54, 32, and 8 percent of total chocolate and nonchocolate candy revenues, respectively, or a dominant 94 percent. Thus, there is much room for expansion by these firms into developing nations whose disposable incomes are increasing, especially nations in Asia and Africa, but also in South America. A comparison of competitors is provided in Exhibits 5 and 6. Note that Mars dominates in nonchocolate candy. Also note that Nestlé is about 10 times larger than Hershey.

EXHIBIT 5 Hershey versus Rival Firms, Market Share (percent)

Product Type	Hershey	Mars	Nestle	Others
USA Chocolate	37	28	5	*30
USA Nonchocolate Candy	21	35	2	42
Global Chocolate and Nonchocolate Candy (non-USA)	5	14	9	**72

Source: Based on information at IBIS and a *Wall Street Journal* article on 2-18-15, p. B6. Numbers are rounded.

* Lindt & Sprungli AG contributed about 10 percent of others market share.

** Mondelez International Inc. and Ferrero SpA contributed 11 and 8 percent market shares, respectively.

EXHIBIT 6 Hershey versus Rival Firms

	Hershey	Nestlé	Tootsie Roll	Industry Avg.
# Employees	20,800	333,000	2,000	1,730
$ Revenue	7.5B	105.47B	541M	3.79B
$ Revenue per Employee	360,575	316,000	270,500	219,000
$ Net Income	840M	11.15B	62.6M	3B
$ Market Capitalization	20.7B	242B	2.08B	675M
% Operating Margin	0.19	0.15	0.15	0.05
Earnings per Share	3.76	3.49	1.03	–0.11

Source: A variety of sources.

Nestlé S.A. (stock symbol = NSRGY)

Headquartered in Vevey, Switzerland, Nestlé is a large food-processing company with 2014 revenues of 96.2 billion U.S. dollars (USD) and a net income of $15.14 billon. According it its website, Nestlé proclaims to be the top global company with respect to nutrition, health, and wellness by providing customers with nutritious and great-tasting food and beverage choices. Nestlé's mission statement is simply "Good Food, Good Life." The company produces a wide array of products ranging from baby foods, chocolate, coffee, juices, dairy, ice cream, pet care, and more. Notable chocolate products include Butterfinger, Crunch, Aero, KitKat, and Toll House chocolate chips. Wonka is also owned by Nestlé and includes Nerds, Sweetarts, Spree, Laffy Taffy, Runts, Gobstopper, Fun Dip, and many other sugary candy options. In 2013, Nestlé reported chocolate sales of $8.5 billion Swiss Francs ($8.5 billion USD) and sugary confectionary sales of 1.2 billion Swiss Francs ($1.4 billion USD). Total chocolate and sugary confectionary sales were around 10 percent of total company revenues. Total sales derived from (1) the Americas, (2) Europe, and (3) Asia, Oceania, and Africa were 44, 28, and 28 percent, respectively.

Nestlé is much more diversified than all of its chocolate competitors, except for Mars, and continues to expand its brands. Recently, Nestlé paid $12 billion to acquire Pfizer Nutrition to bolster its market share in the child nutrition market, as well as Pamlab, a U.S.-based health-care products company. In February 2014, Nestlé sold an 8 percent stake in French cosmetics firm L'Oreal and is currently planning a large share buyback of its own stock. Analysts anticipate that Nestlé will sell its remaining 23 percent stake in L'Oreal. One potential company it might try to acquire is Ferrero, an Italian firm known for producing the chocolate hazelnut spread Nutella. Analysts estimate the value of Ferrero would be around $22 billion USD.

Nestlé and Google agreed in 2014 to name Google's new Android operating system KitKat after Nestlé's world-renown chocolate wafer candy. No money changed hands on the agreement. Google benefits by having more than 50 million specially wrapped KitKat bars in 19 different nations, including the United States, where Nestlé licenses KitKat to Hershey. The 50 million KitKat bars are timed to be released with the launch of Google KitKat. The special wrappers lead consumers to Google-affiliated websites where they can win prizes such as the Google Nexus 7, and credits to spend at Google Play.

Mars, Inc.

Mars is the second-largest candy manufacturer in the United States and the third-largest privately held company in the United States according to *Forbes*. Headquartered in McLean, Virginia, and having annual sales over $30 billion, Mars, like Nestlé, is well diversified with six business units consisting of chocolate, drinks, food, symbioscience, pet care, and Wrigley chewing gum. Mars blockbuster chocolate brands include Snickers, Milky Way, M&Ms, Dove, Bounty, 3 Musketeers, Starburst, and Skittles, among others. The annual revenue of Mars in 2014 was about $35 billion— more than 50 percent higher than in 2007, largely due to the firm's 2008 acquisition of Wrigley. Since patenting recipes is difficult and producing chocolate is secretive, Mars does not allow visitors to its kitchens in its factories and facilities. Mars' first blockbuster product back in 1923 was the Milky Way candy bar, still a big seller today.

Market researcher Euromonitor International recently reported that Mars' market share in the United States rose to 28 percent from 24 percent. To further battle Hershey, in 2014, Mars opened a new 500,000 square-foot chocolate factory in Topeka, Kansas, at a cost of $270 million. The factory cranks out more than 8 million miniature Snickers candy bars and 39 million peanut M&M's every day.

Like Nestlé, Mars advocates global sustainability of the cocoa resource but has received criticism in recent years over purchasing cocoa from West African farms that use child labor. Mars is also one of the world's biggest producers of dog food and pet-care products. Mars' Wrigley division produces chewing gums, confectionery products, and a variety of other products ranging from Uncle Ben's rice to Pamesello grated cheese and Flavia coffee. Mars' pet-food brands include Pedigree, Greenies, Sheba, and Whiskas. Interestingly, chocolate is Mars' second-largest business globally, behind pet care.

Lindt & Sprungli AG

Headquartered in Switzerland, Lindt purchased U.S.-based and privately held Russell Stover in 2014 for an unreported amount, making Lindt the third-largest chocolate company in the United States (with a 10 percent market share), behind Hershey and Mars, and ahead of Nestlé. With the Russell Stover addition, Lindt acquired over 70,000 drugstore outlets for their products in the United States and Canada. Lindt also currently owns Ghirardelli Chocolate, based in San Francisco. Interestingly, Lindt is taking a slightly different strategic path than Hershey, Mars, and Nestlé. Although many top chocolate brands are betting on emerging markets such as China and India that have growth rates over 15 percent, Lindt is betting on North America with growth rates of less than 2 percent in chocolate sales. Lindt cites the main reason for sticking with the United States and Canada are they are safer markets and still will be three times larger chocolate markets than both China and India combined, even as far out as 2018. Lindt also specializes in higher- and middle-end chocolates and these products are not cost-effective options for many of the customers in China and India.

Tootsie Roll Industries (stock symbol = TR)

Headquartered in Chicago, Illinois, Tootsie Roll Industries' CEO and Chairman, Melvin Gordon, died at the age of 95 in January 2015. Gordon, with his wife, Ellen Gordon, who inherited control of the company from her father, were married for 65 years and together created one of the most secretive corporate cultures among publicly traded companies in the United States. The Gordons rarely gave interviews; indeed, they shunned media attention, issued only scant quarterly earnings reports, and tightly restricted visits to its headquarters on Chicago's South Side. An analyst once said, "I think the only way you can get a tour of Tootsie Roll's manufacturing plant is by jumping over the fence and sneaking in."

Over the decades, the Gordans acquired other well-known candy brands, assembling a portfolio of similarly time-worn-but-profitable names, including Charms Blow Pops, Sugar Babies caramels, Junior Mints, and DOTS gumdrops in addition to the eponymous chocolate chews that made Tootsie Roll famous. Tootsie Roll reported earnings of $12.9 million in Q1 of 2015, down from $15.0 million the prior year. The company's sales were $105 million in Q1 of 2015, down from $106 million the prior year. Tootsie Roll Industries became the world's largest maker of lollipops when it bought the Charms Company in 1988. The company later acquired Sugar Daddy and Junior Mints and, in 2004, Concord Confections, adding Dubble Bubble and Wack-o-Wax to the candies it produces. The company was well-known for its commercials. It claims to have received more than 20,000 letters from children trying to answer a question posed by an owl in a 1970s commercial: How many licks does it take to reach the center of a Tootsie Pop?

Tootsie Roll's brands, as well as its real estate assets in Chicago, and the fact that Gordon's children are not directly involved in the business, make the company an attractive firm to acquire, perhaps for Hershey Company, Mars, or Nestlé. Ellen Gordan, age 83, is the largest Tootsie Roll shareholder, and was even prior to her husband's death. The Gordon family holds a controlling stake in the company. Tootsie Roll trades at about 20 times its profit and has about 2,000 employees. That gives it a higher price tag than any other similar-sized public candy maker target in the last decade, even before accounting for a premium. Tootsie Roll's shares rose 8 percent to a 17-month high of $33.28 following the announcement of Mr. Gordon's death, but by May 2015, shares were back down to $30.

Ferrara Candy Company

Ferrara, not to be confused with Italy-based Ferrero maker of Nutella and other chocolate products, was founded in 1908 in Chicago and is a rapidly growing American candy company. Top products include Atomic Fireball, Lemonhead, Now&Later, Fruit Strip, and Boston Baked Beans. The firm has one plant in Mexico and produces almost exclusively nonchocolate candy. Total revenues in 2009 were $563 million, growing to over $1 billion by year end 2013. Ferrara, a rapidly growing company, generally finances through equity over debt to help improve credit ratings.

External Issues

Hershey is replacing high-fructose corn syrup in some of its products with sugar, making the firm a high-profile example of the move away from high-fructose corn syrup that may fuel weight gain and diabetes. Examples of Hershey products that use corn syrup include Almond Joy, Fifth Avenue, Take 5, and York; the American Medical Association has said there is not enough evidence to specifically restrict the use of the syrup. The Corn Refiners Association recently hired market-research firms Mintel and Nielsen to study perceptions of sweeteners, and reported "67% of consumers agree that moderation is more important than specific sweetener types." In the food and beverage industry, soda accounts for a majority of the market for high-fructose corn syrup. Interestingly, Hunt's ketchup is an example product that switched to more sugar but then switched back to corn syrup, seeing no change in the sales of Hunt's. The Food and Drug Administration has denied requests by some companies to have their sweetening agent renamed "corn sugar" on nutrition labels. Chocolate sales in the United States are increasing about 3 percent annually, compared with a 2 percent increase for total packaged food. The chocolate increases are recorded despite a trend toward more healthful eating.

Due to growing consumer demand for healthier food, Nestle SA recently removed artificial flavors and colors from its Crunch and Butterfinger candy bars and other chocolates in the USA. Nestle USA is the first major U.S. candy manufacturer to remove such artificial ingredients, such as Red 40, Yellow 5, and vanillin. For example, natural vanilla flavor is replacing vanillin in Crunch bars, and annatto is replacing artificial food colorings.

Cocoa Prices

When Hershey was founded over 100 years ago, chocolate was generally considered a luxury for the rich and out of the grasp of lower-income customers. Mr. Hershey changed this, at least with respect to U.S. customers, by creating an automated assembly line system and competing on economies of scale. Some 100 years later, once again, chocolate demand is on the increase. This time, however, the increase in demand is not from falling chocolate prices like it was 100 years earlier but rather from millions of new consumers in emerging worldwide markets being able to afford increasingly higher-quality chocolates that require better and higher percentages of cocoa. Unlike other crops, such as corn or soybeans, cocoa is more difficult to produce and cocoa prices are expected to rise substantially moving forward, according to the International Cocoa Organization (ICO).

Typically, cocoa trees take as many as 10 years to mature, and many of today's trees are old, not yielding the same number or quality of beans. Farmers are also switching to more profitable crops, even as the price of cocoa approaches $3,000 per ton. Analysts estimate the cocoa price would need to be $3,500 per ton to maintain current production rates from farmers. In fact, the ICO expects the demand to production ratio to be the highest ever by 2018, since it started keeping records in 1960. In 2013 alone, worldwide consumption of cocoa beans was up 32 percent from 2012 and Chinese demand is projected to rise 5 percent annually through 2018. To help combat the new demand, Mars and Nestlé have spent millions to educate farmers in West Africa on proper techniques and in developing new types of cocoa trees. The Ebola virus outbreak in West Africa threatened hundreds of cocoa farms.

North American–based Blommer Chocolate Company is a top cocoa processor and one of the main suppliers to Hershey and other chocolate-producing companies. Blommer is expanding its processing capacity to meet strong U.S. chocolate demand. Nevertheless, chocolate companies are facing tough choices that include raising prices, reducing portion sizes, or even using less cocoa in its products. As early as 2006, Hershey started using substitutes for cocoa butter in the production of Krackel and Mr. Goodbar, which resulted in the firm having to change the label "milk chocolate" to "made with chocolate" or "chocolate candy" to comply with the Food and Drug Administration (FDA) protocols for the labeling of chocolate food items. Hershey, however, is now switching both Krackel and Mr. Goodbar back to solid milk chocolate, meaning the bars will contain at least 10 percent cocoa per FDA regulations to be called *milk chocolate*. Also hurting Hershey are lower grain prices used in potentially substitute snack products such as pretzels, cookies, and other snacks.

Potential Taxes and Health-Minded Public

There is a growing awareness worldwide of the dangers of unhealthful eating, especially when it comes to sugars, processed foods, and animal fats. Many different governments (local, regional, and national) have increased (or plan to) taxes or have flat out banned unhealthy items. Taxes are viewed by governments much like tobacco taxes as a way not only to curb citizens' consumption but also as an additional means of revenues. For example, Connecticut recently proposed a 2 percent additional tax on all soda, suggesting it would provide $144 million in annual revenues and reduce soda consumption in the state. New York City has banned most sugary drinks 16 ounces and larger from being served. The Navajo Nation, the largest American Indian Reservation in the United States with 300,000 members, is proposing a tax of up to 7 percent on fatty snacks and soda, up from the current level of 5 percent, and excluding healthful food items from taxation. Former NBA star Yao Ming is campaigning in his home country of China to promote healthier eating and exercise habits. Mexico recently passed legislation to significantly tax both sugary drinks and high-calorie items such as candy, and in 2012, Peru, Uruguay, and Costa Rica banned all junk food from public schools, including candy bars. Many other nations in Latin America require red or yellow circles around sugar content on the packaging of items, depending on their sugar content. All of these actions and trends are a threat to Hershey.

Increasing obesity is a major problem among the world's population. Processed sugar negatively impacts the body by increasing chances of tooth decay, obesity, and diabetes, and additionally can significantly increase one's chances of getting heart disease and even cancer. Scientific tests reveal that sugar is basically a food for cancer cells and people who drink 2 soft drinks a week are 87 percent more likely to develop pancreatic cancer. For comparison, a Hershey Milk Chocolate bar contains 24g of sugar, a Hershey Dark Chocolate bar contains 21g of sugar, and a can of cola contains around 39g of sugar. Sugar is also believed to be damaging to one's skin, looks, and overall mood. Moving forward, Hershey could consider increased marketing of dark chocolate, which contain good antioxidants, but is much higher in saturated fat than milk chocolate and contains high levels of sugar. Sugar-free candy has also been linked to cancer and weight gain, partly because artificial sweeteners are not healthy.

Panera Bread Company is removing 150 artificial ingredients from its kitchens by 2017. The types of ingredients being eliminated at Panera include artificial sweeteners, preservatives, and artificial flavor enhancers. Food companies are increasingly eliminating unnatural and unhealthy ingredients. For example, Kraft Foods Group is replacing the artificial orange colorings in its macaroni and cheese product with natural colorings made from spices like turmeric and paprika. PepsiCo is replacing its artificial sweetener aspartame used in Diet Pepsi with sucralose. Dunkin' Donuts is removing titanium dioxide, a whitening agent used in sunscreen, from its powdered doughnut recipes, but only after an environmental advocacy group said it found nanoparticles in the company's white powdered sugar through independent laboratory tests. The environmental group says nanoparticles, such as titanium dioxide, could cause damage to cells and tissues.

Conclusion

Developed in partnership with 3-D Systems (stock symbol = DDD), Hershey Company's new 3-D printing gives consumers nearly endless possibilities for personalizing their chocolate. Hershey has a new 3-D exhibit and 3-D chocolate printer (the most advanced model in operation today) on display at Hershey's Chocolate World Attraction in Hershey, Pennsylvania.

An analyst once said that "strategic planning is more about deciding what strategies not to pursue than it is about deciding what to do." This may be especially true for Hershey Company, which has many good options. Most nations of the world would be pleased to see Hershey extend their product lines into their country. Even in the United States, customers desire to see new Hershey products introduced annually. Hershey could continue to acquire firms in the healthful snacks business such as KRAVE, or acquire firms in the candy business, such as Tootsie Roll Industries, or simply grow more organically by building manufacturing plants and distribution facilities globally. There are more than 150 countries on the planet where Hershey products are still not available. Most people in those countries would welcome chocolate.

Hershey needs a clear strategic plan going forward. Develop a strategic plan that will enable the company to meet its many obligations, not only to the 1,900 girls and boys at the Milton Hershey School but also to its thousands of shareholders who expect to see the company grow both revenues and profits annually.

ASSURANCE OF LEARNING EXERCISES

EXERCISE 1A

Compare Business Strategy with Military Strategy

Purpose

This exercise will enable you to compare and contrast military strategy with business strategy because in many ways, operating a business is similar to conducting a military campaign. Many strategic-management concepts evolved from the military. Napoleon Bonaparte listed 115 maxims for military strategy. U.S. Civil War General Nathan Bedford Forrest, however, had only one strategic principle: "to git thar furst with the most men" (to get there first with the most men). The strategy concepts given as essential in the United States Army's Field Manual (FM-3-0) of Military Operations (sections 4–32 to 4–39) says there are nine key military strategy maxims:

1. Objective—Direct every military operation toward a clearly defined, decisive, and attainable objective.
2. Offensive—Seize, retain, and exploit the initiative.
3. Mass—Concentrate combat power at the decisive place and time.
4. Economy of Force—Allocate minimum essential combat power to secondary efforts.
5. Maneuver—Place the enemy in a disadvantageous position through the flexible application of combat power.
6. Unity of Command—For every objective, ensure unity of effort under one responsible commander.
7. Security—Never permit the enemy to acquire an unexpected advantage.
8. Surprise—Strike the enemy at a time, at a place, or in a manner for which he is unprepared.
9. Simplicity—Prepare clear, uncomplicated plans and clear, concise orders to ensure thorough understanding.

Instructions

Step 1	Consider the extent to which each of the nine maxims listed are applicable in formulating and implementing strategies in a business setting.
Step 2	Rank-order the nine maxims, from 1 = most important to 9 = least important in formulating and implementing strategies in a business setting.
Step 3	Compare your ranking to our (the authors') ranking by getting the difference between each of your rankings and each of the authors' rankings, and summing those differences (i.e., summing the absolute value of those differences).
Step 4	Determine who in the class has the lowest summed difference score. This student(s) scored best in the class on this exercise based on the authors' rankings.

EXERCISE 1B

Gather Strategy Information for the Hershey Company

Purpose

The purpose of this exercise is to get you familiar with strategy terms introduced and defined in this chapter. Let's apply these terms to Hershey (stock symbol = HSY).

Instructions

Step 1	Go to www.thehersheycompany.com (Hershey's website). Along the top of the site, click on *Investors*. Then click *Financial Reports*. Then click on *Annual Reports*. Then print the company's latest *Form 10K*, a document that contains excellent information for developing a list of Hershey's internal strengths and weaknesses.
Step 2	Go to your college library website and print a copy of Standard & Poor's *Industry Surveys* for the confectionery industry. This document will contain excellent information for developing a list of external opportunities and threats facing HSY.

Step 3   Go to the www.finance.yahoo.com website. Enter HSY. Note the wealth of information on Hershey that may be obtained by clicking any item along the left column. Click on *Competitors* down the left column. Print out the resultant tables and information. Note that Hershey's major competitors are Mars, Inc., Mondelez International, Inc., and Nestlé S.A.

Step 4   Using the Hershey Company Cohesion Case, the www.finance.yahoo.com information, the *Form 10K*, and the S&P *Industry Survey* document, on a separate sheet of paper list what you consider to be Hershey's 10 major strengths, 10 major weaknesses, 10 major opportunities, and 10 major threats. Each factor listed for this exercise must include a percentage, number, dollar, or ratio to reveal some quantified fact or trend. These factors provide the underlying basis for a strategic plan because a firm strives to take advantage of strengths, improve weaknesses, avoid threats, and capitalize on opportunities.

Step 5   Through class discussion, compare your lists of external and internal factors to those developed by other students and add to your lists of factors. Keep this information for use in later exercises at the end of other chapters.

Step 6   Whatever case company is assigned to you this semester, update the information on your company by following the steps listed in this Exercise 1B.

EXERCISE 1C
Update the Hershey Cohesion Case

Purpose
Every week Hershey updates its website with News Releases of important strategic decisions and information. Since the time this text was published, more than 100 Hershey News Releases have been posted. In performing strategic planning and classroom strategic-management case analysis, it is important to have the latest information possible on which to base decisions and processes.

Instructions
Step 1   Go to the www.thehersheycompany.com website and across the top of the page, click on *Investors*. Read the most recent Hershey Press Releases.

Step 2   Type a two-page Executive Summary of Hershey's newest strategies being formulated and implemented.

Step 3   Submit your report to your professor.

EXERCISE 1D
Strategic Planning for Your University

Purpose
External and internal factors are the underlying bases of strategies formulated and implemented by organizations. Your college or university faces numerous external opportunities and threats and has many internal strengths and weaknesses. The purpose of this exercise is to illustrate the process of identifying critical external and internal factors.

External influences include trends in the following areas: economic, social, cultural, demographic, environmental, technological, political, legal, governmental, and competitive. External factors could include declining numbers of high school graduates; population shifts; community relations; increased competitiveness among colleges and universities; rising numbers of adults returning to college; decreased support from local, state, and federal agencies; increasing numbers of foreign students attending U.S. colleges; and a rising number of Internet courses.

Internal factors of a college or university include faculty, students, staff, alumni, athletic programs, physical plant, grounds and maintenance, student housing, administration, fund-raising, academic programs, food services, parking, placement, clubs, fraternities, sororities, and public relations.

Instructions
Step 1   On a separate sheet of paper, down the left column, write four headings: External Opportunities, External Threats, Internal Strengths, and Internal Weaknesses.

Step 2   As related to your college or university, list what you consider to be the five most important factors under each of the four headings.

Step 3   Discuss the factors as a class.

Step 4   What new things did you learn about your university from the class discussion? How could this type of discussion benefit an organization?

EXERCISE 1E
Strategic Planning at a Local Company

Purpose

This activity is aimed at giving you practical knowledge about how organizations in your city or town are doing strategic planning. This exercise also will give you experience in interacting on a professional basis with local business leaders.

Instructions

Step 1	Contact several business owners or top managers. Find an organization that does strategic planning. Make an appointment to visit with the strategist (president, chief executive officer, or owner) of that business.
Step 2	Seek answers to the following questions during the interview:

- Does your firm formally conduct strategic planning? If no, why not? If yes, who is involved in the process? Does the firm hold planning retreats? If yes, how often and where?
- Does your firm have a written mission statement? How was the statement developed? When was the statement last changed?
- What are the benefits of engaging in strategic planning?
- What are the major costs or problems in doing strategic planning in your business?
- Do you anticipate making any changes in the strategic-planning process at your company? If yes, please explain.

Step 3	Report your findings to the class.

EXERCISE 1F
Get Familiar with the Strategy Club Website

Purpose

You may use for free all the resources provided at the authors' website, www.strategyclub.com, including the downloadable Excel student template. Thousands of students have found this template to be immensely useful in preparing a strategic management case analysis.

Instructions

Step 1	Go to the www.strategyclub.com website. Review the following free resources:

- Excel student template
- Sample case analysis PowerPoints
- Live author videos
- Live case analysis presentations
- Chapter and case updates

Step 2	Prepare to give your class an overview of your impression of the website.

EXERCISE 1G
Game Plans vs. Strategic Plans: Teams vs. Companies

Purpose

As discussed in the chapter, athletic teams develop elaborate game plans to compete against rival teams. This exercise can familiarize you with how game planning for a football or basketball game compares to strategic planning for a company, organization, or even an institution such as your college or university.

Instructions

Step 1	Make an appointment to visit with a head football, basketball, or soccer coach at your college or university. Ask that person about how he or she develops a game plan for the team's most important rival.
Step 2	Report back to class on your findings. Compare and contrast what the coach told you versus what you read about strategic planning in this textbook.

(Note to Professors—See the Chapter IM for an additional, excellent exercise for this chapter)

STRATEGY FORMULATION

The Business Vision and Mission

LEARNING OBJECTIVES

After studying this chapter, you should be able to do the following:

2-1. Describe the nature and role of vision statements in strategic management.

2-2. Describe the nature and role of mission statements in strategic management.

2-3. Discuss the process of developing a vision and mission statement.

2-4. Discuss how clear vision and mission statements can benefit other strategic-management activities.

2-5. Describe the characteristics of a good mission statement.

2-6. Identify the components of mission statements.

2-7. Evaluate mission statements of different organizations and write effective vision and mission statements.

ASSURANCE OF LEARNING EXERCISES

The following exercises are found at the end of this chapter:

EXERCISE 2A   Develop an Improved BB&T Mission Statement

EXERCISE 2B   Evaluate Three Mission Statements

EXERCISE 2C   Write a Vision and Mission Statement for Hershey Company

EXERCISE 2D   Compare Your College or University's Vision and Mission Statements to That of a Leading Rival Institution

EXERCISE 2E   Conduct Mission Statement Research

This chapter focuses on the concepts and tools needed to evaluate and write business vision and mission statements. It also provides a practical framework for developing and creating effective vision and mission statements. Actual mission statements from large and small organizations and for-profit and nonprofit enterprises are presented and critiqued. The exemplary company examined in the beginning of this chapter, H&R Block, recently broadened its mission to encompass providing health-insurance advice to customers, as well as providing income-tax advice.

We can perhaps best understand vision and mission by focusing on a business when it is first started. In the beginning, a new business is simply a collection of ideas. Starting a new business rests on a set of beliefs that the new organization can offer some product or service to some customers in some geographic area using some type of technology at a profitable price. A new business owner typically believes his or her philosophy of the new enterprise will result in a favorable public image, and the business concept can be effectively communicated to and adopted by important constituencies. When the set of beliefs about a business at its inception is put into writing, the resulting document mirrors the same basic ideas that underlie vision and mission statements. As a business grows, owners or managers find it necessary to revise the founding set of beliefs, but those original ideas usually are reflected in the revised statements of vision and mission.

Vision and mission statements often can be found in the front of annual reports. They often are displayed throughout a firm's premises and are distributed with company information sent to constituencies. The statements are part of numerous internal reports, such as loan requests, supplier agreements, labor relations contracts, business plans, and customer service agreements.

Vision Statements: What Do We Want to Become?

It is especially important for managers and executives in any organization to agree on the basic vision that the firm strives to achieve in the long term. A **vision statement** should answer the basic question, "What do we want to become?" A clear vision provides the foundation for developing a

H&R Block (HRB)

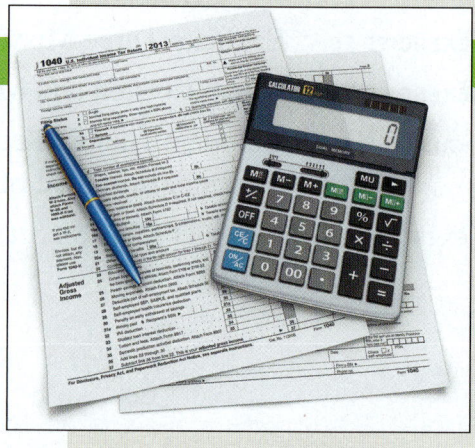

Headquartered in Kansas City, Missouri, H&R Block has more than 10,000 branches across all 50 states—more retail locations than either Dunkin' Donuts or Walgreens. Historically, the company has been a tax-preparation firm, but CEO Bill Cobb recently changed his company's mission to being "in the business of helping citizens comply with government rules." This broadened mission still includes being a tax-preparation firm, but now the company also helps Americans navigate the Affordable Care Act (ACA) provisions. The ACA is closely tied to tax-filing obligations because individuals without employer-provided health insurance must buy coverage, either directly or through an online exchange. Those with incomes below a certain level are eligible for a subsidy, the amount of which will be set and verified through the tax-filing process. In this sense, ACA is technically an "advance tax credit." H&R Block says nearly two-thirds of its clients "seem to be eligible for an ACA subsidy." Also, as part of ACA coverage, individuals who receive a subsidy are required to file a tax return, whether they have worked the prior year or not, expanding H&R Block's pool of potential tax-preparation customers. Those who fail to enroll in a qualified insurance plan will have to pay a penalty, also administered through the tax-reporting process and, in many cases, paid via a reduced refund. For both ACA and H&R Block, 2014 was a transition year, because the early-2015 tax season entailed subsidies and penalties being sorted out in earnest for the first time. H&R Block's broadened mission enables the firm to obtain new customers and revenues, instead of basically being a 14-week-per-year tax-preparation business.

Source: Based on information at http://www.hrblock.com/healthcare/

comprehensive mission statement. Many organizations have both a vision and mission statement, but the vision statement should be established first and foremost. The vision statement should be short, preferably one sentence, and as many managers as possible should have input into developing the statement. Where there is no vision, the people perish (Proverbs 29:18).

For many, if not most, corporations, profit rather than mission or vision is the primary motivator. But profit alone is not enough to motivate people. Profit is perceived negatively by many stakeholders of a firm. For example, employees may see profit as something that they earn and management then uses and even gives away to shareholders. Although this perception is undesired and disturbing to management, it clearly indicates that both profit and vision are needed to motivate a workforce effectively.

When employees and managers together shape or fashion the vision and mission statements for a firm, the resultant documents can reflect the personal visions that managers and employees have in their hearts and minds about their own futures. Shared vision creates a commonality of interests that can lift workers out of the monotony of daily work and put them into a new world of opportunity and challenge.

Although typically a single sentence, vision statements need to be written from a customer perspective. For example, eBay's vision is "To provide a global trading platform where practically anyone can trade practically anything." Vision statements need to do more than identify the product/service a firm offers. The old Ford Motor Company vision, for example, was product-oriented: "To make the automobile accessible to every American," but today Ford has a more effective customer-oriented vision statement: "To provide personal mobility for people around the world." Examples of vision statements are provided in Table 2-1.

Vision Statement Analysis

At a minimum, a vision statement should reveal the type of business the firm engages. For example, to have a vision that says, "to become the best retailing firm in the USA" is much too broad, because that firm could be selling anything from boats to bunnies. Notice here how Starbucks' vision statement is improved.

STARBUCKS VISION STATEMENT (PARAPHRASED)

Starbucks strives to be the premier roaster and retailer of specialty coffee globally.

STARBUCKS "IMPROVED" VISION STATEMENT

Starbucks' vision is to be the most well-known, specialty coffee, tea, and pastry restaurant in the world, offering sincere customer service, a welcoming atmosphere, and unequaled quality.

AUTHOR COMMENTS

- The first vision statement does not state what the company wants to become. Nor does it acknowledge the firm's movement into specialty tea offerings. It is not as customer-oriented as needed.
- The improved vision statement reveals the company's aspirations for the future and acknowledges that upscale tea and pastries complement their premium coffee offerings.

TABLE 2-1 Vision Statement Examples

- General Motors' vision is to be the world leader in transportation products and related services. *(Author comment: Good statement)*
- PepsiCo's responsibility is to continually improve all aspects of the world in which we operate—environment, social, economic—creating a better tomorrow than today. *(Author comment: Statement is too vague; it should reveal how the firm's food and beverage business benefits people)*
- Royal Caribbean's vision is to empower and enable our employees to deliver the best vacation experience for our guests, thereby generating superior returns for our shareholders and enhancing the well-being of our communities. *(Author comment: Statement is good but could end after the word* guests)*

Sources: Courtesy General Motors; © 2013 PepsiCo Inc. Used with permission; Courtesy Royal Caribbean.

Mission Statements: What Is Our Business?

Current thought on mission statements is based largely on guidelines set forth in the mid-1970s by Peter Drucker, who is often called "the father of modern management" for his pioneering studies at General Motors and for his 22 books and hundreds of articles. Drucker believes that asking the question "What is our business?" is synonymous with asking "What is our mission?" An enduring statement of purpose that distinguishes one organization from other similar enterprises, the **mission statement** is a declaration of an organization's "reason for being." It answers the pivotal question "What is our business?" A clear mission statement is essential for effectively establishing objectives and formulating strategies.

Sometimes called a **creed statement**, a statement of purpose, a statement of philosophy, a statement of beliefs, a statement of business principles, or a statement "defining our business," a mission statement reveals what an organization wants to be and whom it wants to serve. All organizations have a reason for being, even if strategists have not consciously transformed this reason into writing. As illustrated with white shading in Figure 2-1, carefully prepared statements of vision and mission are widely recognized by both practitioners and academicians as the

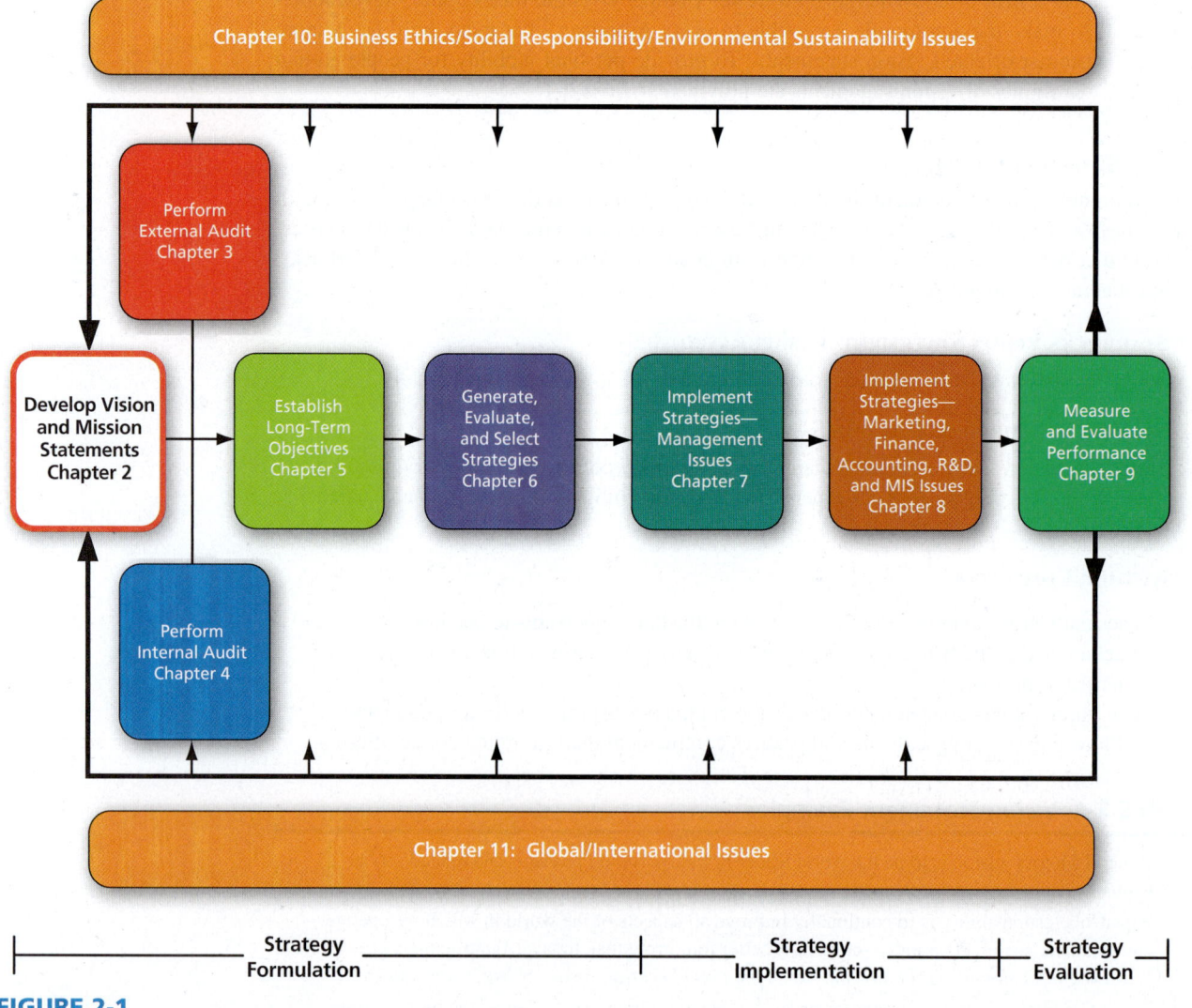

FIGURE 2-1

A Comprehensive Strategic-Management Model

Source: Fred R. David, "How Companies Define Their Mission," *Long Range Planning* 22, no. 3 (June 1988): 40. See also Anik Ratnaningsih, Nadjadji Anwar, Patdono Suwignjo, and Putu Artama Wiguna, "Balance Scorecard of David's Strategic Modeling at Industrial Business for National Construction Contractor of Indonesia," *Journal of Mathematics and Technology,* no. 4 (October 2010): 20.

first step in strategic management. Drucker has the following to say about mission statements (paraphrased):

> A mission statement is the foundation for priorities, strategies, plans, and work assignments. It is the starting point for the design of jobs and organizational structures. Nothing may seem simpler or more obvious than to know what a company's business is. A lumber mill makes lumber, an airline carries passengers and freight, and a bank lends money. But "What is our business?" is almost always a difficult question and the right answer is usually anything but obvious. The answer to this question is the first responsibility of strategists.[1]

Some strategists spend almost every moment of every day on administrative and tactical concerns; those who rush quickly to establish objectives and implement strategies often overlook the development of a vision and mission statement. This problem is widespread even among large organizations. Many corporations in the United States have not yet developed a formal vision or mission statement. An increasing number of organizations, however, are developing these statements.

Some companies develop mission statements simply because owners or top management believe it is fashionable, rather than out of any real commitment. However, as described in this chapter, firms that develop and systematically revisit their vision and mission statements, treat them as living documents, and consider them to be an integral part of the firm's culture realize great benefits. For example, managers at Johnson & Johnson (J&J) meet regularly with employees to review, reword, and reaffirm the firm's vision and mission. The entire J&J workforce recognizes the value that top management places on this exercise, and these employees respond accordingly.

The Process of Developing Vision and Mission Statements

As indicated in the strategic-management model, clear vision and mission statements are needed before alternative strategies can be formulated and implemented. As many managers as possible should be involved in the process of developing these statements because, through involvement, people become committed to an organization.

A widely used approach to developing a vision and mission statement is first to select several articles (such as those listed as Current Readings at the end of this chapter) about these statements and ask all managers to read these as background information. Then, ask managers to individually prepare a vision and mission statement for the organization. A facilitator or committee of top managers should then merge these statements into a single document and distribute the draft statements to all managers. A request for modifications, additions, and deletions is needed next, along with a meeting to revise the document. To the extent that all managers have input into and support the final documents, organizations can more easily obtain managers' support for other strategy formulation, implementation, and evaluation activities. Thus, the process of developing vision and mission statements represents a great opportunity for strategists to obtain needed support from all managers in the firm.

During the process of developing vision and mission statements, some organizations use discussion groups of managers to develop and modify existing statements. Other organizations hire an outside consultant or facilitator to manage the process and help draft the language. At times an outside person with expertise in developing such statements, who has unbiased views, can manage the process more effectively than an internal group or committee of managers. Decisions on how best to communicate the vision and mission to all managers, employees, and external constituencies of an organization are needed when the documents are in final form. Some organizations even create a videotape to explain the statements and how they were developed.

An article by Campbell and Yeung emphasizes that the process of developing a mission statement should create an "emotional bond" and "sense of mission" between the organization and its employees.[2] Commitment to a company's strategy and intellectual agreement on the strategies to be pursued do not necessarily translate into an emotional bond; hence, strategies that have been formulated may not be implemented. These researchers stress that an emotional bond comes when an individual personally identifies with the underlying values and behavior of a firm, thus turning intellectual agreement and commitment to strategy into a sense of mission. Campbell and Yeung also differentiate between the terms *vision* and *mission*, saying that vision is "a possible and desirable future state of an organization" that includes specific goals, whereas mission is more associated with behavior and the present.

The Importance (Benefits) of Vision and Mission Statements

The importance (benefits) of vision and mission statements to effective strategic management is well documented in the literature, although research results are mixed. As indicated in Academic Research Capsule 2-1, there is a positive relationship between mission statements and measures of financial performance.

In actual practice, wide variations exist in the nature, composition, and use of both vision and mission statements. King and Cleland recommend that organizations carefully develop a written mission statement in order to reap the following benefits:

1. To make sure all employees/managers understand the firm's purpose or reason for being.
2. To provide a basis for prioritization of key internal and external factors utilized to formulate feasible strategies.
3. To provide a basis for the allocation of resources.
4. To provide a basis for organizing work, departments, activities, and segments around a common purpose.[3]

Reuben Mark, former CEO of Colgate, maintains that a clear mission increasingly must make sense internationally. Mark's thoughts on vision are as follows:

When it comes to rallying everyone to the corporate banner, it's essential to push one vision globally rather than trying to drive home different messages in different cultures. The trick is to keep the vision simple but elevated: "We make the world's fastest computers" or "Telephone service for everyone." You're never going to get anyone to charge the machine guns only for financial objectives. It's got to be something that makes people feel better, feel a part of something.[4]

ACADEMIC RESEARCH CAPSULE 2-1

The Mission Statement/Firm Performance Linkage

A meta-analysis of 20 years of empirical research on mission statements concluded that "there is a small positive relationship between mission statements and measures of financial organizational performance" (Desmidt et al., 2011, p. 468). However, research in marketing explains that customer satisfaction has a strong positive relationship with organizational performance (Devasagayam et al., 2013). Indeed, researchers have noted that "managers increasingly tend to see customer satisfaction as a valuable intangible asset" (Luo et al., 2012, p. 745). Thus, mission statements designed from a customer perspective could positively impact organizational performance by enhancing customer satisfaction. If written from a customer perspective, mission statements could spur employees, salespersons, and managers to provide exemplary customer service, which arguably would enhance customer loyalty and translate into customers being "on a mission"

to seek out, use, and promote the firm's products and services. Written from a customer perspective, mission statements may indeed "accomplish their mission."

Sources: Based on S. Desmidt, A. Prinzie, & A. Decramer, A. "Looking for the Value of Mission Statements: A Meta-Analysis of 20 Years of Research," *Management Decision*, 49, no. 3 (2011): 468–483; R. Devasagayam, N. R. Stark, & L. S. Valestin, "Examining the Linearity of Customer Satisfaction: Return on Satisfaction as an Alternative," *Business Perspectives and Research* 1, no. 2 (2013): 1–8; X. Luo, J. Wieseke, & C. Homburg, "Incentivizing CEOs to Build Customer- and Employee-Firm Relations for Higher Customer Satisfaction and Firm Value," *Journal of the Academy of Marketing Science* 40, no. 6 (2012): 45–758; M. E. David, Forest R. David, & Fred R. David, "Mission Statement Theory and Practice: A Content Analysis and New Direction," *International Journal of Business, Marketing, and Decision Sciences* 7, no. 1 (Summer 2014): 95–109.

A Resolution of Divergent Views

Another benefit of developing a comprehensive mission statement is that divergent views among managers can be revealed and resolved through the process. The question "What is our business?" can create controversy. Raising the question often reveals differences among strategists in the organization. Individuals who have worked together for a long time and who think they know each other suddenly may realize that they are in fundamental disagreement. For example, in a college or university, divergent views regarding the relative importance of teaching, research, and service often are expressed during the mission statement development process. Negotiation, compromise, and eventual agreement on important issues are needed before people can focus on more specific strategy-formulation activities.

Considerable disagreement among an organization's strategists over vision and mission statements can cause trouble if not resolved. For example, unresolved disagreement over the business mission was one of the reasons for W. T. Grant's bankruptcy and eventual liquidation. Top executives of the firm, including Ed Staley and Lou Lustenberger, were firmly entrenched in opposing positions that W. T. Grant should be like Kmart or JC Penney, respectively. W. T. Grant decided to become a bit like both Kmart and JC Penney; this compromise was a huge strategic mistake. In other words, top executives of W. T. Grant never resolved their vision/mission issue, which ultimately led to the firm's disappearance.[5]

Too often, strategists develop vision and mission statements only when the organization is in trouble. Of course, the documents are needed then. Developing and communicating a clear mission during troubled times indeed may have spectacular results and may even reverse decline. However, to wait until an organization is in trouble to develop a vision and mission statement is a gamble that characterizes irresponsible management. According to Drucker, the most important time to ask seriously, "What do we want to become?" and "What is our business?" is when a company has been successful:

> Success always obsoletes the very behavior that achieved it, always creates new realities, and always creates new and different problems. Only the fairy tale story ends, "They lived happily ever after." It is never popular to argue with success or to rock the boat. It will not be long before success will turn into failure. Sooner or later, even the most successful answer to the question "What is our business?" becomes obsolete.[6]

In multidivisional organizations, strategists should ensure that divisional units perform strategic-management tasks, including the development of a statement of vision and mission. Each division should involve its own managers and employees in developing a vision and mission statement that is consistent with and supportive of the corporate mission. Ten benefits of having a clear mission and vision are provided in Table 2-2.

An organization that fails to develop a vision statement, as well as a comprehensive and inspiring mission statement, loses the opportunity to present itself favorably to existing and

TABLE 2-2 Ten Benefits of Having a Clear Mission and Vision

1. Achieve clarity of purpose among all managers and employees.
2. Provide a basis for all other strategic planning activities, including internal and external assessment, establishing objectives, developing strategies, choosing among alternative strategies, devising policies, establishing organizational structure, allocating resources, and evaluating performance.
3. Provide direction.
4. Provide a focal point for all stakeholders of the firm.
5. Resolve divergent views among managers.
6. Promote a sense of shared expectations among all managers and employees.
7. Project a sense of worth and intent to all stakeholders.
8. Project an organized, motivated organization worthy of support.
9. Achieve higher organizational performance.
10. Achieve synergy among all managers and employees.

potential stakeholders. All organizations need customers, employees, and managers, and most firms need creditors, suppliers, and distributors. Vision and mission statements are effective vehicles for communicating with important internal and external stakeholders. The principal benefit of these statements as tools of strategic management is derived from their specification of the ultimate aims of a firm. Vision and mission statements reveal the firm's shared expectations internally among all employees and managers. For external constituencies, the statements reveal the firm's long-term commitment to responsible, ethical action in providing a needed product and/or service for customers.

Characteristics of a Mission Statement

A mission statement is a declaration of attitude and outlook. It usually is broad in scope for at least two major reasons. First, a good mission statement allows for the generation and consideration of a range of feasible alternative objectives and strategies without unduly stifling management creativity. Excess specificity would limit the potential of creative growth for the organization. However, an overly general statement that does not exclude any strategy alternatives could be dysfunctional. Apple Computer's mission statement, for example, should not open the possibility for diversification into pesticides—or Ford Motor Company's into food processing.

Second, a mission statement needs to be broad to reconcile differences effectively among, and appeal to, an organization's diverse **stakeholders**, the individuals and groups of individuals who have a special stake or claim on the company. Thus, a mission statement should be **reconciliatory**. Stakeholders include employees, managers, stockholders, boards of directors, customers, suppliers, distributors, creditors, governments (local, state, federal, and foreign), unions, competitors, environmental groups, and the general public. Stakeholders affect and are affected by an organization's strategies, yet the claims and concerns of diverse constituencies vary and often conflict. For example, the general public is especially interested in social responsibility, whereas stockholders are more interested in profitability. Claims on any business literally may number in the thousands, and they often include clean air, jobs, taxes, investment opportunities, career opportunities, equal employment opportunities, employee benefits, salaries, wages, clean water, and community services. All stakeholders' claims on an organization cannot be pursued with equal emphasis. A good mission statement indicates the relative attention that an organization will devote to meeting the claims of various stakeholders.

The fine balance between specificity and generality is difficult to achieve, but it is well worth the effort. George Steiner offers the following insight on the need for a mission statement to be broad in scope:

> Most business statements of mission are expressed at high levels of abstraction. Vagueness nevertheless has its virtues. Mission statements are not designed to express concrete ends, but rather to provide motivation, general direction, an image, a tone, and a philosophy to guide the enterprise. An excess of detail could prove counterproductive since concrete specification could be the base for rallying opposition. Precision might stifle creativity in the formulation of an acceptable mission or purpose. Once an aim is cast in concrete, it creates a rigidity in an organization and resists change. Vagueness leaves room for other managers to fill in the details.[7]

As indicated in Table 2-3, in addition to being broad in scope, an effective mission statement should not be too lengthy; recommended length is less than 150 words. An effective mission statement should arouse positive feelings and emotions about an organization; it should be inspiring in the sense that it motivates readers to action. A mission statement should be enduring. All of these are desired characteristics of a statement. An effective mission statement generates the impression that a firm is successful, has direction, and is worthy of time, support, and investment—from all socioeconomic groups of people.

A business mission reflects judgments about future growth directions and strategies that are based on forward-looking external and internal analyses. The statement should provide useful criteria for selecting among alternative strategies. A clear mission statement provides a basis

TABLE 2-3 Characteristics of a Mission Statement

1. Broad in scope; does not include monetary amounts, numbers, percentages, ratios, or objectives
2. Fewer than 150 words in length
3. Inspiring
4. Identifies the utility of a firm's products
5. Reveals that the firm is socially responsible
6. Reveals that the firm is environmentally responsible
7. Includes nine components: customers, products or services, markets, technology, concern for survival/growth/profits, philosophy, self-concept, concern for public image, concern for employees
8. Reconciliatory
9. Enduring

for generating and screening strategic options. The statement of mission should be sufficiently broad to allow judgments about the most promising growth directions and those considered less promising.

A Customer Orientation

An effective mission statement describes an organization's purpose, customers, products or services, markets, philosophy, and basic technology. According to Vern McGinnis, a mission statement should (1) define what the organization is and what the organization aspires to be, (2) be limited enough to exclude some ventures and broad enough to allow for creative growth, (3) distinguish a given organization from all others, (4) serve as a framework for evaluating both current and prospective activities, and (5) be stated in terms sufficiently clear to be widely understood throughout the organization.[8] The mission statement should reflect the anticipations of customers. Rather than developing a product and then trying to find a market, the operating philosophy of organizations should be to identify customers' needs and then provide a product or service to fulfill those needs.

Good mission statements identify the utility of a firm's products to its customers. This is why AT&T's mission statement focuses on communication rather than on telephones; it is why ExxonMobil's mission statement focuses on energy rather than on oil and gas; it is why Union Pacific's mission statement focuses on transportation rather than on railroads; it is why Universal Studios' mission statement focuses on entertainment rather than on movies. A major reason for developing a mission statement is to attract customers who give meaning to an organization.

The following utility statements are relevant in developing a mission statement:

Do not offer me things.

Do not offer me clothes. Offer me attractive looks.

Do not offer me shoes. Offer me comfort for my feet and the pleasure of walking.

Do not offer me a house. Offer me security, comfort, and a place that is clean and happy.

Do not offer me books. Offer me hours of pleasure and the benefit of knowledge.

Do not offer me CDs. Offer me leisure and the sound of music.

Do not offer me tools. Offer me the benefits and the pleasure that come from making beautiful things.

Do not offer me furniture. Offer me comfort and the quietness of a cozy place.

Do not offer me things. Offer me ideas, emotions, ambience, feelings, and benefits.

Please, do not offer me *things*.

Components of a Mission Statement

Mission statements can and do vary in length, content, format, and specificity. Most practitioners and academicians of strategic management feel that an effective statement should include the nine **mission statement components** given here. Because a mission statement is often the most visible and public part of the strategic-management process, it is important that it includes not only the characteristics as summarized in Table 2-3 but also the following nine components:

1. **Customers**—Who are the firm's customers?
2. **Products or services**—What are the firm's major products or services?
3. **Markets**—Geographically, where does the firm compete?
4. **Technology**—Is the firm technologically current?
5. **Survival, growth, and profitability**—Is the firm committed to growth and financial soundness?
6. **Philosophy**—What are the basic beliefs, values, aspirations, and ethical priorities of the firm?
7. **Self-concept (distinctive competence)**—What is the firm's major competitive advantage?
8. **Public image**—Is the firm responsive to social, community, and environmental concerns?
9. **Employees**—Are employees a valuable asset of the firm?[9]

To exemplify how mission statements could be written from a customer perspective, a component-by-component example for a charter boat fishing company is provided in Table 2-4. Note the charter company's customers are "outdoor enthusiasts." "Customers" is a key component to include in a mission statement, but simply including the word *customer* or *consumer* does not qualify that component to be considered "written from a customer perspective." The statement needs to identify more precisely the target groups of customers. All nine components in Table 2-4 are written from a customer perspective. For example, regarding the "product/service" component, the charter fishing company provides "memories for a lifetime"—thus revealing the "utility" of the service offered. Regarding the "distinctive competence" component, whereby the firm reveals the major competitive advantage its products/services provide, the statement says: "for customer enjoyment and safety, we provide the most experienced staff in the industry."

Evaluating and Writing Mission Statements

There is no one best mission statement for a particular organization, so when it comes to evaluating mission statements, good judgment is required. Ideally, the statement will provide more than simply inclusion of a single word such as *products* or *employees* regarding a respective

---

TABLE 2-4 **Mission Statement Components Written from a Customer Perspective**

1. **Customers**—Our customers are outdoor enthusiasts seeking fishing excitement and adventure.
2. **Products or services**—We provide fast, clean boats, all the bait and tackle needed, and friendly first mates to create memories for a lifetime.
3. **Markets**—Our fleet of fast, clean vessels operate all along the Florida Gulf Coast.
4. **Technology**—Our vessels are equipped with the very latest safety and fish finding equipment to ensure that customers comfortably are "catching rather than just fishing."
5. **Survival, growth, and profitability**—Our prices are as low as possible to provide customers great value in conjunction with high employee morale and a reasonable return for our owners.
6. **Philosophy**—We assure customers the upmost courtesy and care as our motto on every vessel is to follow the Golden Rule.
7. **Self-concept**—For customer enjoyment and safety, we provide the most experienced staff in the industry.
8. **Public image**—Our vessels use emission-friendly engines; we strive to bring repeat tourists to all communities where we operate.
9. **Employees**—Our on-the-water and off-the-water employees are "on a mission" to help customers have a great time.

Source: Based on Meredith E. David, Forest R. David, & Fred R. David, "Mission Statement Theory and Practice: A Content Analysis and New Direction," *International Journal of Business, Marketing, and Decision Sciences* 7, no. 1 (Summer 2014): 95–109.

component. Why? Because the statement should motivate stakeholders to action, as well as be customer-oriented, informative, inspiring, and enduring.

Two Mission Statements Critiqued

Perhaps the best way to develop a skill for writing and evaluating mission statements is to study actual company missions. Thus, Table 2-5 provides a component-by-component critique of two actual mission statements from PepsiCo, and Royal Caribbean. The Royal Caribbean statement includes only six of the nine components, comprises 86 words total, and lacks a customer perspective. The Royal Caribbean statement merely includes the word *customer(s)*, which is inadequate to be considered written from a customer perspective.

Five Mission Statements Revised

As additional guidance for practitioners (and students), five actual mission statements are revised/rewritten from a customer perspective and presented in Table 2-6. The improved statements include all nine components written from a customer perspective, and, additionally, are inspiring, concise, and comprised of fewer than 90 words each. Regarding the "customer" component, the new Best Buy statement refers to "individuals and businesses"; the new Lowe's statement refers to "homebuilders and homeowners"; and the improved Crocs statement refers to "men, women, and children." In contrast, the Crocs, Best Buy, Rite Aid, and Lowe's actual statements merely include (or not) the word *customer* or *consumer*. The statements are revised to potentially enhance customer satisfaction, especially if communicated to customers by marketers, and backed by company commitment to and implementation of the mission message. The proposed statement for the footwear company Crocs, Inc., for example, talks about "dependable and lasting comfort all day," whereas the UPS proposed statement talks about "the most timely, dependable, and accurate delivery times in the world."

Two Mission Statements Proposed

The process by which mission statements are developed and the exact language/wording included in the statement can significantly impact their effectiveness as a tool for strategic management and marketing strategy. Firms strive to have customers exhibit an emotional bond with the firm's

TABLE 2-5 Two Mission Statements Critiqued

The numbers in parentheses correspond to the nine mission statement components.

PepsiCo

We aspire to make PepsiCo the world's (3) premier consumer products company, focused on convenient foods and beverages (2). We seek to produce healthy financial rewards for investors (5) as we provide opportunities for growth and enrichment to our employees (9), our business partners and the communities (8) in which we operate. And in everything we do, we strive to act with honesty, openness, fairness and integrity (6). *(Author comment: Statement lacks three components: Customers (1), Technology (4), and Distinctive Competence (7); 62 words)*

Royal Caribbean

We are loyal to Royal Caribbean and Celebrity and strive for continuous improvement in everything we do. We always provide service with a friendly greeting and a smile (7). We anticipate the needs of our customers and make all efforts to exceed our customers' expectations. We take ownership of any problem that is brought to our attention. We engage in conduct that enhances our corporate reputation and employee morale (9). We are committed to act in the highest ethical manner and respect the rights and dignity of others. (6). *(Author comment: Statement lacks six components: Customers (1), Products/ Services (2), Markets (3), Technology (4), Survival/Growth/Profits (5), and Public Image (8); 86 words)*

Source: Based on Meredith E. David, Forest R. David, & Fred R. David, "Mission Statement Theory and Practice: A Content Analysis and New Direction," *International Journal of Business, Marketing, and Decision Sciences* 7, no. 1 (Summer 2014): 95–109. Also based on information found at the various corporate websites. © 2013 PepsiCo Inc. Used with Permission. Courtesy Royal Caribbean.

TABLE 2-6 Five Mission Statements Revised

The numbers in parentheses correspond to the nine mission statement components.

Rite Aid

We are on a mission to offer the best possible drugstore experience for people of all ages (1) around the United States (3). We have a state-of-the-art information system (4) that provides our pharmacists (9) with warnings of any possible drug interactions to help better ensure customer safety (8). We are determined to improve our customers' overall health through our wellness programs (5). We offer an extensive line of other beauty, food, drink, cosmetic, and vitamin products through our alliance with GNC (2). We believe in treating our customers like family (6) and strive to maintain our reputation as the most personable drugstore (7). *(88 words total)*

Best Buy

We are committed to providing individuals and businesses (1) the latest high-tech products (2) at the lowest prices of any retail store (7). Serving North America, China, and other markets (3), all Best Buy employees (9) are exceptionally knowledgeable about the products we offer. We believe good ethics is good business (6) and use business analytics (4) to better understand customer trends. We strive to make a profit for our shareholders (5) and be a good community citizen everywhere we operate (8). *(72 words)*

Lowe's

We are committed to exceeding the expectations of our homebuilder, homeowner, and other customers (1). We offer superior home improvement products (2) and expert advice (7) at nearly 2,000 Lowe's stores in the USA, Canada, and Mexico (3). We have a best-in-class electronic in-store tracking system (4) to help customers. We continue to create jobs (8) in all communities where we operate. Up to 80 percent of our employees work on a full-time basis (9) and have high ethical standards (6). We put the customer first as we strive to grow profitably for our shareholders (8). *(88 words)*

United Parcel Service (UPS)

We strive to be the most timely and dependable parcel and freight forwarding delivery service (2) in the world (3). By implementing the latest tracking technology (4), we are able to profitably grow (5) by offering individuals and businesses (1) dependable and accurate delivery times (7). We promote from within to improve morale among all employees (9). Our philosophy (6) is to responsibly balance the needs of our customers, employees, shareholders, and communities (8) in an exemplary manner. *(68 words)*

Crocs, Inc.

Crocs is committed to providing profound comfort, fun and innovation in all the shoe models (2) we produce. Through our Croslite technology (4) (7), we are able to provide men, women, and children (1) dependable and lasting comfort all day. We strive to expand our brand throughout the world (3) and are able to save on costs (5), while protecting the environment (8) with our package-less shoes. We adhere to the belief that good ethics is good business (6) in all that we do as we strive to take care of our employees and shareholders. *(85 words)*

Source: Based on Meredith E. David, Forest R. David, & Fred R. David, "Mission Statement Theory and Practice: A Content Analysis and New Direction," *International Journal of Business, Marketing, and Decision Sciences* 7, no. 1 (Summer 2014): 95–109.

products/services and be "on a mission" to use and promote those offerings. Mission statements should be developed and used to foster customer satisfaction and create a bond between a firm and its customers. Involving marketers and sales representatives in the mission statement development process, coupled with including the nine components written from a customer perspective, could enable firms to create an emotional bond with customers, and enhance the likelihood that salespersons would be "on a mission" to provide excellent customer service. Avon and L'Oreal's customers, for example, often portray an emotional bond or attachment to the firm's products.

Proposed, exemplary mission statements for Avon and L'Oreal are provided in Table 2-7. These rival firms have uniquely different competitive advantages in that Avon utilizes door-to-door sales representatives to gain competitive advantage, whereas L'Oreal markets products in thousands of retail outlets. The proposed Avon and L'Oreal statements have the characteristics described earlier,

TABLE 2-7 Two Exemplary, Proposed Mission Statements

The numbers in parentheses correspond to the nine mission statement components.

Avon

Our mission is to provide women (1) quality fragrances, cosmetics, and jewelry (2) at reasonable prices backed by outstanding customer service provided by our thousands of door-to-door sales representatives (7, 9) operating globally (3). We use the latest technology (4) to profitably develop and market products desired by women all over the world (5). Avon representatives put integrity first (6) in setting a good example in every community (8) they operate—as they sell beauty. *(58 words)*

L'Oreal

Our mission is to design, produce, and distribute the world's best fragrances, perfumes, and personal care products (2) to women, men, and children (1) by utilizing the latest technological improvements (4). We empower our highly creative team of researchers to develop safe, eco-friendly (7) products that will enable our firm to profitably grow (5) through thousands of retail outlets. We strive to be one of the most socially responsible (8) firms on the planet (3) and appreciate our employees (9) making that happen, while following the "golden rule" in all that we do (6). *(85 words)*

Source: Based on Meredith E. David, Forest R. David, & Fred R. David, "Mission Statement Theory and Practice: A Content Analysis and New Direction," *International Journal of Business, Marketing, and Decision Sciences* 7, no. 1 (Summer 2014): 95–109.

and include the nine components written from a customer perspective. The proposed Avon statement includes the nine components in 58 words, and provides a basis for an emotional bond to be established between the firm and its customers. For example, the Avon statement reveals that if you purchase Avon products, you will be rewarded with "outstanding customer service provided by a personal sales representative who adheres to the highest ethical standards, while providing fragrances, cosmetics, and jewelry that exhibit the highest technological advancements." There is quite a lot in that brief statement that an Avon customer can become loyal to, especially when the Avon marketing representative reinforces the statement with her actions.

Also written from a customer perspective, the proposed L'Oreal mission statement provides a basis for an emotional bond to be formed between the firm and its customers. Potential customers are reassured in the statement that the L'Oreal's fragrances, perfumes, and personal care products are "organic" and developed by excellent teams of researchers. In addition, the statement reveals that L'Oreal does great philanthropy work and follows the "golden rule" in all endeavors. Customers may become more dedicated to L'Oreal when they see the company's marketing communications reinforce the basic content given in the proposed mission statement. Loyal customers are a competitive advantage for any firm.

IMPLICATIONS FOR STRATEGISTS

Figure 2-2 reveals that establishing and nurturing an effective vision and mission is a vital first step in gaining and maintaining competitive advantages. Businesses succeed by attracting and keeping customers, and they do this by providing better value for customers than do their rival firms. Marketers continually assess customers' changing needs and wants and make appropriate adjustments in the design and delivery of products and services to sustain competitive advantage. Developing and communicating a clear business vision and mission is essential because without an effective vision and mission statements, a firm's short-term actions may be counterproductive to long-term interests. A clear vision and mission provides direction for all subsequent activities that endeavor to see customers, employees, and shareholders concurrently "on a mission" to see the firm succeed.

Vision and mission statements are not just words that look nice when framed or engraved; they provide a basis for strategy and action; they reveal the reason a business opens its doors every day, the reason salespersons sell, the reason customers buy, and the reason employees work. The statements ideally are the passion behind the company, the foundation for employee morale, and the basis for customer loyalty. Written from a customer perspective and included in both oral and written communication with customers, the statements could be used to attract and keep customers. Vision and mission statements do matter. Marketers pursue projects and managers make daily decisions mindful of the firm's basic vision, mission, and resources. Managers work hard every day trying to motivate employees. Executives are on a mission to present the firm favorably to many stakeholders. A clear vision and mission enables strategists to lead the way as a firm strives to gain, sustain, and grow its customer base and competitive advantages.

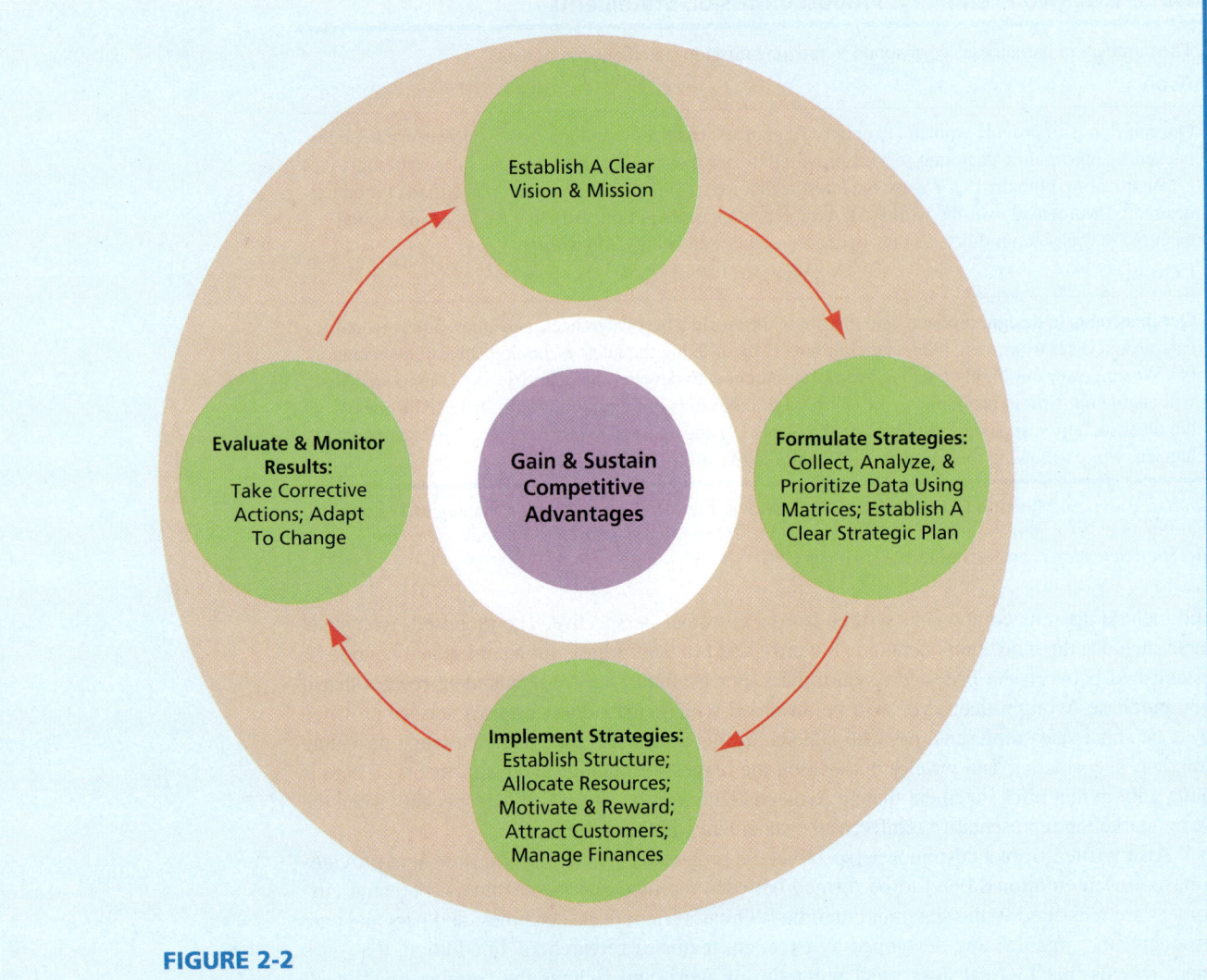

FIGURE 2-2

How to Gain and Sustain Competitive Advantages

IMPLICATIONS FOR STUDENTS

Because gaining and sustaining competitive advantage is the essence of strategic management, when presenting your vision and mission statements as part of a case analysis, be sure to address the "self-concept (distinctive competence)" component. Compare your recommended vision and mission statement with the firm's existing statements, and with rival firms' statements to clearly reveal how your recommendations or strategic plan enables the firm to gain and sustain competitive advantage. Your proposed mission statement should certainly include the nine components and nine characteristics, but in your vision or mission discussion, focus on competitive advantage. In other words, be prescriptive, forward-looking, and insightful—couching your vision/mission overview in terms of how you believe the firm can best gain and sustain competitive advantage. Do not be content with merely showing a nine-component comparison of your proposed statement with rival firms' statements, although that would be nice to include in your analysis.

Chapter Summary

Every organization has a unique purpose and reason for being. This uniqueness should be reflected in vision and mission statements. The nature of a business vision and mission can represent either a competitive advantage or disadvantage for the firm. An organization achieves a heightened sense of purpose when strategists, managers, and employees develop and communicate a clear business vision and mission. Drucker says that developing a clear business vision and mission is the "first responsibility of strategists."

A good mission statement reveals an organization's customers; products or services; markets; technology; concern for survival, growth, and profitability; philosophy; self-concept; concern for public image; and concern for employees. These nine basic components serve as a practical framework for evaluating and writing mission statements. As the first step in strategic management, the vision and mission statements provide direction for all planning activities. As indicated next in the mini-case, even Walt Disney's vision and mission statement can be improved.

Well-designed vision and mission statements are essential for formulating, implementing, and evaluating strategy. Developing and communicating a clear business vision and mission are the most commonly overlooked tasks in strategic management. Without clear statements of vision and mission, a firm's short-term actions can be counterproductive to long-term interests. Vision and mission statements always should be subject to revision, but, if carefully prepared, they will require infrequent major changes. Organizations usually reexamine their vision and mission statements annually. Effective vision and mission statements stand the test of time.

Vision and mission statements are essential tools for strategists—a fact illustrated in a short story told by Porsche's former CEO Peter Schultz (paraphrased):

> Three guys were at work building a large church. All were doing the same job, but when each was asked what his job was, the answers varied: "Pouring cement," the first replied; "Earning a paycheck," responded the second; "Helping to build a cathedral," said the third. Few of us can build cathedrals. But to the extent we can see the cathedral in whatever cause we are following, the job seems more worthwhile. Good strategists and a clear mission help us find those cathedrals in what otherwise could be dismal issues and empty causes.[10]

MyManagementLab®

To complete the problems with the ⭐, go to EOC Discussion Questions in the MyLab.

Key Terms and Concepts

employees (p. 48)
public image (p. 48)
survival, growth, and profitability (p. 48)
creed statement (p. 42)
customers (p. 48)
markets (p. 48)
mission statement (p. 42)
mission statement components (p. 47)

philosophy (p. 48)
products or services (p. 48)
reconciliatory (p. 46)
self-concept (distinctive competence) (p. 48)
stakeholders (p. 46)
technology (p. 48)
vision statement (p. 40)

Issues for Review and Discussion

2-1. Discuss the relative importance of vision and mission documents for managers versus employees versus customers versus shareholders.

⭐ **2-2.** Define "reconciliatory" and give an example of how this "characteristic" can be met in a mission statement.

⭐ **2-3.** Which mission statement component most closely reveals the firm's distinctive competence? Give an example.

⭐ **2-4.** Critique the following vision statement by Stokes Eye Clinic: "Our vision is to take care of your vision."

2-5. For a university, students are the customer. Write a single sentence that could be included in your university's mission statement to reveal the institution's market and product/service components written from a customer perspective.

⭐ **2-6.** Some excellent nine-component mission statements consist of just two sentences. Write a two-sentence mission statement for a company of your choice.

2-7. How do you think an organization can best align company mission with employee mission?

2-8. What are some different names for "mission statement," and where will you likely find a firm's mission statement?

2-9. If your company does not have a vision or mission statement, describe a good process for developing these documents.

2-10. Explain how developing a mission statement can help resolve divergent views among managers in a firm.

2-11. Drucker says the most important time to seriously reexamine the firm's vision or mission is when the firm is successful. Why is this?

⭐ **2-12.** Explain why a mission statement should not include monetary amounts, numbers, percentages, ratios, goals, or objectives.

2-13. Discuss the meaning of the following statement: "Good mission statements identify the utility of a firm's products to its customers."

⭐ **2-14.** Distinguish between the "self-concept" and the "philosophy" components in a mission statement. Give an example of each for your university.

2-15. When someone or some company is "on a mission" to achieve something, many times the person or company cannot be stopped. List three things in prioritized order that you are on a mission to achieve in life.

2-16. Compare and contrast vision statements with mission statements in terms of composition and importance.

2-17. Do local service stations need to have written vision and mission statements? Why or why not?

2-18. Why do you think organizations that have a comprehensive mission tend to be high performers? Does having a comprehensive mission cause high performance?

2-19. What is your college or university's self-concept? How would you state that in a mission statement?

2-20. Explain the principal value of a vision and a mission statement.

2-21. Why is it important for a mission statement to be reconciliatory?

2-22. In your opinion, what are the three most important components that should be included when writing a mission statement? Why?

⭐ **2-23.** How would the mission statements of a for-profit and a nonprofit organization differ?

2-24. Write a vision and mission statement for an organization of your choice.

2-25. Who are the major stakeholders of the bank that you do business with locally? What are the major claims of those stakeholders?

⭐ **2-26.** List eight benefits of having a clear mission statement.

2-27. How often do you think a firm's vision and mission statements should be changed?

MyManagementLab®

Go to the Assignments section of your MyLab to complete these writing exercises.

2-28. Explain why a mission statement should not include strategies and objectives.

2-29. List seven characteristics of a mission statement.

ASSURANCE OF LEARNING EXERCISES

EXERCISE 2A
Develop an Improved BB&T Mission Statement

Purpose

Headquartered in Winston-Salem, North Carolina, Branch Banking and Trust competes every day with hundreds of other banks. The company is a large bank located primarily in the southeastern United States but is expanding nationally. At the bbt.mediaroom.com website, the company states, "At BB&T, we know our business will, and should, experience constant change. Change is necessary for progress. However, our vision, mission, and values are unchanging because these principles are based on basic truths." At the bbt.mediaroom.com website and the *BB&T Philosophy Handbook*, BB&T gives its actual vision and mission statements.

Instructions

Step 1   Develop an improved mission statement for BB&T that complies with (1) the nine components and (2) the nine characteristics presented in this chapter.

Step 2   Based on what you have learned in this chapter, is the BB&T statement about "change" appropriate? Why? Discuss.

EXERCISE 2B
Evaluate Three Mission Statements

Purpose

A business mission statement is an integral part of strategic management. It provides direction for formulating, implementing, and evaluating strategic activities. This exercise will give you practice in evaluating mission statements—a skill that is a prerequisite to writing a good mission statement.

Instructions

Step 1   On a clean sheet of paper, prepare a 9 × 3 matrix. Place the nine mission statement components down the left column and the following three companies across the top of your paper.

Step 2   Write *Yes* or *No* in each cell of your matrix to indicate whether you feel the particular mission statement includes the respective component written from a customer perspective.

Step 3   Turn your paper in to your instructor for a classwork grade.

Mission Statements/Business Purpose

1. **CVS Health Corporation, Headquartered in Woonsocket, Rhode Island**
   "Helping people on their path to better health"
2. **Aflac, Inc. Headquartered in Columbus, Georgia**
   "To combine aggressive strategic marketing with quality products and services at competitive prices
   to pro-vide the best insurance value for consumers."
3. **Bristol-Myers Squibb Company, Headquartered in New York, NY**
   "To discover, develop and deliver innovative medicines that help patients prevail over serious diseases."

*Source: Based on information at http://www.missionstatements.com/fortune_500_mission_statements.html. Courtesy
of CVS Health; Courtesy Aflac; Courtesy Bristol-Myers Squibb Company.*

EXERCISE 2C

Write a Vision and Mission Statement for the Hershey Company

Purpose

Much like a person's curriculum vita (resumé), there is always room for improvement with regard to
an existing vision and mission statement. Hershey does not have a printed vision statement, but the
company's mission statement simply reads as follows: "Bringing sweet moments of Hershey happiness to the world every day."

Instructions

Step 1   Refer to the Cohesion Case (p. 27) after Chapter 1 .

Step 2   On a clean sheet of paper, write a one-sentence vision statement for Hershey.

Step 3   On that same sheet of paper, write a new and improved mission statement for Hershey that
complies with (1) the nine components and (2) the nine characteristics presented in this chapter.

EXERCISE 2D

Compare Your College or University's Vision and Mission Statements to That of a Leading Rival Institution

Purpose

Most universities have a vision and a mission statement. The purpose of this exercise is to give you
practice in comparing the effectiveness of a vision and a mission statement for a university with the
statements from a competing university.

Instructions

Step 1   Determine whether your institution has a vision or a mission statement. Look in the front
of the college handbook. If your institution has a written statement, contact an appropriate
administrator of the institution to inquire as to how and when the statement was prepared.
Share this information with the class. Analyze your college's vision and mission statements
in light of the concepts presented in this chapter.

Step 2   Compare the vision statement and the mission statement of your college or university to
those of a leading institution.

Step 3   Write a one-page analysis comparing the statements.

EXERCISE 2E

Conduct Mission Statement Research

Purpose

This exercise gives you the opportunity to study the nature and role of vision and mission statements
in strategic management.

Instructions

Step 1 Visit the websites of various organizations in your city or county to identify firms that have developed a formal vision or mission statement. Include some websites of nonprofit organizations and government agencies in addition to small and large businesses.

Step 2 Ask to speak with the director, owner, or chief executive officer of several organizations. Explain that you are studying vision and mission statements in class and are conducting research as part of a class activity.

Step 3 Ask several executives the following four questions, and record their answers.
1. When did your organization first develop its vision or mission statement? Who was primarily responsible for its development?
2. How long have your current statements existed? When were they last modified? Why were they modified at that time?
3. By what process are your firm's vision and mission statements altered?
4. How are your vision and mission statements used in the firm?

Step 4 Provide an overview of your findings to the class.

(Note to Professors—See the Chapter IM for an additional, excellent exercise for this chapter)

MINI-CASE ON WALT DISNEY COMPANY (DIS)

WHAT IS DISNEY'S VISION FOR THE FUTURE AND MISSION FOR THE PRESENT?

Source: Alliance/Fotolia

Everyone loves Mickey Mouse and Donald Duck. Walt Disney's two largest segments are Media Networks and Parks and Recreation. Media Networks consists of ABC, ESPN, Disney films, newly acquired Lucasfilm, and 35 radio stations, among others. Parks and Recreation includes the Walt Disney theme parks in the United States, France, China, and Hong Kong, and the more recent Disney cruise line. Disney operates three other divisions: Studio Entertainment, Consumer Products, and Interactive Media.

Walt Disney's actual vision statement is "To make people happy." However, an improved, author-proposed vision statement for Disney is "To offer the best family entertainment in the world through theme parks, cruises, movies, and radio and television coverage of news and sporting events globally."

Walt Disney's actual mission statement is "To be one of the world's leading producers and providers of entertainment and information. Using our portfolio of brands to differentiate our content, services and consumer products, we seek to develop the most creative, innovative and profitable entertainment experiences and related products in the world." However, an improved, author-proposed Disney mission statement is as follows:

> We are on a mission every day to serve customers young and old with outstanding family entertainment. By offering popular theme parks and Disney TV programming to our newly acquired ABC, ESPN, and cruise lines, we provide well-diversified family entertainment worldwide. We use many Disney characters such as Mickey Mouse and Donald Duck to excite customers globally. We produce apps for smartphones in the Interactive Media division. We give back generously to our communities and offer many internships for deserving college students. Everything we do at Disney is possible because of our great employees and fans worldwide.

Questions

1. In what three ways is the proposed vision statement better than Disney's actual vision statement?
2. In what three ways is the proposed mission statement better than Disney's actual mission statement?
3. How would you further improve the proposed new Disney vision and mission statements?

Source: Company documents and a variety of sources.

Current Readings

Bartkus, Barbara, Myron Glassman, and R. Bruce McAfee. "Mission Statements: Are They Smoke and Mirrors?" *Business Horizons* 43, no. 6 (November–December 2000): 23.

Binns, Andy, et al. "The Art of Strategic Renewal." *MIT Sloan Management Review* 55, no. 2 (2014): 21–23.

Birkinshaw, Julian, Nicolai J. Foss, and Siegwart Lindenberg. "Combining Purpose with Profits." *MIT Sloan Management Review* 55, no. 3 (2014): 49–56.

Braun, S., J. S. Wesche, D. Frey, S. Weisweller, & C. Paus. "Effectiveness of Mission Statements in

Organizations—A Review." *Journal of Management & Organization*, 18 (2012): 430–444.

Canton, Andrew M., Chad Murphy, and Jonathan R. Clark. "A (Blurry) Vision of the Future: How Leader Rhetoric about Ultimate Goals Influences Performance." *Academy of Management Journal,* 57 (December 2014): 1,544–1,570.

Church Mission Statements, http://www.missionstatements.com/church_mission_statements.html

Collins, David J., and Michael G. Rukstad. "Can You Say What Your Strategy Is?" *Harvard Business Review* (April 2008): 82. Company Mission Statements, http://www.mission-statements.com/company_mission_statements.html

Conger, Jay A., and Douglas A. Ready. "Enabling Bold Visions." *MIT Sloan Management Review* 49, no. 2 (Winter 2008): 70.

Craig, Nick, and Scott Snook. "From Purpose to Impact." *Harvard Business Review* 92, no. 5 (2014): 104–111.

David, Meredith E., Forest R. David, and Fred R. David. "Mission Statement Theory and Practice: A Content Analysis and New Direction." *International Journal of Business, Marketing, and Decision Sciences* 7, no. 1 (Summer 2014): 95–109.

Day, George S., and Paul Schoemaker. "Peripheral Vision: Sensing and Acting on Weak Signals." *Long Range Planning* 37, no. 2 (April 2004): 117.

Desmidt, S., A. Prinzie, and A. Decramer. "Looking for the Value of Mission Statements: A Meta-Analysis of 20 Years of Research." *Management Decision*, 49 (2011): 468–483.

Devasagayam, R., N. R. Stark, and L. S. Valestin. "Examining the Linearity of Customer Satisfaction: Return on Satisfaction as an Alternative." *Business Perspectives and Research*, 1 (2013): 1–8.

Hollensbe, Elaine, Charles Wookey, Loughlin Hickey, and Gerard George, "Organizations with Purpose." *Academy of Management Journal* 57, no. 5 (October 2014): 1227–1234.

Ibarra, Herminia, and Otilia Obodaru. "Women and the Vision Thing." *Harvard Business Review* (January 2009): 62–71.

Lissak, Michael, and Johan Roos. "Be Coherent, Not Visionary." *Long Range Planning* 34, no. 1 (February 2001): 53.

Luo, X, J. Wieseke, and C. Homburg. "Incentivizing CEOs to Build Customer- and Employee-Firm Relations for Higher Customer Satisfaction and Firm Value." *Journal of the Academy of Marketing Science,* 40 (2012): 745–758.

MacMillan, Martin I. "Managing Your Mission—Critical Knowledge." *Harvard Business Review* (January–February 2015).

Newsom, Mi Kyong, David A. Collier, and Eric O. Olsen. "Using 'Biztainment' to Gain Competitive Advantage." *Business Horizons* (March–April 2009): 167–166.

Nonprofit Organization Mission Statements, http://www.missionstatements.com/nonprofit_mission_statements.html

Palmer, T. B., and J. C. Short. "Mission Statements in U.S. Colleges of Business: An Empirical Examination of Their Content with Linkages to Configurations and Performance." *Academy of Management Learning & Education* 7 (2008): 454–470.

Peyrefitte, Joe, and Forest R. David. "A Content Analysis of the Mission Statements of United States Firms in Four Industries." *International Journal of Management*, 23 (2006): 296–301.

Powers, E. L. "Organizational Mission Statement Guidelines Revisited." *International Journal of Management & Information Systems* 16 (2012): 281–290.

Rarick, C., and J. Vitton. "Mission Statements That Make Cents." *Journal of Business Strategy,* 16 (1995): 11–12.

Restaurant Mission Statements, http://www.missionstatements.com/restaurant_mission_statements.html

School Mission Statements, http://www.missionstatements.com/school_mission_statements.html

Sidhu, J. "Mission Statements: Is It Time to Shelve Them?" *European Management Journal* 21 (2003): 439–446.

Smith, M., R. B. Heady, P. P. Carson, and K. D. Carson. "Do Missions Accomplish Their Missions? An Exploratory Analysis of Mission Statement Content and Organizational Longevity." *The Journal of Applied Management and Entrepreneurship* 6 (2001): 75–96.

Endnotes

1. Peter Drucker, *Management: Tasks, Responsibilities, and Practices* (New York: Harper & Row, 1974), 61.

2. Andrew Campbell and Sally Yeung, "Creating a Sense of Mission," *Long Range Planning* 24, no. 4 (August 1991): 17.

3. W. R. King and D. I. Cleland, *Strategic Planning and Policy* (New York: Van Nostrand Reinhold, 1979), 124.

4. Brian Dumaine, "What the Leaders of Tomorrow See," *Fortune* (July 3, 1989), 50.

5. "How W. T. Grant Lost $175 Million Last Year," *Business Week* (February 25, 1975), 75.

6. Drucker, *Management*, 88.

7. John Pearce II, "The Company Mission as a Strategic Tool," *Sloan Management Review* 23, no. 3 (Spring 1982): 74.

8. George Steiner, *Strategic Planning: What Every Manager Must Know* (New York: The Free Press, 1979), 160.

9. David, Meredith E., David, Forest R., and David, Fred R. "Mission Statement Theory and Practice: A Content Analysis and New Direction," International Journal of Business, Marketing, and Decision Sciences, Vol. 7, No. 1, Summer 2014, 95-109.

10. http://ezinearticles.com/?Elements-of-a-Mission-Statement&id=3846671

3

The External Assessment

LEARNING OBJECTIVES

After studying this chapter, you should be able to do the following:

3-1. Describe the nature and purpose of an external assessment in formulating strategies.

3-2. Identify and discuss 10 external forces that must be examined in formulating strategies: economic, social, cultural, demographic, environmental, political, governmental, legal, technological, and competitive.

3-3. Explain Porter's Five Forces Model and its relevance in formulating strategies.

3-4. Describe key sources of information used for locating vital external information.

3-5. Discuss forecasting tools and techniques.

3-6. Explain how to develop and use an External Factor Evaluation (EFE) Matrix.

3-7. Explain how to develop and use a Competitive Profile Matrix.

ASSURANCE OF LEARNING EXERCISES

The following exercises are found at the end of this chapter:

EXERCISE 3A   Competitive Intelligence (CI) Certification

EXERCISE 3B   Develop an EFE Matrix for Hershey Company

EXERCISE 3C   Perform an External Assessment

EXERCISE 3D   Develop an EFE Matrix for Your University

EXERCISE 3E   Comparing Chipotle Mexican Grill to Panera Bread and Moe's Southwest Grill

EXERCISE 3F   Develop a Competitive Profile Matrix for Hershey Company

EXERCISE 3G   Develop a Competitive Profile Matrix for Your University

This chapter examines the tools and concepts needed to conduct an *external strategic-management* audit (sometimes called **environmental scanning** or **industry analysis**). An **external audit** focuses on identifying and evaluating trends and events beyond the control of a single firm, such as increased foreign competition, population shifts to coastal areas of the United States, an aging society, and taxing Internet sales. An external audit reveals key opportunities and threats confronting an organization, so managers can formulate strategies to take advantage of the opportunities and avoid or reduce the impact of threats. This chapter presents a practical framework for gathering, assimilating, and analyzing external information. The Industrial Organization (I/O) view of strategic management is discussed.

The company showcased here for practicing exemplary strategic management is Chipotle Mexican Grill. Chipotle is a rapidly growing firm with highly motivated employees who execute daily a company strategy to capitalize on the public's increasing concern for animal welfare and preference for organic foods. Chipotle's most recent sales and earnings were reduced somewhat due to its stance on various ethical issues. This chapter addresses whether companies should take a stand on political and societal issues. Do you think companies should?

Chipotle Mexican Grill (CMG)

Headquartered in Denver, Colorado, Chipotle is a chain of about 1,700 restaurants in the United States, the United Kingdom, Canada, Germany, and France, specializing in burritos, tacos, and salads. Chipotle is the Mexican-Spanish name for smoked and dried jalapeno chili pepper. In a recent quarter, Chipotle opened another 45 restaurants, including 17 outside the United States. Chipotle Mexican Grill has a vision statement called *Food with Integrity*, which highlights the company's efforts to use organic ingredients, and to serve more naturally raised meat than any other restaurant chain. Through the company's vision of *Food with Integrity,* Chipotle seeks better food from using ingredients that are fresh and sustainably grown, as well as raised responsibly with respect for the animals, the land, and the farmers who produce the food. Chipotle has reported revenue growth of more than 20 percent annually in the last five years, while rival, traditional, sit-down restaurants are slimming down and growing slowly. The entire restaurant sector is growing about 1 percent annually. Considered to be one of the first so-called fast-casual dining establishments, similar to Panera Bread (stock symbol = PNRA) and Moe's Southwest Grill (private company), Chipotle is rapidly growing, while many mainstream restaurants such as Red Lobster, Applebee's, Olive Garden, and even McDonald's are struggling.

Effective July 1, 2015, Chipotle extended many benefits, including tuition reimbursements, sick pay, and paid vacation, previously available only to salaried employees, to its part-time and entry-level workers. The new benefits are available to all hourly and salaried employees, including cashiers and takeout specialists, who have worked at the company for one year. J. D. Cummings, Chipotle's recruitment strategy manager, states, "We want to invest in the best people we have and keep them with us; we want to recruit and retain high school and college students, a target demographic for entry-level positions."

Chipotle promotes nearly 100 percent of its managers from within, as it did for 9,000 managers in fiscal 2014. The company also uses nontraditional marketing practices such as producing Web videos, sponsoring food and music festivals, and partnering with local farmers' markets. Recently, Chipotle tried to meet customer and societal expectations for the humane treatment of animals by withdrawing a popular pork product, carnitas, (slow-simmered pork) from one third of its restaurants, because a particular supplier "was not treating hogs humanely." Chipotle's actions, however, reveal how healthier, more humane options pose difficulties for any chain trying to balance price, standards, demand, and perception with profitability and growth. Chipotle's guidelines say "Pigs are to be housed in humane conditions with access to the outdoors rather than in pens." The chain also tries to use antibiotic-free and hormone-free meat when it can, consistent with societal expectations.

Source: Based on Ciaran McEvoy, "Fast-Casual Chains Eating Rival's Lunch," *Investor's Business Daily*, March 3, 2014, A1, A6. See also Vance Cariaga, "Chipotle Sticks to Its Own Recipe to Deliver Steady Gains," *Investor's Business Daily*, August 12, 2014, A5.

The Purpose and Nature of an External Audit

The purpose of an external audit is to develop a finite list of opportunities that could benefit a firm as well as threats that should be avoided. As the term *finite* suggests, the external audit is not aimed at developing an exhaustive list of every possible factor that could influence the business; rather, it is aimed at identifying key variables that offer **actionable responses**. Firms should be able to respond either offensively or defensively to the factors by formulating strategies that take advantage of external opportunities or that minimize the impact of potential threats. Figure 3-1 illustrates with white shading how the external audit fits into the strategic-management process.

Key External Forces

External forces can be divided into five broad categories: (1) economic forces; (2) social, cultural, demographic, and natural environment forces; (3) political, governmental, and legal forces; (4) technological forces; and (5) competitive forces. Relationships among these forces and an

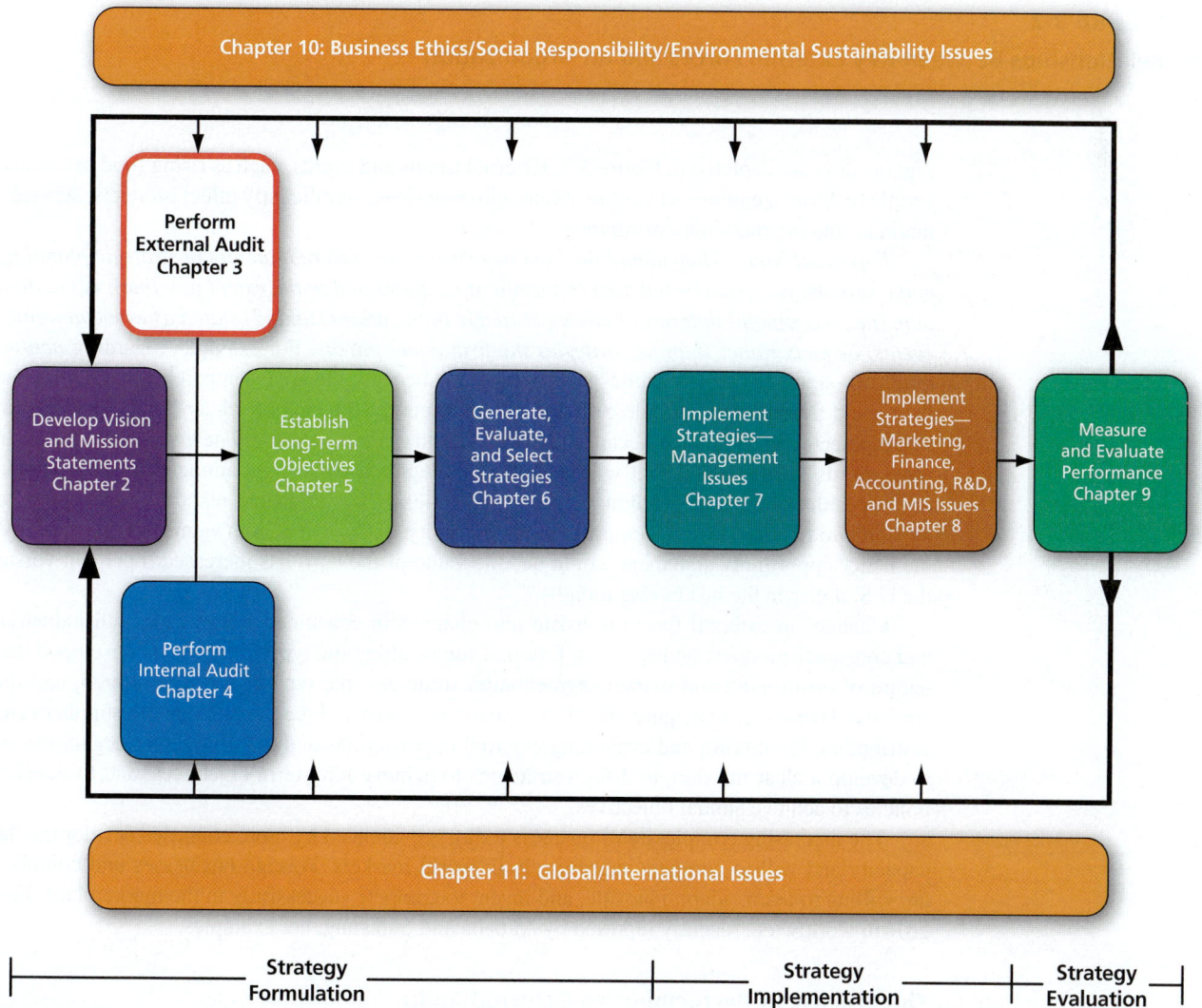

FIGURE 3-1

A Comprehensive Strategic-Management Model

Source: Fred R. David, "How Companies Define Their Mission," *Long Range Planning* 22, no. 3 (June 1988): 40. See also Anik Ratnaningsih, Nadjadji Anwar, Patdono Suwignjo, and Putu Artama Wiguna, "Balance Scorecard of David's Strategic Modeling at Industrial Business for National Construction Contractor of Indonesia," *Journal of Mathematics and Technology,* no. 4 (October 2010): 20.

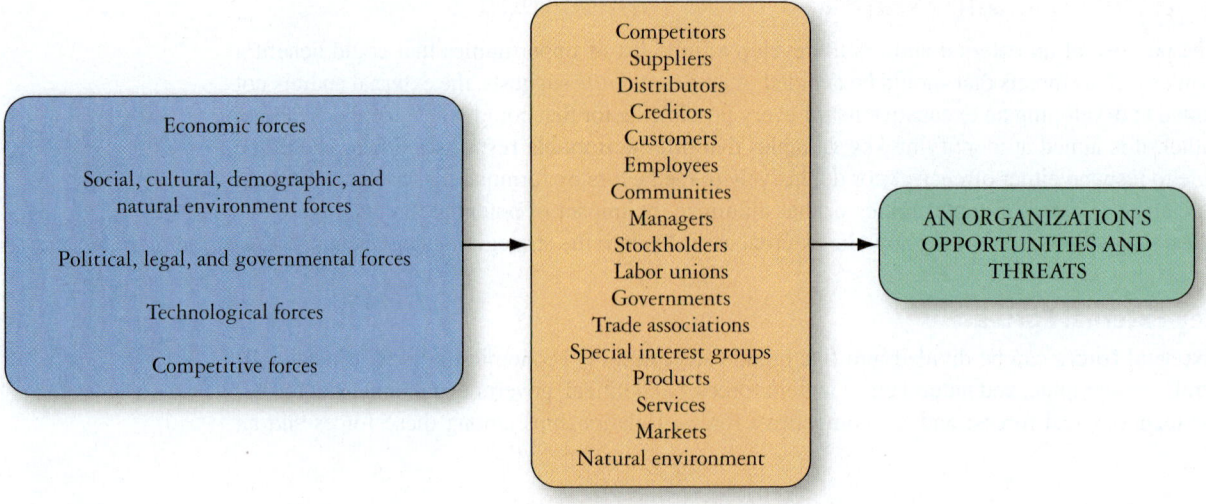

FIGURE 3-2

Relationships Between Key External Forces and an Organization

organization are depicted in Figure 3-2. External trends and events, such as rising food prices and people in African countries learning about online services, significantly affect products, services, markets, and organizations worldwide.

Important Note: When identifying and prioritizing key external factors in strategic planning, make sure the factors selected are (1) specific (i.e., quantified to the extent possible); (2) action-able (i.e., meaningful in terms of having strategic implications) and (3) stated as external trends, events, or facts rather than as strategies the firm could pursue. For example, regarding *action-able,* "the stock market is volatile" is not actionable because there is no apparent strategy that the firm could formulate to capitalize on that factor. In contrast, a factor such as "the GDP of Brazil is 6.8 percent" is actionable because the firm should perhaps open 100 new stores in Brazil. In other words, select factors that will be helpful in deciding what to recommend the firm should do, rather than selecting nebulous factors too vague for an actionable response. Similarly, "to expand into Europe" is not an appropriate opportunity, because it is both vague and is a strategy; the better opportunity statement would be "the value of the euro has increased 5 percent versus the U.S. dollar in the last twelve months."

Changes in external forces translate into changes in consumer demand for both industrial and consumer products and services. External forces affect the types of products developed, the nature of positioning and market segmentation strategies, the type of services offered, and the choice of businesses to acquire or sell. External forces have a direct impact on both suppliers and distributors. Identifying and evaluating external opportunities and threats enables organizations to develop a clear mission, to design strategies to achieve long-term objectives, and to develop policies to achieve annual objectives.

The increasing complexity of business today is evidenced by more countries developing the capacity and will to compete aggressively in world markets. Foreign businesses and countries are willing to learn, adapt, innovate, and invent to compete successfully in the marketplace. Fast growth worldwide, recently reported by Alibaba and Samsung, are examples.

The Process of Performing an External Audit

The process of performing an external audit must involve as many managers and employees as possible. As emphasized in previous chapters, involvement in the strategic-management process can lead to understanding and commitment from organizational members. Individuals appreciate having the opportunity to contribute ideas and to gain a better understanding of their firm's industry, competitors, and markets. Key external factors can vary over time and by industry.

To perform an external audit, a company first must gather competitive intelligence and information about economic, social, cultural, demographic, environmental, political, governmental, legal, and technological trends. Individuals can be asked to monitor various sources of information, such as key magazines, trade journals, and newspapers—and use online sources such as those listed later in this chapter in Table 3-8. These persons can submit periodic scanning reports to the person(s) who coordinate the external audit. This approach provides a continuous stream of timely strategic information and involves many individuals in the external-audit process. Suppliers, distributors, salespersons, customers, and competitors represent other sources of vital information.

After information is gathered, it should be assimilated and evaluated. A meeting or series of meetings of managers is needed to collectively identify the most important opportunities and threats facing the firm. A prioritized list of these factors must be obtained by requesting that all managers individually rank the factors identified, from 1 (for the most important opportunity/threat) to 20 (for the least important opportunity/threat). Instead of ranking factors, managers could simply place a checkmark by their most important "top 10 factors." Then, by summing the rankings, or the number of checkmarks, a prioritized list of factors is revealed. Prioritization is absolutely essential in strategic planning because no organization can do everything that would benefit the firm; tough choices among good choices have to be made.

The Industrial Organization (I/O) View

The **Industrial Organization** view of strategic planning advocates that external (industry) factors are more important than internal ones for gaining and sustaining competitive advantage. Proponents of the I/O view, such as Michael Porter, contend that organizational performance will be primarily determined by industry forces, such as falling gas prices that no single firm can control. Porter's Five-Forces Model, presented later in this chapter, is an example of the I/O perspective, which focuses on analyzing external forces and industry variables as a basis for getting and keeping competitive advantage.

Competitive advantage is determined largely by competitive positioning within an industry, according to I/O advocates. Managing strategically from the I/O perspective entails firms striving to compete in attractive industries, avoiding weak or faltering industries, and gaining a full understanding of key external factor relationships within that attractive industry. I/O theorists contend that external factors—such as economies of scale, barriers to market entry, product differentiation, the economy, and level of competitiveness—are more important than internal resources, capabilities, structure, and operations.

The I/O view has enhanced the understanding of strategic management. However, the authors contend that it is not a question of whether external or internal factors are more important in gaining and maintaining competitive advantage. In contrast, effective integration and understanding of *both* external and internal factors is the key to securing and keeping a competitive advantage. In fact, as discussed in Chapter 6, matching key external opportunities and threats with key internal strengths and weaknesses provides the basis for successful strategy formulation.

Ten External Forces That Affect Organizations

Economic Forces

Economic factors have a direct impact on the potential attractiveness of various strategies. For example, high underemployment (minimum wage-type employment) in the United States bodes well for discount firms such as Dollar Tree, T.J. Maxx, Walmart, and Subway, but hurts thousands of traditional-priced retailers in many industries. Although the Dow Jones Industrial Average is high, corporate profits are high, dividend increases are up sharply, gas prices are low, and emerging markets are growing, millions of people work for minimum wages or are unemployed. As a result of droughts, commodity prices are up sharply, especially food, which is contributing to rising inflation fears. Many firms are switching to part-time rather than full-time employees to avoid having to pay health benefits.

To take advantage of Canada's robust economy and eager-to-spend people, many firms are adding facilities in Canada, including T.J. Maxx opening Marshalls stores and Tanger Outlet

TABLE 3-1 Key Economic Variables to Be Monitored

Shift to a service economy in the USA	Demand shifts for different goods and services
Availability of credit	Income differences by region and consumer groups
Level of disposable income	Price fluctuations
Propensity of people to spend	Foreign countries' economic conditions
Interest rates	Monetary and fiscal policies
Inflation rates	Stock market trends
Gross domestic product trends	Tax rate variation by country and state
Consumption patterns	European Economic Community (EEC) policies
Unemployment trends	Organization of Petroleum Exporting Countries (OPEC) policies
Value of the dollar in world markets	
Import/export factors	

Factory Centers stores opening. Canada is one of the most economically prosperous countries in the world. Although interrelated, every country has its own economic situation, and those situations impact where companies choose to spend money and do business.

Interest rates, stock prices, and discretionary income are slowly rising. As stock prices increase, the desirability of equity as a source of capital increases. When the market rises, consumer and business wealth expands. A few important economic variables that often represent opportunities and threats for organizations are provided in Table 3-1. Be mindful that in strategic planning and case analysis, relevant economic variables such as those listed must be quantified and actionable to be useful.

An example of an economic variable is "value of the dollar" that recently hit a 7-year high compared to the yen, a 9-year high compared to the euro, a 5-year high compared to the Australian dollar, and an 11-year high to some other currencies. The high dollar makes it cheap for Americans to travel abroad, but expensive for foreigners to travel to the United States, thus hurting the U.S. tourism business. Trends in the dollar's value have significant and unequal effects on companies in different industries and in different locations. Agricultural and petroleum industries are hurt by the dollar's rise against the currencies of Mexico, Brazil, Venezuela, and Australia. Generally, a strong or high dollar makes U.S. goods more expensive in overseas markets. This worsens the U.S. trade deficit.

Domestic firms with big overseas sales, such as McDonald's, also are hurt by a strong dollar. Its revenue from abroad is lowered because, for example, 100 euros earned in Europe, when translated back to U.S. dollars for reporting purposes, is worth maybe $75. To combat this "loss," some companies try to raise prices in their European or Mexican stores, but that carries a risk of alienating shoppers, angering retailers, and giving local competitors a price edge. Some advantages of a strong dollar, however, are that (1) companies with substantial outside U.S. operations see their overseas expenses, such as salaries paid in euros, become cheaper; (2) it gives U.S. companies greater firepower for international acquisitions; and (3) companies importing goods have greater buying power because their dollars now go further overseas. Table 3-2 lists 10 advantages of a strong U.S. dollar for U.S. firms.

TABLE 3-2 Ten Advantages of a Strong Dollar for Domestic Firms

1. Leads to lower exports
2. Leads to higher imports
3. Makes U.S. goods expensive for foreign consumers
4. Helps keep inflation low
5. Allows U.S. firms to purchase raw materials cheaply from other countries
6. Allows USA to service its debt better
7. Spurs foreign investment
8. Encourages Americans to travel abroad
9. Leads to lower oil prices because oil globally is priced in U.S. dollars
10. Encourages Americans to spend money because they can buy more for their money

Social, Cultural, Demographic, and Natural Environment Forces

Social, cultural, demographic, and environmental changes impact strategic decisions on virtually all products, services, markets, and customers. Small, large, for-profit, and nonprofit organizations in all industries are being staggered and challenged by the opportunities and threats arising from changes in social, cultural, demographic, and environmental variables. In every way, the United States is much different today than it was yesterday, and tomorrow promises even greater changes.

The United States is becoming older and less white. The oldest among the 76 million baby boomers plan to retire soon, and this has lawmakers and younger taxpayers concerned about who will pay their Social Security, Medicare, and Medicaid. Individuals age 65 and older in the United States as a percentage of the population will rise to 18.5 percent by 2025. The oldest American as of January 1, 2015, is 116-year-old Gertrude Weaver of Little Rock, Arkansas. Weaver is the second-oldest person in the world, behind Misao Okawa of Japan, according to the Gerontology Research Group.

The trend toward an older United States is good news for restaurants, hotels, airlines, cruise lines, tours, resorts, theme parks, luxury products and services, recreational vehicles, home builders, furniture producers, computer manufacturers, travel services, pharmaceutical firms, automakers, and funeral homes. Older Americans are especially interested in health care, financial services, travel, crime prevention, and leisure. The world's longest-living people are the Japanese. By 2050, the Census Bureau projects that the number of Americans age 100 and older will increase to over 834,000 from just under 100,000 centenarians in the country in 2000. Americans age 65 and over will increase from 12.6 percent of the U.S. population in 2000 to 20.0 percent by the year 2050. The aging U.S. population affects the strategic orientation of nearly all organizations.

Retail shoppers in the United States are increasingly buying online, resulting in a persistent 5 to 7 percent decline in store traffic among almost all retail stores, prompting chains to slow or cease store openings.[1] Research reveals that growth in store counts at the 100 largest retailers by revenue slowed to 2 percent in 2014 from more than 12 percent in 2011. Consumer tastes and trends are changing as people wander through stores less, opting more and more to use their mobile phones and computers to research prices and cherry-pick promotions. Sales derived from online purchases are rapidly increasing.

The historical trend of people moving from the Northeast and Midwest to the Sunbelt and West has slowed, but there remains a steady migration to coastal areas. Hard-number data related to this trend can represent key opportunities for many firms and thus can be essential for successful strategy formulation, including where to locate new plants and distribution centers and where to focus marketing efforts.

Fortune recently ranked the largest 100 U.S. cities according to the best managed and worst managed.[2] A variety of factors were included, such as the area's economy, job market, crime level, and welfare of the population. The best-managed city is Irvine, California, followed by Fremont, California; Plano, Texas; Lincoln, Nebraska; Virginia Beach, Virginia; Scottsdale, Arizona; Seattle, Washington; Austin, Texas; Chesapeake, Virginia, and Raleigh, North Carolina.

By 2075, the United States will have no racial or ethnic majority. This forecast is aggravating tensions over issues such as immigration and affirmative action. Hawaii, California, and New Mexico already have no majority race or ethnic group. The population of the world recently surpassed 7 billion; the United States has slightly more than 310 million people. That leaves literally billions of people outside the United States who may be interested in the products and services produced through domestic firms. Remaining solely domestic is an increasingly risky strategy, especially as the world population continues to grow to an estimated 8 billion in 2028 and 9 billion in 2054.

Social, cultural, demographic, and environmental trends are shaping the way Americans live, work, produce, and consume. New trends are creating a different type of consumer and, consequently, a need for different products, new services, and updated strategies. One trend is that there are now more U.S. households with people living alone or with unrelated people than there are households consisting of married couples with children. Another is that U.S. households are making more and more purchases online.

Some important social, cultural, demographic, and environmental variables that represent opportunities or threats for virtually all organizations is given in Table 3-3. Be mindful that in

TABLE 3-3 Key Social, Cultural, Demographic, and Natural Environment Variables

Population changes by race, age, and geographic area	Attitudes toward retirement
Regional changes in tastes and preferences	Energy conservation
Number of marriages	Attitudes toward product quality
Number of divorces	Attitudes toward customer service
Number of births	Pollution control
Number of deaths	Attitudes toward foreign peoples
Immigration and emigration rates	Energy conservation
Social Security programs	Social programs
Life expectancy rates	Number of churches
Per capita income	Number of church members
Social media pervasiveness	Social responsibility issues

strategic planning and case analysis, relevant social, cultural, demographic, and natural environment factors for a particular business must be *quantified* and *actionable* to be useful.

Political, Governmental, and Legal Forces

Political issues and stances do matter for business and do impact strategic decisions, especially in today's world of instant tweeting and emailing. Various industries, such as aerospace and their supplier firms, typically support and lobby for Republicans, whereas other industries, such as automotive and their supplier firms, generally support Democrats. National, state, and local elections impact businesses, with ongoing healthy debate concerning the pros and cons of each party's agenda for business.

For industries and firms that depend heavily on government contracts or subsidies, political forecasts can be the most important part of an external audit. Changes in patent laws, antitrust legislation, tax rates, and lobbying activities can affect firms significantly. The increasing global interdependence among economies, markets, governments, and organizations makes it imperative that firms consider the possible impact of political variables on the formulation and implementation of competitive strategies.

Various countries worldwide are resorting to protectionism to safeguard their own industries. European Union (EU) nations, for example, have tightened their own trade rules and resumed subsidies for their own industries, while barring imports from certain other countries. The EU recently restricted imports of U.S. chicken and beef. India is increasing tariffs on foreign steel. Russia perhaps has instituted the most protectionist measures by raising tariffs on most imports and subsidizing its own exports. Despite these measures taken by other countries, the United States has largely refrained from "Buy American" policies and protectionist measures, although there are increased tariffs on French cheese and Italian water. Many economists say trade constraints will make it harder for global economic growth.

Local, state, and federal laws, as well as regulatory agencies and special-interest groups, can have a major impact on the strategies of small, large, for-profit, and nonprofit organizations. Many companies have altered or abandoned strategies in the past because of political or governmental actions. In the academic world, as state budgets have dropped in recent years, so too has state support for colleges and universities. Resulting from the decline in funds received from the state, many institutions of higher learning are doing more fund-raising on their own—naming buildings and classrooms, for example, for donors.

Some companies take public stands on political issues. For example, Starbucks' recent support of same-sex marriage in its home state of Washington was praised by a number of prominent rights activists. Today, all states allow same-sex marriage. But the Seattle-based coffee chain's outspoken opponents, such as the National Organization for Marriage (NOM), has vowed to make Starbucks (along with other companies that support same-sex marriage) pay a "price" for this stance. "Middle Eastern countries are hostile to lesbian, gay, bisexual, and transgender (LGBT) rights. So, for example, in Qatar, in the Middle East, we've begun working to make sure that there's some price to be paid for this," Brian Brown of the NOM said. "These are not countries that look kindly on same-sex marriage. And this is where Starbucks wants to expand, as well as India."

Recently, CVS Caremark stopped selling tobacco products at its 7,600 stores, becoming the first U.S. drugstore chain to remove cigarettes from the store—and at the same time changed its corporate name to CVS Health. Nontobacco consumers and the medical community in general applauded the CVS announcement. With the announcement, CVS said its tobacco ban will result in the firm losing about $4 billion in annual sales. Euromonitor International reports that cigarette sales in the United States declined 31.3 percent from 2003 to 2013. However, smoking is still cited as the leading cause of preventable death in the country, killing more than 480,000 Americans per year. Within weeks after the CVS announcement, 24 states, Washington DC, and three U.S. territories sent coordinated letters to the CEOs of Walmart, Rite-Aid, Safeway, Kroger, and Walgreens, asking them to stop selling tobacco products.

In mid-2015, the United States normalized relations with Cuba, ending 54 years of hostility. This event represents an opportunity for numerous companies to do business with Cuba. On 7-20-15, Cuba raised its flag over its new embassy in Washington, D.C. For example, Carnival Corporation has won approval to begin cruising to Cuba and back, marking the first time in over 50 years that a cruise line can travel to and from Cuba.

A political debate still rages in the United States regarding sales taxes on the Internet. Walmart, Target, and other large retailers are pressuring state governments to collect sales taxes from Amazon.com. Big brick-and-mortar retailers are backing a coalition called the Alliance for Main Street Fairness, which is leading political efforts to change sales-tax laws in more than a dozen states. According to Walmart's executive Raul Vazquez, "The rules today don't allow brick-and-mortar retailers to compete evenly with online retailers, and that needs to be addressed."

Federal, state, local, and foreign governments are major regulators, deregulators, subsidizers, employers, and customers of organizations. Political, governmental, and legal factors, therefore, can represent major opportunities or threats for both small and large organizations. Politicians decide on tax rates. State and local income taxes and property taxes impact where companies locate facilities and where people desire to live. The five states, in rank order, with the lowest overall state taxes, and the five states with the highest state taxes, are shown here.[3]

Lowest State Taxes	Highest State Taxes
1. Wyoming	1. New York
2. Alaska	2. California
3. Nevada	3. Nebraska
4. Florida	4. Connecticut
5. South Dakota	5. Illinois

Regarding *only* state income taxes (rather than property, local, and sales taxes, too), seven states have zero (0.00) state income taxes: Texas, Nevada, Alaska, Florida, South Dakota, Washington, and Wyoming. States with the highest income tax are California (13.3%), Hawaii (11%), Oregon (9.90%), Minnesota (9.85%), Iowa (8.98%), and New Jersey (8.97%).

The extent that a state is unionized can be a significant political factor in strategic-planning decisions as related to manufacturing plant location and other operational matters. The size of U.S. labor unions has fallen sharply in the last decade as a result in large part of erosion of the U.S. manufacturing base. Organized public-sector labor issues are being debated in many state legislatures. Wisconsin, for example, recently passed a law eliminating most collective-bargaining rights for the state's public-employee unions. That law sets a precedent that many other states may follow to curb union rights as a way to help state budgets become solvent. Ohio is close to passing a similar bill that will curb union rights for 400,000 public workers. Among states, New York continues to have the highest union membership rate (24.1 percent) and North Carolina has the lowest rate (2.9 percent).

Some political, governmental, and legal variables that can represent key opportunities or threats to organizations are provided in Table 3-4, but in stating these for a particular company, the factors should be both *quantitative* and *actionable*.

TABLE 3-4   Some Political, Governmental, and Legal Variables

Environmental regulations	USA vs. other country relationships
Number of patents	Political conditions in foreign countries
Changes in patent laws	Global price of oil changes
Equal employment laws	Local, state, and federal laws
Level of defense expenditures	Import–export regulations
Unionization trends	Tariffs
Antitrust legislation	Local, state, and national elections

Technological Forces

A variety of new technologies such as the Internet of Things, 3D printing, the cloud, mobile devices, biotech, analytics, autotech, robotics, and artificial intelligence are fueling innovation in many industries, and impacting strategic-planning decisions. Businesses are using mobile technologies and applications to better determine customer trends and employing advanced analytics data to make enhanced strategy decisions. The vast increase in the amount of data coming from mobile devices is driving the development of advanced analytics applications. In fact, by 2018, machine-to-machine devices ranging from wearable Web access devices and utility meters and sensors in cars will account for 35 percent of global Internet network-connected devices, up from 18.6 percent today.[4] A primary reason that Cisco Systems has recently entered the data analytics business is that sales of hardware, software, and services connected to the Internet of Things is expected to increase to $7.1 billion by 2020 from about $2.0 billion in 2015.

Rapid technological advances in mobile and electronic banking have led banks to close branch offices at dramatically increasing rates in the United States. The total number of branch locations has dropped below 90,000, the lowest total number in the United States in a decade. Too offset closing branch offices, U.S. banks are ramping up mobile and online services, such as allowing customers to make deposits simply by snapping photos of checks with smartphones and emailing them. Many banks now allow customers to transfer money to other customers via smartphones. At Bank of America, for example, nearly 15 percent of all checks deposited by customers come from snapping pictures on smartphones or tablet computers. Not a single state in the United States reported an increase in the number of branch bank locations in recent years.[5] Florida leads all states in branch bank closures, followed by Pennsylvania. Technology is rapidly changing the competitive landscape in banking, and many other industries characterized by brick-and-mortar stores.

Monitoring online reviews about your business, large or small, has become a burdensome but an essential task, especially given emergence of social-media channels, such as Twitter, that empowers opinionated customers. Research is clear that benign neglect of a company's online reputation could quickly hurt sales, especially given the new normal behavior of customers consulting their smartphones for even the smallest of purchases.[6]

A number of organizations are establishing two positions in their firms: **chief information officer (CIO)** and **chief technology officer (CTO)**, reflecting the growing importance of **information technology (IT)** in strategic management. A CIO and CTO work together to ensure that information needed to formulate, implement, and evaluate strategies is available where and when it is needed. These individuals are responsible for developing, maintaining, and updating a company's information database. The CIO is more a manager, managing the firm's relationship with stakeholders; the CTO is more a technician, focusing on technical issues such as data acquisition, data processing, decision-support systems, and software and hardware acquisition.

Global cybersecurity spending by critical infrastructure industries exceeds $50 billion annually, and is rising more than 10 percent annually.[7] Security is a major concern for all businesses, yet complete security is something most businesses cannot financially afford to install. Hackers recently stole 40 million of Target Corporation's customers' credit- and debit-card numbers, along with passcodes and passwords. Building firewalls and triplicate systems can be expensive. Similarly, J.P. Morgan reported that 76 million of their customers' contact information was recently stolen in a cybersecurity breach. Sony, too, was recently a victim of a massive cyber-attack. Even the federal government employee databanks were recently hacked, reportedly by some entities in China.

Results of technological advancements are varied, as shown in the following list:

1. They represent major opportunities and threats that must be considered in formulating strategies.
2. They can dramatically affect organizations' products, services, markets, suppliers, distributors, competitors, customers, manufacturing processes, marketing practices, and competitive position.
3. They can create new markets, result in a proliferation of new and improved products, change the relative competitive cost positions in an industry, and render existing products and services obsolete.
4. They can reduce or eliminate cost barriers between businesses, create shorter production runs, create shortages in technical skills, and result in changing values and expectations of employees, managers, and customers.
5. They can create new competitive advantages that are more powerful than existing advantages.

No company or industry today is insulated against emerging technological developments. In high-tech industries, identification and evaluation of key technological opportunities and threats can be the most important part of the external strategic-management audit.

Competitive Forces

An important part of an external audit is identifying rival firms and determining their strengths, weaknesses, capabilities, opportunities, threats, objectives, and strategies. George Salk stated, "If you're not faster than your competitor, you're in a tenuous position, and if you're only half as fast, you're terminal."

Collecting and evaluating information on competitors is essential for successful strategy formulation. Identifying major competitors is not always easy because many firms have divisions that compete in different industries. Many multidivisional firms do not provide sales and profit information on a divisional basis for competitive reasons. Also, privately held firms do not publish any financial or marketing information. Addressing questions about competitors, such as those presented in Table 3-5, is important in performing an external audit.

Competition in virtually all industries is intense—and sometimes cutthroat. For example, Walgreens and CVS pharmacies are located generally across the street from each other and battle

TABLE 3-5 Key Questions About Competitors

1. What are the strengths of our major competitors?
2. What are the weaknesses of our major competitors?
3. What are the objectives and strategies of our major competitors?
4. How will our major competitors most likely respond to current economic, social, cultural, demographic, environmental, political, governmental, legal, technological, and competitive trends affecting our industry?
5. How vulnerable are the major competitors to our alternative company strategies?
6. How vulnerable are our alternative strategies to successful counterattack by our major competitors?
7. How are our products or services positioned relative to major competitors?
8. To what extent are new firms entering and old firms leaving this industry?
9. What key factors have resulted in our present competitive position in this industry?
10. How have the sales and profit rankings of our major competitors in the industry changed over recent years? Why have these rankings changed that way?
11. What is the nature of supplier and distributor relationships in this industry?
12. To what extent could substitute products or services be a threat to our competitors?

each other every day on price and customer service. Most automobile dealerships also are located close to each other. Dollar General, Dollar Tree, and Family Dollar compete intensely on price to attract customers away from each other and away from Walmart and Target.

Seven characteristics describe the most competitive companies:

1. Strive to continually increase market share.
2. Use the vision/mission as a guide for all decisions.
3. Realize that the adage "If it's not broke, don't fix it" has been replaced by "Whether it's broke or not, fix it"; in other words, continually strive to improve everything about the firm.
4. Continually adapt, innovate, improve—especially when the firm is successful.
5. Strive to grow through acquisition whenever possible.
6. Hire and retain the best employees and managers possible.
7. Strive to stay cost-competitive on a global basis.[8]

Competitive intelligence (CI), as formally defined by the Society of Competitive Intelligence Professionals (SCIP), is a systematic and ethical process for gathering and analyzing information about the competition's activities and general business trends to further a business's own goals (SCIP website). Good competitive intelligence in business, as in the military, is one of the keys to success. The more information and knowledge a firm can obtain about its competitors, the more likely the firm can formulate and implement effective strategies. Major competitors' weaknesses can represent external opportunities; major competitors' strengths may represent key threats.

Various legal and ethical ways to obtain competitive intelligence include the following:

- Hire top executives from rival firms.
- Reverse engineer rival firms' products.
- Use surveys and interviews of customers, suppliers, and distributors.
- Conduct drive-by and on-site visits to rival firm operations.
- Search online databases.
- Contact government agencies for public information about rival firms.
- Systematically monitor relevant trade publications, magazines, and newspapers.

Information gathering from employees, managers, suppliers, distributors, customers, creditors, and consultants also can make the difference between having superior or just average intelligence and overall competitiveness. The Fuld website explains that competitive intelligence is *not* the following:

Is not spying

Is not a crystal ball

Is not a simple Google search

Is not one-size-fits-all

Is not useful if no one is listening

Is not a job for one, smart person

Is not a fad

Is not driven by software or technology

Is not based on internal assumptions about the market

Is not a spreadsheet.[9]

The three basic objectives of a CI program are (1) to provide a general understanding of an industry and its competitors, (2) to identify areas in which competitors are vulnerable and to assess the impact strategic actions would have on competitors, and (3) to identify potential moves that a competitor might make that would endanger a firm's position in the market.[10] Competitive information is equally applicable for strategy formulation, implementation, and evaluation decisions. An effective CI program allows all areas of a firm to access consistent and verifiable information in making decisions. All members of an organization—from the CEO to custodians—are valuable intelligence agents and should feel themselves to be a part of the CI process. Special characteristics of a successful CI program include flexibility, usefulness, timeliness, and cross-functional cooperation.

Competitive intelligence is not corporate espionage; after all, 95 percent of the information a company needs to make strategic decisions is available and accessible to the public. Sources of competitive information include trade journals, want ads, newspaper articles, and government filings, as well as customers, suppliers, distributors, competitors themselves, and the Internet. Unethical tactics such as bribery, wiretapping, and computer hacking should never be used to obtain information. All the information a company needs can be collected without resorting to unethical tactics.

Porter's Five-Forces Model

Former chair and CEO of PepsiCo Wayne Calloway said, "Nothing focuses the mind better than the constant sight of a competitor that wants to wipe you off the map." As illustrated in Figure 3-3, **Porter's Five-Forces Model** of competitive analysis is a widely used approach for developing strategies in many industries. The intensity of competition among firms varies widely across industries. Table 3-6 reveals the average gross profit margin and earnings per share (EPS) for firms in different industries. Note the substantial variation among industries. For example, note that industry operating margins range from 4 to 34 percent, whereas industry

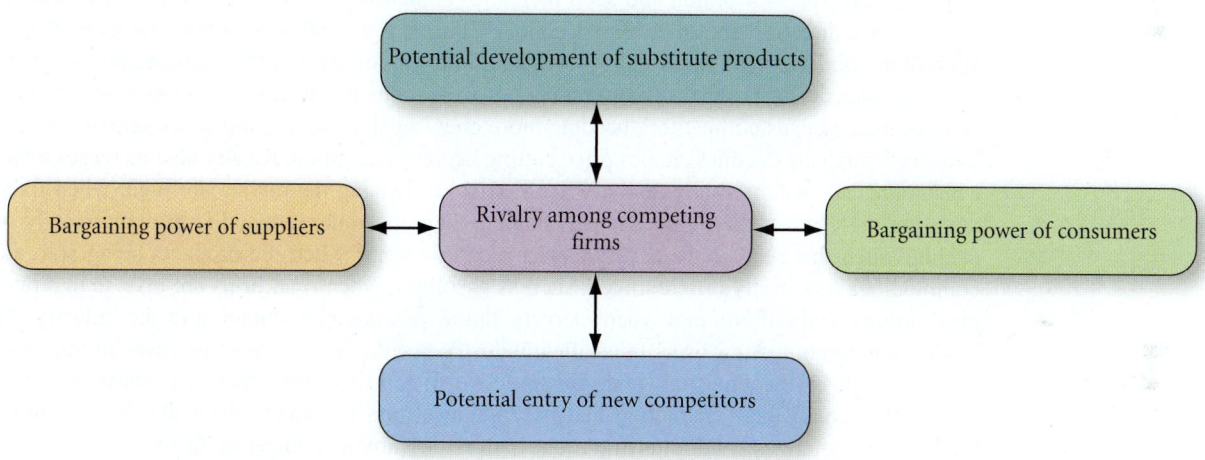

FIGURE 3-3

The Five-Forces Model of Competition

TABLE 3-6 Competitiveness Across a Few Industries (2015 data)

	Operating Margin (%)	EPS ($)
Pharmaceutical	13.0	0.61
Telecommunications	14.0	1.25
Fragrances/Cosmetics	12.0	2.23
Banking	34.0	1.58
Bookstores	6.0	0.16
Food Manufacturers	4.0	0.63
Oil and Gas	10.0	2.03
Airlines	10.0	0.09
Machinery/Construction	7.0	0.96
Paper Products	5.0	0.27

Source: Based on company data.

EPS values range from −16 to 2.23. Note that food manufacturers have the lowest average profit margin (2.3), which implies fierce competition in that industry. Intensity of competition is highest in lower-return industries. The collective impact of competitive forces is so brutal in some industries that the market is clearly "unattractive" from a profit-making standpoint. Rivalry among existing firms is severe, new rivals can enter the industry with relative ease, and both suppliers and customers can exercise considerable bargaining leverage. According to Porter, a Harvard Business School professor, the nature of competitiveness in a given industry can be viewed as a composite of five forces:

1. Rivalry among competing firms
2. Potential entry of new competitors
3. Potential development of substitute products
4. Bargaining power of suppliers
5. Bargaining power of consumers

Rivalry Among Competing Firms

Rivalry among competing firms is usually the most powerful of the five competitive forces. The strategies pursued by one firm can be successful only to the extent that they provide competitive advantage over the strategies pursued by rival firms. Changes in strategy by one firm may be met with retaliatory countermoves, such as lowering prices, enhancing quality, adding features, providing services, extending warranties, and increasing advertising. For example, Verizon recently acquired AOL for $4.4 billion and soon thereafter launched its own video streaming to mobile devices, in a direct attack on rivals Facebook, Google, Sony, Dish Network, and even Apple. With AOL onboard, Verizon also now derives millions of dollars of mobile advertising revenue.

The intensity of rivalry among competing firms tends to increase as the number of competitors increases, as competitors become more equal in size and capability, as demand for the industry's products declines, and as price cutting becomes common. Rivalry also increases when consumers can switch brands easily; when barriers to leaving the market are high; when fixed costs are high; when the product is perishable; when consumer demand is growing slowly or declines such that rivals have excess capacity or inventory; when the products being sold are commodities (not easily differentiated, such as gasoline); when rival firms are diverse in strategies, origins, and culture; and when mergers and acquisitions are common in the industry. As rivalry among competing firms intensifies, industry profits decline, in some cases to the point where an industry becomes inherently unattractive. When rival firms sense weakness, typically they will intensify both marketing and production efforts to capitalize on the "opportunity." Table 3-7 summarizes conditions that cause high rivalry among competing firms.

TABLE 3-7   Conditions That Cause High Rivalry Among Competing Firms

1. When the number of competing firms is high
2. When competing firms are of similar size
3. When competing firms have similar capabilities
4. When the demand for the industry's products is falling
5. When the product or service prices in the industry is falling
6. When consumers can switch brands easily
7. When barriers to leaving the market are high
8. When barriers to entering the market are low
9. When fixed costs are high among competing firms
10. When the product is perishable
11. When rivals have excess capacity
12. When consumer demand is falling
13. When rivals have excess inventory
14. When rivals sell similar products/services
15. When mergers are common in the industry

Potential Entry of New Competitors

Whenever new firms can easily enter a particular industry, the intensity of competitiveness among firms increases. Barriers to entry, however, can include the need to gain economies of scale quickly, the need to gain technology and specialized know-how, the lack of experience, strong customer loyalty, strong brand preferences, large capital requirements, lack of adequate distribution channels, government regulatory policies, tariffs, lack of access to raw materials, possession of patents, undesirable locations, counterattack by entrenched firms, and potential saturation of the market.

Despite numerous barriers to entry, new firms sometimes enter industries with higher-quality products, lower prices, and substantial marketing resources. The strategist's job, therefore, is to identify potential new firms entering the market, to monitor the new rival firms' strategies, to counterattack as needed, and to capitalize on existing strengths and opportunities. When the threat of new firms entering the market is strong, incumbent firms generally fortify their positions and take actions to deter new entrants, such as lowering prices, extending warranties, adding features, or offering financing specials.

The Walt Disney Company is nearing completion of its Shanghai Disneyland, a $4.4 billion complex set to open in China in 2016, complete with hotels, restaurants, retail shops, and other amenities. However, a rival firm, DreamWorks Animation SKG, is nearing completion of a $3.1 billion entertainment district named Dream Center in Shanghai right beside Disneyland and says its facility will also open in 2016. Although expensive to build, theme parks are becoming more popular globally. Time Warner's Warner Brothers is building Harry Potter attractions around the world, including a converted movie studio outside London.

Potential Development of Substitute Products

In many industries, firms are in close competition with producers of substitute products in other industries. Examples are plastic container producers competing with glass, paperboard, and aluminum can producers, and acetaminophen manufacturers competing with other manufacturers of pain and headache remedies. The presence of substitute products puts a ceiling on the price that can be charged before consumers will switch to the substitute product. Price ceilings equate to profit ceilings and more intense competition among rivals. Producers of eyeglasses and contact lenses, for example, face increasing competitive pressures from laser eye surgery. Producers of sugar face similar pressures from artificial sweeteners. Newspapers and magazines face substitute-product competitive pressures from the Internet and 24-hour cable television. The magnitude of competitive pressure derived from the development of substitute products is generally evidenced by rivals' plans for expanding production capacity, as well as by their sales and profit growth numbers.

Competitive pressures arising from substitute products increase as the relative price of substitute products declines and as consumers' costs of switching decrease. The competitive strength of substitute products is best measured by the inroads into the market share those products obtain, as well as those firms' plans for increased capacity and market penetration.

Bargaining Power of Suppliers

The bargaining power of suppliers affects the intensity of competition in an industry, especially when there are few suppliers, when there are few good substitute raw materials, or when the cost of switching raw materials is especially high. It is often in the best interest of both suppliers and producers to assist each other with reasonable prices, improved quality, development of new services, just-in-time deliveries, and reduced inventory costs, thus enhancing long-term profitability for all concerned.

Firms may pursue a backward integration strategy to gain control or ownership of suppliers. This strategy is especially effective when suppliers are unreliable, too costly, or not capable of meeting a firm's needs on a consistent basis. Firms generally can negotiate more favorable terms with suppliers when backward integration is a commonly used strategy among rival firms in an industry.

However, in many industries it is more economical to use outside suppliers of component parts than to self-manufacture the items. This is true, for example, in the outdoor power equipment industry, where producers (such as Murray) of lawn mowers, rotary tillers, leaf blowers, and edgers generally obtain their small engines from outside manufacturers (such as Briggs & Stratton) that specialize in such engines and have huge economies of scale.

In more and more industries, sellers are forging strategic partnerships with select suppliers in an effort to (1) reduce inventory and logistics costs (e.g., through just-in-time deliveries), (2) accelerate the availability of next-generation components, (3) enhance the quality of the parts and components being supplied and reduce defect rates, and (4) squeeze out important cost savings for both themselves and their suppliers.[11]

Bargaining Power of Consumers

When customers are concentrated or large in number or buy in volume, their bargaining power represents a major force affecting the intensity of competition in an industry. Rival firms may offer extended warranties or special services to gain customer loyalty whenever the bargaining power of consumers is substantial. Bargaining power of consumers also is higher when the products being purchased are standard or undifferentiated. When this is the case, consumers often can negotiate selling price, warranty coverage, and accessory packages to a greater extent.

The bargaining power of consumers can be the most important force affecting competitive advantage. Consumers gain increasing bargaining power under the following circumstances:

1. If they can inexpensively switch to competing brands or substitutes
2. If they are particularly important to the seller
3. If sellers are struggling in the face of falling consumer demand
4. If they are informed about sellers' products, prices, and costs
5. If they have discretion in whether and when they purchase the product[12]

Sources of External Information

A wealth of strategic information is available to organizations from both published and unpublished sources. *Unpublished sources* include customer surveys, market research, speeches at professional and shareholders' meetings, television programs, interviews, and conversations with stakeholders. *Published sources* of strategic information include periodicals, journals, reports, government documents, abstracts, books, directories, newspapers, and manuals. A company website is usually an excellent place to start to find information about a firm, particularly on the Investor Relations web pages.

There are many excellent websites for gathering strategic information, but three that the authors use routinely are:

1. http://morningstar.com
2. www.hoovers.com
3. http://globaledge.msu.edu/industries/

An excellent source of industry information is provided by Michigan State University at http://globaledge.msu.edu/industries/. Industry profiles provided at that site are an excellent source for information, news, events, and statistical data for any industry. In addition to a wealth of indices, risk assessments, and interactive trade information, a wide array of global resources are provided.

Most college libraries subscribe to many excellent online business databases that can then be used free by students to gather information to perform a strategic management case analysis. Simply ask your reference librarian. Especially good sources of information are described in Table 3-8.

Forecasting Tools and Techniques

Forecasts are educated assumptions about future trends and events. Forecasting is a complex activity because of factors such as technological innovation, cultural changes, new products, improved services, stronger competitors, shifts in government priorities, changing social values,

TABLE 3-8   Great Online Sources of Company and Industry Information

- **IBISWorld**—Provides online USA Industry Reports (NAICS), U.S. Industry iExpert Summaries, and U.S. Business Environment Profiles. A global version of IBIS is also available.
- **Lexis-Nexis Academic**—Provides online access to newspaper articles (including *New York Times* and *Washington Post*) and business information (including SEC filings).
- **Lexis-Nexis Company Dossier**—Provides online access to extensive, current data on 13 million companies. It collects and compiles information into excellent documents.
- **Mergent Online**—Provides online access to Mergent's (formerly Moody's/FISOnline) Manuals, which include trend, descriptive, and statistical information on hundreds of public companies and industries. Company income statements and balance sheets are provided.
- **Regional Business News**—Provides comprehensive full-text coverage for regional business publications; incorporates coverage of more than 80 regional business publications covering all metropolitan and rural areas within the United States.
- **Standard & Poor's NetAdvantage**—Provides online access to Standard & Poor's *Industry Surveys*, stock reports, corporation records, *The Outlook*, mutual fund reports, and more.
- **Value Line Investment Survey**—Provides excellent online information and advice on approximately 1,700 stocks, more than 90 industries, the stock market, and the economy. Company income statements and balance sheets are provided.

Source: Based on information at www.fmarion.edu/library.

unstable economic conditions, and unforeseen events. Managers often must rely on published forecasts to effectively identify key external opportunities and threats.

A sense of the future permeates all action and underlies every decision a person makes. People eat expecting to be satisfied and nourished in the future. People sleep assuming that in the future they will feel rested. They invest energy, money, and time because they believe their efforts will be rewarded in the future. They build highways assuming that automobiles and trucks will need them in the future. Parents educate children on the basis of forecasts that they will need certain skills, attitudes, and knowledge when they grow up. The truth is we all make implicit forecasts throughout our daily lives. The question, therefore, is not whether we should forecast but rather how we can best forecast to enable us to move beyond our ordinarily unarticulated assumptions about the future. Can we obtain information and then make educated assumptions (forecasts) to better guide our current decisions to achieve a more desirable future state of affairs? Assumptions must be made based on facts, figures, trends, and research. Strive for the firm's assumptions to be more accurate than rival firm's assumptions.

Sometimes organizations must develop their own projections. Most organizations forecast (project) their own revenues and profits annually. Organizations sometimes forecast market share or customer loyalty in local areas. Because forecasting is so important in strategic management and because the ability to forecast (in contrast to the ability to use a forecast) is essential, selected forecasting tools are examined further here.

No forecast is perfect—some are even wildly inaccurate. This fact accents the need for strategists to devote sufficient time and effort to study the underlying bases for published forecasts and to develop internal forecasts of their own. Key external opportunities and threats can be effectively identified only through good forecasts. Accurate forecasts can provide major competitive advantages for organizations. Accurate forecasts are vital to the strategic-management process and to the success of organizations.

Making Assumptions

Planning would be impossible without assumptions. McConkey defines assumptions as the "best present estimates of the impact of major external factors, over which the manager has little if any control, but which may exert a significant impact on performance or the ability to achieve desired results."[13] Strategists are faced with countless variables and imponderables that can be neither controlled nor predicted with 100 percent accuracy. Wild guesses should never be made in formulating strategies, but reasonable assumptions based on available information must *always* be made.

By identifying future occurrences that could have a major effect on the firm and by making reasonable assumptions about those factors, strategists can carry the strategic-management process forward. Assumptions are needed only for future trends and events that are most likely to have a significant effect on the company's business. Based on the best information at the time, assumptions serve as checkpoints on the validity of strategies. If future occurrences deviate significantly from assumptions, strategists know that corrective actions may be needed. Without reasonable assumptions, the strategy-formulation process could not proceed effectively. Firms that have the best information generally make the most accurate assumptions, which can lead to major competitive advantages.

Business Analytics

Business analytics is an MIS technique that involves using software to mine huge volumes of data to help executives make decisions. Sometimes called *predictive analytics, machine learning,* or *data mining,* this software enables a researcher to assess and use the aggregate experience of an organization, which is a priceless strategic asset for a firm. The history of a firm's interaction with its customers, suppliers, distributors, employees, rival firms, and more can all be tapped with **data mining** to generate predictive models. Business analytics is similar to the actuarial methods used by insurance companies to rate customers by the chance of positive or negative outcomes. Every business is basically a risk management endeavor! Therefore, like insurance companies, all businesses can benefit from measuring, tracking, and computing the risk associated with hundreds of strategic and tactical decisions made every day. Business analytics enables a company to benefit from measuring and managing risk.

As more and more products become commoditized (so similar as to be indistinguishable), competitive advantage more and more hinges on improvements to business processes. Business analytics can provide a firm with proprietary business intelligence regarding, for example, which segment(s) of customers choose your firm versus those who defer, delay, or defect to a competitor and why. Business analytics can reveal where competitors are weak so that marketing and sales activities can be directly targeted to take advantage of resultant opportunities (knowledge). In addition to understanding consumer behavior better, which yields more effective and efficient marketing, business analytics also is being used to slash expenses by, for example, withholding retention offers from customers who are going to stay with the firm anyway, or managing fraudulent transactions involving invoices, credit-card purchases, tax returns, insurance claims, mobile phone calls, online ad clicks, and more.

A key distinguishing feature of business analytics is that it enables a firm to learn from experience and to make current and future decisions based on prior information. Deriving robust predictive models from data mining to support hundreds of commonly occurring business decisions is the essence of learning from experience. The mathematical models associated with business analytics can dramatically enhance decision making at all organizational levels and all stages of strategic management. In a sense, art becomes science with business analytics resulting from the mathematical generalization of thousands, millions, or even billions of prior data points to discover patterns of behavior for optimizing the deployment of resources.

Netflix has used business analytics lately to mount a comeback in the industry and to grow dramatically its customer base. Netflix uses data analysis increasingly to refine its movie recommendations to particular customers as well as to identify which movies and television shows to license or develop. A recent article by Willhite defines *business analytics* as "the art and science of collecting and combing through vast amounts of information for insights that aren't apparent on a smaller scale."[14] Data mining, and using an analytical approach to all phases of strategic management, is rapidly burgeoning into a necessary prerequisite for success in hundreds of firms globally. This book advocates a systematic, analytical approach to strategic planning because otherwise emotion, politics, "experience," and subjectivity too often prevent identification and consideration of key facts, figures, and trends in choosing among numerous feasible alternative strategies, and implementing and monitoring the execution of those strategies.

The big data analytics firm, Splunk, reports ever-increasing revenues and profits as it capitalizes on a growing market for helping companies find better ways to manage increasing amounts of data coming in from mobile phones, PCs, global positioning systems, and other electronic devices. Splunk CEO Godfrey Sullivan says companies have "a massive thirst to better understand their customers, as well as the data coming through the enterprise from a variety of sources."

IBM's annual business analytics revenues of about $40 billion are growing about 15 percent every quarter, compared to the industry growing about 15 percent annually. IBM's acquisition of SPSS for $1.2 billion, among other recent acquisitions, launched the firm heavily into the business analytics consulting business. Other business analytics firms are Oracle, Tableau Software, Rocket Fuel, and Cisco Systems.

The External Factor Evaluation Matrix

An **External Factor Evaluation (EFE) Matrix** allows strategists to summarize and evaluate economic, social, cultural, demographic, environmental, political, governmental, legal, technological, and competitive information, illustrated earlier in Figure 3-2. The EFE Matrix can be developed in five steps:

1. List 20 key external factors as identified in the external-audit process, including both opportunities and threats that affect the firm and its industry. List the opportunities first and then the threats. Be as specific as possible, using percentages, ratios, and comparative numbers whenever possible. Recall that Edward Deming said, "In God we trust. Everyone else bring data." In addition, utilize "actionable" factors as defined earlier in this chapter.
2. Assign to each factor a weight that ranges from 0.0 (not important) to 1.0 (very important). The weight indicates the relative importance of that factor to being successful in the firm's industry. Opportunities often receive higher weights than threats, but threats can receive high weights if they are especially severe or threatening. Appropriate weights can be determined by comparing successful with unsuccessful competitors or by discussing the factor and reaching a group consensus. The sum of all weights assigned to the factors must equal 1.0.
3. Assign a rating between 1 and 4 to each key external factor to indicate how effectively the firm's current strategies respond to the factor, where 4 = the response is superior, 3 = the response is above average, 2 = the response is average, and 1 = the response is poor. Ratings are based on effectiveness of the firm's strategies. Ratings are thus company-based, whereas the weights in Step 2 are industry-based. It is important to note that both threats and opportunities can receive a 1, 2, 3, or 4.
4. Multiply each factor's weight by its rating to determine a weighted score.
5. Sum the weighted scores for each variable to determine the total weighted score for the organization.

Regardless of the number of key opportunities and threats included in an EFE Matrix, the highest possible total weighted score for an organization is 4.0 and the lowest possible total weighted score is 1.0. The average total weighted score is 2.5. A total weighted score of 4.0 indicates that an organization is responding in an outstanding way to existing opportunities and threats in its industry. In other words, the firm's strategies effectively take advantage of existing opportunities and minimize the potential adverse effects of external threats. A total score of 1.0 indicates that the firm's strategies are not capitalizing on opportunities or avoiding external threats.

An example of an EFE Matrix is provided in Table 3-9 for a local 10-theater cinema complex. Observe in the table that the most important factor to being successful in this business is "Trend toward healthy eating eroding concession sales," as indicated by the 0.12 weight. Also note that the local cinema is doing excellent in regard to handling two factors, "TDB University is expanding 6 percent annually" and "Trend toward healthy eating eroding concession sales." Perhaps the cinema is placing flyers on campus and also adding yogurt and healthy drinks to its concession menu. Note that you may have a 1, 2, 3, or 4 anywhere down the Rating column. Observe also that the factors are stated in quantitative terms to the extent possible, rather than being stated in vague terms. Quantify the factors as much as possible in constructing an EFE Matrix. Note also that all the factors are "actionable" instead of being something like "The economy is bad." Finally, note that the total weighted score of 2.58 is above the average (midpoint) of 2.5, so this cinema business is doing pretty well, taking advantage of the external opportunities

TABLE 3-9 EFE Matrix for a Local 10-Theater Cinema Complex

Key External Factors	Weight	Rating	Weighted Score
Opportunities			
1. Two new neighborhoods developing within 3 miles	0.09	1	0.09
2. TDB University is expanding 6% annually	0.08	4	0.32
3. Major competitor across town recently closed	0.08	3	0.24
4. Demand for going to cinemas growing 10%	0.07	2	0.14
5. Disposable income among citizens up 5% in prior year	0.06	3	0.18
6. Rowan County is growing 8% annually in population	0.05	3	0.15
7. Unemployment rate in county declined to 3.1%	0.03	2	0.06
Threats			
8. Trend toward healthy eating eroding concession sales	0.12	4	0.48
9. Demand for online movies and DVDs growing 10%	0.06	2	0.12
10. Commercial property adjacent to cinemas for sale	0.06	3	0.18
11. TDB University installing an on-campus movie theater	0.04	3	0.12
12. County and city property taxes increasing 25%	0.08	2	0.16
13. Local religious groups object to R-rated movies	0.04	3	0.12
14. Movies rented at local Red Box's up 12%	0.08	2	0.16
15. Movies rented last quarter from Time Warner up 15%	0.06	1	0.06
TOTAL	**1.00**		**2.58**

and avoiding the threats facing the firm. There is definitely room for improvement, though, because the highest total weighted score would be 4.0. As indicated by ratings of 1, this business needs to capitalize more on the "Two new neighborhoods developing [nearby]" opportunity and the "movies rented from … Time Warner" threat. Notice also that there are many percentage-based factors among the group. Be quantitative to the extent possible! Note, too, that the ratings range from 1 to 4 on both the opportunities and threats.

An actual EFE Matrix for the largest U.S. homebuilder, D. R. Horton, is given in Table 3-10. Note that the most important external threat facing the company, as indicated by a weight of 0.10, deals with labor and supplier costs. The key factors are listed in order beginning with the most important (highest weight). Notice how specific the factors are stated—specificity is essential. Also note that following DRH's EFE Matrix, an "author commentary" is given in Table 3-11, providing the rationale for each factor included.

Author commentary on each factor in the D. R. Horton EFE Matrix is given in Table 3-11 to provide insight on the thinking that needs to support not only inclusion of respective factors but also various weights and ratings assigned. Recall that mathematically, 0.04 is 33 percent more important than 0.03, and a rating of 3 is 50 percent higher than a rating of 2. Small judgments are helpful in moving forward toward larger decisions related to deployment of resources and money across regions and products.

The Competitive Profile Matrix

The **Competitive Profile Matrix (CPM)** identifies a firm's major competitors and its particular strengths and weaknesses in relation to a sample firm's strategic position. The weights and total weighted scores in both a CPM and an EFE have the same meaning. However, *critical success factors* in a CPM include both internal and external issues; therefore, the ratings refer to strengths and weaknesses, where 4 = major strength, 3 = minor strength, 2 = minor weakness, and 1 = major weakness. The critical success factors in a CPM are not grouped

TABLE 3-10   An Actual EFE Matrix for the Homebuilder D. R. Horton

Opportunities	Weight	Rating	Weighted Score
1. The 10 fastest-growing states by population are SC, WA, AZ, FL, SD, NV, TX, CO, UT, and ND.	0.12	3	0.36
2. Most new technological advances in residential building have come in the form of green building.	0.08	2	0.16
3. New home sales are up over 40% (compared to 20% in resales) with the South being up 38% and the West being up 49%.	0.08	3	0.24
4. Lennar's starting prices are about 10% more nationwide.	0.06	3	0.18
5. More than 80% of people over the age of 65 own a home.	0.05	2	0.10
6. Corporate social responsibility pays; 53% of consumers said they would pay up to 10% more for a product from a CSR firm.	0.04	1	0.04
7. It is more affordable to buy than it is to rent in 98 out of 100 U.S. metros.	0.02	2	0.04
8. Interest rates have fallen 0.25% in the last year.	0.02	2	0.04
9. The availability of credit has increased 16%.	0.02	3	0.06
10. The level of disposable income has increased 5%.	0.01	3	0.03

Threats	Weight	Rating	Weighted Score
1. Framing lumber has increased 45%. YTD wages per hour are up 3.1%, cement costs are up 3.8%, and lumber costs are up 6.1%.	0.10	2	0.20
2. Lennar is growing faster than any other top-5 builder; Lennar has built 69% more homes, compared to DRH's 44%.	0.08	3	0.24
3. Lennar operates using an "everything's included" approach (supplying luxury items as standard features).	0.06	2	0.12
4. Lennar is building in just as many, if not more, communities in the South and Southwest (some of the fastest-growing areas).	0.05	2	0.10
5. USA has the lowest number of mortgage applications in 2 years.	0.05	3	0.15
6. 76% of the public are dissatisfied with the direction of the country, with 48% being very dissatisfied.	0.05	3	0.15
7. FHA mortgage insurance premiums increased 5 to 10 basis points and the time until termination significantly increased.	0.04	3	0.12
8. Lennar has a superior website (includes community involvement, how to take care of your home, why buy now).	0.03	2	0.06
9. Homeowner percentage fell from 69% to 65% between 2005 and 2015.	0.02	3	0.06
10. Personal savings rate is 5.7%, up from 4.9% 6 months ago.	0.02	3	0.06
TOTALS	**1.00**		**2.51**

into opportunities and threats as they are in an EFE. In a CPM, the ratings and total weighted scores for rival firms can be compared to the sample firm. This comparative analysis provides important internal strategic information. Avoid assigning the same rating to firms included in your CPM analysis.

A sample CPM is provided in Table 3-12. In this example, the two most important factors to being successful in the industry are "advertising" and "global expansion," as indicated by weights of 0.20. If there were no weight column in this analysis, note that each factor then would be equally important. Thus, having a weight column makes for a more robust analysis because it enables the analyst to assign higher and lower numbers to capture perceived or actual levels of importance. Note in Table 3-12 that Company 1 is strongest on "product quality," as indicated by a rating of 4, whereas Company 2 is strongest on "advertising." Overall, Company 1 is strongest, as indicated by the total weighted score of 3.15 and Company 3 is weakest.

TABLE 3-11 Author Commentary on Each Factor in the D. R. Horton EFE Matrix

Opportunities

1. These states will need more new homes than average because the populations are the fastest growing.
2. Building using more green technologies could result in creating a preference and increased revenue/profit, because customers are increasingly make green requests.
3. Since new homes, especially in the South and the West, are on the rise, there is an opportunity to build more homes, increasing revenue/profit/market share.
4. Building and selling lower-priced homes is a competitive advantage for DRH because consumers are price conscious.
5. Many senior citizens look to downsize, so they could be specifically targeted to increase sales.
6. By increasing its corporate social responsibility position, DRH could build a preference for its homes.
7. If it is more affordable to buy than rent, people will want to build (or buy), and DRH is the largest homebuilder in the USA.
8. With low interest rates, a mortgage is more affordable; therefore, consumers are inclined to build (or buy)—a plus for DRH.
9. If it is easier than before to obtain a mortgage, more consumers will do so. This creates an opportunity for DRH.
10. If consumers have more money to spend, some will want to spend it on a home. This creates an opportunity for DRH.

Threats

1. Increased costs of labor and supplies make new homes less affordable, so fewer people will want one.
2. Lennar is gaining economies of scale on DRH, enabling Lennar to price lower.
3. Lennar creates the perception that they have a higher quality, because they do not "nickel and dime" customers; this hurts DRH.
4. Lennar aims to take market share from DRH by building in more and more communities.
5. If consumers are seeking fewer mortgages, then fewer homes are being sought.
6. As consumers become worried about the country, they become more conservative and are less likely to buy a home.
7. As the FHA becomes less amenable to approving mortgages, this trend hurts DRH.
8. Because everybody does research online, Lennar's superior website could hurt DRH.
9. If the percentage of people that own a home is decreasing, then fewer new homes would be needed.
10. If consumers are saving more, they are spending less, perhaps less even on housing.

TABLE 3-12 An Example Competitive Profile Matrix

Critical Success Factors	Weight	Company 1 Rating	Company 1 Score	Company 2 Rating	Company 2 Score	Company 3 Rating	Company 3 Score
Advertising	0.20	1	0.20	4	0.80	3	0.60
Product Quality	0.10	4	0.40	3	0.30	2	0.20
Price Competitiveness	0.10	3	0.30	2	0.20	1	0.10
Management	0.10	4	0.40	3	0.20	1	0.10
Financial Position	0.15	4	0.60	2	0.30	3	0.45
Customer Loyalty	0.10	4	0.40	3	0.30	2	0.20
Global Expansion	0.20	4	0.80	1	0.20	2	0.40
Market Share	0.05	1	0.05	4	0.20	3	0.15
Total	**1.00**		**3.15**		**2.50**		**2.20**

Note: The ratings values are as follows: 1 = major weakness, 2 = minor weakness, 3 = minor strength, 4 = major strength. As indicated by the total weighted score of 2.20, Company 3 is weakest overall. Only eight critical success factors are included for simplicity; in actuality, however, this is too few.

TABLE 3-13 An Actual CPM for D. R. Horton

Critical Success Factors	Weight	D. R. Horton Rating	D. R. Horton Score	Lennar Rating	Lennar Score	PulteGroup Rating	PulteGroup Score
1. Price	0.16	4	0.64	3	0.48	2	0.32
2. Market Share	0.14	4	0.56	3	0.42	2	0.28
3. Geographical Coverage	0.12	4	0.48	2	0.24	3	0.36
4. Quality	0.10	2	0.20	4	0.40	3	0.30
5. Customer Service	0.09	2	0.18	3	0.27	4	0.36
6. Profitability	0.08	3	0.24	4	0.32	2	0.16
7. Financial Position	0.07	3	0.21	2	0.14	4	0.28
8. Energy Efficiencies	0.06	2	0.12	3	0.18	4	0.24
9. Growth	0.06	3	0.18	4	0.24	2	0.12
10. Website	0.05	3	0.15	4	0.20	2	0.10
11. Warranty Issues	0.04	3	0.12	2	0.08	4	0.16
12. Social Responsibility	0.03	2	0.06	3	0.09	4	0.12
Totals	**1.00**		**3.14**		**3.06**		**2.80**

Other than the critical success factors listed in the sample CPM, factors often included in this analysis include breadth of product line, effectiveness of sales distribution, proprietary or patent advantages, location of facilities, production capacity and efficiency, experience, union relations, technological advantages, and e-commerce expertise.

Just because one firm receives a 3.20 overall rating and another receives a 2.80 in a CPM, it does not necessarily follow that the first firm is precisely 14.3 percent better than the second, but it does suggest that the first firm is better in some areas. Regarding weights in a CPM or EFE Matrix, be mindful that 0.08 is mathematically 33 percent higher than 0.06, so even small differences can reveal important perceptions regarding the relative importance of various factors. The aim with numbers is to assimilate and evaluate information in a meaningful way that aids in decision making.

An actual CPM is provided in Table 3-13, again for the largest homebuilder in the United States, D. R. Horton. Note that the two rival firms, Lennar and PulteGroup, receive higher ratings on "Quality" than D. R. Horton. Also note the factors are listed beginning with the most important (highest weight). D. R. Horton, Lennar, and PulteGroup are headquartered in Fort Worth, Texas; Miami, Florida; and Atlanta, Georgia; respectively.

IMPLICATIONS FOR STRATEGISTS

Figure 3-4 reveals that to gain and sustain competitive advantages, strategists must collect, analyze, and prioritize information regarding the firm's competitors, as well as identify and consider relevant social, demographic, economic, and technology trends and events impacting the firm and its industry. This engineering hunt for the facts is essential because expensive, and sometimes irreversible, strategies are ultimately formulated and implemented based on that information. This chapter reveals that quantified, organized, prioritized, actionable external information is a key ingredient for making decisions that culminate in a winning strategic plan. Increasingly, business analytics is being used to identify key external trends that may otherwise go unnoticed from casual observation. The External Factor Evaluation Matrix and Competitive Profile Matrix presented in this chapter are excellent strategic-planning tools for assimilating and prioritizing information to enhance decision making.

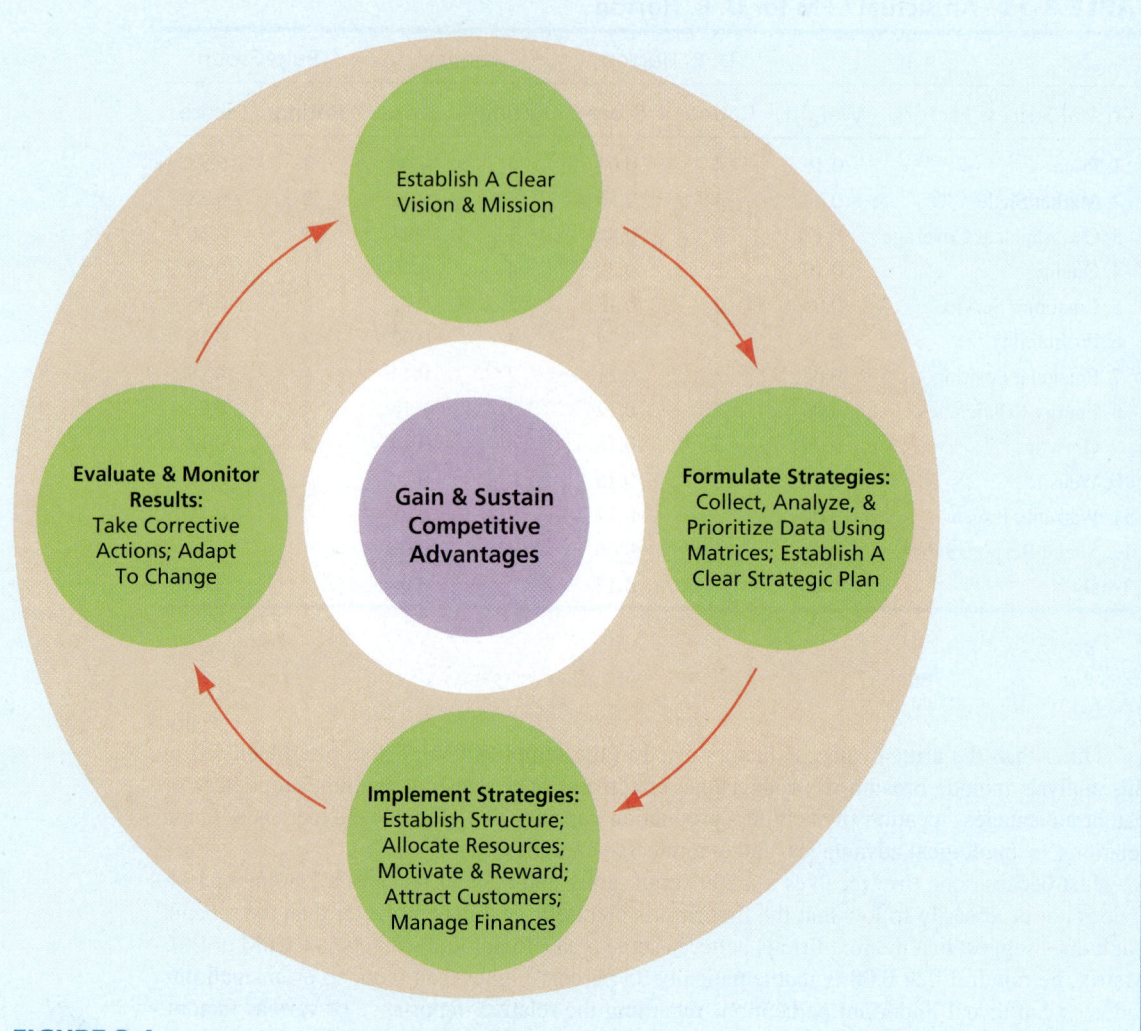

FIGURE 3-4

How to Gain and Sustain Competitive Advantages

IMPLICATIONS FOR STUDENTS

In developing and presenting your external assessment for your firm, be mindful that gaining and sustaining competitive advantage is the overriding purpose of developing the EFE Matrix and CPM. During this section of your written or oral project, emphasize how and why particular factors can yield competitive advantage for the firm. In other words, instead of robotically going through the weights and ratings (which, by the way, are critically important), highlight various factors in light of where you are leading the firm. Make it abundantly clear in your discussion how your firm, with your suggestions, can subdue rival firms or at least profitably compete with them. Showcase during this section of your project the key underlying reasons how and why your firm can prosper among rivals. Remember to be *prescriptive*, rather than *descriptive*, in the manner that you present your entire project. If presenting your project orally, be self-confident and passionate rather than timid and uninterested. Definitely "bring the data" throughout your project, because "vagueness" is the most common downfall of students in case analyses.

Chapter Summary

Increasing turbulence in markets and industries around the world means the external audit has become an explicit and vital part of the strategic-management process. This chapter provided a framework for collecting and evaluating economic, social, cultural, demographic, environmental, political, governmental, legal, technological, and competitive information. Firms that do not mobilize and empower their managers and employees to identify, monitor, forecast, and evaluate key external forces may fail to anticipate emerging opportunities and threats and, consequently, may pursue ineffective strategies, miss opportunities, and invite organizational demise. Firms not taking advantage of e-commerce and social media networks are technologically falling behind.

A major responsibility of strategists is to ensure development of an effective external-audit system. This includes using information technology to devise a competitive intelligence system that works. The external-audit approach described in this chapter can be used effectively by any size or type of organization. Typically, the external-audit process is more informal in small firms, but the need to understand key trends and events is no less important for these firms. The EFE Matrix and Porter's Five-Forces Model can help strategists evaluate the market and industry, but these tools must be accompanied by good intuitive judgment. Multinational firms especially need a systematic and effective external-audit system because external forces among foreign countries vary so greatly.

MyManagementLab®

To complete the problems with the ⭐, go to EOC Discussion Questions in the MyLab.

Key Terms and Concepts

actionable responses (p. 61)
business analytics (p. 76)
chief information officer (CIO) (p. 68)
chief technology officer (CTO) (p. 68)
competitive intelligence (CI) (p. 70)
Competitive Profile Matrix (CPM) (p. 78)
data mining (p. 76)
environmental scanning (p. 60)

external audit (p. 60)
External Factor Evaluation (EFE) Matrix (p. 77)
external forces (p. 61)
Industrial Organization (I/O) (p. 63)
industry analysis (p. 60)
information technology (IT) (p. 68)
Porter's Five-Forces Model (p. 71)

Issues For Review and Discussion

⭐ **3-1.** Define and give an example of business analytics. Why is this technique becoming so widely used in organizations today?

3-2. Do CVS and Target take stances on political issues? Is it good for companies to take stands on political issues? Explain.

3-3. Provide a synopsis of IBISWorld and Mergent Online.

⭐ **3-4.** Mathematically, how much more important is a weight of 0.08 compared to 0.05? Why is this concept important in developing strategic-planning matrices?

⭐ **3-5.** Mathematically, how much more important is a rating of 4 compared to a rating of 3? Why is this concept important in developing strategic-planning matrices?

3-6. Describe union membership trends in the United States. What are the implications for strategic planning in firms such as Boeing or Heinz or Caterpillar?

3-7. List some legal or ethical ways to gather competitive intelligence. List some illegal or unethical ways.

3-8. As the value of the dollar rises, U.S. firms doing business abroad see their profits fall, so some firms raise prices of their products to offset the decrease in profits. What are some risks of raising prices?

3-9. Does McDonald's Corp. benefit from a low or high value of the dollar? Explain why.

3-10. Explain how Facebook, Twitter, and Instagram can represent a major threat or opportunity for a company.

⭐ **3-11.** If your CPM has three firms and they all end up with the same total weighted score, would the analysis still be useful? Why?

3-12. The drop in gas prices benefited thousands of firms. Does this fact confirm that "external factors are more important than internal factors" in strategic planning? Discuss.

3-13. Governments sometimes use "protectionism" to cope with economic problems, imposing tariffs and subsidies on foreign goods as well as placing restrictions and incentives on their own firms to keep jobs at home. What are the strategic implications of protectionism for international commerce?

3-14. What are the three basic objectives of a CI program?

3-15. Let's say you work for McDonald's and you applied Porter's Five-Forces Model to study the fast-food industry. Would information in your analysis provide factors more readily to an EFE Matrix, a CPM, or to neither matrix? Justify your answer.

⭐ **3-16.** Explain why it is appropriate for ratings in an EFE Matrix to be 1, 2, 3, or 4 for any opportunity or threat.

3-17. Why is inclusion of about 20 factors recommended in the EFE Matrix rather than about 10 factors or about 40 factors?

⭐ **3-18.** In developing an EFE Matrix, would it be advantageous to arrange your opportunities according to the highest weight, and do likewise for your threats? Explain.

3-19. In developing an EFE Matrix, would it be best to have 10 opportunities and 10 threats, or would 17 opportunities (or threats) be fine with 3 of the other to achieve a total of 20 factors as desired?

3-20. Could or should critical success factors in a CPM include external factors? Explain.

3-21. Explain how to conduct an external strategic-management audit.

3-22. Identify a recent economic, social, political, or technological trend that significantly affects the local Pizza Hut.

3-23. Discuss the following statement: Major opportunities and threats usually result from an interaction among key environmental trends rather than from a single external event or factor.

3-24. Use Porter's Five-Forces Model to evaluate competitiveness within the U.S. banking industry.

3-25. How does the external audit affect other components of the strategic-management process?

3-26. As the owner of a small business, explain how you would organize a strategic-information scanning system. How would you organize such a system in a large organization?

3-27. Construct an EFE Matrix for an organization of your choice.

3-28. Let's say your boss develops an EFE Matrix that includes 62 factors. How would you suggest reducing the number of factors to 20?

3-29. Discuss the ethics of gathering competitive intelligence.

3-30. Discuss the ethics of cooperating with rival firms.

3-31. Do you agree with I/O theorists that external factors are more important than internal factors to a firm's achieving competitive advantage? Explain both your and their positions.

3-32. Define, compare, and contrast the weights versus ratings in an EFE Matrix.

3-33. Develop a CPM for your university. Include six factors.

3-34. List the 10 external areas that give rise to opportunities and threats.

MyManagementLab®

Go to the Assignments section of your MyLab to complete these writing exercises.

3-35. Describe the "process of performing an external audit" in an organization doing strategic planning for the first time.

3-36. Compare and contrast the duties and responsibilities of a Chief Information Officer (CIO) with a Chief Technology Officer (CTO) in a large firm.

ASSURANCE OF LEARNING EXERCISES

EXERCISE 3A
Competitive Intelligence (CI) Certification

Purpose
This exercise will enhance your knowledge of CI, which is the action of defining, gathering, analyzing, and distributing information about products, customers, and competitors as needed to support executives and managers in making strategic decisions for an organization. With the right information, organizations can avoid unpleasant surprises by anticipating competitors' moves and decreasing response time. Competitive intelligence information is available in newspapers, magazines, and online databases, and also by networking with industry experts, attending trade shows and conferences, gathering information from their own customers and suppliers, and so on. Social-media sources also have become important—providing potential interviewee names, as well as opinions and attitudes, and sometimes breaking news.

Instructions
Step 1   **Examine the following three CI topics and write a short overview of each item.**

1. Strategic & Competitive Intelligence Professionals (SCIP) (**www.scip.org**)
2. The Institute for Competitive Intelligence (**www.institute-for-competitive-intelligence.com**)
3. The Fuld-Gilad-Herring Academy of Competitive Intelligence (**www.academyci.com**)

EXERCISE 3B
Develop an EFE Matrix for Hershey Company

Purpose
This exercise will give you practice in developing an EFE matrix. An EFE Matrix summarizes the results of an external audit. This is an important strategic-planning tool widely used by strategists.

Instructions

Step 1   Join with two other students in class, and jointly prepare an EFE Matrix for Hershey. Refer to the Cohesion Case (p. 26) and to Exercise 1B (p. 35), if necessary, to identify external opportunities and threats. Make sure the factors you include are both specific and actionable. Use the online sources listed in Table 3-8. Be sure not to include strategies as opportunities, but do include as many monetary amounts, percentages, numbers, and ratios as possible.

Step 2   All three-person teams participating in this exercise should record their EFE total weighted scores on the board. Put your initials after your score to identify it as your team's score.

Step 3   Compare the total weighted scores. Which team's score came closest to the instructor's answer? Discuss reasons for variation in the scores reported on the board.

EXERCISE 3C

Perform an External Assessment

Purpose

This exercise will give you practice in performing an external assessment. External opportunities and threats must be identified and evaluated before strategies can be formulated effectively.

Instructions

Step 1   Select a company or business where you currently or previously have worked. Conduct an external audit for this company. Find opportunities and threats in recent issues of newspapers and magazines. Search for information using the Internet. Use the following three websites:

    www.hoovers.com
    http://morningstar.com
    http://globaledge.msu.edu/industries/

Step 2   On a separate sheet of paper, list 10 opportunities and 10 threats that face this company. Be specific in stating each factor.

Step 3   Include a bibliography to reveal where you found the information.

Step 4   Write a three-page summary of your findings, and submit it to your instructor.

EXERCISE 3D

Develop an EFE Matrix for Your University

Purpose

Most colleges and universities do strategic planning. Institutions are consciously and systematically identifying and evaluating external opportunities and threats facing higher education in your state, the nation, and the world.

Instructions

Step 1   Join with two other individuals in class and jointly prepare an EFE Matrix for your institution.

Step 2   Go to the board and record your total weighted score in a column that includes the scores of all three-person teams participating. Put your initials after your score to identify it as your team's score.

Step 3   Which team viewed your college's strategies most positively? Which team viewed your college's strategies most negatively? Discuss the nature of the differences.

EXERCISE 3E

Comparing Chipotle Mexican Grill to Panera Bread and Moe's Southwest Grill

Purpose

The company featured at the beginning of this chapter, Chipotle Mexican Grill, competes with Panera Bread and Moe's Southwest in hundreds of cities. Gaining and sustaining competitive advantage is something that both firms strive to do every day. This exercise gives you practice in identifying competitive advantages that could provide a basis for strategic action.

Instructions

Step 1   Using the online databases mentioned in Table 3-8, and an on-site visit, conduct research aimed at comparing Chipotle versus Panera Bread versus Moe's.

Step 2   Identify four competitive advantages that Chipotle has over the other two firms, and four competitive disadvantages. Give a rationale and source for each of your identified factors.

Step 3   Discuss or write up how Chipotle can best sustain and promote its competitive advantages.

EXERCISE 3F
Develop a Competitive Profile Matrix for Hershey Company

Purpose

Monitoring competitors' performance and strategies is a key aspect of an external audit. This exercise is designed to give you practice in evaluating the competitive position of organizations in a given industry and assimilating that information in a CPM.

Instructions

Step 1	Turn back to the Cohesion Case and review the section on competitors (p. 30-33). Also view on-line resources that compare Hershey with Mars and Nestle. Use the sources listed in Table 3-8.
Step 2	Prepare a CPM that includes Hershey, Mars, and Nestle.
Step 3	Turn in your CPM for a classwork grade.

EXERCISE 3G
Develop a Competitive Profile Matrix for Your University

Purpose

Your college or university competes with all other educational institutions in the world, especially those in your own state. State funds, students, faculty, staff, endowments, gifts, and federal funds are areas of competitiveness. Other areas include athletic programs, dorm life, academic reputation, location, and career services. The purpose of this exercise is to give you practice in thinking competitively about the business of education in your state.

Instructions

Step 1	Identify two colleges or universities in your state that compete directly with your institution for students. Interview several persons, perhaps classmates, who are aware of particular strengths and weaknesses of those universities. Record information about the two competing universities.
Step 2	Prepare a CPM that includes your institution and the two competing institutions. Include the following 10 factors in your analysis:

1. Tuition costs
2. Quality of faculty
3. Academic reputation
4. Average class size
5. Campus landscaping
6. Athletic programs
7. Quality of students
8. Graduate programs
9. Location of campus
10. Campus culture

Step 3	Submit your CPM to your instructor for evaluation.

(Note to Professors—See the Chapter IM for an additional, excellent exercise for this chapter)

MINI-CASE ON COACH, INC. (COH)

Source: ostap25/Fotolia

WHY ARE THE LADIES SHUNNING COACH?

Headquartered in New York City, Coach, Inc. is the leader in North America of women's handbags, but in 2014 and 2015, the company faltered badly due to intense rivalry in the industry. Even though most U.S. stocks rose more than 30 percent in 2014, Coach's stock price declined more than 30 percent. Coach's EPS steeply declined throughout 2015 and the company's net income declined 50 percent in Q1 of 2015. Coach's products are sold worldwide through Coach stores, select department stores and specialty stores, and through Coach's website at www.coach.com. However, competitors such as Michael Kors (KORS), Kate Spade (KATE), and Tory Burch are eroding Coach's market share, and importantly, promotional activity across the category appears to be increasing. In response, Coach is closing dozens of underperforming stores as double-digit sales decline continue. Coach is formulating strategies to protect its market share in the United States, including hiring a new design team, revamping its marketing, remodeling stores, and rethinking its wholesale channels, but it could take an extended period of time to turn around a business so large (more than $3 billion in sales in North America). In 2015, Coach acquired Stuart Weitzman footwear brand for $530 million from private equity firm Sycamore Partners. Coach is spending $570 million through 2017 to improve stores and wholesale locations, plus $50 million to boost advertising.

Coach is impacted by the value of the U.S. dollar and by economic and political conditions globally. The company markets its products to consumers through stores in North America, Japan, Mainland China, Hong Kong, Macau, Singapore, Taiwan, Malaysia, South Korea, the United Kingdom, France, Ireland, Spain, Portugal, Germany, and Italy. It also sells its products to wholesale customers and distributors in approximately 35 countries. Coach operates about 300 retail and 200 outlet stores in North America; 198 coach-operated concession shop-in-shops within department stores, retail stores, and outlet stores in Japan; and 277 coach-operated concession shops within department stores, retail stores, and outlet stores internationally.

Questions

1. Table 3-7 provides a list of 15 conditions that cause high rivalry among competing firms in an industry. In the women's handbag business, what, in your opinion, are the top 5 (among the 15) conditions contributing to Coach's demise?
2. Figure 3-4 reveals Porter's Five Forces Model. Rank order the five forces from 1 = most impact to 5 = least impact to reveal your opinion regarding which forces are contributing most to Coach's demise.
3. In your opinion (ladies), what are the key differentiating features that you look for in handbags, and what could Coach do to re-earn your business? Rank COH, KORS, and KATE in terms of price, style, youthfulness, and quality. Develop a 3 × 4 matrix to reveal your positioning of these rival firms along these dimensions.
4. Does Coach like to see the value of the dollar increase or decrease versus the euro, and versus the yen? Why?

Source: Based on Company documents and a variety of sources.

Current Readings

Howard-Grenville, Jennifer, et al. "Climate Change and Management." *Academy of Management Journal* (June 2014): 615–641.

Kiron, David, et al. "How Serious Is Climate Change to Business?" *MIT Sloan Management Review* 55, no.1 (2013): 75–76.

Roberts, Carter. "Strategy Migration in a Changing Climate." *Harvard Business Review* 92, no. 5 (2014): 42.

Endnotes

1. Shelly Banjo and Paul Ziobro, "Shoppers Flee Physical Stores," *Wall Street Journal,* August 6, 2014, B1.
2. http://247wallst.com/special-report/2014/01/02/the-best-and-worst-run-cities-in-america-2/
3. http://wallethub.com/edu/best-worst-states-to-be-a-taxpayer/2416/#complete-rankings
4. Pete Barlas, "Cisco Systems Dart into Data Analytics," *Wall Street Journal,* December 11, 2014, A5.
5. Saabira Chaudhuri, "Banks Leave More Branches," *Wall Street Journal,* January 28, 2014, C1.
6. Roger Yu, "Online Rep Crucial for Small Companies," *USA Today,* October 30, 2012, 5B.
7. Danny Yadron, "Companies Wrestle with the Cost of Security," *Wall Street Journal,* February 26, 2014, B3.
8. Bill Saporito, "Companies That Compete Best," *Fortune* (May 22, 1989): 36.
9. http://www.fuld.com/what-is-competitive-intelligence
10. John Prescott and Daniel Smith, "The Largest Survey of 'Leading-Edge' Competitor Intelligence Managers," *Planning Review* 17, no. 3 (May–June 1989): 6–13.
11. Arthur Thompson, Jr., A. J. Strickland III, and John Gamble, *Crafting and Executing Strategy: Text and Readings* (New York: McGraw-Hill/Irwin, 2005): 63.
12. Michael E. Porter, *Competitive Strategy: Techniques for Analyzing Industries and Competitors* (New York: Free Press, 1980): 24–27.
13. Dale McConkey, "Planning in a Changing Environment," *Business Horizons* 31, no. 5 (September–October 1988): 67.
14. James Willhite, "Getting Started in 'Big Data,'" *Wall Street Journal*, February 4, 2014, B7.

The Internal Assessment

LEARNING OBJECTIVES

After studying this chapter, you should be able to do the following:

4-1. Describe the nature and role of an internal assessment in formulating strategies.

4-2. Discuss why organizational culture is so important in formulating strategies.

4-3. Identify the basic functions (activities) that make up management and their relevance in formulating strategies.

4-4. Identify the basic functions of marketing and their relevance in formulating strategies.

4-5. Discuss the nature and role of finance/accounting in formulating strategies.

4-6. Discuss the nature and role of production/operations in formulating strategies.

4-7. Discuss the nature and role of research and development (R&D) in formulating strategies.

4-8. Discuss the nature and role of management information systems (MIS) in formulating strategies.

4-9. Explain value chain analysis and its relevance in formulating strategies.

4-10. Develop and use an Internal Factor Evaluation (IFE) Matrix.

ASSURANCE OF LEARNING EXERCISES

The following exercises are found at the end of this chapter:

EXERCISE 4A Apply Breakeven Analysis

EXERCISE 4B Comparing Netflix with Redbox

EXERCISE 4C Perform a Financial Ratio Analysis for Hershey Company

EXERCISE 4D Construct an IFE Matrix for Hershey Company

EXERCISE 4E Construct an IFE Matrix for Your University

EXERCISE 4F Applying Research-Based View (RBV) Theory

This chapter focuses on identifying and evaluating a firm's strengths and weaknesses in the functional areas of business, including management, marketing, finance, accounting, production/operations, research and development (R&D), and management information systems (MIS). Relationships among these areas of business are examined. Also, strategic implications of important functional area concepts are explained. In addition, this chapter describes the process of performing an internal audit. The resource-based view (RBV) of strategic management is introduced, as is value chain analysis (VCA) and benchmarking.

Showcased here for exemplary strategic management, Netflix does an excellent job using its strengths to capitalize on external opportunities. Expanding rapidly globally, Netflix captures demographic information on millions of customers and potential customers globally, and formulates strategies based on that information.

The Nature of an Internal Audit

All organizations have strengths and weaknesses in the functional areas of business. No enterprise is equally strong or weak in all areas. Maytag, for example, is known for excellent production and product design, whereas Procter & Gamble is known for superb marketing. Internal strengths and weaknesses, coupled with external opportunities and threats and clear vision and mission statements, provide the basis for establishing objectives and strategies. Objectives and strategies are established with the intention of capitalizing on internal strengths and overcoming weaknesses. The internal-audit part of the strategic-management process is illustrated in Figure 4-1 with white shading.

EXEMPLARY COMPANY SHOWCASED

Netflix, Inc. (NFLX)

Based in Los Gatos, California, Netflix does an outstanding job analyzing customer buying trends and desires and incorporating that information into its strategic-planning process. Netflix gathers extensive information about its customers' usage and content choices, utilizing voluminous individual data into strategic information. An analyst for Janney Capital Markets recently said, "Netflix understands its viewers by tracking every single thing they do; and develops patterns among its subscribers, and matches them up properly with content offerings." Doing such an excellent job with customer analysis has enabled Netflix to reportedly obtain one-third of all Internet prime-time traffic in the United States. Lately, the company's streaming video services are focusing more on popular TV shows and less on hit movies. Netflix now has 32 percent of the top 75 TV shows from the past 4 years, compared to Amazon's 12 percent, but Amazon is actively promoting its Prime Instant Video service that competes with Netflix. In early 2015, Netflix's stock surged 42 percent in a single day to a 52-week high over $500. Analysts expect Netflix's addressable subscriber base to reach 207 million globally by 2017, as the company grows rapidly across Europe and beyond. Netflix recently entered six European countries: Germany, France, Austria, Switzerland, Belgium, and Luxembourg—after already providing services in the U.K., Ireland, Netherlands, and Scandinavia. Netflix entered Australia and New Zealand in March 2015, followed by Italy, Portugal, Spain, and Japan in October 2015.

Netflix's stock is expected to split in late 2015 for only the second time in the company's 13-year history. With Netflix stock currently being almost $700 per share, a lowered split stock price is expected to widen the pool of people interested in buying the stock, which has been soaring throughout both 2014 and 2015. As of April 1, 2015, Netflix had 20.9 million international subscribers and 41.4 million streaming subscribers in the United States.

Source: Based on Jon Friedman, "Reaching Out to Give What Customers Want: Netflix Offers the Right Movies to the Right People," *Investor's Business Daily,* July 7, 2014, A7.

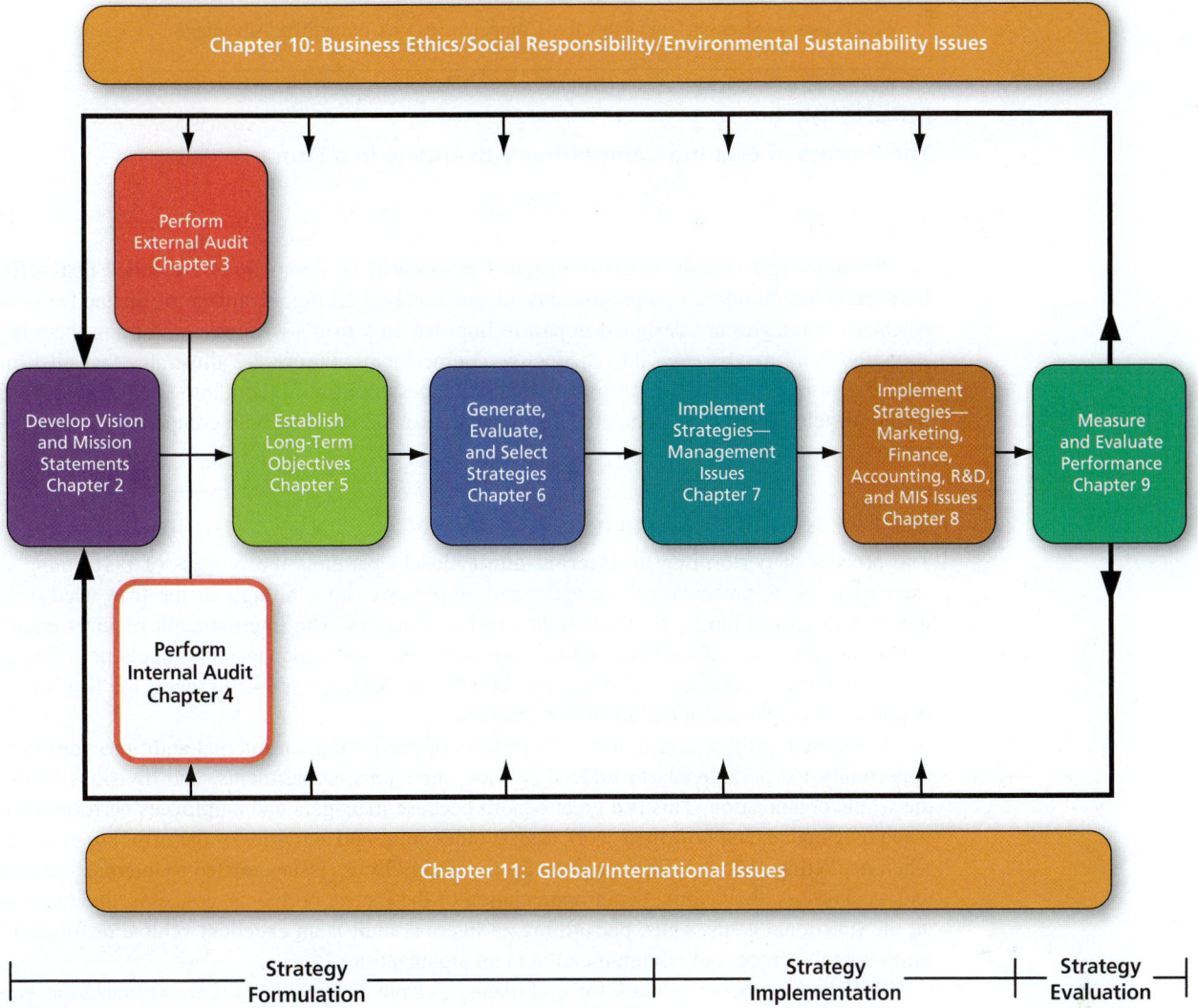

FIGURE 4-1

A Comprehensive Strategic-Management Model

Source: Source: Fred R. David, "How Companies Define Their Mission," *Long Range Planning* 22, no. 3 (June 1988): 40. Also, Ratnaningsih, Anik, and Nadjadji Anwar, Patdono Suwignjo, and Putu Artama Wiguna, "Balance Scorecard of David's Strategic Modeling at Industrial Business for National Construction Contractor of Indonesia," *Journal of Mathematics and Technology* , no. 4, (October 2010): 20.

Key Internal Forces

It is impossible in a strategic-management text to review in depth all the material presented in courses such as marketing, finance, accounting, management, management information systems, and production and operations; there are many subareas within these functions, such as customer service, warranties, advertising, packaging, and pricing under marketing. However, strategic planning must include a detailed assessment of how the firm is doing in all internal areas. A complete internal assessment is vital to help a firm formulate, implement, and evaluate strategies to enable it to gain and sustain competitive advantages.

For different types of organizations, such as hospitals, universities, and government agencies, the functional business areas differ. In a hospital, for example, functional areas may include cardiology, hematology, nursing, maintenance, physician support, and receivables. Functional areas of a university can include athletic programs, placement services, housing, fund-raising, academic research, counseling, and intramural programs. Regardless of the type or size of firm, effective strategic planning hinges on identification and prioritization of internal strengths and weaknesses.

Weaknesses ⇒ Strenghts ⇒ Distinctive Competencies ⇒ Competitive Advantage

FIGURE 4-2

The Process of Gaining Competitive Advantage in a Firm

Strengths that cannot be easily matched or imitated by competitors are called **distinctive competencies**. Building competitive advantages involves taking advantage of distinctive competencies. Strategies are designed in part to improve on a firm's weaknesses, turning them into strengths—and maybe even into distinctive competencies. Figure 4-2 illustrates that all firms should continually strive to improve on their weaknesses, turning them into strengths, and ultimately develop distinctive competencies that can provide the firm with competitive advantages over rival firms.

The Process of Performing an Internal Audit

The process of performing an **internal audit** closely parallels the process of performing an external audit. Representative managers and employees from throughout the firm need to be involved in determining a firm's strengths and weaknesses. The internal audit requires gathering, assimilating, and prioritizing information about the firm's management, marketing, finance and accounting, production and operations, R&D, and MIS operations to reveal the firm's most important strengths and most severe weaknesses.

Compared to the external audit, the process of performing an internal audit provides more opportunity for participants to understand how their jobs, departments, and divisions fit into the whole organization. This is a great benefit because managers and employees perform better when they understand how their work affects other areas and activities of the firm. For example, when marketing and manufacturing managers jointly discuss issues related to internal strengths and weaknesses, they gain a better appreciation of the issues, problems, concerns, and needs of all the functional areas. Thus, performing an internal audit is an excellent vehicle or forum for improving the process of communication in an organization.

William King believes a task force of managers from different units of the organization, supported by staff, should be charged with determining the 20 most important strengths and weaknesses that should influence the future of the firm. According to King,

> The development of conclusions on the 20 most important organizational strengths and weaknesses can be, as any experienced manager knows, a difficult task, when it involves managers representing various organizational interests and points of view. Developing a 20-page list of strengths and weaknesses could be accomplished relatively easily, but a list of the 20 most important ones involves significant analysis and negotiation. This is true because of the judgments that are required and the impact which such a list will inevitably have as it is used in the formulation, implementation, and evaluation of strategies.[1]

Strategic planning is most successful when managers and employees from all functional areas work together to provide ideas and information. Financial managers, for example, may need to restrict the number of feasible options available to operations managers, or R&D managers may develop products for which marketing managers need to set higher objectives. A key to organizational success is effective coordination and understanding among managers from all functional business areas. Through involvement in performing an internal strategic-management audit, managers from different departments and divisions of the firm come to understand the nature and effect of decisions in other functional business areas in their firm. Knowledge of these relationships is critical for effectively establishing objectives and strategies. Financial ratio analysis, for example, exemplifies the complexity of relationships among the functional areas of business. A declining return on investment or profit margin ratio could, for example, be the result of ineffective marketing, poor management policies, R&D errors, or a weak MIS.

The Resource-Based View

Some researchers emphasize the importance of the internal-audit part of the strategic-management process by comparing it to the external audit. Robert Grant, for example, concluded that the internal audit is more important, saying:

> In a world where customer preferences are volatile, the identity of customers is changing, and the technologies for serving customer requirements are continually evolving, an externally focused orientation does not provide a secure foundation for formulating long-term strategy. When the external environment is in a state of flux, the firm's own resources and capabilities may be a much more stable basis on which to define its identity. Hence, a definition of a business in terms of what it is capable of doing may offer a more durable basis for strategy.[2]

The **resource-based view (RBV)** approach to competitive advantage contends that internal resources are more important for a firm than external factors in achieving and sustaining competitive advantage. In contrast to the Industrial Organization (I/O) theory presented in the previous chapter, proponents of the RBV view/theory contend that organizational performance will primarily be determined by internal resources that can be grouped into three all-encompassing categories: physical resources, human resources, and organizational resources.[3] *Physical resources* include all plant and equipment, location, technology, raw materials, and machines; *human resources* include all employees, training, experience, intelligence, knowledge, skills, and abilities; and *organizational resources* include firm structure, planning processes, information systems, patents, trademarks, copyrights, databases, and so on. A firm's resources can be tangible, such as labor, capital, land, plant, and equipment, or resources can be intangible, such as culture, knowledge, brand equity, reputation, and intellectual property. Since tangible resources can more easily be bought and sold, intangible resources are often more important for gaining and sustaining competitive advantage.

Resource-based view theory asserts that resources are actually what helps a firm exploit opportunities and neutralize threats. As indicated in the Academic Research Capsule 4-1, RBV theory may be helpful in identifying diversification targets.

The basic premise of the RBV is that the mix, type, amount, and nature of a firm's internal resources should be considered first and foremost in devising strategies that can lead to sustainable competitive advantage. Managing strategically according to the RBV involves developing and exploiting a firm's unique resources and capabilities, and continually maintaining and strengthening those resources. The theory asserts that it is advantageous for a firm to pursue a strategy that is not currently being implemented by any competing firm. When other firms are unable to duplicate a particular strategy, then the focal firm has a sustainable competitive advantage, according to RBV theorists.

A resource can be considered valuable to the extent that it is (1) rare, (2) hard to imitate, or (3) not easily substitutable. Often called **empirical indicators**, these three characteristics of resources enable a firm to implement strategies that improve its efficiency and effectiveness and lead to a sustainable competitive advantage. The more a resource(s) is rare (not held by many

ACADEMIC RESEARCH CAPSULE 4-1

Does RBV Theory Determine Diversification Targets?

Recent research by Neffke and Henning basically says the answer to this question is *yes*. Their empirical evidence reveals that it is the nature of a firm's human capital, more than any other variable in the firm's value chain, that impacts that firm's choice of diversification targets. Specifically, firms select acquisition targets that offer opportunities to leverage existing human resources. Neffke and Henning report that firms are far more likely to diversify into industries that have ties to the firms' core RBV activities in terms of their existing workforce, rather than into industries without such ties. In fact, the researchers report that "firms are over 100 times more likely to diversify into industries to which the firms' internal human assets are strongly complementary, rather than into industries for which such skill-relatedness linkages are weak."

Source: Based on F. Neffke & M. Henning, "Skill Relatedness and Firm Diversification," *Strategic Management Journal* 34 (2013): 297–316.

firms in the industry), hard to imitate (hard to copy or achieve), and/or not easily substitutable (invulnerable to threat of substitution from different products), the stronger a firm's competitive advantage will be and the longer it will last. See Exercise 4F at the end of this chapter that reveals how an organization can use RBV theory as a tool in formulating strategies to better understand competitive advantages.

Integrating Strategy and Culture

Every business entity has a unique organizational culture that impacts strategic-planning activities. **Organizational culture** is "a pattern of behavior that has been developed by an organization as it learns to cope with its problem of external adaptation and internal integration, and that has worked well enough to be considered valid and to be taught to new members as the correct way to perceive, think, and feel."[4] This definition emphasizes the importance of matching external with internal factors in making strategic decisions. Organizational culture captures the subtle, elusive, and largely unconscious forces that shape a workplace. Remarkably resistant to change, culture can represent a major strength or weakness for any firm. It can be an underlying reason for strengths or weaknesses in any of the major business functions.

Defined in Table 4-1, **cultural products** include values, beliefs, rites, rituals, ceremonies, myths, stories, legends, sagas, language, metaphors, symbols, folktales, and heroes and heroines. These products or dimensions are levers that strategists can use to influence and direct strategy formulation, implementation, and evaluation activities. An organization's culture compares to an individual's personality in the sense that no two organizations have the same culture and no two individuals have the same personality. Both culture and personality are enduring and can be warm, aggressive, friendly, open, innovative, conservative, liberal, harsh, or likable.

At Google and Facebook, for example, the cultures are informal. Google employees are encouraged to wander the halls on employee-sponsored scooters and brainstorm on public whiteboards provided everywhere. In contrast, the culture at Procter & Gamble (P&G) is so rigid that employees jokingly call themselves "Proctoids." Despite this difference, the two companies are swapping employees and participating in each other's staff training sessions. Why? One reason is that P&G spends more money on advertising than any other company and Google desires more of P&G's roughly $8 billion in annual advertising expenses.

TABLE 4-1   **Examples of Cultural Products Defined**

Rites	Planned sets of activities that consolidate various forms of cultural expressions into one event
Ceremonies	Several rites connected together
Rituals	Standardized sets of behaviors used to manage anxieties
Myths	Narratives of imagined events, usually not supported by facts
Sagas	Historical narratives describing the unique accomplishments of a group and its leaders
Legends	Handed-down narratives of some wonderful event, usually not supported by facts
Stories	Narratives usually based on true events
Folktales	Fictional stories
Symbols	Any object, act, event, quality, or relation used to convey meaning
Language	The manner in which members of a group communicate
Metaphors	Shorthand of words used to capture a vision or to reinforce old or new values
Values	Life-directing attitudes that serve as behavioral guidelines
Beliefs	Understanding of particular phenomena
Heroes/Heroines	Individuals greatly respected

Source: Based on H. M. Trice and J. M. Beyer, "Studying Organizational Cultures through Rites and Ceremonials," *Academy of Management Review* 9, no. 4 (October 1984): 655.

Dimensions of organizational culture permeate all the functional areas of business. It is something of an art to uncover the basic values and beliefs that are deeply buried in an organization's rich collection of stories, language, heroes, and rituals, but cultural products can represent both important strengths and weaknesses. Culture is an aspect of an organization that can no longer be taken for granted in performing an internal strategic-management audit, because culture and strategy must work together.

The strategic-management process takes place largely within a particular organization's culture. Lorsch found that executives in successful companies are emotionally committed to the firm's culture, but he concluded that culture can inhibit strategic management in two basic ways. First, managers frequently miss the significance of changing external conditions because they are blinded by strongly held beliefs. Second, when a particular culture has been effective in the past, the natural response is to stick with it in the future, even during times of major strategic change.[5] An organization's culture must support the collective commitment of its people to a common purpose. It must foster competence and enthusiasm among managers and employees.

Organizational culture significantly affects business decisions and must therefore be evaluated during an internal strategic-management audit. If strategies can capitalize on cultural strengths, such as a strong work ethic or highly ethical beliefs, then management often can swiftly and easily implement changes. However, if the firm's culture is not supportive, strategic changes may be ineffective or even counterproductive. A firm's culture can become antagonistic to new strategies, with the result being confusion and disorientation.

Table 4-2 provides some example (possible) aspects of an organization's culture. Note that you might want to ask employees and managers to rate the degree that the dimension characterizes the firm. When one firm acquires another firm, integrating the two cultures effectively can be vital for success. For example, in Table 4-2, one firm may score mostly 1s (low) and the other firm may score mostly 5s (high), which would present a challenging strategic problem.

An organization's culture should infuse individuals with enthusiasm for implementing strategies. Allarie and Firsirotu emphasized the need to understand culture:

> Culture provides an explanation for the insuperable difficulties a firm encounters when it attempts to shift its strategic direction. Not only has the "right" culture become the essence and foundation of corporate excellence, it is also claimed that success or failure of reforms hinges on management's sagacity and ability to change the firm's driving culture in time and in time with required changes in strategies.[6]

Internal strengths and weaknesses associated with a firm's culture sometimes are overlooked because of the interfunctional nature of this phenomenon. This is a key reason why strategists

TABLE 4-2   Fifteen Example (Possible) Aspects of an Organization's Culture

Dimension	Low	Degree			High
1. Strong work ethic; arrive early and leave late	1	2	3	4	5
2. High ethical beliefs; clear code of business ethics followed	1	2	3	4	5
3. Formal dress; shirt and tie expected	1	2	3	4	5
4. Informal dress; many casual dress days	1	2	3	4	5
5. Socialize together outside of work	1	2	3	4	5
6. Do not question supervisor's decision	1	2	3	4	5
7. Encourage whistle-blowing	1	2	3	4	5
8. Be health conscious; have a wellness program	1	2	3	4	5
9. Allow substantial "working from home"	1	2	3	4	5
10. Encourage creativity, innovation, and open-mindedness	1	2	3	4	5
11. Support women and minorities; no glass ceiling	1	2	3	4	5
12. Be highly socially responsible; be philanthropic	1	2	3	4	5
13. Have numerous meetings	1	2	3	4	5
14. Have a participative management style	1	2	3	4	5
15. Preserve the natural environment; have a sustainability program	1	2	3	4	5

need to view and understand their firm as a sociocultural system. Success is oftentimes determined by linkages between a firm's culture and strategies. The challenge of strategic management today is to bring about the changes in organizational culture and individual mind-sets that are needed to support the formulation, implementation, and evaluation of strategies.

Management

The **functions of management** consist of five basic activities: planning, organizing, motivating, staffing, and controlling. An overview of these activities is provided in Table 4-3. These activities must be examined in strategic planning because an organization should continually capitalize on its strengths and improve on its weaknesses in these five areas.

Planning

The only thing certain about the future of any organization is change, and **planning** is the essential bridge between the present and the future that increases the likelihood of achieving desired results. Planning is the process by which a person (1) determines whether to attempt a task, (2) works out the most effective way of reaching desired objectives, and (3) prepares to overcome unexpected difficulties with adequate resources. Planning is the start of the process by which an individual or business may turn empty dreams into achievements. Planning enables one to avoid the trap of working extremely hard but achieving little.

TABLE 4-3 The Basic Functions of Management

Function	Description	Stage of Strategic-Management Process When Most Important
Planning	Planning consists of all those managerial activities related to preparing for the future, such as forecasting, establishing objectives, devising strategies, and developing policies.	Strategy Formulation
Organizing	Organizing includes all those managerial activities that result in a structure of task and authority relationships, such as organizational design, job specialization, job descriptions, span of control, coordination, job design, and job analysis.	Strategy Implementation
Motivating	Motivating involves efforts directed toward shaping human behavior. Specific topics include leadership, communication, work groups, behavior modification, delegation of authority, job enrichment, job satisfaction, needs fulfillment, organizational change, employee morale, and managerial morale.	Strategy Implementation
Staffing	Staffing refers to human resource (HR) activities, such as wage and salary administration, employee benefits, interviewing, hiring, firing, training, management development, employee safety, equal employment opportunity, and union relations.	Strategy Implementation
Controlling	Controlling refers to all those managerial activities directed toward ensuring that actual results are consistent with planned results. Key areas of concern include quality control, financial control, sales control, inventory control, expense control, analysis of variances, rewards, and sanctions.	Strategy Evaluation

Planning is an up-front investment in success. It helps a firm achieve maximum effect from a given effort. It also enables a firm to take into account relevant factors and focus on the critical ones. Planning helps ensure that the firm can be prepared for all reasonable eventualities and for all changes that will be needed. The act of planning allows a firm to gather the resources needed and carry out tasks in the most efficient way possible. It also enables a firm to conserve its own resources, avoid wasting ecological resources, make a fair profit, and be seen as an effective, useful firm. Furthermore, planning enables a firm to identify precisely what is to be achieved and to detail precisely the who, what, when, where, why, and how needed to achieve desired objectives. It empowers a firm to assess whether the effort, costs, and implications associated with achieving desired objectives are warranted.[7] Planning is the cornerstone of effective strategy formulation, and even though it is considered the foundation of management, it is commonly the task that managers neglect most. Planning is essential for successful strategy implementation and strategy evaluation, largely because organizing, motivating, staffing, and controlling activities depend on good planning.

Planning can have a positive impact on organizational and individual performance. It allows an organization to identify and take advantage of external opportunities as well as minimize the impact of external threats. Planning is more than extrapolating from the past and present into the future (long-range planning). It also includes developing a mission, forecasting future events and trends, establishing objectives, and choosing strategies to pursue.

An organization can develop synergy through planning. **Synergy** exists when everyone pulls together as a team that knows what it wants to achieve; synergy is the 2 + 2 = 5 effect. By establishing and communicating clear objectives, employees and managers can work together toward desired results. Synergy can result in powerful competitive advantages. The strategic-management process itself is aimed at creating synergy in an organization.

In addition, planning allows a firm to adapt to changing markets and thus shape its destiny. It enables an organization to be proactive, to anticipate, and to influence, rather than being primarily reactive strategies. Successful organizations strive to control their own futures rather than merely react to external forces and events as they occur. Historically, organisms and organizations that have not adapted to changing conditions have become extinct.

Organizing

The purpose of **organizing** is to achieve coordinated effort by defining task and authority relationships. Organizing means determining who does what and who reports to whom. There are countless examples in history of well-organized enterprises successfully competing against—and in some cases defeating—much stronger but less-organized firms. A well-organized firm generally has motivated managers and employees who are committed to seeing the organization succeed. Resources are allocated more effectively and used more efficiently in a well-organized firm than in a disorganized firm.

The organizing function of management can be viewed as consisting of three sequential activities: breaking down tasks into jobs (work specialization), combining jobs to form departments (departmentalization), and delegating authority. *Breaking down tasks* into jobs requires the development of job descriptions and job specifications. These tools clarify for both managers and employees what particular jobs entail. In *The Wealth of Nations*, published in 1776, Adam Smith cited the advantages of work specialization in the manufacture of pins:

> One man draws the wire, another straightens it, a third cuts it, a fourth points it, a fifth grinds it at the top for receiving the head. Ten men working in this manner can produce 48,000 pins in a single day, but if they had all wrought separately and independently, each might at best produce twenty pins in a day.[8]

Combining jobs to form departments results in an organizational structure, span of control, and a chain of command. Changes in strategy often require changes in structure because positions may be created, deleted, or merged. Organizational structure dictates how resources are allocated and how objectives are established in a firm. Allocating resources and establishing objectives geographically, for example, is much different from doing so by product or customer. The most common types of structure are functional, divisional, strategic business unit, and matrix. These designs are discussed in Chapter 7.

Delegating authority is an important organizing activity, as evidenced in the old saying, "You can tell how good a manager is by observing how his or her department functions when he or she isn't there." Employees today are more educated and more capable of participating in organizational decision making than ever before. In most cases, they expect to be delegated authority and responsibility and to be held accountable for results. Delegation of authority is embedded in the strategic-management process.

Motivating

Motivating is the process of influencing people to accomplish specific objectives.[9] Motivation explains why some people work hard and others do not. Objectives, strategies, and policies have little chance of succeeding if employees and managers are not motivated to implement strategies once they are formulated. The motivating function of management includes at least four major components: leadership, group dynamics, communication, and organizational change.

When managers and employees of a firm strive to achieve high levels of productivity, this indicates that the firm's strategists are good leaders. Good leaders establish rapport with subordinates, empathize with their needs and concerns, set a good example, and are trustworthy and fair. Leadership includes developing a vision of the firm's future and inspiring people to work hard to achieve that vision. Kirkpatrick and Locke reported that certain traits also characterize effective leaders: knowledge of the business, cognitive ability, self-confidence, honesty, integrity, and drive.[10] Stressing the importance of leadership, Sun Tzu stated, "Weak leadership can wreck the soundest strategy."

Research suggests that democratic behavior on the part of leaders results in more positive attitudes toward change and higher productivity than does autocratic behavior. According to Drucker:

> Leadership is not a magnetic personality. That can just as well be demagoguery. It is not "making friends and influencing people." That is flattery. Leadership is the lifting of a person's vision to higher sights, the raising of a person's performance to a higher standard, the building of a person's personality beyond its normal limitations.[11]

Because social media has come to dominate the conversation at all levels of personal and professional life, Frank Guglielmo in *The Social Leader* reports that the best leaders today do not function like generals. Rather, Guglielmo observes, "Leaders today need to be more concerned with their span of influence than their span of control; agendas are negotiated, not dictated; information is shaped, not controlled; and accountability is shared, not monitored."[12] Selladurai and Carraher in *Servant Leadership: Research and Practice* (2014) promote the idea that true leadership requires a dissolution of autocratic thinking in favor of leading by guiding and encouraging.

An organization's system of communication determines whether strategies can be implemented successfully. Good two-way communication is vital for gaining support for departmental and divisional objectives and policies. Top-down communication can encourage bottom-up communication. The strategic-management process becomes a lot easier when subordinates are encouraged to discuss their concerns, reveal their problems, provide recommendations, and give suggestions. A primary reason for instituting strategic management is to build and support effective communication networks throughout the firm.

> The manager of tomorrow must be able to get his [or her] people to commit themselves to the business, whether they are machine operators or junior vice-presidents. The key issue will be empowerment, a term whose strength suggests the need to get beyond merely sharing a little information and a bit of decision making.[13]

Staffing

The management function of **staffing**, or **human resource (HR) management**, includes activities such as recruiting, interviewing, testing, selecting, orienting, training, developing, caring for, evaluating, rewarding, disciplining, promoting, transferring, demoting, and dismissing employees, as well as managing union relations. Staffing activities play a major role in strategy-implementation efforts, and for this reason, HR managers are becoming more actively involved in the strategic-management process. It is important to identify strengths and weaknesses in the staffing area.

The complexity and importance of HR activities have increased to such a degree that all but the smallest organizations generally have a full-time human resource manager. Numerous court cases that directly affect staffing activities are decided each day. Organizations and individuals can be penalized severely for not following federal, state, and local laws and guidelines related to staffing. Line managers simply cannot stay abreast of all the legal developments and requirements regarding staffing. The HR department coordinates staffing decisions in the firm so that an organization as a whole meets legal requirements. This department also provides needed consistency in administering company rules, wages, policies, and employee benefits as well as collective bargaining with unions.

Human resource management is particularly challenging for international companies. For example, the inability of spouses and children to adapt to new surroundings can be a staffing problem in overseas transfers. The problems include premature returns, job performance slumps, resignations, discharges, low morale, marital discord, and general discontent. Firms such as Ford Motors and ExxonMobil screen and interview spouses and children before assigning families to overseas positions. Similarly, 3M Corporation introduces children to peers in the target country and offers spouses educational benefits.

Some companies, such as LRN Corporation and Ruppert Landscape, have recently dissolved their HR departments in order to flatten organizational structures, shift accountability for employees closer to managers, and to take advantage of outsourcing payroll, benefits, and other HR activities for greater efficiency and quality.[14]

Controlling

The **controlling** function of management includes all of those activities undertaken to ensure that actual operations conform to planned operations. All managers in an organization have controlling responsibilities, such as conducting performance evaluations and taking necessary action to minimize inefficiencies. The controlling function of management is particularly important for effective strategy evaluation. Controlling consists of four basic steps:

1. Establishing performance standards
2. Measuring individual and organizational performance
3. Comparing actual performance to planned performance standards
4. Taking corrective actions

Measuring individual performance is often conducted ineffectively or not at all in organizations. Some reasons for this shortcoming are that evaluations can create confrontations that most managers prefer to avoid, can take more time than most managers are willing to give, and can require skills that many managers lack. No single approach to measuring individual performance is without limitations. For this reason, an organization should examine various methods, such as the graphic rating scale, the behaviorally anchored rating scale, and the critical incident method, and then develop or select a performance-appraisal approach that best suits the firm's needs. Increasingly, firms are striving to link organizational performance with managers' and employees' pay.

Management Audit Checklist of Questions

The following checklist of questions can help determine specific strengths and weaknesses in the functional area of business. An answer of *no* to any question could indicate a potential weakness, although the strategic significance and implications of negative answers, of course, will vary by organization, industry, and severity of the weakness. Positive or *yes* answers to the checklist questions suggest potential areas of strength.

1. Does the firm use strategic-management concepts?
2. Are company objectives and goals measurable and well communicated?
3. Do managers at all hierarchical levels plan effectively?
4. Do managers delegate authority well?
5. Is the organization's structure appropriate?

6. Are job descriptions and job specifications clear?
7. Is employee morale high?
8. Are employee turnover and absenteeism low?
9. Are organizational reward and control mechanisms effective?

Marketing

Marketing can be described as the process of defining, anticipating, creating, and fulfilling customers' needs and wants for products and services. There are seven basic **functions of marketing**: (1) customer analysis, (2) selling products and services, (3) product and service planning, (4) pricing, (5) distribution, (6) marketing research, and (7) cost/benefit analysis.[15] Understanding these functions helps strategists identify and evaluate marketing strengths and weaknesses—a vital strategy-formulation activity.

Customer Analysis

Customer analysis—the examination and evaluation of consumer needs, desires, and wants—involves administering customer surveys, analyzing consumer information, evaluating market positioning strategies, developing customer profiles, and determining optimal market segmentation strategies. Customer profiles can reveal the demographic characteristics of an organization's customers. Buyers, sellers, distributors, salespeople, managers, wholesalers, retailers, suppliers, and creditors can all participate in gathering information to successfully identify customers' needs and wants. Successful organizations continually monitor present and potential customers' buying patterns. Business analytics has become an integral part of customer analysis and strategic planning.

Selling Products and Services

Successful strategy implementation generally rests on the ability of an organization to sell some product or service. **Selling** includes many marketing activities, such as advertising, sales promotion, publicity, personal selling, sales force management, customer relations, and dealer relations. The effectiveness of various selling tools for consumer and industrial products varies. Personal selling is most important for industrial goods companies, whereas advertising is most important for consumer goods companies. Determining organizational strengths and weaknesses in the selling function of marketing is an important part of performing an internal strategic-management audit.

Advertising can be expensive, a primary reason marketing is a major business function to be studied carefully. Without marketing, even the best products and services have little chance of being successful. Companies paid in excess of $4 million per 30-second spots during the 2015 Super Bowl. Anheuser-Busch just tallied its 28th year as the exclusive beer advertiser at the Super Bowl, buying a whopping 3.5 minutes of advertising time for Budweiser and Bud Light. George Parker argues that there may be no relationship at all between ads and sales:

> If someone were to do a truly analytical study of the Super Bowls of the last 20 years, I guarantee there would be no correlation between the ads and increases or declines in sales. The only way you can directly measure the effect of advertising is in direct marketing, which is a targeted promotion that provides an immediate point of sale, like an email campaign that encourages recipients to make a direct purchase or inquiry.[16]

Recent research reveals that the most effective marketing methods for firms with fewer than 500 employees is the company website (50%), Facebook and/or other social media sites such as Twitter (27%), and yellow pages and other (23%).[17] Nearly 2 million firms of all sizes now pay to advertise on Facebook, up from about 1 million 18 months ago. Spending on online advertisements globally is increasing about 25 percent annually, according to edMarketer, and represents about 39 percent of total advertising spending in the United States.[18]

Advertising on television is on a downward spiral, according to Time Warner, Discovery Communications, and Comcast. "Upfront" ads for the 2014–2015 TV season declined about 6 percent. Heavy marketers, such as Allstate and Mondelez International, now openly speak about shifting TV ad dollars to digital platforms. Allstate shifted 20 percent of its TV ad dollars to digital from 2013 to 2015 and that is typical. Ad giant Omnicom Group is advising its clients to shift 10 to 25 percent of their TV ad dollars to digital.

Chief marketing officers (CMOs), such as Eduardo Conrado at Motorola, now spend more than 50 percent of their budget on technology to manage activities such as online marketing and social media.[19] Marketing is becoming technical, with software to track and target customers and manage customer relationships, predict consumer behavior, run online storefronts, analyze social media, manage websites, and craft targeted advertisements. In response to this trend, IBM is shifting its attention from CIOs to chief marketing officers (CMOs) as their primary clients.

The world's largest social network, Facebook, may epitomize where the advertising industry is going. Facebook allows a company to "leverage the loyalty" of its best customers. If you have recently gotten engaged and updated your Facebook status, you may start seeing ads from local jewelers who have used Facebook's automated ad system to target you. Facebook enables any firm today to effectively target its exact audience with perfect advertising.[20] In performing a strategic-planning analysis, in addition to comparing rival firms' websites, it is important to compare rival firms' handling of social media issues.

One of the last off-limit advertising outlets has historically been books, but with the proliferation of e-books, marketers are experimenting more and more with advertising to consumers as they read e-books. New ads are being targeted based on the book's content and the demographic profile of the reader. Digital e-book companies such as Wowio and Amazon are trying to insert ads between chapters and along borders of digital pages. Random House says its e-books will soon include ads, but only with author approval.

Product and Service Planning

Product and service planning includes activities such as test marketing; product and brand positioning; devising warranties; packaging; determining product options, features, style, and quality; deleting old products; and providing for customer service. Product and service planning is particularly important when a company is pursuing product development or diversification.

One of the most effective product and service planning techniques is **test marketing**. Test markets allow an organization to test alternative marketing plans and to forecast future sales of new products. In conducting a test market project, an organization must decide how many cities to include, which cities to include, how long to run the test, what information to collect during the test, and what action to take after the test has been completed. Test marketing is used more frequently by consumer goods companies than industrial goods companies. The technique can enable an organization to avoid substantial losses by revealing weak products and ineffective marketing approaches before large-scale production begins.

Pricing

Procter & Gamble is currently embroiled in a shampoo price war with Unilever PLC in the U.S. hair care industry. Unilever's TRESemme, Alberto VO5, Clear, and Dove brands have been taking market share from P&G's Pantene and Old Spice brands, but both firms are now simultaneously cutting prices and spending heavily on advertising to "cripple" the other.

Five major stakeholders affect **pricing** decisions: consumers, governments, suppliers, distributors, and competitors. Sometimes an organization will pursue a forward integration strategy primarily to gain better control over prices charged to consumers. Governments can impose constraints on price fixing, price discrimination, minimum prices, unit pricing, price advertising, and price controls. For example, the Robinson-Patman Act prohibits manufacturers and wholesalers from discriminating in price among channel member purchasers (suppliers and distributors) if competition is injured.

Competing organizations must be careful not to coordinate discounts, credit terms, or condition of sale; not to discuss prices, markups, and costs at trade association meetings; and not to arrange to issue new price lists on the same date, rotate low bids on contracts, or uniformly restrict production to maintain high prices. Strategists should view price from both a short-run and a long-run perspective because competitors can copy price changes with relative ease. Often a dominant firm will aggressively match all price cuts by competitors.

Intense price competition, coupled with Internet price-comparative shopping, has reduced profit margins to bare minimum levels for most companies. Target recently joined Best Buy in offering to match online prices of rival retailers. Both companies are seeking to combat "showrooming" by shoppers who check out products in their stores but buy them on rival's websites. Both Target and Best Buy are matching prices from Amazon.com, Walmart.com, and Toysrus.com.

In contrast to popular opinion, online sales are more expensive for companies than brick-and-mortar sales, after factoring in the cost of shipping, handling, and the higher rates of returns.[21] For example, Kohl's Corporation reports that its profitability online is less than half of its store business, and even WalMart reports that it will lose money online at least through 2016. Primark, the European discount retailer, avoids online retailing "because it deems it to be unprofitable." However, online sales exceeded $294 billion, or 9 percent of all retail sales, in the United States in 2014, but analysts expect those numbers to increase to $414 billion and 11 percent by 2018.

During the 2014 Christmas shopping season, Amazon changed prices on as many as 80 million products during a single day, creating havoc for companies such as Walmart, Best Buy, and Toys "R" Us that had already announced they will not be undersold and would match any competitors' prices in a printed flyer or website. Because of pricing flexibility and variation, retail shopping has become much more challenging for savvy customers, and much more work for brick-and-mortar store managers empowered to meet all competitor prices.

Distribution

Distribution includes warehousing, distribution channels, distribution coverage, retail site locations, sales territories, inventory levels and location, transportation carriers, wholesaling, and retailing. Most producers today do not sell their goods directly to consumers. Various marketing entities act as intermediaries; they bear a variety of names such as wholesalers, retailers, brokers, facilitators, agents, vendors—or simply distributors. Some of the most complex and challenging decisions facing a firm concern product distribution. Intermediaries flourish in our economy because many producers lack the financial resources and expertise to carry out direct marketing. Manufacturers who could afford to sell directly to the public often can gain greater returns by expanding and improving their manufacturing operations.

Successful organizations identify and evaluate alternative ways to reach their ultimate market. Possible approaches vary from direct selling to using just one or many wholesalers and retailers. Strengths and weaknesses of each channel alternative should be determined according to economic, control, and adaptive criteria. Organizations should consider the costs and benefits of various wholesaling and retailing options. They must consider the need to motivate and control channel members and the need to adapt to changes in the future. Once a marketing channel is chosen, an organization usually must adhere to it for an extended period of time.

Marketing Research

Marketing research is the systematic gathering, recording, and analyzing of data about problems relating to the marketing of goods and services. Marketing researchers employ numerous scales, instruments, procedures, concepts, and techniques to gather information; their research can uncover critical strengths and weaknesses. Marketing-research activities support all of the major business functions of an organization. Organizations that possess excellent marketing research skills have a competitive advantage. According to the president of PepsiCo,

> Looking at the competition is the company's best form of market research. The majority of our strategic successes are ideas that we borrow from the marketplace, usually from a small regional or local competitor. In each case, we spot a promising new idea, improve on it, and then out-execute our competitor.[22]

Cost/Benefit Analysis

The seventh function of marketing is **cost/benefit analysis**, which involves assessing the costs, benefits, and risks associated with marketing decisions. Three steps are required to perform a cost/benefit analysis: (1) compute the total costs associated with a decision, (2) estimate the total benefits from the decision, and (3) compare the total costs with the total benefits. When expected benefits exceed total costs, an opportunity becomes more attractive. Sometimes the variables included in a cost/benefit analysis cannot be quantified or even measured, but usually reasonable estimates can be made to allow the analysis to be performed. One key factor to be considered is risk. Cost/benefit analysis should also be performed when a company is evaluating alternative ways to be socially responsible.

The practice of cost/benefit analysis differs among countries and industries. Some of the main differences include the types of impacts that are included as costs and benefits within appraisals, the extent to which impacts are expressed in monetary terms, and differences in the discount rate. Government agencies across the world rely on a basic set of key cost/benefit indicators, including the following:

1. Net present value (NPV)
2. Present value of benefits (PVB)
3. Present value of costs (PVC)
4. Benefit cost ratio (BCR) = PVB/PVC
5. Net benefit = PVB − PVC
6. NPV/k (where k is the level of funds available)[23]

Marketing Audit Checklist of Questions

The following questions about marketing must be examined in strategic planning:

1. Are markets segmented effectively?
2. Is the organization positioned well among competitors?
3. Has the firm's market share been increasing?
4. Are present channels of distribution reliable and cost effective?
5. Does the firm have an effective sales organization?
6. Does the firm conduct market research?
7. Are product quality and customer service good?
8. Are the firm's products and services priced appropriately?
9. Does the firm have an effective promotion, advertising, and publicity strategy?
10. Are marketing, planning, and budgeting effective?
11. Do the firm's marketing managers have adequate experience and training?
12. Is the firm's Internet presence excellent as compared to rivals?

Finance and Accounting

Financial condition is often considered the single-best measure of a firm's competitive position and overall attractiveness to investors. Determining an organization's financial strengths and weaknesses is essential to effectively formulating strategies. A firm's liquidity, leverage, working capital, profitability, asset utilization, cash flow, and equity can eliminate some strategies as being feasible alternatives. Financial factors often alter existing strategies and change implementation plans.

Finance/Accounting Functions

According to James Van Horne, the **functions of finance/accounting** comprise three decisions: the investment decision, the financing decision, and the dividend decision.[24] **Financial ratio analysis** is the most widely used method for determining an organization's strengths and weaknesses in the investment, financing, and dividend areas. Because the functional areas of business are so closely related, financial ratios can signal strengths or weaknesses in management, marketing, production, R&D, and MIS activities. Financial ratios are equally applicable in for-profit and nonprofit organizations. Even though nonprofit organizations obviously would not have return-on-investment or earnings-per-share ratios, they would routinely monitor many other special ratios. For example, a church would monitor the ratio of dollar contributions to the number of members, whereas a zoo would monitor dollar food sales to number of visitors. A university would monitor number of students divided by number of professors. Therefore, be creative when performing ratio analysis for nonprofit organizations, for they strive to be financially sound just as for-profit firms do. Nonprofit organizations need strategic planning just as much as for-profit firms.

The **investment decision**, also called **capital budgeting**, is the allocation and reallocation of capital and resources to projects, products, assets, and divisions of an organization. After strategies are formulated, capital budgeting decisions are required to successfully implement strategies. The **financing decision** determines the best capital structure for the firm and includes examining various methods by which the firm can raise capital (for example, by issuing stock, increasing debt, selling assets, or using a combination of these approaches). The financing decision must consider both short-term and long-term needs for working capital. Two key financial ratios that indicate whether a firm's financing decisions have been effective are the debt-to-equity ratio and the debt-to-total-assets ratio.

Dividend decisions concern issues such as the percentage of earnings paid to stockholders, the stability of dividends paid over time, and the repurchase or issuance of stock. Dividend decisions determine the amount of funds that are retained in a firm compared to the amount paid out to stockholders. Three financial ratios that are helpful in evaluating a firm's dividend decisions are the earnings-per-share ratio, the dividends-per-share ratio, and the price-earnings ratio.

The benefits of paying dividends to investors must be balanced against the benefits of internally retaining funds, and there is no set formula on how to balance this trade-off. In 2014–2016, companies are aggressively boosting their dividends paid to shareholders. Companies are also buying back their own stock (called *Treasury stock*) at record levels. For the reasons listed here, dividends are sometimes paid out even when the firm has incurred a negative annual net income, and/or even if the funds could be better reinvested in the business, and/or even if the firm has to obtain outside sources of capital to pay for the dividends:

1. Paying cash dividends is customary for some firms. Failure to do so could be thought of as a stigma. A dividend change is a signal about the future.
2. Dividends represent a sales point for investment bankers. Some institutional investors can buy only dividend-paying stocks.
3. Shareholders often demand dividends, even in companies with great opportunities for reinvesting all available funds.
4. A myth exists that paying dividends will result in a higher stock price.

Financial Ratios

Financial ratios are computed from an organization's income statement and balance sheet. Computing financial ratios is like taking a photograph—the results reflect a situation at just one point in time. Comparing ratios over time and to industry averages is more likely to result in meaningful statistics that can be used to identify and evaluate strengths and weaknesses. Trend analysis, illustrated in Figure 4-3, is a useful technique that incorporates both the time and industry average dimensions of financial ratios. Note that the dotted lines reveal projected ratios.

Financial ratio analysis should be conducted on three separate fronts:

1. *How has each ratio changed over time?* This information provides a means of evaluating historical trends. Examine whether each ratio has been historically increasing, decreasing, or nearly constant. For example, a 10 percent profit margin could be bad if the trend has been down 20 percent each of the last three years. But a 10 percent profit margin could be excellent if the trend has been up, up, up. Analysts often calculate the percentage change in a ratio from one year to the next to assess historical financial performance on that dimension. Large percent changes can be especially relevant.
2. *How does each ratio compare to industry norms?* A firm's inventory turnover ratio may appear impressive at first glance but may pale when compared to industry standards or norms. Industries can differ dramatically on certain ratios. For example, grocery companies have a high inventory turnover, whereas automobile dealerships have a lower turnover. Therefore, comparison of a firm's ratios within its particular industry can be essential in determining strengths and weaknesses.

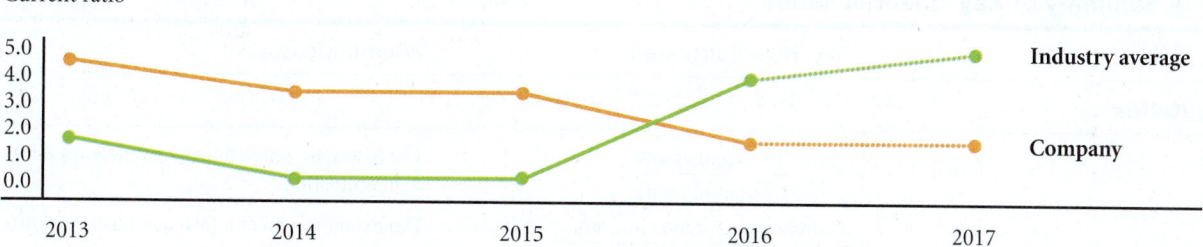

Current ratio

Profit margin (percent)

FIGURE 4-3

The Process of Gaining Competitive Advantage in a Firm

3. *How does each ratio compare with key competitors?* Oftentimes competition is more intense between several competitors in a given industry or location than across all rival firms in the industry. When this is true, financial ratio analysis should include comparison to those key competitors. For example, if a firm's profitability ratio is trending up over time and compares favorably to the industry average, but it is trending down relative to its leading competitor, there may be reason for concern.

Financial ratio analysis is not without some limitations. For example, financial ratios are based on accounting data, and firms differ in their treatment of such items as depreciation, inventory valuation, R&D expenditures, pension plan costs, mergers, and taxes. Also, seasonal factors can influence comparative ratios. Therefore, conformity to industry composite ratios does not establish with certainty that a firm is performing normally or that it is well managed. Likewise, departures from industry averages do not always indicate that a firm is doing especially well or badly. For example, a high inventory turnover ratio could indicate efficient inventory management and a strong working capital position, but it also could indicate a serious inventory shortage and a weak working capital position.

Another limitation of financial ratios in terms of including them as key internal factors in the upcoming IFE Matrix is that financial ratios are not very "actionable" in terms of revealing potential strategies needed (i.e., because they generally are based on performance of the overall firm). For example, to include as a key internal factor that the firm's "current ratio increased from 1.8 to 2.1" is not as "actionable" as "the firm's fragrance division revenues increased 18 percent in Africa in 2015." Recall from the prior chapter the importance of selecting "*actionable responses*" as key factors, both externally and internally, upon which to formulate strategies. Selecting "actionable" key factors is vital to successful strategic planning.

Table 4-4 provides a summary of key financial ratios showing how each ratio is calculated and what each ratio measures. However, all the ratios are not significant for all industries and companies. For example, accounts receivable turnover and average collection period are not meaningful to a company that takes only cash receipts. As indicated in Table 4-4, key financial ratios can be classified into the following five types: liquidity, leverage, activity, profitability, and growth.

TABLE 4-4 A Summary of Key Financial Ratios

Ratio	How Calculated	What It Measures
I. Liquidity Ratios		
Current Ratio	$$\frac{\text{Current assets}}{\text{Current liabilities}}$$	The extent to which a firm can meet its short-term obligations
Quick Ratio	$$\frac{\text{Current assets minus inventory}}{\text{Current liabilities}}$$	The extent to which a firm can meet its short-term obligations without relying on the sale of its inventories
II. Leverage Ratios		
Debt-to-Total-Assets Ratio	$$\frac{\text{Total debt}}{\text{Total assets}}$$	The percentage of total funds provided by creditors
Debt-to-Equity Ratio	$$\frac{\text{Total debt}}{\text{Total stockholders' equity}}$$	The percentage of total funds provided by creditors versus by owners
Long-Term Debt-to-Equity Ratio	$$\frac{\text{Long-term debt}}{\text{Total stockholders' equity}}$$	The balance between debt and equity in a firm's long-term capital structure
Times-Interest-Earned Ratio	$$\frac{\text{Profits before interest and taxes}}{\text{Total interest charges}}$$	The extent to which earnings can decline without the firm becoming unable to meet its annual interest costs
III. Activity Ratios		
Inventory Turnover	$$\frac{\text{Sales}}{\text{Inventory of finished goods}}$$	Whether a firm holds excessive stocks of inventories and whether a firm is slowly selling its inventories compared to the industry average
Fixed Assets Turnover	$$\frac{\text{Sales}}{\text{Fixed assets}}$$	Sales productivity and plant and equipment utilization
Total Assets Turnover	$$\frac{\text{Sales}}{\text{Total assets}}$$	Whether a firm is generating a sufficient volume of business for the size of its asset investment
Accounts Receivable Turnover	$$\frac{\text{Annual credit sales}}{\text{Accounts receivable}}$$	The average length of time it takes a firm to collect credit sales (in percentage terms)
Average Collection Period	$$\frac{\text{Accounts receivable}}{\text{Total credit sales/365 days}}$$	The average length of time it takes a firm to collect on credit sales (in days)
IV. Profitability Ratios		
Gross Profit Margin	$$\frac{\text{Sales minus cost of goods sold}}{\text{Sales}}$$	The total margin available to cover operating expenses and yield a profit
Operating Profit Margin	$$\frac{\text{Earnings before interest and taxes EBIT}}{\text{Sales}}$$	Profitability without concern for taxes and interest
Net Profit Margin	$$\frac{\text{Net income}}{\text{Sales}}$$	After-tax profits per dollar of sales
Return on Total Assets (ROA)	$$\frac{\text{Net income}}{\text{Total assets}}$$	After-tax profits per dollar of assets; this ratio is also called return on investment (ROI)
Return on Stockholders' Equity (ROE)	$$\frac{\text{Net Income}}{\text{Total stockholders' equity}}$$	After-tax profits per dollar of stockholders' investment in the firm
Earnings Per Share (EPS)	$$\frac{\text{Net income}}{\text{Number of shares of common stock outstanding}}$$	Earnings available to the owners of common stock
Price-Earnings Ratio	$$\frac{\text{Market price per share}}{\text{Earnings per share}}$$	Attractiveness of firm on equity markets
V. Growth Ratios		
Sales	Annual percentage growth in total sales	Firm's growth rate in sales
Net Income	Annual percentage growth in profits	Firm's growth rate in profits
Earnings Per Share	Annual percentage growth in EPS	Firm's growth rate in EPS
Dividends Per Share	Annual percentage growth in dividends per share	Firm's growth rate in dividends per share

Breakeven Analysis

Because consumers remain price sensitive, many firms have lowered prices to compete. As a firm lowers prices, its **breakeven (BE) point** in terms of units sold increases, as illustrated in Figure 4-4. The breakeven point can be defined as the quantity of units that a firm must sell for its total revenues (TR) to equal its total costs (TC). Note that the before and after chart in Figure 4-4 reveals that the TR line rotates to the right with a decrease in price, thus increasing the quantity (Q) that must be sold just to break even. Increasing the breakeven point is thus a huge drawback of lowering prices. Of course when rivals are lowering prices, a firm may have to lower prices anyway to compete. However, the breakeven concept should be kept in mind because it is so important, especially in recessionary times.

The before and after charts in Figure 4-5 show that increasing **fixed costs (FC)** raises a firm's breakeven quantity. The figure also reveals that adding fixed costs such as more stores, or more plants, or even more advertising as part of a strategic plan also raises the TC line, which makes the intersection of the TC and TR lines at a point farther down the Quantity axis. Increasing a firm's FC therefore significantly raises the quantity of goods that must be sold to break even. This is not just theory for the sake of theory. Firms with less fixed costs, such as Apple and Amazon.com, have lower breakeven points, which give them a decided competitive advantage in harsh economic times. Figure 4-5 reveals that adding fixed costs—such as plant, equipment, stores, advertising, and land—may be detrimental whenever there is doubt that significantly more units can be sold to offset those expenditures.

Firms must be cognizant of the fact that lowering prices and adding fixed costs could be a catastrophic double whammy because the firm's breakeven quantity needed to be sold is increased dramatically. Figure 4-6 illustrates this double whammy. Note how far the breakeven point shifts with both a price decrease and an increase in fixed costs. If a firm does not break even, then it will of course incur losses, and losses are not good, especially sustained losses.

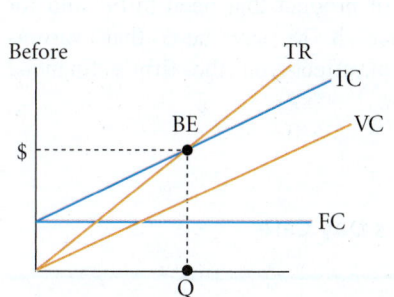
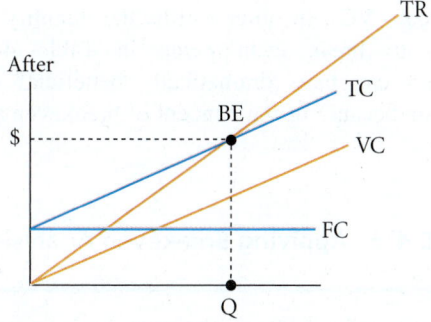

FIGURE 4-4

A Before and After Breakeven Chart When Prices Are Lowered

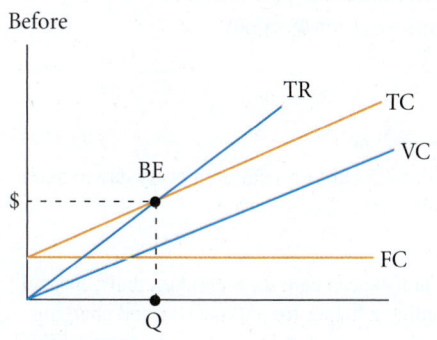
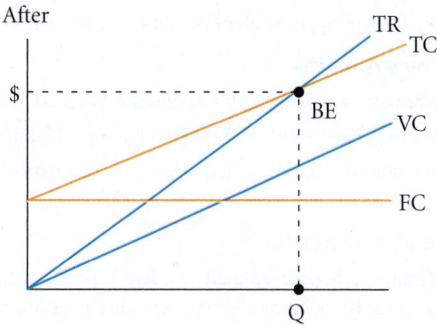

FIGURE 4-5

A Before and After Breakeven Chart When Fixed Costs are Increased

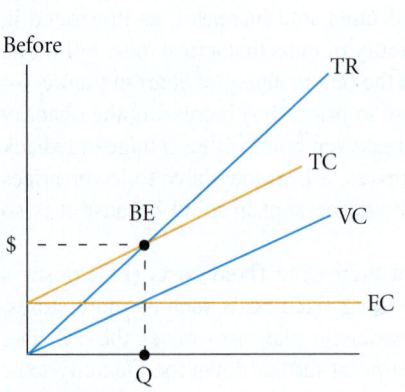
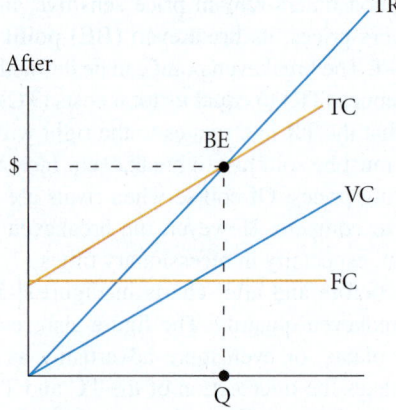

FIGURE 4-6

A Before and After Breakeven Chart When Prices Are Lowered and Fixed Costs Are Increased

Finally, note in Figures 4-4, 4-5, and 4-6 that **variable costs (VC)**, such as labor and materials, when increased, have the effect of raising the breakeven point, too. Raising VC is reflected by the VC line shifting left or becoming steeper. When the TR line remains constant, the effect of increasing VC is to increase TC, which increases the point at which TR = TC = BE.

The formula for calculating the breakeven point is BE Quantity = TFC divided by (price − VC). In other words, the quantity or units of product that need to be sold for a firm to break even given in Table 4-5. Suffice it to say here that various strategies can have dramatically beneficial or harmful effects on the firm's financial condition because of the concept of breakeven analysis.

TABLE 4-5   Applying Breakeven Analysis for Joy's Day Care

Seeing a need for childcare in her town, Joy is considering opening her own day-care service. Joy's Day Care needs to be affordable, so Joy would like to care for each child for $12 a day. But Joy also wants to make money. She needs to know how many children she will have to watch per day to make money. Joy gathered the following information about her potential new business.

- The month of June has 20 workdays, Monday through Friday for 4 weeks.
- Insurance and rent on her business will be $200 and $400, respectively, per month.
- Expenses per student per day will be snacks (2 @ $1.00) + meals (2 @ $3.00).

Joy's Analysis

Breakeven = Operating Expenses ÷ ($12.00 − $8.00)

Breakeven = $600 ÷ $4.00 Breakeven = 150 units (children) in June.

Because there are 20 days in June, Joy must watch 150 ÷ 20 = 7.5 kids, or 8 children every day to make a profit.

Joy's Conclusion

Thanks to breakeven analysis, Joy is pondering whether or not she can care for 8 children daily. Instead of abruptly opening the business, Joy is now considering adding a helper for $50 per day and charging $20 per student per day. How many students now would Joy have to care for to make a profit under this scenario? (Answer 6.6 = 7) What do you think would be an ideal scenario for Joy in planning for her new business?

Finance/Accounting Audit Checklist

Some finance/accounting questions that should be examined in any strategic analysis of the firm are given here:

1. Where is the firm financially strong and weak as indicated by financial ratio analyses?

2. Can the firm raise needed short-term capital?

3. Can the firm raise needed long-term capital through debt or equity?

4. Does the firm have sufficient working capital?

5. Are capital budgeting procedures effective?

6. Are dividend payout policies reasonable?

7. Does the firm have good relations with its investors and stockholders?

8. Are the firm's financial managers experienced and well trained?

9. Is the firm's debt situation excellent?

Production/Operations

The **production/operations function** of a business consists of all those activities that transform inputs into goods and services. production/operations management deals with inputs, transformations, and outputs that vary across industries and markets. A manufacturing operation transforms or converts inputs such as raw materials, labor, capital, machines, and facilities into finished goods and services. The extent to which a manufacturing plant's output reaches its potential output is called **capacity utilization**, a key strategic variable. The higher the capacity utilization, the better; otherwise, equipment may sit idle.

As indicated in Table 4-6, Roger Schroeder suggests that production/operations management comprises five functions or decision areas: process, capacity, inventory, workforce, and quality.

production/operations activities often represent the largest part of an organization's human and capital assets. In most industries, the major costs of producing a product or service are incurred within operations, so production/operations can have great value as a competitive weapon in a company's overall strategy. Strengths and weaknesses in the five functions of production can mean the success or failure of an enterprise.

TABLE 4-6 The Basic Functions (Decisions) within Production/Operations

Decision Areas	Example Decisions
1. Process	These decisions include choice of technology, facility layout, process flow analysis, facility location, line balancing, process control, and transportation analysis. Distances from raw materials to production sites to customers are a major consideration.
2. Capacity	These decisions include forecasting, facilities planning, aggregate planning, scheduling, capacity planning, and queuing analysis. Capacity utilization is a major consideration.
3. Inventory	These decisions involve managing the level of raw materials, work-in-process, and finished goods, especially considering what to order, when to order, how much to order, and materials handling.
4. Workforce	These decisions involve managing the skilled, unskilled, clerical, and managerial employees by caring for job design, work measurement, job enrichment, work standards, and motivation techniques.
5. Quality	These decisions are aimed at ensuring that high-quality goods and services are produced by caring for quality control, sampling, testing, quality assurance, and cost control.

Source: Based on R. Schroeder, *Operations Management* (New York: McGraw-Hill, 1981), p. 12.

Increasingly in production settings, a new breed of robots called **collaborative machines**, are working alongside people. The robots, priced as low as $20,000 and becoming widely used even in small businesses, do not take lunch breaks or sick days or require health insurance, and they can work nonstop all night tirelessly if needed. Unlike larger robots that cost much more, collaborative machines are more flexible, oftentimes doing one task one day and a different task the next day. At Panek Precision Inc., an Northbrook, Illinois-based machine shop, Mr. Panek states, "Having robots has allowed us to move our existing workers into more useful tasks, such as monitoring more-advanced machines that require human tending." Workers are generally quite receptive to collaborative machines, even giving them names, such as "Fred" at Stuller Inc., a jewelry factory in Lafayette, Louisiana, and "Baxter" at K'NEX Brands, a toy maker in Hatfield, Pennsylvania.[25]

Many production/operations managers are finding that cross-training of employees can help their firms respond faster to changing markets. Cross-training can increase efficiency, quality, productivity, and job satisfaction. For example, at General Motors' Detroit gear and axle plant, costs related to product defects were reduced 400 percent in 2 years as a result of cross-training workers. As shown in Table 4-7, James Dilworth has outlined implications of several types of strategic decisions a company might make.

Production/Operations Audit Checklist

Questions such as the following should be examined:

1. Are supplies of raw materials, parts, and subassemblies reliable and reasonable?
2. Are facilities, equipment, machinery, and offices in good condition?
3. Are inventory-control policies and procedures effective?
4. Are quality-control policies and procedures effective?
5. Are facilities, resources, and markets strategically located?
6. Does the firm have technological competencies?

TABLE 4-7 Implications of Various Strategies on Production/Operations

Various Strategies	Implications
1. Become a low-cost provider	Creates high barriers to entry
	Creates larger market
	Requires longer production runs and fewer product changes
2. Become a high-quality provider	Requires more quality-assurance efforts
	Requires more expensive equipment
	Requires highly skilled workers and higher wages
3. Provide great customer service	Requires more service people, service parts, and equipment
	Requires rapid response to customer needs or changes in customer tastes
	Requires a higher inventory investment
4. Be the first to introduce new products	Has higher research and development costs
	Has high retraining and tooling costs
5. Become highly automated	Requires high capital investment
	Reduces flexibility
	May affect labor relations
	Makes maintenance more crucial
6. Minimize layoffs	Serves the security needs of employees and may develop employee loyalty
	Helps attract and retain highly skilled employees

Source: Based on J. Dilworth, *Production/Operations Management: Manufacturing and Nonmanufacturing,* 2nd ed. Copyright © 1983 by Random House, Inc.

Research and Development

The fifth major area of internal operations that should be examined for specific strengths and weaknesses as input into formulating strategies is **research and development (R&D)**. Many firms today conduct no R&D, and yet many other companies depend on successful R&D activities for survival. Firms pursuing a product-development strategy especially need to have a strong R&D orientation. High-tech firms, such as Microsoft, spend a much larger proportion of their revenues on R&D. A key decision for many firms is whether to be a "first mover" or a "late follower" (i.e., spend heavily on R&D to be the first to develop radically new products, or spend less on R&D by imitating/duplicating/improving on products after rival firms develop them).

Organizations invest in R&D because they believe that such an investment will lead to a superior product or service and will give them competitive advantages. Research and development expenditures are directed at developing new products before competitors do, at improving product quality, or at improving manufacturing processes to reduce costs. However, a recent study reported that the stock price appreciation of technology companies in the lowest third of R&D spending have consistently outperformed companies in the highest third over 1, 3, 5, and 10-year periods since 1977, with a 5-year average outperformance of 8 percent.[26] In the study, some big R&D underspenders whose stock price significantly outperformed were Micron Technology, Seagate Technology, Western Digital, and Apple. The study reported in *Investor's Business Daily* accents the need to formulate and implement an effective R&D spending strategy consistent with overall corporate strategy and objectives.

Effective management of the R&D function requires a strategic and operational partnership between R&D and the other vital business functions. A spirit of partnership and mutual trust between general and R&D managers is evident in the best-managed firms today. Managers in these firms jointly explore; assess; and decide the what, when, where, why, and how much of R&D. Priorities, costs, benefits, risks, and rewards associated with R&D activities are discussed openly and shared. The overall mission of R&D has thus become broad based, including supporting existing businesses, helping launch new businesses, developing new products, improving product quality, improving manufacturing efficiency, and deepening or broadening the company's technological capabilities.[27]

Internal and External Research and Development

Four approaches to determining research and development budget allocations commonly are used: (1) financing as many project proposals as possible, (2) using a percentage-of-sales method, (3) budgeting about the same amount that competitors spend for R&D, or (4) deciding how many successful new products are needed and working backward to estimate the required R&D investment. The strengths (capabilities) and weaknesses (limitations) of R&D play a major role in strategy formulation and strategy implementation.

Most firms have no choice but to continually develop new and improved products because of changing consumer needs and tastes, new technologies, shortened product life cycles, and increased domestic and foreign competition. A shortage of ideas for new products, increased global competition, increased market segmentation, strong special-interest groups, and increased government regulations are several factors making the successful development of new products more and more difficult, costly, and risky. In the pharmaceutical industry, for example, only one of every few thousand drugs created in the laboratory ends up on pharmacists' shelves.

Research and Development Audit

Questions such as the following should be asked in performing a research and development audit:

1. Does the firm have R&D facilities? Are they adequate?
2. If outside R&D firms are used, are they cost effective?
3. Are the organization's R&D personnel well qualified?
4. Are R&D resources allocated effectively?
5. Are management information and computer systems adequate?
6. Is communication between R&D and other organizational units effective?
7. Are present products technologically competitive?

Management Information Systems

Billions of bits of information are now "in the cloud." Information ties all business functions together and provides the basis for all managerial decisions. It is the cornerstone of all organizations. Information represents a major source of competitive management advantage or disadvantage. Assessing a firm's internal strengths and weaknesses in information systems is a critical dimension of performing an internal audit.

A purpose of a management information system is to improve the performance of an enterprise by improving the quality of managerial decisions. An effective information system thus collects, codes, stores, synthesizes, and presents information in such a manner that it answers important operating and strategic questions. The heart of an information system is a database containing the kinds of records and data important to managers.

A **management information system (MIS)** receives raw material from both the external and internal evaluation of an organization. It gathers data about marketing, finance, production, and personnel matters internally, and social, cultural, demographic, environmental, economic, political, governmental, legal, technological, and competitive factors externally. Data are integrated in ways needed to support managerial decision making.

Starbucks is an example firm with an outstanding management information system that begins with more than 7 million weekly transactions taking place at Starbucks registers, and 16 percent of those are made from a mobile device. Surprisingly, Starbucks transactions comprise about 90 percent of all mobile pay transactions in the United States. And Starbucks is reportedly developing a stand-alone e-payment system that its customers may use anywhere, anytime, to buy anything. Such a system would compete with Apple Pay, Google's Wallet, eBay's PayPal, and CurrentC used by Walmart and CVS Health.

Managing Voluminous Consumer Data

Recent research by the Pew Research Center reveals that more than 50 percent of all consumers are concerned about the volume of their personal data on the Internet.[28] Basically, every time you get online and do anything at any website with any company or anybody, that information is dissected to determine your patterns of behavior; resultant information is disseminated to marketers. Every time you swipe a card, click, log in, text, tweet, email, or call, your behavior is being tracked. Consider a few facts:

1. The number of times the online activity of an average Internet user is tracked every day is estimated to be 2,000-plus.
2. Facebook and Twitter can track the activity of visitors at 1,205 and 868 of the most popular websites, respectively, on the Internet.
3. The estimated annual value to Facebook of a "very active" versus "relatively inactive" female user is $27.61 and $12.37, respectively, due to their dissemination of the information to marketers.
4. People are so worried about their privacy that 86 percent of them have taken steps to conceal their digital footprints.
5. More than 25 percent of Americans have downloaded advertisement-blocking tools so companies cannot so easily access data about the users.[29]

ACADEMIC RESEARCH CAPSULE **4-2**

New Trends in Managing Big Data

Business analytics can identify and analyze patterns, but perhaps more importantly, they can reveal the likelihood of an event, and that information can be worth millions and even billions of dollars to companies, organizations, and governments. In analyzing big data, two trends in analysis have emerged. First, the typical statistical approach of relying on p values to establish the significance of a finding is becoming less trusted because, with extremely high sample sizes, "almost everything" becomes significant. In contrast, the focus of analysis is shifting more to the size and variance explained (i.e., examining for example R-squared). Stepwise regression and cluster analysis are becoming more widely used to supplement traditional p-value analyses. Second, in analyzing big data, there is a shift from focusing largely on aggregates or averages to focusing also on outliers, because outliers oftentimes reveal (predict) critical innovations, trends, disruptions, and revolutions on the horizon. In essence, knowing more about "who is not your customer and why" may be as (or more) important than knowing about your customer. Perceptual mapping and multidimensional scaling are being more widely used to explore outlier patterns. By 2018, global data analytics software is expected to reach $21.7 billion, a 64 percent increase from 2012. Leading firms providing the software include IBM, SAP, Oracle, Microsoft, Qlik Technologies, Tibco Software, and Tableau Software.

Source: Based on G. George, M. Haas, & A. Pentland, "Big Data and Management," *Academy of Management Journal* 52, no. 2 (April 2014): 321–326. See also P. Barlas, "Data Analytics Gets in the Sports Game," *Investor's Business Daily*, July 11, 2014, A1.

Academic Research Capsule 4-2 reveals key trends in analyzing big data.

Management Information Systems Audit

Questions such as the following should be asked when conducting this audit:

1. Do all managers in the firm use the information system to make decisions?
2. Is there a chief information officer or director of information systems position in the firm?
3. Are data in the information system updated regularly?
4. Do managers from all functional areas of the firm contribute input to the information system?
5. Are there effective passwords for entry into the firm's information system?
6. Are strategists of the firm familiar with the information systems of rival firms?
7. Is the information system user-friendly?
8. Do all users of the information system understand the competitive advantages that information can provide firms?
9. Are computer training workshops provided for users of the information system?
10. Is the firm's information system continually being improved in content and user-friendliness?

Value Chain Analysis

According to Porter, the business of a firm can best be described as a *value chain*, in which total revenues minus total costs of all activities undertaken to develop and market a product or service yields value.[30] All firms in a given industry have a similar value chain, which includes activities such as obtaining raw materials, designing products, building manufacturing facilities, developing cooperative agreements, and providing customer service. A firm will be profitable so long as total revenues exceed the total costs incurred in creating and delivering the product or service. Firms should strive to understand not only their own value chain operations but also those of their competitors, suppliers, and distributors.

Value chain analysis (VCA) refers to the process whereby a firm determines the costs associated with organizational activities from purchasing raw materials to manufacturing product(s) to marketing those products. Value chain analysis aims to identify where low-cost advantages or disadvantages exist anywhere along the value chain from raw material to customer service activities. The VCA process can enable a firm to better identify its own strengths and weaknesses, especially as compared to competitors' value chain analyses and their own data examined over time.

Substantial judgment may be required in performing a VCA because different items along the value chain may impact other items positively or negatively, at times creating complex interrelationships. For example, exceptional customer service may be especially expensive yet may reduce the costs of returns and increase revenues. Cost and price differences among rival firms can have their origins in activities performed by suppliers, distributors, creditors, or even shareholders. The initial step in implementing VCA is to divide a firm's operations into specific activities or business processes. Then the analyst attempts to attach a cost to each discrete activity; the costs could be in terms of both time and money. Finally, the analyst converts the cost data into information by looking for competitive cost strengths and weaknesses that may yield competitive advantage or disadvantage. Conducting a value chain analysis is supportive of the research-based view's examination of a firm's assets and capabilities as sources of distinctive competence.

When a major competitor or new market entrant offers products or services at low prices, this may be because that firm has substantially lower value chain costs or perhaps the rival firm is just waging a desperate attempt to gain sales or market share. Thus, VCA can be critically important for a firm in monitoring whether its prices and costs are competitive. An example value chain is illustrated in Figure 4-7. There can be more than a hundred particular value-creating activities associated with the business of producing and marketing a product or service, and each one of the activities can represent a competitive advantage or disadvantage for the firm. The combined costs of all the various activities in a company's value chain define the firm's cost of doing business. Firms should determine where cost advantages and disadvantages in their value chain occur *relative* to the value chain of rival firms.

Value chains differ immensely across industries and firms. Whereas a paper products company, such as Stone Container, would include on its value chain timber farming, logging, pulp mills, and papermaking, a company such as Hewlett-Packard would include programming, peripherals, software, hardware, and laptops. A motel would include food, housekeeping, check-in and check-out operations, website, reservations system, and so on. However, all firms should use value chain analysis to develop and nurture a core competence and convert this competence into a distinctive competence. A **core competence** is a VCA that a firm performs especially well. When a core competence evolves into a major competitive advantage, then it is called a *distinctive competence*. Figure 4-8 illustrates this process.

More and more companies are using VCA to gain and sustain competitive advantage by being especially efficient and effective along various parts of the value chain. For example, Walmart has built powerful value advantages by focusing on exceptionally tight inventory control and volume purchasing of products. In contrast, computer companies compete aggressively along the distribution end of the value chain. Price competitiveness is a key component of competitiveness for both mass retailers and computer firms.

Benchmarking

Benchmarking is an analytical tool used to determine whether a firm's value chain analysis is competitive compared to those of rivals and thus conducive to winning in the marketplace. Benchmarking entails measuring costs of value chain activities across an industry to determine "best practices" among competing firms for the purpose of duplicating or improving on those best practices. Benchmarking enables a firm to take action to improve its competitiveness by identifying (and improving on) value chain activities where rival firms have comparative advantages in cost, service, reputation, or operation.

A comprehensive survey on benchmarking was recently commissioned by the Global Benchmarking Network, a network of benchmarking centers representing 22 countries. More than 450 organizations responded from over 40 countries. Here are two important results:

1. Mission and vision statements along with customer (client) surveys are the most used (77 percent of organizations) of 20 improvement tools, followed by SWOT (strengths, weaknesses, opportunities, threats) analysis (72 percent), and informal benchmarking (68 percent). Performance benchmarking was used by 49 percent and best practice benchmarking was used by 39 percent of respondents.
2. The tools that are likely to increase the most in popularity over the next 3 years are performance benchmarking, informal benchmarking, SWOT, and best practice benchmarking. More than 60 percent of organizations not currently using these tools indicated they are likely to use them in the next 3 years.[31]

Supplier Costs ————— |
    Raw materials ————— |
    Fuel ————— |
    Energy ————— |
    Transportation ————— |
    Truck drivers ————— |
    Truck maintenance ————— |
    Component parts ————— |
    Inspection ————— |
    Storing ————— |
    Warehouse ————— |
Production Costs ————— |
    Inventory system ————— |
    Receiving ————— |
    Plant layout ————— |
    Maintenance ————— |
    Plant location ————— |
    Computer ————— |
    R&D ————— |
    Cost accounting ————— |
Distribution Costs ————— |
    Loading ————— |
    Shipping ————— |
    Budgeting ————— |
    Personnel ————— |
    Internet ————— |
    Trucking ————— |
    Railroads ————— |
    Fuel ————— |
    Maintenance ————— |
Sales and Marketing Costs ————— |
    Salespersons ————— |
    Website ————— |
    Internet ————— |
    Publicity ————— |
    Promotion ————— |
    Advertising ————— |
    Transportation ————— |
    Food and lodging ————— |
Customer Service Costs ————— |
    Postage ————— |
    Phone ————— |
    Internet ————— |
    Warranty ————— |
Management Costs ————— |
    Human resources ————— |
    Administration ————— |
    Employee benefits ————— |
    Labor relations ————— |
    Managers ————— |
    Employees ————— |
    Finance and legal ————— |

FIGURE 4-7

An Example Value Chain for a Typical Manufacturing Firm

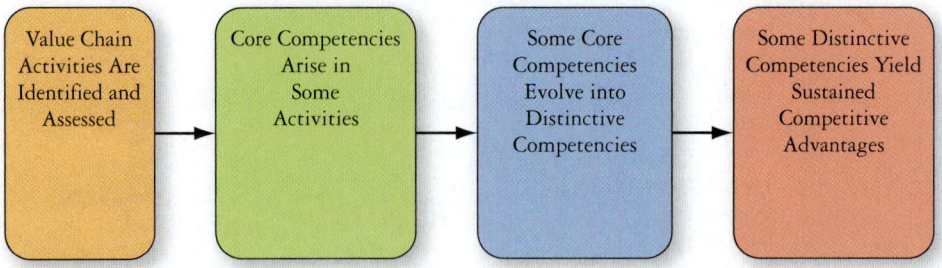

FIGURE 4-8

Transforming Value Chain Activities into Sustained Competitive Advantage

The hardest part of benchmarking can be gaining access to other firms' value chain analyses with associated costs. Typical sources of benchmarking information, however, include published reports, trade publications, suppliers, distributors, customers, partners, creditors, shareholders, lobbyists, and willing rival firms. Some rival firms share benchmarking data. However, the International Benchmarking Clearinghouse provides guidelines to help ensure that restraint of trade, price fixing, bid rigging, bribery, and other improper business conduct do not arise between participating firms.

The Internal Factor Evaluation Matrix

A summary step in conducting an internal strategic-management audit is to construct an **Internal Factor Evaluation (IFE) Matrix**. This strategy-formulation tool summarizes and evaluates the major strengths and weaknesses in the functional areas of a business, and it also provides a basis for identifying and evaluating relationships among those areas. Intuitive judgments are required in developing an IFE Matrix, so the appearance of a scientific approach should not be interpreted to mean this is an all-powerful technique. A thorough understanding of the factors included is more important than the actual numbers. Similar to the EFE Matrix and the Competitive Profile Matrix (CPM) described in Chapter 3, an IFE Matrix can be developed in five steps:

1. List key internal factors as identified in the internal-audit process. Use a total of 20 internal factors, including both strengths and weaknesses. List strengths first and then weaknesses. Be as specific as possible, using percentages, ratios, and comparative numbers. Recall that Edward Deming said, "In God we trust. Everyone else bring data." Include *actionable* factors that can provide insight regarding strategies to pursue. For example, the factor "Our Quick Ratio is 2.1 versus industry average of 1.8" is not actionable, whereas the factor "Our chocolate division's ROI increased from 8 to 15 percent in South America" is actionable. Also, be as *divisional* as possible, because consolidated data oftentimes is not as revealing or useful in deciding among strategies as the underlying by-segment or division data.

2. Assign a weight that ranges from 0.0 (not important) to 1.0 (all-important) to each factor. The weight assigned to a given factor indicates the relative importance of the factor to being successful in the firm's industry. Regardless of whether a key factor is an internal strength or weakness, factors considered to have the greatest effect on organizational performance should be assigned the highest weights. The sum of all weights must equal 1.0.

3. Assign a 1 to 4 rating to each factor to indicate whether that factor represents a major weakness (rating = 1), a minor weakness (rating = 2), a minor strength (rating = 3), or a major strength (rating = 4). Note that strengths must receive a 3 or 4 rating and weaknesses must receive a 1 or 2 rating. Ratings are thus company-based, whereas the weights in step 2 are industry-based.

4. Multiply each factor's weight by its rating to determine a weighted score for each variable.

5. Sum the weighted scores for each variable to determine the total weighted score for the organization.

Regardless of how many factors are included in an IFE Matrix, the total weighted score can range from a low of 1.0 to a high of 4.0, with the average score being 2.5. Total weighted scores well below 2.5 characterize organizations that are weak internally, whereas scores significantly above 2.5 indicate a strong internal position. Like the EFE Matrix, an IFE Matrix should include 20 key factors. The number of factors has no effect on the range of total weighted scores because the weights always sum to 1.0.

When a key internal factor is both a strength and a weakness, the factor may be included twice in the IFE Matrix, and a weight and rating assigned to each statement. For example, the Playboy logo both helps and hurts Playboy Enterprises; the logo attracts customers to *Playboy* magazine, but it keeps the Playboy cable channel out of many markets. Be as quantitative as possible when stating factors. Use monetary amounts, percentages, numbers, and ratios to the extent possible.

An example IFE Matrix is provided in Table 4-8 for a retail computer store. The table reveals that the two most important factors to be successful in the retail computer store business are "Revenues from repair/service in the store" and "Employee morale." Note that the store is doing best on "Average customer purchase" amount and "In-store technical support." The store is having major problems with its carpet, bathroom, paint, and checkout procedures. Note also that the matrix contains substantial quantitative data rather than vague statements; this is excellent. Overall, this store receives a 2.5 total weighted score, which on a 1 to 4 scale is exactly average/halfway, indicating there is definitely room for improvement in store operations, strategies, policies, and procedures.

The IFE Matrix provides important information for strategy formulation. For example, this retail computer store might want to hire another checkout person and repair its carpet, paint, and bathroom problems. Also, the store may want to increase advertising for its repair/services, because that is a really important (weight 0.15) factor to being successful in this business.

An actual IFE Matrix for Forjas Taurus S.A. is provided in Table 4-9. Headquartered in Porto Alegre, Brazil, Taurus manufactures and sells military and civilian pistols, submachine guns, rifles, ammunition, bulletproof vests, motorbike helmets, and more. Note that the total weighted score of 2.53 is barely above the average of 2.50. Note, too, that the most important

TABLE 4-8 Sample Internal Factor Evaluation Matrix for a Retail Computer Store

Key Internal Factors	Weight	Rating	Weighted Score
Strengths			
1. Inventory turnover increased from 5.8 to 6.7.	0.05	3	0.15
2. Average customer purchase increased from $97 to $128.	0.07	4	0.28
3. Employee morale is excellent.	0.10	3	0.30
4. In-store promotions resulted in 20% increase in sales.	0.05	3	0.15
5. Newspaper advertising expenditures increased 10%.	0.02	3	0.06
6. Revenues from repair/service in the store up 16%.	0.15	3	0.45
7. In-store technical support personnel have MIS college degrees.	0.05	4	0.20
8. Store's debt-to-total assets ratio declined to 34%.	0.03	3	0.09
9. Revenues per employee up 19%.	0.02	3	0.06
Weaknesses			
1. Revenues from software segment of store down 12%.	0.10	2	0.20
2. Location of store negatively impacted by new Highway 34.	0.15	2	0.30
3. Carpet and paint in store somewhat in disrepair.	0.02	1	0.02
4. Bathroom in store needs refurbishing.	0.02	1	0.02
5. Revenues from businesses down 8%.	0.04	1	0.04
6. Store has no website.	0.05	2	0.10
7. Supplier on-time delivery increased to 2.4 days.	0.03	1	0.03
8. Often customers have to wait to check out	0.05	1	0.05
Total	**1.00**		**2.50**

TABLE 4-9 An Actual IFE Matrix for Forjas Taurus S.A.

Strengths	Weight	Rating	Weighted Score
1. Taurus offers low prices for pistols and small arms in the USA.	0.09	4	0.36
2. Taurus had a 15.7% increase in net revenue.	0.07	4	0.28
3. Taurus has 51% market share in Brazil's motorcycle helmet industry.	0.06	3	0.18
4. Taurus has reduced the percentage of sales devoted to income tax from 3.11% to 2.82%.	0.06	3	0.18
5. Taurus produces a diverse range of products in different markets.	0.05	3	0.15
6. Taurus is a qualified supplier of products to Brazil's armed forces.	0.05	4	0.20
7. Taurus and ammo-maker Companha Brasileira de Cartuchos dominate Brazil's small arms industry.	0.04	4	0.16
8. Taurus provides weapons for Brazil's military, state, and civil police.	0.03	4	0.12
9. Taurus has good brand recognition within the USA.	0.03	4	0.12
10. Taurus's employee morale is good.	0.02	4	0.08
Weaknesses			
1. Adjusted EBIT is down 23%.	0.08	1	0.08
2. Total revenue in the domestic market is down 10.5%.	0.08	2	0.16
3. Gross margin fell from 38.1% to 29.9%.	0.07	1	0.07
4. Taurus's stock price has plummeted to less than 1.0.	0.07	1	0.07
5. Revenue from products in the metallurgy and plastics segment, excluding helmets, is down 7%.	0.04	2	0.08
6. Taurus has very little presence in Europe and Asia.	0.04	2	0.08
7. Taurus has a reputation for poor customer service.	0.04	2	0.08
8. There was a recent 23.6% increase in operating expenses.	0.03	1	0.03
9. Taurus reported a net income loss of over $32 million.	0.03	1	0.03
10. Taurus has poor quality control—a Taurus pistol discharged in Sao Paulo without pulling the trigger.	0.02	1	0.02
TOTALS	**1.00**		**2.53**

factor in the industry (Weight = 0.09) is price, and Taurus does excellent (Rating = 4) in selling low-priced firearms.

In multidivisional firms, each autonomous division or strategic business unit should construct an IFE Matrix. Divisional matrices then can be integrated to develop an overall corporate IFE Matrix. Be as divisional as possible when developing a corporate IFE Matrix. Also, in developing an IFE Matrix, do not allow more than 30 percent of the key factors to be financial ratios, because financial ratios are generally the result of many factors, so it is difficult to know what particular strategies should be considered based on financial ratios. For example, a firm would have no insight on whether to sell in Brazil or South Africa to take advantage of a high corporate ROI ratio.

IMPLICATIONS FOR STRATEGISTS

Figure 4-9 illustrates that to gain and sustain competitive advantages, a firm must formulate strategies that capitalize on internal strengths across all its products, services, and regions, and continually improve on its internal weaknesses. This must be done in a cost-effective manner, even though large outlays of human and financial capital may be required for various strategies deemed best to pursue. Thus, long-term commitments often accompany a given strategic plan. Breakeven analysis, value chain analysis, and the IFE Matrix are especially useful strategic planning tools in formulating strategies, especially in performing the internal assessment. Coupled with the vision/mission and external audit, the internal audit must be performed methodically and carefully because survival of the firm could hinge on an excellent strategic plan being created. Strategists should follow the guidelines presented in this chapter and throughout this book to help assure that their firm is heading in the right direction for the right reasons, and rewarding the right people, for doing the right things, in the right places.

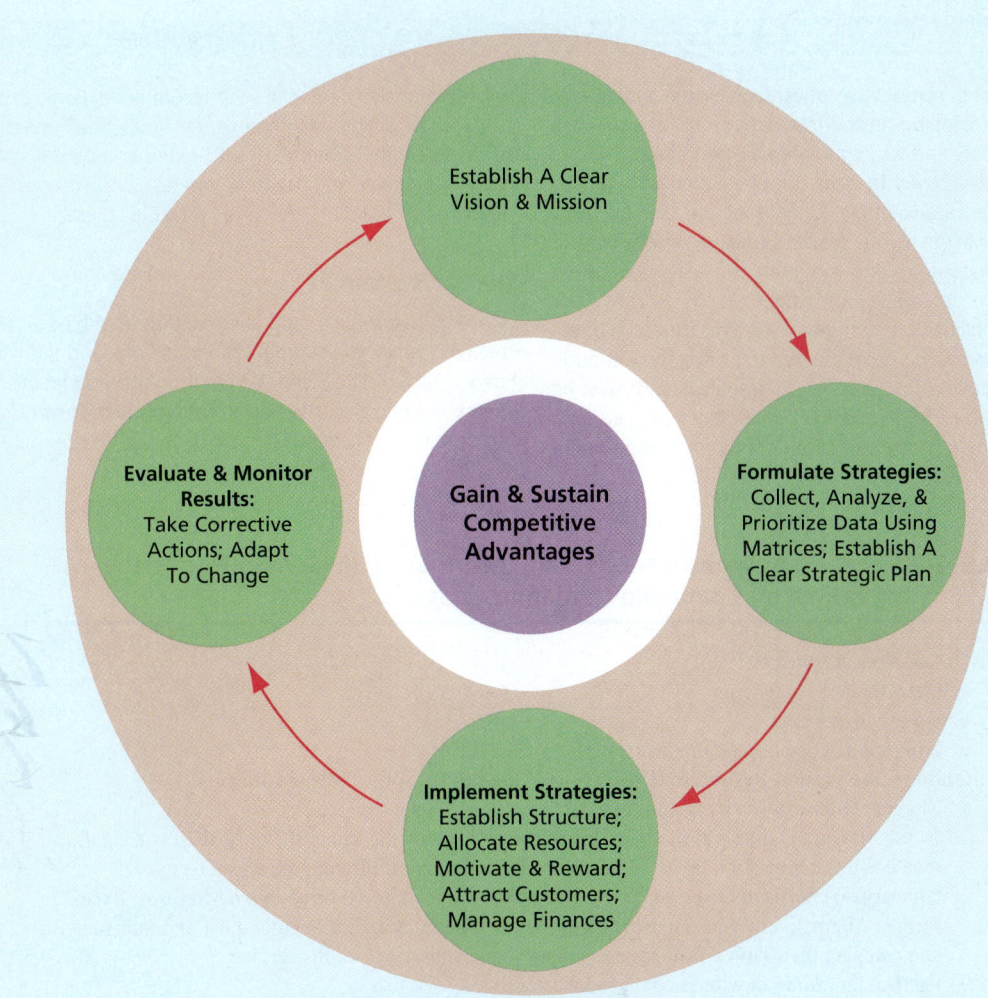

FIGURE 4-9

How to Gain and Sustain Competitive Advantages

Upstream versus Downstream Activities

The primary means for gaining and sustaining competitive advantages for most companies are shifting downstream. Recent research by Dawar reveals that in most industries today, **upstream activities**—such as supply chain management, production, and logistics—are being commoditized or outsourced by firms, whereas **downstream activities** related to consumer behavior are becoming the primary means for gaining and sustaining competitive advantage.[32] Dawar reports that the sources of competitive advantage are shifting away from production processes inside the firm to customers and markets outside the firm. Businesses are increasingly gaining competitive advantage by proactively shaping customers' point-of-purchase behavior, rather than firms using focus groups, surveys, and social media to determine what customers want. An early glimpse of this shift came a few years ago when Apple's Steve Jobs was asked how much market research led to the iPad. Jobs responded, "None. It's not the consumers' job to

know what they want." Activities that attract customers by making it easier, compelling, and convenient for them to purchase the firm's products and services in many ways are leading to sustained competitive advantage much more so than altering internal mechanisms. Figure 4-10 illustrates this shifting source of competitive advantage in most industries.

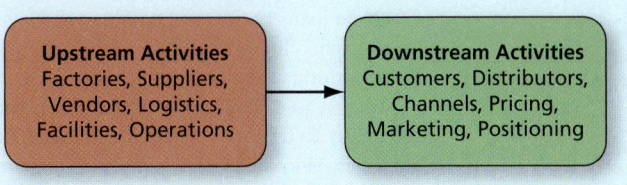

FIGURE 4-10

The Shifting Source of Competitive Advantage

IMPLICATIONS FOR STUDENTS

Gaining and sustaining competitive advantage is the essence or purpose of strategic planning. In the internal portion of your case analysis, emphasize how and why your internal strengths and weaknesses can both be leveraged to gain competitive advantage and overcome competitive disadvantage, in light of the direction you are taking the firm. Maintain your project's upbeat, insightful, and forward-thinking demeanor during the internal assessment, rather than being mundane, descriptive, and vague. Focus on how your firm's resources, capabilities, structure, and strategies, with your recommended improvements, can lead the firm to prosperity. Although the numbers must provide the basis for your analysis and must be accurate and reasonable, do not bore a live audience or class with overreliance on numbers. In contrast, throughout your presentation or written analysis, refer to your recommendations, explaining how your plan of action will improve the firm's weaknesses and capitalize on strengths in light of anticipated competitor countermoves. Keep your audience's attention, interest, and suspense, rather than "reading" to them or "defining" ratios for them.

Special Resources

Excellent free online and subscription (fee-based) resources for obtaining financial information about firms and industries are provided in Table 4-10. Some sources listed provide financial ratios. The free excel template at **www.strategyclub.com** calculates ratios and develops ratio trend lines, once students enter in relevant data.

TABLE 4-10   Excellent Websites to Obtain Information (Including Financial Ratios) on Companies and Industries

1. **Online Free Resources**
   a. http://finance.yahoo.com
   b. www.hoovers.com
   c. http://globaledge.msu.edu/industries/
2. **Online Subscription Resources (Likely Subscribed to by Your College Library)**
   a. Mergent Online: www.mergentonline.com
      At the Mergent Online website, search for companies with the same SIC or NAICS code, and then create a comparison financial ratio report. A number of different ratios can be used as comparison criteria to create a tailored report that can then be exported into a Microsoft Excel format. Alternatively, you can use the Competitors Tab in Mergent to build a list of companies and compare their ratios. Your college library likely subscribes to this service.
   b. Factiva: http://new.dowjones.com/products/factiva/
      At the Factiva website, first use the Companies & Markets tab to search for a company. Next, click "Reports" and choose the "Ratio Comparison Report" to get a company's ratios compared to industry averages. Your college library likely subscribes to this service.
   c. S&P NetAdvantage: http://www.standardandpoors.com
      At the S&P NetAdvantage website, company and industry ratios are provided in two different sections of the database: (1) the Compustat Excel Analytics section of a particular company's information page and (2) in the data from the S&P Industry Surveys. Your college library likely subscribes to this service.
   d. Onesource: www.avention.com/OneSource
      Onesource is a good source for financial ratio information. Search for a particular company and then click on the link for "Ratio Comparisons" on the left side of the company information page. The data in Onesource will compare your company against the industry, against the sector, and against the stock market as a whole.
   e. Yahoo Industry Center: http://biz.yahoo.com/ic/
      The Yahoo Industry Center is an excellent free resource that allows you to browse industries by performance rankings, including ROE, P/E ratio, market cap, price change, profit margin, price-to-book value, long-term debt, and more.
3. **Hardcopy Reference Books for Financial Ratios in Most Libraries**
   a. Robert Morris Associate's *Annual Statement Studies:* An excellent source of financial ratio information.
   b. Dun & Bradstreet's *Industry Norms & Key Business Ratios:* An excellent source of financial ratio information.

Source: Based on a variety of sources.

Chapter Summary

Management, marketing, finance/accounting, production/operations, R&D, and MIS represent the core operations of most businesses and the source of competitive advantages. A strategic-management audit of a firm's internal operations is vital to organizational health. Many companies still prefer to be judged solely on their bottom-line performance. However, it is essential that strategists identify and evaluate internal strengths and weaknesses to effectively formulate and choose among alternative strategies. The Internal Factor Evaluation Matrix, coupled with the Competitive Profile Matrix, the External Factor Evaluation Matrix, and clear statements of vision and mission provide the basic information needed to successfully formulate competitive strategies. The process of performing an internal audit represents an opportunity for managers and employees throughout the organization to participate in determining the future of the firm. Involvement in the process can energize and mobilize managers and employees.

Understanding both external and internal factors and relationships among them (see SWOT analysis in Chapter 6) is the key to effective strategy formulation. Because both external and internal factors continually change, strategists seek to identify and take advantage of positive changes and buffer against negative changes in a continuing effort to gain and sustain a firm's competitive advantage. This is the essence and challenge of strategic management, and often-times survival of the firm hinges on this work.

MyManagementLab®

To complete the problems with the ⭐, go to EOC Discussion Questions in the MyLab.

Key Terms and Concepts

activity ratios (p. 106)
benchmarking (p. 114)
breakeven (BE) point (p. 107)
capacity utilization (p. 109)
capital budgeting (p. 104)
collaborative machines (p. 110)
controlling (p. 99)
core competence (p. 114)
cost/benefit analysis (p. 102)
cultural products (p. 94)
customer analysis (p. 100)
distinctive competencies (p. 92)
distribution (p. 102)
dividend decisions (p. 104)
downstream activities (p. 119)
empirical indicators (p. 93)
financial ratio analysis (p. 103)
financing decision (p. 104)
fixed costs (FC) (p. 107)
functions of finance/accounting (p. 103)
functions of management (p. 96)
functions of marketing (p. 100)
growth ratios (p. 106)
human resource (HR) management (p. 98)

internal audit (p. 92)
Internal Factor Evaluation (IFE) Matrix (p. 116)
investment decision (p. 104)
leverage ratios (p. 106)
liquidity ratios (p. 106)
management information system (MIS) (p. 112)
marketing research (p. 102)
motivating (p. 98)
organizational culture (p. 94)
organizing (p. 97)
planning (p. 96)
pricing (p. 101)
product and service planning (p. 101)
production/operations function (p. 109)
profitability ratios (p. 106)
research and development (R&D) (p. 111)
resource-based view (RBV) (p. 93)
selling (p. 100)
staffing (p. 98)
synergy (p. 97)
test marketing (p. 101)
upstream activities (p. 119)
value chain analysis (VCA) (p. 113)
variable costs (VC) (p. 108)

Issues for Review and Discussion

⭐ **4-1.** The primary means for gaining and sustaining competitive advantages for most companies are shifting downstream. Explain and discuss this statement.

4-2. In analyzing big data, there is a shift from focusing largely on aggregates or averages to also focusing on outliers, because outliers oftentimes reveal (predict) critical innovations, trends, disruptions, and revolutions on the horizon. Explain and discuss this statement.

4-3. What are some limitations of financial ratio analysis?

4-4. Does RBV theory determine diversification targets? Explain and discuss.

⭐ **4-5.** True or False: Recent research reveals that the most effective marketing methods for firms with fewer than 500 employees is the company website (50%). Explain.

4-6. What are "collaborative machines"?

4-7. Identify some excellent online resources for finding financial ratio information.

⭐ **4-8.** Marketing is becoming much more technical, as are the duties and responsibilities of chief marketing officers (CMOs). Give four examples of increasing technical aspects of marketing.

⭐ **4-9.** Is a capacity utilization rate of 50 percent good? Why?

4-10. If Netflix increases its advertising expenses by 30 percent while keeping its price and variable costs the same, does that mean the company's breakeven point will increase 30 percent? Show this calculation for a hypothetical firm.

⭐ **4-11.** What are the limitations of breakeven analysis?

4-12. In the Joy's Daycare breakeven example in the chapter, how would a $1,000 annual advertising expenditure impact the business breakeven point?

4-13. Explain cost/benefit analysis.

4-14. Explain why *communication* may be the most important word in management. What do you think is the most important word in marketing? In finance? In accounting?

4-15. Discuss how the nature of advertisements has changed in the last few years.

⭐ **4-16.** Explain why it is best not to have more than 30 percent of the factors in an IFE Matrix be financial ratios.

4-17. List three firms you are familiar with and give a distinctive competence for each firm.

4-18. Give some key reasons why it is essential to prioritize strengths and weaknesses.

4-19. Why may it be easier in performing an internal assessment to develop a list of 80 strengths and weaknesses than to decide on the top 20 to use in formulating strategies?

4-20. Think of an organization with which you are familiar. List three resources of that entity that are empirical indicators.

4-21. Think of an organization with which you are familiar. Rate that entity's organizational culture on the 15 example dimensions listed in Table 4-2.

4-22. If you and a partner were going to visit a foreign country where you have never been before, how much planning would you do ahead of time? What benefit would you expect that planning to provide?

4-23. Even though planning is considered the foundation of management, why do you think it is commonly the task that managers neglect most?

4-24. Are you more organized than the person sitting beside you in class? If not, what problems could that present in terms of your performance and rank in the class? How analogous is this situation to rival companies?

4-25. List the three ways that financial ratios should be compared or used. Which of the three comparisons do you feel is most important? Why?

4-26. Illustrate how value chain activities can become core competencies and eventually distinctive competencies. Give an example for an organization with which you are familiar.

4-27. In an IFE Matrix, would it be advantageous to list your strengths, and then your weaknesses, in order of decreasing "weight"? Why?

⭐ **4-28.** In an IFE Matrix, a critic may say there is no significant difference between a "weight" of 0.08 and 0.06. How would you respond? What is the mathematical difference?

4-29. Why are so many firms raising their dividend payout amounts?

⭐ **4-30.** When someone says dividends paid are double taxed, to what are they referring?

4-31. Draw a breakeven chart to illustrate a drop in labor costs.

4-32. Draw a breakeven chart to illustrate an increase in advertising expenses.

4-33. Draw a breakeven chart to illustrate closing stores.

4-34. Draw a breakeven chart to illustrate lowering price.

4-35. Explain why prioritizing the relative importance of strengths and weaknesses in an IFE Matrix is an important strategic-management activity.

4-36. How can delegation of authority contribute to effective strategic management?

4-37. Which of the three basic functions of finance and accounting do you feel is most important in a small electronics manufacturing concern? Justify your position.

4-38. Explain how you would motivate managers and employees to implement a major new strategy.

4-39. Why do you think production and operations managers often are not directly involved in strategy-formulation activities? Why can this be a major organizational weakness?

4-40. Give two examples of staffing strengths and two examples of staffing weaknesses of an organization with which you are familiar.

⭐ **4-41.** Define, compare, and contrast weights vs. ratings in an EFE Matrix vs. an IFE Matrix.

4-42. If a firm has zero debt in its capital structure, is that always an organizational strength? Why or why not?

4-43. After conducting an internal audit, a firm discovers a total of 100 strengths and 100 weaknesses. What procedures then could be used to determine the most important of these? Why is it important to reduce the total number of key factors?

4-44. Why do you believe cultural products affect all the functions of business?

4-45. Do you think cultural products affect strategy formulation, implementation, or evaluation the most? Why?

4-46. Explain the difference between *data* and *information* in terms of each being useful to strategists.

4-47. What are the most important characteristics of an effective management information system?

4-48. Do you agree or disagree with the resource-based view theorists that internal resources are more important for a firm than external factors in achieving and sustaining competitive advantage? Explain your and their position.

4-49. Define and discuss empirical indicators.

4-50. Define and explain value chain analysis.

4-51. List five financial ratios that may be used by your university to monitor operations.

4-52. Explain benchmarking.

MyManagementLab®

Go to the Assignments section of your MyLab to complete these writing exercises.

4-53. List three ways that financial ratios should be compared or used. Which of the three comparisons do you feel is most important? Why?

4-54. Would you ever pay out dividends when your firm's annual net profit is negative? Why or why not? What effect could this have on a firm's strategies?

ASSURANCE OF LEARNING EXERCISES

EXERCISE 4A
Apply Breakeven Analysis

Purpose

Breakeven analysis is one of the simplest yet underused analytical tools in management. It helps provide a dynamic view of the relationships among sales, costs, and profits. A better understanding of breakeven analysis can enable an organization to formulate and implement strategies more effectively. This exercise will show you how to calculate breakeven points mathematically.

The formula for calculating breakeven point is BE Quantity = TFC/P − VC. In other words, the quantity (Q) or units of product that need to be sold for a firm to break even is total fixed costs (TFC) divided by (Price per Unit − Variable Costs per Unit).

Instructions

Step 1   Let's say an airplane company has fixed costs of $100 million and variable costs per unit of $2 million. Planes sell for $3 million each. What is the company's breakeven point in terms of the number of planes that need to be sold just to break even?

Step 2   If the airplane company wants to make a profit of $99 million annually, how many planes will it have to sell?

Step 3   If the company can sell 200 airplanes in a year, how much annual profit will the firm make?

EXERCISE 4B
Compare Netflix with Redbox

Purpose

Showcased at the beginning of this chapter, Netflix and rival Expedia rely almost exclusively on their website for business. Thus, it is obviously essential in this industry to have the most effective, efficient, and user-friendly website possible. This exercise gives you practice in identifying key strengths and weaknesses for two rival firms.

Instructions

Step 1	Visit the Netflix and the Redbox websites and study their features, prices, ease of navigation, user friendliness, and general layout.
Step 2	Which of the two companies' websites reveal most effectively "the best movies" for the week? What are the best movies being rented this week?
Step 3	Prepare an analysis and report for Netflix's website manager to reveal how her company can improve its performance by improving its website.

EXERCISE 4C

Perform a Financial Ratio Analysis for Hershey Company

Purpose

Financial ratio analysis is one of the best techniques for identifying and evaluating internal strengths and weaknesses. Potential investors and current shareholders look closely at firms' financial ratios, making detailed comparisons to industry averages and to previous periods of time. Financial ratio analyses provide vital input information for developing an IFE Matrix.

Instructions

Step 1	Using the resources listed in Table 4-10, find as many Hershey financial ratios as possible. Record your sources. Report your research to your classmates and your professor.

EXERCISE 4D

Construct an IFE Matrix for Hershey Company

Purpose

This exercise will give you experience in developing an IFE Matrix. Identifying and prioritizing factors to include in an IFE Matrix fosters communication among functional and divisional managers. Preparing an IFE Matrix allows human resource, marketing, production and operations, finance and accounting, R&D, and MIS managers to articulate their concerns and thoughts regarding the business condition of the firm. This results in an improved collective understanding of the business.

Instructions

Step 1	Join with two other individuals to form a three-person team. Develop a team IFE Matrix for Hershey. Use information from Exercise 1B on page 35.
Step 2	Compare your team's IFE Matrix to other teams' IFE matrices. Discuss any major differences.
Step 3	What strategies do you think would allow Hershey to capitalize on its major strengths? What strategies would allow Hershey to improve on its major weaknesses?

EXERCISE 4E

Construct an IFE Matrix for Your University

Purpose

This exercise gives you the opportunity to evaluate your university's major strengths and weaknesses. As will become clearer in the next chapter, an organization's strategies are largely based on striving to take advantage of strengths and improving on weaknesses.

Instructions

Step 1	Join with two other individuals to form a three-person team. Develop a team IFE Matrix for your university. You may use the strengths and weaknesses determined in Exercise 1D on page 36.
Step 2	What was your team's total weighted score?
Step 3	Compare your team's IFE Matrix to other teams' IFE matrices. Discuss any major differences.
Step 4	What strategies do you think would allow your university to capitalize on its major strengths? What strategies would allow your university to improve on its major weaknesses?

EXERCISE 4F
Applying Research-Based View (RBV) Theory

Purpose

This exercise reveals how a firm can utilize RBV theory to identify, gain, and sustain competitive advantages.

Instructions

Step 1   Develop a "Resources" by "Empirical Indicators" Matrix. Place on the left side 10 key resources of a firm with which you are familiar. Across the top are the three empirical indicators: Rare, Nonimitatable, and Nonsubstitutable. Along the far bottom and far right of your matrix, add a row and a column to record "Total Summed Values."

Step 2   Within your matrix, rate each resource on each indicator on a 1 to 5 scale, where 1 is exceptionally low and 5 is exceptionally high in terms that the resource is Rare, Nonimitatable, and/or Nonsubstitutable.

Step 3   Sum the rows and columns to determine the extent that each resource and empirical indicator is being utilized effectively.

Step 4   Discuss implications of your analysis.

(Note to Professors—See the Chapter IM for an additional, excellent exercise for this chapter)

MINI-CASE ON BUFFALO WILD WINGS, INC. (BWLD)

WHAT DO OUTSTANDING MANAGEMENT, MARKETING, AND FINANCE EXECUTIVES DO TOGETHER?

Source: Timolina/Fotolia

One answer to this question is that they work for Buffalo Wild Wings (BWW). Founded in 1982 and headquartered in Minneapolis, Minnesota, BWW is a fast-growing owner, operator, and franchisor of restaurants featuring Buffalo- and New York-style chicken wings and more. The menu offers 21 signature sauces and seasonings with flavor sensations ranging from Sweet BBQ to Blazin'. Each restaurant features an extensive multimedia system for watching favorite sporting events. The company has received hundreds of "Best Wings" and "Best Sports Bar" awards from across the country. There are currently more than 1,100 Buffalo Wild Wings locations in the United States, Canada, and Mexico.

Management, marketing, and finance executives at BWW recently celebrated the college football bowl season by sponsoring the inaugural BWW Citrus Bowl on New Year's Day. The company launched the "Million Dollar Bowl Pick 'Em Challenge," whereby from December 8 through December 19, guests can visit the GameBreak gaming platform in BWW restaurants and, on their mobile devices or desktop, pick the winners of all 39 college football bowl games. If a guest picks all games correctly, he or she will win $1,000,000, and if there is no million-dollar winner, the player with the most correct picks will win $10,000. Also, as a promotion, customers can access the GameBreak app and play a game called "Gametime Pick 'Em." This game asks fans to predict the winner of any bowl game yet to be played for a chance to win B-Dubs prize packs, which include a $125 BWW gift card and additional Dr Pepper merchandise.

During the recent BWW Citrus Bowl, when the Missouri Tigers played the Minnesota Golden Gophers, thousands of fans made their local Buffalo Wild Wings their headquarters to "tablegate" and enjoy the game with flavorful wings, cold beverages, and an all-day, in-restaurant GameBreak Live competition. Guests competed to score the most points on GameBreak Live—earning triple points during the BWW Citrus Bowl (1 pm to 4 pm ET). The guest earning the most points that day won a grand prize trip for four to the 2016 BWW Citrus Bowl, while those who came in 2nd through 75th received a $50 BWW gift card.

Buffalo Wild Wings had significant brand presence during the game—for example, 100 kids from the local Orlando Boys and Girls Clubs received tickets to the game to be a part of the action. Between quarters during the game, BWW presented its annual contribution to their charitable partner, the Boys and Girls Club of America. Buffalo Wild Wings President and CEO, Sally Smith, presented the winning team with the newly designed BWW Citrus Bowl trophy.

Questions

1. From a management perspective, do you think the college football expenditures by BWW are warranted? Why?
2. From a marketing perspective, do you think the college football expenditures by BWW are warranted? Why?
3. From a finance perspective, do you think the college football expenditures by BWW are warranted? Why?
4. Management, marketing, and finance executives do not always agree, so how could differences in opinion be resolved?
5. As BWW spends more on advertising, does its breakeven point go up or down? Illustrate.
6. How does BWW's approach to marketing compare to recent trends regarding how to best spend advertising dollars?

Source: Company documents and a variety of sources.

Current Readings

Acito, Frank, and Vijay Khatri. "Business Analytics: Why Now and What Next?" *Business Horizons* 57, no. 5 (2014): 565–570.

Chen, Chien-Ming, Magali A. Delmas, and Marvin B. Lieberman. "Production Frontier Methodologies and Efficiency as a Performance Measure in Strategic Management Research." *Strategic Management Journal* 36, no. 1 (January 2015): 19–36.

Davenport, Thomas H. "What Businesses Can Learn from Sports Analytics." *MIT Sloan Management Review* 55, no. 4 (2014): 10–13.

George, Gerard, Martine R. Haas, and Alex Pentland. "Big Data and Management." *Academy of Management Journal* (April 2014): 321–338.

Hayashi, Alden M. "Thriving in a Big Data World." *MIT Sloan Management Review* 55, no. 2 (2014): 35–39.

Howard, Dana, W. Glynn Mangold, and Tim Johnston. "Managing Your Social Campaign Strategy Using Facebook, Twitter, Instagram, YouTube & Pinterest: An Interview with Dana Howard, Social Media Marketing Manager." *Business Horizons* 57, no. 5 (2014): 657–665.

Kiron, David, Pamela Kirk Prentice, and Renee Boucher Ferguson. "Raising the Bar with Analytics." *MIT Sloan Management Review* 55, no. 2 (2014): 29–33.

Kuratko, Donald F., Jeffrey S. Hornsby, and Jeffrey G. Covin. "Diagnosing a Firm's Internal Environment for Corporate Entrepreneurship." *Business Horizons* 57, no.1 (2014): 37–47.

Ross, Jeanne W., Cynthia M. Beath, and Anne Quaadgras. "You May Not Need Big Data After All." *Harvard Business Review* 91, no.11 (2013).

Sampler, Jeffrey L., and Michael J. Earl. "What's Your Information Footprint?" *MIT Sloan Management Review* 55, no. 2 (2014): 96–97.

Thomas, Roberta J., et al. "Developing Tomorrow's Global Leaders." *MIT Sloan Management Review* 55, no. 1 (2013): 12–13.

Wuyts, Stefan, and Shantanu Dutta. "Benefiting from Alliance Portfolio Diversity: The Role of Past Internal Knowledge Creation Strategy." *Journal of Management* 40 (2014).

Endnotes

1. Reprinted by permission of the publisher from "Integrating Strength–Weakness Analysis into Strategic Planning," by William King, *Journal of Business Research* 2, no. 4: 481. Copyright 1983 by Elsevier Science Publishing Co., Inc.
2. Robert Grant, "The Resource-Based Theory of Competitive Advantage: Implications for Strategy Formulation," *California Management Review* (Spring 1991): 116.
3. J. B. Barney, "Firm Resources and Sustained Competitive Advantage," *Journal of Management* 17 (1991): 99–120; J. B. Barney, "The Resource-Based Theory of the Firm," *Organizational Science* 7 (1996): 469; J. B. Barney, "Is the Resource-Based 'View' a Useful Perspective for Strategic Management Research? Yes." *Academy of Management Review* 26, no. 1 (2001): 41–56.
4. Edgar Schein, *Organizational Culture and Leadership* (San Francisco: Jossey-Bass, 1985), 9.
5. John Lorsch, "Managing Culture: The Invisible Barrier to Strategic Change," *California Management Review* 28, no. 2 (1986): 95–109.
6. Y. Allarie and M. Firsirotu, "How to Implement Radical Strategies in Large Organizations," *Sloan Management Review* (Spring 1985): 19.

7. www.mindtools.com/plfailpl.html
8. Adam Smith, *The Wealth of Nations* (New York: Modern Library, 1937), 3–4.
9. Richard Daft, *Management*, 3rd ed. (Orlando, FL: Dryden Press, 1993), 512.
10. Shelley Kirkpatrick and Edwin Locke, "Leadership: Do Traits Matter?" *Academy of Management Executive* 5, no. 2 (May 1991): 48.
11. Peter Drucker, *Management Tasks, Responsibilities, and Practice* (New York: Harper & Row, 1973), 463.
12. Michael Mink, "Stay Atop Social Media," *Investor's Business Daily*, October 7, 2014, A4.
13. Brain Dumaine, "What the Leaders of Tomorrow See," *Fortune, July 3, 1999*, 51.
14. Lauren Weber and Rachael Feintzeig, "Is It a Dream or a Drag? Companies without HR," *Wall Street Journal*, April 9, 2014, B1.
15. J. Evans, and B. Bergman, *Marketing* (New York: Macmillan, 1982), 17.
16. http://www.ibtimes.com/super-bowl-ads-2014-what-does-4-million-really-buy-you-1551884
17. Sarah Needleman and Jack Marshall, "Small Businesses Grapple with Facebook," *Wall Street Journal,* August 7, 2014, B5.
18. Jack Marshall, "Online Ads Lure Cash, But Losses Still Mount," *Wall Street Journal,* August 18, 2014, B1.
19. Spencer Ante, "As Economy Cools, IBM Furthers Focus on Marketers," *Wall Street Journal,* July 18, 2012, B3.
20. Brad Stone, "See Your Friends," *Bloomberg Businessweek* (September 27–October 3, 2010): 65–69.
21. Suzanne Kapner, "Higher Web Sales Drag on Retailers," *Wall Street Journal,* December 2, 2014, B1.
22. Quoted in Robert Waterman, Jr., "The Renewal Factor," *BusinessWeek* (September 14, 1987): 108.
23. http://en.wikipedia.org/wiki/Cost-benefit_analysis
24. J. Van Horne, *Financial Management and Policy* (Upper Saddle River, NJ: Prentice-Hall, 1974): 10.
25. Timothy Aeppel, "Robots Work Their Way into Small Factories," *Wall Street Journal,* September 18, 2004, B1.
26. Patrick Seitz, "Largest Tech R&D Spenders Not Top Stock Performers," *Investor's Business Daily,* July 8, 2014, A5.
27. Philip Rousebi, Kamal Saad, and Tamara Erickson, "The Evolution of Third Generation R&D," *Planning Review* 19, no. 2 (March–April 1991): 18–26.
28. Based on Elizabeth Dwoskin, "Big Data: Give Me Back My Privacy," *Wall Street Journal,* March 24, 2014, R1–R4.
29. Ibid.
30. Michael Porter, *Competition Strategy: Techniques for Analyzing Industries and Competitors* (New York: Free Press, 1980), 34–44.
31. http://en.wikipedia.org/siki/Benchmarking
32. Niraj Dawar, "When Marketing Is Strategy," *Harvard Business Review* (December 2013): 101–108.

Source: shock/Fotolia

Strategies in Action

Hundreds of companies today have embraced strategic planning in their quest for higher revenues and profits. Kent Nelson, former chair of UPS, explains why his company created a new strategic-planning department: "Because we're making bigger bets on investments in technology, we can't afford to spend a whole lot of money in one direction and then find out five years later it was the wrong direction."[1]

This chapter brings strategic management to life with many contemporary examples. Sixteen types of strategies are defined and exemplified, including Michael Porter's generic strategies: cost leadership, differentiation, and focus. Guidelines are presented for determining when each strategy is most appropriate to pursue. An overview of strategic management in nonprofit organizations, governmental agencies, and small firms is provided. As showcased next, Signet Jewelers is an example company that for many years has exemplified excellent strategic management, especially of late in its use of a horizontal integration strategy (defined in Table 5-4).

Long-Term Objectives

Long-term objectives represent the results expected from pursuing certain strategies. Strategies represent the actions to be taken to accomplish long-term objectives. The time frame for objectives and strategies should be consistent, usually from 2 to 5 years. Without long-term objectives, an organization would drift aimlessly toward some unknown end. It is hard to imagine an organization or an individual being successful without clear objectives. You probably have worked hard the last few years striving to achieve an objective to graduate with a business degree. Success only rarely occurs by accident; rather, it is the result of hard work directed toward achieving certain objectives.

Long-term objectives are needed at the corporate, divisional, and functional levels of an organization. They are an important measure of managerial performance. Many practitioners and academicians attribute a significant part of U.S. industry's competitive decline to the short-term, rather than long-term, strategy orientation of managers in the United States. Arthur D. Little argues that bonuses or merit pay for managers today must be based to a greater extent on long-term objectives and strategies. An example framework for relating objectives to performance

Signet Jewelers Limited (SIG)

Signet Jewelers, parent company of mall-based Kay Jewelers, Jared the Galleria of Jewelry, and Zale Corporation, is the largest specialty jewelry retailer in the United States, the United Kingdom, and Canada. Signet's Sterling Jewelers division operates over 1,500 stores in all 50 states, primarily under the name brands of Kay Jewelers and Jared The Galleria of Jewelry. Signet's U.K. division operates about 500 stores, primarily under the name brands H. Samuel and Ernest Jones. Signet's Zale division operates nearly 1,600 locations in the United States and Canada, primarily under the name brands Zales, Peoples, and Piercing Pagoda. Signet recently removed from Zale stores 10 percent of its inventory, deemed to be slow-turning, and replaced it with faster-turning inventory, such as Vera Wang and Unstoppable Love Collections.

Headquartered in Hamilton, Bermuda, Signet does an outstanding job in strategic planning, using primarily a horizontal integration strategy to grow globally. Signet's same-store sales for the company's fiscal 2015 holiday season increased 2.5, 3.5, and 9.7 percent, respectively, for the company's Sterling Jewelers, Zale, and United Kingdom divisions.

Company sales increased 3.6 percent overall. For Q1 (first quarter) of fiscal 2016, Signet reported a 3.6 percent same-store sales growth overall, led by a 6.2 percent increase in the company's United Kingdom division and a 5.6 percent same-store sales increase in the Zale division. During Q1 of 2016, Signet repurchased $21.9 million of its own stock, expecting the stock price to increase further. Signet's Q1 of 2016 sales were $1.530.6 million, up 44.9 percent from fiscal Q1 of the prior year. Signet is on a roll, led by excellent strategists and strategies.

Source: A variety of sources.

TABLE 5-1 Varying Performance Measures by Organizational Level

Organizational Level	Basis for Annual Bonus or Merit Pay
Corporate	75% based on long-term objectives
	25% based on annual objectives
Division	50% based on long-term objectives
	50% based on annual objectives
Function	25% based on long-term objectives
	75% based on annual objectives

evaluation is provided in Table 5-1. A particular organization could tailor these guidelines to meet its own needs, but incentives should be attached to both long-term and annual objectives.

Characteristics and Benefits of Objectives

Objectives should be quantitative, measurable, realistic, understandable, challenging, hierarchical, obtainable, and congruent among organizational units. Each objective should also be associated with a timeline. Objectives are commonly stated in terms such as *growth in assets, growth in sales, profitability, market share, degree and nature of diversification, degree and nature of vertical integration, earnings per share*, and *social responsibility*. Clearly established objectives offer many benefits. They provide direction, allow synergy, assist in evaluation, establish priorities, reduce uncertainty, minimize conflicts, stimulate exertion, and aid in both the allocation of resources and the design of jobs. Objectives provide a basis for consistent decision making by managers whose values and attitudes differ. Objectives serve as standards by which individuals, groups, departments, divisions, and entire organizations can be evaluated.

Table 5-2 reveals the desired characteristics of objectives, and Table 5-3 summarizes the benefits of having clear objectives.

Financial versus Strategic Objectives

Two types of objectives are especially common in organizations: financial and strategic objectives. **Financial objectives** include those associated with growth in revenues, growth in earnings, higher dividends, larger profit margins, greater return on investment, higher earnings per share, a rising stock price, improved cash flow, and so on; whereas **strategic objectives** include things such as a larger market share, quicker on-time delivery than rivals, shorter design-to-market times than rivals, lower costs than rivals, higher product quality than rivals, wider geographic coverage than rivals, achieving technological leadership, consistently getting new or improved products to market ahead of rivals, and so on.

Although financial objectives are especially important in firms, oftentimes there is a trade-off between financial and strategic objectives such that crucial decisions have to be made. For example, a firm can do certain things to maximize short-term financial objectives that would harm long-term strategic objectives. To improve financial position in the short run through higher

TABLE 5-2 Eight Desired Characteristics of Objectives

1. Quantitative
2. Measurable
3. Realistic
4. Understandable
5. Challenging
6. Hierarchical
7. Obtainable
8. Congruent across departments

TABLE 5-3 Ten Benefits of Having Clear Objectives

1. Provide direction by revealing expectations
2. Allow synergy
3. Assist in evaluation by serving as standards
4. Establish priorities
5. Reduce uncertainty
6. Minimize conflicts
7. Stimulate exertion
8. Aid in allocation of resources
9. Aid in design of jobs
10. Provide basis for consistent decision making

prices may, for example, jeopardize long-term market share. The dangers associated with trading off long-term strategic objectives with near-term bottom-line performance are especially severe if competitors relentlessly pursue increased market share at the expense of short-term profitability. Amazon, for example, went many years operating without profits but gaining market share. And there are other trade-offs between financial and strategic objectives, related to riskiness of actions, concern for business ethics, the need to preserve the natural environment, and social responsibility issues. Both financial and strategic objectives should include both annual and long-term performance targets. Ultimately, the best way to sustain competitive advantage over the long run is to relentlessly pursue strategic objectives that strengthen a firm's business position over rivals. Financial objectives can best be met by focusing first and foremost on achieving strategic objectives that improve a firm's competitiveness and market strength.

Avoid Not Managing by Objectives

Mr. Derek Bok, former President of Harvard University, once said, "If you think education is expensive, try ignorance." The idea behind this saying also applies to establishing objectives, because strategists should avoid the following ways of "not managing by objectives."

- *Managing by Extrapolation* —Adheres to the principle "If it ain't broke, don't fix it." The idea is to keep on doing the same things in the same ways because things are going well.
- *Managing by Crisis* —Based on the belief that the true measure of a really good strategist is the ability to solve problems. Because there are plenty of crises and problems to go around for every person and organization, strategists ought to bring their time and creative energy to bear on solving the most pressing problems of the day. Managing by crisis is actually a form of reacting, letting events dictate the *what* and *when* of management decisions.
- *Managing by Subjectives* —Built on the idea that there is no general plan for which way to go and what to do; just do the best you can to accomplish what you think should be done. In short, "Do your own thing, the best way you know how" (sometimes referred to as *the mystery approach to decision making* because subordinates are left to figure out what is happening and why).
- *Managing by Hope* —Based on the fact that the future is laden with great uncertainty and that if we try and do not succeed, then we hope our second (or third) attempt will succeed. Decisions are predicated on the hope that they will work and that good times are just around the corner, especially if luck and good fortune are on our side![2]

Types of Strategies

The model illustrated in Figure 5-1 provides a conceptual basis for applying strategic management. Defined and exemplified in Table 5-4, alternative strategies that an enterprise could pursue can be categorized into 11 actions: forward integration, backward integration, horizontal integration, market penetration, market development, product development, related diversification,

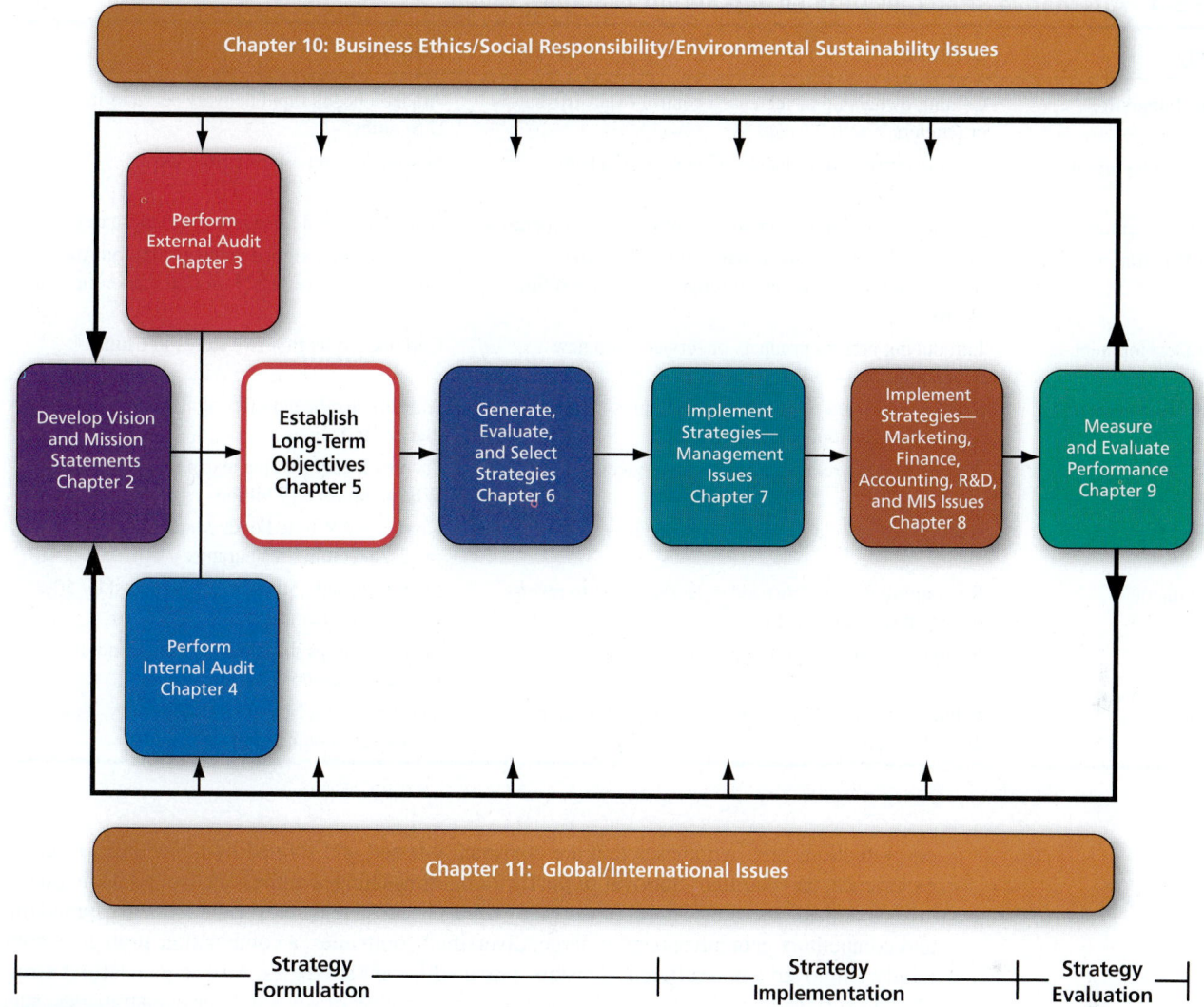

FIGURE 5-1

A Comprehensive Strategic-Management Model

Source: Fred R. David, "How Companies Define Their Mission," *Long Range Planning* 22, no. 3 (June 1988): 40. See also Anik Ratnaningsih, Nadjadji Anwar, Patdono Suwignjo, and Putu Artama Wiguna, "Balance Scorecard of David's Strategic Modeling at Industrial Business for National Construction Contractor of Indonesia," *Journal of Mathematics and Technology,* no. 4 (October 2010): 20.

unrelated diversification, retrenchment, divestiture, and liquidation. Each alternative strategy has countless variations. For example, market penetration can include adding salespersons, increasing advertising expenditures, couponing, and using similar actions to increase market share in a given geographic area.

Most organizations simultaneously pursue a combination of two or more strategies, but a **combination strategy** can be exceptionally risky if carried too far. No organization can afford to pursue all the strategies that might benefit the firm. Difficult decisions must be made. Priorities must be established. Organizations, like individuals, have limited resources. Both organizations and individuals must choose among alternative strategies and avoid excessive indebtedness.

Hansen and Smith explain that strategic planning involves "choices that risk resources and trade-offs that sacrifice opportunity." In other words, if you have a strategy to go north, then you must buy snowshoes and warm jackets (spend resources) and forgo the opportunity of "faster population growth in southern states." You cannot have a strategy to go north and then take a step east, south, or west "just to be on the safe side." Firms spend resources and focus on a finite number of opportunities in pursuing strategies to achieve an uncertain outcome in the future. Strategic planning is much more than a roll of the dice; it is an educated wager based

TABLE 5-4 Alternative Strategies Defined and Recent Examples Given

Strategy	Definition	Example
Forward Integration	Gaining ownership or increased control over distributors or retailers	Amazon began rapid delivery services in some U.S. cities.
Backward Integration	Seeking ownership or increased control of a firm's suppliers	Starbucks purchased a coffee farm.
Horizontal Integration	Seeking ownership or increased control over competitors	BB&T acquired Susquehanna Bancshares.
Market Penetration	Seeking increased market share for present products or services in present markets through greater marketing efforts	Under Armour signed tennis champion Andy Murray to a 4-year, $23 million marketing deal.
Market Development	Introducing present products or services into new geographic area	Gap opened its first five stores in China.
Product Development	Seeking increased sales by improving present products or services or developing new ones	Amazon just began offering its own line of baby diapers and wipes.
Related Diversification	Adding new but related products or services	Facebook acquired the text-messaging firm WhatsApp for $19 billion.
Unrelated Diversification	Adding new, unrelated products or services	Kroger and Whole Foods Market are cooking meals, becoming restaurants.
Retrenchment	Regrouping through cost and asset reduction to reverse declining sales and profit	Staples closed 250 stores and reduced by 50% the size of other stores.
Divestiture	Selling a division or part of an organization	Sears Holdings divested its Land's End division to Sears' shareholders.
Liquidation	Selling all of a company's assets, in parts, for their tangible worth	The Trump Taj Mahal in Atlantic City, New Jersey, faces liquidation.

on predictions and hypotheses that are continually tested and refined by knowledge, research, experience, and learning. Survival of the firm oftentimes hinges on an excellent strategic plan.[3]

Organizations cannot excel in too many things because resources and talents get spread thin and competitors gain advantage. In large, diversified companies, a combination strategy is commonly employed when different divisions pursue different strategies. Also, organizations struggling to survive may simultaneously employ a combination of several defensive strategies, such as divestiture, liquidation, and retrenchment.

Levels of Strategies

Strategy making is not just a task for top executives. Middle- and lower-level managers also must be involved in the strategic-planning process to the extent possible. In large firms, there are actually four levels of strategies: corporate, divisional, functional, and operational—as illustrated in Figure 5-2. However, in small firms, there are three levels of strategies: company, functional, and operational.

The persons primarily responsible for having effective strategies at the various levels include the CEO or business owner at the corporate level; the president or executive vice president at the divisional level; the chief finance officer (CFO), chief information officer (CIO), human resource manager (HRM), chief marketing officer (CMO), and so on at the functional level; and the plant manager, regional sales manager, and so on at the operational level. It is important that all managers at all levels participate and understand the firm's strategic plan to help ensure coordination, facilitation, and commitment, while avoiding inconsistency, inefficiency, and miscommunication.

Integration Strategies

Forward integration and backward integration are sometimes collectively referred to as **vertical integration**. Vertical integration strategies allow a firm to gain control over distributors and suppliers, whereas **horizontal integration** refers to gaining ownership and/or control over competitors. Vertical and horizontal actions by firms are broadly referred to as **integration strategies**.

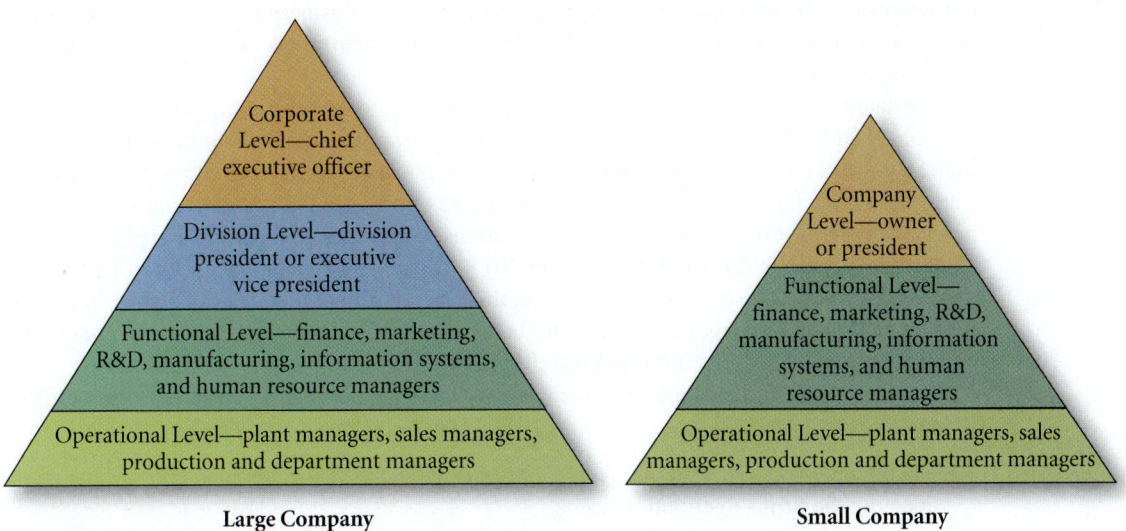

FIGURE 5-2
Levels of Strategies with Persons Most Responsible

Forward Integration

Forward integration involves gaining ownership or increased control over distributors or retailers. Increasing numbers of manufacturers (suppliers) are pursuing a forward integration strategy by establishing websites to sell their products directly to consumers.

In a forward integration move, Coca-Cola recently signed a 10-year partnership with Green Mountain Coffee Roasters, maker of the Keurig single-serve coffeemaker, to offer for the first time a Coca-Cola drink through a K-Cup. Coca-Cola thus plans to sell Coke through the at-home beverage system Keurig K-Cup. With the partnership, Coca-Cola also acquired 10 percent of the Green Mountain company for about $1.25 billion. Green Mountain now has a similar partnership with Campbell Soup to brew a cup of chicken broth in a K-Cup.

Based in Cincinnati and having more than 2,600 grocery stores, Kroger recently acquired Viatcost.com to expand its push into online groceries, partly so as not to concede the same-day food delivery market to Amazon.com. FedEx and UPS are both using forward integration, paying the United States Post Office (USPS) to ship their packages. Today, USPS delivers about 2.5 million packages daily for FedEx, or about one third of FedEx's express-mail U.S.-bound mailings.

Amazon is forward integrating into the "installation business." When you buy, for example, a ceiling fan or car stereo from Amazon, the company now wants to install it for you for a fee—at least in three cities (Los Angeles, New York, and Seattle). Amazon's new program is called Amazon Local Services and is another step by the company to erode brick-and-mortar's 90 percent market share of retail sales in the United States. In addition, Amazon is developing a new mobile application that recruits and pays ordinary people to be carriers of packages as they travel, doing away with the need for FedEx, UPS, and even the United States Postal Service. This new Amazon forward integration strategy is known as "On My Way" and is still being tested to resolve potential issues such as what happens if the package is damaged, or even stolen, by the transporter.

Taco Bell also wants to ring your doorbell and deliver you the goods. Fast food delivery is already a strategy at some rival firms, such as Jimmy John's sandwich shop; Burger King has been offering delivery in select markets for a couple of years now; Starbucks is testing delivery.

An effective means of implementing forward integration is **franchising**. Approximately 2,000 companies in about 50 different industries in the United States use franchising to distribute their products or services. Businesses can expand rapidly by franchising because costs and opportunities are spread among many individuals. Total sales by franchises in the United States are annually about $1 trillion. There are about 800,000 franchise businesses in the United States. However, a growing trend is for franchisees, who, for example, may operate 10 franchised restaurants, stores, or whatever, to buy out their part of the business from their franchiser (corporate owner). A growing rift between franchisees and franchisers is escalating as the offspring often outperforms the parent.

Restaurant chains are increasingly being pressured to own fewer of their locations. For example, TGI Fridays recently sold its 250 company-owned restaurants in the United States to franchisees as well as its 63 company-owned restaurants in the United Kingdom. Applebee's also is becoming much more a franchisee-owned business. Burger King is converting virtually all of its company-owned outlets to franchised operations, with revenue from franchisees going from 30 percent of sales in 2011 to 90 percent in 2015. This change results in a drop in Burger King revenues, since franchisees show revenues on their own personal income statements. In contrast, rival Yum Brands owns virtually all of its outside-U.S. restaurants and says that policy gives greater control and benefits if things go well (or bad).

The following six guidelines indicate when forward integration may be an especially effective strategy:[4]

1. An organization's present distributors are especially expensive, unreliable, or incapable of meeting the firm's distribution needs.
2. The availability of quality distributors is so limited as to offer a competitive advantage to those firms that promote forward integration.
3. An organization competes in an industry that is growing and is expected to continue to grow markedly; this is a factor because forward integration reduces an organization's ability to diversify if its basic industry falters.
4. An organization has both the capital and human resources needed to manage the new business of distributing its own products.
5. The advantages of stable production are particularly high; this is a consideration because an organization can increase the predictability of the demand for its output through forward integration.
6. Present distributors or retailers have high profit margins; this situation suggests that a company could profitably distribute its own products and price them more competitively by integrating forward.

Backward Integration

Backward integration is a strategy of seeking ownership or increased control of a firm's suppliers. This strategy can be especially appropriate when a firm's current suppliers are unreliable, too costly, or cannot meet the firm's needs. Starbucks recently purchased its first coffee farm—a 600-acre property in Costa Rica. This backward integration strategy was utilized primarily to develop new coffee varieties and to test methods to combat a fungal disease known as coffee rust that plagues the industry. Manufacturers as well as retailers purchase needed materials from suppliers.

The huge wine and beer producer, Constellation Brands, recently purchased several glass-bottle factories after experiencing problems with several suppliers of their bottles. Constellation acquired a controlling interest in a Mexican Anheuser-Busch glass-bottle factory, giving Constellation ownership now of more than 50 percent of the glass bottles it uses.

Some industries, such as automotive and aluminum producers, are reducing their historical pursuit of backward integration. Instead of owning their suppliers, companies negotiate with several outside suppliers. Ford and Chrysler buy more than half of their component parts from outside suppliers such as TRW, Eaton, General Electric (GE), and Johnson Controls. **De-integration** makes sense in industries that have global sources of supply. Companies today shop around, play one seller against another, and go with the best deal. Global competition is also spurring firms to reduce their number of suppliers and to demand higher levels of service and quality from those they keep. Although traditionally relying on many suppliers to ensure uninterrupted supplies and low prices, many U.S. firms now are following the lead of Japanese firms, which have far fewer suppliers and closer, long-term relationships with those few. "Keeping track of so many suppliers is onerous," said Mark Shimelonis, formerly of Xerox.

Seven guidelines when backward integration may be an especially effective strategy are:[5]

1. An organization's present suppliers are especially expensive, unreliable, or incapable of meeting the firm's needs for parts, components, assemblies, or raw materials.

2. The number of suppliers is small and the number of competitors is large.

3. An organization competes in an industry that is growing rapidly; this is a factor because integrative-type strategies (forward, backward, and horizontal) reduce an organization's ability to diversify in a declining industry.

4. An organization has both capital and human resources to manage the new business of supplying its own raw materials.

5. The advantages of stable prices are particularly important; this is a factor because an organization can stabilize the cost of its raw materials and the associated price of its product(s) through backward integration.

6. Present suppliers have high profit margins, which suggest that the business of supplying products or services in a given industry is a worthwhile venture.

7. An organization needs to quickly acquire a needed resource.

Horizontal Integration

Seeking ownership of or control over a firm's competitors, horizontal integration is arguably the most common growth strategy. Thousands of mergers, acquisitions, and takeovers among competitors are consummated annually. Nearly all these transactions aim for increased economies of scale and enhanced transfer of resources and competencies. Kenneth Davidson makes the following observation about horizontal integration:

> The trend towards horizontal integration seems to reflect strategists' misgivings about their ability to operate many unrelated businesses. Mergers between direct competitors are more likely to create efficiencies than mergers between unrelated businesses, both because there is a greater potential for eliminating duplicate facilities and because the management of the acquiring firm is more likely to understand the business of the target.[6]

In the cigarette industry, Reynolds American recently acquired Lorillard for $25 billion. The merger combined Reynolds' Pall Mall and Camel brands (with 8.1 percent market share each in the United States) with Lorillard's Newport brand (with 12.2 market share) to combat industry leader Altria's Marlboro brand that commands 40.2 percent market share in the United States. As part of the transaction, to combat antitrust concerns, Reynolds CEO Susan Cameron said her company will divest Lorillard's Blu e-cigarette to Imperial Tobacco (another rival firm), while keeping and growing Reynolds' Vuse e-cigarette. Reynolds also divested its Kool, Winston, Salem, and Maverick brands to Imperial.

Both Dollar General and Dollar Tree recently competed for months to acquire Family Dollar. The winner, Dollar Tree, is reducing prices and converting Family Dollar stores into bright, clean, friendly places. Dollar Tree still sells more items for a dollar or less, whereas Family Dollar sells more branded merchandise. About 5,000 Dollar Tree stores and 8,300 Family Dollar stores now compete with industry leader Dollar General's 11,500 stores.

Charter Communications (CHTR) recently acquired (1) Time Warner Cable (TWC) for $55.33 billion and (2) Bright House Networks for $10.4 billion, creating a giant U.S. TV and Internet firm. The new Charter has nearly 24 million customers, below the leader Comcast's (CMCSK) 27.2 million customers. Comcast owns NBCUniversal. Charter also lags AT&T (T), whose recent merger with DirecTV (DTV) gave AT&T 26.4 million TV customers and 16.1 million fixed Internet customers, as well as tens of millions of wireless customers. Several major factors are spurring horizontal integration in the TV and Internet business, including that cable providers are rapidly losing TV subscribers, and pressure from online video services such as Netflix (NFLX), Hulu, and Amazon is increasing dramatically.

The following five guidelines indicate when horizontal integration may be an especially effective strategy:[7]

1. An organization can gain monopolistic characteristics in a particular area or region without being challenged by the federal government for "tending substantially" to reduce competition.

2. An organization competes in a growing industry.

3. Increased economies of scale provide major competitive advantages.

4. An organization has both the capital and human talent needed to successfully manage an expanded organization.

5. Competitors are faltering as a result of a lack of managerial expertise or a need for particular resources that an organization possesses; note that horizontal integration would not be appropriate if competitors are doing poorly because in that case overall industry sales are declining.

Intensive Strategies

Market penetration, market development, and product development are sometimes referred to as **intensive strategies** because they require intensive efforts if a firm's competitive position with existing products is to improve.

Market Penetration

A **market penetration** strategy seeks to increase market share for present products or services in present markets through greater marketing efforts. This strategy is widely used alone and in combination with other strategies. Market penetration includes increasing the number of salespersons, increasing advertising expenditures, offering extensive sales promotion items, or increasing publicity efforts. For example, Anheuser annually purchases several $4.5+ million, 30-second advertising slots during the Super Bowl.

Tiffany & Co. recently began using same-sex couples in advertising, preceded by J. Crew casting one of its designers and his boyfriend in a catalogue. Gap uses a handsome couple in a billboard, and Jeremiah Brent and Nate Berkus appear in a Banana Republic advertising campaign.

The following five guidelines indicate when market penetration may be an especially effective strategy:[8]

1. Current markets are not saturated with a particular product or service.
2. The usage rate of present customers could be increased significantly.
3. The market shares of major competitors have been declining while total industry sales have been increasing.
4. The correlation between dollar sales and dollar marketing expenditures historically has been high.
5. Increased economies of scale provide major competitive advantages.

Market Development

Market development involves introducing present products or services into new geographic areas. For example, Whirlpool recently acquired Indesit, an Italian company that sells appliances, in order to double Whirlpool's size in Europe, where the company has struggled to compete against Electrolux AB of Sweden, LG Electronics Inc. of South Korea, and Haier Group of China. Indesit had 13 percent of the major appliance market share in eastern Europe and Whirlpool had 5 percent, so now 18 percent of the major appliances sold in eastern Europe are Whirlpool. In western Europe, the Indesit acquisition gave Whirlpool a 17 percent market share behind the leader, BSH Bosch & Siemens Hausgerate GmbH's 20 percent.

The largest online video-streaming company, Netflix, recently launched it services into France, Germany, Belgium, and Switzerland, as well as eastern and southern Europe, and expects to be a global service provider by 2018. Netflix's major rival in Europe is Vivendi SA's pay-TV unit Canal Plus that offers Netflix-like services through its Canal Play services.

These six guidelines indicate when market development may be an especially effective strategy:[9]

1. New channels of distribution are available that are reliable, inexpensive, and of good quality.
2. An organization is successful at what it does.
3. New untapped or unsaturated markets exist.
4. An organization has the needed capital and human resources to manage expanded operations.
5. An organization has excess production capacity.
6. An organization's basic industry is rapidly becoming global in scope.

Product Development

Product development is a strategy that seeks increased sales by improving or modifying present products or services. Product development usually entails large research and development expenditures. Walt Disney Company recently developed a Disney Baby line of products and services that it expects to become a powerful baby brand for customers ages 0 to 2. Bob Chapek, president of Disney Consumer Products, stated, "This gives Disney the opportunity to reach out to moms when magical moments begin; there is no more special occasion than the birth of a baby."

The action camera company, GoPro, recently unveiled new high- and low-end cameras. GoPro is the leading producer of wearable and durable high-definition video cameras used by outdoor enthusiasts such as scuba divers and surfers. Based in San Mateo, California, GoPro's rival firms include Sony, Canon, Garmin, and Polaroid, but GoPro is doing great by selling products in more than 100 countries and through more than 25,000 retail outlets.

The new Apple Watch is actually a wrist-top computer, and now competes with various Android-powered devices from Motorola and Samsung Electronics. "Wearable computers" are good for the people to monitor their healthiness among countless other things. The firm Sensoria is making smart garments, including smart socks, which yes, are washable. Opportunities for product development strategies are endless, given rapid technological changes occurring daily.

These following five guidelines indicate when product development may be an especially effective strategy to pursue:[10]

1. An organization has successful products that are in the maturity stage of the product life cycle; the idea here is to attract satisfied customers to try new (improved) products as a result of their positive experience with the organization's present products or services.
2. An organization competes in an industry that is characterized by rapid technological developments.
3. Major competitors offer better-quality products at comparable prices.
4. An organization competes in a high-growth industry.
5. An organization has especially strong research and development capabilities.

Diversification Strategies

The two general types of **diversification strategies** are **related diversification** and **unrelated diversification**. Businesses are said to be *related* when their value chains possess competitively valuable cross-business strategic fits; businesses are said to be *unrelated* when their value chains are so dissimilar that no competitively valuable cross-business relationships exist.[11] Most companies favor related diversification strategies to capitalize on synergies as follows:

- Transferring competitively valuable expertise, technological know-how, or other capabilities from one business to another
- Combining the related activities of separate businesses into a single operation to achieve lower costs
- Exploiting common use of a well-known brand name
- Cross-business collaboration to create competitively valuable resource strengths and capabilities[12]

Diversification strategies are becoming less popular because organizations are finding it more difficult to manage diverse business activities. In the 1960s and 1970s, the trend was to diversify to avoid being dependent on any single industry, but the 1980s saw a general reversal of that thinking. Diversification is still on the retreat. Michael Porter, of the Harvard Business School, commented, "Management found it couldn't manage the beast." Businesses are still selling, closing, or spinning off less profitable or "different" divisions to focus on their core businesses. For example, ITT recently divided itself into three separate, specialized companies. At one time, ITT owned everything from Sheraton hotels and Hartford Insurance to the maker of Wonder Bread and Hostess Twinkies. About the ITT breakup, analyst Barry Knap said, "Companies generally are not very efficient diversifiers; investors usually can do a better job of that by purchasing stock in a variety of companies." Rapidly appearing new technologies, new products, and fast-shifting buyer preferences make diversification difficult.

Diversification must do more than simply spread business risks across different industries; after all, shareholders could accomplish this by simply purchasing equity in different firms across different industries or by investing in mutual funds. Diversification makes sense only to the extent that the strategy adds more to shareholder value than what shareholders could accomplish acting individually. Any industry chosen for diversification must be attractive enough to yield consistently high returns on investment and offer potential across the operating divisions for synergies greater than those entities could achieve alone. Many strategists contend that firms should "stick to the knitting" and not stray too far from the firms' basic areas of competence.

A few companies today, however, pride themselves on being conglomerates, from small firms such as Pentair Inc. and Blount International to huge companies such as Textron, Berkshire Hathaway, Allied Signal, Emerson Electric, GE, Viacom, Amazon, Google, Disney, and Samsung. Conglomerates prove that focus and diversity are not always mutually exclusive. In an unattractive industry, for example, diversification makes sense, such as for Philip Morris, because cigarette consumption is declining, product liability suits are a risk, and some investors reject tobacco stocks on principle.

Related Diversification

Alcoa recently diversified further into the jet-engine parts industry by acquiring Firth Rixson Ltd. for nearly $3 billion. The move away from total reliance on aluminum puts Alcoa in position to become a major player in the aerospace jet-engine market. Jet engines utilize a lot of aluminum but still this strategy is best classified as related diversification rather than forward integration due to the new high-tech competencies required.

With its new Apply Pay product being linked with iBeacon so stores can detect and locate iPhone users via a Bluetooth wireless signal as they enter the premises, Apple recently entered the online payments business, competing directly with PayPal. Using their iPhone and/or Apple Watch, consumers can now make retail purchases by tapping their device at participating checkout registers. Apple is basically diversifying into the banking business with these new products, but the threat to PayPal in particular is spurring eBay and Google to cooperate in this arena.

The guidelines for when related diversification may be an effective strategy are as follows.[13]

1. An organization competes in a no-growth or a slow-growth industry.
2. Adding new, but related, products would significantly enhance the sales of current products.
3. New, but related, products could be offered at highly competitive prices.
4. New, but related, products have seasonal sales levels that counterbalance an organization's existing peaks and valleys.
5. An organization's products are currently in the declining stage of the product's life cycle.
6. An organization has a strong management team.

Unrelated Diversification

Privately held Mars Inc., best known for its M&M chocolates and its Mars and Snickers candy bars, recently became the world's largest pet-food company, purchasing 80 percent of Procter & Gamble's pet-food brands for $2.9 billion, to go with its own Whiskas, Pedigree, and Royal Canin pet brands. Mars has over 25 percent market share in the global pet-food industry, slightly ahead of Nestle S.A., which owns Purina and Friskies.

Google now offers an electric-powered driverless car that has no steering wheel, brake, or gas pedal; rather, the car is equipped with buttons for go and stop, and travels at a top speed of 25 mph. Further diversifying, Google recently acquired Skybox Imaging to collect and provide data from the sky using satellites that collect daily photos and video of the Earth. With the acquisition, Google is also trying to cover the globe with fast Internet access from the sky, using balloons, drones, and satellites.

Honda Motor Company diversified in 2015 by developing, producing, and marketing its first business jet, named the HondaJet HA-420 that has a range of 1,180 miles and a top speed of 420 knots, and can carry seven passengers. This new product competes directly with the Cessna Citation M2 and Embraer Phenom 100E business jets. These business jets sell for about $4.5 million each.

An unrelated diversification strategy favors capitalizing on a portfolio of businesses that are capable of delivering excellent financial performance in their respective industries, rather than striving to capitalize on value chain strategic fits among the businesses. Firms that employ unrelated diversification continually search across different industries for companies that can be acquired for a deal and yet have potential to provide a high return on investment. Pursuing unrelated diversification entails being on the hunt to acquire companies whose assets are undervalued, companies that are financially distressed, or companies that have high-growth prospects but are short on investment capital.

Given below are 10 guidelines when unrelated diversification may be an especially effective strategy.[14]

1. Revenues derived from an organization's current products or services would increase significantly by adding the new, unrelated products.
2. An organization competes in a highly competitive or a no-growth industry, as indicated by low industry profit margins and returns.
3. An organization's present channels of distribution can be used to market the new products to current customers.
4. New products have countercyclical sales patterns compared to an organization's present products.
5. An organization's basic industry is experiencing declining annual sales and profits.
6. An organization has the capital and managerial talent needed to compete successfully in a new industry.
7. An organization has the opportunity to purchase an unrelated business that is an attractive investment opportunity.
8. Financial synergy exists between the acquired and acquiring firm. (Note that a key difference between related and unrelated diversification is that the former should be based on some commonality in markets, products, or technology, whereas the latter is based more on profit considerations.)
9. Existing markets for an organization's present products are saturated.
10. Antitrust action could be charged against an organization that historically has concentrated on a single industry.

Defensive Strategies

In addition to integrative, intensive, and diversification strategies, organizations also could pursue defensive strategies such as retrenchment, divestiture, or liquidation.

Retrenchment

Retrenchment occurs when an organization regroups through cost and asset reduction to reverse declining sales and profits. Sometimes called a *turnaround* or *reorganizational strategy*, retrenchment is designed to fortify an organization's basic distinctive competence. During retrenchment, strategists work with limited resources and face pressure from shareholders, employees, and the media. Retrenchment can involve selling off land and buildings to raise needed cash, pruning product lines, closing marginal businesses, closing obsolete factories, automating processes, reducing the number of employees, and instituting expense control systems.

Levi Strauss & Co. recently cut 20 percent of its nonretail and nonmanufacturing workforce as part of a retrenchment strategy aimed at streamlining the firm's operations and generating cost savings of nearly $200 million per year. The 160-year-old company headquartered in San Francisco is having trouble competing in the intensely competitive retail clothing industry, marked by fleeting fashions and "sale only" shoppers.

Cisco Systems recently removed 6,000 employees from its payrolls, comprising 8 percent of the company's total workforce. The routing and switching system company is experiencing declining revenue and profits. The Turner Broadcasting division of Time Warner recently deleted 1,475 jobs, or 10 percent of its workforce. The Turner division generates about half of Time Warner's operating profit and has more than 5,000 full-time employees in its home city of Atlanta. Staples closed 170 stores in North America in 2014, and closed another 55 stores in 2015.

In some cases, declaring **bankruptcy** can be an effective retrenchment strategy. Bankruptcy can allow a firm to avoid major debt obligations and to void union contracts. There are five major types of bankruptcy: Chapter 7, Chapter 9, Chapter 11, Chapter 12, and Chapter 13. The first type, *Chapter 7 bankruptcy*, is a liquidation procedure used only when a corporation sees no hope of being able to operate successfully or to obtain the necessary creditor agreement. All the organization's assets are sold in parts for their tangible worth. Several hundred thousand companies declare Chapter 7 bankruptcy annually.

Chapter 9 bankruptcy applies to municipalities. Detroit, Michigan, is the largest U.S. city to declare bankruptcy, but others include Stockton, California, and Birmingham, Alabama.

Chapter 11 bankruptcy allows organizations to reorganize and come back after filing a petition for protection. Quiznos recently filed Chapter 11 bankruptcy as its 2,100 stores simply cannot compete with rival Subway's 41,000 stores. Quiznos collects a 7 percent royalty fee and another 4 percent advertising from is disgruntled franchisees, compared to the industry average 6 percent royalty fee and 2 percent marketing fee. The average Quiznos store has about $300,000 in annual revenue, down from $425,000 a few years ago.

Also, Sbarro recently filed Chapter 11 bankruptcy for a second time in less than three years. The pizza chain blamed its recent financial troubles on "an unprecedented decline in mall traffic." Based in Melville, New York, Sbarro is a privately held firm with about 800 stores in more than 40 countries.

An artificial-sapphire producer for Apple, GT Advanced Technologies, recently filed for bankruptcy, soon after Apple decided to go with glass screens rather than sapphire. GT's stock price dropped 93 percent the same day the bankruptcy news released. By using sapphire, Apple was hoping for a more scratch- and shatter-resistant cover for its smartphones, but decided instead to use hardened glass.

Chapter 12 bankruptcy was created by the Family Farmer Bankruptcy Act of 1986. This law provides special relief to family farmers with debt equal to or less than $1.5 million.

Chapter 13 bankruptcy is a reorganization plan similar to Chapter 11, but it is available only to small businesses owned by individuals with unsecured debts of less than $100,000 and secured debts of less than $350,000. The Chapter 13 debtor is allowed to operate the business while a plan is being developed to provide for the successful operation of the business in the future.

Five guidelines for when retrenchment may be an especially effective strategy to pursue are as follows:[15]

1. An organization has a clearly distinctive competence but has failed consistently to meet its objectives and goals over time.
2. An organization is one of the weaker competitors in a given industry.
3. An organization is plagued by inefficiency, low profitability, poor employee morale, and pressure from stockholders to improve performance.
4. An organization has failed to capitalize on external opportunities, minimize external threats, take advantage of internal strengths, and overcome internal weaknesses over time; that is, when the organization's strategic managers have failed (and possibly will be replaced by more competent individuals).
5. An organization has grown so large so quickly that major internal reorganization is needed.

Divestiture

Selling a division or part of an organization is called **divestiture**. It is often used to raise capital for further strategic acquisitions or investments. Divestiture can be part of an overall retrenchment strategy to rid an organization of businesses that are unprofitable, that require too much capital, or that do not fit well with the firm's other activities. Divestiture has also become a popular strategy for firms to focus on their core businesses and become less diversified.

The largest consumer-products company in the world, Procter & Gamble (P&G), is in the process of divesting (selling) more than half of its brands (nearly 100) in order to focus on its core brands (about 80). With brands such as Pampers, Tide, Era, Cheer, Metamucil, Clairol, Wella, Oral-B, Duracell, Fixodent, Ivory, and Clearblue (pregnancy tests), P&G has 23 brands that have more than $1 billion annual sales each. Ivory might be divested, as Americans have increasingly opted for body washes and liquid hand soap over plain bar soaps.

Airbus Group NV is in the process of divesting its defense assets in order to focus solely on its commercial-airplane business. Airbus is selling its secure-communications business, Fairchild Controls, as well as Rostock System-Technik, AvDef, ESG, and its Atlas Elektronik naval-technology joint venture with ThyseenKrupp AG. Airbus is also divesting its 46 percent nonvoting interest in Dassault Aviation SA that makes France's Rafale combat jets and Falcon business jets.

A version of divestiture occurs when a corporation splits into two or more parts. For example, Hewlett-Packard (HP) recently separated its personal computer and printer businesses from its corporate hardware and services operations. Most often, divested segments become separate, publically traded companies. Many large conglomerate firms are employing this strategy. Sometimes this strategy is a prelude to the firm selling the separated part(s) to a rival firm, such as HP's corporate hardware and services business perhaps merging with EMC Corporation. PepsiCo is under pressure to split its soft drinks division away from its snacks operations. Even General Electric is facing pressure from investors to spin off some of its diverse operations ranging from power plants to locomotives to MRI machines. Dupont is splitting off a segment that generates 20 percent of its revenue. Gannet Company, owner of *USA Today* and *Wall Street Journal*, recently split their print-publishing business from their television-film business.

In 2014 alone, corporations globally split off about $2 trillion worth of subsidiaries. Part of the reason for splitting diversified firms is that the homogenous parts are generally much more attractive for potential buyers. Most times, the acquiring firms desire to promote homogeneity to complement their own operations, rather than heterogeneity, and are willing to pay for homogeneity. For example, Fiat Chrysler Automobiles NV recently "spun off" its Ferrari segment into a separate IPO, possibly raising as much as $10 billion for Fiat. In the United States, Ferrari sports cars are priced between $190,000 and $400,000, with limited edition models exceeding $3 million each.

Germany's huge power utility, E.ON SE, recently split into two companies, one focusing on the utility's green energy initiatives, while the other company is comprised of the firm's conventional power-generation operations. Germany is in the midst of an aggressive policy to phase out all of its nuclear energy power plants by 2025.

Here are some guidelines for when divestiture may be an especially effective strategy to pursue:[16]

1. An organization has pursued a retrenchment strategy and failed to accomplish needed improvements.
2. To be competitive, a division needs more resources than the company can provide.
3. A division is responsible for an organization's overall poor performance.
4. A division is a misfit with the rest of an organization; this can result from radically different markets, customers, managers, employees, values, or needs.
5. A large amount of cash is needed quickly and cannot be obtained reasonably from other sources.
6. Government antitrust action threatens an organization.

Liquidation

Selling all of a company's assets, in parts, for their tangible worth is called **liquidation**; it is associated with Chapter 7 bankruptcy. Liquidation is a recognition of defeat and consequently can be an emotionally difficult strategy. However, it may be better to cease operating than to continue losing large sums of money. For example, based in New York City, Crumbs Bake Shop, the nation's largest cupcake company, filed for Chapter 7 bankruptcy liquidation of its 65 stores in 12 states and Washington, DC. Crumbs Bake Shop was famous for selling giant cupcakes in flavors such as Red Velvet, Cookie Dough, and Girl Scouts Thin Mints. The company notified all its 165 full-time employees and 655 part-time hourly employees that the business was closing. Crumbs' last day on the Nasdaq was June 30, 2014, at a stock price of 11 cents.

The midwestern retailer, Alco Stores, in early 2015 liquidated (closed) all its stores after earlier operating under Chapter 11 bankruptcy. Founded in 1901 as a general-merchandising store in Abilene, Kansas, Alco had major offices both in Abilene and in Coppell, Texas. More than 3,000 employees lost their job as Alco liquidated its assets.

Based in Bonita Springs, Florida, one of the largest distributors of magazines in the United States, Source Interlink Distribution, recently liquidated, laying off its 6,000 employees and forgoing its $750 million a year in revenue. Source Interlink had played a major role in arranging for printed magazines to be distributed to retailers, large and small.

These three guidelines indicate when liquidation may be an especially effective strategy to pursue:[17]

1. An organization has pursued both a retrenchment strategy and a divestiture strategy, and neither has been successful.
2. An organization's only alternative is bankruptcy. Liquidation represents an orderly and planned means of obtaining the greatest possible amount of cash for an organization's assets. A company can legally declare bankruptcy first and then liquidate various divisions to raise needed capital.
3. The stockholders of a firm can minimize their losses by selling the organization's assets.

Michael Porter's Five Generic Strategies

Probably the three most widely read books on competitive analysis in the 1980s were Michael Porter's *Competitive Strategy* (1980), *Competitive Advantage* (1985), and *Competitive Advantage of Nations* (1989). According to Porter, strategies allow organizations to gain competitive advantage from three different bases: cost leadership, differentiation, and focus. Porter calls these bases **generic strategies**.

Cost leadership emphasizes producing standardized products at a low per-unit cost for consumers who are price sensitive. Two alternative types of cost leadership strategies can be defined. Type 1 is a *low-cost* strategy that offers products or services to a wide range of customers at the lowest price available on the market. Type 2 is a *best-value* strategy that offers products or services to a wide range of customers at the best price-value available on the market. The best-value strategy aims to offer customers a range of products or services at the lowest price available compared to a rival's products with similar attributes. Both Type 1 and Type 2 strategies target a large market.

Porter's Type 3 generic strategy is **differentiation**, a strategy aimed at producing products and services considered unique to the industry and directed at consumers who are relatively price insensitive.

Focus means producing products and services that fulfill the needs of small groups of consumers. Two alternative types of focus strategies are Type 4 and Type 5. Type 4 is a low-cost focus strategy that offers products or services to a small range (niche group) of customers at the lowest price available on the market. Examples of firms that use the Type 4 strategy include Jiffy Lube International and Pizza Hut, as well as local used car dealers and hot dog restaurants. Type 5 is a best-value focus strategy that offers products or services to a small range of customers at the best price-value available on the market. Sometimes called "focused differentiation," the best-value focus strategy aims to offer a niche group of customers the products or services that meet their tastes and requirements better than rivals' products do. Both Type 4 and Type 5 focus strategies target a small market. However, the difference is that Type 4 strategies offer products or services to a niche group at the lowest price, whereas Type 5 offers products and services to a niche group at higher prices but loaded with features so the offerings are perceived as the best value. Bed-and-breakfast inns and local retail boutiques are examples of Type 5 firms.

Porter's five strategies imply different organizational arrangements, control procedures, and incentive systems. Larger firms with greater access to resources typically compete on a cost leadership or differentiation basis, whereas smaller firms often compete on a focus basis. Porter's five generic strategies are illustrated in Figure 5-3. Note that a differentiation strategy (Type 3) can be pursued with either a small target market or a large target market. However, it is not effective to pursue a cost leadership strategy in a small market because profits margins are generally too small. Likewise, it is not effective to pursue a focus strategy in a large market because economies of scale would generally favor a low-cost or best-value cost leadership strategy to gain or sustain competitive advantage.

Porter stresses the need for strategists to perform cost-benefit analyses to evaluate "sharing opportunities" among a firm's existing and potential business units. Sharing activities and

Type 1: Cost Leadership—Low Cost
Type 2: Cost Leadership—Best Value
Type 3: Differentiation
Type 4: Focus—Low Cost
Type 5: Focus—Best Value

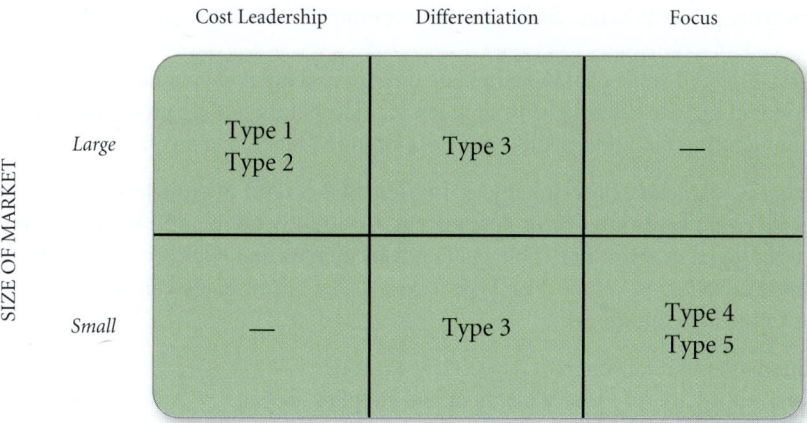

FIGURE 5-3

Porter's Five Generic Strategies

Source: Based on Michael E. Porter, *Competitive Strategy: Techniques for Analyzing Industries and Competitors* (New York: Free Press, 1980), 35–40.

resources enhances competitive advantage by lowering costs or increasing differentiation. In addition to prompting sharing, Porter stresses the need for firms to effectively "transfer" skills and expertise among autonomous business units to gain competitive advantage. Depending on factors such as type of industry, size of firm, and nature of competition, various strategies could yield advantages in cost leadership, differentiation, and focus.

Cost Leadership Strategies (Type 1 and Type 2)

A primary reason for pursuing forward, backward, and horizontal integration strategies is to gain low-cost or best-value cost leadership benefits. But cost leadership generally must be pursued in conjunction with differentiation. A number of cost elements affect the relative attractiveness of generic strategies, including economies or diseconomies of scale achieved, learning and experience curve effects, the percentage of capacity utilization achieved, and linkages with suppliers and distributors. Other cost elements to consider in choosing among alternative strategies include the potential for sharing costs and knowledge within the organization, research and development (R&D) costs associated with new product development or modification of existing products, labor costs, tax rates, energy costs, and shipping costs.

Striving to be the low-cost producer in an industry can be especially effective when the market is composed of many price-sensitive buyers, when there are few ways to achieve product differentiation, when buyers do not care much about differences from brand to brand, or when there are a large number of buyers with significant bargaining power. The basic idea is to under-price competitors and thereby gain market share and sales, entirely driving some competitors out of the market. Companies employing a low-cost (Type 1) or best-value (Type 2) cost leadership strategy must achieve their competitive advantage in ways that are difficult for competitors to copy or match. If rivals find it relatively easy or inexpensive to imitate the leader's cost leadership methods, the leaders' advantage will not last long enough to yield a valuable edge in the marketplace. Recall that for a resource to be valuable, it must be either rare, hard to imitate, or not easily substitutable. To employ a cost leadership strategy successfully, a firm must ensure that its total costs across its overall value chain are lower than competitors' total costs. There are two ways to accomplish this:[18]

1. Perform value chain activities more efficiently than rivals and control the factors that drive the costs of value chain activities. Such activities could include altering the plant layout, mastering newly introduced technologies, using common parts or components in different products, simplifying product design, finding ways to operate close to full capacity year-round, and so on.

2. Revamp the firm's overall value chain to eliminate or bypass some cost-producing activities. Such activities could include securing new suppliers or distributors, selling products online, relocating manufacturing facilities, avoiding the use of union labor, and so on.

When employing a cost leadership strategy, a firm must be careful not to use such aggressive price cuts that its own profits are low or nonexistent. Constantly be mindful of cost-saving technological breakthroughs or any other value chain advancements that could erode or destroy the firm's competitive advantage. A Type 1 or Type 2 cost leadership strategy can be especially effective under the following conditions:[19]

1. Price competition among rival sellers is especially vigorous.
2. Products of rival sellers are essentially identical and supplies are readily available from any of several eager sellers.
3. There are few ways to achieve product differentiation that have value to buyers.
4. Most buyers use the product in the same ways.
5. Buyers incur low costs in switching their purchases from one seller to another.
6. Buyers are large and have significant power to bargain down prices.
7. Industry newcomers use introductory low prices to attract buyers and build a customer base.

A successful cost leadership strategy usually permeates the entire firm, as evidenced by high efficiency, low overhead, limited perks, intolerance of waste, intensive screening of budget requests, wide spans of control, rewards linked to cost containment, and broad employee participation in cost control efforts. Some risks of pursuing cost leadership are that competitors may imitate the strategy, thus driving overall industry profits down; technological breakthroughs in the industry may make the strategy ineffective; or buyer interest may swing to other differentiating features besides price. The dollar stores are well known for their low-cost leadership strategies.

Differentiation Strategies (Type 3)

Different strategies offer different degrees of differentiation. Differentiation does not guarantee competitive advantage, especially if standard products sufficiently meet customer needs or if rapid imitation by competitors is possible. Durable products protected by barriers to quick copying by competitors are best. Successful differentiation can mean greater product flexibility, greater compatibility, lower costs, improved service, less maintenance, greater convenience, or more features. Product development is an example of a strategy that offers the advantages of differentiation.

A differentiation strategy should be pursued only after a careful study of buyers' needs and preferences to determine the feasibility of incorporating one or more differentiating features into a unique product that showcases the desired attributes. A successful differentiation strategy allows a firm to charge a higher price for its product and to gain customer loyalty because consumers may become strongly attached to the differentiation factors. Special features that differentiate one's product can include superior service, spare parts availability, engineering design, product performance, useful life, gas mileage, or ease of use.

A risk of pursuing a differentiation strategy is that the unique product may not be valued highly enough by customers to justify the higher price. When this happens, a cost-leadership strategy easily will defeat a differentiation strategy. Another risk of pursuing a differentiation strategy is that competitors may quickly develop ways to copy the differentiating features. Firms thus must find durable sources of uniqueness that cannot be imitated quickly or cheaply by rival firms.

Common organizational requirements for a successful differentiation strategy include strong coordination among the R&D and marketing functions and substantial amenities to attract scientists and creative people. Firms can pursue a differentiation (Type 3) strategy based on many different competitive aspects. Differentiation opportunities exist or can potentially be developed anywhere along the firm's value chain, including supply chain activities, product R&D activities, production and technological activities, manufacturing activities, human resource management activities, distribution activities, or marketing activities.

The most effective differentiation bases are those that are hard or expensive for rivals to duplicate. Competitors are continually trying to imitate, duplicate, and outperform rivals along any differentiation variable that has yielded competitive advantage. For example, when U.S. Airways cut its prices, Delta quickly followed suit. When Caterpillar instituted its quick-delivery-of-spare-parts policy, John Deere soon followed suit. To the extent that differentiating attributes are tough for rivals to copy, a differentiation strategy will be especially effective, but the sources of uniqueness must be time consuming, cost prohibitive, and simply too burdensome for rivals to match. A firm, therefore, must be careful when employing a differentiation (Type 3) strategy. Buyers will not pay the higher differentiation price unless their perceived value exceeds the price they are currently paying.[20] Based on such matters as attractive packaging, extensive advertising, quality of sales presentations, quality of website, list of customers, professionalism, size of the firm, or profitability of the company, perceived value may be more important to customers than actual value.

A Type 3 differentiation strategy can be especially effective under the following four conditions:[21]

1. There are many ways to differentiate the product or service and many buyers perceive these differences as having value.
2. The buyer's needs and uses are diverse.
3. Few rival firms are following a similar differentiation approach.
4. Technological change is fast paced and competition revolves around rapidly evolving product features.

Focus Strategies (Type 4 and Type 5)

A successful focus strategy depends on an industry segment that is of sufficient size, has good growth potential, and is not crucial to the success of other major competitors. Strategies such as market penetration and market development offer substantial focusing advantages. Midsize and large firms can effectively pursue focus-based strategies only in conjunction with differentiation or cost leadership–based strategies. All firms essentially follow a differentiated strategy. Because only one firm can differentiate itself with the lowest cost, the remaining firms in the industry must find other ways to differentiate their products.

Focus strategies are most effective when consumers have distinctive preferences or requirements and when rival firms are not attempting to specialize in the same target segment. For example, Clorox Company, which obtains 80 percent of its revenue from the United States, is focusing on brands viewed as environmentally friendly. Marriott continues to focus on its hotel business by announcing plans to double its hotels in Asia to 275 by 2017, especially growing its China-based hotels to about 125 from 60 and covering nearly 75 percent of Chinese provinces. Reasoning for Marriott's strategy is that Chinese tourists are traveling at home and abroad in dramatically increased numbers, up 21 percent on average year after year.

Risks of pursuing a focus strategy include the possibility that numerous competitors will recognize the successful focus strategy and copy it or that consumer preferences will drift toward the product attributes desired by the market as a whole. An organization using a focus strategy may concentrate on a particular group of customers, geographic markets, or particular product-line segments to serve a well-defined but narrow market better than competitors who serve a broader market.

A low-cost (Type 4) or best-value (Type 5) focus strategy can be especially attractive under these conditions:[22]

1. The target market niche is large, profitable, and growing.
2. Industry leaders do not consider the niche to be crucial to their own success.

3. Industry leaders consider it too costly or difficult to meet the specialized needs of the target market niche while taking care of their mainstream customers.
4. The industry has many different niches and segments, thereby allowing a focuser to pick a competitively attractive niche suited to its own resources.
5. Few, if any, other rivals are attempting to specialize in the same target segment.

Means for Achieving Strategies

Cooperation among Competitors

Fierce competitors for decades, Apple and IBM recently formed an alliance to cooperate in developing apps and selling iPhones and iPads. For Apple, the alliance allows the company to expand the reach of its products into the business world, whereas for IBM the alliance allows the firm to move more of its business software onto mobile devices. In a joint interview with IBM CEO Virginia Rometty, Apple's CEO Tim Cook observed, "In 1984, we were competitors, but today, I don't think you can find two more complementary companies." Apple and IBM are today developing more than 100 apps together.

Also fierce competitors for decades, Apple and Google recently agreed to share rights to digital content with any consumer who buys a Disney movie using the Disney Movies Anywhere app. Previously, both Apple and Google had restricted movies, TV shows, and other content to its own family of iOS or Android-powered devices, respectively. Now, both Apple and Google pay Walt Disney Company a wholesale rate for each copy of a Disney film that they sell, regardless of the type device people use.

Strategies that stress cooperation among competitors are being used more. For collaboration between competitors to succeed, both firms must contribute something distinctive, such as technology, distribution, basic research, or manufacturing capacity. But a major risk is that unintended transfers of important skills or technology may occur at organizational levels below where the deal was signed.[23] Information not covered in the formal agreement often gets traded in the day-to-day interactions and dealings of engineers, marketers, and product developers. Firms often give away too much information to rival firms when operating under cooperative agreements! Tighter formal agreements are needed.

Perhaps the best example of rival firms in an industry forming alliances to compete against each other is the airline industry. Today, there are three major alliances: Star, SkyTeam, and Oneworld. Joint ventures and cooperative arrangements among competitors demand a certain amount of trust if companies are to combat paranoia about whether one firm will injure the other. Increasing numbers of domestic firms are joining forces with competitive foreign firms to reap mutual benefits. Kathryn Harrigan at Columbia University contends, "Within a decade, most companies will be members of teams that compete against each other."

Often, U.S. companies enter alliances primarily to avoid investments, being more interested in reducing the costs and risks of entering new businesses or markets than in acquiring new skills. In contrast, *learning from the partner* is a major reason why Asian and European firms enter into cooperative agreements. American firms, too, should place learning high on the list of reasons to be cooperative with competitors. Companies in the United States often form alliances with Asian firms to gain an understanding of their manufacturing excellence, but Asian competence in this area is not easily transferable. Manufacturing excellence is a complex system that includes employee training and involvement, integration with suppliers, statistical process controls, value engineering, and design. In contrast, U.S. know-how in technology and related areas can be imitated more easily. Therefore, U.S. firms need to be careful not to give away more intelligence than they receive in cooperative agreements with rival Asian firms.

Academic Research Capsule 5-1 examines whether international alliances are more effective with competitors or noncompetitors.

Joint Venture and Partnering

Joint venture is a popular strategy that occurs when two or more companies form a temporary partnership or consortium for the purpose of capitalizing on some opportunity. Often, the two or more sponsoring firms form a separate organization and have shared equity ownership in the new entity.

ACADEMIC RESEARCH CAPSULE 5-1

Are International Alliances More Effective with Competitors or Noncompetitors?

Recent research reveals that small- and medium-size firms expanding into other countries should form alliances with noncompetitors rather than with rival firms. Alliances with competitors are more costly, directly and indirectly, and provide redundant knowledge and resources, leading researchers to conclude that small- and medium-size firms should strive to form alliances with noncompetitors rather than competitors whenever possible. Researchers report that the benefits of allying with competitors are offset by higher monitoring and control costs. Also, competing firms oftentimes share less knowledge than they could or should. Even though small- and medium-size firms typically have resource constraints as they expand globally and need alliances to grow, research shows that alliances with noncompetitors are positively associated with international performance, whereas alliances with competitors are negatively related. These findings are based on a recent study involving 162 British and U.S. private small- and medium-sized businesses.

Source: Based on K. Brouthers & P. Dimitratos, "International Alliances with Competitors and Non-Competitors: The Disparate Impact on SME International Performance," *Strategic Entrepreneurship Journal*, 8, no. 2 (June 2014): 167–182.

Other types of cooperative arrangements include research and development partnerships, cross-distribution agreements, cross-licensing agreements, cross-manufacturing agreements, and joint-bidding consortia. Although joint ventures and partnerships are increasingly preferred over mergers as a means for achieving strategies, they are not always successful, for four primary reasons:

1. Managers who must collaborate daily in operating the venture are not involved in forming or shaping the venture.
2. The venture may benefit the partnering companies but may not benefit customers, who then complain about poorer service or criticize the companies in other ways.
3. The venture may not be supported equally by both partners. If supported unequally, problems arise.
4. The venture may begin to compete more with one of the partners than the other.[24]

Joint ventures are being used increasingly because they allow companies to improve communications and networking, to globalize operations, and to minimize risk. They are formed when a given opportunity is too complex, uneconomical, or risky for a single firm to pursue alone, or when an endeavor requires a broader range of competencies and know-how than any one firm can marshal. Kathryn Rudie Harrigan, summarizes the trend toward increased joint venturing:

In today's global business environment of scarce resources, rapid rates of technological change, and rising capital requirements, the important question is no longer "Shall we form a joint venture?" Now the question is "Which joint ventures and cooperative arrangements are most appropriate for our needs and expectations?" followed by "How do we manage these ventures most effectively?"[25]

In a global market tied together by the Internet, joint ventures, partnerships, and alliances are proving to be a more effective way to enhance corporate growth than mergers and acquisitions.[26] Strategic partnering takes many forms, including outsourcing, information sharing, joint marketing, and joint research and development. There are today more than 10,000 joint ventures formed annually—more than all mergers and acquisitions. Walmart's successful joint venture with Mexico's Cifra is indicative of how a domestic firm can benefit immensely by partnering with a foreign company to gain substantial presence in that new country. Technology also is a major reason behind the need to form strategic alliances, with the Internet linking widely dispersed partners. For example, IBM recently signed partnerships with both Twitter and Facebook, enabling IBM to mine information from Twitter's 302 million monthly active users and Facebook's 1.4 billion users. With data from those partnerships, IBM is using its cloud analytics and data analytics services to help companies create social data-enabled apps. The leading data analytics, or business analytics, company is Tableau Software, followed by Qlik Technologies.

Although evidence is mounting that firms should use partnering as a means for achieving strategies, most U.S. firms in many industries—such as financial services, forest products, metals, and retailing—still operate in a merge or acquire mode to obtain growth. Partnering is not yet taught at most business schools and is often viewed within companies as a financial issue rather than a strategic issue. However, partnering has become a core competency, a strategic issue of such high importance.

Six guidelines for when a joint venture may be an especially effective means for pursuing strategies are:[27]

1. A privately owned organization is forming a joint venture with a publicly owned organization. There are some advantages to being privately held, such as closed ownership. There are also some advantages of being publicly held, such as access to stock issuances as a source of capital. Sometimes the unique advantages of being privately and publicly held can be synergistically combined in a joint venture.

2. A domestic organization is forming a joint venture with a foreign company. A joint venture can provide a domestic company with the opportunity for obtaining local management in a foreign country, thereby reducing risks such as expropriation and harassment by host country officials.

3. The distinct competencies of two or more firms complement each other especially well.

4. Some project is potentially profitable but requires overwhelming resources and risks.

5. Two or more smaller firms have trouble competing with a large firm.

6. There is a need to quickly introduce a new technology.

Merger/Acquisition

Merger and acquisition are two commonly used ways to pursue strategies. A **merger** occurs when two organizations of about equal size unite to form one enterprise. An **acquisition** occurs when a large organization purchases (acquires) a smaller firm or vice versa. If a merger or acquisition is not desired by both parties, it is called a **hostile takeover**, as opposed to a **friendly merger**. Most mergers are friendly, but the number of hostile takeovers is on the rise. Not all mergers are effective and successful. For example, soon after Halliburton acquired Baker Hughes, Halliburton's stock price declined 11 percent. So, a merger between two firms can yield great benefits, but the price and reasoning must be right. Some key reasons why many mergers and acquisitions fail are provided in Table 5-5.

There were far more global mergers and acquisitions in 2014 than in any year since 2007, exceeding $3.5 billion. Three contributory reasons for this trend are (1) the desire of diversified firms to "spin off" segments into separate companies that are then acquired by other firms, (2) the desire of firms to acquire similar companies in countries with low corporate tax rates and to shift company profits from the United States through those countries, and (3) the desire of shareholders for firms to continually grow revenues. Often, growth is most effective through acquisition, as opposed to internal (organic) growth.

In the United States, mergers and acquisitions totaled $1.52 trillion in 2014, comprising 45 percent of global deals, up from $998 billion, or 43 percent, the prior year. The data firm Dealogic reported in mid-2015 that global mergers and acquisitions in 2015 likely will hit an all-time record of $4.58 trillion.

TABLE 5-5   Nine Reasons Why Many Mergers and Acquisitions Fail

1. Integration difficulties
2. Inadequate evaluation of target
3. Large or extraordinary debt
4. Inability to achieve synergy
5. Too much diversification
6. Managers overly focused on acquisitions
7. Too large an acquisition
8. Difficult to integrate different organizational cultures
9. Reduced employee morale due to layoffs and relocations

However, the U.S. Treasury Department's new rules cracking down on tax inversions, where a company acquires a foreign company in order to avoid paying federal taxes, will likely somewhat curtail the number of mergers and acquisitions going forward. More than 10,000 mergers transpire annually in the United States, with same-industry combinations predominating. A general market consolidation is occurring in many industries, especially energy, banking, insurance, defense, and health care, but also in pharmaceuticals, food, airlines, accounting, publishing, computers, retailing, financial services, and biotechnology. Table 5-6 presents the potential benefits of merging with or acquiring another firm.

A **leveraged buyout (LBO)** occurs when a corporation's shareholders are bought (hence *buyout*) by the company's management and other private investors using borrowed funds (hence *leverage*). Besides trying to avoid a hostile takeover, other reasons for initiating an LBO include whenever a particular division(s) does not fit into an overall corporate strategy, or whenever selling a division could raise needed cash. An LBO converts a public firm into a private company.

Private-Equity Acquisitions

Private equity (PE) firms are acquiring and taking private a wide variety of companies almost daily in the business world. For example, one of the world's largest private-equity firms, Apollo Global Management LLC, recently acquired 577 Chuck E. Cheese stores, the party pizza and arcade game venues, in 47 states and 10 foreign countries or territories. Apollo paid about $950 million for the parent company, CEC Entertainment, or a 12 percent premium over the company's stock price. Chuck E. Cheese's profit and revenue has been on the decline of late and the number of birthday parties hosted falling. Another large PE firm, Carlyle Group LP, recently acquired Johnson & Johnson's blood-testing business for $4.15 billion.

Private equity firms are an integral part of the business world, especially in the United States but also in Europe, Asia, and, more recently, Latin America. Private equity firms such as Kohlberg Kravis Roberts (KKR) have jumped aggressively back into the business of acquiring and selling firms, and releasing new initial public offerings (IPO). A large PE firm, Cerberus Capital Management, recently bought the second-largest U.S. grocery store chain, Safeway Inc., based in Pleasanton, California, for $9.4 billion. Cerberus already owns Albertsons, the fifth-largest U.S. grocery store chain. Cerberus plans to unite the two companies' distribution and purchasing operations to save money and compete better with major rivals, Wal-Mart Stores and Kroger.

Headquartered in Phoenix, Arizona, PetSmart was acquired in December 2014 by London-based PE firm BC Partners for $8.8 billion, the largest U.S. private equity deal of the year. PetSmart reportedly had received a joint bid offer from KKR and Clayton Dubilier & Rice, and a bid from Apollo, all PE firms. PetSmart operates 1,387 retail pet stores in the United States, Canada, and Puerto Rico. BC Partners paid $83 per share for PetSmart, a 6.86 percent premium over PetSmart's closing stock price.

TABLE 5-6   **Eleven Potential Benefits of Merging with or Acquiring Another Firm**

1. To provide improved capacity utilization
2. To make better use of the existing sales force
3. To reduce managerial staff
4. To gain economies of scale
5. To smooth out seasonal trends in sales
6. To gain access to new suppliers, distributors, customers, products, and creditors
7. To gain new technology
8. To gain market share
9. To enter global markets
10. To gain pricing power
11. To reduce tax obligations

The intent of virtually all PE acquisitions is to buy firms at a low price and sell them later at a high price, arguably just good business. Private equity firms also are buying companies from other PE firms, such as Clayton, Dubilier & Rice's recent purchase of David's Bridal from Leonard Green & Partners LP for $1.05 billion. Such PE-to-PE acquisitions are called **secondary buyouts**. In addition, PE firms especially, but other firms too, sometimes borrow money simply to fund dividend payouts to themselves, a controversial practice known as **dividend recapitalizations**. Critics say dividend recapitalization saddles a company with debt, thus burdening its operations.

Tactics to Facilitate Strategies

Strategists use numerous tactics to accomplish strategies, including being a "first mover," outsourcing, and reshoring. There are advantages and disadvantages of such tactics, as discussed next.

First Mover Advantages

First mover advantages refer to the benefits a firm may achieve by entering a new market or developing a new product or service prior to rival firms. As indicated in Table 5-7, some advantages of being a first mover include securing access to rare resources, gaining new knowledge of key factors and issues, and carving out market share and a position that is easy to defend and costly for rival firms to overtake. First mover advantages are analogous to taking the high ground first, which puts one in an excellent strategic position to launch aggressive campaigns and to defend territory. Being the first mover can be an excellent strategy when such actions (1) build a firm's image and reputation with buyers; (2) produce cost advantages over rivals in terms of new technologies, new components, new distribution channels, and so on; (3) create strongly loyal customers, and (4) make imitation or duplication by a rival difficult or unlikely.

To sustain the competitive advantage gained by being the first mover, a firm needs to be a fast learner. There are, however, risks associated with being the first mover, such as unexpected and unanticipated problems and costs that occur from being the first firm doing business in the new market. Therefore, being a slow mover (also called *fast follower* or *late mover*) can be effective when a firm can easily copy or imitate the lead firm's products or services. If technology is advancing rapidly, slow movers can often leapfrog a first mover's products with improved second-generation products. Samsung is an example in the smartphone business. Apple has always been a good example of a first mover firm.

First mover advantages tend to be greatest when competitors are roughly the same size and possess similar resources. If competitors are not similar in size, then larger competitors can wait while others make initial investments and mistakes, and then respond with greater effectiveness and resources. Lenovo has done this of late, as has Volkswagen.

Outsourcing and Reshoring

The second largest U.S. airline by traffic, United Continental Holdings, recently outsourced its check-in, baggage-handling, and customer service jobs to vendors who perform the duties at a lower cost. **Outsourcing** involves companies hiring other companies to take over various parts of

---

TABLE 5-7   Five Benefits of a Firm Being the First Mover

1. Secure access and commitments to rare resources.
2. Gain new knowledge of critical success factors and issues.
3. Gain market share and position in the best locations.
4. Establish and secure long-term relationships with customers, suppliers, distributors, and investors.
5. Gain customer loyalty and commitments.

their functional operations, such as human resources, information systems, payroll, accounting, customer service, and even marketing.

For more than a decade, U.S. and European companies have been outsourcing their manufacturing, tech support, and back-office work, but most insisted on keeping research and development activities in-house. However, an ever-growing number of firms today are outsourcing their product design to Asian developers. China and India are becoming increasingly important suppliers of intellectual property. The details of what work to outsource, to whom, where, and for how much can challenge even the biggest, most sophisticated companies. And some outsourcing deals do not work out, such as the J. P. Morgan Chase deal with IBM and Dow Chemical's deal with Electronic Data Systems. Both outsourcing deals were abandoned after several years. India has become a booming place for outsourcing.

Table 5-8 reveals some of the potential benefits that firms strive to achieve through outsourcing. Notice that benefit #1 is that outsourcing is oftentimes used to access lower wages in foreign countries.

Reshoring is the new term that refers to U.S. companies planning to move some of their manufacturing back to the United States. Many U.S. companies plan to *reshore* in 2016–2017 for the following reasons: a desire to get products to market faster and respond rapidly to customer orders, savings from reduced transportation and warehousing, improved quality and protection of intellectual property, pressure to increase U.S. jobs.[28] "Made in the USA" is making a comeback. Walmart, for example, is spending an added $250 billion in the next 10 years on USA-made goods. Consequently, numerous Walmart suppliers, such as Element Electronics based in Eden Prairie, Minnesota, are bringing manufacturing and assembly operations back to the United States. Element now assembles flat screen televisions in Winnsboro, South Carolina. Whirlpool and General Electric have also reshored some of their production operations back to the United States. However, the management consulting firm A. T. Kearney reports that reshoring has stalled, and that U.S. firms are increasingly producing goods in lower-cost countries.[29] The strength of the dollar also has led U.S. firms to look outside the United States more and more to produce goods. The high value of the dollar makes U.S. goods more expensive overseas and

TABLE 5-8 Thirteen Potential Benefits of Outsourcing

1. *Cost savings:* Access lower wages in foreign countries.
2. *Focus on core business:* Focus resources on developing the core business rather than being distracted by other functions.
3. *Cost restructuring:* Outsourcing changes the balance of fixed costs to variable costs by moving the firm more to variable costs. Outsourcing also makes variable costs more predictable.
4. *Improve quality:* Improve quality by contracting out various business functions to specialists.
5. *Knowledge:* Gain access to intellectual property and wider experience and knowledge.
6. *Contract:* Gain access to services within a legally binding contract with financial penalties and legal redress. This is not the case with services performed internally.
7. *Operational expertise:* Gain access to operational best practice that would be too difficult or time consuming to develop in-house.
8. *Access to talent:* Gain access to a larger talent pool and a sustainable source of skills, especially science and engineering.
9. *Catalyst for change:* Use an outsourcing agreement as a catalyst for major change that cannot be achieved alone.
10. *Enhance capacity for innovation:* Use external knowledge to supplement limited in-house capacity for product innovation.
11. *Reduce time to market:* Accelerate development or production of a product through additional capability brought by the supplier.
12. *Risk management:* Manage risk by partnering with an outside firm.
13. *Tax benefit:* Capitalize on tax incentives to locate manufacturing plants to avoid high taxes in various countries.

makes imports to the United States cheaper. However, seven benefits of reshoring back into the United States are as follows:

1. Stable wages
2. Reduced gas and electricity costs
3. Excellent security to protect designs from overseas copycats
4. Enable closer tabs on quality control and supply chains
5. Excellent economy with consumers purchasing more
6. Less shipment costs with consumers nearby
7. Excellent human rights, education, legal, and political systems that promote freedom and opportunity for citizens

Strategic Management in Nonprofit, Governmental, and Small Firms

Nonprofit organizations are basically just like for-profit companies except for two major differences: (1) nonprofits do not pay taxes and (2) nonprofits do not have shareholders to provide capital. In virtually all other ways, these two types of organizations are like one another. Nonprofits have employees, customers, creditors, suppliers, and distributors as well as financial budgets, income statements, balance sheets, cash flow statements, and so on. Nonprofit organizations embrace strategic planning just as much as for-profit firms, and perhaps even more, because equity capital is not an alternative source of financing. Nonprofits also have competitors that want to put them out of business.

The strategic-management process is being used effectively by countless nonprofit and governmental organizations, such as the Girl Scouts, Boy Scouts, the Red Cross, chambers of commerce, educational institutions, medical institutions, public utilities, libraries, government agencies, zoos, cities, and churches. The nonprofit sector, surprisingly, is by far the largest employer in the United States. Many nonprofit and governmental organizations outperform private firms and corporations on innovativeness, motivation, productivity, and strategic management.

Compared to for-profit firms, nonprofit and governmental organizations may be totally dependent on outside financing. Especially for these organizations, strategic management provides an excellent vehicle for developing and justifying requests for needed financial support. Nonprofits and governmental organizations owe it to their constituencies to garner and use monies wisely; that requires excellent strategy formulation, implementation, and evaluation.

Educational Institutions

The world of higher education is rapidly moving to online courses and degrees. The American Council on Education, an association for higher education presidents, is considering allowing free, online courses to be eligible for credit toward a degree and eligible for transfer credit. Educational institutions are more frequently using strategic-management techniques and concepts. Richard Cyert, former president of Carnegie Mellon University, said, "I believe we do a far better job of strategic management than any company I know." Population shifts nationally from the Northeast and Midwest to the Southeast and West are but one factor causing trauma for educational institutions that have not planned for changing enrollments. Ivy League schools in the Northeast are recruiting more heavily in the Southeast and West. This trend represents a significant change in the competitive climate for attracting the best high school graduates each year. Online degrees are a threat to traditional colleges and universities. "You can put the kids to bed and go to law school," says Andrew Rosen, chief operating officer of Kaplan Education Centers, a subsidiary of the Washington Post Company. Reduced state and federal funding for higher education has resulted in more aggressive fund raising by colleges and universities. President Obama's call for free community college education for all could also erode attendance in four-year colleges' 100 and 200-level courses. All institutions of higher learning need an excellent strategic plan to survive and prosper.

Medical Organizations

Declining occupancy rates, deregulation, and accelerating growth of health maintenance organizations, preferred provider organizations, urgent care centers, outpatient surgery centers, diagnostic centers, specialized clinics, and group practices are other major threats facing hospitals today. Many private and state-supported medical institutions are in financial trouble as a result of traditionally taking a reactive rather than a proactive approach in dealing with their industry. Originally intended to be warehouses for people dying of tuberculosis, smallpox, cancer, pneumonia, and infectious disease, hospitals are creating new strategies today as advances in the diagnosis and treatment of chronic diseases are undercutting that previous mission. Hospitals are beginning to bring services to the patient as much as bringing the patient to the hospital; health care is more and more being concentrated in the home and in the residential community rather than on the hospital campus. Current strategies being pursued by many hospitals include creating home health services, establishing nursing homes, and forming rehabilitation centers. Backward integration strategies that some hospitals are pursuing include acquiring ambulance services, waste disposal services, and diagnostic services. Millions of people annually research medical ailments online, causing a dramatic shift in the balance of power between doctor, patient, and hospitals.

Governmental Agencies and Departments

Federal, state, county, and municipal agencies and departments, such as police departments, chambers of commerce, forestry associations, and health departments, are responsible for formulating, implementing, and evaluating strategies that use taxpayers' dollars in the most cost-effective way to provide services and programs. Strategic-management concepts are generally required and thus widely used to enable governmental organizations to be more effective and efficient.

Strategists in governmental organizations operate with less strategic autonomy than their counterparts in private firms. Public enterprises generally cannot diversify into unrelated businesses or merge with other firms. Governmental strategists usually enjoy little freedom in altering the organizations' missions or redirecting objectives. Legislators and politicians often have direct or indirect control over major decisions and resources. Strategic issues get discussed and debated in the media and legislatures. Issues become politicized, resulting in fewer strategic choice alternatives. There is now more predictability in the management of public sector enterprises.

Government agencies and departments are finding that their employees get excited about the opportunity to participate in the strategic-management process and thereby have an effect on the organization's mission, objectives, strategies, and policies. In addition, government agencies are using a strategic-management approach to develop and substantiate formal requests for additional funding.

Small Firms

"Becoming your own boss" is a dream for millions of people and a reality for millions more. Almost everyone wants to own a business—from teens and college students, who are signing up for entrepreneurial courses in record numbers, to those older than age 65, who are forming more companies every year. However, the January 3, 2015, issue of the *Wall Street Journal* (page A1) reported that the percentage of people under age 30 who own private businesses has reached a 24-year low in the United States, to about 3.6 percent, down from 10.6 percent in 1989. The stereotype that 20-somethings are entrepreneurial risk-takers is simply false, as millions of young adults struggle in underpaid jobs to maintain their own household, rather than living with their parents. Reasons for the decline vary, but reduced bank lending for small business startups, more indebtedness among young people, and increasing numbers of competitors due to the Internet, all contribute to a more risk-averse, under-30 age group for becoming entrepreneur strategists.

The strategic-management process is just as vital for small companies as it is for large firms. From their inception, all organizations have a strategy, even if the strategy just evolves from day-to-day operations. Even if conducted informally or by a single owner or entrepreneur, the strategic-management process can significantly enhance small firms' growth and prosperity. However, a lack of strategic-management knowledge is a serious obstacle for many small business owners, as is a lack of sufficient capital to exploit external opportunities and a day-to-day cognitive frame of reference. Research indicates that strategic management in small firms is more informal than in large firms, but small firms that engage in strategic management generally outperform those that do not.

Academic Research Capsule 5-2 reveals the key attributes of great entrepreneurs, many of whom never went to college and never were an expert at their trade.

ACADEMIC RESEARCH CAPSULE 5-2

What Attributes Do Great Entrepreneurs Possess?

Many people dream of becoming a professional football player, musician, doctor, or entrepreneur, but many of us do not think we have the perceived special skills required to become greatly successful. Most aspiring entrepreneurs mistakenly believe those special skills are mandatory versus other skill sets we devalue. Baron and Henry carefully examined what attributes most great entrepreneurs possess, and found that many great strategists began as great entrepreneurs, including Michael Dell, Steve Jobs, Milton Hershey, Walt Disney, Henry Ford, and Bill Gates. Baron and Henry report that neither "years of experience" nor "God given natural ability" are top attributes that explain the success of most entrepreneurs. There does indeed need to be some level of natural "special" competence, but importantly, most of us are competent enough to become surprisingly successful at any endeavor we choose.

Baron and Henry found that most aspiring entrepreneurs can gain or already have the necessary experience in a particular area, and additional experience yields only incremental improvements; they contend that experience, in fact, can become an inhibiting factor. This finding is surprising because experience is highly valued in most professions, especially by those making hiring decisions. Many students, for example, when applying for jobs, are told, "You don't have enough work experience." So, if innate talent (special skills) and experience are not overriding keys to entrepreneurial success, what is? Baron and Henry provide the answer, reporting that the dominating, overriding factor accounting for the success of most great entrepreneurs is that they possess a high level of **deliberate practice**. Deliberate practice is best described as "an intense focusing on all aspects related to a subject matter or business idea." Deliberate practice goes well beyond hard work or routine practice, so much so that even the most successful entrepreneurs cannot engage in deliberate practice for more than a few hours each day. This characteristic includes examining yourself as a person, your competition, and a wide array of factors related to the entrepreneurial endeavor at hand. Several antecedents of deliberate practice include strong motivation, self-efficacy, self-discipline, delayed gratification, and self-control. Other factors are determination, strong work ethic, goal-oriented, dedication, time management, and "being on a mission."

Deliberate practice entails working "hard and smart" simultaneously; it is all about developing and utilizing a strategic mental approach to the endeavor at hand, rather than having a special innate talent or gaining 20 years of experience. Mr. Disney, Ford, Dell, Gates, Hershey, and Jobs utilized deliberate practice right out of the gate, rather than waiting to obtain innate talent or work experience. These great entrepreneurs (strategists) generally had neither innate talent nor years of work experience. Baron and Henry assert that anyone can become great through deliberate practice. Thus, do not get discouraged by having minimal innate talent or work experience. Rather, use the deliberate practice process to become successful in your chosen endeavor.

Source: Based on R. A. Baron & R. Henry, "How Entrepreneurs Acquire the Capacity to Excel: Insights from Research on Expert Performance," *Strategic Entrepreneurship Journal*, 4 (2019): 49–65. (*Note:* This is the most downloaded article in this journal in the last five years.)

IMPLICATIONS FOR STRATEGISTS

Figure 5-4 reveals that to gain and sustain competitive advantages, firms must collect, analyze, and prioritize large amounts of information in order to make excellent decisions. A "strategic plan" is very much akin to an athletic team's "game plan" in the sense that both a strategic plan and a game plan are developed after carefully studying rival firms (teams); success of the firm (or team) depends greatly on that plan being a better plan than the rival's plan. Any strategist, much like any coach, puts his or her firm in great jeopardy of failure if the opposing strategist (coach) has a better strategic plan.

Substantial deliberate practice, as discussed in Academic Research Capsule 5-2, is required to create, identify, nurture, and exploit competitive advantages that can lead to success. Parity (and commoditization) is becoming commonplace in both business and athletics; as parity increases, the intrinsic value of the overarching strategic plan, or game plan, increases exponentially.

For example, in college football, great parity exists among teams such as Auburn, Alabama, Ohio State, Florida State, Kansas State, Oregon, Arizona State, Michigan State, and Michigan, so the game plan can make the difference between winning and losing.

Most of the strategies described in this chapter would separately yield substantial benefits for firms, but no firm has sufficient resources to pursue more than a few basic strategies. Thus, strategists must select from a number of excellent alternatives, eliminate other excellent options, and consider risks, tradeoffs, costs, and other key factors. Any strategist, or coach, that gets "outstrategized" by his or her opposing strategist (or coach) puts his or her firm (or team) at a major disadvantage. Being outcoached can doom even a superior team (or firm). Therefore, in Chapter 6 we examine six additional analytical tools being widely used by strategists to help develop a winning strategic plan.

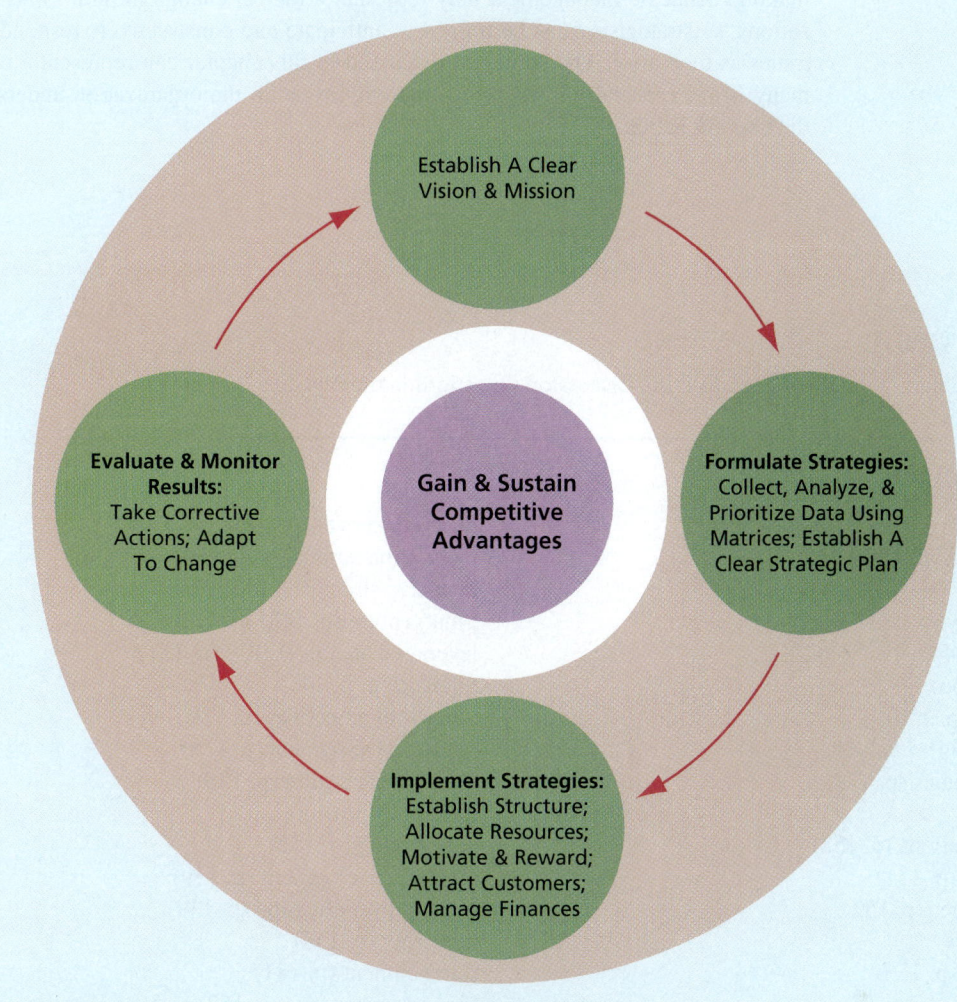

FIGURE 5-4

How to Gain and Sustain Competitive Advantages

Numerous alternative strategies could benefit any firm, but your strategic-management case analysis should result in specific recommendations that you decide will best provide the firm with competitive advantages. Because company recommendations with costs comprise the most important pages or slides in your case project, introduce bits of that information early in the presentation as relevant supporting material is presented to justify your expenditures. Your recommendations page(s) itself should therefore be a summary of suggestions mentioned throughout your paper or presentation, rather than being a surprise shock to your reader or audience. You may even want to include with your recommendations insight as to why certain other feasible strategies were not chosen for implementation. That information, too, should be anchored in the notion of competitive advantage and disadvantage with respect to perceived costs and benefits. If someone asks, "What is the difference between recommendations and strategies?", respond with "Recommendations are alternative strategies actually selected for implementation."

Chapter Summary

The main appeal of any managerial approach is the expectation that it will enhance organizational performance. This is especially true of strategic management. Through involvement in strategic-management activities, managers and employees achieve a better understanding of an organization's priorities and operations. Strategic management allows organizations to be efficient, but more important, it allows them to be effective. Although strategic management does not guarantee organizational success, the process allows proactive rather than reactive decision making. Strategic management may represent a radical change in philosophy for some organizations, so strategists must be trained to anticipate and constructively respond to questions and issues as they arise. The strategies discussed in this chapter can represent a new beginning for many firms, especially if managers and employees in the organization understand and support the plan for action.

MyManagementLab®

To complete the problems with the ⭐, go to EOC Discussion Questions in the MyLab.

Key Terms and Concepts

acquisition (p. 150)
backward integration (p. 136)
bankruptcy (p. 142)
combination strategy (p. 133)
cost leadership (p. 144)
de-integration (p. 136)
deliberate practice (p. 156)
differentiation (p. 144)
diversification strategies (p. 139)
divestiture (p. 142)
dividend recapitalizations (p. 152)
financial objectives (p. 131)
first mover advantages (p. 152)
focus (p. 144)
forward integration (p. 135)
franchising (p. 135)
friendly merger (p. 150)
generic strategies (p. 144)
horizontal integration (p. 134)

hostile takeover (p. 150)
integration strategies (p. 134)
intensive strategies (p. 138)
joint venture (p. 148)
leveraged buyout (LBO) (p. 151)
liquidation (p. 143)
long-term objectives (p. 130)
market development (p. 138)
market penetration (p. 138)
merger (p. 150)
outsourcing (p. 152)
product development (p. 139)
related diversification (p. 139)
reshoring (p. 153)
retrenchment (p. 141)
secondary buyouts (p. 152)
strategic objectives (p. 131)
unrelated diversification (p. 139)
vertical integration (p. 134)

Issues for Review and Discussion

⭐ **5-1.** According to the Baron and Henry article discussed in Academic Research Capsule 5-2, what is "deliberate practice" and why is this important in strategic management?

⭐ **5-2.** True or False? The strength of the dollar has led to U.S. firms outsourcing more and more, rather than reshoring. Explain.

5-3. Give three reasons why so many companies are divesting (spinning off) key segments/divisions of the firm.

⭐ **5-4.** Are international alliances more effective with competitors or noncompetitors? Why?

5-5. Give actual examples of how Amazon is forward integrating and diversifying at the same time.

5-6. Define and give an example of *reshoring*. What are three reasons why reshoring is becoming more popular? What are three reasons many companies expect "never" to reshore (as Steve Jobs once told President Obama)?

5-7. Define and give a hypothetical example of a *secondary buyout*.

5-8. The number and dollar value of *hostile takeovers* are on the rise. Give two reasons for this trend.

5-9. What do you believe are the eight most important benefits of outsourcing?

5-10. Define and give an example of a *dividend recapitalization*. List some pros and cons of doing this in a business.

5-11. How are for-profit firms different from nonprofit firms in terms of business? What are the implications for strategic planning?

5-12. If the CEO of a beverage company such as Dr. Pepper Snapple asked you whether backward or forward integration would be better for the firm, how would you respond?

⭐ **5-13.** In order of importance, list six characteristics of objectives.

⭐ **5-14.** In order of importance, list six benefits of objectives.

5-15. Called de-integration, there appears to be a growing trend for firms to become less forward integrated. Discuss why.

5-16. Called de-integration, there appears to be a growing trend for firms to become less backward integrated. Discuss why.

5-17. What conditions, externally and internally, would be desired or necessary for a firm to diversify?

5-18. There is a growing trend of increased collaboration among competitors. List the benefits and drawbacks of this practice.

5-19. List four major benefits of forming a joint venture to achieve desired objectives.

⭐ **5-20.** List six major benefits of acquiring another firm to achieve desired objectives.

5-21. List five reasons why many mergers or acquisitions historically have failed.

5-22. Can you think of any reasons why not-for-profit firms would benefit less from doing strategic planning than for-profit companies?

5-23. Discuss how important it is for a college football or basketball team to have a good game plan for the big rival game this coming weekend. How much time and effort do you feel the coaching staff puts into

developing that game plan? Why is such time and effort essential?

⭐ **5-24.** How does strategy formulation differ for a small versus a large organization? How does it differ for a for-profit versus a nonprofit organization?

5-25. Give hypothetical examples of market penetration, market development, and product development.

5-26. Give hypothetical examples of forward integration, backward integration, and horizontal integration.

5-27. Give hypothetical examples of related and unrelated diversification.

5-28. Give hypothetical examples of joint venture, retrenchment, divestiture, and liquidation.

⭐ **5-29.** Are hostile takeovers unethical? Why or why not?

5-30. What are the major advantages and disadvantages of diversification?

5-31. What are the major advantages and disadvantages of an integrative strategy?

5-32. How does strategic management differ in for-profit and nonprofit organizations?

5-33. Why is it not advisable to pursue too many strategies at once?

⭐ **5-34.** Compare and contrast financial objectives with strategic objectives. Which type is more important in your opinion? Why?

5-35. How do the levels of strategy differ in a large firm versus a small firm?

5-36. List 11 types of strategies. Give a hypothetical example of each strategy listed.

5-37. Define and explain first mover advantages.

5-38. Define and explain outsourcing.

5-39. Give some advantages and disadvantages of cooperative versus competitive strategies.

⭐ **5-40.** What are the two major differences between for-profit and not-for-profit organizations?

MyManagementLab®

Go to the Assignments section of your MyLab to complete these writing exercises.

5-41. If a company has $1 million to spend on a new strategy and is considering market development versus product development, what determining factors would be most important to consider?

5-42. Discuss five reasons why many mergers or acquisitions historically have failed.

ASSURANCE OF LEARNING EXERCISES

EXERCISE 5A
Develop Hypothetical Hershey Company Strategies

Purpose
Table 5-4 identifies, defines, and exemplifies 11 key types of strategies available to firms. This exercise will give you practice formulating possible strategies within each broad category.

Instructions

Step 1   Develop an 11 × 2 matrix where Hershey's (1) North American and (2) International segments are along the top and the 11 strategies listed in Table 5-4 are along the left.

Step 2   Review the Hershey divisional information provided in the Cohesion Case (pages 28–29).

Step 3   In each of the 22 cells within your 11 × 2 matrix, write in a hypothetical strategy for the respective business segment indicated. Be specific with numbers .

EXERCISE 5B
Horizontal Integration in Practice

Purpose

As showcased at the beginning of this chapter, Signet Jewelers Limited (SIG) is successfully pursuing horizontal integration. This exercise gives you practice analyzing whether a firm should or could acquire a rival firm.

Instructions

Step 1   Review material about Signet at the beginning of this chapter and at the www.signetjewelers.com website. Review current news articles about Signet as posted on the www.finance.yahoo.com website.

Step 2   Review information about a major rival to Signet, Tiffany & Co. (stock symbol TIF). Determine whether you believe Signet could or should try to acquire Tiffany. Give the pros and cons of such a horizontal integration strategy. Recall that Signet recently acquired rival Zale Corporation.

EXERCISE 5C
What Strategies Should Hershey Pursue in 2017?

Purpose

In performing strategic-management case analysis, you can find information about the respective company's actual and planned strategies. Comparing *what is planned* versus *what you recommend* is an important part of case analysis. Do not recommend what the firm actually plans, unless in-depth analysis of the situation reveals those strategies to be best among all feasible alternatives. This exercise gives you experience conducting library and Internet research to determine what Hershey is doing in 2015–16 and should do in 2017.

Instructions

Step 1   Go to the www.hersheycompany.com website and click on Newsroom. Read through the most recent 10 press releases.

Step 2   Determine two strategies that Hershey is actually pursuing. Give some pros and cons of those two new Hershey strategies.

EXERCISE 5D
Examine Strategy Articles

Purpose

Strategy articles can be found weekly in journals, magazines, and newspapers. By reading and studying strategy articles, you can gain a better understanding of the strategic-management process. Several of the best journals in which to find corporate strategy articles are *Advanced Management Journal, Business Horizons, Long Range Planning, Journal of Business Strategy*, and *Strategic Management Journal.* These journals are devoted to reporting the results of empirical research in management. They apply strategic-management concepts to specific organizations and industries, and they introduce new strategic-management techniques and provide short case studies on selected firms. Other good journals in which to find strategic-management articles are *Harvard Business Review, Sloan Management Review, California Management Review, Academy of Management Review, Academy of Management Journal, Academy of Management Executive, Journal of Management*, and *Journal of Small Business Management.*

In contrast to journals, several of the best magazines in which to find applied strategy articles are *Dun's Business Month, Fortune, Forbes, BusinessWeek, Inc.,* and *Industry Week.* Newspapers such as *USA Today, Wall Street Journal, New York Times*, and *Barron's* cover strategy events when they occur—for example, a joint venture announcement, a bankruptcy declaration, a new advertising campaign start, acquisition of a company, divestiture of a division, a chief executive officer's hiring or firing, or a hostile takeover attempt.

In combination, journal, magazine, and newspaper articles can make the strategic-management course more exciting. They allow current strategies of for-profit and nonprofit organizations to be identified and studied.

Instructions

Step 1 Use your college's online databases to find a recent journal article that focuses on a strategic-management topic. Select your article from one of the journals just mentioned (not from a magazine). Copy the article and bring it to class.

Step 2 Give a 3-minute oral report summarizing the most important information in your journal article. Include comments giving your personal reaction to the article. Pass your article around in class.

EXERCISE 5E

Classify Some Recent Strategies

Purpose

This exercise can improve your understanding of various strategies by giving you experience in classifying strategies. This skill will help you use the strategy-formulation tools presented in Chapter 6. Consider the following recent strategies by various firms:

1. Amazon started producing and selling its own line of diapers.
2. MillerCoors offers free delivery of Miller Lite in four U.S. cities for customers who order through its online store.
3. Sears is closing about 235 stores annually.
4. The largest toymaker in the United States, Mattel, is struggling; therefore, it is introducing flashier and more educative toys.
5. German power utility E.ON SE sold its Spanish assets to Australia's Macquarie Group and Kuwait's sovereign-wealth fund for $3.1 billion.
6. Target Corporation is closing all of its 133 stores in Canada and China.
7. Coca-Cola recently axed 1,600 white-collar jobs globally as part of a cost-cutting move.
8. Nissan has totally revamped its Titan full-size pickup truck with new features and options and style.
9. General Motors just introduced a sports car version of its electric car, the Chevrolet Volt, and is introducing an all-electric vehicle in 2017 called the Chevrolet Bolt, capable of driving 200 miles without recharging.
10. SolarWinds acquired Pingdom, Confio, and N-Able Technologies to obtain different products and services since the solar business has slowed as oil prices have dropped.
11. Amazon Studios is branching out from television series to movies, with plans to begin producing and acquiring original movies for theatrical release and video streaming.
12. ZF Friedrichshafen AG of Germany recently acquired TRW Automotive Holdings in the United States to create the world's second-largest auto-parts supplier behind Germany's Robert Bosch GmbH and ahead of Japan's Denso Corp.
13. Southwest Airlines recently began flying outside the United States, with flights to various Caribbean, Central America, and Mexico destinations.
14. Amazon is pushing aggressively into the same-day grocery delivery service with its AmazonFresh business along the west coast of the United States.
15. USPS has begun delivering groceries for Amazon.com within the AmazonFresh grocery-delivery service, especially in San Francisco and other markets.
16. USPS also recently launched Access Point, a strategy that allows customers to pick up their packages at dry cleaners, convenience stores, and pharmacies.
17. The huge food company General Mills recently acquired Annies's Inc. for $820 million, paying a 37 percent premium for the firm, in order to expand its presence in the rapidly growing organic and natural foods category.
18. Google recently entered the hotel-booking industry by acquiring the firm called Room 77 and expanding its ties with big hotel firms such as Hilton Worldwide Holdings and Radisson Hotels that now offer virtual tours on Google. Google now allows hotels to list their rooms on their site, in effect bypassing travel search sites such as Priceline Group, Expedia, and TripAdvisor.

19. Google recently partnered with the medical firm Novartis to develop high-tech contact lenses that monitor glucose levels and other body functions.
20. Amazon recently entered the mobile payments business and is now competing with PayPal, ApplePay, and all charge cards.
21. The world's largest furniture retailer, IKEA, recently diversified into the insurance business, providing child, pregnancy, and home insurance products at its stores.
22. Office Depot closed nearly 500 stores in the last three years.
23. The drug maker, Dendreon Corporation, recently filed for Chapter 11 bankruptcy. Its major drug, Provenge, which treats prostate cancer, never gained traction in the market.
24. Symantec Corporation, known for its antivirus software, recently split its $4.2 billion cybersecurity business away from its $2.5 billion management information business, making them two publicly traded companies.
25. eBay recently split into two companies, with PayPal being one and the eBay Marketplace segment being the other.

Instructions

Step 1	On a separate sheet of paper, number from 1 to 25. These numbers correspond to the strategies described.
Step 2	What type of strategy best describes the 25 actions cited?
Step 3	Exchange papers with a classmate, and grade each other's paper as your instructor gives the right answers.

EXERCISE 5F
How Risky Are Various Alternative Strategies?

Purpose

This exercise focuses on how risky various alternative strategies are for organizations to pursue. Different degrees of risk are based largely on varying degrees of *externality*, defined as movement away from present business into new markets and products. In general, the greater the degree of externality, the greater the probability of loss resulting from unexpected events. High-risk strategies generally are less attractive than low-risk strategies.

Instructions

Step 1	On a separate sheet of paper, number vertically from 1 to 10. Think of 1 as "most risky," 2 as "next most risky," and so forth to 10, "least risky."
Step 2	Write the following strategies beside the appropriate number to indicate how risky you believe the strategy is to pursue: horizontal integration, related diversification, liquidation, forward integration, backward integration, product development, market development, market penetration, retrenchment, and unrelated diversification.
Step 3	Grade your paper as your instructor gives you the right answers and supporting rationale. Each correct answer is worth 10 points.

EXERCISE 5G
Develop Alternative Strategies for Your University

Purpose

It is important for representatives from all areas of a college or university to identify and discuss alternative strategies that could benefit faculty, students, alumni, staff, and other constituencies. As you complete this exercise, notice the learning and understanding that occurs as people express differences of opinion. Recall that *the process of planning is more important than the document*.

Instructions

Step 1	Recall or locate the external opportunity and threat and internal strength and weakness factors that you identified as part of Exercise 1D (p. 36). If you did not do that exercise, discuss now as a class important external and internal factors facing your college or university.
Step 2	Identify and put on the screen 10 alternative strategies that you feel could benefit your college or university. Your proposed actions should allow the institution to capitalize on

particular strengths, improve on certain weaknesses, avoid external threats, or take advantage of particular external opportunities. Number the strategies as they are written on the screen from 1 to 10. State each strategy in specific terms, such as "Build two new dormitories," rather than in vague terms, such as "Do market penetration."

Step 3   On a separate sheet of paper, number from 1 to 10. Everyone in class individually should rate the strategies identified, using a 1 to 3 scale, where 1 = *I do not support implementation*, 2 = *I am neutral about implementation*, and 3 = *I strongly support implementation*. In rating the strategies, recognize that no institution has sufficient funds to do everything desired or potentially beneficial.

Step 4   Your professor will now pick up the rating sheets and have a student add up the scores for each strategy. That is, sum the ratings for each strategy, so that a prioritized list of recommended strategies is obtained. The higher the sum, the more attractive the strategy. This prioritized list reflects the collective wisdom of your class. Strategies with the highest score are deemed best.

Step 5   Discuss how this process could enable organizations to achieve understanding and commitment from individuals.

Step 6   Share your class results with a university administrator, and ask for comments regarding the process and top strategies recommended.

(Note to Professors—See the Chapter IM for an additional, excellent exercise for this chapter)

MINI-CASE ON LINKEDIN CORPORATION (LNKD)

SHOULD LINKEDIN COOPERATE WITH FACEBOOK?

Source: Alphaspirit/Fotolia.

This chapter discussed rival firms cooperating. Headquartered in Mountain View, California, LinkedIn is an online professional network designed to help members find jobs, connect with other professionals, and locate business opportunities. There are currently more than 160 million LinkedIn members in 200 countries. Launched in 2003, LinkedIn is free to join, but the company offers a paid premium membership with additional features. LinkedIn sells advertising and earns revenue through its job-listing service. Companies post job openings on LinkedIn and search for candidates on LinkedIn—particularly advantageous for students nearing graduation. Members of LinkedIn tend to be white collar and highly educated; more than 40 percent of LinkedIn visitors earn more than $100,000 per year.

LinkedIn's major rival, Facebook, recently launched "professional" rather than personal features to its business, thus trying to take market share from LinkedIn, whose primary strategy is product development. LinkedIn continually develops new and improved, visible and invisible, business analytics models to gather and assimilate data. LinkedIn has developed a big-data framework dubbed Gobblin that helps the social network collect tons of data from a variety of sources, so that it can be analyzed in its Hadoop-based data warehouses. The company also houses a variety of internal data (information pertaining to member profiles, user actions such as comments and clicking, and so on) in databases such as Espresso and event-logging systems such as Kafka. Also, LinkedIn takes in data from outside sources—for instance, Salesforce and Twitter. Advertisers increasingly are using LinkedIn to more effectively promote various products and services to businesspersons globally.

Questions

1. Examine Facebook's new professional features and access that company's potential to affect LinkedIn's business.
2. Rival firms are increasingly forming partnerships and cooperative agreements. Perhaps LinkedIn and Facebook should cooperate. Identify and describe three ways the two rival firms could perhaps cooperate in mutually beneficial ways.
3. Other than product development, identify and describe four other strategies that LinkedIn should/could pursue, from the most attractive (#1) to the least attractive (#4).

Source: Company documents and a variety of sources.

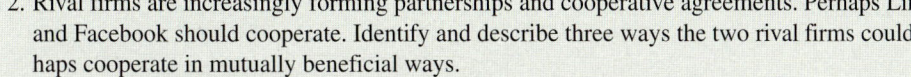

Current Readings

Cabral, Sandro, Bertrand Quelin, and Walmir Maia. "Outsourcing Failure and Reintegration: The Influence of Contractual and External Factors." *Long Range Planning* 47, no. 6 (December 2014): 365–378.

Dobni, C. Brooke, Mark Klassen, and W. Thomas Nelson. "Innovation Strategy in the US: Top Executives Offer Their Views." *Journal of Business Strategy* 36, no. 1 (2015): 3–13.

Fogarty, David, and Peter C. Bell. "Should You Outsource Analytics?" *MIT Sloan Management Review* 55, no. 2 (2014): 41–45.

MacCormack, Alan, Fiona Murray, and Erika Wagner. "Spurring Innovation through Competitions." (Cover Story). *MIT Sloan Management Review* 55, no. 1 (2013): 25–32.

Martinez-Jerez, F. Asis. "Rewriting the Playbook for Corporate Partnerships." *MIT Sloan Management Review* 55, no. 2 (2014): 63–70.

Mckinley, William, Scott Latham, and Michael Braun. "Organizational Decline and Innovation: Turnarounds and Downward Spirals." *Academy of Management Review* 39, no. 1 (2014): 88–110.

Nadkarni, Sucheta, and Jianhong Chen. "Bridging Yesterday, Today, and Tomorrow: CEO Temporal Focus, Environmental Dynamism, and Rate of New Product Introduction." *Academy of Management Journal* 57 (December 2014): 1,810–1,833.

Roloff, Julia, Michael S. Ablander, and Dilek Z. Nayir. "The Supplier Perspective: Forging Strong Partnerships with Buyers." *Journal of Business Strategy* 36, no. 1 (2015): 25–32.

Rubera, Gaia, and Gerard J. Tetlis. "Spinoffs versus Buyouts: Profitability of Alternate Routes for Commercializing Innovations." *Strategic Management Journal*, 35, no. 13 (December 2014): 2,043–2,052.

Smith, Wendy K. "Dynamic Decision Making: A Model of Senior Leaders Managing Strategic Paradoxes." *Academy of Management Journal* 57 (December 2014): 1,592–1,623.

Trahms, Cheryl A., Hermann Achidi Ndofor, and David G. Sirmon. "Organizational Decline and Turnaround: A Review and Agenda for Future Research." *Journal of Management* 39, no. 5 (2013): 1,277–1,307.

Endnotes

1. John Byrne, "Strategic Planning—It's Back," *BusinessWeek* (August 26, 1996): 46.
2. Steven C. Brandt, *Strategic Planning in Emerging Companies* (Reading, MA: Addison-Wesley, 1981). Reprinted with permission of the publisher.
3. F. Hansen and M. Smith, "Crisis in Corporate America: The Role of Strategy," *Business Horizons* (January–February 2003): 9.
4. Based on F. R. David, "How Do We Choose among Alternative Growth Strategies?" *Managerial Planning* 33, no. 4 (January–February 1985): 14–17, 22.
5. Ibid.
6. Kenneth Davidson, "Do Megamergers Make Sense?" *Journal of Business Strategy* 7, no. 3 (Winter 1987): 45.
7. David, "How Do We Choose."
8. Ibid.
9. Ibid.
10. Ibid.
11. Arthur Thompson Jr., A. J. Strickland III, and John Gamble, *Crafting and Executing Strategy: Text and Readings* (New York: McGraw-Hill/Irwin, 2005), 241.
12. Michael E. Porter, *Competitive Strategy: Techniques for Analyzing Industries and Competitors* (New York: Free Press, 1980), 53–57, 318–319.
13. David, "How Do We Choose."
14. Ibid.
15. Ibid.
16. Ibid.
17. Ibid.
18. Michael Porter, *Competitive Advantage* (New York: Free Press, 1985), 97. See also Arthur Thompson Jr., A. J. Strickland III, and John Gamble, *Crafting and Executing Strategy: Text and Readings* (New York: McGraw-Hill/Irwin, 2005), 117.
19. Arthur Thompson Jr., A. J. Strickland III, and John Gamble, *Crafting and Executing Strategy: Text and Readings* (New York: McGraw-Hill/Irwin, 2005), 125–126.
20. Porter, *Competitive Advantage,* 160–162.
21. Thompson, Strickland, and Gamble, *Crafting and Executing Strategy,* 129–130.
22. Ibid., 134.

23. Gary Hamel, Yves Doz, and C. K. Prahalad, "Collaborate with Your Competitors—and Win," *Harvard Business Review* 67, no. 1 (January–February 1989): 133.
24. Matthew Schifrin, "Partner or Perish," *Forbes* (May 21, 2001): 32.
25. Kathryn Rudie Harrigan, "Joint Ventures: Linking for a Leap Forward," *Planning Review* 14, no. 4 (July–August 1986): 10.
26. Schifrin, "Partner or Perish," p. 26.
27. David, "How Do We Choose."
28. James Hagerty, "Some Firms Opt to Bring Manufacturing Back to USA," *Wall Street Journal,* July 18, 2012, B8.
29. James Hagerty, "Offshoring Outpaces 'Reshoring,'" *Wall Street Journal*, December 15, 2014, B3.

6

Strategy Analysis and Choice

LEARNING OBJECTIVES

After studying this chapter, you should be able to do the following:

6-1. Describe the strategy analysis and choice process.

6-2. Diagram and explain the three-stage strategy-formulation analytical framework.

6-3. Diagram and explain the Strengths-Weaknesses-Opportunities-Threats (SWOT) Matrix.

6-4. Diagram and explain the Strategic Position and Action Evaluation (SPACE) Matrix.

6-5. Diagram and explain the Boston Consulting Group (BCG) Matrix.

6-6. Diagram and explain the Internal-External (IE) Matrix.

6-7. Diagram and explain the Grand Strategy Matrix.

6-8. Diagram and explain the Quantitative Strategic Planning Matrix (QSPM).

6-9. Discuss the role of organizational culture in strategic analysis and choice.

6-10. Identify and discuss important political considerations in strategy analysis and choice.

6-11. Discuss the role of a board of directors (governance) in strategic planning.

ASSURANCE OF LEARNING EXERCISES

The following exercises are found at the end of this chapter:

EXERCISE 6A   Perform a SWOT Analysis for Hershey Company

EXERCISE 6B   Develop a SPACE Matrix for Hershey

EXERCISE 6C   Develop a BCG Matrix for Hershey

EXERCISE 6D   Develop a QSPM for Hershey

EXERCISE 6E   Formulate Individual Strategies

EXERCISE 6F   Develop a BCG Matrix for Your University

EXERCISE 6G   The Role of Boards of Directors

EXERCISE 6H   Locate Companies in a Grand Strategy Matrix

Strategy analysis and choice largely involve making subjective decisions based on objective information. This chapter introduces important concepts that can help strategists generate feasible alternatives, evaluate those alternatives, and choose a specific course of action. Behavioral aspects of strategy formulation are featured, including politics, culture, ethics, and social responsibility considerations. Modern tools for formulating strategies are described, and the appropriate role of a board of directors is discussed. As showcased next, Smith & Wesson Holding Corporation is successfully vertically integrating after using a number of the strategic planning tools described in this chapter.

The Strategy Analysis and Choice Process

As indicated by Figure 6-1 with white shading, this chapter focuses on generating and evaluating alternative strategies, as well as selecting strategies to pursue. Strategy analysis and choice seek to determine alternative courses of action that could best enable the firm to achieve its mission and objectives. The firm's present strategies, objectives, vision, and mission, coupled with the external and internal audit information, provide a basis for generating and evaluating feasible alternative strategies. This systematic approach is the best way to avoid an organizational crisis. Rudin's Law states, "When a crisis forces choosing among alternatives, most people choose the worst possible one."

Unless a desperate situation confronts the firm, alternative strategies will likely represent incremental steps that move the firm from its present position to a desired future position. Alternative strategies do not come out of the wild blue yonder; they are derived from the firm's vision, mission, objectives, external audit, and internal audit; they are consistent with, or build on, past strategies that have worked well.

The Process of Generating and Selecting Strategies

Strategists never consider all feasible alternatives that could benefit the firm because there are an infinite number of possible actions and an infinite number of ways to implement those actions. Therefore, a manageable set of the most attractive alternative strategies must be developed, examined, prioritized, and selected. The advantages, disadvantages, trade-offs, costs, and benefits of these strategies should be determined. This section discusses the process that many

EXEMPLARY COMPANY SHOWCASED

Smith & Wesson Holding Corporation (SWHC)

After performing a SWOT analysis as described in this chapter, Smith & Wesson (S&W) is vertically integrating, gaining some control over both its suppliers and distributors. The company's stock price soared 17 percent in the first four weeks of 2015 while the overall stock market declined 3 percent. Headquartered in Springfield, Massachusetts, and having 1,800 full-time employees, S&W acquired Battenfeld Technologies for $130 million on December 11, 2014, adding a broad manufacturing and distribution network for expanding in the firearm accessories market. Based in Columbia, Missouri, Battenfeld is a maker of shooting, reloading, and gun-cleaning supplies under several brands sold through sporting-goods retailers, including Cabella's and Dick's Sporting Goods. Smith & Wesson expects the Battenfeld acquisition to contribute revenue of more than $55 million in 2016. Leading firearm manufacturer S&W also recently formed a partnership with General Dynamics' Ordinance and Tactical Systems division to compete for the U.S. Army's Modular Handgun System (MHS) that will replace the M9 standard Army sidearm.

The two partners are developing a Modular Handgun System based on Smith & Wesson's M&P Polymer Pistol platform. The M&P pistols are extensively used by the United States and other law-enforcement bodies throughout the world and have been in production for the last 11 years. The Army expects the first batch of the new Modular Handgun Systems to be available in 2017. Smith and Wesson's revenues for fiscal fourth quarter (Q4) of 2015 increased 6.2 percent year-over-year, partly due to the company's new Accessories division that was created after the acquisition of Battenfeld.

Source: Based on a variety of sources.

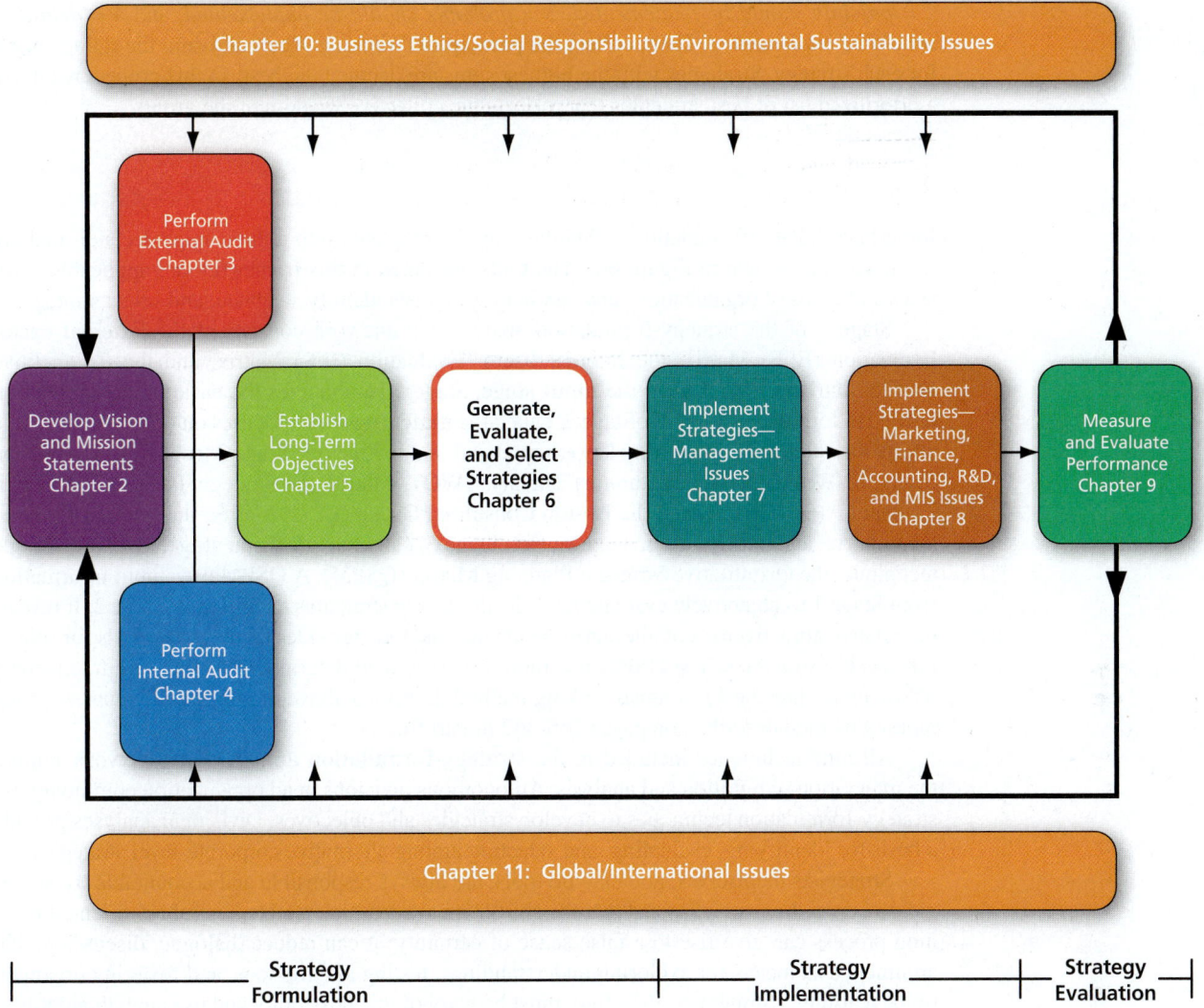

FIGURE 6-1

A Comprehensive Strategic-Management Model

Source: Fred R. David, "How Companies Define Their Mission," *Long Range Planning* 22, no. 3 (June 1988): 40. See also Anik Ratnaningsih, Nadjadji Anwar, Patdono Suwignjo, and Putu Artama Wiguna, "Balance Scorecard of David's Strategic Modeling at Industrial Business for National Construction Contractor of Indonesia," *Journal of Mathematics and Technology*, no. 4 (October 2010): 20.

firms use to determine an appropriate set of alternative strategies. Recommendations (strategies selected to pursue) come from alternative strategies formulated.

Identifying and evaluating alternative strategies should involve many of the managers and employees who previously assembled the organizational vision and mission statements, performed the external audit, and conducted the internal audit. Representatives from each department and division of the firm should be included in this process, as was the case in previous strategy-formulation activities. Involvement provides the best opportunity for managers and employees to gain an understanding of what the firm is doing and why and to become committed to helping the firm accomplish its objectives.

All participants in the strategy analysis and choice activity should have the firm's external and internal audit information available. This information, coupled with the firm's vision and mission statements, will help participants crystallize in their own minds particular strategies that they believe could benefit the firm most. Creativity should be encouraged in this thought process.

Alternative strategies proposed by participants should be considered and discussed in a meeting or series of meetings. Proposed strategies should be listed in writing. When all feasible strategies identified by participants are given and understood, the strategies should be individually ranked in order of attractiveness by each participant, with 1 = *should not be implemented*,

2 = *possibly should be implemented*, 3 = *probably should be implemented*, and 4 = *definitely should be implemented*. Then, collect the participants' ranking sheets and sum the ratings given for each strategy. Strategies with the highest sums are deemed the best, so this process results in a prioritized list of best strategies that reflects the collective wisdom of the group.

The Strategy-Formulation Analytical Framework

Important strategy-formulation techniques can be integrated into a three-stage decision-making framework, as shown in Figure 6-2. The tools presented in this framework are applicable to all sizes and types of organizations and can help strategists identify, evaluate, and select strategies.

Stage 1 of the strategy-formulation analytical framework consists of the External Factor Evaluation (EFE) Matrix, the Internal Factor Evaluation (IFE) Matrix, and the Competitive Profile Matrix (CPM). Called the **input stage**, Stage 1 summarizes the basic input information needed to formulate strategies. Stage 2, called the **matching stage**, focuses on generating feasible alternative strategies by aligning key external and internal factors. Stage 2 techniques include the Strengths-Weaknesses-Opportunities-Threats (SWOT) Matrix, the Strategic Position and Action Evaluation (SPACE) Matrix, the Boston Consulting Group (BCG) Matrix, the Internal-External (IE) Matrix, and the Grand Strategy Matrix. Stage 3, called the **decision stage**, involves a single technique, the Quantitative Strategic Planning Matrix (QSPM). A QSPM uses input information from Stage 1 to objectively evaluate feasible alternative strategies identified in Stage 2. It reveals the relative attractiveness of alternative strategies and thus provides an objective basis for selecting specific strategies. The QSPM is a more robust way to determine the relative attractiveness of strategies than the 1) summed ranking method described above, or the 2) individual vs group ranking method described on pages 366-367 in Part 6).

All nine techniques included in the **strategy-formulation analytical framework** require the integration of intuition and analysis. Autonomous divisions in an organization commonly use strategy-formulation techniques to develop strategies and objectives. Divisional analyses provide a basis for identifying, evaluating, and selecting among alternative corporate-level strategies.

Strategists themselves, not analytic tools, are always responsible and accountable for strategic decisions. Lenz emphasized that the shift from a words-oriented to a numbers-oriented planning process can give rise to a false sense of certainty; it can reduce dialogue, discussion, and argument as a means for exploring understandings, testing assumptions, and fostering organizational learning.[1] Strategists, therefore, must be wary of this possibility and use analytical tools to facilitate, rather than to diminish, communication. Without objective information and analysis, personal biases, politics, prejudices, emotions, personalities, and halo error (the tendency to put too much weight on a single factor) oftentimes play a dominant role in the strategy-formulation process, undermining effectiveness. Thus, an analytical approach is essential for achieving maximum effectiveness in strategic planning.

STAGE 1: THE INPUT STAGE				
External Factor Evaluation (EFE) Matrix		Competitive Profile Matrix (CPM)		Internal Factor Evaluation (IFE) Matrix
STAGE 2: THE MATCHING STAGE				
Strengths-Weaknesses-Opportunities-Threats (SWOT) Matrix	Strategic Position and Action Evaluation (SPACE) Matrix	Boston Consulting Group (BCG) Matrix	Internal-External (IE) Matrix	Grand Strategy Matrix
STAGE 3: THE DECISION STAGE				
Quantitative Strategic Planning Matrix (QSPM)				

FIGURE 6-2

The Strategy-Formulation Analytical Framework

The Input Stage

Procedures for developing an EFE Matrix, an IFE Matrix, and a CPM were presented in Chapters 3 and 4. Information derived from the EFE Matrix, IFE Matrix, and CPM provides basic input information for the matching and decision stage matrices described in this chapter.

The input tools require strategists to quantify subjectivity during early stages of the strategy-formulation process. Making small decisions in the input matrices regarding the relative importance of external and internal factors allows strategists to more effectively generate, prioritize, evaluate, and select among alternative strategies. Good intuitive judgment is always needed in determining appropriate weights and ratings, but keep in mind that a rating of 3, for example, is mathematically 50 percent more important than with a rating of 2, so small differences matter.

The Matching Stage

Strategy is sometimes defined as the match an organization makes between its internal resources and skills and the opportunities and risks created by its external factors.[2] The matching stage of the strategy-formulation framework consists of five techniques that can be used in any sequence: the SWOT Matrix, the SPACE Matrix, the BCG Matrix, the IE Matrix, and the Grand Strategy Matrix. These tools rely on information derived from the input stage to match external opportunities and threats with internal strengths and weaknesses. **Matching** external and internal key factors is the essential for effectively generating feasible alternative strategies. For example, a firm with excess working capital (an internal strength) could take advantage of the cell phone industry's 20 percent annual growth rate (an external opportunity) by acquiring Cellfone, Inc. This example portrays simple one-to-one matching. In most situations, external and internal relationships are more complex, and the matching requires multiple alignments for each strategy generated. Successful matching of key external and internal factors depends on those underlying key factors being *specific, actionable, and divisional* to the extent possible. The basic concept of matching is illustrated in Table 6-1.

The Decision Stage

As indicated above, participants could individually rate strategies on a 1-to-4 scale as to desirability, and then sum the ratings from all participants, so that a prioritized list of the best strategies could be achieved. However, the QSPM, described later in this chapter, offers a more robust procedure to determine the relative attractiveness of alternative strategies.

The SWOT Matrix

The **Strengths-Weaknesses-Opportunities-Threats (SWOT) Matrix** is an important matching tool that helps managers develop four types of strategies: SO (strengths-opportunities) strategies, WO (weaknesses-opportunities) strategies, ST (strengths-threats) strategies, and WT (weaknesses-threats) strategies.[3] Matching key external and internal factors is the most difficult part of developing a SWOT Matrix, as it requires good judgment—and there is no one best set of matches. Note in Table 6-1 that the first, second, third, and fourth strategies are SO, WO, ST, and WT strategies, respectively.

SO strategies use a firm's internal strengths to take advantage of external opportunities. All managers would like their organization to be in a position in which internal strengths can be used to take advantage of external trends and events. Organizations generally will pursue WO, ST,

---

TABLE 6-1 Matching Key External and Internal Factors to Formulate Alternative Strategies

Key Internal Factor	Key External Factor	Resultant Strategy
Excess working capital (an internal strength)	+ Annual growth of 20 percent in the cell phone industry (an external opportunity)	= Acquire Cellfone, Inc.
Insufficient capacity (an internal weakness)	+ Exit of two major foreign competitors from the industry (an external opportunity)	= Pursue horizontal integration by buying competitors' facilities
Strong research and development expertise (an internal strength)	+ Decreasing numbers of younger adults (an external threat)	= Develop new products for older adults
Poor employee morale (an internal weakness)	+ Rising health-care costs (an external threat)	= Develop a new wellness program

or WT strategies to get into a situation in which they can apply SO strategies. When a firm has major weaknesses, it will strive to overcome them and make them strengths. When an organization faces major threats, it will seek to avoid them to concentrate on opportunities.

WO strategies aim at improving internal weaknesses by taking advantage of external opportunities. Sometimes key external opportunities exist, but a firm has internal weaknesses that prevent it from exploiting those opportunities. For example, there may be a high demand for electronic devices to control the amount and timing of fuel injection in automobile engines (opportunity), but a certain auto parts manufacturer may lack the technology required for producing these devices (weakness). One possible WO strategy would be to acquire this technology by forming a joint venture with a firm having competency in this area. An alternative WO strategy would be to hire and train people with the required technical capabilities.

ST strategies use a firm's strengths to avoid or reduce the impact of external threats. This does not mean that a strong organization should always meet threats in the external environment head-on. An example ST strategy occurred when Texas Instruments used an excellent legal department (a strength) to collect nearly $700 million in damages and royalties from nine Japanese and Korean firms that infringed on patents for semiconductor memory chips (threat). Rival firms that copy ideas, innovations, and patented products are a threat in many industries.

WT strategies are defensive tactics directed at reducing internal weakness and avoiding external threats. An organization faced with numerous external threats and internal weaknesses may indeed be in a precarious position. In fact, such a firm may have to fight for its survival, merge, retrench, declare bankruptcy, or choose liquidation.

A schematic representation of the SWOT Matrix is provided in Figure 6-3. Note that a SWOT Matrix is composed of nine cells. As shown, there are four key factor cells, four strategy cells, and one cell that is always left blank (the upper-left cell). The four strategy cells, labeled *SO, WO, ST,* and *WT*, are developed after completing four key factor cells, labeled *S, W, O,* and *T*. The process of constructing a SWOT Matrix can be summarized in eight steps, as follows:

1. List the firm's key external opportunities.
2. List the firm's key external threats.
3. List the firm's key internal strengths.
4. List the firm's key internal weaknesses.
5. Match internal strengths with external opportunities, and record the resultant SO strategies in the appropriate cell.
6. Match internal weaknesses with external opportunities, and record the resultant WO strategies.
7. Match internal strengths with external threats, and record the resultant ST strategies.
8. Match internal weaknesses with external threats, and record the resultant WT strategies.

Some important aspects of a SWOT Matrix are evidenced in Figure 6-3. For example, note that both the internal and external factors and the SO, ST, WO, and WT strategies are stated in quantitative terms. This is important! For example, regarding the second SO number 2 and ST number 1 strategies, if the analyst just said, "Add new repair and service persons," the reader might think that 20 new repair and service persons are needed. Actually only 2 are needed. So, with strategies, as with the underlying key external and internal factors, *be specific, actionable, and divisional* to the extent possible.

It is also important to include the "S1, O2" type notation after each strategy in a SWOT Matrix. This notation reveals the rationale for each alternative strategy. Strategies do not appear out of the blue. Note in Figure 6-3 how this notation reveals the internal and external factors that were matched to formulate desirable strategies. For example, note that this retail computer store business may need to "purchase land to build new store" because a new Highway 34 will make its location less desirable. The notation (W2, O2) and (S8, T3) in Figure 6-3 exemplifies this matching process.

The purpose of SWOT analysis and each Stage 2 matching tool is to generate feasible alternative strategies, not to select or determine which strategies are best. Not all of the strategies developed in the SWOT Matrix will be selected for implementation. No firm has sufficient capital or resources to implement every strategy formulated.

The strategy-formulation guidelines provided in Chapter 5 can enhance the process of matching key external and internal factors. For example, when an organization has both the capital and human resources needed to distribute its own products (internal strength) and distributors are unreliable, costly, or incapable of meeting the firm's needs (external threat), forward integration can be an attractive ST strategy. When a firm has excess production capacity (internal weakness)

	Strengths	Weaknesses
	1. Inventory turnover up 5.8 to 6.7 2. Average customer purchase up $97 to $128 3. Employee morale is excellent 4. In-store promotions = 20 percent increase in sales 5. Newspaper advertising expenditures down 10 percent 6. Revenues from repair and service in store up 16 percent 7. In-store technical support persons have MIS degrees 8. Store's debt-to-total-assets ratio down 34 percent	1. Software revenues in store down 12 percent 2. Location of store hurt by new Hwy 34 3. Carpet and paint in store in disrepair 4. Bathroom in store needs refurbishing 5. Total store revenues down 8 percent 6. Store has no website 7. Supplier on-time-delivery up to 2.4 days 8. Customer checkout process too slow 9. Revenues per employee up 19 percent
Opportunities	**SO Strategies**	**WO Strategies**
1. Population of city growing 10 percent 2. Rival computer store opening one mile away 3. Vehicle traffic passing store up 12 percent 4. Vendors average six new products a year 5. Senior citizen use of computers up 8 percent 6. Small business growth in area up 10 percent 7. Desire for websites up 18 percent by realtors 8. Desire for websites up 12 percent by small firms	1. Add four new in-store promotions monthly (S4, O3) 2. Add two new repair and service persons (S6, O5) 3. Send flyer to all seniors over age 55 (S5, O5)	1. Purchase land to build new store (W2, O2) 2. Install new carpet, paint, and bath (W3, W4, O1) 3. Up website services by 50 percent (W6, O7, O8) 4. Launch mailout to all realtors in city (W5, O7)
Threats	**ST Strategies**	**WT Strategies**
1. Best Buy opening new store in one year nearby 2. Local university offers computer repair 3. New bypass Hwy 34 in 1 year will divert traffic 4. New mall being built nearby 5. Gas prices up 14 percent 6. Vendors raising prices 8 percent	1. Hire two more repair persons and market these new services (S6, S7, T1) 2. Purchase land to build new store (S8, T3) 3. Raise out-of-store service calls from $60 to $80 (S6, T5)	1. Hire two new cashiers (W8, T1, T4) 2. Install new carpet, paint, and bath (W3, W4, T1)

FIGURE 6-3

A SWOT Matrix for a Retail Computer Store

and its basic industry is experiencing declining annual sales and profits (external threat), related diversification can be an effective WT strategy.

Although the SWOT Matrix is widely used in strategic planning, the analysis does have some limitations.[4] First, SWOT does not show how to achieve a competitive advantage, so it must not be an end in itself. The matrix should be the starting point for a discussion on how proposed strategies could be implemented as well as cost/benefit considerations that ultimately could lead to competitive advantage. Second, SWOT is a static assessment (or snapshot) in time. A SWOT Matrix can be like studying a single frame of a motion picture where you see the lead characters and the setting but have no clue as to the plot. As circumstances, capabilities, threats, and strategies change, the dynamics of a competitive environment may not be revealed in a single matrix. Third, SWOT analysis may lead the firm to overemphasize a single internal or external factor in formulating strategies. There are interrelationships among the key internal and external factors that SWOT does not reveal that may be important in devising strategies. Fourth, there are no weights, ratings, or numbers in a SWOT analysis. Finally, the relative attractiveness of alternative strategies is not provided.

The Strategic Position and Action Evaluation (SPACE) Matrix

The **Strategic Position and Action Evaluation (SPACE) Matrix**, another important Stage 2 matching tool, is illustrated in Figure 6-4. Its four-quadrant framework indicates whether aggressive, conservative, defensive, or competitive strategies are most appropriate for a given organization. The axes of the SPACE Matrix represent two internal dimensions (**financial position [FP]** and **competitive position [CP]**) and two external dimensions (**stability position [SP]** and **industry position [IP]**). These four factors are perhaps the most important determinants of an organization's overall strategic position.[5]

It is helpful here to elaborate on the difference between the SP and IP axes. The term *SP* refers to the volatility of profits and revenues for firms in a given industry. Thus, SP volatility (stability) is based on the expected impact of changes in core external factors such as technology, economy, demographic, seasonality, and so on. The higher the frequency and magnitude of changes in a given industry, the more unstable the SP becomes. An industry can be stable or unstable on SP, yet high or low on IP. The smartphone industry, for instance, would be unstable (−6 or −7) on SP yet high growth on IP, whereas the canned food industry would be stable (−1 or −2) on SP yet low growth on IP.

Depending on the type of organization, numerous variables could make up each of the dimensions represented on the axes of the SPACE Matrix. Factors that were included in the firm's EFE

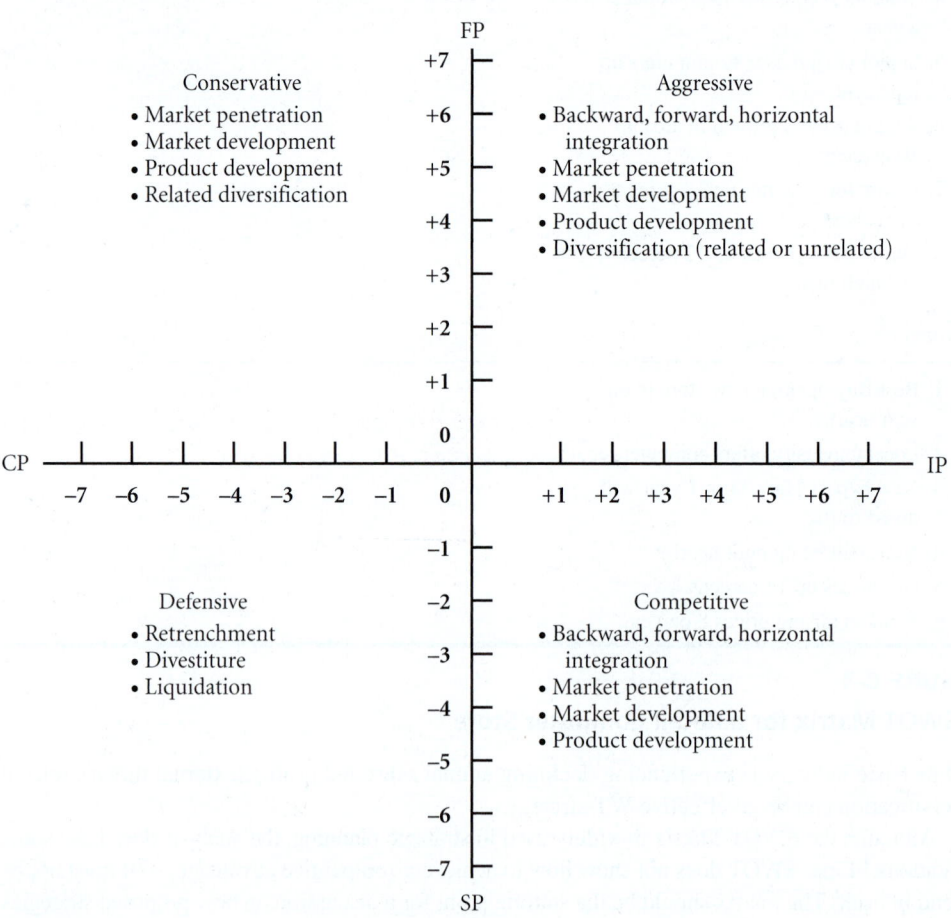

FIGURE 6-4

The SPACE Matrix

Source: Based on H. Rowe, R. Mason, and K. Dickel, *Strategic Management and Business Policy: A Methodological Approach* (Reading, MA: Addison-Wesley Publishing Co. Inc., © 1982), 155.

and IFE Matrices should be considered in developing a SPACE Matrix. Other variables commonly included are given in Table 6-2. For example, return on investment, leverage, liquidity, working capital, and cash flow are commonly considered to be determining factors of an organization's financial position (FP). Like the SWOT Matrix, the SPACE Matrix should be both tailored to the particular organization being studied and based on factual information to the extent possible.

The process of developing a SPACE Matrix can be summarized in six steps, as follows:

1. Select a set of variables to define financial position (FP), competitive position (CP), stability position (SP), and industry position (IP).
2. Assign a numerical value ranging from +1 (worst) to +7 (best) to each of the variables that make up the FP and IP dimensions. Assign a numerical value ranging from –1 (best) to –7 (worst) to each of the variables that make up the SP and CP dimensions. On the FP and CP axes, make comparisons to competitors. On the IP and SP axes, make comparisons to other industries. On the SP axis, know that a –7 denotes highly unstable industry conditions, whereas –1 denotes highly stable.
3. Compute an average score for FP, CP, IP, and SP by summing the values given to the variables of each dimension and then by dividing by the number of variables included in the respective dimension.
4. Plot the average scores for FP, IP, SP, and CP on the appropriate axis in the SPACE Matrix.
5. Add the two scores on the *x*-axis and plot the resultant point on X. Add the two scores on the *y*-axis and plot the resultant point on Y. Plot the intersection of the new (*x*, *y*) coordinate.
6. Draw a **directional vector** from the origin of the SPACE Matrix (0,0) through the new (*x*, *y*) coordinate. That vector, being located in a particular quadrant, reveals particular strategies the organization should consider.

Some example strategy profiles that can emerge from SPACE analysis are shown in Figure 6-5. The directional vector associated with each profile suggests the type of strategies to pursue: aggressive, conservative, defensive, or competitive. Specifically, when a firm's directional vector is located in the **Aggressive Quadrant** (upper right) of the SPACE Matrix, an organization is in an excellent position to use its internal strengths to (1) take advantage of external opportunities, (2) overcome internal weaknesses, and (3) avoid external threats. Therefore, market penetration, market

TABLE 6-2 **Example Factors That Make Up the SPACE Matrix Axes**

Internal Strategic Position	External Strategic Position
Financial Position (FP)	*Stability Position (SP)*
Return on investment	Technological changes
Leverage	Rate of inflation
Liquidity	Demand variability
Working capital	Price range of competing products
Cash flow	Barriers to entry into market
Inventory turnover	Competitive pressure
Earnings per share	Ease of exit from market
Price earnings ratio	Risk involved in business
Competitive Position (CP)	*Industry Position (IP)*
Market share	Growth potential
Product quality	Profit potential
Product life cycle	Financial stability
Customer loyalty	Extent leveraged
Capacity utilization	Resource utilization
Technological know-how	Ease of entry into market
Control over suppliers and distributors	Productivity, capacity utilization

Source: Based on H. Rowe, R. Mason, & K. Dickel, *Strategic Management and Business Policy: A Methodological Approach* (Reading, MA: Addison-Wesley Publishing Co. Inc., © 1982), 155–156.

development, product development, backward integration, forward integration, horizontal integration, or diversification, can be feasible, depending on the specific circumstances that face the firm.

When a particular company is known, the analyst must be much more specific in terms of recommended strategies. For example, instead of saying market penetration is a recommended

Aggressive Profiles

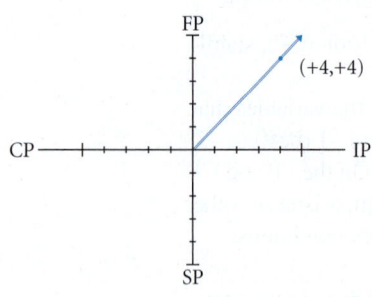

A financially strong firm that has achieved major competitive advantages in a growing and stable industry

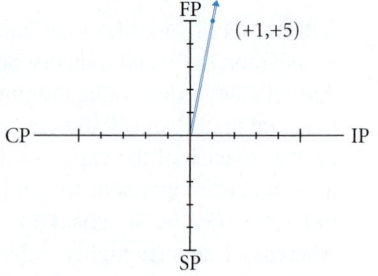

A firm whose financial strength is a dominating factor in the industry

Conservative Profiles

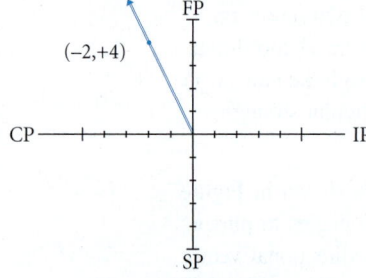

A firm that has achieved financial strength in a stable industry that is not growing; the firm has few competitive advantages

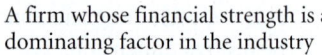

A firm that suffers from major competitive disadvantages in an industry that is technologically stable but declining in sales

Competitive Profiles

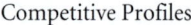

A firm with major competitive advantages in a high-growth industry

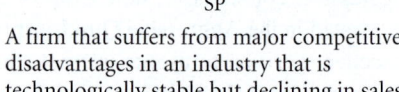

An organization that is competing fairly well in an unstable industry

Defensive Profiles

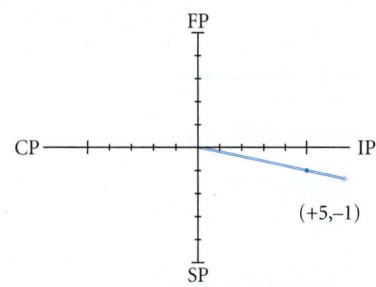
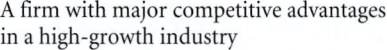

A firm that has a very weak competitive position in a negative growth, stable industry

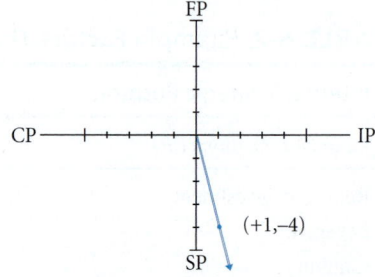

A financially troubled firm in a very unstable industry

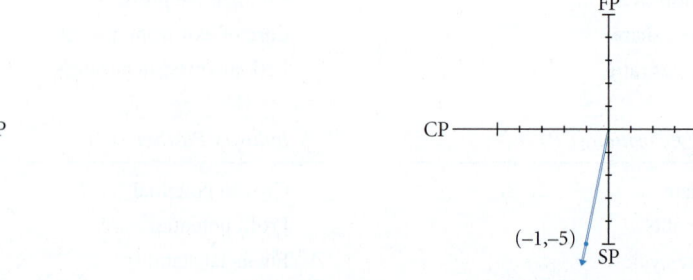
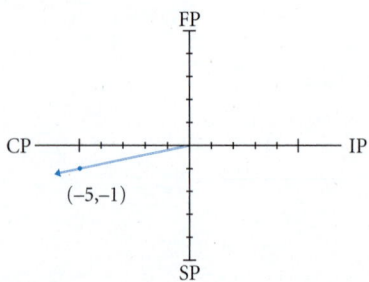

FIGURE 6-5

Example Strategy Profiles

Source: Based on H. Rowe, R. Mason, and K. Dickel, *Strategic Management and Business Policy: A Methodological Approach* (Reading, MA: Addison-Wesley Publishing Co. Inc., © 1982), 155.

strategy when your vector is located in the Conservative Quadrant, say that adding 34 new stores in India is a recommended strategy. This is an important point for students doing case analyses because whenever a particular company is known, then terms such as *market development* are too vague to use. That term could refer to adding a manufacturing plant in Thailand or Mexico or South Africa. Thus, be *specific* to the extent possible regarding implications of all the matrices presented herein this chapter. Vagueness can be disastrous in strategic management. Avoid terms such as *expand, increase, decrease,* and *grow*—be more specific than that! *Reveal how your proposed strategies could enable your company to rotate/shift its SPACE vector more toward the Aggressive Quadrant.*

The directional vector may appear in the **Conservative Quadrant** (upper left) of the SPACE Matrix, which implies staying close to the firm's basic competencies and not taking excessive risks. Conservative strategies most often include market penetration, market development, product development, and related diversification. The directional vector may be located in the **Defensive Quadrant** (lower left) of the SPACE Matrix, which suggests the firm should focus on improving internal weaknesses and avoiding external threats. Defensive strategies include retrenchment, divestiture, liquidation, and related diversification. Finally, the directional vector may be located in the **Competitive Quadrant** (lower right) of the SPACE Matrix, indicating competitive strategies. Competitive strategies include backward, forward, and horizontal integration; market penetration; market development; and product development.

Note that a SPACE Matrix has some limitations:

1. It is a snapshot in time.
2. There are more than four dimensions that firms could/should be rated on.
3. The directional vector could fall directly on an axis, or could even go nowhere if the coordinate is (0,0).
4. Implications of the exact angle of the vector within a quadrant are unclear.
5. The relative attractiveness of alternative strategies generated is unclear.
6. Key underlying internal and external factors are not explicitly considered.

A SPACE Matrix for Domino's Pizza, Inc. is provided in Figure 6-6. Note the SPACE vector for Domino's is located in the Competitive Quadrant (lower right), based primarily on

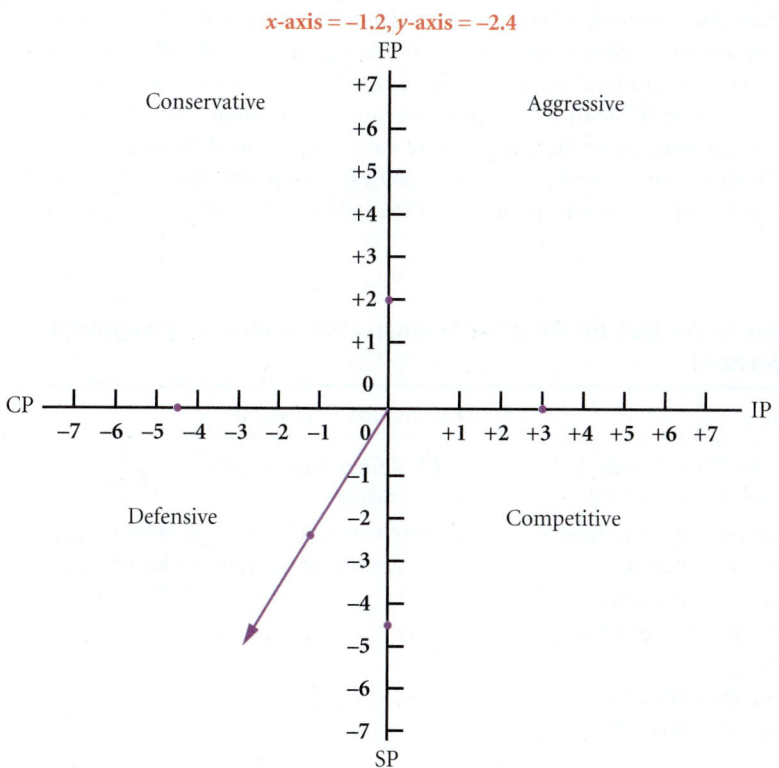

FIGURE 6-6

A SPACE Matrix for Domino's Pizza

three factors: (1) the company's $1.5 billion in long-term debt, (2) intense competition within the fast-food industry, and (3) offering products that are generally not a healthy food choice. Domino's should consider adding a line of salads to their menu to shift the SPACE vector into the Aggressive Quadrant (upper right); adding salads would likely benefit Domino's financially, thus moving the SPACE point on the vertical (y-axis) up.

In performing strategic-management case analysis, prepare the SPACE Matrix (and all matrices) based on the point in time of your analysis rather than a desired future point in time. However, in your discussion of implications, be sure to comment on what you recommend the firm should do to improve its situation. Focus more on implications of matrices than on "number crunching" in your actual oral delivery of a case analysis.

The Boston Consulting Group (BCG) Matrix

Based in Boston and having 6,200 consultants worldwide, the Boston Consulting Group (BCG) has 87 offices in 45 countries, and annually ranks in the top five of *Fortune*'s list of the "100 Best Companies to Work For." The Boston Consulting Group is a private management consulting firm that specializes in strategic planning.

Autonomous divisions (also called *segments* or *profit centers*) of an organization make up what is called a **business portfolio**. When a firm's divisions compete in different industries, a separate strategy often must be developed for each business. The **Boston Consulting Group (BCG) Matrix** and the Internal-External (IE) Matrix are designed specifically to enhance a multidivisional firm's efforts to formulate strategies. Allocating resources across divisions is arguably the most important strategic decision facing multidivisional firms. Multidivisional firms range in size from small, three-restaurant, mom-and-pop firms, to huge conglomerates such as Walt Disney Company, to universities that have various schools or colleges—and they all need to use portfolio analysis.

In a *Form 10K* or *Annual Report*, some companies do not disclose financial information by segment, in which case a BCG portfolio analysis may not be possible by persons external to the firm. However, reasons to disclose by segment financial information in a *Form 10K* more than offset the reasons not to disclose, as indicated in Table 6-3.

The BCG Matrix graphically portrays differences among divisions based on two dimensions: (1) relative market share position on the *x*-axis and (2) industry growth rate on the *y*-axis. The BCG Matrix allows a multidivisional organization to manage its portfolio of businesses by examining these two dimensions for each division relative to other divisions in the organization. **Relative market share position (RMSP)** is defined as the ratio of a division's own market share (or revenues) in a particular industry to the market share (or revenues) held by the largest rival firm in that industry. Other variables can be used in this analysis besides revenues. For example, number of stores, or number of restaurants, or, in the airline industry, number of airplanes could

TABLE 6-3 Reasons to (or Not to) Disclose Financial Information by Segment (by Division)

Reasons to Disclose	Reasons Not to Disclose
1. Transparency is a good thing in today's world of Sarbanes-Oxley Act of 2002.	1. Rival firms can obtain free competitive information.
2. Investors will better understand the firm, which can lead to greater support.	2. Performance failures can be hidden.
3. Managers and employees will better understand the firm, which should lead to greater commitment.	3. Rivalry among segments can be reduced.
4. Disclosure enhances the communication process both within the firm and with outsiders.	

TABLE 6-4 **Current Market Share Data for Cigarette and Beer Brands**

What Percentage of People Smoke What Cigarette Brands in the USA?		What Beer Brands Annually Sell the Most Million Barrels in the USA?	
Marlboro	40.2 %	Bud Light	381
Newport	12.2	Coors Light	182
Pall Mall	8.1	Budweiser	160
Camel	8.1	Miller Lite	137
Winston	2.4	Corona Extra	74
Pyramid	2.3	Samuel Adams	23
Doral	2.0	Sierra Nevada	10
USA Gold	1.9	New Belgium	8
Kool	1.8		
Other	21.0		
Total	100.0		

Source: Based on M. Esterl & P. Evans, "Reynolds, Lorillard Strike a Match," *Wall Street Journal*, July 6, 2014, B4. See also M. Esterl & T. Mickle, "Beer Conglomerates Cultivate Their Crafty Side," *Wall Street Journal*, December 29, 2014, B1.

be used for comparative purposes to determine relative market share position. In the cigarette industry, for example, Newport's relative market share position is 12.2/40.2 = 0.303, and Miller Lite's relative market share position is 137/381 = 0.359 (see Table 6-4).

Relative market share position is given on the *x*-axis of the BCG Matrix. The midpoint on the *x*-axis usually is set at 0.50, corresponding to a division that has half the market share of the leading firm in the industry. The *y*-axis represents the **industry growth rate (IGR)** in sales, measured in percentage terms—that is, the average annual increase in revenue for all firms in an industry. The growth rate percentages on the *y*-axis could range from −20 to +20 percent, with 0.0 being the midpoint. The average annual increase in revenues for several leading firms in the industry would be a good estimate of the value. Also, various sources such as the *S&P Industry Surveys* and www.finance.yahoo.com (click on Competitors) would provide this value. These numerical ranges on the *x*- and *y*-axes are often used, but other numerical values could be established as deemed appropriate for particular organizations, such as −10 to +10 percent on the *y*-axis.

Based on each division's respective (*x, y*) coordinate, each segment can be properly positioned (centered) in a BCG Matrix. Divisions located in Quadrant I (upper right) of the BCG Matrix are called "Question Marks," those located in Quadrant II (upper left) are called "Stars," those located in Quadrant III (lower left) are called "Cash Cows," and those divisions located in Quadrant IV (lower right) are called "Dogs." The following list describes the four BCG quadrants.

- *Question Marks*—Divisions in Quadrant I (upper right) have a low relative market share position, yet they compete in a high-growth industry. Generally these firms' cash needs are high and their cash generation is low. These businesses are called **question marks** because the organization must decide whether to strengthen them by pursuing an intensive strategy (market penetration, market development, or product development) or to sell them.
- *Stars*—Divisions in Quadrant II (upper left) represent the organizations' best long-run opportunities for growth and profitability, and are therefore called **stars**. Divisions with a high relative market share and a high industry growth rate should receive substantial investment to maintain or strengthen their dominant positions. Forward, backward, and horizontal integration; market penetration; market development; and product development are appropriate strategies for these divisions to consider, as indicated in Figure 6-7.
- *Cash Cows*—Divisions in Quadrant III (lower left) have a high relative market share position but compete in a low-growth industry. Called **cash cows** because they generate cash in excess of their needs, they are often milked. Many of today's cash cows were

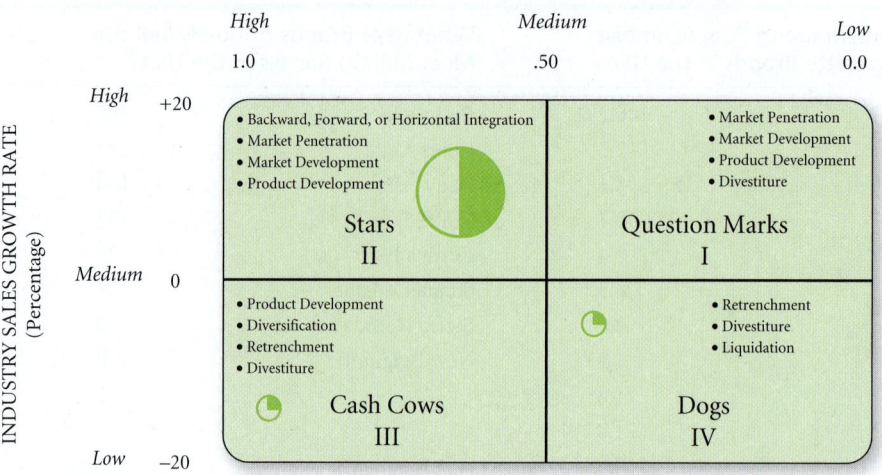

FIGURE 6-7

The BCG Matrix

Source: Based on the BCG Portfolio Matrix from the Product Portfolio Matrix, © 1970, The Boston Consulting Group.

yesterday's stars. Cash cow divisions should be managed to maintain their strong position for as long as possible. Product development or diversification may be attractive strategies for strong cash cows. However, as a cash cow division becomes weak, retrenchment or divestiture can become more appropriate.

- *Dogs*—Divisions in Quadrant IV (lower right) have a low relative market share position and compete in a slow- or no-market-growth industry; they are **dogs** in the firm's portfolio. Because of their weak internal and external position, these businesses are often liquidated, divested, or trimmed down through retrenchment. When a division first becomes a dog, retrenchment can be the best strategy to pursue because many dogs have bounced back, after strenuous asset and cost reduction, to become viable, profitable divisions.

The basic BCG Matrix appears in Figure 6-7. Each circle represents a separate division. The size of the circle corresponds to the proportion of corporate revenue generated by that business unit, and the pie slice indicates the proportion of corporate profits generated by that division.

The major benefit of the BCG Matrix is that it draws attention to the cash flow, investment characteristics, and needs of an organization's various divisions. The divisions of many firms evolve over time: dogs become question marks, question marks become stars, stars become cash cows, and cash cows become dogs in an ongoing counterclockwise motion. Less frequently, stars become question marks, question marks become dogs, dogs become cash cows, and cash cows become stars (in a clockwise motion). In some organizations, no cyclical motion is apparent. Over time, organizations should strive to achieve a portfolio of divisions that are stars.

An example of a BCG Matrix is provided in Figure 6-8, which illustrates an organization composed of five divisions with annual sales ranging from $5,000 to $60,000. Division 1 has the greatest sales volume, so the circle representing that division is the largest one in the matrix. The circle corresponding to Division 5 is the smallest because its sales volume ($5,000) is least among all the divisions. The pie slices within the circles reveal the percent of corporate profits contributed by each division. As shown, Division 1 contributes the highest profit percentage, 39 percent, as indicated by 39 percent of the area within circle 1 being shaded. Notice in the diagram that Division 1 is considered a star, Division 2 is a question mark, Division 3 is also a question mark, Division 4 is a cash cow, and Division 5 is a dog.

The BCG Matrix, like all analytical techniques, has some limitations. For example, viewing every business as a star, cash cow, dog, or question mark is an oversimplification; many businesses

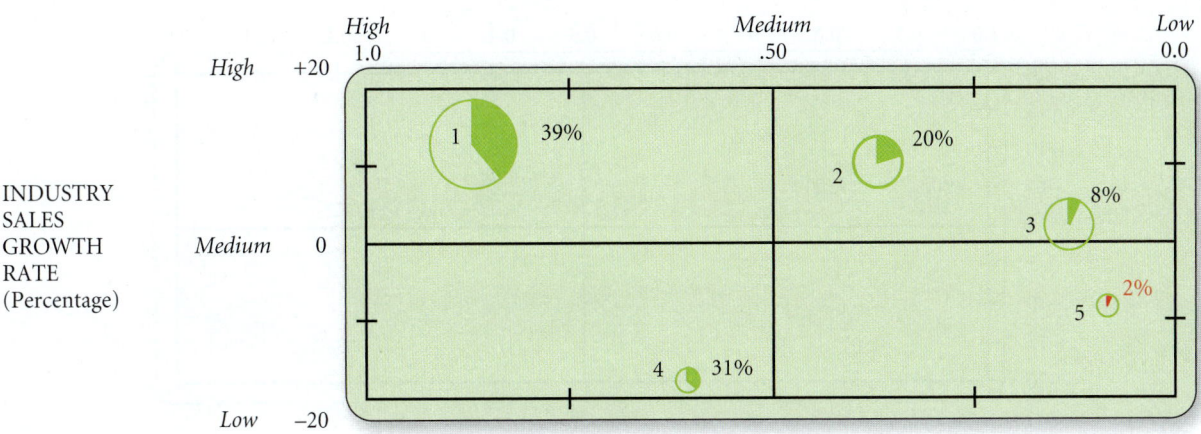

Division	Revenues	Percent Revenues	Profits	Percent Profits	Relative Market Share	Industry Growth Rate (%)
1	$60,000	37	$10,000	39	.80	+15
2	40,000	24	5,000	20	.40	+10
3	40,000	24	2,000	8	.10	+1
4	20,000	12	8,000	31	.60	−20
5	5,000	3	−500	2	.05	−10
Total	$165,000	100	$25,500	100	—	—

FIGURE 6-8

An Example BCG Matrix

fall right in the middle of the BCG Matrix and thus are not easily classified. Furthermore, the BCG Matrix does not reflect if various divisions or their industries are growing over time; that is, the matrix has no temporal qualities, but rather it is a snapshot of an organization at a given point in time. Finally, other variables besides relative market share position and industry growth rate in sales, such as size of the market and competitive advantages, are important in making strategic decisions about various divisions.

Another example BCG Matrix is provided in Figure 6-9. As you can see, Division 5 had an operating loss of $188 million.

The Internal-External (IE) Matrix

The **Internal-External (IE) Matrix** positions an organization's various divisions (segments) in a nine-cell display, illustrated in Figure 6-10. The IE Matrix is similar to the BCG Matrix in that both tools involve plotting a firm's divisions in a schematic diagram; this is why they are both called *portfolio matrices*. Also, in both the BCG and IE Matrices, the size of each circle represents the percentage of sales contribution of each division, and pie slices reveal the percentage of profit contribution of each division. But there are four important differences between the BCG Matrix and the IE Matrix, as follows:

1. The *x* and *y* axes are different.
2. The IE Matrix requires more information about the divisions than does the BCG Matrix.
3. The strategic implications of each matrix are different. For these reasons,
4. The IE Matrix has nine quadrants versus four in a BCG Matrix.

For the previous four reasons, strategists in multidivisional firms often develop both the BCG Matrix and the IE Matrix in formulating alternative strategies. A common practice is to develop a BCG Matrix and an IE Matrix for the present, and then develop projected matrices to reflect expectations of the future. This before-and-after analysis can be very effective in an oral presentation, enabling students (or strategists) to pave the way for (justify or give some rationale for) their recommendations across divisions of the firm.

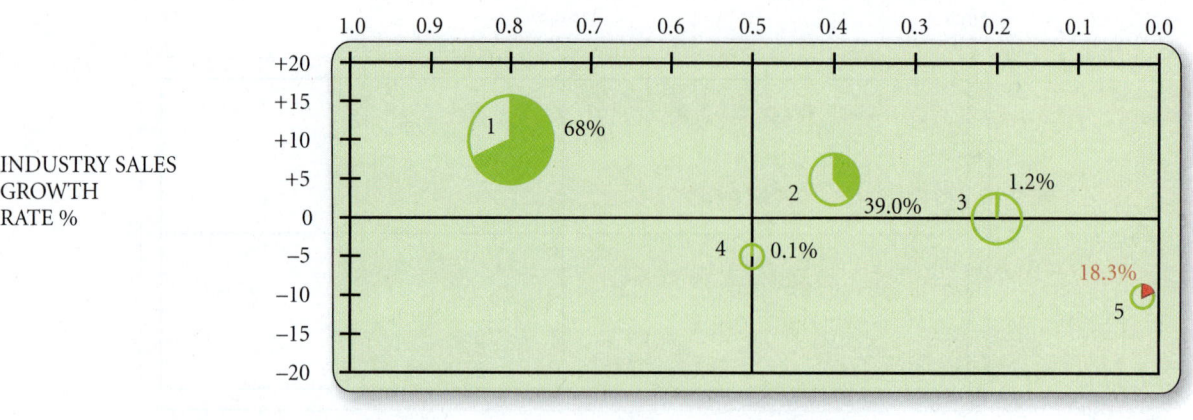

Division	$ Sales (millions)	% Sales	$ Profits (millions)	% Profits	RMSP	IG Rate %
1	$5,139	51.5	$799	68.0	0.8	10
2	2,556	25.6	400	39.0	0.4	05
3	1,749	17.5	12	1.2	0.2	00
4	493	4.9	4	0.1	0.5	−05
5	42	0.5	−188	(18.3)	.02	−10
Total	**$9,979**	**100.0**	**$1,027**	**100.0**		

FIGURE 6-9

An Example BCG Matrix

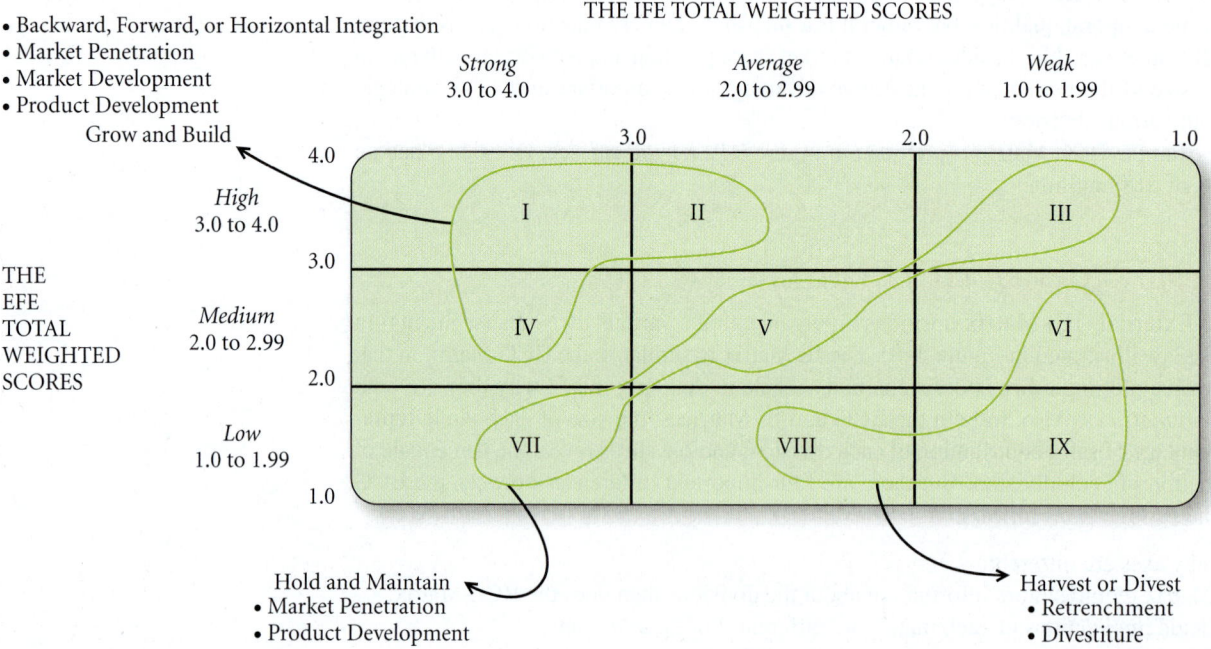

FIGURE 6-10

The Internal-External (IE) Matrix

Source: Based on: The IE Matrix was developed from the General Electric (GE) Business Screen Matrix. For a description of the GE Matrix, see Michael Allen, "Diagramming GE's Planning for What's WATT," in R. Allio and M. Pennington, eds., *Corporate Planning: Techniques and Applications* l par; New York: AMACOM, 1979.

The IE Matrix is based on two key dimensions: (1) the IFE total weighted scores on the *x*-axis and (2) the EFE total weighted scores on the *y*-axis. Recall that each division of an organization should construct an IFE Matrix and an EFE Matrix for its part of the organization, but oftentimes in performing case analysis, strategic-management students are asked to simply estimate divisional IFE and EFE scores, rather than prepare those underlying matrices for every division. Anyway, the total weighted scores derived from the divisions allow construction of the corporate-level IE Matrix. On the *x*-axis of the IE Matrix, an IFE total weighted score of 1.0 to 1.99 represents a weak internal position; a score of 2.0 to 2.99 is considered average; and a score of 3.0 to 4.0 is strong. Similarly, on the *y*-axis, an EFE total weighted score of 1.0 to 1.99 is considered low; a score of 2.0 to 2.99 is medium; and a score of 3.0 to 4.0 is high. Circles, representing divisions, are positioned in an IE Matrix based on their (*x, y*) coordinate.

Despite having nine cells (or quadrants), the IE Matrix has three major regions that have different strategy implications, as follows:

- *Region 1*—The prescription for divisions that fall into cells I, II, or IV can be described as *grow and build*. Intensive (market penetration, market development, and product development) or integrative (backward integration, forward integration, and horizontal integration) strategies can be most appropriate for these divisions. This is the best region for divisions, given their high IFE and EFE scores. Successful organizations are able to achieve a portfolio of businesses positioned in Region 1.
- *Region 2*—The prescription for divisions that fall into cells III, V, or VII can be described as *hold and maintain* strategies; market penetration and product development are two commonly employed strategies for these types of divisions.
- *Region 3*—The prescription for divisions that fall into cells VI, VIII, or IX can be described as *harvest or divest*.

An example of a four-division IE Matrix is given in Figure 6-11. As indicated by the positioning of the four circles, *grow and build* strategies are appropriate for Divisions 1, 2, and 3. But Division 4 is a candidate for *harvest or divest*. Division 2 contributes the greatest percentage of company sales and thus is represented by the largest circle. Division 1 contributes the greatest proportion of total profits; it has the largest-percentage pie slice.

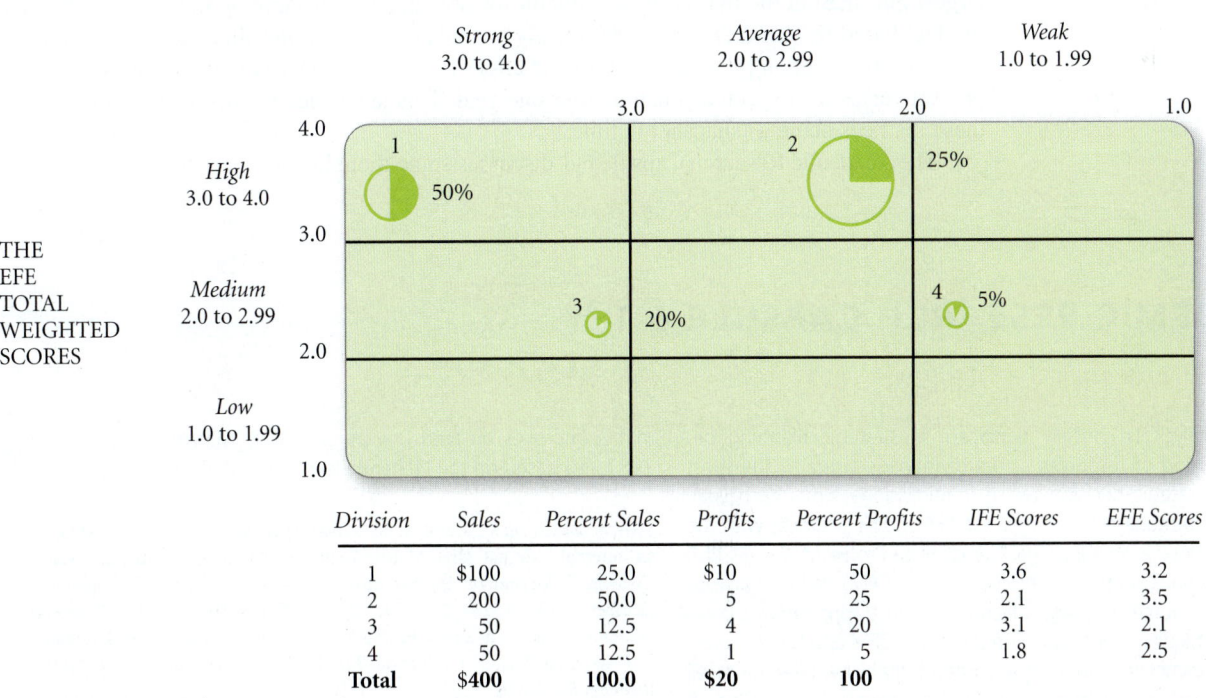

Division	Sales	Percent Sales	Profits	Percent Profits	IFE Scores	EFE Scores
1	$100	25.0	$10	50	3.6	3.2
2	200	50.0	5	25	2.1	3.5
3	50	12.5	4	20	3.1	2.1
4	50	12.5	1	5	1.8	2.5
Total	**$400**	**100.0**	**$20**	**100**		

FIGURE 6-11

An Example IE Matrix

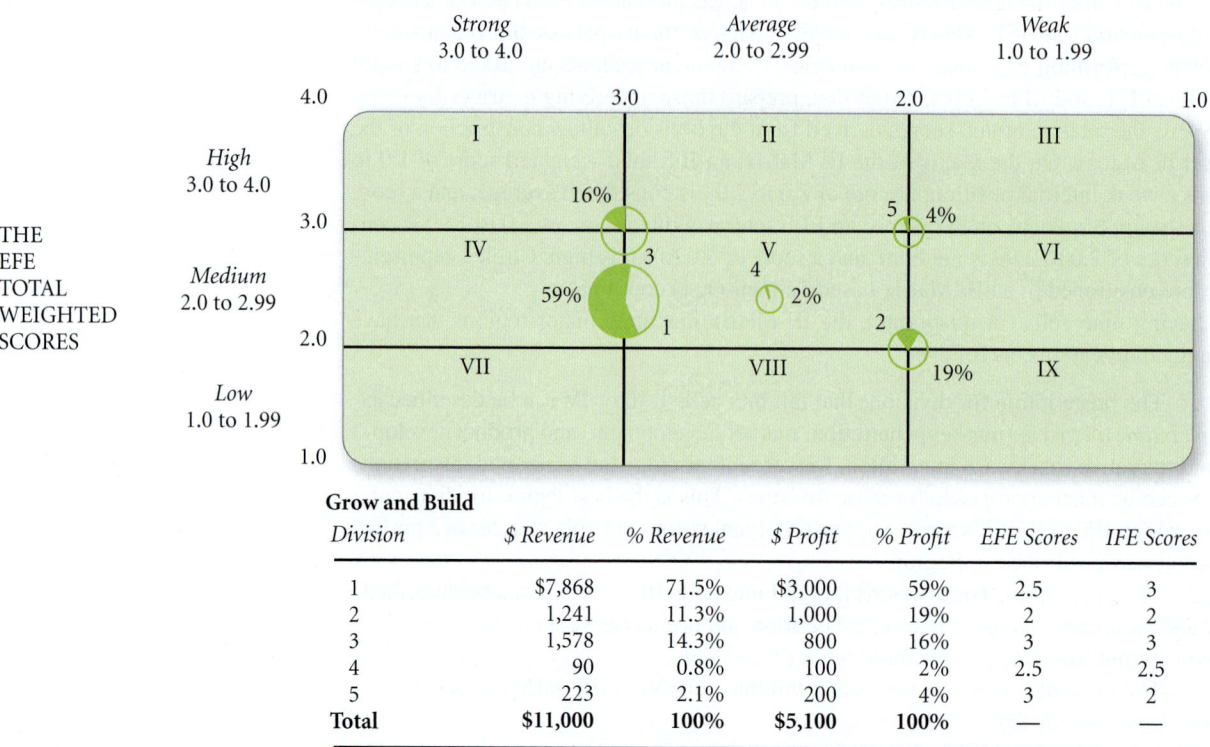

FIGURE 6-12

The IE Matrix

An example five-division IE Matrix is given in Figure 6-12. Note that Division 1 has the largest revenues (as indicated by the largest circle) and the largest profits (as indicated by the largest pie slice) in the matrix. It is common for organizations to develop both geographic and product-based IE Matrices to more effectively formulate strategies and allocate resources among divisions. Firms often prepare a "before and after" IE (or BCG) Matrix to reveal the situation at present versus the expected situation after one year. This latter idea minimizes the limitation of these matrices being a "snapshot in time."

The Academic Research Capsule 6-1 discusses some thoughts on a new IE Matrix.

ACADEMIC RESEARCH CAPSULE 6-1

A New IE Matrix

Portfolio analysis is critically significant in strategic planning because allocation of resources across divisions is arguably the most important strategic decision facing multidivisional firms each year. Two recent journal articles merged the EFE and IFE Matrices with the CPM to propose a new External Competitive Profile Matrix (ECPM) and an Internal Competitive Profile Matrix (ICPM). In their articles cited in the source, Cassidy, Glissmeyer, and Capps present a revised IE Matrix developed based on the new ECPM and ICPM scores. Cassidy, Glissmeyer, and Capps contend that the new nine-cell matrix improves on Fred David's original IE Matrix, first offered in 1987 and based on the General Electric (GE) Business Screen.

Source: Based on C. Cassidy, M. Glissmeyer, & C. Capps III, "Mapping an Internal-External (IE) Matrix Using Tradition and Extended Matrix Concepts," *Journal of Applied Business Research*, 29, no. 5 (September/October 2013): 1523–1528. See also C. Capps III and M. Glissmeyer, "Extending the Competitive Profile Matrix Using Internal Factor Evaluation and External Factor Evaluation Matrix Concepts," *Journal of Applied Business Research*, 28, no. 5 (2012): 1062

The Grand Strategy Matrix

In addition to the SWOT Matrix, SPACE Matrix, BCG Matrix, and IE Matrix, the **Grand Strategy Matrix** has become a popular tool for formulating alternative strategies. All organizations can be positioned in one of the Grand Strategy Matrix's four strategy quadrants. A firm's divisions likewise could be positioned. As illustrated in Figure 6-13, the Grand Strategy Matrix is based on two evaluative dimensions: (1) competitive position on the *x*-axis and (2) market (industry) growth on the *y*-axis. Any industry whose annual growth in sales exceeds 5 percent could be considered to have rapid growth. Appropriate strategies for an organization to consider are listed in sequential order of attractiveness in each quadrant of the Grand Strategy Matrix.

Firms located in Quadrant I of the Grand Strategy Matrix are in an excellent strategic position. For these companies, continued concentration on current markets (market penetration and market development) and products (product development) is an appropriate strategy. It is unwise for a Quadrant I firm to shift notably from its established competitive advantages. When a Quadrant I organization has excessive resources, then backward, forward, or horizontal integration may be effective strategies. When a Quadrant I firm is too heavily committed to a single product, then related diversification may reduce the risks associated with a narrow product line. Quadrant I firms can afford to take advantage of external opportunities in several areas. They can take risks aggressively when necessary.

Firms positioned in Quadrant II need to evaluate their present approach to the marketplace seriously. Although their industry is growing, they are unable to compete effectively; they need to determine why the firm's current approach is ineffective and how the company can best change to improve its competitiveness. Because Quadrant II organizations are in a rapid market growth industry, an intensive strategy (as opposed to integrative or diversification) is usually the first option that should be considered. However, if the firm is lacking a distinctive competence

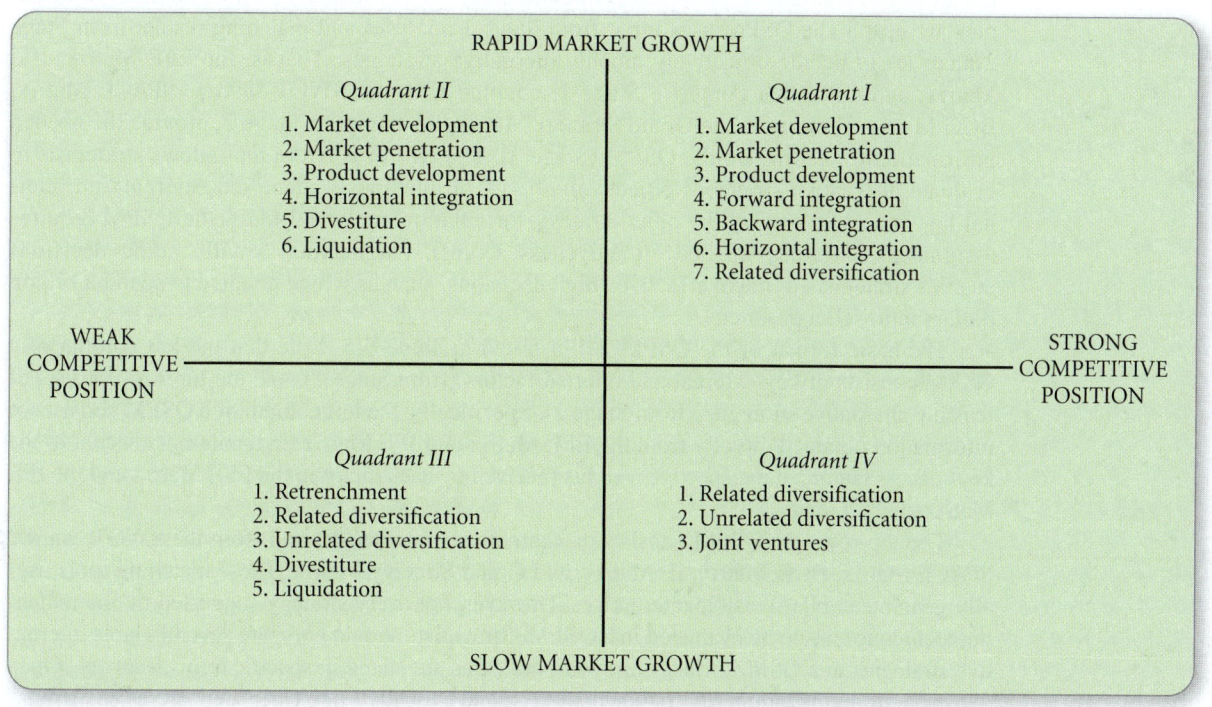

FIGURE 6-13

The Grand Strategy Matrix

Source: Based on Roland Christensen, Norman Berg, and Malcolm Salter, *Policy Formulation and Administration* (Homewood, IL: Richard D. Irwin, 1976), 16–18.

or competitive advantage, then horizontal integration is often a desirable alternative. As a last resort, divestiture or liquidation should be considered. Divestiture can provide funds needed to acquire other businesses or buy back shares of stock.

Quadrant III organizations compete in slow-growth industries and have weak competitive positions. These firms must make some drastic changes quickly to avoid further decline and possible liquidation. Extensive cost and asset reduction (retrenchment) should be pursued first. An alternative strategy is to shift resources away from the current business into different areas (diversify). If all else fails, the final options for Quadrant III businesses are divestiture or liquidation.

Finally, Quadrant IV businesses have a strong competitive position but are in a slow-growth industry. These firms have the strength to launch diversified programs into more promising growth areas: Quadrant IV businesses have characteristically high cash-flow levels and limited internal growth needs and often can pursue related or unrelated diversification successfully. Quadrant IV firms also may pursue joint ventures.

Even with the Grand Strategy Matrix, be certain that you always, whenever possible, state your alternative strategies in *specific, actionable, and divisional* terms to the extent possible. When you know the particular firm, such as in strategic-management case analysis, avoid using terms such as *divestiture,* for example. Rather, specify the exact division to be sold. Also, be sure to use the free Excel student template at www.strategyclub.com that facilitates construction of all strategic planning matrices.

The Decision Stage: The Quantitative Strategic Planning Matrix (QSPM)

Other than ranking strategies to achieve the prioritized list, there is only one analytical technique in the literature designed to determine the relative attractiveness of feasible alternative actions. The **Quantitative Strategic Planning Matrix (QSPM)**, which comprises Stage 3 of the strategy-formulation analytical framework, objectively indicates which alternative strategies are best.[6] The QSPM uses input from Stage 1 analyses and matching results from Stage 2 analyses to decide objectively among alternative strategies. That is, the EFE Matrix, IFE Matrix, and CPM that comprise Stage 1, coupled with the SWOT Matrix, SPACE Matrix, BCG Matrix, IE Matrix, and Grand Strategy Matrix that comprise Stage 2, provide the needed information for setting up the QSPM (Stage 3). The QSPM is a tool that allows strategists to evaluate alternative strategies objectively, based on previously identified external and internal key success factors. Like other strategy-formulation analytical tools, the QSPM requires assignment of ratings (called attractiveness scores), but making "small" rating decisions enables strategists to make effective "big" decisions, such as which country to spend a billion dollars in to sell a product.

The basic format of the QSPM is illustrated in Table 6-5. Note that the left column of a QSPM consists of key external and internal factors (from Stage 1), and the top row consists of feasible alternative strategies (from Stage 2). Specifically, the left column of a QSPM consists of information obtained directly from the EFE Matrix and IFE Matrix. In a column adjacent to the key success factors, the respective weights received by each factor in the EFE Matrix and the IFE Matrix are recorded.

The top row of a QSPM consists of alternative strategies derived from the SWOT Matrix, SPACE Matrix, BCG Matrix, IE Matrix, and Grand Strategy Matrix. These matching tools usually generate similar feasible alternatives. However, not every strategy suggested by the matching techniques has to be evaluated in a QSPM. Strategists should compare several viable alternative strategies in a QSPM. Make sure your strategies are stated in specific terms, such as "Open 275 new stores in Indonesia" rather than "Expand globally" or "Open new stores in Africa." Ultimately, a dollar value must be established for each recommended strategy; it would be impossible to establish a dollar value for "expand globally."

Conceptually, the QSPM determines the relative attractiveness of various strategies based on the extent that key external and internal factors are capitalized on or improved. The relative attractiveness of each strategy within a set of alternatives is computed by determining the cumulative impact of each external and internal factor. Any number of sets of alternative strategies can

TABLE 6-5 The Quantitative Strategic Planning Matrix (QSPM)

		Strategic Alternatives		
Key Factors	Weight	Strategy 1	Strategy 2	Strategy 3
Key External Factors				
Economy				
Political/Legal/Governmental				
Social/Cultural/Demographic/ Environmental				
Technological				
Competitive				
Key Internal Factors				
Management				
Marketing				
Finance/Accounting				
Production/Operations				
Research and Development				
Management Information Systems				

be included in the QSPM, and any number of strategies can make up a given set, but only strategies within a given set are evaluated relative to each other. For example, one set of strategies may include diversification, whereas another set may include issuing stock and selling a division to raise needed capital. These two sets of strategies are totally different, and the QSPM evaluates strategies only within sets. Note in Table 6-5 that three strategies are included, and they make up just one set.

A Quantitative Strategic Planning Matrix for a retail computer store is provided in Table 6-6. This example illustrates all the components of the QSPM: strategic alternatives, key factors, weights, attractiveness scores (AS), total attractiveness scores (TAS), and the sum total attractiveness score. The three new terms just introduced—(1) attractiveness scores, (2) total attractiveness scores, and (3) the sum total attractiveness score—are defined and explained as the six steps required to develop a QSPM are discussed:

Step 1: ***Make a list of the firm's key external opportunities and threats and internal strengths and weaknesses in the left column of the QSPM.*** This information should be taken directly from the EFE Matrix and IFE Matrix. (The Excel template at www.strategyclub.com can facilitate this process.)

Step 2: ***Assign weights to each key external and internal factor.*** These weights are identical to those in the EFE Matrix and IFE Matrix. The weights are presented in a straight column just to the right of the external and internal factors.

Step 3: ***Examine the Stage 2 (matching) matrices, and identify alternative strategies that the organization should consider implementing.*** Record these strategies in the top row of the QSPM. Group the strategies into mutually exclusive sets if possible.

Step 4: ***Determine the Attractiveness Scores (AS),*** defined as numerical values that indicate the relative attractiveness of each strategy considering a single external or internal factor. **Attractiveness Scores (AS)** are determined by examining each key external or internal factor, one at a time, and asking the question, "Does this factor affect the choice of strategies being made?" If the answer to this question is *yes,* then the strategies should be compared relative to that key factor. Specifically, AS should be assigned to each strategy to indicate the relative attractiveness of one strategy over others, considering the particular factor. The range for AS is 1 = *not attractive,* 2 = *somewhat attractive,* 3 = *reasonably attractive,* and 4 = *highly attractive.* By "attractive," we mean the extent

TABLE 6-6 A QSPM for a Retail Computer Store

Key Factors	Weight	STRATEGIC ALTERNATIVES			
		1 Buy New Land and Build New Larger Store		2 Fully Renovate Existing Store	
		AS	TAS	AS	TAS
Opportunities					
1. Population of city growing 10%	0.10	4	0.40	2	0.20
2. Rival computer store opening one mile away	0.10	2	0.20	4	0.40
3. Vehicle traffic passing store up 12%	0.08	1	0.08	4	0.32
4. Vendors average six new products/year	0.05	—		—	
5. Senior citizen use of computers up 8%	0.05	—		—	
6. Small business growth in area up 10%	0.05	—		—	
7. Desire for websites up 18% by realtors	0.04	—		—	
8. Desire for websites up 12% by small firms	0.03	—		—	
Threats					
1. Best Buy opening new store nearby in one year	0.15	4	0.60	3	0.45
2. Local university offers computer repair	0.08	—		—	
3. New bypass for Hwy 34 in one year will divert traffic	0.12	4	0.48	1	0.12
4. New mall being built nearby	0.08	2	0.16	4	0.32
5. Gas prices up 14%	0.04	—		—	
6. Vendors raising prices 8%	0.03	—		—	
Total	**1.00**				
Strengths					
1. Inventory turnover increased from 5.8 to 6.7	0.05	—		—	
2. Average customer purchase increased from $97 to $128	0.07	2	0.14	4	0.28
3. Employee morale is excellent	0.10	—		—	
4. In-store promotions resulted in 20% increase in sales	0.05	—		—	
5. Newspaper advertising expenditures increased 10%	0.02	—		—	
6. Revenues from repair/service segment of store up 16%	0.15	4	0.60	3	0.45
7. In-store technical support personnel have MIS college degrees	0.05	—		—	
8. Store's debt-to-total-assets ratio declined to 34%	0.03	4	0.12	2	0.06
9. Revenues per employee up 19%	0.02	—		—	
Weaknesses					
1. Revenues from software segment of store down 12%	0.10	—		—	
2. Location of store negatively impacted by new Highway 34	0.15	4	0.60	1	0.15
3. Carpet and paint in store somewhat in disrepair	0.02	1	0.02	4	0.08
4. Bathroom in store needs refurbishing	0.02	1	0.02	4	0.08
5. Revenues from businesses down 8%	0.04	3	0.12	4	0.16
6. Store has no website	0.05	—		—	
7. Supplier on-time delivery increased to 2.4 days	0.03	—		—	
8. Often customers have to wait to check out	0.05	2	0.10	4	0.20
Total	**1.00**		**3.64**		**3.27**

that one strategy, compared to others, enables the firm to either capitalize on the strength, improve on the weakness, exploit the opportunity, or avoid the threat. Work row by row in developing a QSPM. If the answer to the previous question is *no*, indicating that the respective key factor has no effect on the specific choice being made, then do not assign AS to the strategies in that set. Use a dash to indicate that the key factor does not affect the choice being made. *Note:* If you assign an AS score to one strategy, then assign an AS score(s) to the other—in other words, if one strategy receives a dash—then all others must receive a dash in a given row. Also, in the Excel template provided at www. strategyclub.com, zeros are used instead of dashes.

Step 5: *Compute the Total Attractiveness Scores.* Total Attractiveness Scores (TAS) are defined as the product of multiplying the weights (Step 2) by the AS (Step 4) in each row. The TAS indicate the relative attractiveness of each alternative strategy, considering only the impact of the adjacent external or internal critical success factor. The higher the TAS, the more attractive the strategic alternative (considering only the adjacent critical success factor).

Step 6: *Compute the Sum Total Attractiveness Score.* Add TAS in each strategy column of the QSPM. The **Sum Total Attractiveness Scores (STAS)** reveal which strategy is most attractive in each set of alternatives. Higher scores indicate more attractive strategies, considering all the relevant external and internal factors that could affect the strategic decisions. The magnitude of the difference between the STAS in a given set of strategic alternatives indicates the relative desirability of one strategy over another.

In Table 6-6, two alternative strategies—(1) buy new land and build new larger store and (2) fully renovate existing store—are being considered by a computer retail store. Note by the Sum Total Attractiveness Scores of 3.64 versus 3.27 that the analysis indicates the business should buy new land and build a new larger store. Note the use of dashes to indicate which factors do not affect the strategy choice being considered. If a particular factor affects one strategy, but not the other, it affects the choice being made, so AS should be recorded for both strategies. Never rate one strategy and not the other. Note also in Table 6-6 that there are no consecutive 1s, 2s, 3s, or 4s across any row in a QSPM; never assign the same AS score across a row. Always prepare a QSPM working row by row. Also, if you have more than one strategy in the QSPM, then let the AS scores range from 1 to "the number of strategies being evaluated." This will enable you to have a different AS score for each strategy. These are all important guidelines to follow in developing a QSPM. In actual practice, the store did purchase the new land and build a new store; the business also did some minor refurbishing until the new store was operational.

There should be a rationale for each AS score assigned. Note in the first row of Table 6-6 that the "Population of city growing 10 percent" opportunity could be capitalized on best by Strategy 1, "Buy New Land and Build New, Larger Store," so an AS score of 4 was assigned to Strategy 1. Attractiveness Scores, therefore, are not mere guesses; they should be rational, defensible, and reasonable. Mathematically, the AS score of 4 in row 1 suggests Strategy 1 is 100 percent more attractive than Strategy 2, whose AS score was 2 (since $4 - 2 = 2$ and 2 divided by $2 = 100$ percent).

Positive Features and Limitations of the QSPM

A positive feature of the QSPM is that sets of strategies can be examined sequentially or simultaneously. For example, corporate-level strategies could be evaluated first, followed by division-level strategies, and then function-level strategies. There is no limit to the number of strategies that can be evaluated or the number of sets of strategies that can be examined at once using the QSPM.

Another positive feature of the QSPM is that it requires strategists to integrate pertinent external and internal factors into the decision process. Developing a Quantitative Strategic Planning Matrix makes it less likely that key factors will be overlooked or weighted inappropriately. It draws attention to important relationships that affect strategy decisions. Although developing a QSPM requires Attractiveness Scores (AS) decisions, those small decisions enhance the probability that the final strategic decisions will be best for the organization. A QSPM can be used by small and large, for-profit and nonprofit organizations.[7]

The Quantitative Strategic Planning Matrix has two limitations. First, it always requires informed judgments regarding AS scores, but quantification is helpful throughout the strategic-planning process to minimize halo error and various biases. Attractiveness Scores are not mere guesses. Be reminded that a 4 is 33 percent more important than a 3; making good small decisions is important for making good big decisions, such as deciding among various strategies to implement. Second, a limitation of the QSPM is that it can be only as good as the prerequisite information and matching analyses on which it is based.

Cultural Aspects of Strategy Analysis and Choice

As defined in Chapter 4, organizational culture includes the set of shared values, beliefs, attitudes, customs, norms, rites, rituals, personalities, heroes, and heroines that describe a firm. Culture is the unique way an organization does business. It is the human dimension that creates solidarity and meaning, and it inspires commitment and productivity in an organization when strategy changes are made. All human beings have a basic need to make sense of the world, to feel in control, and to make meaning. When events threaten meaning, individuals react defensively. Managers and employees may even sabotage new strategies in an effort to recapture the status quo. For these reasons, it is beneficial to view strategy analysis and choice from a cultural perspective, because success often rests on the degree of support that strategies receive from a firm's culture. If a firm's strategies are supported by an organization's culture, then managers often can implement changes swiftly and easily. However, if a supportive culture does not exist and is not cultivated, then strategy changes may be ineffective or even counterproductive. A firm's culture can become antagonistic to new strategies, and the result of that antagonism may be confusion and disarray.

Strategies that require fewer cultural changes may be more attractive because extensive changes can take considerable time and effort. Whenever two firms merge, it becomes especially important to evaluate and consider culture-strategy linkages. Organizational culture can be the primary reason for difficulties a firm encounters when it attempts to shift its strategic direction, as the following statement explains:

> Not only has the "right" corporate culture become the essence and foundation of corporate excellence, but success or failure of needed corporate reforms hinges on management's sagacity and ability to change the firm's driving culture in time and in tune with required changes in strategies.[8]

The Politics of Strategy Analysis and Choice

All organizations are political. Unless managed, political maneuvering consumes valuable time, subverts organizational objectives, diverts human energy, and results in the loss of some valuable employees. Sometimes political biases and personal preferences get unduly embedded in strategy choice decisions. Internal politics affect the choice of strategies in all organizations. The hierarchy of command in an organization, combined with the career aspirations of different people and the need to allocate scarce resources, guarantees the formation of coalitions of individuals who strive to take care of themselves first and the organization second, third, or fourth. Coalitions of individuals often form around key strategy issues that face an enterprise. A major responsibility of strategists is to guide the development of coalitions, to nurture an overall team concept, and to gain the support of key individuals and groups of individuals.

In the absence of objective analyses, strategy decisions too often are based on the politics of the moment. With development of improved strategy-formation analytical tools, political factors become less important in making strategic decisions. In the absence of objectivity, political factors sometimes dictate strategies, and this is unfortunate. Managing political relationships is an integral part of building enthusiasm and esprit de corps in an organization.

A classic study of strategic management in nine large corporations examined the political tactics of successful strategists.[9] Successful strategists were found to let weakly supported ideas and proposals die through inaction and to establish additional hurdles or tests for strongly supported ideas considered unacceptable but not openly opposed. Successful strategists kept a low political profile on unacceptable proposals and strived to let most negative decisions come from subordinates or a group consensus, thereby reserving their personal vetoes for big issues and crucial moments. Successful strategists did a lot of chatting and informal questioning to stay abreast of how things were progressing and to know when to intervene. They led strategy but did not dictate it. They gave few orders, announced few decisions, depended heavily on informal questioning, and sought to probe and clarify until a consensus emerged.

Successful strategists generously and visibly rewarded key thrusts that succeeded. They assigned responsibility for major new thrusts to **champions**, the individuals most strongly identified with the idea or product and whose futures were linked to its success. They stayed alert to the symbolic impact of their own actions and statements so as not to send false signals that could stimulate movements in unwanted directions.

Successful strategists ensured that all major power bases within an organization were represented in, or had access to, top management. They interjected new faces and new views into considerations of major changes. This is important because new employees and managers generally have more enthusiasm and drive than employees who have been with the firm a long time. New employees do not see the world the same old way; nor do they act as screens against changes. Successful strategists minimized their own political exposure on highly controversial issues and in circumstances in which major opposition from key power centers was likely. In combination, these findings provide a basis for managing political relationships in an organization.

Because strategies must be effective in the marketplace and capable of gaining internal commitment, the following tactics used by politicians for centuries can aid strategists:

1. Achieving desired results is more important that imposing a particular method; therefore, consider various methods and choose, whenever possible, the one(s) that will afford the greatest commitment from employees/managers.
2. Achieving satisfactory results with a popular strategy is generally better than trying to achieve optimal results with an unpopular strategy.
3. Often, an effective way to gain commitment and achieve desired results is to shift from specific to general issues and concerns.
4. Often, an effective way to gain commitment and achieve desired results is to shift from short-term to long-term issues and concerns.
5. Middle-level managers must be genuinely involved in and supportive of strategic decisions, because successful implementation will hinge on their support.[10]

Boards of Directors: Governance Issues

A **board of directors** is a group of individuals elected by the ownership of a corporation to have oversight and guidance over management and to look out for shareholders' interests. The act of oversight and direction is referred to as **governance**. The National Association of Corporate Directors defines *governance* as "the characteristic of ensuring that long-term strategic objectives and plans are established and that the proper management structure is in place to achieve those objectives, while at the same time making sure that the structure functions to maintain the corporation's integrity, reputation, and responsibility to its various constituencies." Boards are held accountable for the entire performance of an organization. Boards of directors are increasingly sued by shareholders for mismanaging their interests. New accounting rules in the United States and Europe now enhance corporate-governance codes and require much more extensive financial disclosure among publicly held firms. The roles and duties of a board of directors can be divided into four broad categories, as indicated in Table 6-7.

Shareholders are increasingly wary of boards of directors. Most directors globally have ended their image as rubber-stamping friends of CEOs. Boards are more autonomous than

TABLE 6-7 Board of Director Duties and Responsibilities

1. CONTROL AND OVERSIGHT OVER MANAGEMENT
   a. Select the Chief Executive Officer (CEO).
   b. Sanction the CEO's team.
   c. Provide the CEO with a forum.
   d. Ensure managerial competency.
   e. Evaluate management's performance.
   f. Set management's salary levels, including fringe benefits.
   g. Guarantee managerial integrity through continuous auditing.
   h. Chart the corporate course.
   i. Devise and revise policies to be implemented by management.
2. ADHERENCE TO LEGAL PRESCRIPTIONS
   a. Keep abreast of new laws.
   b. Ensure the entire organization fulfils legal prescriptions.
   c. Pass bylaws and related resolutions.
   d. Select new directors.
   e. Approve capital budgets.
   f. Authorize borrowing, new stock issues, bonds, and so on.
3. CONSIDERATION OF STAKEHOLDERS' INTERESTS
   a. Monitor product quality.
   b. Facilitate upward progression in employee quality of work life.
   c. Review labor policies and practices.
   d. Improve the customer climate.
   e. Keep community relations at the highest level.
   f. Use influence to better governmental, professional association, and educational contacts.
   g. Maintain good public image.
4. ADVANCEMENT OF STOCKHOLDERS' RIGHTS
   a. Preserve stockholders' equity.
   b. Stimulate corporate growth so that the firm will survive and flourish.
   c. Guard against equity dilution.
   d. Ensure equitable stockholder representation.
   e. Inform stockholders through letters, reports, and meetings.
   f. Declare proper dividends.
   g. Guarantee corporate survival.

ever and continually mindful of and responsive to legal and institutional-investor scrutiny. Boards are more cognizant of auditing and compliance issues and more reluctant to approve excessive compensation and perks. Boards stay much more abreast today of public scandals that attract shareholder and media attention. Increasingly, boards of directors monitor and review executive performance carefully without favoritism to executives, representing shareholders rather than the CEO. Boards are more proactive today, whereas in years past they were often merely reactive. These are all reasons why the chair of the board of directors should not also serve as the firm's CEO. In North America, the number of new incoming CEOs that also serve as Chair of the Board has declined to about 10 percent today from about 50 percent in 2001. Academic Research Capsule 6-2 reveals "how many" board of director members are ideal.

Until recently, individuals serving on boards of directors did most of their work sitting around polished mahogany tables. However, Hewlett-Packard's directors, among many others, now log on to their own special board website twice a week and conduct business based on

ACADEMIC RESEARCH CAPSULE 6-2

How Many Board of Directors Members Are Ideal?

Recent research reveals that companies with fewer board members outperform larger boards, largely because having fewer directors facilitates deeper debates, more nimble decision making, and greater accountability. For example, there are only 8 members on Apple's board, and Apple is doing great. Recent research reveals that among companies with a market capitalization of at least $10 billion, smaller boards produced substantially higher shareholder returns between 2011 and 2014. Research also shows that 9-person boards perform much better, for example, than 14- to 15-member boards. As a result of this recent research, many companies are reducing their number of board members. Another benefit of fewer board members is that CEOs are more often reprimanded (or dismissed) if needed. Dr. David Yermack, a finance professor at New York University's business school, reports that smaller boards are generally more decisive, more cohesive, more hands-on, and have more informal meetings and fewer committees. Netflix is another example of a company with a small board,

only 7 members, who debate extensively before approving important management moves. Netflix is doing great. In contrast, Eli Lilly & Co. has 14 board members who find it "too big to encourage the kinds of discussions you want, because drilling down on different issues simply takes too long; members feel constrained even asking a second or third question." Bank of America has 15 directors—too many to be efficient. In addition, the chair of the board should rarely, if ever, be the same person as the CEO, as discussed. In summary, companies should seek to reduce their board of directors to fewer than 10 persons, whenever possible—and strategy students should examine this issue in their assigned case companies.

Source: Based on Joann Lublin, "Are Smaller Boards Better for Investors?" *Wall Street Journal*, August 27, 2014. Also based on Den Favaro, Per-Ola Karlsson, and Gary Neilson, "The $112 Billion CEO Succession Problem," *Strategy + Business*, PwC Strategy (May 4, 2015).

extensive confidential briefing information posted there by the firm's top management team. Then the board members meet face-to-face fully informed every two months to discuss the biggest issues facing the firm. New board involvement policies are aimed at curtailing lawsuits against board members.

Today, boards of directors are composed mostly of outsiders who are becoming more involved in organizations' strategic management. The trend in the United States is toward much greater board member accountability with smaller boards, now averaging 12 members rather than 18 as they did a few years ago. *BusinessWeek* recently evaluated the boards of most large U.S. companies and provided the following "principles of good governance":

1. Never have more than two of the firm's executives (current or past) on the board.
2. Never allow a firm's executives to serve on the board's audit, compensation, or nominating committee.
3. Require all board members to own a large amount of the firm's equity.
4. Require all board members to attend at least 75 percent of all meetings.
5. Require the board to meet annually to evaluate its own performance, without the CEO, COO, or top management in attendance.
6. Never allow the CEO to be chairperson of the board.
7. Never allow interlocking directorships (where a director or CEO sits on another director's board).[11]

Jeff Sonnerfeld, associate dean of the Yale School of Management, comments, "Boards of directors are now rolling up their sleeves and becoming much more closely involved with management decision making." Company CEOs and boards are required to personally certify financial statements; company loans to company executives and directors are illegal; and there is faster reporting of insider stock transactions. Just as directors place more emphasis on staying informed about an organization's health and operations, they are also taking a more active role in ensuring that publicly issued documents are accurate representations of a firm's status. Failure to accept responsibility for auditing or evaluating a firm's strategy is considered a serious breach of a director's duties. Legal suits are becoming more common against directors for fraud, omissions, inaccurate disclosures, lack of due diligence, and culpable ignorance about a firm's operations.

IMPLICATIONS FOR STRATEGISTS

This chapter has revealed six new matrices widely used by strategists to gain and sustain a firm's competitive advantages, the core purpose of strategic planning, as illustrated in Figure 6-14. Five of the six are matching tools, SWOT, SPACE, BCG, IE, and GRAND, coupled with the single decision-making tool, QSPM. Whereas some consulting firms and some textbooks advocate using only one or two matrices in strategic planning, our experience is that all six tools introduced in this chapter are uniquely valuable. Coupled with the External Factor Evaluation Matrix, the Competitive Profile Matrix, and the Internal Factor Evaluation Matrix from earlier

chapters, the nine tools together give strategists the best means for leading a firm down the narrow path to success. Rarely is the path to success wide or easy, due to parity, commoditization, imitation, duplication, substitute products, global competitors, and the willingness and ability of consumers to switch allegiances and loyalties. Employees expect strategists to formulate a superior "game plan," so their hard work implementing the strategic plan will yield job security, good compensation, and ultimately happiness for employees.

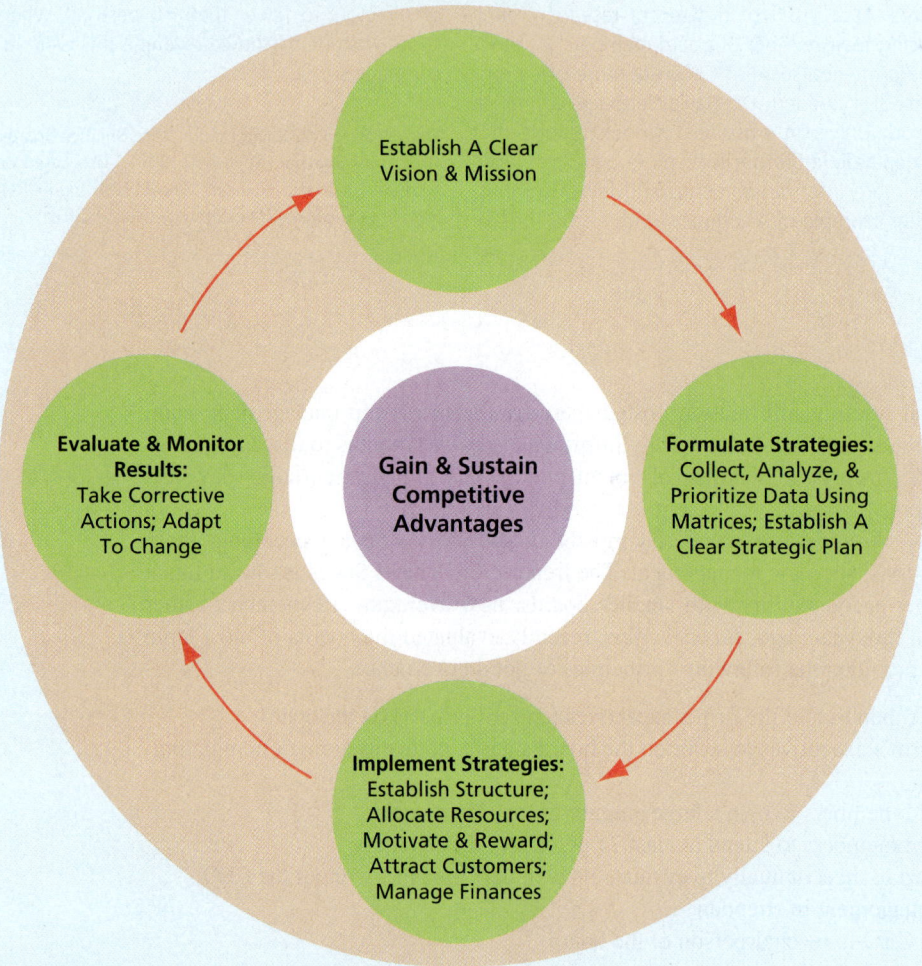

FIGURE 6-14

How to Gain and Sustain Competitive Advantages

IMPLICATIONS FOR STUDENTS

In preparing the strategy-formulation matrices presented in this chapter, it is important to avoid "wild guesses," but at the same time to become comfortable with "excellent estimates," as needed, based on research, to move forward with appropriate matrices. Sometimes students are so accustomed (due to their accounting and finance classes especially) to being counted wrong if their answer is

off at the third decimal place, that it takes a while in a strategic management class to realize that businesses make "excellent estimates based on research" all the time, because no one is sure what tomorrow will bring. So, if you can make reasonable estimates, move forward with particular matrices. For example, with the BCG Matrix, if segment information is not provided, enter only a single circle in the matrix for the overall firm, rather than two or more circles for the divisions. But be mindful that multiple circles could be included based on the number of stores, or the number of customers, rather than traditional dollar revenue numbers, so do not rush to the conclusion that portfolio information is not available.

To generate and decide on alternative strategies that will best gain and sustain competitive advantages, your SWOT, SPACE, BCG, IE, Grand, and QSPM need to be developed accurately. However, in covering those matrices in an oral presentation, focus more on the implications of those analyses than the nuts-and-bolts calculations. In other words, as you go through those matrices in a presentation, your goal is not to prove to the class that you did the calculations correctly. They expect accuracy and clarity and certainly you should

have that covered. It is the implications of each matrix that your audience will be most interested in, so use these matrices to pave the way for your recommendations with costs, which generally come just a page or two deeper into the project. A good rule of thumb is to spend at least an equal amount of time on the implications as the actual calculations of each matrix when presented. This approach will improve the delivery aspect of your presentation or paper by maintaining the high interest level of your audience. Focusing on implications rather than calculations will also encourage questions from the audience when you finish. Silence from an audience is a bad sign because silence could mean your audience was asleep, disinterested, or did not feel you did a good job. Also, utilize the free Excel student template at www.strategyclub.com as needed.

The Sarbanes-Oxley Act resulted in scores of boardroom overhauls among publicly traded companies. Board audit committees must now have at least one financial expert as a member, and meet 10 or more times per year, rather than 3 of 4 times as they did prior to the act. The act put an end to the "country club" atmosphere of most boards and shifted power from CEOs to directors. Although aimed at public companies, the act has also had a similar impact on privately owned companies. A board of directors should conduct an annual strategy audit in much the same fashion that it reviews the annual financial audit.

Recent research reveals that about 31 percent of boards of directors have served a decade or longer, and there is a movement nationwide to replace highly tenured board members with fresh, new talent.[12] Many companies have a mandatory retirement age of 75 for board members, but analysts expect that age limit to drop due to new technological prowess and the tendency to investigate new ideas.

Women make up only 19.2 percent of board members at companies in the S&P 500, but in 2014, 29 percent of new board members appointed were women, and the number of companies with no women on the board dropped to 18 from 25 the prior year.[13] Analysts say it is no longer acceptable for a company to have zero board members who are women. For example, Twitter's board was all men at the time of its initial public offering (IPO) and this fact drew widespread criticism, and makes a firm more vulnerable to discrimination lawsuits.

Chapter Summary

The essence of strategy formulation is an assessment of whether an organization is doing the right things and how it can be more effective in what it does. Every organization should be wary of becoming a prisoner of its own strategy, for even the best strategies become obsolete sooner or later. Regular reappraisal of strategy helps management avoid complacency. Objectives and strategies should be consciously developed and coordinated and should not merely evolve out of day-to-day operating decisions.

An organization with no sense of direction and no coherent strategy precipitates its own demise. When an organization does not know where it wants to go, it usually ends up some place it does not want to be. Every organization needs to consciously establish and communicate clear objectives and strategies. Any organization, whether military, product-oriented, service-oriented, governmental, or even athletic, must develop and execute good strategies to win. A good offense without a good defense, or vice versa, usually leads to defeat. Developing strategies that use strengths to capitalize on opportunities could be considered an offense, whereas strategies designed to improve on weaknesses while avoiding threats could be termed defensive. Every organization has some external opportunities and threats and internal strengths and weaknesses that can be aligned to formulate feasible alternative strategies.

Modern strategy-formulation tools and concepts described in this chapter are integrated into a practical three-stage framework. Tools such as the SWOT Matrix, SPACE Matrix, BCG Matrix, IE Matrix, and QSPM can significantly enhance the quality of strategic decisions, but they should never be used to dictate the choice of strategies. Behavioral, cultural, and political aspects of strategy generation and selection are always important to consider and manage. Because of increased legal pressure from outside groups, boards of directors are assuming a more active role in strategy analysis and choice. This is a positive trend for organizations.

MyManagementLab®

To complete the problems with the ⭐, go to EOC Discussion Questions in the MyLab.

Key Terms And Concepts

Aggressive Quadrant (p. 175)
Attractiveness Scores (AS) (p. 187)
board of directors (p. 191)
Boston Consulting Group (BCG) Matrix (p. 178)
business portfolio (p. 178)
cash cows (p. 179)
champions (p. 191)
competitive position (CP) (p. 174)
Competitive Quadrant (p. 177)
Conservative Quadrant (p. 177)
decision stage (p. 170)
Defensive Quadrant (p. 177)
directional vector (p. 175)
dogs (p. 180)
financial position (FP) (p. 174)
governance (p. 191)
Grand Strategy Matrix (p. 185)
halo error (p. 170)
industry growth rate (p. 179)
industry position (IP) (p. 174)

input stage (p. 170)
Internal-External (IE) Matrix (p. 181)
matching (p. 171)
matching stage (p. 170)
Quantitative Strategic Planning Matrix (QSPM) (p. 186)
question marks (p. 179)
relative market share position (RMSP) (p. 178)
SO strategies (p. 171)
stability position (SP) (p. 174)
stars (p. 179)
Strategic Position and Action Evaluation (SPACE) Matrix (p. 174)
strategy-formulation analytical framework (p. 170)
Strengths-Weaknesses-Opportunities-Threats (SWOT) Matrix (p. 171)
ST strategies (p. 172)
Sum Total Attractiveness Scores (STAS) (p. 189)
Total Attractiveness Scores (TAS) (p. 189)
WO strategies (p. 172)
WT strategies (p. 172)

Issues For Review and Discussion

⭐ **6-1.** A *Wall Street Journal* article (July 12, 2014, p. B3) said Apple's smartphone market share in China is 6.0 percent, behind the two leaders Samsung (17.8%) and Lenovo (11.4%). With regard to a BCG Matrix, what are the three firms' relative market share position?

⭐ **6-2.** List five limitations of a SPACE Matrix.

6-3. List the pros and cons of a firm disclosing by-segment corporate information in a *Form 10K*.

6-4. What are some key differences between the BCG and the IE portfolio matrices?

6-5. What is an ideal number of persons to have on a board of directors? Why?

6-6. Smith & Wesson is vertically integrating. What does this mean? How could S&W vertically integrate further?

6-7. Minorities and women each hold less than 15 percent of board seats of many S&P 500 companies. Why is this not good?

6-8. In developing a QSPM, if 10 strategies are being compared simultaneously, what would be a good scale for the AS scores? Why?

6-9. In developing a BCG Matrix or an IE Matrix, what would be a good surrogate for revenues for Target Corp., Burger King, Bank of America, and Spirit Airlines?

6-10. In developing a SPACE Matrix, what would you expect the SP average to be for Apple, Heinz, Verizon, Amazon, and Kroger? Diagram and explain.

6-11. Rather than developing a QSPM, what is an alternative procedure for prioritizing the relative attractiveness of alternative strategies?

6-12. Overlay a BCG Matrix with a Grand Strategy Matrix and discuss similarities in terms of format and implications. Diagram and explain.

6-13. Why should a board not consist of all men, or all women, or all whites, or all minorities?

6-14. Define halo error. How can halo error inhibit selecting the best strategies to pursue?

6-15. List six drawbacks of using only subjective information in formulating strategies.

6-16. For a firm that you know well, give an example of SO strategy, showing how an internal strength can be matched with an external opportunity to formulate a strategy.

6-17. For a firm that you know well, give an example WT strategy, showing how an internal weakness can be matched with an external threat to formulate a strategy.

6-18. List three limitations of the SWOT matrix and analysis.

6-19. For the following three firms using the given factors, calculate a reasonable stability position (SP) coordinate to go on their SPACE Matrix axis, given what you know about the nature of those industries.

Factors	Winnebago	Apple	U.S. Postal Service
Barriers to entry into market			
Seasonal nature of business			
Technological changes			
SP Score			

6-20. Would the angle or degrees of the vector in a SPACE Matrix be important in generating alternative strategies? Diagram and explain.

6-21. On the competitive position (CP) axis of a SPACE Matrix, what level of capacity utilization would

be necessary for you to give the firm a negative 1? Negative 7? Why? Diagram and explain.

6-22. If a firm has weak financial position and competes in an unstable industry, in which quadrant will the SPACE vector lie? Diagram and explain.

6-23. Describe a situation where the SPACE analysis would have no vector. In other words, describe a situation where the SPACE analysis coordinate would be (0,0). What should an analyst do in this situation?

6-24. Develop a BCG Matrix for your university. Because your college does not generate profits, what would be a good surrogate for the pie slice values? How many circles do you have and how large are they? Explain.

6-25. In a BCG Matrix, would the question mark quadrant or the cash cow quadrant be more desirable? Diagram and explain.

6-26. Would a BCG Matrix and analysis be worth performing if you do not know the profits of each segment? Why?

6-27. What major limitations of the BCG Matrix does the IE Matrix overcome? Diagram and explain.

6-28. In an IE Matrix, do you believe it is more advantageous for a division to be located in cells II or IV? Why? Diagram and explain.

6-29. Develop a 2 × 2 × 2 × 2 × 2 QSPM for an organization of your choice (i.e., two strengths, two weaknesses, two opportunities, two threats, and two strategies). Follow all the QSPM guidelines presented in the chapter.

6-30. How would application of the strategy-formulation analytical framework differ from a small to a large organization?

6-31. What types of strategies would you recommend for an organization that achieves total weighted scores of 3.6 on the IFE Matrix and 1.2 on the EFE Matrix? Diagram and explain.

6-32. Given the following information, develop a SPACE Matrix for the XYZ Corporation: FP = +2; SP = – 6; CP = –2; IP = +4. Diagram and explain.

6-33. Given the information in the following table, develop a BCG Matrix and an IE Matrix:

Divisions	1	2	3
Profits	$10	$15	$25
Sales	$100	$50	$100
Relative Market Share	0.2	0.5	0.8
Industry Growth Rate	+.20	+.10	–.10
IFE Total Weighted Scores	1.6	3.1	2.2
EFE Total Weighted Scores	2.5	1.8	3.3

6-34. How would you develop a portfolio matrix for your school of business?

6-35. What do you think is the appropriate role of a board of directors in strategic management? Why?

6-36. Discuss the limitations of various strategy-formulation analytical techniques.

6-37. Explain why cultural factors should be an important consideration in analyzing and choosing among alternative strategies.

6-38. How would for-profit and nonprofit organizations differ in their applications of the strategy-formulation analytical framework?

6-39. Develop a SPACE Matrix for a company that is weak financially and is a weak competitor. The industry for this company is pretty stable, but the industry's projected growth in revenues and profits is not good. Label all axes and quadrants.

6-40. List four limitations of a BCG Matrix. Diagram and explain.

6-41. Make up an example to show clearly and completely that you can develop an IE Matrix for a three-division company, where each division has $10, $20, and $40 in revenues and $2, $4, and $1 in profits. State other assumptions needed. Label axes and cells.

6-42. What procedures could be necessary if the SPACE vector falls right on the axis between the competitive and defensive quadrants? Diagram and explain.

6-43. In a BCG Matrix or the Grand Strategy Matrix, what would you consider to be a rapid market (or industry) growth rate?

6-44. How did the Sarbanes-Oxley Act of 2002 impact boards of directors?

6-45. Rank *BusinessWeek*'s "principles of good governance" from 1 to 14 (1 being most important and 14 least important) to reveal your assessment of these new rules.

6-46. Why is it important to work row by row instead of column by column in preparing a QSPM?

6-47. Why should one avoid putting double 4s in a row in preparing a QSPM?

6-48. Envision a QSPM with no weight column. Would that still be a useful analysis? Why or why not? What do you lose by deleting the weight column?

6-49. Prepare a BCG Matrix for a two-division firm with sales of $5 and $8 versus profits of $3 and $1, respectively. State assumptions for the RMSP and IGR axes to enable you to construct the diagram.

6-50. Consider developing a before-and-after BCG or IE Matrix to reveal the expected results of your proposed strategies. What limitation of the analysis would this procedure overcome somewhat?

6-51. If a firm has the leading market share in its industry, where on the BCG Matrix would the circle lie? Diagram and explain.

6-52. If a firm competes in an unstable industry, such as telecommunications, where on the SP axis of the SPACE Matrix would you plot the appropriate point? Diagram and explain.

6-53. Why do you think the SWOT Matrix is the most widely used of all strategy matrices?

6-54. Nestlé's market share of bottled water in the United States is 29.8%, followed by Niagara (23.3%), Coke's Dasani (5.8%), DS Waters (5.7%), Pepsi's Aquafina (4.1%), and Premium Waters (3.1%). Calculate Dasani's RMSP and Aquafina's RMSP. What are Dasani and Aquafina's relative market share position (RMSP)? (*Note:* Nestlé brands include Poland Springs, Perrier, and Pure Life. Nestlé's water home-delivery revenues are growing twice as fast as their shipments to stores/businesses.)

6-55. What are two limitations of the QSPM discussed in the chapter?

6-56. What percentage of new, incoming CEOs in North America, also serve as chair of the board of directors? In this regard, what is the trend and why?

MyManagementLab®

Go to the Assignments section of your MyLab to complete these writing exercises.

6-57. Explain the steps involved in developing a QSPM.

6-58. How are the SWOT Matrix, SPACE Matrix, BCG Matrix, IE Matrix, and Grand Strategy Matrix similar? How are they different?

ASSURANCE OF LEARNING EXERCISES

EXERCISE 6A

Perform a SWOT Analysis for Hershey Company

Purpose

The SWOT Matrix is the most widely used of all strategic planning tools and techniques because it is conceptually simple and lends itself readily to discussion among executives and managers.

The SWOT Matrix is effective in formulating strategies because it clearly matches a firm's internal strengths and weaknesses with the firm's external opportunities and threats to generate feasible strategies that should be considered. This exercise gives you practice in developing a SWOT for a large corporation.

Instructions

Step 1	Join with two other students in class. Together, develop a SWOT Matrix for Hershey Company. Follow all the SWOT guidelines provided in the chapter, including notation (for example, S4, T3) at the end of each strategy. Include two strategies in each of the four (SO, ST, WT, WO) quadrants. Be specific regarding your strategies, avoiding generic terms such as *forward integration*. Use the Cohesion Case material and your answers to Assurance of Learning Exercise 1B on page 35.
Step 2	Turn in your team-developed SWOT Matrix to your professor for a classwork grade.

EXERCISE 6B
Develop a SPACE Matrix for Hershey

Purpose

The SPACE Matrix is one of five matching strategic management tools widely used to formulate feasible strategies. Used in conjunction with the SWOT, BCG, IE, and GRAND, the SPACE can be helpful in devising a strategic plan because hard choices normally must be made between attractive strategic options. This exercise gives you practice in developing a SPACE Matrix.

Instructions

Step 1	Review Hershey's business as described in the Cohesion Case as well as the company's most recent *Form 10K*.
Step 2	Review industry and competitive information pertaining to Hershey.
Step 3	Develop a SPACE Matrix for Hershey. Write a one-page executive overview summarizing strategies that you recommend for this business segment, given your SPACE analysis. Avoid generic, vague terms such as *market development*.

EXERCISE 6C
Develop a BCG Matrix for Hershey

Purpose

Portfolio matrices are widely used by multidivisional organizations to help identify and select strategies to pursue. A BCG analysis identifies particular divisions that should receive fewer resources than others. It may identify some divisions that need to be divested. This exercise can give you practice in developing a BCG Matrix.

Instructions

Step 1	Place the following five column headings at the top of a separate sheet of paper: Divisions, Revenues, Profits, Relative Market Share Position, Industry Growth Rate. Down the far left of your page, list Hershey's two geographic divisions. Now turn back to the Cohesion Case and find information to fill in all the cells in your data table from page 24.
Step 2	Based on Hershey's year-end 2014 segment data given in the Cohesion Case (p. 29), complete a BCG Matrix for Hershey.
Step 3	Compare your BCG Matrix to other students' matrices. Discuss any major differences.

EXERCISE 6D
Develop a QSPM for Hershey

Purpose

This exercise can give you practice in developing a QSPM to determine the relative attractiveness of various strategic alternatives.

Instructions

Step 1   Join with two other students in class to develop a joint QSPM for Hershey.
Step 2   Compare your team's QSPM to those of other teams.
Step 3   Discuss any major differences.

EXERCISE 6E
Formulate Individual Strategies

Purpose

Individuals and organizations are alike in many ways. Each has competitors, and each should plan for the future. Every individual and organization faces some external opportunities and threats and has some internal strengths and weaknesses. Both individuals and organizations establish objectives and allocate resources. These and other similarities make it possible for individuals to use many strategic-management concepts and tools. This exercise is designed to demonstrate how the SWOT Matrix can be used by individuals to plan their futures. As one nears completion of a college degree and begins interviewing for jobs, planning can be particularly important.

Instructions

Construct a SWOT Matrix. Include what you consider to be your major external opportunities, your major external threats, your major strengths, and your major weaknesses. An internal weakness may be a low grade point average. An external opportunity may be that your university offers a graduate program that interests you. Match key external and internal factors by recording in the appropriate cell of the matrix alternative strategies or actions that would allow you to capitalize on your strengths, overcome your weaknesses, take advantage of your external opportunities, and minimize the impact of external threats. Be sure to use the appropriate matching notation in the strategy cells of the matrix. Because every individual (and organization) is unique, there is no one right answer to this exercise.

EXERCISE 6F
Develop a BCG Matrix for Your University

Purpose

Developing a BCG Matrix for many nonprofit organizations, including colleges and universities, is a useful exercise. Of course, there are no profits for each division or department—and in some cases no revenues. However, be creative in performing a BCG Matrix. For example, the pie slice in the circles can represent the number of majors receiving jobs on graduation, the number of faculty teaching in that area, or some other variable that you believe is important to consider. The size of the circles can represent the number of students majoring in particular departments or areas.

Instructions

Step 1   Develop a BCG Matrix for your university. Include all academic schools, departments, or colleges.
Step 2   Diagram your BCG Matrix on the blackboard.
Step 3   Discuss differences among the BCG Matrices on the board.

EXERCISE 6G
The Role of Boards of Directors

Purpose

This exercise will give you a better understanding of the role of boards of directors in formulating, implementing, and evaluating strategies.

Instructions

Identify a person in your community who serves on a board of directors. Make an appointment to interview that person, and seek answers to the following questions. Summarize your findings in a 5-minute oral report to the class.

- On what board are you a member?
- How often does the board meet?

- How long have you served on the board?
- What role does the board play in this company?
- How has the role of the board changed in recent years?
- What changes would you like to see in the role of the board?
- To what extent do you prepare for the board meeting?
- To what extent are you involved in strategic management of the firm?
- How many person serve on the board?
- Is the business owner or CEO also the chair of the board?

EXERCISE 6H
Locate Companies in a Grand Strategy Matrix

Purpose
The Grand Strategy Matrix is a popular tool for formulating alternative strategies. All organizations can be positioned in one of the Grand Strategy Matrix's four strategy quadrants. The divisions of a firm could likewise be positioned. The Grand Strategy Matrix is based on two evaluative dimensions: competitive position and market growth. Appropriate strategies for an organization to consider are listed in sequential order of attractiveness in each quadrant of the matrix. This exercise gives you experience in using a Grand Strategy Matrix.

Instructions
Using the year-end 2014 financial information provided, prepare a Grand Strategy Matrix on a separate sheet of paper. Write the respective company names in the appropriate spots on the matrix. Based on this analysis, what strategies are recommended for each company?

Company	Gross Margin/EPS	Industry	Industry & Its Revenue Growth %
Polaris Industries	0.30/6.24	Recreational Vehicles	0.00
Spirit Airlines	0.30/2.90	Major Airlines	0.25
PepsiCo	0.54/4.52	Beverages	0.14
Papa John's Int.	0.34/1.65	Restaurants	0.09

Source: Based on information at www.finance.yahoo.com on December 5, 2014, under the Competitor section of the various companies.

(Note to Professors—See the Chapter IM for an additional, excellent exercise for this chapter)

MINI-CASE ON THE STARBUCKS CORPORATION (SBUX)

WHAT STARBUCKS STRATEGIES ARE BEST?

There is only so much revenue that coffee, lattes, and pastries can bring in, so Starbucks performed SWOT and QSPM analyses and decided to spend millions on three new strategies: (1) provide beer and wine, (2) provide expanded lunch and dinner menus, and (3) provide advanced mobile ordering. Several key factors that entered into this decision were (1) there have been long wait times for customers to get served at many of its locations, (2) company business had fallen off 30 percent after morning breakfast, and (3) rivals Panera Bread, Atlanta Bread, and Dunkin Donuts were expanding their menus and growing revenue 15 percent faster than Starbucks. Starbucks' five-year strategic plan is to double its U.S. food revenue to more than $4 billion, with wine and beer alone adding $1 billion in 2015. Starbucks' new food items include truffle macaroni and cheese, Parmesan crusted chicken skewers, bacon-wrapped dates with balsamic glaze, artichoke and goat cheese flatbread, and chocolate espresso, champagne, and raspberry truffles. Starbucks' new wines include a variety of sparkling, red, white, and rose choices. Starbucks' new mobile app

Source: Racorn/123rf

and coffee truck and delivery trucks help stores anticipate demand, so customer orders are often available immediately.

Questions

1. Develop a SWOT Matrix for Starbucks that includes the three strategies and three factors cited in the case.
2. Develop a 3 × 3 QSPM for Starbucks that includes the three strategies and three factors cited in the case. Which of your three factors received the highest weight? Which of your three strategies was most attractive? Explain.

Source: Company documents and a variety of sources.

Current Readings

Barton, Dominic, and Mark Wiseman. "Where Boards Fall Short." *Harvard Business Review* (January–February 2015).

Beckman, Christine M., et al. "Relational Pluralism in De Novo Organizations: Boards of Directors as Bridges or Barriers to Diverse Alliance Portfolios?" *Academy of Management Journal* 57, no. 2 (2014): 460–483.

Donaldson, Lex, Steven D. Charlier, and Jane X. J. Qiu. "Corrigendum to Organizational Portfolio Analysis: Focusing on Risk Inside the Corporation." *Long Range Planning* 45, no. 4 (2012): 235–257.

Hacklin, F., B. Battistini, and G. Von Krogh. "Strategic Choices in Converging Industries." *MIT Sloan Management Review* 55, no. 1 (2013): 65–73.

Joseph, John, William Ocasio, and Mary-Hunter McDonnell. "The Structural Elaboration of Board Independence: Executive Power, Institutional Logics, and the Adoption of CEO-Only Board Structures in U.S. Corporate Governance." *Academy of Management Journal* 57 (December 2014): 1834–1858.

Misangyi, Vilmos F., and Abhijith G. Acharya. "Substitutes or Complements? A Configurational Examination of Corporate Governance Mechanisms." *Academy of Management Journal* 57 (December 2014): 1681–1705.

Reuer, J. J., E. Klijn, and C. S. Lioukas. "Board Involvement in International Joint Ventures." *Strategic Management Journal*, 35, no. 11 (November 2014): 1626–1644.

Tihanyi, Laszio, Scott Graffin, and Gerard George. "Rethinking Governance in Management Research." *Academy of Management Journal* 57 (December 2014): 1535–1543.

Zhu, David H., and James D Westphal. "How Directors' Prior Experience with Other Demographically Similar CEOs Affects Their Appointments onto Corporate Boards and the Consequences for CEO Compensation." *Academy of Management Journal* 57, no. 3 (2014): 791–813.

Endnotes

1. R. T. Lenz, "Managing the Evolution of the Strategic Planning Process," *Business Horizons* 30, no. 1 (January–February 1987): 37.
2. Robert Grant, "The Resource-Based Theory of Competitive Advantage: Implications for Strategy Formulation," *California Management Review* (Spring 1991): 114.
3. Heinz Weihrich, "The TOWS Matrix: A Tool for Situational Analysis," *Long Range Planning* 15, no. 2 (April 1982): 61. *Note:* Although Dr. Weihrich first modified SWOT analysis to form the TOWS matrix, the acronym SWOT is much more widely used than TOWS in practice. See also Marilyn Helms and Judy Nixon, "Exploring SWOT Analysis—Where Are We Now?" *Journal of Strategy and Management* 3, no. 3 (2010): 215–251.
4. Greg Dess, G. T. Lumpkin, and Alan Eisner, *Strategic Management: Text and Cases* (New York: McGraw-Hill/Irwin, 2006), 72.
5. Adapted from H. Rowe, R. Mason, and K. Dickel, *Strategic Management and Business Policy: A Methodological Approach* (Reading, MA: Addison-Wesley, 1982), 155–156.
6. Fred David, "The Strategic Planning Matrix—A Quantitative Approach," *Long Range Planning* 19, no. 5 (October 1986): 102; Andre Gib and Robert Margulies, "Making Competitive Intelligence Relevant to the User," *Planning Review* 19, no. 3 (May–June 1991): 21.

7. Meredith E. David, Forest R. David, and Fred R. David, "The QSPM: A New Marketing Tool," Presented at the International Academy of Business and Public Administration Disciplines (IABPAD) Meeting in Dallas, Texas, April 2015.

8. Y. Allarie and M. Firsirotu, "How to Implement Radical Strategies in Large Organizations," *Sloan Management Review* 26, no. 3 (Spring 1985): 19. Another excellent article is P. Shrivastava, "Integrating Strategy Formulation with Organizational Culture," *Journal of Business Stratgegy* 5, no. 3 (Winter 1985): 103–111.

9. James Brian Quinn, *Strategies for Changes: Logical Incrementalism* (Homewood, IL: Irwin, 1980), 128–145.

These political tactics are listed in A. Thompson and A. Strickland, *Strategic Management: Concepts and Cases* (Plano, TX: Business Publications, 1984), 261.

10. William Guth and Ian Macmillan, "Strategy Implementation versus Middle Management Self-Interest," *Strategic Management Journal* 7, no. 4 (July–August 1986): 321.

11. Louis Lavelle, "The Best and Worst Boards," *BusinessWeek,* October 7, 2002, 104–110.

12. Joann Lublin, "Boards' Longtimers Face Pressure to Move On," *Wall Street Journal*, December 24, 2014, B6.

13. Rachel Feintzeig, "Changes Ahead for Women on Boards," *Wall Street Journal*, January 13, 2015, B1.

PART 3

STRATEGY IMPLEMENTATION

7

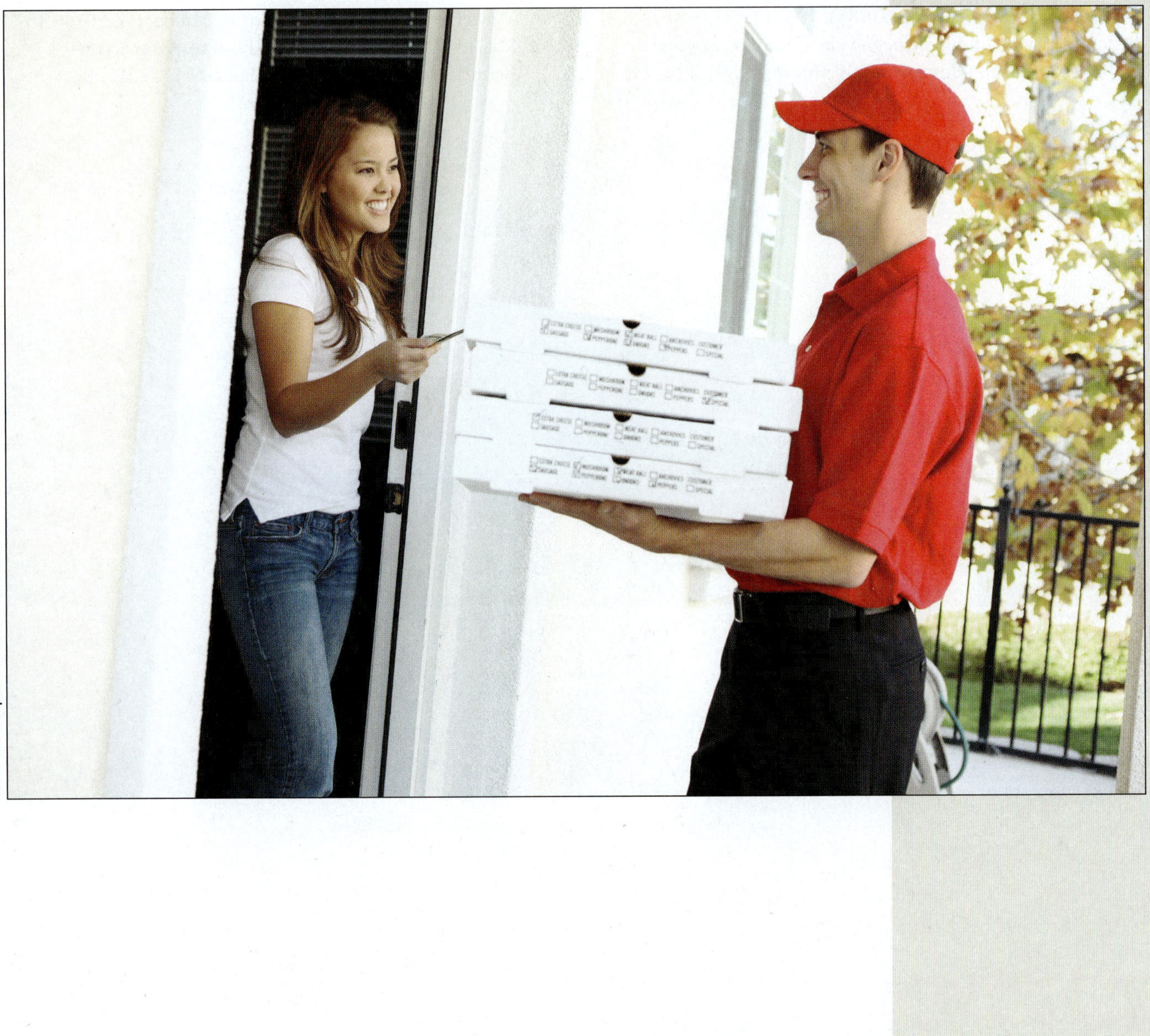

Source: Stephen Coburn/Fotolia

Implementing Strategies: Management, Operations, and Human Resource Issues

LEARNING OBJECTIVES

After studying this chapter, you should be able to do the following:

7-1. Describe the transition from formulating to implementing strategies

7-2. Discuss five reasons why annual objectives are essential for effective strategy implementation.

7-3. Identify and discuss six reasons why policies are essential for effective strategy implementation.

7-4. Explain the role of resource allocation and managing conflict in strategy implementation.

7-5. Discuss the need to match a firm's structure with its strategy.

7-6. Identify, diagram, and discuss seven different types of organizational structure.

7-7. Identify and discuss fifteen dos and don'ts in constructing organizational charts.

7-8. Discuss four strategic production/operations issues vital for successful strategy implementation.

7-9. Discuss seven strategic human resource issues vital for successful strategy implementation.

ASSURANCE OF LEARNING EXERCISES

The following exercises are found at the end of this chapter:

EXERCISE 7A Critique Corporate Organizational Charts

EXERCISE 7B Draw an Organizational Chart for Hershey Company Using a Free, Online Template

EXERCISE 7C Do Organizations Really Establish Objectives?

EXERCISE 7D Understanding Your University's Culture

The strategic-management process does not end with deciding what strategy or strategies to pursue. There must be a translation of strategic thought into action. This translation is much easier if managers and employees of the firm understand the business, feel a part of the company, and through involvement in strategy-formulation activities have become committed to helping the organization succeed. Without understanding and commitment, strategy-implementation efforts face major problems. Vince Lombardi commented, "The best game plan in the world never blocked or tackled anybody."

Implementing strategy affects an organization from top to bottom, including all the functional and divisional areas of a business. This chapter focuses on management, operations, and human resource issues most critical for successful strategy implementation, whereas Chapter 8 focuses on marketing, finance/accounting, R&D, and management information systems (MIS) strategic issues. As showcased next, Papa John's is a company with exemplary strategic management, especially by motivating its franchisees to own and operate excellent restaurants.

Even the most technically perfect strategic plan will serve little purpose if it is not implemented. Many organizations tend to spend an inordinate amount of time, money, and effort on developing the strategic plan, treating the means and circumstances under which it will be implemented as afterthoughts! Change comes through implementation and evaluation, not through the plan. A technically imperfect plan that is implemented well will achieve more than the perfect plan that never gets off the paper on which it is typed.[1]

Transitioning from Formulating to Implementing Strategies

The strategy-implementation stage of strategic management is revealed in Figure 7-1, as illustrated with white shading. Successful strategy formulation does not guarantee successful strategy implementation. It is always more difficult to do something (strategy implementation) than to say you are going to do it (strategy formulation)! Although inextricably linked, strategy implementation is fundamentally different from strategy formulation.

EXEMPLARY COMPANY SHOWCASED

Papa John's International, Inc. (PZZA)

The world's third-largest pizza delivery company and headquartered in Louisville, Kentucky, Papa John's is a pizza delivery and dine-in chain of restaurants. For 13 of the past 15 years, consumers have rated Papa John's No. 1 in customer satisfaction among all national pizza chains in the American Customer Satisfaction Index (ACSI). That distinction reveals highly motivated franchisees, managers, and employees at the company—a tribute to excellent management policies, incentives, and compensation. Papa John's is one of the most financially accessible for franchise owners; the total investment is between $129,910 and $644,210, depending on where the franchise is located and the size. Franchisees pay royalties of 5 percent, agree to a 10-year term, and must also have a net worth of at least $150,000, with at least $50,000 available in cash.

Papa John's operates 4,500 restaurants, 750 company-owned and 3,750 franchised, in 50 states in the United States and in 35 countries. In 2015, Papa John's added hickory-smoked bacon to its Cheeseburger Pizza, and began offering a new Double Chocolate Chip Brownie; the company trails Pizza Hut and Domino's in sales in the United States. Two of Papa John's seven members of the Board of Director are female, Olivia Kirtley and Laurette Koellner.

Along with Avan Projects and Global Franchise Architects (GFA), Papa John's recently acquired Pizza Corner stores in southern India.

Papa John's is converting the existing Pizza Corner stores to Papa John's branded restaurants, as part of Papa John's commitment to expand its presence in India, specifically in Bangalore, Chennai, and Hyderabad. Pizza Corner, part of the GFA brands, is the third largest pizza chain in southern India, with special focus on the city of Chennai. Prior to the acquisition, Papa John's operated 15 restaurants across India through its Master Franchisee for the region, Om Pizza and Eats. Through this merger, Papa John's added 40 restaurants in India with conversions continuing monthly.

Papa John's is spending $100 million annually to eliminate 14 artificial ingredients, preservatives, and additives from its menu, including all artificial colors and corn syrup. All 14 will be totally banished by the end of 2016 from Papa John's. Monosodium glutamate (MSG) and trans fats were removed from the company's menu in 2015.

Source: Based on a variety of sources.

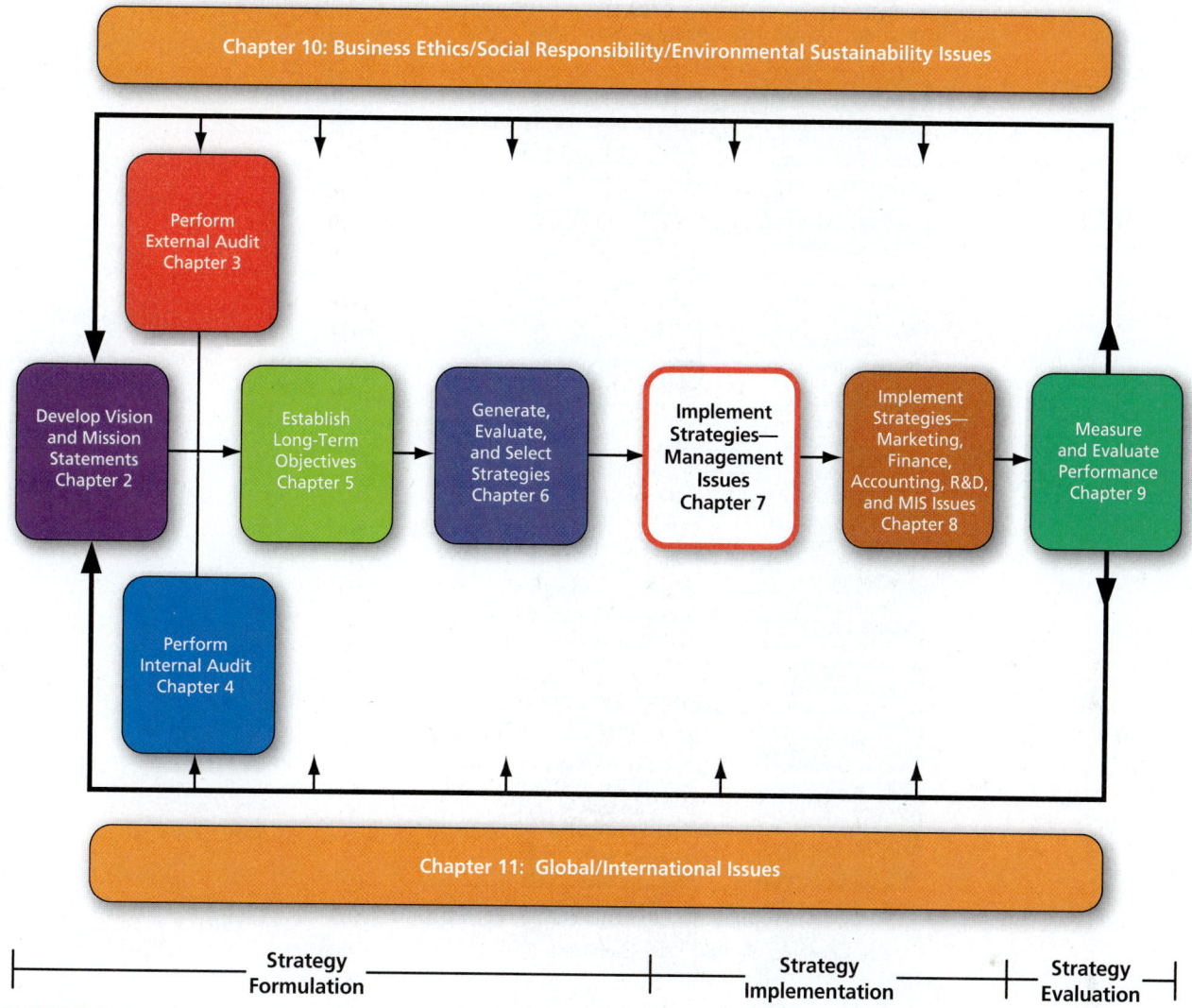

FIGURE 7-1

Comprehensive Strategic-Management Model

Source: Fred R. David, "How Companies Define Their Mission," *Long Range Planning* 22, no. 3 (June 1988): 40. See also Anik Ratnaningsih, Nadjadji Anwar, Patdono Suwignjo, and Putu Artama Wiguna, "Balance Scorecard of David's Strategic Modeling at Industrial Business for National Construction Contractor of Indonesia," *Journal of Mathematics and Technology*, no. 4, (October 2010): 20.

In all but the smallest organizations, the transition from strategy formulation to strategy implementation requires a shift in responsibility from strategists to divisional and functional managers. Implementation problems can arise because of this shift in responsibility, especially if strategy-formulation decisions come as a surprise to middle- and lower-level managers. Managers and employees are motivated more by perceived self-interests than by organizational interests, unless the two coincide. This is a primary reason why divisional and functional managers should be involved as much as possible in both strategy-formulation and strategy-implementation activities. Strategy formulation and implementation can be contrasted in the ways illustrated in Figure 7-2.

Strategy-formulation concepts and tools do not differ greatly for small, large, for-profit, or nonprofit organizations. However, strategy implementation varies substantially among different types and sizes of organizations. Implementing strategies requires such actions as altering sales territories, adding new departments, closing facilities, hiring new employees, changing an organization's pricing strategy, developing financial budgets, developing new employee benefits, establishing cost-control procedures, changing advertising strategies, building new facilities, training new employees, transferring managers among divisions, and building a better management information system. These types of activities obviously differ greatly among manufacturing, service, and governmental organizations.

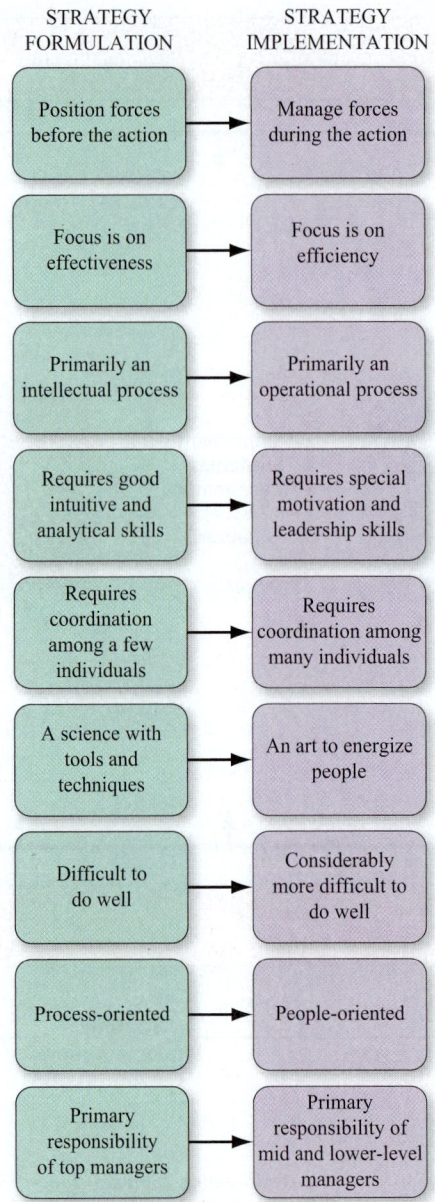

STRATEGY FORMULATION → STRATEGY IMPLEMENTATION

STRATEGY FORMULATION	STRATEGY IMPLEMENTATION
Position forces before the action	Manage forces during the action
Focus is on effectiveness	Focus is on efficiency
Primarily an intellectual process	Primarily an operational process
Requires good intuitive and analytical skills	Requires special motivation and leadership skills
Requires coordination among a few individuals	Requires coordination among many individuals
A science with tools and techniques	An art to energize people
Difficult to do well	Considerably more difficult to do well
Process-oriented	People-oriented
Primary responsibility of top managers	Primary responsibility of mid and lower-level managers

FIGURE 7-2

Contrasting Strategy Formulation with Strategy Implementation

The Need for Clear Annual Objectives

Annual objectives are desired milestones an organization needs to achieve to ensure successful strategy implementation. Annual objectives are essential for strategy implementation for five primary reasons:

1. They represent the basis for allocating resources.
2. They are a primary mechanism for evaluating managers.
3. They enable effective monitoring of progress toward achieving long-term objectives.
4. They establish organizational, divisional, and departmental priorities.
5. They are essential for keeping a strategic plan on track.

Considerable time and effort should be devoted to ensuring that annual objectives are well conceived, consistent with long-term objectives, and supportive of strategies to be implemented. Active participation in establishing annual objectives is needed for the preceding reasons listed.

Approving, revising, or rejecting annual objectives is much more than a rubber-stamp activity. The purpose of annual objectives can be summarized as follows:

Annual objectives serve as guidelines for action, directing and channeling efforts and activities of organization members. They provide a source of legitimacy in an enterprise by justifying activities to stakeholders. They serve as standards of performance. They serve as an important source of employee motivation and identification. They give incentives for managers and employees to perform. They provide a basis for organizational design.[2]

Clearly stated and communicated objectives are critical to success in all types and sizes of firms. Annual objectives are often stated in terms of profitability, growth, and market share by business segment, geographic area, customer groups, and product. Figure 7-3 illustrates how

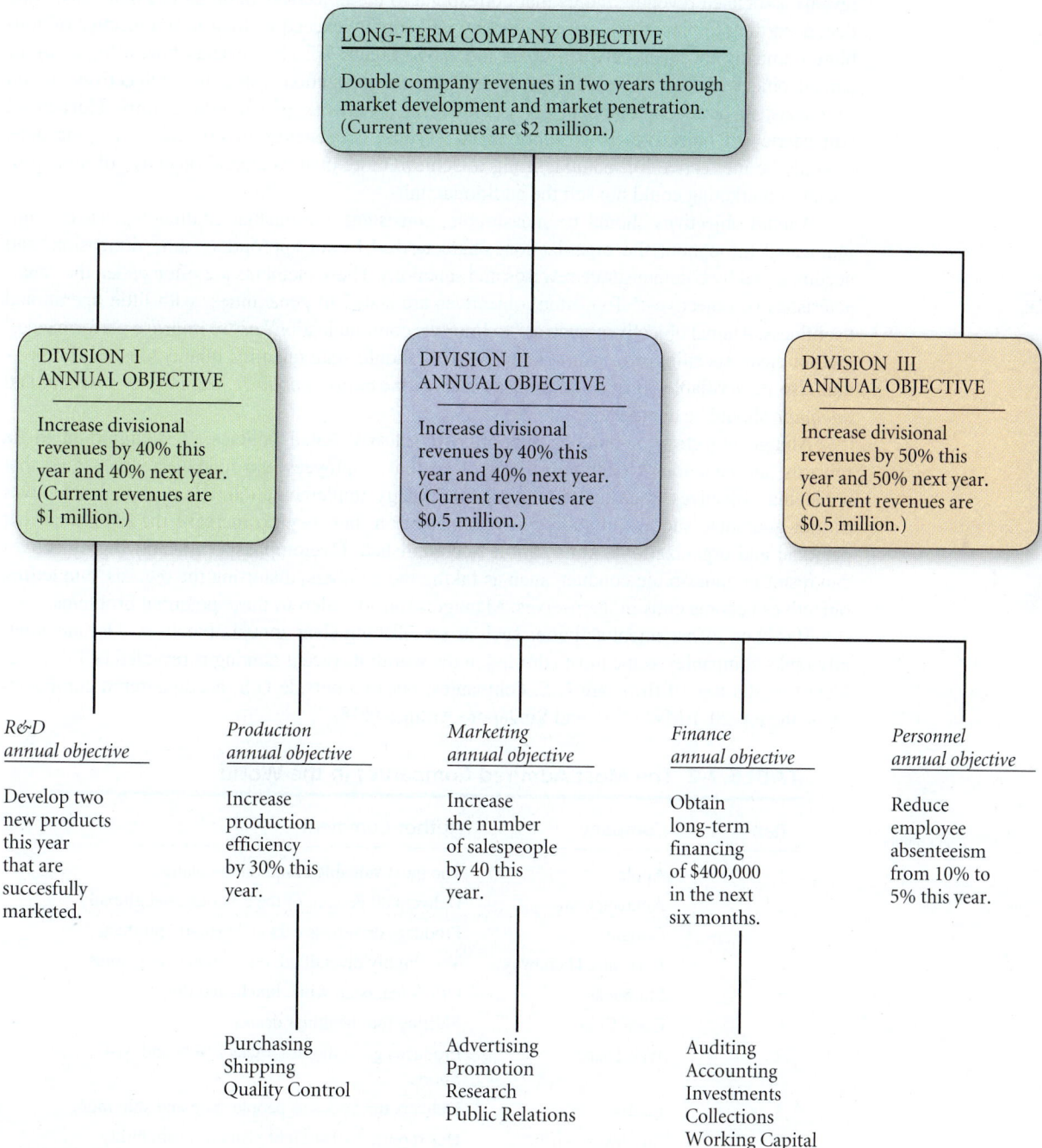

FIGURE 7-3

The Stamus Company's Hierarchy of Aims

TABLE 7-1 The Stamus Company's Revenue Expectations (in $ millions)

	2016	2017	2018
Division I Revenues	1.0	1.400	1.960
Division II Revenues	0.5	0.700	0.980
Division III Revenues	0.5	0.750	1.125
Total Company Revenues	**2.0**	**2.850**	**4.065**

the Stamus Company could establish annual objectives based on long-term objectives. Table 7-1 reveals associated revenue figures that correspond to the objectives outlined in Figure 7-3. Note that, according to plan, the Stamus Company will slightly exceed its long-term objective of doubling company revenues between 2016 and 2018. Figure 7-3 also reflects how a hierarchy of annual objectives can be established based on an organization's structure. Objectives should be consistent across hierarchical levels and form a network of supportive aims. **Horizontal consistency of objectives** is as important as **vertical consistency of objectives**. For instance, it would be ineffective for manufacturing to achieve more than its annual objective of units produced, if marketing could not sell the additional units.

Annual objectives should be measurable, consistent, reasonable, challenging, clear, communicated throughout the organization, characterized by an appropriate time dimension, and accompanied by commensurate rewards and sanctions. These elements are often called the "characteristics of objectives." Too often, objectives are stated in generalities, with little operational usefulness. Annual objectives, such as "to improve communication" or "to improve performance," are not clear, specific, or measurable. Objectives should state quantity, quality, cost, and time—and also be verifiable. Terms and phrases such as *maximize, minimize, as soon as possible*, and *adequate* should be avoided.

Annual objectives should be supported by clearly stated policies. It is important to tie rewards and sanctions to annual objectives so that employees and managers understand that achieving objectives is critical to successful strategy implementation. Clear annual objectives do not guarantee successful strategy implementation, but they do increase the likelihood that personal and organizational aims can be accomplished. Overemphasis on achieving objectives can result in undesirable conduct, such as faking the numbers, distorting the records, and letting objectives become ends in themselves. Managers must be alert to these potential problems.

Based on management activities such as establishing clear annual objectives, *Fortune* annually ranks companies as the most admired in the world; its recent ranking is revealed in Table 7-2. Note that the top 10 firms are U.S. companies, but two outside-U.S.-headquartered companies made the top 20: BMW (#14) and Singapore Airlines (#18).

TABLE 7-2 The Most Admired Companies in the World

Rank	Company	Author Comment
1	Apple	The most valuable brand on the planet
2	Amazon.com	Delivers 80 percent of the e-books read globally
3	Google	Produces driverless cars and "smart" products
4	Berkshire Hathaway	Very highly diversified; owns many companies
5	Starbucks	Offers tea, beer, wine, lunch, and dinner
6	Coca-Cola	Shifting into healthier drinks
7	Walt Disney	Produces great movies; owns ESPN and ABC Sports
8	FedEx	Delivers the goods as people shop and ship more
9	Southwest Airlines	Has reported 40 straight years of profitability
10	General Electric	Highly diversified; competes in many industries

Source: Based on information at http://fortune.com/worlds-most-admired-companies/apple-1/

The Need for Clear Policies

Policies refer to specific guidelines, methods, procedures, rules, forms, and administrative practices established to support and encourage work toward stated goals. Changes in a firm's strategic direction do not occur automatically. On a day-to-day basis, policies are needed to make a strategy work. Policies facilitate solving recurring problems and guide the implementation of strategy. Policies are essential instruments for strategy implementation, for at least six reasons:

1. Policies set boundaries, constraints, and limits on the kinds of administrative actions that can be taken to reward and sanction behavior.
2. Policies let both employees and managers know what is expected of them, thereby increasing the likelihood that strategies will be implemented successfully.
3. Policies provide a basis for management control and allow coordination across organizational units.
4. Policies reduce the amount of time managers spend making decisions. Policies also clarify what work is to be done and by whom.
5. Policies promote delegation of decision making to appropriate managerial levels where various problems usually arise.
6. Policies clarify what can and cannot be done in pursuit of an organization's objectives.

As an example, some companies have a policy that bans employees from accessing their personal social media sites during work hours. Some companies are more stringent than others regarding social media policy. An excerpt from Gap, Inc.'s social media policy asserts, "Unless you are an authorized Social Media Manager for Gap, do not let social media affect your job performance." Many organizations have a policy manual that serves to guide and direct behavior. Policies can apply to all divisions and departments (such as, "We are an equal opportunity employer"). Some policies apply to a single department ("Employees in this department must take at least one training and development course each year"). Whatever their scope and form, policies serve as a mechanism for implementing strategies and obtaining objectives. Policies should be stated in writing whenever possible. They represent the means for carrying out strategic decisions. Sometimes policies can be controversial, as described in the mini-case at the end of this chapter for Hilton Hotels.

Examples of policies that support a company strategy, a divisional objective, and a departmental objective are given in Table 7-3. Some example issues that may require a management policy are provided in Table 7-4.

Allocate Resources and Manage Conflict

Allocate Resources

All organizations have at least four types of resources (or assets) that can be used to achieve desired objectives: (1) financial resources, (2) physical resources, (3) human resources, and (4) technological resources. **Resource allocation** can be defined as distributing an organization's "assets" across products, regions, and segments according to priorities established by annual objectives. Allocating resources is a vital strategy-implementation activity. Strategic management itself is sometimes referred to as a "resource allocation process."

In organizations that do no strategic planning, resource allocation is often based on political or personal factors and bias, rather than being based on clear analysis and thought. Strategists should be wary of a number of factors that commonly prohibit effective resource allocation, including an overprotection of resources, too great an emphasis on short-run financial criteria, organizational politics, vague strategy targets, a reluctance to take risks, and a lack of sufficient knowledge. Below the corporate level, there often exists an absence of systematic thinking about resources allocated and strategies of the firm. Effective resource allocation does not guarantee successful strategy implementation because programs, personnel, controls, and commitment must breathe life into the resources provided. Yavitz and Newman explain why:

Managers normally have many more tasks than they can do. Managers must allocate time and resources among these tasks. Pressure builds up. Expenses are too high. The CEO wants a good financial report for the third quarter. Strategy formulation and implementation

TABLE 7-3 A Hierarchy of Policies

Company Strategy
Acquire a chain of retail stores to meet our sales growth and profitability objectives.

Supporting Policies
1. "All stores will be open from 8 AM to 8 PM Monday through Saturday." (This policy could increase retail sales if stores currently are open only 40 hours a week.)
2. "All stores must submit a Monthly Control Data Report." (This policy could reduce expense-to-sales ratios.)
3. "All stores must support company advertising by contributing 5 percent of their total monthly revenues for this purpose." (This policy could allow the company to establish a national reputation.)
4. "All stores must adhere to the uniform pricing guidelines set forth in the Company Handbook." (This policy could help assure customers that the company offers a consistent product in terms of price and quality in all its stores.)

Divisional Objective
Increase the division's revenues from $10 million in 2016 to $15 million in 2018.

Supporting Policies
1. "Beginning in January 2017, each one of this division's salespersons must file a weekly activity report that includes the number of calls made, the number of miles traveled, the number of units sold, the dollar volume sold, and the number of new accounts opened." (This policy could ensure that salespersons do not place too great an emphasis in certain areas.)
2. "Beginning in January 2017, this division will return to its employees 5 percent of its gross revenues in the form of a Christmas bonus." (This policy could increase employee productivity.)
3. "Beginning in January 2017, inventory levels carried in warehouses will be decreased by 30 percent in accordance with a just-in-time (JIT) manufacturing approach." (This policy could reduce production expenses and thus free funds for increased marketing efforts.)

Production Department Objective
Increase production from 20,000 units in 2016 to 30,000 units in 2018.

Supporting Policies
1. "Beginning in January 2017, employees will have the option of working up to 20 hours of overtime per week." (This policy could minimize the need to hire additional employees.)
2. "Beginning in January 2017, perfect attendance awards in the amount of $100 will be given to all employees who do not miss a workday in a given year." (This policy could decrease absenteeism and increase productivity.)
3. "Beginning in January 2017, new equipment must be leased rather than purchased." (This policy could reduce tax liabilities and thus allow more funds to be invested in modernizing production processes).

TABLE 7-4 Some Issues That May Require a Management Policy

- To offer extensive or limited management development workshops and seminars
- To centralize or decentralize employee-training activities
- To recruit through employment agencies, college campuses, or newspapers
- To promote from within or to hire from the outside
- To promote on the basis of merit or on the basis of seniority
- To tie executive compensation to long-term or annual objectives
- To offer numerous or few employee benefits
- To negotiate directly or indirectly with labor unions
- To delegate authority for large expenditures or to centrally retain this authority
- To allow much, some, or no overtime work
- To establish a high- or low-safety stock of inventory
- To use one or more suppliers
- To buy, lease, or rent new production equipment
- To greatly or somewhat stress quality control
- To establish many or only a few production standards
- To operate one, two, or three shifts
- To discourage using insider information for personal gain
- To discourage sexual harassment
- To discourage smoking at work
- To discourage insider trading
- To discourage moonlighting

activities often get deferred. Today's problems soak up available energies and resources. Scrambled accounts and budgets fail to reveal the shift in allocation away from strategic needs to currently squeaking wheels.[3]

Manage Conflict

Honest differences of opinion, turf protection, and competition for limited resources can inevitably lead to conflict. **Conflict** can be defined as a disagreement between two or more parties on one or more issues. Establishing annual objectives can lead to conflict because individuals have different expectations, perceptions, schedules, pressures, obligations, and personalities. Misunderstandings between line managers (such as production supervisors) and staff managers (such as human resource specialists) can occur. For example, a collection manager's objective of reducing bad debts by 50 percent in a given year may conflict with a divisional objective to increase sales by 20 percent. Conflict must be managed for strategy implementation to be successful. Managing conflict is a strategic issue in most, if not all, organizations.

Establishing objectives can lead to conflict because managers and strategists must make trade-offs, such as whether to emphasize short-term profits or long-term growth, profit margin or market share, market penetration or market development, growth or stability, high risk or low risk, and social responsiveness or profit maximization. Trade-offs are necessary because no firm has sufficient resources to pursue all strategies that would benefit the firm. Table 7-5 reveals some important management trade-off decisions required in strategy implementation. Strategic planning necessitates making effective trade-off decisions.

Conflict is not always bad. An absence of conflict can signal indifference and apathy. Conflict can serve to energize opposing groups into action and may help managers identify problems. General George Patton once said, "If everyone is thinking alike, then somebody isn't thinking."

Various approaches for managing and resolving conflict can be classified into three categories: avoidance, defusion, and confrontation. **Avoidance** includes such actions as ignoring the problem in hopes that the conflict will resolve itself or physically separating the conflicting individuals (or groups). **Defusion** can include playing down differences between conflicting parties while accentuating similarities and common interests, compromising so that there is neither a clear winner nor loser, resorting to majority rule, appealing to a higher authority, or redesigning present positions. **Confrontation** is exemplified by exchanging members of conflicting parties so that each can gain an appreciation of the other's point of view or holding a meeting at which conflicting parties present their views and work through their differences.

Match Structure with Strategy

Changes in strategy often require changes in the way an organization is structured, for two major reasons. First, structure largely dictates how objectives and policies will be established. For example, objectives and policies established under a geographic organizational structure are

TABLE 7-5 **Some Management Trade-Off Decisions Required in Strategy Implementation**

To emphasize short-term profits or long-term growth

To emphasize profit margin or market share

To emphasize market development or market penetration

To lay off or furlough

To seek growth or stability

To take high risk or low risk

To be more socially responsible or more profitable

To outsource jobs or pay more to keep jobs at home

To acquire externally or to build internally

To restructure or reengineer

To use leverage or equity to raise funds

To use part-time or full-time employees

TABLE 7-6 Symptoms of an Ineffective Organizational Structure

1. Too many levels of management
2. Too many meetings attended by too many people
3. Too much attention being directed toward solving interdepartmental conflicts
4. Too large a span of control
5. Too many unachieved objectives
6. Declining corporate or business performance
7. Losing ground to rival firms
8. Revenue or earnings divided by number of employees or number of managers is low compared to rival firms

couched in geographic terms. Objectives and policies are stated largely in terms of products in an organization whose structure is based on product groups. The structural format for developing objectives and policies can significantly impact all other strategy-implementation activities.

The second major reason why changes in strategy often require changes in structure is that structure dictates how resources will be allocated. If an organization's structure is based on customer groups, then resources will be allocated in that manner. Similarly, if an organization's structure is set up along functional business lines, then resources are allocated by functional areas. Unless new or revised strategies place emphasis in the same areas as old strategies, structural reorientation commonly becomes a part of strategy implementation.

Alfred Chandler promoted the notion that "changes in strategy lead to changes in organizational structure." Structure should be designed to facilitate the strategic pursuit of a firm and, therefore, follow strategy. Without a strategy or reasons for being (mission), companies find it difficult to design an effective structure. There is no one optimal organizational design or structure for a given strategy or type of organization. What is appropriate for one organization may not be appropriate for a similar firm, although successful firms in a given industry do tend to organize themselves in a similar way. For example, consumer goods companies tend to emulate the divisional structure-by-product form of organization. Small firms tend to be functionally structured (centralized). Medium-sized firms tend to be divisionally structured (decentralized). Large firms tend to use a **strategic business unit (SBU) structure** or matrix structure.

When a firm changes its strategy, the existing organizational structure may become ineffective. As indicated in Table 7-6, symptoms of an ineffective organizational structure include too many levels of management, too many meetings attended by too many people, too much attention being directed toward solving interdepartmental conflicts, too large a span of control, and too many unachieved objectives. Changes in structure can facilitate strategy-implementation efforts, but changes in structure should not be expected to make a bad strategy good, to make bad managers good, or to make bad products sell.

Structure undeniably can and does influence strategy. Strategies formulated must be workable, so if a certain new strategy requires massive structural changes, it may not be an attractive choice. In this way, structure can shape the choice of strategies. But a more important concern is determining what types of structural changes are needed to implement new strategies and how these changes can best be accomplished.

Types of Organizational Structure

Structure matters! There are seven basic types of organizational structure: (1) functional, (2) divisional by geographic area, (3) divisional by product, (4) divisional by customer, (5) divisional by process, (6) strategic business unit (SBU), and (7) matrix. Companies, like people and armies, strive to be better organized/structured than rivals, because better organization can yield tremendous competitive advantages. There are countless examples throughout history of incidents, battles, and companies where superior organization overcame massive odds against the entity.

The Functional Structure

The most widely used structure is the functional or centralized type because this structure is the simplest and least expensive of the seven alternatives. A **functional structure** groups tasks and

TABLE 7-7 Advantages and Disadvantages of a Functional Organizational Structure

Advantages	Disadvantages
1. Simple and inexpensive	1. Accountability forced to the top
2. Capitalizes on specialization of business activities such as marketing and finance	2. Delegation of authority and responsibility not encouraged
3. Minimizes need for elaborate control system	3. Minimizes career development
4. Allows for rapid decision making	4. Low employee and manager morale
	5. Inadequate planning for products and markets
	6. Leads to short-term, narrow thinking
	7. Leads to communication problems

activities by business function, such as production and operations, marketing, finance and accounting, research and development, and management information systems. A university may structure its activities by major functions that include academic affairs, student services, alumni relations, athletics, maintenance, and accounting. Besides being simple and inexpensive, a functional structure also promotes specialization of labor, encourages efficient use of managerial and technical talent, minimizes the need for an elaborate control system, and allows rapid decision making. Some disadvantages of a functional structure are that it forces accountability to the top, minimizes career development opportunities, and is sometimes characterized by low employee morale, line or staff conflicts, poor delegation of authority, and inadequate planning for products and markets. Table 7-7 summarizes the advantages and disadvantages of a functional organizational structure.

A functional structure often leads to short-term and narrow thinking that may undermine what is best for the firm as a whole. For example, the research and development department may strive to overdesign products and components to achieve technical elegance, whereas manufacturing may argue for low-frills products that can be mass produced more easily. Thus, communication is often not as good in a functional structure. Schein gives an example of a communication problem in a functional structure:

> The word "marketing" will mean product development to the engineer, studying customers through market research to the product manager, merchandising to the salesperson, and constant change in design to the manufacturing manager. Then when these managers try to work together, they often attribute disagreements to personalities and fail to notice the deeper, shared assumptions that vary and dictate how each function thinks.[4]

Most large companies have abandoned the functional structure in favor of decentralization and improved accountability. However, a large company that still operates from a functional type of organizational design is Nucor. Headquartered in Charlotte, North Carolina, Nucor's executive management team consists of eight white, male persons (lack of diversity is not good; see http://www.nucor.com/governance/executives/). A large producer of steel products, Nucor has no apparent division heads, and John Ferriola is both CEO and Chairman of the Board (holding those two titles is not good).

The Divisional Structure

The **divisional (decentralized) structure** is the second-most common type. Divisions are sometimes referred to as *segments, profit centers,* or *business units.* As a small organization grows, it has more difficulty managing different products and services in different markets. Some form of divisional structure generally becomes necessary to motivate employees, control operations, and compete successfully in diverse locations. The divisional structure can be organized in one of four ways: (1) by geographic area, (2) by product *or* service, (3) by customer, or (4) by process. With a divisional structure, functional activities are performed both centrally and in each separate division.

Sun Microsystems recently reduced the number of its business units from seven to four. Kodak recently reduced its number of business units from seven by-customer divisions to five by-product divisions. As consumption patterns become increasingly similar worldwide, a by-product structure is becoming more effective than a by-customer or a by-geographic type of divisional structure. In the restructuring, Kodak eliminated its global operations division and distributed those responsibilities across the new by-product divisions.

A divisional structure has some clear advantages. First and perhaps foremost, accountability is clear. That is, divisional managers can be held responsible for sales and profit levels. Because a divisional structure is based on extensive delegation of authority, managers and employees can easily see the results of their good or bad performances. As a result, employee morale is generally higher in a divisional structure than it is in a centralized structure. Other advantages of the divisional design are that it creates career development opportunities for managers, allows local control of situations, leads to a competitive climate within an organization, and allows new businesses and products to be added easily.

The divisional design is not without some limitations, however. Perhaps the most important limitation is that a divisional structure is costly, for a number of reasons. First, each division requires functional specialists who must be paid. Second, there exists some duplication of staff services, facilities, and personnel; for instance, functional specialists are also needed centrally (at headquarters) to coordinate divisional activities. Third, managers must be well qualified because the divisional design forces delegation of authority; better-qualified individuals require higher salaries. A divisional structure can also be costly because it requires an elaborate, headquarters-driven control system. Fourth, competition between divisions may become so intense that it is dysfunctional and leads to limited sharing of ideas and resources for the common good of the firm. Table 7-8 summarizes the advantages and disadvantages of divisional organizational structure.

A *divisional structure by geographic area* is appropriate for organizations whose strategies need to be tailored to fit the particular needs and characteristics of customers in different geographic areas. This type of structure can be most appropriate for organizations that have similar branch facilities located in widely dispersed areas. A divisional structure by geographic area allows local participation in decision making and improved coordination within a region. Due to steady declines in revenues among its U.S. restaurants, McDonald's recently created a new organizational structure for its operations in the United States, replacing three regions with four geographic zones to better respond to local tastes. McDonald's U.S. President Mike Andres said, "What has worked for McDonald's USA for the past decade is not sufficient to propel the business forward in the future." The footwear maker, Crocs, Inc., also uses the divisional-by-region type of structure, as illustrated in Figure 7-4.

The *divisional structure by product (or services)* is most effective for implementing strategies when specific products or services need special emphasis. Also, this type of structure is widely used when an organization offers only a few products or services or when an organization's products or services differ substantially. The divisional structure allows strict control over and attention to product lines, but it may also require a more skilled management force and reduced top management control.

TABLE 7-8 Advantages and Disadvantages of a Divisional Organizational Structure

Advantages	Disadvantages
1. Clear accountability	1. Can be costly
2. Allows local control of local situations	2. Duplication of functional activities
3. Creates career development chances	3. Requires a skilled management force
4. Promotes delegation of authority	4. Requires an elaborate control system
5. Leads to competitive climate internally	5. Competition among divisions can become so intense as to be dysfunctional
6. Allows easy adding of new products or regions	6. Can lead to limited sharing of ideas and resources
7. Allows strict control and attention to products, customers, or regions	7. Some regions, products, or customers may receive special treatment

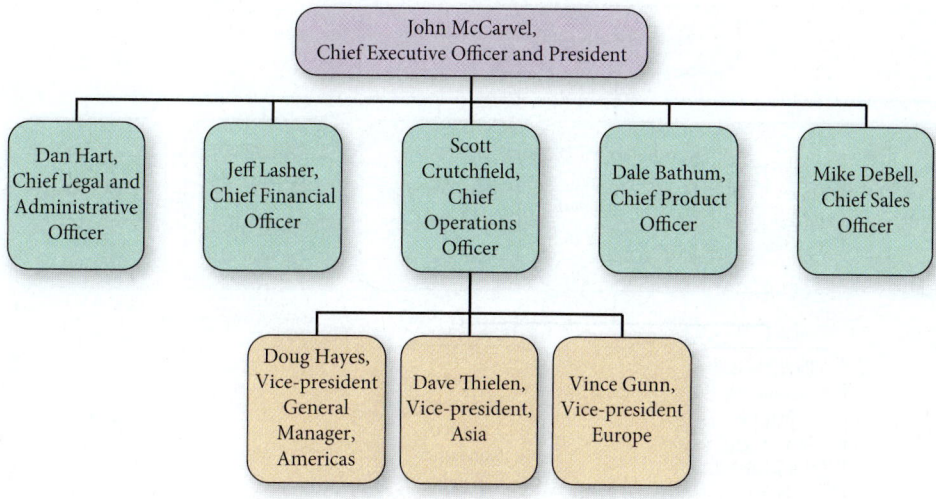

FIGURE 7-4

Divisional Organizational Structure of Crocs, Inc.

When a few major customers are of paramount importance and many different services are provided to these customers, then a *divisional structure by customer* can be the most effective way to implement strategies. This structure allows an organization to cater effectively to the requirements of clearly defined customer groups. For example, book-publishing companies often organize their activities around customer groups, such as colleges, secondary schools, and private commercial schools. Some airline companies have two major customer divisions: (1) passengers and (2) freight or cargo services. Utility companies often use (1) commercial, (2) residential, and (3) industrial as their divisions by customer.

Headquartered in New York City, Time Warner Cable (TWC) recently changed its organizational structure from a divisional-by-geographic region to a divisional-by-customer design. Time Warner is now organized by reference to its customer groups served (residential, business, or media clients) and the functions necessary to serve those customers. The company now has three business units—(1) Residential Services, (2) Business Services, and (3) Media Services—reporting to the chief operating officer (COO) Rob Marcus.

A *divisional structure by process* is similar to a functional structure, because activities are organized according to the way work is actually performed. However, a key difference between these two designs is that functional departments are not accountable for profits or revenues, whereas divisional process departments are evaluated on these criteria. An example of a divisional structure by process is a manufacturing business organized into six divisions: electrical work, glass cutting, welding, grinding, painting, and foundry work. In this case, all operations related to these specific processes would be grouped under the separate divisions. Each process (division) would be responsible for generating revenues and profits. The divisional structure by process can be particularly effective in achieving objectives when distinct production processes represent the thrust of competitiveness in an industry.

The Strategic Business Unit (SBU) Structure

As the number, size, and diversity of divisions in an organization increase, controlling and evaluating divisional operations become increasingly difficult for strategists. Increases in sales often are not accompanied by similar increases in profitability. The span of control becomes too large at top levels of the firm. For example, in a large conglomerate organization composed of 90 divisions, such as ConAgra, the chief executive officer could have difficulty even remembering the first names of divisional presidents. In multidivisional organizations, an SBU structure can greatly facilitate strategy-implementation efforts. ConAgra has put its many divisions into two primary SBUs: (1) consumer foods and (2) private brands and commercial foods. ConAgra's SBU structure is illustrated in Figure 7-5. Commercial foods are "food for restaurants," whereas consumer foods are "food in grocery stores."

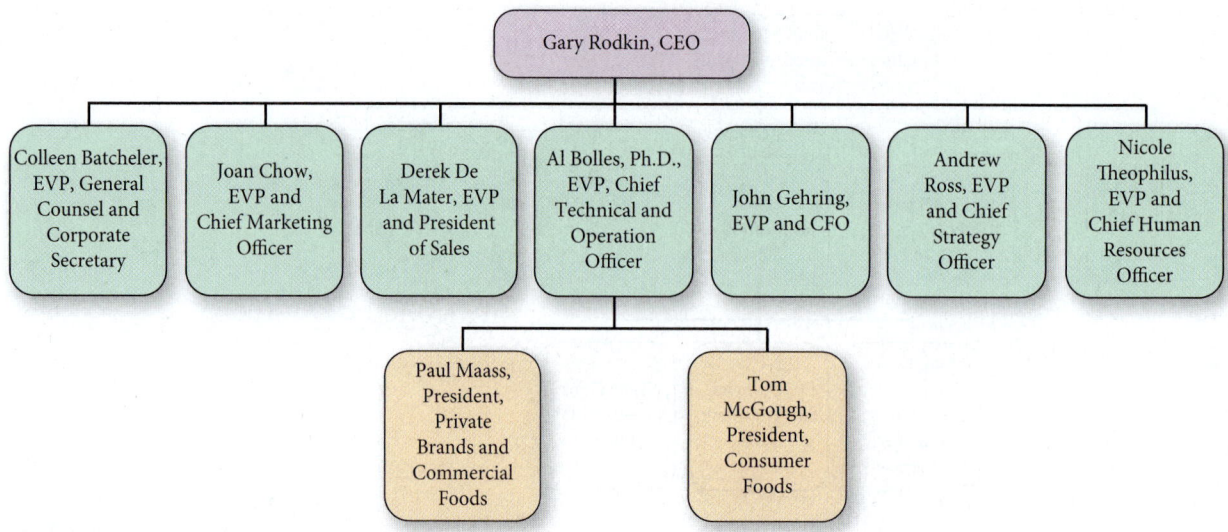

FIGURE 7-5

ConArgra's SBU Organizational Structure

Source: Based on information at the company's *Form 10k.*

The strategic business unit structure groups similar divisions into SBUs and delegates authority and responsibility for each unit to a senior executive who reports directly to the chief executive officer. This change in structure can facilitate strategy implementation by improving coordination between similar divisions and channeling accountability to distinct business units. In a 100-division conglomerate, the divisions could perhaps be regrouped into 10 SBUs according to certain common characteristics, such as competing in the same industry, being located in the same area, or having the same customers.

Two disadvantages of an SBU structure are that it requires an additional layer of management, which increases salary expenses. Also, the role of the group vice president is often ambiguous. However, these limitations often do not outweigh the advantages of improved coordination and accountability. Another advantage of the SBU structure is that it makes the tasks of planning and control by the corporate office more manageable. Halliburton operates from an SBU structure with the divisions based on process, as described at www.halliburton.com (click on About Us, then click Company Profile). In June 2015, Microsoft changed its organizational structure to become three by-product strategic business units: (1) Windows and Devices Group (WDG), (2) Cloud and Enterprise (C+E), and (3) Applications and Services Group (ASG).

The Matrix Structure

A **matrix structure** is the most complex of all designs because it depends on both vertical and horizontal flows of authority and communication (hence the term *matrix*). In contrast, functional and divisional structures depend primarily on vertical flows of authority and communication. A matrix structure can result in higher overhead because it creates more management positions. Other disadvantages of a matrix structure that contribute to overall complexity include dual lines of budget authority (a violation of the unity-of-command principle), dual sources of reward and punishment, shared authority, dual reporting channels, and a need for an extensive and effective communication system.

Despite its complexity, the matrix structure is widely used in many industries, including construction, health care, research, and defense. As indicated in Table 7-9, some advantages of a matrix structure are that project objectives are clear, there are many channels of communication, workers can see the visible results of their work, shutting down a project can be accomplished relatively easily, and it facilitates the use of specialized personnel, equipment, and facilities. Functional resources are shared in a matrix structure, rather than duplicated as in a divisional structure. Individuals with a high degree of expertise can divide their time as needed among projects, and they in turn develop their own skills and competencies more than in other structures.

TABLE 7-9 Advantages and Disadvantages of a Matrix Structure

Advantages	Disadvantages
1. Clear project objectives	1. Requires excellent vertical and horizontal flows of communication
2. Results of their work clearly seen by employees	2. Costly because creates more manager positions
3. Easy to shut down a project	3. Violates unity of command principle
4. Facilitates uses of special equipment, personnel, and facilities	4. Creates dual lines of budget authority
5. Shared functional resources instead of duplicated resources, as in a divisional structure	5. Creates dual sources of reward and punishment
	6. Creates shared authority and reporting
	7. Requires mutual trust and understanding

A typical matrix structure is illustrated in Figure 7-6. Note that the letters (A through Z4) refer to managers. For example, if you were manager A, you would be responsible for financial aspects of Project 1, and you would have two bosses: the Project 1 Manager on site and the CFO off site.

For a matrix structure to be effective, organizations need participative planning, training, clear mutual understanding of roles and responsibilities, excellent internal communication, and mutual trust and confidence. The matrix structure is being used more frequently by U.S. businesses because firms are pursuing strategies that add new products, customer groups, and technology to their range of activities. Out of these changes are coming product managers, functional managers, and geographic-area managers, all of whom have important strategic responsibilities. When several variables, such as product, customer, technology, geography, functional area, and line of business, have roughly equal strategic priorities, a matrix organization can be an effective structural form.

Dos and Don'ts in Developing Organizational Charts

Students analyzing strategic-management cases (and actual corporate executives) oftentimes revise and improve a firm's organizational structure. This section provides some basic guidelines for this endeavor. There are some basic dos and don'ts in regard to devising or constructing organizational charts, especially for midsize to large firms. First of all, reserve the title *CEO* for the top executive of the firm. Don't use the title *president* for the top person; use it for the division top managers if there are divisions within the firm. Also, do not use the title *president* for functional business executives. They should have the title *chief*, or *vice president*, or *manager*, or *officer*, such as "Chief Information Officer," or "VP of Human Resources." Furthermore, do not recommend a dual title (such as *CEO and president*) for just one executive.

Do not let a single individual be both chairman of the board and CEO of a company, although Seifi Ghasemi was recently named as the new CEO, President, and Chairman of the large industrial-gas provider Air Products & Chemicals Inc. Also, Home Depot recently appointed their CEO Craig Menear to also be the company's chairman of the board. Menear is the first person to hold both CEO and chairman titles of Home Depot since the company's co-founder, Bernie Marcus. Actually, *chairperson* is much better than *chairman* for a top board person's title. A significant movement among corporate America is to split the chairperson of the board and the CEO positions in publicly held companies.[5] The movement includes asking the New York Stock Exchange and Nasdaq to adopt listing rules that would require separate positions. About 50 percent of companies in the S&P 500 stock index have separate positions, up from 22 percent in 2002, but this still leaves plenty of room for improvement. Among European and Asian companies, the split in these two positions is much more common. For example, 79 percent of British companies split the positions, and all virtually German and Dutch companies split the position.

Directly below the CEO, it is best to have a COO (chief operating officer) with any division presidents reporting directly to the COO. On the same level as the COO and also reporting to the CEO, draw in your functional business executives, such as a CFO (chief financial officer), VP of human resources, a CSO (chief strategy officer), a CIO (chief information officer), a CMO (chief marketing officer), a VP of R&D, a VP of legal affairs, an investment relations officer, maintenance officer, and so on. Note in Figure 7-6 that these positions are labeled and placed

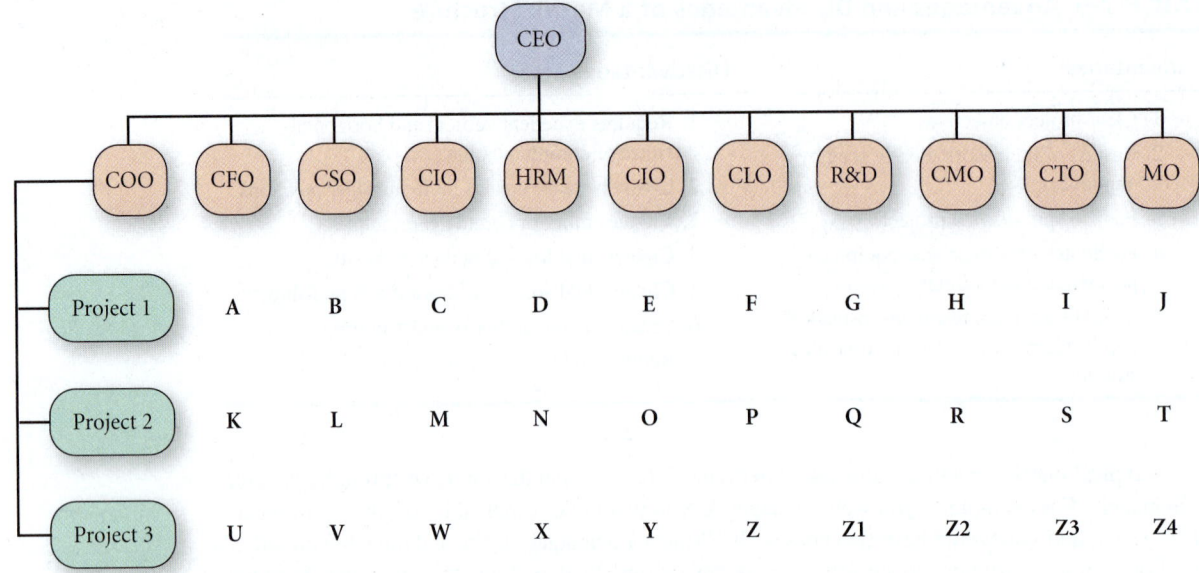

Note: Titles spelled out as follows.

Chief Executive Officer (CEO)
Chief Finance Officer (CFO)
Chief Strategy Officer (CSO)
Chief Information Officer (CIO)
Human Resources Manager (HRM)
Chief Operating Officer (COO)
Chief Legal Officer (CLO)
Research & Development Officer (R&D)
Chief Marketing Officer (CMO)
Chief Technology Officer (CTO)
Competitive Intelligence Officer (CIO)
Maintenance Officer (MO)

FIGURE 7-6

Typical Top Managers of a Large Firm

appropriately in a matrix structure, which, as shown, generally include project managers rather than division presidents reporting to a COO. However, note in Academic Research Capsule 7-1 the COO position is losing favor in North America.

In developing an organizational chart, avoid having a particular person reporting to more than one person in the chain of command. This would violate the unity-of-command principle of management that "every employee should have just one boss." Also, do not have the CFO, CIO, CSO, human resource officer, or other functional positions report to the COO. All these positions report directly to the CEO.

A recent article (*WSJ*, 8-25-15, p. B5) reveals that since 2009 there has been a 40 percent rise in the number of chief accounting officers (CAO) among American companies. CAO's now do much more than just manage the company's books and prepare financial statements. Companies increasingly need a CAO that can stand up and debate strategic issues related to how best to balance the balance sheet, and know when and how to recognize revenue, and know how to report results using both USA and foreign standards (GAAP vs IFRS). CAO's are more and more signing the company's financial filings, making them personally liable for any mistakes or improprieties – along with the CFO and CEO. As more and more firms acquire foreign firms and even relocate their headquarters offshore (inversion), a CAO is needed who knows both USA and foreign insurance and accounting practices. Gary Kabureck, former CAO at Xerox Corp. says: "I think what happened over the last 15 years in the USA is that the accounting function started to separate from the controller function." In a firm, a controller is typically more focused on budgeting and planning, whereas the CAO is responsible for the in's and out's of global bookkeeping. The CAO also interacts closely with the board's audit committee, as well with outside firms auditing the company.

A relatively new, but increasingly popular, top management position, is the Chief Design Officer (CDO). Johnson & Johnson (J&J), for example, just hired a chief design officer, Ernesto

ACADEMIC RESEARCH CAPSULE 7-1

Why Is the COO Position Being Deleted in Many Organizations?

The COO position is increasingly being deleted in U.S. companies. Twitter recently divided the duties of its COO among all managers. McDonald's, Tiffany & Co., and Yahoo recently deleted their COO position. In fact, the percentage of large companies in the United States with COOs has declined almost every year for a decade, to about 36 percent today. Health-care and industrial companies are least likely to have a COO today. A senior executive search firm, Crist Kolder Associates, reports that the percentage of Fortune 500 and S&P 500 companies with a COO has declined steadily from 48 percent in 2000 to 36 percent in 2014. An accounting firm, PricewaterhouseCoopers, suggests there are four reasons why companies are phasing out the COO position: (1) flatten their structure, (2) eliminate a layer of management, (3) reduce costs, and (4) expand the CEO's authority and responsibility. Digital communications and even social media today enable a CEO oftentimes to perform COO duties. However, three situations that especially warrant having a COO include (1) whenever the CEO lacks operational experience, (2) whenever the firm desires to be transparent about their CEO succession plans, and (3) whenever the CEO needs to lead a restructuring or transformation of the

firm. Although historically a stepping-stone position to the CEO position, many companies now delegate the traditional duties of a COO to the CEO or to other positions, such as the CFO or to the chief brand officer. Deleting the COO position does increase the span of control of the CEO, spreading him or her thinly, which is not a good idea for many companies.

Interestingly, as the COO position has declined, the chief financial officer (CFO) position has increased in responsibility and prevalence. An example is the CFO position at Twitter Inc., where Anthony Noto is being groomed perhaps to become that company's CEO. Noto was recently also given head responsibility for marketing at Twitter. In the last year, it was Noto who initiated and coordinated the major business deals and acquisitions at Twitter.

Source: Based on Feintzeig, Rachel, "COOs Join Endangered Species List," *Wall Street Journal*, June 13, 2014, B1. Also based on Crist Kolder Associates, "Trends in CEO Recruiting and Succession," *Volatility Report 2014;* http://strategy-business.com/article/00328 published by PricewaterhouseCoopers; and Yoree Koh, "Ascent of Twitter CFO Creates a Power Center," *Wall Street Journal*, June 15, 2015, B1 and B4.

Quinteros, to be a liaison between the chief marketing officer (CMO) and R&D. The CDO position has equal status with the CMO position at J&J, PepsiCo, and Phillips Electronics NV— because "a product that is wonderfully designed sells itself, and has a huge benefit on the marketing side," said J&J's Sandi Peterson, who created the CDO position at J&J.

If a firm is large with numerous divisions, an SBU type of structure would be more appropriate to reduce the span of control reporting to the COO. One never knows for sure if a proposed or actual structure is indeed most effective for a particular firm. Declining financial performance signals a need for altering the structure. Some important guidelines to follow in devising organizational charts for companies are provided in Table 7-10.

TABLE 7-10 Fifteen Guidelines for Developing an Organizational Chart

1. Instead of *chairman* of the board, make it *chairperson* of the board.
2. Make sure the board of directors reveals diversity in race, ethnicity, gender, and age.
3. Make sure the chair of the board is not also the CEO or president of the company.
4. Make sure the CEO of the firm does not also carry the title *president*.
5. Reserve the title *president* for the division heads of the firm.
6. Make sure the firm has a COO.
7. Make sure only presidents of divisions report to the COO.
8. Make sure functional executives such as CFO, CIO, CMO, CSO, R&D, CLO, CTO, and HRM report to the CEO, not the COO.
9. Make sure every executive has one boss, so lines in the chart should be drawn accordingly, assuring unity of command.
10. Make sure span of control is reasonable, probably no more than 10 persons reporting to any other person.
11. Make sure diversity in race, ethnicity, gender, and age is well represented among corporate executives.
12. Avoid a functional type structure for all but the smallest firms.
13. Decentralize, using some form of divisional structure, whenever possible.
14. Use an SBU type structure for large, multidivisional firms.
15. Make sure executive titles match product names as best possible in division-by-product and SBU-designated firms.

Strategic Production/Operations Issues

Production/operations capabilities, limitations, and policies can significantly enhance or inhibit the attainment of objectives. Production processes typically constitute more than 70 percent of a firm's total assets. Thus, a major part of the strategy-implementation process takes place at the production site. Strategic production-related decisions on plant size, plant location, product design, choice of equipment, kind of tooling, size of inventory, inventory control, quality control, cost control, use of standards, job specialization, employee training, equipment and resource utilization, shipping and packaging, and technological innovation can determine the success or failure of strategy-implementation efforts.

Four production/operations issues—(1) restructuring/reengineering, (2) managing resistance to change, (3) deciding where/how to produce goods, and (4) managing an ESOP—are especially important for successful strategy implementation and are therefore discussed next.

Restructuring and Reengineering

Restructuring and reengineering are becoming commonplace on the corporate landscape across the United States and Europe. **Restructuring** involves reducing the size of the firm in terms of number of employees, number of divisions or units, and number of hierarchical levels in the firm's organizational structure. This reduction in size is intended to improve both efficiency and effectiveness. Restructuring is concerned primarily with shareholder well-being rather than employee well-being.

The primary benefit sought from restructuring is cost reduction. For some highly bureaucratic firms, restructuring can actually rescue the firm from global competition and demise. But the downside of restructuring can be reduced employee commitment, creativity, and innovation that accompanies the uncertainty and trauma associated with pending and actual employee layoffs. Avon Products recently restructured, reducing its six commercial business units down to two—(1) Developed Markets and (2) Developing Markets—essentially going to a divisional by geographic region type structure.

The recent falling euro and weak economy in Europe forced many European companies to downsize, laying off managers and employees. This practice was historically rare in Europe because labor unions and laws required lengthy negotiations or huge severance checks before workers could be terminated. In contrast to the United States, labor union executives of large European firms sit on most boards of directors. Job security in European companies is slowly moving toward a U.S. business model, in which firms lay off almost at will. From banks in Milan to factories in Mannheim, European employers are starting to show people the door in an effort to streamline operations, increase efficiency, and compete against already slim and trim U.S. firms. European firms still prefer to downsize by attrition and retirement, rather than by blanket layoffs because of culture, laws, and unions.

In contrast to restructuring, reengineering is concerned more with employee and customer well-being than shareholder well-being. **Reengineering** involves reconfiguring or redesigning work, jobs, and processes for the purpose of improving cost, quality, service, and speed. Reengineering does not usually affect the organizational structure or chart, nor does it imply job loss or employee layoffs. Whereas restructuring is concerned with eliminating or establishing, shrinking or enlarging, and moving organizational departments and divisions, the focus of reengineering is changing the way work is actually carried out. Reengineering is characterized by many tactical (short-term, business-function-specific) decisions, whereas restructuring is characterized by strategic (long-term, affecting all business functions) decisions.

Developed by Motorola in 1986 and made famous by CEO Jack Welch at General Electric and more recently by Robert Nardelli, former CEO of Home Depot, **Six Sigma** is a quality-boosting process improvement technique that entails training several key persons in the firm in the techniques to monitor, measure, and improve processes and eliminate defects. Six Sigma has been widely applied across industries from retailing to financial services. For example, CEO Dave Cote at Honeywell and CEO Jeff Immelt at General Electric spurred acceptance of Six Sigma, which aims to improve work processes and eliminate waste by training "select" employees who are given judo titles such as Master Black Belts, Black Belts, and Green Belts. Target Corp. claims more than $100 million in savings over the past six years resulting from its Six Sigma program.

Six Sigma was criticized in a *Wall Street Journal* article that cited many example firms whose stock price fell for a number of years after adoption of Six Sigma. The technique's reliance on the special group of trained employees is problematic and its use within retail firms such as Home Depot has not been as successful as in manufacturing firms.[6]

Manage Resistance to Change

No organization or individual can escape change. But the thought of change raises anxieties because people fear economic loss, inconvenience, uncertainty, and a break in normal social patterns. Almost any change in structure, technology, people, or strategies has the potential to disrupt comfortable interaction patterns. For this reason, people resist change. The strategic-management process can impose major changes on individuals and processes. Reorienting an organization to get people to think and act strategically is not an easy task. Strategy implementation can pose a threat to many managers and employees. New power and status relationships are anticipated and realized. New formal and informal groups' values, beliefs, and priorities may be largely unknown. Managers and employees may become engaged in resistance behavior as their roles, prerogatives, and power in the firm change. Disruption of social and political structures that accompany strategy execution must be anticipated and considered during strategy formulation and managed during strategy implementation.

Resistance to change may be the single-greatest threat to successful strategy implementation. Resistance regularly occurs in organizations in the form of sabotaging production machines, absenteeism, filing unfounded grievances, and an unwillingness to cooperate. People often resist strategy implementation because they do not understand what is happening or why changes are taking place. In that case, employees may simply need accurate information. Successful strategy implementation hinges on managers' ability to develop an organizational climate conducive to change. Change must be viewed by managers and employees as an opportunity for the firm to compete more effectively, rather than being seen as a threat to everyone's livelihood.

Resistance to change can emerge at any stage or level of the strategy-implementation process. Although there are various approaches for implementing changes, three commonly used strategies are a force change strategy, an educative change strategy, and a rational or self-interest change strategy. A **force change strategy** involves giving orders and enforcing those orders; this strategy has the advantage of being fast, but it is plagued by low commitment and high resistance. The **educative change strategy** is one that presents information to convince people of the need for change; the disadvantage of an educative change strategy is that implementation becomes slow and difficult. However, this type of strategy evokes greater commitment and less resistance than does the force change strategy. Finally, a **rational change strategy** or **self-interest change strategy** is one that attempts to convince individuals that the change is to their personal advantage. When this appeal is successful, strategy implementation can be relatively easy. However, implementation changes are seldom to everyone's advantage.

Strategists can take a number of positive actions to minimize managers' and employees' resistance to change. For example, individuals who will be affected by a change should be involved in the decision to make the change and in decisions about how to implement the change. Strategists should anticipate changes and develop and offer training and development workshops so that managers and employees can adapt to those changes. They also need to effectively communicate the need for changes. Strategy implementation is basically a process of managing change.

The most successful organizations today continuously adapt to changes in the competitive environment. It is not sufficient today to simply react to change. Managers need to anticipate change and be the creator of change. Viewing change as a continuous process is in stark contrast to an old management doctrine regarding change, which was to unfreeze behavior, change the behavior, and then refreeze the new behavior. The new "continuous organizational change" philosophy should mirror the popular "continuous quality improvement philosophy."

Decide Where and How to Produce Goods

In China, about 700,000 assembly workers at manufacturing contractors such as Foxconn put together Apple products. It would be virtually impossible to bring those jobs to the United States for at least three reasons. First of all, Foxconn—China's largest private employer and

TABLE 7-11 **Production Management and Strategy Implementation**

Type of Organization	Strategy Being Implemented	Production System Adjustments
Hospital	Adding a cancer center (Product Development)	Purchase specialized equipment and add specialized people.
Bank	Adding 10 new branches (Market Development)	Perform site location analysis.
Beer brewery	Purchasing a barley farm operation (Backward Integration)	Revise the inventory control system.
Steel manufacturer	Acquiring a fast-food chain (Unrelated Diversification)	Improve the quality control system.
Computer company	Purchasing a retail distribution chain (Forward Integration)	Alter the shipping, packaging, and transportation systems.

the manufacturer of an estimated 40 percent of the world's consumer electronic devices—pays its assembly workers far less than U.S. labor laws would allow. A typical salary is about $18 a day. Second, unlike U.S. plants, Foxconn and other Chinese manufacturing operations house employees in dormitories and can send hundreds of thousands of workers to the assembly lines at a moment's notice. On the lines, workers are subjected to what most Americans would consider unbearable long hours and tough working conditions. That system gives tech companies the efficiency needed to race products out the door, so speed is a bigger factor than pay. Finally, most of the component suppliers for Apple and other technology giants are also in China or other Asian countries. That geographic clustering gives companies the flexibility to change a product design at the last minute and still ship on time.

Examples of adjustments in production systems that could be required to implement various strategies are provided in Table 7-11 for both for-profit and nonprofit organizations. For instance, note that when a bank formulates and selects a strategy to add 10 new branches, a production-related implementation concern is site location. The largest bicycle company in the United States, Huffy, recently ended its own production of bikes and now contracts out those services to Asian and Mexican manufacturers. Huffy focuses instead on the design, marketing, and distribution of bikes, but it no longer produces bikes itself. The Dayton, Ohio, company closed its plants in Ohio, Missouri, and Mississippi.

Just-in-time (JIT) production approaches have withstood the test of time. Just-in-time significantly reduces the costs of implementing strategies. Parts and materials are delivered to a production site just as they are needed, rather than being stockpiled as a hedge against later deliveries. Harley-Davidson reports that at one plant alone, JIT freed $22 million previously tied up in inventory and greatly reduced reorder lead time.

Factors that should be studied before locating production facilities include the availability of major resources, the prevailing wage rates in the area, transportation costs related to shipping and receiving, the location of major markets, political risks in the area or country, and the availability of trainable employees. Some of these factors explain why many manufacturing operations in China are moving back to Mexico, or to Vietnam, or even back to the United States. Table 7-12 lists ways that companies today are reducing labor, production, and operations costs to stay financially sound.

Employee Stock Ownership Plans (ESOPs)

Besides reducing worker alienation and stimulating productivity, **employee stock ownership plans (ESOPs)** allow firms other benefits, such as substantial tax savings. An ESOP is a tax-qualified, defined-contribution, employee-benefit plan whereby employees purchase stock of the company through borrowed money or cash contributions. These plans empower employees to work as owners; this is a primary reason why the number of ESOPs have grown dramatically to more than 10,000 firms covering more than 14 million employees. Today, ESOPs control more than $600 billion in corporate stock in the United States. "The ownership culture really makes a difference, when management is a facilitator, not a dictator," observes Corey Rosen, executive

TABLE 7-12 Labor Cost-Saving Tactics

Salary freeze

Hiring freeze

Salary reductions

Reduction of employee benefits

Increase in employee contribution to health-care premiums

Reduction of employee 401(k)/403(b) match

Reduction of employee workweek

Mandatory furlough (temporary layoff)

Voluntary furlough

Temporary instead of full-time employees

Contract employees instead of full-time employees

Volunteer buyouts (Walt Disney is doing this)

Production halt for three days a week (Toyota Motor is doing this)

Layoffs

Early retirement

Reducing or eliminating bonuses

Source: Based on Mattioli, Dana, "Employers Make Cuts Despite Belief Upturn Is Near," *Wall Street Journal*, April 23, 2009, B4.

TABLE 7-13 The Ten Largest ESOP Companies in the United States

Company	Headquarters Location	# Employees (in thousands)
Publix Super Markets	Lakeland, Florida	160
Daymon Worldwide	Stamford, Connecticut	35
CH2M Hill	Englewood, Colorado	26
Lifetouch	Eden Prairie, Minnesota	25
Price Chopper	Schenectady, New York	23
Penmac	Springfield, Missouri	18
Amsted Industries	Chicago, Illinois	16
Houchens Industries	Bowling Green, Kentucky	15
WinCo Foods	Boise, Idaho	15
Parsons	Pasadena, California	15

director of the National Center for Employee Ownership. The 10 largest employee-owned companies are listed in Table 7-13.

Strategic Human Resource Issues

Any organization is only as good as its people! Thus, human resource issues can make or break successful strategy implementation. Thus, seven human resource issues are discussed further in this section, as follows: (1) linking performance and pay to strategy, (2) balancing work life with home life, (3) developing a diverse work force, (4) using caution in hiring a rival's employees, (5) creating a strategy-supportive culture, (6) using caution in monitoring employees' social media, and (7) developing a corporate wellness program.

Linking Performance and Pay to Strategy

An organization's compensation system needs to be aligned with strategic outcomes. Decisions on salary increases, promotions, merit pay, and bonuses need to support the long-term and annual objectives of the firm. A dual bonus system based on both annual and long-term objectives can be helpful in linking performance and pay to strategies. The percentage of a manager's annual bonus attributable to short-term versus long-term results should vary by hierarchical level in the organization. It is important that bonuses not be based solely on short-term results, because such a system ignores long-term company strategies and objectives.

To better link performance and pay to strategies, many companies have recently instituted policies to allow their shareholders to vote on executive compensation policies. Back in 2007, Aflac was the first U.S. firm to voluntarily give shareholders an advisory vote on executive compensation. Apple did the same in 2008, as did H&R Block. Several companies that instituted say-on-pay policies more recently were Ingersoll-Rand, Verizon, Motorola, Occidental Petroleum, and Hewlett-Packard. Firms are also establishing profit sharing, gain sharing, and bonus systems. More than 30 percent of U.S. companies have profit-sharing plans, but critics emphasize that too many factors affect profits for this to be a good criterion. Taxes, pricing, or an acquisition would wipe out profits, for example. Also, firms try to minimize profits in a sense to reduce taxes.

For employee (rather than executive) bonuses and incentives, only 16 percent of U.S. companies are now using stock price, down from 29 percent in 2009.[7] Instead, companies are using profit in order to more closely link employees' incentives to spending and budget decisions. PepsiCo, for example, recently began using profit and cash flow instead of stock price to focus managers on profit and cash-flow targets. PepsiCo's CFO, Hugh Johnston, remarked, "The change allows our employees to make decisions about spending and profit trade-offs themselves, rather than simply being handed a budget to follow; it's something they can wrap their arms around and say, 'Now I understand how I can impact PepsiCo's stock price.'" For upper-level executives, stock price is still the major variable used for compensation incentives, but for mid- and lower-level managers and employees, stock price is dependent on too many extraneous variables for it to be an effective compensation variable.

Gain sharing requires employees or departments to establish performance targets; if actual results exceed objectives, all members get bonuses. More than 26 percent of U.S. companies use some form of gain sharing; about 75 percent of gain-sharing plans have been adopted since 1980. Carrier, a subsidiary of United Technologies, has had excellent success with gain sharing in its six plants in Syracuse, New York; Firestone's tire plant in Wilson, North Carolina, has experienced similar success with gain sharing.

Criteria such as sales, profit, production efficiency, quality, and safety could also serve as bases for an effective **bonus system**. If an organization meets certain understood, agreed-on profit objectives, every member of the enterprise should share in the harvest. A bonus system can be an effective tool for motivating individuals to support strategy-implementation efforts. BankAmerica, for example, recently overhauled its incentive system to link pay to sales of the bank's most profitable products and services. Branch managers receive a base salary plus a bonus based both on the number of new customers and on sales of bank products. Every employee in each branch is also eligible for a bonus if the branch exceeds its goals. Thomas Peterson, a top BankAmerica executive, says, "We want to make people responsible for meeting their goals, so we pay incentives on sales, not on controlling costs or on being sure the parking lot is swept."

A combination of reward strategy incentives, such as salary raises, stock options, fringe benefits, promotions, praise, recognition, criticism, fear, increased job autonomy, and awards, can be used to encourage managers and employees to push hard for successful strategic implementation. The range of options for getting people, departments, and divisions to actively support strategy-implementation activities in a particular organization is almost limitless. Merck, for example, recently gave each of its 37,000 employees a 10-year option to buy 100 shares of Merck stock at a set price of $127.

In an effort to cut costs and increase productivity, more and more Japanese companies are switching from seniority-based pay to performance-based approaches. Toyota has switched to a full merit system for 20,000 of its 70,000 white-collar workers. Fujitsu, Sony, Matsushita Electric Industrial, and Kao also have switched to merit pay systems. This switching is hurting morale at some Japanese companies, which have trained workers for decades to cooperate rather than to compete and to work in groups rather than individually.

Richard Brown, CEO of Electronic Data Systems (EDS), once said,

You have to start with an appraisal system that gives genuine feedback and differentiates performance. Some call it ranking people. That seems a little harsh. But you can't have a manager checking a box that says you're either stupendous, magnificent, very good, good, or average. Concise, constructive feedback is the fuel workers use to get better. A company that doesn't differentiate performance risks losing its best people.[8]

Balance Work Life and Home Life

More women than men earn both undergraduate and graduate degrees in the United States, but a wage disparity still persists between genders at all education levels.[9] Women, on average, make 25 percent less than men. The average age today for U.S. women to get married is 30 years old for those with a college degree, and 26 years old for those with only a high school degree. About 29 percent of both men and women in the United States today have a college degree, whereas in 1970, only 8 percent of women and 14 percent of men had college degrees. In March 2015, the U.S. Census Bureau and American Association of University Women revealed that among full-time, year-round workers, women are paid, on average, 78 percent as much as men. The pay gap discrepancy between genders has not moved much in a decade. Catherine Rampell at the *Washington Post* reports that among 342 professions, women earn more than men in only *nine*. (For more information, see the two charts given at http://jobs.aol.com/articles/2015/03/24/charts-illustrate-gender-wage-gap/)

Work and family strategies now represent a competitive advantage for those firms that offer such benefits as elder care assistance, flexible scheduling, job sharing, adoption benefits, on-site summer camp, employee help lines, pet care, and even lawn service referrals. New corporate titles such as Work and Life Coordinator and Director of Diversity are becoming common. Globally, it is widely acknowledged that the best countries for working women are Iceland, Norway, Sweden, Finland, and Denmark, all of which rate above the United States. According to the World Economic Forum's 2014 report on the global gender gap overall, the United States, in fact, ranked number 20 overall.

Working Mother magazine annually published its listing of "The 100 Best Companies for Working Mothers" (www.workingmother.com). Three especially important variables used in the ranking were availability of flextime, advancement opportunities, and equitable distribution of benefits. Other important criteria are compressed weeks, telecommuting, job sharing, childcare facilities, maternity leave for both parents, mentoring, career development, and promotion for women. *Working Mother's* top 10 best companies for working women in 2014 are provided in Table 7-14. *Working Mother* also conducts extensive research to determine the best U.S. firms for women of color.

A corporate objective to become more lean and mean must today include consideration for the fact that a good home life contributes immensely to a good work life. The work and family issue is no longer just a women's issue. Some specific measures that firms are taking to address this issue are providing spouse relocation assistance as an employee benefit; supplying company resources for family recreational and educational use; establishing employee country clubs, such

TABLE 7-14 Top Ten Companies for Working Women

Company	# Employees	% Women	Headquarters
1. Abbott	18,400	47	Abbott Park, Illinois
2. Deloitte	45,900	42	New York, New York
3. Discovery Communications	3,600	53	Silver Spring, Maryland
4. Ernst & Young LLP	31,500	46	New York, New York
5. General Mills	16,500	40	Minneapolis, Minnesota
6. IBM	430,000	30	Armonk, New York
7. Prudential Financial	19,800	51	Newark, New Jersey
8. PwC	36,500	45	New York, New York
9. WellStar Health System	13,200	82	Marietta, Georgia
10. Zoetis	4,200	40	Florham Park, New Jersey

Source: Based on information at the Working Mother website, January 1, 2015.

TABLE 7-15 The 26 Fortune 500 Women CEOs in 2015 (up from 21 in 2013)

CEO	Company	Fortune 500 Rank
Mary Barra	GM	(#7)
Meg Whitman	HP	(#17)
Virginia Rometty	IBM	(#23)
Patricia Woertz	Archer Daniels Midland	(#27)
Indra Nooyi	PepsiCo, Inc.	(#43)
Marillyn Hewson	Lockheed Martin	(#59)
Safra Catz (co-CEO)	Oracle	(#82)
Ellen Kullman	DuPont	(#86)
Irene Rosenfeld	Mondelez International	(#89)
Phebe Novakovic	General Dynamics	(#99)
Carol Meyrowitz	TJX Companies	(#108)
Lynn Good	Duke Energy	(#123)
Ursula Burns	Xerox Corporation	(#137)
Deanna Mulligan	Guardian	(#245)
Kimberly Bowers	CST Brands	(#266)
Debra Reed	Sempra Energy	(#267)
Barbara Rentler	Ross Stores	(#277)
Sheri McCoy	Avon Products	(#282)
Denise M. Morrison	Campbell Soup	(#315)
Susan Cameron	Reynolds American	(#329)
Heather Bresch	Mylan	(#377)
Ilene Gordon	Ingredion	(#412)
Jacqueline Hinman	CH2M Hill	(#437)
Kathleen Mazzarella	Graybar Electric	(#449)
Lisa Su	Advanced Micro Devices	(#474)
Gracia Martore	Gannett	(#481)

Source: Fortune, http://fortune.com/2013/05/09/women-ceos-in-the-fortune-500/.

as those at IBM and Bethlehem Steel; and creating family and work interaction opportunities. A study by Joseph Pleck of Wheaton College found that in companies that do not offer paternity leave for fathers as a benefit, most men take short, informal paternity leaves anyway by combining vacation time and sick days.

Some organizations have developed family days, when family members are invited into the workplace, taken on plant or office tours, dined by management, and given a chance to see exactly what other family members do each day. Family days are inexpensive and increase the employee's pride in working for the organization. Flexible working hours during the week are another human resource response to the need for individuals to balance work life and home life.

There is great room for improvement in removing the glass ceiling domestically, especially considering that women make up 47 percent of the U.S. labor force. **Glass ceiling** refers to the invisible barrier in many firms that bars women and minorities from top-level management positions. The United States is a leader globally in promoting women and minorities into mid- and top-level managerial positions in business. However, only 5.2 percent (26/500) of Fortune 500 firms have a woman CEO. Academic Research Capsule 7-2 reveals that women CEOs more often than men lead firms to be more philanthropic (giving). Table 7-15 gives the 26 Fortune 500 Women CEOs in 2015. These women are excellent role models for women globally.

Develop a Diverse Workforce

Chief Executive Officer Rosalind Brewer, the first African American woman to lead a Walmart business unit, is turning Walmart's SAM's Club into a $100 billion business. A recent study by McKinsey & Co. revealed that Asian companies' average return on equity improves from 15

ACADEMIC RESEARCH CAPSULE 7-2

How Do Women vs. Men CEOs Perform?

It is widely acknowledged in the literature that increased presence of women executives and directors leads firms to make greater philanthropic contributions. Marquis and Lee concluded that women executives and directors seek to strengthen external relationships of the firm through corporate philanthropy. Recent research also indicates that firms need to be much more proactive in public relations efforts announcing a new female CEO, due to a "guilt by association" effect. Specifically, female CEOs, unlike their male counterparts, are subject to criticism simply by being among a small group for such top executive women. Thus, a firm should actively take steps to bring legitimacy to a female CEO by highlighting her qualifications and accomplishments, while minimizing gender-related stereotypes. Investors react more negatively to the appointment of female CEOs than to male counterparts, partly because of media reports, rather than any legitimate performance differences. Recent research also reveals that women (and people of color) are more likely than white men to be promoted CEO of weakly performing firms.

Source: Based on Marquis, Christopher, & Matthew Lee, "Who Is Governing Whom? Executives, Governance, and the Structure of Generosity in Large U.S. Firms." *Strategic Management Journal*, 34 (2013): 483–497. See also Dixon-Fowler, Heather, Alan Ellstrand, and Jonathan Johnson, "Strength in Numbers or Guilt by Association? Intragroup Effects of Female Chief Executive Announcements," *Strategic Management Journal*, 34 (April 2013): 1488–1501; and Cook, Alison, and Christy Glass, "Above the Glass Ceiling: When Are Women and Racial/Ethnic Minorities Promoted to CEO?" *Strategic Management Journal*, 7 (July 2014): 1080–1089.

to 22 percent when more and more women hold high-level positions.[10] Wang Jin at McKinsey remarks, "Women tend to be stronger in terms of collaboration and people development, while men tend to be stronger in individual decision making. By having more women at the senior level, companies are helping to improve organizational health as well as financial performanc*e*."[11]

An organization can perhaps be most effective when its workforce mirrors the diversity of its customers. For global companies, this goal can be optimistic, but it is a worthwhile goal. The customer base in every country includes gay persons. Thus, retailers are increasingly using gay couples in advertisements. Tiffany recently promoted the company's first same-sex couples in advertising, preceded by J. Crew. Gap, and Banana Republic using gay couples in advertising campaigns.

Six benefits of having a diverse workforce are as follows:

1. Women and minorities have different insights, opinions, and perspectives that should be considered.
2. A diverse workforce portrays a firm committed to nondiscrimination.
3. A workforce that mirrors a customer base can help attract customers, build customer loyalty, and design/offer products/services that meet customer needs/wants.
4. A diverse workforce helps protect the firm against discrimination lawsuits.
5. Women and minorities represent a huge additional pool of qualified applicants.
6. A diverse workforce strengthens a firm's social responsibility and ethical position.

The percentage of women on corporate boards in Australia increased from 8.3 in 2010 to more than 16 percent in 2016.[12] Malaysia and South Korea are also making excellent progress integrating women into upper levels of management and subsidizing companies that build child-care facilities and help women juggle work and family life. In contrast, women in India still are expected to care for their family and extended family; many women in India often have an abortion if they know their fetus is a girl. Overall, in Asia, women comprise only 6 percent of corporate board seats, compared to 17 percent in Europe and 15 percent in the United States. However, there are currently 24 countries globally with female presidents, chancellors, or prime ministers – the 22 pictured in Table 7-16, plus Switzerland (Simonetta Sommaruga) and Croatia (Kolinda Grabar-Kitarovic).

Use Caution in Hiring a Rival's Employees

A recent article titled "Dos and Don'ts of Poaching Workers" in *Investor's Business Daily* gives guidelines to consider before hiring a rival firm's employees.[13] The practice of hiring employees from rival firms has a long tradition, but increasingly in our lawsuit-happy environment, firms must consider whether that person(s) had access to the "secret sauce formula, customer list, programming algorithm, or any proprietary or confidential information" of the rival firm. If the

TABLE 7-16 Female Presidents, Chancellors, and Prime Ministers of Countries (as of 2015)

#	Country	Pic	Leader	In office since:	Notes
1	Germany		Chancellor **Angela Merkel**	Nov. 22, 2005 -	elected
2	Liberia		President **Ellen Johnson-Sirleaf**	Jan. 16, 2006 -	elected
3	Argentina		President **Cristina Fernandez de Kirchner**	Dec. 10, 2007 -	elected
4	Bangledesh		Prime Minister **Sheikh Hasina Wajed**	Jan. 6, 2009 -	elected
5	Lithuania		President **Dalia Grybauskaite**	Jul. 12, 2009 -	elected
6	Costa Rica		President **Laura Chinchilla**	May 8, 2010 -	elected
7	Trinidad and Tobago		Prime Minister **Kamla Persad-Bissessar**	May 26, 2010 -	elected
8	Brazil		President **Dilma Rousseff**	Jan. 1, 2011 -	elected
9	Kosovo		President **Atifete Jahjaga**	Apr. 7, 2011 -	elected
10	Denmark		Prime Minister **Helle Thorning-Schmidt**	Oct. 3, 2011 -	elected
11	Jamaica		Prime Minister **Portia Simpson Miller**	Jan. 5, 2012 -	elected
12	Malawi		President **Joyce Banda**	Apr. 7, 2012 -	succeeded

#	Country	Pic	Leader	In office since:	Notes
13	**South Korea**		President **Park Geun-hye**	Feb. 25, 2013 -	elected
14	**Slovenia**		Prime Minister **Alenka Bratusek**	Mar. 20, 2013 -	elected
15	**Cyprus (North)**		Prime Minister **Sibel Siber**	Jun. 13, 2013 -	appointed
16	**Senegal**		Prime Minister **Aminata Touré**	Sep. 3, 2013 -	appointed
17	**Norway**		Prime Minister **Erna Solberg**	Oct. 16, 2013 -	elected
18	**Latvia**		Prime Minister **Laimdota Straujuma**	Jan. 22, 2014 -	elected
19	**Central African Republic**		President **Catherine Samba-Panza**	Jan. 23, 2014 -	appointed
20	**Chile**		President **Michelle Bachelet**	Mar. 11, 2014 -	elected
21	**Malta**		President **Marie-Louise Coleiro Preca**	Apr. 7, 2014 -	elected
22	**Poland**	Not Available	Prime Minister **Ewa Kopacz**	Apr. 7, 2014 -	elected

Source: Based on information at http://www.jjmccullough.com/charts_rest_female-leaders.php. Used with permission.

person has that information and joins your firm, lawsuits could follow that hiring, especially if the person was under contract at the rival firm or had signed a "noncompete agreement." The article says that to help safeguard the firm from this potential problem, a "well-written employee handbook" addressing the issue is necessary. The article talks about Hewlett-Packard (HP) recently hiring an IBM general manager, and IBM suing HP over the hiring, and in that case lost, but this type of legal action is becoming more commonplace.

According to Wayne Perrett, human resource manager for ComAp in Roscoe, Illinois, "A company does not want to become known as one that "steals" employees from competitors; that is bad for ethics and bad for business." Thus, it is not illegal to interview and hire employees from rival firms, and it has been done for centuries, but increasingly this is becoming a strategic issue to be managed, to avoid litigation.

TABLE 7-17 Ways and Means for Altering an Organization's Culture

1. Recruitment
2. Training
3. Transfer
4. Promotion
5. Restructuring
6. Reengineering
7. Role modeling
8. Positive reinforcement
9. Mentoring
10. Revising vision and/or mission
11. Redesigning physical spaces/facades
12. Altering reward system
13. Altering organizational policies, procedures, and practices

Create a Strategy-Supportive Culture

All organizations have a unique **culture**. For example, at Facebook, Inc., employees are given unusual freedom to choose and change assignments. Even low-level employees are encouraged to question and criticize managers. Facebook employees are rated on a normal distribution curve (Bell curve), which creates a hectic, intense work environment, where past accomplishments mean little, compared to what you have done lately for the firm. Managers are not revered at Facebook as bosses; rather, they are regarded as helpers.

Strategists should strive to preserve, emphasize, and build on aspects of an existing culture that support proposed new strategies. Aspects of an existing culture that are antagonistic to a proposed strategy should be identified and changed. Changing a firm's culture to fit a new strategy is usually more effective than changing a strategy to fit an existing culture. As indicated in Table 7-17, numerous techniques are available to alter an organization's culture, including recruitment, training, transfer, promotion, restructure of an organization's design, role modeling, positive reinforcement, and mentoring.

Schein indicated that the following elements are most useful in linking culture to strategy:

1. Formal statements of organizational philosophy, charters, creeds, materials used for recruitment and selection, and socialization
2. Designing of physical spaces, facades, and buildings
3. Deliberate role modeling, teaching, and coaching by leaders
4. Explicit reward and status system and promotion criteria
5. Stories, legends, myths, and parables about key people and events
6. What leaders pay attention to, measure, and control
7. Leader reactions to critical incidents and organizational crises
8. How the organization is designed and structured
9. Organizational systems and procedures
10. Criteria used for recruitment, selection, promotion, leveling off, retirement, and "excommunication" of people[14]

When Volkswagen AG recently acquired Porsche, there was concern that the autocratic style of 75-year-old Volkswagen Chairman Ferdinand Piech would be at odds with Porsche's informal culture. Porsche had for a long time placed a premium on individual effort among its engineers and designers, often encouraging competition among groups to come up with new design ideas and innovations. Time will tell if Volkswagen and Porsche can meld their cultures into a competitive advantage.

In the personal and religious side of life, the impact of loss and change is easy to see.[15] Memories of loss and change often haunt individuals and organizations for years. Ibsen wrote, "Rob the average man of his life illusion and you rob him of his happiness at the same stroke."[16] When attachments to a culture are severed in an organization's attempt to change direction, employees and managers often experience deep feelings of grief. This phenomenon commonly occurs when external conditions dictate the need for a new strategy. Managers and employees often struggle to find meaning in a situation that changed many years before. Some people find comfort in memories; others find solace in the present. Weak linkages between strategic management and organizational culture can jeopardize performance and success. Deal and Kennedy emphasized that making strategic changes in an organization always threatens a culture:

> People form strong attachments to heroes, legends, the rituals of daily life, the hoopla of extravaganza and ceremonies, and all the symbols of the workplace. Change strips relationships and leaves employees confused, insecure, and often angry. Unless something can be done to provide support for transitions from old to new, the force of a culture can neutralize and emasculate strategy changes.[17]

Use Caution in Monitoring Employees' Social Media

Many companies monitor employees' and prospective employees' social media activities, and have the legal right to do so, but there are many pros and cons of this activity. Proponents of companies monitoring employees' social media activities emphasize that (1) a company's reputation in the marketplace can easily be damaged by disgruntled employees venting on social media sites and (2) social media records can be subpoenaed, like email, and used as evidence against the company. Proponents say companies have a responsibility to know the nature of employees' communication through social media as related to clients, patients, suppliers, distributors, coworkers, managers, technology, patents, procedures, policies, and much more. To ignore social media communication by employees, proponents say, is irresponsible and too risky for the firm. Using social media to research and screen job candidates, various companies report finding provocative/inappropriate photos and information related to potential employees' bias, stereotypes, prejudices, drinking, and using drugs that led to rejection of the candidate. Companies should never use social media to discriminate based on age, race, ethnic background, religion, sexuality, or handicapped issues.

However, arguments against the practice of companies monitoring employees' social media activities say it is an invasion of privacy and too often becomes "a fishing expedition" sifting through tons of personal information irrelevant to a company or its business. Positions on political issues, gun rights, or immigration are all examples topics where company researchers may "not like" individuals with different belief systems than their own. In a recent study, 77 percent of employers said they conduct Internet searches of prospective employees, and 35 percent have rejected job applicants because of information they found.[18] Rejecting potential employees because of private behavior unrelated to work is unfair. In addition, whenever a company discovers through social media that an employee or potential employee is Muslim, disabled, gay, or over 40 years old, for example, and then denies a promotion or hires someone else, that "social media discovery information" could be the basis of a discrimination suit against the firm. For some jobs, such as law enforcement, due diligence may require firms to monitor social media activities to help assure their entire workforce is not involved in drugs, child pornography, gangs, and so on.

On balance, companies generally should monitor employee and potential employee's social media activities whenever they have a reason to believe the person is engaged in illegal or unethical conduct—but to systematically investigate every employee and job candidate's social media activities is arguably counterproductive. The bottom line is that companies have the *legal right* to monitor employees' conduct, but have the *legal duty* to do so only if there is sufficient reason for concern.

Develop a Corporate Wellness Program

Corporate wellness has become a major strategic issue in companies. If you owned a company and paid the health insurance of employees, would you desire to have a healthy workforce? Your likely answer is *yes*, because health insurance premiums are more costly for an unhealthy workforce.

Corporate wellness programs have proliferated in recent years due in part to the Affordable Care Act, which increased the maximum incentives and penalties employers may use to encourage employee well-being.[19] Most companies therefore now have both "carrots," such as giving employee discounts on insurance premiums or even extra cash, and "sticks," such as imposing surcharges on premiums for those who do not make progress towards getting healthy. For example, the state of Maryland installed penalties up to $450 per person for 2017 on any employee who fails to undergo certain screenings or treatment plans. Similarly at CVS Health, employees pay an extra $600 if they do not comply with certain health policies. Some employers, however, face lawsuits for violating the Americans with Disabilities Act that forbids employers from requiring medical exams and making disability-related inquiries. At Caesars, employees may reduce their insurance premiums by $40 per paycheck if they participate in the firm's wellness program, and additionally can obtain a $250 annual bonus if they improve their healthiness over the year. Companies are increasingly instituting wellness programs to curtail growing health-care costs.

JetBlue has a corporate wellness program called LifeVest, where the firm gives $500 to employees who improve their body mass index. However, a recent report from the Bipartisan Policy Center's CEO Council on Health and Innovation concluded that "results from studies examining the return on investment of wellness programs are mixed." Despite mixed results, 74 percent of firms with wellness programs are increasing incentives "paid and charged" to employees to be and stay healthy, up from 57 percent a few years ago.

About 2.1 billion people globally, or 29 percent of the world's population, are obese, with most of those people living in developed countries.[20] From 1980 to 2013, the prevalence of obesity rose by 27.5 percent for adults and 47.1 percent for children. The percentage of a nation's population that is obese, from the most obese countries, are the United States, China, India, Russia, Brazil, Mexico, Egypt, Germany, Pakistan, and Indonesia.[21] Corporate wellness programs are largely aimed at reducing workforce obesity.

Recent articles detail how companies such as Johnson & Johnson (J&J), Lowe's Home-Improvement, the supermarket chain H-E-B, and Healthwise report impressive returns on investment of comprehensive, well-run employee wellness programs, sometimes as high as six to one.[22] A recent study by Fidelity Investments and the National Business Group on Health reports that nearly 90 percent of employers today offer some kind of wellness incentives or prizes to employees who "get healthier," up from 59 percent in 2009. For example, JetBlue Airways offers employees money—$25 for teeth cleanings, $400 for completing an Ironman triathlon, and so forth. Furniture company KI has all its employees divided into four groups based on "healthiness" with the most healthy people paying $1,000 less on health insurance premiums than the least healthy employees.

Chevron and Biltmore provide exemplary wellness programs that think beyond diet and exercise and focus also on stress management by assisting employees with such issues as divorce, serious illness, death and grief recovery, child rearing, and care of aging parents. Biltmore's two-day health fairs twice a year focus on physical, financial, and spiritual wellness. At Lowe's headquarters, an impressive spiral staircase in the lobby makes climbing the stairs more appealing than riding the elevator. Such practices as "providing abundant bicycle racks," "conducting walking meetings," and "offering five-minute stress breaks" are becoming common at companies to promote a corporate wellness culture.

Whole Foods Market, headquartered in Austin, Texas, is another outstanding corporate wellness company with its employees receiving a 30 percent discount card on all products sold in their stores "if they maintain and document a healthy lifestyle." In addition, Wegman's Food Markets, headquartered in Rochester, New York, has an excellent corporate wellness program. Scotts Miracle-Gro Company (based in Marysville, Ohio), IBM, and Microsoft are implementing wellness programs, requiring employees to get healthier or pay higher insurance premiums. Employees who do get healthier win bonuses, free trips, and pay lower premiums; nonconforming employees pay higher premiums and receive no "healthy" benefits. Wellness of employees has become a strategic issue for many firms. Most firms require a health examination as a part of an employment application, and healthiness is more and more becoming a hiring factor. Michael Porter, coauthor of *Redefining Health Care*, says, "We have this notion that you can gorge on hot dogs, be in a pie-eating contest, and drink every day, and society will take care of you. We can't afford to let individuals drive up company costs because they're not willing to address their own health problems."

TABLE 7-18 Seven Keys to Staying Healthy, Living to 100, and Being a "Well" Employee

1. Eat nutritiously—Eat a variety of fruits and vegetables daily because they have ingredients that the body uses to repair and strengthen itself.
2. Stay hydrated—Drink plenty of water to aid the body in eliminating toxins and to enable body organs to function efficiently; the body is mostly water.
3. Get plenty of rest—The body repairs itself during rest, so get at least seven hours of sleep nightly, preferably eight hours.
4. Get plenty of exercise—Exercise vigorously at least 30 minutes daily so the body can release toxins and strengthen vital organs.
5. Reduce stress—The body's immune system is weakened when one is under stress, making the body vulnerable to many ailments, so keep stress to a minimum.
6. Do not smoke—Smoking kills, no doubt about it anymore.
7. Take vitamin supplements—Consult your physician, but because it is difficult for diet alone to supply all the nutrients and vitamins needed, supplements can be helpful in achieving good health and longevity.

Source: Based on Etter, Lauren, "Trans Fats: Will They Get Shelved?" *Wall Street Journal*, December 8, 2006, A6. See also Fuhrman, Joel, MD, *Eat to Live* (Boston: Little, Brown, 2003).

Seven key lifestyle habits listed in Table 7-18 may significantly improve health and longevity.

The Equal Employment Opportunity Commission (EEOC) is presently investigating Honeywell International because the firm recently asked employees to participate in a voluntary health screening of their cholesterol, body mass index, and other health measures as part of the firm's corporate wellness program. The EEOC has a problem with the Honeywell provision that employees choosing not to sit for the medical screenings could face up to $4,000 in surcharges and lost incentives in 2015. This is only the third EECO investigation of any company's corporate wellness program, the other two being Flamgea Inc, owned by Nordic Group, and Orion Energy Systems, when employees were fired for not participating or their insurance cancelled for not participating in the firm's corporate wellness program. The EEOC got involved in the Honeywell matter when two employees filed discrimination charges under the Americans with Disabilities Act, after being requested to participate in the firm's health screenings. The Affordable Care Act specifically encourages firms to reward as well as penalize employees who do or do not meet specific health goals, such as lowering blood sugar, weight, or cholesterol. Honeywell's program applies to spouses of employees when those persons are covered too by the firm's health insurance plans. Health insurance is expensive and companies desire a healthy workforce.

About 38 percent of companies now cover weight-loss bariatric surgery for employees, according to the Society for Human Resource Management (SHRM). Many companies now promote weight-reduction programs under the banner of wellness programs. Some companies are promoting and even paying for newly approved weight-loss drugs, such as Belviq, Qsymia, and Contrave. The Equal Employment Opportunity Commission (EEOC) is set to release guidance to employers regarding dos and don'ts related to corporate wellness programs.

IMPLICATIONS FOR STRATEGISTS

Figure 7-7 reveals that to gain and sustain competitive advantages, firms must be exceptionally well organized, and must allocate resources appropriately across products, services, and regions. Employees must know clearly what rewards and benefits they will receive if the firm does well; this knowledge will help motivate the workforce to work hard. As indicated in this chapter, other management policies and procedures also are needed to facilitate superior strategic implementation, including respect for women and minorities, linking compensation to firm performance, encouraging corporate wellness, and nurturing an organizational culture that treats all people with respect. If strategists do an exceptional job with the management, production/operations, and human resource issues related to strategy implementation, as described in this chapter, the firm is well on its way to success. But there are also critically important marketing and financial strategy implementation issues, as examined in the next chapter.

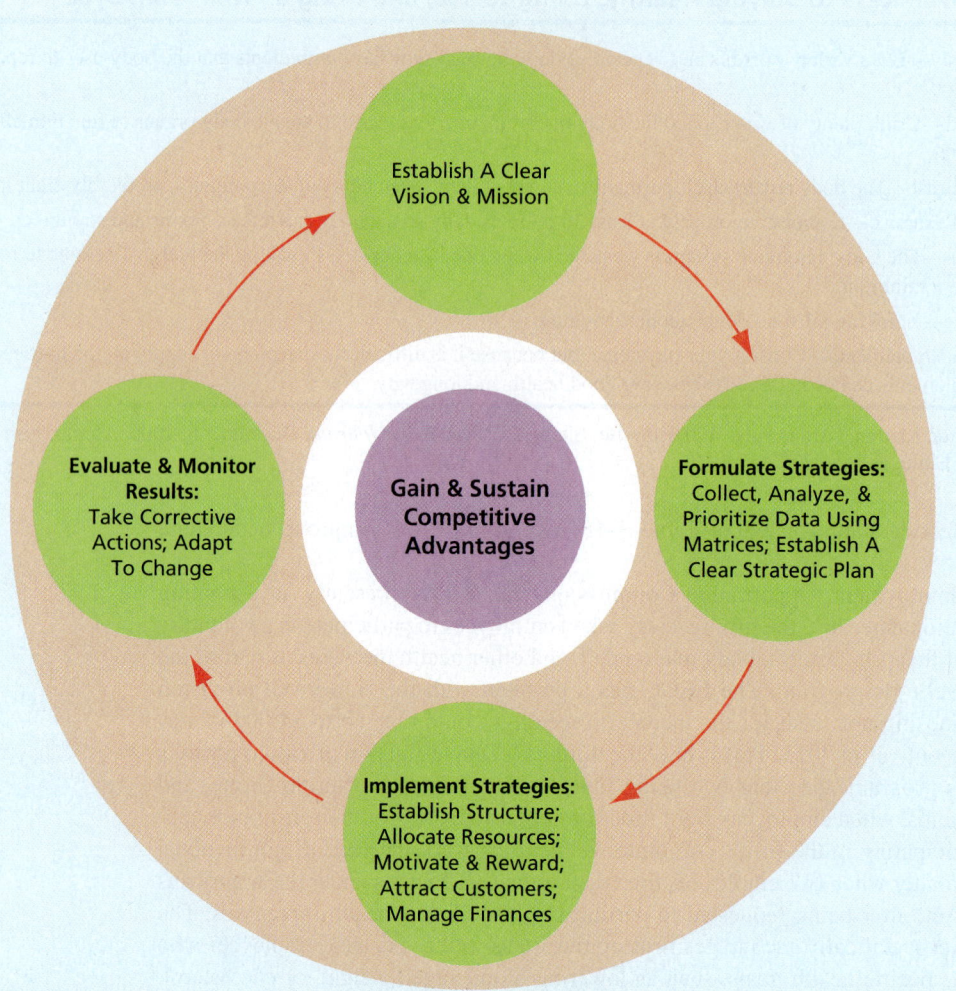

FIGURE 7-7

How to Gain and Sustain Competitive Advantages

IMPLICATIONS FOR STUDENTS

An integral part of managing a firm is continually and systematically seeking to gain and sustain competitive advantage through effective planning, organizing, motivating, staffing, and controlling. Rival firms engage in these same activities, so emphasize in your strategic-management case analysis how your firm can best implement your recommendations. Remember to be prescriptive rather than descriptive on every page or slide in your project, meaning to be insightful, forward-looking, and analytical, rather than just describing operations. It is easy to *describe* a company but it is difficult to *analyze* a company. Strategic-management case analysis is about *analyzing* a company and its industry, uncovering ways and means for the firm to best gain and sustain competitive advantage. So, communicate throughout your project how your firm, and especially your recommendations, will lead to improved growth and profitability versus rival firms. Avoid vagueness and generalities throughout your project, as your audience or reader seeks great ideas backed up by great analyses. Be analytical and prescriptive rather than vague and descriptive in highlighting every slide you show an audience.

A key consideration in devising an organizational structure concerns the divisions. Note whether the divisions (if any) of a firm presently are established based on geography, customer, product, or process. If the firm's organizational chart is not available, you often can devise a chart based on the titles of executives. An important case analysis activity is for you to decide how the divisions of a firm should be organized for maximum effectiveness. Even if the company presently has no divisions, determine whether it would operate better with divisions. In other words, which type of divisional breakdown do you (or your group or team) feel would be best for the firm in allocating resources, establishing objectives, and devising compensation incentives? This important strategic decision faces many midsize and large firms (and teams of students analyzing a strategic-management case).

Be mindful that all firms have functional staff below their top executive and often readily provide this information, so be wary of concluding prematurely that a particular firm uses a functional structure. If you see the word *president* in the titles of executives, coupled with financial-reporting segments, such as by product or geographic region, then the firm is currently divisionally structured.

Chapter Summary

Successful strategy formulation does not at all guarantee successful strategy implementation. Although inextricably interdependent, strategy formulation and strategy implementation are characteristically different. In a single word, strategy implementation means *change*. It is widely agreed that *the real work begins after strategies are formulated*. Successful strategy implementation requires the support of, as well as discipline and hard work, from motivated managers and employees. It is sometimes frightening to think that a single individual can irreparably sabotage strategy-implementation efforts.

Formulating the right strategies is not enough because managers and employees must be motivated to implement those strategies. Management issues considered central to strategy implementation include matching organizational structure with strategy, linking performance and pay to strategies, creating an organizational climate conducive to change, managing political relationships, creating a strategy-supportive culture, adapting production and operations processes, and managing human resources. Establishing annual objectives, devising policies, and allocating resources are central strategy-implementation activities common to all organizations. Depending on the size and type of the organization, other management issues could be equally important to successful strategy implementation.

MyManagementLab®

To complete the problems with the ⭐, go to EOC Discussion Questions in the MyLab..

Key Terms and Concepts

annual objectives (p. 208)
avoidance (p. 213)
bonus system (p. 226)
conflict (p. 213)
confrontation (p. 213)
culture (p. 232)
defusion (p. 213)
divisional (decentralized) structure by geographic area,
    product, customer, or process (p. 215)
educative change strategy (p. 223)
employee stock ownership plans (ESOPs) (p. 224)
force change strategy (p. 223)
functional structure (p. 214)
furloughs (p. 225)
gain sharing (p. 226)

glass ceiling (p. 228)
horizontal consistency of objectives (p. 210)
just-in-time (JIT) (p. 224)
matrix structure (p. 218)
policies (p. 211)
rational change strategy (p. 223)
reengineering (p. 222)
resistance to change (p. 223)
resource allocation (p. 211)
restructuring (p. 222)
self-interest change strategy (p. 223)
Six Sigma (p. 222)
strategic business unit (SBU) structure (p. 214)
vertical consistency of objectives (p. 210)

Issues for Review and Discussion

7-1. What policy do you recommend for companies regarding employees spending time on their personal Facebook and other social media accounts? Could your policy be enforced? How? Why?

⭐ **7-2.** What are some advantages and disadvantages of Nucor's organizational structure as discussed under "The Functional Structure" heading on page 214?

7-3. What do you like and dislike about the Crocs' organizational chart illustrated in the chapter, in terms of guidelines and dos and don'ts presented in the chapter?

⭐ **7-4.** List five important benefits of a company or organization having a diverse workforce.

7-5. Given the list of female Fortune 500 CEOs and the list of 25 countries with female presidents, chancellors, or prime ministers, is there any reason why women cannot perform equally or better than men as top-level strategists in companies? Discuss.

⭐ **7-6.** Discuss the "Dos and Don'ts of Poaching Workers" from rival firms.

7-7. Discuss recent trends and facts regarding corporate wellness programs in the United States.

7-8. What was the impact of the Affordable Care Act on corporate wellness programs?

7-9. Should companies monitor employees' social media? Why or why not? If yes, how?

7-10. Discuss the glass ceiling in the United States, giving your ideas and suggestions.

7-11. Discuss three ways for linking performance and pay to strategies.

7-12. List the different types of organizational structure. Diagram what you think is the most complex of these structures and label your chart clearly.

7-13. List the advantages and disadvantages of a functional versus a divisional organizational structure.

7-14. Discuss recent trends in women and minorities becoming top executives in the United States.

7-15. Discuss recent trends in firms downsizing family-friendly programs.

7-16. List seven guidelines to follow in developing an organizational chart.

7-17. Women comprise only 6 percent of corporate board seats in Asia, compared to 17 percent in Europe and 15 percent in the United States. Why is this a problem globally for many companies and countries?

7-18. Some head football coaches get paid millions, presumably because there is so much money involved in college football, the need to win is paramount. However, head coaches are often fired when a season goes badly, with huge payouts to the coach by contract. How could a head coach's compensation package be better structured to encourage winning, and at the same time not be so potentially costly to a university?

7-19. *Businessweek* says firms should "base executive compensation on actual company performance, rather than on the company's stock price." For example, Target Corp. bases executive pay on same-store sales growth rather than stock price. Discuss.

7-20. Advertising agencies are an example of an industry transitioning from specialist Hispanic, African American, and Asian firms to multicultural, generalist agencies. Why is this occurring? What other industries or institutions may follow suit? Why?

7-21. Describe three conflict situations in which to resolve the problems you would use (1) avoidance, (2) defusion, and (3) confrontation, respectively.

7-22. The chapter says strategy formulation focuses on effectiveness, whereas strategy implementation focuses on efficiency. Which is more important, effectiveness or efficiency? Give an example of each concept.

7-23. In stating objectives, why should terms such as *increase, minimize, maximize, as soon as possible, adequate*, and *decrease* be avoided?

7-24. Considering avoidance, defusion, and confrontation, which method of conflict resolution do you prefer most? Why? Which do you prefer least? Why?

7-25. Explain why Alfred Chandler's strategy–structure relationship commonly exists among firms.

7-26. If you owned and opened three restaurants after you graduated, would you operate from a functional or divisional structure? Why?

7-27. Explain how to choose between a divisional-by-product and a divisional-by-region organizational structure.

7-28. Think of a company that would operate best, in your opinion, by a division-by-services organizational structure. Explain your reasoning.

7-29. Identify and discuss four reasons why companies are phasing out the COO position.

7-30. In order of importance, in your opinion, list six advantages of a matrix organizational structure.

7-31. Why should division head persons have the title *president* rather than *vice president*?

7-32. Compare and contrast profit sharing with gain sharing as employee performance incentives.

7-33. List three resistance-to-change strategies. Give an example when you would use each method or approach.

7-34. In order of importance, in your opinion, list six techniques or activities widely used to alter an organization's culture.

7-35. What are the benefits of establishing an ESOP in a company?

7-36. List reasons why it is important for an organization not to have a "glass ceiling."

7-37. Allocating resources can be a political and an ad hoc activity in firms that do not use strategic management. Why is this true? Does adopting strategic management ensure easy resource allocation? Why?

7-38. Describe the relationship between annual objectives and policies.

7-39. Identify and discuss three policies that apply to your present strategic-management class.

7-40. Explain the following statement: Horizontal consistency of goals is as important as vertical consistency.

7-41. Describe several reasons why conflict may occur during objective-setting activities.

7-42. In your opinion, what approaches to conflict resolution would be best for resolving a disagreement between a personnel manager and a sales manager over the firing of a particular salesperson? Why?

7-43. Describe the organizational culture of your college or university.

7-44. Explain why organizational structure is so important in strategy implementation.

7-45. In your opinion, how many separate divisions could an organization reasonably have without using an SBU-type organizational structure? Why?

7-46. Identify and discuss three situations in the corporate world that especially warrant having a COO within the firm.

7-47. Do you believe expenditures for child-care or fitness facilities are warranted from a cost/benefit perspective? Why or why not?

7-48. Explain why successful strategy implementation often hinges on whether the strategy-formulation process empowers managers and employees.

7-49. Identify and discuss four primary reasons why annual objectives are so essential for effective strategy implementation.

7-50. Identify and discuss eight characteristics of objectives.

MyManagementLab®

Go to the Assignments section of your MyLab to complete these writing exercises.

7-51. What are the two major disadvantages of an SBU-type organizational structure? What are the two major advantages? At what point in a firm's growth do you feel the advantages offset the disadvantages? Explain.

7-52. Would you recommend a divisional structure by geographic area, product, customer, or process for a medium-sized bank in your local area? Why?

ASSURANCE OF LEARNING EXERCISES

EXERCISE 7A

Critique Corporate Organizational Charts

Purpose

There are tremendous benefits for a company (and an individual) to be well organized. Students know that being better organized usually yields higher grades. Competitiveness is so intense among companies in various industries that being well organized can make the difference between success and failure. This exercise gives you practice critiquing various organizational charts so that improved organizational designs for those companies can be devised.

Instructions

Step 1 In this chapter, refer to the Nucor organizational chart discussion on page 215. Visit the Nucor website. Click on Governance and then click on Executives. Prepare an effective organizational chart for Nucor.

Step 2 Discuss why you believe your new chart will be effective for Nucor.

EXERCISE 7B

Draw an Organizational Chart for Hershey Company Using a Free, Online Template

Purpose

Strategic-management students and business executives are oftentimes asked to construct an organizational chart. This exercise will make you aware of various online websites that provide free software for developing an organizational chart. Some websites in particular are as follows:

> www.vertex42.com/ExcelTemplates/organizational-chart.html
> http://office.microsoft.com/en-us/templates/business-organizational-chart-TC006088976.aspx
> www.edrawsoft.com
> www.smartdraw.com/specials/orgchart.asp
> www.orgchart.net

Instructions

Do a Google search for "organizational charts" and examine various free templates for constructing a chart. Decide which template you think is most user-friendly and effective. List some reasons why you decided on that particular template. Develop a sample organizational chart using the template you selected. Include 12 positions in your chart. Follow all guidelines provided in the chapter. In addition, use your template to develop an improved organizational chart for Hershey, as illustrated in the Cohesion Case.

EXERCISE 7C

Do Organizations Really Establish Objectives?

Purpose

Objectives provide direction, allow synergy, aid in evaluation, establish priorities, reduce uncertainty, minimize conflicts, stimulate exertion, and aid in both the allocation of resources and the design of jobs. This exercise will enhance your understanding of how organizations use or misuse objectives.

Instructions

Step 1 Join with one other person in class to form a two-person team.

Step 2   Contact the owner or manager of an organization in your city or town. Request a 15-minute personal interview or meeting with that person for the purpose of discussing "business objectives." During your meeting, seek answers to the following questions:

1. Do you believe it is important for a business to establish and clearly communicate long-term and annual objectives? Why or why not?
2. Does your organization establish objectives? If yes, what type and how many? How are the objectives communicated to individuals? Are your firm's objectives in written form or simply communicated orally?
3. To what extent are managers and employees involved in the process of establishing objectives?
4. How often are your business objectives revised and by what process?

Step 3   Take good notes during the interview. Let one person be the note taker and one person do most of the talking.

Step 4   Prepare a 5-minute oral presentation for the class, reporting the results of your interview. Turn in your typed report.

EXERCISE 7D

Understanding Your University's Culture

Purpose

It is something of an art to uncover the basic values and beliefs that are buried deeply in an organization's rich collection of stories, language, heroes, heroines, and rituals, yet culture can be the most important factor in implementing strategies.

Instructions

Step 1   On a separate sheet of paper, list the following terms: *hero/heroine, belief, metaphor, language, value, symbol, story, legend, saga, folktale, myth, ceremony, rite,* and *ritual.*

Step 2   For your college or university, give examples of each term. If necessary, speak with faculty, staff, alumni, administration, or fellow students of the institution to identify examples of each term.

Step 3   Report your findings to the class. Tell the class how and why cultural products can be managed to help implement strategies.

(Note to Professors—See the Chapter IM for an additional, excellent exercise for this chapter)

MINI-CASE ON HILTON WORLDWIDE HOLDINGS (HLT)

Source: Olgavolodina/Fotolia

IS THE NEW HILTON POLICY WARRANTED?

Headquartered in McLean, Virginia, Hilton Worldwide (and Marriott) on January 1, 2015, implemented a new policy that requires customers to notify the hotel the day before their scheduled arrival to avoid having to pay for the room. This policy reverses a long tradition of allowing customers to cancel their reservation "up to 6pm the day of arrival without penalty." Bob Gilbert, CEO of the Hospitality Sales and Marketing Association International, a hotel industry group, said of the Hilton move, "It's not surprising. The hotel business is one of the last places where you can hold inventory with no commitment." Hotel demand in 2014–2015 has exceeded supply in many cities, giving hoteliers the upper hand. Another motivation for the new policy is that hoteliers desire to stifle the use of apps such as Yapta that track hotel prices and, whenever a rate dips, apparently a growing number of travelers rebook at a lower rate and cancel the costlier reservation, literally right up until check-in time. Penny-pinching travelers are increasingly using such tools, and Hilton is seeking to stifle this practice. Big rivals to Hilton (and Marriott) are staying the course, however, with traveler-friendly cancellation policies, including Starwood, Sheraton, Westin, Four Points, Intercontinental, Crowne Plaza, Hotel Indigo, Holiday Inn, and others. Some customers now say they will avoid making a reservation at all if they will be charged for a room they did not use when, for instance, their plane gets delayed. Other customers say they will now simply use last-day booking services such as HotelTonight. Other customers say they will just book with Sheraton or Westin. Yet, Hilton says the industry needs to prevent the rapidly growing practice of travelers booking a hotel at the last minute after checking online for last-minute deals in the area. As discussed in this chapter, policies are often needed to effectively implement strategies.

Questions

1. Do you think the benefits will offset the costs of the new Hilton cancellation policy? Why?
2. Do you think the new Hilton cancellation policy is ethical? Is it legal? Is it practical?
3. What would be a more effective cancellation policy for Hilton?
4. How should a company such as Hilton decide on new policies?

Source: Company documents and a variety of sources.

Current Readings

Brinker, Scott, and Laura McLellan. "The Rise of the Chief Marketing Technologist." *Harvard Business Review* 92, no. 7/8 (2014): 82–85.

Ganster, Daniel C., and Christopher C. Rosen. "Work Stress and Employee Health: A Multidisciplinary Review." *Journal of Management* 39, no. 5 (2013): 1085–1122.

Gedmin, Jeffrey. "Our Mania for Measuring (and Remeasuring) Well-Being." *Harvard Business Review* 91, no. 9 (2013): 38.

Hewlett, Sylvia Ann, Melinda Marshall, and Laura Sherbin. "How Diversity Can Drive Innovation." *Harvard Business Review* 91, no.12 (2013): 30.

Hirsch, Peter. B. "Being Awkward: Creating Conscious Culture Change." *Journal of Business Strategy* 36, no. 1 (2015): 52–55.

Hoobler, Jenny M., Grace Lemmon, and Sandy J. Wayne. "Women's Managerial Aspirations: An Organizational Development Perspective." *Journal of Management* 40, no. 3 (2014): 703–730.

Ibarra, Herminia, Robin Ely, and Deborah Kolb. "Women Rising: The Unseen Barriers." (Cover Story). *Harvard Business Review* 91, no. 9 (2013): 60–67.

Krause, Ryan, Matthew Semadeni, and Albert A. Cannella. "CEO Duality: A Review and Research Agenda." *Journal of Management* 40, no. 1 (2014): 256–286.

Puranam, Phanish, Oliver Alexy, and Markus Reitzig. "What's 'New' about New Forms of Organizing?" *Academy of Management Review* 39, no. 2 (2014): 162–180.

Riccò, Rossella and Marco. "Diversity Challenge: An Integrated Process to Bridge the 'Implementation Gap.'" *Business Horizons* 57, no. 2 (2014): 235–245.

Wagner, Stephan, M. Kristoph, K. R. Ullrich, and Sandra Transchel. "The Game Plan dor Aligning the Organization." *Business Horizons* 57, no. 2 (2014): 189–201.

Endnotes

1. Dale McConkey, "Planning in a Changing Environment," *Business Horizons* (September–October 1988): 66.

2. A. G. Bedeian and W. F. Glueck, *Management,* 3rd ed. (Chicago: Dryden, 1983), 212.

3. Boris Yavitz and William Newman, *Strategy in Action: The Execution, Politics, and Payoff of Business Planning* (New York: The Free Press, 1982), 195.

4. E. H. Schein, "Three Cultures of Management: The Key to Organizational Learning," *Sloan Management Review* 38, 1 (1996): 9–20.

5. Joann Lublin, "Chairman-CEO Split Gains Allies," *Wall Street Journal*, March 30, 2009, B4.

6. Karen Richardson, "The 'Six Sigma' Factor for Home Depot," *Wall Street Journal*, January 4, 2007, C3.

7. Emily Chasan, "Stock Loses Some Sway on Pay," *Wall Street Journal,* October 30, 2012. B4.

8. Richard Brown, "Outsider CEO: Inspiring Change with Force and Grace," *USA Today,* July 19, 1999, 3B.

9. Conor Dougherty, "Strides by Women, Still a Wage Gap," *Wall Street Journal*, March 1, 2011, A3. See also David Jackson and Mimi Hall, "Women Gain in Education and Longevity," *USA Today*, March 2, 2011, 5A.

10. Kathy Chu, "Asian Women Fight Barriers," *Wall Street Journal,* July 2, 2012, B4.

11. Ibid.

12. Ibid.

13. Sheila Riley, "The Dos and Don'ts of Poaching Workers," *Investor's Business Daily*, March 31, 2014, A10.

14. E. H. Schein, "The Role of the Founder in Creating Organizational Culture," *Organizational Dynamics* (Summer 1983): 13–28.

15. T. Deal and A. Kennedy, "Culture: A New Look Through Old Lenses," *Journal of Applied Behavioral Science* 19, no. 4 (1983): 498–504.

16. H. Ibsen, "The Wild Duck," in O. G. Brochett and L. Brochett (Eds.), *Plays for the Theater* (New York: Holt, Rinehart and Winsstron, 1967); R. Pascale, "The Paradox of 'Corporate Culture': Reconciling Ourselves to Socialization," *California Management Review* 28, no. 2 (1985): 26, 37–40.

17. T. Deal and A. Kennedy, *Corporate Cultures: The Rites and Rituals of Corporate Life* (Reading, MA: Addison-Wesley, 1982), 256.

18. Nancy Flynn and Lewis Maltby, "Should Companies Monitor Their Employees' Social Media?" *Wall Street Journal*, May 12, 2014, R1.

19. Lauren Weber, "A Health Check for Wellness Programs," *Wall Street Journal,* October 8, 2014, B1, B8.

20. Betsy McKay, "About 30% of Word Is Overweight," *Wall Street Journal,* May 30, 2014.

21. Ibid.

22. Leonard Berry, Ann Mirabito, and William Baun, "What's the Hard Return on Employee Wellness Programs?" *Harvard Business Review,* December 210, 104–112. See also Jen Wieczner, "Your Company Wants to Make You Healthy," *Wall Street Journal,* December 17, 2014, B1.

Implementing Strategies: Marketing, Finance/ Accounting, R&D, and MIS Issues

LEARNING OBJECTIVES

After studying this chapter, you should be able to do the following:

8-1. Identify and describe strategic marketing issues vital for strategy implementation.

8-2. Explain why social media marketing is an important strategy-implementation tool.

8-3. Explain why market segmentation is an important strategy-implementation tool.

8-4. Explain how to use product positioning (perceptual mapping) as a strategy-implementation tool.

8-5. Identify and describe strategic finance/accounting issues vital for strategy implementation.

8-6. Perform EPS/EBIT analysis to evaluate the attractiveness of debt versus stock as a source of capital to implement strategies.

8-7. Develop projected financial statements to reveal the impact of strategy recommendations.

8-8. Determine the cash value of any business using four corporate evaluation methods.

8-9. Discuss IPOs, keeping cash offshore, and issuing corporate bonds as strategic decisions that face many firms.

8-10. Discuss the nature and role of research and development (R&D) in strategy implementation.

8-11. Explain how management information systems (MISs) impact strategy-implementation efforts.

ASSURANCE OF LEARNING EXERCISES

The following exercises are found at the end of this chapter:

EXERCISE 8A Develop a Product-Positioning Map for Hershey Company

EXERCISE 8B Gain Practice Developing Perceptual Maps

EXERCISE 8C Perform an EPS/EBIT Analysis for Hershey Company

EXERCISE 8D Prepare Projected Financial Statements for Hershey Company

EXERCISE 8E Determine the Cash Value of Hershey Company

EXERCISE 8F Develop a Product-Positioning Map for Your University

EXERCISE 8G Do Banks Require Projected Financial Statements?

Strategies can be implemented successfully only when an organization markets its goods and services effectively and raises needed working capital. This chapter examines marketing, finance/accounting, research and development (R&D), and management information systems (MIS) issues that are central to effective strategy implementation. Special topics include market segmentation, market positioning, evaluating the worth of a business, determining to what extent debt or stock should be used as a source of capital, developing projected financial statements, contracting R&D outside the firm, and creating an information support system. Manager and employee involvement and participation are essential for success in marketing, finance and accounting, R&D, and MIS activities.

A football quarterback can call the best play possible in the huddle, but that does not mean the play will go for a touchdown. The team may even lose yardage unless the play is executed (implemented) well. Headquartered in New York City, Foot Locker is implementing strategies especially well, as described below.

Strategy implementation generally impacts the lives of everyone in an organization. In some situations, individuals may not have participated in the strategy-formulation process at all and may not appreciate or understand the thought that went into strategy formulation, nor accept the work required for strategy implementation. There may even be foot dragging or resistance on their part. Managers and employees who do not understand the business and are not committed to the business may attempt to sabotage strategy-implementation efforts in hopes that the organization will return to its old ways. The strategy-implementation stage of the strategic-management process is highlighted in Figure 8-1 as illustrated with white shading.

Strategic Marketing Issues

Countless marketing variables affect the success or failure of strategy implementation efforts. Some strategic marketing issues or decisions are as follows:

1. How to make advertisements more interactive to be more effective
2. How to take advantage of Facebook and Twitter conservations about the company and industry

Foot Locker, Inc. (FL)

The athletic-footwear retailer Foot Locker is doing a great job managing debt versus equity, while aggressively growing globally. With over 3,500 stores in 23 countries, Foot Locker is adding about 25 stores quarterly, as the company implements an excellent strategic plan to grow its "kids business" globally, while also expanding into emerging markets. As rivals such as Finish Line, Hibbett, and Dick's Sporting Goods falter, Foot Locker's comparable store sales are growing mid-single digit year after year. The company's CEO, Ken Hicks, recently revealed the opening of many new Kids Foot Lockers globally, especially in Europe, where the company recently acquired German athletic store chain Runners Point Group's 200 stores and online sales business. Even as traffic in malls has declined in recent years, Foot Locker has done great, with apparel now comprising 24 percent of the company's revenues and online sales comprising 10 percent. Fully 30 percent of Foot Locker stores are located outside the United States. Customers are especially buying the company's colorful basketball shoes, the fastest-growing category in the athletic footwear market. Foot Locker operates about 1,050 stores in the United States, 610 in Europe, 140 in Canada, and 100 in the Asia-Pacific region. In addition, the company has about 350 Kids Foot Locker stores, 245 Lady Foot Locker stores, 550 Champs Sports stores, and 280 Footaction stores.

Foot Locker is adding more stores across Europe as basketball becomes more and more popular. To spur its women's business, Foot Locker recently opened nine fitness stores called Six:02 that offer yoga pants, workout gear, and related apparel.

Foot Locker recently introduced the Adidas D Lillard 1 shoe, named for Portland Trail Blazers point guard Damian Lillard, and supported the shoe with heavy marketing.

Source: Based on James Detar, "Foot Locker Steps Up Profit, Sales Gains as Broad Sporting Goods Chains Falter," *Investor's Business Daily*, May 27, 2014, A2, A7. Also based on Lawrence Carrel, "Foot Locker: Stepping into a Strategic Pivot," *Investor's Business Daily*, May 12, 2014, A6; and Marilyn Alva, "America's Sneaker Culture Powers Foot Locker," *Investor's Business Daily*, July 3, 2014, A5.

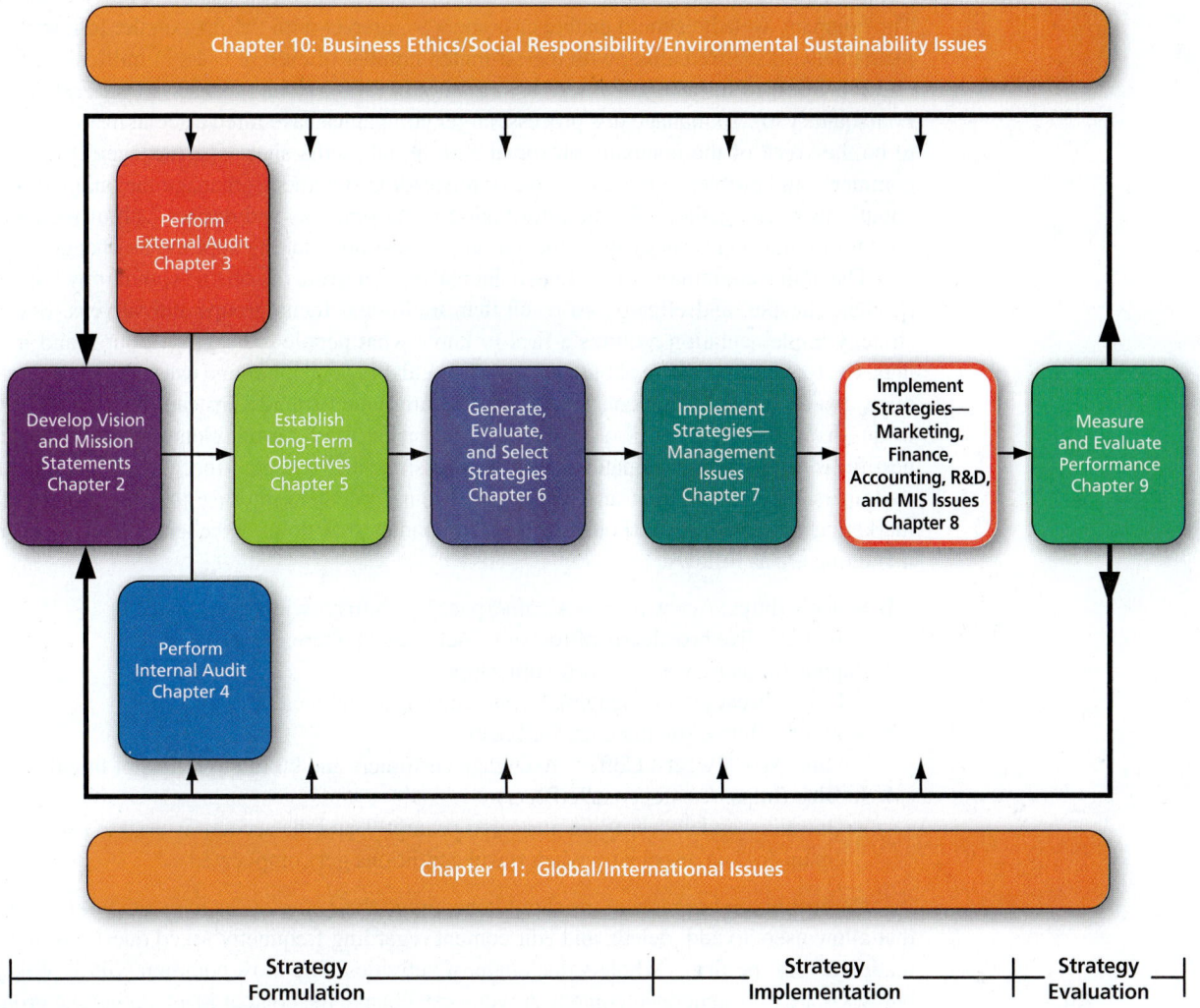

FIGURE 8-1

A Comprehensive Strategic-Management Model

Source: Fred R. David, "How Companies Define Their Mission," *Long Range Planning* 22, no. 3 (June 1988): 40. See also Anik Ratnaningsih, Nadjadji Anwar, Patdono Suwignjo, and Putu ArtamaWiguna, "Balance Scorecard of David's Strategic Modeling at Industrial Business for National Construction Contractor of Indonesia," *Journal of Mathematics and Technology*, no. 4 (October 2010): 20.

3. To use exclusive dealerships or multiple channels of distribution
4. To use heavy, light, or no TV advertising versus online advertising
5. To limit (or not) the share of business done with a single customer
6. To be a price leader or a price follower
7. To offer a complete or limited warranty
8. To reward salespeople based on straight salary, commission, or a combination salary and commission

Three marketing activities especially important in strategy implementation are listed below and then discussed:

1. Engage customers in social media.
2. Segment markets effectively.
3. Develop and use product-positioning/perceptual maps.

Social Media Marketing

Social media marketing has become an important strategic issue. Marketing has evolved to be more about building a two-way relationship with consumers than just informing consumers about a product or service. Marketers increasingly must get customers involved in the company website and solicit suggestions in terms of product development, customer service, and ideas. The company website should enable customers to interact with the firm on the following social media networks (listed along with the estimated number of current users in millions): Facebook (1,200), Google Plus (500), Twitter (400), LinkedIn (300), Instagram (200), Pinterest (100), and Foursquare (50). To manage this process, larger companies have hired a social media manager(s) to be the voice of the company on social and digital media sites. The manager(s) responds to comments and problems, track negative or misleading statements, manage the online discussion about a firm, and gather valuable information about opinions and desires—all of which can be vital for monitoring strategy implementation progress and making appropriate changes.

The online community of customers increasingly mirrors the offline community but is much quicker, cheaper, and effective to reach than traditional focus groups and surveys. Successful strategy implementation requires a firm to know what people are saying about it and its products. Customers are talking about and creating valuable content around every brand through blog posts, tweets, e-mails, and conversations with family and friends. Instead of ignoring or trying to quash "amateur content," or trying to drown it out with "professional advertisements," the best firms today embrace amateurs' opinions, desires, and feelings—because they are the firms' customers. They learn from and leverage amateur content to improve the authenticity of their marketing communication. Four example companies that do an excellent job of social media marketing are as follows:

1. SpaceX (https://www.facebook.com/SpaceX); (https://twitter.com/SpaceX)
   - Includes live broadcasts of rocket launches and pictures from space.
2. Zappos (https://www.facebook.com/zappos)
   - Does a great job of engaging its audience on social media.
3. Starbucks (https://twitter.com/Starbucks)
   - Launched "Tweet a Coffee" to engage customers and build awareness of brand.
4. JetBlue (https://twitter.com/JetBlue/)
   - Questions and concerns are answered promptly, and the account is used to keep customers up-to-date, especially when travel conditions get complicated.

Companies and organizations should encourage their employees to create **wikis**—websites that allow users to add, delete, and edit content regarding frequently asked questions and information across the firm's whole value chain of activities. The most common wiki is Wikipedia, but wikis are user-generated content. Anyone can change the content in a wiki but the group and other editors can change the content submitted.

Firms benefit immensely by providing incentives to customers to share their thoughts, opinions, and experiences on the company website. Encourage customers to network among themselves on topics of their choosing on the company website. The company website must not be just about the company—it must be all about the customer too. Perhaps offer points, discounts, or coupons on the website for customers who provide ideas, suggestions, or feedback. Drive traffic to the company website, and then keep customers at the website for as long as possible with daily new material, updates, excitement, and offers. Encourage and promote customer participation and interaction. Customers trust other customers' opinions more than a company's marketing pitch, and the more they talk freely, the more the firm can learn how to improve its product, service, and marketing. Marketers should monitor blogs daily to determine, evaluate, and influence opinions being formed by customers. Customers must not feel like they are a captive audience for advertising at a firm's website. Table 8-1 provides new principles of marketing according to Parise, Guinan, and Weinberg.[1]

Wells Fargo and Bank of America **tweet** (Twitter.com) customers to describe features of bank products. Some banks are placing marketing videos on YouTube. UMB Financial of Kansas City, Missouri, tweets about everything from the bank's financial stability to the industry's prospects. Steve Furman, Discover's director of e-commerce, says the appeal of social networking is that it provides "pure, instant" communication with customers.[2]

Although the exponential increase in social networking has created huge opportunities for marketers, it also has produced some severe threats. Perhaps the greatest threat is that any kind of negative publicity travels fast online. Seemingly minor ethical and questionable actions can catapult these days into huge public relations problems for companies as a result of the monumental online social and business communications.

TABLE 8-1 The New Principles of Marketing

1. Do not just talk at consumers—work with them throughout the marketing process.
2. Give consumers a reason to participate.
3. Listen to—and join—the conversation outside your company's website.
4. Resist the temptation to sell, sell, sell. Instead attract, attract, attract.
5. Do not control online conversations; let it flow freely.
6. Find a "marketing technologist," a person who has three excellent skill sets (marketing, technology, and social interaction).
7. Embrace instant messaging and chatting.

Source: Based on Salvatore Parise, Patricia Guinan, and Bruce Weinberg, "The Secrets of Marketing in a Web 2.0 World," *Wall Street Journal*, December 15, 2008, R1.

Increasingly, people living in underdeveloped and poor nations around the world have smartphones, but oftentimes no computers. This is opening up even larger markets to online marketing. People in remote parts of Indonesia, Egypt, and Africa represent the fastest-growing customer base for many companies, including Opera Software ASA, a Norwegian maker of Internet browsers for mobile devices.

People ages 18 to 27 spend more time weekly on the Internet than watching television, listening to the radio, and watching DVDs combined. Most companies have come to the realization that social networking and video sites are better means of reaching customers than spending so many marketing dollars on traditional yellow pages, television, magazine, radio, or newspaper ads.

New companies such as Autonet Mobile based in San Francisco are selling new technology equipment for cars so that everyone in the vehicle can be online except, of course, the driver. This technology is accelerating the movement from hard media to web-based media. With this technology, when the vehicle drives into a new location, information on shows, museums, hotels, and other attractions in the location can be instantly downloaded.

Digital advertising spending on social media and mobile devices increased nearly 17 percent to $50 billion in the United States in 2014, comprising 28 percent of total ad spending in the nation; however, about 36 percent of all traffic on the Internet is fake, being the result of bogus computers programmed to visit websites to take advantage of marketers who typically pay for ads whenever they are loaded when a user visits a webpage, regardless if the user is an actual person.[3] Criminals can erect websites and deliver phony traffic and collect payments from advertisers through middlemen, oftentimes in third-world countries. This fraud problem is becoming so severe that Bob Liodice, CEO of the Association of National Advertisers, observes, "The total digital-media ad budget is being questioned and totally challenged; marketers want to spend more money in digital, but until there is more transparency on how their money is being spent, many hold back."[4]

The ad-fraud detection firm White Ops reports that more than $6 billion of online ads in the USA annually are paid to "fraudsters." Digital advertising is here to stay, no doubt, but there is a need to be increasingly careful of automated (fake) systems/websites/individuals securing your ad monies.

Market Segmentation

Market segmentation and product positioning rank as marketing's most important contributions to strategic management. **Market segmentation** can be defined as the subdividing of a market into distinct subsets of customers according to needs and buying habits. For example, eBay recently initiated a new market segmentation strategy to target consumers under 18 years old. "We're definitely looking at ways to legitimately bring younger people in," said Devin Wenig at eBay. "We won't allow a 15-year-old unfettered access to the site. We would want a parent, an adult, as a ride-along. But the age 18 and up group [is] an increasingly savvy and desirable consumer segment for us."

Market segmentation is important in strategy implementation for at least three major reasons. First, strategies such as market development, product development, market penetration,

TABLE 8-2 The Marketing Mix Component Variables

Product	Place	Promotion	Price
Quality	Distribution channels	Advertising	Level
Features and options	Distribution coverage	Personal selling	Discounts and allowances
Style	Outlet location	Sales promotion	Payment terms
Brand name	Sales territories	Publicity	
Packaging	Inventory levels and locations		
Product line	Transportation carriers		
Warranty			
Service level			
Other services			

Source: Based on E. Jerome McCarthy, *Basic Marketing: A Managerial Approach,* 9th ed. (Homewood, IL: Richard D. Irwin, Inc., 1987), 37–44. Used with permission.

and diversification require increased sales through new markets and products. To implement these strategies successfully, new or improved market-segmentation approaches are required. Second, market segmentation allows a firm to operate with limited resources because mass production, mass distribution, and mass advertising are not required. Market segmentation enables a small firm to compete successfully with a large firm by maximizing per-unit profits and per-segment sales. And third, market segmentation decisions directly affect **marketing mix variables**: product, place, promotion, and price, as indicated in Table 8-2. Geographic and demographic bases for segmenting markets are the most commonly employed, as illustrated in Table 8-3.

Evaluating potential market segments requires strategists to determine the characteristics and needs of consumers, to analyze consumer similarities and differences, and to develop consumer group profiles. Segmenting consumer markets is generally much simpler and easier than segmenting industrial markets, because industrial products, such as electronic circuits and forklifts, have multiple applications and appeal to diverse customer groups.

Segmentation is a key to matching supply and demand, which is one of the thorniest problems in customer service. Segmentation often reveals that large, random fluctuations in demand actually consist of several small, predictable, and manageable patterns. Matching supply and demand allows factories to produce desirable levels without extra shifts, overtime, and subcontracting. Matching supply and demand also minimizes the number and severity of stock-outs. The demand for hotel rooms, for example, can be dependent on foreign tourists, businesspersons, and vacationers. Focusing separately on these three market segments, however, can allow hotel firms to more effectively predict overall supply and demand.

Banks now are segmenting markets to increase effectiveness. "You're dead in the water if you aren't segmenting the market," observes Anne Moore, president of a bank consulting firm in Atlanta. The Internet makes market segmentation easier today because consumers naturally form "communities" on the Web.

To aid in segmenting markets and targeting specific groups of customers, companies commonly tag each of their active customers with three "retention" values:

- Tag 1: Is this customer at high risk of canceling the company's service? One of the most common indicators of high-risk customers is a drop off in usage of the company's service. For example, in the credit card industry this could be signaled through a customer's decline in spending on his or her card.
- Tag 2: Is this customer worth retaining? This determination boils down to whether the postretention profit generated from the customer is predicted to be greater than the cost incurred to retain the customer. Customers need to be managed as investments.
- Tag 3: What retention tactics should be used to retain this customer? For customers who are deemed "save-worthy," it is essential for the company to know which save tactics are most likely to be successful. Tactics commonly used range from providing "special" customer discounts to sending customers communications that reinforce the value proposition of the given service.[5]

TABLE 8-3 Alternative Bases for Market Segmentation

Variable	Typical Breakdowns
Geographic	
Region	Pacific, Mountain, West North Central, West South Central, East North Central, East South Central, South Atlantic, Middle Atlantic, New England
County Size	A, B, C, D
City Size	Under 5,000; 5,000–20,000; 20,001–50,000; 50,001–100,000; 100,001–250,000; 250,001–500,000; 500,001–1,000,000; 1,000,001–4,000,000; 4,000,001 or over
Density	Urban, suburban, rural
Climate	Northern, southern
Demographic	
Age	Under 6, 6–11, 12–19, 20–34, 35–49, 50–64, 65+
Gender	Male, female
Family Size	1–2, 3–4, 5+
Family Life Cycle	Young, single; young, married, no children; young, married, youngest child under 6; young, married, youngest child 6 or over; older, married, with children; older, married, no children under 18; older, single; other
Income	Under $10,000; $10,001–$15,000; $15,001–$20,000; $20,001–$30,000; $30,001–$50,000; $50,001–$70,000; $70,001–$100,000; over $100,000
Occupation	Professional and technical; managers, officials, and proprietors; clerical and sales; craftspeople; foremen; operatives; farmers; retirees; students; housewives; unemployed
Education	Grade school or less; some high school; high school graduate; some college; college graduate
Religion	Catholic, Protestant, Jewish, Islamic, other
Race	White, Asian, Hispanic, African American
Nationality	American, British, French, German, Scandinavian, Italian, Latin American, Middle Eastern, Japanese
Psychographic	
Social Class	Lower lowers, upper lowers, lower middles, upper middles, lower uppers, upper uppers
Personality	Compulsive, gregarious, authoritarian, ambitious
Behavioral	
Use Occasion	Regular occasion, special occasion
Benefits Sought	Quality, service, economy
User Status	Nonuser, ex-user, potential user, first-time user, regular user
Usage Rate	Light user, medium user, heavy user
Loyalty Status	None, medium, strong, absolute
Readiness Stage	Unaware, aware, informed, interested, desirous, intending to buy
Attitude toward Product	Enthusiastic, positive, indifferent, negative, hostile

Source: Adapted from Philip Kotler, *Marketing Management: Analysis, Planning and Control,* © 1984: 256. Adapted by permission of Prentice-Hall, Inc., Upper Saddle River, New Jersey.

The idea with retention-based segmentation is to examine and compare the attributes of active customers with the attributes of prior customers in order to better target potential customers with similar attributes. Using the theory that "birds of a feather flock together," the approach is based on the assumption that active customers will have similar retention outcomes as those of their comparable predecessor. This whole process is possible through business analytics or **data mining**.

People all over the world are congregating into virtual communities on the web by becoming members, customers, and visitors of websites that focus on an endless range of topics. People essentially segment themselves by nature of the websites that comprise their "favorite places," and many of these websites sell information regarding their "visitors." Businesses and groups of individuals all over the world pool their purchasing power in websites to get volume discounts. Through its Connect feature, Facebook uses a type of mobile advertising that targets consumers based on the apps they use from their phones. Connect lets users log into millions of websites and apps with their Facebook identity, so the company then targets ads based on that data. Facebook can also track what people do on their apps. Google uses similar means to gather (and sell) market segmentation data.

Product Positioning and Perceptual Mapping

After markets have been segmented so that the firm can target particular customer groups, the next step is to find out what customers want and expect. This takes analysis and research. A severe mistake is to assume the firm knows what customers want and expect. Countless research studies reveal large differences between how customers define service and rank the importance of different service activities versus how companies view services. Many firms have become successful by filling the gap between what customers versus companies see as good service. What the customer believes is good service is paramount, not what the producer believes service should be.

Product positioning (sometimes called **perceptual mapping**) entails developing schematic representations that reflect how products or services compare to those of the competitors on dimensions most important to success in the industry. Product positioning is widely used for deciding how to meet the needs and wants of particular consumer groups. The technique can be summarized in five steps:

1. Select key criteria that effectively differentiate products or services in the industry.
2. Diagram a two-dimensional product-positioning map with specified criteria on each axis.
3. Plot major competitors' products or services in the resultant four-quadrant matrix.
4. Identify areas in the positioning map where the company's products or services could be most competitive in the given target market. Look for vacant areas (niches).
5. Develop a marketing plan to position the company's products or services appropriately.

Because just two criteria can be examined on a single product-positioning (perceptual) map, multiple maps are often developed to assess various approaches to strategy implementation. **Multidimensional scaling** could be used to examine three or more criteria simultaneously, but this technique is beyond the scope of this text. Some rules for using product positioning as a strategy-implementation tool are the following:

1. Look for the hole or **vacant niche**, which is a segment of the market currently not being served.
2. Do not serve two segments with the same strategy. Usually, a strategy successful with one segment cannot be directly transferred to another segment.
3. Do not position yourself in the middle of the map. The middle usually indicates a strategy that is not clearly perceived to have any distinguishing characteristics. This rule can vary with the number of competitors. For example, when there are only two competitors, as in U.S. presidential elections, the middle becomes the preferred strategic position.[6]

An effective product-positioning strategy meets two criteria: (1) it uniquely distinguishes a company from the competition and (2) it leads customers to expect slightly less service than a company can deliver. Network Equipment Technology is an example of a company that keeps customer expectations slightly below perceived performance. This is a constant challenge for marketers. Firms need to inform customers about what to expect and then exceed the promise. Underpromise and overdeliver! That is a key for excellent strategy implementation.

The product positioning map, or perceptual map, in Figure 8-2 shows consumer perceptions of various automobiles on the two dimensions of sporty and conservative and classy and affordable. This sample of consumers felt Porsche was the sportiest and classiest of the cars in the study (top right corner) and Plymouth was the most practical and conservative (bottom left corner). Car manufacturers focus their marketing efforts on various target groups, or design features in their vehicles, based on research and survey information illustrated in perceptual maps. Perceptual maps can aid marketers in being more effective in spending money to promote products. Products, brands, or companies positioned close to one another are perceived as similar

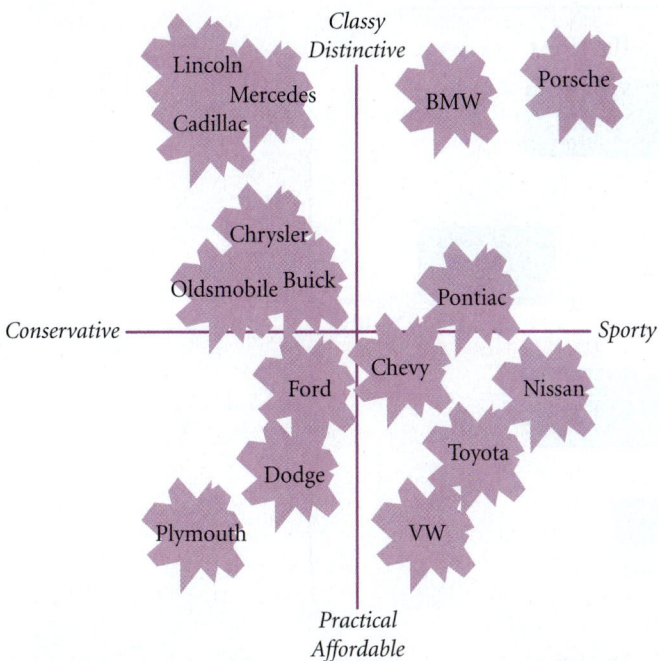

FIGURE 8-2

A Perceptual Map for the Automobile Industry

Source: Based on info at http://en.wikipedia.org/wiki/Perceptual_mapping.

on the relevant dimensions. For example, in Figure 8-2, consumers see Lincoln, Mercedes, and Cadillac as similar. They are close competitors and form a competitive grouping. A company considering the introduction of a new or improved model may look for a vacant niche on a perceptual map. Some perceptual maps use different size circles to indicate the sales volume or market share of the various competing products.

Perceptual maps may also display consumers' ideal points. These points reflect ideal combinations of the two dimensions as seen by a consumer. Dots are often used to represent one respondent's ideal combination of the two dimensions. Areas where there is a cluster of ideal points indicates a **market segment**. Areas without ideal points are sometimes referred to as **demand voids**. A company considering introducing a new product will look for areas with a high density of ideal points. They will also look for areas without competitive rivals (a vacant niche), perhaps best done by placing both the (1) ideal points and (2) competing products on the same map.

Companies commonly develop several perceptual maps to better understand competitive advantages and disadvantages versus rival companies. For example, the largest homebuilder in the United States, D. R. Horton (DRH), competes with Pulte, Lennar, KB Home, and other homebuilders. Figures 8-3, 8-4, and 8-5 reveal recently developed D. R. Horton perceptual maps. Note the author commentary provided for each illustration.

Author Commentary

AUTHOR COMMENTARY ON FIGURE 8-3 Price versus Quality is used in a perceptual map because these two factors are often viewed as the most important considerations when purchasing a home. The average sale price per DRH home is lower than any other major homebuilders in the United States, which is why they are the lowest on the perceptual map. Oftentimes, however, being the low-cost provider can mean actual, or perceived, low quality. The map reveals that DRH is above only KB Home in quality. Quality was determined through interpreting online ratings of the companies, as well as reviewing all of the competitor's websites for proof that quality was being provided. Note that Lennar is the closet to DRH on the Price versus Quality perceptual map.

AUTHOR COMMENTARY ON FIGURE 8-4 When buying or building a new home, consumers not only want to make sure it can be built where they want it but also with the layout or options they desire. By comparing coverage maps of the largest homebuilders in the United States, it was concluded that DRH has the highest geographical coverage of all the competitors. Additionally,

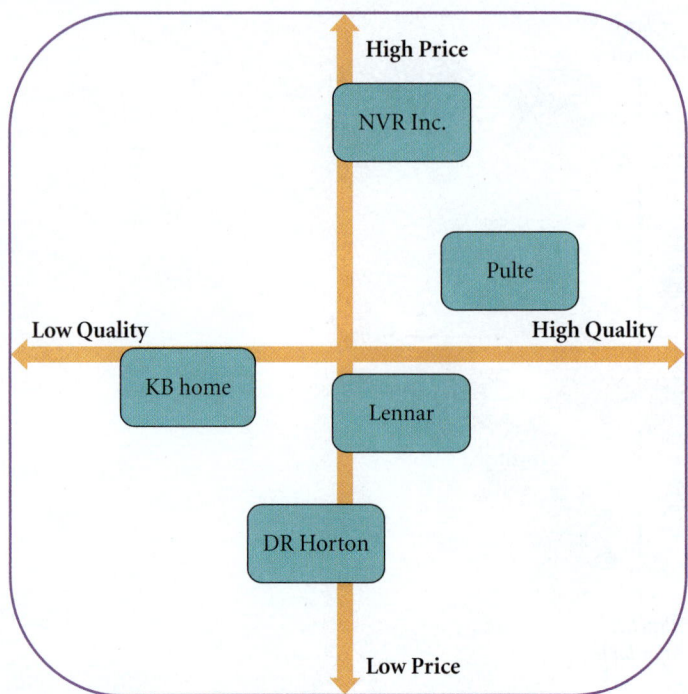

FIGURE 8-3
A DRH Perceptual Map—Price versus Quality

through a review of the homebuilder's websites, it was determined that DRH has the largest quantity of options and layouts for new homes. Neither of these facts should come as a surprise, as DRH does hold the title of "Largest Home Builder in the USA." Rival firms are placed accordingly on the perceptual map. Note that Lennar is the closest to DRH on the Number of Options and Layouts versus Geographical Coverage perceptual map.

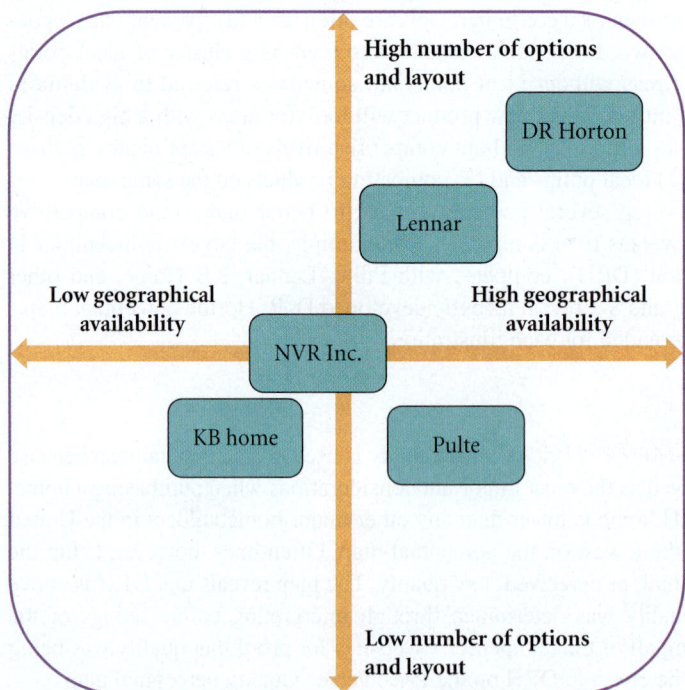

FIGURE 8-4
A DRH Perceptual Map—Number of Options/Layouts versus Geographical Availability

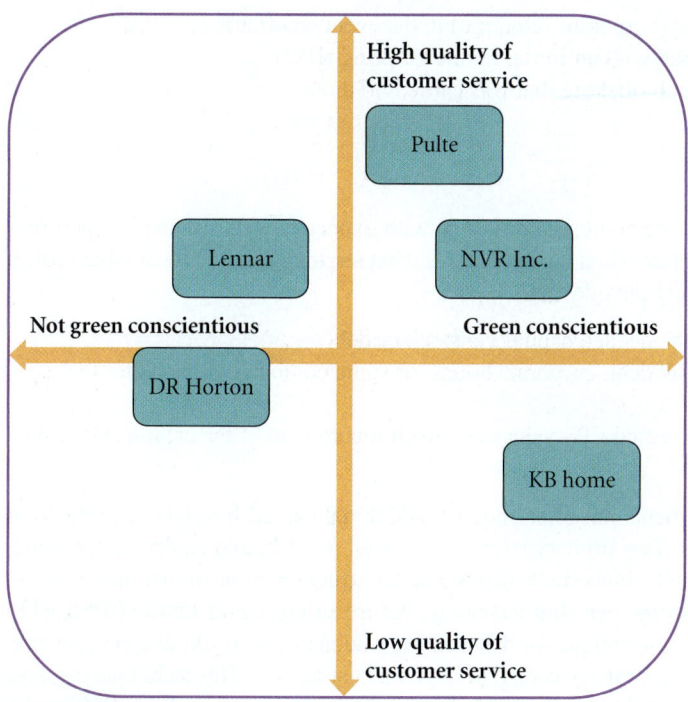

FIGURE 8-5
A DRH Perceptual Map—Quality of Customer Service versus Extent the Firm is Green Conscientious

AUTHOR COMMENTARY ON FIGURE 8-5 Consumers increasingly are concerned with what and from whom they are purchasing. Thus, customer service and green conscientiousness are often key factors considered by consumers. After examining online ratings of the largest homebuilders and reviewing competitor's websites, it was determined that DRH has, at best, average customer service. There were numerous complaints at several websites, and not very many resolutions, or ways to find resolutions. Furthermore, through a review of the competitors' websites, it appears that DRH is the least green conscientious builder among the major players. It had very little, if any, mention of green considerations, whereas some firms had very involved and detailed sections on their web pages about green building. Note that Lennar is the closest to DRH on the Quality of Customer Service versus Extent the Firm is Green Conscientious perceptual map.

Strategic Finance/Accounting Issues

Several finance/accounting concepts central to strategy implementation are acquiring needed capital, developing projected financial statements, preparing financial budgets, and evaluating the worth of a business. Some examples of decisions that may require finance and accounting policies are:

1. To raise capital with short-term debt, long-term debt, preferred stock, or common stock
2. To lease or buy fixed assets
3. To determine an appropriate dividend payout ratio
4. To use last-in, first-out (LIFO), first-in, first-out (FIFO), or a market-value accounting approach
5. To extend the time of accounts receivable
6. To establish a certain percentage discount on accounts within a specified period of time
7. To determine the amount of cash that should be kept on hand

Five especially important finance/accounting activities central to strategy implementation are listed below and then discussed:

1. Acquire needed capital to implement strategies; perform EPS/EBIT analysis
2. Develop projected financial statements to show expected impact of strategies implemented

3. Determine the firm's value (corporate valuation) in the event an offer is received
4. Decide whether to go public with an Initial Public Offering (IPO)
5. Decide whether to keep cash offshore that was earned offshore

EPS/EBIT Analysis: Acquire Needed Capital

When students complete their recommendations page with expected costs summed as part of a case analysis, or in actual practice when a firm decides what strategies to pursue at what cost, it is necessary to address the following questions:

1. Can the company obtain the needed capital via stock or debt?
2. Would common stock, bank debt, corporate bonds, or some combination be better to raise needed capital?
3. What would the firm's projected EPS values be, given securement of the capital and implementation of the strategies?

Successful strategy implementation often requires additional capital beyond net profit from operations or the sale of assets. Two primary sources of capital are debt and equity. Determining an appropriate mix of debt and equity in a firm's capital structure is an important strategy-implementation decision. **Earnings per share/earnings before interest and taxes (EPS/EBIT) analysis** is the most widely used technique for determining whether debt, stock, or a combination of the two is the best alternative for raising capital to implement strategies. This technique involves an examination of the impact that debt versus stock financing has on earnings per share (EPS) under various expectations for EBIT, given specific recommendations (strategies to be implemented).

Theoretically, an enterprise should have enough debt in its capital structure to boost its return on investment by applying debt to products and projects earning more than the cost of the debt. In low-earning periods, too much debt in the capital structure of an organization can endanger stockholders' returns and jeopardize company survival. Fixed debt obligations generally must be met, regardless of circumstances. This does not mean that stock issuances are always better than debt for raising capital. When the cost of capital (interest rates) is low, debt may be better than stock to obtain capital, but the analysis still must be performed because high stock prices usually accompany low interest rates, making stock issuances attractive for obtaining capital. Some special concerns with stock issuances are dilution of ownership, effect on stock price, and the need to share future earnings with all new shareholders.

Another popular way for a company to raise capital is to issue corporate bonds, which is analogous to going to the bank and borrowing money, except that with bonds, the company obtains the funds from investors rather than banks. Especially when a company's balance sheet is strong and its credit rating excellent, issuing bonds can be an effective, and certainly an alternative way to raise needed capital. In 2014, companies around the world issued more than $1 trillion in corporate bonds, more than 4 percent higher than the prior year. Thus, even with high stock prices, the low interest rate environment enticed companies to increasingly use debt to (1) finance growth, (2) pay dividends, and (3) buy back their own stock (called **treasury stock**). In fact, in 2014, companies sold corporate bonds at the fastest pace ever, led by Apple, Numericable Group (a French firm), Oracle, Petrobras, Cisco, and Bank of America. Twitter recently raised $1.5 billion by offering **convertible bonds** in two chunks of $650 million. The word *convertible* means the bonds can be converted into shares of stock in some cases. Companies lately have been flocking to the convertible bond market to raise cash, as many investors look for less volatility in their investments. Medtronic, the Minneapolis medical-device-maker, recently eclipsed even Apple's $12 billion bond sale and Alibaba's $8 billion bond sale. Medtronic raised $17 billion selling bonds, enabling the company to finance its $43 billion purchase of Ireland's Covidien PLC. Companies are selling bonds at a hectic rate in order to finance strategies at low interest rates, since rates are expected to climb in 2016–2017.

Before explaining EPS/EBIT analysis, it is important to know that EPS is *earnings per share,* which is net income divided by number of shares outstanding. Another term for *shares outstanding* is *shares issued.* In addition, know that the denominator of EPS is reduced when a firm buys its own stock (treasury stock), thus increasing the overall EPS value. Also know that EBIT is earnings before interest and taxes, or as it is sometimes called, operating income. EBT is earnings before tax. EAT is earnings after tax.

The purpose of EPS/EBIT analysis is to determine whether all debt, all stock, or some combination of debt and stock yields the highest EPS values for the firm. Earnings per share is perhaps the best measure of success of a company, so it is widely used in making the capital acquisition decision. It reflects the common "maximizing shareholders' wealth" overarching corporate objective. By chance if profit maximization is the company's goal, then in performing an EPS/EBIT analysis, you may focus more on the EAT row than the EPS row. Large companies may have millions of shares outstanding, so even small differences in EPS across different financing options can equate to large sums of money saved by using that highest EPS value alternative. Any number of combination debt/stock (D/S) scenarios, such as 70/30 D/S or 30/70 D/S, may be examined in an EPS/EBIT analysis. The free Excel template at www.strategyclub.com can enable easy calculation of various scenarios of financing options.

Perhaps the best way to explain EPS/EBIT analysis is by working through an example for the XYZ Company, as provided in Table 8-4. Note that 100 percent stock is the best financing alternative as indicated by the EPS values of 0.0279 and 0.056. An EPS/EBIT chart can be constructed to determine the breakeven point, where one financing alternative becomes more attractive than another. Figure 8-4 reveals that issuing common stock is the best financing alternative for the XYZ Company. As noted in Figure 8-6, the top row (EBIT) on the *x*-axis is graphed with the bottom row (EPS) on the *y*-axis, and the highest plotted line reveals the best method. Sometimes the plotted lines will interact, so a graph is especially helpful in making the capital acquisition decision, rather than solely relying on a table of numbers.

All analytical tools have limitations and EPS/EBIT analysis is no exception. But unless you have a compelling reason to overturn the highest last row EPS values dictating the best financing option, then indeed those highest values along the bottom row should dictate the financing decision, because EPS is arguably the best measure of organizational performance, and thus is the best variable to examine in deciding which financing option is best. Seven potential limitations of EPS/EBIT analysis are here:

1. **Flexibility is a limitation.** As an organization's capital structure changes, so does its flexibility for considering future capital needs. Using all debt or all stock to raise capital in the

TABLE 8-4 EPS/EBIT Analysis for the XYZ Company

Input Data	The Number	How Determined
$ Amount of Capital Needed	$100 million	Estimated $ cost of recommendations
EBIT Range	$20 to $40 million	Estimate based on prior year EBIT and recommendations for the coming year(s)
Interest Rate	5 percent	Estimate based on cost of capital
Tax Rate	30 percent	Use prior year %: taxes divided by income before taxes, as given on income statement
Stock Price	$50	Use most recent stock price
# Shares Outstanding	500 million	For the debt columns, enter the existing # shares outstanding. For stock columns, use the existing # shares outstanding + the # new shares that must be issued to raise the needed capital (i.e., based on stock price). So divide the stock price into the $ amount of capital needed.

	100% Debt		100% Stock		50/50 Debt/Stock Combo	
$ EBIT *range*	20,000,000	40,000,000	20,000,000	40,000,000	20,000,000	40,000,000
$ Interest	5,000,000	5,000,000	0	0	2,500,000	2,500,000
$ EBT	15,000,000	35,000,000	20,000,000	40,000,000	17,500,000	37,500,000
$ Taxes	4,500,000	10,500,000	6,000,000	12,000,000	5,250,000	11,250,000
$ EAT	10,500,000	24,500,000	14,000,000	28,000,000	12,250,000	26,250,000
# Shares	500,000,000	500,000,000	502,000,000	502,000,000	501,000,000	501,000,000
$ EPS	0.0210	0.049	0.0279	0.056	0.0245	0.0523

Conclusion: The best financing alternative is 100% stock because the EPS values are largest; the worst financing alternative is 100% debt because the EPS values are lowest.

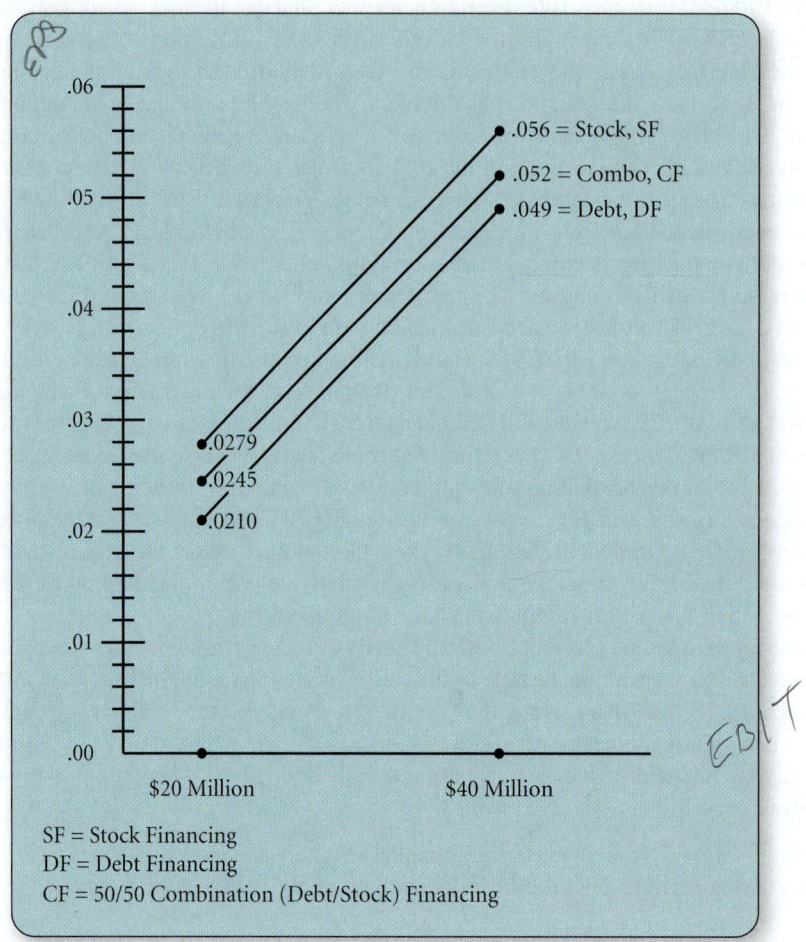

FIGURE 8-6
An EPS/EBIT Chart for the XYZ Company

present may impose fixed obligations, restrictive covenants, or other constraints that could severely reduce a firm's ability to raise additional capital in the future.

2. *Control is a limitation.* When additional stock is issued to finance strategy implementation, ownership and control of the enterprise are diluted. This can be a serious concern in today's business environment of hostile takeovers, mergers, and acquisitions. Dilution of ownership could be a problem, and if so, debt could be better than stock regardless of determined EPS values in the analysis.

3. *Timing is a limitation..* If interest rates are expected to rise, then debt could be better than stock, regardless of the determined EPS values in the analysis. In times of high stock prices, stock may prove to be the best alternative from both a cost and a demand standpoint.

4. *Extent leveraged is a limitation.* If the firm is already too highly leveraged versus industry average ratios, then stock may be best regardless of determined EPS values in the analysis.

5. *Continuity is a limitation.* The analysis assumes stock price, tax rate, and interest rates are constant during all economic conditions.

6. *EBIT ranges are a limitation.* The estimated EBIT low and high values are estimated based on the prior year, plus the impact of strategies to be implemented.

7. *Dividends are a limitation.* If EPS values are highest for the "all-stock scenario," and if the firm pays dividends, then more funds will leave the firm due to dividends if the all stock scenario is selected.

Table 8-5 provides an EPS/EBIT analysis for Boeing Company. Notice in the analysis that the combination stock/debt options vary from 30/70 to 70/30. Any number of combinations

TABLE 8-5 EPS/EBIT Analysis for Boeing Company (M = in millions)

Amount Needed: $10,000 M
Interest Rate: 5%
Tax Rate: 7%
Stock Price: $53.00
# of Shares Outstanding: 826 M

	Common Stock Financing			Debt Financing		
	Recession	*Normal*	*Boom*	*Recession*	*Normal*	*Boom*
EBIT	1,000.00	2,500.00	5,000.00	1,000.00	2,500.00	5,000.00
Interest	0.00	0.00	0.00	500.00	500.00	500.00
EBT	1,000.00	2,500.00	5,000.00	500.00	2,000.00	4,500.00
Taxes	70.00	175.00	350.00	35.00	140.00	315.00
EAT	930.00	2,325.00	4,650.00	465.00	1,860.00	4,185.00
# Shares	1,014.68	1,014.68	1,014.68	826.00	826.00	826.00
EPS	0.92	2.29	4.58	0.56	2.25	5.07

	70% Stock—30% Debt			70% Debt—30% Stock		
	Recession	*Normal*	*Boom*	*Recession*	*Normal*	*Boom*
EBIT	1,000.00	2,500.00	5,000.00	1,000.00	2,500.00	5,000.00
Interest	150.00	150.00	150.00	350.00	350.00	350.00
EBT	850.00	2,350.00	4,850.00	650.00	2,150.00	4,650.00
Taxes	59.50	164.50	339.50	45.50	150.50	325.50
EAT	790.50	2,185.50	4,510.50	604.50	1,999.50	4,324.50
# Shares	958.08	958.08	958.08	882.60	882.60	882.60
EPS	0.83	2.28	4.71	0.68	2.27	4.90

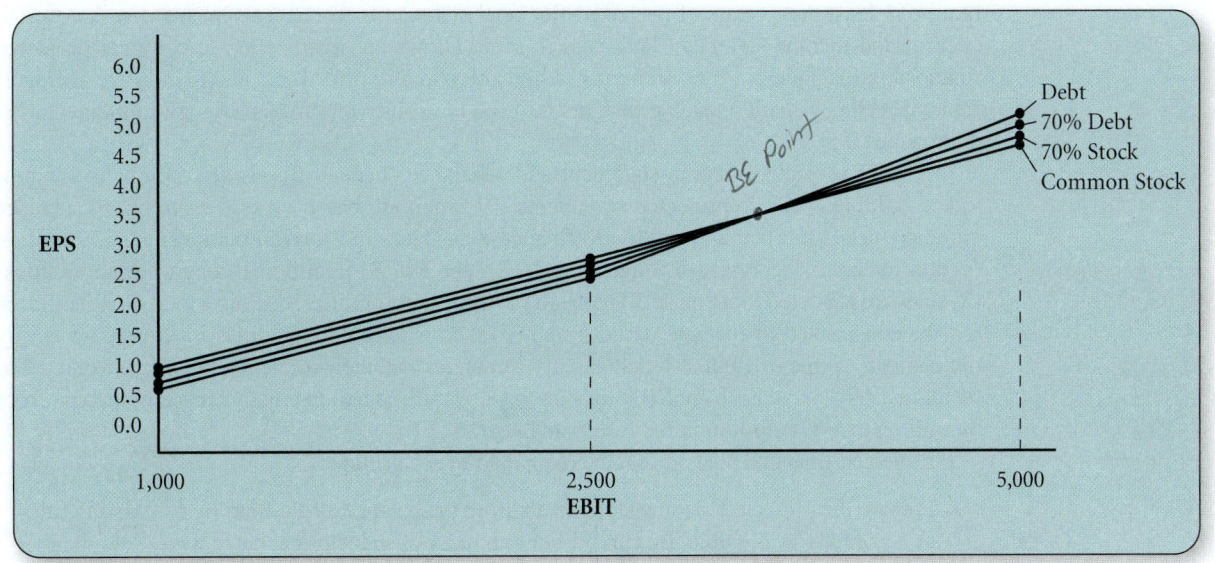

Conclusion: Boeing should use common stock to raise capital in a recession (see 0.92) or a normal (see 2.29) economic conditions but should use debt financing under boom conditions (see 5.07).

could be explored. However, sometimes in preparing the EPS/EBIT graphs, the lines will intersect, thus revealing breakeven points at which one financing alternative becomes more or less attractive than another. The slope of these lines will be determined by a combination of factors, including stock price, interest rate, number of shares, and amount of capital needed. Also, it

should be emphasized here that the best financing alternatives are indicated by the highest EPS values. In Table 8-5, the 7 percent tax rates was computed from Boeing's income statement by dividing taxes paid by income before taxes. Always calculate the tax rate in this manner.

In Table 8-5, note that Boeing should use stock to raise capital in a recession (see 0.92) or in normal (see 2.29) economic conditions but should use debt financing under boom conditions (see 5.07). Let us calculate here the "# Shares" figure of 1,014.68 given under Boeing's stock alternative. Divide $10,000 M funds needed by the stock price of $53 = 188.68 M new shares to be issued + the 826 M shares outstanding already = 1014.68 M shares under the stock scenario. Along the final row, EPS is the number of shares outstanding divided by EAT in all columns.

Note in Table 8-5 that a dividends row is absent from the Boeing analysis. The more shares outstanding, the more dividends to be paid (if the firm indeed pays dividends). To consider dividends in an EPS/EBIT analysis, simply insert another row for "Dividends" right below the "EAT" row and then insert an "Earnings After Taxes and Dividends" row. Considering dividends would make the analysis more robust.

In the Boeing graph, notice that there is a breakeven point between the normal and boom range of EBIT where the debt option overtakes the 70/30 D/S option as the best financing alternative. A breakeven point (where two lines cross each other) is the EBIT level where various financing alternatives represented by lines crossing are equally attractive in terms of EPS. The Boeing graph indicates that EPS values are highest for the 100 percent debt option at high EBIT levels. The graph also reveals that the EPS values for 100 percent debt increase faster than the other financing options as EBIT levels increase beyond the breakeven point. At low levels of EBIT, however, the Boeing graph indicates that 100 percent stock is the best financing alternative because the EPS values are highest.

Projected Financial Statements

Projected financial statement analysis is a technique that allows an organization to examine the expected results of strategies being implemented. This analysis can be used to forecast the impact of various implementation decisions (for example, to increase promotion expenditures by 50 percent to support a market-development strategy or to increase research and development expenditures by 70 percent to support product development). Most financial institutions require at least three years of projected financial statements whenever a business seeks capital. A projected income statement and balance sheet allows an organization to compute projected financial ratios under various scenarios. When compared to prior years and to industry averages, financial ratios provide valuable insights into the feasibility of various strategy-implementation approaches.

A 2017 projected income statement and a balance sheet for the Litten Company are provided in Table 8-6. The projected statements for Litten are based on five assumptions: (1) The company needs to raise $45 million to finance expansion into foreign markets; (2) $30 million of this total will be raised through increased debt and $15 million through common stock; (3) sales are expected to increase 50 percent; (4) three new facilities, costing a total of $30 million, will be constructed in foreign markets; and (5) land for the new facilities is already owned by the company. Note in Table 8-6 that Litten's strategies and their implementation are expected to result in a sales increase from $100 million to $150 million and in a net increase in income from $6 million to $9.75 million in the forecasted year.

Projected financial analysis can be explained in seven steps:

1. Prepare the projected income statement before the balance sheet. Start by forecasting sales as accurately as possible. Be careful not to blindly push historical percentages into the future with regard to revenue (sales) increases. Be mindful of what the firm did to achieve those past sales increases, which may not be appropriate for the future unless the firm takes similar or analogous actions (such as opening a similar number of stores, for example). If dealing with a manufacturing firm, also be mindful that if the firm is operating at 100 percent capacity running three 8-hour shifts per day, then probably new manufacturing facilities (land, plant, and equipment) will be needed to increase sales further.

2. Use the percentage-of-sales method to project cost of goods sold (CGS) and the expense items in the income statement. For example, if CGS is 70 percent of sales in the prior year

TABLE 8-6 A Projected Income Statement and Balance Sheet for the Litten Company (in millions)

	Prior Year 2016	Projected Year 2017	Remarks
PROJECTED INCOME STATEMENT			
Sales	$100	$150.00	50% increase
Cost of Goods Sold	70	105.00	70% of sales (70% also in prior yr)
Gross Margin	30	45.00	
Selling Expense	10	15.00	10% of sales
Administrative Expense	5	7.50	5% of sales
Earnings Before Interest and Taxes	15	22.50	
Interest	3	3.00	
Earnings Before Taxes	12	19.50	
Taxes	6	9.75	50% rate
Net Income	**6**	**9.75**	
Dividends	2	5.00	
Retained Earnings	4	4.75	
PROJECTED BALANCE SHEET			
Assets			
Cash	5	7.75	Plug figure
Accounts Receivable	2	4.00	100% increase
Inventory	20	45.00	
Total Current Assets	27	56.75	
Land	15	35.00	Purchased land
Plant and Equipment	50	80.00	Add three new plants at $10 million each
Less Depreciation	10	20.00	
Net Plant and Equipment	40	60.00	
Total Fixed Assets	55	75.00	
Total Assets	**82**	**151.75**	
Liabilities			
Accounts Payable	10	10.00	
Notes Payable	10	10.00	
Total Current Liabilities	20	20.00	
Long-Term Debt	40	70.00	Borrowed $30 million
Additional Paid-in-Capital	20	35.00	Issued 100,000 shares at $150 each
Retained Earnings	2	6.75	$2 + $4.75
Total Liabilities and Net Worth	**82**	**151.75**	

(as it is in Table 8-6), then use that same percentage to calculate CGS in the future year—unless there is a reason to use a different percentage. Items such as interest, dividends, and taxes must be treated independently and cannot be forecasted using the percentage-of-sales method.

3. Calculate the projected net income.
4. Subtract from the net income any dividends to be paid for that year. This remaining net income is retained earnings (RE). Bring this retained earnings amount for that year (NI – DIV = RE) over to the balance sheet by adding it to the prior year's RE shown on the balance sheet. In other words, every year, a firm adds its RE for that particular year (from the income statement) to its historical RE total on the balance sheet. Therefore, the RE amount on the balance sheet is a cumulative number rather than money available for

strategy implementation. Note that retained earnings is the first projected balance sheet item to be entered. As a result of this accounting procedure in developing projected financial statements, the RE amount on the balance sheet is usually a large number. However, it also can be a low or even negative number if the firm has been incurring losses. The only way for RE to decrease from one year to the next on the balance sheet is (1) if the firm incurred an earnings loss that year or (2) the firm had positive net income for the year but paid out dividends more than the net income. Be mindful that RE is the key link between a projected income statement and balance sheet, so be careful to make this calculation correctly.

5. Project the balance sheet items, beginning with retained earnings and then forecasting shareholders' equity, long-term liabilities, current liabilities, total liabilities, total assets, fixed assets, and current assets (in that order), working from the bottom to the top of the balance sheet.

6. Use the cash account as the plug figure—that is, use the cash account to make the assets total the liabilities and net worth. Then make appropriate adjustments. For example, if the cash needed to balance the statements is too small (or too large), make appropriate changes to borrow more (or less) money than planned. If the projected cash account number is too high, a firm could reduce the cash number and concurrently reduce a liability or equity account the same amount to keep the statement in balance. Rarely is the cash account number perfect on the first pass-through, so adjustments are needed and made.

7. List commentary (remarks) on the projected statements. Any time a significant change is made in an item from a prior year to the projected year, an explanation (comment) should be provided. Comments/remarks are essential because otherwise changes can be difficult to understand.

The U.S. Securities and Exchange Commission (SEC) conducts fraud investigations if projected numbers are misleading or if they omit information that is important to investors. Projected statements must conform with generally accepted accounting principles (GAAP) and must not be designed to hide poor expected results. The Sarbanes-Oxley Act requires CEOs and CFOs of corporations to personally sign their firms' financial statements attesting to their accuracy. These executives could thus be held personally liable for misleading or inaccurate statements. Some firms still "inflate" their financial projections and call them "pro formas," so investors, shareholders, and other stakeholders must still be wary of different companies' financial projections.[7]

On financial statements, different companies use different terms for various items, such as *revenues* or *sales* used for the same item. *Net income, earnings,* or *profits* can refer to the same item on an income statement, depending on the company.

Projected Financial Statement Analysis for D. R. Horton

Because so many strategic management students have limited experience developing projected financial statements, let us apply the steps outlined on the previous pages to the largest American homebuilder company by revenues, D. R. Horton (DRH). The projected statements, developed on January 14, 2014, considered that D.R. Horton would go forward with the following four recommendations in 2014–2016, and incur the following expected costs:

1. Acquire four building products firms: (a) Universal Forest Products, (b) Scotch and Gulf Lumber, (c) United Plywood and Lumber, and (d) Dixie Plywood. **Total Cost = $850 million**

2. Expand home-building services to North and South Dakota to gain 5% of the market by the end of 2016. (Start with an office in Bismarck, ND, the second-largest city in ND. It is close enough to the ND/SD border to serve both states, and it is located where Bismarck and Minneapolis can both help serve Fargo/Moorhead. If all goes well, place a second location in Rapid City, SD, the second-largest city in SD. It is located where Rapid City and Minneapolis can both help serve Sioux Falls, and is located close enough to Casper, WY, and Scottsbluff, NE, for possible future service expansions.) **Total Cost = $232 million**

3. Increase the number of communities that DRH services by 50% in California and Nevada by 2016 (20 more communities in California and 10 more communities in Nevada). **Total Cost = $290 million**

4. Develop and launch a nationwide marketing campaign. Topics should include D. R. Horton's low prices in the industry (while still stressing they provide value),

TABLE 8-7 DRH's Actual and Projected Income Statements (in millions)

	Actual Year 2013	Projected 2014	Projected 2015	Projected 2016
Sales	$6,259.00	$10,607.94	$12,520.69	$14,776.03
Costs of Goods Sold	$4,854.00	$8,570.14	$10,115.44	$11,937.52
Gross Margin	$1,405.00	$2,037.81	$2,405.25	$2,838.50
Selling & Administrative	$766.00	$1,298.24	$1,532.33	$1,808.35
Other Operating	–$15.00	–$25.42	–$30.01	–$35.41
EBIT	$654.00	$764.99	$902.93	$1,065.57
Interest	$5.00	$8.47	$10.00	$11.80
Other Income	$9.00	$15.25	$18.00	$21.25
EBT	$658.00	$771.77	$910.93	$1,075.01
Taxes	$195.00	$228.72	$269.96	$318.58
Net Income	**$463.00**	**$543.05**	**$640.97**	**$756.43**
Dividends	$60.20	$70.45	$72.57	$74.74
Retained Earnings	$402.80	$472.60	$568.41	$681.69

home owning is still more cost effective than renting, green solutions offered by DRH, corporate social responsibility efforts by DRH, and targeting the 55 to 75 age group for buying homes. **Total Cost = $35 million**

Based on these recommendations, DHR's actual and projected income statements are given in Table 8-7. Note the large increase in sales in 2014 were due to DRH potentially acquiring four smaller homebuilder companies. Note also at the bottom of Table 8-7 the dividends to be paid and resultant annual retained earnings to be carried forward to the DRH projected balance sheets. Commentary regarding DRH's actual and projected income statements is provided in Table 8-8.

Table 8-9 reveals DRH's actual and projected balance sheets given the four recommendations listed earlier and the annual retained earnings carried forward to the balance sheet. Table 8-10 provides commentary regarding the projected balance sheet changes.

Note in Table 8-9 that DRH increased its retained earnings on the projected balance sheets correctly, expecting to pay out the dividend amounts indicated in Table 8-8. Note in Table 8-9

TABLE 8-8 Comments Regarding DRH's Actual and Projected Income Statements

In millions	Comments
Sales	New home building up 18% in last year. 15% increase year to year seems fair (works out to about 15% in the housing market and 10% in building supplies). Plus, the goal of 1% increase in market share (0.33%/yr). Plus, $3,000 in year 1 from acquisitions.
Costs of Goods Sold	80.8% of sales after acquisitions
Gross Margin	
Selling and Admin. Expense	12.25% of sales
Other Operating Expenses	0.25% of sales
EBIT	
Interest	0.08% of sales
Other Income	0.14% of sales
EBT	
Taxes	29.65% of EBT
Net Income	
Dividends	3% increase year to year. Plus, $8.2M in year 1 from acquisitions.
Retained Earnings	NI – Dividends

TABLE 8-9 DRH's Actual and Projected Balance Sheets (in millions)

	Actual Year 2013	Projected Year 2014	Projected Year 2015	Projected Year 2016
Assets				
Cash	$937.00	$1,091.30	$891.72	$652.53
Inventory	$6,197.00	$7,955.96	$9,390.52	$11,082.02
Deferred Income Taxes	$587.00	$994.87	$1,174.25	$1,385.77
Other Current Assets	$77.00	$99.00	$99.00	$99.00
Total Current Assets	$7,798.00	$10,141.12	$11,555.49	$13,294.06
Land, Plant, and Equipment	$237.00	$924.76	$943.40	$962.98
Less Depreciation	$130.00	$500.00	$530.00	$560.00
Goodwill	$39.00	$199.00	$199.00	$199.00
Other Long-Term Assets	$913.00	$981.40	$1,053.23	$1,128.64
Total Fixed Assets	$1,059.00	$1,605.16	$1,665.63	$1,730.62
Total Assets	**$8,857.00**	**$11,746.28**	**$13,221.12**	**$14,949.94**
Liabilities				
Accounts Payable	$400.00	$583.44	$688.64	$812.68
Taxes Payable	$60.00	$60.00	$60.00	$60.00
Accrued Liabilities	$211.00	$318.24	$375.62	$443.28
Other Current Liabilities	$615.00	$615.00	$615.00	$615.00
Total Current Liabilities	$1,286.00	$1,576.68	$1,739.26	$1,930.96
Long-Term Debt	$3,509.00	$4,959.00	$5,702.85	$6,558.28
Minority Interest	$3.00	$3.00	$3.00	$3.00
Total Noncurrent Liabilities	$3,512.00	$4,962.00	$5,705.85	$6,561.28
Total Liabilities	$4,798.00	$6,538.68	$7,445.11	$8,492.24
Additional Paid-in Capital	$2,042.00	$2,218.00	$2,218.00	$2,218.00
Common Stock	$3.00	$3.00	$3.00	$3.00
Retained Earnings	$2,146.00	$3,118.60	$3,687.01	$4,368.70
Treasury Stock	–$134.00	–$134.00	–$134.00	–$134.00
Other Accumulated Income	$2.00	$2.00	$2.00	$2.00
Total Stockholders' Equity	$4,059.00	$5,207.60	$5,776.01	$6,532.44
Total Liabilities and Net Worth	**$8,857.00**	**$11,746.28**	**$13,221.12**	**$14,949.94**

that the projections show DRH not buying back any of its own stock (treasury stock), as indicated by the $134 number staying unchanged. Many companies lately have been aggressively buying their own stock, reflecting optimism about their future. However, some analysts argue that stock buybacks eat cash that a firm could better use to grow the firm. Stock buybacks do however reduce a firm's number of shares outstanding, which increases a firm's EPS, so firms reap this "intangible benefit" with stock buybacks. Sometimes firms will thus increase their treasury stock near the end of the quarter, or near the end of the year, to "artificially" inflate their EPS, which oftentimes makes the stock price go up. For example, FedEx bought $2.8 billion worth of its own stock in its 2014 fiscal fourth quarter, contributing 15 cents to the company's EPS of $2.10, thus beating Wall Street's expectation of $1.95. In fact, 25 percent of the S&P 500 companies in the third quarter of 2014 alone increased their EPS by 4 percent or more simply by buying back their own stock.

Corporate Valuation

Evaluating the worth of a business is central to strategy implementation because numerous strategies are often implemented by acquiring other firms. In addition, some strategies, such as retrenchment and divestiture, may result in the sale of a division of an organization or of the firm itself. Thus, thousands of transactions occur each year in which businesses are bought or sold in

TABLE 8-10 Comments Regarding DRH's Actual and Projected Balance Sheets

	Comments
Assets	
Cash	Plug Variable
Inventory	75% of sales after acquisitions
Deferred Income Taxes	9.4% of sales
Other Current Assets	$22 increase in year one due to acquisition
Total Current Assets	
Land, Plant, and Equipment	Currently 63 locations, Average = 3.75 million. Upgrading 5 facilities at 50% and adding 2 new facilities in the next 3 years. Plus 5% average increase with market share per year. Plus $670 in year 1 from acquisitions
Less Depreciation	$340 increase in year 1 from acquisitions plus 30 million per year
Goodwill	$160 increase due to acquisitions
Other Long-Term Assets	Increase at the same percentage as Land, Plant, and Equipment, less acquisitions
Total Fixed Assets	
Total Assets	
Liabilities	
Accounts Payable	5.5% of sales after acquisitions
Taxes Payable	
Accrued Liabilities	3.0% of sales after acquisitions
Other Current Liabilities	
Total Current Liabilities	
Long-Term Debt	Borrowed $1450 for acquisitions and expansions in year 1. Plus 15% thereafter.
Minority Interest	
Total Noncurrent Liabilities	
Total Liabilities	
Additional Paid-in Capital	$176 increase in year one due to acquisitions
Common Stock	
Retained Earnings	Prior RE + the new annual RE
Treasury Stock	
Other Income	
Total Stockholders' Equity	
Total Liabilities and SE	

the United States. In all these cases, it is necessary to establish the financial worth or cash value of a business to successfully implement strategies.

Corporate valuation is not an exact science; value is sometimes in the eye of the beholder. Companies desire to sell high and buy low, and negotiation normally takes place in both situations. The valuation of a firm's worth is based on financial facts, but common sense and good judgment enter into the process because it is difficult to assign a monetary value to some factors—such as a loyal customer base, a history of growth, legal suits pending, dedicated employees, a favorable lease, a bad credit rating, or good patents—that may not be reflected in a firm's financial statements. Also, different valuation methods will yield different totals for a firm's worth, and no prescribed approach is best for a certain situation. Evaluating the worth of a business truly requires both qualitative and quantitative skills.

Before we examine four methods widely used for corporate valuation, let's examine the concepts of goodwill, premium, and discount a bit further because these issues directly relate to corporate valuation. FASB Rule 142 requires companies to admit once a year if the premiums they paid for acquisitions, called **goodwill**, were a waste of money. Goodwill is not a good thing

ACADEMIC RESEARCH CAPSULE 8-1

When Should We Overpay to Acquire a Firm?

Scholars have long been interested in the decision-making process regarding when firms pay premiums versus discounts for acquired firms. Paying high acquisition premiums inflate a firm's goodwill, and has often been criticized in research. Acquisition premiums the last few years have averaged 25 to 40 percent, but sometimes exceed 100 percent. Prior research suggests that high premiums generally have negative impacts on acquisition performance. Scholars have explored the how and why of excessive premium decisions to determine if overconfidence or hubris on the part of chief executive officers (CEOs) is the culprit. Specifically, Zhu recently reported that board members' influence on premium versus discount decisions

may not always be beneficial. In particular, Zhu reports a tendency for directors to support low premiums when their average prior premium was low, but directors tend to support paying high premiums when their average prior premium was relatively high. Due to this "group bias," Zhu questions the extent (or whether) members of a firm's board of directors should be involved with acquisition purchase decisions.

Source: Based on Zhu, David, "Group Polarization on Corporate Boards: Theory and Evidence on Board Decisions about Acquisition Premiums," *Strategic Management Journal*, 34 (2013): 800–822.

to have on a balance sheet. J. Crew Group Inc., for example, recently wrote down the value of the goodwill on its balance sheet by 57 percent, or $536 million. Hewlett-Packard, Boston Scientific, Frontier Communications, and Republic Services carry more goodwill on their balance sheet than their market (or book) value. This is a signal that their goodwill should be "written down," which means "reduced and recorded as an expense on the income statement." Jack Ciesielski, publisher of Analyst's Accounting Observer, says, "Writing down goodwill is an admission that the company screwed up when it budgeted what an acquired firm is worth." Sometimes it is OK to pay more for a company than its book value if the firm has technology or patents you need or economies of scale you desire or even to reduce competitive pricing pressure, but, like buying a house, paying a "premium" for a company is almost always not a good thing. Acquiring at a "discount" is far better for shareholders. Because goodwill write-down accounting rules involve projections and judgments, companies have leeway for when to write down goodwill, and by how much. If the purchase price is less than the stock price times the number of shares outstanding (rather than more), that difference is called a **discount**. For example, Clayton Doubilier & Rice LLC recently acquired Emergency Medical Services (EMS) Corp. for $2.9 billion, a 9.4 percent discount below EMS's stock price of $64.00. Academic Research Capsule 8-1 addresses the premium versus discount issue.

Corporate Valuation Methods

Four methods are often used to determine the monetary value of a company; these four methods are described below.

METHOD 1 The Net Worth Method = Total Shareholders' Equity (SE) – (Goodwill + Intangibles) Other terms for Total Shareholders' Equity are Total Owners' Equity or Net Worth, but this line item near the bottom of a balance sheet represents the sum of common stock, additional paid-in capital, and retained earnings. After calculating total SE, subtract goodwill and intangibles if these items appear as assets on the firm's balance sheet. Whereas intangibles include copyrights, patents, and trademarks, goodwill arises only if a firm acquires another firm and pays more than the book value for that firm.

METHOD 2 The Net Income Method = Net Income × Five
The second approach for measuring the monetary value of a company grows out of the belief that the worth of any business should be based largely on the future benefits its owners may derive through net profits. A conservative rule of thumb is to establish a business's worth as five times the firm's current annual profit. A 5-year average profit level could also be used. When using this approach, remember that firms normally suppress earnings in their financial statements to minimize taxes. Note in Table 8-11 that Method 2 results in the lowest corporate valuation of all methods for all three firms. If you were acquiring a business, this might be a good first offer, but likely Method 2 does not produce a value you would want to begin with if you are selling your business.

TABLE 8-11 Company Worth Analysis for Amazon.com, Ross Stores, and Panera Bread Company (in millions, except stock price and EPS)

Input Data	Amazon.com	Ross Stores	Panera Bread
$ Shareholders' Equity (SE)	9,746	2,007	699
$ Net Income (NI)	274	837	196
$ Stock Price (SP)	307	90	160
$ EPS	7.59	4.24	6.80
# of Shares Outstanding	463	205	27
$ Goodwill	2,656	0	123
$ Intangibles	0	0	79
$ Total Assets	40,159	3,896	1,180
Company Worth Analyses			
1. SE – Goodwill – Intangibles	7,090	2,007	497
2. Net Income × 5	1,370	4,185	980
3. (Stock Price/EPS) × NI	142,572	17,766	4,611
4. # of Shares Out × Stock Price	142,141	18,450	4,320
5. Four Method Average	$73,293	$10,604	$2,602
$ Goodwill/$ Total Assets	6.6%	0	10.4%

If a firm's net income is negative, theoretically Method 2 yields a negative number, implying that the firm would pay you to acquire them. Of course, when you acquire another firm, you obtain all of the firm's debt and liabilities, so theoretically this would be possible.

METHOD 3 **Price-Earnings Ratio Method** = (Stock Price ÷ EPS) × NI
To use this method, divide the market price of the firm's common stock by the annual earnings per share (EPS) and multiply this number by the firm's average net income for the past five years. Notice in Table 8-12 this method yields an answer close to Method 4. Algebraically, this method is identical to Method 4, if earnings and # of shares figures are taken at the same point in time.

METHOD 4 **Outstanding Shares Method** = # of Shares Outstanding × Stock Price
To use this method, simply multiply the number of shares outstanding (or issued) by the market price per share. If the purchase price is more than this amount, the additional dollars are called a **premium**. The outstanding shares method may also be called the **market value** or **market capitalization** or **book value** of the firm. The premium is a per-share dollar amount that a person or firm is willing to pay beyond the book value of the firm to control (acquire) the other company.

Table 8-11 provides the cash value analyses for three companies—Amazon.com, Ross Stores, and Panera Bread Company at year-end 2014. Note in Table 8-11 that Panera Bread Company's $ Goodwill to $ Total Assets is high at 10.4 percent, indicating that a tenth of the company's assets are "Goodwill," which is not good.

Notice in Table 8-11 there is significant variation among the four methods used to determine cash value. For example, the worth of Amazon ranged from $1.3 billion to $142 billion. Obviously, if you were selling your company, you would seek the larger values, whereas if purchasing a company you would seek the lower values. In practice, substantial negotiation takes place in reaching a final compromise (or averaged) amount.

In addition to preparing to buy or sell a business, corporate valuation analysis is oftentimes performed when dealing with the following issues: bank loans, tax calculations, retirement packages, death of a principal, divorce, partnership agreements, and IRS audits. Practically, it is just good business to have a reasonable understanding of what a firm is worth. This knowledge protects the interests of all parties involved.

TABLE 8-12 The Top 20 College Football Programs in Terms of Monetary Value (all numbers are in millions of $)

Team	Revenue	Net Income	Team Value
1. Texas Longhorns	109	82	139
2. Notre Dame Fighting Irish	78	46	117
3. Alabama Crimson Tide	89	47	110
4. LSU Tigers	74	48	105
5. Michigan Wolverines	81	58	104
6. Florida Gators	75	49	94
7. Oklahoma Sooners	70	45	92
8. Georgia Bulldogs	66	40	91
9. Ohio State Buckeyes	61	38	83
10. Nebraska Cornhuskers	56	35	80
11. Auburn Tigers	75	39	77
12. Arkansas Razorbacks	61	32	74
13. USC Trojans	58	35	73
14. Texas A&M Aggies	54	36	72
15. Penn State Nittany Lions	59	30	71
16. Wisconsin Badgers	51	19	70
17. Washington Huskies	56	33	66
18. South Carolina Gamecocks	49	24	65
19. Oregon Ducks	54	33	64
20. Tennessee Volunteers	55	28	63

Source: Based on information from the U.S. Department of Education as of February 1, 2014, and www .forbes.com.

Table 8-12 provides a list of U.S. college football teams ranked in terms of their monetary value. Note that the Texas Longhorns are Number 1, followed by the Notre Dame Fighting Irish. Also observe that there are eight Southeastern Conference (SEC) teams among the top 20. In calculating the team value amounts, analysts made various cash flow adjustments, so the amounts are generally less than the "net income times five" formula described in Method 2. Net income times two (or three) is much closer to actual figures reported for the monetary value of college football programs.

IPOs, Cash Management, and Corporate Bonds

Go Public With An IPO?

Hundreds of companies annually hold **initial public offerings (IPOs)** to move from being private to being public. In 2014, the number of firms going public was at its fastest pace in years, as investors bid aggressively for new shares of new companies, paying on average 14.5 times annual sales for firms. The average U.S. IPO stock price in 2014 increased 19 percent, rewarding investors.[8] However, nearly three quarters of the firms going public in 2014 were unprofitable, and most had annual sales of less than $50 million. In addition to Alibaba, some of the most successful IPOs in 2014 were GoPro, maker of the popular action photography camera, whose stock hit the market mid-year priced at $24 and rose to $71 for a 195 percent total return. Also in 2014, the IPO from Immune Design, a large pharmaceutical firm, saw its initial stock price of $12 rise to $34, up 184 percent. There were 275 IPOs on the U.S. stock markets in 2014, up from 222 the prior year. However, not all initial public offering stock prices increased. Even Facebook's stock dropped dramatically after its IPO, although it eventually recovered nicely.

"Going public" means selling off a percentage of a company to others to raise capital; consequently, it dilutes the owners' control of the firm. Going public is not recommended for companies with less than $10 million in sales because the initial costs can be too high for the firm to generate sufficient cash flow to make going public worthwhile. One dollar in four is the average total cost paid to lawyers, accountants, and underwriters when an initial stock issuance is under $1 million; $1 in $20 will go to cover these costs for issuances over $20 million. In addition to initial costs involved with a stock offering, there are costs and obligations associated with reporting and management in a publicly held firm. For firms with more than $10 million in sales, going public can provide major advantages. It can allow the firm to raise capital to develop new products, build plants, expand, grow, and market products and services more effectively.

Keep Cash Offshore is Earned Offshore?

Many U.S. firms have most of the cash on their balance sheet in overseas accounts, since a large percentage of their revenues are derived in foreign countries. Many such firms prefer to leave their cash outside the United States because to use those funds to pay dividends or purchase treasury stock, for example, would trigger a big U.S. corporate income tax payment. During calendar year 2014, U.S.-based companies added $206 billion to their stockpiles of offshore profits, recorded as "Cash" on their balance sheet. Keeping earnings (cash) in banks in low-tax countries has resulted in U.S. multinational companies having now accumulated $1.95 trillion in cash held outside the United States, up 11.8 percent from a year earlier, according to securities filings from 307 corporations reviewed by Bloomberg News. Three U.S.-based companies in particular—Microsoft, Apple, and IBM—added $37.5 billion, or 18.2 percent of the total increase in 2014. So, when you see "Cash" on a firm's balance sheet, that cash may not be readily available, given the firm may prefer not to pay U.S. taxes on those "foreign" earnings. The federal government is currently considering legislation to tax those foreign cash accounts, such as pay a one-time tax of 10 percent and bring all that cash back to U.S. banks, but nothing has been decided so far.

Issue Corporate Bonds for What Purpose?

Corporations normally issue bonds to raise capital for acquisitions, to refinance debt, and to fund various strategies expected to yield long-term profits. However, increasingly, companies are issuing bonds to buy back their own stock and to pay cash dividends to shareholders. This practice has become a concern. For example, in the first half of 2015, at least ten junk-rated or B-rated companies, including Sirius XM Holdings, Nathan's Famous (Hotdogs), and McGraw-Hill Education, issued more than $5.4 billion in bonds at least in part to finance paying out cash dividends and buying back company stock. For all of 2014, 30 companies issued more than $14.8 billion of bonds for the same purpose. Companies in the S&P 500 in 2014 paid out a record $93.4 billion in dividends and repurchased $148 billion worth of stock— partly (or largely) by issuing corporate bonds. Stock buybacks in 2015 are on pace to exceed $600 billion, a huge increase. The CFO of Legg Mason says "debt analysts hate companies' practice of using debt to fund buybacks."[9] A strategic decision facing corporations therefore, is whether to issue bonds to raise capital to pacify shareholders with cash dividends and purchase company stock, or to issue bonds to finance strategies carefully formulated to yield greater revenues and profits.

Strategic Research and Development (R&D) Issues

Research and development (R&D) personnel can play an integral part in strategy implementation. These individuals are generally charged with developing new products and improving old products effectively. R&D persons perform tasks that include transferring complex technology, adjusting processes to local raw materials, adapting processes to local markets, and altering products to particular tastes and specifications. Strategies such as product development, market penetration, and related diversification require that new products be successfully developed and that old products be significantly improved.

Technological improvements that affect consumer and industrial products and services shorten product life cycles. Companies in virtually every industry rely on the development of new products and services to fuel profitability and growth. Surveys suggest that the most successful

TABLE 8-13 R&D Involvement in Selected Strategy-Implementation Situations

Type of Organization	Strategy Being Implemented	R&D Activity
Pharmaceutical company	Product development	Test the effects of a new drug on different subgroups.
Boat manufacturer	Related diversification	Test the performance of various keel designs under various conditions.
Plastic container manufacturer	Market penetration	Develop a biodegradable container.
Electronics company	Market development	Develop a telecommunications system in a foreign country.

organizations use an R&D strategy that ties external opportunities to internal strengths and is linked with objectives. Well-formulated R&D policies match market opportunities with internal capabilities. Strategic R&D issues include the following:

1. To emphasize product or process improvements.
2. To stress basic or applied research.
3. To be a leader or follower in R&D.
4. To develop robotics or use manual-type processes.
5. To spend a high, average, or low amount of money on R&D.
6. To perform R&D within the firm or contract R&D to outside firms.
7. To use university researchers or private-sector researchers.

Research and development policy among rival firms often varies dramatically. Various pharmaceutical firms, for example, have a philosophical disagreement over the merits of heavy investment to discover new drugs, versus waiting for others to spend the money and then follow up with similar products. Table 8-13 gives some examples of R&D activities that could be required for successful implementation of various strategies. Many U.S. utility, energy, and automotive companies have charged their R&D departments with determining how the firm can effectively reduce its gas emissions.

Many firms wrestle with the decision to acquire R&D expertise from external firms or to develop R&D expertise internally. The following guidelines can be used to help make this decision:

1. If the rate of technical progress is slow, the rate of market growth is moderate, and there are significant barriers to possible new entrants, then in-house R&D is the preferred solution. The reason is that R&D, if successful, will result in a temporary product or process monopoly that the company can exploit.
2. If technology is changing rapidly and the market is growing slowly, then a major effort in R&D may be risky because it may lead to the development of an ultimately obsolete technology or one for which there is no market.
3. If technology is changing slowly but the market is growing quickly, there generally is not enough time for in-house development. The prescribed approach is to obtain R&D expertise on an exclusive or nonexclusive basis from an outside firm.
4. If both technical progress and market growth are fast, R&D expertise should be obtained through acquisition of a well-established firm in the industry.[10]

There are at least three major R&D approaches for implementing strategies, as discussed here:

1. The first approach is to be the first firm to market new technological products. This is a glamorous and exciting strategy but also a dangerous one. Firms such as 3M, Apple, and General Electric have been successful with this method, but many other pioneering firms have fallen, with rival firms seizing the initiative.
2. The second approach is to be an innovative imitator of successful products, thus minimizing the risks and costs of a "startup." This approach entails allowing a pioneer firm to develop the first version of the new product and to demonstrate that a market exists. Then, laggard firms develop a similar product. This strategy requires excellent R&D and marketing personnel.

3. The third approach is to be a low-cost producer by mass-producing products similar to but less expensive than products recently introduced. As a new product is accepted by customers, price becomes increasingly important in the buying decision. Also, mass marketing replaces personal selling as the dominant selling strategy. This approach requires substantial investment in plant and equipment, but fewer expenditures in R&D than the other two approaches. Dell and Lenovo have utilized this third approach to gain competitive advantage.

R&D spending in China increased to about $285 billion in 2014, up 22 percent from 2012. In contrast, R&D spending in the United States grew about 4 percent to $465 billion during the same period. Analysts expect R&D spending in China to surpass U.S. R&D spending by 2022.[11] For example, Shenzhen-based Huawei Technologies, the second-largest telecom-equipment firm in the world behind Ericsson, spends almost $6 billion annually on R&D. Huawei's R&D center in Shanghai employs more than 10,000 engineers, many of whom have computer science advanced degrees. Lenovo, another Chinese firm spending billions on R&D, just opened its huge new hub for R&D in the central Chinese city of Wuhan. China's Fuzhou Rockchip Electronics and Allwinner Technology are rapidly trying to catch up in the mobile processor chips industry with the U.S. Qualcomm and Nvidia Corp. Generally speaking, Chinese firms are "on a mission" to eventually lead the world in technological advancements.

Perhaps the most current trend in R&D has been lifting the veil of secrecy whereby firms, even major competitors, join forces to develop new products. Collaboration is on the rise as a result of new competitive pressures, rising research costs, increasing regulatory issues, and accelerated product development schedules. Companies are also turning to consortia at universities for their R&D needs; more than 600 research consortia are now in operation in the United States.

Strategic Management Information Systems (MIS) Issues

Firms that gather, assimilate, and evaluate external and internal information most effectively are gaining competitive advantages over other firms. Having an effective **management information system (MIS)** may be the most important factor in differentiating successful from unsuccessful firms. The process of strategic management is facilitated immensely in firms that have an effective information system. Information collection, retrieval, and storage can be used to create competitive advantages in ways such as cross-selling to customers, monitoring suppliers, keeping managers and employees informed, coordinating activities among divisions, and managing funds. Like inventory and human resources, information is now recognized as a valuable organizational asset that can be controlled and managed. Firms strive to implement strategies using the best information.

A good information system can allow a firm to reduce costs. For example, online orders from salespersons to production facilities can shorten materials ordering time and reduce inventory costs. Direct communications between suppliers, manufacturers, marketers, and customers can link together elements of the value chain as though they were one organization. Improved quality and service often result from an improved information system.

Firms are increasingly concerned about computer hackers and are taking specific measures to secure and safeguard corporate communications, files, orders, and business. Thousands of companies today are plagued by computer hackers, who may include disgruntled employees, competitors, sociopaths, thieves, spies, and hired agents. Computer vulnerability is a huge, strategic, expensive headache. The first big hacking of 2015 happened at the health insurer Anthem Inc., exposing 80 million customers' personal information. Two recent hackings occurred at Home Depot, exposing 56 million customers' information, and a month later, at J.P. Morgan Chase, exposing 76 million customers' information. Millions of companies are vulnerable to hackers.

In many firms, information technology is allowing employees to work at home or anywhere, anytime. The mobile concept of work allows employees to work the traditional 9-to-5 workday across any of the 24 time zones around the globe. Desktop videoconferencing allows employees to "beam in" whenever needed. Any manager or employee who travels a lot away from the office is a good candidate for working at home. Salespersons and consultants are good examples, but any person whose job largely involves talking to others or handling information could operate at home with the proper MIS.[12]

Mobile Tracking of Employees

Mobile devices and inexpensive monitoring software now enable companies to know where employees are, eavesdrop on their phone calls, and do other things such as know whether or not a driver is wearing his/her seatbelt. More than 40 percent of businesses that send employees out on service calls today track the location and movement of those employees by their company-owned/provided hand-held devices or vehicles.[13] Some employees complain that various monitoring practices are an invasion of privacy, but businesses contend that such measures improve workplace safety and productivity, while also reducing theft and protecting against discrimination.

No federal laws currently prevent businesses from using GPS devices to monitor employees, nor does federal law require businesses to disclose to employees whether they are using such techniques. In fact, in the United States, only two states currently require businesses to tell employees if their electronic communications—including e-mails, instant messages, texts,

IMPLICATIONS FOR STRATEGISTS

Figure 8-7 reveals that to gain and sustain competitive advantages, firms must attract customers and manage their finances better than the best rival firms. Thus, being good is most usually not good enough; being superior is often required. Perceptual mapping and market segmentation, as described in this chapter, are vitally important tools for strategists to make sure that monies devoted to advertising, promotion, publicity, and selling are wisely used. Marketing expenditures can be unnecessarily exorbitant if not based on clear product positioning analyses, target marketing, and customer analysis.

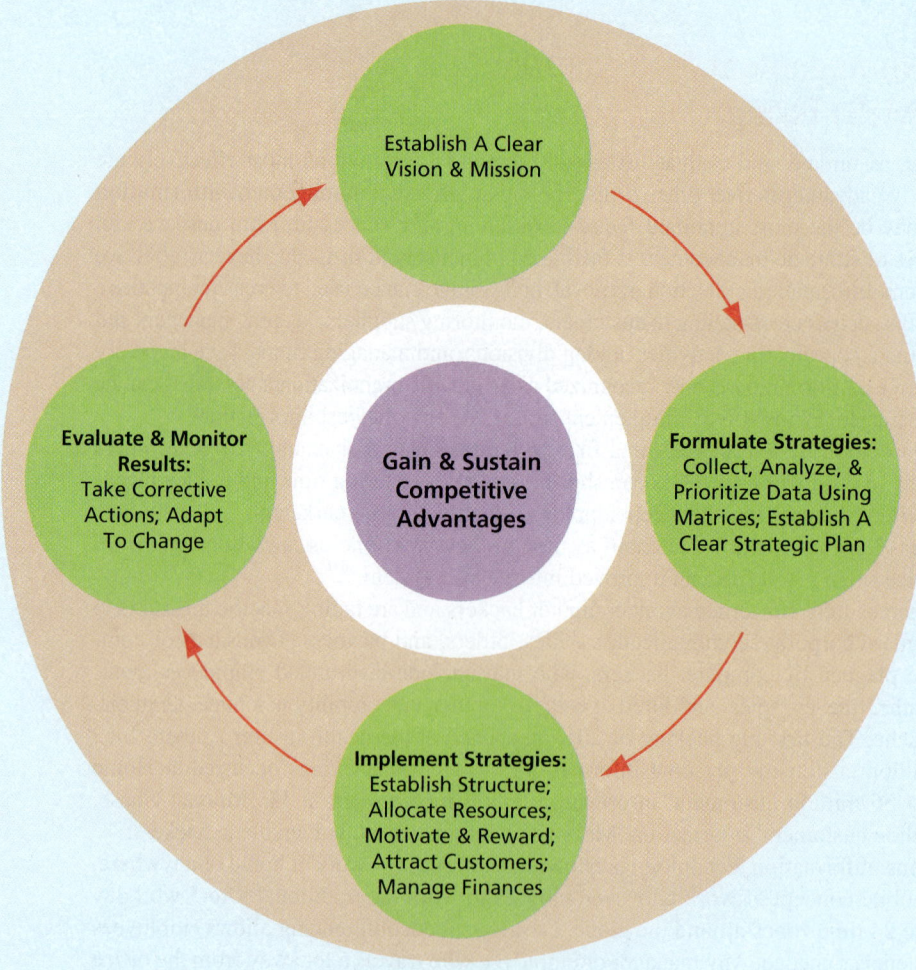

FIGURE 8-7
How to Gain and Sustain Competitive Advantages

According to Figure 8-7, strategists must manage the firm's financial resources exceptionally well, better than strategists at rival firms, especially using corporate valuation analysis, EPS/EBIT analysis, and projected financial statement analysis. It is difficult to make a dollar of profit; every dollar saved is like a dollar earned. Dollars matter and successful strategy implementation is dependent on superior "dollar management." Its take dollars to gain and sustain competitive advantage, and strategists are entrusted with dollar management.

IMPLICATIONS FOR STUDENTS

Regardless of your business major, be sure to capitalize on that special knowledge in delivering your strategic-management case analysis. Whenever the opportunity arises in your oral or written project, reveal how your firm can gain and sustain competitive advantage using your marketing, finance and accounting, or MIS recommendations. Continuously compare your firm to your firm's rivals and draw insights and conclusions so that your recommendations come across as well conceived. Never shy away from the EPS/EBIT or projected financial statement analyses, because your audience must be convinced that what you recommend is financially feasible and worth the dollars to be spent. Spend sufficient time on the nuts-and-bolts of those analyses, so fellow students (and your professor) will be assured that you did them correctly and reasonably. Too often, when students rush at the end, it means their financial statements are overly optimistic or incorrectly developed—so avoid that issue. The marketing, finance and accounting, R&D, and MIS aspects of your recommended strategies must ultimately work together to gain and sustain competitive advantage for the firm—so point that out frequently. By the way, the free student Excel template at www.strategyclub.com can help immensely in performing EPS/EBIT analysis.

photos, and websites visited—are being monitored; the two states are Delaware and Connecticut. MIS tracking technology today has permeated many industries and is utilized by thousands of businesses ranging from landscaping firms to restaurants. And, in many of the businesses, employees do not realize that their actions, location, and habits are being monitored whenever they are on the job.

Mobile Apps for Customers

Companies are increasingly developing mobile apps for customers and using resultant data to devise improved strategies for attracting customers. For example, hotels are rapidly developing apps to help speed up check-in for travelers, including letting customers go straight to their rooms by using their smartphone to unlock doors. In November 2014, Starwood Hotels and Resorts became the first hotel to let guests unlock doors with their phones. Starwood Hotels requires the phone to actually touch a pad on the outside of the door to open it—to make sure if there is a knock on the door late at night and a guest goes to the peephole to see who is there, the guest's phone in his or her pocket will not accidently unlock the door. Some hotel chains, such as Marriott, are holding off on using smartphones as keys until potential security issues can be resolved.

Hilton Worldwide is the second hotel chain, behind Starwood, to announce plans for mobile room keys, which it plans to roll out at the end of 2015 at some U.S. properties. In all 4,000 Hilton properties worldwide, guests can also use maps on the Hilton app to select a specific room. However, guests who like personal interaction at check-in, such as to ask about pool hours or whatever, can still opt for a more leisurely check-in. Hotels eventually would like all travelers to be comfortable using mobile apps on their iPad, smartphone, or smartwatch to request a wakeup call, purchase suite upgrades, book spa treatments, request room service, and open their room door.

Chapter Summary

Successful strategy implementation depends on cooperation among all functional and divisional managers in an organization. Marketing departments are commonly charged with implementing strategies that require significant increases in sales revenues in new areas and with new or improved products. Finance and accounting managers must devise effective strategy-implementation approaches at low cost and minimum risk to that firm. Research and development managers have to transfer complex technologies or develop new technologies to successfully implement strategies. Information systems managers are being called on more and more to provide leadership and training for all individuals in the firm. The nature and role of marketing, finance/accounting, R&D, and MIS activities, coupled with the management, production/operations, and human resource activities described in Chapter 7, largely determine organizational success.

MyManagementLab®

To complete the problems with the ⭐, go to EOC Discussion Questions in the MyLab.

Key Terms and Concepts

book value (p. 265)
convertible bonds (p. 254)
data mining (p. 249)
demand void (p. 251)
discount (p. 264)
EPS/EBIT analysis (p. 254)
goodwill (p. 263)
initial public offering (IPO) (p. 266)
management information system (MIS) (p. 269)
market capitalization (p. 265)
market segment (p. 251)
market segmentation (p. 247)
market value (p. 265)

marketing mix variables (p. 248)
multidimensional scaling (p. 250)
outstanding shares method (p. 265)
perceptual mapping (p. 250)
premium (p. 265)
price-earnings ratio method (p. 265)
product positioning (p. 250)
projected financial statement analysis (p. 258)
treasury stock (p. 254)
tweet (p. 246)
vacant niche (p. 250)
wikis (p. 246)

Issues for Review and Discussion

⭐ **8-1.** True or False? Acquisition premiums the last few years have averaged 25 to 40 percent, but sometimes exceed 100 percent; prior research suggests that high premiums generally have negative impacts on acquisition performance. Explain.

8-2. Define and give an example of multidimensional scaling.

⭐ **8-3.** Explain why increasing treasury stock will increase EPS in any corporation.

8-4. Some analysts say that huge New York Stock Exchange IPOs from companies such as Alibaba, headquartered in China, should be illegal in the United States, since under communist governments there are not sufficient safeguards in place for financial transactions. Do you agree or disagree? Why?

⭐ **8-5.** True or False? In the United States, no federal laws prevent businesses from using GPS devices to monitor employees, nor does federal law require businesses to disclose to employees whether they are using such techniques. What are the implications for employees and companies?

8-6. Do you agree with privacy advocates who contend that Facebook should provide ways for users to opt out of the mobile ad targeting? Why or why not?

8-7. Develop a perceptual map for the six colleges and universities closest to your institution. Illustrate a *market*

segment and a *demand void* in your map. What are the strategic implications of your map?

8-8. To raise capital, what are the pros and cons of selling bonds compared to issuing stock or borrowing money from a bank?

8-9. Many companies are aggressively buying their own stock. What are situations when this practice is recommended or especially beneficial? What are the pros and cons of increasing treasury stock on the balance sheet?

⭐ **8-10.** Hewlett-Packard has more $ goodwill than the $ book value of the firm. Explain what this means, how it could occur, and what can be done about this situation.

8-11. Give a hypothetical example where Company A buys Company B for a 15.0 percent premium.

⭐ **8-12.** Give a hypothetical example where Company A buys Company B for a 15.0 percent discount.

8-13. What is treasury stock? When should a company purchase treasury stock?

8-14. What is an IPO? When is an IPO good for a company? Why did Facebook use an IPO? Was that a wise strategic move? Why?

8-15. Discuss the new principles of marketing according to Parise, Guinan, and Weinberg.

8-16. For companies in general, identify and discuss three opportunities and three threats associated with social networking activities on the Internet.

8-17. Generally speaking, how large should a firm be to justify having an IPO? Explain the IPO process.

8-18. Explain how and why the Internet makes market segmentation easier.

8-19. A product-positioning rule given in the chapter is that "When there are only two competitors, the middle becomes the preferred strategic position." Illustrate this for the cruise ship industry, where two firms, Carnival and Royal Caribbean, dominate. Illustrate this for the commercial airliner building industry, where Boeing and Airbus dominate.

8-20. How could or would dividends affect an EPS/EBIT analysis? Would it be correct to refer to "earnings after taxes, interest, and dividends" as retained earnings for a given year?

8-21. In performing an EPS/EBIT analysis, where do the first-row (EBIT) numbers come from?

8-22. In performing an EPS/EBIT analysis, where does the tax rate percentage come from?

8-23. For the Litten Company in Table 8-6, what would the Retained Earnings value have to have been in 2016 on the balance sheet, given that the 2017 NI-DIV value was $4?

8-24. Show algebraically that the price-earnings ratio formula is identical to the number of shares outstanding times stock price formula. Why are the values obtained from these two methods sometimes different?

8-25. In accounting terms, distinguish between intangibles and goodwill on a balance sheet. Why do these two items generally stay the same on projected financial statements?

8-26. Explain four methods often used to calculate the total worth of a business.

8-27. Diagram and label clearly a product-positioning map that includes six fast-food restaurant chains.

8-28. Explain why EPS/EBIT analysis is a central strategy-implementation technique.

8-29. Identify *and* discuss the limitations of EPS/EBIT analysis.

8-30. Explain how marketing, finance and accounting, R&D, and MIS managers' involvement in strategy formulation can enhance strategy implementation.

8-31. True or False? Retained earnings on the balance sheet are not monies available to finance strategy implementation. Explain.

8-32. Explain why projected financial statement analysis is considered both a strategy-formulation and a strategy-implementation tool.

8-33. Complete the following EPS/EBIT analysis for a company whose stock price is $20, interest rate on funds is 5 percent, tax rate is 20 percent, number of shares outstanding is 500 million, and EBIT range is $100 million to $300 million. The firm needs to raise $200 million in capital. Use the following table to complete the work.

	100% Common Stock	100% Debt Financing	20% Debt 80% Stock Financing
EBIT			
Interest			
EBT			
Taxes			
EAT			
#Shares			
EPS			

8-34. Under what conditions would retained earnings on the balance sheet decrease from one year to the next?

8-35. In your own words, list all the steps in developing projected financial statements.

8-36. Based on the financial statements provided for Hershey (pp. 29–30), how much dividends in dollars did Hershey pay in 2013? In 2014?

8-37. Based on the financial statements provided in this chapter for Litten Company, calculate the value of this company if you know that its stock price is $20 and it has 1 million shares outstanding. Calculate four different ways and average.

8-38. Why should you be careful not to use historical percentages blindly in developing projected financial statements?

8-39. In developing projected financial statements, what should you do if the dollar amount you must put in the cash account (to make the statement balance) is far more (or less) than desired?

8-40. Why is it both important and necessary to segment markets and target groups of customers, rather than market to all possible consumers?

8-41. In full detail, explain the following EPS/EBIT chart.

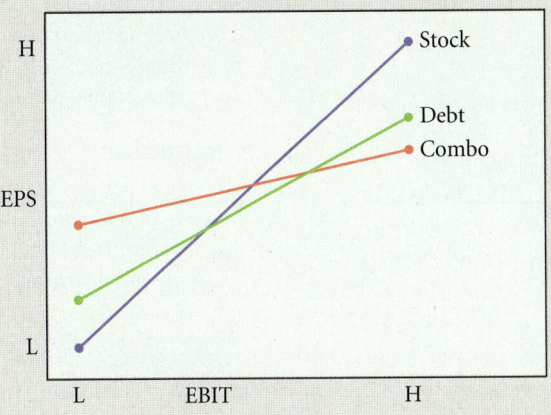

MyManagementLab®
Go to the Assignments section of your MyLab to complete these writing exercises.

8-42. Why is it essential for organizations to segment markets and target particular groups of consumers?

8-43. Explain how you would estimate the total worth of a business.

ASSURANCE OF LEARNING EXERCISES

EXERCISE 8A
Develop a Product-Positioning Map for Hershey Company

Purpose

Organizations continually monitor how their products and services are positioned relative to those of competitors. Product-positioning maps, often called *perceptual maps*, provide useful strategic information for marketing managers as well as corporate executives responsible for strategic planning. Hershey uses perceptual maps in strategic planning.

Headquartered in McClean, Virginia, Mars, Inc. is the third-largest privately held company in the United States and a major rival to Hershey. Five of Mars' leading candies are 3 Musketeers, Snickers, Twix, Milky Way, and M&M's. Headquartered in Vevey, Switzerland, Nestle's is the largest food company in the world and also a major rival to Hershey. Four of Nestle's leading candies are Kit Kat, Baby Ruth, Nestle Crunch, and Butterfinger. Four of Hershey's leading candies are Mr. Goodbar, Krackel, Hershey's Kiss, and Almond Joy. All 13 of these candies compete for market share, shelf space, and customer loyalty.

Instructions

Step 1	Do some research that can enable you to develop a perceptual map based on High/Low Quality and High/Low Price including the 13 candy bars just identified. How could this information be helpful for Hershey? Which company's products do you prefer? Why?
Step 2	Do some research that can enable you to develop a perceptual map based on High/Low Calories and High/Low Nutrition including the 13 candy bars just identified. How could this information be helpful for Hershey?

EXERCISE 8B
Gain Practice Developing Perceptual Maps

Purpose

In product (or market) positioning, an important point is to use various dimensions of a product that are most important to consumers. A positioning map with price and quality is obvious, but other dimensions may be more important. Think strategically. Here are some possible positioning dimensions for beer and shampoo:

> **Beer**—high or low calorie, dark or light, domestic or imported, brand name or store brand
> **Shampoo**—dandruff control, harsh or light, perfume level, conditioner included or not

Instructions

For (1) beer and (2) shampoo products that you are familiar with, do some research that can enable you to develop positioning (perceptual) maps that reveal competitive information for products in these categories. Include four products in both your beer map and your shampoo map. Below each map, give a reason why one is your favorite brand.

EXERCISE 8C
Perform an EPS/EBIT Analysis for Hershey Company

Purpose

An EPS/EBIT analysis is one of the most widely used techniques for determining the extent that debt or stock should be used to finance strategies to be implemented. This exercise can give you practice performing EPS/EBIT analysis.

Instructions

Amount Hershey needs: $1 billion to build four new manufacturing plants outside the United States
Interest rate: 3%
Tax rate: 430/1,251 = 34%
Stock price: $106 as of January 1, 2015
Number of shares outstanding: 220 million

1. Prepare an EPS/EBIT analysis for Hershey. Determine whether Hershey should use all debt, all stock, or a 50-50 combination of debt and stock to finance this market-development strategy.
2. Develop an EPS/EBIT chart after completing the EPS/EBIT table.
3. Next, give a 3-sentence recommendation for Hershey's CFO, Mr. David Tacka.

EXERCISE 8D
Prepare Projected Financial Statements for Hershey Company

Purpose

This exercise is designed to give you experience preparing projected financial statements. This analysis is a strategic finance/accounting issue because it allows managers to anticipate and evaluate the expected results of various strategy-implementation approaches.

Instructions

Step 1   Work with a classmate. Develop a projected 2016 income statement and balance sheet for Hershey. Assume that Hershey plans to raise $900 million to increase its market share, and plans to obtain 50 percent financing from a bank and 50 percent financing from a stock issuance. Make other assumptions as needed, and state them clearly in written form.

Step 2   Compute Hershey's projected current ratio, debt-to-equity ratio, and return-on-investment ratio. How do your projected ratios compare to prior year ratios? Why is it important to make this comparison? To begin your analysis, start with the Hershey's 2015 actual financial statements given at http://finance.yahoo.com or the company website.

Step 3   Bring your projected statements to class and discuss any problems or questions you encountered.

Step 4   Compare your projected statements to the statements of other students. What major differences exist between your analysis and the work of other students?

EXERCISE 8E
Determine the Cash Value of Hershey Company

Purpose

It is simply good business to continually know the cash value (corporate valuation) of your company. This exercise gives you practice in determining the total worth of a company using several methods. To perform this analysis, use Hershey's 2014 financial statements as given in the Cohesion Case.

Instructions

Step 1   Calculate the financial worth of Hershey based on four approaches: (1) the net worth method, (2) the net income method, (3) the price-earnings ratio method, and (4) the outstanding shares method.

Step 2   Get an average of the four methods. In a dollar amount, how much is Hershey worth?

Step 3   Compare your analyses and conclusions with those of other students.

EXERCISE 8F
Develop a Product-Positioning Map for Your University

Purpose

The purpose of this exercise is to give you practice in developing product-positioning maps. Nonprofit organizations, such as universities, are increasingly using product-positioning maps to determine effective ways to implement strategies.

Instructions

Step 1	Join with two other people in class to form a group of three.
Step 2	Jointly prepare a product-positioning map that includes your institution and four other colleges or universities in your state.
Step 3	At the chalkboard, diagram your product-positioning map.
Step 4	Discuss differences among the maps diagrammed on the board.
Step 5	How can your college/university best take advantage of the information revealed in the diagrams developed?

EXERCISE 8G
Do Banks Require Projected Financial Statements?

Purpose

The purpose of this exercise is to explore the practical importance and use of projected financial statements in the banking business.

Instructions

Visit with two local bankers and seek answers to the questions that follow. Record the answers you receive, and report your findings to the class.

1. Does your bank require projected financial statements as part of a business loan application?
2. How does your bank use projected financial statements when they are part of a business loan application?
3. What special advice do you give potential business borrowers in preparing projected financial statements?

(Note to Professors—See the Chapter IM for an additional, excellent exercise for this chapter)

MINI-CASE ON ALIBABA GROUP HOLDING LTD. (BABA)

Source: Rido/Fotolia

IS SELLING STOCK OR BONDS BEST TO RAISE CAPITAL?

Headquartered in Hangzhou, China, Alibaba is an Internet-based e-commerce retailer that is twice as large as eBay and Amazon combined. Handling about half of all online transactions in China, Alibaba does in China what PayPal and Amazon do in the United States. Alibaba operates Taobao, a consumer marketplace with millions of small Chinese merchants. Recently, Alibaba acquired Silicon Valley startup company, TangoMe Inc., a mobile-messaging firm in the United States that offers popular apps used to make free video calls. TangoMe competes with WhatsApp, recently acquired by Facebook. Alibaba is also an online bank and cloud-computing firm similar to E-Trade and Google. Alibaba's largest website, Taobao, has about 760 million product listings from 7 million Chinese sellers. It is free for merchants to sell products through Alibaba, but they pay Alibaba an advertising fee to get exposure. The no-fee strategy is very popular in China. Taobao is mostly for small merchants, whereas Tmall, another shopping site owned by Alibaba, caters to large merchants. Together, Taobao and Tmall account for more than half of all parcel deliveries in China. Alibaba is much more profitable than Amazon but has less revenues because it does not sell products.

Recently, Alibaba launched the largest Internet IPO by a Chinese firm in the history of the United States and the largest IPO ever by any firm, raising $21.8 billion in its single-day IPO. Alibaba's stock price rose 38 percent in its trading debut on the New York Stock Exchange (NYSE). Alibaba broke with tradition by offering five banks equal billing to host their IPO: Credit Suisse Group AG, Deutsche Bank AG, Goldman Sachs Group, P. Morgan Chase, and Morgan Stanley.

Alibaba is growing both organically (internally) and externally through acquisitions, continually diversifying into related high-tech industries. With 80 percent of China's entire e-commerce market business, Alibaba recently acquired AutoNavi for $1.13 billion and ChinaVision Media Group for $804 million. Alibaba is spending heavily to adapt its e-commerce platform to mobile apps. The company has also turned its Taobao Travel business into an Alitrip online travel website than now competes heavily with Bellevue, Washington-based Expedia and Shanghai-based Ctrip.com.

In late 2014, Alibaba sold about $8 billion in bonds, the largest Chinese corporate-debt offering of the year, and equals the $8 billion bond sale by Walgreen in late 2014 to help finance its acquisition of European drugstore chain Alliance Boots GmbH. Companies such as Alibaba (and Walgreen) desire to take advantage of low interest rates to lock in favorable borrowing costs.

Questions

1. How does a company decide among common stock, corporate bonds, and bank debt to raise needed capital?
2. Diagram the relationship between $ equity financing and $ bond financing for Alibaba, Amazon, and Google. What is the relationship on average for large, Internet-based technology companies? Discuss procedure and implications.

Source: Based on Douglas MacMillan, "China's Alibaba Invests $215 Million in Startup Tango," *Wall Street Journal,* March 20, 2014, B3. See also Bradley Hope, "NYSE Leads Race to Host Alibaba's IPO," *Wall Street Journal*, March 19, 2014, C1; and Juro Osawa, "Meet Alibaba: China's Mix of Amazon, eBay, and PayPal," *Wall Street Journal*, March 17, 2014, B1.

Current Readings

Bell, R. Greg, Igor Filatotchev, and Ruth V. Aguilera. "Corporate Governance and Investors' Perceptions of Foreign IPO Value: An Institutional Perspective." *Academy of Management Journal* 57, no. 1 (2014): 301–320.

Changhyun, Kim, and Richard A. Bettis. "Cash Is Surprisingly Valuable as a Strategic Asset." *Strategic Management Journal*, 35, issue 13 (December 2014): 2053–2063.

Dawar, Niraj. "When Marketing Is Strategy." *Harvard Business Review* 91, no. 12 (2013): 100–108.

Glen, Roy, Christy Suciu, and Christopher Baughn. "The Need for Design Thinking in Business Schools." *Academy of Management Journal Learning and Education* 13 (December 2014): 653–667.

Kodama, Matt, and Bill Ladd. "Mapping the Cyberwar Battlefield." *Harvard Business Review* 91, no. 9 (2013): 32–33.

Wang, R. D., and J. M. Shaver, "Competition-Driven Repositioning," *Strategic Management Journal* 35, no. 11 (November 2014): 1,585–1,604.

Yang, Yi, Vadake K. Narayanan, and Donna M. De Carolis. "The Relationship between Portfolio Diversification and Firm Value: The Evidence from Corporate Venture Capital Activity." *Strategic Management Journal* 35, no. 13 (December 2014): 1993–2011.

Endnotes

1. Salvatore Parise, Patricia Guinan, and Bruce Weinberg, "The Secrets of Marketing in a Web 2.0 World," *Wall Street Journal*, December 15, 2008, R1.
2. Kathy Chu and Kim Thai, "Banks Jump on Twitter Wagon," *USA Today*, May 12, 2009, B1.
3. Suzanne Vranica, "Man vs. Bot: The Online-Ad Wars," *Wall Street Journal*, March 24, 2014, B1 & B5.
4. Ibid.
5. Gupta, Sunil, and Donald R. Lehmann, *Managing Customers as Investments: The Strategic Value of Customers in the Long Run* ("Customer Retention" section) (Upper Saddle River, NJ: Pearson Education/ Wharton School Publishing, 2005).
6. Ralph Biggadike, "The Contributions of Marketing to Strategic Management," *Academy of Management Review* 6, no. 4 (October 1981): 627.
7. Michael Rapoport, "Pro Forma Is a Hard Habit to Break," *Wall Street Journal*, September 18, 2003, B3A.
8. Telis Demos, "Companies Rush to Join IPO Surge," *Wall Street Journal*, March 7, 2014, p. A1.
9. Based on Maxwell Murphy and Mike Cherney, "Bond-Funded Buybacks Draw Skeptics," *Wall Street Journal*, June 16, 2015, p. B6.
10. Pier Abetti, "Technology: A Key Strategic Resource," *Management Review* 78, no. 2 (February 1989): 38.
11. Juro Osawa and Paul Mozur, "The Rise of China's Innovation Engine," *Wall Street Journal*, January 17, 2004, B1.
12. Adapted from Edward Baig, "Welcome to the Officeless Office," *Businessweek*, June 26, 1995.
13. Spencer Ante and Lauren Weber, "Memo to Workers: The Boss Is Watching," *Wall Street Journal*, October 28, 2013, B1, B6.

## PART 4

STRATEGY EVALUATION

9

Source: Burmakin Andrey/123rf

Strategy Review, Evaluation, and Control

The best formulated and best implemented strategies become obsolete as a firm's external and internal environments change. It is essential, therefore, that strategists systematically review, evaluate, and control the execution of strategies. This chapter presents a framework that can guide managers' efforts to evaluate strategic-management activities, to make sure they are working, and to make timely changes. Guidelines are presented for formulating, implementing, and evaluating strategies. Nike is the exemplary company showcased because the firm continually evaluates its strategies and takes prompt corrective actions as needed, posting higher and higher revenues and profits every year.

The Strategy-Evaluation Process, Criteria, and Methods

The strategic-management process results in decisions that can have significant, long-lasting consequences. Erroneous strategic decisions can inflict severe penalties and can be exceedingly difficult, if not impossible, to reverse. Therefore, most strategists agree that strategy evaluation is vital to an organization's well-being; timely evaluations can alert management to problems or potential problems before a situation becomes critical. The strategy-evaluation process includes three basic activities:

1. Examine the underlying bases of a firm's strategy.
2. Compare expected results with actual results.
3. Take corrective actions to ensure that performance conforms to plans.

Figure 9-1 illustrates the strategy-evaluation stage of the strategic-management process (see white shading). Adequate and timely feedback is the cornerstone of effective strategy evaluation. Strategy evaluation can be no better than the information on which it is based. Too much pressure from top managers may result in lower managers contriving numbers they think will be satisfactory. Strategy evaluation can be a complex and sensitive undertaking. Too much emphasis on evaluating strategies may be expensive and counterproductive. No one likes to be evaluated too closely! The more managers attempt to evaluate the behavior of others, the less control they have. Yet too little or no evaluation can create even worse problems. Strategy evaluation is essential to

Nike, Inc. (NKE)

The sportswear clothing giant, Nike, is running away from rival firms with both sales and earnings increases. Headquartered in Beaverton, Oregon, Nike's first-quarter (Q1) 2015 revenues rose 25 percent in western Europe, 12 percent in North America, and 20 percent in greater China. Analyst Laurent Vasilescu recently announced. "Nike is eating Adidas' lunch, especially in western Europe." Nike is doing an excellent job implementing its strategy to focus more on higher-margin products, higher average prices, and direct-to-consumer sales (includes Nike stores and Nike website). The company is capitalizing on the trend for people to wear gym clothes (called *activewear*) outside the gym. Nike recently secured the endorsement of NBA superstar Kevin Durant, beating out rival Under Armour's bid for that athlete.

Nike's strategy evaluation activities have resulted in the company offering premium stores called NIKETOWNs, the largest Nike stores in the fleet. Each NIKETOWN store features six or seven NIKE brand categories, providing the very best innovative product and services. For example, the NIKE Running Store in New York City caters to the complete needs of the runner, and Nike's House of Hoops for Basketball with Foot Locker is available, as well as the NIKE Track Club for runners with Finish Line and the Field House with Dick's Sporting Goods Store. Nike store variation strategies allow for premium pricing. In addition, Nike has factory stores that provide a premium product to consumers shopping for value. These stores attract higher customer shopper volumes.

Revenues for Nike's 2015 Q2 rose 15 percent to $7.4 billion, while the company's earnings per share increased 25 percent to $0.74. For that quarter, revenues for the Nike brand rose 17 percent to $7.0 billion, while the company's Converse revenues rose 24 percent to $434 million. The company's net income for the quarter increased 23 percent to $655 million.

Source: Based on Elaine Low, "Nike Sales Surge on Europe, Internet," *Investor's Business Daily*, September 26, 2014, A2.

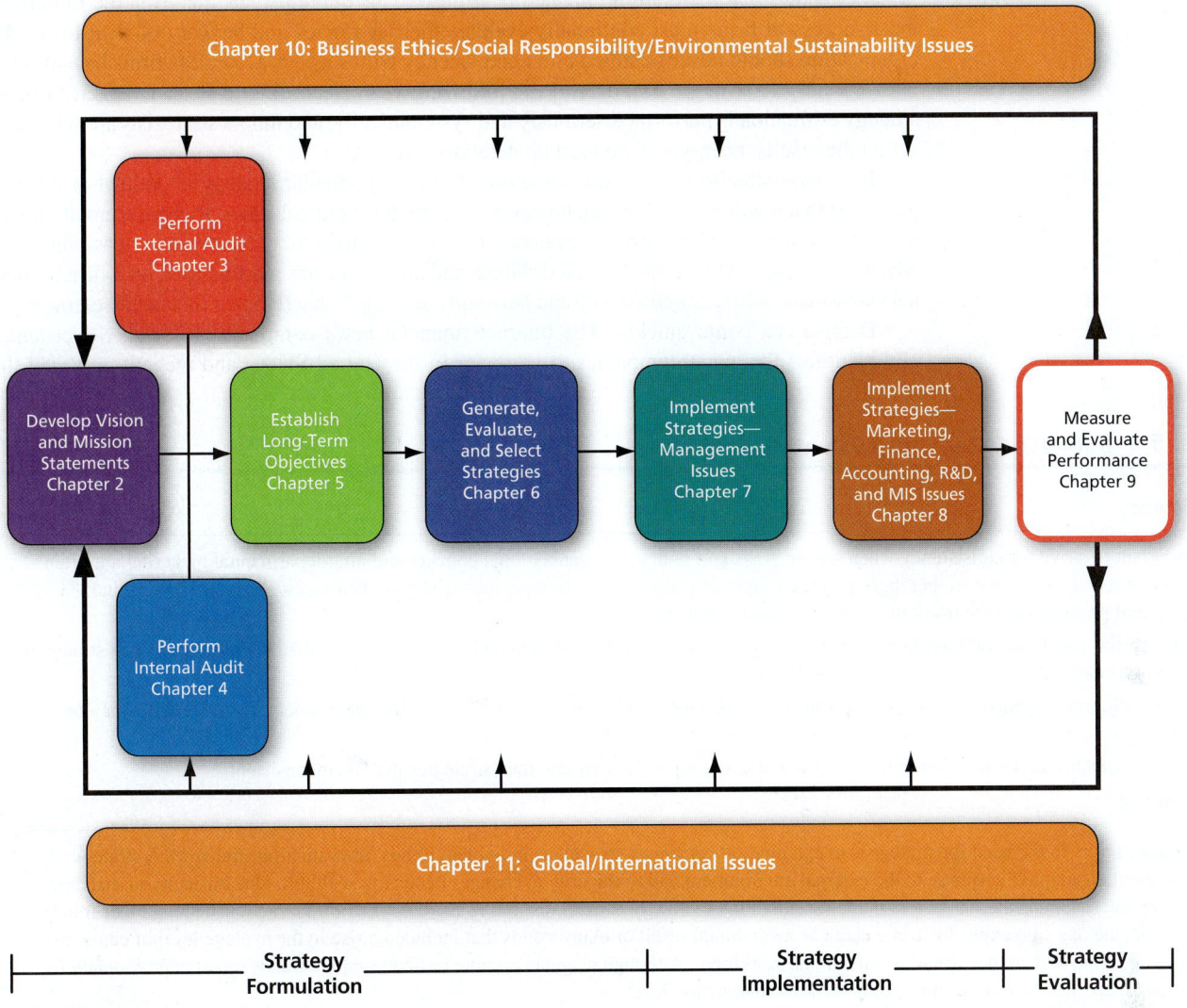

FIGURE 9-1

A Comprehensive Strategic-Management Model

Source: Fred R. David, "How Companies Define Their Mission," *Long Range Planning* 22, no. 3 (June 1988): 40. See also Anik Ratnaningsih, Nadjadji Anwar, Patdono Suwignjo, and Putu Artama Wiguna, "Balance Scorecard of David's Strategic Modeling at Industrial Business for National Construction Contractor of Indonesia," *Journal of Mathematics and Technology*, no. 4 (October 2010): 20.

ensure that stated objectives are being achieved. Strategists need to create an organizational culture where strategy evaluation is viewed as an opportunity to make the firm better, so the firm can compete better, so everyone in the firm can do better, sharing in the firm's increased profitability.

In many organizations, strategy evaluation is simply an appraisal of how well an organization has performed. Have the firm's assets increased? Has there been an increase in profitability? Have sales increased? Have productivity levels increased? Have profit margin, return on investment, and earnings-per-share ratios increased? Some firms argue that their strategy must have been correct if the answers to these types of questions are affirmative. Well, the strategy or strategies may have been correct, but this type of reasoning can be misleading because strategy evaluation must have both a long-run and short-run focus. Strategies often do not affect short-term operating results until it is too late to make needed changes.

Strategy evaluation is important because organizations face dynamic environments in which key external and internal factors often change quickly and dramatically. Success today is no guarantee of success tomorrow! Joseph Stalin was a ruthless leader (from 1928 on) and premier (from 1941 on) of the Soviet Union until his death in 1953. A famous quote from Stalin was:

"History shows that there are no invincible armies." This quote reveals that even the mightiest, most successful firms must continually evaluate their strategies and be wary of rival firms. An organization should never be lulled into complacency with success. Countless firms have thrived one year only to struggle for survival the following year. According to Peter Drucker, "Unless strategy evaluation is performed seriously and systematically, and unless strategists are willing to act on the results, energy will be used up defending yesterday."

It is impossible to demonstrate conclusively that a particular strategy is optimal or even to guarantee that it will work. One can, however, evaluate it for critical flaws. Richard Rumelt offered four criteria that could be used to evaluate a strategy: consistency, consonance, feasibility, and advantage. Described in Table 9-1, *consonance* and *advantage* are mostly based on a firm's external assessment, whereas *consistency* and *feasibility* are largely based on an internal assessment.

Demise can come quickly. The Internet financial news company 24/7 Wall Street annually identifies the worst companies to work for in the United States, and recently reported the

TABLE 9-1 Rumelt's Criteria for Evaluating Strategies

Consistency

It is important to strive for **consistency** when setting goals and policies. Organizational conflict and interdepartmental bickering are often symptoms of managerial disorder, but these problems may also be a sign of strategic inconsistency. Three guidelines help determine if organizational problems are the result of inconsistencies in strategy:

- If managerial problems continue despite changes in personnel and if they tend to be issue-based rather than people-based, then strategies may be inconsistent.
- If success for one organizational department means, or is interpreted to mean, failure for another department, then strategies may be inconsistent.
- If policy problems and issues continue to be brought to the top for resolution, then strategies may be inconsistent.

Consonance

Consonance refers to the need for strategists to examine *sets of trends*, as well as individual trends, in evaluating strategies. A strategy must represent an adaptive response to the external environment and to the critical changes occurring within it. One difficulty in matching a firm's key internal and external factors in the formulation of strategy is that most trends are the result of interactions among other trends. For example, the day care explosion came about as a combined result of many trends that included a rise in the average level of education, increased inflation, and an increase in women in the workforce. Although single economic or demographic trends might appear steady for many years, there are waves of change going on at the interaction level.

Feasibility

A strategy must neither overtax available resources nor create unsolvable subproblems. The final broad test of strategy is its **feasibility**; that is, can the strategy be attempted within the physical, human, and financial resources of the enterprise? The financial resources of a business are the easiest to quantify and are normally the first limitation against which strategy is evaluated. It is sometimes forgotten, however, that innovative approaches to financing are often possible. Devices, such as captive subsidiaries, sale-leaseback arrangements, and tying plant mortgages to long-term contracts, have all been used effectively to help win key positions in suddenly expanding industries. A less quantifiable, but actually more rigid, limitation on strategic choice is that imposed by individual and organizational capabilities. In evaluating a strategy, it is important to examine whether an organization has demonstrated in the past that it possesses the abilities, competencies, skills, and talents needed to carry out a given strategy.

Advantage

A strategy must provide for the creation or maintenance of a competitive **advantage** in a selected area of activity. Competitive advantages normally are the result of superiority in one of three areas: (1) resources, (2) skills, or (3) position. The idea that the positioning of one's resources can enhance their combined effectiveness is familiar to military theorists, chess players, and diplomats. Position can also play a crucial role in an organization's strategy. Once gained, a good position is defensible—meaning that it is so costly to capture that rivals are deterred from full-scale attacks. Positional advantage tends to be self-sustaining so long as the key internal and environmental factors that underlie it remain stable. This is why entrenched firms can be almost impossible to unseat, even if their raw skill levels are only average. Although not all positional advantages are associated with size, it is true that larger organizations tend to operate in markets and use procedures that turn their size into advantage, whereas smaller firms seek product or market positions that exploit other types of advantage. The principal characteristic of good position is that it permits the firm to obtain advantage from policies that would not similarly benefit rivals without the same position. Therefore, in evaluating strategy, organizations should examine the nature of positional advantages associated with a given strategy.

Source: Adapted from Richard Rumelt, "The Evaluation of Business Strategy," in W. F. Glueck (ed.), *Business Policy and Strategic Management* (New York: McGraw-Hill, 1980), 359–367. Used with permission.

worst company to be Books-A-Million, followed by Express Scripts, Frontier Communications, Jos. A. Bank Clothiers, Brookdale Senior Living, Dillards, ADT, hhgregg, Family Dollar Stores, Children's Place, and, the 11th worst, Radio Shack.[1]

Strategy evaluation is becoming increasingly difficult with the passage of time, for many reasons. Domestic and world economies were more stable in years past, product life cycles were longer, product development cycles were longer, technological advancement was slower, change occurred less frequently, there were fewer competitors, foreign companies were generally weak, and there were more regulated industries. Other reasons why strategy evaluation is more difficult today include the following trends:

1. A dramatic increase in the environment's complexity
2. The increasing difficulty of predicting the future with accuracy
3. The increasing number of variables
4. The rapid rate of obsolescence of even the best plans
5. The increase in the number of both domestic and world events affecting organizations
6. The decreasing time span for which planning can be done with any degree of certainty[2]

A fundamental problem facing managers today is how to effectively manage a workforce in light of modern organizational demands for greater flexibility, innovation, creativity, and initiative from employees.[3] Managers need empowered employees acting responsibly and never putting the well-being of the business at risk. The potential costs to companies in terms of damaged reputations, fines, missed opportunities, and diversion of management's attention are enormous, and bad news oftentimes spreads like wildfire over social media. Too much pressure to achieve specific goals can lead to dysfunctional behavior. For example, Nordstrom, the upscale fashion retailer known for outstanding customer service, was subjected to lawsuits and fines when employees underreported hours worked to increase their sales per hour—the company's primary performance criterion.

The Process of Evaluating Strategies

Strategy evaluation is necessary for all sizes and kinds of organizations. Strategy evaluation should initiate managerial questioning of expectations and assumptions, should trigger a review of objectives and values, and should stimulate creativity in generating alternatives and formulating criteria of evaluation.[4] Regardless of the size of the organization, a certain amount of "management by wandering around" at all levels is essential to effective strategy evaluation. Strategy-evaluation activities should be performed on a continuing basis, rather than at the end of specified periods of time or just after problems occur. Waiting until the end of the year, for example, could result in a firm closing the barn door after the horses have already escaped.

Evaluating strategies on a continuous rather than on a periodic basis allows benchmarks of progress to be established and more effectively monitored. Some strategies take years to implement; consequently, associated results may not become apparent for years. Successful strategies combine patience with a willingness to promptly take corrective actions when necessary. There always comes a time when corrective actions are needed in an organization! Centuries ago, a writer (perhaps Solomon) made the following observations about change:

> There is a time for everything,
> A time to be born and a time to die,
> A time to plant and a time to uproot,
> A time to kill and a time to heal,
> A time to tear down and a time to build,
> A time to weep and a time to laugh,
> A time to mourn and a time to dance,
> A time to scatter stones and a time to gather them,
> A time to embrace and a time to refrain,
> A time to search and a time to give up,
> A time to keep and a time to throw away,
> A time to tear and a time to mend,
> A time to be silent and a time to speak,
> A time to love and a time to hate,
> A time for war and a time for peace.[5]

Managers and employees of the firm should be continually aware of progress being made toward achieving the firm's objectives. As key success factors change, organizational members should be involved in determining appropriate corrective actions. If assumptions and expectations deviate significantly from forecasts, then the firm should renew strategy-formulation activities, perhaps sooner than planned. In strategy evaluation, like strategy formulation and strategy implementation, people make the difference. Through involvement in the process of evaluating strategies, managers and employees become committed to keeping the firm moving steadily toward achieving objectives.

The Three Strategy-Evaluation Activities

Table 9-2 summarizes the three strategy-evaluation activities in terms of key questions that should be addressed, alternative answers to those questions, and appropriate actions for an organization to take. Notice that corrective actions are almost always needed except when (1) external and internal factors have not significantly changed and (2) the firm is progressing satisfactorily toward achieving stated objectives. Relationships among strategy-evaluation activities are illustrated in Figure 9-2.

Reviewing Bases of Strategy

As shown in Figure 9-2, **reviewing the underlying bases of an organization's strategy** could be approached by developing a revised EFE Matrix and IFE Matrix. A **revised IFE Matrix** should focus on changes in the organization's management, marketing, finance and accounting, production and operations, research and development (R&D), and management information systems (MIS) strengths and weaknesses. A **revised EFE Matrix** should indicate how effective a firm's strategies have been in response to key opportunities and threats. This analysis could also address such questions as the following:

1. How have competitors reacted to our strategies?
2. How have competitors' strategies changed?
3. Have major competitors' strengths and weaknesses changed?
4. Why are competitors making certain strategic changes?
5. Why are some competitors' strategies more successful than others?
6. How satisfied are our competitors with their present market positions and profitability?
7. How far can our major competitors be pushed before retaliating?
8. How could we more effectively cooperate with our competitors?

Numerous external and internal factors can prevent firms from achieving long-term and annual objectives. Externally, actions by competitors, changes in demand, changes in technology, economic

TABLE 9-2 A Strategy-Evaluation Assessment Matrix

Have Major Changes Occurred in the Firm's Internal Strategic Position?	Have Major Changes Occurred in the Firm's External Strategic Position?	Has the Firm Progressed Satisfactorily Toward Achieving Its Stated Objectives?	Result
No	No	No	Take corrective actions
Yes	Yes	Yes	Take corrective actions
Yes	Yes	No	Take corrective actions
Yes	No	Yes	Take corrective actions
Yes	No	No	Take corrective actions
No	Yes	Yes	Take corrective actions
No	Yes	No	Take corrective actions
No	No	Yes	Continue present strategic course

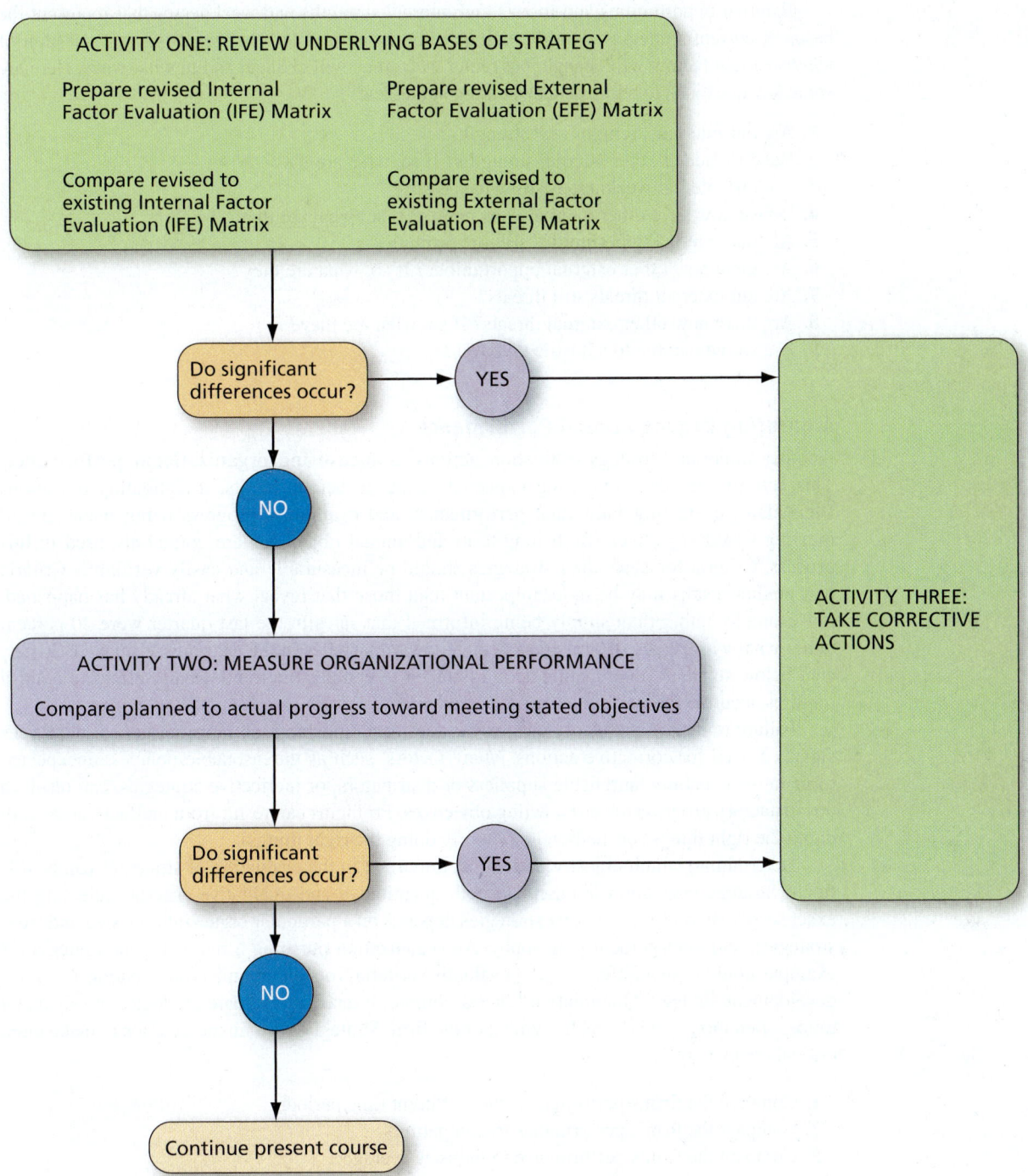

FIGURE 9-2

A Strategy-Evaluation Framework

changes, demographic shifts, and governmental actions may prevent objectives from being accomplished. Internally, ineffective strategies may have been chosen or implementation activities may have been poor. Objectives may have been too optimistic. Thus, failure to achieve objectives may not be the result of unsatisfactory work by managers and employees. All organizational members need to know this to encourage their support for strategy-evaluation activities. Organizations desperately need to know as soon as possible when their strategies are not effective. Sometimes managers and employees on the front lines discover this well before strategists.

External opportunities and threats and internal strengths and weaknesses that represent the bases of current strategies should continually be monitored for change. It is not a question of *whether* these factors will change, but rather *when* they will change, and in what ways. Here are some key questions to address in evaluating strategies:

1. Are our internal strengths still strengths?
2. Have we added other internal strengths? If so, what are they?
3. Are our internal weaknesses still weaknesses?
4. Do we now have other internal weaknesses? If so, what are they?
5. Are our external opportunities still opportunities?
6. Are there now other external opportunities? If so, what are they?
7. Are our external threats still threats?
8. Are there now other external threats? If so, what are they?
9. Are we vulnerable to a hostile takeover?

Measuring Organizational Performance

Another important strategy-evaluation activity is **measuring organizational performance**. This activity includes comparing expected results to actual results, investigating deviations from plans, evaluating individual performance, and examining progress being made toward meeting stated objectives. Both long-term and annual objectives are commonly used in this process. Criteria for evaluating strategies should be measurable and easily verifiable. Criteria that predict results may be more important than those that reveal what already has happened. For example, rather than simply being informed that sales in the last quarter were 20 percent under what was expected, strategists need to know that sales in the next quarter may be 20 percent below standard unless some action is taken to counter the trend. Really effective control requires accurate forecasting.

Failure to make satisfactory progress toward accomplishing long-term or annual objectives signals a need for corrective actions. Many factors, such as unreasonable policies, unexpected turns in the economy, unreliable suppliers or distributors, or ineffective strategies, can result in unsatisfactory progress toward meeting objectives. Problems can result from ineffectiveness (not doing the right things) or inefficiency (poorly doing the right things).

Determining which objectives are most important in the evaluation of strategies can be difficult. Strategy evaluation is based on both quantitative and qualitative criteria. Selecting the exact set of criteria for evaluating strategies depends on a particular organization's size, industry, strategies, and management philosophy. An organization pursuing a retrenchment strategy, for example, could have a different set of evaluative criteria from an organization pursuing a market-development strategy. Quantitative criteria commonly used to evaluate strategies are financial ratios, often monitored for each segment of the firm. Strategists use financial ratios to make three critical comparisons:

1. Compare the firm's performance over different time periods.
2. Compare the firm's performance to competitors.
3. Compare the firm's performance to industry averages.

Many variables can and should be included in measuring organizational performance. As indicated in Table 9-3, typically a favorable or unfavorable variance is recorded monthly, quarterly, and annually, and resultant actions needed are then determined.

Some potential problems are associated with using only quantitative criteria for evaluating strategies. First, most quantitative criteria are geared to annual objectives rather than long-term objectives. Also, different accounting methods can provide different results on many quantitative criteria. Third, intuitive judgments are almost always involved in deriving quantitative criteria. Thus, qualitative criteria are also important in evaluating strategies. Human factors such as high absenteeism and turnover rates, poor production quality and quantity rates, or low employee satisfaction can be underlying causes of declining performance. Marketing, finance and accounting, R&D, or MIS factors can also cause financial problems. The need for a "balanced" quantitative/qualitative approach in evaluating strategies gives rise in a moment to discussion of the balanced scorecard.

TABLE 9-3 A Sample Framework for Measuring Organizational Performance

Factor	Actual Result	Expected Result	Variance	Action Needed
Corporate Revenues				
Corporate Profits				
Corporate ROI				
Region 1 Revenues				
Region 1 Profits				
Region 1 ROI				
Region 2 Revenues				
Region 2 Profits				
Region 2 ROI				
Product 1 Revenues				
Product 1 Profits				
Product 1 ROI				
Product 2 Revenues				
Product 2 Profits				
Product 2 ROI				

Some additional key questions that reveal the need for qualitative judgments in strategy evaluation are as follows:

1. How good is the firm's balance of investments between high-risk and low-risk projects?
2. How good is the firm's balance of investments between long-term and short-term projects?
3. How good is the firm's balance of investments between slow-growing markets and fast-growing markets?
4. How good is the firm's balance of investments among different divisions?
5. To what extent are the firm's alternative strategies socially responsible?
6. What are the relationships among the firm's key internal and external strategic factors?
7. How are major competitors likely to respond to particular strategies?

Taking Corrective Actions

The final strategy-evaluation activity, **taking corrective actions,** requires making changes to competitively reposition a firm for the future. As indicated in Table 9-4, examples of changes that may be needed are altering an organization's structure, replacing one or more key individuals, selling a division, or revising a business mission. Other changes could include establishing or revising objectives, devising new policies, issuing stock to raise capital, adding additional salespersons, differently allocating resources, or developing new performance incentives. Taking corrective actions does not necessarily mean that existing strategies will be abandoned or even that new strategies must be formulated.

The probabilities and possibilities for incorrect or inappropriate actions increase geometrically with an arithmetic increase in personnel. Any person directing an overall undertaking must check on the actions of the participants as well as the results they have achieved. If either the actions or results do not comply with preconceived or planned achievements, then corrective actions are needed.[6]

McDonald's is currently taking extensive corrective actions after recently reporting steep declines in its revenues and profits. A company spokesman said, "We will diligently work to enhance our marketing, simplify our menu, and implement a more locally driven organizational structure to increase relevance with consumers." In taking corrective actions, McDonald's recently fired a CEO, hired another CEO, shuffled its management ranks, created a new organizational structure, and revamped its menu.

TABLE 9-4   Corrective Actions Possibly Needed to Correct Unfavorable Variances

 1. Alter the firm's structure.
 2. Replace one or more key individuals.
 3. Divest a division.
 4. Alter the firm's vision or mission.
 5. Revise objectives.
 6. Alter strategies.
 7. Devise new policies.
 8. Install new performance incentives.
 9. Raise capital with stock or debt.
10. Add or terminate salespersons, employees, or managers.
11. Allocate resources differently.
12. Outsource (or rein in) business functions.

No organization can survive as an island; no organization can escape change. Taking corrective actions is necessary to keep an organization on track toward achieving stated objectives. In his thought-provoking books *Future Shock* and *The Third Wave*, Alvin Toffler argued that business environments are becoming so dynamic and complex that they threaten people and organizations with **future shock,** which occurs when the nature, types, and speed of changes overpower an individual's or organization's ability and capacity to adapt. Strategy evaluation enhances an organization's ability to adapt successfully to changing circumstances.

Taking corrective actions raises employees' and managers' anxieties. Research suggests that participation in strategy-evaluation activities is one of the best ways to overcome individuals' resistance to change. According to Erez and Kanfer, individuals accept change best when they have a cognitive understanding of the changes, a sense of control over the situation, and an awareness that necessary actions are going to be taken to implement the changes.[7]

Strategy evaluation can lead to strategy-formulation and/or strategy-implementation changes, or no changes at all. Strategists cannot escape having to revise strategies and implementation approaches sooner or later. Hussey and Langham offered the following insight on taking corrective actions:

> Resistance to change is often emotionally based and not easily overcome by rational argument. Resistance may be based on such feelings as loss of status, implied criticism of present competence, fear of failure in the new situation, annoyance at not being consulted, lack of understanding of the need for change, or insecurity in changing from well-known and fixed methods. It is necessary, therefore, to overcome such resistance by creating situations of participation and full explanation when changes are envisaged.[8]

Corrective actions should place an organization in a better position to capitalize on internal strengths; to take advantage of key external opportunities; to avoid, reduce, or mitigate external threats; and to improve internal weaknesses. Corrective actions should have a proper time horizon and an appropriate amount of risk. They should be internally consistent and socially responsible. Perhaps most important, corrective actions strengthen an organization's competitive position in its basic industry. Continuous strategy evaluation keeps strategists close to the pulse of an organization and provides information needed for an effective strategic-management system. Carter Bayles described the benefits of strategy evaluation as follows:

> Evaluation activities may renew confidence in the current business strategy or point to the need for actions to correct some weaknesses, such as erosion of product superiority or technological edge. In many cases, the benefits of strategy evaluation are much more far-reaching, for the outcome of the process may be a fundamentally new strategy that will lead, even in a business that is already turning a respectable profit, to substantially increased earnings. It is this possibility that justifies strategy evaluation, for the payoff can be very large.[9]

The Balanced Scorecard

Do a Google search using the keywords *balanced scorecard images* and you will see more than 100 currently used balanced scorecards. Note the wide variation in format evidenced through the images. Developed in the early 1990s by Harvard Business School professors Robert Kaplan and David Norton, and refined continually through today, the **Balanced Scorecard** is a strategy evaluation and control technique. Balanced Scorecard derives its name from the perceived need of firms to "balance" financial measures that are oftentimes used exclusively in strategy evaluation and control with nonfinancial measures such as product quality and customer service. An effective Balanced Scorecard contains a carefully chosen combination of strategic and financial objectives tailored to the company's business.

As a tool to manage and evaluate strategy, the Balanced Scorecard is currently in use at Sears, United Parcel Service, 3M Corporation, Heinz, and hundreds of other firms. For example, 3M Corporation has a financial objective to achieve annual growth in earnings per share of 10 percent or better, as well as a strategic objective to have at least 30 percent of sales come from products introduced in the past four years. The overall aim of the Balanced Scorecard is to "balance" shareholder objectives with customer and operational objectives. Obviously, these sets of objectives interrelate and many even conflict. For example, customers want low price and high service, which may conflict with shareholders' desire for a high return on their investment. The Balanced Scorecard concept is consistent with the notions of continuous improvement in management (CIM) and total quality management (TQM).

The Balanced Scorecard basic premise is that firms should establish objectives and evaluate strategies on criteria other than financial measures. Financial measures and ratios are vitally important in strategic planning, but of equal importance are factors such as customer service, employee morale, product quality, pollution abatement, business ethics, social responsibility, community involvement, and other such items. In conjunction with financial measures, these "softer" factors comprise an integral part of both the objective-setting process and the strategy-evaluation process. A Balanced Scorecard for a firm is simply a listing of all key objectives to work toward, along with an associated time dimension of when each objective is to be accomplished, as well as a primary responsibility or contact person, department, or division for each objective.

The Balanced Scorecard is an important strategy-evaluation tool that allows firms to evaluate strategies from four perspectives: financial performance, customer knowledge, internal business processes, and learning and growth. Its analysis requires that firms seek answers to the following questions and use that information, in conjunction with financial measures, to adequately and more effectively evaluate strategies being implemented:

1. Is the firm continually improving and creating value along measures such as innovation, technological leadership, product quality, operational process efficiencies, and so on?
2. Is the firm sustaining and even improving on its core competencies and competitive advantages?
3. How satisfied are the firm's customers?

A sample Balanced Scorecard is provided in Table 9-5. Notice that the firm examines six key issues in evaluating its strategies: (1) Customers, (2) Managers/Employees, (3) Operations/Processes, (4) Community/Social Responsibility, (5) Business Ethics/Natural Environment, and (6) Financial. The basic form of a Balanced Scorecard may differ for different organizations. The Balanced Scorecard approach to strategy evaluation aims to balance long-term with short-term concerns, to balance financial with nonfinancial concerns, and to balance internal with external concerns. The Balanced Scorecard would be constructed differently—that is, adapted to particular firms in various industries with the underlying theme or thrust being the same, which is to evaluate the firm's strategies based on both key quantitative and qualitative measures.

The Balanced Scorecard Institute has a Certification Program that includes two levels of certification: Balanced Scorecard Master Professional (BSMP) and Balanced Scorecard Professional (BSP), both of which are offered in association with George Washington University and are achievable through public workshop participation. The website for this program is http://www.balancedscorecard.org/

The Graphic Communications Group Limited (GCGL), Ghana's leading print media organization, recently adopted the Balanced Scorecard to monitor quantitative and qualitative targets set by itself and its staff. A recent article reports that the Balanced Scorecard is used by 65 percent of

TABLE 9-5 An Example Balanced Scorecard

Area of Objectives	Measure or Target	Time Expectation	Primary Responsibility
Customers			
1.			
2.			
3.			
4.			
Managers/Employees			
1.			
2.			
3.			
4.			
Operations/Processes			
1.			
2.			
3.			
4.			
Community/Social Responsibility			
1.			
2.			
3.			
4.			
Business Ethics/Natural Environment			
1.			
2.			
3.			
4.			
Financial			
1.			
2.			
3.			
4.			

Fortune 500 companies.[10] Other companies using the Balanced Scorecard in Ghana are the Social Security and National Insurance Thrust (SSNIT), the Volta River Authority (VRA), Electricity Company of Ghana (ECG), and the Ghana Revenue Authority (GRA). The Managing Director of GCGL, Mr. Kenneth Ashigbey, sees the Balanced Scorecard as a roadmap that will help his company connect its strategy to its vision. The vision of the GCGL "to become the dominant multimedia group in West Africa, telling the African story." Along with adopting the Balanced Scorecard system, GCGL's mission was rewritten "to empower our audience and customers everywhere with authentic information and excellent products through visionary leadership and strong brands." Ashigbey says with the introduction of the Balanced Scorecard, the ultimate objective of GCGL is "to be a leading and top-of-the-mind multimedia company in English-speaking West Africa by 2017." He also says about the BSC: "We will maintain our leadership position in print media and become one of the top three multimedia organizations in terms of circulation, audience reach, advert spend and sales revenue." Ashigbey refers to the Balanced Scorecard as "a tool for employees to understand how their respective day-to-day work contributes to the company's success." As part of the Balanced Scorecard, GCGL set for itself eight core values, which include leadership in all that it does, exhibition of high level of professionalism and integrity, commitment to excellence, customer focus, and working as a team. The firm also set four strategic themes: business growth, operational excellence, service excellence, and innovation.

Published Sources of Strategy-Evaluation Information

Sydney Finkelstein, professor of management at the Tuck School of Business at Dartmouth, annually releases his list of the worst CEOs each year.[11] For the year 2014, Finkelstein reported that among the worst CEOs were Dick Costolo, CEO of Twitter; Eddie Lampert, CEO of Sears Holdings; Phillip Clarke, CEO of Tesco, a British supermarket chain; Dov Charney, CEO of American Apparel; and Ricardo Espírito Santo Silva Salgado, CEO of Banco Espírito, the second largest bank in Portugal.

A number of publications are helpful in evaluating a firm's strategies. For example, *Fortune* annually identifies and evaluates the Fortune 1000 (the largest manufacturers) and the Fortune 50 (the largest retailers, transportation companies, utilities, banks, insurance companies, and diversified financial corporations in the United States). *Fortune* ranks the best and worst performers on various factors, such as return on investment, sales volume, and profitability. Annually, the publication publishes its strategy-evaluation research in an article titled "World's Most Admired Companies." Nine key attributes serve as evaluative criteria: people management, innovativeness, products quality, financial soundness, social responsibility, use of assets, long-term investment, global competitiveness, and quality of management. *Fortune's* 2014 evaluation in Table 9-6 reveals the most admired companies.

Businessweek, Industry Week, and *Dun's Business Month* periodically publish detailed evaluations of U.S. businesses and industries. Although published sources of strategy-evaluation information focus primarily on large, publicly held businesses, the comparative ratios and related information are widely used to evaluate small businesses and privately owned firms as well.

Characteristics of an Effective Strategy Evaluation System

The strategy-evaluation process must exhibit several characteristics to be effective. First, strategy-evaluation activities must be economical; too much information can be just as bad as too little information, and too many controls can do more harm than good. Strategy-evaluation activities also should be meaningful; they should specifically relate to a firm's objectives. They should

TABLE 9-6 Fortune's 20 Most Admired Companies in 2014

1. Apple
2. Amazon.com
3. Google
4. Berkshire Hathaway
5. Starbucks
6. Coca-Cola
7. Walt Disney
8. FedEx
9. Southwest Airlines
10. General Electric
11. American Express
12. Costco Wholesale
13. Nike
14. BMW
15. Procter & Gamble
16. IBM
17. Nordstrom
18. Singapore Airlines
19. Johnson & Johnson
20. Whole Foods Market

Source: Based on information at http://www.haygroup.com/ww/best_companies/index.aspx?id=155

provide managers with useful information about tasks over which they have control and influence. Strategy-evaluation activities should provide timely information; on occasion and in some areas, managers may need information on a daily or even continuous basis. For example, when a firm has diversified by acquiring another firm, evaluative information may be needed frequently. In contrast, in an R&D department, daily or even weekly evaluative information could be dysfunctional. Approximate information that is timely is generally more desirable as a basis for strategy evaluation than accurate information that does not depict the present. Frequent measurement and rapid reporting may frustrate control rather than give better control. The time dimension of control must coincide with the time span of the event being measured.

Strategy-evaluation processes should be designed to provide a true picture of what is happening. For example, in a severe economic downturn, productivity and profitability ratios may drop alarmingly, although employees and managers are actually working harder. Strategy evaluations should fairly portray this type of situation. Information derived from the strategy-evaluation process should facilitate action and should be directed to those individuals in the organization who need to take action based on it. Managers commonly ignore evaluative reports that are provided only for informational purposes; not all managers need to receive all reports. Controls need to be action-oriented rather than information-oriented. The strategy-evaluation process should not dominate decisions; it should foster mutual understanding, trust, and common sense. No department should fail to cooperate with another in evaluating strategies. Strategy evaluations should be simple, not too cumbersome, and not too restrictive. Complex strategy-evaluation systems often confuse people and accomplish little. The test of an effective evaluation system is its usefulness, not its complexity.

Large organizations require a more elaborate and detailed strategy-evaluation system because it is more difficult to coordinate efforts among different divisions and functional areas. Managers in small companies often communicate daily with each other and their employees and do not need extensive evaluative reporting systems. Familiarity with local environments usually makes gathering and evaluating information much easier for small organizations than for large businesses. But the key to an effective strategy-evaluation system may be the ability to convince participants that failure to accomplish certain objectives within a prescribed time is not necessarily a reflection of their performance.

There is no one ideal strategy-evaluation system. The unique aspects of an organization, including its size, management style, purpose, problems, and strengths, can determine a strategy-evaluation and control system's final design. Robert Waterman offered the following observation about successful organizations' strategy-evaluation and control systems:

> Successful companies treat facts as friends and controls as liberating. Morgan Guaranty and Wells Fargo not only survive but thrive in the troubled waters of bank deregulation, because their strategy evaluation and control systems are sound, their risk is contained, and they know themselves and the competitive situation so well. Successful companies have a voracious hunger for facts. They see information where others see only data. Successful companies maintain tight, accurate financial controls. Their people don't regard controls as an imposition of autocracy but as the benign checks and balances that allow them to be creative and free.[12]

Contingency Planning

A basic premise of good strategic management is that firms strive to be proactive, planning ways to deal with unfavorable and favorable events before they occur. Too many organizations prepare contingency plans just for unfavorable events; this is a mistake, because both minimizing threats and capitalizing on opportunities can improve a firm's competitive position.

Regardless of how carefully strategies are formulated, implemented, and evaluated, unforeseen events, such as strikes, boycotts, natural disasters, arrival of foreign competitors, and government actions, can make a strategy obsolete. To minimize the impact of potential threats, organizations should develop contingency plans as part of their strategy-evaluation process. **Contingency plans** can be defined as alternative plans that can be put into effect if certain key events do not occur as expected. Only high-priority areas require the insurance of contingency plans. Strategists cannot and should not try to cover all bases by planning for all possible contingencies. But in any case, contingency plans should be as simple as possible.

Some contingency plans commonly established by firms include the following:

1. If a major competitor withdraws from particular markets as intelligence reports indicate, what actions should our firm take?
2. If our sales objectives are not reached, what actions should our firm take to avoid profit losses?
3. If demand for our new product exceeds plans, what actions should our firm take to meet the higher demand?
4. If certain disasters occur—such as loss of computer capabilities; a hostile takeover attempt; loss of patent protection; or destruction of manufacturing facilities because of earthquakes, tornadoes, or hurricanes—what actions should our firm take?
5. If a new technological advancement makes our new product obsolete sooner than expected, what actions should our firm take?

Too many organizations discard alternative strategies not selected for implementation although the work devoted to analyzing these options would render valuable information. Alternative strategies not selected for implementation can serve as contingency plans in case the strategy or strategies selected do not work. When strategy-evaluation activities reveal the need for a major change quickly, an appropriate contingency plan can be executed in a timely way. Contingency plans can promote a strategist's ability to respond quickly to key changes in the internal and external bases of an organization's current strategy. For example, if underlying assumptions about the economy turn out to be wrong and contingency plans are ready, then managers can make appropriate changes promptly. Sometimes, external or internal conditions present unexpected opportunities. When such opportunities occur, contingency plans could allow an organization to quickly capitalize on them. Linneman and Chandran report that contingency planning gives users, such as DuPont, Dow Chemical, Consolidated Foods, and Emerson Electric, three major benefits, as follows:

1. It enables quick responses to change.
2. It prevents panic in crisis situations.
3. It makes managers more adaptable by encouraging them to appreciate just how variable the future can be.

In addition, Linneman and Chandran suggest that effective contingency planning involves a five-step process, as follows:

1. Identify both good and bad events that could jeopardize strategies.
2. Determine when the good and bad events are likely to occur.
3. Determine the expected pros and cons of each contingency event.
4. Develop contingency plans for key contingency events.
5. Determine early warning trigger points for key contingency events.[13]

Auditing

A frequently used tool in strategy evaluation is the audit. **Auditing** is defined by the American Accounting Association (AAA) as "a systematic process of objectively obtaining and evaluating evidence regarding assertions about economic actions and events to ascertain the degree of correspondence between these assertions and established criteria, and communicating the results to interested users."[14]

Auditors examine the financial statements of firms to determine whether they have been prepared according to **generally accepted accounting principles (GAAP)** and whether they fairly represent the activities of the firm. Independent auditors use a set of standards called **generally accepted auditing standards (GAAS).** Public accounting firms often have a consulting arm that provides strategy-evaluation services.

The new era of **international financial reporting standards (IFRS)** is approaching in the United States, and businesses need to go ahead and get ready to use IFRS. Many U.S. companies now report their finances using both the old GAAP and the new IFRS. "If companies don't prepare, if they don't start three years in advance," warns business professor Donna Street at the University of Dayton, "they're going to be in big trouble." The GAAP standards are comprised of 25,000 pages, whereas the IFRS comprises only 5,000 pages, so in that sense IFRS is less cumbersome.

This accounting switch from GAAP to IFRS in the United States will cost businesses millions of dollars in fees and upgraded software systems and training. Certified public accountants in the United States need to study global accounting principles, and business schools should go ahead and begin teaching students the new accounting standards. Most large accounting firms and multinational firms favor the switch to IFRS, saying it will simplify accounting, make it easier for investors to compare firms across countries, and make it easier to raise capital globally. But many smaller firms oppose the upcoming change, believing it will be too costly; some firms are uneasy about the idea of giving an international body the authority to write accounting rules for the United States. Some firms also would pay higher taxes because last in, first out (LIFO) inventory methods are not allowed under IFRS. The International Accounting Standards Board (IASB) has publicly expressed "regret" over the slowness in the United States of adopting IFRS.

The U.S. Chamber of Commerce supports a change, saying it will lead to much more cross-border commerce and will help the United States compete in the world economy. Already the European Union and 113 nations have adopted or soon plan to use international rules, including Australia, China, India, Mexico, and Canada. So, the United States is likely to adopt IFRS rules, but this switch could unleash a legal and regulatory nightmare. A few U.S. multinational firms already use IFRS for their foreign subsidiaries, such as United Technologies (UT), which derives more than 60 percent of its revenues from abroad and is already training its entire staff to use IFRS.

Movement to IFRS from GAAP encompasses a company's entire operations, including auditing, oversight, cash management, taxes, technology, software, investing, acquiring, merging, importing, exporting, pension planning, and partnering. Switching from GAAP to IFRS is also likely to be plagued by gaping differences in business customs, financial regulations, tax laws, politics, and other factors. One critic of the upcoming switch is Charles Niemeier of the Public Company Accounting Oversight Board, who says the switch "has the potential to be a Tower of Babel," costing firms millions when they do not even have thousands to spend.

Others say the switch will help U.S. companies raise capital abroad and do business with firms abroad. Perhaps the biggest upside of the switch is that IFRS rules are more streamlined and less complex than GAAP. Lenovo is a big advocate of IFRS, as it desires to be a world company rather than a U.S. or Chinese company, so the faster the switch to IFRS, the better for them. The bottom line is that IFRS is coming to the United States, likely sooner rather than later.

Twenty-First-Century Challenges in Strategic Management

Three particular challenges or decisions that face all strategists today are (1) deciding whether the process should be more an art or a science, (2) deciding whether strategies should be visible or hidden from stakeholders, and (3) deciding whether the process should be more top-down or bottom-up in their firm.[15]

The Art or Science Issue

This book is consistent with most of the strategy literature in advocating that strategic management be viewed more as a science than an art. This perspective contends that firms need to systematically assess their external and internal environments, conduct research, carefully evaluate the pros and cons of various alternatives, perform analyses, and then decide on a particular course of action. In contrast, Mintzberg's notion of "crafting" strategies embodies the artistic model, which suggests that strategic decision making be based primarily on holistic thinking, intuition, creativity, and imagination.[16] Mintzberg and his followers reject strategies that result from objective analysis, preferring instead subjective imagination. "Strategy scientists" reject strategies that emerge from emotion, hunch, creativity, and politics. Proponents of the artistic view often consider strategic planning exercises to be time poorly spent. The Mintzberg philosophy insists on informality, whereas strategy scientists (and this text) insist on more formality.

Mintzberg refers to strategic planning as an "emergent" process, whereas strategy scientists use the term *deliberate* process.[17]

The answer to the art-versus-science question is one that strategists must decide for themselves, and certainly the two approaches are not mutually exclusive. The CEO of Williams-Sonoma, Laura Alber, recently stated, "I've found that the very best solutions arise from a willingness to blend art with science, ideas with data, and instinct with analysis." In deciding which approach is more effective, however, consider that the business world today has become increasingly complex and more intensely competitive. There is less room for error in strategic planning. Recall that Chapter 1 discussed the importance of intuition, experience, and subjectivity in strategic planning, and even the weights and ratings discussed in Chapters 3, 4, and 6 certainly require good judgment. But the idea of deciding on strategies for any firm without thorough research and analysis, at least in the mind of these authors, is unwise. Certainly, in smaller firms there can be more informality in the process compared to larger firms, but even for smaller firms, a wealth of competitive information is available on the Internet and elsewhere and should be collected, assimilated, and evaluated before deciding on a course of action on which survival of the firm may hinge. The livelihood of countless employees and shareholders may hinge on the effectiveness of strategies selected. Too much is at stake to be less than thorough in formulating strategies. It is not wise for a strategist to rely too heavily on gut feeling and opinion instead of research data, competitive intelligence, and analysis in formulating strategies.

The Visible or Hidden Issue

An interesting aspect of any competitive analysis discussion is whether strategies themselves should be secret or open within firms. The mini-case near the end of this chapter examines this issue for TJX Companies, a secretive company. The Chinese warrior Sun Tzu and military leaders today strive to keep strategies secret, because war is based on deception. But for business organizations, secrecy may not be best. Keeping strategies secret from employees and stakeholders at large could severely inhibit employee and stakeholder communication, understanding, and commitment, as well as forgo valuable input that these persons could have regarding formulation or implementation of that strategy. Thus, strategists in a particular firm must decide for themselves whether the risk of rival firms easily knowing and exploiting a firm's strategies is worth the benefit of improved employee and stakeholder motivation and input. Most executives agree that some strategic information should remain confidential to top managers, and that steps should be taken to ensure that such information is not disseminated beyond the inner circle. For a firm that you may own or manage, would you advocate openness or secrecy in regard to strategies being formulated and implemented?

There are certainly good reasons to keep the strategy process and strategies themselves visible and open rather than hidden and secret. There are also good reasons to keep strategies hidden from all but top-level executives. Strategists must decide for themselves what is best for their firms. This text comes down largely on the side of being visible and open, but certainly this may not be best for all strategists and all firms. As pointed out in Chapter 1, Sun Tzu argued that all war is based on deception and that the best maneuvers are those not easily predicted by rivals. Business and war are analogous in many respects.

Four reasons to be completely open with the strategy process and resultant decisions are these:

1. Managers, employees, and other stakeholders can readily contribute to the process. They often have excellent ideas. Secrecy would forgo many excellent ideas.
2. Investors, creditors, and other stakeholders have greater basis for supporting a firm when they know what the firm is doing and where the firm is going.
3. Visibility promotes democracy, whereas secrecy promotes autocracy. Domestic firms and most foreign firms prefer democracy over autocracy as a management style.
4. Participation and openness enhance understanding, commitment, and communication within the firm.

However, four reasons why some firms prefer to conduct strategic planning in secret and keep strategies hidden from all but the highest-level executives are as follows:

1. Free dissemination of a firm's strategies may easily translate into competitive intelligence for rival firms who could exploit the firm given that information.
2. Secrecy limits criticism, second guessing, and hindsight.
3. Participants in a visible strategy process become more attractive to rival firms who may lure them away.
4. Secrecy limits rival firms from imitating or duplicating the firm's strategies and undermining the firm.

The obvious benefits of the visible versus hidden extremes suggest that a working balance must be sought between the apparent contradictions. Parnell says that in a perfect world all key individuals both inside and outside the firm should be involved in strategic planning, but in practice, particularly sensitive and confidential information should always remain strictly confidential to top managers.[18] This balancing act is difficult but essential for survival of the firm.

The Top-Down or Bottom-Up Approach

Proponents of the top-down approach contend that top executives are the only persons in the firm with the collective experience, acumen, and fiduciary responsibility to make key strategy decisions. In contrast, bottom-up advocates argue that lower- and middle-level managers and employees who will be implementing the strategies need to be actively involved in the process of formulating the strategies to ensure their support and commitment. Recent strategy research and this text emphasize the bottom-up approach, but earlier work by Schendel and Hofer stressed the need for firms to rely on perceptions of their top managers in strategic planning.[19] Strategists must reach a working balance of the two approaches in a manner deemed best for their firms at a particular time, while being cognizant of the fact that current research supports the bottom-up approach, at least among U.S. firms. Increased education and diversity of the workforce at all levels are reasons why middle- and lower-level managers—and even nonmanagers—should be invited to participate in the firm's strategic planning process, at least to the extent that they are willing and able to contribute.

Guidelines for Effective Strategic Management

Failing to follow certain guidelines in conducting strategic management can foster criticisms of the process and create problems for the organization. Issues such as "Is strategic management in our firm a people process or a paper process?" should be addressed. Some organizations spend an inordinate amount of time developing a strategic plan, but then fail to follow through with effective implementation. Change and results in a firm come through implementation, not through formulation, although effective formulation is critically important for successful implementation. Continual evaluation of strategies is also essential because the world changes so rapidly that existing strategies can need modifying often.

Strategic management must not become a self-perpetuating bureaucratic mechanism. Rather, it must be a self-reflective learning process that familiarizes managers and employees in the organization with key strategic issues and feasible alternatives for resolving those issues. Strategic management must not become ritualistic, stilted, orchestrated, or too formal, predictable, and rigid. Words supported by numbers, rather than numbers supported by words, should represent the medium for explaining strategic issues and organizational responses. A key role of strategists is to facilitate continuous organizational learning and change.

R. T. Lenz offers six guidelines for effective strategic management:

1. Keep the process simple and easily understandable.
2. Eliminate vague planning jargon.
3. Keep the process nonroutine; vary assignments, team membership, meeting formats, settings, and even the planning calendar.
4. Welcome bad news and encourage devil's advocate thinking.

5. Do not allow technicians to monopolize the planning process.

6. To the extent possible, involve managers from all areas of the firm.[20]

An important guideline for effective strategic management is open-mindedness. A willingness and eagerness to consider new information, new viewpoints, new ideas, and new possibilities is essential; all organizational members must share a spirit of inquiry and learning. Strategists such as chief executive officers, presidents, owners of small businesses, and heads of government agencies must commit themselves to listen to and understand managers' positions well enough to be able to restate those positions to the managers' satisfaction. In addition, managers and employees throughout the firm should be able to describe the strategists' positions to the satisfaction of the strategists. This degree of discipline will promote understanding and learning.

No organization has unlimited resources. No firm can take on an unlimited amount of debt or issue an unlimited amount of stock to raise capital. Therefore, no organization can pursue all the strategies that potentially could benefit the firm. Strategic decisions, then, always have to be made to eliminate some courses of action and to allocate organizational resources among others. Most organizations can afford to pursue only a few corporate-level strategies at any given time. It is a critical mistake for managers to pursue too many strategies at the same time, thereby spreading the firm's resources so thin that all strategies are jeopardized.

Strategic decisions require trade-offs such as long-range versus short-range considerations or maximizing profits versus increasing shareholders' wealth. There are ethics issues, too. Strategy trade-offs require subjective judgments and preferences. In many cases, a lack of objectivity in formulating strategy results in a loss of competitive posture and profitability. Most organizations today recognize that strategic-management concepts and techniques can enhance the effectiveness of decisions. Subjective factors such as attitudes toward risk, concern for social responsibility, and organizational culture will always affect strategy-formulation decisions, but organizations need to be as objective as possible in considering qualitative factors. Table 9-7 summarizes important guidelines for the strategic-planning process to be effective.

TABLE 9-7 Seventeen Guidelines for the Strategic-Planning Process to Be Effective

1. It should be a people process more than a paper process.
2. It should be a learning process for all managers and employees.
3. It should be words supported by numbers rather than numbers supported by words.
4. It should be simple and nonroutine.
5. It should vary assignments, team memberships, meeting formats, and even the planning calendar.
6. It should challenge the assumptions underlying the current corporate strategy.
7. It should welcome bad news.
8. It should welcome open-mindedness and a spirit of inquiry and learning.
9. It should not be a bureaucratic mechanism.
10. It should not become ritualistic, stilted, or orchestrated.
11. It should not be too formal, predictable, or rigid.
12. It should not contain jargon or arcane planning language.
13. It should not be a formal system for control.
14. It should not disregard qualitative information.
15. It should not be controlled by "technicians."
16. Do not pursue too many strategies at once.
17. Continually strengthen the "good ethics is good business" policy.

IMPLICATIONS FOR STRATEGISTS

Figure 9-3 reveals on the far left that strategists must systematically, continuously, and carefully evaluate and monitor results by product, region, territory, segment, store, department, and even by individual, so that timely corrective actions can be taken to keep the firm on track. Quarterly, weekly, and even daily, companies have to adapt to changes that occur externally and internally, because even the best strategic plan needs periodic adjusting as rival firms adjust and launch new initiatives and products in new areas. As described in this chapter, the balanced scorecard is widely used by strategists to help manage the strategy evaluation process.

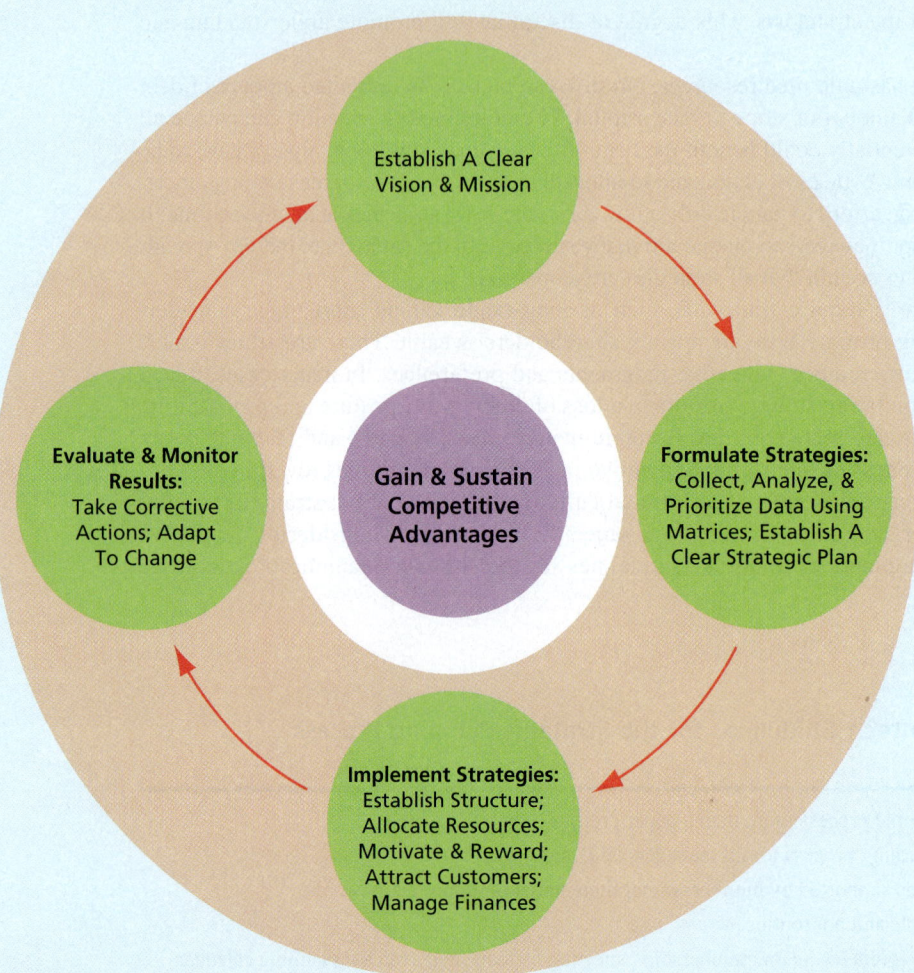

FIGURE 9-3

How to Gain and Sustain Competitive Advantages

IMPLICATIONS FOR STUDENTS

In performing your case analysis, develop and present a Balanced Scorecard that you recommend to help your firm monitor and evaluate progress toward stated objectives. Effective, timely evaluation of strategies can enable a firm to adapt quickly to changing conditions, and a Balanced Scorecard can assist in this endeavor. Couch your discussion of the Balanced Scorecard in terms of competitive advantage versus rival firms.

Chapter Summary

Effective strategy evaluation allows an organization to capitalize on internal strengths as they develop, to exploit external opportunities as they emerge, to recognize and defend against threats, and to mitigate internal weaknesses before they become detrimental.

Strategists in successful organizations take the time to formulate, implement, and then evaluate strategies deliberately and systematically. Good strategists move their organization forward with purpose and direction, continually evaluating and improving the firm's external and internal strategic positions. Strategy evaluation allows an organization to shape its own future rather than allowing it to be constantly shaped by remote forces that have little or no vested interest in the well-being of the enterprise.

Although not a guarantee for success, strategic management allows organizations to make effective long-term decisions, to execute those decisions efficiently, and to take corrective actions as needed to ensure success. Computer networks and the Internet help to coordinate strategic-management activities and to ensure that decisions are based on good information. A key to effective strategy evaluation and to successful strategic management is an integration of intuition and analysis:

A potentially fatal problem is the tendency for analytical and intuitive issues to polarize. This polarization leads to strategy evaluation that is dominated by either analysis or intuition, or to strategy evaluation that is discontinuous, with a lack of coordination among analytical and intuitive issues.[21] Strategists in successful organizations realize that strategic management is first and foremost a people process. It is an excellent vehicle for fostering organizational communication. People are what make the difference in organizations.

The real key to effective strategic management is to accept the premise that the planning process is more important than the written plan, that the manager is continuously planning and does not stop planning when the written plan is finished. The written plan is only a snapshot as of the moment it is approved. If the manager is not planning on a continuous basis—planning, measuring, and revising—the written plan can become obsolete the day it is finished. This obsolescence becomes more of a certainty as the increasingly rapid rate of change makes the business environment more uncertain.[22]

MyManagementLab®

To complete the problems with the ⭐, go to EOC Discussion Questions in the MyLab.

Key Terms and Concepts

advantage (p. 283)
auditing (p. 293)
Balanced Scorecard (p. 289)
consistency (p. 283)
consonance (p. 283)
contingency plans (p. 292)
feasibility (p. 283)
future shock (p. 288)
generally accepted accounting principles (GAAP) (p. 293)

generally accepted auditing standards (GAAS) (p. 293)
international financial reporting standards (IFRS) (p. 293)
measuring organizational performance (p. 286)
reviewing the underlying bases of an organization's strategy (p. 284)
revised EFE Matrix (p. 284)
revised IFE Matrix (p. 284)
taking corrective actions (p. 287)

Issues for Review and Discussion

9-1. Give several hypothetical situations whereby a company should establish contingency plans.

9-2. Explain why companies continually evaluate their strategies, rather than waiting for the end of the quarter or fiscal year to engage in the three core strategy evaluation activities discussed in this chapter.

9-3. Which of the three core strategy-evaluation activities do you think is most critical to be performed well? Why?

⭐ **9-4.** If a firm has two regions and two products, develop a sample framework for measuring organizational performance.

⭐ **9-5.** Compare strategy formulation with strategy implementation in terms of each being an art or a science.

9-6. Do an Internet search using the keywords *Balanced Scorecard Images*. Choose two images among the hundred available. Compare and contrast the two images and processes regarding effectiveness.

9-7. Do an Internet search using the keywords *GAAP to IFRS* to update yourself on this important transition coming soon in the United States.

9-8. How does an organization know if it is pursuing "optimal" strategies?

9-9. Discuss the nature and implications of the upcoming accounting switch from GAAP to IFRS in the United States.

9-10. Ask an accounting professor at your college or university the following question and report back to the class: "To what extent would my learning the IFRS standards on my own give me competitive advantage in the job market?"

9-11. Give an example of "consonance" other than the one provided by Rumelt in the chapter.

9-12. Evaluating strategies on a continuous rather than a periodic basis is desired. Discuss the pros and cons of this statement.

9-13. Why has strategy evaluation become so important in business today?

9-14. What types of quantitative and qualitative criteria should be used to evaluate a company's strategy?

9-15. As owner of a local, independent barbecue restaurant, explain how you would evaluate the firm's strategy.

⭐ **9-16.** Under what conditions are corrective actions not required in the strategy-evaluation process?

9-17. Identify types of organizations that may need to evaluate strategy more frequently than others. Justify your choices.

9-18. As executive director of the local Chamber of Commerce, in what way and how frequently would you evaluate the organization's strategies?

9-19. Identify some key financial ratios that would be important in evaluating a bank's strategy.

⭐ **9-20.** Strategy evaluation allows an organization to take a proactive stance toward shaping its own future. Discuss the meaning of this statement.

⭐ **9-21.** Diagram and discuss the Balanced Scorecard.

9-22. Develop a Balanced Scorecard for a local movie cinema complex.

9-23. Do you feel strategic management should be more a top-down or bottom-up process in a firm? Explain.

9-24. Do you believe strategic management is more an art or a science? Explain.

⭐ **9-25.** Regarding the strategic-planning process, give four "should be" guidelines and four "should not be" guidelines.

⭐ **9-26.** Researchers say contingency planning is a five-step process. Identify and discuss the five steps.

⭐ **9-27.** Identify and discuss five characteristics of effective strategy evaluation.

⭐ **9-28.** Identify and discuss four reasons to be open (visible) in regard to the strategic-planning process and outcomes.

⭐ **9-29.** Identify and discuss four reasons to be closed (secret) in regard to the strategic-planning process and outcomes.

MyManagementLab®

Go to the Assignments section of your MyLab to complete these writing exercises.

9-30. Why is the Balanced Scorecard an important topic both in devising objectives and in evaluating strategies?

9-31. Do you believe strategic management should be more visible or hidden as a process in a firm? Explain.

ASSURANCE OF LEARNING EXERCISES

EXERCISE 9A
Examine 100 Balanced Scorecards

Purpose

The Army Surgeon General and Commander of the U.S. Army Medical Command use the Balanced Scorecard as "the principal tool by which they improve operational and fiscal effectiveness and better meet the needs of patients and stakeholders." This exercise will give your experience in evaluating many different formats for the Balanced Scorecard. It will also give you exposure to many different organizations that currently use the Balanced Scorecard as part of their strategic planning.

Instructions

Step 1   Do a Google search using the terms *Balanced Scorecard images*. Review the many different formats of the Balanced Scorecard currently being used by organizations. Decide on three formats that you believe are particularly effective.

Step 2   Do a Google search using the terms *Balanced Scorecard Adopters*. Review the many different organizations currently using the Balanced Scorecard as part of their strategic planning. Select three different companies or organizations. Compare and contrast their use of the Balanced Scorecard technique.

Step 3   Prepare a three-page Executive Summary of your Balanced Scorecard analysis and recommendations.

EXERCISE 9B
Prepare a Strategy-Evaluation Report for Hershey Company

Purpose

This exercise can give you practice in developing a strategy-evaluation report.

Instructions

Step 1   Locate strategy-evaluation information regarding Hershey's performance last quarter and analysts' thoughts on Hershey's overall strategy going forward.

Step 2   Summarize your research findings by preparing a strategy-evaluation report. Include a summary of Hershey's strategies and performance of late, and a summary of your conclusions regarding the effectiveness of Hershey's strategies going forward.

Step 3   Is Hershey pursuing effective strategies? What recommendations would you offer to Hershey's CEO?

EXERCISE 9C
Evaluate Your University's Strategies

Purpose

An important part of evaluating strategies is determining the nature and extent of changes in an organization's external opportunities and threats as well as internal strengths and weaknesses. Changes in these underlying key factors can indicate a need to change or modify the firm's strategies.

Instructions

As a class, discuss positive and negative changes in your university's external and internal factors during your college career. Begin by listing on the board new or emerging opportunities and threats. Then identify strengths and weaknesses that have changed significantly during your college career. In light of the external and internal changes that were identified, discuss whether your university's strategies need modifying. Are there any new strategies that you would recommend? Make a list to recommend to your department chair, dean, president, or chancellor.

(Note to Professors—See the Chapter IM for an additional, excellent exercise for this chapter)

MINI-CASE ON TJX COMPANIES, INC. (TJX)

IS SECRET STRATEGIC PLANNING BEST FOR TJX?

Headquartered in Framingham, Massachusetts, TJX Companies is a discount apparel and home fashions retailer in the United States and abroad. The company owns T. J. Maxx, Marmaxx, Home Goods, TJX Canada, TJX Europe, and Sierra Trading Post. It operates about 1,100 T. J. Maxx stores, 950 Marshalls, 450 Home Goods, and 4 Sierra Trading Posts in the United States alone. TJX's annual sales of nearly $30 billion are up 50 percent over the past 6 years and company profits have tripled to over $2.1 billion.

Source: Pressmaster/Fotolia

Regarding its corporate strategic planning and evaluating process, TJX is one of the most secretive of all publically held retailers. As discussed in this chapter, there are numerous advantages and disadvantages of being secretive rather than open in revealing corporate strategy. TJX's CEO, Carol Meyrowitz, as well as her top executives, rarely give interviews and never discuss corporate strategy. TJX does not talk about its corporate strategy in part because rival firms are eager to learn this information in order to duplicate, imitate, undermine, and replicate. However, recent research by *Fortune* reveals that "excellent inventory control" is a secret to the strategic success of TJX, including the following practices:

1. Turn inventory over quickly. According to Morningstar, TJX turns over inventory every 55 days, versus 85 days for its peer group. TJX is structured to buy quickly and sell merchandise. The company shipped about 2 billion units to its stores in its 2014 fiscal year (which ended on February 1), up from 1.6 billion in fiscal 2010. Oftentimes, merchandise is sold before TJX has paid its vendors. Quick inventory turnover keeps new merchandise on the floor so customers rarely see the same items on repeat visits. TJX trains employees to "buy when you see it; otherwise it will be gone."
2. Provide "value, trendy merchandise," not "cheap, leftover merchandise."
3. Promote the "treasure hunt" experience rather than catering to lower-income customers. Even high-income customers love the treasure hunt experience in TJX stores.
4. Train buyers extensively and then give buyers autonomy to negotiate millions of dollars of purchases from suppliers. Purchase inventory year-round, continuously rather than seasonally, and purchase as close to the time of need as possible to negotiate a better price and be assured of the latest fashion trend. Negotiate low prices for purchases even if it means oftentimes purchasing "all available items in a category."

Despite performing considerably better than it rival firms, TJX faces heightened competition in the off-price retail industry. For example, Nordstrom (JWN) is rapidly expanding its Rack stores, opening 27 off-price new stores in 2016. Macy's (M) opened four pilot off-price stores in fall 2015, and Neiman Marcus, Saks, and Ross Stores (ROST) are boosting their presence in off-price retailing.

Questions

1. What are the advantages and disadvantages of keeping the strategic-planning process secret versus placing the firm's strategic plan on the corporate website and discussing strategies and planning publically?
2. What are three types of industries where secrecy is warranted and three industries where secrecy is not warranted, or does type of industry even matter?
3. Many colleges and universities have their strategic plan posted on their website. What are the advantages and disadvantages of this practice?
4. Rank order the four "secret" practices listed in terms of how important you think the items are to TJX's overall success. Rank the four items from 1 = most important to 4 = least important.

Source: Based on information at http://fortune.com/2014/07/24/t-j-maxx-the-best-retail-store/?icid=maing-grid7%7Chtmlws-main-bb%7Cdl30%7Csec1_lnk3%26pLid%3D508272

Current Readings

DaSilva, Carlos M., and Peter Trkman. "Business Model: What It Is and What It Is Not." *Long Range Planning* 47, issue 6 (December 2014): 379–389.

Drummond, Helga. "Escalation of Commitment: When to Stay the Course?" *Academy of Management Perspectives* 28 (November 2014): 430–446.

Kownatzki, Maximilian, et al. "Corporate Control and the Speed of Strategic Business Unit Decision Making." *Academy of Management Journal* 56, no. 5 (2013): 1295–1324.

Endnotes

1. Based on information at http://finance.yahoo.com/news/america-worst-companies-152240176.html
2. Dale McConkey, "Planning in a Changing Environment," *Business Horizons* (September–October 1988): 64.
3. Robert Simons, "Control in an Age of Empowerment," *Harvard Business Review* (March–April 1995), 80.
4. Dale Zand, "Reviewing the Policy Process," *California Management Review* 21, no. 1 (Fall 1978): 37.

5. Ecclesiastes. 3:1–8.

6. Claude George Jr., *The History of Management Thought* (Upper Saddle River, NJ: Prentice Hall, 1968), 165–166.

7. M. Erez and F. Kanfer, "The Role of Goal Acceptance in Goal Setting and Task Performance," *Academy of Management Review* 8, no. 3 (July 1983): 457.

8. D. Hussey and M. Langham, *Corporate Planning: The Human Factor* (Oxford, England: Pergamon, 1979), 138.

9. Carter Bayles, "Strategic Control: The President's Paradox," *Business Horizons* 20, no. 4 (August 1977): 18.

10. Based on information at http://graphic.com.gh/archive/Business-News/graphic-adopts-balanced-scorecard.html

11. Based on information at http://finance.yahoo.com/news/the-worst-ceos-of-2014-191156277.html

12. Robert Waterman, Jr., "How the Best Get Better," *BusinessWeek*, September 14, 1987, 105.

13. Robert Linneman and Rajan Chandran, "Contingency Planning: A Key to Swift Managerial Action in the Uncertain Tomorrow," *Managerial Planning* 29, no. 4 (January–February 1981): 23–27.

14. American Accounting Association, *Report of Committee on Basic Auditing Concepts*, 1971, 15–74.

15. John Parnell, "Five Critical Challenges in Strategy Making," *SAM Advanced Management Journal* 68, no. 2 (Spring 2003): 15–22.

16. Henry Mintzberg, "Crafting Strategy," *Harvard Business Review* (July–August 1987): 66–75.

17. Henry Mintzberg and J. Waters, "Of Strategies, Deliberate and Emergent," *Strategic Management Journal* 6, no. 2 (1985): 257–272.

18. Parnell, "Five Critical Challenges," 15–22.

19. D. E. Schendel and C. W. Hofer (Eds.), *Strategic Management* (Boston: Little, Brown, 1979).

20. R. T. Lenz, "Managing the Evolution of the Strategic Planning Process," *Business Horizons* 30, no. 1 (January–February 1987): 39.

21. Michael McGinnis, "The Key to Strategic Planning: Integrating Analysis and Intuition," *Sloan Management Review* 26, no. 1 (Fall 1984): 49.

22. McConkey, "Planning in a Changing Environment," 72.

KEY STRATEGIC-MANAGEMENT TOPICS

10

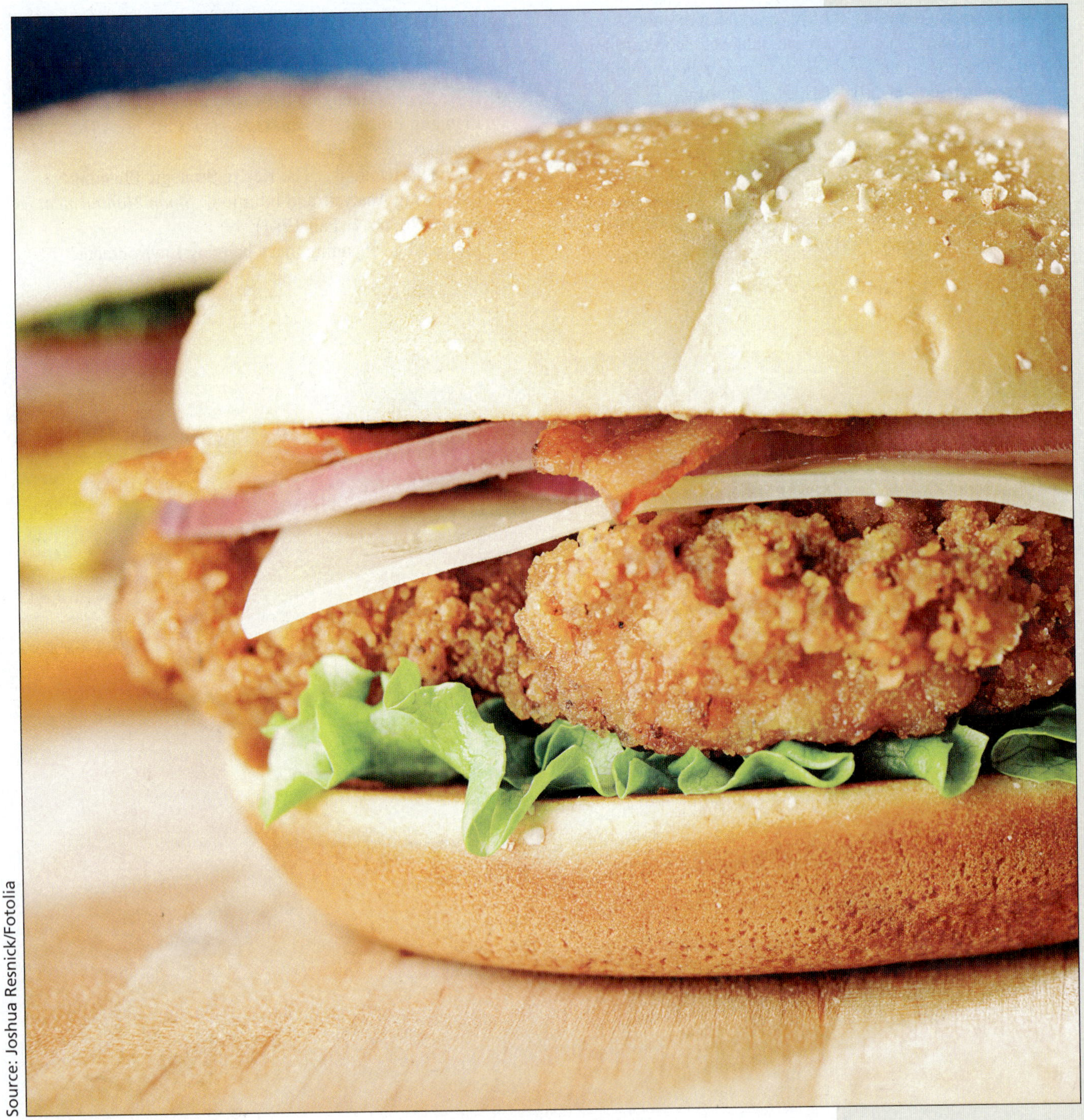

Source: Joshua Resnick/Fotolia

Business Ethics, Social Responsibility, and Environmental Sustainability

LEARNING OBJECTIVES

After studying this chapter, you should be able to do the following:

10-1. Explain why good ethics is good business in strategic management.

10-2. Explain why whistle-blowing, bribery, and workplace romance are strategic issues.

10-3. Discuss why social responsibility and policy are key issues in strategic planning.

10-4. Discuss the nature of environmental sustainability and why it is a key issue in strategic planning.

10-5. Explain why animal welfare is a strategic issue for firms.

ASSURANCE OF LEARNING EXERCISES

The following exercises are found at the end of this chapter:

EXERCISE 10A How Does Your Municipality Compare to Others on Being Pollution-Safe?

EXERCISE 10B Does Hershey Company or Mars, Inc. Win on Sustainability?

EXERCISE 10C The Ethics of Spying on Competitors

EXERCISE 10D Who Prepares a Sustainability Report?

Although the three sections of this chapter [(1) business ethics, (2) social responsibility, and (3) environmental sustainability] are distinct, the topics are quite related. For example, many people consider it unethical for a firm to be socially irresponsible or to treat animals inhumanely. **Business ethics** can be defined as principles of conduct within organizations that guide decision making and behavior. Good business ethics is a prerequisite for good strategic management; good ethics is just good business! **Social responsibility** refers to actions an organization takes beyond what is legally required to protect or enhance the well-being of living things. **Sustainability** refers to the extent that an organization's operations and actions protect, mend, and preserve rather than harm or destroy the natural environment. Polluting the environment, for example, is unethical, irresponsible, and in many cases illegal, as is treating pigs, cows, chickens, and turkeys inhumanely. Business ethics, social responsibility, and environmental sustainability issues therefore are interrelated and impact all areas of the strategic-management process, as illustrated in Figure 10-1 with white shading.

An example of a high-performing, highly ethical, privately held company is Chick-fil-A, the popular restaurant that is closed on Sundays out of respect for the Sabbath. Another high-performing, highly ethical, publicly held company is Chipotle Mexican Grill, which recently stopped selling a pork product at one third of its U.S. restaurants because one of its suppliers failed an animal welfare audit. That particular supplier could not ensure that pigs have outdoor access or "deeply bedded barns" instead of being raised in tight cages. In response, Chipotle stopped offering carnitas, or pork meat, in its burritos or bowls. An increasing number of firms like Chipotle are raising their standards for animal welfare in terms of its beef, pork, and poultry suppliers raising animals with respect and also avoid using various antibiotics and growth hormones. A Chipotle spokesman remarked, "This is fundamentally an animal welfare decision and is rooted in our unwillingness to compromise our standards where animal welfare is concerned; we hope the vendor will solve its problems and return as a regular supplier for Chipotle."

Why "Good Ethics Is Good Business"

The Institute of Business Ethics (IBE) recently did a study titled "Does Business Ethics Pay?" and concluded that companies displaying a "clear commitment to ethical conduct" consistently outperform companies that do not display ethical conduct. Philippa Foster Black of the IBE

EXEMPLARY COMPANY SHOWCASED

Chick-Fil-A

Headquartered in Atlanta, Georgia, Chick-fil-A prides itself on demonstrating high business ethics. Although all Chick-fil-A restaurants are closed on Sundays out of respect for the Sabbath, the company recently surpassed Kentucky Fried Chicken (KFC) as the largest chicken quick-service restaurant (QSR) in the United States. This is shocking because there are only about 2,000 Chick-fil-A outlets in the nation, compared to KFC's 4,500. Total annual revenues for Chick-fil-A exceed $5 billion, whereas all of KFC's U.S. restaurants have revenues under $5 billion. Each Chick-fil-A restaurant averages $3.2 million in annual sales, more than three times the average KFC at $938,000.

Over the last 10 years, the average Chick-fil-A restaurant sales increased steadily, compared to the average KFC's sales being unchanged, or down. Chick-fil-A added 100 restaurants in the United States in 2014, whereas the number of KFCs is declined. Most Chick-fil-A restaurants are located in the southern United States, but the company is expanding north rapidly. For example, there are 270, 200, and 161 Chick-fil-A outlets in Texas, Georgia, and Florida, respectively, but only 1 in the state of New York, and none in Montana, North Dakota, South Dakota, Vermont, Maine, or Connecticut—but that is to change soon.

The old saying that "good ethics is good business" seems to be especially true for Chick-fil-A.

Source: Based on http://www.dailyfinance.com/2014/03/28/chick-fil-a-stole-kfcs-chicken-crown-with-a-fraction-of-the-sto/?icid=maing-grid7%7Clegacy%7Cdl1%7Csec1_lnk3%26pLid%3D458929

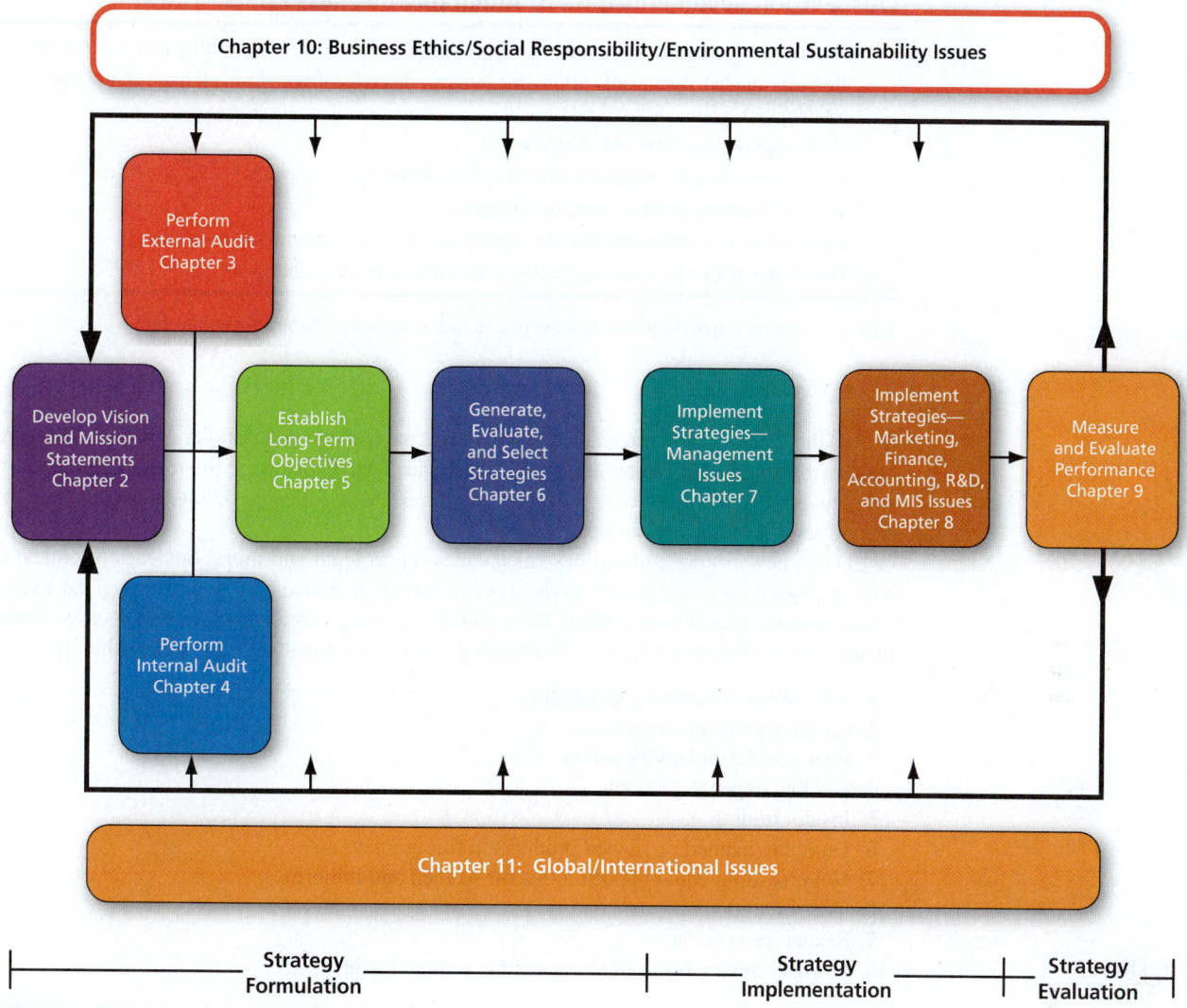

FIGURE 10-1

A Comprehensive Strategic-Management Model

Source: Fred R. David, "How Companies Define Their Mission," *Long Range Planning* 22, no. 3 (June 1988): 40. See also Anik Ratnaningsih, Nadjadji Anwar, Patdono Suwignjo, and Putu Artama Wiguna, "Balance Scorecard of David's Strategic Modeling at Industrial Business for National Construction Contractor of Indonesia," *Journal of Mathematics and Technology*, no. 4 (October 2010): 20.

stated, "Not only is ethical behavior in business life the right thing to do in principle, it pays off in financial returns." Alan Simpson remarked, "If you have integrity, nothing else matters. If you don't have integrity, nothing else matters." Good ethics is good business. Bad ethics can derail even the best strategic plans. This chapter provides an overview of the importance of business ethics in strategic management. Table 10-1 provides some results of the IBE study.

Does It Pay to Be Ethical?

A rising tide of consciousness about the importance of business ethics is sweeping the United States and the rest of the world. Strategists such as CEOs and business owners are the individuals primarily responsible for ensuring that high ethical principles are espoused and practiced in an organization. All strategy formulation, implementation, and evaluation decisions have ethical ramifications.

As indicated in Academic Research Capsule 10-1, it does pay to be ethical; high-performing companies generally exhibit high business ethics. *Investor's Business Daily* reported on 7-20-15

TABLE 10-1 Seven Principles of Admirable Business Ethics

1. Be trustworthy; no individual or business wants to do business with an entity it does not trust.
2. Be open-minded, continually asking for "ethics-related feedback" from all internal and external stakeholders.
3. Honor all commitments and obligations.
4. Do not misrepresent, exaggerate, or mislead with any print materials.
5. Be visibly a responsible community citizen.
6. Utilize your accounting practices to identify and eliminate questionable activities.
7. Follow the motto: Do unto others as you would have them do unto you.

Source: Based on http://sbinformation.about.com/od/bestpractices/a/businessethics.htm

(p. A4) that character-driven leaders deliver five times greater profitability results and 26 percent higher workforce engagement than self-focused leaders. Those were the results of a seven-year study by Fred Kiel, author of "*Return on Character*," who followed 8,000 employees and 84 top executives of Fortune 500 companies.

Daily, newspapers and business magazines report legal and moral breaches of ethical conduct by both public and private organizations. Being unethical can be expensive. For example, Cisco Systems in 2015 sued Arista Networks for copying verbatim sections of its user manuals. In addition to plagiarism, literally hundreds of business actions are unethical, including:

1. Misleading advertising or labeling
2. Causing environmental harm
3. Poor product or service safety
4. Padding expense accounts
5. Insider trading
6. Dumping banned or flawed products in foreign markets
7. Not providing equal opportunities for women and minorities
8. Overpricing
9. Sexual harassment
10. Using company funds or resources for personal gain

Increasingly, executives' and managers' personal and professional decisions are placing them in the crosshairs of angry shareholders, disgruntled employees, and even their own boards

---

ACADEMIC RESEARCH CAPSULE 10-1

What Can We Learn from High-Performance Companies?

Research at DePaul University in Chicago by Frigo and Litman found a pattern of strategic activities of high-performance companies. Their research involved screening the financial performance of more than 15,000 public companies using 30 years of financial data and identifying about 100 high-performance companies. Here are three lessons from high-performance companies studied:

1) **Commitment to Return on Investment and Ethical Business Conduct**: High-performance companies demonstrate a strong commitment to creating shareholder value by focusing on sustainable return on investment (ROI). These companies achieve superior ROI and growth while adhering to ethical business conduct, such as Johnson & Johnson, which is famous for its credo as a foundation for ethical business conduct at the company.

2) **Focus on Unmet Customer Needs in Growing Market Segments**: To avoid commoditization, high-performance companies concentrate on fulfilling unmet customer needs and target growing market segments. Harley-Davidson targets customer needs (lifestyle, freedom, community) with their unique Harley experience while pursuing a growing customer group (the Baby Boom generation).

3) **Innovate Offerings**: High-performance companies constantly reexamine their products and services (their offerings), modifying existing ones and developing new ones that will better fulfill customers' unmet needs. For example, Apple demonstrate this characteristic through its innovation strategy.

Source: Based on Mark L. Frigo and Joel Litman, *DRIVEN: Business Strategy, Human Actions and the Creation of Wealth, Strategy and Execution* (Chicago: Strategy & Execution LLC, 2008).

of directors—making the imperious CEO far more vulnerable to personal, public, and corporate missteps than ever before. "Certainly, anybody who is doing something that can be construed as unethical, immoral or greedy is being taken to task," says Paul Dorf of Compensation Resources, a consultant to boards of directors.[1]

Social media and business-centric websites such as glassdoor.com and vault.com as well as disclosure mandates required under Sarbanes-Oxley are just several among hundreds of outlets that today quickly spread fact and rumor about the inside dealings of corporations and organizations, revealing ethical breaches and internal business practices that may never have surfaced years ago. Wendy Patrick, who teaches business ethics at San Diego State University, states, "God forbid anyone who isn't squeaky-clean these days or misrepresents their credentials. Anything embarrassing and you begin to question everything. If you aren't making good decisions in your personal life, it can bleed over to your career (professional life)."

How to Establish an Ethics Culture

A new wave of ethics issues has recently surfaced related to product safety, employee health, sexual harassment, AIDS in the workplace, smoking, acid rain, affirmative action, waste disposal, foreign business practices, cover-ups, takeover tactics, conflicts of interest, employee privacy, inappropriate gifts, and security of company records. A key ingredient for establishing an ethics culture is to develop a clear **code of business ethics**. Internet fraud, hacking into company computers, spreading viruses, and identity theft are other unethical activities that plague every sector of online commerce.

As indicated in Academic Research Capsule 10-2, anyone is prone to be unethical in a business, so Donald Palmer provides six procedures to establish an ethics culture.

Merely having a code of ethics, however, is not sufficient to ensure ethical business behavior. A code of ethics can be viewed as a public relations gimmick, a set of platitudes, or window dressing. To ensure that the code is read, understood, believed, and remembered, periodic ethics workshops are needed to sensitize people to workplace circumstances in which ethics issues may arise.[2] If employees see examples of punishment for violating the code as well as rewards for upholding the code, this reinforces the importance of a firm's code of ethics. The website www.ethicsweb.ca/codes provides guidelines on how to write an effective code of ethics.

Reverend Billy Graham once said, "When wealth is lost, nothing is lost; when health is lost, something is lost; when character is lost, all is lost." An ethics "culture" needs to permeate organizations! To help create an ethics culture, Citicorp developed a business ethics board game that is played by thousands of employees worldwide. Called "The Word Ethic," this game asks players business ethics questions, such as "How do you deal with a customer who offers you football tickets in exchange for a new, backdated IRA?" Diana Robertson at the Wharton School

ACADEMIC RESEARCH CAPSULE 10-2

Who Is Prone to Be Unethical in a Business?

Prior research suggests that being unethical is abnormal, rare, and most often perpetrated by people who are abhorrent. However, Donald Palmer recently reported that misconduct is a normal phenomenon and that wrongdoing is as prevalent as "rightdoing," and that misconduct is most often done by people who are primarily good, ethical, and socially responsible. Palmer reports that individuals engage in unethical activities due to a plethora of structure, processes, and mechanisms inherent in the functioning of organizations—and, importantly, all of us are candidates to be unethical under the right circumstances in any organization. Implications of this new research abound for managers. In light of his findings, Palmer concludes that organizations should implement the following six procedures as soon as possible:

1) Punish wrongdoing swiftly and severely when it is detected.
2) Be careful to hire employees who possess high ethical standards.
3) Develop socialization programs to reinforce desired cultural values.
4) Alter chains of command so subordinates report to more than one superior.
5) Develop a culture whereby subordinates may challenge their superior's orders when they seem questionable.
6) Develop a better understanding of internal policies, procedures, systems, and mechanisms that could lead to misconduct.

Source: Based on Donald Palmer, "The New Perspective on Organizational Wrongdoing," *California Management Review*, 56, no. 1 (2013): 5–23.

of Business believes the game is effective because it is interactive. Many organizations have developed a code-of-conduct manual outlining ethical expectations and giving examples of situations that commonly arise in their businesses.

One reason strategists' salaries are high is that they must take the moral risks of the firm. Strategists are responsible for developing, communicating, and enforcing the code of business ethics for their organizations. Although primary responsibility for ensuring ethical behavior rests with a firm's strategists, an integral part of the responsibility of all managers is to provide ethics leadership by constant example and demonstration. Managers hold positions that enable them to influence and educate many people. This makes managers responsible for developing and implementing ethical decision making. Gellerman and Drucker, respectively, offer some good advice for managers:

> All managers risk giving too much because of what their companies demand from them. But the same superiors who keep pressing you to do more, or to do it better, or faster, or less expensively, will turn on you should you cross that fuzzy line between right and wrong. They will blame you for exceeding instructions or for ignoring their warnings. The smartest managers already know that the best answer to the question "How far is too far?" is don't try to find out.[3]

> A man (or woman) might know too little, perform poorly, lack judgment and ability, and yet not do too much damage as a manager. But if that person lacks character and integrity—no matter how knowledgeable, how brilliant, how successful—he destroys. He destroys people, the most valuable resource of the enterprise. He destroys spirit. And he destroys performance. This is particularly true of the people at the head of an enterprise because the spirit of an organization is created from the top. If an organization is great in spirit, it is because the spirit of its top people is great. If it decays, it does so because the top rots. As the proverb has it, "Trees die from the top." No one should ever become a strategist unless he or she is willing to have his or her character serve as the model for subordinates.[4]

No society anywhere in the world can compete long or successfully with people stealing from one another or not trusting one another, with every bit of information requiring notarized confirmation, with every disagreement ending up in litigation, or with government having to regulate businesses to keep them honest. Being unethical is a recipe for headaches, inefficiency, and waste. History has proven that the greater the trust and confidence of people in the ethics of an institution or society, the greater its economic strength. Business relationships are built mostly on mutual trust and reputation. Short-term decisions based on greed and questionable ethics will preclude the necessary self-respect to gain the trust of others. More and more firms believe that ethics training and an ethics culture create strategic advantage. According to Max Killan, "If business is not based on ethical grounds, it is of no benefit to society, and will, like all other unethical combinations, pass into oblivion."

Whistle-Blowing, Bribery, and Workplace Romance

As social media and technology have become commonplace globally, three business ethics topics—whistle-blowing, bribery, and workplace romance—have become important strategic issues facing companies. Missteps in any of these three areas can severely harm an organization.

Whistle-Blowing

Whistle-blowing refers to employees reporting any unethical violations they discover or see in the firm. Employees should practice whistle-blowing, and organizations should have policies that encourage whistle-blowing. Three individuals recently received $170 million for helping investigators obtain a record $16.65 billion penalty against Bank of America for inflating the value of mortgage properties and selling defective loans to investors. The whistle-blower payouts are among the highest ever in financial institution cases. Thousands of firms warn managers and employees that failing to report an ethical violation by others could bring discharge. The Securities and Exchange Commission (SEC) recently strengthened its whistle-blowing policies, virtually mandating that anyone seeing unethical activity report such behavior.

Whistle-blowers in the corporate world receive up to 25 percent of the proceeds of legal proceedings against firms for wrongdoing. Such payouts are becoming more and more common. J.P. Morgan Chase employee Keith Edwards recently received a $63.9 million payout for his whistle-blowing tips that led J.P. Morgan to pay $614 million to the U.S. government for illegally approving thousands of FHA loans and hundreds of VA loans that did not meet underwriting requirements. The SEC recently paid $30 million to a non-U.S. citizen whistle-blower who reported an ongoing fraud matter. Sean McKessy, the SEC's whistle-blower top executive, commented about the case, "Whistleblowers from all over the world should feel similarly incentivized to come forward with credible information about potential violations of the U.S. securities laws."

An accountant who recently tipped off the IRS that his employer was skimping on taxes received $4.5 million in the first IRS whistle-blower award. The accountant's tip netted the IRS $20 million in taxes and interest from the errant financial-services firm. The award represented a 22 percent cut of the taxes recovered. The IRS program, designed to encourage tips in large-scale cases, mandates awards of 15 to 30 percent of the amount recouped. "It's a win-win for both the government and taxpayers. These are dollars that are being returned to the U.S. Treasury that otherwise wouldn't be," said lawyer Eric Young.

Ethics training programs should include messages from the CEO or owner of the business, emphasizing ethical business practices, the development and discussion of codes of ethics, and procedures for discussing and reporting unethical behavior. Firms can align ethical and strategic decision making by incorporating ethical considerations into strategic planning, by integrating ethical decision making into the performance appraisal process, by encouraging whistle-blowing, and by monitoring departmental and corporate performance regarding ethical issues.

Avoid Bribery

Managers, employees, and firms must avoid bribery. **Bribery** is defined by *Black's Law Dictionary* as the offering, giving, receiving, or soliciting of any item of value to influence the actions of an official or other person in discharge of a public or legal duty. A **bribe** is a gift bestowed to influence a recipient's conduct. The gift may be any money, goods, actions, property, preferment, privilege, emolument, object of value, advantage, or merely a promise or undertaking to induce or influence the action, vote, or influence of a person in an official or public capacity. Bribery is a crime in most countries of the world, including the United States.[5] As indicated in the minicase near the end of this chapter, Avon Products has been plagued by bribery charges over the last 8 years. French engineering firm Alstom SA recently pleaded guilty to criminal charges that the company paid tens of millions of dollars in a "widespread" bribery scheme to win energy contracts globally. Alstom paid a fine of $772 million for falsifying financial records and paying bribes to win contracts around the world.

The U.S. Foreign Corrupt Practices Act (FCPA) governs bribery in the United States and has stepped up enforcement. This act, and a new provision in the Dodd-Frank financial-regulation law, allows company employees or others who bring cases of financial fraud, such as bribery, to the government's attention to receive up to 30 percent of any sum recovered. Bribery suits against a company also expose the firm to shareholder lawsuits. Hewlett-Packard (HP) recently paid $108 million to resolve bribery investigations in Russia, Poland, and Mexico. The HP bribery activities included the use of slush funds and shell companies to funnel monies to politicians, as well as free trips to Las Vegas with free cash to gamble.

A recent *Wall Street Journal* article titled "Bribery Law Dos and Don'ts" provides a synopsis of the recent 130-page document released by the U.S. Justice Department and the SEC to respond to complaints from companies that ambiguity in the FCPA has forced them to abandon business in high-risk countries and spend millions of dollars investigating themselves.[6] Numerous examples of bribery are given, such as "providing a $12,000 birthday trip for a government official from Mexico that includes visits to wineries and museums" and "$10,000 spent on a government official for drinks, dinners, and entertainment." The U.S. Justice Department and the SEC each file about 100 bribery cases annually.

The United Kingdom Bribery Law forbids any company doing any business in the United Kingdom from bribing foreign or domestic officials to gain competitive advantage. The British law is more stringent even than the similar U.S. FCPA. The British Bribery Law carries a maximum 10-year prison sentence for those convicted of bribery. The law stipulates that "failure to prevent bribery" is an offense and stipulates that facilitation payments, or payments to gain access, are not a valid defense to prevent bribery. The United Kingdom law applies even to bribes between private businesspersons, and if the individual who makes the payment does not realize the transaction was a bribe, he or she is still liable. The new bribery law is being enforced by Britain's Serious Fraud Office (SFO) and boosts the maximum penalty for bribery from 7 years to 10 years in prison, and sets no limits on fines. More and more nations are taking a tougher stance against corruption, and companies worldwide are installing elaborate programs to avoid running afoul of the FCPA or the SFO.

In some foreign countries, paying bribes and kickbacks has historically been acceptable. But now, antibribery and extortion initiatives are advocated by many organizations, including the World Bank, the International Monetary Fund, the European Union (EU), the Council of Europe, the Organization of American States, the Pacific Basin Economic Council, the Global Coalition for Africa, and the United Nations. Tipping is even now considered bribery in some countries. Taking business associates to lavish dinners and giving them expensive holiday gifts and even outright cash may have been expected in some countries, such as South Korea and China, but there is now stepped-up enforcement of bribery laws virtually everywhere. The world's third-largest commercial aircraft manufacturer, Embraer SA, headquartered in Brazil, is currently being investigated for allegedly paying a $3.5 million bribe to a Dominican Republic Air Force colonel, who then pressured Dominican legislators to approve a $92 million contract for Embraer to provide attack planes to that country.

Several pharmaceutical companies, including Merck, AstraZeneca PLC, Bristol-Myers Squibb, and GlaxoSmithKline PLC, are currently being investigated for allegedly paying bribes in certain foreign countries to boost sales and speed approvals. Four types of violations are being reviewed: bribing government-employed doctors to purchase drugs, paying company sales agents commissions that are passed along to government doctors, paying hospital committees to approve drug purchases, and paying regulators to win drug approvals. Johnson & Johnson recently paid $70 million to settle allegations that it paid bribes to doctors in Greece, Poland, and Romania to use their surgical implants and to prescribe its drugs. Pfizer paid $60 million to resolve similar probes to win business overseas.

Workplace Romance

Workplace romance is an intimate relationship between two consenting employees, as opposed to **sexual harassment**, which the Equal Employment Opportunity Commission (EEOC) defines broadly as unwelcome sexual advances, requests for sexual favors, and other verbal or physical conduct of a sexual nature. Sexual harassment (and discrimination) is illegal, unethical, and detrimental to any organization and can result in expensive lawsuits, lower morale, and reduced productivity.

Workplace romance between two consenting employees simply happens, so the question is generally not whether to allow the practice, or even how to prevent it, but rather how best to manage the phenomena. An organization probably should not strictly forbid workplace romance because such a policy could be construed as an invasion of privacy, overbearing, or unnecessary. Some romances actually improve work performance, adding a dynamism and energy that translates into enhanced morale, communication, creativity, and productivity.[7]

However, it is important to note that workplace romance can be detrimental to workplace morale and productivity, for a number of reasons that include:

1. Favoritism complaints can arise.
2. Confidentiality of records can be breached.
3. Reduced quality and quantity of work can become a problem.
4. Personal arguments can lead to work arguments.
5. Whispering secrets can lead to tensions and hostilities among coworkers.
6. Sexual harassment (or discrimination) charges may ensue, either by the involved female or a third party.
7. Conflicts of interest can arise, especially when well-being of the partner trumps well-being of the company.

In some states, such as California, managers can be held personally liable for damages that arise from workplace romance. Organizations should establish guidelines or policies that address workplace romance, for at least six reasons:

1. Guidelines can enable the firm to better defend against and avoid sexual harassment or discrimination charges.

2. Guidelines can specify reasons (such as the seven listed previously) why workplace romance may not be a good idea.
3. Guidelines can specify resultant penalties for romancing partners if problems arise.
4. Guidelines can promote a professional and fair work atmosphere.
5. Guidelines can help assure compliance with federal, state, and local laws and recent court cases.
6. Lack of any guidelines sends a lackadaisical message throughout the firm.

Workplace romance guidelines should apply to all employees at all levels of the firm and should specify certain situations in which affairs are especially discouraged, such as supervisor and subordinate. Company guidelines or policies in general should discourage workplace romance because "the downside risks generally exceed the upside benefits" for the firm. Best Buy CEO Brian Dunn recently resigned when directors learned of his inappropriate relationship with a young subordinate, which was a violation of that company's code of ethics. Based in Fremont, California, IGate Corp. fired its CEO, Phaneesh Murthy, recently for allegedly failing to report a workplace romance relationship that turned into a sexual harassment issue with a subordinate.

Flirting is a step down from workplace romance, but a full-page *Wall Street Journal* article titled "The New Rules of Flirting" reveal the dos and don'ts of flirting.[8] Flirting is defined by researchers as "romantic behavior that is ambiguous and goal oriented," or said differently, "ambiguous behavior with potential sexual or romantic overtones that is goal-oriented." A few flirting rules given in the article are:

1. Do not flirt with someone you know is looking for a relationship if you are not interested in a new relationship.
2. Do flirt within a relationship that you want to strengthen.
3. Do not flirt to make your partner jealous because this is manipulative behavior.
4. Flirting between power differences, such as boss and employee or professor and student, usually leads to trouble, as many defendants in sexual harassment complaints know.
5. Do not make physical contact with the person you are flirting with, unless it is within a desired relationship.

Among colleges and universities, the federal Office of Civil Rights (OCR) has stepped up its investigation of sexual harassment cases brought forward by female students against professors. Numerous institutions are currently being investigated. At no charge to the student, the OCR will investigate a female student's claim if evidence is compelling.

A *Wall Street Journal* article recapped U.S. standards regarding boss and subordinate love affairs at work.[9] Only 5 percent of all firms sampled had no restrictions on such relationships; 80 percent of firms have policies that prohibit relationships between a supervisor and a subordinate. Only 4 percent of firms strictly prohibited such relationships, but 39 percent of firms had policies that required individuals to inform their supervisors whenever a romantic relationship begins with a coworker. Only 24 percent of firms required the two persons to be in different departments.

In Europe, romantic relationships at work are largely viewed as private matters and most firms have no policies on the practice. However, European firms are increasingly adopting explicit, U.S.-style sexual harassment laws. The U.S. military strictly bans officers from dating or having sexual relationships with enlistees. At the World Bank, sexual relations between a supervisor and an employee are considered "a de facto conflict of interest which must be resolved to avoid favoritism." World Bank president Paul Wolfowitz recently was forced to resign as a result of a relationship he had with a bank staff person.

A recent *Bloomberg Businessweek* article reports that employees are filing sexual harassment complaints as a way to further their own job security. Many of these filings are increasingly third-party individuals not even directly involved in the relationship but alleging their own job was impacted. Largely the result of the rise of third-party discrimination claims, the EEOC recovers about $500 million on behalf of office romance victims.[10]

Social Responsibility and Policy

Some strategists agree with Ralph Nader, who proclaims that organizations have tremendous social obligations. Nader points out, for example, that ExxonMobil has more assets than most countries, and because of this, such firms have an obligation to help society cure its many ills.

ACADEMIC RESEARCH CAPSULE 10-3

Does It Pay to Be Socially Responsible?

Economists generally say *no*, and philanthropists say *yes* to this question. Recent research by Barnett and Salomon examined the relationship between corporate social performance (CSP) and corporate financial performance (CFP). They hypothesized, and then confirmed, that the CSP–CFP relationship is U-shaped. Specifically, Barnett and Salomon reported that firms with low CSP have higher CFP than firms with moderate CSP, but firms with high CSP have the highest CFP. They also found that firms with the highest CSP generally have the highest CFP. In addition, the researchers reported that the accrual of social responsibility deeds causes the benefits of CSP to increase at a higher rate than the costs, producing an eventual upturn in the CSP–CFP relationship.

Source: Based on Michael Barnett and Robert Salomon, "Does It Pay to Be Really Good? Addressing the Shape of the Relationship Between Social and Financial Performance," *Strategic Management Journal*, 33 (2012): 1304–1320.

Other people, however, agree with the economist Milton Friedman, who asserts that organizations have no obligation to do any more for society than is legally required. Friedman may contend that it is irresponsible for a firm to give monies to charity.

Do you agree more with Nader or Friedman? Surely we can all agree that the first social responsibility of any business must be to make enough profit to cover the costs of the future, because if this is not achieved, no other social responsibility can be met. Indeed, no social need can be met if the firm fails. Strategists should examine social problems in terms of potential costs and benefits to the firm and focus on social issues that could benefit the firm most. For example, if a firm avoids cutting jobs to protect employees' livelihood, and that decision forces the firm to liquidate, then all the employees lose their jobs. As indicated in Academic Research Capsule 10-3, most economists suggest that firms should not engage much, if any, in philanthropy, because simply making a profit is difficult, and shareholders expect a high return on their investment.

Design and Articulate a Social Policy

The term **social policy** embraces managerial philosophy and thinking at the highest level of the firm, which is why the topic is covered in this text. Social policy concerns what responsibilities the firm has to employees, consumers, environmentalists, minorities, communities, shareholders, and other groups. After decades of debate, many firms still struggle to determine appropriate social policies. The impact of society on business and vice versa is becoming more pronounced each year. Corporate social policy should be designed and articulated during strategy formulation, set and administered during strategy implementation, and reaffirmed or changed during strategy evaluation.[11]

Firms should strive to engage in social activities that have economic benefits. Merck & Co. once developed the drug ivermectin for treating river blindness, a disease caused by a fly-borne parasitic worm endemic in poor tropical areas of Africa, the Middle East, and Latin America. In an unprecedented gesture that reflected its corporate commitment to social responsibility, Merck then made ivermectin available at no cost to medical personnel throughout the world. Merck's action highlights the dilemma of orphan drugs, which offer pharmaceutical companies no economic incentive for profitable development and distribution. Merck did, however, garner substantial goodwill among its stakeholders for its actions.

Social Policies on Retirement

Some countries around the world are facing severe workforce shortages associated with their aging populations. The percentage of persons age 65 or older exceeds 20 percent in Japan, Italy, and Germany—and will reach 20 percent in 2018 in France. In 2036, the percentage of persons age 65 or older will reach 20 percent in the United States and China. Unlike the United States, Japan is reluctant to rely on large-scale immigration to bolster its workforce. Instead, Japan provides incentives for its elderly to work until ages 65 to 75. Western European countries are doing the opposite, providing incentives for its elderly to retire at ages 55 to 60. The International Labor Organization says 71 percent of Japanese men ages 60 to 64 work, compared to 57 percent of American men and just 17 percent of French men in the same age group.

TABLE 10-2 The Ten Best Socially Responsible Companies in the World

1. Microsoft
2. Google
3. Walt Disney Company
4. BMW
5. Apple
6. Daimler (Mercedes-Benz)
7. Volkswagen
8. Sony
9. Colgate-Palmolive
10. LEGO Group

Source: Based on information at http://www.forbes.com/pictures/efkk45mmlm/no-1-microsoft/

Sachiko Ichioka, a typical 67-year-old man in Japan, says, "I want to work as long as I'm healthy. The extra money means I can go on trips, and I'm not a burden on my children." Better diet and health care have raised Japan's life expectancy now to 82, the highest in the world. Japanese women are having, on average, only 1.28 children compared to 2.04 in the United States. Keeping the elderly at work, coupled with reversing the old-fashioned trend of keeping women at home, are Japan's two key remedies for sustaining its workforce in factories and businesses. This prescription for dealing with problems associated with an aging society should be considered by many countries around the world. The Japanese government is phasing in a shift from age 60 to age 65 as the date when a person may begin receiving a pension, and premiums paid by Japanese employees are rising while payouts are falling. Unlike the United States, Japan has no law against discrimination based on age.

Worker productivity increases in Japan are not able to offset declines in number of workers, thus resulting in a decline in overall economic production. Like many countries, Japan does not view immigration as a good way to solve this problem. Japan's shrinking workforce has become such a concern that the government just recently allowed an unspecified number of Indonesian and Filipino nurses and caregivers to work in Japan for two years. The number of working-age Japanese—those between ages 15 and 64—is projected to shrink to 70 million by 2030. Using foreign workers is known as *gaikokujin roudousha* in Japanese. Many Filipinos have recently been hired now to work in agriculture and factories throughout Japan.

Forbes best companies globally in regard to being socially responsible are listed in Table 10-2. Former CEO Bill Gates, of the number-one ranked firm Microsoft, established the well-known Bill and Melinda Gates Foundation, which sets a high standard for any person or company.

Environmental Sustainability

The ecological challenge facing all organizations requires managers to formulate strategies that preserve and conserve natural resources and control pollution. Special natural environment issues include ozone depletion, global warming, depletion of rain forests, destruction of animal habitats, protecting endangered species, developing biodegradable products and packages, waste management, clean air, clean water, erosion, destruction of natural resources, and pollution control. Firms increasingly are developing green product lines that are biodegradable or are made from recycled products. Green products sell well. Managing the health of the planet requires an understanding of how international trade, competitiveness, and global resources are connected. Managing environmental affairs, for example, can no longer be simply a technical function performed by specialists in a firm; more emphasis must be placed on developing an environmental perspective among all employees and managers of the firm.

Businesses must not exploit and decimate the natural environment. Mark Starik at George Washington University believes, "Halting and reversing worldwide ecological destruction and deterioration is a strategic issue that needs immediate and substantive attention by all businesses and managers." According to the International Standards Organization, the word **environment** is defined as "surroundings in which an organization operates, including air, water, land, natural resources, flora, fauna, humans, and their interrelation." This chapter illustrates how many firms are gaining competitive advantage by being good stewards of the natural environment.

Employees, consumers, governments, and societies are especially resentful of firms that harm rather than protect the natural environment. Conversely, people today are especially appreciative of firms that conduct operations in a way that mends, conserves, and preserves the natural environment. Consumer interest in businesses preserving nature's ecological balance and fostering a clean, healthy environment is high.

What Firms Are the Best Stewards?

Lennar Corporation, the nation's second-largest homebuilder, now offers solar panels as standard equipment on thousands of its new homes, especially in the southwestern United States. Homeowners can either lease the solar panels from Lennar or purchase the panels outright. Even with oil and gas prices at decade lows, solar panels have become quite cost effective, and "exhumes good ethics rather than bad fumes." Walmart is installing solar panels on its stores in California and Hawaii, providing as much as 30 percent of the power in some stores. It may go national with solar power if this test works well. Also moving to solar energy is department-store chain Kohl's Corp., which is converting 64 of its 80 California stores to use solar power. There are big subsidies for solar installations in some states.

In October of every year, three world-renowned corporate sustainability rankings are published: (1) the Dow Jones Sustainability Index (DJSI), (2) the Carbon Disclosure Project, and (3) *Newsweek's* "Green" rankings. The DJSI annually reveals the best corporations in the world in various industries in terms of sustainability. Note in Table 10-3 that Sodexo, for example,

TABLE 10-3 **The Best "Environmental Sustainability" Company in Various Industries (2014–2015)**

Company	Industry
BMW AG	Automobiles & Components
AG Westpac Banking	Banks
Siemens AG	Capital Goods
SGS SA	Commercial & Professional Services
LG Electronics Inc	Consumer Durables & Apparel
Sodexo	Consumer Services
ING Group NV	Diversified Financials
Thai Oil PCL	Energy
Woolworths Ltd	Food & Staples Retailing
Unilever NV	Food, Beverage & Tobacco
Abbott Laboratories	Health Care Equipment & Services
Kao Corp	Household & Personal Products
Swiss Re AG	Insurance
Akzo Nobel NV	Materials
Telenet Group Holding NV	Media
Roche Holding AG	Pharmaceuticals & Biotechnology
GPT Group	Real Estate
Lotte Shopping Co Ltd	Retailing
Taiwan Semiconductor Manufacturing	Semiconductors
Wipro Ltd	Software & Services
Alcatel Lucent	Technology Hardware & Equipment
Telecom Italia SpA	Telecommunication Services
Air France-KLM	Transportation
EDP Energias de Portugal SA	Utilities

Source: Based on information at http://www.sustainability-indices.com/review/annual-review-2014.jsp

leads all "consumer services" companies in "environmental sustainability"; consumer services includes providing food services in the cafeteria at many colleges and universities.

The strategies of both companies and countries are increasingly scrutinized and evaluated from a natural environment perspective. Companies (e.g., Walmart) now monitor not only the price their vendors offer for products but also how those products are made in terms of environmental practices, as well as safety and infrastructure soundness—particularly of Southeast Asia factories. A growing number of business schools offer separate courses and even a concentration in environmental management.

In terms of megawatts of wind power generated by various states in the nation, Texas's 8,000 megawatts dwarfs all other states. Minnesota also is making substantial progress in wind power generation. New Jersey recently outfitted 200,000 utility poles with solar panels. A *Wall Street Journal* (6-29-15, p. B1) article says Hawaii leads all states in the most electricity per capita (21%) generated from solar or wind. A new Hawaii mandates that 100 percent of the state's electricity be supplied by wind turbines and solar panels by 2045. States that get the most electricity per capita from residential solar panels are Hawaii 168 watts per capita, followed by California at 47, Arizona at 44, and New Jersey at 25.

Sustainability Reports

A **sustainability report** reveals how a firm's operations impact the natural environment. This document discloses to shareholders information about the firm's labor practices, product sourcing, energy efficiency, environmental impact, and business ethics practices.

No business wants a reputation as being a polluter. A bad sustainability record will hurt the firm in the market, jeopardize its standing in the community, and invite scrutiny by regulators, investors, and environmentalists. Governments increasingly require businesses to behave responsibly and require, for example, that businesses publicly report the pollutants and wastes their facilities produce. It is simply good business for any business to provide a sustainability report annually to the public.

With 60,000 suppliers and more than $350 billion in annual sales, Walmart works with its suppliers to make sure they provide such reports. Many firms use the Walmart sustainability report as a benchmark guideline, and model to follow in preparing their own report. Walmart encourages and expects its 1.35 million U.S. employees to adopt what it calls Personal Sustainability Projects, which include such measures as organizing weight-loss or smoking-cessation support groups, biking to work, or starting recycling programs. Employee wellness can be a part of sustainability. Home Depot, the world's second-largest retailer behind Walmart, recently more than doubled its offering of environmentally friendly products such as all-natural insect repellent. Home Depot has made it much easier for consumers to find its organic products by using special labels similar to Timberland's (the outdoor company) Green Index tags.

The Global Reporting Initiative recently issued a set of detailed reporting guidelines specifying what information should go into sustainability reports. The proxy advisory firm Institutional Shareholder Services reports that an increasing number of shareholder groups are pushing firms to provide sustainability information annually. Two companies that released sustainability reports for the first time were Hyatt Hotels & Resorts and Las Vegas Sands Corporation. Rival firm Hilton Worldwide does not have a stand-alone sustainability report, but Marriott and Wyndham Worldwide do release annual sustainability reports and report excellent reductions in energy, water, waste, and carbon dioxide emissions.

Managers and employees of firms must be careful not to become scapegoats blamed for company environmental wrongdoings. Harming the natural environment can be unethical, illegal, and costly. When organizations today face criminal charges for polluting the environment, they increasingly turn on their managers and employees to win leniency. Employee firings and demotions are becoming common in pollution-related legal suits. Managers were fired at Darling International, Inc., and Niagara Mohawk Power Corporation for being indirectly responsible for their firms polluting water. Managers and employees today must be careful not to ignore, conceal, or disregard a pollution problem, or they may find themselves personally liable.

A few years ago, firms could get away with placing "green" terminology on their products and labels, using such terms as *organic, green, safe, earth-friendly, nontoxic,* or *natural* because there were no legal or generally accepted definitions. Today, however, these terms carry much more specific connotations and expectations. Uniform standards defining environmentally responsible company actions are rapidly being incorporated into the legal landscape. It has become more and more difficult for firms to make "green" claims when their actions are not substantive, comprehensive, or even true. Lack of standards once made consumers cynical about corporate environmental claims, but those claims today are increasingly being challenged in courts. According to Joel Makower, "One of the main reasons to truly become a green firm is for your employees. They're the first group that needs assurance than any claims you make hold water."[12]

Around the world, political and corporate leaders now realize that the "business green" topic is not going away and in fact is gaining ground rapidly. Strategically, companies more than ever must demonstrate to their customers and stakeholders that their green efforts are substantive and set the firm apart from competitors. A firm's social performance (facts and figures) must back up their rhetoric and be consistent with sustainability standards.

The Office of Environmental Affairs

Many companies are moving environmental affairs from the staff side of the organization to the line side, thus making the corporate environmental group report directly to the chief operating officer. Firms that manage environmental affairs will enhance relations with consumers, regulators, vendors, and other industry players, substantially improving their prospects of success. Environmental strategies could include developing or acquiring green businesses, divesting or altering environment-damaging businesses, striving to become a low-cost producer through waste minimization and energy conservation, and pursuing a differentiation strategy through green-product features. In addition, firms could include an environmental representative on their board of directors, conduct regular environmental audits, implement bonuses for favorable environmental results, become involved in environmental issues and programs, incorporate environmental values in mission statements, establish environmentally oriented objectives, acquire environmental skills, and provide environmental training programs for company employees and managers.

Preserving the environment should be a permanent part of doing business, for the following reasons:

1. Consumer demand for environmentally safe products and packages is high.
2. Public opinion demanding that firms conduct business in ways that preserve the natural environment is strong.
3. Environmental advocacy groups now have more than 20 million Americans as members.
4. Federal and state environmental regulations are changing rapidly and becoming more complex.
5. More lenders are examining the environmental liabilities of businesses seeking loans.
6. Many consumers, suppliers, distributors, and investors shun doing business with environmentally weak firms.
7. Liability suits and fines against firms having environmental problems are on the rise.

More firms are becoming environmentally proactive—doing more than the bare minimum to develop and implement strategies that preserve the environment. The old undesirable alternative of being environmentally reactive—changing practices only when forced to do so by law or consumer pressure—more often today leads to high clean-up costs, liability suits, reduced market share, reduced customer loyalty, and higher medical costs. In contrast, a proactive policy views environmental pressures as opportunities and includes such actions as developing green products and packages, conserving energy, reducing waste, recycling, and creating a corporate culture that is environmentally sensitive.

ISO 14000/14001 Certification

Based in Geneva, Switzerland, the International Organization for Standardization (ISO) is a network of the national standards institutes of 147 countries, with one member per country. The ISO is the world's largest developer of sustainability standards. Widely accepted all over the world, ISO standards are voluntary because it has no legal authority to enforce their implementation; the organization itself does not regulate or legislate. Governmental agencies in various countries, such as the Environmental Protection Agency (EPA) in the United States, have adopted ISO standards as part of their regulatory framework, and the standards are the basis of much legislation. Adoptions are sovereign decisions by the regulatory authorities, governments, or companies concerned. Businesses and municipalities should consider becoming ISO certified to help attract business.

ISO 14000 refers to a series of voluntary standards in the environmental field. The ISO 14000 family of standards concerns the extent to which a firm minimizes harmful effects on the environment caused by its activities and continually monitors and improves its own environmental performance. These standards have been adopted by thousands of firms and municipalities worldwide to certify to their constituencies that they are conducting business in an environmentally friendly manner; these standards offer a universal technical benchmark for environmental compliance that more and more firms are requiring not only of themselves but also of their suppliers and distributors. Included in the ISO 14000 series are the ISO 14001 standards in fields such as environmental auditing, environmental performance evaluation, environmental labeling, and life-cycle assessment.

ISO 14001 is a set of standards adopted by thousands of firms worldwide to certify to their constituencies that they are conducting business in an environmentally friendly manner. The ISO 14001 standard offers a universal technical standard for environmental compliance that more and more firms are requiring not only of themselves but also of their suppliers and distributors.

According to the ISO 14001 standard, a community or organization is required to put in place and implement a series of practices and procedures that, when taken together, result in an **environmental management system (EMS)**. The ISO 14001 is not a technical standard and as such does not in any way replace technical requirements embodied in statutes or regulations. It also does not set prescribed standards of performance for organizations. Not being certified with ISO 14001 can be a strategic disadvantage for towns, counties, and companies because people today expect organizations to minimize or, even better, to eliminate environmental harm they cause.[13] There are six major requirements of an EMS under ISO 14001:

1. Show commitments to prevention of pollution, continual improvement in overall environmental performance, and compliance with all applicable statutory and regulatory requirements.
2. Identify all aspects of the organization's activities, products, and services that could have a significant impact on the environment, including those that are not regulated.
3. Set performance objectives and targets for the management system that link back to three policies: (a) prevention of pollution, (b) continual improvement, and (c) compliance.
4. Meet environmental objectives that include training employees, establishing work instructions and practices, and establishing the actual metrics by which the objectives and targets will be measured.
5. Conduct an audit operation of the EMS.
6. Take corrective actions when deviations from the EMS occur.

Wildlife Welfare

Consumers globally are becoming increasingly intolerant of any business or nation that directly or indirectly destroys wildlife, especially endangered wildlife, such as tigers, elephants, whales, songbirds, and coral reefs. Affected businesses range from retailers that sell ivory chess pieces to restaurants that sell whale meat. The United States recently crushed over 6 tons of elephant ivory as part of a global effort to combat elephant poaching; one elephant is killed every 16 minutes.[14] The Chinese government recently destroyed more than 6.1 tons of elephant ivory to help stop illegal ivory smuggling that is fueling poaching and decimating elephant populations in Africa. There are today less than 100,000 elephants in Africa, down from more than 300,000 in 2002, primarily because the demand for ivory remains robust in Asia, particularly China.

African giraffes are in danger of becoming extinct due to hunting and poaching in Africa that has decimated the giraffe population. There are only about 80,000 giraffes left in the wild, down from 140,000 giraffes 15 years ago. Fewer than 300 West African giraffes remain in Niger, and only 700 Rothschild's giraffes remain in Uganda and Kenya. Poaching is especially detrimental in eastern and central Africa, partly because some people (in Tanzania) erroneously believe the giraffe's meat and/or bone marrow is an HIV cure.

Many New Zealanders, supported by Australians, are outraged about Japan's large-scale whaling operations in the Antarctic. Japan recently issued permits allowing its whalers to kill up to 935 Antarctica minkes, 50 fin whales, and 50 humpbacks as part of "research into sustainable hunting." Whale meat is regarded as a delicacy in Japan and can fetch up to US$38 for 100 grams. Japan ironically is a member of the International Whaling Commission that has banned commercial whaling in a 31 million square-mile area around Antarctica known as the Southern Ocean Whale Sanctuary. Unfortunately, South Korea recently resumed whaling, despite a 1986 moratorium on commercial whaling. Many countries are upset with whaling, including Australia, where the Prime Minister Julia Gillard asserted, "We are completely opposed to whaling; there's no excuse for scientific whaling." Only a few countries—such as Norway, Japan, and Russia—favor and engage in commercial whaling. Norway was soundly criticized globally in mid-2015 for launching whale-hunting expeditions, to follow up on their killing 729 whales the prior year, the most annual whale killings by Norway in two decades. Countries, municipalities, and companies increasingly run the risk of being boycotted and exposed for direct or indirect wildlife endangering practices.

About 50 million sharks are killed every year solely to cut off (and sell) their fins.[15] Although "shark-finning" was outlawed in U.S. waters in 2000, the law does not ban fin imports or serving the fins in food, so about 57 metric tons of fins are imported in the United States annually. Only eight U.S. states have laws banning the sale of shark fins in food: Hawaii, Oregon, Washington, Illinois, California, Maryland, New York, and Delaware. The problem is much worse in some countries, especially China. More than 25 percent of the world's shark species now face extinction, according to the International Union for Conservation of Nature.

Table 10-4 reveals the impact that bad environmental policies have on songbirds and coral reefs, two of nature's many ecosystems.

TABLE 10-4 **Songbirds and Coral Reefs Need Help**

Songbirds

Please be a good steward of the natural environment to save our songbirds. Bluebirds are one of 76 songbird species in the United States that have dramatically declined in numbers in the last two decades. Not all birds are considered songbirds, and why birds sing is not clear. Some scientists say they sing when calling for mates or warning of danger, but many scientists now contend that birds sing for sheer pleasure. Songbirds include chickadees, orioles, swallows, mockingbirds, warblers, sparrows, vireos, and the wood thrush. "These birds are telling us there's a problem, something's out of balance in our environment," says Jeff Wells, bird conservation director for the National Audubon Society. Songbirds may be telling us that their air or water is too dirty or that we are destroying too much of their habitat. People collect Picasso paintings and save historic buildings. "Songbirds are part of our natural heritage. Why should we be willing to watch songbirds destroyed any more than allowing a great work of art to be destroyed?" asks Wells. Whatever message songbirds are singing to us today about their natural environment, the message is becoming less and less heard nationwide. Listen when you go outside today. Each of us as individuals, companies, states, and countries should do what we reasonably can to help improve the natural environment for songbirds.[16] A recent study concludes that 67 of the 800 bird species in the United States are endangered, and another 184 species are designated of "conservation concern." The birds of Hawaii are in the greatest peril.

Coral Reefs

Please be a good steward of the natural environment to save our coral reefs. The ocean covers more than 71 percent of the earth. The destructive effect of commercial fishing on ocean habitats coupled with increasing pollution runoff into the ocean and global warming of the ocean have decimated fisheries, marine life, and coral reefs around the world. The unfortunate consequence of fishing over the last century has been overfishing, with the principal reasons being politics and greed. Trawl fishing with nets destroys coral reefs and has been compared to catching squirrels by cutting down forests because bottom nets scour and destroy vast areas of the ocean. The great proportion of marine life caught in a trawl is "by-catch" juvenile fish and other life that are killed and discarded. Warming of the ocean as a result of carbon dioxide emissions also kills thousands of acres of coral reefs annually. The total area of fully protected marine habitats in the United States is only about 50 square miles, compared to some 93 million acres of national wildlife refuges and national parks on the nation's land. A healthy ocean is vital to the economic and social future of the nation—and, indeed, all countries of the world. Everything we do on land ends up in the ocean, so we all must become better stewards of this last frontier on earth to sustain human survival and the quality of life.[17]

Food Suppliers and Animal Welfare

Humane treatment of animals matters! Walmart, other retailers, and restaurants are demanding that food suppliers treat animals better, and consumers are flocking to organic foods. Thus, numerous food companies, such as Tyson Foods, the largest U.S. meatpacker, are phasing out use of human antibiotics and are "housing" animals more humanely. Walmart says its suppliers must begin to "raise animals with sufficient space for them to express normal behaviors and freedom from discomfort." Walmart wants the use of battery cages for chickens, gestation crates for hogs, and veal crates for cows to be eliminated, although such small confined areas are currently used to raise many chickens, pigs, and cows in the United States. Wayne Pacelle, CEO of the Humane Society of the United States, wants Walmart to set a timeline for compliance. Parents want their children to eat food raised without use of growth hormones and antibiotics. Sales of organic milk, eggs, and other food products are booming, even at the higher prices. Walmart is by far the largest grocer in the United States, with grocery accounting for 56 percent of the company's $288 billion in sales in 2014.[18]

IMPLICATIONS FOR STRATEGISTS

Figure 10-2 reveals that the whole strategic-management process is designed to gain and sustain competitive advantages, but all can be lost with ethical violations, ranging from bribery to sexual harassment to selling whale meat. Trees die from the top; strategists are at the top of the firm. Consequently, strategists must set an exemplary example personally and professionally to establish and continually reinforce an organizational culture for "doing the right thing." Social responsibility and environmental sustainability policies, practices, and procedures must reinforce that good ethics is good business," and that good ethics is the foundation for everything we do and say."

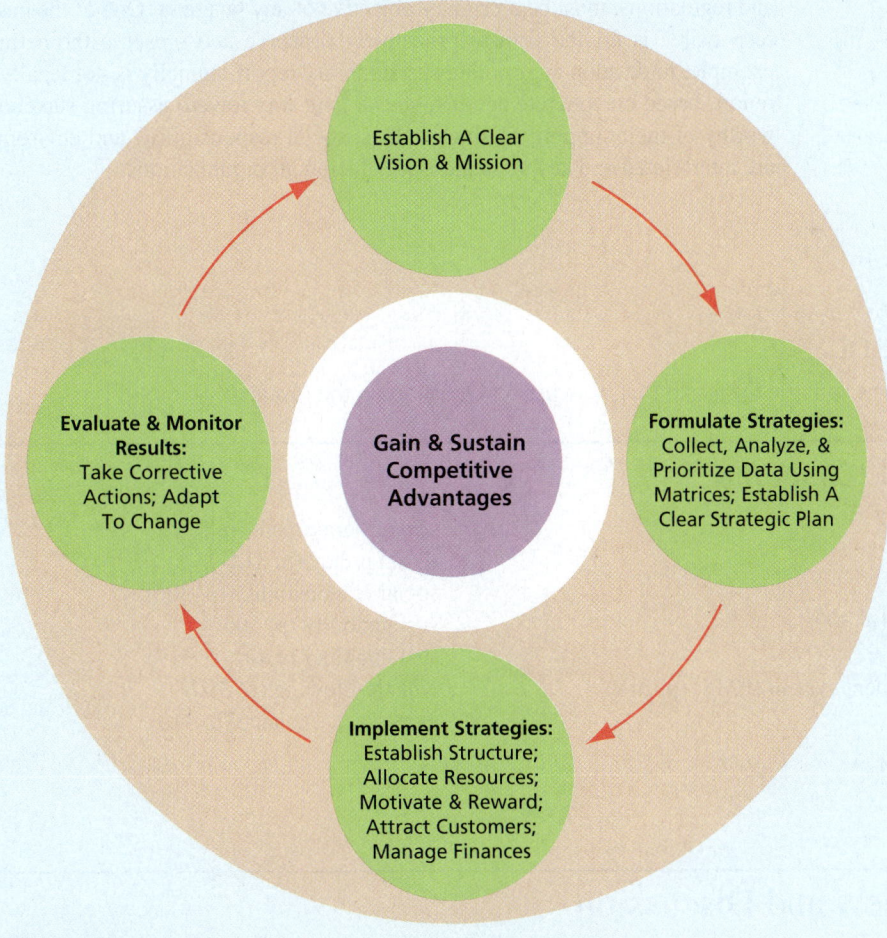

FIGURE 10-2

How to Gain and Sustain Competitive Advantages

IMPLICATIONS FOR STUDENTS

No company or individual wants to do business with someone who is unethical or is insensitive to natural environment concerns. It is no longer admirable simply to be environmentally proactive; today, it is expected, and in many respects is the law. Firms are being compared to rival firms every day on sustainability and ethics behavior, actually every minute on Facebook, Twitter, LinkedIn, and YouTube. Issues presented in this chapter therefore comprise a competitive advantage or disadvantage for all organizations. Thus, you should include in your case analysis recommendations for your firm to exceed stakeholder expectations on ethics, sustainability, and social responsibility. Make comparisons to rival firms to show how your firm can gain or sustain competitive advantage on these issues. Reveal suggestions for the firm to be a good corporate citizen and promote that for competitive advantage. Be mindful that the first responsibility of any business is to stay in business, so use cost/benefit analysis as needed to present your recommendations effectively.

Chapter Summary

In a final analysis, ethical standards come out of history and heritage. Our predecessors have left us with an ethical foundation on which to build. Even the legendary football coach Vince Lombardi knew that some things were worth more than winning, and he required his players to have three kinds of loyalty: to God, to their families, and to the Green Bay Packers, "in that order." Employees, customers, and shareholders have become less and less tolerant of business ethics violations in firms, and more and more appreciative of model ethical firms. Information-sharing across the Internet increasingly reveals such model firms versus irresponsible firms.

Consumers across the country and around the world appreciate firms that do more than is legally required to be socially responsible. But staying in business, while adhering to all laws and regulations, must be a primary objective of any business. One of the best ways to be socially responsible is for the firm to proactively conserve and preserve the natural environment. For example, to develop a corporate sustainability report annually is not legally required, but such a report, based on concrete actions, goes a long way toward assuring stakeholders that the firm is worthy of their support. Business ethics, social responsibility, and environmental sustainability are interrelated and key strategic issues facing all organizations.

MyManagementLab®

To complete the problems with the ⭐, go to EOC Discussion Questions in the MyLab.

Key Terms and Concepts

bribe (p. 311)
bribery (p. 311)
business ethics (p. 306)
code of business ethics (p. 309)
environment (p. 315)
environmental management system (EMS) (p. 319)
ISO 14000 (p. 319)
ISO 14001 (p. 319)

sexual harassment (p. 312)
social policy (p. 314)
social responsibility (p. 306)
sustainability (p. 306)
sustainability report (p. 317)
whistle-blowing (p. 310)
workplace romance (p. 312)

Issues for Review and Discussion

 10-1. What do whales, giraffes, sharks, songbirds, and coral reefs have in common? What are the implications for companies?

 10-2. Does it pay to be socially responsible? In general, economists say *no* and philanthropists say *yes*. What do you say? Why? What are the implications for companies?

10-3. Summarize Donald Palmer's research regarding "Who Is Prone to Be Unethical in a Business?" What are the implications for companies?

10-4. Chick-fil-A is closed on Sundays. Is that wise management or irresponsible activism? Discuss.

10-5. List five reasons why workplace romance can be detrimental to workplace morale and productivity.

10-6. List five benefits of having workplace romance guidelines in a workplace.

10-7. Discuss the ethics of workplace romance.

10-8. Explain why concern for wildlife is a strategic issue for firms.

10-9. Explain why whistle-blower payouts by the federal government to informants are becoming more and more common.

10-10. Compare and contrast the British Bribery Law with the U.S. bribery law.

10-11. Compare procedures in the corporate world versus a university setting in terms of how sexual harassment complaints are investigated outside the organization.

10-12. Compare the EEOC with the OCR in terms of mission and scope of operations.

10-13. AOL has 100 lobbyists on its payroll and spends about $20 million on lobbying in Washington, DC, annually. Is this ethical?

10-14. If you owned a small business, would you develop a code of business conduct? If yes, what variables would you include? If no, how would you ensure that ethical business standards were being followed by your employees?

10-15. What do you feel is the relationship between personal ethics and business ethics? Are they or should they be the same?

10-16. How can firms best ensure that their code of business ethics is read, understood, believed, remembered, and acted on, rather than ignored?

10-17. Why is it important *not* to view the concept of whistle-blowing as "tattle-telling" or "ratting" on another employee?

10-18. List six desired results of "ethics training programs" in terms of recommended business ethics policies and procedures in the firm.

10-19. Discuss bribery. Would actions such as politicians adding earmarks in legislation or pharmaceutical salespersons giving away drugs to physicians constitute bribery? Identify three business activities that would constitute bribery and three actions that would not.

10-20. How could a strategist's attitude toward social responsibility affect a firm's strategy? On a 1-to-10 scale ranging from Nader's view to Friedman's view, what is your attitude toward social responsibility?

10-21. How do social policies on retirement differ in various countries around the world?

10-22. How are policies and procedures changing regarding growing animals for slaughter for supermarkets?

10-23. Is it a conflict of interest for companies to encourage employee whistle-blowing since the firm could be fined heavily or incur worse penalties? Explain.

MyManagementLab®

Go to the Assignments section of your MyLab to complete these writing exercises.

10-24. Firms should formulate and implement strategies from an environmental perspective. List eight ways firms can do this.

10-25. Discuss the major requirements of an EMS under ISO 14001.

ASSURANCE OF LEARNING EXERCISES

EXERCISE 10A

How Does Your Municipality Compare to Others on Being Pollution-Safe?

Purpose

Sometimes it is difficult to know how safe a particular municipality or county is regarding industrial and agricultural pollutants. A website that provides consumers and businesses excellent information in this regard is http://scorecard.goodguide.com/. This type of information is often used in assessing where to locate new business operations.

Instructions

Go to http://scorecard.goodguide.com/. Put in your zip code. Print off the information available for your city or county regarding pollutants.

Step 1   Prepare a comparative analysis of your municipality versus state and national norms on pollution issues. Does your locale receive an A, B, C, D, or F?

Step 2   Prepare a report of your findings for your professor.

EXERCISE 10B
Does Hershey Company or Mars, Inc. Win on Sustainability?

Purpose

Sustainability reports are increasingly becoming expected or even required by business organizations. This exercise will give you practice in comparing and evaluating sustainability reports. At the www.thehersheycompany.com website, click on "Responsibility" and view the 2-minute video by clicking on "Shared Goodness." Then click on "Cocoa Sustainability" and read the information. Next, click on "Nutrition & Well-Being" and read through that information. A major rival of Hershey is Mars, Inc. Go to the Mars' website at http://www.mars.com/global/about-mars/the-five-principles-of-mars. aspx and read about Mars, Inc.'s five principles: Quality, Responsibility, Mutuality, Efficiency, and Freedom. Compare and contrast Hershey's business ethics, social responsibility, and environmental sustainability efforts with Mars' efforts.

Instructions

Step 1   Determine the six best aspects of Hershey's business ethics, social responsibility, and environmental sustainability efforts.

Step 2   Determine the six best aspects of Mars' business ethics, social responsibility, and environmental sustainability efforts.

Step 3   Develop a report comparing and contrasting the two companies with regard to business ethics, social responsibility, and environmental sustainability. In your opinion, does Hershey or Mars receive a grade of A on their business ethics, social responsibility, and sustainability efforts? Grade each company on the three dimensions, and give each an overall grade. Justify your grades.

EXERCISE 10C
The Ethics of Spying on Competitors

Purpose

This exercise gives you an opportunity to discuss in class ethical and legal issues related to methods being used by many companies to spy on competing firms. Gathering and using information about competitors is an area of strategic management that Japanese firms do more proficiently than U.S. firms.

Instructions

On a separate sheet of paper, number from 1 to 18. For the 18 spying activities listed as follows, indicate whether or not you believe the activity is ethical or unethical and legal or illegal. Place either an *E* for ethical or *U* for unethical, and either an *L* for legal or an *I* for illegal for each activity. Compare your answers to those of your classmates and discuss any differences.

1. Buying competitors' garbage
2. Dissecting competitors' products
3. Taking competitors' plant tours anonymously
4. Counting tractor-trailer trucks leaving competitors' loading bays
5. Studying aerial photographs of competitors' facilities
6. Analyzing competitors' labor contracts
7. Analyzing competitors' help-wanted ads
8. Quizzing customers and buyers about the sales of competitors' products
9. Infiltrating customers' and competitors' business operations
10. Quizzing suppliers about competitors' level of manufacturing
11. Using customers to buy out phony bids
12. Encouraging key customers to reveal competitive information
13. Quizzing competitors' former employees

14. Interviewing consultants who may have worked with competitors
15. Hiring key managers away from competitors
16. Conducting phony job interviews to get competitors' employees to reveal information
17. Sending engineers to trade meetings to quiz competitors' technical employees
18. Quizzing potential employees who worked for or with competitors

EXERCISE 10D
Who Prepares a Sustainability Report?

Purpose
The purpose of this activity is to determine the nature and prevalence of sustainability reports among companies in your state.

Instructions
Visit the websites of at least five different large businesses in your area. Seek answers to the following questions. Follow up with a phone call(s) or actually visit the business if needed. Present your findings in a written report to your instructor.

1. Does your company prepare a sustainability report? If yes, please describe the nature and scope of the report.
2. Are environmental criteria included in the performance evaluation of managers? If yes, please specify the criteria.
3. Are environmental affairs more a technical function or a management function in your company?
4. Does your firm offer any environmental workshops for employees? If yes, please describe them.

(Note to Professors—See the Chapter IM for an additional, excellent exercise for this chapter)

MINI-CASE ON AVON PRODUCTS, INC. (AVP)

WOULD CLAIMS OF ETHICAL WRONGDOING BY A COMPANY IMPACT YOUR BUYING THE FIRM'S PRODUCTS?

Source: Kurhan/123rf

Headquartered in New York City, Avon Products is the world's largest direct-seller firm, and by far the largest direct seller of cosmetics and beauty-related items. Avon is the fifth-largest cosmetics and fragrance firm in the world. The company receives sales from catalogs and online, but the vast majority of its sales come from about six million independent sales representatives in 110 countries. Since 1892, Avon has empowered women to be their own boss and become leaders in communities and business. Avon is struggling to recover from poor management and global bribery investigations. Specifically, law firm Zamansky LLC is investigating Avon's employee personal savings account plan (the "Plan") for potential violations of the federal Employee Retirement Income Security Act ("ERISA"). This federal act imposes fiduciary duties to prudently manage and invest plan assets. According to the claim, Avon allegedly violated ERISA guidelines by its continued offering of company stock during a pending federal investigation for violations of the Foreign Corrupt Practices Act ("FCPA"). Between 2010 and 2015, Avon's stock price fell from over $40 per share to below $10 per year. The collapse in stock price relates to the FCPA investigation by the U.S. Department of Justice and Securities and Exchange Commission that makes it illegal for U.S. companies operating in foreign countries to pay bribes or kickbacks. Separate shareholder lawsuits have alleged that Avon engaged in systemic FCPA violations, and misrepresented its revenues from various foreign countries. One lawsuit alleges that Avon made numerous misrepresentations about the extent, reach, and costs of the investigations against the company. According to Zamansky, Avon employees who purchased and held company stock through the Plan since 2010 suffered substantial losses to their retirement savings. Zamansky says FCPA investigation and shareholder lawsuits raise serious issues over the prudent monitoring and oversight of the Plan by Avon under ERISA.

Questions

1. According to the chapter, who in a company is most prone to engaging in unethical practices? What are the implications for companies?
2. Why do ethics and integrity matter in a company? How can a company best ensure highly ethical practices?
3. Review recent news releases about Avon. Does the company seem to have recovered from its ethical problems?

Source: Company documents and a variety of sources.

Current Readings

Barnett, Michael L. "Why Stakeholders Ignore Firm Misconduct: A Cognitive View." *Journal of Management* 40, no. 3 (2014): 676–702.

Hanson, William R., and Jeffrey R. Moore, "Business Student Moral Influencers: Unseen Opportunities for Development?" *Academy of Management Journal Learning and Education* 13 (December 2014): 525–546.

Hess, Megan F., and Earnest Broughton. "Fostering an Ethical Organization from the Bottom Up and the Outside In." *Business Horizons* (July 2014): 541–561.

Jones, David A., Chelsea R. Willness, and Sarah Madey. "Why Are Job Seekers Attracted by Corporate Social Performance? Experimental and Field Tests of Three Signal-Based Mechanisms." *Academy of Management Journal* 57, no. 2 (2014): 383–404.

Lubin, David A., and Daniel C. Esty. "Bridging the Sustainability Gap." *MIT Sloan Management Review* 55, no. 4 (2014): 18–21.

Paine, Lynn S. "Sustainability in the Boardroom." *Harvard Business Review* 92, no. 7/8 (2014): 86–94.

Perrott, Bruce E. "Building the Sustainable Organization: An Integrated Approach." *Journal of Business Strategy* 36, no. 1 (2015): 41–51.

Rangan, Kasturi, Lisa Chase, and Sohel Karim. "The Truth about CSR." *Harvard Business Review* (January–February 2015).

Reilly, Anne H., and Katherine A. Hynan. "Corporate Communication, Sustainability, and Social Media: It's Not Easy (Really) Being Green," *Business Horizons* 57, no. 6 (January–February 2015): 747–758.

Scott, Brent A., Adela S. Garza, Donald E. Conlon, and You Jin Kim. "Why Do Managers Act Fairly in the First Place? A Daily Investigation of "Hot" and "Cold" Motives and Discretion," *Academy of Management Journal,* December 1, 2014, vol. 47, no. 6, pp. 1571–1591.

Sonenshein, Scott, Katherine A., Decelles, and Jane E. Dutton. "It's Not Easy Being Green: The Role of Self-Evaluations in Explaining Support of Environmental Issues." *Academy of Management Journal* 57, no. 1 (2014): 7–37.

Unruh, Gregory. "The Sweet Spot of Sustainability Strategy." *MIT Sloan Management Review* 55, no. 1 (2013): 16–19.

Washburn, Nathan T., and Donald Lange. "Does Your Company Seem Socially Irresponsible?" *MIT Sloan Management Review* 55, no. 1 (2013): 10–11.

Endnotes

1. http://www.usatoday.com/money/companies/management/story/2012-05-14/ceo-firings/54964476/1
2. Joann Greco, "Privacy—Whose Right Is It Anyhow?" *Journal of Business Strategy* (January–February 2001): 32.
3. Ashby Jones and JoAnn Lublin, "New Law Prompts Blowing Whistle," *Wall Street Journal,* November 1, 2010, B1.
4. Saul Gellerman, "Why 'Good' Managers Make Bad Ethical Choices," *Harvard Business Review* 64, no. 4 (July–August 1986): 88.
5. www.wikipedia.org
6. Joe Palazzolo and Christopher Matthews, "Bribery Law Do's and Don'ts," *Wall Street Journal* (November 15, 2012): B1.
7. http://www.businessknowhow.com/manage/romance.htm
8. Elizabeth Bernstein "The New Rules of Flirting," *Wall Street Journal,* November 13, 2012, D1.

9. Phred Dvorak, Bob Davis, and Louise Radnofsky, "Firms Confront Boss-Subordinate Love Affairs," *Wall Street Journal,* October 27, 2008, B5.
10. Spencer Morgan, "The End of the Office Affair," *Bloomberg Businessweek,* September 20–26, 2010, 74.
11. Archie Carroll and Frank Hoy, "Integrating Corporate Social Policy into Strategic Management," *Journal of Business Strategy* 4, no. 3 (Winter 1984): 57.
12. Kerry Hannon, "Businesses' Green Opportunities Are Wide, But Complex," *USA Today,* January 2, 2009, 5B.
13. Adapted from the www.iso14000.com website and the www.epa.gov website.
14. Ana Campoy, "Crushing Illegal Ivory Trade," *Wall Street Journal,* November 15, 2013, p. A3. See also, Dinny McMahon, "Chinese Officials Destroy Tons of Illegal Ivory," *Wall Street Journal,* January 7, 2014, p. A10.

15. Zusha Elinson, "Shark-Fin Bans Hard to Police," *Wall Street Journal*, February 25, 2014, A3.

16. Tom Brook, "Declining Numbers Mute Many Birds' Songs," *USA Today*, September 11, 2001, 4A.

17. John Ogden, "Maintaining Diversity in the Oceans," *Environment*, April 2001, 29–36.

18. Based on Sarah Nassauer, "Wal-Mart: Food Suppliers Must Treat Animals Better," *Wall Street Journal,* May 23–24, 2015, p. B3.

11

Global and International Issues

LEARNING OBJECTIVES

After studying this chapter, you should be able to do the following:

11-1. Discuss the nature of doing business globally, including language and labor union issues.

11-2. Explain the advantages and disadvantages of doing business globally.

11-3. Discuss the global challenge facing firms and why this is a strategic issue.

11-4. Discuss tax rates and tax inversions as strategic issues.

11-5. Compare and contrast American business culture versus foreign business cultures; explain why this is a strategic issue.

11-6. Discuss the business culture found in Mexico, Japan, China, and India; explain why this is a strategic issue.

11-7. Discuss the business climate in Africa, China, Indonesia, India, Japan, Mexico, and Vietnam; explain why this is a strategic issue.

ASSURANCE OF LEARNING EXERCISES

The following exercises are found at the end of this chapter:

EXERCISE 11A   Business Cultures across Countries: A Hershey Company Analysis

EXERCISE 11B   Hershey Company Wants to Enter Africa. Help Them.

EXERCISE 11C   Does Your University Recruit in Foreign Countries?

EXERCISE 11D   Assess Differences in Culture across Countries

EXERCISE 11E   How Well Traveled Are Business Students at Your University?

Global considerations impact virtually all strategic decisions, as illustrated in Figure 11-1 with white shading. The boundaries of countries no longer can define the limits of our imaginations. To see and appreciate the world from the perspective of others has become a matter of survival for businesses. The underpinnings of strategic management hinge on managers gaining an understanding of competitors, markets, prices, suppliers, distributors, governments, creditors, shareholders, and customers worldwide. The price and quality of a firm's products and services must be competitive on a worldwide basis, not just on a local basis. Shareholders expect substantial revenue growth, so doing business globally is one of the best ways to achieve this end. As indicated in the exemplary company shown next, the huge aluminum corporation, Alcoa Inc., effectively and successfully does business globally.

The Nature of Doing Business Globally

Exports of goods and services from the United States account for only 13.5 percent of U.S. gross domestic product, so the nation is still largely a domestic, continental economy. What happens inside the United States largely determines the strength of the economic recovery. In contrast, as a percent of gross domestic product (GDP), exports comprise 45.6 percent of the German economy, 22.6 percent of the Chinese economy, and 187 percent of the Singapore economy (http://data.worldbank.org/indicator/NE.EXP.GNFS.ZS). Singapore's number is so high because it imports oil and other products and then re-exports them globally. A point here is that the United States has substantial room for improvement in doing business globally based on the 11 percent exports to the GDP number.

EXEMPLARY COMPANY SHOWCASED

Alcoa, Inc. (AA)

Headquartered in New York City, Alcoa has been doing great following a global strategy of supplying aluminum products to automobile, aerospace, and other firms. In a forward integration move, Alcoa recently acquired jet-engine parts maker Firth Rixson Ltd. based in the United Kingdom. Alcoa now supplies Boeing and Airbus with aluminum sheet and plate products, and supplies engine parts for Pratt & Whitney jet engines. Alcoa's Davenport, Iowa, plant supplies Ford Motor Company with new, military-grade aluminum alloy products for the new 2015, all-aluminum frame F-150 pickup truck. As aluminum prices have risen to more than $2,000 a ton, Alcoa has also closed unprofitable smelters in high-cost areas such as Tennessee and Australia. Alcoa's Q3 of 2014 earnings per share climbed 182 percent as revenues increased 7.5 percent to $6.2 billion.

Alcoa's strategy is to lower its cost base and create a globally competitive business, so the company recently divested its Alcoa World Alumina and Chemicals (AWAC) segment. Alcoa had part ownership of the Jamalco (located in Jamaica) bauxite mining and alumina refinery joint venture with Noble Group Ltd. The AWAC segment continues as Jamalco's managing operator for three years and workers remain employed by Jamalco. Alcoa World Alumina and Chemicals was the joint venture owned 60 percent by Alcoa and 40 percent by Alumina Limited of Australia.

Aerospace companies are one of Alcoa's most profitable segments. Alcoa expects the demand from the aerospace industry to grow 10 percent in 2015, given the huge order backlog in the aerospace industry from Boeing and Airbus. In early 2015, Alcoa opened its expanded wheels manufacturing plant in Hungary. The larger facility doubles Alcoa's capacity to produce its Dura-Bright® EVO surface-treated wheels, compared to 2014 production levels, and enables Alcoa to meet growing European demand for its lightweight, durable, low-maintenance aluminum truck wheels. "This expansion positions Alcoa to capture increasing demand for our innovative aluminum truck wheels in Europe, including our easiest-to-clean wheels that look new longer, reduce maintenance costs, and increase payload and fuel efficiency," said Tim Myers, president of Alcoa Wheel and Transportation Products. "Sales of aluminum truck wheels are expected to increase from 30 percent of global sales in 2010 to 50 percent in 2018."

Source: Based on John Miller and Tess Stynes, "Alcoa Lifted by Higher Prices, New Customers," *Wall Street Journal*, October 9, 2014, B8.

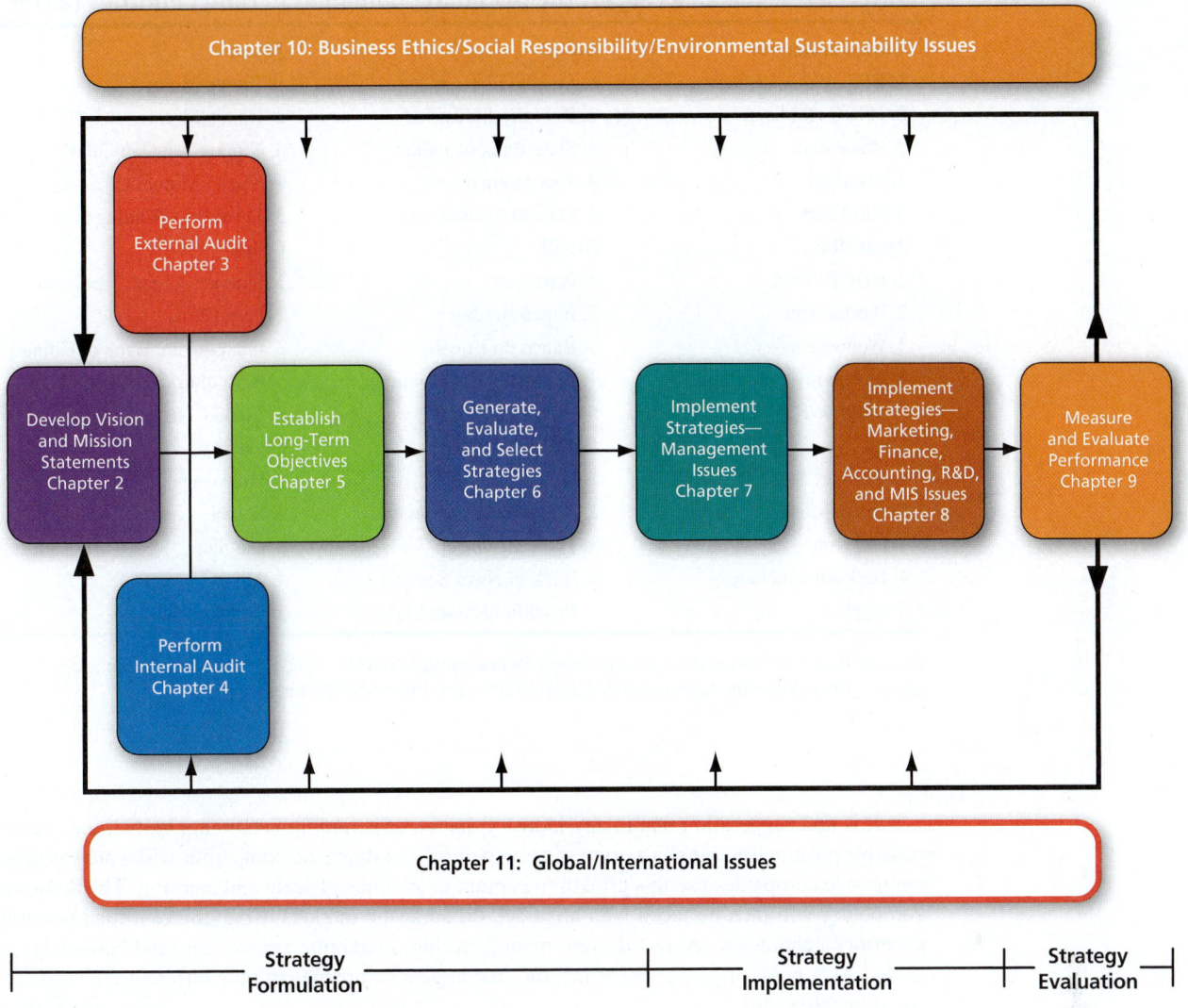

FIGURE 11-1

A Comprehensive Strategic-Management Model

Source: Fred R. David, "How Companies Define Their Mission," *Long Range Planning* 22, no. 3 (June 1988): 40. See also Anik Ratnaningsih, Nadjadji Anwar, Patdono Suwignjo, and Putu Artama Wiguna, "Balance Scorecard of David's Strategic Modeling at Industrial Business for National Construction Contractor of Indonesia," *Journal of Mathematics and Technology*, no. 4 (October 2010): 20.

A world market has emerged from what previously was a multitude of distinct national markets, and the climate for international business today is more favorable than in years past. Mass communication and high technology have created similar patterns of consumption in diverse cultures worldwide. This means that many companies may find it difficult to survive by relying solely on domestic markets.

Globalization is a process of doing business worldwide, so strategic decisions are made based on global profitability of the firm rather than just domestic considerations. A global strategy seeks to meet the needs of customers worldwide, with the highest value at the lowest cost. This may mean locating production in countries with the lowest labor costs or abundant natural resources, locating research and complex engineering centers where skilled scientists and engineers can be found, and locating marketing activities close to the markets to be served.

A **global strategy** includes designing, producing, and marketing products with global needs in mind, instead of considering individual countries alone. A global strategy integrates actions against competitors into a worldwide plan. Today, there are global buyers and sellers and the instant transmission of money and information across continents.

TABLE 11-1 The Five Largest (by revenue) Companies in Nine Countries (2015)

United Kingdom	India	Japan
1. BP	1. Indian Oil	1. Toyota Motor
2. HSBC Holdings	2. Reliance Industries	2. Honda Motor
3. Prudential	3. State Bank of India	3. Nippon TeleG & TeleP
4. Vodafone	4. Tata Motors	4. Nissan Motor
5. Rio Tinto	5. Oil and Natural Gas	5. Japan Post Holdings
Australia	**Brazil**	**China**
1. BHP Billiton	1. Petrobras	1. Sinopec–China Petroleum
2. Wesfarmers	2. Banco Bradesco	2. PetroChina
3. Woolworths	3. Banco do Brasil	3. Ind. & Com. Bank of China
4. Commonwealth Bank	4. Itau Unibanco Holding	4. Agricultural Bank of China
5. Westpac Banking	5. Vale	5. China Construction Bank
USA	**Canada**	**Germany**
1. Walmart Stores	1. Suncor Energy	1. Volkswagen
2. ExxonMobil	2. Royal Bank of Canada	2. E. ON
3. Chevron	3. TD Bank Group	3. Daimier
4. Berkshire Hathaway	4. Bank of Nova Scotia	4. Allianz
5. Apple	5. Brookfield Asset Mgt.	5. BMW Group

Source: Based on information at http://www.forbes.com/global2000/#page:4_sort:0_direction:asc_search:_filter:All%20industries_filter:United%20States_filter:All%20states

It is no exaggeration that in any industry that is, or is rapidly becoming, global, the riskiest possible posture is to remain a domestic competitor. The domestic competitor will watch as more aggressive companies use this growth to capture economies of scale and learning. The domestic competitor will then be faced with an attack on domestic markets using different (and possibly superior) technology, product design, manufacturing, marketing approaches, and economies of scale.[1] As a point of global reference, the five largest companies in nine different countries are listed in Table 11-1.

Multinational Firms

Organizations that conduct business operations across national borders are called **international firms** or **multinational corporations**. The strategic-management process is conceptually the same for multinational firms as for purely domestic firms; however, the process is more complex for international firms as a result of more variables and relationships. The social, cultural, demographic, environmental, political, governmental, legal, technological, and competitive opportunities and threats that face a multinational corporation are almost limitless, and the number and complexity of these factors increase dramatically with the number of products produced and the number of geographic areas served. Millions of small businesses do business everyday outside their home country by interacting with customers though websites, smartphones, and social media. All of Africa, and places such as Cuba and Iran, are becoming more desirable for business every day.

More time and effort are required to identify and evaluate external trends and events in multinational corporations than in domestic corporations. Geographic distance, cultural and national differences, and variations in business practices often make communication between domestic headquarters and overseas operations difficult. Strategy implementation can be more difficult because different cultures have different norms, values, and work ethics. Multinational corporations (MNCs) face unique and diverse risks, such as expropriation of assets, currency losses through exchange rate fluctuations, unfavorable foreign court interpretations of contracts and agreements, social/political disturbances, import/export restrictions, tariffs, and trade barriers. Strategists in MNCs are often confronted with the need to be globally competitive and nationally responsive at the same time. With the rise in world commerce, government and regulatory bodies are more closely monitoring foreign business practices. The U.S. Foreign Corrupt Practices Act, for example, monitors business practices in many areas.

Before entering international markets, firms should scan relevant journals and patent reports, seek the advice of academic and research organizations, participate in international trade fairs, form partnerships, and conduct extensive research to broaden their contacts and diminish the risk of doing business in new markets. Firms can also offset some risks of doing business internationally by obtaining insurance from the U.S. government's Overseas Private Investment Corporation (OPIC). The decision to expand operations into foreign markets—that is, to globalize—is one of the most important strategic decisions made by companies. Thus, variables that influence how, when, where, and why to internationalize have attracted much attention in scholarly journals. Recent research reveals that countries are attractive not only because of their own institutions but also as a function of their serving as a platform for entry into other regions.[2] Therefore, multinational firms make globalization decisions with special consideration in mind for how a particular region/country will facilitate the firm's further globalization into other regions/countries.

Different Languages Globally

A strategic issue facing many firms is whether to publish their website material in different languages, given that most of the world's population does not speak English. Pioneering work to document the number of different languages spoken has been done by the Summer Institute of Linguistics (SIL) International. That organization today publishes 2,508 translations of the Christian Bible, and has compiled a catalogue of the world's languages, called the *Ethnologue,* which lists 6,909 distinct languages being spoken. Of that total, only 230 are spoken in Europe and 2,197 in Asia. But in Papua, New Guinea, 830 different languages are spoken by 3.9 million people, and in France, the *Ethnologue* cites 10 languages being spoken, including Picard, Gascon, Provençal, Allemannisch, Alsace, Breton, and French. Academic Research Capsule 11-1 reveals that most languages will permanently disappear by the end of this century.

Labor Unions across Europe

Prevalence of unions is a relevant factor in many strategic decisions, such as where to locate stores or factories. There is great variation across Europe in regards to levels of union membership, ranging from 74 percent of employees in Finland and 71 percent in Sweden to 9 percent in Lithuania and 8 percent in France. However, percentage of union membership is not the only indicator of strength. In France, for example, unions have repeatedly shown that despite low levels of membership, they are able to mobilize workers in mass strikes and demonstrations to great effect.

ACADEMIC RESEARCH CAPSULE 11-1

How Many Languages Are There Globally?

When businesses consider offering their products or services globally, or manufacturing and securing resources outside their own country, language barriers arise. Interacting with people who speak a different language is one of many variables that complicate doing business globally—yet millions of businesses need to do more business globally. Thankfully, translations to and from most mainstream languages such as English, Spanish, French, German, and Chinese are easily done with online programs, and there are millions of multilingual people.

The implication for businesses doing business globally is that the total number of languages spoken globally is decreasing quite dramatically. For example, in North America, many Native American languages are disappearing yearly, a common phenomenon all over the world. Whenever any language ceases to be learned by young children, that language generally does not survive the death of current native speakers. In North America, about 75 languages are spoken by only a handful of older people, and those languages are expected to become extinct. About 25 percent of the world's languages have fewer than a thousand remaining speakers. By the year 2099, analysts estimate that roughly one half of the 6,909 languages listed by *Ethnologue* will disappear. By 2115, researchers say there will be only 600 left on the planet.

Source: Based on information from the website http://www.linguisticsociety.org/content/how-many-languages-are-there-world; and John McWhorter, "What the World Will Speak in 2115," *Wall Street Journal,* January 4, 2015, C1–C2.

The average level of union membership across the whole of the European Union (EU), weighted by the numbers employed in the different member states, is 23 percent, compared to about 11 percent in the United States. The European average is held down by relatively low levels of membership in some of the larger EU states: Germany with 18 percent, France with 8 percent, Spain with 19 percent, and Poland with 12 percent. The three smallest states—Cyprus, Luxembourg, and Malta—have levels well above the average.

The four Nordic countries of Denmark, Sweden, Finland, and Norway have 67, 70, 74, and 52 percent, respectively, of all employees as members of unions. In part this is because, as in Belgium, which also has above-average levels of union density, unemployment and other social benefits are normally paid out through the union. High union density in the Nordic countries also reflects an approach that sees union membership as a natural part of employment. Central and Eastern Europe nations generally have below-average levels of union membership. In Poland, for example, 12 percent of employees are estimated to be union members. Level of union membership is clearly trending downward all over Europe. The two exceptions appear to be Ireland and Italy, where union membership is slowly growing.

Advantages and Disadvantages of Doing Business Globally

Firms have numerous reasons for formulating and implementing strategies that initiate, continue, or expand involvement in business operations across national borders. Perhaps the greatest advantage is that firms can gain new customers for their products and services, thus increasing revenues. Growth in revenues and profits is a common organizational objective and often an expectation of shareholders because it is a measure of organizational success. Potential advantages to initiating, continuing, or expanding international operations are as follows:

1. Firms can gain new customers for their products.
2. Foreign operations can absorb excess capacity, reduce unit costs, and spread economic risks over a wider number of markets.
3. Foreign operations can allow firms to establish low-cost production facilities in locations close to raw materials or cheap labor.
4. Competitors in foreign markets may not exist, or competition may be less intense than in domestic markets.
5. Foreign operations may result in reduced tariffs, lower taxes, and favorable political treatment.
6. Joint ventures can enable firms to learn the technology, culture, and business practices of other people and to make contacts with potential customers, suppliers, creditors, and distributors in foreign countries.
7. Economies of scale can be achieved from operation in global rather than solely domestic markets. Larger-scale production and better efficiencies allow higher sales volumes and lower-price offerings.
8. A firm's power and prestige in domestic markets may be significantly enhanced if the firm competes globally. Enhanced prestige can translate into improved negotiating power among creditors, suppliers, distributors, and other important groups.

The availability, depth, and reliability of economic and marketing information in different countries vary extensively, as do industrial structures, business practices, and the number and nature of regional organizations. There are also numerous potential disadvantages of initiating, continuing, or expanding business across national borders, such as the following:

1. Foreign operations could be seized by nationalistic factions.
2. Firms confront different and often little-understood social, cultural, demographic, environmental, political, governmental, legal, technological, economic, and competitive forces when doing business internationally. These forces can make communication difficult in the firm.

3. Weaknesses of competitors in foreign lands are often overestimated, and strengths are often underestimated. Keeping informed about the number and nature of competitors is more difficult when doing business internationally.

4. Language, culture, and value systems differ among countries, which can create barriers to communication and problems managing people.

5. Gaining an understanding of regional organizations such as the European Economic Community, the Latin American Free Trade Area, the International Bank for Reconstruction and Development, and the International Finance Corporation is difficult but is often required in doing business internationally.

6. Dealing with two or more monetary systems can complicate international business operations.

The Global Challenge

Few companies can afford to ignore the presence of international competition. Firms that seem insulated and comfortable today may be vulnerable tomorrow; for example, foreign banks do not yet compete or operate in most of the United States, but this too is changing. Thomson Reuters annually compiles a list of the world's most innovative companies, using metrics that include patent activity, R&D investment, success rate, globalization, and influence. For the first time ever, Japan (39 percent) overtook the United States (36 percent) in 2014 as having the most innovative companies in the world. Top U.S. firms making the list included Apple, Lockheed Martin, Google, Microsoft, Intel, and IBM, whereas some top Asian companies on the top-100 list included Samsung, Fujitsu, Hitachi, Canon, and for the first time, a Chinese company, Huawei.

The U.S. economy is becoming much less American. A world economy and monetary system are emerging. Corporations in every corner of the globe are taking advantage of the opportunity to obtain customers globally. Markets are shifting rapidly and, in many cases, converging in tastes, trends, and prices. Innovative transport systems are accelerating the transfer of technology. Shifts in the nature and location of production systems, especially to China and India, are reducing the response time to changing market conditions. China has more than 1.3 billion residents and a dramatically growing middle class anxious to buy goods and services.

More and more countries around the world are welcoming foreign investment and capital. As a result, labor markets have steadily become more international. East Asian countries are market leaders in labor-intensive industries, Brazil offers abundant natural resources and rapidly developing markets, and Germany offers skilled labor and technology. The drive to improve the efficiency of global business operations is leading to greater functional specialization. This is not limited to a search for the familiar low-cost labor in Latin America or Asia. Other considerations include the cost of energy, availability of resources, inflation rates, tax rates, and the nature of trade regulations.

Many countries are quite protectionist, and this position can impact companies' strategic plans. **Protectionism** refers to countries imposing tariffs, taxes, and regulations on firms outside the country to favor their own companies and people. Most economists argue that protectionism harms the world economy because it inhibits trade among countries and invites retaliation.

Advancements in telecommunications are drawing countries, cultures, and organizations worldwide closer together. Foreign revenue as a percentage of total company revenues already exceeds 50 percent in hundreds of U.S. firms, including ExxonMobil, Gillette, Dow Chemical, Citicorp, Colgate-Palmolive, and Texaco. A primary reason why most domestic firms do business globally is that growth in demand for goods and services outside the United States is considerably higher than inside. For example, the domestic food industry is growing just 3 percent per year, so Kraft Foods, the second-largest food company in the world behind Nestlé, is focusing on foreign acquisitions. Shareholders and investors expect sustained growth in revenues from firms; satisfactory growth for many firms can only be achieved by capitalizing on demand outside the United States. Joint ventures and partnerships between domestic and foreign firms are becoming the rule rather than the exception!

Fully 95 percent of the world's population lives outside the United States, and this group is growing 70 percent faster than the U.S. population. The lineup of competitors in virtually all industries is global. General Motors and Ford compete with Toyota and Hyundai. General Electric and Westinghouse battle Siemens and Mitsubishi. Caterpillar and John Deere compete with Komatsu. Goodyear battles Michelin, Bridgestone/Firestone, and Pirelli. Boeing competes with Airbus. Only a few U.S. industries—such as furniture, printing, retailing, consumer packaged goods, and retail banking—are not yet greatly challenged by foreign competitors. But many products and components in these industries too are now manufactured in foreign countries. International operations can be as simple as exporting a product to a single foreign country or as complex as operating manufacturing, distribution, and marketing facilities in many countries.

New research examined in Academic Research Capsule 11-2 sheds some light on how firms decide where to expand.

It is clear that different industries become global for different reasons. The need to amortize massive research and development (R&D) investments over many markets is a major reason why the aircraft manufacturing industry became global. Monitoring globalization in one's industry is an important strategic-management activity. Knowing how to use that information for one's competitive advantage is even more important. For example, firms may look around the world for the best technology and select one that has the most promise for the largest number of markets. When firms design a product, they design it to be marketable in as many countries as possible. When firms manufacture a product, they select the lowest-cost source, which may be Japan for semiconductors, Sri Lanka for textiles, Malaysia for simple electronics, and Europe for precision machinery.

Tax Rates and Tax Inversions

Tax Rates

Tax rates in countries are important in strategic decisions regarding where to build manufacturing facilities or retail stores or even where to acquire other firms. High corporate tax rates deter investment in new factories and also provide strong incentives for corporations to avoid and evade taxes. Corporate tax rates vary considerably across countries and companies. As indicated in Table 11-2, the top national statutory corporate tax rates in 2015 among sample countries ranged from 0 percent in Bermuda to 55 percent in the United Arab Emirates (UAE). Note that some countries have a flat tax, which often, on adoption, triggers a surge in foreign direct investment. Signet Jewelers Ltd., owner of Kay's Jewelers, Zale Corporation, and Jared the Galleria of Jewelry, is headquartered in Bermuda for a reason: zero corporate taxes.

The United States requires companies to pay the difference between lower foreign taxes and the U.S. corporate-tax rate of 35 percent when they bring their international earnings home. In contrast, the territorial system that many other countries use allows companies to pay little to no taxes on foreign profits above what they have already paid abroad. The United States is the only nation that imposes taxes on foreign earnings. Thus, to avoid paying U.S. taxes on income made in other countries, many U.S. companies are cash-rich outside the USA, but cash-poor inside

ACADEMIC RESEARCH CAPSULE 11-2

How Do Firms Decide Where to Expand?

Considerable prior research has examined the relative attractiveness of various countries to expand operations, quite often from a "need to exploit resources in host countries" perspective. A recent article focused on the nature of institutions, such as schools, laws, and health care, rather than resources, such as oil, gas, minerals, and labor, in the decision to expand operations to other countries. Arregle and colleagues report that it does indeed matter which region(s) are chosen for expansion. More specifically, Arregle and colleagues have found that companies seek to expand primarily to regions that have institutions similar to their own institutions, or at least similar to the institutions in other regions where the firm already has operations. The "institutions factor" may be more important than the "resources factor" in internationalization decisions.

Source: Based on Jean-Luc Arregle, Tuyah Miller, Michael Hitt, and Paul Beamish, "Do Regions Matter?" An Integrated Institutional and Semi-Globalization Perspective on the Internationalization of MNEs," *Strategic Management Journal* 34 (2013): 910–934.

TABLE 11-2 Corporate Tax Rates across Countries in 2015 (from high to low)

Country	Corporate Tax Rate (%)
United Arab Emirates (UAE)	55.00
Chad	40.00
USA	35.00
Brazil	34.00
France	33.33
Germany	33.00
India	30.00
Mexico	30.00
Italy	27.50
Japan	25.50
Israel	25.00
Austria	25.00
China	25.00
Portugal	25.00
Finland	24.50
U.K.	23.00
Ukraine	21.00
Estonia	21.00
Russia	20.00
Greece	20.00
Croatia	20.00
Libya	20.00
Netherlands	20.00
Turkey	20.00
Poland	19.00
Czech Republic	19.00
Hungary	19.00
Singapore	17.00
Canada	15.00
Hong Kong	16.50
Romania	16.00
Latvia	15.00
Lithuania	15.00
Ireland	12.50
Serbia	10.00
Bulgaria	10.00
Cyprus	10.00
Bermuda	0.00

Source: Based on information at http://www.worldwide-tax.com/#partthree, retrieved January 1, 2015.

the USA, and they bring cash back to the United States only as needed. For example, Microsoft has $15+ billion in cash reserves on its balance sheet, but only about 15 percent of that money is housed in the United States. General Electric and Apple have a similar policy to avoid paying U.S. corporate taxes. Emerson Electric has $2 billion in cash with almost all of it in Europe and Asia, so the firm borrows money in the United States rather than bringing its cash back and paying a 35 percent corporate U.S. tax on corporate profits minus whatever tax it has already paid overseas. Johnson & Johnson keeps virtually all of its $24+ billion in cash outside the United States, as does Illinois Tool Works Inc. Whirlpool has 85 percent of its cash offshore. Bruce Nolop, former CFO of Pitney Bowes, explains it this way: "You end up with the really peculiar result where you are borrowing money in the USA, while you show cash on the balance sheet that is trapped overseas. It is a totally inefficient capital structure." The U.S. tax system, unfortunately for Americans, is structured so that companies can cut their tax bill by shifting income offshore to lower-tax countries.

Since the 1980s, most countries have been steadily lowering their tax rates, but the United States has not cut its top statutory corporate tax rate since 1993. Canada recently achieved its goal of having the most business-friendly tax system of the Group of Seven (G-7) nations, which include Canada, France, Germany, Italy, Japan, the United Kingdom and the United States. In January 2014, Canada's federal corporate tax rate automatically fell to 15 percent from 16.5 percent as the last installment of a series of corporate rate cuts launched in 2006 by the administration of Prime Minister Stephen Harper, who had campaigned on the promise to lower Canada's overall federal corporate tax rate by one third. More recently, the United Kingdom lowered its federal tax rate to 23 percent.

Other factors besides the corporate tax rate obviously affect companies' decisions of where to locate plants and facilities and whether to acquire other firms. For example, the large, affluent market and efficient infrastructure in both Germany and Britain attract companies, but the high labor costs and strict labor laws there keep other companies away. The rapidly growing GDP in Brazil and India attracts companies, but violence and political unrest in Middle East countries deter investment. Perhaps the United States should lower its rate to reward companies that invest in jobs domestically. Lowering the U.S. corporate tax rate should also reduce unemployment and spur growth domestically.

Tax Inversions

An increasing number of U.S. companies are reincorporating in foreign countries to reduce their tax burden, and doing this typically by acquiring a foreign firm. For example, Illinois-based AbbVie recently acquired Dublin-based Shire PLC for $54 billion and Pennsylvania-based Mylan acquired Abbott Laboratories' overseas generic drugs segment for $5.3 billion. Whenever a U.S. firm acquires a foreign firm and adopts that firm's lower tax rate or establishes a holding company in a foreign country and adopts that firm's lower tax rate, the transaction is called an **inversion**. Inversions are becoming common out of fear that politicians will soon eliminate that cross-border tax strategy. The U.S. Treasury Department installed some new rules in September 2014 to curtail inversions, but those rules had little effect. Under consideration currently are U.S.-based Pfizer and Medtronic bidding for Actavis (based in Ireland) and Covidien (based in Ireland), respectively, and Chiquita (based in Charlotte, NC) recently acquiring Fyffes (based in Ireland). Ireland in particular is taking steps to close the best-known corporate tax loophole.

Tax inversions have led to a higher dollar value of mergers and acquisitions in the United States in 2014–2015 than in the past 10 years. Inversions are common because the old alternative strategy of simply reincorporating in, say Bermuda or the Cayman Islands, has been virtually eliminated by politicians. Mylan, like many firms, used its foreign acquisition to reincorporate in the Netherlands, and then transfer pretax income from their domestic operations to their foreign parent through intercompany debt. Similarly, Salix Pharmaceuticals in North Carolina recently acquired an Italian drug company and reincorporated in Ireland in the process. Congress's Joint Committee on Taxation says eliminating inversions would yield $19.46 billion more in tax revenue for the United States over 10 years, but this will likely not get done for several years.

American Versus Foreign Business Culture

To be successful in world markets, U.S. managers must obtain a better knowledge of historical, cultural, and religious forces that motivate and drive people in other countries. For multinational firms, knowledge of business culture variation across countries can be essential for gaining and sustaining competitive advantage. An excellent website to visit on this topic is www.worldbusinessculture. com, where you may select any country in the world and check out how business culture varies in that country versus other lands. In Japan, for example, business relations operate within the context of **Wa**, which stresses group harmony and social cohesion. In China, business behavior revolves around **guanxi**, or personal relations. In South Korea, activities involve concern for **inhwa**, or harmony based on respect of hierarchical relationships, including obedience to authority.[3]

In Europe, it is generally true that the farther north on the continent, the more participatory the management style. Most European workers are unionized and enjoy more frequent vacations and holidays than U.S. workers. A 90-minute lunch break plus 20-minute morning and afternoon breaks are common in European firms. Many Europeans resent pay-for-performance, commission salaries, and objective measurement and reward systems. This is true especially of workers in southern Europe. Many Europeans also find the notion of team spirit difficult to grasp because the unionized environment has dichotomized worker–management relations throughout Europe.

A weakness of some U.S. firms in competing with Pacific Rim firms is a lack of understanding of Asian cultures, including how Asians think and behave. Spoken Chinese, for example, has more in common with spoken English than with spoken Japanese or Korean. U.S. managers consistently put more weight on being friendly and liked, whereas Asian and European managers often exercise authority without this concern. Americans tend to use first names instantly in business dealings with foreigners, but foreigners find this presumptuous. In Japan, for example, first names are used only among family members and intimate friends; even longtime business associates and coworkers shy away from the use of first names. Table 11-3 lists other cultural differences or pitfalls that would benefit U.S. managers.

Managers from the United States place greater emphasis on short-term results than do foreign managers. In marketing, for example, Japanese managers strive to achieve "everlasting customers," whereas many Americans strive to make a one-time sale. Marketing managers in Japan see making a sale as the beginning, not the end, of the selling process. This is an important distinction. Japanese managers often criticize U.S. managers for worrying more about shareholders, whom they do not know, than employees, whom they do know. Americans refer to "hourly employees," whereas many Japanese companies still refer to "lifetime employees."

Rose Knotts summarized some important cultural differences between U.S. and foreign managers.[4] Awareness and consideration of these differences can enable a manager to be more effective, regardless of his or her own nationality.

1. Americans place an exceptionally high priority on time, viewing time as an asset. Many foreigners place more worth on relationships. This difference results in foreign managers often viewing U.S. managers as "more interested in business than people."
2. Personal touching and distance norms differ around the world. Americans generally stand about three feet from each other when carrying on business conversations, but Arabs and

TABLE 11-3 Cultural Pitfalls That May Help You Be a Better Manager

- Waving is a serious insult in Greece and Nigeria, particularly if the hand is near someone's face.
- Making a "good-bye" wave in Europe can mean "No," but it means "Come here" in Peru.
- In China, last names are written first.
- A man named Carlos Lopez-Garcia should be addressed as Mr. Lopez in Latin America but as Mr. Garcia in Brazil.
- Breakfast meetings are considered uncivilized in most foreign countries.
- Latin Americans are, on average, 20 minutes late to business appointments.
- Direct eye contact is impolite in Japan.
- Do not cross your legs in any Arab or many Asian countries—it is rude to show the sole of your shoe.
- In Brazil, touching your thumb and first finger—an American "Okay" sign—is the equivalent of raising your middle finger.
- Nodding or tossing your head back in southern Italy, Malta, Greece, and Tunisia means "No." In India, this body motion means "Yes."
- Snapping your fingers is vulgar in France and Belgium.
- Folding your arms across your chest is a sign of annoyance in Finland.
- In China, leave some food on your plate to show that your host was so generous that you could not finish.
- Do not eat with your left hand when dining with clients from Malaysia or India.
- One form of communication works the same worldwide. It is the smile—so take that along wherever you go.

Africans stand about one foot apart. Touching another person with the left hand in business dealings is taboo in some countries.

3. Family roles and relationships vary in different countries. For example, males are valued more than females in some cultures, and peer pressure, work situations, and business interactions reinforce this phenomenon.

4. Business and daily life in some societies are governed by religious factors. Prayer times, holidays, daily events, and dietary restrictions, for example, need to be respected by managers not familiar with these practices in some countries.

5. Time spent with the family and the quality of relationships are more important in some cultures than the personal achievement and accomplishments espoused by the traditional U.S. manager.

6. Many cultures around the world value modesty, team spirit, collectivity, and patience much more than competitiveness and individualism, which are so important in the United States.

7. Punctuality is a valued personal trait when conducting business in the United States, but it is not revered in many of the world's societies.

8. Eating habits also differ dramatically across cultures. For example, belching is acceptable in some countries as evidence of satisfaction with the food that has been prepared. Chinese culture considers it good manners to sample a portion of each food served.

9. To prevent social blunders when meeting with managers from other lands, one must learn and respect the rules of etiquette of others. Sitting on a toilet seat is viewed as unsanitary in most countries, but not in the United States. Leaving food or drink after dining is considered impolite in some countries, but not in China. Bowing instead of shaking hands is customary in many countries. Some cultures view Americans as unsanitary for locating toilet and bathing facilities in the same area, whereas Americans view people of some cultures as unsanitary for not taking a bath or shower every day.

10. Americans often do business with individuals they do not know, unlike businesspersons in many other cultures. In Mexico and Japan, for example, an amicable relationship is often mandatory before conducting business.

In many countries, effective managers are those who are best at negotiating with government bureaucrats, rather than those who inspire workers. Many U.S. managers are uncomfortable with nepotism, which is practiced in some countries. The United States defends women from sexual harassment, defends minorities from discrimination, and allows gay marriage, but not all countries embrace the same values. American managers in China have to be careful about how they arrange office furniture because Chinese workers believe in **feng shui**, the practice of harnessing natural forces. Also, U.S. managers in Japan have to be careful about **nemaswashio**, whereby Japanese workers expect supervisors to alert them privately of changes rather than informing them in a meeting. Japanese managers have little appreciation for versatility, expecting all managers to be the same. In Japan, "If a nail sticks out, you hit it into the wall," says Brad Lashbrook, an international consultant for Wilson Learning.

Probably the biggest obstacle to the effectiveness of U.S. managers—or managers from any country working in another—is the fact that it is almost impossible to change the attitude of a foreign workforce. "The system drives you; you cannot fight the system or culture," says Bill Parker, president of Phillips Petroleum in Norway. For example, in the Middle East, gifts should not be made of pigskin, and should not be any type of alcohol, because Muslins do not eat pork or drink alcohol. In India, cows are revered, so no leather gifts.

Communication Differences across Countries

Communication may be the most important word in strategic management. Americans increasingly interact with managers in other countries, so it is important to understand communication differences across countries. Americans sometimes come across as intrusive, manipulative, and garrulous; this impression may reduce their effectiveness in communication. Asian managers view extended periods of silence as important for organizing and evaluating one's thoughts, whereas U.S. managers have a low tolerance for silence. Sitting through a conference without talking is unproductive in the United States, but it is viewed as positive in Japan if one's silence helps preserve unity. Managers from the United States are much more action-oriented than their counterparts around the world; they rush to appointments, conferences, and meetings—and then feel the day has been productive. But for many foreign managers, resting, listening, meditating, and thinking is considered productive.

Most Japanese managers are reserved, quiet, distant, introspective, and other oriented, whereas most U.S. managers are talkative, insensitive, impulsive, direct, and individual-oriented. Americans often perceive Japanese managers as wasting time and carrying on pointless conversations, whereas U.S. managers often use blunt criticism, ask prying questions, and make quick decisions. These kinds of communication differences have disrupted many potentially productive Japanese–American business endeavors. Viewing the Japanese communication style as a prototype for all Asian cultures is a stereotype that must be avoided.

Like many Asian and African cultures, the Japanese are nonconfrontational. They have a difficult time saying "no," so you must be vigilant at observing their nonverbal communication. Rarely refuse a request, no matter how difficult or nonprofitable it may appear at the time. In communicating with Japanese, phrase questions so that they can answer *yes*—for example, "Do you disagree with this?" Group decision making and consensus are vitally important. The Japanese often remain silent in meetings for long periods of time and may even close their eyes when they want to listen intently.

Business Culture across Countries[5]

Managers, marketers, salespersons, and virtually all businesspersons can be more effective in doing business with persons and companies in other countries if they have an understanding and appreciation of business culture variation across countries. Thus, let's focus here on a few countries to compare and contrast their business cultures with the U.S. business culture.

Mexico's Business Culture

Mexico is an authoritarian society in terms of schools, churches, businesses, and families. Employers seek workers who are agreeable, respectful, and obedient, rather than innovative, creative, and independent. Mexican workers tend to be activity-oriented rather than problem solvers. When visitors walk into a Mexican business, they are impressed by the cordial, friendly atmosphere. This is almost always true because Mexicans desire harmony rather than conflict; desire for harmony is part of the social fabric in worker–manager relations. There is a much lower tolerance for adversarial relations or friction at work in Mexico as compared to that in the United States.

Mexican employers are paternalistic, providing workers with more than a paycheck, but in return they expect allegiance. Weekly food baskets, free meals, free bus service, and free day care are often part of compensation. The ideal working condition for a Mexican worker is the family model, with people all working together, doing their share, according to their designated roles. Mexican workers do not expect or desire a work environment in which self-expression and initiative are encouraged. American business embodies individualism, achievement, competition, curiosity, pragmatism, informality, spontaneity, and doing more than expected on the job, whereas Mexican businesses stress collectivism, continuity, cooperation, belongingness, formality, and doing exactly what is told.

In Mexico, business associates rarely entertain each other at their homes, which are places reserved exclusively for close friends and family. Business meetings and entertaining are nearly always done at a restaurant. Preserving one's honor, saving face, and looking important are also exceptionally important in Mexico. This is why Mexicans do not accept criticism and change easily; many find it humiliating to acknowledge having made a mistake. A meeting among employees and managers in a business located in Mexico is a forum for giving orders and directions rather than for discussing problems or participating in decision making. Mexican workers want to be closely supervised, cared for, and corrected in a civil manner. Opinions expressed by employees are often regarded as back talk in Mexico. Mexican supervisors are viewed as weak if they explain the rationale for their orders to workers.

In general, Mexicans do not feel compelled to follow rules that are not associated with a particular person in authority they work for or know well. Thus, signs to wear earplugs or safety glasses, or attendance or seniority policies, and even one-way street signs are often ignored. Whereas Americans follow the rules, Mexicans often do not. Life is simply slower in Mexico than in the United States. The first priority is often assigned to the last request, rather than to the first. Telephone systems break down. Banks may suddenly not have pesos. Phone repair can take a month. Electricity for an entire plant or town can be down for hours or even days. Business and government offices may open and close at odd hours. Buses and taxis may be hours off schedule. Meeting times for appointments are not rigid. Tardiness is common everywhere. Effectively doing business in Mexico requires knowledge of the Mexican way of life, culture, beliefs, and customs.

When greeting others, Mexican women normally pat each other on the right forearm or shoulder rather than shake hands. Men normally shake hands or, if close friends, use the traditional hug and back slapping upon greeting. If visiting a person's home in Mexico, bring a gift such as flowers or sweets, but avoid both marigolds and red flowers because they symbolize negativity. White flowers are an excellent choice. Arrive up to 30 minutes late, but definitely not early. If you receive a gift, open it immediately and react enthusiastically. At dinner, do not sit until you are invited to, and wait to be told where to sit. This is true in most foreign countries as well as in the United States. Do not begin eating until the hostess starts. Only men give toasts in Mexico. It is also polite to leave some food on your plate after a meal. For business appointments, as opposed to home visits, it is best to arrive on time, although your Mexican counterparts may be up to 30 minutes late. Do not get irritated at their lack of punctuality.

Mexicans often judge or stereotype a person by who introduces them, and changing that first impression is difficult in business. Expect to answer questions about personal background, family, and life interests—because Mexicans consider trustworthiness and character to be of upmost importance. Mexicans are status conscious, so business titles and rank are important. Face-to-face meetings are preferred over telephone calls, letters, or e-mail. Negotiations in Mexico include a fair amount of haggling, so do not give a best offer first.

Japan's Business Culture

Due to its dwindling workforce and aging population, Japan is increasingly promoting women into managerial positions. Recent statistics show that only 10 only percent of managers in Japan are currently women, compared with 31 percent in Singapore, 38 percent in Germany, and 43 percent in the United States.[6] Therefore, Prime Minister Shinzo Abe of Japan has proclaimed a goal to fill 30 percent of leadership positions in Japan with women by 2020. Abe recently filled five open positions in his own cabinet with women. A key reason that Japanese women have historically not advanced to managerial positions is the business culture of notorious long work hours. Although Japan's powerful business lobby, Keidanren, currently has no women on its 24-member board of directions, the body has mandated its member companies to publicize their gender equity strategies and progress—and Keidanren itself plans to appoint women into board positions. Suppression, exploitation, and even persecution of women are severe problems in many countries, especially in the Middle East and to a lesser extent in the Far East. However, Japan is taking a leadership role by aggressively reversing its historical underutilization of women in business.

The Japanese people place great importance on group loyalty and consensus—a concept called *Wa*. Nearly all corporate activities in Japan encourage Wa among managers and employees. Wa requires that all members of a group agree and cooperate; this results in constant discussion and compromise. Japanese managers evaluate the potential attractiveness of alternative business decisions in terms of the long-term effect on the group's Wa. This is why silence, used for pondering alternatives, can be a plus in a formal Japanese meeting. Discussions potentially disruptive to Wa are generally conducted in informal settings, such as at a bar, so as to minimize harm to the group's Wa. Entertaining is an important business activity in Japan because it strengthens Wa. Formal meetings are often conducted in informal settings. When confronted with disturbing questions or opinions, Japanese managers tend to remain silent, whereas Americans tend to respond directly, defending themselves through explanation and argument.

Americans have more freedom to control their own fates than do the Japanese. The United States offers more upward mobility to its people, as indicated below:

> America is not like Japan and can never be. America's strength is the opposite: It opens its doors and brings the world's disorder in. It tolerates social change that would tear most other societies apart. This openness encourages Americans to adapt as individuals rather than as a group. Americans go west to California to get a new start; they move east to Manhattan to try to make the big time; they move to Vermont or to a farm to get close to the soil. They break away from their parents' religions or values or class; they rediscover their ethnicity. They go to night school; they change their names.[7]

In Japan, a person's age and status are of paramount importance, whether in the family unit, the extended family, or a social or business situation. Schoolchildren learn early that the oldest person in the group is to be honored. Older folks are served first and their drinks are poured for them. Greetings in Japan are formal and ritualized, so wait to be introduced, because it may be viewed as impolite to introduce yourself, even in a large gathering. Foreigners may shake hands, but the traditional form of greeting in Japan is to bow. The deeper you bow, the more respect you show, but at least bow the head slightly in greetings.

Chocolates or small cakes are excellent gifts in Japan, but do not give lilies, camellias, lotus blossoms, or white flowers, because they all are associated with funerals. Do not give potted plants because they encourage sickness, although a bonsai tree is always acceptable. Give items in odd numbers, but avoid the number 9. Gifts are not opened when received. If going to a Japanese home, remove your shoes before entering and put on the slippers left at the doorway. Leave shoes pointing away from the doorway you are about to walk through. If going to the toilet in a Japanese home, put on the toilet slippers and remove them when you exit.

Learn how to use chopsticks before visiting Japan and do not pierce food with chopsticks. Never point the chopsticks. Japanese oftentimes slurp their noodles and soup, but mixing other food with rice is inappropriate. Instead of mixing, eat a bit of rice and then a bit of food. To signify that you do not want more rice or drink, leave some in the bowl or glass. Conversation over dinner is generally subdued because the Japanese prefer to savor their food.

Unlike Americans, Japanese prefer to do business on the basis of personal relationships rather than impersonally speaking over the phone or by written correspondence. Therefore, build and maintain relationships by sending greeting, thank-you, birthday, and seasonal cards. You need to be a good "correspondent" to effectively do business with the Japanese. Punctuality is important, so arrive on time for meetings and be mindful that it may take several meetings to establish a good relationship. The Japanese are looking for a long-term relationship. Always give a small gift as a token of your appreciation, and present it to the most senior person at the end of any meeting.

Business cards are exchanged in Japan constantly and with excitement. Invest in quality business cards and keep them in pristine condition. Do not write on them. Have one side of your card translated in Japanese and give it to the person with the Japanese side facing the recipient. Business cards are generally given and received with two hands and a slight bow. Examine any business card you receive carefully.

China's Business Culture

In China, greetings are formal and the oldest person is always greeted first. Like in the United States, handshakes are the most common form of greeting. Many Chinese will look toward the ground when greeting someone. The Chinese have an excellent sense of humor, oftentimes laughing at themselves if they have a comfortable relationship with the other person. In terms of gifts, a food basket makes an excellent gift, but do not give scissors, knives, or other cutting utensils, because these objects indicate severing of the relationship. Never give clocks, handkerchiefs, flowers, or straw sandals, because they are associated with funerals. Do not wrap gifts in white, blue, or black paper. In China, the number 4 is unlucky, so do not give four of anything. Eight is the luckiest number, so giving eight of something is a great idea.

If invited to a Chinese person's home, consider this a great honor and arrive on time. Remove your shoes before entering the house and bring a small gift to the hostess. Wait to be told where to sit, and eat heartily to demonstrate that you are enjoying the food. You should use chopsticks and try everything that is offered; never eat the last piece from the serving tray. Hold the rice bowl close to your mouth while eating. Do not be offended if a Chinese person makes slurping or belching sounds; it merely indicates that they are enjoying their food.

The Chinese rarely do business with companies or people they do not know. Your position on an organizational chart is extremely important in business relationships. Gender bias is generally not an issue. Meals and social events are not the place for business discussions. There is a demarcation between business and socializing in China, so try to be careful not to intertwine the two. Like in the United States and Germany, punctuality is important in China. Arriving late to a meeting is an insult and could negatively affect your relationship. Meetings require patience because mobile phones ring frequently and conversations tend to be boisterous. Never ask the Chinese to turn off their mobile phones because this causes you both to lose face. The Chinese are nonconfrontational and virtually never overtly say *no*. Rather, "they will think about it." The Chinese are shrewd negotiators, so an initial offer or price should leave room for negotiation.

India's Business Culture

According to statistics from the United Nations, India's rate of female participation in the labor force is 34.2 percent, which is quite low, especially because women make up 42 percent of college graduates in India. But even Indian women with a college degree are expected to let their careers take a back seat to caring for their husband, children, and elderly parents. "The measures of daughterly guilt are much higher in Indian women than in other countries," says Sylvia Ann Hewlett, president of the Center for Work-Life Policy, a Manhattan think tank, who headed a recent study on the challenges Indian women face in the workplace.[8] Hewlett adds, "Since taking care of elderly parents usually becomes a reality later in a woman's career, it takes them out of the workplace just when they should be entering top management roles." That is why gender disparities at Indian companies unfortunately grow more pronounced at higher levels of management.

Like in many Asian cultures, people in India do not like to say *no*, verbally or nonverbally. Rather than disappoint you, they often will say something is not available, will offer you the response that they think you want to hear, or will be vague with you. This behavior should not be considered dishonest. Shaking hands is common in India, especially in the large cities among the more educated who are accustomed to dealing with westerners. Men may shake hands with other men and women may shake hands with other women; however, there are seldom handshakes between men and women because of religious beliefs.

Indians believe that giving gifts eases the transition into the next life. Gifts of cash are common, but do not give frangipani or white flowers, because they represent mourning. Yellow, green, and red are lucky colors, so remember that when you wrap gifts. Because Hindus consider cows to be sacred, do not give gifts made of leather. Before entering an Indian's house, take off your shoes, just as you would in China or Japan. Politely turn down the host's first offer of tea, coffee, or snacks. You will be asked again and again. Saying no to the first invitation is part of the protocol. Be mindful that neither Hindus nor Sikhs eat beef, and many are vegetarians. Muslims do not eat pork or drink alcohol. Lamb, chicken, and fish are the most commonly served main courses. Table manners are somewhat formal, but much Indian food is eaten with the fingers. Like most places in the world, wait to be told where and when to sit at dinner. Women in India typically serve the men and eat later. You may be asked to wash your hands before and after sitting down to a meal. Always use your right hand to eat, whether using utensils or your fingers. Leave a small amount of food on your plate to indicate that you are satisfied. Finishing all your food means that you are still hungry, which is true in Egypt, China, Mexico, and many countries.

Indians prefer to do business with those with whom they have established a relationship built on mutual trust and respect. Punctuality is important. Indians generally do not trust the legal system, and someone's word is often sufficient to reach an agreement. Do not disagree publicly with anyone in India. Titles such as professor, doctor, or engineer are important in India, as is a person's age, university degree, caste, and profession. Use the right hand to give and receive business cards. Business cards need not be translated into Hindi but always present your business card so the recipient may read the card as it is handed to him or her. This is a nice, expected gesture in most countries around the world.

Business Climate across Countries

The World Bank and the International Finance Corporation annually rank 189 countries in terms of their respective ease of doing business (http://www.doingbusiness.org/rankings). The index ranks nations from 1 (best) to 189 (worst). For each nation, the ranking is calculated as the simple average of the percentile rankings on how easy is it to (1) start a business, (2) deal with construction permits, (3) register property, (4) get credit, (5) protect investors, (6) pay taxes, (7) trade across borders, (8) enforce contracts, (9) resolve insolvency, and (10) get electricity.

Table 11-4 reveals the 2014 "Ease of Doing Business" rankings for the top 10 nations in six regions of the world. Note, for example, that Norway is rated the sixth best country on the planet for doing business, the United States is ranked seventh, and Colombia is the best country in South America. This information can be helpful for strategists (and students) deciding where to locate new operations, and where to focus new efforts.

TABLE 11-4 The Top 10 Nations That Are Easiest To Do Business With Across Continents

Overall Best	East Asia Pacific	East Europe Central Asia	Latin America Caribbean	Mid-East & North Africa	Sub-Saharan Africa	South Asia
1. Singapore	Singapore	Georgia	Colombia	UAE	Mauritius	Sri Lanka
2. New Zealand	Hong Kong	Latvia	Peru	S. Arabia	S. Africa	Nepal
3. Hong Kong	Malaysia	Lithuania	Mexico	Qatar	Rwanda	Maldives
4. Denmark	Taiwan	Macedonia	Puerto Rico	Bahrain	Botswana	Bhutan
5. South Korea	Thailand	Montenegro	Jamaica	Tunisia	Seychelles	Pakistan
6. Norway	Samoa	Bulgaria	Guatemala	Oman	Nambia	India
7. USA	Tonga	Armenia	Trinidad/Tobago	Morocco	Swaziland	Bangladesh
8. UK	Mongolia	Romania	Uruguay	Kuwait	Zambia	Afghanistan
9. Finland	Vanuatu	Hungary	Costa Rica	Malta	Cabo Verde	NA
10. Australia	Vietnam	Turkey	Dom. Republic	Lebanon	Mozambique	NA

Source: Based on information at http://www.doingbusiness.org/rankings, retrieved on January 1, 2005.

Africa's Business Climate

Recently, 25 African countries held democratic elections, whereas two decades ago only 3 African countries were considered democracies. Currencies in Africa are stabilizing and many countries are fund-raising to build modern highways, ports, and power grids. Many African and non-African companies are launching operations in Africa due to the rapidly growing middle class and an average GDP growth of 5 percent for the continent through 2017. Also, the World Bank says food demand across Africa will double between 2012 and 2020.

Morocco has the highest Internet penetration among all countries in Africa, with 51 percent, followed by Egypt (36%), Kenya (tied with Nigeria at 28%), Senegal (18%), South Africa (17%), Angola (15%), Algeria (14%), Ghana (14%), and Tanzania (12%).[9] All other African countries have less than 6 percent Internet penetration among their residents. The article was based on research published by the consulting firm McKinsey, which estimates that only 16 percent of Africans have access to the Internet. McKinsey predicts that by 2025, 50 percent of Africans will be online.

Nigeria (GDP = $510B) recently surpassed South Africa (GDP = $320B) as having the continent's largest gross domestic product.[10] In 2014, Nissan Motor assembled thousands of cars in Nigeria, General Electric began building $10 billion worth of new turbines for power plants, and Procter & Gamble opened a second diaper factory. Nigeria's population will be seven times larger than South Africa by 2050, even though the country still has problems with infrastructure, unemployment, crime, and poverty.

A recent article in the *Wall Street Journal* (7-13-15, p. B1) reported that Ethiopia is the newest country where garment companies are shifting manufacturing work; Kenya also is receiving numerous new "clothing" factories. VF Corporation that makes such brands as Lee, Wrangler, and Timberland, as well as Calvin Klein and PVH Corporation that makes Tommy Hilfiger, are all mentioned in the article as increasingly shifting their production operations to Africa. Such companies are shifting work to Africa from China, Bangladesh, Vietnam, Cambodia, India, Sri Lanka, and Turkey, primarily due to exceptionally low wages. For example, the article reports that Chinese garment workers earn between $155 to $297 a month, compared to workers in Bangladesh and Ethiopia that earn about $67 and $21 a month respectively. Many African countries also grow cotton and that is a plus for textile companies, but the lowest wages on the planet, coupled with improving infrastructure and stability, is the real draw.

Table 11-5 provides a summary of the economic situation in 12 African countries. Note that Angola is rated lowest in terms of doing business, whereas South Africa is rated highest. Recent regime changes in Egypt, Tunisia, Libya, and Algeria may spur further investment in Africa as democracy and capitalism strengthens. Many multinational companies are now gaining first mover advantages by engaging Africa at all levels. Today, 40 percent of Africans live in the cities—a proportion close to China and India. *The general stereotype of Africa is rapidly changing from subsistence farmers avoiding lions to millions of smartphone-carrying consumers in cities purchasing products.*

Africa has the world's largest deposits of platinum, chrome, and diamonds—and many Chinese companies in particular are investing there. Africa's largest food retailer, Shoprite Holdings, has more than 1,000 stores in 17 countries. Shoprite is a potential acquisition target being considered by European retailers Carrefour and Tesco. Diageo PLC sells Guinness beer,

TABLE 11-5 Sampling of African Countries: Ease-of-Doing-Business Rankings

	Population in Millions	Ease of Doing Business among All Countries	Capital City
South Africa	49	43 out of 183	Pretoria
Tunisia	11	60 out of 183	Tunis
Ghana	24	70 out of 183	Accra
Morocco	32	71 out of 183	Rabat
Kenya	39	136 out of 183	Nairobi
Egypt	79	112 out of 183	Cairo
Ethiopia	86	132 out of 183	Addis Ababa
Uganda	33	150 out of 183	Kampala
Nigeria	150	170 out of 183	Abuja
Sudan	41	160 out of 183	Khartoum
Mozambique	22	127 out of 183	Maputo
Angola	13	181 out of 183	Luanda

Source: Based on information at http://www.doingbusiness.org/rankings, retrieved on January 1, 2015.

Smirnoff vodka, Baileys liqueur, and Johnnie Walker whiskey in more than 40 countries across Africa. Nestlé SA now has more than 25 factories in Africa.

All of Africa is coming online, representing huge opportunities for countless companies. McKinsey & Co. estimates that within 5 years another 220 million Africans that today can meet only basic needs will join the middle class as consumers.[11] There are more than 950 million people who live in Africa.

China's Business Climate

The International Monetary Fund (IMF) recently reported that China, the world's most populous country, has overtaken the United States as the world's number-one economic powerhouse. China's economic output in 2014 reached $17.6 trillion, compared to the USA's $17.4 trillion. China now accounts for 16.5 percent of the world economy, compared to the 6.3 percent recorded by the United States. Experts have predicted this monumental shift in economic power for years, but it has come much faster than expected. Hundreds of companies are scurrying to set up business in China.

China's economic growth has slowed to 6.8 percent, led especially by a domestic-property slump that has dented construction activity and demand for materials such as steel and cement. Ruling Communist Party leaders are calling the situation the "new normal" of slower growth as the government tries to reduce widespread pollution and conserve energy. Fixed-asset investment in China is poised to fall to 12.8 percent in 2015, down from 15.5 percent the prior year. Cantonese-speaking demonstrators in Hong Kong, supported by millions of Mandarin-speaking main land Chinese, still hold out for democracy. More than 40 million Chinese visit Hong Kong (population 7 million) annually."[12]

For many decades, low wage rates in China helped keep world prices low on hundreds of products—but that is changing, because all 31 Chinese provinces and regions recently boosted their minimum wage for the third consecutive year. Demand for workers in China now outstrips supply, and this is contributing to rapidly rising wage rates and worldwide inflation. Commercial and industrial development in China's west has turned interior cities such as Chongqing into production centers that compete for labor with coastal factories. In fact, Chinese labor laws limiting student interns to 8 work hours a day and no night shifts are widely disregarded by factories.[13] Many of China's vocational schools "dump students for long internships (up to one year) at factories." Intern students are generally paid about the same as regular workers, about $212 a month before overtime, but students often have to pay most of their base wages to their school.

As indicated in Table 11-6, China ranks 90 out of 189 countries in terms of doing business. That ranking is relatively low for a variety of reasons, ranging from human rights issues to substantial disregard for copyright, patent, and trademark rules of law. Best Buy and Home Depot are examples of companies that are closing stores in China. In contrast, luxury handbag maker Coach Inc. has made China the cornerstone of its international strategy, adding more products for men and opening men's stores in China. However, Coach is struggling to compete with Hong Kong–based Michael Kors. Note also in Table 11-6 that Singapore is rated the best country on the planet for doing business.

Brazil's Business Climate

Brazil's biggest trading partner is China, but as China's economy has slowed, Brazil's economy has deteriorated. In August 2015, consumer confidence in Brazil is at a record low, unemployment has increased to 8.3 percent, inflation is nearing 10 percent, and corruption scandals have left President Dilma Rouseseff with approval ratings below 10 percent. Demand for Brazil's commodities, especially soybeans and iron ore, has declined sharply, so Brazilian businesses are laying off workers and cutting spending. Lower commodity prices cost Brazil $12 billion in foreign sales through the first half of 2015 alone. Brazil's currency, the real, declined 30 percent versus the US dollar in the last twelve months; Brazil's stock market is down 22 percent in the last twelve months; Brazil's economy is shrinking at about 1.7 percent annually. Economists now predict prolonged stagnation for Brazil. Marcos Troyjo, a former Brazilian diplomat who now is at Columbia University, says: "We went from Brazil mania to Brazil nausea; we are now looking at a lost decade." Instead of negative growth, Brazil reported 7+ percent annual GDP growth in 2010–2012 making it a BRIC (Brazil, Russia, India, China) high performer. But that was then. Also hurting Brazil now has been the fall in oil prices since that country is (or was) a big exporter of oil.

Indonesia's Business Climate

A Pacific archipelago comprised of thousands of islands, Indonesia's stock market was the top performer in 2014 among all Asian countries, and was also the top performer in five out of the last seven years in Asia. Indonesia's currency is the rupiah and its economy is one of the fastest growing in Asia, behind China and the Philippines. Indonesia's GDP is expected to grow 5.7 percent in 2015 As Southeast Asia's largest economy, Indonesia elected a new legislature and president in 2014. Despite its large population and densely populated regions, Indonesia has the world's second-highest level of biodiversity, with vast areas of wilderness and abundant natural resources.

India's Business Climate

The GDP of India in 2015 is expected to reach 8.3 percent, making it the world's fastest-growing large economy, and the first time that India's growth rate has exceeded that of China since the 1990s. China's GDP for 2015 is expected to slow to 6.8 percent.

By a landslide, India elected a new prime minister in May 2014, Narendra Modi. Modi has introduced excellent policies to jump-start India's economy, boosting profits at companies ranging from banks to cement makers. In support of Modi and India's future, money managers worldwide poured more than $17 billion into Indian stocks in 2014—the most of any developing country tracked by the Institute of International Finance. India's S&P Index grew nearly 40 percent in 2014. The country is the world's tenth-largest economy, but its economy pre-Modi was stagnant due to cumbersome bureaucracy and poor infrastructure. India grew faster (5.6%) in 2014 than any BRIC (Brazil, Russia, India, and China) country. India's economy is expected to grow 6.4

TABLE 11-6 Sampling of Asian Countries: Ease-of-Doing-Business Rankings

	Population in Millions	Ease of Doing Business among All Countries	Capital City
Singapore	5	1 out of 189	Singapore
South Korea	49	5 out of 189	Seoul
Malaysia	26	18 out of 189	Kuala Lumpur
Thailand	66	26 out of 189	Bangkok
Japan	127	29 out of 189	Tokyo
Taiwan	23	19 out of 189	Taipei
China	1,500	90 out of 189	Beijing
Pakistan	175	128 out of 189	Islamabad
Russia	140	62 out of 189	Moscow
Indonesia	241	114 out of 189	Jakarta
India	1,160	142 out of 189	New Delhi
Philippines	98	95 out of 189	Manila

Source: Based on information at http://www.doingbusiness.org/rankings, retrieved on January 1, 2015.

percent in 2015. Modi's political party has the ruling majority in the India legislature for the first time in 30 years. India is benefiting greatly from low prices for oil and gas, India's biggest import.

India's state Parliament of Rajasthan recently overhauled its local labor laws by making it easier for companies with as many as 300 employees to fire workers and avoid other contentious provisions of strict labor-protection laws. Modi is using various Indian states where his Bharatiya Janata Party has control to test his greater economic openness policies. He believes, for example, that manufacturers will now relocate to Rajasthan, and the neighboring state of Haryana has suggested it may follow Rajasthan. Modi is trying to revitalize India's manufacturing sector by taking the following steps immediately: reducing the powers of labor inspectors, replacing onerous paperwork with digital submissions, removing restrictions on women working at night, improving factory conditions for workers, easing regulations on hiring apprentices, and facilitating overtime.

Foreign firms may now own 100 percent of some Indian retail ventures, up from a previous 51 percent a few years ago. One company taking advantage of this change in the law is IKEA, which recently opened 25 new stores in India. India has also greatly reduced the expensive government subsidies on diesel fuel. Indian banks are lowering interest rates to spur growth. The country is implementing a 5-year road map to improve its finances, aiming to narrow its budget deficit of 5.3 percent of GDP to 3 percent by 2017. Complicating matters in India are high interest rates and budget deficits. The Indian Parliament recently approved higher overseas ownership in their insurance and pension investments sectors of the economy.

The Indian government is slowly improving the country's education system, but an enormous amount of work remains. Only 74 percent of Indian men and 48 percent of Indian women are literate, compared to 96 percent of men and 88 percent of women in China. India's "knowledge economy" employs only about 2.23 million people out of 750 million available.

At present, only 15 percent of India's citizens enter higher education, and the government hopes to increase this to 21 percent by 2017. The Indian Institutes of Technology—a group of universities focused on engineering and technology—are world renowned, but offer only a miniscule 7,000 places to students each year. There is elaborate red tape required to establish and operate any business in India. Also, the country's tax code is archaic and many new sectors are not even open to foreign direct investment. However, India will surpass China as the most populated country in 2030. Its highest density growth and population is in the northwest and east-central areas of the country. India has a literacy rate now of 74 percent, up from 65 percent a decade ago.

Japan's Business Climate

Japan's new Prime Minister Shinzo Abe was reelected on a mandate to revive the economy. Hopes for Abe's "Three Arrows" of hyper-easy monetary policy, government spending, and reforms such as deregulation were tarnished after Japan's economy slipped into a recession in Q3 2014, following a national sales tax increase from 5 to 8 percent aimed primarily at reducing Japan's huge public debt, the worst among advanced nations. But the sales tax increase hurt ordinary Japanese citizens. However, the falling yen has hurt small businesses and consumers by raising the cost of imported goods. Abe is pushing hard now for Japanese companies to raise wages of their employees, because company stock prices and profits are up and ordinary citizens are suffering. Abe says if wages do not rise as quickly as prices, households will cut back on spending, endangering a desired economic recovery in Japan.

Prime Minister Abe wants to restart nuclear reactors that were taken offline after the 2011 Fukushima disaster. As of 2015, all 48 of Japan's reactors are offline. Abe likely will stay in power in Japan through 2018, becoming one of Japan's rare long-term leaders. His historically pro-business Liberal Democratic Party (LBD), together with its junior coalition partner, the Komeito party, now controls more than two thirds of the lower house. Abe also wants to revitalize Japan's military to help confront growing aggression from China and North Korea, and to be able to respond to incidents such as the recent ISIS beheading of two Japanese journalists.

Mexico's Business Climate

South Korea's Kia Motors is building a $1 billion assembly near Monterrey, Mexico, joining Mazda Motors, Honda Motors, Audi AG, BMW AG, Renault SA, Nissan Motors, and Daimler AG, all of which are shifting automobile assembly operations to Mexico. The country of Mexico is now (2015) the fourth-largest auto exporter in the world, behind Japan, Germany, and South Korea. Mexico's auto industry now employs one of every six Mexican factor workers and comprises one third of all exports from Mexico.

No country was hurt more in the last decade by the rise of China than Mexico, but Chinese policy today is to boost wages and therefore boost consumer spending. The Boston Consulting Group estimates that "China's average manufacturing wage exceeded Mexico's in 2012 for the first time, when accounting for differences in productivity; Mexican workers typically produce more per hour than Chinese workers."[14] The average wage plus benefits across Mexico is $3.50 an hour. This fact, coupled with China's rising wages and slowing growth and Mexico's close proximity to the United States, represents a great opportunity for Mexico to recoup much of the manufacturing prowess it lost in the last decade to China.

Foreign direct investment (FDI) in Mexico has surged to exceed $30 billion annually, led by automobile manufacturers such as Volkswagen AG building new factories, and auto-parts suppliers such as Delphi Automotive PLC following. Home Depot will soon have 150 stores in Mexico. The FDI surge is expected to last at least through 2018, spurred by low wages, government policies that allow foreign companies to import raw materials without paying duties or tariffs, a 30 percent corporate tax rate, and rising wages in China. Note in Table 11-7 that Mexico rose to 39th place (from 53rd place) in the last two years among all nations in terms of ease of doing business.

Mexico is especially attractive for manufacturing products that are bulky or costly to transport, such as automobiles. However, a key variable hurting Mexico is drug-related violence. Mexico's homicide rate exceeds 15 people per 100,000, compared with a per capita rate of about 5.0 in the United States and 1.1 in China. If Mexico can improve its security situation as it intends, then hundreds of additional firms may consider returning to Mexico from China (and India).

Vietnam's Business Climate

Internet penetration has grown to 44 percent among Vietnam's 90 million people, up from 12 percent a decade ago.[15] Unlike another communist country, North Korea, Vietnam is booming for business. The market for e-commerce in Vietnam generates $4 billion in revenue annually and is growing dramatically. Telecommunications companies in Vietnam, such as Viettel Mobile and Vietnam Mobile Telecom Services, provide the lowest data prices in the world at just over $3 per gigabyte. The Vietnamese are among the most prevalent watchers of videos on smartphones in the world. The number of active mobile social-media accounts in Vietnam rose 41 percent from January 2014 to January 2015—a higher growth rate than China, India, or Brazil. Facebook has over 30 million active users in Vietnam, up from 8.5 million in 2012. Even the smallest businesses in the United States (and elsewhere) can easily reach and sell to consumers in Vietnam, who yearn for new products and services. (Interestingly, the most recent foreign translation of this textbook, *Strategic Management,* has been translated into Vietnamese).

TABLE 11-7 **Sampling of North and South American Countries: Ease-of-Doing-Business Rankings**

	Population in Millions	Ease of Doing Business among All Countries	Capital City
USA	308	7 out of 183	Washington, DC
Canada	34	16 out of 183	Ottawa
Chile	17	41 out of 183	Santiago
Peru	30	35 out of 183	Lima
Mexico	112	39 out of 183	Mexico City
Argentina	41	124 out of 183	Buenos Aires
Brazil	199	120 out of 183	Brasilia
Ecuador	15	115 out of 183	Quito
Bolivia	10	157 out of 183	La Paz
Venezuela	27	182 out of 183	Caracas

Source: Based on information at http://www.doingbusiness.org/rankings, retrieved on January 1, 2015.

IMPLICATIONS FOR STRATEGISTS

Figure 11-2 reveals that doing business globally is increasingly a prerequisite for success even for the smallest of firms. An estimated 95 percent of consumers globally live outside the United States; firms can grow and gain economies of scale by serving these consumers. Staying domestic oftentimes gives rival firms major competitive advantages. There are about 190 countries on seven continents.

Whatever product/service your company has to offer, it would likely be well received in many nations, and it may be strategically best for your firm to outsource operations, procure resources, and use a labor force away from home, to gain and sustain competitive advantages at home.

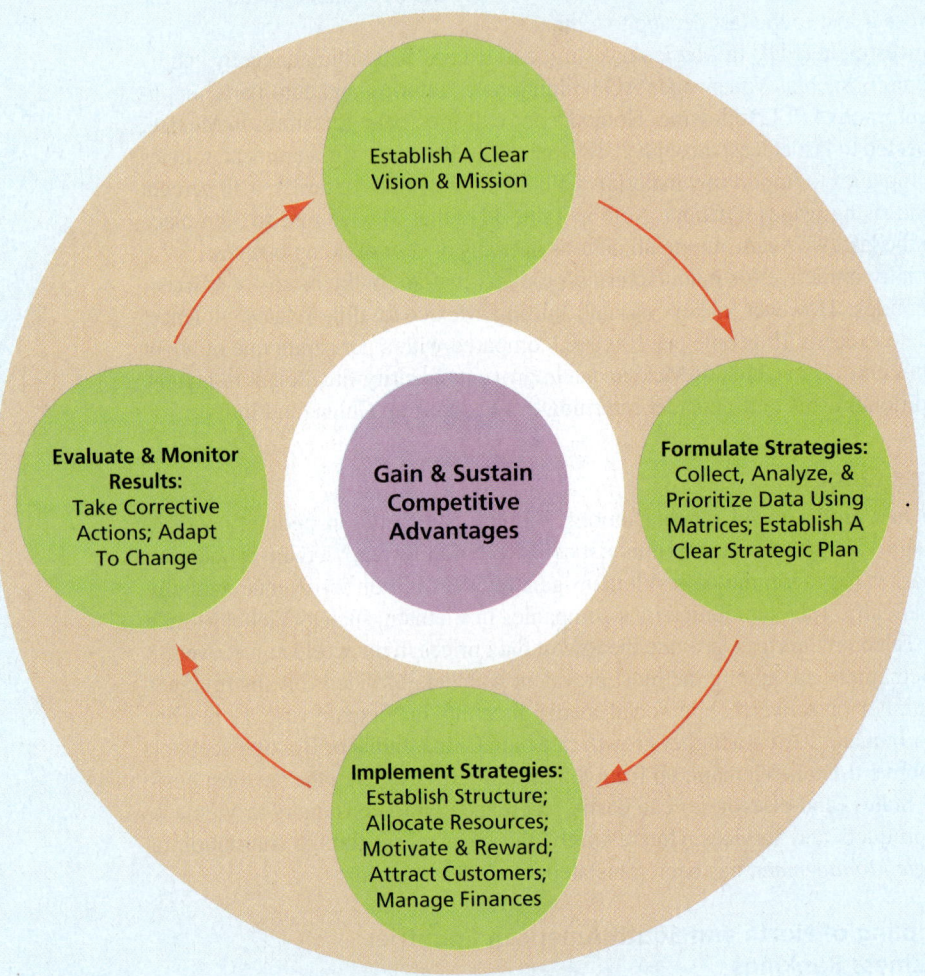

FIGURE 11-2

How to Gain and Sustain Competitive Advantages

IMPLICATIONS FOR STUDENTS

Even the smallest businesses today regularly serve customers globally and gain competitive advantages and economies of scale by doing so. Many iconic U.S. businesses, such as Tupperware, obtain more than 80 percent of their revenue from outside the United States. Therefore, in performing a strategic-management case analysis, you must evaluate the scope, magnitude, and nature of what your company is doing globally compared to rival firms. Then, determine what your company should be doing to garner global business. Continuously throughout your presentation or written report, compare your firm to rivals in terms of global business and make recommendations based on careful analysis. Be "prescriptive and insightful" rather than "descriptive and mundane" with every slide presented to pave the way for your specific recommendations with costs regarding global reach of your firm. Continually compare and contrast what you are recommending versus what the company is actually doing or planning to do.

Chapter Summary

The population of the world has surpassed 7 billion. Just as they did for centuries before Columbus reached America, businesses search for new opportunities beyond their national boundaries for centuries to come. There has never been a more internationalized and economically competitive society than today's model. Some U.S. industries, such as textiles, steel, and consumer electronics, are in disarray as a result of the international challenge.

Success in business increasingly depends on offering products and services that are competitive on a world basis, not just on a local basis. If the price and quality of a firm's products and services are not competitive with those available elsewhere in the world, the firm may soon face extinction. Global markets have become a reality in all but the most remote areas of the world. Certainly throughout the United States, even in small towns, firms feel the pressure of world competitors.

This chapter has provided some basic global information that can be essential to consider in developing a strategic plan for any organization. The advantages of engaging in international business may well offset the drawbacks for most firms. It is important in strategic planning to be effective, and the nature of global operations may be the key component in a plan's overall effectiveness.

MyManagementLab®

To complete the problems with the ⭐, go to EOC Discussion Questions in the MyLab.

Key Terms and Concepts

feng shui (p. 340)

global strategy (p. 331)

globalization (p. 331)

guanxi (p. 338)

international firms (p. 332)

inhwa (p. 338)

inversion (p. 338)

multinational corporations (p. 332)

nemaswashio (p. 340)

protectionism (p. 335)

Wa (p. 338)

Issues for Review and Discussion

⭐ **11-1.** The total number of languages spoken globally is decreasing. Is this good news for business? In what sense it is bad news for business?

⭐ **11-2.** Compare the climate for doing business in India pre-Prime Minister Modi versus post-Prime Minister Modi. What are the implications for companies?

⭐ **11-3.** According to the International Monetary Fund (IMF), which country on the planet generates more economic output than any other? What are the implications for companies?

⭐ **11-4.** What nation is Southeast Asia's largest economy and what is that country's percent GDP (gross domestic product) growth annually? What are the implications for companies?

⭐ **11-5.** What country in Africa recently surpassed South Africa in annual GDP? What are the implications for companies?

⭐ **11-6.** Recent statistics show that only 10 percent of managers in Japan are currently women, compared with 31 percent in Singapore, 38 percent in Germany, and 43 percent in the United States. What specifically is Japan doing about this "problem," if anything? What

are the implications for companies?

⭐ **11-7.** What country in Africa has the highest Internet penetration among all countries? *Hint:* Its Internet penetration rate is 51 percent versus Egypt's 36 percent and South Africa's 17 percent. What are the implications for companies?

⭐ **11-8.** According to the chapter, which country recently achieved its goal of having the most business-friendly tax system of the Group of Seven (G-7) nations (Canada, France, Germany, Italy, Japan, the United Kingdom and the United States)? What are the implications for companies?

⭐ **11-9.** True or False: The United States requires companies to pay the difference between lower foreign taxes and the U.S. corporate-tax rate of 35 percent when they bring their international earnings home. In contrast, a territorial system that many other countries use allows companies to pay little to no taxes on foreign profits above what they have already paid abroad. The United States is the only nation that imposes taxes on foreign earnings. Discuss the implications of your answer.

11-10. For the first time in 2014, what country, with 39 percent, overtook the United States, with 36 percent, of "the most innovative companies in the world"? What are the implications for companies?

11-11. Why are some U.S. companies, such as Eaton, reincorporating in foreign countries, such as Dublin, Ireland? What are the pros and cons of that strategy?

11-12. Give specifics regarding the nature and role of "Union Membership across Europe." What are the strategic implications of these facts and figures?

11-13. Give specifics regarding income tax rates and practices across countries, and associated strategic implications.

11-14. Exports from the United States comprise about 13.5 percent of GDP, compared to about 45 percent of Germany's GDP. What are implications of this for U.S. firms doing business globally?

11-15. A company is planning to begin operations in Switzerland. That company's EFE Matrix includes 20 factors. How much weight (1.0 to 0.01) would you place on the corporate tax rate factor? Discuss.

11-16. Explain how awareness of business culture across countries can enhance strategy implementation.

11-17. Describe the business culture in China.

11-18. Describe the business culture in India.

11-19. Describe the business culture in Mexico.

11-20. Describe the business culture in Japan.

11-21. List in prioritized order the top four countries in Africa that are safe, worthwhile, and potentially lucrative for opening new business operations. Give a rationale for each.

11-22. What percentage of the people living in Vietnam have and use the Internet? Why is this a strategic issue?

11-23. Do some research on Singapore to determine whether you agree that the country merits its number-1 ranking globally in attractiveness for doing business.

11-24. To what extent do you feel political unrest in the Middle East will spread outside the region? Would that be a good or bad thing for global business? What countries do you feel may experience political unrest? Why?

11-25. About 53 percent of people in Belgium are members of a labor union. Compare and contrast the labor union situation across European countries and comment on the positive or negative impact this factor has on attracting business investment into those countries.

11-26. Explain why consumption patterns are becoming similar worldwide. What are the strategic implications of this trend?

11-27. What are the major differences between U.S. and multinational operations that affect strategic management?

11-28. Why is globalization of industries a common factor today?

11-29. Compare and contrast the United States versus foreign cultures in terms of doing business.

11-30. List six reasons that strategic management is more complex in a multinational firm.

11-31. Do you feel that protectionism is good or bad for the world economy? Why?

11-32. Why are some industries more "global" than others? Discuss.

11-33. *Wa, guanxi*, and *inhwa* are important management terms in Japan, China, and South Korea, respectively. What would be analogous terms to describe U.S. management practices?

11-34. Why do many Europeans find the notion of "team spirit" in a work environment difficult to grasp?

11-35. In China, *feng shui* is important in business, whereas in Japan, *nemaswashio* is important. What are analogous U.S. terms and practices?

11-36. Compare tax rates in the United States versus other countries. What impact could these differences have on "keeping jobs at home"?

11-37. Discuss the business climate in Vietnam.

MyManagementLab®

Go to the Assignments section of your MyLab to complete these writing exercises.

11-38. Make a good argument for keeping the statutory corporate tax rate in the United States the highest in the world. Make the counterargument.

11-39. What are the advantages and disadvantages of beginning export operations in a foreign country?

ASSURANCE OF LEARNING EXERCISES

EXERCISE 11A

Business Cultures across Countries: A Hershey Company Analysis

Purpose

Various websites give excellent detail that compare and contrast business culture across countries. One excellent website is http://www.kwintessential.co.uk/resources/country-profiles.html, where you can click on more than 100 countries and obtain a synopsis of a country's business culture. After clicking on a country at that website, you may scroll down to reach the section titled "Business Etiquette and Protocol."

This exercise will expand your knowledge about how business culture varies across countries. Being knowledgeable of various countries' business culture can make you a more effective manager and communicator with people and organizations globally. This knowledge is especially helpful for firms that desire to grow globally, such as Hershey. Less than 15 percent of Hershey's revenues come from outside the United States. Hershey wants to aggressively grow globally, but there are more than 180 different countries with different business cultures, creating many options. Business culture is an important variable in global expansion decisions.

Step 1	Go to http://www.kwintessential.co.uk/resources/country-profiles.html. Click on any three countries located on different continents. Scroll down to the "Business Etiquette and Protocol" section of each country.
Step 2	Come to class prepared to give an oral presentation that compares the business culture in the three countries you selected. Frame your presentation as if you are giving advice to Hershey top managers regarding expansion into those three countries.

EXERCISE 11B
Hershey Company Wants to Enter Africa. Help Them.

Purpose
More and more companies every day decide to launch operations in Africa. Hershey Company sees millions of people with a sweet tooth in Africa. Research is necessary to determine the best strategy for being the first mover in many African countries.

Instructions
Step 1	Print a map of Africa.
Step 2	Print the demographic data on eight African countries.
Step 3	Gather competitive information regarding the presence of Mars candies and Nestlé in Africa.
Step 4	Develop a prioritized list of eight African countries in which you would recommend Hershey build distribution warehouses. Country 1 is your best, and country 2 is your next best. List in prioritized order three cities in each of your eight African countries where you believe Hershey should focus distribution and retail efforts. Justify your choices.

EXERCISE 11C
Does Your University Recruit in Foreign Countries?

Purpose
A competitive climate is emerging among colleges and universities around the world. Colleges and universities in Europe and Japan are increasingly recruiting U.S. students to offset declining enrollments. Foreign students already make up more than a third of the student body at many U.S. universities. The purpose of this exercise is to identify particular colleges and universities in foreign countries that recruit U.S. students.

Instructions
Step 1	Select a foreign country. Conduct research to determine the number and nature of colleges and universities in that country. What are the major educational institutions in that country? What programs are those institutions recognized for offering? What percentage of undergraduate and graduate students attending those institutions are U.S. citizens? Do these institutions actively recruit U.S. students? Are any of the schools of business at the various universities AACSB International accredited?
Step 2	Prepare a report that summarizes your research findings. Present your report to the class.

EXERCISE 11D
Assess Differences in Culture across Countries

Purpose
Americans can be more effective in dealing with businesspeople from other countries if they have some awareness and understanding of differences in cultures across countries.

Instructions
Step 1	Identify three individuals who either grew up in a foreign country or who have lived in a foreign country for more than one year. Interview those persons. Try to have three different countries represented. During each interview, develop a list of eight key differences between

U.S. style and custom and that particular country's style and custom in terms of various aspects of speaking, meetings, meals, relationships, friendships, and communication that could impact business dealings.

Step 2   Develop a 15-minute PowerPoint presentation for your class and give a talk summarizing your findings. Identify in your talk the persons you interviewed, as well as the length of time those persons lived in the respective countries.

EXERCISE 11E
How Well Traveled Are Business Students at Your University?

Purpose

How well traveled are students at your university? To what extent do students consider their travels to be helpful in becoming an effective businessperson? Generally speaking, the more one has traveled, especially outside the United States, the more tolerant, understanding, and appreciative one is for diversity. Many students even state on their résumé the extent to which they have traveled, both across the United States and perhaps around the world.

Instructions

Administer the following survey to at least 30 business students, including your classmates in the strategic-management course. Analyze the results. Give a 15-minute presentation to your class regarding your findings.

The Survey

1. How many states in the United States have you visited?
2. How many states in the United States have you lived in for at least three months?
3. How many countries outside the United States have you visited?
4. List the countries outside the United States that you have visited.
5. How many countries outside the United States have you lived in for at least three months?
6. List the countries outside the United States that you have lived in for at least three months.
7. To what extent do you feel that traveling across the United States can make a person a more effective businessperson? Use a 1-to-10 scale, where 1 is "Does Not Make a Difference" and 10 is "Makes a Tremendous Difference."
8. To what extent do you feel that visiting countries outside the United States can make a person a more effective businessperson? Use a 1-to-10 scale, where 1 is "Does Not Make a Difference" and 10 is "Makes a Tremendous Difference."
9. To what extent do you feel that living in another country can make a person a more effective businessperson? Use a 1-to-10 scale, where 1 is "Does Not Make a Difference" and 10 is "Makes a Tremendous Difference."
10. What three important ways do you feel that traveling or living outside the United States would be helpful to a person in being a more effective businessperson?

Source: wavebreakmedia/Shutterstock

(Note to Professors—See the Chapter IM for an additional, excellent exercise for this chapter)

MINI-CASE ON DOMINO'S PIZZA, INC. (DPZ)

Source: Edyta Pawlowska/Fotolia

TO GROW GLOBALLY THE RIGHT WAY = FOLLOW DOMINO'S?

Headquartered in Ann Arbor, Michigan, Domino's is the second-largest pizza chain in the United States behind Pizza Hut. Domino's has over 10,000 delivery-only stores in about 70 countries and in all 50 states. Among the 5,000+ Domino's in the United States, only about 400 are company-owned; all others are franchised. Between 2011 and 2015, Domino's opened 1,800 stores in 10 countries. Many of the business communication, culture, and climate facts, figures, and information presented in this chapter impact the choices made by companies deciding where on the planet to launch new endeavors. Currently, Domino's has reported 85 consecutive quarters of positive same-store sales in its international business. Domino's earnings and revenues are rising dramatically. The company remains committed to accelerate its presence in high-growth international markets to boost its business. Domino's clearly is growing globally the right way.

In addition to building new stores and adding new franchisees, Domino's has also recently revitalized its menu with Pan Pizza and Specialty Chicken. In addition, it has instituted mandatory reimaging of stores, which has received an overwhelming positive response from franchisees. The company has completed redesigning almost 15 percent of its U.S. stores and just over 25 percent of international stores. Given the response of customers at the reimaged stores, Domino's intends to continue remodeling both its company-owned and franchised stores. Furthermore, Domino's is investing heavily in technology-driven initiatives such as digital ordering to boost sales.

However, like other food chains, Domino's margins have suffered due to higher commodity costs. Costs of cheese, pork, and other meats have recently risen sharply. Prices of food commodities are expected to continue rising due to worldwide agricultural supply and demand imbalance and other macroeconomic factors. These rising costs are expected to continue to hurt margins further.

Questions

1. How does a company such as Domino's decide what countries to begin operating in next?
2. How concerned should Domino's be about rising commodity prices? Why?
3. Why would the franchise approach potentially be better for global expansion than the company-owned approach? What are the pros and cons of each approach?

Source: Company documents and a variety of sources.

Current Readings

Alessandri, Todd M., and Anju Seth. "The Effects of Managerial Ownership on International and Business Diversification: Balancing Incentives and Risks." *Strategic Management Journal*, 35, issue 13 (December 2014): 2064–2075.

Berman, Jonathan, Brad Smith, and Eniola Ladapo. "Seven Reasons Why Africa's Time Is Now: Interaction." *Harvard Business Review* 91, no. 12 (2013): 22.

Bremmer, Ian. "The New Rules of Globalization." *Harvard Business Review* 92, no. 1/2 (2014): 103–107.

Chand, Masud, and Rosalie L. Tung. "The Aging of the World's Population and Its Effects on Global Business." *Academy of Management of Perspectives* 28 (November 2014): 409–429.

Mazrouei, Hanan A., and Richard J. Pech. "The Expatriate as Company Leader in the UAE: Cultural Adaptation." *Journal of Business Strategy*, no. 1 (2015): 33–40.

Schneckenberg, Dirk. "Open Innovation and Knowledge Networking in a Multinational Corporation." *Journal of Business Strategy* 36, no. 1 (2015): 14–24.

Tate, Wendy L., et al. "Global Competitive Conditions Driving the Manufacturing Location Decision." *Business Horizons* 57, no. 3 (2014): 381–390.

Endnotes

1. Frederick Gluck, "Global Competition in the 1990s," *Journal of Business Strategy* (Spring 1983): 22–24.
2. Arregle, Jean-Luc, Toyah Miller, Michael Hitt, and Paul Beamish, "Do Regions Matter? An Integrated Institutional and Semiglobalization Perspective on the Internationalization of MNEs," *Strategic Management Journal*, 34 (2013): 910–934.
3. Jon Alston, "Wa, Guanxi, and Inhwa: Managerial Principles in Japan, China and Korea," *Business Horizons* 32, no. 2 (March–April 1989): 26.
4. Rose Knotts, "Cross-Cultural Management: Transformations and Adaptations," *Business Horizons* (January–February 1989): 29–33.
5. Some of the narrative in this section is based on information at http://kwintessential.co.uk/resources/country-profiles.html and http://www.kwintessential.co.uk/resources/global-etiquette/
6. Toko Sekiguchi, "Japan Seeks New Salarywomen," *Wall Street Journal,* September 12, 2014, A9.
7. Stratford Sherman, "How to Beat the Japanese?" *Fortune* (April 10, 1989): 45.
8. Mehul Srivastava, "Keeping Women on the Job in India," *Bloomberg Businessweek,* March 7–13, 2011, 11–12.
9. Sarah Childress, "Telecom Giants Battle for Kenya," *Wall Street Journal*, January 14, 2011, B1.
10. Drew Hinshaw, "Nigeria Economy Takes Lead in Continent," *Wall Street Journal,* April 7, 2014, A13.
11. Emmanuel Tumanjong, "Prying Open Africa's Web Reach," *Wall Street Journal,* January 10, 2014, B6.
12. Gordon Corvitz, "China 'Voids' Hong Kong Rights," *Wall Street Journal,* December 10, 2014, A11.
13. Eva Dou, "China Fills Tech Factories with Student Labor," *Wall Street Journal,* September 25, 2014, B1.
14. David Luhnow and Bob Davis, "For Mexico, an Edge on China," *Wall Street Journal,* September 17, 2012, A12.
15. James Hookway, "Vietnam's Mobile Revolution," *Wall Street Journal,* June 15, 2015, B4.

How to Prepare and Present a Case Analysis

LEARNING OBJECTIVES

After studying Part 6, you should be able to do the following:

1. Describe the case method for learning strategic-management concepts.

2. Identify the steps in preparing a comprehensive written case analysis.

3. Describe how to give an effective oral case analysis presentation.

4. Discuss special tips for doing a case analysis.

The purpose of this section is to help you analyze strategic-management cases. Numerous guidelines and suggestions are presented as well as steps to follow. Be sure to use the author website (www.strategyclub.com), which provides sample case analyses, sample presentations, author videos, case and chapter updates, and especially the free Excel student template.

What Is a Strategic-Management Case?

A *strategic-management case* describes an organization's external and internal conditions and raises issues concerning the firm's vision, mission, strategies, objectives, and policies. Most of the information in a strategic-management case is established fact, but some information may be opinions, judgments, and beliefs. Strategic-management cases are more comprehensive than those you may have studied in other courses. They generally include a description of important internal (management, marketing, finance/accounting, production/operations, research and development (R&D), management information systems) and external issues. A case puts you at the scene of the action by describing a firm's situation at some point in time. Strategic-management cases are written to give you practice applying strategic-management concepts. The case method for studying strategic management is often called *learning by doing*.

Guidelines for Preparing Case Analyses

The Need for Practicality

There is no such thing as a complete case, and no case ever gives you all the information you need for conducting analyses and making recommendations. Likewise, in the business world, strategists never have all the information they need to make decisions: Information may be unavailable or too costly to obtain, or it may take too much time to obtain. So, in analyzing cases, do what strategists do every day—make reasonable assumptions about unknowns, perform appropriate analyses, and make decisions. *Be practical.* For example, in performing a projected financial analysis, make reasonable assumptions and proceed to show what impact your recommendations are expected to have on the organization's financial position. Avoid saying, "I don't have enough information." Always supplement the information provided in a case with Internet and library research.

The Need for Justification

There is no single best solution or one right answer to a case, so it is important to give ample justification for your recommendations. In the business world, strategists oftentimes do not know if their decisions are right until resources have been allocated and consumed. Then it is often too late to reverse a decision. Therefore, in your project, amply justify your recommendations, from the beginning to the end of your written or oral presentation.

The Need for Realism

Avoid recommending a course of action beyond an organization's means. *Be realistic.* No organization can possibly pursue all the strategies that could potentially benefit the firm. Estimate how much capital will be required to implement your recommendation. Determine whether debt, stock, or a combination of debt and stock could be used to obtain the capital. Make sure your suggestions are feasible. Do not prepare a case analysis that omits all arguments and information not supportive of your recommendations. Rather, present the major advantages and disadvantages of several feasible alternatives. Try not to exaggerate, stereotype, prejudge, or overdramatize. Strive to demonstrate that your interpretation of the evidence is reasonable and objective.

The Need for Specificity

Do not make broad generalizations such as, "The company should pursue a market penetration strategy." Be specific by telling *what, why, when, how, where*, and *who*. Failure to use specifics is the single major shortcoming of most oral and written case analyses. For example, in an internal audit, say, "The firm's current ratio fell from 2.2 in 2015 to 1.3 in 2016, and this is considered to be a major weakness," instead of "The firm's financial condition is bad." But recall from what you have read that selected external and internal factors need to be "*actionable*" to the extent possible, and financial ratios in general are not actionable. Rather than concluding from a Strategic Position and Action Evaluation (SPACE) Matrix that a firm should be defensive be more specific, saying, "The firm should consider closing three plants, laying off 280 employees, and divesting itself of its chemical division, for a net savings of $20.2 million in 2017." Use ratios, percentages, numbers, and dollar estimates. Businesspeople dislike generalities and vagueness.

The Need for Originality

Do not necessarily recommend the course of action that the firm plans to take or actually undertook, even if those actions resulted in improved revenues and earnings. The aim of case analysis is for you to consider all the facts and information relevant to the organization at the time, to generate feasible alternative strategies, to choose among those alternatives, and to defend your recommendations. Support your position with charts, graphs, ratios, analyses, and the like. *Be original.* Compare and contrast what you recommend versus what the company plans to do or is doing.

The Need to Contribute

Strategy formulation, implementation, and evaluation decisions are commonly made by a group of individuals rather than by a single person. (See the individual versus group decision-making exercise at the end of this Part 6.) Your professor will likely divide the class into three- or four-person teams and ask you to prepare written or oral case analyses. Members of a team, in class or in the business world, differ on their aversion to risk, their concern for short-run versus long-run benefits, their attitudes toward social responsibility, and their views concerning globalization. There are no perfect people, so there are no perfect strategies. Be open-minded to others' views. *Be a good listener and a good contributor.*

Your professor may ask the whole class to prepare a case for class discussion. Preparing a case for class discussion means that you need to read the case before class, make notes regarding the organization's external opportunities and threats as well as internal strengths and weaknesses, perform appropriate analyses, and come to class prepared to offer and defend some specific recommendations. Be excited about strategic management. Be a class leader.

The Case Method Versus Lecture Approach

The *case method* of teaching involves a classroom situation in which students do most of the talking; your professor facilitates discussion by asking questions and encouraging student interaction regarding ideas, analyses, and recommendations. Be prepared for a discussion along the lines of "What would you do, why would you do it, when would you do it, and how would you do it?" Prepare answers to the following types of questions:

- What are the firm's most important external opportunities and threats?
- What are the organization's major strengths and weaknesses?
- How would you describe the organization's financial condition?
- What are the firm's existing strategies and objectives?
- Who are the firm's competitors, and what are their strategies?
- What objectives and strategies do you recommend for this organization? Explain your reasoning. How does what you recommend compare to what the company plans?
- How could the organization best implement what you recommend? What implementation problems do you envision? How could the firm avoid or solve those problems?

The Cross-Examination

Take a stand on the issues and support your position with objective analyses and outside research. Strive to apply strategic-management concepts and tools in preparing your case for class discussion. Seek defensible arguments and positions. Support opinions and judgments with facts, reasons, and evidence. Crunch the numbers before class! Be willing to describe your recommendations to the class without fear of disapproval. Respect the ideas of others, but be willing to go against the majority opinion when you can justify a better position.

Case analysis gives you the opportunity to learn more about yourself, your colleagues, strategic management, and the decision-making process in organizations. The rewards of this experience will depend on the effort you put forth. Discussing cases in class is exciting and challenging. Expect views counter to those you present. Different students will place emphasis on different aspects of an organization's situation and submit different recommendations for scrutiny and rebuttal. Cross-examination discussions commonly arise, just as they occur in a real business organization. Avoid being a silent observer.

Preparing a Written Case Analysis

In addition to asking you to prepare a case for class discussion, your professor could ask you to prepare a written case analysis. Written reports are generally more structured and more detailed than an oral presentation. Always avoid using jargon, vague or redundant words, acronyms, abbreviations, sexist language, and ethnic or racial slurs. And watch your spelling! Use short sentences and paragraphs and simple words and phrases. Use quite a few subheadings. Arrange issues and ideas from the most important to the least important. Use the active voice rather than the passive voice for all verbs; for example, say "Our team recommends that the company diversify" rather than "It is recommended by our team to diversify." Use many examples to add specificity and clarity. Tables, figures, pie charts, bar charts, timelines, and other kinds of exhibits help communicate important points and ideas. Sometimes a picture *is* worth a thousand words.

The Executive Summary

Your professor could ask you to focus the written case analysis on a particular aspect of the strategic-management process, such as (1) to identify and evaluate the organization's existing vision, mission, objectives, and strategies; or (2) to propose and defend specific recommendations for the company; or (3) to develop an industry analysis by describing the competitors, products, selling techniques, and market conditions in a given industry. These types of written reports are sometimes called *executive summaries*. An executive summary usually ranges from three to five pages of text in length, plus exhibits.

The Comprehensive Written Analysis

If asked to develop a *comprehensive written analysis*, picture yourself as a consultant who has been asked by a company to conduct a study of its external and internal environment and to make specific recommendations for its future. Prepare exhibits to support your recommendations. Highlight exhibits with discussion in the paper. Comprehensive written analyses are usually about 20 pages in length, plus 20 exhibits. Throughout your written analysis, emphasize how your proposed strategies will enable the firm to gain and sustain competitive advantage. Visit www.strategyclub.com for examples.

Steps in Preparing a Comprehensive Written Analysis

In preparing a *written* case analysis, you should follow the steps outlined here, which correlate to the stages in the strategic-management process and the chapters in this text. (Note—More detailed steps, including a minute-by-minute breakdown, are given later in this Part 6.)

Step 1   Identify the firm's existing vision, mission, objectives, and strategies.

Step 2   Develop vision and mission statements for the organization.

Step 3   Identify the organization's external opportunities and threats.

Step 4   Construct a Competitive Profile Matrix (CPM).

Step 5   Construct an External Factor Evaluation (EFE) Matrix.

Step 6   Identify the organization's internal strengths and weaknesses.

Step 7   Construct an Internal Factor Evaluation (IFE) Matrix.

Step 8   Prepare a Strengths-Weaknesses-Opportunities-Threats (SWOT) Matrix, Strategic Position and Action Evaluation (SPACE) Matrix, Boston Consulting Group (BCG) Matrix, Internal-External (IE) Matrix, Grand Strategy Matrix, and Quantitative Strategic Planning Matrix (QSPM) as appropriate. Give advantages and disadvantages of alternative strategies.

Step 9   Recommend specific strategies and long-term objectives. Show how much your recommendations will cost. Clearly itemize these costs for each projected year. Compare your recommendations to actual strategies planned by the company.

Step 10   Specify how your recommendations can be implemented and what results you can expect. Prepare forecasted ratios and projected financial statements. Present a timetable or agenda for action.

Step 11   Recommend specific annual objectives and policies.

Step 12   Recommend procedures for strategy review and evaluation.

Making an Oral Presentation

Your professor may ask you to prepare a case analysis, individually or as a group, and present your analysis to the class. Oral presentations are usually graded on two parts: content and delivery. *Content* refers to the quality, quantity, correctness, and appropriateness of analyses presented, including such dimensions as logical flow through the presentation, coverage of major issues, use of specifics, avoidance of generalities, absence of mistakes, and feasibility of recommendations. *Delivery* includes such dimensions as audience attentiveness, clarity of visual aids, appropriate dress, persuasiveness of arguments, tone of voice, eye contact, and posture. Great ideas are of no value unless others can be convinced of their merit through clear communication. The guidelines presented here can help you make an effective oral presentation. Present a united front when presenting as a team. Always say "we did such and such" and "we recommend such and such," rather than, "I did the financial ratios" or "I recommend such and such." A light or humorous introduction can be effective at the beginning of a presentation.

Controlling Your Voice

An effective rate of speaking ranges from 100 to 125 words per minute. Practice your presentation aloud to determine if you are talking too fast. Individuals commonly speak too fast when they are nervous. Breathe deeply before and during the presentation to help yourself slow down. Have a cup of water available; pausing to take a drink will wet your throat, give you time to collect your thoughts, control your nervousness, slow you down, and signal to the audience a change in topic.

Avoid a monotone voice by placing emphasis on different words or sentences. Speak loudly and clearly, but do not shout. Silence can be used effectively to break a monotone voice. Stop at the end of each sentence, rather than running sentences together with *and* or *uh*.

Managing Body Language

Be sure not to fold your arms, lean on the podium, put your hands in your pockets, or put your hands behind you. Maintain a straight posture, with one foot slightly in front of the other. Do not turn your back to the audience; doing so is not only rude but it also prevents your voice from projecting well. Avoid using too many hand gestures, too. On occasion, leave the podium or table and walk toward your audience, but do not walk around too much. Never block the audience's view of your visual aids.

Maintain good eye contact throughout the presentation. This is the best way to persuade your audience. There is nothing more reassuring to a speaker than to see members of the audience nod in agreement or smile. Try to look everyone in the eye at least once during your presentation, but focus more on individuals who look interested than on those who seem bored. To stay in touch with your audience, use humor and smiles as appropriate throughout your presentation. No presentation should ever be dull!

Speaking from Notes

Be sure not to read to your audience; doing so puts people to sleep. Perhaps worse than reading is merely reciting what you have memorized. Do not try to memorize anything. Rather, practice unobtrusively using notes. Make sure your notes are written clearly so you will not flounder when trying to read your own writing. Include only main ideas on your note cards. Keep note cards on a podium or table if possible so that you will not drop them or get them out of order; walking with note cards tends to be distracting.

Constructing Visual Aids

Make sure your visual aids are legible to individuals in the back of the room. Using color to highlight special items is a good idea. Avoid putting complete sentences on visual aids; rather, use short phrases and then orally elaborate on issues as you make your presentation. Generally, there should be no more than four to six lines of text on each visual aid. Use clear headings and subheadings. Do not use many handouts or your audience may concentrate on them instead of you during the presentation.

Answering Questions

It is best to field questions at the end of your presentation, rather than during the presentation itself. Encourage questions, and take your time to respond to each one. Answering questions can be persuasive because it involves you with the audience. If a team is giving the presentation, the audience should direct questions to a specific person. During the question-and-answer period, be polite, confident, and courteous. Avoid verbose responses. Do not get defensive with your answers, even if a hostile or confrontational question is asked. Staying calm during potentially disruptive situations, such as a cross-examination, reflects self-confidence, maturity, poise, and command of the particular company and its industry. Stand up throughout the question-and-answer period.

Tips for Success in Case Analysis

Strategic-management students who have used this text over 15 editions offer you the following tips for success in doing case analysis.

1. Use the www.strategyclub.com website resources. The free Excel student template is especially useful as are the sample PowerPoint case analyses.
2. In preparing your external assessment, use the online databases subscribed to by your college library.
3. Go to http://finance.yahoo.com and enter your company's stock symbol. Also, enter your firm's major rival's stock symbol. Become knowledgeable about key trends and issues in your industry.
4. View your case analysis and presentation as a product that must have some competitive factor to favorably differentiate it from the case analyses of other students.
5. Develop a mind-set of *why*, continually questioning your own and others' assumptions and assertions.
6. Seek the help of professors in other specialty areas when necessary, and mention them by name in your presentation.
7. A goal of case analysis is to improve your ability to think clearly in ambiguous and confusing situations; do not get frustrated that there is no single best answer.
8. Work hard to develop the ability to formulate reasonable, consistent, and creative plans; put yourself in the strategist's position.
9. Develop confidence in using quantitative tools for analysis.
10. Strive for excellence in writing and in the technical preparation of your case. Prepare informative and neat charts, tables, diagrams, and graphs.
11. Pay attention to detail.
12. Think through alternative implications fully and realistically. The consequences of decisions are not always apparent. They often impact many different aspects of a firm's operations.
13. Provide answers to such fundamental questions as *what, when, where, why, who,* and *how.*

14. Do not merely recite ratios or present figures. Rather, develop ideas and conclusions concerning the possible trends. Use figures to support what your team is recommending.
15. Your analysis should be as detailed and specific as possible.
16. Emphasize the Recommendations and Strategy Implementation sections. A common mistake is to spend too much time on the external or internal analysis parts of your paper or presentation. The recommendations and implementation sections are the most important part.
17. Throughout your case analysis, emphasize how your proposed strategic plan will enable the firm to gain and sustain competitive advantage.
18. When working as a team, do most of the work individually. Use team meetings mostly to assimilate work. This approach is most efficient.
19. During the presentation, keep good posture, eye contact, and voice tone, and project confidence. Do not get defensive under any conditions or with any questions.
20. Prepare your case analysis in advance of the due date to allow time for reflection and practice. Do not procrastinate.
21. Other students will have strengths in functional areas that will complement your weaknesses, so develop a cooperative spirit that moderates competitiveness in group work.
22. When preparing a case analysis as a group, divide into separate teams to work on the external analysis and internal analysis.
23. Maintain a good sense of humor.
24. Capitalize on the strengths of each member of the group; volunteer your services in your areas of strength.
25. Set goals for yourself and your team; budget your time to attain them.
26. Foster attitudes that encourage group participation and interaction. Do not be hasty to judge group members.
27. Be prepared to work. There will be times when you will have to do more than your share. Accept it, and do what you have to do to move the team forward.
28. Think of your case analysis as if it were really doing this for a company.
29. To uncover flaws in your analysis let one person in the group actively play the devil's advocate.
30. Do not schedule excessively long group meetings; two-hour sessions are about right.
31. Push your ideas hard enough to get them listened to, but then let up; listen to others and try to follow their lines of thinking; follow the flow of group discussion, recognizing when you need to get back on track.
32. Develop a case-presentation style that is direct, assertive, and convincing; be concise, precise, fluent, and correct.
33. Have fun when at all possible. Preparing a case is frustrating at times, but enjoy it while you can; it may be several years before you are playing CEO again.
34. Get things written down (drafts) as soon as possible.
35. Neatness is a real plus; your case analysis should look professional.
36. Let someone else read and critique your presentation several days before you present it.
37. Make special efforts to get to know your group members. This leads to more openness in the group and allows for more interchange of ideas.
38. Be constructively critical of your group members' work. Do not dominate group discussions. Be a good listener and contributor.
39. Include this project on your resume as class work is accomplished.
40. Apply for a full-time job at the case company for which you prepared this strategic plan.
41. For every slide you show in an oral presentation, point out how the information supports your recommendations for the firm.
42. Make certain that your key external and internal factors are quantitative, divisional, and actionable to the extent possible.

Sample Case Analysis Outline

There are musicians who play wonderfully without notes and there are chefs who cook wonderfully without recipes, but most of us prefer a more orderly cookbook approach, at least in the first attempt at doing something new. Therefore, the eight minute-by-minute steps shown in Table 1

TABLE 1 Recommended Outline for Delivering a 27-Minute Oral Case Presentation
_____

I. INTRODUCTION (1 MINUTE)

a. Introduce yourselves by name and major. Establish the time setting of your case and analysis. Prepare your strategic plan for the three years forthcoming.

b. Introduce your company and its products or services; capture interest.

c. Show the outline of your presentation and tell who is doing what parts.

II. VISION AND MISSION (2 MINUTES)

a. Show existing vision and mission statements if available from the firm's website, annual report, or elsewhere.

b. Show your "improved" vision and mission and tell how and why it is different.

c. Compare your vision and mission to a leading competitor's statements.

III. INTERNAL ASSESSMENT (5 MINUTES)

a. Give your financial ratio analysis. Highlight especially good and bad ratios. Do not give definitions of the ratios and do not highlight all the ratios.

b. Show the firm's organizational chart found or "created based on executive titles." Identify the type of chart as well as good and bad aspects. Unless all white males comprise the chart, peoples' names are generally not important because positions reveal structure.

c. Present your improved organizational chart. Tell how and why it is different.

d. Show a market positioning map with firm and competitors. Discuss the map in light of strategies you envision for firm versus competitors' strategies.

e. Identify the marketing strategy of the firm in terms of good and bad points versus competitors and in light of strategies you envision for the firm.

f. Show a map locating the firm's operations. Discuss in terms of strategies you envision. Perhaps show a value chain analysis chart.

g. Discuss (and perhaps show) the firm's website and Facebook page in terms of good and bad points compared to rival firms.

h. Show your "value of the firm" analysis.

i. List the firm's 20 most important strengths and weaknesses. Go over highly rated factors without "reading" any verbatim. Make sure your key internal factors are quantitative, divisional, and actionable to the extent possible.

j. Show and highlight your Internal Factor Evaluation (IFE) Matrix.

IV. EXTERNAL ASSESSMENT (5 MINUTES)

a. Identify and discuss major competitors. Use pie charts, maps, tables, or figures to show the intensity of competition in the industry. Pave the way for your recommendations.

b. Show your Competitive Profile Matrix. Include 15 factors and two competitors.

c. Summarize key industry trends citing Standard & Poor's *Industry Survey* and IBIS World information. Highlight key external (economic, social, cultural, demographic, geographic, technological, political, legal, governmental, and natural environment) trends as they impact the firm.

d. List the firm's 20 most important opportunities and threats. Make sure your opportunities are not stated as strategies. Go over highly weighted factors without "reading" any verbatim. Make sure your key external factors are quantitative, divisional, and actionable to the extent possible.

e. Show and highlight your External Factor Evaluation (EFE) Matrix.

V. STRATEGY FORMULATION (7 MINUTES)

a. Show and highlight your SWOT Matrix, focusing on the strategies you ultimately will recommend.

b. Show and explain your SPACE Matrix. Focus more on the implications than the numbers. Strategies must be specific; avoid vague terms such as *market penetration*.

c. Show your Boston Consulting Group (BCG) Matrix. Focus more on the implications than the numbers. Do multiple BCG Matrices if possible, including domestic versus global, or another geographic breakdown. Develop a product BCG if at all possible. Comment on each matrix as per strategies you recommend. Develop this matrix even if you do not know the profits per division and even if you have to estimate the axes information. However, make no wild guesses on axes or revenue/profit information.

d. Show and highlight your Internal-External (IE) Matrix.

e. Show and highlight your Grand Strategy Matrix.

f. Show your Quantitative Strategic Planning Matrix (QSPM). Be sure to explain your strategies. Do not go back over the internal and external factors.

g. Present your recommendations page. This is the most important page in your presentation. Be specific in terms of both strategies and estimated costs of those strategies. *Total your estimated costs.* You should have 10 or more strategies. Divide your strategies into two groups: (1) Existing Strategies to Be Continued and (2) New Strategies to Be Started.

VI. STRATEGY IMPLEMENTATION (4 MINUTES)

   a. Show and highlight your earnings per share/earnings before interest and taxes (EPS/EBIT) analysis to reveal whether stock, debt, or a combination is best to finance your recommendations. Graph the analysis.
   b. Show your projected income statement and balance sheet. Relate changes in the items to your recommendations rather than blindly going with historical percentage changes. Be sure to show the retained earnings calculation and the results of your EPS/EBIT decision.
   c. Show your projected financial ratios and highlight several key ratios to show the benefits of your strategic plan.

VII. STRATEGY EVALUATION (1 MINUTE)

   a. Prepare a Balanced Scorecard to show your expected financial and nonfinancial objectives recommended for the firm.

VIII. CONCLUSION (2 MINUTES)

   a. Compare and contrast your strategic plan versus the company's own plans for the future.
   b. Thank audience members for their attention. Genuinely seek and gladly answer questions.

---

may serve as a basic outline for you in presenting a strategic plan for your firm's future. This outline is not the only approach used in business and industry for communicating a strategic plan, but this approach is time-tested, it does work, and it does cover all of the basics. You may amend the content, tools, and concepts given to suit your own company, audience, assignment, and circumstances, but it helps to know and understand the rules before you start breaking them.

Recommended Time Allocation for Presenting a Case Analysis

Your professor may allow between 15 and 40 minutes for your case presentation; the outline in Table 1 is provided for a 27-minute presentation. Be sure in an oral presentation to manage time, knowing that your recommendations and associated costs are the most important part. If you are only allowed 15 minutes of presentation time, prepare (1) a condensed slide show and (2) a full slide show of your case analysis, using the condensed for presentation purposes and the full to submit to your professor. Good luck.

ASSURANCE OF LEARNING EXERCISE

Strategic Planning for Gruma SAB

Purpose

Strategic-management classes are usually composed of a team of students who perform case analysis as described in the text. The purpose of this exercise is to examine whether individual decision making is better than group decision making. Academic research suggests that groups make better decisions than individuals about 80 percent of the time. No company has sufficient resources to implement all strategies that would benefit the firm. Thus, tough choices have to be made. Ranking strategies as to their relative attractiveness (1 = most attractive, 2 = next most attractive, etc.) is a commonly used procedure to help determine which actions to fund. Oftentimes, a group of managers will jointly rank strategies and compare their ranking to other groups. This ranking process may be used to determine the relative attractiveness of feasible alternative strategies.

Completing this exercise will reveal whether you as an individual make better strategic decisions than your group or team. This is a fun exercise that also gives you experience selecting among feasible alternative strategies for a company.

The Situation

Headquartered in Monterrey, Gruma is the largest tortilla producer in the world. Gruma uses corn and wheat flour and other ingredients to produce grits, cereals, tortilla chips, taco shells, sauces, snacks, pasta, potato chips, and more. Top Gruma food brand names are Mission, Guerrero, Calidad,

Maseca, and Tortimasa. The company also produces Tortec and Batitech machines that produce tortilla and tortilla chips that are sold to restaurants, supermarkets, and other food service providers. One special feature of Gruma's machines and products is the use of a dry production method rather than using wet dough. Gruma's method yields lower costs and superior product uniformity. Over the last 10 years, Gruma has acquired several competing firms, including Albuquerque Tortilla Company, Casa de Oro Foods, and Archer Daniels Midlands stake in Azteca Milling. Gruma operates 101 production facilities serving over 113 countries and employs 18,000. On July 22, 2015, the company announced excellent results for its second quarter of 2015 (2Q15). During the course of 2Q15, Gruma made capital investments worth 33 million U.S. dollars, most of which was spent on technology improvements, expanding the installed capacity of the firm's tortilla and corn flour production plants in Mexicali, building a new plant to produce tostadasin in Tijuana, Mexico, and building a tortilla plant in Russia. Despite doing really well, Gruma wants to do better. It is trying to decide what strategies would be best for the company going forward. Following are 12 strategies that are being considered.

The Strategies

1. **Backward integration.** Purchase a 10,000-acre corn and wheat farm to gain better control over supplies needed for production operations.
2. **Forward integration (a).** Acquire Chipotle Mexican Grill (CMG). Chipotle is a chain of about 1,700 restaurants in the United States, United Kingdom, Canada, and Europe, specializing in burritos, tacos, and salads. *Chipotle* is Spanish for "smoked or fried jalapeno chili pepper."
3. **Forward integration (b).** Acquire Chuy's (CHUY). Chuy's is a chain of 59 small Mexican restaurants in the United States. Chuy's is not "fast casual" like Chipotle, but rather is a sit-down table-service restaurant that is uniquely festive. Chuy's revenue soared 20 percent to $64.1 million in its latest quarter. Chuy's opened 11 more locations in the last year.
4. **Horizontal integration.** Acquire Grupo Bimbo, S.A.B. de C.V. Founded in 1945 in Mexico City, Grupo Bimbo employs over 129,000 and does business worldwide with 167 plants, but the company's principal operations are in Mexico and the United States. Top brands in Mexico include Bimbo, Marinela, Barcel, and Ricolino.
5. **Market development (a).** Build a manufacturing plant in China to begin servicing that country.
6. **Market development (b).** Build a manufacturing plant in South Africa to begin servicing all of Africa.
7. **Market penetration (a).** Launch an advertising, promotion, and publicity campaign in Mexico to increase market share in Mexico.
8. **Market penetration (b).** Launch an advertising, promotion, and publicity campaign in the United States to increase market share in the country.
9. **Product development (a).** Develop, produce, and launch a full line of organic tortillas, chips, and taco shells.
10. **Product development (b).** Develop, produce, and launch new products, including spaghetti, linguine, and bread.
11. **Related diversification.** Acquire the Prego trademark brand name pasta sauce from Campbell Soup Company. Prego pasta sauce is available in 19 different flavors, including marinara, traditional, mini meatball, zesty mushroom, and roasted garlic parmesan. Several Prego flavors are made with all organic ingredients.
12. **Unrelated diversification.** Acquire a construction company in Mexico, such as one of the following companies: Cemex, Grupo Villacero, Tubacero, Lamosa, or ICA.

The Task

Your task is to rank the 12 preceding strategies in terms of their relative attractiveness for Gruma, where 1 = the most attractive strategy to pursue, 2 = the next most attractive strategy, and so on to 12 = the least attractive strategy to pursue. Rank the strategies first as an individual, and then as part a group. Then, listen to the EXPERT ranking and rationale. In this manner, this exercise enables you to determine what individual(s) and what group(s) in class make the best strategic decisions (i.e., that come closest to the expert ranking).

TABLE 2 Strategic Planning for Gruma: Individual versus Group Decision Making

	Column Number				
Strategy	(1) My Rank	(2) Group Rank	(3) EXPERT Rank	(4) Absolute Value 1–3	(5) Absolute Value 2–3
1. Backward integration					
2. Forward integration (a)					
3. Forward integration (b)					
4. Horizontal integration					
5. Market development (a)					
6. Market development (b)					
7. Market penetration (a)					
8. Market penetration (b)					
9. Product development (a)					
10. Product development (b)					
11. Related diversification					
12. Unrelated diversification					
Sum of Columns 1, 2, 4, & 5					

Note: The expert ranking and rationale are given in the *Chapter Instructor's Manual.*

The Steps

1. Fill in Column 1 in Table 2 to reveal your individual ranking of the relative attractiveness of the proposed strategies. For example, if you feel backward integration is the seventh-best option, then enter 7 into Column 1 beside backward integration.
2. Fill in Column 2 in the table to reveal your group's ranking of the relative attractiveness of the proposed strategies. For example, if your group believes backward integration is the third-best option, then enter 3 into Column 2 beside backward integration.
3. Fill in Column 3 in the table to reveal the expert's ranking of the relative attractiveness of the proposed strategies.
4. Fill in Column 4 in the table to reveal the absolute difference between Column 1 and Column 3 to reveal how well you performed as an individual in this exercise. (Note: Absolute difference disregards negative numbers.)
5. Fill in Column 5 in the Table to reveal the absolute difference between Column 2 and Column 3 to reveal how well your group performed in this exercise.
6. Sum Column 4. Sum Column 5.
7. Compare the Column 4 sum with the Column 5 sum. If your Column 4 sum is less than your Column 5 sum, then you performed better as an individual than as a group. If you did better than your group, your performance was especially good.
8. The Individual Winner(s): The individual(s) with the lowest Column 4 sum is the WINNER.
9. The Group Winners(s): The group(s) with the lowest Column 5 score is the WINNER.

Strategic Management Cases

Dunkin' Brands Group, Inc., 2015

www.dunkinbrands.com, DNKN

Headquartered in Canton, Massachusetts, Dunkin' Brands (Dunkin') sells hot and cold coffee and baked goods, as well as hard-serve ice cream, using a near-100 percent franchised business model. With 11,300 Dunkin' Donuts restaurants in 40 states and 32 foreign countries, and 7,500 Baskin-Robbins restaurants in 43 states and 46 foreign countries, Dunkin' is one of the world's largest franchisors of quick-service restaurants (QSR). All but 36 Dunkin' Donuts and Baskin-Robbins are franchisee-owned. In the last few years, more and more customers are coming into Dunkin' restaurants and spending more and more money when they are there. About 70 percent of all Dunkin' stores have a drive thru, which caters to consumers in a hurry. Dunkin' is a speed leader among QSR, even given increased ticket volume and menu complexity.

Dunkin' recently launched a loyalty and rewards program that enables the company to collect data from customers to determine their habits. For example, if you normally visit Dunkin' Donuts in the morning, the firm may soon send you offers to purchase some donuts in the afternoon or evening. Companies increasingly are using business analytics to make strategic decisions. Major rival firms in the coffee retailing business include Starbucks, Krispy Kreme Doughnuts, and Tim Hortons. Dunkin' especially caters to the on-the-go consumer looking for a quick coffee and breakfast. One potential weakness for Dunkin' is that the firm does not offer many healthy food options for health-conscious customers.

Coffee prices rose 50 percent in 2014 due to drought conditions in South America, especially since Brazil endured its worst drought in decades. The 2014 coffee harvest in Brazil was the lowest in three years. To take up the slack, Colombia, the world's number-two Arabica grower, was increasing production, but Colombia only produces about one quarter as much coffee as Brazil.

Dunkin' Brands is performing quite well. In mid-2015, Dunkin' announced agreements with seven franchise groups to open 51 new restaurants in Virginia and West Virginia over the next several years. Of the seven groups, only one is a new franchisee while the rest are existing franchisees/franchise groups. For Q1 of 2015, the company's revenues increased 8.1 percent year-over-year to $185.9 million, driven partly by revenue from the Dunkin' K-Cup pack licensing agreement with Keurig Green Mountain, Inc.

Copyright by Fred David Books LLC. www.strategyclub.com (Written by Meredith E. David)

History

Independently in the 1940s, Bill Rosenberg founded the first Dunkin' Donut restaurant, and Burt Baskin and Irv Robbins each founded a chain of ice cream shops that eventually combined to form Baskin-Robbins. Baskin-Robbins and Dunkin' Donuts were acquired by Allied Domecq in 1973 and 1989, respectively, and renamed Dunkin' Brands, Inc. in 2004. Allied was acquired in 2005 by Pernod Ricard, who soon sold the firm to Bain Capital Partners, LLC, The Carlyle Group, and Thomas H. Lee Partners, L.P. In 2011, Dunkin' Brands became listed on the NASDAQ Global Select Market under the symbol "DNKN."

Dunkin' Donuts

Bill Rosenberg opened his first donut restaurant, Kettle Donuts, in 1948, in Quincy, Massachusetts. The name changed to Dunkin' Donuts in 1950. Rosenberg sold franchisees to others as early as 1955. The 100th restaurant opened in 1963, the 1,000th in 1979, and the 3,000th in 1992. In 1996, bagels were introduced to the Dunkin' Donuts menu and breakfast sandwiches the following year.

In 2013, Dunkin' Donuts received the No. 1 ranking for customer loyalty in the coffee category by Brand Keys for eight years running, and was rated by CREST in December 2013 as number-one in iced regular/decaf/flavored coffee, number-one in hot regular/decaf/flavored coffee, number-one in donut category, and number-one in bagel and muffin category.

The following year, Dunkin' Donuts reentered the United Kingdom, 20 years after it exited the country, with its first store opening in Harrow, London. In Canada, Dunkin' Donuts has lost a substantial percent of its market share in recent years, and now has only five restaurants, all in Quebec. Dunkin's Canadian decline is largely due to rival donut firm Tim Hortons.

Baskin-Robbins

In 1945, brothers-in-law Burt Baskin and Irv Robbins owned different ice cream parlors, Burton's Ice Cream and Snowbird Ice Cream, both in Glendale, California. The separate companies merged in 1953 and the number of ice cream flavors increased to 31. That year, Baskin-Robbins hired Carson-Roberts Advertising who recommended adoption of the number 31 as well as the pink (cherry) and brown (chocolate) polka dots and typeface. In the 1970s, the company went international, opening stores in Japan, Saudi Arabia, Korea, and Australia. Baskin-Robbins was the first company to introduce ice cream cakes to the public, and the first to offer both hand scooped and Soft Serve ice cream. In some places, such as Malaysia, Baskin-Robbins gives 31 percent off their hand-packed ice cream on the 31st of a month.

Today, Baskin-Robbins is the world's largest chain of ice cream specialty shops serving premium ice cream, specialty-frozen desserts, and beverages to more than 300 million customers annually. In 2014, the company was named the top U.S. ice cream and frozen dessert franchise by *Entrepreneur* magazine.

Vision/Mission

Dunkin's vision statement is given on the corporate website as follows: "Serving Responsibly— To be recognized as a company that responsibly serves our guests, franchisees, employees, communities, business partners, and the interests of our planet."

Dunkin's mission statement is also given on the corporate website, but it is titled "Our Priorities." The statement has four parts: Our People, Our Guests, Our Neighborhoods, and Our Planet. For example, regarding Our People, the statement reads: "From our employees and franchisees to the farmers who grow our coffee, we believe in treating everyone with respect and fairness so they are empowered to reach their goals."

Organizational Structure

In 2014, Dunkin' extended Chairman and CEO Nigel Travis's employment contract through December 2018. Mr. Travis, age 64, joined Dunkin' Brands as CEO in December 2008; his contract was to expire in 2016. Besides Mr. Travis, other top executives at Dunkin' are listed in Exhibit 1. Notice there is no Chief Operating Officer and Mr. Travis is both the Chairman and CEO. Also notice there are no women or minorities among the top nine executives.

Regarding Dunkin's number of employees, since the company is nearly 100 percent franchised, workers are employed and paid by the franchisee, rather than by Dunkin'. Dunkin' has no unionized employees.

EXHIBIT 1 **Dunkin' Brands' Organizational Chart**

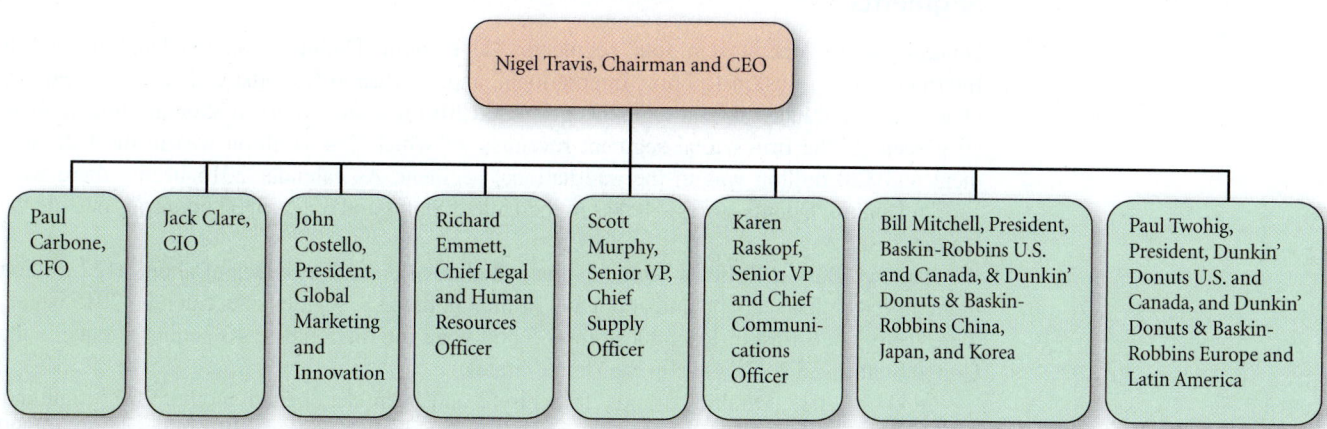

Source: Based on information at Dunkin' Brands' corporate website.

Internal Issues

Strategy

Dunkin' is opening 65 Dunkin' Donuts stores in Brazil's capital of Brasilia and surrounding states by 2016, through a licensing agreement with OLH Group. The new stores will be primarily in the capital city of Brasilia and the state of Goias. Dunkin' also has plans to open an additional 80 stores in Brazil outside of the capital area by 2018. Dunkin's largest South American presence to date is in Colombia with 171 restaurants. In 2014, Dunkin' opened about 700 Dunkin' Donuts and Baskin-Robbins stores worldwide. Store cannibalization is becoming a problem in some areas as the firm increasingly opens new stores in close proximity to existing stores. Dunkin' restaurants are most heavily concentrated in the New England region of the United States. Dunkin' franchisees are currently overhauling restaurant décor into a "sip and sit" atmosphere, with over 100 restaurants now offering soft seating areas, as well as high and low tables and stools. The new décor features earthy colors, contemporary lights, coffee-housed themed artwork, free Wi-Fi, power outlets, flat panel televisions, and digital menus.

To keep revenues flowing around the clock, Dunkin' Donuts (and rival Starbucks) now offer more dinner-friendly foods. "Though breakfast remains our core, today people are seeking all-day dining, and they want to eat what they want, when they want it and where they want it," says John Costello, Dunkin' Donuts president of global marketing and innovation. Thus, Dunkin' Donuts in late 2014 introduced a dinner staple (steak) and made a steak sandwich as well as a wrap with eggs permanent additions to its menu. Only 40 percent of Dunkin' Donuts' sales come after 11 AM, leaving a lot of room for growth in that arena, especially at the more than 2,300 Dunkin' Donuts in the United States that are open 24 hours. Most Dunkin' Donuts, Costello said, are open until 10 PM.

Sustainability

Dunkin' Brands has a current Corporate Sustainability Report (CSR) posted on their website. The CSR details how Dunkin' is progressing toward improving on its environmental goals and objectives. For example, the Dunkin' Donuts & Baskin-Robbins Community Foundation (DDBRCF) recently partnered with Feeding America to support such initiatives as the BackPack Program to provide hungry children with nutritious and easy-to-prepare food to take home on weekends, and to support the School Pantry Program, which helps alleviate child hunger in America.

Franchise Fees

In the United States, Dunkin' Donuts franchisees pay a royalty of about 5.4 percent of gross sales to the company, and Baskin-Robbins franchisees pay about 5.0 percent. However, outside the United States, Dunkin' Donut franchisees, on average, pay a royalty rate of only 2.1 percent. For the Baskin-Robbins brand outside the United States, Dunkin' does not generally receive royalty payments from franchisees; instead, it earns revenue from such franchisees by selling ice cream products to them, so the royalty rate in this segment is about 0.7 percent. Dunkin' franchisees in the United States also pay advertising fees of about 5 percent of gross sales.

Segments

Dunkin' Brands operates in four segments: (1) Dunkin' Donuts U.S., (2) Dunkin' Donuts International, (3) Baskin-Robbins International, and (4) Baskin-Robbins U.S. The two Dunkin' Donuts U.S. and International segments generated 2014 revenues of about $568 million, or about 76 percent of the firm's total segment revenues, of which $549 million was in the U.S. segment and $20 million was in the international segment. As calendar 2015 began, there were 11,275 Dunkin' Donuts stores—8,047 in the United States and 3,228 in 32 countries outside the United States.

The two Baskin-Robbins segments generated 2014 annual revenues of about $122 million in the international segment and about $43 million in the U.S. segment. As calendar 2015 began, there were 7,546 Baskin-Robbins stores—5,068 were international in 46 countries outside the United States, and 2,478 were in the United States.

In Q4 of 2015, Dunkin' Brands' franchisees and licensees opened another 260 restaurants worldwide, including 141 Dunkin' Donuts U.S. locations, 75 Baskin-Robbins International

EXHIBIT 2 Dunkin' Brands' Number of Restaurants at Year-End

	2014	2013	2012
Dunkin' Donuts U.S.	8,047	7,677	7,306
Dunkin' Donuts International	3,228	3,181	3,043
Baskin-Robbins U.S.	2,478	2,467	2,463
Baskin-Robbins International	5,068	4,833	4,556
Total	**18,821**	**18,158**	**17,368**

outlets, 46 Dunkin' Donuts International units. Also, two Baskin-Robbins U.S. locations were closed. Additionally, Dunkin' Donuts U.S. franchisees remodeled 172 restaurants during the quarter. Exhibit 2 provides a breakdown of Dunkin' Brands' restaurants.

Since Dunkin' Brands is nearly 100 percent franchised, revenues derived from selling both ice cream and donuts to consumers is reported on the franchisees' financial statements, rather than on Dunkin's financial statements. Thus, the company generates revenue from five primary sources: royalty income and fees, rental income from restaurant properties leased, sales of ice cream products to franchisee, retail store revenue at company-owned stores, and licensing of the Dunkin' Donuts brand for products sold in nonfranchised outlets (such as retail packaged coffee).

Outside the United States, Dunkin' stores are predominantly located in Asia and the Middle East, which accounted for about 70 and 16 percent, respectively, of international franchisee-reported sales in 2014.

Dunkin' Donuts

The Dunkin' Donuts brand has evolved into a predominantly coffee-based concept, with approximately 57 percent of Dunkin' Donuts' U.S. franchisee-reported sales for fiscal year 2013 generated from coffee and other beverages. Dunkin' Donuts has centralized manufacturing locations (CMLs) that are franchisee-owned and operated for producing donuts and bakery goods. The CMLs deliver freshly baked products to Dunkin' Donuts restaurants on a daily basis with consistent quality. At year-end 2013, there were 114 Dunkin' CMLs of varying size and capacity in the United States. However, some Dunkin' Donuts restaurants produce donuts and bakery goods on-site rather than relying on CMLs. Some of those stand-alone Dunkin' Donuts restaurants supply other local Dunkin' Donuts restaurants that do not have access to CMLs.

Dunkin's coffee supplier, National DCP LLC, hedges coffee prices with farmers, protecting Dunkin' from rapid swings in coffee price. Coffee prices have been rising of late, due to inclement weather, especially a drought in South America. Consequently, the price of Robusta coffee beans is high, whereas Arabica coffee bean prices are lower. Dunkin' is positioned well somewhat because on the Dunkin' website, it says, "We use 100% Arabica coffee beans."

Exhibit 3 provides a breakdown of Dunkin' Donuts' restaurants outside the United States, and income globally.

Baskin-Robbins

Dunkin' Brands outsources all its manufacturing and distribution of ice cream products for the domestic Baskin-Robbins brand franchisees to Dean Foods. Dunkin's Baskin-Robbins U.S. segment has reported comparable store sales growth in each of the last three fiscal years. The company's "31 flavors" offer consumers a different flavor for each day of the month. Baskin-Robbins USA franchise system has sales of about $520 million, or 5.5 percent of Dunkin's global franchisee-reported sales.

About 65 percent of Baskin-Robbins restaurants are located outside of the United States and operate primarily through joint ventures and country or territorial license arrangements with "master franchisees." The Baskin-Robbins international franchise system, predominantly located across Asia and the Middle East, generated franchisee-reported sales of $2.0 billion in 2013, or 22.1 percent of Dunkin' Brands' global franchisee-reported sales.

The number of Baskin-Robbins outside of the United States are revealed in Exhibit 4, as well as the segment's income globally.

EXHIBIT 3 The Number of Dunkin' Donuts Outside the United States and Income Globally (in thousands of USD)

	2014 # Stores	2013 # Stores
South Korea	902	827
Middle East	338	386
Other	1,941	2,015
Total	**3,181**	**3,228**
Dunkin' Donuts U.S.		
Income		
Royalty income	$362,342	$337,170
Franchise fees	36,192	29,445
Rental income	91,918	92,049
Sales at company-owned stores	24,976	22,765
Other revenues	5,751	3,970
Total revenues	**521,179**	**485,399**
Segment profit	**379,751**	**355,274**
Dunkin' Donuts International		
Income		
Royalty income	$14,249	$13,474
Franchise fees	3,531	1,715
Rental income	133	179
Other revenues	403	117
Total revenues	**18,316**	**15,485**
Segment profit	**7,479**	**9,670**

EXHIBIT 4 The Number of Baskin-Robbins Outside the United States and Income Globally (in thousands of USD)

	2014 # Stores	2013 # Stores
South Korea	1,065	1,106
Japan	1,157	1,170
Middle East	706	754
Other	1,805	2,030
Total	**4,833**	**5,068**
Baskin-Robbins U.S.		
Income		
Royalty income	$25,728	$25,768
Franchise fees	1,160	775
Rental income	3,420	3,949
Sales of ice cream products	3,808	3,942
Sales at company-owned stores	—	157
Other revenues	8,036	7,483
Total revenues	**42,152**	**42,074**
Segment profit	**27,081**	**26,274**
Baskin-Robbins International		
Income		
Royalty income	$9,109	$9,301
Franchise fees	1,665	1,292
Rental income	535	561
Sales of ice cream products	108,435	90,717
Other revenues	589	104
Total revenues	**120,333**	**101,975**
Segment profit	**54,321**	**42,004**

Finance

Dunkin' Brands' revenues in 2014 were $748.7 million, up 4.9 percent year over year. Adjusted earnings per share were $1.74, up 13.7 percent over the prior year. For that quarter, Dunkin' Brands declared a quarterly dividend of 26.5 cents per share of common stock, an increase of 15 percent from the prior quarter. The increased dividend was paid on March 18, 2015 of record as of March 9.

Dunkin' Brands' income statement and balance sheet are provided in Exhibits 5 and 6, respectively.

EXHIBIT 5 **Dunkin' Brands' Income Statement (in thousands of USD)**

Report Date	December 27, 2014	December 28, 2013
Revenues	$748,709	$713,840
Operating expenses	432,535	436,631
Operating income	22,684	27,527
EBIT	338,858	304,736
Interest	83,125	86,648
EBT	255,733	218,088
Tax	80,170	71,784
Other items	794	599
Net income	**176,357**	**146,903**

Source: Based on p. 52 in Dunkin's 2014 *Form 10K*.

EXHIBIT 6 **Dunkin' Brands' Balance Sheet (in thousands of USD)**

Report Date	December 27, 2014	December 27, 2013
Cash	$208,080	$256,933
Accounts receivable	105,060	79,765
Inventories	—	—
Other current assets	129,478	125,062
Total current assets	442,618	461,760
Property, plant & equipment	182,061	182,858
Equity investments	164,493	170,644
Goodwill & intangibles	2,317,167	2,343,803
Other assets	71,044	75,625
Total assets	**3,177,383**	**3,234,690**
Short-term debt	3,852	5,000
Accounts payable	13,814	12,445
Other current liabilities	337,853	326,853
Total current liabilities	355,519	344,298
Long-term debt	1,807,081	1,818,609
Deferred income taxes	540,339	561,714
Other liabilities	99,494	97,781
Total liabilities	**2,802,433**	**2,822,402**
Noncontrolling interest	6,991	4,930
Common stock	104	107
Retained earnings	(711,531)	(779,741)
Treasury stock	—	(10,773)
Paid in capital and other	1,079,386	1,197,765
Total equity	**367,959**	**407,358**
Total liabilities, noncontrolling interest, & equity	**3,177,383**	**3,234,690**

Source: Based on p. 51 in Dunkin's 2014 *Form 10K*.

Competitors

There are thousands of "mom-and-pop" doughnut shops globally. However, Krispy Kreme Doughnuts (KKD), Starbucks, Dunkin' Brands Group, and Tim Hortons (now owned by Restaurant Brands) are dominant rivals, and have been increasing coffee and doughnuts sales annually. For example, total sales in 2014 for KKD, Starbucks, and Dunkin' Brands Group, increased 6.5, 10.1, and 4.9 percent, respectively. All four companies have aggressive expansion plans. Krispy Kreme Doughnuts is in an aggressive growth mode and plans to expand in a way similar to that of Dunkin' Brands, which plans to double its Dunkin' Donuts store count to around 15,000 in the United States alone. Krispy Kreme plans to increase its 800 stores worldwide to 1,300 by 2017.

Exhibit 7 provides some comparative information about Dunkin' Brands, Krispy Kreme Doughnuts, and Starbucks. Revenue per employee is not really applicable due to franchising, whereas the persons are employees of the franchisee and not Dunkin'.

Starbucks Corporation (SBUX)

Starbucks is the world's largest specialty coffee retailer with more than 18,000 coffee shops in 60 countries. It offers coffee drinks and pastries, roasted beans, coffee accessories, and teas. The company owns about 9,400 of its own shops (mostly in the United States), while licensees and franchisees operate roughly 8,650 units worldwide (primarily in shopping centers and airports). In 2014, Starbucks began offering beer and wine, as well as fancy snacks, chicken skewers, chocolate fondue, and other items. By year-end 2014, only 40 Starbucks offered these new items. The company also owns the Seattle's Best Coffee and Torrefazione Italia coffee brands. Starbucks markets its coffee through grocery stores and licenses its brand for other food and beverage products. The company is determined to get the afternoon and evening customer, whereas historically it has mainly been a breakfast place. That is why the beer, wine, and more food is being rolled out at more and more Starbucks outlets.

The company sees afternoon and dinner also as a way to differentiate itself from Dunkin' Donuts and Krispy Kreme Doughnuts that historically have been more about quick service than sit down and stay, which is the venue Starbucks plans to enter aggressively globally. Starbucks now offers 10 standard small dinner plates as part of its evening menu, such as truffle macaroni and cheese. There are also five choices of red wine, three white wines, a sparkling rose, and prosecco.

Krispy Kreme Doughnuts (KKD)

Krispy Kreme Doughnuts is chain of doughnut outlets with about 695 locations throughout the United States and in about 20 other countries. The shops are popular for their glazed doughnuts that are served fresh and hot out of the fryer, as well as cake and filled doughnuts, crullers, and fritters. Hot coffee and other beverages also are sold. KKD outlets are almost all owned and operated by franchisees; the company owns and operates 90 locations. Aside from doughnuts and coffee, no other food items of substance are offered. The company markets its doughnuts through grocery stores and supermarkets.

Green Mountain Coffee Roasters Inc. (GMCR) and KKD have agreed to widen the homemade single-serve coffee options for Keurig users, whereby KKD's upcoming coffees—Smooth and Decaf—will be available in K-Cup packs for Keurig brewers. Krispy Kreme's K-Cup packs

EXHIBIT 7 Dunkin' Donuts versus Rival Firms

	Dunkin'	Krispy Kreme	Starbucks
# Employees	1,150	2,500	191,000
$ Net Income	$176 M	$34 M	$2,068 M
$ Revenue	$748 M	$460 M	$16,447 M
$ Revenue/Employee	NA	$184,000	$86,110
$ EPS Ratio	$1.65	$0.55	$3.30
Market Cap.	$5.0 B	$1.4 B	$66.7 B

will be available at the online shopping sites of Keurig and KKD, along with the participating KKD shops, grocery, and many other retail outlets. The convenience of Keurig brewers will enhance the popularity of KKD coffee among Keurig fans.

The fiscal fourth-quarter results for KKD on March 12, 2014, saw revenue rise 3.3 percent to $112.7 million. Company-owned same-store sales rose 1.6 percent, and franchise same-store sales soared 6.7 percent. Adjusted net income grew 37 percent to $8.3 million. It was the fifth full year and 21st quarter in a row of same-store KKD sales gains.

Tim Hortons, Inc.

Tim Hortons is Canada's leading quick-service restaurant brand, having more than 4,250 coffee and donut shops across the country, and in several U.S. states. Tim Hortons was acquired by Burger King Worldwide in late 2014 in an $11 billion deal, and BKW immediately created Restaurant Brands International (RBI). RBI is now the second largest global quick-service restaurant in the world. Today, BKW is headquartered in Oakville, outside of Toronto, Canada.

The Tim Horton menu features a variety of coffees and cappuccino, along with donuts, Dutchies, bagels, and other baked goods. In addition, Tim Hortons serves a lunch menu of soup, sandwiches, and chili. The chain includes freestanding as well as kiosk and mall-based outlets; all but about 20 of the locations are operated by franchisees. The company owns the Cold Stone Creamery ice cream shop chain. Tim Hortons' revenues in a recent quarter increased 10.7 percent, and adjusted earnings-per-share grew 6 percent.

External Issues

Barriers to Entry

Barriers to entry are relatively low for the restaurant industry, but rivalry (competitiveness) among firms is exceptionally high. One large contributing factor for the low barriers to entry is many small entrepreneurs can open mom-and-pop establishments and bypass the franchise fees, royalties, selection process, and so on, of owning a franchised restaurant and lease an existing building at a relatively low price. There are thousands of mom-and-pop donut shops across the United States and likely tens of thousands of small ice cream places. However, even avoiding high fixed costs, variable costs are often high, and small-scale entrepreneurs are not able to compete with larger franchise stores that can better negotiate pricing on food, packaging, and other supplies. In the QSR industry, the bargaining power of consumers is quite powerful, availability of restaurant options in most places is abundant, and consequently there is intense price competitiveness among rival firms. Even if you are sure you want a donut or ice cream, you likely have many options.

Future

Dunkin' Brands reported slower sales growth slow in Q4 of 2014 as it faced intensifying competition for on-the-go customers in the mornings. Sales for Dunkin' Donuts USA edged up 1.4 percent in the period, down from the growth of 3.5 percent a year ago. Analysts say the slowdown comes as more competitors have pushed into the breakfast category, a relative bright spot in the fast-food industry. For example, Yum Brands' Taco Bell segment recently reported that its quarterly sales rose 7 percent in its U.S. locations, boosted by its national breakfast launch. Dunkin' CEO Nigel Travis says, "If you think about it, everyone's getting into the breakfast space."

Rival Burger King provides breakfast and coffee to millions of customers through thousands of restaurants located near Dunkin' Donuts restaurants. Now, in addition, Burger King owns Tim Hortons, and looks to put those restaurants near Dunkin' Donuts restaurants, especially in the northeastern United States. CEO Nigel Travis at Dunkin' Brands needs a three-year strategic plan. Do you have any suggestions to help Mr. Travis?

Krispy Kreme Doughnuts, Inc., 2015

www.krispykreme.com, KKD

Headquartered in Winston-Salem, North Carolina, Krispy Kreme Doughnuts (KKD) serves doughnuts and coffee as well as other snack items. The company has locations in 23 different countries. Many Krispy Kreme shops are factory shops where customers can watch doughnuts being made and purchase fresh hot doughnuts as well. The factory stores are responsible for servicing local grocery stores and convenience stores. The KK Supply Chain provides raw materials for both franchise and company-owned stores in the doughnut-making process. Krispy Kreme storeowners must purchase all materials from KK Supply Chain. Krispy Kreme reported total revenues in fiscal year end February 2015 of $490 million (up from $460 million the prior year) with about 90 percent of revenues derived from the United States.

For the fiscal first quarter (Q1) of 2015, Krispy Kreme's revenue rose 9 percent year-over-year to $132.5 million, driven almost entirely by a 17.3 percent increase in Krispy Kreme's store count. For that quarter, the company's domestic same-store sales rose 5.2 percent, but its international franchise same-store sales declined 1.7 percent. Overall for Q1 of 2015, the company's adjusted net income was $16.6 million, or $0.24 per share. The company's EPS number was up at least by the KKD buying back 391,300 shares of its stock for $7.4 million.

Copyright by Fred David Books LLC. www.strategyclub.com (Written by Forest R. David)

History

Krispy Kreme traces its roots back to 1933 when Vernon Rudolph bought a doughnut shop in Paducah, Kentucky. After selling doughnuts in Kentucky, Tennessee, and West Virginia, the store known today as Krispy Kreme was moved to Winston-Salem. Krispy Kreme doughnuts were sold to grocery stores at first, but became so popular with customers that they requested the option to buy the doughnuts fresh and hot from the store, thus launching the doughnut factory retail store and selling directly to the public.

Krispy Kreme grew quickly over the next four decades before being sold to Beatrice Foods Company in 1976. Shortly after the purchase by Beatrice, in 1982, several Krispy Kreme franchisees purchased the company back from Beatrice Foods and quickly established the current Doughnut Theater style of factory stores where by customers can watch doughnuts being made. It was not until 1996 that KKD finally expanded outside the Southeast by opening a store in New York City, followed in 2001 by opening its first store outside the United States, in Canada. The company went public with its IPO launch in April 2000.

In the United Kingdom, KKD just concocted a single, gigantic box that holds 2,400 doughnuts. The box (11.4 feet by 3 feet) was filled with doughnuts and required eight KKD employees to deliver it to 360 Resourcing Solutions. The box was part of a promotion for the new "Krispy Kreme Occasions" division that customizes doughnut offerings for corporate events or special occasions such as weddings and other celebrations. The division sells doughnut "towers" for special events or even personalized doughnuts with customized, chocolate nameplates or corporate logos. The company has no plans to create another box, but it is happy to sell 100 of the so-called double-dozen boxes for about $2,600.

Krispy Kreme opened its first store in India in 2013 in Bangalore, Karnataka, and now there are seven in that city. Also in 2013, KKD began opening stores in Colombia, with a total of 25 planned, as the first South American country for the company. In late 2013, KKD opened its first store in Taipei, Taiwan. In 2014, KKD opened its first shop in Chennai in southern India.

Internal Issues

Vision/Mission

Krispy Kreme Doughnuts does not appear to have a published vision statement. The company's mission statement, however, is given as follows:

> Consumers are our lifeblood, the center of the doughnut
> There is no substitute for quality in our service to consumers
> Impeccable presentation is critical wherever Krispy Kreme is sold
> We must produce a collaborative team effort that is unexcelled
> We must cast the best possible image in all that we do
> We must never settle for "second best;" we deliver on our commitments
> We must coach our team to ever-better results. (*Source:* Company documents)

Distribution

Krispy Kreme doughnuts are sold in KKD stores, grocery stores, convenience stores, gas stations, Walmart, and Target stores in the United States. Internationally, the doughnuts are sold in Loblaws supermarkets, Petro-Canada gas stations, and as freestanding stores in Canada, along with BP Service Stations and BP Travel Centers and 7-Eleven stores in Australia. In the United Kingdom, Tesco supermarkets, Tesco Extra, and most Tesco service stations carry KKD products, and service stations Moto, Welcome Break, and Road Chef also carry self-service KKD cabinets. Today, KKD has locations in the United Kingdom, Australia, Turkey, the Dominican Republic, Kuwait, Mexico, Puerto Rico, Taiwan, South Korea, Malaysia, Thailand, Indonesia, the Philippines, Japan, China, the United Arab Emirates, Qatar, Saudi Arabia, Bahrain, Hong Kong, and Ethiopia.

Organizational Structure

As illustrated in Exhibit 1, KKD basically has two segments: USA and International. Note the company does not have a Chief Operating Officer (COO), Chief Administrative Officer (CAO), or Chief Strategy Officer (CSO). However, KKD reports revenues by geographic region, but is not structured geographically. In fact, the company appears to be structurally functionally, rather than divisionally.

EXHIBIT 1 KKD's Organizational Structure

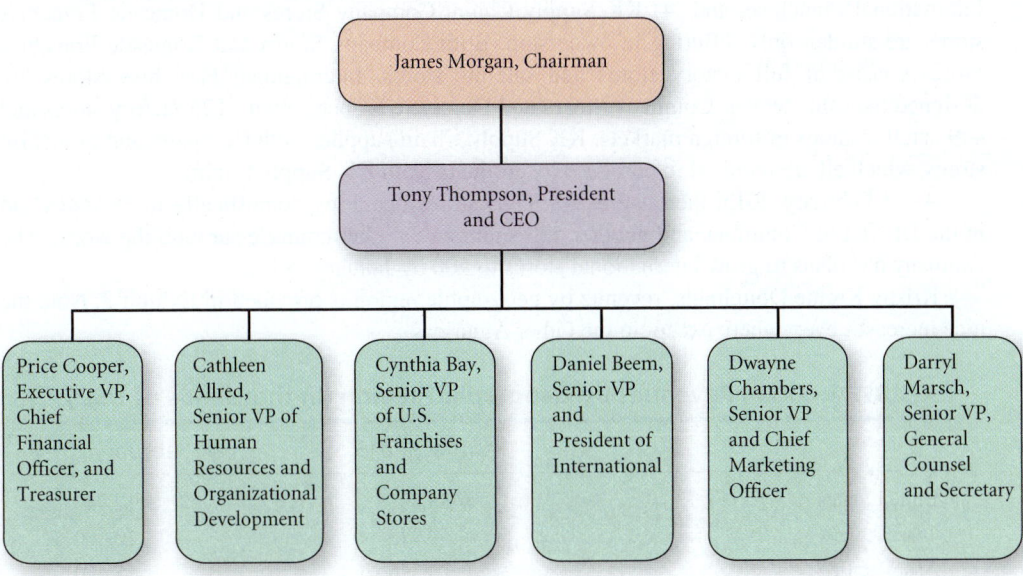

Source: A depiction based on author's best judgment.

Strategy

Krispy Kreme Doughnuts has long prided itself on hot fresh doughnuts and a one of a kind taste. As you can easily watch at a KKD factory store Doughnut Theater, the original glazed doughnut is fried before it heads toward a glazing waterfall to be covered in a sugary signature glaze. There is only one supplier of KKD's signature glaze. In addition to entertaining guests, KKD feels the Doughnut Theater also reveals the firm's commitment to quality and freshness. To help attract customers into the store, the original hot doughnuts sign is lit during peak production hours, generally early in the mornings and late at night, when customers are most likely to visit the stores. In essence, KKD's strategy is hot fresh doughnuts, but the firm also sells its products in gas stations, grocery stores, and other retail outlets. About 50 percent of all KKD revenue is derived from wholesale outlets, so the firm plans to work on ways to improve the freshness and quality of its doughnuts sold in various retail locations.

The company is transitioning toward smaller factory shops that will focus on retail rather than wholesale customers. This strategy appears more in line with the firm's new marketing approach. Many new stores in the southeastern United States will be company owned, whereas new smaller factory stores outside the southeast are more likely to be operated under franchisee agreements.

Krispy Kreme Doughnuts has long helped the communities with fund-raisers, even offering special packaging at times. Fund-raisers are under the firm's "local relationship marketing" strategy. The company does a good job attracting customers from local businesses and families. About 55 percent of all domestic transactions are for doughnut orders of 1 dozen or more. However, this is also partly explained by the volume discount provided for such orders. International orders of a dozen or more doughnuts at a time are a significant portion of sales as well, indicating that doughnut consumption habits are more homogeneous globally than some may believe. The company likes to mention homogeneity as a part of its "sharing concept," which is a key aspect of the firm's global marketing strategy.

In early 2014, KKD and Keurig Green Mountain Coffee agreed to create both decaf and regular Krispy Kreme coffee for Keurig coffee makers. Customers can purchase the products at both Keurig and KKD websites as well as at KKD factory stores, grocery, retail, and other channels throughout the United States. Krispy Kreme also has a new line of iced coffee. About 89 percent of all KKD's retail sales are derived from doughnuts, with the industry average closer to 50 percent of sales being derived from doughnuts. KKD is late to capitalize on selling coffee and other drinks, but the company is making efforts.

Segments

Krispy Kreme Doughnuts is broken down into (1) Company Stores, (2) Domestic Franchise, (3) International Franchise, and (4) KK Supply Chain. Company Stores and Domestic Franchise stores are similar, only differing in ownership. Both Company Stores and Domestic Franchise Stores consist of full factory stores and satellite stores. International Franchise Stores are designed the same way as Company Stores and Domestic Franchise with 125 factory stores and 449 satellite shops in foreign markets. KK Supply Chain supplies both Company and Franchise stores, which all are required to purchase its products from KK Supply Chain.

As of February 2015, there were 278 KKD stores operating domestically in 38 states and in the District of Columbia, and another 523 shops in 23 other countries around the world. The company has plans to grow international stores to 900 by January 2017.

Krispy Kreme Doughnuts' revenue by geographic region is provided in Exhibit 2. Note the nice increases everywhere except in the Other Americas.

EXHIBIT 2 KKD's Revenues by Geographic Region (in thousands of USD)

	February 2015	February 2014
United States	$438,801	$412,743
Other Americas	9,973	10,000
Asia/Pacific	28,575	25,460
Middle East & Europe	12,985	12,128
Total Revenues	**490,334**	**460,331**

Source: Based on KKD *Annual Report*, 2015, page 23.

EXHIBIT 3 KKD's Revenues by Company-Owned versus Franchise (in thousands of USD)

	Revenues		Operating Income	
	February 2015	February 2014	February 2015	February 2014
Company Stores	$325,306	$306,825	$9,287	$11,334
Domestic Franchise	13,450	11,839	8,103	8,083
International Franchise	28,598	25,607	20,026	17,977
KKD Supply Chain After Adjustments	122,980	116,060	41,823	36,953
Totals	**490,334**	**460,331**	**79,239**	**74,347**

Source: Based on KKD *Annual Report*, 2015 page 41.

Revenues and operating income by company-owned versus franchised stores are provided in Exhibit 3. Notice nice increases across the board, with international franchise lagging slightly.

Krispy Kreme Doughnuts' revenues by retail versus wholesale are provided in Exhibit 4. Note that retail sales are the highest, accounting for 49 percent of 2014 revenues. However, collectively, wholesale sales accounted for 51 percent of total revenues led by grocers and mass merchants such as Walmart at 31 percent of total sales.

Finance

The fiscal year for Krispy Kreme Doughnuts ends in February. The company had an outstanding 2013 (ending February 1, 2014) on most financial areas. The firm's stock price was up over 100 percent, revenues increased 6 percent, and the company reported a 65 percent increase in net income. Much of the increases can be attributed to opening 80 new locations around the world, but KKD also reported 6.7 percent increase in comparable store sales. The company's CEO indicated in the spring of 2014 that overseas markets remain strong for the firm, with many new store openings having long lines for up to 3 months after opening. The CFO, Douglas Muir, retired in 2015, turning the reins over to Price Cooper. Also, KKD is increasing its $80 million stock buyback to $105 million in 2015.

The company's most recent income statement and balance sheet are provided in Exhibits 5 and 6, respectively.

External Issues

The doughnut market in the United States is a $13 billion industry, with about 25 percent of sales coming from bulk doughnuts in the 1 dozen-size box and up. Another 40 percent of sales come from drinks with half of this being derived from coffee. Major rival Dunkin' Brands accounts for much of these sales with their popular coffee offerings. Yeast doughnuts account for about 10 percent of industrywide sales. Doughnut holes and other varieties account for about 10 percent. There are thousands of "mom-and-pop" doughnut and coffee shops globally.

EXHIBIT 4 KKD's Revenues by Retail versus Wholesale

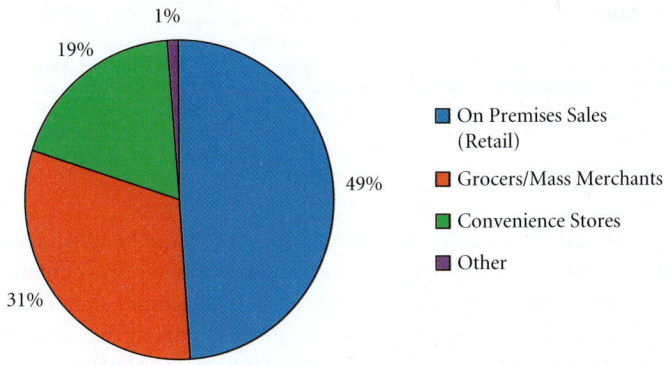

Source: Based on KKD *Annual Report*, 2014, page 44.

EXHIBIT 5 Income Statement (in millions of USD)

Report Date	February 2, 2015	February 2, 2014
Revenues	$490	$460
Operating expenses	441	413
EBIT	49	47
Interest and other benefit	0.8	1.5
EBT	48	45
Tax	18	10
Net income	**30**	**34**

Source: Based on KKD's 2015 *Annual Report*.

EXHIBIT 6 Balance Sheet (in millions of USD)

Report Date	February 2, 2015	February 2, 2014
Assets		
Cash and equivalents	$51	$56
Accounts receivable	28	25
Inventories	18	17
Deferred tax	23	23
Other current assets	8	6
Total current assets	128	127
Property, plant, & equipment	116	93
Goodwill and intangibles	30	24
Deferred tax	68	83
Other assets	11	11
Total assets	**353**	**338**
Liabilities		
Short-term debt	—	—
Accounts payable	49	17
Taxes	1	2
Other current liabilities	0	27
Total current liabilities	50	46
Long-term debt	9	2
Other liabilities	26	25
Total liabilities	**85**	**73**
Common stock	311	338
Retained earnings	(43)	(73)
Total equity	**268**	**265**
Total liabilities & equity	**353**	**338**

Source: Based on KKD's 2015 *Annual Report*, and Yahoo Finance.

Eating Healthy

Both in the United States and globally, people are becoming more health conscious in their diet and food choices. In addition, as society becomes more litigious, firms competing in the fast-food industry, including doughnut shops, have become much more mindful of product labeling and ingredients used. Low-carb diets are still extremely popular worldwide and many have even made low-carb eating a lifestyle. Some cities and other governments around the world, for example, are imposing laws that restrict portion sizes of soft drinks and other sugary-laden snack sizes. Competitors of KKD, including Dunkin' Brands and Starbucks, have already diversified their menu options to include healthier choices. However, still, when most people want a doughnut, they want it to taste good and view it as a treat, so the outlook for doughnut shops remains positive, especially outside of North America, where the market is not saturated.

Coffee Prices

Like many commodities, the price of coffee is subject to wild price fluctuations. Brazil accounts for about 40 percent of worldwide coffee production. Droughts in Brazil, fungal infections, and deforestation of the rain forest have caused prices to swing greatly. The fungal infection in 2014 accounted for $1 billion in lost revenues; coffee production could drop as much as 40 percent in the coming years. Also, a global acceptance to "fair trade" providing farmers a fair wage and educational programs for their farming efforts has also contributed to higher prices. In addition, a growing middle class in developing countries has provided upward pressure on coffee prices. In total, coffee prices doubled from 2013 to 2014. The good news for consumers is that coffee prices paid will not be felt much more than a nickel or dime per cup at a restaurant, according to most analysts.

Competitors

Top doughnut competitors are Dunkin' Brands, Tim Hortons, as well as Starbucks for coffee and other snacks. The global market looks promising for American donut firms and Canadian-based Tim Hortons. Dunkin' Brands accounts for about 54 percent of the total doughnut shop market share. Krispy Kreme and Tim Hortons each account for about 5 percent of the U.S. doughnut market share. Regarding coffee shops, Starbucks accounts for 35 percent, Dunkin' Brands for 25 percent, and Tim Hortons and KKD 2 percent each of the U.S. coffee shop market share in total revenues. Exhibit 7 shows the summary financial information for KKD and its rival firms.

Dunkin' Brands Group (DNKN)

Headquartered in Canton, Massachusetts, Dunkin' Brands is a global distributor of coffee, baked goods, and their famous ice cream served under the Baskin Robbins name brand. There are 11,000 Dunkin' Donuts restaurants in 40 states and 32 foreign countries, as well as 7,300 Baskin-Robbins restaurants in 43 states and 46 foreign countries. Many Dunkin' Donuts restaurants also contain a Baskin-Robbins within them, and all but 36 Dunkin' Donuts and Baskin-Robbins stores are franchisee owned. About two thirds of all Dunkin' restaurants in the United States have a drive-through that caters to customers, especially morning customers on their way to work. The majority of Dunkin' Donuts and Baskin-Robbins stores outside the United States are located in Asia and the Middle East, with South Korea and Japan having the most stores.

After an infusion of cash from going public with its IPO in 2011, Dunkin' started to aggressively expand within the United States and internationally, opening 700 Dunkin' Donuts and Baskin-Robbins worldwide in 2014 alone. Dunkin' is opening 65 stores in Brazil between 2014 and 2016. The company is also introducing a European flavor to over 100 restaurants that now offer soft seating areas with low tables in earthy colors and contemporary lights. Implemented in 2014 was a company rewards program that enables Dunkin' to understand its customers better and learn ways to meet their demand and desires more efficiently.

EXHIBIT 7 **Summary Financial Information for KKD versus Rival Firms**

	Krispy Kreme	Dunkin' Brands	Starbucks
# Employees	2,800	1,584	191,000
$ Net Income	30 M	176 M	2,068 M
$ Revenue	490 M	749 M	16,477 M
$ Revenue/Employee	175,000	473,000	86,000
$ EPS Ratio	0.46	1.70	1.69
Market Cap.	1.24 B	5.32 B	81.83 B

Source: Based on company documents.

With 99 percent of all Dunkin' Donuts stores under the franchisee system, most of Dunkin's revenues are derived from a 5.4 percent royalty payment franchisees pay on gross sales to the company. Baskin-Robbins franchisees pay around 5.0 percent. These numbers are U.S.-based only, as international based Dunkin' and Baskin-Robbins pay 2.1 percent and 0.7 percent royalty rates, with Baskin-Robbins stores also paying for certain ice cream products. U.S.-based stores also pay advertising fees of 5 percent of gross sales.

Financially, 2014 was a banner year for Dunkin' Brands with revenues increasing 5 percent to $748 million, buoyed by 790 new restaurants that were opened worldwide in 2013 with 439 of these outside the United States. With new additions and improving business and prospects in foreign markets, Dunkin', like KKD, also experienced a large increase in net income of around 17 percent in 2014. Also noteworthy of late is Dunkin's increases in royalty income, franchise fees, and higher margins on Baskin Robbins ice cream products.

Tim Hortons

Tim Hortons is the largest doughnut and coffee retailer in Canada. Founded in Hamilton, Ontario, in 1964, the firm sells premium coffee, espresso, teas, and many other hot and cold beverages including fruit smoothies. Food items sold include soups, sandwiches, wraps, and many other choices. The company's mainstay, however, is donuts for which the firm was founded. There are over 850 Tim Hortons locations throughout the United States. The company also offers its products in self-service kiosk machines. In 2014, the company generated over $634 million in the United States alone. Tim Hortons was recently acquired by Burger King Worldwide.

Starbucks

Starbucks is the world's largest specialty coffee retailer with over 18,000 stores in 60 different countries. In addition to offering a variety of hot and cold coffee drinks, Starbucks also offers pastries, muffins, cookies, and other dessert-type items. As of 2014, Starbucks expanded its line of products to include beer, wine, chocolate fondue, and even chicken skewers at around 40 of its locations. The company also owns Seattle's Best Coffee and Torrefazione Italia coffee brands. Customers frequently purchase Starbucks coffee and ready-made coffee drinks at grocery stores, gas stations, and department stores.

An important way Starbucks has historically differentiated itself from rivals KKD and Dunkin' Brands was by its perception as a more premium coffee offered in a variety of flavors. With Dunkin' Brands responding similarly with its product line, Starbucks is now using sales of beer, wine, and upgraded snacks and food as a means of attracting customers in the late afternoon and early evening—a time when sales are historically slower. Starbucks also maintains its position as more of a sit-down-and-relax establishment, unlike most KKD and Dunkin' Donuts stores. Starbucks has enjoyed over a 100 percent stock price increase from January 2013 to the summer 2015 and a new income increase of 50 percent from fiscal year end 2012 to fiscal year end 2014.

Future

Krispy Kreme Doughnuts is slowly shifting its focus from wholesale to more of a retail presence. Currently around 50 percent of revenues are derived from each source. However, KKD has always prided itself on hot fresh doughnuts that customers purchase directly from factory stores. As a result, the firm is building smaller-sized factory stores to better serve the retail customer directly. The company is also expanding its footprint internationally. In December 2014, KKD opened its 100th store in South Korea, a 3,200-square-foot doughnut theater facility with the full viewing area and the famous "Hot Doughnuts Now" sign. Also, in early 2015, KKD agreed with Doughnuts Café to establish 15 Krispy Kreme facilities in the greater Saint Petersburg, Russia, area by 2020.

As KKD has expanded and become a global brand, rival firms and other food-producing companies are eyeing the possibility of acquiring the company. In early 2015, Jollibee Foods Corp., based in the Philippines, was considered by many analysts to be a serious contender to purchase KKD, as Jollibee management looks to add an American-based food company to its portfolio. Between growing both domestically and internationally, moving into a more retail-focused strategy, hedging off potential takeovers, and a growing awareness of a healthy eating public, KKD needs a clear strategic plan. Devise a three-year plan for CEO Morgan moving forward.

Marriott International, Inc., 2015

www.marriott.com, MAR

Marriott International is the largest hotel company in the world with more than 4,100 properties in over 80 countries and territories around the world, over 700,000 rooms, and an additional 200,000 rooms in the development pipeline. In June 2014, Marriott opened its 4,000th hotel, the Marriott Marquis in Washington, DC, and opened its 4,200th property in the summer of 2015. The majority of rooms and properties are franchised out, with 2,673 franchised properties containing a total of 360,451 rooms. About 1,057 Marriott properties with 283,029 rooms are company-owned with long-term management agreements. In total, about 97 percent of all Marriott rooms are either managed or franchised, as the company is opposed to owning the rooms outright.

The firm's flagship brand is Marriott Hotels, designed to serve business and leisure travelers as well as meeting groups. Courtyard is another popular Marriott-owned property designed around transient business travelers. Courtyard hotels are smaller, often with 90 to 150 rooms, and upper moderately priced. Fairfield Inn & Suites are also designed for business travelers, but are priced below Courtyard. Marriott's Residents Inn is designed for extended stay customers. Marriott's Ritz Carlton hotels offer luxury accommodations.

Beginning in 2016 at many Marriott hotels you can unlock your room door with your phone, log into your Netflix account from your room television, and charge your wireless mobile device. Marriott's Q1 2015 earnings were $207 million, up from $197 million the prior quarter, while company revenues dropped slightly to $3.513 billion from $3.559 billion the previous quarter.

Copyright by Fred David Books LLC. www.strategyclub.com (Written by Forest R. David)

MyManagementLab®

For additional assurance of learning questions which prove you understand and are able to apply the strategic concepts in this case, go to the assignment section of your MyLab.

History

Marriott traces its roots to an A&W root beer stand founded by Willard Marriott and his wife Alice in 1927 in Washington, DC. The following year, the Marriotts added hot food items to their menu and the new business name became Hot Shoppes. By 1957, the business had grown large enough to become a public offering selling out of stock within 2 hours at the opening price of $10.25 per share. Using capital from the sale of stock, Marriott opened its first hotel the same year in Arlington, Virginia, with 325 rooms. The firm experienced growth in the domestic market and international market over the next two decades, even opening an additional fast-food restaurant and forming a partnership with Sun Line cruise ships.

In 1983, Marriott introduced its Courtyard properties designed for business travelers. In 1987, Marriott introduced Fairfield Inn and acquired Residence Inn and Renaissance Hotel properties. Marriott is noted for including copies of the Book of Mormon in addition to the Holy Bible in its rooms. U.S. Republican Presidential candidate Mitt Romney, a Mormon, recently reported $260,390 in director's fees from Marriott. Guinness World Records recently recognized the 5-Star JW Marriott Marquis Hotel Dubai as the world's tallest hotel. In 2013, Marriott International introduced Vacations by Marriott, the company's official travel deal website.

In 2014, Marriott began a new initiative titled "The Envelope Please" whereby its hotels leave an envelope in every room for customers to tip the housekeeper who cleans their room. Since cleaning is oftentimes performed by women working for minimum wages, tipping these individuals is a way to show your appreciation for their services. Marriott now places envelopes in 160,000 hotel rooms in the United States and Canada, urging its customers to tip the housekeepers. Roughly 750 to 1,000 hotels take part in the envelope campaign from Marriott brands such as Courtyard, Residence Inn, J. W. Marriott, Ritz-Carlton, and Renaissance hotels.

EXHIBIT 1 Marriott's Executives and Structure

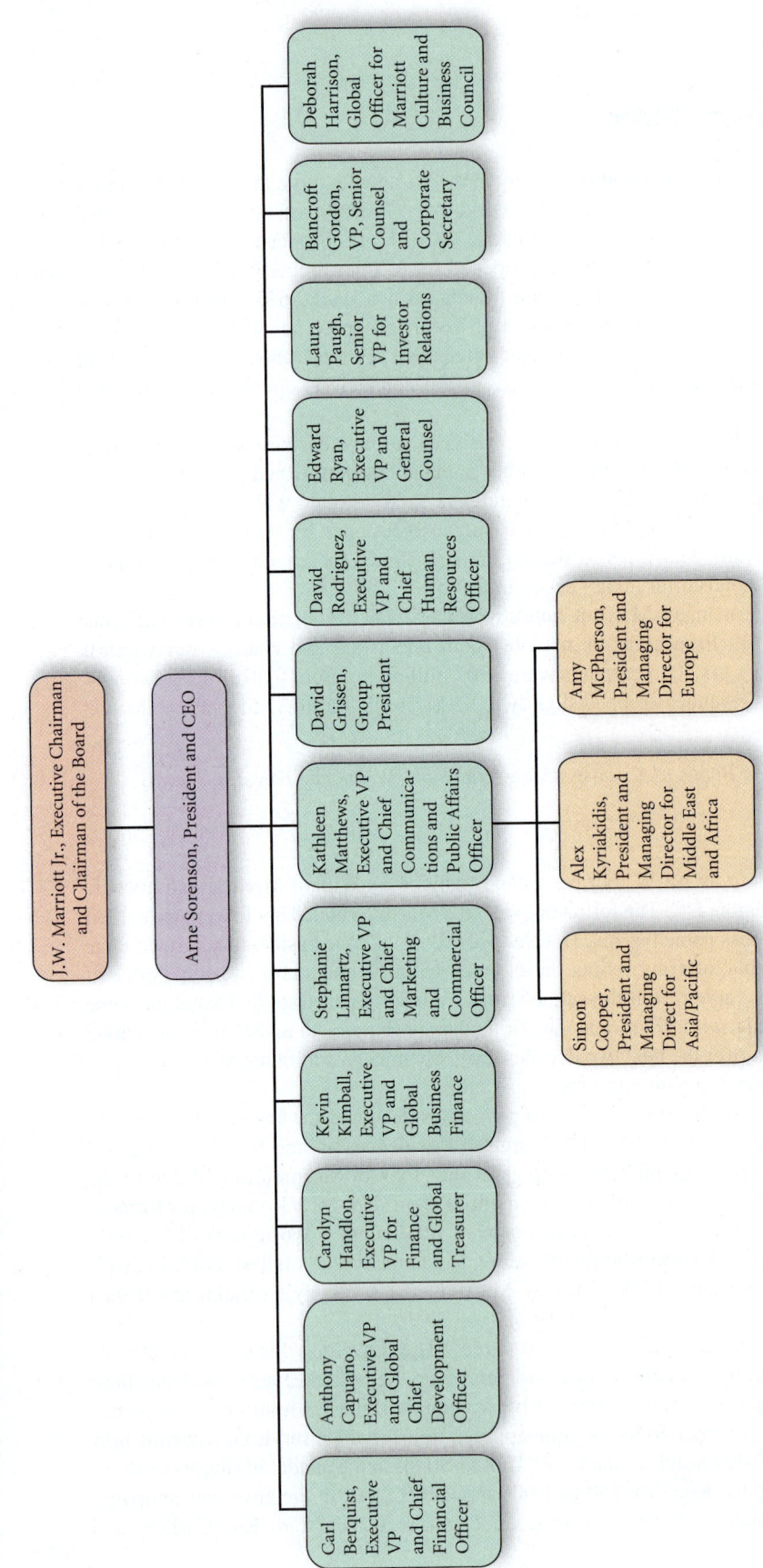

Source: Based on author's judgment as to reporting relationships.

Mission, Vision, Values

Marriott does not report a vision or mission statement. However, the firm does state its core values and the founder's philosophy. Marriott's philosophy is to "Take care of associates and they will take care of the customers." Marriott's values are as follows:

1. We put people first.
2. We pursue excellence.
3. We embrace change.
4. We act with integrity.
5. We serve our world.

Internal Issues

Exhibit 1 Organizational Structure

As illustrated in Exhibit 1, Marriott operates from a divisional-by-region organizational chart. Notice the firm has numerous female executives, consistent with its exemplary record on workplace equality.

New Policy

On January 1, 2015, Marriott, and rival Hilton Worldwide, implemented a new policy that requires customers to notify them the day before their scheduled arrival to avoid having to pay for the room. This policy reverses a long tradition of allowing customers to cancel their reservation "up to 6 pm the day of arrival without penalty." Bob Gilbert, CEO of the Hospitality Sales and Marketing Association International, a hotel industry group, said of the Marriott move: "It's not surprising. The hotel business is one of the last places where you can hold inventory with no commitment." Hotel demand in 2014–2015 has exceeded supply in many cities, giving hoteliers the upper hand. Another motivation for the new policy is hoteliers' desire to stifle the use of apps such as Yapta or HotelTonight that track hotel prices and, whenever a rate dips, apparently a growing number of travelers rebook at a lower rate and cancel the costlier reservation, literally right up until check-in time. Penny-pinching travelers are increasingly using such tools, and Marriott seeks to deter this practice. Big most rival hotels are staying the course with traveler-friendly cancellation policies.

Segment Information

Marriot provides detailed financial breakdowns based on hotel type and location, with three reporting business segments: North American Full-Service, North American Limited-Service, and International.

1. **North American Full-Service** includes *Ritz-Carlton, EDITION, Marriott Hotels, J. W. Marriott, Renaissance Hotels, Gaylord Hotels,* and *Autograph Collection Hotels.*
2. **North American Limited-Service** includes *AC Hotels by Marriott, Courtyard, Fairfield Inn & Suites, SpringHill Suites, Residence Inn,* and *TownePlace Suites.*
3. **International** includes *Ritz-Carlton, Bulgari Hotels & Resorts, EDITION, Marriott Hotels, J. W. Marriott, Renaissance Hotels, Autograph Collection, Courtyard, AC Hotels by Marriott, Fairfield Inn & Suites, Residence Inn,* and *Marriott Executive Apartments* located outside the United States and Canada.

Revenue and net income information for Marriott's various brands and businesses is provided in Exhibits 2 and 3. Note, the North American Full-Service segment has twice the revenue of the Limited-Service segment, yet the Limited-Service segment net income was slightly more in both 2012 and 2014.

Exhibit 4 reveals Marriott's hotel ownership type by percent of total properties. Note the majority of Marriott's properties are franchised.

Notable brands by property type are provided in Exhibit 5. Note Courtyard is the most common hotel by number of properties followed by Fairfield.

Marriott's properties and rooms by geographic region are reported in Exhibit 6.

EXHIBIT 2 Marriott's Revenue Data by Segments (in millions of USD)

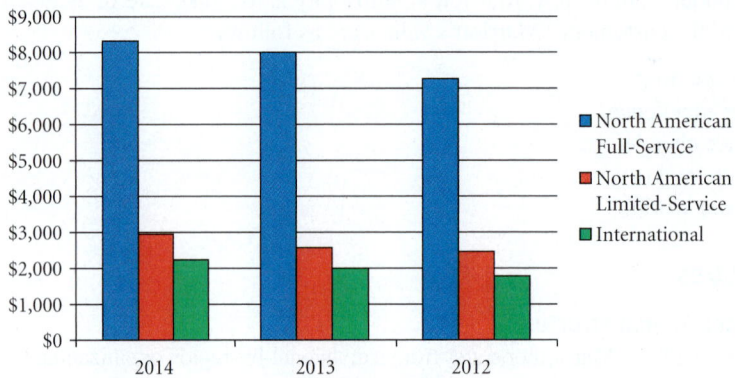

Source: Based on Marriott's 2015 *Annual Report,* p. 84.

EXHIBIT 3 Marriott's Net Income Data by Segments (in millions of USD)

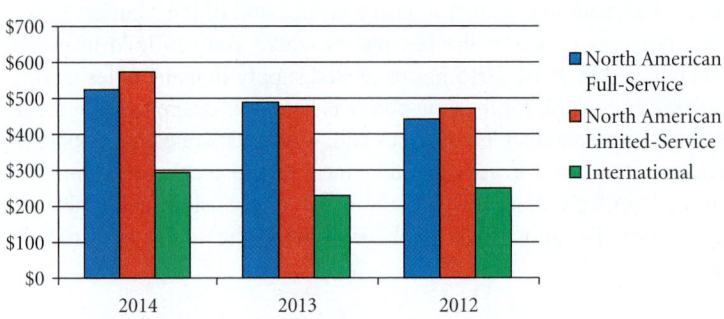

Source: Based on Marriott's 2015 *Annual Report,* p. 85.

Finance

RevPAR is "Revenue Per Available Room = Average price of room × occupancy rate × number of rooms available." In 2014, Marriott reported worldwide a RevPAR increase of 6.6 percent with a worldwide average daily price of $150.23. For 2014, Marriott reported net income of $753 million, up from $198 million in 2011. Luxury demand worldwide continues to be the strongest segment, and leisure destinations in the United States also experienced strong demand. Marriott reported that Eastern Europe, Russia, and the United Kingdom had strong demand for Marriott properties, but Western Europe only experienced moderate RevPAR growth. The company reported stronger RevPAR growth in the United Arab Emirates, Thailand, and Indonesia in 2014. Marriott's properties in China, Egypt, and other regions in Asia Pacific reported numbers average to below average on RevPAR.

Marriott's recent income statements and balance sheets are provided in Exhibits 7 and 8, respectively.

Strategy

Marriott plans to add over 5,000 hotels worldwide to its portfolio by the year 2017 with a focus on overseas markets, in particular Asia, where Marriott plans to double its exposure by 2017. The Middle East and Africa are also key areas of growth. With the recent acquisition of Protea in South Africa, Marriott expects to have a compounded growth rate of 25 percent from 2013 to 2017 in this region and also a 25 percent compounded growth rate in the Middle East over the same time frame.

EXHIBIT 4 **Marriott's Properties by Ownership Type**

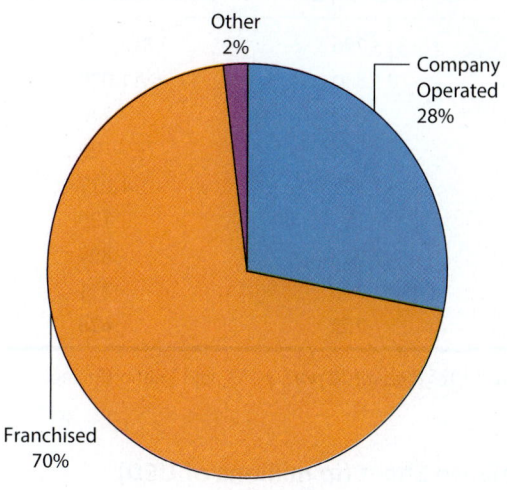

Source: Based on company documents.

EXHIBIT 5 **Marriott's Top Brand Hotels in 2014**

Courtyard	988
Fairfield Inn & Suites	721
Residence Inn	675
Marriott Hotels	499
Ritz-Carlton	131
All Others	1,079
Total	4,093

Source: Based on Marriott's 2015 *Annual Report*, p. 3.

EXHIBIT 6 **Marriott's Properties by Geographic Region**

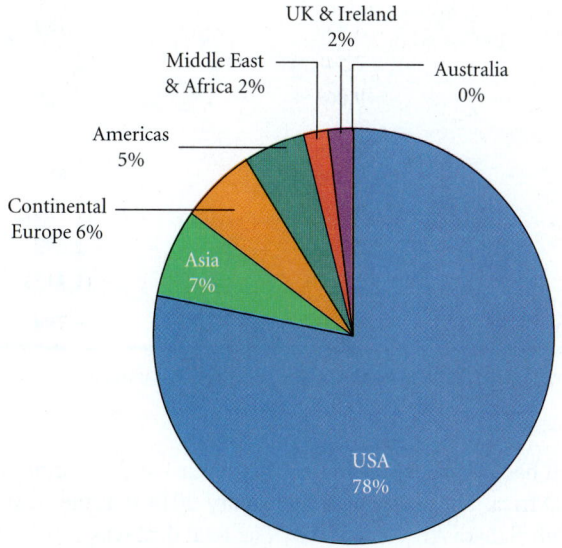

Source: Based on company documents.

EXHIBIT 7 Marriott's Income Statement (in millions of USD)

Report Date	December 31, 2014	December 31, 2013
Revenues	$13,796	$12,784
Cost of revenue	11,830	11,020
Operating expenses	807	776
Other income	44	29
EBIT	1,203	1,017
Interest and others	115	120
EBT	1,088	897
Tax	335	271
Net income	**753**	**626**

Source: Based on Marriott's 2015 *Annual Report,* p. 53, and Yahoo Finance.

EXHIBIT 8 Marriott's Balance Sheet (in millions of USD)

Report Date	December 31, 2014	December 31, 2013
Assets		
Cash and equivalents	$104	$126
Accounts receivable	1,100	1,081
Inventories	—	—
Other current assets	484	346
Assets held for sale	233	350
Total current assets	1,921	1,903
Property, plant, & equipment	1,460	1,543
Goodwill	894	874
Intangible assets	1,351	1,131
Other assets	1,239	1,343
Total assets	**6,865**	**6,794**
Liabilities		
Short-term debt	324	6
Accounts payable	605	557
Other current liabilities	2,131	2,112
Total current liabilities	3,060	2,675
Long-term debt	3,457	3,147
Other liabilities	2,548	2,387
Total liabilities	**9,065**	**8,209**
Common stock	5	5
Retained earnings	4,286	3,837
Treasury stock	(9,223)	(7,929)
Paid in capital and other	2,732	2,672
Total equity	**(2,200)**	**(1,415)**
Total liabilities & equity	**6,865**	**6,794**

Source: Based on Marriott's 2015 *Annual Report,* p. 56, and Yahoo Finance.

At year-end 2014, Marriott had 46 properties in the Middle East and in northern Africa, and 104 properties in Sub-Sahara Africa, but announced in January 2014 that the firm was adding 116 hotels in seven different Sub-Sahara African nations. The total deal was worth $187 million. Africa is a strategic focus for Marriott moving forward, citing the continent's growing middle class and higher growth rates than the United States. Africa tourism grew 6 percent in 2013 and is expected to continue at this rate over the long term. The acquisition of Protea Hospitality Group makes Marriott the largest hotel company in Africa. However, the Ebola virus outbreak in western Africa is a primary concern for Marriott.

Marriott is the largest hotel operator in Beijing and Shanghai, but not in China as a whole. The company plans to open a new hotel in China every few weeks for the next several years. Marriott is more focused on the luxury market in China, but has plans to get into the more middle-class market as this demographic in China grows.

External Issues

Technology

Hotels are rapidly developing smartphone apps to help speed up check-in for travelers, including letting customers go straight to their rooms by using their smartphone to unlock doors. In November 2014, Starwood Hotels and Resorts (HOT) became the first hotel to let guests unlock doors with their phones. The feature is available at 140 Aloft, Element, and W hotels at mid-2015. "Guests want this because it makes their lives simpler," says Mark Vondrasek, who oversees the loyalty program and digital initiatives for Starwood. "The ability to go right to your room gives them back time."

In 2013, Marriott International (MAR) launched its check-in app at 330 North American hotels last year. By the end of 2014, that Marriott app was live at all 4,000 of its hotels world-wide. When a room becomes available, a message is sent to the guest's phone. Traditional room keys are preprogrammed and waiting at the front desk. A special express line allows guests to bypass crowds, flash their IDs, and get keys. Marriott guests made $1.25 billion in bookings in 2013 through its mobile app, according to George Corbin, senior vice president of digital for the company. However, Marriott is holding off on using smartphones as keys until security issues can be resolved.

With brands Hilton, Waldorf Astoria, Conrad, and Canopy, Hilton Worldwide (H) is the second hotel chain, behind Starwood, to announce plans for mobile room keys, which it plans to roll out at the end of 2015 at some U.S. properties. Guests can use also use maps on the Hilton app to select a specific room.

Guests who like personal check-in attention, such as to ask about pool hours, restaurant hours, and so on, can still opt for the traditional check-in. Hotel companies say new technologies are not about cutting jobs. Many hotel chains desire travelers to eventually be comfortable using their mobile apps to interact, such as using an iPad, phone, or smartwatch to request a wakeup call or purchase suite upgrades, spa treatments, and room service. InterContinental Hotels Group (IGH) is testing express check-in at 60 hotels.

The top 15 hotel companies have more than 42,000 properties worldwide with a combined 5.2 million rooms, according to travel research firms STR and STR Global. Thus, some hotels have made smart app technology updates over the past few years, but they remain the minority. One reason for reluctance is security. Starwood, for example, requires the phone to actually touch a pad on the outside of the door to open it. This is to assure the guests that if there is knock on the door late at night and guests go to the peephole to see who is there, their phones in their pockets will not accidently unlock the door.

Industry Fragmentation

The overall hotel industry is quite fragmented with only around 51 percent of the total hotel market being derived from the major brand's properties. The top five hotel brand companies in the world account for only 41 percent of all branded hotels, leaving many other brands (and "mom-and-pop" hotels) divided among the remaining 59 percent of the branded hotel market. However, the future outlook appears much more positive for branded hotel companies in general, as 72 percent of hotels currently being developed belong to major hotel companies. Hotel industry fragmentation is even much more pronounced in markets outside the United States. For example, in the United States about 70 percent of all hotel rooms available are branded, leaving only 30 percent to independent operators. However, in regions such as China and India, branded penetration can be as low as 20 percent of the total rooms available. Analysts expect a great increase in branded penetration in developing markets such as China and India moving forward, as customers become more affluent, have increased disposable income, and are able to travel more. Many consumers prefer particular brands being assured generally of better security and consistency from one hotel to another of the same brand.

The overall hotel industry is also expected to see modest gains moving toward 2018, enhanced by limited (but positive) supply growth, an improving economy, higher room rates, and a willingness for both businesses and individuals to travel. A key area of revenue growth for hotels is add-on fees, much like airlines charge. Hotel fees have doubled in the last 10 years with luxury hotels often charging the lion's share of the industry's total fees. Internet and mini-bars have historically been prone to fees, but in addition now, business centers, in-room safes, and even mandatory valet parking are being added at some hotels to help improve the bottom line.

Different Business Models

Different firms in the hotel industry operate under some combination of four general business models that are (1) owned, (2) leased, (3) managed model, or (4) franchised. Hilton even structures its operations under the four models, whereas Marriott structures are based more on geographic region. Most all hotel firms provide segment data for both ownership type and geographic region breakdowns. Owned hotels are majority or even 100 percent owned by the parent company. Under the leased model, common in large cities, the major hotel brand leases space but otherwise has total control over hotel operations. The managed model consists of a third-party manager operating the hotel on the parent company's behalf. In return, the branded hotel pays the manager fees, usually based on some combination of revenues and profits. Finally, a franchised hotel is owned and operated by an individual or group of individuals who benefit from the brand name of the company, yet have the luxury of owning and operating their own business. The individuals who run the hotel are required to pay franchise fees and usually a percentage of sales to the major brand company. Hotel brands enjoy franchising to third parties, as this drastically reduces initial capital. However, reduced risks in initial capital can be offset by loss of quality control in franchised properties.

Industry Growth Globally

The hotel industry as a whole enjoyed 4.4 percent overall RevPAR growth in 2013, but growth rates varied greatly between different regions and price points. The top-grossing region was the Americas, with RevPAR growing 6.6 percent attributed mostly to hotels being able to charge higher prices. Higher-end segments also enjoyed much better RevPAR numbers than middle- or lower-tier hotel properties.

Growth in the Eurozone lagged many other global regions with industrywide RevPAR of only 3.2 percent in 2013 with hotel rooms available increasing only 0.9 percent. RevPAR in the InterContinental home market of the U.K. increased 3.9 percent. Germany was a laggard in Europe, only reporting an increase in RevPAR of 1.7 percent.

Asia, Middle East, and Africa (AMEA) enjoyed an overall RevPAR of 6.1 percent. This region does not have the number of developed hotels as other regions; therefore, the numbers are a bit misleading because it is easier to achieve a higher percent gain when working off an initial revenue base much less than that of Europe and the United States. The 6.1 percent increase in RevPAR was buoyed by a 5 percent growth in the average daily rate charged and an increase in total hotel rooms of 2.6 percent. The Middle East and South East Asia enjoyed the largest percent gains of RevPAR at 11.4 and 7.9 percent, respectively. The Middle East numbers are especially impressive considering the ongoing civil unrest the region has experienced recently. Hotel rooms available increased by 4.6 percent in India in 2013, but demand did not rise as fast, resulting in a decrease of RevPAR of 3.3 percent.

The hotel industry in China experienced a similar pattern as India in 2013, with an increase in available hotel rooms of 4.6 percent resulting in prices dropping 3.1 percent and total RevPAR falling 4.2 percent. Analysts blame not only the increase in available rooms but also the slowest growth in China this millennium at only 7.7 percent GDP in 2013. With a large population, a growing middle-class population, and China's growing tourism, the long-term outlook remains positive for China's hotel industry.

Competitors

Many thousands of hotel/motels compete for travelers' dollars. Some major rival firms to Marriott are InterContinental, Wyndham Worldwide, Hilton Hotels, Accor S.A., Best Western, Choice Hotels, and Starwood Hotels & Resorts. Exhibit 9 provides a comparison of Marriott and two other competitors, and Exhibit 10 provides additional data regarding some competitors.

EXHIBIT 9 Marriott versus Rival Firms

	Marriott	Hilton	Starwood
# Fulltime Employees	123,000	152,000	180,000
$ Net Income	$753 M	$673	$633 M
$ Revenue	$13,795 M	$10,502 M	$5,983 M
$ Revenue/Employee	$112,000	$69,000	$33,200
$ EPS Ratio	$2.35	$0.56	$3.41
Market Cap.	$23.5 B	$27.9 B	$13.86 B

Source: The creation of this table is based on Yahoo Finance and company websites.

Note in Exhibit 9 that Marriott leads both Hilton and Starwood on both total revenues and net income. Starwood has a significantly higher earnings-per-share (EPS) ratio but trails both rivals on market capitalization.

Hotel occupancy rates vary by location. Hotels located in urban areas and airports tend to have higher occupancy rates than other areas, such as resorts and suburban and highway properties. These properties benefit from both tourism and business travel. Exhibit 11 provides the 2013 occupancy rates for hotels in the United States based on quality of hotel property. Note that higher-end hotels, at least in the United States, enjoyed higher occupancy rates in 2013, with the

EXHIBIT 10 Marriott and Rival Firms Number of Properties and Rooms

Parent Firm	Major Brands	Number of Properties	Number of Rooms
InterContinental	InterContinental, Holiday Inn, Crowne Plaza	4,700	687,000
Marriott International	Marriott, Courtyard Residence Inn, Fairfield Inn, Renaissance	3,900	360,450
Wyndham Worldwide	Days Inn, Ramada, Super 8, Travelodge	7,350	627,000
Hilton Hotels	Hilton, DoubleTree, Embassy Suites, Hampton Inn, Waldorf Astoria and Conrad	4,000	678,000
Starwood Hotels & Resorts	Sheraton, Westin	1,200	350,000

Source: Based on information at S&P Survey 2014.

EXHIBIT 11 USA Hotel Occupancy Rates in 2013 by Property Type

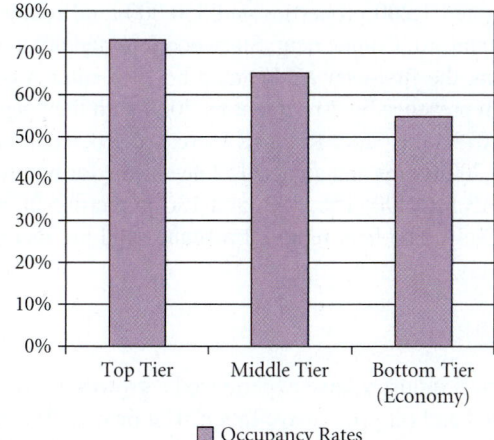

Source: Based on information at S&P Survey.

most luxurious hotels (average rate over $200) enjoying the highest occupancy rates of all. The overall trend toward higher-end hotels and occupancy rates was similar in international markets as well. Generally, top tier, middle tier, and bottom tier are considered to be hotels with prices over $120, $85, and below $60, respectively.

Hilton Worldwide Holdings (HLT)

Headquartered in McLean, Virginia, Hilton is a large worldwide hotel chain with 10 brand names and properties in 91 countries. Hilton operates and/or franchises 4,000 hotels and timeshares with over 678,000 rooms and around 40 million customers in its rewards program; it employs over 150,000. Hilton's vision is "to fill the earth with the light and warmth of hospitality" and its mission is "To be the preeminent global hospitality company—the first choice of guests, team members, and owners alike." Notable properties Hilton operates include Waldorf Astoria and Conrad in the luxury segment, Hilton, Double Tree, and Embassy Suites in the Full-Service line, and Hilton Garden Inn, Hampton, Homewood Suites, and Home 2 in the Focused-Service segment.

Hilton's three primary business segments for Hilton are (1) ownership, (2) management and franchise, and (3) timeshare. Year-end financial results were $4,075 million with EBIT of $926 million, $1,271 million with EBIT of $1,271 million, and $1,109 million with EBIT of 297 million for each of the three segments, respectively. Hilton reported overall net income of $415 million in 2013, up from $253 million just two years earlier. However, Hilton reported net income of $673 million in 2014, up 62 percent from 2013, while revenues increased 8 percent to $10,502 million.

InterContinental Hotels Group plc (IHG)

Headquartered in Denham, United Kingdom, InterContinental is world famous for its InterContinental flagship branded hotel. The company's brands include Hotel Indigo, Crowne Plaza, Holiday Inn, Holiday Inn Express, EVEN, and several others. The firm's rewards program is considerably larger than that of rival Hilton, with over 77 million members worldwide. The company owns, leases, or franchises over 4,700 hotels with over 687,000 rooms in 100 different nations around the world. In 2013, InterContinental opened an additional 237 properties and signed contracts to put 444 more in the pipeline. Key markets moving forward for InterContinental are the United States, the Middle East, Germany, the U.K., Canada, Greater China, India, Russia, Mexico, and Indonesia. Intercontinental reports earnings based on geographic region and broken down further by company-owned versus franchised-owned by each geographic segment.

Starwood Hotels and Resorts Worldwide (HOT)

Starwood operates luxury hotels, full-service hotels, resorts, select-service hotels, and extended-stay hotels under a variety of brand names, but the company primarily focuses on upper-end hotel offerings. Branded hotels by Starwood include the W, Westin, Le Meridien, Sheraton, Four Points, Aloft, and Element. Starwood is expanding its footprint with both management and franchise contracts; it doubled its international footprint between 2008 and 2013. As of March 2014, the hotel owned and operated 1,200 properties and 350,000 total rooms in 100 different countries. Headquartered in Stamford, Connecticut, Starwood reported net income of $635 million in 2013. Starwood is building the first-ever Aloft brand hotel to enter Australia by 2016 and will expand its Latin American presence by 20 percent by 2016 with the opening of 17 new hotels in that region. Starwood's 2013 same-store RevPAR increased 5 percent and the company opened 74 new hotels totaling 16,200 rooms and signed 152 new deals for hotels—the most since 2007. Starwood at year-end 2013 had 590, 158, 133, and 130 properties in North America, Europe, Asia, and China, respectively. The firm reported revenues and net income of $5,983 and $633 million in 2014, respectively.

Future

Marriott and the entire travel industry have experienced a growth in sales as the economy in the United States has improved and oil prices have fallen. The firm in 2015 announced plans to buy back 25 million shares or around 9 percent of total shares outstanding. Marriott also announced in January 2015 that it plans to buy Canadian-based Delta Hotels and Resorts for $125 million. The acquisition of Delta Hotels is in line with Marriott's plans to expand internationally; however, the firm is mostly focused on emerging markets. In 2015, CEO Sorenson reiterated these plans in particular to India, where the firm currently operates 24 hotels with plans to operate 50 by 2020. Currently, Marriott has 40 hotels in the long-term pipeline for India; however, infrastructure issues continue to hamper expansion into India as rapidly as Marriott and other rivals would like. In addition to India, Marriott has 150 properties in Asia (not including China or India), with more than 200 in the pipeline. Chinese properties currently total 70, with more than 80 additional hotels scheduled to be operating by 2020. Marriott is opening a hotel every two weeks in China, and plans to increase the number of its properties in the Middle East and Africa by 75 percent and Latin America by 50 percent through 2020.

Currently many emerging markets are struggling and the strong dollar hurts overseas sales that are converted back to dollars. There are also many regions of the world in which Marriott and rivals would like to position their properties. Help CEO Sorenson develop a three-year strategic plan moving forward that most effectively uses Marriott's resources.

Wynn Resorts Limited, 2015

www.wynnresorts.com, WYNN

Headquartered in Paradise, Nevada, Wynn Resorts is a large upscale casino with properties in Las Vegas and Macau. Wynn's properties offer many high-end gaming options and world-class entertainment through shows, shopping, spas, dining, and more. Wynn's Las Vegas properties include Wynn and Encore, which offer nightclubs, a beach club, Ferrari and Maserati dealerships, and even a golf course. Wynn Resorts has 4,748 hotel rooms in Las Vegas and 1,008 rooms in Macau. Wynn Macau (located on an island just off the coast of Hong Kong) has an agreement with the Chinese government to use 51 acres of land in the Cotai area of Macau to build an exclusive $4 billion resort. Wynn expects the project to be completed in the first half of 2016. The company owns 72 percent of its Chinese operations and employs 16,500. However, gambling revenue in Macau fell 2.6 percent in 2014 to 351.5 billion patacas ($44 billion USD), the first decline in Macau since 2002. December 2014 gambling revenues in Macau dropped a record 30 percent from a year earlier to 23.29 billion patacas. Wynn generates much of its revenue from premium customers who gamble on credit. Its lax credit policy leaves the firm at a higher credit risk than rival firms. All Macau companies are struggling, primarily due to a crackdown on corruption in China and that country's tighter visa policies, which undermined gambling in Macau.

Copyright by Fred David Books LLC. www.strategyclub.com (Written by Forest R. David)

History

Wynn Resorts traces its history back to 2002 when Mr. Steve Wynn and Japanese billionaire Kazuo Okada agreed to terms on the Wynn Resort property in Las Vegas. The two purchased the Desert Inn for $270 million and had its IPO the same year, a full three years before the Wynn opened its doors for business. Three other properties followed with Wynn Macau, Encore in Las Vegas, and the Encore in Macau opening their doors in 2006, 2009, and 2010, respectively. The Wynn Macau property's construction began over a year before the Wynn Las Vegas opened for business. In September 2014, the Massachusetts Gaming Commission voted to approve Wynn Resorts' proposed $1.6 billion casino to be located in Everett, Massachusetts, just north of Boston.

For Q3 of 2014, Wynn's revenues from its Las Vegas operations increased 9 percent year-over-year to $427.8 million, due to higher casino and room revenues. Casino revenues increased 10.5 percent from the prior-year period, while room revenues were up 7.2 percent to $102.5 million. Wynn reports its Macau table games results under two categories: the VIP segment and the mass market segment. For Q3 of 2014, Wynn Macau's revenues declined 5.6 percent year-over-year to $942.3 million, owing to a decline in revenues generated from the VIP market. Wynn's overall Q3 2014 results were good, so the company increased its quarterly dividend by 20 percent, and approved an additional cash dividend of $1.00 per share.

Internal Issues

Wynn's organizational structure is found in Exhibit 1. The company has two primary reporting segments: Las Vegas and Macau. There is substantial duplication of titles in the firm's structure, including two different executives with the title president of Wynn Macau. Top management is well compensated, with Steven Wynn's reported annual salary being $19 million, and the top 6 other executives' salary plus options ranging between $5 and $9 million.

Vision/Mission

The authors could not find either a vision or mission statement for Wynn Resorts.

Strategy

CEO Steve Wynn has excellent expertise in developing and operating high-quality casino properties. Wynn employees are thoroughly trained to provide guests with the luxury service they expect. An extensive reward system also attracts and keeps guests returning. The

EXHIBIT 1 Wynn Resorts' Organizational Structure

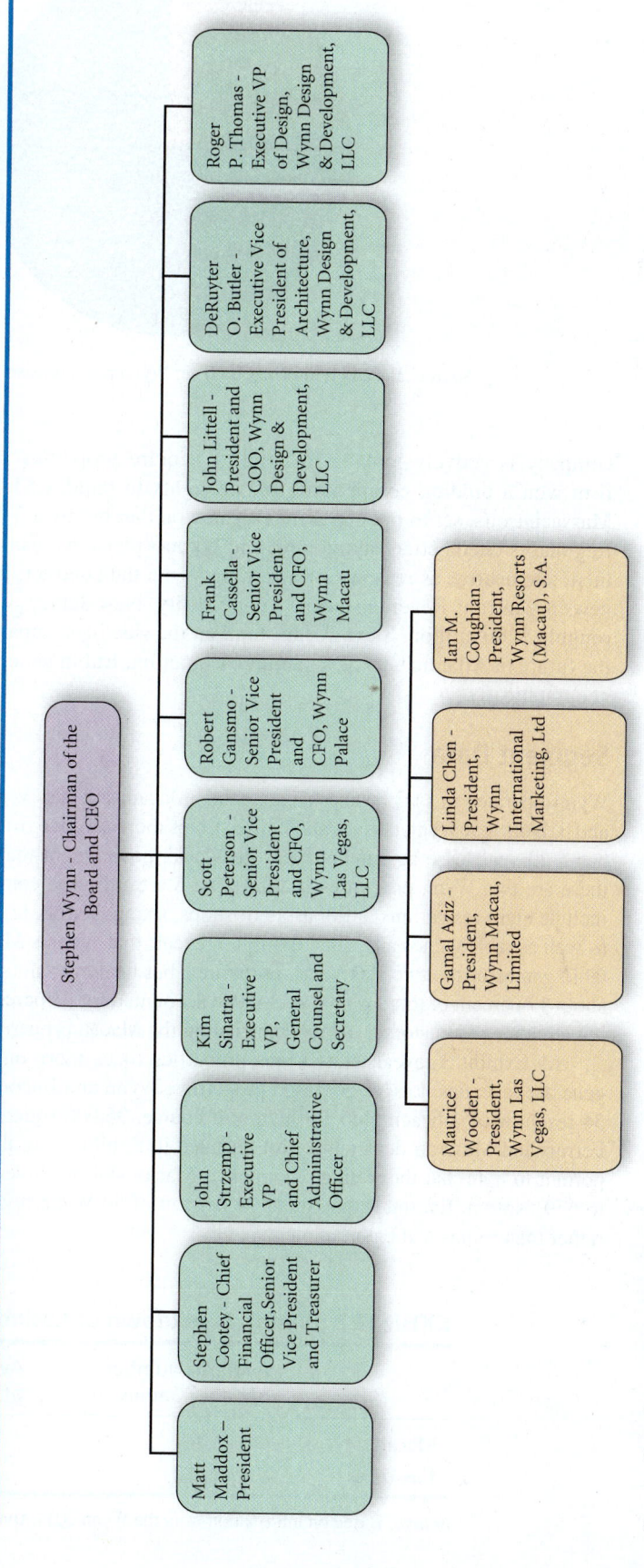

Source: Based on company documents.

EXHIBIT 2 Wynn's 2014 Operating Income by Location

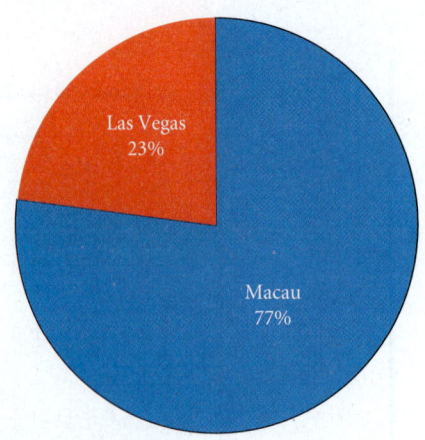

Source: Based on information from Wynn press release 2015.

company is actively looking to build or acquire properties in new markets. In 2013, the firm won a bidding competition for the rights to build a $1.6 billion casino near Boston, Massachusetts, set to open in 2017. Wynn won that bid by a 3-1 vote over the Mohegan Sun. Regulators cited better-paying jobs, and Wynn's plans to clean up an industrial land development site nearby, as reasons for awarding Wynn the contract. Interestingly, as the $2 billion, new, oceanfront Revel casino in Atlantic City, New Jersey, was auctioned off in 2014 for roughly $200 million, Steve Wynn stood on the sidelines, apparently having no confidence in the future of Atlantic City as a gaming destination. But in general, Wynn is looking to expand geographically.

Segment Data

Wynn operates in two business segments—Macau and Las Vegas—as revealed in Exhibits 2 and 3. Note that Wynn derives about three times more revenue from Macau than Las Vegas. Wynn has a 20-year lease agreement with the Macau government that runs through 2022. Currently there are two Wynn properties in Macau with a third to be completed in 2016. The properties include eight restaurants, a full array of shops, spa, poker pit, high-end private gambling salons, as well as table games and slots. Exhibit 3 reveals that Wynn's Macau properties have double the table games of the two Las Vegas properties, but far fewer slots. Macau properties account for about 17 percent of total rooms, yet Macau accounted for 61 percent of revenues in 2013, reflecting a higher end customer on average visiting the Macau properties.

As Exhibit 3 reveals, Las Vegas properties focus more on slot than Macau properties to generate revenues. Las Vegas based properties, Wynn and Encore, have a total of 3 night clubs, 34 restaurants, a beach club, 18-hole golf course, 96,000 square feet of high-end shops, and a Ferrari and Maserati dealership. Not revealed in Exhibit 3 are the data from 2013, but it is important to note that the average number of Macau slot machines declined 21 percent from 866 to 679. Note in Exhibit 4 that about 79 percent of all Wynn revenues are derived from gaming rather than rooms and entertainment.

EXHIBIT 3 Wynn's Breakdown of Casino Properties

	Average Number of Table Games	Average Number of Slots
Macau	461	679
Las Vegas	232	1,858

Source: Based on information from the Wynn 2014 *Annual Report*, p. 44.

EXHIBIT 4 **Product Revenues (in millions of USD)**

	2014	2013	2012
Casino	$4,274	$4,490	$4,035
Rooms	543	492	480
Entertainment and retail	401	419	417
Food and beverage	605	587	588
(Promotional allowances)	(369)	(367)	(366)
Total revenues	5,434	5,621	5,154

Source: Based on information from Wynn press release, 2015.

Finance

Wynn Resorts is engaged in developing the Wynn Palace Project on the Cotai land in Macau. The opening of this new casino was scheduled ahead of the Chinese New Year in February 2016, however, it has been reportedly postponed owing to a delay in timing of permits and will open sometime later in the first half of 2016. Currently, the company expects the project to cost around $4.1 billion. The company spent around $428.7 million on the Cotai project in the quarter.

For Q4 of 2014, Wynn Resorts' revenues from Las Vegas operations declined 5.8 percent year over year to $376.8 million due to a decline in casino revenues. Net casino revenues fell 15.5 percent from the prior-year period to $171.0 million. Table games win percentage was 24 percent. However, room revenues were up 6.3 percent to $95.5 million, due to improved average daily rate and occupancy rate. During Q4 2014, RevPAR was up 7.2 percent.

For all of 2014, Wynn's earnings per share were $7.58, down 0.8 percent year over year. Revenues were $5.43 billion, down 3.3 percent year over year. Wynn's recent income statement is provided in Exhibit 5, and the company's balance sheet is provided in Exhibit 6.

Competitors

Wynn competes with Caesars Entertainment and MGM Resorts in Las Vegas, and competes with Las Vegas Sands in both Las Vegas and Macau. Caesars and MGM have hotels around the United States and are larger than Wynn, based on total U.S. revenues. Growth expected in the U.S. gaming industry is projected to be close to 2 percent from 2015 to 2019, a slight increase from the 1.5 percent growth rate from 2010 to 2014. Competition is fierce, however—not only between rival firms but also between local and state governments, and with online gaming companies. In 2014 alone, 4 casinos shut down in Atlantic City, partly blamed for new casinos opening in neighboring Philadelphia, Baltimore, and West Virginia, drastically reducing the number of persons driving to Atlantic City to gamble.

Especially in areas with many casinos, like Las Vegas or Atlantic City, casino companies are have to continually update their properties, amenities, and games. New slot machines that are cashless, larger gambling promotions, larger jackpot prizes, and other strategies are being used to

EXHIBIT 5 **Wynn's Income Statement (in millions of USD)**

Report Date	December 31, 2014	December 31, 2013
Revenues	$5,433	$5,620
Operating expenses	4,159	4,334
EBIT	1,274	1,286
Interest	315	299
EBT	959	987
Tax	4	18
Other items	(223)	(240)
Net income	**732**	**729**

Source: Based on Wynn's 2014 *Annual Report,* p. 70, and Yahoo Finance.

EXHIBIT 6 Wynn's Balance Sheet (in millions of USD)

Report Date	December 31, 2014	December 31, 2013
Assets		
Cash and equivalents	2,422	$2,609
Accounts receivable	238	242
Inventories	72	75
Other current assets	50	43
Assets held for sale	—	—
Total current assets	2,782	2,969
Property, plant, & equipment	5,856	4,934
Goodwill	—	—
Intangible assets	112	31
Other assets	312	443
Total assets	**9,062**	**8,377**
Liabilities		
Short-term debt	—	$1
Accounts payable	303	273
Taxes	137	211
Other current liabilities	873	970
Total current liabilities	1,313	1,455
Long-term debt	7,345	6,588
Deferred income taxes	25	14
Other liabilities	169	188
Minority interest	239	317
Total liabilities	**9,091**	**8,562**
Common stock	1	1
Retained earnings	164	66
Treasury stock	(1,145)	(1,143)
Paid in capital and other	951	891
Total equity	**(29)**	**(185)**
Total liabilities & equity	**9,062**	**8,377**

Source: Based on Wynn's 2014 *Annual Report,* p. 69, and Yahoo Finance.

attract customers. The casino hotel industry also faces competition from external players such as racetracks and riverboats. Although American citizens can still easily gamble online, the United States has legislated against such operations, though many of these casinos are often based in the Caribbean. Lotteries are also a competitor in the industry.

Exhibit 7 reveals that both Caesars and MGM reported negative net income and have significantly lower market caps than Wynn.

Caesars Entertainment Corporation (CZR)

Headquartered in Las Vegas, Caesars is one of the largest casino companies in the world with brand names including Harrah's, Caesars, Bally's, Rio, and Horseshoe. The firm employs 70,000 worldwide, with notable properties in Las Vegas, Atlantic City, New Orleans, Mississippi, several other states, and the London Clubs International family of casinos. The company operates in three main geographic segments: (1) Las Vegas, accounting for 40 percent of domestic revenues, (2) Atlantic City, and (3) an "Other," focusing on properties in states mostly bordering the Mississippi River.

Caesars also manages several Native American casinos. In total, Caesars controls about 13 percent of the total U.S. market share and reported worldwide revenues in Q3 of 2014 to be $1.395 billion, up 0.3 percent from the prior year-over-year period. However, the company's net

EXHIBIT 7 **A Comparative Analysis of Wynn versus Rival Firms**

	Wynn	Las Vegas Sands	Caesars	MGM
# Employees	16,800	48,500	68,000	50,000
$ Net Income	732 M	2,306 M	(2,948 M)	(156 M)
$ Revenue	5,433 M	13,770 M	8,560 M	9,809 M
$ Revenue/Employee	323,000	284,000	125,882	196,180
$ EPS Ratio	7.18	3.52	(25)	0.30
$ Market Cap.	16 B	48 B	1.5 B	10.6 B

Source: Based on various company reports.

income for that Q3 was negative $908 million, compared to a negative $761 million the prior year-over-year period. Caesars is having to spend excessively to modernize outdated Las Vegas properties. As of October 2014, Caesars and its lenders were negotiating terms to provide a path for Caesars to de-leverage and more effectively pay off its debt.

MGM Resorts International (MGM)

MGM is one of the largest hotel casino corporations in the world, with an 11 percent market share in the United States. Originally named MGM Mirage, the firm changed its name to MGM Resorts International in 2010 to better reflect its strategy of international expansion. MGM primarily still operates in Las Vegas, but also has properties along the Mississippi Gulf Coast, in Detroit, and in Macau. Unlike Caesars, which has recently been remodeling many of its properties, MGM is known for continually investing in properties to keep them up-to-date. The firm earns around 43 percent of sales from gaming activities and 57 percent from hotels, food, and entertainment. In late 2014, MGM was allowed to reclaim its 50 percent stake in the Atlantic City-based Borgata, after its share was held in a trust since 2010 awaiting a potential buyer. To diversify its assets, MGM recently purchased a $400 million stake for a 55 percent share in Mark Burnett's Ventures. Mr. Burnett has produced such television shows as *Survivor, The Bible, Shark Tank,* and *The Apprentice,* among others.

Las Vegas Sands (LVS)

The Las Vegas Sands accounts for about 4 percent of the hotel casino industry in the United States and has an overall profile most similar to the Wynn than any other casino corporations. Top properties of the Sands include The Venetian, The Palazzo, and The Sands casinos in Las Vegas. Total Vegas properties include 7,100 rooms and over 225,000 square feet of gaming space. In Macau, the Las Vegas Sands operates the Sands Macau, the Venetian Macau, and the Four Seasons Macau. The Sands reported 2013 revenues of $13.8 billion, up 45 percent from two years prior.

Interestingly, the Las Vegas Sands was in discussion with the government in Spain to build a "EuroVegas" project for $30 billion in Madrid, but it was cancelled in December 2013 due to disagreements between the Spanish government and the Sands. The Sands also recently paid $47 million to the U.S. government to settle a money-laundering case. Even though the settlement is not large in relation to the Sands finances, the settlement has caused the Sands to work diligently to strengthen their compliance globally.

External Issues

Internet Gaming and Poker

Online gambling is currently legal in Nevada, Delaware, New Jersey, and Washington, DC. The industry is expected to generate annual revenues of $10 billion by 2017. The market is primarily focused on 25- to 35-year-old customers. To facilitate entering the market, the top firms, such as MGM and Caesars, have acquired online gaming firms that produce apps for use on phones and tablets. Competitors such as PokerStars, Full Tilt Poker, and Absolute Poker pose a risk to traditional casinos with their online operations. However, in 2011, the United States Federal Government shut the sites down on the basis of fraud. But in 2012, a U.S. judge in New York ruled that Texas Holdem Poker is more of a game of skill than luck, and running Texas Holdem

Poker games technically does not violate any U.S. gambling laws. The ruling only legally applies for the judge's district, but it does serve as a precedent, and could open the door for possibly online gambling returning, or even smaller "mom-and-pop" physical poker locations.

Industry Outlook

About 85 percent of Americans now say gambling is an acceptable activity; this increasing approval rate should help the industry moving forward. Wynn relies on middle-class Americans, but targets upscale clients—more so than any rival firm. Outside the United States, there is fierce competition for high-end customers in Macau, Dubai, and Singapore. With the high-end market in Macau, table games tend to be the largest driver of casino operations, exceeding all other forms of gaming, as well as revenue from food, rooms, and other entertainment provided. The annual growth rates from Asia's middle-class customers have exceeded U.S. growth rates in each year from 2010 to 2014. However, high-end customers remain a top priority, even in the U.S. market with 30 percent of U.S. industrywide revenue coming from households with $150,000 or more in income. With household incomes between $35,000 to $99,000, middle-class customers comprise about 46 percent of total U.S. casino revenues. High-stakes gamblers comprise about 22 percent of worldwide casino revenues.

The first half of 2014 saw revenues 5 percent below revenues for the same prior period in Macau, but revenues on the Las Vegas strip were up 4 percent from the first half of 2013 to the first half of 2014. A revitalization of the Las Vegas strip may be near, as casinos are updating their offerings and Australian Billionaire James Packer announced a new 34-acre project along the Las Vegas strip to be finished in 2018.

In the United States, slot machines, poker machines, and various other gaming machines account for 55 percent of industrywide revenue, while table games account for 15 percent and accommodations account for 11 percent of industrywide revenues. However, the percentages depend on location. In Iowa and South Dakota, for example, slot revenues can be in excess of 90 percent of casino revenues, because most of these customers are drive-in folks with a limited budget, thereby making slots an attractive choice for their entertainment dollars. The Las Vegas strip now receives over 60 percent of its revenue from nongaming activities such as food, drinks, shopping, and shows. Many customers in Las Vegas visit for reasons other than primarily to gamble. There is also a growing trend among younger customers to favor table games over slots. Younger customers also value nongaming amenities like bars, clubs, shopping, and food. According to the American Gaming Association, about 34 percent of Americans visit casinos annually.

Industrywide Revenue Volatility

The hotel casino industry has relatively stable revenues, regardless of the economy. Caesars, for example, experienced revenue increases of 6 percent between 2011 and 2013, and Wynn Resorts revenues increased 7 percent over the same time period. Overall, the U.S. casino hotel market saw annual revenue increases of only 0.5 percent between 2010 and 2014. Several reasons cited as to why revenues are relatively stable include (1) high-stakes gamblers are not affected by the economy to the same degree as smaller-stakes gamblers, (2) people with a gambling problem are likely to gamble regardless, and (3) many tourists still desire to gamble while on vacation.

Gambling Regulations

The casino industry is a highly regulated industry in the United States as well as internationally. States have jurisdiction in the country to regulate or even prohibit the practice. Currently, the only two states with gambling allowed statewide are Nevada and Louisiana. In total, 17 American states have legally operating casinos, including states with riverboat casinos. Kansas recently opened 4 casinos operated by the Kansas Lottery, and Massachusetts has recently accepted the bid from Wynn Resorts to open a casino near Boston. The high degree of regulation is a burden for firms like Wynn, MGM, and Caesars from expanding into other possible gaming locations such as Myrtle Beach, South Carolina, where casinos are prohibited.

Nevada accounts for about 50 percent of casino hotels in the United States and earns nearly 30 percent of U.S. casino revenues. Las Vegas first opened casinos in the 1930s and enjoyed nearly 50 years of uncontested market space, until Atlantic City's first casino in 1978. In the last 40 years however, many states have added casinos, including American Indian reservations, putting increased pressure on Las Vegas in addition to large international markets like Dubai, Macau, and Singapore. For example, Pennsylvania now accounts for 8 percent of total U.S. casino revenues, mostly from slot machines, and future projections predict New York and Massachusetts as significant players as casinos are set to soon open in these states. Florida has casinos, as does Mississippi and North Carolina.

Macau Developments

Macau overtook the Las Vegas Strip in 2006 as the world's largest casino market. Macau gaming revenues increases were 58, 42, 13, and 19 percent from 2010 to 2013, respectively. However, in 2014, Macau revenues declined by 2 percent. The long-term outlook for Macau is positive because of the growing middle class in China, but the slowdown has some industry experts pointing to Las Vegas as a new profit driver. Nevertheless, casino revenues in Macau in 2013 were seven times that of the Las Vegas strip. Part of the slowdown in Macau during 2014 was blamed on a Chinese crackdown on corruption on the mainland, as well as pro-democracy political unrest in Hong Kong. Macau is a one-hour ferry ride from Hong Kong. Also dragging down Macau casinos are tighter visa policies for Chinese people traveling to Macau, increased oversight on UnionPay cards many gamblers use to access funds in Macau, new smoking restrictions, and China's crackdown on corruption has prompted high-rollers to shy away from Macau.

In 2014, Macau experienced over a 6 percent decline in revenue from the same time period in 2013. Macau has heavily relied on junkets to bring high-rolling customers to Macau from mainland China. The Chinese government limits the amount of money that can leave the mainland, so the junkets serve as an intermediary, arranging to take high-rollers to Macau, loan them credit, and collect on the credit once back in China. Many of the junket organizers are speculated to be associated with organized crime as well, and many casinos—such as Las Vegas Sands and Wynn Resorts—have refused to do business with several junket outfits, and require extensive background checks on others suspected of organized crime.

A new $5 billion bridge linking Hong Kong to Macau will cut travel time from over an hour (and in some cases, 4 hours) to only 40 minutes, saving a 40-mile ferry ride. The bridge should be completed in 2016. Other infrastructure improvements such as rapid transit rails from highly populated areas to Macau, and upgrades to the airport to double its capacity by 2017, should bode well for casino properties in Macau, practically the Cotai Strip area of Macau, which will see a new Wynn property and MGM property open in 2016.

Japan is a potential new gaming industry player in the Asia region moving forward. Ahead of the 2020 Olympics, Japan is aggressively seeking legislation to legalize gambling.

Future

Wynn Resorts concluded its fourth quarter of 2014 with a 32 and 5.8 percent decrease in revenues from fourth quarter 2013 in Macau and Las Vegas, respectively—blamed on a poor economy and a government crackdown on high-end gambling in China. A new smoking ban proposed in 2015 in Macau is also expected to hinder revenues if formally passed. Wynn currently has two main projects in the works: Wynn Palace in Macau with a cost totaling $4.1 billion and expected to open on Cotai in 2016, and the Wynn Project in Massachusetts. Wynn's Massachusetts project is proceeding forward after the purchase of 33 acres of land in Everett, Massachusetts, along the Mystic River. Falling revenues and intense competition have plagued the industry over the last 3 years. Help CEO Steve Wynn develop a 3-year strategic plan to move his company forward.

Cinemark Holdings, Inc., 2015

www.cinemark.com, CNK

Headquartered in Plano, Texas, Cinemark Holdings is one of the leaders in the movie theater business with over 465 theaters and 5,000 screens in the United States and Latin America (and Taiwan), making it the third-largest in the United States and the largest in Brazil and Argentina. The company operates in two segments—United States and International, with all international business contained within Mexico, Central America, South America, and Taiwan. In total, Cinemark operates 334 theaters in the United States with 4,457 screens in 39 states and 148 theaters, and over 1,106 in 13 Latin American nations, including a presence in 14 of the top 15 South American markets. Cinemark competes with AMC Entertainment and Regal Entertainment in the United States, along with a host of other smaller competitors, in addition to Cable TV, Satellite TV, Netflix, and Hulu. Cinemark had 2014 year-end revenues of $2.6 billion and employs 6,000.

Following an 11 percent decline between 2004 and 2014, the number of movie-going tickets sold in the United States shrank again in 2013, 1.5 percent to $1.34 billion. Box office revenue was down 4 percent in 2014. However, receipts were far better overseas, especially in China, where theaters reported a 27 percent growth in 2013, following a 36 percent growth in 2012. Movie theater companies overall are building, on average, 14 new screens per day in China. In the United States, movie theaters are raising prices, with the average movie ticket price in 2013 increasing to $8.13, up from $7.96 in 2012. 3-D and IMAX movie ticket prices ranged from $10 to $20 each.

An interesting development in summer 2015 for Cinemark, Regal and AMC was all three major players received formal inquiries from the U.S. Department of Justice on antitrust. The principle argument accuses the three large players of signing deals with large film studios to limit the number of theaters showing blockbuster movies. This has the effect of shutting out smaller independent chains from showing blockbusters until well after the movies have been released. As of July 2015, all three firms believe they are not in violation of the U.S. Sherman Act and are in the process of supplying information to the U.S. authorities in hopes of resolving the matter.

Copyright by Fred David Books LLC. www.strategyclub.com (Written by Forest R. David)

History

Founded by Lee Roy Mitchell in 1984 and initially building movie theaters in Texas, Utah, and California, Cinemark was one of the pioneers in the stadium seating design that began in the 1990s. In 2006, Cinemark acquired Century Theaters, which added 80 theaters to its portfolio. In 2009 and 2012, respectively, Cinemark acquired Oakland Park, Florida-based Muvico and Dallas-based Rave Cinemas. The Rave acquisition helped the firm further expand into the New England market with 32 theaters located in 12 states, providing 483 screens.

Cinemark needs "movie going" to be much more of an "experience" than sitting at home watching Netflix or cable television. So, in October 2014, Cinemark filled its theater seats in Texas, Illinois, and Washington, in the middle of the night, by streaming a video game competition, the Riot Games League of Legends Championships, being held in South Korea. Cinemark is also following some rivals, such as Regal Cinemas, which has been adding luxury recliners to as many as 350 theater locations by 2015. AMC's Dine-in-Theaters now allow patrons at some locations to purchase beer and wine, as well as lunch, dinner, or some snacks, while watching a movie. In June 2014, the first 4D theater in the United States opened in Los Angeles, with artificial wind, fog, scents, and sensor-equipped seats, adding another dimension to 3D films.

Internal Issues

Organizational Structure

Based on the company's website and most recent *Form 10K*, Cinemark has no divisions by region and in fact no divisions at all, yet the firm has a COO, as indicated in Exhibit 1. Analysts do not consider the Cinemark structure to be effective or efficient.

EXHIBIT 1 Cinemark Organizational Chart

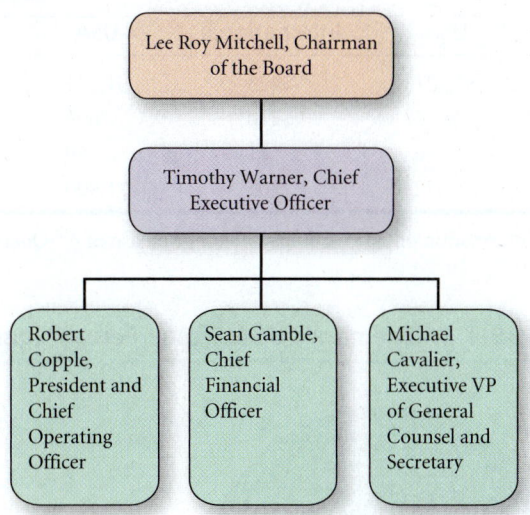

Source: Based on company documents.

Vision/Mission

Cinemark does not provide a written vision statement. However the following mission statement was taken from its website:

> Cinemark has a unique operating philosophy which combines finding the right markets in which to expand, having high-quality, right-sized theatres, and a strong operating discipline, resulting in strong operating performance. We have grown through organic expansion and selective acquisitions, creating a diverse footprint of high quality theatres in high growth markets with superior demographics.

Strategy

Cinemark currently serves 23 of the top 30 U.S. markets, including San Francisco, Dallas, Atlanta, and Salt Lake City, among others. The company also has a market presence in 14 of the top 15 metro areas in South America, and is the industry leader in Brazil and Argentina. Cinemark has 148 theaters with 1,106 screens in 12 Latin American nations. International sales were 29 percent of total revenues for 2013.

Like rivals AMC and Regal, Cinemark has a clear commitment to building new state-of-the-art theaters, remodeling existing theaters, and/or acquiring new theater rivals in select markets. In 2013 alone, Cinemark opened 709 new state-of-the-art screens worldwide and has plans to open another 263 by 2016. There is a trend in the market to shift from film to digital technology. All U.S. and international auditoriums have digital projection technology, and over 50 percent of screens in both the United States and international segments are 3-D compatible. Cinemark had approximately 150 XD auditoriums in 2013 and 200 in 2014 to lead the industry. XD auditoriums are considered premium in nature, with customer sound and wall-to-wall and ceiling-to-floor screens, surround sound, and plush seating.

The firm opened its first Cinemark Movie Bistro in 2013, offering fresh wraps, burgers, gourmet pizza along with beers, wines, and frozen cocktails. These premium concept theaters charge higher prices, but the company waited until 2014 to raise prices, much like their competitors Regal and AMC did with their more premium theater experiences.

Segment Data

Cinemark's sales derived from U.S. and Latin American operations in 2013 were 71 and 29 percent, respectively. Exhibits 2 and 3 reveal the breakdown in U.S. and Latin American locations. Even though 29 percent of revenues were derived from Latin America in 2013, only 20 percent of wide screens are located in this region, revealing the revenue strength generated from these regions.

EXHIBIT 2 Cinemark's Revenues by Segment (in millions of USD)

Revenues	2014		2013	
	USA	International	USA	International
Admissions	$1,221	$423	$1,231	$475
Concessions	$636	$210	$609	$236
Other	66	71	59	72
Total Revenues	1,922	705	1,900	783

Source: Based on information on 2015 Company News Release of 4th Quarter 2014 data.

EXHIBIT 3 Cinemark's USA Screen Percentages

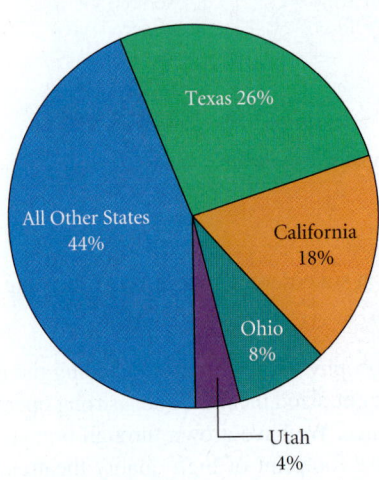

Source: Based on information on page 8 of the Cinemark 2013 *Annual Report.*

Note in Exhibit 2 that Cinemark derived 63 percent of its revenues in 2014 from admissions, but experienced a 3.6 percent decline in total consolidated admissions from 2013. However, international admission revenues declined 11 percent and total revenues from the international division declined 10 percent. Cinemark's average U.S. ticket price was $7.02 in 2014, up only 7 cents from 2013. Average ticket prices outside the United States in 2014 were $6.23 for Cinemark. Note in Exhibit 3 that 44 percent of Cinemark's screens in the United States are in California and Texas. Not revealed in Exhibit 3, 2014, total screen allocations in the US did not meaningfully change from 2013. Despite being the largest movie theater firm in Argentina, Cinemark actually has more locations in Colombia, albeit with fewer screens. As indicated by Exhibit 4, despite being the largest Brazil alone accounts for 45 percent of all Cinemark screens in Latin America.

EXHIBIT 4 Cinemark's South American Operations

South America	Locations	Screens
Brazil	65	516
Colombia	28	144
Argentina	19	168
All Other Latin America	48	349
Latin America Totals	160	1,177

Source: Based on information on page 9 of the Cinemark 2014 *Annual Report.*

Finance

Exhibit 5 reveals that Cinemark's total revenues decreased 2 percent from 2013 to 2014, yet net income rose an impressive 30 percent—mostly explained by a $72 million loss the firm took in 2013 on an early retirement of debt. This number is consolidated into the other income (loss) line in Exhibit 5. Cinemark's $2.7 billion in 2013 revenues includes 32 theaters acquired during that fiscal year. Through its acquisition strategy, however, Cinemark has accumulated over $1.2 billion in goodwill and $356 million in intangibles, exceeding total stockholders' equity by over $500 million, as revealed in Exhibit 6. The firm also has total long-term debt of over $2 billion, or twice the total equity of the firm.

As of 2013, 292 Cinemark USA theaters were leased and 42 were company owned. Leases generally are on a long-term basis ranging from 20 to 45 years. Approximately 81 percent of current theaters on lease have terms in excess of 15 years. Leases charge a fixed monthly rent payment with an additional percentage if certain revenue levels are reached. All properties outside the United States are under lease agreements.

Competitors

In December 2014, Redbox raised prices on movies rented at its 40,000 kiosks in the United States, with daily rental rates for DVDs going from $1.20 to $1.50 (up 25 percent) and Blu-ray rentals going from $1.50 to $2 (up 33 percent). In January 2015, Redbox raised prices on its daily video game rentals from $2 to $3 (up 50 percent). Even at $1.50 a day on DVDs, Redbox remains "the best value in new-release home entertainment," says CEO J. Scott Ki Valerio of parent company Outerwall (OUTR). Redbox (and Cinemark) faces mounting competition from video streamers Netflix and Amazon. Redbox's Q3 2014 revenue dropped 5 percent to $1.4 billion, and same-store sales fell nearly 12 percent. By the end of 2014, Redbox plans to remove 500 to 700 underperforming kiosks. This was the first time Redbox has raised prices on Blu-ray discs and video games, and only the second time in more than 12 years that the company raised prices on DVDs.

The movie theater industry is dominated by three major companies: AMC Entertainment, Regal Entertainment, and Cinemark. Carmark is also a large competitor, but its strategy is to focus on small- to medium-sized markets. Exhibit 7 reveals a comparison of Cinemark versus top rival firms. Note AMC's EPS is significantly higher than those of rival firms. The industry also faces stiff competition from concerts, amusement parks, cable television, home video systems, Netflix, Hulu, and other forms of entertainment.

Regal Entertainment Group (RGC)

The largest motion picture exhibitor company in the United States, Regal Entertainment Group employs 25,000 people and has properties in 42 states with 7,394 total screens. Headquartered in Knoxville, Tennessee, about 78 percent of Regal's properties feature stadium seating, with close to 100 percent of screens outfitted in digital format and 50 percent being 3D. Key brands

EXHIBIT 5 Cinemark's Income Statement (in millions of USD)

Report Date	December 31, 2014	December 31, 2013
Revenues	$2,627	$2,683
Operating expenses	2,264	2,268
EBIT	363	415
Interest	73	152
EBT	290	263
Tax	96	113
Income from continuing operations	194	150
Other items	(1)	(2)
Net income	**193**	**148**

Source: Based on Cinemark's 2014 *Annual Report* Page F-4 and Yahoo Finance

EXHIBIT 6 **Cinemark's Balance Sheet (in millions of USD)**

Report Date	December 31, 2014	December 31, 2013
Assets		
Cash and equivalents	$639	$599
Accounts receivable	48	81
Inventories	13	14
Other current assets	41	36
Total current assets	741	730
Property, plant, & equipment	1,451	1,427
Goodwill	1,277	1,288
Intangible assets	348	356
Other assets	335	343
Total assets	**4,152**	**4,144**
Liabilities		
Short-term debt	8	10
Accounts payable	119	93
Other current liabilities	287	293
Total current liabilities	414	396
Long-term debt	1,814	1,823
Deferred income taxes	149	168
Other liabilities	651	655
Total liabilities	**3,028**	**3,042**
Common stock	120	119
Retained earnings	224	148
Treasury stock	(62)	(52)
Paid in capital and other	842	887
Total equity	**1,124**	**1,102**
Total liabilities & equity	**4,152**	**4,144**

Source: Based on Cinemark's 2014 *Annual Report* Page F-3 and Yahoo Finance.

operated by Regal include Regal Cinemas, United Artist, Edwards, Great Escape Theaters, and Hollywood Theatres. In 2013, close to 70 percent of profits came from admissions, but Regal is expanding into offering meals and beer to help boost concession revenues. Popular food items offered include Cinnabon Gooey Bites, gourmet pizza, chicken nuggets, corn dog nuggets, ice cream, and normal movie snack foods. The firm's geographic position strategy is to locate in midsize metro areas and in the suburbs of larger metro areas.

EXHIBIT 7 **Cinemark versus Rival Firms**

	Cinemark	Regal	AMC
# Full-Time Employees	6,253	23,168	900
$ Net Income	193 M	105 M	64 M
$ Revenue	2,627 M	2,990 M	2,695 M
$ Revenue/Employee	420,011	129,000	2,994,444
$ EPS Ratio	1.38	0.68	3.38
$ Market Cap.	4.81 B	3.67 B	3.17 B

Source: Based on company documents.

Regal is aggressively acquiring smaller theater companies, such as Hollywood Theatres and Great Escape Theaters, and divesting others. Regal even has recently swapped several properties with top competitor AMC. Regal, AMC, and Cinemark are partners in CineMedia, a company specializing in marketing and advertising, with Regal currently having a 20 percent stake in the firm. Regal had revenues in 2013 of over $3 billion with $157 million net income. However, 2014 net income was only $105 million, with revenues totaling just under $3 billion.

AMC Entertainment Holdings (AMC)

Founded in 1920 and headquartered in Kansas City, Missouri, AMC operates over 330 theaters and 5,000+ screens and focuses on urban markets in the United States, with a small market share in Canada, United Kingdom, and Hong Kong. The firm has the largest or second-largest market share in many of the top U.S. cities, including New York City, Los Angles, Atlanta, Chicago, Dallas, and more. AMC also operates four of the top five-highest grossing theaters in the United States, and 22 of the top 50. AMC estimates that over 200 million guests visit their properties each year. Historically, the company operated many theaters around the world, but started divesting overseas properties in 2009. All AMC theaters are digital and 3D enabled. AMC offers IMAX at 150 locations, and dine in and premium seating at 11 and 35 locations. respectively.

AMC has over 18,000 employees, many of whom are part time. The company had revenues of $2.7 billion in 2013 with net income of $364 million. Dalian Wanda Group, a Chinese-based firm, acquired AMC for $2.6 billion in 2013.

Key properties include Kerasotes, Loews, and General Cinema. Like its rivals, AMC is also upgrading its concession offerings to include typical fast-food options such as chicken tenders, mozzarella sticks, curly fries, and hot dogs, in addition to candy and popcorn. The theaters also offer beer, wine, and mixed drinks. AMC is also remodeling many of its theaters with larger La-Z-Boy–type seats. Many theaters face the problem of having large outdated theaters that are too expensive to tear down, so expensive remodeling efforts are being pursued. AMC experienced a 60 percent increase in sales in Q1 of 2014 from Q1 2013 in newly renovated theaters with the larger seats.

In October 2014, AMC reported a Q3 net income decline of 78 percent to $7.4 million from $335 million a year earlier, while revenues declined 8.9 percent to $633 million. However, 2014 net income for AMC was $64 million down from $364 million in 2013 largely due to a $263 million tax benefit the firm received in 2013.

Netflix, Inc. (NFLX)

Headquartered in Los Gatos, California, Netflix has 50+ million customers in 50 countries and provides over two billion hours of movies and TV shows each month for $8.99 in the U.S. market. Customers watch their programs on demand anywhere in the world with their television, computers, tablets, phones, or nearly any device connected to the Internet, all commercial free and with the ability to pause and rewind as needed. Netflix employs 2,000+ people and had revenues of $4.3 billion in 2013.

Although Netflix does not compete with movie theaters directly, it is a large competitor for customers' entertainment dollars. Larger HD screens at affordable prices serve as a substitute for customers going to the movies. In a way, Netflix is competing on convenience, whereas the traditional movie theaters are competing on the "outing." For customers simply wanting to watch a movie, Netflix must be viewed as a serious competitor, especially since many customers already have a Netflix account and can watch movies free, since Netflix offers a one-price unlimited plan. One problem plaguing Netflix is that many of the top movies are not available until 2 years after their release dates on the live streaming. Customers, however, can pay an additional $8.99 for DVD rental service from Netflix with access to the top movies much sooner, generally the same year the movie is released.

iTunes, Red Box, and Hulu are also top competitors of the movie industry. Customers can download movies for a per-movie fee basis from iTunes within months of the movie coming out. Nevertheless, the movie theater industry still is able to control when secondary markets have access to the top films for the time being. However, in October 2014, Netflix partnered with Weinstein Co. and IMAX to show the film "Crouching Tiger, Hidden Dragon: The Green Legend" that was shown only to Netflix subscribers and in selected IMAX theaters.

External Issues

The Summer 2014 total box office receipts for movies in the United States were down nearly 15 percent from the prior year, with receipts of $4.06 billion being the lowest since 2006. The largest movie theater chain, Regal, then announced its desire to be acquired, as the company's most recent quarter's revenue declined 15 percent to $694 million. Firms possibly interested in Regal include China Film Group or Mexico's Cinepolis theater chain. AMC is already owned by China's Dalian Wanda Group.

In 2009, the movie theater industry began a shift from film to digital projection technology. The advantages of digital for the industry are numerous, including (1) better-quality movies with realism and detail; (2) the ability to send the feed via satellite, physical media, or by fiber optic networks; and (3) no risk of degrading, film tears, or film shipping costs. By 2013, the movie industry in the United States generated $15 billion in revenue, but had an annual growth rate of only 0.5 percent over the time period from 2008 to 2013. The growth rate is expected to increase to 1.5 percent over the next years through 2018.

Barriers to entry are high for domestic firms because the industry is mature, but internationally, the industry still has much opportunity for growth in emerging markets; however, barriers to entry are high in these markets as well. The industry also has experienced rapid technological change in recent years with the shift from film technology to digital movies. Virtually all of the theaters in the United States owned by AMC, Regal, or Cinemark had switched to fully digital by 2014, and most international theaters owned by the three giants have as well.

To better compete in the industry, many competitors are closing underperforming theaters and reinvesting in better food options, stadium seating, plush seating, improved sound and digital technology, and an overall upgrade in atmosphere at better performing theaters with subsequent price increases. Currently, admissions account for 67 percent of U.S. industrywide sales, and concessions account for 29 percent of sales.

Most hurt by recent shifts in the market are smaller movie theater firms that make up 40 percent of the total market. Many of these firms do not have the capital resources available to shift to digital technology and upgrade their facilities. It is estimated that up to 20 percent of this class of theater will close by 2019. Despite the pressures on smaller movie firms, merger and acquisition activity has been limited over the last 5 years, possibly because many of these firms are located in smaller markets—the same markets the larger movie theaters are divesting.

Expenses

The movie theater industry is plagued by low margins, generally anywhere from 3.5 to 4.5 percent, on average, depending on the size of the firm. Larger firms tend to have higher margins. The shift to digital technologies and upgrading existing theaters has significantly contributed to the low margins, along with flat attendance and many other costs associated with the industry. One of the largest expenses for the industry is rental of films, which accounts for around 32 percent of revenues on average. The 32 percent number is only an average, however, and many high-grossing films may receive 80 percent of admission revenues on the opening weekend, with a sliding scale lowering the royalty rate paid.

Since many theaters rent or lease their properties, rent expense is high and accounts for an average of 34 percent of total revenues when adding in utilities. Most workers are considered part time in a movie theater; therefore, wages account for only around 10 percent of total revenues. Concessions receipts comprise about 5 percent of total industrywide revenues on average.

Movie Decline

Summer 2014 witnessed a 20+ percent decline in box office revenue from the prior summer. This trend has been ongoing since 2011 with below-average ticket sales. This also comes at a time when the economy and employment rates are improving in the United States. Hollywood Studios, for example, had their worst summer since 1997 in 2014, and it was the first summer since 2001 that no American film generated $300 million in sales. International markets such as Japan and larger nations in Europe have also seen sales slip. However, revenues have been increasing in regions relatively new to big box American movies, such as China, Russia, and Brazil. As of 2014, around 70 percent of all U.S. box office revenues are generated outside the United States, with some films generating over 80 percent of all revenues in foreign markets.

Future

Cinemark experienced a 2 percent decline in revenues in fiscal year 2014 as the movie industry continues to face increasing pressure from Netflix, Hulu, and other movie providers. In addition, many consumers now have 50-inch and larger TVs at home, providing even further incentive to skip expensive movie outings. Regal also experienced a slight decline in 2014 revenues and AMC experienced a 9 percent decline in revenues. Sales for Cinemark in South America were down significantly, accounting for much of the 10 percent drop in revenues in non-U.S. markets.

Cinemark continues to be dependent on top movie hits. To the extent popular movies are produced and released, customers have shown they will go to a movie theater, but for average movies, many customers wait for Netflix or other mediums to get rights for the movie. Cinemark has a large presence in South America, but this market is not the best place to have resources. CEO Mitchell is in desperate need of a well-constructed 3-year strategic plan to more effectively position Cinemark for future success.

Facebook, Inc., 2015

www.facebook.com, FB

Headquartered in Menlo Park, California, Facebook is the largest social media network in the world, with over 1.3 billion current active users of its website. Facebook ended 2014 with record numbers: a total of 890 million users, 745 million daily active mobile users, and $3,851 million in revenue. Facebook's revenues from advertising totaled $3.6 billion, and $257 million in collected payments and other fees. The company spent 29 percent of its revenue dollars on research and development (R&D) in 2014, and spent a record $1,831 billion on purchasing new property and equipment.

Facebook launched its audience network in 2014, which allowed advertisers to run their Facebook ads on third-party mobile applications. Then in 2015, Facebook unveiled its own mobile advertising distributor, similar to rival Twitter's MoPub aimed at attracting more business. CEO Mark Zukerberg spent much of early 2015 personally traveling the world, to India, Latin America, Africa, Jakarta, and elsewhere, meeting with groups who petition their governments for Internet access. Given that Facebook wants to grow globally, Mr. Zukerberg describes his travels as "really cool." He wants to aggressively help phone companies build Internet connections globally. Only about half of Facebook's revenues currently come from outside the United States and Canada. Reportedly, more than 10 percent of Facebook accounts are fake.

Copyright by Fred David Books LLC. www.strategyclub.com (Written by Jason R. Willoughby, Elizabethtown Community College)

History

Facebook was founded in February 2004 by Mark Zuckerberg and his Harvard University roommates. Initially, it was to be used only by Harvard University students, but eventually Zuckerberg and the other founders gave access to the Ivy League universities and Stanford University. As Facebook grew popular, user access was given to other universities, as well as Boston area high school students. Today, Facebook has grown into a phenomenon and anyone over the age of 13 can have access to Facebook, a social media platform loved by millions.

After launching his initial (Thefacebook.com) website, three Harvard University seniors accused Zuckerberg of taking their idea to create a social network called HarvardConnection.com to create a competitive product. After the three individuals made a complaint, an investigation was initiated, and a lawsuit filed, which was settled in 2008 for 1.2 million shares ($300 million) of Facebook's IPO offering.

Facebook's initial big investment was given by the co-founder of PayPal, Peter Thiel. In 2005, the company bought the domain name facebook.com for $200,000 and dropped "the" from the original name. The investments began to grow as in 2005, as Accel invested $12.7 million and Jim Breyer added $1 million of his own money. Facebook has recently surpassed both Google and Amazon in percent market share and number of users in the social media industry.

Internal Issues

Vision and Mission

Facebook's mission statement is "to give people the power to share and make the world more open and connected." Although Facebook does not have an explicit vision statement, Zuckerberg mentions three items that reveal his desire for the company: "(1) stay connected with friends and family, (2) discover what is going on in the world, and (3) share and express what matters to the individual."

EXHIBIT 1   Facebook's Organizational Structure

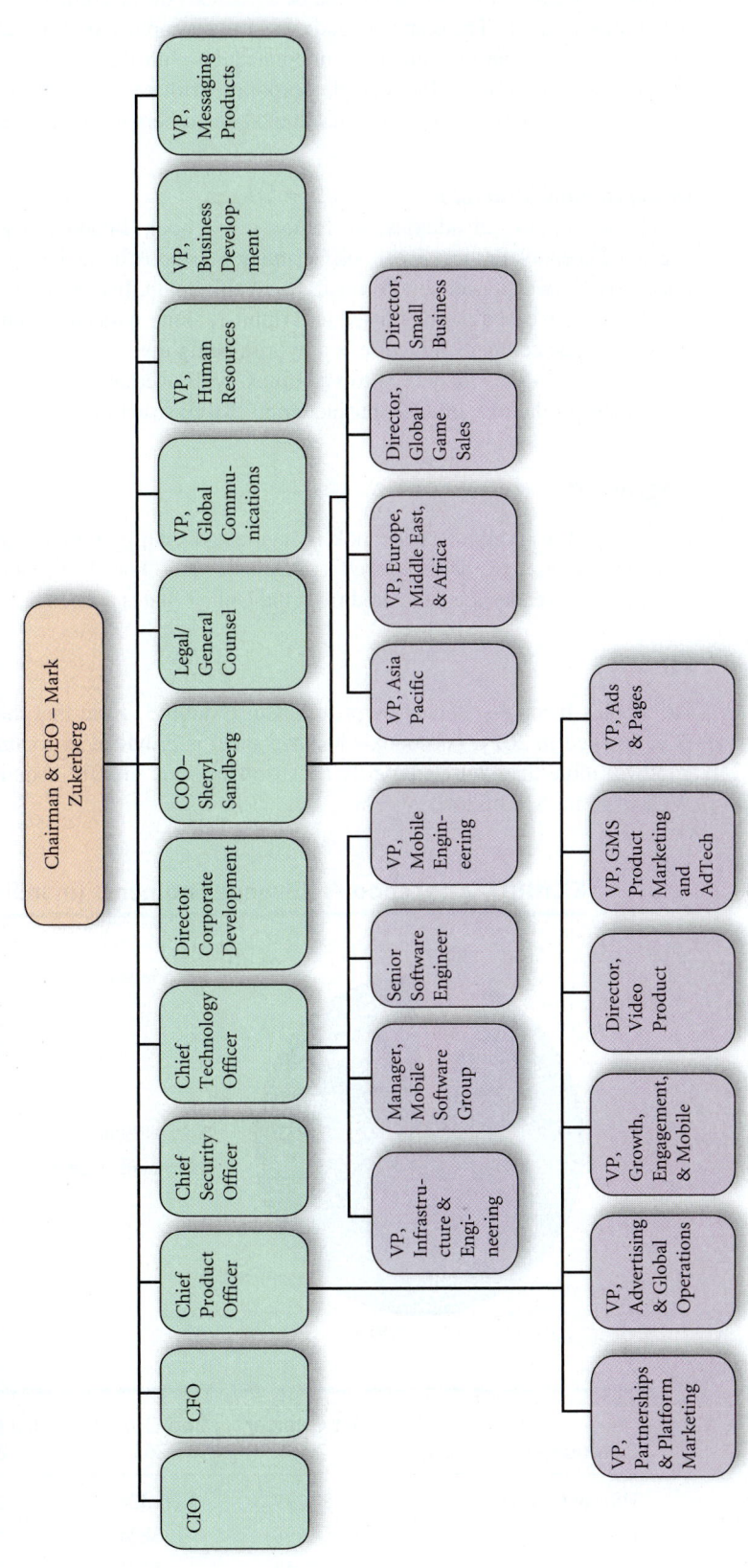

Source: Based on Facebook's organizational chart (http://www.theofficialboard.com/org-chart/facebook).

Code of Conduct

According to Facebook's corporate governance report, "Facebook Personnel" are expected to act lawfully, honestly, ethically, and in the best interests of the company while performing duties on behalf of Facebook. The company code of conduct applies to all Facebook personnel, including members of the board of directors (in connection with their work for Facebook), officers, and employees of Facebook, Inc. and its corporate affiliates, as well as contingent workers (e.g., agency workers, contractors, and consultants) and others working on Facebook's behalf.

Organizational Structure

Facebook has 14 subsidiaries, as follows: Facebook Benelux, Facebook Brazil, Facebook Canada, Facebook France, Facebook Germany, Facebook India, Facebook Italy, Facebook Korea, Facebook Norway, Facebook Portugal, Facebook Spain, Instagram, Oculus VR, and WhatsApp. Facebook's top executives are listed in Exhibit 1, along with an organizational chart of the company. Note the company structure is a hybrid, being divisional by region and by product. Some analysts suggest the structure is too complex, with overlapping duties, and would prefer to see something similar to a strategic business unit (SBU) structure.

Segments

As indicated in Exhibit 2, Facebook is segmented both by region, having four regions, and by revenue source, Advertising as well as Payments and Other Fees. Note that roughly one half of Facebook's revenues are generated from the United States and Canada.

Finance

Facebook's income statement is provided in Exhibit 3. Note that the firm's net income more than doubled in 2014. Facebook's balance sheet is provided in Exhibit 4. Note the company's goodwill more than doubled, partly because Facebook in 2014 acquired the messaging service WhatsApp for $19 billion.

EXHIBIT 2 Facebook's Revenue Segments (in millions of USD)

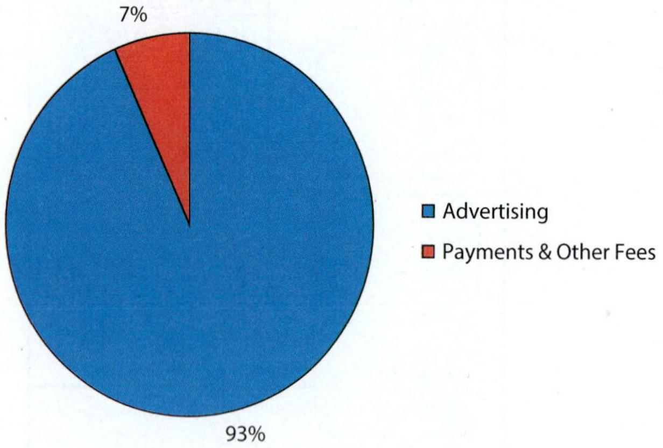

Revenue - Geography	1st Quarter 2014	2nd Quarter 2014	3rd Quarter 2014	4th Quarter 2014
USA & Canada	$1,179	$1,308	$1,514	$1,864
Europe	$698	$824	$844	$1,030
Asia-Pacific	$354	$431	$492	$554
Rest of the World	$271	$347	$353	$403

Source: Based on Facebook's 2014 *Form 10-K*.

EXHIBIT 3 Facebook's Income Statements (in millions of USD)

Report Date	December 31, 2014	December 31, 2013
Revenues	$12,466	$7,872
Operating expenses	7,472	5,068
EBIT	4,994	2,804
Interest	84	50
Other income (loss)	—	—
EBT	4,910	2,754
Tax	1,970	1,254
Income from continuing operations	2,940	1,500
Other items	(15)	(9)
Net income	**2,925**	**1,491**

Source: Based on Facebook's 2014 *Annual Report* Page 57 and Yahoo Finance.

EXHIBIT 4 Facebook's Balance Sheets (in millions of USD)

Report Date	December 31, 2014	December 31, 2013
Assets		
Cash and equivalents	$11,199	$11,449
Accounts receivable	1,678	1,109
Other current assets	793	512
Total current assets	13,670	13,070
Property, plant & equipment	3,967	2,882
Goodwill	17,981	839
Intangible assets	3,929	883
Other assets	638	221
Total assets	**40,184**	**17,895**
Liabilities		
Short-term debt	180	277
Accounts payable	378	268
Other current liabilities	866	555
Total current liabilities	1,424	1,100
Long-term debt	119	237
Other liabilities	2,545	1,088
Total liabilities	**4,088**	**2,425**
Common stock	—	—
Retained earnings	6,099	3,159
Paid in capital and other	29,997	12,311
Total equity	36,096	15,470
Total liabilities & equity	**40,184**	**17,895**

Source: Based on Facebook's 2014 *Annual Report* Page 56 and Yahoo Finance.

Marketing Strategy

Until November 2014, most Facebook users obtained free marketing and advertising of a product or service by creating posts on their "wall" to their mass audience. But a new system was installed toward the end of 2014. Individuals now wanting to gain exposure based on free advertising and marketing will no longer obtain the high-traffic distribution to their page "fans." The only way entrepreneurs and small business owners can receive high volumes of distribution of their materials is to pay Facebook for their product service exposure. The more money paid by the individual or business, the more reach their message will be distributed.

Another marketing item Facebook has initiated is product ads, which show users pictures of products and prices, once the user has visited the specific product's website, based on the users' interests and/or location. Facebook now also offers a work-oriented product similar to LinkedIn and rivals Microsoft, Google, and Salesforce.com. The new Facebook "professional" service enables users to keep their personal postings, pictures, and identity separate from the professional and work content. The new service includes online chatting with professional colleagues, which is a serious challenge to LinkedIn, the leading business-oriented social network. The new service comes with tools to share and store documents, taking aim at products and services from Microsoft, Google, and Salesforce.com. Facebook has a significant advantage in any competition, given its reported 1.35 billion users who are active monthly and 864 million who use it daily, compared to LinkedIn's claims of 332 million registered users, but only 90 million persons visited the site from July through September 2014.

Facebook's wide following is its main competitive advantage, because of what is commonly referred to as the *network effect* in business and economics. Much of the value comes from the availability of other people with similar interests that you may want to market to or interact with professionally or personally. Two disadvantages of Facebook, however, and reasons many companies have banned employees from using the service at work, is that (1) many persons lose significant productivity at work by spending too much time on Facebook and (2) Facebook has faced privacy criticisms for years. Information leaked through employees "communicating" on Facebook could potentially land in the hands of competitors, causing damage to the business. It is unclear yet whether the new Facebook "professional" service will charge users or be paid for by advertising.

For a decade, digital marketers have been constrained to an increasingly outdated technology known as the *cookie*, which are still used to measure and target digital ads. Best described as bits of code dropped into web browsers, cookies generate poor approximations of how many people view a digital ad and provides inaccurate estimates of how many times any given individual sees an ad. Cookies give unreliable measures of clicks and sales and are not used on mobile apps. However, from 2015 to 2017, Facebook-owned Atlas aims to take digital marketing beyond the cookie to (1) correct cookies' inaccuracies and (2) discover what's happening within the cookie-less world of mobile apps. Atlas strives to be able to connect offline purchases and conversions to digital ads shown across mobile apps and the Web. In essence, Facebook's Atlas is an ad server that allows ad buyers to measure, target, and optimize digital and mobile ads across digital apps (i.e., not just on Facebook).

For Facebook, Google, Yahoo!, Microsoft, and AOL, the primary revenue sources are Internet advertising. Exhibit 5 reveals the percentage of total digital display ad revenues for each company.

EXHIBIT 5 Digital Display Ad Revenues: Facebook versus Rivals

	2010	2011	2012	2013	2014
Google	12.1%	13.5%	15.4%	18.0%	21.2%
Facebook	11.5%	14.1%	14.4%	15.2%	15.5%
Yahoo!	14.0%	11.0%	9.3%	8.0%	7.0%
Microsoft	5.2%	4.9%	4.5%	4.3%	4.0%
AOL	4.7%	4.3%	3.6%	3.1%	2.7%

*These data include advertising on desktop and laptop computers, mobile phones, and tablets.

Source: Based on http://www.quora.com/Who-are-facebooks-biggest-competitors-and-why

Instagram

Facebook recently acquired Instagram, whose primary customer base is teenagers. Instagram is the Web's leading photo-sharing and video-sharing social media service and is on pace to top 100 million users in the United States by 2018. Instagram surpassed Twitter in early 2015 as the second-most used social media service in the region after its parent company, Facebook. The number of U.S. users of Instagram climbed by nearly 60 percent to 64.2 million in 2014 versus the year-earlier. Twitter ended 2014 with 48.4 million users in the United States, an increase of 12 percent. However, Instagram's user growth is expected to climb to 21 percent in 2015, 15 percent in 2016, and 10 percent in 2017, whereas Twitter's user growth is expected to decline to 9 percent in 2015, 8 percent in 2016, and 7 percent in 2017. Analysts expect that by 2018, Instagram will have 106.2 million users in the United States, up 7 percent, compared to Twitter, which is projected to have 66 million users and year-over-year growth of 6 percent. Although Instagram has customers of all ages, roughly 62 percent of all teens in the 12 to 17 age group used Instagram regularly in 2014.

Competitors

Although there are hundreds of online social media websites, the major competitors of Facebook include Instagram, Snapchat, LinkedIn, Google+, and Twitter. Snapchat is a more private medium than Facebook, which is why it's growing in popularity. Snapchat only lets you send "snaps" to the friends selected by the user. Compared to Snapchat, LinkedIn is not as nearly as popular with social media usage, but LinkedIn is gaining users and platform time from Facebook due to the professional nature of LinkedIn. Google+ and Twitter compete with Facebook for users and time spent on social media.

Snapchat

Three Stanford University students created the Snapchat photo messaging system in July 2011. In 2013, Snapchat launched an application named Snapkidz for users 13 years of age and younger, with those users only being able to save photos on their local drive; they are not able to send pictures to anyone. In October 2014, with the demand to raise more funds and users for this application, Snapchat released their first 20-second movie trailer for the film *Ouija*. This was their first paid advertising venture into the market. Currently, Snapchat caters to sending over 700 million videos and photos for current users. Snapchat is a photo messaging application whereby users can take photos, record videos, add text and drawings, and send them to a controlled list of recipients. These sent photographs and videos are known as "Snaps." Users set a time limit for how long recipients can view their Snaps (as of April 2014, the range is from 1 to 10 seconds), after which they are hidden from the recipient's device and deleted from Snapchat's servers. According to Snapchat in May 2014, the app's users were sending 700 million photos and videos per day, and Snapchat Stories content was being viewed 500 million times per day. The company has a valuation of $10 to $20 billion, depending on various sources.

LinkedIn Corporation (LNKD)

LinkedIn is a professional social networking service that has over 260 million users in 200 countries. Headquartered in Mountain View, California, LinkedIn has three major business units: talent solutions, marketing solutions, and premium subscriptions. Companies can utilize LinkedIn talent solutions for employee procurement. Individuals seeking employment can pay a premium subscription to find job openings. LinkedIn continues to acquire competing firms to help complement its current product offerings. A key recent acquisition was Digg, a social news site, in 2012. As its growth continues, LinkedIn's 2014 market penetration was highest in the United States, the United Kingdom, Canada, and Australia. India was the fastest-growing country of LinkedIn users that grew to 20 million during 2014.

Google, Inc. (GOOG)

Google+ is an identity service and a social network with up to 540 million active users. About 30 percent of Google+ customers use the application on their smartphones. Beginning at age 13,

EXHIBIT 6 Facebook vs Rival Firms

	Facebook	LinkedIn	Twitter
# Full-Time Employees	9,200	6,900	3,900
$ Net Income	$2,900 M	($15.7 M)	($578 M)
$ Revenue	$12,400 M	$2,218 M	$1,403 M
$ Revenue/Employee	$1,348,000	$321,000	$360,000
$ EPS Ratio	$1.03	$(0.37)	$(0.98)
$ Market Cap.	$251 B	$26.9 B	$24.6 B

Source: Based on Yahoo Finance 2014 data and other sources.

teens may create a Google+ account. There are services that set Google+ apart from its competitors such as circles, streams, Hangouts, Hangouts on Air, and the +1 button. One item that Google+ users and advertisers will benefit from is SEO (Search Engine Optimization), as being on Google+ will boost search results rankings.

Twitter, Inc. (TWTR)

Headquartered in San Francisco, Twitter is a social networking service that allows individuals to send tweets within their network. Tweets are 140-character messages and can be posted only by registered users. By the end of 2014, Twitter had more than 500 million users. The company has several revenue services to generate income, such as paid advertising to companies that can be compared to Google Adwords. Twitter offers a self-service advertising system for small business owners. Total revenue for 2014 was $1.4 billion compared to $664.89 million the prior year.

Exhibit 6 provides comparative data for Facebook and its direct competitors. Note both LinkedIn and Twitter reported negative net income in 2014.

External Issues

Pinning, tweeting, posting, tagging, texting, liking, and other social media lingo have become a major part of daily lives, with almost two billion people in the world being active users of social media applications. However, social media users increasingly feel commercialized when pop-up ads cover their computer screens while surfing social media platforms. Companies must figure out a way to utilize advertising that creates comfort when seen by individuals.

The age of users continues to be an external issue. Facebook currently has a policy that children age 13 or younger must have parent consent to create a page on their platform, which parallels with the Children's Online Privacy Protection Act (COPPA). Approximately 1 of 8 Americans show signs of having a social media addiction, which consists of declining social relationships, anger and depression when the Internet is not available for use, lying about usage, and experiencing high levels of happiness when using the Internet. Other characteristics of this addiction consist of waking up in the middle of the night to check Facebook, checking social media before getting out of bed, and using social media to cover up everyday life problems.

A new Facebook application enables users to comment on political debates and issues. Users connecting via the Facebook platform and the company pushing the idea of political impact caused the Egyptian government to ban Facebook in their country. Facebook created a political action committee in 2011 with the Federal Election Commission. It was named the FB PAC. Google+ is banned by the People's Republic of China and Iran. Currently, in Mainland China, it is not blocked, but government intervention has slowed down the loading of the Google+ program enough to where users have to wait a large amount of time to utilize the program.

Social Media and Personal Branding

A new trend is the idea of using social media platforms to create a person brand whereby individuals are combining their social media applications to create a personal brand or image that directly relates to future employment. A common practice for human resource managers is to perform a search on potential employees. One company, Klout, has grasped the idea that society has become aware of individual brands, and has made it easier for human resource managers to review a potential employee's social media influence. Headquartered in San Francisco, Klout is a private company that measures social media analytics to rank an individual's social influence. One's Klout score can be between 1 and 100. As President Obama's score is 99, the likes of Justin Bieber and actress Zooey Deschanel have scores of 92 and 86, respectively. To put a Klout score into perspective, my (the case author) clout score is currently 53. The higher the score, the better it is for individuals looking to be hired at large corporations in the United States. Klout uses Bing, Facebook, Foursquare, Google+, Instagram, LinkedIn, Twitter, and Wikipedia data to create Klout user profiles that are assigned a unique "Klout Score."

The Future

Social media use is growing exponentially. A key question moving forward is: Where will the large amounts of data be stored? Who will control the stored data? Will government intervention play a part of using the stored data? Does Facebook have a right to store and even sell this information?

Google and Facebook are becoming closer friends. Both companies want more people online, searching around and clicking on ads. Both firms are finding new ways to make it happen—from selling smartphone data plans, to using solar-powered drone aircraft as floating cell towers, to partnering with telecom providers in the developing world to get people hooked on apps. Both companies recently gave updates on their efforts at the Mobile World Congress wireless show in Barcelona, Spain, in March 2015. At the meeting, Facebook CEO Mark Zuckerberg and Google Vice President Sundar Pichai told attendees they plan to collaborate more, but are taking very different approaches to getting the world connected. Internet.org is Facebook's fledgling effort to create new users in countries with little or low Internet use. Zuckerberg revealed at the meeting that his company has launched apps with basic free services in six countries: Zambia, Ghana, Kenya, Tanzania, Colombia, and most recently, India. The app is customized for each country and telecom operator, in order to attract new users while not hurting the telecoms' already existing base of customers. Facebook offers free versions of services users already pay for— a primary reason why Internet.org does not include the WhatsApp messaging service.

Develop a three-year strategic plan for Facebook's CEO, Mr. Mark Zukerberg.

Zynga, Inc., 2015

www.zynga.com, ZNGA

Headquartered in San Francisco, California, Zynga is a social network game-development company recognized as one of the top five companies in the industry. The Internet game industry is rapidly evolving as technology changes and new firms enter the business. Creation of new games and enhancements to existing games are crucial to Zynga's success. International expansion requires that the company adapt games to multiple languages, cultures, and customs. Zynga relies on a small number of games that generate a majority of its revenue and has posted a net loss for the past three years. Zynga has a high level of dependence on Facebook to market games.

Zynga develops, operates, and markets social games that are played on the Internet, at social networking sites and on mobile platforms such as Apple's App Store and Google's Play App Store, as well as the company's website. Typically, the games are free and revenue is generated through the sale of in-game virtual goods, mobile game download fees, and advertising services. Zynga has become a leader in the industry and has gained a competitive advantage through its investment in its people, game content, brand technology, and infrastructure. In reports released by AppData, Zynga had 3 of the top 10 games on Facebook based on daily active users (DAUs).

Recently Zynga entered the sports game category with its new sports brand, Zynga Sports 365 and its "NFL Showdown," both being available on multiple mobile devices. Zynga also updated its popular "Zynga Poker," "New Words with Friends," "FarmVille 2: Country Escape," "Hit It Rich!," "Slots," "Mafia Wars," and "CSR Classics" games. As of this writing (Fall 2015), Zynga has been out of favor on Wall Street since 2012. However, Zynga's business has started to move slightly higher, but it still has a long way to go to its revenue peaks in 2012. Some good news for Zynga is that the company has plenty of cash. Moving forward, Zynga desperately needs a new hit product to have a chance to keep pace with its rival King Digital Entertainment (NYSE: KING).

Copyright by Fred David Books LLC. www.strategyclub.com (Written by Debora J. Gilliard and David Lynn Hoffman, Metropolitan State University of Denver)

History

Founded in April 2007 by Mark Pincus, Zynga completed an initial public offering (IPO) in December 2011. Shares of Zynga rose nicely in late 2014 after the company launched its entry into the mobile Action Strategy category with an early beta of a new mobile game: "Empires & Allies." This release marks the first step for Zynga and its commitment to this category throughout 2015. Zynga says its new "Empires & Allies" completely reimagines the brand for today's mobile audience. In June 2011, "Empires & Allies" began on Facebook (FB) and within a month had nearly 40 million users. That version ended on Facebook in April 2013.

Despite recent good news, TheStreet Ratings team rates Zynga stock as a "Sell" with a ratings score of D because of the company's deteriorating 2015 net income and disappointing return on equity. The team says Zynga has significantly underperformed when compared to that of the S&P 500 and the software industry, and the company's net income recently decreased by significantly when compared to the same quarter one year ago, falling from –$0.07 million to –$57.06 million.

Internal Issues

Vision/Mission

Zynga has no stated vision statement. Zynga's mission is to "connect the world through games" which is supported by its passion for games and for family and friends playing together. It is important for Zynga to continually create a compelling game experience for its players.

EXHIBIT 1 Zynga's Organizational Chart

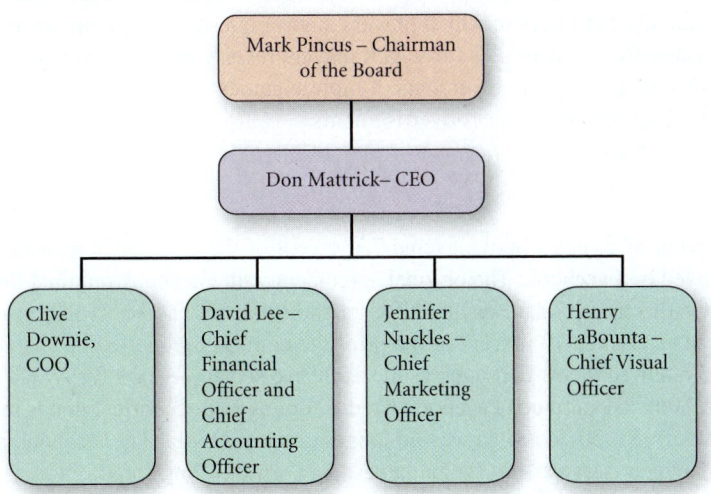

Source: Based on company documents.

Organizational Structure
Zynga's organizational chart is provided in Exhibit 1.

Research and Development/Technology
Zynga must continually enhance existing games and develop new games, so it invests heavily in R&D. Allocations of $396 million in 2014, $413 million in 2013, $645.6 million in 2012, and $727 million in 2011 were made for software development. Investment has been made in developing a proprietary technology stack that has the ability to handle sudden bursts of activity from millions of players. The technology stack includes a data center and cloud computing management, shared code base, network and cross-promotional features, and proprietary data analysis. It also supports the growth of 2D and 3D game engines across the mobile business and provides high-level security and antifraud infrastructure.

Intellectual Property
Software games are highly dependent on intellectual property in the form of software code, patented technology, and trade secrets that are used to develop games and run them on multiple platforms. The company creates product and feature names, and audiovisual elements that include graphics, music, story lines, and interface design. The company protects its intellectual property through contractual agreements, trade secrets, copyrights, trademarks, trade dress, domain names, and patents. Typically, there is a high level of protection through federal and state laws in the United States. However, this same protection may not be as strong or even available in some countries in which games are available.

Marketing
Players (customers) are acquired by cross-promoting new games to the existing audience. The company has fan pages on Facebook to connect to players and uses social media, such as Twitter, to communicate with players. Zynga hosts live and online player events. In 2013, the company spent $60.6 million on advertising.

In October 2014, Zynga had 1.3 million monthly unique players (MUPs), down from the 1.6 million at October 2013. Daily active players (DAUs) in the third quarter of 2014 were 26 million, compared to 30 million in the third quarter of 2013. There were 112 million monthly active users (MAUs) third quarter 2014, compared to 133 million third quarter of 2013. Monthly unique users (MUUs) were 77 million in the first quarter of 2014, compared to 97 million third quarter of 2013 (Globe Newswire, November 6, 2014).

Advertising revenue is generated in the following ways:

- Branded virtual goods and sponsorships that integrate advertising within games
- Engagement ads and offers in which players answer questions, sign up for third-party services or watch-to-earn activities for which players receive virtual currency
- Mobile ads that are in the free versions of mobile games
- Display ads that include banner advertisements
- Licensing the brand

Facebook

In 2013, 69 percent of Zynga's bookings and 75 percent of the company's revenue were derived from games played on Facebook. The original agreement with Facebook required the company to use Facebook Credits as a primary payment for its games on the Facebook platform and required Facebook to remit to Zynga 70 percent of the price the company requested be charged to players. Zynga was also required to use Facebook as the exclusive social platform for Zynga properties. In June 2012, Facebook discontinued Facebook Credits, opting to price virtual goods in local currencies, so as of March 31, 2013, Zynga was no longer obligated to display Facebook advertising or use Facebook payment services on Zynga games. As a result, Zynga could process its own payments and Facebook no longer had the right to receive 30 percent of the proceeds from payments. In addition, as of March 31, 2013, Zynga was no longer required to use Facebook as its exclusive social platform for games. These agreements and amendments with Facebook expired in May 2015.

Products

In June 2014, Zynga had 39 games available. Its most popular games are "Farmville 2: Country Escape," "CityVille," "ChefVille," "Zynga Poker," "Hidden Chronicles," "Bubble Safari," and "Words with Friends." In September 2014, Zynga announced its launch of "NFL Showdown," which is the first mobile-based football manager simulation game. It provides football fans a new way to connect and compete with friends every day. Licensing agreements with the National Football League and NFL Players, Inc., allows Zynga to bring real NFL teams and players to the mobile gaming arena. This game is the first addition to Zynga Sports 365.

To date, Zynga has relied on a small number of games for a majority of its revenue. Bookings from existing games decline over time. In 2013, bookings declined 38 percent from 2012. In addition, only about 2 percent of all players are paying players. Thus, it is imperative for the company to consistently launch new games and update existing games in order to retain current players and attract new players. Exhibit 2 reveals the percent breakdown in 2014 revenues for Zynga's two business segments.

Human Resources

Zynga's game designers, product managers, engineers, and executives are in high demand and highly sought by competitors, so it's no surprise that Zynga experiences high turnover rates. At the end of the 2013 fiscal year, 22 percent of Zynga's employees had been with the company for

EXHIBIT 2 Percent Revenues by Segment

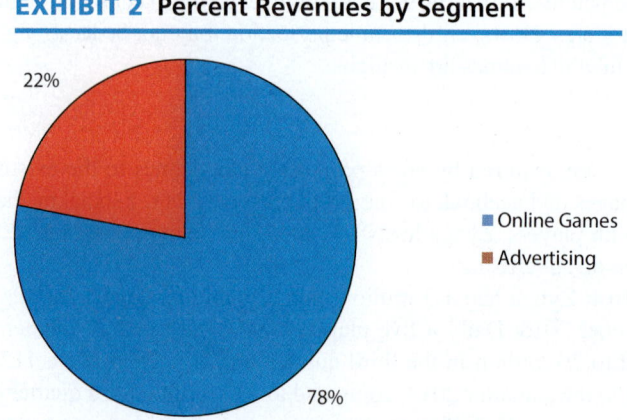

Source: Based on company documents.

less than 1 year and 52 percent had been with the company less than 2 years. The company relies on its culture and competitive compensation in order to attain and retain employees. Its culture is entrepreneurial and execution-focused. Zynga uses stock ownership to entice employees to join and stay with the company. At fiscal year-end 2014, the company had 1,974 employees.

Social Responsibility

Zynga.org is a nonprofit organization whose mission is to make the world a better place through games. It has raised over $18 million since its inception from over 1 million players through 150 in-game campaigns to support many causes. The nonprofit started as a result of "passion projects" when a small group of employees saw an opportunity to use games to connect players with social causes. Zynga.org works with Zynga Inc. to engage players and encourage social impact through campaigns integrated into its games. Its first attempt was "Sweet Seeds for Haiti," an in-game campaign that allowed FarmVille players to purchase and plant special seeds. Over $1 million was raised, which was used to build a new school for children in Haiti after the country was hit with an earthquake in January 2010.

In March 2014, Zynga.org reached a milestone $1 million in total contributions to support water.org, an organization that leads innovative, community-driven, and market-based initiatives to ensure that all people have access to safe water. The most recent in-game campaign raised $100,000 as "Zynga Poker" players contributed 15 percent of the in-game winnings to a Helping Hands charity pot.

Other initiatives recently undertaken by Zynga.org include:

- Working with "ed-tech" start-ups to build stronger learning games and apps through co.labs and in partnership with New Schools Venture Fund
- In a partnership with San Francisco Unified School District, Zynga aims to help public schools to develop a game design curriculum and experienced based learning to encourage students to consider technology careers
- Partnering with Zynga Inc., code.org, Girls Who Code, and Techbridge to host visits with Zynga tech professionals to help students understand the connection between games and STEM elements and encouraging students to consider STEM-related careers.
- Addressing hunger and food security issues throughout the world by developing partnerships with World Food Programme, Save the Children, Heifer International, and Feeding America and receiving player donations through in-game campaigns in "FarmVille," "FarmVille 2," "ChefVille," and "Café World."

Finance

Zynga had a disappointing fiscal 2014 with revenues down 21 percent and net income falling from a $37 to a $226 million loss from 2013 to 2014. Zynga's stock price fell over 20 percent from the day before earnings to the day after earnings were reported. The company's income statement and balance sheet are provided in Exhibits 3 and 4. Notice in Exhibit 5 that Zynga's profit margins are all negative versus its major rivals.

EXHIBIT 3 Zynga's Income Statement (in millions of USD)

Report Date	December 31, 2014	December 31, 2013
Revenues	$690	$873
Operating expenses	935	939
EBIT	(245)	(66)
Interest income	3	4
Other income	8	(3)
EBT	(233)	(65)
Tax benefit	7	28
Net income	**(226)**	**(37)**

Source: Based on Zynga's 2014 *Annual Report,* p. 76, and Yahoo Finance.

EXHIBIT 4 Zygna's Balance Sheet (in millions of USD)

Report Date	December 31, 2014	December 31, 2013
Assets		
Cash and equivalents	$916	$1,125
Accounts receivable	90	66
Other current assets	77	50
Total current assets	1,083	1,241
Property, plant, & equipment	298	349
Goodwill	651	228
Intangible assets	67	18
Long-term securities	231	416
Other assets	19	26
Total assets	**2,349**	**2,278**
Liabilities		
Accounts payable	15	21
Deferred revenue	190	187
Other current liabilities	164	69
Total current liabilities	369	277
Deferred income taxes	5	—
Deferred revenue	4	3
Other liabilities	74	122
Total liabilities	**452**	**402**
Common Stock and Paid in Capital	3,097	2,823
Other	(1,200)	(947)
Total equity	**1,897**	**1,876**
Total liabilities & equity	**2,349**	**2,279**

Source: Based on Zynga's 2014 *Annual Report,* p. 75, and Yahoo Finance.

EXHIBIT 5 Zynga's 2014 Profitability versus Electronic Arts

	Zynga	Electronic Arts
# Full-Time Employees	1,974	8,400
$ Net Income	(226 M)	875 M
$ Revenue	690 M	4,515 M
$ Revenue/Employee	350,000	538,000
$ EPS Ratio	(0.24)	2.69
$ Market Cap.	2.5 B	22.5 B

Source: Based on Yahoo Finance 2014 data and other sources.

Exhibit 6 reveals ratio comparisons of Zynga versus its top competitors based on 2013 data. However, at fiscal year-end 2014, Zynga's current ratio fell to 2.9 from 4.5 in 2013.

Recent Strategies

In Q2 of 2013, Zynga decreased its workforce by 520 employees and in early 2014 decreased the workforce by an additional 314 employees. In addition, the company closed a data center and other office facilities. On February 14, 2014, Zynga completed its acquisition of NaturalMotion, a U.K. company, expanding its game titles and international offerings, and bringing new technology to the company.

EXHIBIT 6 Ratio Comparison 2013

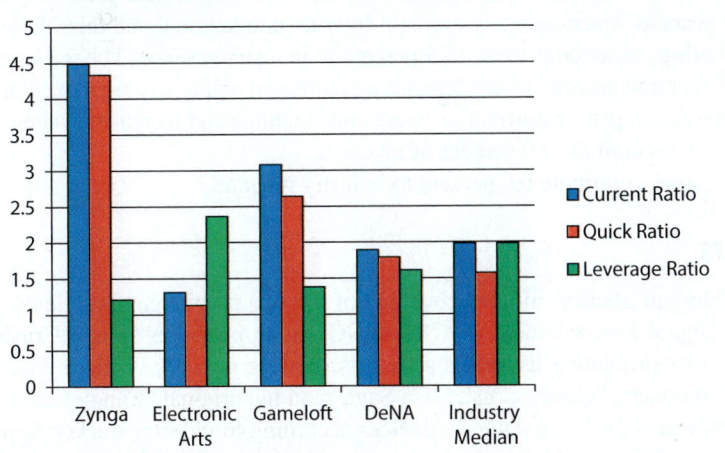

Source: Based on company documents.

In 2014, Zynga focused on global expansion and offering its games on mobile devices. The "Hit It Rich!" slots game was launched in May 2014 and is available in 7 languages worldwide on Google Play (Globe Newswire, May 12, 2014). In April 2014, Zynga launched "FarmVille 2: Country Escape," giving its global players new choices in how they play the game by offering a social experience that allows players more ways to work together to build a farm, adding a Connected Rewards Program, allowing the ability to play offline, and adding new graphics and animation (Globe Newswire, April 17, 2014).

External Issues

The Social Network Game Development industry revenues reached $6 billion in 2013 with industry growth of 29.7 percent, and going forward an annual growth rate of 16.9 percent annually expected through 2018, reaching a revenue of $13.1 billion. There are 2,086 companies in the industry with 38,426 employees. By 2018, it is expected that there will be 4,542 companies in the industry, employing 89,289 employees. The industry is in its growth stage, has few barriers to entry, does not require substantial capital investment, but does experience a high rate of technological innovation.

External Industry Drivers

Increased broadband Internet connections and the increased purchase of mobile devices such as tablets and smartphones (due to increased disposable incomes) has increased player access to social games. Although video game consoles continue to be popular, it is expected that competitive pressure from them will decrease. Because video games consoles are traditionally used at home, there are limited playing opportunities, whereas social network games can be available to players anywhere, anytime.

Typical Customers

It is reported that one in five Americans over the age of 6 play some type of social game. The fastest-growing demographic of players is women over age 40. Women typically begin social gaming through their participation in social network sites, where they are often invited to play a game. Women, comprising 54 percent of the players in the industry, tend to play more puzzle and word games. Women over age 40 account for 27.9 percent of the industry, women under the age of 40 account for 14.4 percent, while men over age 40 account for 23.9 percent, and men over age 40 12.2 percent. Information Solutions Group (Schmidt, 2013) reports that 36.0 percent of U.S. online gamers visit social network games more than once each day.

Product Segments

IBISWorld (Schmidt, 2013) identifies 5 major product segments in the social network game industry:

1. The fastest-growing category is the role-playing game segment and it accounts for 49.0 percent of industry revenue.

2. Dating games account for 17.2 percent of industry revenue. The games are social and offer potential for off-Internet interaction among players. This segment is predicted to grow in the next 5 years as Americans rely more on Internet interaction to aid their dating options.
3. Content-sharing games contribute 15.9 percent to industry revenue. The segment has grown in the past year and customers are demanding increased ability to customize the content giving game developers opportunities to enhance features and increase revenues.
4. Puzzle games account for 9.9 percent of revenue.
5. Gambling games contribute 6.6 percent to industry revenue.

Competitors

In July 2015, Morgan Stanley initiated coverage of the two mobile gaming giants, Zynga, and its rival, King Digital Entertainment (NYSE: KING). King publishes "Sugar Crush Saga" and is excellent at cross-promoting its games across its growing network of more than 350 million players. King's products, "Candy Crush Soda Saga" and the original "Candy Crush Saga," rank third and fourth, respectively, on Android devices according to industry tracker AppAnnie.com. King is also on the list of providing the highest grossing games with its "Farm Heroes Saga at 11," "Pet Rescue Saga at 24," and "Bubble Witch 2 Saga at 26." Morgan Stanley also likes the fact that King is also flush in cash with franchise-widening updates in the pipeline to keep rolling in the near future.

The social network game industry has a low level of concentration, as the four top companies account for 26.2 percent of industry revenue. In order to be successful in this industry, companies must be able to react quickly to consumers' changing tastes, preferences, and demands. They must continually update and add features to existing games and offer new games to play. Today's games are much more detailed than games of the past. They require a lot of people to develop the worlds, characters, and complexity demanded by today's players, so games cost millions to create and make. As a result, major companies no longer create many games and hope that one will be a major success. Companies now release fewer games each year, but each game is more complex and challenging. For example, Electronic Arts released 36 games in 2011 but only 11 games in 2014.

Companies must attain and retain a skilled workforce. Because game developers are scarce, companies often compete with other firms to hire the best employees. Company games and websites must be easy to access and offer a high level of security to players. Successful firms consistently watch consumer trends and analyze market data, so they can predict future trends and prepare games that will catch the eye of the player. Increasingly, game companies must look to the international market for expansion opportunities. This creates additional challenges as games need to be localized via translation to local languages, adapted to local customs and culture, and meet local legal requirements.

Electronic Arts, Inc. (EA)

Headquartered in Redwood City, California, EA Games was founded in 1982 by Trip Hawkins as a home gaming company developing social network games, and then made a big leap into the industry with its purchase of London-based Playfish in 2009. Popular games owned by Electronic Arts include "PopCap Games," "Pet Society," "Restaurant City," "EA Sports FIFA Superstars," "SCRABBLE," "Madden NFL Superstars," "World Series Superstars," "The Sims Social," and "Bejeweled." Electronic Arts made another major acquisition in 2011 with its purchase of PopCap Games. The company had roughly $4,515 million in revenues and $875 million in net income in 2014.

Playdom

Playdom, the social network game subsidiary of Walt Disney Company, was founded in 2008, has a 4.2 market share, and has grown through the acquisitions of Three Melons, Acclaim Games, Hive7, and Metaplace. Its popular games include "Gardens of Time," "Wild Ones," "Bola, City of Wonder," "Sorority Life," "Social City," "ESPNU College Town," "Mobsters," and "NBA Dynasty," which allows players to build and manage their NBA dreams by choosing from more than 9,000 player seasons. The company had roughly $252.6 million in revenues and $65.1 million in operating income in 2013.

Gameloft

Founded in 1999, in Paris, France, by Michael Guillemot and his four brothers, Gameloft in 2008 began focusing on games for smartphones and touchscreen interfaces. Over 1 million of its games are downloaded every day. About 5,200 Gameloft developers create games for over 4,000 different smartphone/tablet devices and 350 feature phone models. With over 6,000 employees working in 27 studios in Europe, the Americas, and Asia, Gameloft is expected to continue its rapid growth in the future. The company's top games include "Asphalt 8," "Captain America," "The Amazing Spiderman 2," "World at Arms," "The Dark Knight Rises," "Green Farm 3," "Despicable Me," "Heroes of Order and Chaos," and "Modern Combat 4." Gameloft reported revenues of 233.3 million euros ($318.207 million) and operating income of 28.4 million euros ($38.7 million) in 2013.

DeNA

DeNA was founded in 1999, in Tokyo, Japan, as an online auction service, but the company expanded its product line and entered the mobile games industry in 2009. DeNA originally launched on the Mobage platform but today has over 2,000 games with game developers located in offices around the world. Its popular social network games include "Ninja Royale," "Blood Brothers," and "Hellfire." DeNA's fiscal 2014 revenues for social network games were about 181 million Yen ($1.76 million) and operating profit was about 53 million Yen ($0.517 million).

Crowdstar

Headquartered in Burlingame, California, and Dublin, Ireland, Crowdstar has less than 5 percent market share but has grown rapidly with revenue in 2013 of about $100.0 million. The company has received $23 million in funding from Intel Capital, Time Warner, China's The9, and NVInvestments. Crowdstar's most popular games include "Happy Aquarium," "Happy Pets," and "It Girl."

Future

There are some positive signs at Zynga (Graham, December 4, 2014): (1) The company is beginning to reposition itself from Facebook to mobile games, (2) the Zynga brand is well established, (3) the acquisition of NaturalMotion provides the company with new games, and (4) the move into the sports ventures with NFL Showdown and its upcoming Tiger Woods golf title provide the company with a new revenue source. But will this be enough? In a highly competitive market, Zynga is the only major company that is not operating at a profit. What should CEO Don Mattrick do next?

The Priceline Group, Inc., 2015

www.priceline.com, PCLN

Headquartered in Norwalk, Connecticut, Priceline is the world's leading travel services company, achieving an impressive $50.3 billion in gross bookings in 2014. Renamed The Priceline Group, Inc. in 2014 to reflect its multiple, independently owned brands, this successful, fast-growing company provides travel-related services in 200 countries, through six popular brands:

1. Booking.com
2. Priceline.com
3. Agoda.com
4. KAYAK
5. Rentalcars.com
6. OpenTable

With its unique *Name Your Own Price* service, travelers can name their price for airline tickets, hotel rooms, car rentals, and vacation packages. The purchaser can select a general location, service level, price, hotel, rental car company, and airline, but the customer cannot cancel after the purchase has gone through. Priceline's mobile products have been featured multiple times by Apple in iTunes, highlighted by Google, and voted as some of the best tools for travelers by several leading media reports, including Travel+Leisure, Conde Nast, and *USA Today*.

In July 2015, Priceline paid $60 million to enter into a strategic partnership with the Brazilian online travel company, Hotel Urbano. The 2016 Olympic Games are to be held in Rio de Janeiro, Brazil. Priceline now offers Hotel Urbano customers access to lodging outside of Latin America from the Priceline worldwide network of over 680,000 affiliates. Also, as part of the agreement, Priceline's Booking.com will be Hotel Urbano's exclusive provider for its non-Latin American retail hotels product, and Priceline will be the preferred provider for Urbano's global packages. Based in Rio, Urbano has commercial deals with 8,000 hotels—more than its competitors such as Decolar.com and CVC. Priceline has been steadily adding affiliates and forming alliances in emerging international markets. The agreement with Urbano is Priceline's first investment in Brazil.

Copyright by Fred David Books LLC; www.strategyclub.com (Written by Raj Selladurai, Indiana University Northwest, and Roshan Selladurai, a student at Indiana University's Kelley School of Business)

History

Mr. Jay Walker founded priceline.com in 1997 with its famous *Name Your Own Price* service. In 1999, Priceline had an initial public offering (IPO) and on the very first day reached a $12.9 billion market value, the highest first-day value for a corporation at that time. In 2004, Priceline entered the retail hotel business by acquiring a major share in TravelWeb and ActiveHotels.com, a leading online hotel-booking service in Europe. In 2005, Priceline acquired Booking.com, the leading hotel-booking website in Europe, and the world's largest accommodations website today, and combined it with ActiveHotels. In 2010, Priceline surpassed Expedia as the world's largest online hotel service, and in 2013, it acquired KAYAK, a travel search company.

Priceline named Mr. Darren Huston as the President and Chief Executive Officer in 2014, the same year the company received special recognition as a *Fortune* Most Admired Company. Among the company's spokespersons over the years, William Shatner of *Star Trek* fame has remained a constant, enduring celebrity synonymous with Priceline as "Priceline Negotiator," while being featured in its advertising from its early days in 1997 through today.

Internal Issues

Vision/Mission/Ethics Statements

Priceline's vision statement is "to continue the company's geographic expansion and expansion of hotel supply around the world, and to coordinate collaboration among the company's different brands, all while maintaining the company's market-leading growth and operating leverage." The company's mission statement is "to be the leading on-line travel business for value-conscious leisure travelers in North America."

The company has a detailed Code of Business Conduct and Ethics policy, which focuses on several issues, including corporate governance practices related to reporting and investigation, workplace respect, antibribery and corruption, and financial integrity and reporting. It also includes gifts and conflict of interest; fair competition/antitrust; international trade; insider trading; privacy and data security; protection of company assets; fair dealing; and communications with public, investors, and the media.

Organizational Structure

As shown in Exhibit 1, Priceline is divisionally structured by product.

Business Segments

Priceline provides financial statements for three key business segments: (1) agency revenues, (2) merchant revenues, and (3) advertising and other revenues. Agency revenues are those generated from travel-related transactions conducted by third parties. These include all travel commissions, Global Distribution System (GDS) reservation booking fees related to certain travel services, and customer processing fees. Most of the revenue for Booking.com is agency revenue, which the company has generated from travel commissions.

EXHIBIT 1 Priceline's Organizational Structure

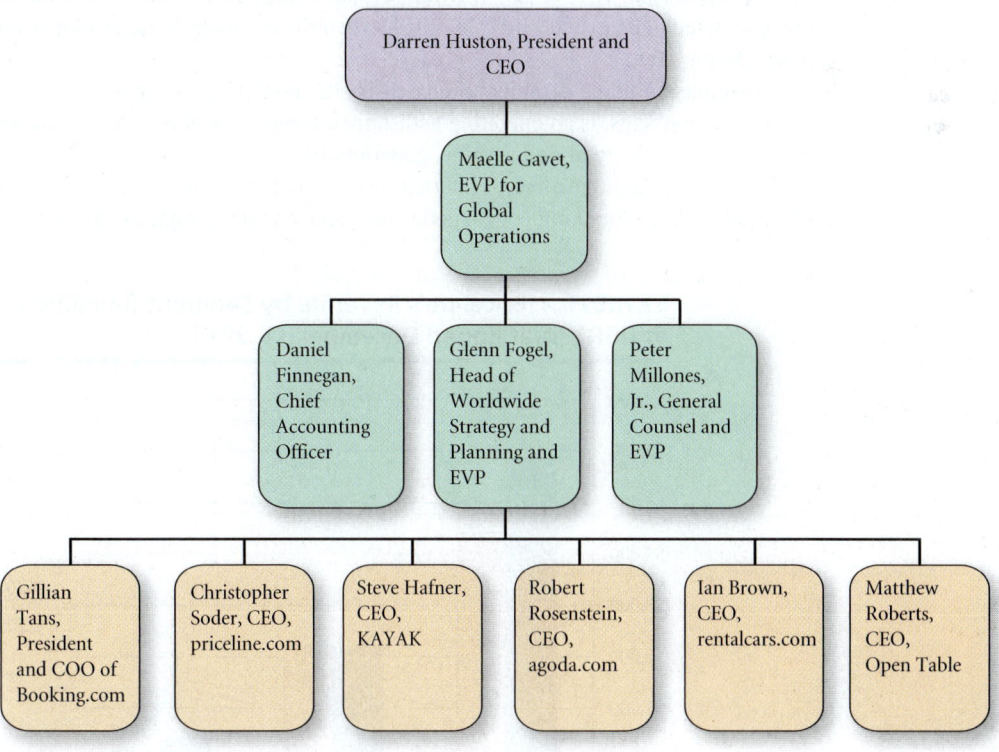

Source: Based on company documents.

Priceline's merchant revenues are from services where the company is not the merchant of record, and therefore charges the customer's credit card for the travel services provided. Merchant revenues include the following:

1. Transaction revenues that represent the selling price of *Name Your Own Price* ® hotel room night, rental car and airline ticket reservations, and vacation packages.
2. Transaction revenues that represent the amount charged to a customer, minus the amount charged by travel service providers. These providers offer (a) the accommodation room reservations provided through its merchant price-disclosed hotel service at agoda.com and priceline.com; and (b) the reservations provided through its merchant rental car service at rentalcars.com and merchant *Express Deals* ® hotel service at priceline.com.
3. Customer processing fees charged in connection with the sale of *Name Your Own Price* ® hotel room night, rental car and airline ticket reservations, and merchant price-disclosed hotel reservations.
4. Ancillary fees, including GDS reservation booking fees related to certain of the services listed.

Exhibit 2 shows that agency revenues in 2014 increased 32.5 percent compared to the prior year, mainly because of the growth in the business of Booking.com. The revenues resulted from growth in its retail rental car, agency airline ticket, and hotel reservation businesses. In addition, merchant revenues for 2014 decreased 1.1 percent compared to 2013, because of decreases in revenues from priceline.com's *Name Your Own Price* reservation services. However, increases in its agoda.com business, rentalcars.com business, priceline.com's *Express Deals* and retail merchant hotel reservation services, and priceline.com's *Express Deals* rental car reservation services made up for the decreases.

Priceline's advertising and other revenues during 2014 were derived primarily from restaurant reservation revenues and subscription revenues for restaurant reservation management services. Advertising and other revenues are obtained primarily from KAYAK for sending referrals to travel service providers and online travel agents, as well as from advertising placements on KAYAK's websites and mobile applications. These showed a substantial increase of 139.6 percent from 2013 to 2014. Other revenues for 2014 include $100.6 million of OpenTable revenue, which came since July 24, 2014, when the company acquired OpenTable, a restaurant reservation system.

Priceline's volume of units purchased by its travel reservation services customers, referred to as gross bookings, is an operating and statistical metric widely used in the travel business. The metric captures the total dollar value, generally inclusive of taxes and fees, of all travel services booked by Priceline customers. International gross bookings reflect gross bookings generated principally by its Booking.com, agoda.com, and rentalcars.com businesses; and the domestic

EXHIBIT 2 **Priceline's Revenue by Segment (in millions of USD); Year Ended December 31, 2014**

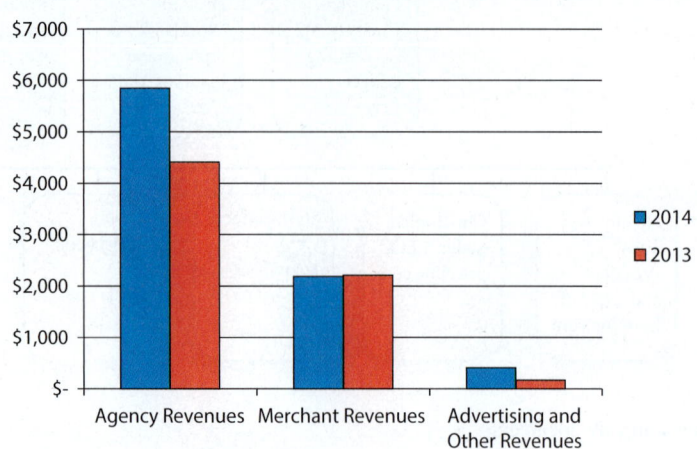

Source: Based on Priceline's 2014 *Annual Report.*

EXHIBIT 3 Priceline's Gross Bookings by Region (in millions of USD)

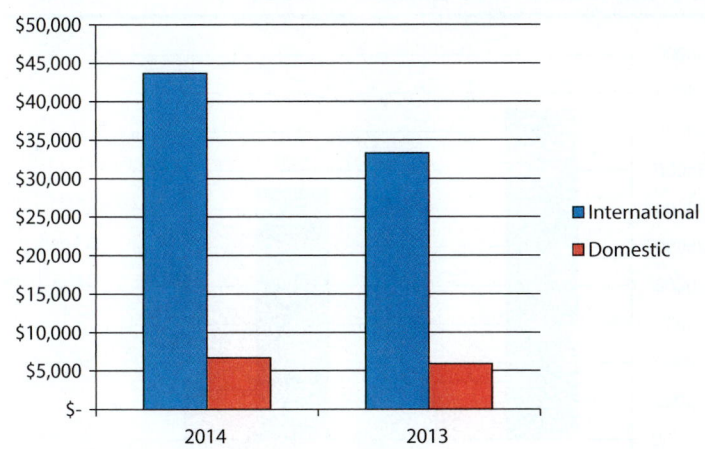

Source: Based on Priceline's 2014 *Annual Report.*

gross bookings reflect gross bookings generated principally by the priceline.com business, in each case regardless of where the consumer resides, where the consumer is physically located while making a reservation, or the location of the travel service provider or restaurant. Gross bookings resulting from accommodation room nights, rental car days, and airline tickets reserved through the company's international and U.S. operations for 2014 and 2013 are given in Exhibit 3.

Exhibit 3 reveals that gross bookings increased by 28.4 percent for 2014, compared to 2013, primarily due to growth of 27.9 percent in accommodation room night reservations, growth of 18.1 percent in rental car day reservations, and 12.0 percent growth in airline ticket reservations. International gross bookings grew by 31.0 percent in 2014, primarily due to growth in accommodation room night reservations for the company's Booking.com and agoda.com businesses, as well as growth in rental car day reservations for its rentalcars.com business.

Priceline's domestic gross bookings increased by 13.4 percent for 2014, primarily due to increases in Priceline's retail airline ticket, retail hotel, *Express Deals* ® hotel, and retail rental car services. However, declines in priceline.com's *Name Your Own Price* ® reservation services offset these increases. Travel service providers—especially hotels—typically provide a limited amount of availability to opaque services such as Priceline, usually during periods of healthy travel demand. As a result, the recent healthy travel environment in the United States has had an adverse impact on its access to availability for Priceline's opaque reservation services.

Exhibit 4 gives Priceline's gross bookings resulting from reservations of accommodation room nights, rental car days, and airline tickets made through Priceline agency and merchant models for 2014. Agency gross bookings increased 31.3 percent for 2014, due primarily to growth in Booking.com hotel reservations, priceline.com's retail airline ticket, rental car and hotel reservation services, and rentalcars.com reservation service. Merchant gross bookings increased 14.0 percent in 2014. This was mainly because of increases in agoda.com hotel reservation services, rentalcars.com rental car reservation services, and priceline.com *Express Deals* hotel and retail hotel reservation services, which were partially offset by declines in priceline.com's *Name Your Own Price* services.

Priceline helps connect consumers wishing to make travel reservations with providers of travel services around the world, offering consumers accommodation reservations (including hotels, bed and breakfasts, hostels, apartments, vacation rentals, and other properties) through its Booking.com, priceline.com, and agoda.com brands. Priceline.com offers reservations for rental cars, airline tickets, vacation packages, and cruises, all through six major brands/segments as follows:

1. **Booking.com**: Headquartered in the Netherlands, booking.com is the world's leading brand for booking online accommodation reservations with operations worldwide for more than 600,000 properties in over 200 countries and territories on its various websites and in 42 languages, which includes over 245,000 vacation rental properties. Booking.com has begun to offer website and other marketing services to accommodation providers as part of its BookingSuite initiative.

EXHIBIT 4 Priceline's Gross Bookings by Agency and Merchant Models (in millions of USD)

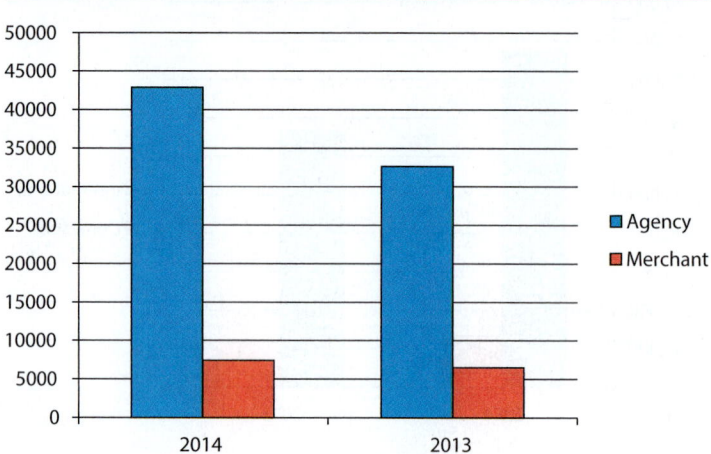

Source: Based on Priceline's 2014 *Annual Report.*

2. **Priceline.com**: This online travel reservation service provider primarily operates in the United States, providing hotel, rental car, and airline ticket reservations services, as well as vacation packages and cruises. Priceline.com is a leader in the "opaque" travel reservation business (not disclosing service provider identity until after reservation completed) through its pioneering *Name Your Own Price* and *Express Deals* hotel, rental car, and airline reservation services.

3. **Agoda.com**: Headquartered in Singapore, agoda.com is a leading online accommodation reservation service catering primarily to consumers in the Asia-Pacific region, with operations in Bangkok, Thailand, and throughout the region. Agoda.com operates primarily under a merchant model, by filing rates and information about the property in agoda.com's proprietary extranet.

4. **Rentalcars.com**: Headquartered in Manchester, England, rentalcars.com is a leading worldwide online rental car reservation service offering merchants online retail and opaque rental car reservation service. It allows consumers to make rental car reservations in more than 28,000 locations throughout the world, with excellent customer support provided in 40 languages.

5. **KAYAK**: Headquartered in Stamford, Connecticut, KAYAK provides an online price comparison service (often referred to as "meta-search") that allows consumers to easily search and compare travel itineraries and prices, including airline tickets, accommodation reservations, and rental car reservation information from hundreds of travel websites all at once. KAYAK derives revenues from advertising placements on its websites and mobile apps, and from sending referrals to travel service providers. KAYAK does business primarily in the United States, but has plans to expand globally.

6. **OpenTable**: Headquartered in San Francisco, California, OpenTable provides online restaurant reservation services to consumers and to restaurants. OpenTable does business primarily in the United States, although plans are to grow globally.

Strategies

Priceline wants to aggressively grow globally while continuing to offer excellent customer service through its call centers and websites. The company focuses on developing mutually beneficial relationships with travel service providers and restaurants around the world. Travel service providers and restaurants can benefit from participating in its services. For example, an independent hotel may not have the means or expertise to market itself to international travelers, including the use of other languages, building and operating effective desktop and mobile websites and online reservation services, or engaging in sophisticated online marketing techniques. The company maintains multiple, independently managed brands to appeal to a variety of target audiences while maintaining an entrepreneurial, competitive spirit among its brands.

EXHIBIT 5 Priceline's Income Statement (in millions of USD)

Report Date	December 31, 2014	December 31, 2013
Revenues	$8,442	$6,793
Operating expenses	5,365	4,413
EBIT	3,077	2,380
Interest	88	83
EBT	2,989	2,297
Tax	568	403
Other items	—	(2)
Net income	**2,421**	**1,892**

Source: Based on company documents and Yahoo Finance.

Marketing

Priceline has established widely used and recognized e-commerce brands through aggressive marketing and promotion campaigns. As a result, the company's online and offline advertising expense has increased significantly in recent years, a trend most likely to continue. During 2014, Priceline's total online advertising expense was approximately $2.4 billion, and the company spent a substantial portion of it internationally through Internet search engines (primarily Google), meta-search and travel research services, and affiliate marketing. The company also invested $231 million in offline advertising, and it plans to continue a strategy of aggressively promoting brand awareness, primarily through online means, as well as expanding offline campaigns into additional markets. For example, building on its first offline advertising campaign, which it launched in the United States in 2013, Booking.com has begun offline advertising campaigns in other markets, including Australia, Canada, the United Kingdom, and Germany.

Finance

Priceline's recent income statement and balance sheet are provided in Exhibits 5 and 6, respectively. Priceline's revenues increased 24 percent in 2014, but the firm's goodwill almost doubled (increased by 88 percent).

Competitors

Priceline competes with hundreds of online and traditional travel agencies and reservation services, including even Google, Apple, Alibaba, Amazon, and Facebook, all of which have access to significantly greater and more diversified resources than Priceline does. Social media and search engine sites continue to leverage other aspects of Priceline's business. Google has entered various aspects of the online travel market through its ITA Software, Inc., a major flight information software company, its hotel meta-search service known as "Hotel Finder," and its license of hotel-booking software known as Room 77.

Priceline faces strong competition from online travel services including Expedia, Hotwire, Hotels.com, Travelocity, Orbitz, and others. Traditional travel service companies such as American Express, Thomas Cook, Tui Travel, and others also pose major threats to Priceline. Meta-search companies—for example, TripAdvisor, Google, and Trivago—compete with Priceline. Even Apple has acquired a patent for "iTravel" that would enable consumers to make quick and convenient travel arrangements on their phones. With "Passbook" being in its repertoire of products, Apple seems ready and eager to offer some new services to its many users worldwide to penetrate the travel services industry in the near future.

Priceline's closest and most intense rival firm is Expedia. Exhibit 7 provides a comparative analysis of Priceline with Expedia and Orbitz. Notice that Priceline is the best company on all measures.

EXHIBIT 6 Priceline's Balance Sheet (in millions of USD)

Report Date	December 31, 2014	December 31, 2013
Assets		
Cash and equivalents	$3,149	$1,300
Accounts receivable	797	610
Other current assets	1,321	5,570
Total current assets	5,267	7,480
Long-term investments	3,756	—
Property, plant, & equipment	199	135
Goodwill	3,326	1,768
Intangible assets	2,334	1,020
Other assets	58	41
Total assets	**14,940**	**10,444**
Liabilities		
Short-term debt	37	152
Accounts payable	882	793
Other current liabilities	461	437
Total current liabilities	1,380	1,382
Long-term debt	3,850	1,751
Other liabilities	1,144	402
Total liabilities	**6,374**	**3,535**
Common stock	0	0
Retained earnings	6,640	4,219
Treasury stock	(2,737)	(1,987)
Paid in capital and other	4,663	4,677
Total equity	**8,566**	**6,909**
Total liabilities & equity	**14,940**	**10,444**

Source: Based on company documents and Yahoo Finance.

EXHIBIT 7 Priceline's 2014 Profitability versus Rival Firms

	Priceline	Expedia	Orbitz
$ Revenues	8.5 B	5.8 B	940 M
# Employees	13 K	19 K	NA
$ Revenues per Employee	654,000	305,000	NA
$ Net Income	2.4 B	400 M	18 M
$ EPS	46	3.0	0.16
$ Market Capitalization	64 B	12 B	1.3 B

Source: A variety of sources.

Expedia (EXPE)

Headquartered in Bellevue, Washington, Expedia owns Travelocity and plans to acquire Orbitz. Expedia's brands include Expedia.com, Hotels.com, Hotwire.com, Classic Vacations, Travelocity, Expedia Local Expert, Egencia, Expedia CruiseShipCenters, eLong, and Venere.com, as well as Trivago, CarRentals.com, Wotif.com, lastminute.com.au, travel.com.au, Asia Web Direct, LateStays.com, GoDo.com.au, and Arnold Travel Technology. Both Priceline and Expedia have been aggressively acquiring smaller competitors for years, as the online travel booking industry has rapidly consolidated. Expedia has about 3,000 employees in Bellevue, but is running out of space in its building, so is considering moving out of the city to a new location, possibly in Seattle. Expedia currently owns over an 8 percent market share in the travel industry, making it the largest player with rival Priceline owning a 5 percent market share. Expedia is heavily expanding its presence outside the United States and now generates approximately 50 percent of its revenues from outside the country.

External Issues

Rapid consumer adoption and use of mobile devices globally creates new challenges for Priceline because such trends enable device companies such as Apple to offer travel services. The iPhone and Android-enabled smartphones, coupled with improved web browsing functionality and development of thousands of useful "apps" available on these devices, is driving substantial online traffic and commerce to mobile platforms. Priceline has experienced a significant shift of business to mobile platforms; its advertising partners are also seeing a rapid shift of traffic to mobile platforms.

Priceline's business is dependent on leisure travel. People booking hotels, bed and breakfasts, hostels, apartments, vacation rentals, rental car and airline ticket reservations, and so on, are dependent on discretionary spending levels. The U.S. economy and most global economies are improving, and so long as that trend continues, Priceline benefits. The company also benefits from lower gasoline prices.

Unforeseen events such as oil prices, terrorist attacks, unusual weather patterns, earthquakes, hurricanes, tsunamis, floods, and volcanic eruptions can affect travel. Further, travel-related health concerns—including pandemics and epidemics such as Ebola, Influenza H1N1, avian bird flu, and SARS, as well as political instability, regional hostilities, imposition of taxes or surcharges by regulatory authorities or travel related accidents—can disrupt travel or otherwise result in declines in travel demand.

The value of the U.S. dollar affects Priceline's business because millions of their customers reside outside the United States. In March 2015, the U.S. dollar hit an 11-year high to the Euro.

Market Segmentation

Historically, customers were forced to book travel accommodations through a travel agent or directly through an airline, often at high commissions for the customer. However, customers today are increasingly using websites, such as Priceline and Expedia, that control 5 and 8 percent, respectively, of the market, to book their travel arrangements, generally at a great cost savings for the customer. There are over 10,000 travel agencies in the United States, and even though Priceline and Expedia make up 13 percent of the total revenues generated, the market is still quite fragmented, potentially leaving large market shares to be gained by top firms. Overall, the industry growth rate remains sluggish, with growth of less than 2 percent expected through 2020.

Exhibit 8 reveals the percent breakdown between the most common markets for the industry. It is interesting to note that among U.S. travel industry revenues, approximately 50 percent of

EXHIBIT 8 Most Common Revenue Sources for the U.S. Travel Industry

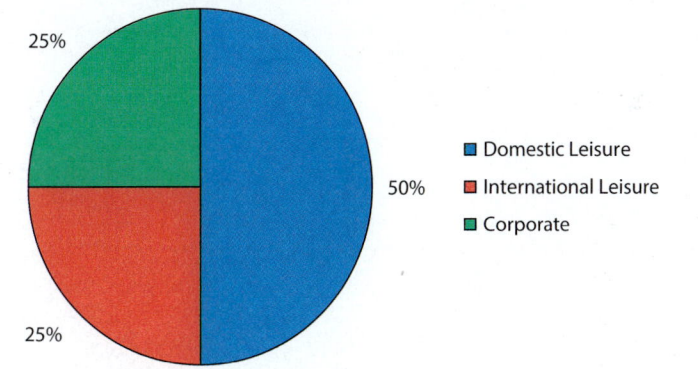

- Domestic Leisure
- International Leisure
- Corporate

Source: Based on a variety of sources.

revenues are derived from international-based travel. As international travel becomes more affordable, many customers are venturing overseas. In addition, a significant portion of international travel is booked through traditional travel agencies, as many tourists who are visiting overseas for the first time appreciate and value the one-on-one service a traditional travel agent provides.

Aside from customer type, the industry is fairly well split between service type among customers. Tour packages account for 30 percent of total revenues, and, like international travel packages, they are routinely booked through traditional travel agencies. U.S. cruises and airline bookings account for 50 percent of the total, with approximately equal weight between them. Surprisingly, rental car bookings account for little more than 2 percent of all travel revenues, yet on any travel site such as Priceline and Expedia, offering a car is almost always forced on the customer to accept or opt out of before continuing with their desired transaction of a hotel, flight, or whatever they may be purchasing. International-based market segmentation has a profile similar to that of the United States, with tours being the most popular, followed by cruises and airline bookings.

Future

Priceline's year-over-year growth rates have generally decelerated in recent years. For example, in 2014, Priceline's accommodation room night reservation growth was 28 percent, a deceleration from 37, 40, and 53 percent in the years prior, respectively. Given the size of its hotel reservation business, the company expects that its year-over-year growth rates will continue to decelerate.

Priceline's mobile offerings have received strong reviews and achieved solid download trends, and are driving an increasing share of its business. Mobile bookings present an opportunity for growth and are necessary to maintain and grow its business as consumers increasingly turn to mobile devices instead of a personal computer and to mobile applications in addition to a web browser.

Several factors affect online advertising efficiency, including costs per click, cancellation rates, foreign exchange rates, the ability to convert paid traffic to booking customers, and the extent to which consumers come directly to websites or mobile apps for bookings. KAYAK and OpenTable spend significantly less on advertising that the other brands, so Priceline expects its online advertising efficiency to increase dramatically.

Typically, hotels make available only a limited number of hotel rooms for opaque services such as Priceline's, especially during periods of high occupancy. As a result, recent high hotel occupancy levels in the United States have had an adverse impact on its access to hotel rooms for its opaque hotel reservation services, which has negatively affected the company's opaque hotel reservation gross profits.

Priceline's shareholders are accustomed to high growth rates. The company needs a clear three-year strategic plan. Prepare this document for CEO Darren Huston.

The TJX Companies, Inc., 2015

www.tjx.com, TJX

A treasure hunt in a department store? This is the experience that CEO Carol Meyrowitz of TJX wants customers to have when they come into any of the company's 3,200-plus stores in the United States, Canada, and Europe. TJX is a huge retail conglomerate of off-price brands, including TJMaxx, Marshalls, HomeGoods, and Sierra Trading Post—with stores in all 50 states of the USA, 10 provinces of Canada, as well as the European nations the United Kingdom, Ireland, Germany, and Poland. Headquartered in Framingham, Massachusetts, TJX's revenue increased to $29 billion in fiscal 2014 that ended January 31, 2015, while the company's net income increased to $2.2 billion. TJX has about 195,000 employees who often work right across the street from rival companies such as Ross Stores, Stein Mart, Gap, and Cato.

TJX reported 2016 Q1 EPS of $0.69, up 8 percent from Q1 of the previous fiscal year, despite a 4 cent per share foreign exchange rate loss. Same store sales also grew 5 percent. CEO Meyrowitz attributed the increased EPS to increased consumer traffic and merchandise margins in nearly all of the company's Canadian and U.S. stores. Part of the increase in consumer traffic is a new trend where consumers are not as willing to drive to outlet stores that are often far from their homes in search of deals. If this trend continues, firms like TJX and rivals such as Ross should continue to benefit as they siphon sales away from outlet malls.

Copyright by Fred David Books LLC. www.strategyclub.com (Written by Diana Tsaw and Forest R. David)

History

In 1919, two brothers, Max and Morris Feldberg, established the New England Trading Company in Boston, Massachusetts, and by 1929, devoted the business to selling ladies hosiery, a luxury during that time. By 1949, the Feldberg brothers were owners of a chain of women's apparel stores along the East Coast of the United States.

When the next generation of Feldbergs, Stanley and Sumner, took over in the 1950s, they changed the business model to one that offered discounted merchandise to the entire family. They also changed the company name to Zayne Discount Department Store (Zayne) and listed it on the New York Stock Exchange.

In 1976, Ben Cammarata (who recently retired in June 2015), chairman of the Board of Directors, created the brand TJMaxx and officially changed the name of the company to TJX. A few milestones in TJX's history are given below.

USA

1992	TJX launched HomeGoods, a brand consisting of items for the home.
1995	TJX acquired Marshalls and grouped it with TJMaxx to form The MarMaxx Group, the largest division/product line in the TJX stable.
2012	TJX acquired Sierra Trading Post of Wyoming, an off-price store selling goods for most outdoors activities.

Canada

1990	TJX acquired Winners, an off-price chain in Canada that offers many of the same goods as TJMaxx.
2001	Winners launched HomeSense, similar to HomeGoods in USA.
2011	TJX launched Marshalls in Canada.

Europe

1994	TJX established TJMaxx in United Kingdom (UK), which later expanded to Ireland.
2007	TJMaxx began its business in Germany.

| **2008** | TJMaxx brings HomeSense from Canada to the UK. |
| **2009** | TJMaxx opens its first store in Poland. |

Internal Issues

Corporate Values

The top part of the "X" in the TJX logo is a "V" that represents the VALUES believed in by TJX. In broad strokes, each alphabet represents vital parts of its business model, and each alphabet in VALUE translates into more specific codes of conduct:

V = Vendor Relationships are unequivocally built on high standards of ethics

A = TJX pays **Attention** in governance and to integrity, fairness, and openness in treatment of others.

L = TJX **Leverages** the diversity and inclusion among employees, customers, and vendors.

U = TJX **Unites** with the communities in which its stores are in to enrich the lives of employees, customers, and people who live in these communities.

E = TJX follows the motto of "smart for business, good for the **Environment**" by being deliberate in controlling waste/pollution and in managing energy sources.

Organizational Structure

TJX's organizational chart is provided in Exhibit 1. The company appears to operate using a strategic-business unit (SBU) design, but it is not clear from the titles of executives what the groups are or what the divisions underneath the group heads are. Analysts suggest that improvements are needed in the design or at least in the titles of executives to more clearly reveal reporting relationships and areas of responsibility. The company's CEO, Carol Meyrowitz, was also elected to be Chairman of the Board in mid-2015.

EXHIBIT 1 TJX's Organizational Structure.

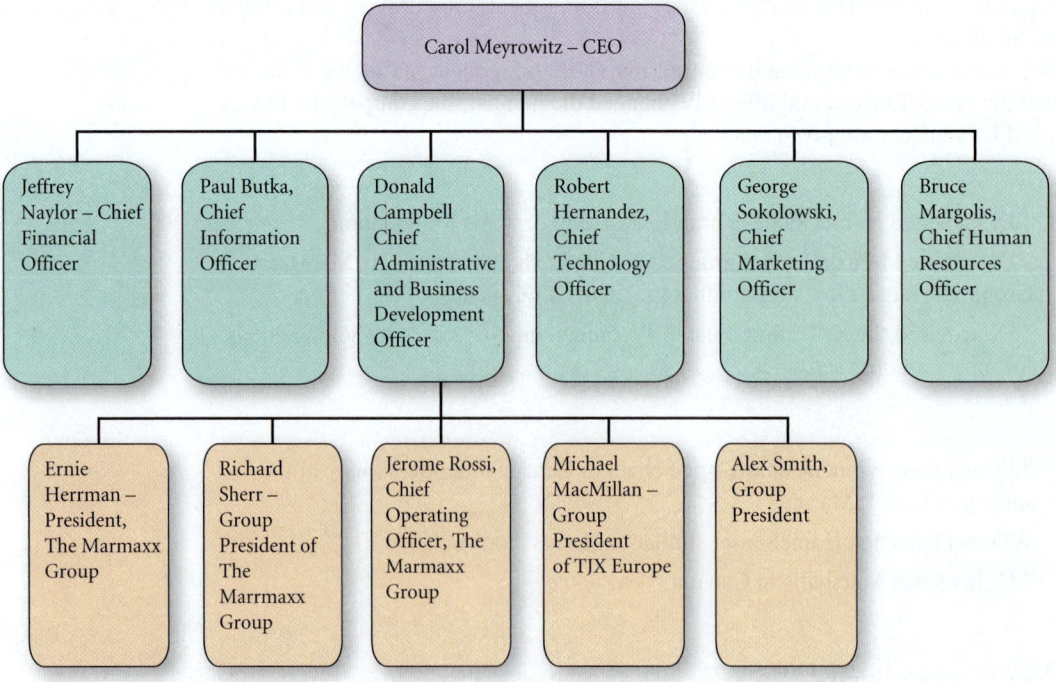

Source: Based on company documents.

Business Segments

Formed after the acquisition of Marshalls in 1995, The MarMaxx Group is the division that consists of the T.J. Maxx and Marshalls brands. Both T.J. Maxx and Marshalls sell similar items, consisting of home goods, furniture, laps, rugs, giftware, snack foods, and much more. TJMaxx offers off-price brand names in family apparel, fine jewelry, accessories, and beauty products. The term *off-price* translates to prices 20 to 60 percent less than that of the major department and/or specialty stores. The Runway, a high-end house designer line, is offered in some T.J. Maxx stores. In fact, T.J. Maxx considers The Runway, and other higher-end selections, as a way it differentiates itself from Marshalls.

There are nearly 1,200 T.J. Maxx stores in the United States, with an average size of 29,000 square feet. Marshalls offers merchandise similar to T.J. Maxx and was purchased partly as a means to remove a competitor from the industry, along with growing the T.J. Maxx's brand. Marshalls' signature difference from T.J. Maxx is The CUBE designed for juniors. The CUBE is a store within a store, an A-level boutique offering higher-end selections targeted for juniors. There were 942 Marshalls stores in the United States in 2014, up 4.5 percent from 2013, with an average size of 31,000 square feet. In total, there are over 2,000 T.J. Maxx and Marshalls stores in the country, with a long-range outlook to expand to 3,000 stores.

TJX's other U.S.-based business is HomeGoods, which focuses on furniture, laps, rugs, giftware, wall décor, and bath and bedding through 450 stores in the United States, with an average store size of 26,000 square feet. The firm has a vision to increase its HomeGoods store presence to 850 stores long term.

TJX's newly acquired Sierra Trading Post is a small Wyoming-based business specializing in outdoor equipment, family apparel, footwear, and many other items, including expensive suits, shirts, and slacks. Sierra Trading Post currently operates four stores in the United States, with plans to add two additional stores. Being a super-discount seller of overstocked goods, it is not uncommon to find products for as much as 70 percent off retail prices, but equally as common, it can be difficult to find your size or the exact product you wish to purchase from Sierra Trading Post. The store is best known for its website, www.sierratradingpost.com, rather than its physical stores.

TJX's Winners segment is a leading off-priced retail chain in Canada. The offerings are similar to T.J. Maxx, but with brand names familiar to Canadian customers in apparel and home goods. TJX recently added fine jewelry and The Runway to selected Winners stores. There are 227 Winners stores located in 10 provinces, the majority of which are in Ontario (104), Quebec (41), and British Columbia (80). Winners owns HomeSense, a chain of 91 stores that offer similar merchandise as HomeGoods USA for the kitchen, dining room, living room, and bedroom. The majority of HomeSense stores (42) are found in Ontario.

TJX brought Marshalls into Canada in 2011 with the establishment of 27 stores, the majority (20) of which are found in Ontario. Other than the usual Marshalls merchandise, the Canadian stores offer brand name footwear. TJX plans to add an additional 100 Marshalls stores in Canada.

Unique to TJMaxx in Europe are two in-house brands: The Mod Box is a line of apparel aimed specifically at young adults, and the Gold label consists of European high-end designer brands. As of fiscal 2014, there were 371 stores spread over the UK and Ireland (270), Germany (63), and Poland (38). Currently, there are 28 HomeSense stores in Europe offering merchandise for the living room, dining room, bedroom, kitchen, and garden. The average T.J. Maxx and HomeSense store in Europe is 31,000 and 21,000 square feet, respectively. The company plans to have 900 stores total in Europe.

Exhibit 2 reveals the locations and types of TJX stores worldwide. Note that approximately 13 percent of stores are located in Europe in fiscal 2015, but no stores in Asia, Middle East, or Africa. Exhibit 3 shows revenues per geographic region. The United States accounts for 77 percent of all store locations and 76 percent of all revenue. TJX reported revenues of $27.4 and $25.8 billion in fiscal 2014 and 2013, respectively.

Exhibit 3 provides a revenue and profit breakdown for TJX's segments. Not revealed in Exhibit 3, fiscal 2015 produced modest gains across every business operated by TJX. Total sales companywide were up 6 percent. Canada, which experienced a small decline in sales from 2013 to 2014, had a small increase in fiscal 2015 to $2,884 million. The largest percent increase was

EXHIBIT 2 TJX's Total Number of Stores

Business	2015	2014
Marmaxx		
USA T.J. Maxx	1,119	1,079
USA Marshalls	975	942
HomeGoods	487	450
Sierra Trading Post	6	4
TJX Canada		
Winners	234	227
HomeSense	96	91
Marshalls	38	27
TJX Europe		
T.K. Maxx	407	371
HomeSense	33	28
TJX Totals	3,395	3,219

Source: Based on a TJX Q4 2015 press release.

EXHIBIT 3 TJX's Revenue and Profits (in thousands of USD)

Revenues	2014	2013
USA Marmaxx	$17,929,576	$17,011,409
USA HomeGoods	2,993,718	2,657,111
TJX Canada	2,877,834	2,925,991
TJX Europe	3,621,568	3,283,861
Totals	$27,422,696	$25,878,372

Profits	2014	2013
USA Marmaxx	$2,612,693	$2,486,274
USA HomeGoods	386,541	324,623
TJX Canada	405,363	414,914
TJX Europe	275,453	215,713
Totals*	$3,319,489	$3,077,351

*Adjusted to reflect interest and corporate expenses.
Source: TJX's 2014 *Annual Report*, p. F-19.

in USA HomeGoods, increasing sales to over $3 billion with Marmaxx (combination of TJ Maxx and Marshalls) increasing to $18 billion for the largest net dollar change.

Exhibit 4 reveals TJX's revenues by product category across all stores. The firm does not reveal profit details by products. TJX's revenue mix has remained stable over the last 3 years, with the only minor trend being clothing, which dropped from 60 percent of revenues in 2012 (not shown in Exhibit 4) to 58 percent in fiscal 2014.

Finance
TJX's income statement and balance sheet are provided in Exhibits 5 and 6, respectively. Note the nice increases in revenue and net income.

Supply Chain Management
The beginning point of TJX's supply chain is the acquisition of inventory by its approximately 900 associates (buyers) in 13 buying offices in 10 countries. TJX associates maintain close relationships with vendors, and are constantly looking out for opportunistic purchases—close-out

EXHIBIT 4 TJX's 2014 Percent Revenue by Product

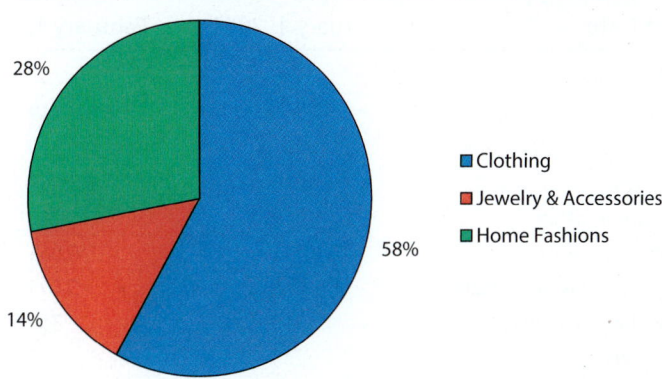

Source: Based on 2014 *Annual Report*, page F-19.

sales, order cancellations, and manufacturing overruns. TJX buys on an ongoing basis, keeping track of customers' preferences, trends, and seasonal needs in merchandise.

There are about 16,000 vendors around the world, mainly manufacturers and other retailers. TJX purchases "less-than-full" assortment items, of quantity from small to large, and in different styles and sizes. TJX pays vendors promptly and therefore has no need for any retail concessions like promotion or mark-down allowances, or delivery concessions like discount on shipment cost, or reliance on a "return policy" discount. When appropriate, TJX will purchase inventory to sell at a future time, in spite of its usual policy of adhering to a lean and rapid turnover of inventory.

The next point in the supply chain is warehousing where inventory is collected, sorted, and processed for distribution. Thus, the various distribution centers can be viewed as TJX production facilities. Although many of TJX retail outlets are leased, many of its distribution centers are owned and located near, or as part of, corporate offices in order to facilitate the centrally controlled decisions on pricing, mark-downs, and inventory replenishment.

In the United States, TJX distribution centers are located in Massachusetts, Indiana, Georgia, North Carolina, Pennsylvania, Nevada, and Arizona. In Canada, they are located in Ontario, and in Europe, they are located in England, Germany, and Poland.

Marketing

The one key success factor for TJX is pricing, as in offering merchandise at least 20 to 60 percent off the prices charged by major retail and specialty department stores. TJX claims it serves a wide spectrum of customers with annual household income from $50,000 to millions of dollars. Given their business model, one area where TJX does save is in advertising and customer service. Customers are encouraged to explore in a "treasure hunt" in its stores, where no walls separate

EXHIBIT 5 TJX's Income Statement (in millions of USD)

Report Date	February 1, 2015	February 1, 2014
Revenues	$29,078	$27,423
Cost of sales	20,777	19,605
Operating expenses	4,712	4,468
EBIT	3,589	3,350
Interest	40	31
EBT	3,549	3,319
Tax	1,334	1,182
Net income	**2,215**	**2,137**

Source: Based on TJX's 2014 *Annual Report*, page F-3.

EXHIBIT 6 TJX's Balance Sheet (in millions of USD)

Report Date	February 1, 2015	February 1, 2014
Assets		
Cash and equivalents	$2,494	$2,149
Accounts receivable	283	210
Inventories	3,218	2,967
Other current assets	720	742
Total current assets	6,715	6,068
Property, plant & equipment	3,868	3,595
Goodwill & intangibles	310	313
Other assets	235	225
Total assets	**11,128**	**10,201**
Liabilities		
Accounts payable	2,008	1,771
Other current liabilities	1,922	1,747
Total current liabilities	3,930	3,518
Long-term debt	1,624	1,274
Other liabilities	1,310	1,179
Total liabilities	**6,864**	**5,971**
Common stock	685	705
Retained earnings	4,134	3,724
Other equity	(554)	(200)
Paid in capital	—	—
Total equity	**4,264**	**4,230**
Total liabilities & equity	**11,128**	**10,201**

Source: Based on TJX's 2014 *Annual Report*, page F-5.

the different departments. Customers roam freely about the open-spaced layout without staff "hovering around," yet the customers are able to seek assistance from such staff when needed. TJX has a generous return policy. It encourages customers to apply for and obtain a TJX credit card.

TJX marketers work closely with TJX buyers to identify customers' preferences, and in recent years, they have worked with the product development people to produce its own in-house and licensed brands. TJX's primary advertising strategy is its stores—a visible and physical representation of its brands. In Europe, especially with the younger generation, TJX engages in TV, radio, and social media advertising, pushing its "tri-branding" campaigns. Starting in 2013, TJX launched www.tjmaxx.com in the United States and www.tkmaxx.com in the United Kingdom and officially entered in e-commerce arena.

Competitors

The family clothing business in the United States is highly fragmented, with over 20,000 businesses, ranging in size from a mom-and-pop to TJX, which is the largest clothing business based on total revenues. Profit margins are slim in the industry that is valued at $100 billion in annual sales, with profits slightly above $3 billion and a growth rate of less than 2.5 percent. Top competitors in the industry include TJX, Ross Stores, L Brands, Gap, Cato, Stein Mart, and many more. Notable newcomers to the U.S. market include H&M, based in Sweden and popular throughout Europe, specializing in inexpensive but quality clothing. Also, Zara, a fashionable clothing store with inexpensive prices based in Spain, now has U.S. stores.

Note in Exhibit 7, TJX has a larger market cap, net income, and revenues than Ross and Gap combined. However, Ross is worth more per share than TJX.

EXHIBIT 7 Comparative Analysis of TJX versus Rival Firms

	TJX	Ross	Gap
# Employees	198,000	71,400	141,000
$ Net Income	2,215 M	837 M	1,280 M
$ Revenue	29,078 M	10,230 M	16,148 M
$ Revenue/Employee	147,000	143,000	115,000
$ EPS Ratio	3.15	4.42	2.87
Market Cap.	47.5 B	21.5 B	17.7 B

Source: Based on Yahoo Finance 2014 data and other sources.

Ross Stores, Inc. (ROST)

Based in Dublin, California, Ross Stores is a discount clothing and home fashions store offering products at prices generally 20 to 60 percent off typical retail department store prices. The firm's main slogan is "Ross, Dress for Less." The firm operates under two segments: Ross, Dress for Less and dd's Discounts. The firm employs over 17,000 people, and reported revenues were over $10 billion in fiscal year-end February 2014. In total, Ross operates over 1,100 stores in 36 states with product offerings similar to TJX—including women's clothing, lingerie, maternity clothing, shoes, accessories, handbags, watches, jewelry, luggage, and more. Ross operates under a no-frills policy that extends to having no window displays, no mannequins, nor other fancy marketing and advertising displays. In Q4 of 2014, Ross's sales advanced 10.6 percent to over $3 billion, and the company's comparable-store sales jumped 6 percent year over year.

Arguably TJX's primary competitor, Ross operates 130 discounts stores in 10 states, offering products similar to TJX, but in generally lesser-known name brands. There are about 315, 189, and 156 stores in California, Texas, and Florida, respectively. Ross has no stores yet in much of the Midwest and Northeast, including no stores in Michigan, Ohio, or New York. Exhibit 8 reveals the breakdown in sales from various products in Ross Stores.

The Gap Inc. (GPS)

Headquartered in San Francisco, California, Gap's notable brands include Gap, Banana Republic, Old Navy, Piperlime, Athleta, and Intermix. Gap's stores are generally considered full-retail–priced stores, unlike TJX and Ross, both of which are off-priced–retail stores. GAP sells a variety of casual apparel, including men's, women's, children's, and baby's clothing in all styles and fashions, as well as various accessories and luxury and contemporary products. Gap operates over 3,600 stores worldwide on every inhabited continent. The company reported fiscal year-end February 2014 revenues in excess of $16 billion, with the bulk of revenues being derived from Gap, Banana Republic, and Old Navy, as revealed in Exhibit 9 by geographic region. In 2013,

EXHIBIT 8 Ross Stores' Percent Revenue 2014 Fiscal Year

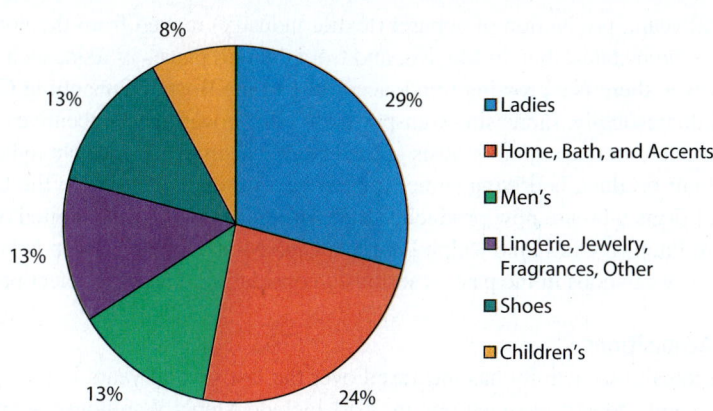

Source: Based on Ross Stores' 2014 *Annual Report,* page 3.

EXHIBIT 9 Gap's Fiscal 2013 (year-end February 1, 2014) Revenues (in millions of USD)

Region	Gap	Old Navy	Banana Republic	Other	Total
US	$3,800	$5,698	$2,365	$668	$12,531
Canada	404	482	238	4	1,128
Europe	809	–	82	–	891
Asia	1,165	77	155	–	1,397
Other	173	–	28	–	201
Total	6,351	6,257	2,868	672	16,148

Source: Based on various tables from Gap's 2013 *Annual Report.*

Gap reported 15 percent of its sales from outside the United States and Canada. The firm controls approximately 14 percent of the U.S. market share for retail appeal stores.

Burlington Stores Inc. (BURL)

Headquartered in Burlington, New Jersey, Burlington Stores is a large apparel company that reported net sales of $4.4 billion in fiscal year-end February 2014. Better known as Burlington Coat Factory, the company operates 521 stores in 44 states, with merchandise often priced up to 70 percent below department store prices. Burlington Stores offers clothing for men, women, children, and babies, as well as home décor, jewelry, and much more.

For its fourth quarter ending January 31, 2015, the company sales increased about 10 percent, whereas its comparable store sales increases about 5.5 percent. BURL's full fiscal year 2014 (the 52 weeks ending January 31, 2015) revealed a sales increase of about 8.3 percent, with comparable store sales for the full year to be approximately 4.5 percent. Thus, Burlington Stores is performing quite well and is a qualified competitor to TJX.

External Issues

Product Segmentation

Women's clothing accounts for 62 percent of all clothing sold in the United States. Men's clothing accounts for 30 percent, and children's about 8 percent. Casual clothing for both men and women have twice the sales volumes as formal wear, with other types of clothing being a distant third in total sales. In general, formal wear includes business attire, church attire, and other such settings. Sales in formal wear have been relatively stable over the last 5 years. Casual wear, including shorts, jeans, and even athletic wear, has increased slightly over the last several years, due in part to businesses becoming more lax on what employees can wear to work, and also the increasing trend of athletic wear being included in casual wear. Some estimates place 30 percent of all women's casual wear to be categorized as athletic wear.

Reshoring

Over the last 50 years, production of apparel (textile industry) moved from the northern United States to the southern states, then to Mexico, and from there to places in Asia, such as China and Vietnam. However, there is a growing trend, according to the Boston Consulting Group, to produce products domestically. Increasing transportation cost, government incentives, being closer to the end consumer, increasing labor costs abroad, and just simply being able to have "Made in the USA" on your product, is driving some firms to start production again in the United States. Several apparel firms who are now producing some of their brands in the United States include Abercrombie & Fitch, J. Crew, and Ralph Lauren's Club Monaco brand. Even Nike, plagued by its operations in sweatshops in the past, is seriously considering reshoring select products.

Mergers and Acquisitions

Mergers and acquisitions activity has increased over the last several years in the apparel industry. Notable apparel industry acquisitions in 2014 include Men's Warehouse acquiring Jos. A. Banks, and Sycamore Partners LLC acquiring the Jones Group Inc. for $1.8 and $2.2 billion, respectively. The largest two acquisitions from 2010 through 2014 were TPG Capital's acquisition of J Crew Group for $3 billion in 2011, and Phillips Van-Huesen's acquisition of Tommy Hilfiger Group B.V. for $3.2 billion in 2010. From 2012 through the Summer of 2014, there were five acquisitions in the industry at over $1 billion.

Future

TJX reported that its fiscal year 2015 comparable store sales increased 2 percent, compared to a 3 percent increase the prior year. In the United States, Marmaxx comps were up 3 percent. HomeGoods reported an outstanding quarter that ended January 31, 2015, with comparable stores sales up 11 percent.

TJX's plans for 2015 include remodeling about 225 stores and adding 181 stores globally. At Marmaxx, the company plans to increase their store base by over 40 percent to about 3,000 stores, partly because in 2014, Marmaxx's segment profit margin was a strong 14.6 percent. The company recently raised TJX Canada's long-term store estimate to around 500 stores—50 more than their prior estimate. The company plans to grow the Marshalls chain to about 100 stores.

TJX Europe's adjusted segment profit margin, excluding foreign currency, increased to 8.1 percent in 2014, another divisional record. Thus, the company raised their long-term store growth potential estimates for TJX Europe to about 975 stores, more than double the early 2015 number of stores. In fact, in the Spring of 2015, TJX added their seventh country, Austria, with their first store opening in March. In the Fall of 2015, TJX added their eighth country, the Netherlands.

At HomeGoods, TJX recently raised their estimates for its long-term growth store potential to approximately 1,000 stores. This is double the current base and 175 more stores than TJX's prior estimates. The HomeGoods profit margin hit a divisional record of 13.6 percent.

Based on key external and internal factors, develop a 3-year strategic plan for TJX Companies. How aggressively should TJX expand globally, and where, and when, to maximize the value of the company for shareholders?

Tiffany & Co., Inc., 2015

www.tiffany.com, TIF

Headquartered in New York City, Tiffany is a jeweler and specialty retailer that manufactures and sells an extensive offering of jewelry, timepieces, sterling silverware, china, crystal, stationery, fragrances, and accessories. Tiffany employs 10,600 employees worldwide. As of December 31, 2014, Tiffany operated 296 stores (123 in the Americas, 73 in Asia-Pacific, 56 in Japan, 38 in Europe, 5 in the United Arab Emirates, and 1 in Russia) versus 286 stores (121 in the Americas, 69 in Asia-Pacific, 54 in Japan, 37 in Europe, and 5 in the United Arab Emirates) on December 31, 2013.

The Tiffany name conjures a vision of a tiny blue box topped with a perfect white bow. Inside is a Tiffany diamond, a sight that brings exquisite delight, romance, and a sparkle in the eyes of the beholder. To the discernable eye, the Tiffany blue box holds unparalleled quality and luxury. But to many others, the price of a Tiffany diamond is exorbitant, and a look-alike diamond can bring just as much happiness at a fraction of the cost.

In January 2015, Tiffany reported its sales for the two-month holiday period ending December 31, 2014. Worldwide net sales of $1.02 billion were 1 percent below the prior year. In terms of regional performance, Asia-Pacific reported sales growth of 10 percent, led by China and Singapore where sales increased 7 percent to $210 million. Tiffany's sales in Japan for the period declined 16 percent to $113 million and the company's European sales rose 1 percent to $133 million. The company's Americas declined 1 percent to $544 million, while the company's "Other sales" rose 14 percent to $24 million, led by Tiffany's new store in Moscow.

For the first quarter of Tiffany's fiscal 2015 that ended April 30, 2015, company sales dropped 5 percent year-over-year, led down by a 30 percent drop in sales in Japan to $122 million. In Tiffany's Asia-Pacific region, Q1 sales declined 1 percent to $259 million, but in other regions, sales decreased a disturbing 6 percent to $35 million. The company's Q1 sales in the Americas grew 1 percent to $444 million, but that too was disappointing since the company generates more than half of its revenues from this region. To combat its weak global performance, Tiffany is expanding its distribution network by adding stores in both new and existing markets. The company is opening smaller stores that offer selected collections of lower priced higher-margin product, which in turn boosts store productivity. In addition, Tiffany is putting more emphasis on improving sales per square foot by increasing customer traffic through targeted advertising, sales training and customer-oriented initiatives.

Copyright by Fred David Books LLC. www.strategyclub.com (Written by Lori Radulovich)

History

Charles L. Tiffany founded Tiffany & Co. in 1837 when he opened a store at 259 Broadway in downtown Manhattan and earned first-day receipts totaling $4.98. The world-famous New York flagship store, featured in the film *Breakfast at Tiffany's,* on the corner of 57th Street and Fifth Avenue, was opened in 1910. Today, Tiffany's headquarters are located at 727 Fifth Avenue in New York City. The Tiffany legacy began with the legendary 287-carat fancy yellow Tiffany Diamond purchased by Charles Tiffany in 1878, which was then cut by master craftsmen to 128.54 carats. Tiffany celebrated its 175th-year anniversary in 2012 by touring a necklace with the Tiffany Diamond suspended from more than 100 carats of white diamonds. Tiffany is also known for its trademarked ring called *Tiffany Setting* introduced in 1886, and the astounding purchase of the French Crown jewels. Tiffany is world renowned for iconic designs and diamonds of breathtaking brilliance, and has also introduced to the world previously unknown colored gemstones.

Internal Issues

Vision/Mission

A recent Tiffany & Co. letter to shareholders says the company is engaged in "designing and crafting products of inspiring beauty and legendary style, engaging our customers with warmth and elegance, and doing so in stores that radiate the energy and excitement of New York City. Our objective remains to deliver the promise of the Blue Box."

Tiffany's unofficial company mission statement is "To be the world's most respected and successful designer, manufacturer and retailer of the finest jewelry."

Organizational Structure

Tiffany's corporate structure is depicted in Exhibit 1. Notice there is no COO and no divisional Presidents by region or type of product.

Marketing

Tiffany's single-most important asset is its brand. The Tiffany brand signifies high-quality gemstone jewelry, especially diamond jewelry, excellent customer service, an elegant and upscale store environment and location, and the distinctive, sophisticated style and romance, packaged in the Tiffany Blue Box. To protect its brand, Tiffany has obtained proprietor trademark registrations for TIFFANY and TIFFANY & CO., the TIFFANY BLUE BOX®, and the color TIFFANY BLUE®. Tiffany aggressively pursues unauthorized use of its trademarked assets, such as in 2013 when Tiffany took legal steps to halt Costco's use of a "Tiffany Setting" label displayed on a Costco ring, stating that "Tiffany" and "Tiffany Setting" are not generic terms and are exclusive registered trademarks of Tiffany & Co.

To maintain the brilliance of the Tiffany brand, the company invests significantly in diamond and gemstone inventory, professional knowledgeable staff, and expensive "high street" locations that provide eye-popping showcase displays of fine jewelry. In 2014, a new store opened on the Champs-Elysées in Paris.

The expenses to implement a luxury brand strategy entail high retail space costs, lower gross margins, limited display space for new product introductions, and high advertising and packaging costs. Tiffany's marketing expenses for 2013 totaled $247,466,000, or 6.1 percent of worldwide net sales. The company's Internet sales across all 13 countries accounted for 6 percent of its worldwide net sales in 2013, 2012, and 2011.

Tiffany's sales are seasonal and dependent on economic conditions. Its policy is not to engage in price promotional activities. However, Tiffany in 2014 made its first foray into featuring same-sex couples in its advertising with its new engagement campaign. The ad features a real-life New York couple and follows a few other retailers such as J. Crew and Banana Republic that have featured similar marketing to the gay community.

Manufacturing

Tiffany manufactures approximately 60 percent of its jewelry in New York, Kentucky, and Rhode Island. Tiffany processes, cuts, and polishes diamonds at facilities outside the United States. The majority of rough and polished diamonds are purchased from Australia, Botswana, Canada, Namibia, Russia, and Sierra. Tiffany owns diamond-processing operations in Belgium, Botswana, Mauritius, Namibia, South Africa, Vietnam, and Cambodia. The locations in Botswana, Namibia, and South Africa provide access to rough diamond allocations reserved for local manufacturers and third parties who own minority, noncontrolling interests in mining companies.

To secure access to a supply of rough diamonds, mixed assortments of rough diamonds are purchased that contain diamonds that do not meet Tiffany's standards. Sub-par diamonds are sold to third parties at a marginal profit. Tiffany also enters into contractual agreements to purchase a specified portion of a diamond mine's output at a market price at the time of production. For example, Tiffany entered into agreements to purchase $200,000,000 of rough diamonds in 2014. Up to 70 percent of finished diamonds are produced from the rough diamonds that Tiffany has purchased. The remaining 30 percent is purchased from diamond dealers. Although Tiffany prefers to acquire diamonds by purchasing and polishing rough diamonds, the company does purchase polished diamonds mainly from four key vendors by securing agreements to buy fixed quantities; however, either party may terminate the agreements at any time. Periodically, Tiffany also provides financing to diamond mining and exploration companies to obtain first rights to acquire the mine's output.

There has been substantial volatility in the prices of both rough and polished diamonds. The supply and price of diamonds depend on several factors, including global demand, political stability in diamond-producing countries, the number of new mines, the supply and arrangements for rough diamonds, and industry liquidity. The Diamond Trading Company (DTC), owned by the De Beers Group, maintains an influence over the supply and price of diamonds since it continues to remain a large supplier of the world supply of rough, gem-quality diamonds. Tiffany

EXHIBIT 1 Tiffany's Organizational Structure

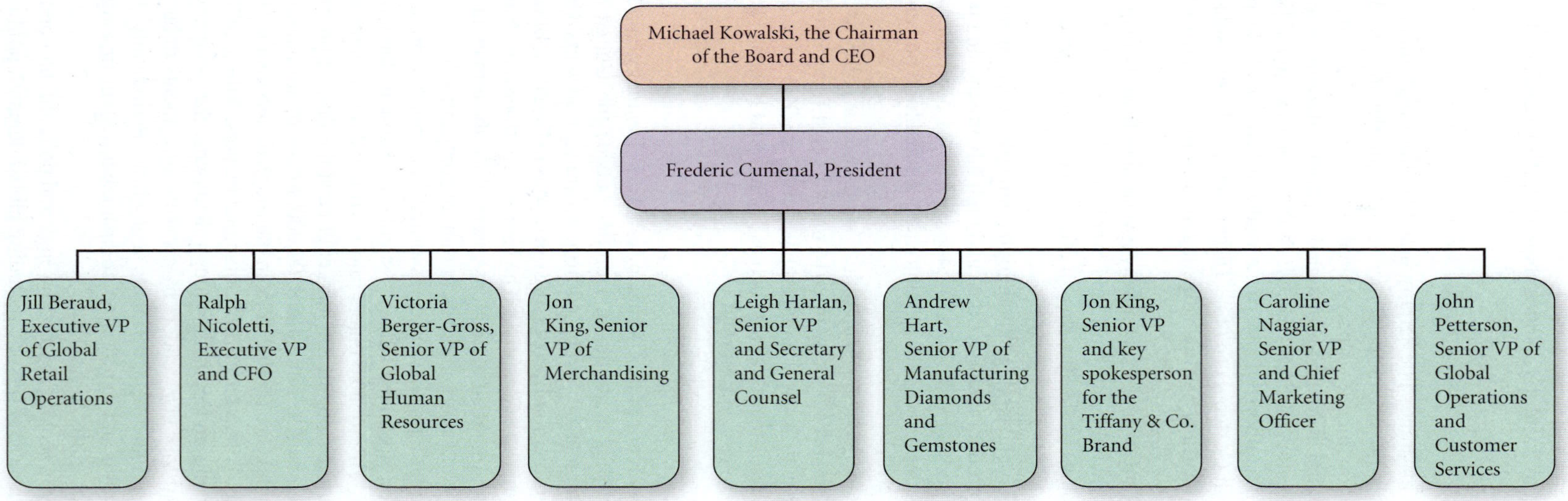

Source: Extrapolated based on executive titles provided on the corporate website.

has also experienced substantial price volatility of precious metals. Even though finished jewelry is purchased from 60 manufacturers, Tiffany seeks alternative suppliers of high-demand jewelry designs to mitigate disruptions.

Segments

Regions

Upon examination of the number of stores in Exhibit 2, the United States possesses the greatest number of Tiffany locations, with 94 stores, or 32.5 percent of worldwide store locations, and garners 48 percent of worldwide net sales. The Asia-Pacific region, second-largest with 72 store locations, generates 23 percent of worldwide net sales.

For calendar year 2013, Tiffany's sales in the United States garnered 88 percent of the total net sales. The 121 stores in the Americas are located as follows: United States (94), Canada (12), Mexico (10), and Brazil (5). Within the Asia-Pacific region, sales in Greater China represent more than half of Asia-Pacific's net sales. The 72 Tiffany store locations in Asia-Pacific are dispersed as follows: China (26), Korea (14), Hong Kong (9), Taiwan (8), Australia (6), Singapore (5), Macau (2), and Malaysia (2). Japanese sales were transacted in 54 Tiffany stores, 50 of which are located within department stores that account for 77 percent of Japan's net sales. Japan is unique in that there are four large department store groups in Japan. Tiffany also has 14 store locations in other department stores. Sales earned in the United Kingdom account for more than 40 percent of total European net sales. Store locations range as follows: the United Kingdom (10), Germany (7), Italy (7), France (4), Spain (2), Switzerland (2), Austria (1), Belgium (1), the Czech Republic (1), Ireland (1), and the Netherlands (1). Tiffany has recently entered emerging markets by opening five stores in the United Arab Emirates and one store in Russia.

Tiffany plans to open new stores in prestigious high-rent areas across the world to extend the reach of its brand into untapped markets. The average sales per gross square foot generated by all stores in 2013 were $3,100. Tiffany's net sales and earnings by country region for 2013 and 2014 are provided in Exhibit 3.

Americas   Sales from 121 stores in the United States, Canada, and Latin America accounted for 48 percent of worldwide net sales in 2013; U.S. sales represented 88 percent of net sales in the Americas. In 2013, the Americas sales via the Internet, independent distributors, and catalog sales increased 5 percent due to an increase in the average price per jewelry sold. Store sales increased 3 percent in 2013 led by growth in the New York flagship store.

Asia-Pacific   Sales in 72 stores and products sold through the Internet and wholesale operations accounted for 23 percent of worldwide net sales in 2013. Sales in Greater China represented more

EXHIBIT 2   Percent of Tiffany Stores by Geographic Region

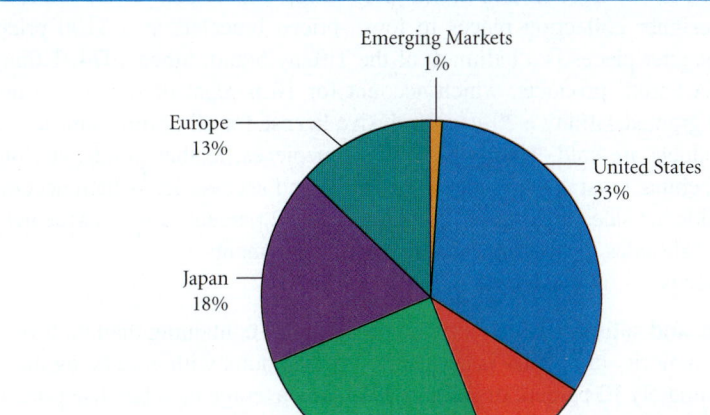

Source: Based on Tiffany's 2014 *Annual Report*, pages 4–5.

EXHIBIT 3 Tiffany's Earnings per Country Region Segment (in millions of USD)

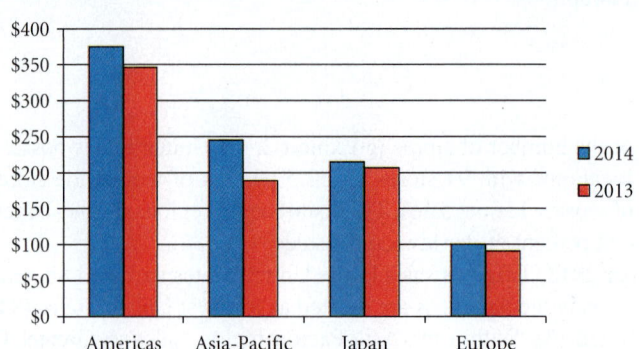

Source: Based on Tiffany's 2014 *Annual Report*.

than half of Asia-Pacific's net sales in the same periods. In 2013, total sales in Asia-Pacific increased 17 percent due to both an increase in the number of jewelry units and the average price per unit sold.

Japan   Sales in 54 company-operated Tiffany stores, as well as sales of Tiffany products through business-to-business, Internet, and wholesale operations represented 14 percent of worldwide net sales in 2013. The decline in 2013 was due to a negative translation effect from the Japanese yen weakening against the U.S. dollar. In 2013, total sales in Japan decreased 9 percent and comparable store sales decreased 10 percent due to currency translation. However, on a constant-exchange-rate basis, Japanese sales actually increased 11 percent and comparable store sales increased 10 percent.

Europe   Sales from Europe's 37 stores, including sales via the Internet and wholesale operations, represented 12 percent of worldwide net sales in 2013. UK sales accounted for more than 40 percent of European net sales. In 2013, total sales in Europe increased 9 percent due to increased units sold and a higher average price per unit sold. Store sales increased $21,653,000 or 6 percent, nonstore sales increased $10,927,000, and Internet sales increased $5,047,000.

Other   "Other" sales include the emerging markets stores in the U.A.E., wholesale sales of merchandise to independent distributors for resale in the Middle East and Russia, and the sale of wholesale purchases of bulk diamonds that are deemed not suitable for sale. In 2013, sales of this segment increased 53 percent.

Products

Tiffany offers an extensive selection and broad price range of branded jewelry ranging from exclusive Gatsby designer collection pieces to lower-priced bracelets at a $100 price point. Selling exclusive designer pieces is a hallmark of the Tiffany brand. Since 1974, Tiffany is the sole licensee of Elsa Peretti products, which account for 10 percent of worldwide net sales. In 2012, Ms. Peretti granted Tiffany a 20-year exclusive license for all of the countries in which her jewelry and products are sold. Tiffany also sells timepieces, leather goods, sterling silver goods (nonjewelry), china, crystal, stationery, fragrances, and accessories, which accounted for 7 percent of worldwide net sales in 2013. The remaining 1 to 2 percent of worldwide net sales is attributable to wholesale sales of diamonds and licensing agreements.

Tiffany sells three types of jewelry:

1. **Statement, fine, and solitaire jewelry** encompasses items containing diamonds or gemstones. The majority of jewelry is constructed of platinum, with gold being the primary metal in approximately 12 percent of sales in 2013. The average merchandise price is $4,600.
2. **Engagement jewelry** often contains diamonds and is largely comprised of platinum, although gold was used in 7 percent of sales in 2013. The average price of engagement merchandise in 2013 was $3,600.

EXHIBIT 4 Tiffany's 2014 Percent Revenues from Jewelry Segments

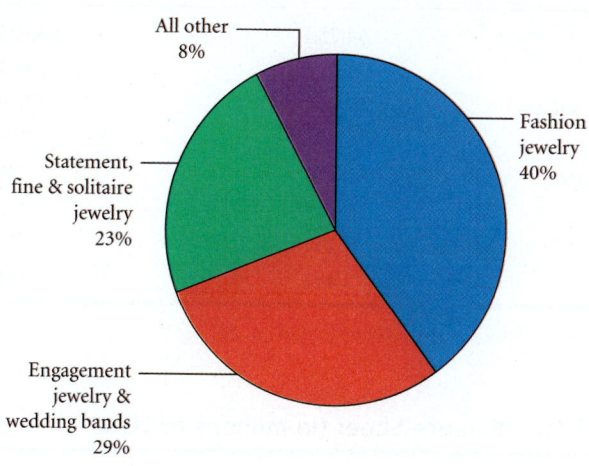

Source: Based on Tiffany's 2014 *Annual Report*, p. 88.

3. **Fashion jewelry** is nongemstone, sterling silver, gold or metal jewelry, although small gemstones may be used as accents. The average merchandise price in this category is $300. Jewelry containing one or more diamonds, including accent diamonds, accounted for 58 percent of worldwide net sales in 2013. Sales of jewelry containing one or more diamonds of one carat or larger accounted for 15 percent of worldwide net sales.

Exhibit 4 reveals Tiffany's recent sales by jewelry category.

Finance

Tiffany's income statement are provided in Exhibit 5 and Tiffany's balance sheet are given in Exhibit 6.

Competitors

Competition for engagement jewelry sales is intense, particularly in the fourth quarter of every year, when sales garner one third of total annual sales. Tiffany's retail price of diamond jewelry is perhaps the highest in the industry. According to a recent study conducted by Wakefield Research, a diamond engagement ring purchased from a traditional jewelry store is overpriced by as much as 72 percent if obtained at a leading luxury jewelry chain, 40 percent at a traditional mall jeweler, and 18 percent at independent local jewelers, compared to the same quality diamond purchased online from rival Blue Nile, Inc.

Large retail jewelers, such as Blue Nile and Signet Jewelers, do not manufacture but instead purchase a majority of their finished goods from manufacturers in India, Southeast Asia, and Italy. Exhibit 7 provides comparative information among Blue Nile, Signet, and Tiffany.

Blue Nile, Inc. (Nile)

Headquartered in Seattle, Washington, Blue Nile is a large online diamond retailer with operations in over 40 countries. It is the world's largest online retailer of independently certified diamonds and fine jewelry, offering custom design jewelry through websites in the United States, Canada, the United Kingdom, and China. In fiscal 2014, sales in the United States accounted for 83.7 percent of total revenues. Blue Nile's expansion into international markets has been led by its recent 25 percent growth in the Asia-Pacific region, which accounts for about 50 percent of the company's of international revenue.

Blue Nile offers over 50,000 diamond choices and the ability to build and customize your diamond rings, pendants, and earrings. Products offered include loose diamonds and gold or platinum engagement rings with diamond center stones. Blue Nile is positioned as a simple, nonintimidating shopping experience where consumers educate themselves about diamonds

EXHIBIT 5 Tiffany's Income Statement (in millions of USD)

Report Date	January 31, 2015	January 31, 2014
Revenues	$4,250	$4,031
Cost of sales	1,713	1,691
Operating expenses	1,646	2,036
EBIT	891	304
Interest & others	153	49
EBT	738	255
Tax	254	74
Net income	**484**	**181**

Source: Based on Tiffany's 2014 *Annual Report*, p. 51.

EXHIBIT 6 Tiffany's Balance Sheet (in millions of USD)

Report Date	January 31, 2015	January 31, 2014
Assets		
Cash and equivalents	$732	$367
Accounts receivable	195	189
Inventories	2,362	2,326
Other current assets	322	346
Total current assets	3,611	3,228
Property, plant & equipment	900	855
Goodwill	—	—
Other assets	670	669
Total assets	**5,181**	**4,752**
Liabilities		
Short-term debt	234	252
Accounts payable	318	342
Taxes	40	32
Other current liabilities	66	71
Total current liabilities	658	697
Long-term debt	883	751
Retirement benefits	524	268
Other liabilities	265	302
Total liabilities	**2,330**	**2,018**
Common stock	1	1
Retained earnings	1,951	1,682
Comprehensive loss	(290)	(58)
Paid in capital and other	1,189	1,109
Total equity	**2,851**	**2,734**
Total liabilities & equity	**5,181**	**4,752**

Source: Based on Tiffany's 2014 *Annual Report*, p. 50.

with online materials and purchase diamonds at wholesale prices. The unique benefit of Blue Nile's "made-to-order" business model is that the company holds no inventory. Once a consumer designs a diamond product, Blue Nile then sources its suppliers and sets the stone in its Seattle plant; thus, inventory is minimized. Blue Nile also owns a fulfillment center in Washington and Ireland, and two facilities in China.

EXHIBIT 7 A Financial Comparison of Tiffany versus Rival Firms

	Tiffany	Blue Nile	Signet
# Employees	12,000	288	28,949
$ Net Income	484 M	9.8 M	381 M
$ Revenue	4,249 M	474 M	5,700 M
$ Revenue/Employee	354,000	1,646,000	196,897
$ EPS Ratio	3.57	0.80	5.03
Market Cap.	12.04 B	366 M	9.64 B

Source: Based on Yahoo Finance 2014 data and company documents.

Signet Jewelers (SIG)

Headquartered in Bermuda, Signet Jewelers does business under the brand names of Kay Jewelers, Jared, Zale Jewelers, Ultra Diamonds, Sterling Jewelers, and Piercing Pagoda. Originating from the United Kingdom in 1862, Signet is the largest specialty jewelry retailer, boasting revenue of $5.7 billion in fiscal 2015. In 2014, Signet acquired Zale Corporation, which doubled the number of Signet stores to 3,600. Signet competes with Tiffany in the lower-tier market with 84.0 percent of revenue generated in the United States. Kay Jewelers, typically located inside malls, targets households with annual incomes between $35,000 and $100,000. According to Signet, this segment accounts for 50.0 percent of U.S. jewelry sales. Jared, a higher-end retailer, targets households with incomes between $50,000 and $150,000. Signet's U.S. revenue is expected to grow to $5.6 billion by 2015. Similar to Tiffany, Signet's sales have risen due to branding and the use of designer jewelry lines, such as the Neil Lane Bridal collection. Signet is opening new stores and remodeling existing locations.

External Issues

Selling jewelry is a $36.0 billion industry that analysts expect to grow at a 2.4 percent annual rate in revenues over the next few years. Most people buy jewelry when they have disposable income—that is, when the economy is doing well. Low gas prices increase disposable income; falling unemployment rates do also. Individuals earning over $100,000 account for 45.0 percent of all retail jewelry sales revenue. Household incomes over $60,000 account for 66.0 percent of industry sales, and households with incomes less than $24,000 garner 11.0 percent of sales. The profile of jewelry purchasers indicates that consumers aged 45 to 64 are the highest-frequency purchasers with consumers aged 20 and 30 in a close second. With the aging baby boomer population, jewelry purchases are expected to increase over the next five years.

Within the jewelry industry, the *diamond jewelry* segment accounts for approximately 45.0 percent of industry sales This segment includes rings, necklaces, bracelets, and other items containing diamonds. Although the diamond jewelry segment has shown a small increase, the declining number of marriages over the past five years has counteracted recent growth.

The second-largest segment, *gold jewelry,* earned 15.0 percent of industry revenue and encompasses all karat gold jewelry items in which diamonds, colored stones, or pearls make up less than 50.0 percent of the value. Gold jewelry sales have remained stable for the past 5 years. *Watches*, the third-largest segment, earned 14.0 percent of industry revenue. This segment has slightly declined over the past 5 years as a result of substitution by cell phones. Sales of *sterling and plated silverware*, the fourth-largest segment, garner 4.4 percent of industry revenue and continue to decline due to the products' high maintenance and lack of dishwasher-safe feature. In contrast, platinum jewelry, which accounts for less than 2.0 percent of revenue, has slightly increased over the past 5 years and is expected to continue to do so as a result of the increase in consumer preference for platinum rings over gold.

Given the industry structure, demand in the United States is expected to continue to increase, partly due to a 1.5 percent increase in the number of U.S. households earning more than $100,000. Since consumers in this income group engage in greater discretionary spending and are brand conscious, they are willing to pay premium prices for prestige products. Consequently, revenue earned by Tiffany, the largest industry retailer, is expected to increase at an annualized rate of 9.3 percent to $1.8 billion through 2019.

Purchases of precious metals and stones, including platinum, gold, diamonds, and pearls, constitute the largest expense at 58.0 percent of jewelry companies' revenue. Skyrocketing costs and the increasing price of gold have negatively affected profit margins. The cost of gold has increased an average 4.5 percent per year over the past 5 years. Furthermore, manufacturers have been unable to pass on increasing costs to consumers due to decreasing demand, and competition from Internet wholesalers and retailers has compounded the deflationary price environment.

Technology

Online sales have continued to rise over the past decade as online retailers become savvy in using social media to engage consumers and deploy behavioral tracking to gain insight into consumer purchase motivations. A significant privacy breach in Tiffany's information systems or security breach of customers' data would tarnish Tiffany's corporate reputation and potentially result in a substantial loss of income. Data and information protection has become a priority and increasingly a more demanding and costly corporate challenge given the recent security breaches of well-known retailers such as eBay, Target, Sony, and Kmart.

The online marketing strategy of Tiffany incorporates the use of analytics, which tracks and integrates online and offline consumer behavior. In tandem with its website redesign, Tiffany uses data analytics to track and optimize e-commerce. Analytics enables Tiffany to improve the effectiveness of ads, content, offers, visitor engagement, and product purchases. Search engine marketing using keywords "optimization," "lead nurturing," "engagement," and "funnel visualization" enhance the effectiveness of Tiffany's website and online marketing strategy

Future

Tiffany is adding to existing stores in Japan and new stores in Russia, and is targeting China, where plans call for opening three stores per year for the foreseeable future. Tiffany plans to grow sales between 10 and 12 percent per year with strategic initiatives that call for growing sales per square retail foot and opening at least three to four stores per year for the foreseeable future. How rapidly and where should Tiffany add stores? Is Tiffany an enduring luxury brand of unprecedented quality, or has the lower-priced Tiffany trinkets and online diamond retailers tarnished the Tiffany brand? Can the Tiffany brand continue to fulfill the promise of the Blue Box, or is the Tiffany Blue Box just an overpriced, blue box? These are but a few of the many strategic planning questions that management must address.

Citigroup Inc., 2015

www.citigroup.com, C

Headquartered in New York City, Citigroup is a diversified financial services holding company formally divided into Citicorp and Citi Holdings. Citi Holdings contains the noncore businesses and comprises only about 6 percent of the overall company. The Citicorp segment provides global banking, advisory services, derivative services, brokerage, mortgages, auto loans, and much more. Citigroup is the largest banking enterprise in the world based on geographic coverage with operations in 160 nations and over 16,000 offices worldwide with 251,000 full-time employees. Citigroup is world's largest credit card issuer with over 900 million retail accounts with various well-known brands.

Senator Elizabeth Warren in December 2014 took to the Senate floor and gave a barn-burning speech attacking Citigroup for being unethical. Warren's rhetoric called out by name Citigroup for economic problems in the United States, and blamed Citi for costing millions of Americans their jobs and homes. Warren stated that Citi was bailed out with half a trillion dollars of taxpayer money, and then used their fortunes to buy Congress, and make it more likely they will be bailed out again. There are numerous business ethics issues associated with Citigroup, but Senator Warren pointed out that five top economic advisors to Presidents Bush and Obama were/are Citi alumni.

During Q2 of 2015, Citigroup continued to wind down its Citi Holdings division by reducing that segment's assets another $32 billion, or 22 percent, from the prior-year period. In Q2, Citi sold about $32 billion of the remaining assets in Citi Holdings, including OneMain Financial, the largest business remaining in Citi Holdings. Citi Holdings maintained profitability in Q2 of 2015, contributing to Citigroup's reported net income of $4.8 billion, compared to $181 million in the prior-year period. Citicorp revenues, net of interest expense, increased 2 percent from the prior-year period to $17.8 billion.

Copyright by Fred David Books LLC. www.strategyclub.com (Written by Forest R. David)

History

Citigroup traces its roots to 1812 when the Citi Bank of New York was formed with $2 million in assets. The bank was founded by Samuel Osgood, who served as the nation's first postmaster-general as well as a soldier, and legislator, and is associated with the founding fathers of the United States. Osgood was keen on foreign trade with nations. His bank financed much of the War of 1812 against England and also the railroad advancement in the middle 1800s. Citi was instrumental in financing the transatlantic cable that brought New York and London instant communication in 1866. By 1895, the bank was the largest in the United States. Citi was the first American bank to surpass $1 billion in assets and eventually became the largest bank in the world in 1929. In 1976, the bank was officially named Citibank and in 1998 it merged with Travelers Group to create a $140 billion firm with assets of $700 billion, changing its name to Citigroup. However, Travelers Group was divested in 2002. Still under government oversight following the subprime mortgage crisis in 2008, Citi failed Federal Reserve stress tests in 2012 and 2014. Citi reported net income of $13.7 billion in 2013 and had a market capitalization of $162 billion in late 2014.

In 2015, Citigroup sold its Japanese retail operations to Sumitomo Mitsui Banking Corp. for $400 million, ending this Citigroup problematic, money-losing segment. With this divestiture, Citigroup lost 740,000 customers in Japan.

Internal Issues

Organizational Structure

Citigroup operates from a hybrid, complex organizational structure, but it most resembles a strategic business unit (SBU) design, with the two groups being Institutional Clients and Global Consumer Banking. Citigroup's probable chain of command is illustrated in Exhibit 1.

EXHIBIT 1 Citigroup's Organizational Structure

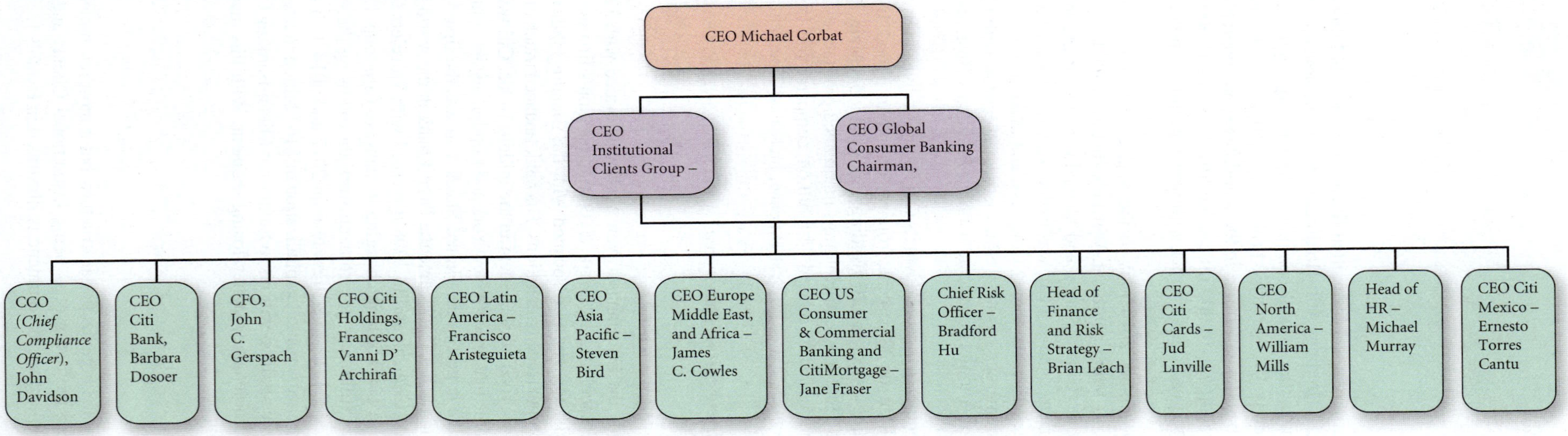

CEO Michael Corbat

CEO Institutional Clients Group –

CEO Global Consumer Banking Chairman,

CCO (Chief Compliance Officer), John Davidson

CEO Citi Bank, Barbara Dosoer

CFO, John C. Gerspach

CFO Citi Holdings, Francesco Vanni D' Archirafi

CEO Latin America – Francisco Aristeguieta

CEO Asia Pacific – Steven Bird

CEO Europe Middle East, and Africa – James C. Cowles

CEO US Consumer & Commercial Banking and CitiMortgage – Jane Fraser

Chief Risk Officer – Bradford Hu

Head of Finance and Risk Strategy – Brian Leach

CEO Citi Cards – Jud Linville

CEO North America – William Mills

Head of HR – Michael Murray

CEO Citi Mexico – Ernesto Torres Cantu

Source: Based on information from Citigroup's recent *Annual Report.*

456

Vision/Mission

Citigroup does not have a vision statement. However, at the corporate website, Citigroup provides a mission statement, as follows: "Citi works tirelessly to serve individuals, communities, institutions and nations. With 200 years of experience meeting the world's toughest challenges and seizing its greatest opportunities, we strive to create the best outcomes for our clients and customers with financial solutions that are simple, creative, and responsible. An institution connecting over 1,000 cities, 160 countries, and millions of people, we are your global bank; we are Citi."

Strategy

Citigroup has recently resolved a significant portion of its mortgage litigation, and cut Citi Holdings annual loss in half. Citi Holdings now accounts for only 6 percent of the balance sheet. CEO Corbat has shifted his strategy from selling assets in Citi Holdings to cutting costs, in an attempt to break even in the near future. Recently, all 101 countries Citi does business in were sorted into four categories, or buckets, to better help prioritize resources.

In late 2014, Citigroup was close to fully spinning off OneMain Financial, which would remove Citi's exposure to its U.S. subprime-lending unit. Although the unit suffered major losses during the financial crisis, it has been profitable since 2012. OneMain targets customers that may not qualify for traditional bank loans, so divesting this business would help Citi avoid any unnecessary scrutiny from the government or stakeholders. This is the second time since 2009 that Citi has tried to sell OneMain, but the price was not right at the time. Subprime lending, contrary to public opinion, has become a more attractive business of late. If Citi is successful in the divesture, it will take several years to fully divest 100 percent of its holdings in OneMain.

Ethical Issues

Citigroup incurred charges of $3.5 billion in Q4 of 2014 to cover legal and restructuring costs. The bank allocated $2.7 billion of that amount to cover legal costs associated with investigations into currency trading, the manipulation of a key interest rate, as well as anti-money laundering and related probes. The remaining $800 million was spent reducing the bank's headcount and reducing the number of its physical branch offices. Investigators at Citi recently found $235 million in falsified invoices reported through a financing program in Mexico. Citi's problems in Mexico go hand in hand with the Federal Reserve in 2014 citing Citi for failing a stress test. In late 2014, it was speculated that Mr. Medina-Mora, the head of the consumer-banking unit in Mexico, plans to step down amid further scandal at Banamex (Citi's Mexico Unit). Citigroup was stricken with another $400 million in fraud by the oil services firm Oceanografia (also tied to Banamex) in 2014. Citi fired 12 Banamex employees over the Oceanografia incident. Banamex remains one of Citigroup's best assets and is the second largest bank in Mexico. Banamex has earned Citi over $1 billion in net income over the last several years, even during the financial crisis.

Segments

Citigroup reports in two segments: Citicorp and Citi Holdings. The Citicorp business includes Global Consumer Banking, Securities and Banking, and Transaction Services. Citi Holdings accounts for only 6 percent of the total balance sheet for Citigroup and the firm is currently cutting costs further in this segment. Note in Exhibit 2 that Citi Holdings had a loss of $3.3 billion in 2014. Citicorp specializes in providing global bank operations for consumers and businesses and is also closely tied to many emerging markets, with a heavy focus on Latin America.

Citigroup's Global Consumer Banking (GCB) segment is the largest in terms of revenues of any other segment and includes Citigroup's four geographical Regional Consumer Banking (RCB) businesses. The segment reported $37,753 million in sales during fiscal 2014. These banks provide services to retail customers, commercial banking, credit cards, and other financial services. As of January 2014, Citi had 3,729 branches in 36 different countries. As of January 2015, Citi operated 3,280 branches in 35 countries. The main strategy of the GCB is to become the top bank of choice among the affluent worldwide, with a focus on metropolitan areas. Retail banking accounted for $17 billion and cards accounted for $21 billion in 2013 across all geographic markets in GCB.

Citigroup's Institutional Clients group consists of Securities and Banking (S&B) and Transaction Services. The segment focuses on offering products for corporations, governments,

EXHIBIT 2 Segment Data for Citigroup (in millions of USD)

	2014		2013	
	Revenues	Income	Revenues	Income
Global Consumer Banking				
North America	$ 19,645	$ 4,421	$19,778	$ 3,910
EMEA	1,358	(7)	1,449	35
Latin America	· 9,204	1,204	9,318	1,337
Asia	7,546	1,320	7,624	1,481
Total	37,753	6,938	38,169	6,763
Institutional Clients Group				
North America	12,345	3,896	11,473	3,143
EMEA	9,513	1,984	10,020	2,432
Latin America	4,237	1,337	4,692	1,628
Asia	7,172	2,304	7,382	2,211
Total	33,267	9,521	33,567	9,414
Corporate/Other	47	(5,593)	121	(630)
Citi Holdings	5,815	(3,366)	4,566	(1,917)
Citi Totals*	$76,882	$ 7,313	$76,419	$13,673

*Reflects discontinued operations removed.

Based on Citigroup Financial Supplement, http://www.citigroup.com/citi/investor/qer.htm

institutions, and high net worth individuals and reported $33,267 million in revenues for fiscal year 2014. S&B offers customers cash, fixed income, foreign currency, equity, and commodity products. The segment also offers corporate lending, prime brokerage, derivative services, and many other services. Fixed income markets earned $13 billion, followed by total investment banking and equity markets earning $4 and $3 billion, respectively, in 2013 across all geographic markets in S&B. The Transaction Services business serves corporations, financial institutions, and the public sector worldwide. Most all business in the segment is related to foreign transactions, with most income coming from fees and the spread in interest revenue on trade loans. In total, the Transaction Services business serves institutions in the United States and 140 countries, with $3 trillion in global transactions daily. The business serves 85 percent of the Fortune 500 companies, through 10 regional processing centers.

Finance

Citigroup's recent income statement and balance sheet are provided in Exhibits 3 and 4, respectively. Note the decline in net income in 2014. The statements are condensed somewhat from the company's actual statements in its *Annual Report*.

Competitors

A comparative analysis of Citigroup with rivals J. P. Morgan and Bank of America is provided in Exhibit 5. Note that Citigroup trails both J. P. Morgan and Bank of America on every statistic presented, except total number of employees, with all three banks roughly equal on employment numbers.

J. P. Morgan Chase (JPM)

Founded in 1799 and headquartered in New York City, JPM is the largest bank in the United States, with 2013 revenues of $96 billion and assets over $2.4 trillion. The firm employs over 242,000 people. The firm divides its operations in two distinct areas: (1) Consumer and Community Banking and (2) Corporate and Investment Bank. Services offered under the consumer and community banking include credit cards, auto loans, student loans, home mortgage, business mortgages, and banking for both individuals and businesses. J. P. Morgan's Corporate

EXHIBIT 3 Citigroup's Income Statement (in millions of USD)

	December 31, 2014	December 31, 2013
Revenues	$76,882	$76,419
Operating expenses	55,051	48,408
Operating income	21,831	28,011
Other expenses	7,467	8,514
EBIT	14,364	19,497
Interest expense	–	–
EBT	14,364	19,497
Tax	6,864	5,867
EAT	7,500	13,630
Other items	(187)	43
Net income	**7,313**	**$13,673**

Source: Based on Citigroup's 2014 *Annual Report* p. 134.

EXHIBIT 4 Citigroup's Balance Sheet (in millions of USD)

Report Date	December 31, 2014	December 31, 2013
Cash	$402,767	$455,927
Accounts receivable	28,419	25,674
Total current assets	431,186	481,601
Property, plant & equipment	–	–
Goodwill	23,592	25,009
Intangibles	4,566	5,056
Trading account	296,786	285,928
Total investments	333,443	308,980
Net loans	628,641	645,824
Other assets	124,316	127,984
Total assets	**1,842,530**	**1,880,382**
Current debt	231,773	262,456
Accounts payable	52,180	53,707
Other current liabilities	899,332	968,273
Total current liabilities	1,183,285	1,284,436
Long-term debt	362,116	329,878
Other liabilities	85,084	59,935
Total liabilities	**1,630,485**	**1,674,249**
Common stock	31	31
Preferred stock	10,468	6,738
Retained earnings	118,201	111,168
Treasury stock	(2,929)	(1,658)
Paid in capital and other	86,274	89,854
Total equity	**212,045**	**206,133**
Total liabilities & equity	**1,842,530**	**1,880,382**

Source: Based on Citigroup's 2014 *Annual Report* p. 136.

EXHIBIT 5 Citigroup versus Rival Firms (Net Income, Revenue, and Market Cap., (in millions of USD))

	Citigroup	J. P. Morgan	Bank of America
# Employees	241,000	241,000	223,000
$ Net Income	7,313	17,923	11,431
$ Revenue	76,882	96,381	101,697
$ Revenue/Employee	319,012	399,921	456,040
$ EPS Ratio	2.20	5.29	0.36
Market Cap.	142,000	202,000	159,000

Source: Based on company documents and a variety of sources.

and Investment Bank deals with investment banking, securities, equity markets, fixed income, and other corporate related financing related activities.

Exhibit 6 reveals JPM's 2013 financial breakdown by segment. The largest revenue and income driver is the Consumer & Community Banking. Top services provided here are ATMs, online banking, business banking, mortgage banking, credit cards, student loans, among others. The worst performing segment was Corporate/Private Equity, which serves to monitor the four other segments. The bank was scheduled to divest $3.5 billion of is physical commodities business to Swiss trading firm Mercuria in 2014, but the deal was cut to an all-cash $800 million deal, including JPM's Henry Bath & Sons Ltd., which is a chain of metals warehouses. JPM is actively looking to divest the full $3.5 billion of its physical commodity assets and is currently in search of potential suitors. Despite the sale, JPM plans to remain trading commodities, including storing precious metals.

J. P. Morgan continues to pay out $4 billion in consumer aid required with its settlement with the Justice Department in 2013 largely over the subprime mortgage issues. The bank announced in 2014 it should receive credit for $869 million from actions that include lower mortgage debts for low-income homeowners and lending to similar potential buyers. The $869 million in credit steams from providing $7.6 billion in mortgage relief.

In 2014, JPM suffered a security breach that released contact information for 76 million households and 7 million small businesses. Fortunately, no sensitive account data was breached. CEO Dimon has pledged to double the bank's security measures in the next 5 years from $250 million to $500 million. Although a potential risk for other big banks, there is no evidence any other large banks were affected by breaches.

Bank of America

Headquartered in Charlotte, North Carolina, Bank of America is a huge bank in the both the United States and the global banking industry. Its top brand name is Merrill Lynch. Bank of America does business in all 50 states and in 40 countries, with 230,000 full-time employees. The bank had year-end 2013 revenues of over $100 billion and total assets over $2 trillion. The bank's real estate segment has lately been the poorest performing, with a net loss in 2013 of over

EXHIBIT 6 JPM's Segment Data (in millions of USD)

Segment	2013 Revenues	2013 Income
Consumer and Community Banking	$46,026	$10,749
Corporate and Investment Bank	34,225	8,546
Commercial Banking	6,973	2,575
Asset Management	11,320	2,031
Corporate/Private Equity	1,254	(5,978)
Total	**99,798**	**17,923**

Source: Based on J. P. Morgan's 2013 *Annual Report*, page 85.

$5 billion. The bank's Global Banking segment is its investment bank and the Global Markets segment focuses on fixed income and equity markets. The Global Markets segment also includes a high concentration in energy and commodities markets.

Bank of America continues to be plagued by litigation stemming from the subprime era. The bank has faced nearly twice the litigation than either J. P. Morgan or Citigroup. The bank estimates that litigation demands have cannibalized 30 percent of profit in 2013 and 2014. Further troubling for Bank of America is the SEC debating on whether the bank should face further business restrictions after meeting its agreed upon litigation requirements. In particular, the SEC is considering how quickly Bank of America should be able to issue stocks and bonds without a SEC review. As of 2014, the bank had spent $75 billion to settle lawsuits, pay fines, and other litigation processes, much related to the 2008 purchase of Countrywide Financial and in the process acquiring many bad loans.

Online Banks

Online banks are growing rapidly in number and taking market share from large banks. The website http://www.mybanktracker.com/best-online-banks rates 30-plus online banks in the United States in terms of having low fees, low interest rates, excellent technology, and great customer service. Exhibit 7 reveals in rank order the top 5 Internet banks in the United States. The only bank to remain in the top 5 since 2011 is Ally Bank, which held the #1 spot in 2011. With low interest rates, some online banks such as Ally Bank are offering interest payments on money market funds around 1,000 percent more than many brick-and-mortar banks. As of November 2014, Ally was offering 0.80 percent on money market funds with many tradition banks offering interest rates of 0.01 percent.

External Issues

U.S. Investment Banking and Securities

The investment banking and securities business is a $148 billion operation in the United States, dominated by Bank of America, J. P. Morgan Chase, Citigroup, Morgan Stanley, and Goldman Sachs, with U.S. market shares of 12, 11, 8, 8, and 8 percent, respectively. Approximately 53 percent of the industry revenues are derived from other firms. The industry is currently improving from the subprime loan era where, from 2009 to 2014, revenues declined industry wide at an annualized rate of over 4 percent. However, the outlook moving forward from 2014 to 2019 is for a growth rate over 4 percent. Replacing the subprime loan market as key growth initiatives are underwriting of equity services and mergers and acquisitions (M&A) advising fees. Large banks have enjoyed many new IPOs and a high level of M&A activity in the last 2 years. Underwriting equities and M&A advising fees account for around 15 and 17 percent of total U.S. bank revenues. Underwriting debt and trading and related services account for about 30 and 24 percent of total U.S. industrywide revenues.

Firms also use investment banks to aid in raising capital by issuing bonds (debt). Trading services account for 24 percent of the investment banking and securities business and include principal trading and market making, proprietary trading, and prime brokerage. Principle trading and market making is what most people think of when they think of trading. Here, the bank takes the client's money and buys a stock or some other security and the client then waits for the security to appreciate (hopefully) in value before selling. Banks charge a fee for this service, much like any online stockbroker would. The investment banks also are able to capitalize on the differences in the "ask and bid," known as the *spread prices*. Proprietary trading is also considered part of the trading services portfolio of many banks; however, its use is declining. Simply, proprietary

EXHIBIT 7 **The Top Five Online Banks in the United States**

1. Sally Mae Bank
2. Ally Bank
3. Bank of Internet
4. Capital One 360
5. Discover Bank

trading is when the bank places its trades on a particular security before the trades of its clients, ensuring a better price for itself. However, the Volcker Rule in the Dodd-Frank Wall Street Reform and Consumer Protection Act of 2010 places limitations on proprietary trading and the future of proprietary trading impact on overall revenues for investment banks should be greatly reduced. Banks also engage in lending to hedge funds in order to buy securities on margin.

With the increase in mergers and acquisitions in recent years, along with divestitures and other restructurings, investment banks have made significant profits on financial advisory services. Mergers and acquisitions alone account for over 17 percent of U.S. banking and securities revenues, and other advisory fees account for about 5 percent of total revenues. Corporate financial services on various loans generate 9 percent of industry revenue. Low rates worldwide have limited higher returns in this business.

Unlike commercial banks, many U.S. investment banks also control a significant portion of the global investment banking business. Bank of America, Citigroup, and J. P. Morgan all account for approximately 12 percent each of total revenues. Two large non-U.S.-based banks, Barclays and Deutsche Bank AG, each account for around 6 percent of total revenues.

U.S. Commercial Banking

The U.S. commercial banking industry provides loans to commercial and consumers from funds deposited in the bank. The industry makes money from fees and from the spread on money deposited compared to a higher interest rate of the same money loaned back out. Interest rates are affected by Federal Funds Rate, Prime Rate, and the respective consumers' credit scores. In the United States, there is a $426 billion industry that is just now starting to grow gain, after annualized growth rates less than 2 percent from 2009 to 2014. Approximately 40 percent of all loans are considered to be based on real estate, and another 27 percent for depository services (bank accounts and other similar services). Individual loans and loans to commercial operations account for about 15 percent each of the market. Most loans to individuals are in the form of auto, marine, or recreational vehicles. Personal loans for housing are not included under this industry.

In the global commercial banking industry, large U.S. players have very little market share, and no single player has more than a 4 percent market share. Key players include the Industrial and Commercial Bank of China, Bank of America, J. P. Morgan, and Wells Fargo. The balance of competitors account for over 85 percent of total revenues generated.

U.S. Credit Card Industry

The U.S. credit card business is a $90 billion industry with profits in excess of $30 billion and growth rates expected to be around 2.5 percent annualized through 2020. The industry is slowly recovering from an annual negative growth rate of 3.5 percent from 2009 to 2014. The six major players in the market control nearly 85 percent of revenues, with American Express being the single market leader with a 20 percent market share. Capital One, Bank of America, and J. P. Morgan all enjoy market shares between 15 and 18 percent; Citigroup and Discovery have market shares of 9 and 7 percent, respectively. The industry makes money from three key areas: interest income, interchange fees, and cardholder fees. All three revenue streams account for approximately one third each of total revenues. Interest charged on U.S. credit cards now ranges from 12 to 19 percent and is largely dependent on the customer's credit score. Interchange fees are the fees firms like MasterCard and Visa charge merchants for accepting a customer's card. The higher the fees, the higher the profits for banks, and MasterCard and Visa often raise fees to attract banks into selecting their particular card. The United States has some of the highest credit card fees in the world, and with increased competition from other credit card players, there is expected to be downward pressure on card fees in the future.

A growing trend in the United States is the use of mobile payments through providers such as Apple and Google, which use processing firms Visa and MasterCard. It remains to be seen if new players such as Apple and Google can create their own brands and bypass the banks in gaining access directly to the major credit card companies. However, consumers in Europe have been using mobile phone payments for around a decade now with growing popularity and use. The new technology does bring growing awareness to security issues and the perceived dangers of a digital currency as data is increasingly stored on Internet accessible systems. Recent security breaches, such as Home Depot and J. P. Morgan, are examples of potential problems that could escalate in the future. New competitors—for example, Bitcoin and PayPal—also may increasingly take market share away from the larger banks, along with possibly Apple and Google, if they can enter into direct agreements with MasterCard and Visa, and totally bypass the banks all together.

U.S. Loans

The loan business in the United States is a $90 billion industry with profits of $14 billion. The industry is largely dependent on the health of the housing market. With low interest rates, many homeowners have refinanced lately. The extended outlook for the industry is to generate $95 billion by 2019. The industry is heavily fragmented with Bank of America, Citigroup, J. P. Morgan, and Wells Fargo, all accounting for just over 26 percent of the total industrywide revenues, fairly evenly distributed among the four. The balance of 75 percent is comprised of thousands of other banks, mostly regional in nature. There are currently over 5,500 different commercial banks in the United States.

Latin America Growth Slows

Latin America is expected to have its slowest growth in 2014 at 1.2 percent having grown only 2.5 and 3 percent, respectively, in 2012 and 2013. The World Bank projects 2015 growth of 2.2 percent. Much of the drawdown can be explained by a rising U.S. dollar and lower commodity prices, which many Latin American nations rely on heavily. Slowdown is also contributed to China, a large buyer of many Latin American commodities, along with the United States tapering and then ending its Quantitative Easing programs. Venezuela, largely dependent on oil, is experiencing inflation of over 60 percent, and Argentina has double-digit inflation itself. Both nations are expected to experience gross domestic product contractions of 2.9 and 1.5 percent, respectively. Highlights in the region include Mexico, which grew 2.5 percent in 2014. Mexico is also a large business partner for Citigroup and should remain strong moving forward. The largest-growing country in Latin America, with respect to gross domestic product, is Colombia, with nearly 5 percent growth in 2014.

Future

Banks, including Citigroup, are largely dependent on the spread between short- and long-term interest rates, referred to as the yield curve. When short-term rates are low, and long-term rates are high, bank profits tend to be higher, as they are able to pay relatively low interest rates on CDs and savings, while charging higher rates on automobile, housing, business and other loans. This spread is where the banks make money. In 2015, interest rates have been rising slowly in the United States.

Automobile sales were up in both 2014 and 2015 as customers are buying new and larger vehicles as the price of oil has dropped. This is a potential windfall for banks but only to the extent that rates start to increase. With the European Central Bank, Japan, Australia, and other top economies are engaging in their own quantitative easing programs, rates will not likely move higher in these regions throughout 2015. While the U.S. Federal Reserve plans to start raising rates in late 2015, they may be unable to do so because the increasing dollar value has already put a burden on U.S. corporations, hurting profits in overseas markets. One aspect that is positive for Citigroup moving forward is that the firm receives over 50 percent of revenues from its Global Consumer segment from the United States, with rates likely to rise in the nation quicker than in overseas markets.

JetBlue Airways Corporation, 2015

www.jetblue.com, JBLU

Headquartered in Long Island City, New York, JetBlue is a passenger airline carrier company operating a fleet of 13 Airbus A321 aircrafts, 130 Airbus A320 aircrafts, and 60 EMBRAER 190 aircrafts. JetBlue serves 90 destinations in 27 states, the District of Columbia, Puerto Rico, the U.S. Virgin Islands, and 17 countries in the Caribbean and Latin America. JetBlue is sometimes called New York's Hometown Airline, and is the leading carrier in Boston, Fort Lauderdale/ Hollywood, Los Angeles (Long Beach), Orlando, and San Juan.

JetBlue reported a 1.5 percent decrease in yield per passenger per mile as the company's average airfare decreased to $166.17 in 4Q 2014 from $168.94 in 4Q 2013. For 4Q 2014, JetBlue's revenue passenger miles (or RPM) increased 8.5 percent to 9,392 million miles. Capacity, or available seat miles (or ASM), and load factor (or capacity utilization) drive RPM growth for an airline. For 4Q 2014, JetBlue's capacity increased 7 percent to 11,436 million, and seat occupancy increased to 82.1 percent from 80.9 percent in 4Q 2013.

Lower fuel prices have helped airlines' performance metrics, but JetBlue competes with many aggressive, growing rival companies, including Spirit Airlines, Southwest, American Airlines, Delta Air Lines, United Continental, and even rapidly growing Virgin America. On April 22, 2014, JetBlue's pilots voted to unionize, for the first time since the airline was founded in 1999, with 71 percent of the airline's pilots voting in favor of joining the Air Line Pilots Association (ALPA).

For Q2 2015, JetBlue's number of revenue passengers grew by 8 percent year-over-year, indicating growing demand for the airline's services. JetBlue's traffic grew by 9.8 percent year-over-year for the first half of 2015. The airline improved its load factor, or aircraft utilization, by 1 percent to 85.6 percent for Q2 2015. JetBlue also increased its capacity in Q2 2015—measured by available seat miles (or ASM)—by 7.5 percent year-over-year. This was the second-highest capacity increase among the six major airlines. In 2Q 2015, JetBlue's competitors notched the following capacity increases:

1. Alaska Air Group (ALK): 10.7%
2. Southwest Airlines (LUV): 7%
3. Delta Air Lines (DAL): 6%
4. United Continental (UAL): 2.3%
5. American Airlines (AAL): 1.5%

JetBlue needs a clear strategic plan for the future.

Copyright by Fred David Books LLC. www.strategyclub.com (Written by Fred R. David)

History

Former Southwest Airlines employee, David Neeleman, incorporated "NewAir" in Delaware in August 1998 but later changed its name. JetBlue started by following Southwest's approach of offering low-cost travel, with the exception that JetBlue would offer amenities, such as in-flight entertainment—for instance, a TV at every seat and Sirius satellite radio. Neeleman's vision for JetBlue was "to bring humanity back to air travel."

In September 1999, JetBlue was awarded 75 initial take off/landing slots at JFK International Airport in New York City. The airline started operations on February 11, 2000, with service to Buffalo and Ft. Lauderdale.

In 2012, for the eighth year in a row, JetBlue was ranked "Highest in Customer Satisfaction Among Low Cost Carriers in North America" by J. D. Power and Associates. In 2013, JetBlue introduced Mint, a premium cabin service on transcontinental flights. The service began in 2014, using the Airbus A321-200 aircraft ordered by JetBlue. These planes are outfitted with winglets, as well as "lie flat" seats and moveable partitions that can create small suites on the airplane.

Called "Mint" by JetBlue, these planes are configured with 16 business-class seats and 143 economy seats, instead of an all-economy configuration of 190 seats.

On September 18, 2014, JetBlue's CEO, Dave Barger, announced his resignation from the company effective February 16, 2015, following reports that investors and the board were unhappy with his performance. Mr. Barger was replaced on the board, and as CEO, by Robin Hayes.

In late July 2015, JetBlue reported Q2 operating income of $282 million, compared to $141 million in Q2 the prior year. The company's 2015 Q2 net income was $152 million, compared to $61 million the prior year. JetBlue's 2015 Q2 operating revenues were $1.6 billion. Its revenue passenger miles for Q2 increased 8.7 percent to 10.5 billion on a capacity increase of 7.5 percent, resulting in a Q2 load factor of 85.6 percent—an increase of 1.0 points year-over-year. The company's yield per passenger mile in Q2 also increased 0.2 percent to 14.28 cents, while passenger revenue per available seat mile (PRASM) for Q2 of 2015 increased 1.4 percent year-over-year to 12.22 cents, and operating revenue per available seat mile (RASM) increased 0.4 percent year-over-year to 13.17 cents. Given all these increases, and with oil prices falling in August 2015, JetBlue seems to have a bright future.

Internal Issues

Vision/Mission

JetBlue has a combined vision/mission that reads: "JetBlue Airways exists to provide superior service in every aspect of our customers' air travel experience." The company also has a customer bill of rights on the corporate website.

Organizational Structure

JetBlue lists nine top executives on its corporate website. The company appears to operate using a functional design, as illustrated in Exhibit 1.

Segments

JetBlue has two reportable segments: (1) revenue from passengers filling seats and (2) revenue from ancillary amenity offerings. JetBlue's ancillary amenity revenue, the higher-margin source, increased 3 percent to $25 per customer in 4Q 2014. The airline's total ancillary revenue increased to $745 million in 2014, a year-over-year increase of 11 percent.

Adding to its ancillary revenue, JetBlue in 2015 began adding baggage fees. To increase the company's passenger revenue, JetBlue in 2015 cut the leg-room in some of its planes. These changes come even though JetBlue has long been one of the most enviable brands around, winning travelers' hearts with free snacks and other amenities rarely found on rival airlines. Partly because providing amenities was the founder's initial vision for the company, a recent poll

EXHIBIT 1 **JetBlue's Organizational Structure**

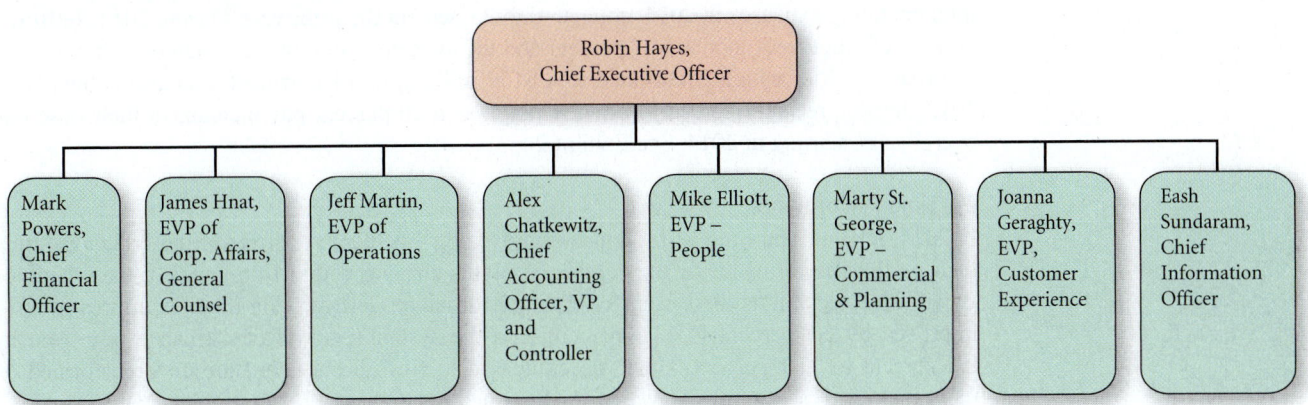

Source: Based on the company's website.

revealed that the percentage of people polled who say they are positive about the JetBlue brand fell almost 8 points to 56.2 from 63.8 percent (based on information at YouGov, a research firm that surveys consumers about brand perceptions).

Passenger Load

JetBlue's revenue passenger miles increased by 14.3 percent year-over-year to 3,183 million in January 2015, compared to 2,785 million the prior year. The company's revenue passengers increased by 13.4 percent as its number of departures rose to 25,107 in January 2015 from 21,986 in January 2014. JetBlue's passenger revenue per available seat mile (or PRASM) for January 2015 increased by 3 percent. The company's available seat miles increased by 15.5 percent that month, but its load factor decreased by 0.9 percent to 81.9 percent.

JetBlue's traffic and capacity growth increased during January 2015 to record the highest growth among its peers. Alaska Air Group (ALK), for example, recorded the second-highest traffic and capacity growth of 7.9 percent and 10.4 percent, followed by Southwest Airlines' (LUV) 8.6 percent and 10.2 percent, respectively. Following those positions are Delta Air Lines' (DAL) 3.6 percent and 6.2 percent and United Continental Holdings' (UAL) 1.1 percent and 1.4 percent. Only American Airlines (AAL) recorded negative traffic and capacity growth of –2.8 percent and –0.2 percent, respectively.

Capacity Utilization

JetBlue had 203 aircraft at the end of 2014, including 138 A320s, 60 E190s, and 13 A321s. The company expects to take delivery of an additional 12 A321s in 2015. JetBlue's total capital expenditure for 2015 is planned to range from $810 million to $860 million. However, to increase its cash flow, JetBlue deferred 18 Airbus aircraft deliveries, which will be delivered about 2022–2023, instead of in 2016–2018.

JetBlue's overall capacity increased about 12 percent in 1Q 2015 and is expected to increase about 8 percent for the full year 2015. A high 16 percent growth is expected in JetBlue's transcontinental flights, which comprise 30 percent of the company's total capacity. Another 30 percent of the capacity is expected to be deployed in the Caribbean and Latin America, with another 29 percent deployed in Florida.

Fuel

Aircraft fuel is JetBlue's largest expense category, representing 36 percent of total operating expenses in 2014, compared to 38 percent in 2013. The company's average price paid for fuel decreased 5 percent in 2014 to $2.99 per gallon, but the company consumed 35 million more gallons of aircraft fuel in 2014 compared to 2013. In 2014, JetBlue recorded fuel hedge losses of $30 million compared to $10 million in fuel hedge losses in 2013. However, fuel and taxes expenses were down 6.5 percent from Q3 to Q4 thanks to a 50 percent drop in oil prices over the last quarter of 2014.

Salaries, Wages, and Benefits

Salaries, wages, and benefits are JetBlue's second-largest expense, representing 24 percent of total operating expenses in 2014, compared to 23 percent the prior year. During 2014, JetBlue's number of employees increased 7 percent and the average tenure of crew members increased to 6.2 years, both of which contributed to a $159 million, or 14.1 percent, increase compared to 2013. JetBlue recently agreed to provide its pilots a 20 percent pay increase in their base rate over 3 years starting in 2014. See Exhibit 2.

On-Time Performance

In 2014, JetBlue's on-time performance improved by 4 percent year-over-year. Airlines measure their on-time performance by the number of flights arriving within 14 minutes of the scheduled arrival time, as well as the system's arrival performance. JetBlue's on-time departures in 2014 improved by 2.7 percent to 63.5 percent, and the system's arrival performance improved by 2.5 percent to 77.1 percent. However, compared to rival airlines, JetBlue underperformed on these metrics. For example, Hawaiian Airlines had the highest 2014 on-time arrival rate of 92.3 percent, followed by Alaska Air's 86.6, Delta's 83, American's 76.4, and United's 76.1 percent, respectively, ranked slightly better than JetBlue.

EXHIBIT 2 Notable Expenses for JetBlue

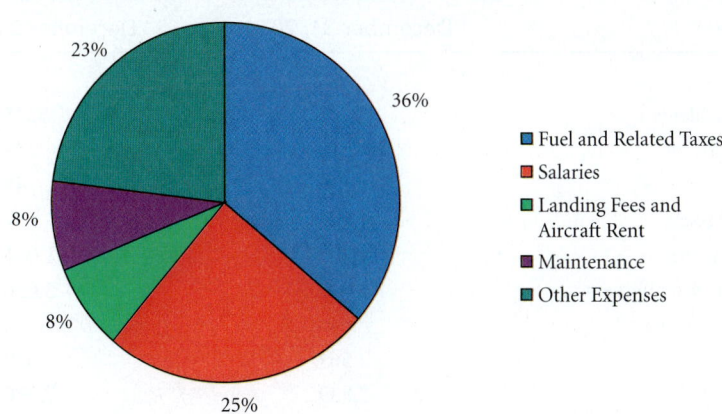

- Fuel and Related Taxes
- Salaries
- Landing Fees and Aircraft Rent
- Maintenance
- Other Expenses

Source: A variety of sources.

EXHIBIT 3 JetBlue's Income Statement (in millions of USD)

Report Date	December 31, 2014	December 31, 2013
Revenues	$5,817	$5,441
Cost of revenue	2,775	2,764
Gross profit	3,042	2,677
Operating expenses	2,285	2,250
EBIT	757	427
Interest	134	148
EBT	623	279
Tax	222	111
Net income	**401**	**168**

Source: Based on company documents.

Finance

JetBlue reported its highest net income ever in 2014—$401 million—an increase of $233 million over 2013, but the $401 million number includes an after-tax gain on the sale of a JetBlue subsidiary, LiveTV, of $169 million. LiveTV was JetBlue's leading provider of inflight entertainment and connectivity systems for its planes. In 2014, JetBlue reported over $5.8 billion in operating revenue, led by rapid ancillary revenue growth. About 80 percent of JetBlue's operations come from the northeastern corridor of the United States, which in 2014 and 2015 experienced very harsh winters, leading to 4,100 flight cancellations in 2014 alone, compared to about 2,100 cancellations in 2013.

JetBlue's recent income statement and balance sheet are provided in Exhibits 3 and 4, respectively.

Competitors

For 2014, JetBlue and Delta Air Lines (DAL) reported the highest revenue growth of 6.9 percent, followed by Southwest Airline's, 5.1 percent, Alaska Air Group's (ALK) 4.1 percent, and United Continental Holdings' 1.6 percent. Exhibit 5 provides some comparative metrics of JetBlue and other airlines. Notice that JetBlue's revenue per employee is much less than United Continental, and its EPS is lowest among the sample air carriers.

The domestic airline business is highly competitive, led by Delta, American, and United Continental, with market shares ranging from 20 to 15 percent, respectively. Southwest's U.S. market share is approximately 11 percent, with JetBlue and Spirit enjoying 3 and 1 percent

EXHIBIT 4 JetBlue's Balance Sheet (in millions of USD)

Report Date	December 31, 2014	December 31, 2013
Assets		
Cash and equivalents	$341	$225
Accounts receivable	310	249
Inventories	46	48
Other current assets	503	534
Total current assets	1,200	1,056
Property, plant & equipment	6,072	5,656
Goodwill	—	—
Other assets	567	638
Total assets	**7,839**	**7,350**
Liabilities		
Short-term debt	265	469
Accounts payable	698	580
Other current liabilities	973	825
Total current liabilities	1,936	1,874
Long-term debt	1,968	2,116
Deferred liabilities	832	605
Other liabilities	574	621
Total liabilities	**5,310**	**5,216**
Common stock	4	3
Retained earnings	1,002	601
Treasury stock	(125)	(43)
Paid in capital and other	1,648	1,573
Total equity	**2,529**	**2,134**
Total liabilities & equity	**7,839**	**7,350**

Source: Based on company documents.

EXHIBIT 5 JetBlue versus Rival Airlines on Key Metrics

	JetBlue	American	Southwest	United Continental
$ Revenue	6 B	43 B	19 B	40 B
# Employees	16 K	115 K	47 K	85 K
$ Revenue per Employee	375,000	374,000	404,000	470,000
$ Net Income	400 M	3 B	1.2 B	1.2 B
$ EPS	1.20	3.95	1.66	2.95
$ Market Capitalization	5.4 B	33.5 B	29 B	25 B

Source: Based on a variety of sources.

market shares, respectively. The airline industry generates about $150 billion in annual revenues with the big 4 airlines (shown in Exhibit 5) accounting for over 50 percent of all revenue. In total, there are over 300 airline businesses in the United States.

It is fairly easy to begin an airline business; there are low barriers to entry because many airplanes are leased not owned by the carriers. However, ironically, it is often expensive to exit the industry, as airlines have long-term lease agreements in place. Airlines are notorious for low margins. The outlook moving forward is for the airline industry to grow about 2 percent annually. However, with the lower fuel costs, airlines may become more profitable as a group. In fact, American Airlines' earnings per share was up 25 percent from Q3 2013 to Q3 2014, to $1.28, for an all-time record.

Spirit Airlines, Inc. (SAVE)

Headquartered in Miramar, Florida, Spirit is the nation's deepest discount airline, offering customers numerous for-pay options, including bags, seat assignment, and refreshments. Spirit derives nearly 40 percent of its revenue from nonticket product purchases. To maximize efficiency, Spirit has all-Airbus, single-aisle planes, operating more than 325 daily flights to 57 destinations in the United States, Latin America, and the Caribbean. The nation's "Ultra-Low Cost Carrier," Spirit Airlines received a respected, independent endorsement recently in that *Air Transport World* named Spirit as the "Value Airline of the Year" at its 41st Annual Industry Achievement Awards ceremony.

Virgin America (VA)

Headquartered in Burlingame, California, Virgin America is a low-cost airline that provides air travel services in the United States and Mexico. Founded in 2004, Virgin America has a fleet of 53 Airbus single-aisle aircraft. The company performed exceedingly well in the final quarter of 2014, reporting better-than-expected earnings and revenues in the quarter. Virgin America is adding flights monthly, striving to keep costs low by flying a single aircraft type (Airbus A320 family) and outsourcing many activities such as baggage delivery, maintenance, and reservations.

Southwest Airlines (LUV)

Headquartered in Dallas, Texas, Southwest in 2015 began flying nonstop to eight new cities out of its main hub, Dallas Love Field, with 180 departures a day from Dallas Love Field to 50 destinations in the United States and near-international markets. At year-end 2014, Southwest operated 665 Boeing 737 aircraft and had 12 Boeing 717 aircraft. Southwest flies to 93 destinations in 40 states, the District of Columbia, and Puerto Rico, as well as Mexico, Jamaica, the Bahamas, Aruba, and the Dominican Republic.

United Continental Holding, Inc. (UAL)

Headquartered in Chicago, Illinois, United Airlines, the wholly owned subsidiary of United Continental Holdings, provides air transportation services all over the planet. UAL transports both people and cargo, using a fleet of 1,260 aircraft and having more than 84,000 full-time employees.

External Issues

According to SITA, a specialist in air transport communications and information technology solutions, the airline industry will soon see a major transformation in the way passengers interact with airlines. SITA says there are four major trends that will shape the future of global air travel in 2015 and beyond, as follows:

1. Passengers will expect more personal service and airlines will deliver, primarily using smartphones and apps much more. For example, Alaska Airlines already has a travel app that alerts fliers to airfare deals from their hometowns and to cities where their friends live.
2. Nearly every airline will offer mobile check-in—up from 50 percent today. Passengers will use 2-dimensional boarding passes or contactless technology on their phones, at different stages of their journey, such as at boarding gates to fast-track security zones.
3. Customer services will become more mobile and social. Nearly every airline and airport will provide flight updates using smartphone apps. The industry is also exploring apps to improve the customer experience.
4. Almost every airport and airline will offer business intelligence solutions aimed at improving customer service and satisfaction, often through personalized services. For example, a European airline, Vueling, researches customers via social media in order to better understand their behavior and then integrates this information into their own intelligence program to improve customer loyalty.

Market Segmentation

The airlines cater to a variety of customers but generally customers are categorized as coach, first class, business class, and freight. Coach passenger revenue tends to account for 80 percent of all revenue generated by air service companies. This revenue includes extra bag fees, food and drink, and all other fees associated with coach class passengers. Business class and first class passengers account for 10 and 5 percent of total revenues, respectively, with freight accounting for 3 percent of total industrywide revenues.

Airlines Hoarding Cash

Fearing economic downturns, airlines generally keep substantial cash on their balance represents. For example, Delta reported $5 billion in 2014 cash and short-term investments to 2013 revenues of $37 billion or 14 percent of revenue. American Airlines reported 2014 cash and equivalents of $8 billion, about 30 percent of revenue. JetBlue, for example, from 2012 to 2014 increased its cash position by 87 percent to $341 million. Delta increased its cash balance by 25 percent over the same time frame. Overall, the industry's 2014 revenue passenger miles were up 2.5 percent, with passenger revenues rising 5 percent. Another area driving up cash balances and revenues for airlines are ancillary fees. Currently, 16 U.S. airlines charge baggage fees, totaling $3.4 billion in 2013. Reservation change fees generated another $2.8 billion in 2013 revenues for the airline industry. Generally met with great distaste and resistance among passengers, after being customary in the industry for a number of years now, most customers are now accustomed to the ancillary fees charged by airlines.

Airline Pollution Concerns

Airlines for years have fought the perception they are a major source of greenhouse gasses. Most airlines routinely list the ways in which they have reduced jet fuel usage and as a result greenhouse gases. Many of the ways listed, however, are often through higher fees on customers. Baggage fees, heavy bag surcharges, lack of free drinks and food, tighter seating arrangements, and smaller more fuel-efficient plans all have helped to reduce weight at the direct expense of customer comfort. So the jury remains out on the true motives of airlines in the battle against greenhouse gas emissions. Another interesting development in the industry is the use of biofuels instead of traditional jet fuel. Several firms, such as Continental and KLM Royal Dutch Airlines, have experimented with biofuels since 2009, but there does not appear to be industrywide acceptance or a hurry to switch in the foreseeable future.

Airline Taxes

Airlines pay high taxes. Delta, Spirit, JetBlue, and Southwest all paid taxes between 35 and 38.5 percent in 2014. However, American Airlines paid taxes of 11 percent and United Continental received a tax credit in 2014. President Obama recently proposed raising taxes on airlines to help reduce the federal deficit, improve immigration, improve airports, and reduce the wait-time for processing foreign visitors. Obama's new airline tax plan would add between $2.50 and $9 per ticket one way. The cost of any new taxes is expected to be passed on to the consumer. Tax increases may not seem like much in absolute terms, but one analyst suggested a $300 domestic ticket's taxes that are currently $61 would increase to $75, amounting to a staggering 23 percent tax increase. To compare what a 23 percent tax high relates to, the inflation rate in the United States during 2014 was around 1.5 percent.

Mergers Dominate the Industry

Two notable recent mergers include United and Continental and US Airways and American Airlines. While possibly attractive, at least in the short term for the airlines, the mergers came at the expense of substantial goodwill on the balance sheets. American, for example, reported no goodwill in 2012, yet after the merger with US Air, the new firm reported over $4 billion in goodwill. United Continental reports over $4 billion in goodwill on its balance sheet. The likely benefit for these firms is with reduced competition will come the ability to more easily raise airline ticket prices. In addition to higher prices facing airline passengers, airline CEOs are also altering their market-share–grabbing strategy by focusing on the most profitable area routes, reducing redundant routes, no longer serving certain routes, and being able to charge more for ancillary fees.

Future

For the full year 2015, JetBlue projects that its operating capacity will increase by approximately 8 percent over 2014, with the addition of 12 Airbus A321 aircraft to its operating fleet. The company projects that its cost per available seat mile, excluding fuel and profit sharing, will increase 1 percent over 2014.

The airline industry is intensely competitive, and is becoming more and more like a commodity. JetBlue is backing away from its amenities in order to compete and stay profitable, yet customers are expecting more personalized services and amenities. JetBlue needs a clear strategic plan. Help the company prepare this document.

FedEx Corporation, 2015

FDX, www.fedex.com

Headquartered in Memphis, Tennessee, and founded in 1971, FedEx is one of the largest express freight delivery companies in the world, having about 57,000 drop-off locations, 700 aircraft, and 62,000 vehicles. FedEx does business in over 220 countries and employs over 220,000 workers. The company is comprised of subsidiaries: FedEx Ground, FedEx Express, FedEx Freight, and FedEx Services. Revenues for fiscal year-end of May 2014 were $45 billion, or about $10 billion less than top competitor United Parcel Service (UPS). In fact, rival UPS is spending $2 billion to expand internationally in Asia, Europe, and the Americas, and is modernizing its U.S. operations to automatically sort packages. UPS expects its revenues to rise 7 percent annually through 2018, so FedEx needs an excellent strategic plan going forward.

In April 2015, FedEx offered to acquire Dutch delivery firm TNT Express N.V. (TNTEY) for approximately $8.75 per share, or $4.8 billion (€4.4 billion). However on July 13, 2015, the European Commission (EC) raised concerns about competition being restrained in the event of the deal materializing. As the antitrust watchdog of the European Union, the EC is investigating whether the impending deal, involving two key global players in the field of small package delivery, abides by the EU Merger Regulation. The EC is concerned that the combined entity, if approved, would dominate the market for small packages, thereby stifling competition in the space and causing prices to soar.

Copyright by Fred David Books LLC. www.strategyclub.com (Written by Forest R. David)

History

FedEx traces its history to 1971, when Frederick Smith (the current CEO) bought a controlling interest in Arkansas Aviation Sales. The frustration of being unable to effectively deliver packages in 2 days created the idea of determining a more effective way to handle freight. Smith named his new company Federal Express in hopes of obtaining a contract with the Federal Reserve Bank and to draw public interest though the term *Federal.* The contract proposal with the Federal Reserve was denied, but the company officially began operating in 1973 with 14 small aircraft from Memphis, Tennessee, by delivering 186 packages to 25 different U.S. cities. Federal Express did not officially change its name to FedEx until 1994.

FedEx first turned a profit in 1975 and was instrumental in lobbying for the deregulation of air cargo that was passed in 1977. Deregulation allowed FedEx to use larger aircraft, and today, FedEx is the world's largest all cargo fleet. The firm reached $1 billion in sales in 1983, marking the first ever for a U.S. company to reach this level of revenues without mergers or acquisitions within 10 years of operations. After a series of international acquisitions, FedEx starting offering services to Europe, Asia, and China through a 1995 acquisition.

In 2014, about 90 percent of FedEx's $1.2 billion investments were to boost capacity or infrastructure. As Christmas approached, the company hired about 50,000 seasonal workers, up from 40,000 the prior year. The investment is designed to address the rapid growth of consumer goods ordered online. Peak volume, referring to the busiest day of the year, had climbed dramatically in recent years for FedEx, to 26-plus million packages on one day near Christmas. That busiest day recently jumped 40 percent at rival UPS, to 31 million packages. Last-minute, holiday online free shipping deals have proliferated in recent years.

Internal Issues

Organizational Structure

FedEx uses a divisional-by-product organizational structure, but the firm does not appear to have executives with popular titles such as COO, CTO, CSO, HRM, or R&D. Exhibit 1 provides a probable schematic of the company structure.

EXHIBIT 1 FedEx's Organizational Structure

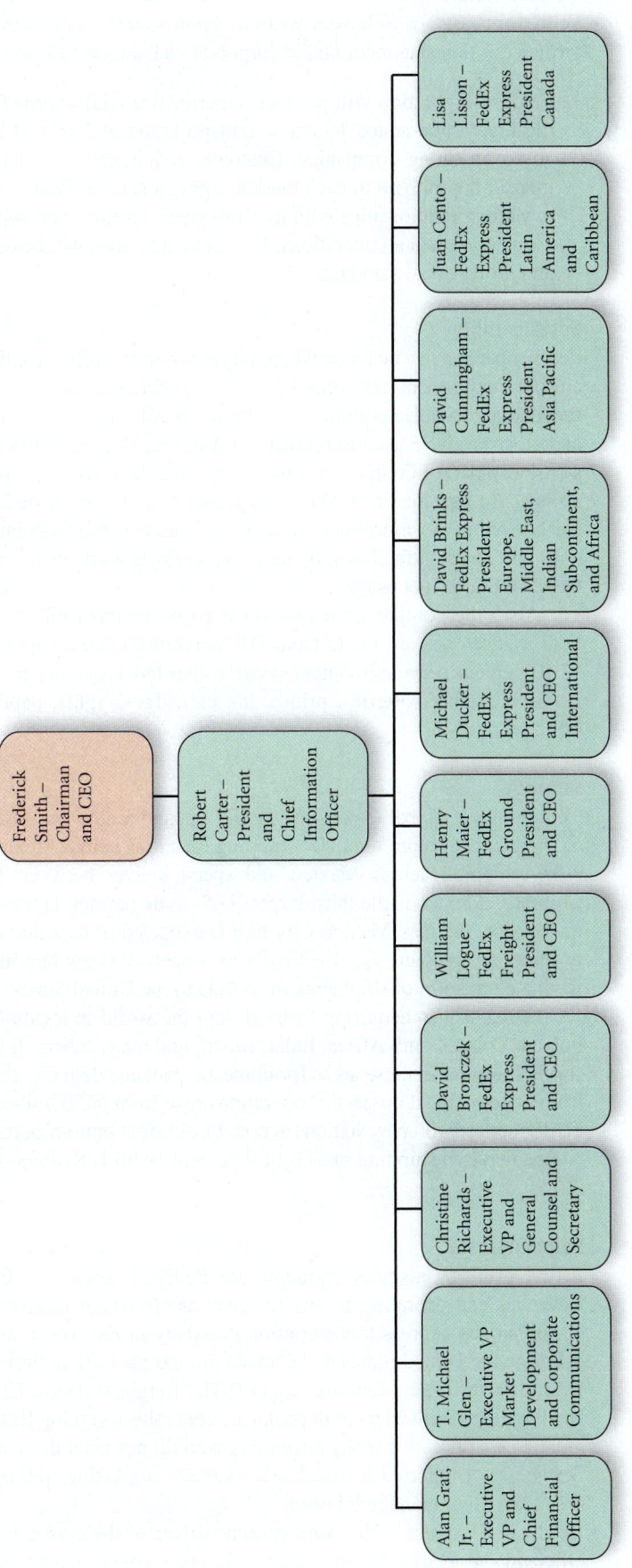

Source: Based on FedEx's 2014 *Annual Report.*

Vision/Mission

FedEx appears not to have a written vision statement. However, the company does provide a written mission statement on the corporate website, as follows:

> FedEx Corporation will produce superior financial returns for its shareowners by providing high value-added logistics, transportation and related business services through focused operating companies. Customer requirements will be met in the highest quality manner appropriate to each market segment served. FedEx will strive to develop mutually rewarding relationships with its employees, partners and suppliers. Safety will be the first consideration in all operations. Corporate activities will be conducted to the highest ethical and professional standards.

Sustainability

FedEx operates in a business where large carbon footprints are the norm. Operating a fleet of 700 aircraft, and over 60,000 vehicles, many of which are trucks, results in a large consumption of fuel and added noise pollution. In addition, FedEx is fraught with excess packaging boxes, tape, and other products used to protect items during shipment. Efforts made to reduce carbon emissions are a part of FedEx's overall strategy and the company reports its fleet miles per gallon has dropped 14 percent since 2005 with a goal of a 20 percent reduction by 2020. The declines are partly from newer more fuel-efficient engines, but also from building more strategically located hubs and dispatch facilities. In addition, working with customers on their own supply chain has helped reduced fuel usage.

Also, the company uses recycled paper in most all of their shipping packaging. Most FedEx envelopes are made from 100 percent recycled paper, and boxes contain a minimum of 40 percent recycled content. FedEx also has recycling programs in place for a variety of items, including batteries, printer ink cartridges, lights, paper, oil, tires, plastics, and many other products.

Strategy

Continuing its global expansion, FedEx opened a new hub in Mexico City in 2014 to help aid in shipments to more than 800 shipping locations across Mexico. The hub should better enable 2-day shipping across Mexico and speed deliver between Mexico and the United States. Currently, Mexico is the third-largest U.S. trade partner, accounting for 13.5 percent of all U.S. trade. Also, the new Mexico City hub is expected to expedite service to Latin America, where revenues are growing rapidly. FedEx also opened a new hub in Osaka, Japan, in 2014 to better facilitate transport of shipments from Asia to the United States.

FedEx is also acquiring firms around the world in locations such as the United Kingdom, Poland, China, South Africa, India, Brazil, and many others. It is FedEx's strategy to establish a strong footprint in these areas for domestic package delivery. Between 2011 and 2014, revenues from "international domestic" operations rose from $650 million to $1.4 billion. Across Europe, FedEx opened 100 new stations across 11 different nations between 2011 and May of 2014. The company raised shipping rates by 4.9 percent on all U.S. domestic and imported mail in January 2015.

Segment Data

FedEx primary business segments are FedEx Express, FedEx Ground, and FedEx Freight. Revenues and operating profits for each are provided in Exhibit 2. FedEx Express claims to be the largest express transportation company in the world, and FedEx Ground is a principle player in the United States and Canada ground package delivery system. FedEx Freight is a top U.S. provider of less-than-truckload (LTL) freight services. LTL includes shipments on trucks smaller than 18 wheelers with packages generally weighing less than 150 pounds. This provides great cost savings for many customers who do not need the volume of a full-size truck. FedEx Services, not reported in Exhibit 2, oversees marketing, information technology, communications, and other managerial needs.

FedEx Express is the main revenue driver of the company although it does not operate as efficiently as FedEx Ground. FedEx Express covers many services focused on timely delivery but also on cost savings if expenses are more important than time. The business segment

EXHIBIT 2 FedEx's Revenues and Operating Income by Segment (in millions of USD)

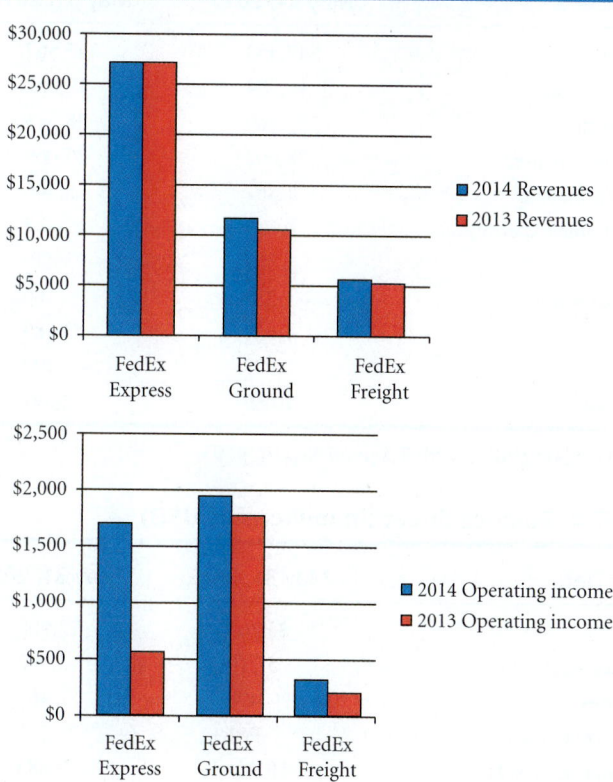

Source: Based on company documents.

provides worldwide delivery in anywhere from 1 to 5 business days based on client needs. Total U.S. and international revenues from FedEx Express were $11.6 billion and $8.7 billion, respectively, in 2014. In addition to $8.7 billion in international revenues, FedEx Express also reported $1.4 billion in revenues from "international domestic." FedEx Express is continuing its acquisition of foreign companies to establish domestic services for those areas. Freight accounted for $4.1 billion of FedEx Express's 2014 revenues. FedEx Express plans on an increase in expenses in 2015 and 2016 as the segment modernizes its airline and trucking fleet.

FedEx Ground offers services to nearly 100 percent of all U.S. residences and most Canadian residences as well. The segment specializes in package delivery. FedEx SmartPost business uses the United States Postal Service (USPS) to deliver smaller packages that are less time sensitive. However, SmartPost only generated $983 million of the $11,617 million the segment reported in 2014. Daily average package volume for FedEx Ground and FedEx SmartPost are $4,588 and $2,186 million, respectively. FedEx Ground receives on average $9.10 per package, whereas SmartPost generates $1.78 of revenue per package.

FedEx Freight, like FedEx Express and FedEx Ground, reported improved financial numbers in each of the last three years, as revealed in Exhibit 2.

Finance

FedEx reported 2015 revenues of $47.4 billion with net income of over $1 billion (down from over $2 billion in 2014), as revealed in Exhibit 3. The firm paid 35 percent taxes in fiscal year 2015, and has over $3 billion in goodwill on the balance sheet, as indicated in Exhibit 4. FedEx has been in an aggressive share buyback program, buying back 2.7 million shares in fiscal 2013 for an average price of $90.96 and 36.8 million shares in fiscal 2014 (ended in May) for an average price of $131.83. The company's stock price was trading for over $173 a share in February of 2015. FedEx has cash of $2.9 billion and expects enough liquidly moving forward without needing additional debt.

EXHIBIT 3 Income Statement (in millions of USD)

Report Date	May 31, 2015	May 31, 2014
Revenues	$47,453	$45,567
Cost of revenue	16,984	17,052
Gross profit	30,469	28,515
Operating expenses	28,602	25,069
Operating income	1,867	3,446
Other income/expenses	(5)	3
EBIT	1,862	3,449
Interest expense	235	160
EBT	1,627	3,289
Tax	577	1,192
Net income	**1,050**	**2,097**

Source: Based on FedEx's 2015 *Annual Report*, p. 93.

EXHIBIT 4 Balance Sheet (in millions of USD)

Report Date	May 31, 2015	May 31, 2014
Cash	$3,763	$2,908
Accounts receivable	5,719	5,982
Inventories	498	463
Other current assets	961	330
Total current assets	**10,941**	**9,683**
Property, plant & equipment	20,875	19,550
Goodwill	3,810	—
Intangible assets	—	—
Other assets	1,443	1,047
Total assets	**37,069**	**33,070**
Current debt	19	1
Accounts payable	5,948	5,311
Total current liabilities	**5,957**	**5,312**
Long-term debt	7,249	4,736
Deferred liabilities	2,639	3,078
Other liabilities	6,231	4,667
Total liabilities	**22,076**	**17,793**
Common stock	32	32
Retained earnings	16,900	20,429
Treasury stock	(4,897)	(4,133)
Paid in capital and other	2,958	(1,051)
Total equity	**14,993**	**15,277**
Total liabilities & equity	**37,069**	**33,070**

Source: Based on FedEx's 2015 *Annual Report*, p. 91.

Competitors

A summary of key statistics for large package delivery firms is provided in Exhibit 5. Note that FedEx has nearly double the earnings per share (EPS) as UPS, despite having half the net income.

FedEx competes primarily with UPS and the U.S. Postal Service in the United States, and with UPS and Deutsche Post internationally. The U.S. Mail Delivery Services segment accounts

EXHIBIT 5 FedEx versus Rival Firms

	FedEx	UPS	U.S. Postal Service
# Employees	231,500	213,200	488,000
$ Net Income	$2.1 B	$4.4 B	($5.5 B)
$ Revenue	$45.5 B	$55.4 B	$67.8 B
$ Revenue/Employee	$196,544	$259,849	$128,9344
$ EPS Ratio	$7.89	$4.02	—
Market Cap.	$49 B	$91 B	—

Source: Based on FedEx's 2014 company documents.

EXHIBIT 6 Percent Market Share of Key Global Players

	FedEx	UPS	Others
USA Mailbox Rentals	6%	13%	*81%
USA Mail Delivery	26%	38%	*46%
Cargo Airplanes (Non USA)	19%	10%	**71%
Mail Delivery (Non USA)	20%	24%	***56%

*United States Postal Service not included in this data.

**Air France-KLM SA, Deutsche Lufthansa AG, Emirates account for approximately 16% total with approximately equal market shares.

***Deutsche Post (parent to DHL International) accounts for around 19%.

Source: From various company reports (such as IBIS, headings changed).

for over $90 billion in annual revenues, with a 3 percent projected annual growth rate over the next 5 years. Approximately 55 percent of the $90 billion is derived from ground delivery services, whereas 29 and 8 percent, respectively, are derived from domestic and international air delivery services. Delivery services outside the United States currently are a $200 billion industry with 3 to 4 percent annual growth expected through 2020, taking the overall projected industry revenues to over $250 billion by 2020.

Traditionally, FedEx, UPS, US Postal Service, Deutsche Post, TNT International, and large national postal services in other nations were the main drivers of package delivery, along with many smaller local companies. However, with e-commerce growing, new delivery competitors such as Google, eBay, and Amazon are offing delivery services. As of now, many of these delivery services are same day and only in large cities such as Manhattan, Los Angeles, and San Francisco. It is unclear whether Amazon and Alibaba can also become package delivery giants; however, they have eroded into margins of the big transport firms such as UPS and FedEx. With Amazon's size and package volume, the firm can negotiate attractive shipping prices for its customers. Exhibit 6 reveals market share data for rival firms in the package delivery industry.

United Parcel Service (UPS)

Headquartered in Atlanta, Georgia, UPS was founded in 1907 and competes in the package delivery business as well as providing logistics and financial services in both the United States and internationally. UPS is broken down into three operating segments: U.S. Domestic Package, International Package, and Supply Chain & Freight. UPS's Package segments deliver packages to over 220 countries and the Supply Chain & Freight Segment aids businesses in financing, risk mitigation, supply chain design, consulting services, and much more in 195 countries.

United Parcel Service has reported total revenues of $58.2 billion in 2015, up from $55.4 billion the prior year. The company's 2014 net income, however, declined to $3.0 billion from $4.3 billion the prior year. About 75 percent of company revenues are derived from U.S. operations. By segments, U.S. Packaging, International Packaging, and Supply Chain & Freight account for about 62, 22, and 16 percent of total revenues, respectively. Total revenues associated from air package delivery are about $6 billion, or 11 percent, of total revenues, leaving UPS ground the single-largest driver of corporate revenues.

UPS operates over 103,000 vehicles and owns 33,000 package containers. Kentucky-based UPS Airlines, a division of UPS, operates the world's second-largest cargo aircraft fleet with 240 aircraft. UPS Airlines processes 416,000 packages per hour and has hubs in Hong Kong, China, Germany, Canada, and many states. In 2012, UPS was denied permission to acquire competitor TNT Express on monopolistic concerns. UPS is actively expanding internally, and completed a 70 percent expansion of its hub in Cologne, Germany, in November 2012. In addition, UPS has acquired multiple firms in Latin America, Europe, and Asia-Pacific over the last several years.

In 2014, UPS announced it is expanding its service that allows customers to pick up packages at convenience stores, dry cleaners, UPS shops, and many other businesses. UPS has found many customers browse online, then shop in stores, because they are unable to sign for packages delivered to their home during working hours. For $5 per package or $40 annual membership, customers can have packages dropped off at a specified pick-up location. The strategy has worked well in Europe, which currently has over 12,000 pick-up locations with plans to expand to over 20,000 in Europe alone by year-end 2015. Receiving a fee to drop off at central locations is a bonanza for UPS. The firm has determined that saving 1 second per driver per day will result in $14.5 million in savings annually.

CEO David Abney in Fall 2014 outlined UPS's commitment to becoming more a global player, especially with respect to China and Vietnam. Abney also indicated Africa will become more of a global player in the future and possibly Mexico will become a larger player as manufacturing plants want to relocate closer to the United States, as fuel prices and labor wages in Asia increase.

United States Postal Service (USPS)

Beginning with the Pony Express and stagecoaches, the United States Postal Service (USPS) is the oldest postal service in the country, existing for over 235 years. Currently, USPS employs 488,000 workers, making it the third-largest employer in the United States, behind Walmart and the federal government. USPS daily reaches over 150 million residences, businesses, and post office boxes, delivering about 155 billion pieces of mail to 971,000 delivery points. USPS delivers around 40 percent of the world's total mail volume with its fleet of over 218,000 vehicles.

The United States Postal Service is divided into five business segments: (1) First Class Mail, (2) Standard Mail, (3) Packages, (4) International, and (5) Periodicals. Revenues for the segments in 2013 were $28, $17, $12.5, $3, and $1.6 billion, respectively. Total revenues for 2014 were $67.8 billion, about the same as in 2013. Operating expenses were $73 billion in 2014, resulting in a $5.5 billion loss. The USPS lost $4.9 billion in 2013 and $15.9 billion in 2012.

The USPS continues to consolidate mail-processing centers and reduce delivery days on Standard Mail offerings. The firm also is aggressively training employees better to reduce waste, making many rural post offices part-time post offices, and offering discounts up to 58 percent to customers who mail 50,000 parcels a year. These cost saving plans are expected to save the USPS around $500 million annually. However, UPS and FedEx have questions regarding how the USPS can offer discounts to customers, when both UPS and FedEx are being forced to raise prices. With respect to USPS' lower prices, UPS's management recently stated in that it should "raise a red flag," especially since the organization is currently operating at a loss. UPS management went further, accusing USPS of charging higher rates on first-class letters, where customers have little choice or bargaining power on who to do business with. In addition, both UPS and FedEx have accused USPS of offering subsidies to customers to ship with them and even charging less for package deliver than revenues derived. USPS's proprietary pricing information does not allow FedEx or UPS to get a clear picture of the situation, but both FedEx and UPS are threating antitrust lawsuits against USPS. As a result of USPS' moves, its package business has grown over 20 percent annually from 2009 to 2014. By law, the USPS must pay its own way, and does not receive tax payer support.

The USPS workforce is heavily unionized, being represented by four labor unions: (1) American Postal Workers Union (APWU); (2) National Association of Letter Carriers (NALC); (3) National Rural Letter Carriers Association (NRLCA); and (4) National Postal Mail Handlers Union (NPMHU). All jobs at USPS not in one of the three main categories of employment are covered with the clerks by the APWU. Some union policies are quite restrictive on the postal service. For example, it is standard policy after a letter carrier has served 360 days, he or she may be represented by the NALC for reduced working hours, or for "just cause" any issue determined to be unfavorable by the union member. As mail volume continues to decrease, due to the increased use of email, bank draft billing, and the transition from junk mail advertising to Internet, USPS is constantly downsizing operations, replacing many positions with machines and consolidating mail routes. The forced pre-funding requirements for retirement benefits costs the USPS about $5.5 billion annually.

Deutsche Post (DPW.DE)

Considered the world's largest courier company, Deutsche Post employs 488,000 workers and reported 2014 revenues of €29.4 billion, or approximately $35 billion USD (up 8.1 percent from the prior year), and profits of €1.38 billion, or approximately $1.65 billion USD (down 9.1 percent from prior year). Headquartered in Bonn, Germany, Deutsche Post serves customers in over 220 countries. The company currently trades under the ticker symbol DPW on the Xetra in Germany. The company most directly competes with FedEx and UPS through DHL Express, a shipping company it acquired in 2005.

External Issues

Air Freight Demand

Demand for air cargo rose over 2 percent from May 2013 to May 2014. High jet fuel prices historically was to blame for many customers switching to trucking and slower means of transportation, favoring lower cost over more timely arrival of products. However, with oil prices falling dramatically in 2014–2015, demand for air freight is rising. Domestic freight accounts for about 20 percent of total air cargo ton-mile revenues, with FedEx Express and UPS accounting for 80 percent of this total. International freight demand was up less than 1 percent between both the United States and Europe as well as the United States and Asia in early 2014, improving from 3 to 4 percent declines in 2013. Even with an improving economy and lower oil prices, freight demand outlook for international packages by air travel is murky due to competition from large ocean shipping companies, new ports, and quicker shipping times.

International Markets

International markets continue to be important for future growth in the airfreight industry. In 2014, international markets accounted for over 50 percent of the airfreight ton-miles and have been increasing steadily since then. Domestic volumes are growing around 4 percent a year, whereas volumes in Asia are growing nearly 20 percent a year. Both FedEx and UPS have capitalized on these trends, especially in China, but also in Germany, to help facilitate a growing European market as well. International rates tend to offer a higher margin as well, since many customers internationally disproportionally use next day service, which carries a significant price premium.

Less than Truck Load (LTL)

FedEx Ground and UPS both compete in the LTL segment that accounts for about 6 percent of the total trucking industry. Annual revenues in the LTL are over $50 billion with both FedEx Ground and UPS accounting for the majority shares. The LTL typical haul consists of 1,000 to 1,500 pounds and is normally used by business-to-business or retail-to-consumer segments, such as Amazon sending shipments to customers. The LTL system also requires a large hub structure, which both UPS and FedEx Ground have. In LTL, labor costs are high, with many drivers being represented by the International Brotherhood of Teamsters Union.

Natural Gas Powered Trucks

The trucking industry had high hopes for natural gas powered trucks, especially in the United States, where natural gas is plentiful but sales have lagged expectations. In 2013, sales were around 8,700 trucks and around 10,000 in 2014. However, analysts were expecting 16,000 natural gas powered trucks to be sold in 2014. Premiums on the trucks upwards of 33 percent have caused pause with potential customers, combined with cheaper diesel fuel prices during the same time. Also, only in select parts of the South and West are there reliable natural-gas fueling stations. Natural gas powered trucks do save around $1.70 per equivalent gallon on fuel after taking into account diesel trucks are 20 percent more fuel efficient. In the end, it takes around

4 years at current fuel prices to recover the price premium paid for a natural gas powered truck. However, UPS has a fleet of around 300 gas-powered trucks and 700 tractors. In addition, UPS has helped finance several natural-gas filling stations.

Future

From Summer 2014 into early 2015, oil prices fell nearly 60 percent in the United States, in what many would consider a boom for trucking companies such as FedEx. But as CEO of Old Dominion Trucking pointed out, much of the oil price is passed on to consumers, and rising or falling prices do not directly impact trucking business. FedEx, in fact, missed its second quarter 2014 earnings estimates, reporting $2.14 EPS versus Wall Street estimates of $2.22 EPS. The difference was blamed mostly on reduced fuel surcharges stemming from the drop in oil prices, which FedEx was unable to pass along to consumers as the price of oil dropped. Nevertheless, FedEx is still doing great; second-quarter 2014 profits were up 23 percent from the same quarter in 2013, and revenue was up 5 percent over the same period. UPS's stock price dropped nearly 15 percent in one week in January 2015 after reporting flat earnings and a 6 percent sales gain. In response to UPS's news and growing concerns, FedEx's CEO was quoted as saying "We are not UPS."

FedEx acquired GENCO Distribution System, Inc. in January 2015. The GENCO acquisition is expected to further FedEx's commitment to its customers by improving logistics offerings. GENCO is a large third-party logistic provider in the United States and Canada. FedEx plans to allow GENCO to operate as a subsidiary and keep its management team. The new subsidiary will, however, report through FedEx's Ground business segment.

FedEx is flying high. In mid-2015, the company signed a deal to buy 50 additional Boeing Co (BA.N) 767-300 freighters in the biggest order ever for the plane, allowing Boeing to extend its production line well into the next decade. The deal includes options for another 50 767Fs and is worth $9.97 billion at list prices. The new aircraft are being delivered to FedEx Express over the fiscal years 2018 to 2023. This deal brings FedEx's orders for 767Fs to 106 and extends the company's drive to modernize its fleet.

FedEx needs a clear strategic plan moving forward. Help CEO Smith prepare this document.

Tyson Foods, Inc., 2015

www.tyson.com, TSN

Headquartered in Springdale, Arkansas, Tyson Foods has about 115,000 employees and is the world's second-largest meat-producing company, trailing only Brazil-based JBS S.A., the parent to Pilgrim's Pride. Tyson has international operations in Mexico, Brazil, China, and India. Although commonly and inaccurately thought of in its home market of the United States as a chicken-only company, Tyson actually derives higher sales from beef than chicken, although operating income from poultry operations is significantly higher. Tyson also produces significant pork and prepared foods, including deli meats, pizza toppings, pizza crust, and tortilla chips, among others.

Tyson is one of the largest U.S. marketers of value-added chicken, beef, and pork to retail grocers, food-service distributors, and fast-food and full-service restaurant chains. Tyson supplies all KFC, Taco Bell, McDonald's, Burger King, Wendy's, Walmart, Kroger, IGA, Beef O'Brady's, and other restaurants with their meat. Tyson has 123 food-processing plants, making Buffalo wings, boneless Buffalo wings, chicken nuggets and tenders, and more. The company's largest meat-packing facility is its beef plant in Dakota City, Nebraska. Other facilities include feed mills, hatcheries, and tanneries.

Tyson has aggressively expanded its operations in China by building more than 40 chicken farms out of a planned 90 to ensure better quality and safer chicken products for Chinese customers. Tyson recently acquired Don Juilo Foods, a tortilla and snack firm; Circle Foods, a producer of frozen Mexican food; and Bosco's Pizza. Tyson continues to expand into prepared foods.

The company is fully integrated in its poultry business, especially in overseas markets. In the United States, however, Tyson relies on contract growers to a large extent, since they are regulated and standards are more consistent from grower to grower. Tyson is engaged in feed production, and through its wholly owned subsidiary Cobb-Vantress (Cobb) is one of the leading poultry breeding stock suppliers in the world.

About 20 percent of all beef, chicken, and pork in the United States is provided by Tyson. With relationships with 5,500 chicken farms, Tyson each week handles 41 million chickens, 135 thousand cattle, and 319 thousand pigs. Tyson has 57, 13, 9, and 25 production plants for chicken, beef, pork, and prepared foods, respectively.

For the quarter that ended June 30, 2015, Tyson reported its fiscal Q3 revenue up 4 percent year-over-year to $10.1 billion, and adjusted operating income up 40 percent year-over-year to a record high of $568 million. For that period, Tyson's total adjusted operating margin was 5.6 percent, led by their Chicken segment operating margin of 11.4 percent and Prepared Foods segment at a record adjusted operating margin of 10.9 percent. During the quarter, Tyson had synergies of $87 million that resulted from the integration of Hillshire Brands.

Copyright by Fred David Books LLC. www.strategyclub.com (Written by Forest R. David)

History

Back in 1929, John Tyson moved his family from Missouri to Arkansas and began transporting cheap southern chickens to cities such as Chicago, Detroit, and St. Louis, where Tyson could command a high price. His business was so successful that he quickly began to backward integrate by purchasing and operating his own chicken farms. By the 1960s, Tyson had divested its chicken farms to focus on meat processing, establishing an elaborate system of buying from contract famers and paying each farmer based on timely and quality chicken production. Recently, however, Tyson has backward integrated again by purchasing its own farms to gain better control of sanitation and quality of chickens, especially in China.

In 2001, Tyson Foods acquired IBP, Inc., the largest beef packer and second-largest pork processor in the United States, for $3.2 billion. It also acquired in the last decade companies such as Hudson Foods, Garrett Poultry, Washington Creamery, Franz Foods, Prospect Farms,

Krispy Kitchens, Ocoma Foods, Cassady Broiler, Vantress Pedigree, Wilson Foods, Honeybear Foods, Mexican Original, Valmac Industries, Heritage Valley, Lane Processing, Cobb-Vantress, Holly Farms, Wright Brand Foods, and Don Julio Foods. In June 2014, Tyson acquired Hillshire Brands for $7.7 billion. Hillshire produces Jimmy Dean sausage and Ball Park hot dogs and more. In July 2014, Tyson sold its Mexican and Brazilian poultry businesses to JBS S.A. for $575 million to help pay for Hillshire.

Vision/Mission

Tyson Foods has quite an elaborate written mission statement on the corporate website. The mission statement is divided into three parts: Who We Are, What We Do, and How We Do It. Basically, the Tyson mission statement says "We are a company of people engaged in the production of food, seeking to pursue truth and integrity, and committed to creating value for our shareholders, our customers, our team members, and our communities."

Organizational Structure

Exhibit 1 reveals that Tyson Foods uses a divisional-by-product organizational structure. Note there is only one female among 14 top executives.

Tyson's Chicken Strategy

China

Historically, Tyson has purchased chicken from independent farmers in close proximity to Tyson's chicken processors. This remains the firm's main strategy in the United States. However, due to recent food safety concerns in China, Tyson is spending millions to backward integrate in China by building its own chicken farms. In early 2014, Tyson operated around 20 farms in China and expects to operate 90 by late 2015. Tyson's CEO, Donnie Smith, was quoted as saying, "We just can't build the chicken houses (in China) fast enough, and we're going absolutely as fast as we know how to go." This is likely an important strategy for Tyson, considering that traditionally many chicken farms in China are nothing more than mom-and-pop homesteads producing a few hundred birds at a time in open-air farms that are subject to bird droppings from above. Research shows bird droppings could lead to increased cases of the bird flu. For example, in the United States, a single covered, climate-controlled farm may supply Tyson with 100,000 birds at a time. In markets such as China, where there are many small suppliers, it makes monitoring the sheer volume of farms for sanitation and excessive use of food additives to promote chicken growth difficult and expensive. In contrast, one Tyson farm in China typically can house over 330,000 chickens in 16 climate-controlled buildings each the size of two Olympic swimming pools. Trucks are sprayed three times before entering the facility. Numerous sanitation procedures are followed by workers on the floor.

With the recent safety concerns on meat products in China, Chinese consumers have reduced their meat consumption considerably. Thus, building trust with the Chinese consumer in the Tyson brand could go a long way to creating a sustainable competitive advantage by providing dependable and safe chicken for Chinese consumers. Chinese consumers for the first time exceeded U.S. consumers as the largest chicken consumers in the world in 2012. The United States remains the largest chicken consumption nation per capita by over 3-1 ratio. Even firms such as Walmart in China have taken notice of Tyson's commitment to delivering safe chicken products, thus reducing Walmart's own risk. Although Tyson does not report sales by geographic region, analysts estimated Tyson's revenue in China was $715 million in fiscal year 2013 and projections of revenues topping $1.1 billion by fiscal year 2015. However, Tyson has not produced a profit in recent years stemming from the large expensive backward integration strategy. Management expects by 2015 to enjoy profits from the new strategy in China.

United States

To help maintain its supply of chicken, Tyson pays chicken farmers in the United States on an incentive-based system with farmers who produce the largest quantity of healthy birds earning more. To keep chicken from different farms as constant as possible, Tyson provides farmers with both the chickens and chicken feed. This also protects farmers from volatile prices of corn

EXHIBIT 1 Tyson's Organizational Structure

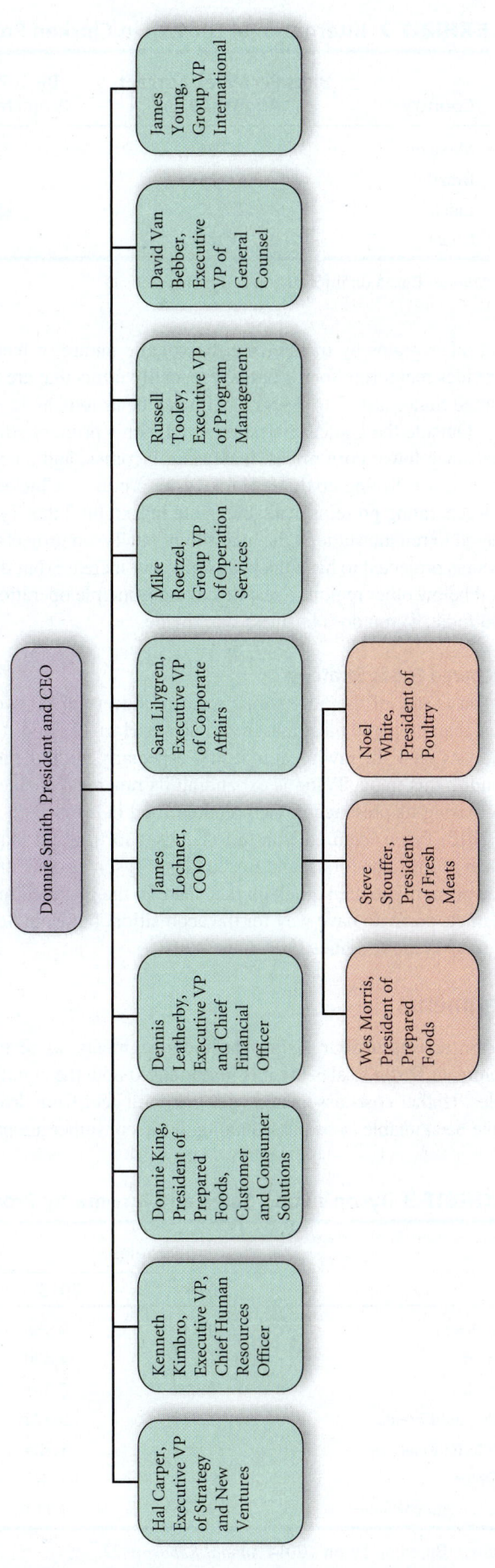

Source: Based on the author's depiction given executives' titles.

EXHIBIT 2 International Growth in Chicken Production by Year-End 2014

Country	Birds Per Week Current August 2013	Birds Per Week Projected in 2014	Percent Increase
Mexico	2.7 M	2.7 M	0%
Brazil	1.3 M	2 M	54%
India	275 K	450 K	61%
China	1.5 M	3 M	50%

Source: Based on information at Tyson's website.

and other grains by transferring the volatile nature of feed prices to Tyson. In addition, Tyson provides mentoring for all farms, especially farms that are struggling. The typical contract in the United States lasts 3 to 7 years, but it can be as long as 15 years for excellent farms.

Outside the United States, one of Tyson's primary strategies is to increase chicken production since lower corn prices, increasing incomes, and a demand for safe foods in many foreign markets are driving up demand for Tyson products. Chicken also remains one of the higher margin-generating proteins available. Note in Exhibit 2 that Tyson's chicken sales in Mexico are expected to remain static in the near future but Tyson projects large gains in both China and Brazil. India is projected to have the largest percent increase, but the volume of chicken in India remains well below other regions. Despite having principle operations in the U.S., Mexico, Brazil, China, and India, Tyson does business worldwide.

Prepared Foods Strategy

Tyson is one of the largest raw meat producers in the world, but raw meats have lower margins than prepared meat that firms such as Hormel Foods (and Hillshire Brands) produce. Many analysts view the raw meat industry, especially in the United States, to have limited growth. To counter this trend, Tyson is expanding its raw meat business outside the United States, but also increasing its presence in the prepared food industry both in the U.S. and globally. This is why, in 2013, Tyson acquired Don Juilo Foods, a tortilla and snack manufacturer; Circle Foods, a producer of Mexican foods; and Bosco Pizza. Tyson's acquisition of Hillshire Brands for $7.7 billion was primarily to gain quick market share in the prepared meat industry. Tyson sold Heinold Hog Markets partly to pave way for the acquisition, but Heinold accounted for only around 1 percent of total Tyson revenues.

Segments

Tyson reports in four distinct business segments, as revealed in Exhibit 3. Chicken and beef dominate Tyson's sales but it is important to note the significantly lower margins on beef-related sales. Higher costs associated with pork and beef from drought, increased feed, and disease that have been unable to be passed along to the consumer are partly to blame.

EXHIBIT 3 Tyson's Food Sales and Income by Product (in millions of USD)

	Sales		Operating Income	
	2014	2013	2014	2013
Chicken	$11,116	$10,988	$883	$683
Beef	16,177	14,400	347	296
Pork	6,304	5,408	455	332
Prepared Foods	3,927	3,322	(60)	101
International	1,381	1,324	(121)	(37)
Other	—	46	(74)	—
Intersegment Sales	(1,325)	(1,114)	—	—

Source: Based on Tyson's 2014 *Annual Report* p. 27.

EXHIBIT 4 Tyson's Sales by Geographic Region

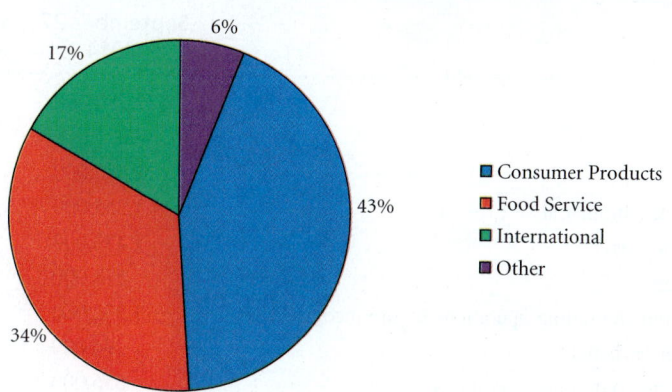

Legend:
- Consumer Products
- Food Service
- International
- Other

Source: Based on company documents.

Tyson does not provide a detailed breakdown based on international sales and revenues, but Exhibit 4 indicates about 17 percent of all sales are derived from foreign markets. With Tyson's commitment to build 90 full-scale chicken farms in China and their further commitments to other regions, it is expected international sales percentage will increase in the future. Tyson has yet to turn a profit on its Chinese backward integration strategy, and CEO Donnie Smith indicated it may take until early 2015 before a profit is reached from these operations.

Finance

For the quarter that ended June 30, 2015, Tyson reported its fiscal Q3 segment revenue as follows:

Chicken: Sales decreased 2.5 percent year-over-year to $2.75 billion due to a 5.3 percent decline in average sales price (ASP). Sales volume increased 2.9 percent.

Beef: Sales climbed 2.7 percent year-over-year to $4.3 billion. Average sales price went up 6.9 percent due to lower domestic availability of fed cattle supplies.

The segment suffered an operating loss partly due to reduced consumption of beef.

Pork: Sales plunged 31.7 percent year-over-year to $1.20 billion due to a 4.8 percent decline in volumes and 28.2 percent decrease in ASP.

Prepared Foods: Sales increased to $1.81 billion from $901 million a year ago, primarily due to a 77.4 percent increase in volumes as well as an ASP increase of 13.2 percent.

International: Sales declined 33.2 percent to $244 million due to a 25.3 percent drop in volume and a 10.5 percent ASP decline due to supply imbalances as a result of weak demand in China.

Tyson's income statement and balance sheet are provided in Exhibits 5 and 6, respectively. Unlike their fiscal Q3 data just summarized, Tyson's sales and net income increased nicely in 2014.

Competitors

Exhibit 7 reveals a comparative analysis of Tyson Foods versus rival firms. The rival firms in Exhibit 7 compete mostly on chicken with Tyson; however, Tyson also produces substantial beef and pork products indicated by Exhibits 9 and 10.

Pilgrim's Pride

The Brazilian food giant, JBS, owns 75 percent of Pilgrim's Pride. JBS is the second-largest producer of chicken products in the world, trailing only Tyson Foods. The firm's largest U.S.-based business is Pilgrim's Pride, which has operations in the states, Mexico, and Puerto Rico, with its global headquarters in Greeley, Colorado. Pilgrim's Pride sells its products to over 100 countries, employs 38,000 people, and processes 36 million chickens per week compared to Tyson's

EXHIBIT 5 Income Statement for Tyson Foods (in thousands of USD)

	September 27, 2014	September 28, 2013
Sales	$37,580,000	$34,374,000
Cost of sales	34,895,000	32,016,000
Gross profit	2,685,000	2,358,000
Selling, general & administrative expenses	1,255,000	983,000
Operating income (loss)	1,430,000	1,375,000
Interest and other	178,000	118,000
Income (loss) from continuing operations before income taxes	1,252,000	1,257,000
Income tax expense (benefit)	396,000	409,000
Income (loss) from continuing operations	856,000	848,000
Income (loss) from discontinued operations, net	8,000	(70,000)
Net income (loss)	864,000	778,000

Source: Based on company documents.

EXHIBIT 6 Balance Sheet for Tyson Foods (in thousands of USD)

	September 27, 2014	September 28, 2013
Cash & cash equivalents	$438,000	$1,145,000
Accounts receivable	1,684,000	1,497,000
Inventories	3,274,000	2,817,000
Other current assets	825,000	145,000
Total current assets	6,221,000	5,604,000
Net property, plant & equipment	5,130,000	4,053,000
Goodwill	6,706,000	1,902,000
Intangible assets	5,276,000	138,000
Other assets	623,000	480,000
Total assets	**23,956,000**	**12,177,000**
Current debt	643,000	513,000
Accounts payable	1,806,000	1,359,000
Other current liabilities	1,348,,000	1,138,000
Total current liabilities	3,797,000	3,010,000
Long-term debt	7,535,000	1,895,000
Deferred income taxes	2,450,000	479,000
Other liabilities	1,284,000	592,000
Total liabilities	**15,066,000**	**5,976,000**
Common stock	42,000	39,000
Paid in capital	4,257,000	2,292,000
Retained earnings	5,748,000	4,999,000
Treasury stock	(1,010,000)	(1,021,000)
Other	(147,000)	(108,000)
Total shareholders' equity	**8,890,000**	**6,201,000**
Total liabilities & equity	**23,956,000**	**12,177,000**

Source: Based on company documents.

41 million. Pilgrim's contracts out much of its chicken growing to independent farmers with over 3,900 contract farmers on record. Pilgrim's is currently in the process of buying Tyson's poultry operations in Brazil and Mexico for about $600 million, after losing the bidding battle for Hillshire Brands with Tyson.

EXHIBIT 7 Tyson versus Rival Firms

	Tyson	Pilgrim's Pride	Sanderson Farms
# Employees	124,000	35,400	11,400
$ Net Income	$856 M	$549 M	$249 M
$ Revenue	$37.6 B	$8.4 B	$2.8 B
$ Revenue/Employee	$303,225	$237,288	$245,614
$ EPS Ratio	$2.41	$2.65	$10.80
Market Cap.	$15 B	$6.6 B	$1.9 B

Source: Based on company documents.

Smithfield Foods, Inc.

Headquartered in Smithfield, Virginia, Smithfield is the largest pork producer and processor in the United States. Located in Tar Hill, North Carolina, it is the largest slaughterhouse and meat-processing plant in the world—a Smithfield facility. Purchased by Chinese WH Group in 2013 for $7.1 billion, Smithfield is listed on the Hong Kong Stock Exchange. Packaged meats are the largest revenue-generating segment of Smithfield, increasing to about $1.75 billion in mid-year 2014, up from $1.45 billion the previous year. Fresh pork sales also increased to $1.6 billion from $1.3 billion over the same time frame. Total sales were up 14 percent with a profit of over $32 million.

Hormel Foods Corporation

Headquartered in Austin, Minnesota, Hormel is a Fortune 500 American food company that produces Spam luncheon meat and many other products under brand names such as Farmer John, Lloyd's, and Muscle Milk. As Tyson moves more into prepared foods, it is moving into Hormel's territory. Hormel has 40 manufacturing and distribution facilities. The company has about 20,000 employees and generates about $9 billion annually in revenue. In 2013, Hormel acquired Skippy, the best-selling brand of peanut butter in China and the second-best-selling brand in the world—from Unilever for $700 million; the sale included Skippy's U.S. and China factories. Hormel produces a brand of wrapped tortilla-type snacks dubbed *REV.* These wraps are essentially miniature burritos, available in several flavors such as pepperoni pizza, ham and cheese, peppered turkey, meat lovers' pizza, Italian-style ham, along with several others. In 2014, Hormel bought the CytoSport Company for about $450 million, including the Muscle Milk protein supplement brand.

External Issues

An Oligopoly

Exhibits 8, 9, and 10 pertain to U.S. chicken, beef, and pork production, respectively, and indicate an oligopoly "meat industry," with the top 4 or 5 firms producing most of all meat consumed by Americans. However, chicken production, dominated by Tyson and Pilgrim's Pride, is quite fragmented, with 46 percent of all chicken production in the United States coming from smaller

EXHIBIT 8 USA Chicken Production

Company	Market Share
Tyson	21%
Pilgrim's Pride	19%
Sanderson Farms	7%
Perdue Farms	7%
Other	46%

Source: Based on information at Watt Poultry USA, March 2013.

EXHIBIT 9 USA Beef Production

Company	Market Share
Tyson	26%
JBS	23%
Cargill	23%
National Beef	13%
Other	15%

Source: Based on information at Cattle Buyers Weekly 2012.

EXHIBIT 10 USA Pork Production

Company	Market Share
Smithfield	26%
Tyson	17%
JBS Swift	11%
Cargill	9%
Hormel	8%
Other	29%

Source: Based on information at Tyson's Website 2013.

companies. Note in the exhibits that Tyson Foods is the U.S. leader in both chicken and beef production and trails only Smithfield (bought by China Shuanghui International Holdings Ltd. in 2013) in pork production.

Beef Trends

Meatpackers across the United States were paying the highest prices on record for live cattle in January 2014, due to droughts in much of America's Great Plains (and in Mexico) that led to higher corn prices. Cattle numbers in the United States in 2014 were at 60-year lows and prices were up 26 percent from just 5 years earlier. While potentially good news for Tyson's beef segment, the higher prices and healthier eating trends have also been met with reduced red meat consumption. In the United States, consumption rates of red meat are down 25 percent over the last three decades. Many customers now prefer chicken, pork, fish, and increasingly a totally vegetarian diet.

Mexico has also experienced a decline in red meat consumption per capita over the last decade. On average, beef tends to be a much more expensive meat product to produce and is met with much lower margins. One interesting way firms such as Tyson and its rivals are increasing profit margins from beef is by slicing areas of beef carcasses traditionally used for ground beef into thinly sliced steaks. The overall beef industry is also benefiting from increased exports to Asia and Russia, and is benefiting from the waning paranoia of the mad cow disease from a decade earlier.

Despite reductions in red meat consumption, Americans still account for the largest beef-eating nation, averaging a whopping 77 pounds per person of beef annually, compared to citizens of Europe at 34 and China at 10 pounds per person. Mexico, Japan, and Canada are the three top beef export destinations for U.S.-produced beef. The three nations have rotated their respective absolute positions over the last 10 years, with Mexico reclaiming the top spot (of the three) recently, likely do to the droughts in the U.S.

Chicken Trends

Chicken is the most commonly eaten animal in the United States; it is also popular around the world as an affordable way to obtain lean protein (assuming one does not eat the skin). As of early 2014, China was the largest chicken consumer in the world, but the United States still leads considerably in per capita consumption. Per capita chicken consumption in the United States,

European Union (EU), and China are around 99, 41, and 22 pounds per person annually, respectively. Mexico, Brazil, Argentina, and Canada all consume about 70 pounds per person, and many other nations in Central America and South America also consume more chicken per capita than Europe or China. Peru, Paraguay, and Bolivia significantly lag their South American counterparts in chicken consumption and offer possible opportunities for exporting chicken producers.

Despite great popularity, chicken is also more likely to be contaminated than other meats and cross-contaminate other food products. A report in *Consumer Reports* in December 2013 claimed that 97 percent of all U.S. chicken breasts contain harmful bacteria, sparking a snap reply from the National Chicken Counsel that "99.99%" of chicken in the United States is eaten safely each day. Taken literally, that would indicate 1 in 10,000 people become sick each day, so hopefully the number is considerably higher than 99.99%, but one way for consumers to ensure their chicken is safe is to heat to at least 165 F° (74 C°), avoid contact with other foods, and wipe down all countertops thoroughly. It is probable that most of U.S. consumers getting sick from chicken were negligent in the preparation process.

The principle concerns are with Escherichia coli (E. coli) and salmonella. In the *Consumer Reports* study, it was reported that half of 316 breasts sampled (U.S. only) contained significant bacteria resistant to multiple antibiotics. The U.S. Food and Drug Administration (FDA) is currently pushing for farmers to reduce the amount of antibiotics used in chicken feed to help reduce producing bacteria that are resistant to antibiotics. Interestingly enough, there is no set standard in the United States by either the FDA or the United States Department of Agriculture (USDA) to officially bar food containing E. coli, so variation remains quite high in chicken from one producer to another. Interestingly, Europe avoids U.S. chicken, reportedly because in America, chicken is submerged in chlorine briefly to assure cleanliness. This procedure is not done in Europe.

China has also dealt with its fair share of chicken-associated illnesses in recent years, so many Chinese consumers have reduced their chicken consumption considerably. China has far fewer standards than those in the United States. Farmers in China may sell only a few hundred chickens at a time to the processor and their farms are open air, at risk for bird droppings from above, and may be fed diets excessive in growth hormones at a rate much higher than other farmers.

Pork Trends

China blows everyone else in the world away when it comes to total pork consumption, but Europe is not far behind in per capita consumption. Data from 2013 revealed per capita pork consumption in pounds for China, EU, and United States was 90, 88, and 62, respectively. Pork production has risen in the United States, but consumption has declined in recent years due partly to huge demand in foreign markets. The main recipient of U.S. pork is Japan, where about 35 percent of all American-exported pork is shipped. Mexico is second, acquiring about 20 percent of all U.S.-exported pork. Pork growth rates remain moderate per capita at around 2.5 percent in Mexico, 3 percent in China, 2.6 percent in South Korea, and 1.3 percent in Japan. Mexico might be the real future star out of this above list, as Mexico has a population growth of 1.6 percent, resulting in over 4 percent total pork consumption. Unlike Mexico, most developed nations worldwide are experiencing declining or stable populations.

The cost of pork continues to rise for pork processors. From the low in 2009 to March 2014, lean hog prices are up over 100 percent, which is not necessarily good news for firms such as Tyson, which, at times, has difficulty passing on the increased cost to the consumer. This situation is slowly changing, however, as pork demand is rising faster than prices and Tyson is more able to pass on increased cost to the consumer. One strategy to help margins would be to backward integrate into raising pigs. However, there have been numerous illnesses associated with pigs in recent years, just as with chickens and cattle. A new swine virus discovered in 2013 quickly spread to 25 states in less than a year, killing millions of pigs. Europe, in 2014, was experiencing a virus dubbed the "African Swine Virus" that was killing pigs but was harmless to humans. Nevertheless, the virus caused Russia to block all European pig imports, creating quite a political ruckus between the two global powers.

Aside from consumption patterns, rising prices, and potential viruses, the pig industry is plagued by inhumane treatment of pigs in the United States and probably other geographic locations as well. Tyson urges American farmers to improve the quality of housing for all pigs, especially pregnant sows, but has not terminated contracts with farmers that use stalls where sows are unable to stand, turnaround, or stretch. Such stalls are still present and even common on some farms in the United States. Tyson is also concerned about the problem with sick pigs often being killed by blunt force, likely resulting in increased suffering.

Required Meat ID Labels

Since 2013, the USDA requires all meat producers to accurately label from where the meat was derived. The labeling should make it easier to track the source of contaminated meat. Firms such as Tyson complain it is an unnecessary step that adds additional expenses. In addition, all ground meat must now come from the same country. Historically, it was possible for ground beef or pork to come not only from different individual animals but also from different countries. In addition to meat-producing firms such as Tyson, some countries (e.g., Canada and Mexico) have expressed concern that American customers may be prejudiced toward meat grown in their respective countries for various reasons such as not being patriotic and not trusting the quality of the meats from other countries. Tyson even stopped buying cattle form Canada in late 2013, citing the additional costs associated with the new USDA rule. U.S.-based firms are also fearful that Canada and Mexico will now start to impose tariffs on American-grown meats.

Geopolitical Concerns to Growing Livestock

Meat, poultry, and fish products were once only affordable to the wealthy, but as incomes have grown worldwide, so has meat consumption, and the resulting increase in raising livestock to feed this new growing population. Some of the statistics below are startling, considering how many hungry people remain in the world. For example, it is estimated that over one third of all grain harvested is used to feed livestock, with around 75 percent of all grain in the United States being used to feed livestock. To grow this amount of feed grain, according to one published report, around half of all water consumed in the United States goes into keeping crops grown for livestock feed well watered and healthy. It is estimated that for every 1 gram of meat protein a cow yields, the cow consumed 5.6 grams of plant/grain protein. As populations demand more meat products, especially beef products, there has been widespread deforestation of old growth forest in parts of the Amazon and top-soil erosion and other monopolization of valuable grazing land that could be used for crops. Organizations such as People for the Ethical Treatment of Animals (PETA) at times have suggested that all raising of livestock is unethical. So, while many people enjoy eating meat, and while meat production creates many jobs, there remain geopolitical headwinds from environmentalists in the overall livestock industry for companies such as Tyson to navigate.

Future

Many U.S.-based companies were hurt on 2014 revenues because of the rising dollar in overseas markets. Tyson, which does significant business in China and other foreign markets, indicated that cheaper chicken and pork prices globally offset many of the currency headwinds facing the firm and allowed for rising profits in U.S. markets. Operating income for chicken alone was up 29 percent for Tyson in 2014. Lower feed costs also helped boost profits as well as a reduction in the viruses that killed many pigs over 2012 through much of 2014. CEO Donnie Smith has recently expressed concerns over a number of slowdowns at ports along the U.S. West Coast and the uncertainty it will bring Tyson. Two other areas that are potentially prone to help Tyson moving forward include consumers becoming more health conscious and switching from red meat to more chicken and even processed chicken items. Chicken products tend to have significantly higher margins than beef, as shown in Exhibit 3. Tyson's successful launches of Nature Raised Farms and Jimmy Dean's frozen sandwiches and bowls also boosted profits. Nature Raised Farms markets chicken as "no antibiotics ever" for health-minded consumers and the new Jimmy Dean frozen food items are designed around lunch and dinner, moving away from Jimmy Dean's traditional breakfast line-up of product offerings.

Considering the heavy competition in the meat industry, prepare a 3 year strategic plan to help CEO Smith moving forward.

Constellation Brands Inc., 2015

www.cbrands.com, STZ

Headquartered in Victor, New York, Constellation Brands is the third-largest producer and marketer of beer in the United States and the second-largest producer of wine in the United States, Canada, and New Zealand, with operations also in Mexico and Italy. The firm holds 14 and 2.7 percent of the total wine market share in the United States and worldwide, respectively. Top wine brands include Arbor Mist, Blackstone, Clos du Bois, Franciscan Estate, and many others. Constellation's spirit (liquor) brands are limited to Black Velvet Canadian Whiskey and Svedka Vodka. Spirits only account for 5 percent of total company sales, with wine and beer fairly evenly accounting for the remaining 95 percent. Constellation Brands acquired Grupo Modelo's U.S. beer business from Anheuser-Busch InBev for $4.75 billion in 2013, and has rights to sell Corona Extra, Corona Light, Modelo Especial, Pacifico, Negra Modelo, and Victoria brands of beers in all 50 states. The company reported fiscal year-end 2014 revenues of $4.8 billion, and employs 6,300 in the United States, Mexico, and Canada.

In August 2015, Constellation Brands successfully closed its previously announced acquisition of luxury wine brand Meiomi for $315 million from Copper Cane LLC. Constellation now owns all rights to the Meiomi trademark and associated stock of pinot noir and chardonnay. Interestingly, Meiomi's pinot noir has been regarded as the best in terms of sales growth across all pinot noir price points over the last 3 months. The integration of Meiomi enhances Constellation Brands' robust brand portfolio of well-known brands like Robert Mondavi, Clos du Bois, Arbor Mist, and Blackstone. Launched in 2006, Meiomi sold about 60,000 cases in the United States in 2010 and has grown to become a nearly 600,000 case brand in 2015. Meiomi is currently the fastest-growing major pinot noir at the $20 luxury price point and has experienced dollar sales growth of more than 50 percent over the last 12 months. In calendar 2014, Meiomi generated more than $65 million in net sales with an excellent operating profit margin profile.

Constellation in 2015 has been entering into agreements and joint ventures such as their venture with Owens-Illinois to gain possession and operational rights of a glass plant. With this transaction, Constellation Brands supplies more than 50 percent of its own glass demand. The stock of Constellation Brands, Inc. has risen 30 percent through the first 8 months of 2015. The beverage alcohol company topped analysts' estimates for both earnings and quarterly revenue in mid-2015, with earnings per share of $1.26 and net revenues of $1.63 billion.

Copyright by Fred David Books LLC. www.strategyclub.com (Written by Forest R. David)

History

Constellation Brands traces its history back to 1945 when Marvin Sands, at age 21, formed the Canandaigua Industries Company with only eight employees. By 1980, the company reported $50 million in sales and was the eighth-largest wine producer in the United States. Sales expanded to $250 million by 1992 when the company acquired Barton Inc., adding to its portfolio the beer brands Corona, Peroni, and Tsingtao, along with gin, vodka, bourbon, and tequila products. Canandaigua Industries changed its name in 1997 to Canandaigua Brands, to better reflect its expanding alcoholic drink business, and to Constellation Brands in 2000.

After experiencing trouble with glass in bottles from suppliers, Constellation in October 2014 acquired a state-of-the-art glass production plant located beside its brewery in Nava, Mexico, for approximately $300 million. The acquisition included the purchase of a high-density warehouse, land, and rail infrastructure. Constellation also formed an equally owned joint venture with Owens-Illinois to own and operate the glass production plant to provide bottles exclusively for the Constellation brewery. The glass plant currently has one operational glass furnace and plans are in place to expand it to four furnaces by 2018, when this facility will supply more than 50 percent of Constellation's glass requirements for the company's beer segment. Also in October 2014, Constellation announced a 5 million hectoliter expansion of its

EXHIBIT 1 Constellation Brands' Organizational Structure

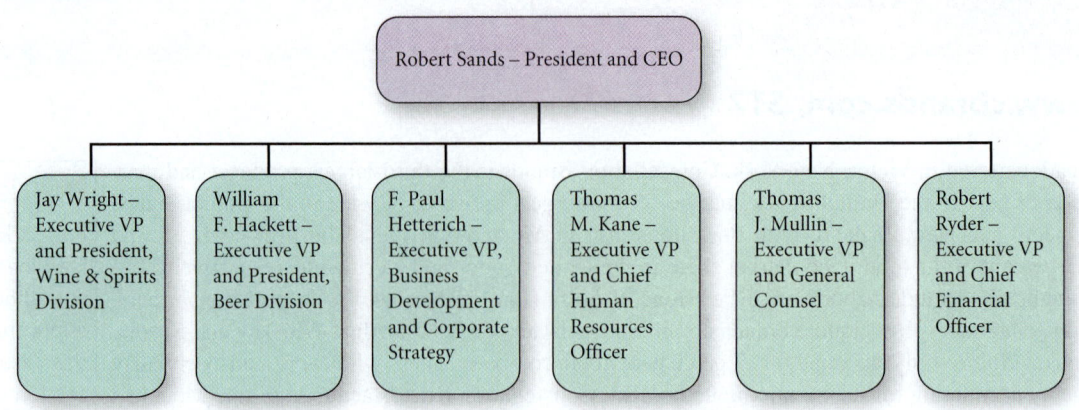

Source: Based on company documents.

Nava brewery that will increase production capacity to 25 million hectoliters when completed by the end of 2017.

Internal Issues

Organizational Structure

Constellation appears to operate from a divisional-by-product type organizational structure, but there is no chief operating officer, chief strategy officer, chief technology officer, R&D officer, chief information officer, or chief marketing officer. The company's organizational chart is depicted in Exhibit 1.

Vision/Mission/Values

Constellation's vision statement is "To elevate life with every glass raised." This statement is not provided with the company's *Annual Report* or *Form 10K*, but is listed within the About Us section on the company website under Vision and Values.

At the company website, a mission statement is given as follows: "At Constellation, we're building brands that people love: *Artfully*—with a passion for premium winemaking and industry-leading standards for quality. *Smartly*—through leading innovations, consumer insights and marketing that help grow our business and the business of our partners. *Responsibly*—by caring for the land, people and communities where we live and work." The company also publishes a set of core values based on key words: People, Quality, Entrepreneurship, Customer, Focus, and Integrity.

Sustainability

Sustainability is at the forefront of operations at Constellation Brands. Being an agricultural company, the livelihood of the firm depends directly on the natural environment. In 2011, Constellation became the largest solar user of any wine company, with 17,000 solar panels. The panels will eventually power all the wineries' needs. Constellation has been recognized by the California Department of Fish and Game as having fish-friendly farming practices, meaning runoff from the wineries are not substantially harmful to fish stocks that inhabit the surrounding water supply or lakes on vineyard properties.

Napa Green Program has certified Constellation for its efforts to ensure water conservation, energy conservation, preventing pollution, and reducing solid waste at its Robert Mondavi Winery and Franciscan Estate, the two properties owned by Constellation that are located in the Napa region. In Canada, grape rinds are provided by Constellation to help produce energy in the region. Constellation has received numerous accolades for its conservation efforts in New Zealand, and 380 acres of vineyards in San Joaquin County, California, are certified by Lodi Rules. Lodi Rules Certification is peer reviewed by scientists, academics, and environmentalists and has a mission to improve the ecosystem health, society at large, and wine quality.

Production

Just over half of all "Constellation" beer demand is produced in Nava, Mexico, located only 10 minutes south of the Texas border. With the new addition of 10 million extra hectoliters expected to be completed by 2017, Constellation expects all of its beer to be produced at this facility. As of now, the remaining Mexican beer is produced with Anheuser-Busch through a 3-year agreement. Constellation operates 18 wineries in the United States, with most of the grapes grown in California, 9 wineries in Canada, 4 in New Zealand, and 5 in Italy. Grapes are crushed and stored as wine at the wineries until branded and sold in bottles or bulk. By having wineries in New Zealand, Constellation can provide new wines year round by taking advantage of the opposite season in the Southern Hemisphere. Canadian Whiskey is produced by Constellation in Canada.

Constellation receives its water for beer from a mountain aquifer and the firm believes it will have a steady supply of quality water moving forward. About 78 percent of beer produced is bottled in glass bottles, with 21 and 1 percent, respectively, stored in cans and kegs. Constellation now owns or controls over 50 percent of the glass bottles it needs to meet demand.

The company owns or leases approximately 20,000 acres of vineyards worldwide and uses grapes from these locations to produce fine wines. In addition, Constellation purchases grapes from over 1,000 vineyards in the United States, 100 in Canada, 80 in New Zealand and 10 in Italy.

Strategy

Constellation competes in an industry that is undergoing extensive consolidation of suppliers, wholesalers, and retailers. Constellation has used both acquisition and divesture over many years to vertically integrate. Constellation's most notable acquisition was Grupo Modelo's U.S. beer segment in 2013. Other notable acquisitions include Mark West and Ruffino, which strengthened Constellation's Italian wine focus in the United States. After recalling $37 million of beer in August 2014 for possibly having small shards of glass in the bottles, Constellation later that year agreed to acquire a controlling interest in a Mexican Anheuser-Busch glass bottle factory. Called Crown Imports before the acquisition of Grupo Modelo's U.S. distribution rights from Anheuser-Busch, Constellation's beer segment reported revenues in fiscal 2014 of over $2.8 billion.

Segments

Exhibit 2 reveals that Constellation receives equal revenues from both (1) Beer and (2) Wine and Spirit segments. However, only 11 percent of fiscal 2014 Wine and Spirit revenues were derived from Spirits. With the completion of the Crown Imports segment acquisition, Constellation has the exclusive rights to market Corona Extra, Corona Light, Modelo Especial, Pacifico, Negra Modelo, and Victoria beers in all 50 states. In total, Constellation has 5 of the top 15 best-selling imported beers in the United States, with Corona Extra leading the way. In addition to the beers listed, a new beer called Modelo Especial Chelada was introduced in 2014 that contains tomato, salt, and lime. Constellation also has rights to produce Tsingtao, a Chinese beer, in the U.S. market. To help meet growing demand of Mexican beers in the United States, Constellation plans to increase the capacity of its brewery from 10 million hectoliters to 20 million hectoliters by 2017 at a cost of $1 billion.

Constellation claims to be the world's leading producer and marketer of premium wine. The firm has wine products across all price ranges and categories: table wine, sparkling wine,

EXHIBIT 2 A Segment Breakdown of Constellation Brands' Beverages (in millions of USD)

	2015		2014	
	Revenues	Gross Profit	Revenues	Gross Profit
Beer	3,189	$1,466	$2,836	$1,132
Wine & Spirits	2,839	1,172	2,846	1,117
Other	—	(60)	(813)	(257)
Totals	6,028	2,578	4,868	1,992

Source: Based on Constellation Brands' 2015 *Annual Report*, pp. 31–37.

and dessert wine. In the United States, the firm sells 14 of the top 100 wines and sells its wines worldwide. The firm is also the top wine company in Canada, offering 6 of the top 25 table wines there. Top brands include Arbor Mist, Robert Mondavi, Blackstone, Mark West, Ruffino, Franciscan Estate, Clos du Bois, and others. Most Constellation-produced wines are priced between $5 and $20, but the firm is growing toward obtaining an increased market share on higher-end wines. Constellation imports Svedka Vodka from Sweden and Black Velvet Canadian Whisky form Canada.

Finance

Constellation's income statement and balance sheet are provided in Exhibits 3 and 4, respectively.

Competitors

Many beer companies have struggled over the last decade as numerous consumers switched to sprits, wine, and more premium beers. Industrywide consolidations also have increased competition, especially for distribution rights. Firms have often had to pay well in excess of book value (a premium) for distribution firms. Constellation competes with rivals on brand names, price, and distribution networks. Anheuser-Busch InBev, Miller Coors, Boston Beer (Sam Adams), and Heineken are rival beer firms. Wine competitors include E&J Gallo, The Wine Group, and Trinchero, among others in the United States, and Pernod Ricard, Lion Natham, and Kruger internationally. Top spirit producers are Diageo, Beam, and Bacardi, but spirits are a very small part of Constellation's sales.

The U.S. wine industry is a $20 billion industry that has enjoyed growth rates of over 5 percent annualized from 2009 to 2014. Growth rates are expected to increase to an annual rate of 6.5 percent from 2015 through 2019. The industry is extremely fragmented with over 3,500 different businesses; however, the three key players are E&J Gallo Winery, Constellation Brands, and The Wine Group with market shares based on revenues of 18, 14, and 7 percent, respectively. Over 60 percent of all revenue is derived from smaller firms, many of which are mom-and-pop size businesses, although Bronco Wine Company and Treasury Wine Estates each account for 3.5 percent of the market.

As of 2014, 20 states allowed direct wine sales to the consumer, providing smaller wineries the freedom to ship directly to customers, removing the huge advantage larger wineries had over smaller wineries through extensive distribution channels. Partly as a result of the new distribution laws, new wineries, many small, increased at a rate of 11 percent between 2009 and 2014.

Exhibit 5 reveals the top wine types in the United States. Both white and red wine are fairly equally popular, with Chardonnay, a white wine, being the single-most popular wine by a wide margin in the United States. The least popular in the United States is the sparkling wine category, which many people incorrectly call champagne. Champagne is a sparkling wine, but it must come from the Champagne region of France to be classified as Champagne.

EXHIBIT 3 Constellation's Income Statement (in millions of USD)

Report Date	February 28, 2015	February 28, 2014
Revenues	$6,028	$4,868
Cost of revenue	3,449	2,876
Gross profit	2,579	1,992
Operating expenses	1,079	1,196
Gain on investments	—	1,642
EBIT	1,500	2,438
Interest & other	320	236
EBT	1,180	2,202
Tax	341	259
Net income	**839**	**1,943**

Source: Based on Constellation Brands' 2015 *Annual Report,* p. 53.

EXHIBIT 4 Constellation's Balance Sheet (in millions of USD)

Report Date	February 28, 2015	February 28, 2014
Assets		
Cash and equivalents	$110	$64
Accounts receivable	599	626
Inventories	1,827	1,744
Other current assets	374	313
Total current assets	2,910	2,747
Property, plant & equipment	2,682	2,014
Goodwill	6,208	6,147
Intangible assets	3,181	3,231
Other assets	163	163
Total assets	**15,144**	**14,302**
Liabilities		
Short-term debt	158	590
Accounts payable	338	295
Other current liabilities	635	1,141
Total current liabilities	1,131	2,026
Long-term debt	7,137	6,373
Deferred income taxes	819	763
Other liabilities	176	159
Total liabilities	**9,263**	**9,321**
Common stock	2	28
Retained earnings	5,277	4,438
Treasury stock	(1,649)	(1,662)
Paid in capital and other	2,251	2,177
Total equity	**5,881**	**4,981**
Total liabilities & equity	**15,144**	**14,302**

Source: Based on Constellation Brands' 2015 *Annual Report,* p. 52.

EXHIBIT 5 USA Market Share of Wine Types

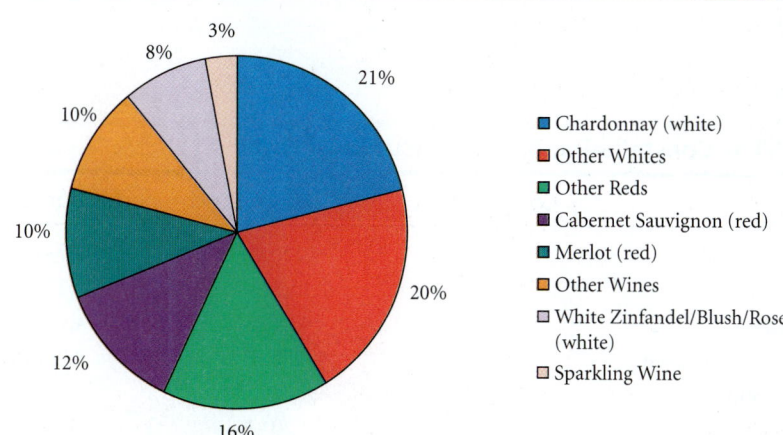

■ Chardonnay (white)
■ Other Whites
■ Other Reds
■ Cabernet Sauvignon (red)
■ Merlot (red)
■ Other Wines
□ White Zinfandel/Blush/Rose (white)
□ Sparkling Wine

Source: Based on various IBIS Reports.

The spirit (liquor) market share in the United States is dominated by Diageo, Beam, and Brown Forman with U.S. market shares of 33, 18, and 18 percent, respectively. Based in the United Kingdom, Diageo is a publically traded company with total revenues near $3 billion. Top Diageo brands include Johnnie Walker, Captain Morgan, Crown Royal, J&B, Smirnoff, Ciroc, and Ketel One. Beam was purchased by Japan-based Suntory in 2014 for $16 billion and officially renamed Beam Suntory Inc. Top brands include Jim Beam, Effen Vodka, Skinny Girl, Maker's Mark, and Pinnacle Vodka. Total 2014 revenues for Beam Suntory were $1.6 billion.

Brown Forman Corporation is the third-largest distillery in the United States, but only fractionally smaller than Beam Suntory. Brown Forman's top product is Jack Daniels. Other top products include Gentleman Jack, Southern Comfort, and Canadian Mist, among others. Total 2014 revenues for Brown Foreman are $1.6 billion. Campari is a fourth major player in the U.S. market with around a 5 percent market share. Top brands of Campari include Wild Turkey, Jameson, Seagram's, and Skyy Vodka. Constellation Brands' market share in both the U.S. and world spirit business is negligible.

Exhibit 6 provides an overview of Constellation and its rival firms in terms of basic financial variables. Note both E&J Gallo and The Wine Group are privately held companies. Therefore the table compares Constellation to two main beer rivals.

E&J Gallo Winery

E&J Gallo is the largest winery in the United States, with an 18 percent wine market share and a 3.4 percent global wine market share. Gallo has over 60 brands that include table, sparkling, and dessert as well as a few spirits. Top brands include Andre, Barefoot, and Carlo Rossi. Gallo is also extensively involved in research and development and even operates a research winery. On the contrary, Constellation shows no R&D expenses on its income statement. Gallo reported revenues of $3.8 billion in 2014 with $652 million in operating income.

The Wine Group

Like rival Gallo, The Wine Group (TWG) is also privately held and based in California. Top brands for the company include Cupcake, Flipflop, Mogen David, Jewel Box, Trapiche, and others. With the growing demand for chillable red wines, the Mogen David Winery in upstate New York has enjoyed strong sales growth with its concord and blackberry table wines. TWG and Constellation are proactive with solar energy attracting many environmentally conscious customers. In 2008, TWG acquired Almaden and Inglenook from Constellation for $134 million. Revenues in 2014 for The Wine Group were $1.4 billion with operating profits of $180 million.

Perceptual Mapping

Two product-positioning maps for Constellation could be prepared for its (1) wine and spirits and (2) beer businesses. The maps could use the dimensions Many Varieties versus Fewer Varieties and Budget versus Premium brands. Diageo, United Spirits, and Brown Forman have many offerings in the spirits category that are recognized as premium brands. However, Constellation has the most variety in terms of wine at more affordable prices than its competitors.

EXHIBIT 6 **Constellation Brands versus Rival Firms**

	Constellation	Anheuser-Busch	Molson Coors
# Employees	6,300	155,000	17,400
$ Net Income	1,943 M	15,518 M	514 M
$ Revenue	4,867 M	43,195 M	4,146 M
$ Revenue/Employee	772,540	278,677	238,275
$ EPS Ratio	3.89	5.53	2.76
Market Cap. $	22.2 B	201 B	14.1 B

Source: Based on 2014 company documents.

The beer market is highly competitive in the United States, with the craft beer segment growing more than 13 percent annually. However, Constellation has a niche market as it imports three of the top five imported beers in the United States. These beers are perceived as Mexican beers and have a strong following among those who relate to them. The growing Hispanic population in the United States and creative marketing will help ensure the growth of the Grupo Modelo brands that Constellation produces. Competitors such as SAB and AB InBev have the largest market cap in the United States, but they are perceived as less-quality brands. Sam Adams is the largest countrywide craft brewer to offer many varieties, whereas most other craft breweries are regional.

External Issues

California Drought
A three-year dry spell in California ending in 2014 has produced some of the best wine-making grapes in recent memory. Droughts wreaked havoc on most all crops in California over the three-year period from 2012 to 2014, but warm days, cool nights, and dry air produce a high-quality grape. Less water means smaller grapes; while possibly not as good for the table, smaller grapes are more concentrated in sugars and much less risky to mold and mildew on the vine during wetter seasons. Also, grapes can take on a grassy flavor during wet seasons. Cabernet Sauvignons scored ratings of 96 in both 2012 and 2013, significantly up from a score of 78 in a wetter 2011. In 2013, the California wine industry had sales of $23 billion, up 5 percent from a year earlier. To illustrate just how impactful droughts, or warmer than normal summers, can be, take the price of Cabernet Sauvignon grapes that are grown in the Napa Valley, California, versus the same species of grapes grown in Fresno, California. Typically, the grapes from the Napa Valley fetch up to 15 times more than their counterpart grapes in Fresno. The principle reason cited is the 5-degree Fahrenheit temperate difference between the two locations.

Napa Increases Sauvignon Blanc Production
The Napa Valley has long been known for producing excellent Riesling and Cabernet Sauvignon wines, but there has been an increasing shift toward production of Sauvignon Blanc. Traditionally, Sauvignon Blanc was viewed as a cash crop, a grape that could be turned into wine ready to be sold in less than 6 months, saving millions on storage and aging and helping to pay the bills for wine makers despite its cheaper price. The crop was also looked down on in Napa for its "inferior" quality. In 2013, for example, Napa vineyards planted 2,800 acres of Sauvignon Blanc compared to 20,000 acres of Cabernet Sauvignon. However, the trend is changing, as some Napa vineyards are using their best plots of land for Sauvignon Blanc and are now able to obtain prices from $50 to over $100 per bottle.

Beer Industry Trends
Beer sales in the United States have declined much of the last 5 years, especially the traditional American-style beers such as Budweiser and Miller. Shipments of Anheuser Busch products fell 2.5 percent in 2013, Miller Coors sales fell 3 percent, and overall industry sales fell 1.2 percent. Constellation Brands beer segment shipments, however, rose 5.7 percent, and sales were up also. One of the worst performing product lines were light beers. Spirits and wine shipments sales have increased slightly. Based on U.S. shipments, the leading U.S. players in the beer industry are Anheuser Busch, Miller Coors, Constellation Brands, Heineken USA, Pabst, and Boston Beer (Sam Adams), with market shares of 46, 27, 6, 4, 2.7, and 1.3 percent, respectively. The two top brands in the United States are Bud Light and Coors Light, selling 38 and 18 million gallons, respectively, in 2013. The only Constellation product to make the top 10 was Corona Extra by selling 7.4 million gallons in 2013.

The strongest two areas in the beer industry are imports and craft beers. Import shipments rose 4 percent in 2013 and total revenues increased 7 percent, as consumers are willing to pay more for imported beers. Mexican beers, led by Constellation Brands product lines, dominate the imports. Craft beers as a whole experienced an 18 percent increase in volume and a 20 percent increase in sales during 2013. The lead craft beer company in the United States is Boston Beer, better known by its product name Sam Adams, with a 16 percent market share in the craft beer category. Sierra Nevada is second with a 6 percent market share. Hard cider is also growing in this segment. Miller Coors paid $40 million to acquire Crispin Cider Company in 2012.

Spirit Industry Trends

Spirit (liquor) volume rose 2 percent in 2013 with sales up nearly 5 percent, as consumers traded up from light beers. Anytime a country's economy improves, consumers generally are willing to pay a premium for quality spirits, especially higher-end spirits. Higher spirits reported 7 percent volume increases in 2013, whereas cheaper spirits declined 1 percent. Irish Whiskey experienced the largest growth in 2013, with a 20 percent volume increase. The shift from beer to spirits has been ongoing since 2000, when the U.S. market share for beer, spirits, and wine was 55.5, 28.7, and 15.7 percent, respectively. Today, total market shares are 48.3, 34.7, and 17 percent, respectively. Domestically, one of the strongest-growing spirit areas are flavored drinks. Internationally, American whiskey continues to grow in popularity.

Wine Industry Trends

High-end wine sales continue to increase in the United States, led by the Millennial generation (people considered to be born from about 1980 to 2000, meaning about half of the generation is not even old enough to currently purchase alcohol). High-end wine buyers are often considered consumers who purchase a bottle of wine that costs more than $20 at least once a month. In addition, there is a growing trend in the United States of people wanting to try newer wine varieties other than the standard Chardonnay and Merlot varieties. Other trends in the industry include wine companies packaging wine in plastic containers, boxes, and even aluminum cans. Such packaging is cheaper than glass wine bottles, and younger wine consumers are more readily accepting of alternative packing options. Of the three classifications of wine—table, dessert, and sparkling—table wine is the fastest-growing and most popular in the United States. About 75 percent of all wine consumed in this country is domestically produced table wine.

Wine Types

Cabernet Sauvignon is one of the world's most popular red grape wines, although the actual grape is black in color. The name *Sauvignon* is believed to be derived from the French word for "wild." One of the reasons leading to the popularity of this grape is the wide range of climates in which it can be grown around the world. Cabernet Sauvignon grapes are now grown for wine in Canada, Lebanon, France, Australia, Chile, and California, including the famous Napa Valley. Often, Cabernet Sauvignon is blended with Merlot and other wines as well. The grape was considered the most premium in the world for hundreds of years until Merlot replaced it in the 1990s. Overall, however, Cabernet Sauvignon remains more popular worldwide than Merlot.

Merlot is considered by many to be the most premium of the wines. The word *Merlot* is believed to be derived from the French word *merle,* which translates to "blackbird" in English, as the grapes have a deep blue to black outer appearance. The grapes are grown worldwide and are especially common in eastern Europe, France, United States, Australia, New Zealand, South Africa, and parts of South America. Merlot generally comes in two styles, a Bordeaux wine that is harvested early to produce a more medium body taste and what wine experts refer to as a "International Style" of Merlot that is harvested later in the year to produce a fuller body.

Chardonnay also traces its roots to France, but now is the second-most commonly grown white grape in the world. The grape is greenish to white in color and is used to make white wine. Many new wine-growing regions start with Chardonnay, as it is an easier grape and wine to produce than some of the fancier reds. Chardonnay grapes are also used to make many sparkling wines, including champagne. Chardonnay grapes grown in cooler climates are said to have a light, crisp taste. Chardonnay wine remains extremely popular, as shown earlier in Exhibit 5.

Wine Health Benefits

Research has revealed that red wine can help reduce the risk of depression for those drinking two to seven glasses of wine per week. Some research suggests that red wine consumption may reduce bowel tumors by 50 percent, helping to prevent colon cancer. Red wine has also been shown to help prevent breast cancer, while most other alcoholic beverages increase the risk of breast cancer. However, researchers on breast cancer are quick to point out that raw natural red grapes are more powerful in reducing breast cancer than red wine. Despite all the studies on red wine, most scientists agree, the key health benefits of red wine derive from resveratrol, which is a compound found in grapes, blueberries, raspberries, peanuts, and several other plants. The bulk of resveratrol content is found in the rinds and seeds of grapes, and with red wine using the rinds in the fermentation process, unlike white wine, it explains where most of the red wine health benefits are derived.

Future

Constellation Brands is a rapidly growing firm enjoying approximately a 45 percent increase in stock price in 2014, and nearly 1,000 percent since the 2009 stock market bottomed. The firm currently owns 14 percent of the U.S. wine market, but only 2.7 percent of the wine market worldwide. Constellation reported revenues of $4.8 billion in fiscal 2014, with nearly half of the revenues being derived from beer and the other half from wine and spirits. Spirits are a small part of the overall business, accounting for around 5 percent of total revenues. Constellation's beer segment is focused on the United States, where it has rights to Grupo Modelo's U.S. beer business from Anheuser-Busch InBev. So, while doing great financially, the firm is heavily focused on U.S. markets and has over $9 billion in goodwill and intangibles on the balance sheet, accounting for 65 percent of total assets, largely from the Grupo Modelo business acquisition. CEO Sands is in need of a well-developed strategic plan moving forward. Key areas to consider in how best to allocate resources are expanding further into international markets, growing the spirit business further, and renting versus owning vineyards. Develop a 3-year plan for CEO Sands.

GoPro, Inc., 2015

www.gopro.com, GPRO

Headquartered in San Mateo, California, GoPro produces cameras, accessories, and software for outdoor enthusiasts, such as rock climbers, hikers, scuba divers, surfers, mountain bikers, snow skiers, and others who need waterproof, small, lightweight cameras. The firm also sells its cameras to many who value the convenience of a smaller camera. To service its customers, GoPro develops a wide range of accessories, including camera mounts for helmets, handlebars, roller bars, and tripod mounts. In addition, spare batteries, charging accessories, cables, microphones, flotation devices, dive filters, anti-fogging strips, and many other accessories are available for purchase. GoPro products are sold through retailers, wholesalers, and through its website. The company is aggressively trying to develop its GoPro Channel App on a new line of smart TVS from LG Electronics. GoPro wants its customers to showcase their videos and is therefore soon releasing software to edit and publish content captured by its cameras. GoPro cameras are not yet available in all nations. In fact, GoPro's global market share for stand-alone digital cameras and camcorders is only 7 percent.

GoPro is looking good lately. In August 2015, the IDC (International Data Corporation) reported that GoPro has 30.40 percent of the camcorder market share, followed by Sony (SNE) with 20.80 percent share. GoPro's new HERO4 and HERO + LCD boosted its overall revenue from $363.1 million in 1Q 2015 to $419.9 million in 2Q 2015. However, GoPro is facing competition from ION America, Sony, and Garmin (GRMN). Garmin offers the VIRB X and VIRB XE camcorders, whereas ION offers the Air Pro. During Q2 2015, GoPro expanded further to the EMEA (Europe, the Middle East and Africa) and APAC (Asia-Pacific) countries and now has 40,000 retail outlets. GoPro's revenue rose 126 percent in 2Q 2015 compared to the same quarter the previous year. The company's Q2 2015 revenue generated from APAC tripled to $70.4 million from $24.9 million over the same quarter the previous year. For GoPro, China is in the top 10 revenue generating countries, but the company's Europe's revenue rose to $137.2 million in 2Q 2015 from $67 million in 2Q 2014. In the United States, GoPro's revenue rose 39 percent in 2Q 2015 to $212.3 million.

Copyright by Fred David Books LLC. www.strategyclub.com (Written by Forest R. David)

History

GoPro was founded in 2004 but traces its roots back to 2002, when current CEO Nick Woodman was on a surfing trip in Australia and was unable to capture quality action of himself surfing, due to expensive wide-angle equipment and amateur photographers' inability to get close enough to create quality video or photos. After this vacation, Nick Woodman envisioned a better system—a camera that most could afford and that would take quality, close shots. Woodman came up with the name GoPro, as this was what his vision was, professional quality video and photos for the average person. In 2004, the company was known as Woodman Labs, Inc. By 2012, GoPro had a 21.5 percent market share of digital camcorders in the United States, up 6 percent from 2011. Later in 2012, Foxconn Technology purchased an 8.9 percent stake in GoPro, giving it a total valuation of $2.25 billion; the firm's engineering team had increased fivefold from 20 to 100. By 2013, Woodman had gone from sleeping and living in his van to a billionaire worth $1.3 billion. A key driver of the firm's success was that consumers no longer needed a point-and-shoot camera, as smartphones were more than capable. Many competitors viewed GoPro as a niche camera maker just for sports enthusiasts and to date have missed out on the popularity the camera has had with the masses. GoPro went public in 2013 and a year later appointed Tony Bates, a former Microsoft executive, to be president, reporting to CEO Woodman. GoPro earnings rebounded in the first quarter of 2015, up 52 percent thanks in large part to the general public's increasing interest.

Internal Issues

GoPro currently has only one main product: the Hero 4 line of cameras with accessories to support the device. GoPro cameras with their cases are rugged yet lightweight and small, ideal for transport and extreme environments, such as the ocean or mountains. Even today, the most expensive model is less than $500, so GoPro products are affordable to most. One attribute about GoPro cameras is the free software that is downloadable to smartphones and tablets where consumers can control settings and receive a live feed wirelessly of their video. As of September 2014, since producing high definition (HD) cameras in 2009, GoPro has sold over 10 million cameras in over 100 countries. As of 2013, GoPro had a staggering 45 percent market share in the United States on camcorders, and was the number-one seller in both dollars and units, and the number-six seller in accessories. To help support the camera, GoPro provides free desktop software that enables users to edit their videos in many different ways. Customers shooting in ProTune can adjust color, speed, contrast, and many other aspects. The software also supports the camera's slow motion and time-lapse options. Users can also easily share their experiences on YouTube, Facebook, Instagram, and many other social network platforms.

Organizational Structure

GoPro appears to operate from a functional organizational chart with 15 top executives, as illustrated in Exhibit 1. Some analysts say GoPro should consider using a divisional-by-product or divisional-by-region type structure.

Vision/Mission

It is not clear that GoPro has a vision statement, but the company uses the slogans "Be a Hero" and also "GoPro" quite often, so one of these may be the vision. GoPro wants to enable their customers to be heroes and to look professional. Some company narrative that might be considered a GoPro mission statement is as follows: "Enabling engaging content is at the core of our business. We develop hardware and software solutions to alleviate consumer pain points associated with capturing, managing, sharing and enjoying engaging content."

Strategy

GoPro has established strong marketing relationships with celebrities, athletes, and through sporting events such as the X games, Supercross, and ASP world surfing championships. Top extreme athletes such as Shaun White and Kelly Slater, along with entertainers Alton Brown, the Foo Fighters, and others all endorse and use GoPro products. However, perhaps the best endorsers of all for GoPro products are the users themselves because the company allows customers to submit videos for the GoPro website. Just posting your personal videos on YouTube, often with the GoPro advertisement as the lead into their video, has aided tremendously in marketing. In fact, it is difficult to find a self-made video on YouTube now that does not feature a GoPro product.

In helping to advance the product, GoPro acquired General Things, Inc. in 2013 to help advance its editing and sharing software capabilities. GoPro is focused increasingly on international markets, which offers significant growth, but maintains a key focus on the U.S. market. GoPro recently increased its store space in Best Buy stores in the United States. GoPro products are designed in the United States but are manufactured by Chicony and Sky Light, both located in Shenzhen, China.

GoPro announced in 2015 that it plans on selling helicopter drones equipped with GoPro cameras in late 2015 for prices between $500 and $1,000. It is an interesting development, considering there are many well-established drone producers currently in the market that fit GoPro cameras for consumers. Analysts suggest, though, that the world's largest consumer drone marker, Chinese-based SZ DJI, has started selling drones with its own cameras, possibly cutting GoPro out of one of its largest drone-producing customers.

Exhibit 2 provides data for GoPro sales by geographic region. Note that company sales are growing rapidly and 63 percent of all 2014 sales were derived from the Americas.

EXHIBIT 1 GoPro's Organizational Structure

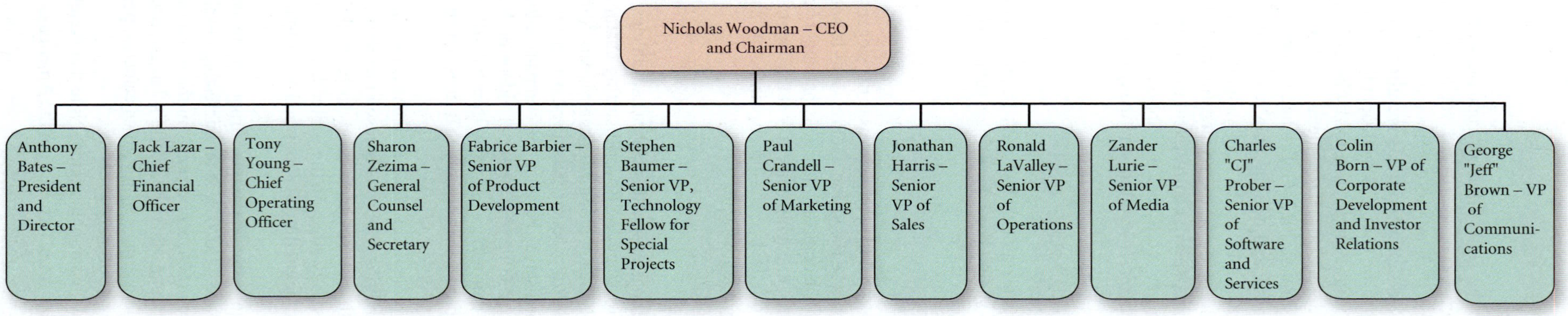

Nicholas Woodman – CEO and Chairman

- Anthony Bates – President and Director
- Jack Lazar – Chief Financial Officer
- Tony Young – Chief Operating Officer
- Sharon Zezima – General Counsel and Secretary
- Fabrice Barbier – Senior VP of Product Development
- Stephen Baumer – Senior VP, Technology Fellow for Special Projects
- Paul Crandell – Senior VP of Marketing
- Jonathan Harris – Senior VP of Sales
- Ronald LaValley – Senior VP of Operations
- Zander Lurie – Senior VP of Media
- Charles "CJ" Prober – Senior VP of Software and Services
- Colin Born – VP of Corporate Development and Investor Relations
- George "Jeff" Brown – VP of Communications

Source: Based on Authors Best Interpretation from Company Documents.

EXHIBIT 2 Segment Data for GoPro (in millions of USD)

	2014	2013
Americas	$890	$557
Europe, Middle East, and Africa	371	322
Asia Pacific	133	106

Source: Based on GoPro's Q4 2014 Earnings Summary.

Products

GoPro makes one principle product, its Hero camcorder, and then a multitude of accessories to complement the camera. As of early 2015, customers could purchase GoPro's Hero, Hero 3, Hero 3+, and Hero 4 cameras. Typically, each design has cases—white, silver, and black—with black costing more and having several extra features. As of early 2015, the Hero retailed for $129, up to the Hero Black at $499. GoPro is unique in that it continues to sell older products, and many customers wait for the newer products to arrive, knowing they can receive a substantial discount on older camcorders. All GoPro cameras have fixed lens configurations, meaning they cannot be zoomed in or out. Cameras have a small LCD screen where users can adjust settings, but many users prefer to use the wireless application on their mobile phone or tablet to adjust camera settings. GoPro also offers a LCD back screen as an accessory, but this feature is not standard except on the Hero 4 Silver camera. Without an LCD back screen, users either shoot blind or use their mobile or tablet to get a visual on what exactly is being filmed in the view finder. Surprisingly, this drawback is often not a problem for many applications, such as surfing, diving, and mountain biking. When the camera is on wide angle, generally everything desired is in the field of view, and without an LCD screen, battery life is much extended.

Hero cameras come with a polycarbonate housing that is waterproof to 131 feet and also a skeleton backdoor that can replace the solid backdoor for filming in less challenging environments to aid better sound quality. The Hero 4 was released in September 2014 for $399 and $499 for the silver and black, respectively. The Hero is also available at a price point of $129, a budget camera of sorts. The new Hero 4 Black provides 12 mega pixels with an f/2.8 fixed maximum aperture. In addition, it has Bluetooth connectivity and has a new processor that is twice as fast as the former Hero3 + Black. In addition, the Hero 4 can record in 4k video with frame rates limited to 24, 25, and 30 frames per second. GoPro claims the battery life is 65 minutes shooting in 4k and up to 2 hours in 720p with the Wi-Fi disabled in both instances. The Hero 4 Silver is practically the Hero 3+ Black repackaged, and this has been the trend with many GoPro products over their development of new releases.

GoPro offers many accessories, including battery packs, remotes, and LCD screens. These products retail from $49.99 to $79.99 in the United States. In addition, the firm provides a wide array of mounting devices for bikes, surfboards, and head mounts. Prices range from $7.99 to $79.99, depending on the mount. Many customers who purchase a GoPro camera are often forced to buy a mount designed for the special application they desire to use. The company also sells extra cases, chargers, filters for scuba diving, and much more. All GoPro cameras come with free access to GoPro studio, a software-editing platform, and free apps for smartphones and tablets.

Finance

GoPro's largest single customer, Best Buy, accounts for about 19 percent of total revenue. The company's top 10 customers account for about 50 percent of total revenue. GoPro reported net income of over $128 million in 2014, as indicated in Exhibit 3, up from $32 million in 2012. GoPro's recent balance sheet are provided in Exhibit 4.

Competitors

The camera and video markets are highly competitive with major players including Sony, Canon, Apple, Samsung, GoPro, and others. Many competitors such as Sony and Canon were caught somewhat by surprise by quality point-and-shoot cameras built into smartphones by new rivals Apple, Samsung, and others. Digital camera sales fell globally about 50 percent from 2011 to

EXHIBIT 3 GoPro's Income Statement (in millions of USD)

Report Date	December 31, 2014	December 31, 2013
Revenues	$1,394	$986
Cost of revenue	767	624
Gross profit	627	362
Operating expenses	440	263
Operating Income	187	99
Other expense	6	7
EBT	181	92
Tax	53	31
Net income	**128**	**61**

Source: Based on GoPro's 2014 *Annual Report,* p. 51.

EXHIBIT 4 GoPro's Balance Sheet (in millions of USD)

Report Date	December 31, 2014	December 31, 2013
Assets		
Cash and equivalents	$422	$101
Accounts receivable	184	123
Inventories	153	112
Other current assets	64	22
Total current assets	823	358
Property, plant & equipment	42	32
Goodwill & intangibles	17	17
Other assets	36	33
Total assets	**918**	**440**
Liabilities		
Short-term debt	0	60
Accounts payable	126	127
Other current liabilities	133	114
Total current liabilities	259	301
Long-term debt	0	53
Other liabilities	18	14
Total liabilities	**277**	**368**
Common stock	533	15
Retained earnings	108	(20)
Convertible stock		77
Paid in capital and other		
Total equity	**641**	**72**
Total liabilities & equity	**918**	**440**

Source: Based on GoPro's 2014 *Annual Report,* p. 50.

2013. GoPro was largely viewed as a niche player for outdoor enthusiasts only, but sales show many consumers value GoPro's products over traditional video cameras by Sony, Canon, and others. However, for more professional quality video and more control from the user, products from Canon, Sony, Nikon, Olympus, and others still are likely better options than GoPro.

Major players in the camera industry have extensive networks and diversified product lines along with robust supply and distribution systems worldwide creating substantial threats to GoPro.

EXHIBIT 5 GoPro versus Rival Firms

	GoPro	Canon	Apple
# Employees	970	190,000	92,000
$ Net Income	128 M	2,200 M	39,500 M
$ Revenue	1.4 B	35.5 B	182.8 B
$ Revenue/Employee	1.44 M	186,842	$2 M
$ EPS Ratio	0.92	1.91	7.39
Market Cap.	5.7 B	36.0 B	692.7 B

Source: Based on company documents.

Smartphones are also increasingly becoming the choice for casual video users. Apple's iPhone, for example, now has image stability and even allows for slow motion video production. However, phones to date are not constructed as rugged or durable as GoPro's products, but for many, the extra protection is not warranted and the convenience of having all in one piece phone, camera, and video is a substantial threat moving forward for GoPro. Camcorder sales fell 33 percent from 2011 to 2013. In addition, the ability of smartphones in the future to be constructed in a manner that is a substitute for challenging environments would likely further erode GoPro's profits. To date, however, GoPro is the top option for a durable small frame camcorder with little direct competition. See Exhibit 5.

Sony

Headquartered within a few miles of Nikon and Canon in Tokyo, Japan, Sony manufactures LCD televisions; cameras; audio and video equipment; personal computers (PCs); personal navigation systems; game consoles and software; audio, video, and monitors for broadcast and commercial use; image sensors and other semi-conductors; optical pickups; batteries; data recording media and systems; movie software; and animation works. Sony also has a Finance segment that provides life and nonlife insurance, banking services, and credit finance services, and a new Sony Mobile segment provides mobile phones. In 2013, Sony reported revenues of $75 billion with net income totaling to a $1.2 billion net loss. The firm was founded in 1946.

Canon

Headquartered within a few miles of Nikon in Tokyo, Japan, Canon makes cameras, LCD projectors, lenses, LCDs, and binoculars— competing against Nikon on all these products. But Canon has diversified and also manufactures printers, multifunction document equipment, and other computer peripherals for home and office use. Canon generates only 20 percent of its revenues in Japan. It manufactures digital single-lens reflex cameras; compact digital cameras; interchangeable lenses; digital video cameras; ink-jet multifunction devices; single-function ink-jet printers; image scanners; television lenses for broadcasting use; office network, color network, and personal multifunction devices; office, color, and personal copy machines; laser printers; large-sized ink-jet printers and digital production printers; exposure equipment used in semi-conductor and liquid crystal displays (LCDs); medical image recording equipment; ophthalmic instruments; magnetic heads; micro motors; computers; handy terminals; and document scanners.

In early 2013, Canon released three stylish, feature-packed PowerShot Digital Cameras: the PowerShot ELPH 330 HS, ELPH 115 IS, and A2500. These new models offer great photo quality and excellent video performance in compact, powerful point-and-shoot designs while providing advanced wireless connectivity for easy sharing and great performance in dimly lit situations. It is interesting that Canon is still aggressively producing point-and-shoot cameras despite falling industry sales. Exhibit 6 reveals that Canon reported approximately $32 billion in revenue in each of the last two years with $12 billion from Imaging Systems. The company's Imaging Systems division includes camcorders, EOS line of cameras, smaller point-and-shoot cameras, projectors, camera lens, and printers.

To compete with GoPro, Canon's top product is the Canon VIXIA mini. This camcorder allows for hands-free place-and-shoot and self-shooting from many different positions. The product is

EXHIBIT 6 Canon's Revenue by Segment (in billions of USD)

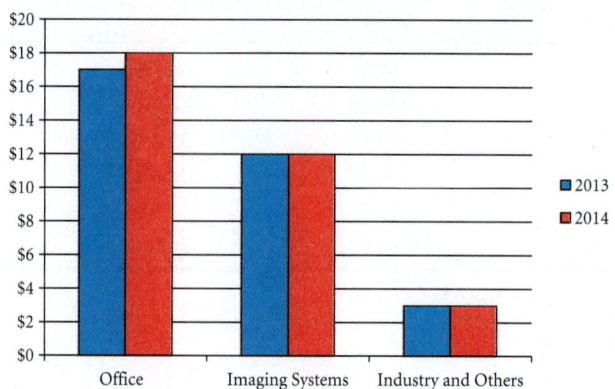

Source: Based on company reports.

excellent to set up on a chair, table, or window and film dance routines, recitals, or sports. The cameras are also equipped with ultra-wide-angle lens, allowing for full coverage in even tight spaces. Wi-Fi capabilities also allow seamless syncing with mobile devices.

Samsung

Headquartered in South Korea, Samsung has five R&D centers located in China. In 2013, Samsung smartphones were 21 percent of the total smartphone market for sales volume, making Samsung the industry leader. Today, Samsung produces a wide range of consumer electronics in addition to smartphones with built-in cameras. Top Samsung products include tablets, televisions, Blu-rays, DVD players, cameras, refrigerators, air conditioners, washing machines, ovens, PC notebooks, printers, storage devices, and more. All Samsung phones are capable of extensive video and photo capabilities, often more than capable enough for most photo and video needs for consumers. Samsung reported revenues of over $212 billion in 2013.

Apple

The world's largest corporation based on market capitalization with a net worth of over $633 billion and over $200 billon more than Exxon, the world's second-largest company, Apple designs, manufacturers, and markets the world's single-most popular smartphone—the iPhone—even though Apple only has around a 15 percent market share in the smartphone market. In addition, Apple produces the iPad, iPod, iCloud, Mac computers, and other accessory devices. Apple also owns iTunes, the popular app and store where customers can download music. New for Apple with the release of the iPhone 6 and 6 Plus is Apple Pay, where customers can pay at merchants by scanning their phone. Apple currently operates 450 Apple stores and employs 98,000 people. Apple is headquartered in Cupertino, California.

Apple's release of the iPhone 6 and 6+ broke tradition with the firm by finally producing larger screen smartphones to better compete with rivals such as Samsung. Initial sales for the iPhone 6 and 6+ broke records, with the higher margin 6+ doing best of all. Apple phones also include advanced photo capabilities; currently people take more photos with the iPhone every day than any other camera available. Key features include the ability to shoot video at 1080p at 60fps and 240 fps slow motion, including time lapse video. In January 2015, Apple was awarded a patent for a wearable camera system that the company claims improves on the susceptibility to vibration on many GoPro cameras.

Outdoor Recreation

The scuba industry in the United States is a $420 million industry with a growth rate of near 3 percent. Training accounts for nearly 55 percent of all revenue, 14 percent equipment rentals, and the remaining 31 percent spent on travel. Disposable income increased 1.2 percent annually from 2010 through 2014, and an overall increase in consumer sentiment helped industry growth.

Scuba divers in the United States becoming certified as Open Water divers in 2009 totaled 141,000; this increased to 146,000 by 2013. A declining unemployment rate and increased consumer spending are such that the scuba industry is expected to see growth rates of 2.7 percent. The average age of a certified diver is 29 years old, and over 75 percent of divers are younger than age 45, and generally are adapt with technology and more likely to possibly purchase additional equipment such as GoPro cameras to film their adventures. It is difficult to go on a dive boat today without at least one third of the divers on the boat owning a GoPro camera.

As Americans have become more health-conscious, they are also spending more time enjoying outdoor sports and activities. It is estimated that nearly 20 percent of the population in the United States will engage in outdoor sports by 2020. Visitors to national and state parks and other top outdoor recreation areas are also projected to rise through 2020. As of 2014, the hiking and equipment stores to help serve this demand were valued at a $4 billion business in the United States.

The ski and snowboard resorts totaled $3 billion in sales in 2014. The industry is largely dependent on disposable income, snowfall, and people's willingness to spend vacation time during the winter as opposed to the summer months. Despite the challenges, ski resort operators are expecting an increase in revenues of over 2 percent through the next several years. Part of the rise in popularity is from price cuts making lessons more affordable to new skiers. Ski equipment has also become cheaper as quality imports have become increasingly available. Unlike scuba, where the sport is dominated by younger individuals, skiing is a sport dominated by the children of baby boomers, who also have higher disposable incomes. GoPro cameras are popular among snow skiers.

Future

GoPro made significant strides in 2014, establishing its European sales and marketing headquarters in Munich, Germany, starting a product assembly plant in Brazil for South American products, and forming partnerships with two large online retailers in China. The firm also shipped 5.2 million cameras in 2014 with 2.4 million being shipped in the fourth quarter alone, which totaled to more than the entire year of shipments in 2013. The company currently does not have a formal competitor competing with a similar product, but rival camera makers such as Sony and Canon should be expected to introduce similar products in the future. In addition, Apple and other smartphone manufacturers are offering excellent quality in still and video cameras on their phones, which are acceptable for many users of GoPro products. GoPro's earnings in fourth quarter 2014 were less than analysts expected. COO Nina Richardson abruptly resigned in early 2015 but was replaced with Informatica Corp. executive Tony Young. Young will be serving as Chief Information Officer. There were no plans at the time to replace the COO position. The firm's stock has fallen over 50 percent lately. GoPro is in the early stages of producing drones to carry their cameras. Prepare a 3-year strategic plan for CEO Woodman as GoPro moves forward.

Arctic Cat Inc., 2015

www.arcticcat.com, ACAT

Based in Thief River Falls, Minnesota, with its principle office in Plymouth, Minnesota, Arctic Cat designs, engineers, and produces snowmobiles, side-by-sides, and all-terrain vehicles (ATVs) under the Arctic Cat brand name. With 1,670 employees, Arctic Cat also makes garments and accessories for its products, including wheels, shocks, snow blowers, and luggage racks, among many others. Artic Cat's major rival, Polaris Industries, had two founders, and when they disagreed, one of the founders left Polaris and founded Arctic Cat. The two companies even today make similar products, are structured similarly, and are located in the same region of the United States. Arctic Cat does business in the United States, Canada, and Europe through independent dealers, whereas customers in South America, the Middle East, and Asia can purchase products through third-party distributers.

In the fiscal year ending March 2014, Arctic Cat reported revenues of $730 million and profits of $39 million. Sales were up from $580 million in fiscal 2012. However, Arctic Cat's sales dropped to $699 million in fiscal 2015, with profits falling to $5 million. Rival Polaris is much larger and has performed significantly better than Arctic Cat for the three years leading into 2016.

In March 2015, Arctic Cat completed its acquisition of privately held MotorFist, LLC, a manufacturer of high-performance technical riding gear. The acquisition complements Arctic Cat's garment and riding-gear business. Sales of MotorFist-branded products will add to the company's PG&A (Parts, Garments, and Accessories) sales in fiscal 2016.

For Arctic Cat's first quarter of 2016 that ended June 30, 2015, the company reported a net loss of $1.1 million on net sales of $134.4 million. In the prior year period, the company had reported net earnings of $3.6 million on net sales of $143.6 million. Thus, it has been a bad 12 months for the company. For fiscal Q1 of 2016, the company's snowmobile sales totaled $58.2 million, up 3.7 percent versus $56.2 million in the prior-year quarter. However, the company's ATV/ROV sales in the fiscal 2016 first quarter totaled $52.9 million, down 17.2 percent compared to prior-year sales of $63.8 million, although sales of Wildcat ROVs remained strong. The company's PG&A sales in its fiscal 2016 first quarter decreased 1.6 percent to $23.3 million versus $23.7 million in the prior-year quarter.

Copyright by Fred David Books LLC. www.strategyclub.com (Written by Forest R. David)

History

The father of the snowmobile is considered to be Edgar Hetteen, who, in 1955, with employees David Johnson, Paul Knochenmus, and Orlen Johnson, created a vehicle to ride through the snow. The primary use of the craft was to access better hunting areas that traditionally had required wearing snowshoes. The first Polaris snowmobile, which was called the Polaris Sno Traveler, rolled off the assembly line in Minnesota in 1956. Edgar displayed his snowmobile on a 1,200-mile trek across Alaska in 1960. However, unhappy with the performance of his Polaris vehicle, Edgar left the company in 1960 and started Polar Manufacturing, which was later changed to Arctic Enterprises, and ultimately went bankrupt in the 1980s. Arctic emerged from bankruptcy and continues today under the name Arctic Cat, producing ATVs, side-by-sides, snowmobiles, and other accessories. The firm also experimented with snow blowers, generators, mini-bikes, and two-wheel vehicles. Artic Cat released its first ATV in 1995 and in 2007 introduced the industry's first diesel ATV.

Vision/Mission

Arctic Cat has no vision statement, but does have a "passion" statement that could count as the firm's mission statement. The passion statement is as follows:

Passion. It's in everything we do. Within every turn of a screw. Every hole drilled. Every knuckle bloodied. It's what makes us Arctic Cat. From the assembly line workers to

EXHIBIT 1 Arctic Cat's Organizational Chart

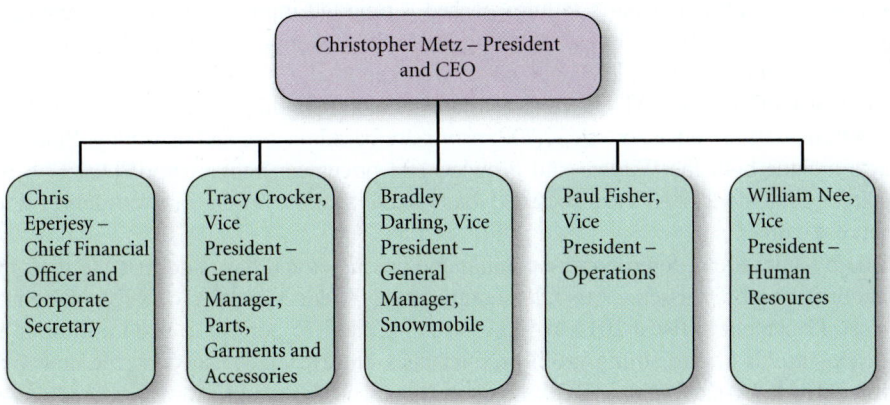

Source: Based on information at the company's website.

the R&D engineers, we all share a common bond tougher than steel. Forged of sweat and raw determination. It's a commitment to making the best ATVs, Side by Sides, and Snowmobiles around. Arctic Cat Passion. Three big words no one else can dare claim. It's what separates us from all the rest. (cited from www.arcticcat.com)

Organizational Structure

In June 2014, Claude Jordan stepped down as Chairman and CEO of Arctic Cat and was replaced on an interim basis by Chris Twomey, who had served previously as CEO of Arctic Cat for 24 years. In November 2014, Christopher Metz was hired as the company's new CEO, while Twomey remains as Chairman. Arctic Cat appears to operate using a functional organizational design, because there is no chief operating officer and no divisional presidents, as illustrated in Exhibit 1. Note also there are no women among the company's top executives.

Segments

For reporting purposes, Arctic Cat separates its ATVs and side-by-sides into one segment, and its Snowmobiles, and Parts and Garments, into separate segments. Sales in 2014 grew across all three segments but sales dropped in fiscal 2015 in both Parts and Garments and ATVs.

Snowmobiles

Arctic Cat produces 60 brands of snowmobiles tailored to serve most all market segments. Retail prices in 2014 ranged from $7,300 to $15,700, with one youth model priced at $2,700. While Arctic Cat products are sold worldwide, the firm's snowmobiles are primarily sold in the United States, Canada, Scandinavia, and Russia. Products are produced for several functions and generally labeled performance, cross-over, mountain, touring, and utility. Arctic Cat snowmobiles can cost more than some cars and include turbo-charged, four-stroke engines, heated seats, and 150-mile fuel ranges.

Snowmobile innovation is continually improving as many customers are sports enthusiasts and demand higher-quality products. Arctic Cat has partnered with Yamaha and other firms to help supply top-of-the-line engines and parts. Awards from SnowTrax Television and Supertrax Magazine in recent years reveal the appeal, awareness, and quality of Arctic Cat snowmobiles. Brands winning awards include the 6000 El Tigre, ZR 70000 SP, Bearcat GS, and many others.

Arctic Cat is also active in the racing industry and sponsors Tucker Hibbert, the most winning snowmobile rider of all time, winning seven consecutive sno-cross gold medals at the Winter X Games. Arctic Cat competes in many other competitions as well with both men and women participants. Jolene Bute has won multiple female events. Snowmobile sales have increased each of the last four years and represent 43 percent of the company's total sales.

ATVs and Side-by-Sides

Arctic Cat is committed to safety in all the products. However, in 2014, the firm was forced to recall 40,000 ATVs after parts failures caused 4 reported injuries. In total, 44 reports were received of front gear case failings, including 10 vehicles stopping instantly. No one was seriously injured, but broken ribs, knee, and backs were reported.

Arctic Cat offers many ATV options for customers ranging in price from $4,300 to $14,500 with youth models priced as low as $2,700; prices are based on size and durability. Side-by-side products include both the Wildcat and Prowler, and prices can range from $11,000 to nearly $25,000 for 2015 models. ATVs, also called *four wheelers*, allow for one or two riders to ride one in front of the other.

Side-by-sides are becoming more popular and are larger and have bucket-style seats allowing one driver with a passenger to ride shotgun style. Arctic Cat sales of ATVs and side-by-sides rose 11 percent in fiscal 2014 to $333 million but fell 15 percent to $284 million in fiscal 2015. Sales in 2014 were strong in all product lines but especially aided by the new Wildcat Trail model side-by-side vehicle. ATVs only experienced 4 percent growth, but side-by-sides did much better, enjoying 19 percent growth in 2014. In total, four new Wildcat models were introduced in fiscal 2014, including the high-horsepower Wildcat X. One feature that makes the Wildcat Trail so popular is its narrower 50-inch wide platform. With growing regulations and bans on ATVs and side-by-sides in many parks and trails, the smaller profile allows riders access to more authorized ATV trails that have restrictions on size of the ATVs allowed. The new Wildcat Trail includes the industry-leading horsepower and suspension in its class and the lowest price 50-plus horsepower segment.

The Prowler line includes engines ranging in size from 550cc to 1,000cc. Other Prowler products include extended chassis, larger cargo box, bench seating, and electronic power steering. Arctic Cat has won numerous awards for producing best-in-class products. In total, Arctic Cat now offers 28 ATVs and 17 side-by-side models.

Parts, Garments, and Accessories

Arctic Cat generated $114 million from its Parts, Garments, and Accessory's segment in 2015 for a total of 16 percent of revenues. Replacement parts and maintenance supplies include fuel additives, bumpers, cabs, luggage racks, snowplows, windshields, wheels, and other add-on features. The company is even providing airbags now for select products. In addition to parts and accessories, the company also capitalizes on its brand by offering jackets, coats, plants, and other sportswear sold in many different styles and sizes. Another clothing brand the company has is its Drift Racing line of products that is worn by snowmobile racers and recreational users alike.

Exhibit 3 reveals the percent breakdown of Arctic Cat's 2015 revenues.

Internal Issues

Production/Operations and Research and Development (R&D)

Arctic Cat manufactures most of its products in St. Cloud, MN, but its smaller ATVs in the 90cc to 450cc range are manufactured in Taiwan. The firm is vertically integrated with its parts, and also has developed relationships with suppliers for select parts often in cooperation with Arctic Cat. Many of the vertically integrated operations include manufacturing of seats, and welding and painting components. The firm also manufactures many ATV engines to control quality and limit exposure to the Japanese yen. However, in 2013, Arctic Cat agreed with Yamaha to purchase

EXHIBIT 2 Segment Data for Arctic Cat (in millions of USD)

	2015 Revenue	2014 Revenue
Snowmobiles	$301	$282
ATV & Side-by-Sides	284	333
Parts, Garments, Accessories	114	115
Total Revenue	$699	$730

Source: Based on Arctic Cat's 2015 *Annual Report*, p. 16.

EXHIBIT 3 Arctic Cat's Percent Segment Data by Product

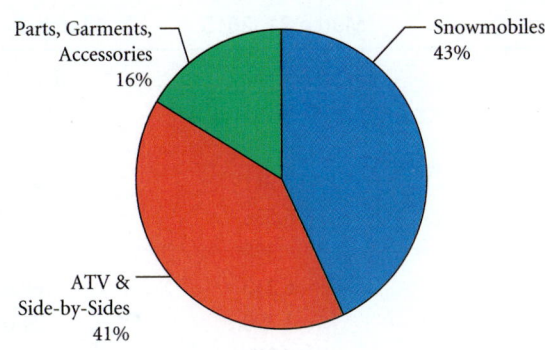

Based on information in the 2015 *Annual Report*, p. 16.

select engines for its snowmobiles while other snowmobile engines are made in St. Cloud. The actual snowmobiles themselves are made in Thief River Falls, MN. Snowmobile production starts in late spring and continues through late fall, while ATVs and side-by-sides are built throughout the year. In both 2014 and 2015, Arctic Cat reported cost of revenue of $579 million.

Snowmobiles and ATVs historically were for utility purposes only, but many people now enjoy them for recreation and expect better-quality engines and frills such as heated seats, better suspensions, and more trendy design. Arctic Cat currently employs 160 people in design of new products and 23 solely involved in the testing of snowmobiles, ATVs, and ORVs (off-road vehicles) in all environmental conditions. In fiscal 2014 and 2015, Arctic Cat spent nearly $24 million on R&D activities, compared to top rival Polaris that spent $139 million in 2014, or 5.7 times the amount spent by Arctic Cat. Polaris has 5 times the 2014 revenues of Arctic Cat.

Marketing

Arctic Cat products are sold through networks of independent dealers across the United States, Canada, and Europe. In other international markets, products are sold through other distributors and in the United States, Canada, and Europe, Arctic Cat has a team of sales managers to help generate new dealerships. Dealerships typically enter into a 3-year agreement and are required to order a sufficient number of products to service their markets. Many Arctic Cat dealers also sell lawn and garden, marine, motorcycles, and other products from a variety of companies. One of Arctic Cat's top distributers is Bass Pro Shops. Top rival Cabalas sells Coleman ATVs.

Finance

Arctic Cat reported net sales in 2014 of $730 million up from $672 and $585 in 2013 and 2012, respectively. Despite the 8.6 percent increase in sales, net income dropped from $39.7 million in 2013 to $39.4 million in 2014 (see Exhibit 4). However, sales did grow across all three product lines. The company has zero long-term debt and also zero goodwill on its balance sheet (see Exhibit 5). The firm reported in August 2014 that it was authorizing a $25 million share repurchase program. With 13 million shares outstanding, at the time of the announcement, it would require Arctic Cat to repurchase approximately 700,000 shares, or 5 percent of total shares outstanding. The firm also increased its dividend in May 2014 by 25 percent to $0.125 per share. However, fiscal 2015 was a poor year for Arctic Cat with revenues falling over 5 percent and net income dropping 87 percent.

Competitors

The ATV, side-by-side, and snowmobile markets are fiercely competitive with companies offering a wide range of products. Yamaha, for example, produces ATVs, side-by-sides, outboard marine engines, motorcycles, and many other products. Honda Motor Company produces everything Yamaha does in addition to vehicles. John Deere produces side-by-side products and lawn mowers all the way to heavy machinery for farming. Polaris and Arctic Cat dominate the snowmobile industry, but Bombardier Recreational Products (BRP) and Yamaha also make snowmobiles. Polaris also produces motorcycles.

EXHIBIT 4 **Income Statement (in thousands of USD)**

Report Date	March 31, 2015	March 31, 2014
Revenues	$698,756	$730,491
Cost of revenue	579,307	579,412
Gross profit	119,449	151,079
Operating expenses	112,911	90,583
EBIT	6,538	60,496
Interest	328	92
EBT	6,210	60,404
Tax	1,290	21,000
Net income	**4,920**	**39,404**

Source: Based on Arctic Cat's 2015 *Annual Report,* p. 30.

EXHIBIT 5 **Balance Sheet (in thousands of USD)**

Report Date	March $31, 2015	March 31, 2014
Cash	$40,253	$22,524
Short-term investments	1,009	60,008
Net accounts receivable (less uncollectable accounts)	28,695	42,003
Inventories	152,443	140,652
Other current assets	24,999	20,109
Total current assets	247,399	285,296
Property, plant, & equipment	62,868	55,931
Goodwill & intangibles	6,579	1,067
Total assets	**316,846**	**342,294**
Current debt	—	—
Accounts payable	124,633	148,541
Total current liabilities	124,633	148,541
Long-term debt	—	—
Deferred income taxes	11,151	8,710
Other liabilities	690	—
Total liabilities	**136,474**	**157,251**
Common stock	130	129
Retained earnings	185,444	187,024
Treasury stock	—	—
Paid in capital and other	(5,202)	(2,110)
Total equity	**180,372**	**185,043**
Total liabilities & equity	**316,846**	**342,294**

Source: Based on Arctic Cat's 2015 *Annual Report,* p. 29.

Exhibit 6 provides a comparison of Arctic Cat with Polaris and Deere. Note that Arctic Cat is significantly smaller than its main rival Polaris and even Deere & Company reported revenues of $800 million from ATV and Snowmobile sales. Arctic Cat's EPS ratio also decreased from nearly $2.00 to $0.02 from fiscal 2014 to fiscal 2015.

Polaris Industries, Inc. (PII)

Headquartered in Medina, Minnesota, Polaris (named after the North Star) designs, engineers, manufactures, and markets off-road vehicles (ORVs), snowmobiles, motorcycles, and electric on-road vehicles primarily in the United States, Canada, and Europe (and a few other nations),

EXHIBIT 6 Arctic Cat versus Rival Firms

	Arctic Cat	Polaris	Deere & Company
# Employees	1,670	7,000	59,600
$ Net Income	4.9 M	454 M	2.58 B
$ Revenue	699 M	4,479 M	32,900 M
$ Revenue/Employee	419,000	640,000	625,000
$ EPS Ratio	0.02	6.83	7.33
Market Cap.	383 M	9,880 M	32,100 M

Source: Based on company documents.

with revenues generated from these regions of 75, 10, and 15 percent, respectively in 2014. It was a record year for Polaris based on sales and the fifth consecutive year of annual revenue increases of 15 percent or greater. Net income grew over 20 percent annually over the same time frame.

Polaris does business in over 130 different nations and outside-U.S. sales were up 18 percent in 2013 and another 23 percent in 2014. Products are sold through 1,750 independent dealers in North America and through 22 subsidiaries and 85 distributors in over 100 countries worldwide. Approximately 750 dealers in the United States are located in areas where snowmobiles are not sold and Polaris prides itself on selling ORVs in lawn and garden dealers as well as in motorcycle dealerships throughout the United States. Many top rivals do not sell products through lawn and garden dealers. Completion of a 425,000-square-foot manufacturing facility in Monterrey, Mexico, in 2011 serves as a platform for better Polaris penetration in Latin and South America. Polaris also produces replacement parts and other accessories such as oils, chrome accessories, electric starters, covers, cargo box accessories, and much more. Polaris opened a new manufacturing facility in Poland in the spring of 2015 that employs 300.

Polaris receives about 65 percent of its revenues from ORVs, as revealed in Exhibit 7. Off-road vehicles have been a consistent revenue generator for the firm. Even though Polaris generates only 8 percent of total revenues from snowmobiles, this amounts to $20 million more in sales of snowmobiles than rival Arctic Cat. Motorcycle brands include both Victory and Indian. Notable ATV brands include the Ranger and the Ace. Polaris also makes products for military and governments. In total, Polaris has five times the revenues of Arctic Cat and has approximately a 23 percent market share in the industry, based on North American sales, nearly four times the market share of Arctic Cat.

Deere & Company (DE)

Deere manufactures a wide range of agriculture, construction, and forestry equipment and sells its products worldwide. Notable products in agriculture include tractors of all sizes; combines; corn, cotton, and sugar cane harvesters; and irrigation equipment. Deere also lumps in lawn mowers, golf course equipment, and ARVs into this segment. The Construction and Forestry

EXHIBIT 7 Polaris' Segment Data in Percent Revenue

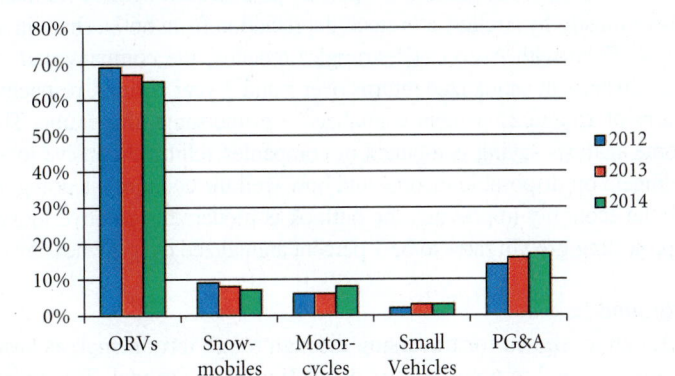

Source: Based on information in the 2014 Polaris *Annual Report*, p. 3.

EXHIBIT 8 Deere & Company's Segment Data (in millions of USD)

Segment	2014 Revenues	2013 Revenues
Agriculture and Turf	$26,380	$29,132
Construction and Forestry	6,581	5,866
Financial Services	2,577	2,347
Other	529	448
Total	**36,067**	**37,795**

Source: Based on information at http://www.deere.com/en_US/docs/Corporate/investor_relations/pdf/financialdata/reports/2014/2014_fourthquarter.pdf (page 10).

segment produces heavy earth-moving equipment, timber harvesting products, excavators, dump trucks, and much more. Deere also has a well-organized Financial Services segment to provide easy financing and insurance options to customers.

While Deere does not provide breakdowns on product sales, the products most closely related to Arctic Cat's can be found in the Agriculture and Turf segment. It is estimated that Deere had approximately $850 million in revenues from ATV and snowmobiles in 2014. Revenues in this segment, as revealed by Exhibit 8 below, fell nearly 10 percent in fiscal year end October 2014 and the company anticipates farming machinery to fall 20 percent in 2015, due partly to lower crop prices. Deere remains the world's leader in sales of tractors and harvesting combines and heavily dominates the U.S. and Canadian markets, especially in large farming equipment. The firm's construction and forestry segment experienced revenue gains of 12 percent in fiscal 2014 and the outlook remains positive moving forward.

Honda Motor Company, Ltd. (HMC)

Founded in 1946 and headquartered in Tokyo, Japan, Honda develops and sells motorcycles, ATVs, automobiles, snow blowers, lawn mowers, weed eaters, generators, and many other power products. Honda is the world's largest motorcycle company and one of the world's largest automakers. It has recently initiated a new strategy with its motorcycles to target the "fun segment." Honda's research reveals there is a growing demand for motorcycles in the smaller 125cc and 700cc sizes used for leisure, enjoyment, and everyday use. These products cost less and are cheaper to operate, having excellent fuel economy. The 125cc size is targeted primarily at Asian and Indian customers.

In fiscal 2014, Honda reported that 14 percent of all their revenue was derived from motorcycles and ATVs, with total revenues of around $14 billion. Approximately $78 billion were derived from automobiles and $2.5 billion from power products, which include outboard motors, generators, lawn mowers, and other products. Honda also generated $6 billion in financing. In total, Honda reported net income of 11,842 billion yen or approximately $100 billion.

External Issues

The recreational vehicle industry has been one of the most consistent performers in terms of stock price over the last 5 years, led by Polaris. However, in 2014, the industry lagged the SP-500 with an annual return of 5 percent compared to 17 percent as of December 2014. Financial performance was dragged down mostly by Arctic Cat's stock depreciation from $60 a share in late 2013 to $30 a share in late 2014. Even with Artic Cat's struggles recently, the company and industry has done well, with 24 and 29 percent annualized returns over 5 and 3-year periods, respectively, compared to the SP-500 returns of 15 and 21 percent annualized over the same time frame. That's pretty amazing for what some analysts saying is a bunch of companies selling expensive toys. The industry is very much contingent on disposable income and how well the economy is doing, as well as ease of financing. With the economy improving, the outlook is moderately positive moving forward, with some analysts projecting growth rates to be 1 percent annualized over the next 5 years.

Industry Background

Off-road vehicles are designed for traversing through rough terrain such as swamps and marshlands and can often carry 2 to 6 passengers depending on the model. Their main purpose is for hunting and fishing, but they are also used on farms, ranches, and the military, as well as for mud-riding or other rough-riding activities. Off-road vehicles were introduced into the United States in 1970 by Honda, followed later by Yamaha, Kawasaki, and Suzuki. Polaris entered the ATV market in 1985, followed by Arctic Cat in 1995 and Bombardier in 1998. Both the United States and Western Europe, also a primary market for ATVs, have experienced a sales decline in ATVs as customers prefer side-by-side ORVs. Currently, the main competitors of Arctic Cat in the side-by-side market are Deere, Kawasaki, Yamaha, and Polaris. Industrywide side-by-side sales were 238,000 in 2013, up 11 percent from 2012. The U.S. ATV and side-by-side market is a $5 billion market based on revenues.

The novelty of snowmobiles peaked in the 1960s with over 100 producers and 495,000 units produced in 1971. Today, the only makers of snowmobiles are Yamaha, BRP, Arctic Cat, and Polaris. U.S. industrywide sales are around $1.2 billion, with 102,000 industry wide units produced in 2014.

Safety Regulations

Arctic Cat products can be dangerous, especially because they are often used by youth. Both the federal and state governments continually promulgate laws to increase product safety and awareness with regard to ORVs, ATVs, and snowmobiles. International governments have taken similar measures. Two key commissions in the United States are the Consumer Product Safety Commission (CPSC), which has oversight on ATVs, snowmobile, and side-by-side vehicles, and the National Highway Transportation Safety Administration (NHTSA), which has oversight on motorcycles and other small electric vehicles that Arctic Cat produces. Governmental oversight puts increased pressure on Arctic Cat to closely monitor their dealers and ensure all dealers are in compliance with safety regulations. Many states require that snowmobiles and ORVs be regulated and that operators have licenses on them much like a boat or car.

Environmental Concerns

Recent governmental oversight has restricted the amount of lead paint that can be used on products aimed at youth 12 years of age and younger. In addition, to better protect the environment, the federal government and many state governments have restricted the use or banned all together the use of ATVs, ORVs, and snowmobiles from some national parks, federal lands, and state lands.

The Environmental Protection Agency (EPA) continues to adopt and revise more stringent emission regulations for ATVs and ORVs. Europe is also establishing new laws on emissions that could take effect as early as 2016. The laws require firms in the industry to increase their R&D expenditures to improve on emission technologies to meet not only current regulations but future regulations as well.

Future

In November 2014, Arctic Cat formally introduced Chris Metz as its new CEO, only a month after the company recalled all its ATVs manufactured in 2008 and a portion of ATVs produced in 2009 over front gear box concerns. Arctic Cat had a rough year in 2014 with its stock price falling nearly 50 percent, while rival Polaris enjoyed stock price appreciation of approximately 25 percent. In early 2015, Arctic Cat slashed its 2015 sales projections from $745 million to as low as $705 million. Net sales of $705 million in 2015 would be a decrease of 3.5 percent from fiscal year end 2014 sales of $730 million.

CEO Metz predicts a challenging 2015/2016 based on high inventories and a poor exchange rate with the Canadian dollar. Arctic Cat currently derives 33 percent of its annual sales from Canada. Arctic Cat's best-selling product in Q4 of 2014 was the Wildcat off-road vehicle, increasing over 7 percent. However, Polaris's similar product enjoyed a 19 percent increase over Q4 of 2014. Snowmobile shipments fell slightly for the firm in Q4, whereas snowmobile sales increased 2 percent for rival Polaris. It appears Arctic Cat has slipped further behind rival Polaris in 2014 and the trend continued throughout 2015. Specifically, in August 2015, Arctic Cat said it expects full-year earnings to be 80 to 95 cents per share, with revenue in the range of $690 million to $705 million. Due to declining sales and profits, the company's stock has declined 11 percent since the beginning of 2015, and has dropped 17 percent in the last 12 months.

Arctic Cat needs a clear strategic plan to reverse its demise and to catch up with Polaris. Design a 3-year strategic plan for new CEO Metz. Use the template at the www.strategyclub.com website to prepare matrices and analyses.

Tesla Motors, Inc., 2015

www.teslamotors.com, TSLA

Headquartered in Palo Alto, California, Tesla Motors designs, develops, manufactures, and sells fully electric vehicles and advanced powertrain components. Well known for its one-of-a-kind Roadster sports car vehicle, Tesla operates 80 dealerships and galleries in North America, Europe, and Asia, and sells vehicles directly from the corporate website.

During Q4 of 2014, Tesla introduced an all-wheel drive Model S, produced a record 11,627 vehicles, delivered 9,834 vehicles, and announced that its new Model X would ship in 6 months. However, the company's Q4 performance fell far short of expectations because Tesla's net income for Q4 decreased 561.8 percent, compared to the same quarter a year earlier, falling from –$16.26 million to –$107.63 million. Tesla's net operating cash flow decreased to –$86.40 million or 166.58 percent, compared to the same quarter the prior year. Furthermore, the company reported a steep decline in earnings per share to $2.36, versus –$0.71 the prior year. Tesla attributed the poor performance to bad weather, shipping problems, currency headwinds, and customer vacations that prevented planned deliveries.

As of February 19, 2015, Tesla's stock was trading at $211.71, up 27.4 percent below its 52-week high of $291.42, and 19.5 percent above its 52-week low of $177.22. Investors are nervous about Tesla's future, due to the (1) impact of lower gasoline prices on customer demand, (2) speed with which the company can ramp up production, (3) high value of the dollar, and (4) company's primary interest in growing market share at the expense of profitability.

In August 2015, *Reuters'* analysis revealed that Tesla was actually losing more than $4,000 on every model S Sedan sold as the company reported operating losses of $359 million during the second quarter of 2015. Tesla's losses are beginning to worry analysts. However, CEO Elon Musk has promised to deliver profits by the first quarter of 2016 and is looking to expand Tesla's energy storage business. The company's model S Sedan sold a mere 11,532 vehicles during the second quarter of 2015, but the company is planning to launch its Model X SUV in September 2015. Tesla still says it will deliver 500,000 autos by 2020, but critics are skeptical. A bright spot for the company is the grid battery business, dubbed "Tesla Energy," that may provide future profit. Shares of Tesla in August 2015 sold for $241, having dropped about 9 percent in the last 30 days.

History

Founded in 2003 by a group of engineers, Jeffrey Straubel, Elon Musk, and Marc Tarpenning, Tesla manufactured its first electric vehicle, the Tesla Roadster, in 2008. The vehicle offered instant torque, incredible power, and zero emissions. The Roadster featured a sports car powertrain built around an AC induction motor, patented in 1888 by Nikola Tesla, the inventor who inspired the company's name. The Roadster accelerates from 0 to 60 mph in 3.7 seconds and has a range of 245 miles per charge of its lithium ion battery. To date, Tesla has sold more than 2,400 Roadsters, now on the road in more than 30 countries.

In 2012, Tesla launched a fully electric sedan named the Model S, with room for seven passengers and more than 64 cubic feet of storage. The Model S provides the comfort and utility of a family sedan while achieving the acceleration of a sports car: 0 to 60 mph in about 5 seconds. With a range of 265 miles per charge, the Model S was named Motor Trend's 2013 Car of the Year and achieved a 5-star safety rating from the U.S. National Highway Traffic Safety Administration.

In late 2014, Tesla released its two dual-motor, all-wheel drive configurations of the Model S, named the P85D and featuring a high-efficiency motor at the front and rear. The P85D can achieve a 0 to 60 mph time of 3.2 seconds—the fastest four-door production car ever made. With more than 50,000 vehicles on the road worldwide at year-end 2014, Tesla is preparing to launch

Model X, a cross-over vehicle that enters volume production in 2015. For long-distance journeys, Tesla's Supercharger network provides convenient and free access to high-speed charging, replenishing half a charge in as little as 20 minutes. Superchargers now connect popular routes in North America, Europe, and Asia Pacific.

Internal Issues

Vision/Mission/Values
Tesla has an elaborate code of business conduct and ethics posted at the corporate website. Its mission is to "accelerate the world's transition to sustainable transport."

Organizational Structure
As illustrated in Exhibit 1, Tesla uses a functional organizational design, with no apparent divisions, no COO, and no women among top management.

Manufacturing
Tesla produces up to 1,000 vehicles per week at its factory in Fremont, California, but the company is building additional manufacturing facilities in Tilburg, the Netherlands, where it has an assembly facility, and Lathrop, California, where it has a specialized production plant. Along with partners such as Panasonic, Tesla is building a Gigafactory near Reno, Nevada, that will produce a mass-market affordable vehicle, named the Model 3. By 2020, the Gigafactory will produce more high-tech lithium ion cells than all of the world's combined output in 2013. The Gigafactory will also produce battery packs intended for use in stationary storage, helping to improve robustness of the electrical grid, reduce energy costs for businesses and residences, and provide a backup supply of power. The Gigafactory reveals that Tesla is not just an automaker but a technology and design company with a focus on energy innovation.

Strategy
In 2014, Tesla increased its number of dealerships and service centers by over 40 percent, expanded its Supercharger network by 400 percent, started construction of the Gigafactory, and introduced numerous advances on Model S. The company entered 2015 with over 10,000 orders for its Model S and almost 20,000 reservations for its Model X.

In Q4 of 2014, Tesla built 11,627 vehicles, achieving its production target of 35,000 Model S vehicles for the entire year. The company launched the Model S P85D in November 2014. *Motor Trend* called this vehicle the "quickest sedan in the world" and a YouTube video of thrilled passengers went viral.

Tesla has started selling vehicles in Australia, and four other countries/regions, doubling its number of sales and service locations internationally. Tesla remains convinced that China is a key country for the company, and thus is simplifying the buying process in China by having Tesla personnel install charging points at customer homes or businesses well before vehicle delivery.

EXHIBIT 1 Tesla's Organizational Structure

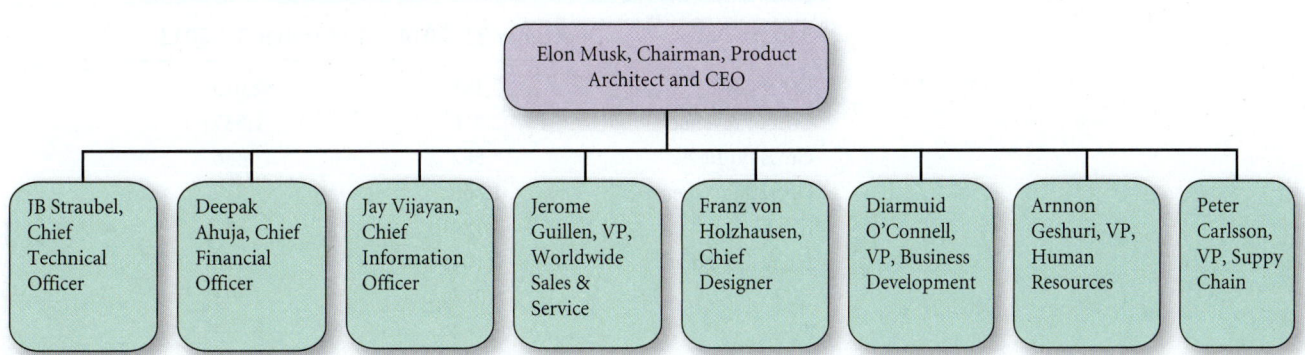

Source: Based on the author's depiction given current executives listed at Tesla's corporate website.

In Q4 of 2014, Tesla installed a quarterly record 125 Supercharger stations, increasing the total to 380 Supercharger stations energized globally. As an extension of the company's Supercharger network, hotels and popular destinations have been installing high-powered wall connectors at such a rapid pace that Tesla is now coordinating these efforts as a Destination Charging program. In early 2015, about 900 locations in Asia and North America have 1,600 Tesla connectors installed. Tesla is expanding the Destination Charging program into Europe in Q2 of 2015.

Tesla's Model X deliveries are on schedule to begin in Q3 of 2015. To meet this demand, the company is expanding its Lathrop manufacturing facility in central California and installing a state of the art, highly automated casting and machining operation for various aluminum components used on both Model S and Model X.

In Q4 of 2014, Tesla leased 647 cars to customers with $65 million of transaction value. Q4 revenue was $1.1 billion, up 44 percent from a year ago, to $957 million. Automotive revenue for Q4 included $42 million of powertrain sales primarily to Daimler. In 2014, about 55 percent of Tesla's new Model S vehicles were delivered in North America, while deliveries in Asia/Pacific (APAC) were flat. The APAC region represented about 15 percent of Tesla deliveries in 2014, with the remaining 30 percent of deliveries going to Europe, where delivery volume more than doubled from a year ago.

Tesla opened a record 21 new sales and service locations during Q4 of 2014. The company's Q4 net loss was $16 million, contributing to the company's full year net income loss of $2.36 per share.

Segments

Tesla did not provide by-segment data for 2014. However, starting in 2015, Tesla is reorganizing its revenue and cost of revenue sections of its income statement, so that automotive revenue and gross margin reflect only new car sales activities. Revenues and gross margin for all the company's other businesses, such as powertrain sales, services, trade-in sales, and stationary storage will be reported in the "Services and Other" section of the income statement. Tesla says this change will "provide clearer disclosure of our core business of new car production and deliveries."

Finance

Tesla's recent income statement and balance sheet are provided in Exhibits 2 and 3, respectively.

Competitors

The automobile industry includes General Motors (GM), Ford Motor Company (F), and Chrysler. This group is commonly referred to as Detroit's Big Three. In addition, BMW, Daimler (DAI), Honda (HMC), Hyundai, Mazda, Nissan (NSANY), Subaru, and Toyota (TM) are other competitors developing and producing electric vehicles.

EXHIBIT 2 Tesla's Income Statement (in millions of USD)

Report Date	December 31, 2014	December 31, 2013
Revenues	$3,198	$2,013
Cost of revenue	2,316	1,557
Gross profit	882	456
Operating expenses	1,066	517
EBIT	(184)	(61)
Interest & other	(101)	(10)
EBT	(285)	(71)
Tax	9	3
Net income	**(294)**	**(74)**

Source: Based on company documents.

EXHIBIT 3 Tesla's Balance Sheet (in millions of USD)

Report Date	December 31, 2014	December 31, 2013
Assets		
Cash and equivalents	$1,923	$849
Accounts receivable	226	49
Inventories	954	340
Other current assets	95	28
Total current assets	3,198	1,266
Property, plant & equipment	1,829	738
Operating lease vehicles	766	383
Goodwill & intangibles	—	—
Other assets	56	30
Total assets	**5,849**	**2,417**
Liabilities		
Accounts payable	1,047	412
Other current liabilities	763	457
Total current liabilities	1,810	869
Long-term debt	2,408	586
Other liabilities	661	294
Total liabilities	**4,879**	**1,749**
Common stock	—	—
Retained earnings	(1,434)	(1,140)
Treasury stock	—	—
Paid in capital and other	2,404	1,808
Total equity	**970**	**668**
Total liabilities & equity	**5,849**	**2,417**

Source: Based on company documents.

In a recent period, Tesla topped U.S. sales of electric and plug-in hybrid cars with 1,100 units sold, followed by Nissan with its all-electric Leaf at 1,070 units sold, and then came the BMW i3 at 670. The Chevrolet Volt hybrid was next in units sold with 542, followed by the Ford Fusion Energi with 426, and then the Toyota Prius PHV hybrid at 401.

Rumors are that Apple plans to start production of an electric car by 2020 under the code name Project Titan. That timeline would put Apple in line to compete head to head with various automakers that have plans to introduce a self-driving or fully electric car in 2020. For example, Nissan has set 2020 as a deadline to market a self-driving car. And Google says it might be ready sooner with a self-driving car. Tesla plans to have its Model 3, a middle-market advanced electric car, on the road by about 2017, about the same time that GM says it will have its Chevrolet Bolt ready, an all-electric car with 200-mile range.

A comparative analysis of Tesla with GM and Ford is provided in Exhibit 4.

General Motors (GM)

The fully electric Chevrolet Bolt vehicle was shown at the North American International Auto Show in Detroit in January 2015. Some analysts confused GM's Bolt with the company's Volt, the Chevy extended-range hybrid car. "Some people think it's confusing," said Alan Batey, president of GM North America. "But the Volt and Bolt are different vehicles for people with different needs," he said.

Ford (F)

The Fusion Energi is a plug-in hybrid car that began selling in the United States in February 2013. Initially, the Energi was priced at $39,495, but in January 2014 the starting price was reduced to $35,525. Sales of hybrid electric cars in the United States in 2014 declined

EXHIBIT 4 Tesla versus Rival Firms

	Tesla	Ford	GM
# Employees	10,000	187,000	216,000
$ Net Income	(294)	3,187 M	3,949
$ Revenue	3,198 M	144,077 M	155,929 M
$ Revenue/Employee	320,000	770,000	722,000 M
$ EPS Ratio	(2.36)	0.80	1.65
Market Cap.	25.6 B	64.6 B	60 B

Source: Based on company documents.

8.8 percent from 2013, while sales of the Fusion Hybrid declined 5.0 percent. The Fusion, however, continued to rank as the fourth top-selling hybrid in the United States. Sales of Ford's Lincoln MKZ Hybrid, however, continued its growth trend in 2014, with sales up 34.3 percent from a year earlier.

Audi AG

Headquartered in Ingolstadt, Bavaria, Germany, Audi is a subsidiary of the Volkswagen Group. Regarding electric or hybrid vehicles, the Audi 2016 Audi R8 e-tron debuted at the 2015 Geneva Motor Show and featured a 92kWh t-shaped lithium-ion battery pack capable of delivering 280 miles of electric range. That immediately put the R8 e-tron vehicle in a class occupied only by Tesla's Model S. The new electric Audi vehicle can accelerate from 0 to 62 mph in just 3.9 seconds, and hit an artificially restricted top speed of 155.3 mph. Audi says the battery can be charged in "significantly less than two hours." The new Audi R8 e-tron numbers match up favorably to the high-performance version Model S range of 270 miles and 0 to 60 in 3.2 seconds' acceleration time. The two-seat Audi R8 e-tron is more of a direct competitor to Tesla's discontinued Roadster in terms of passenger capacity and its sporting nature, than it is the four-door Model S. Audi says it is now in the electric are business for the long term.

External Issues

Electric and hybrid cars remain a very small fraction of overall car sales, and no company yet has actually turned a profit making electric cars. Tesla does have a significant head start with its battery technology and the distance its cars are able to go per charge, but gas prices are low and customers are actually trending toward larger rather than smaller cars.

Tesla serves an international market and has a global supply chain, but most of the Model S vehicles are built in North America, so a strong dollar has a slightly negative net effect on the company's profitability. In markets where the local currency has declined significantly versus the U.S. dollar, Tesla recently increased prices by only about half that decline. The price increase, however, applies only to new orders and is not retroactive to the existing orders.

Lithium Batteries

Many automobile producers are also now producing lithium batteries, and the industry was valued at over $3 billion in 2014. There are only 50 producers of lithium batteries in the United States, and revenue growth is expected to approach 20 percent through 2020. Key players include Nissan, with a 13 percent market share, followed by Ford, GM, and Tesla, with market shares around 8 percent each, leaving approximately 60 percent of the revenues outside the these four firms, opening the possibly of industry consolidation. In addition, as technology, economies of scale, and further developments reduce production cost, more competitors may enter the market. However, for the next 5 years, demand is expected to top supply, keeping prices attractive for manufacturers.

About 70 percent of all lithium battery revenue today is derived from automobiles, according to IBIS, with consumer goods and medical products accounting for approximately 8 percent each. The switch into battery production for automobiles has been aided of late by government incentives to produce green hybrid and electric vehicles. China in particular is providing heavy incentives for customers, including tax exemptions for customers choosing to purchase electric vehicles, attracting many companies interest to China. Tesla and Panasonic recently agreed to terms on a $5 billion factory to be completed in 2020 in Nevada that will produce 500,000 Tesla batteries annually.

Some car manufacturers still produce lead-acid batteries for hybrid cars, but these have a distinct disadvantage, as lithium batteries have twice the energy density of the rival lead-acid batteries, and also are not plagued by the same memory issues lead-acid batteries have. Lead-acid batters, when partially discharged, have a tendency to only recharge to the previously discharged positions; this is not a concern with lithium batteries.

Oil Prices

From 2011 to the summer of 2014, Light Sweet Crude prices were relatively stable, ranging from $75 to $114 per barrel. However, from the summer of 2014 through March 2015, Light Sweet Crude fell 60 percent from $107 to less than $45. Long-term forecasts expect oil prices to be around $75 per barrel by 2020, but with oil, projecting price is risky. An OPEC executive in early 2015 joked the price of oil will finish the year between $30 and $150 per barrel, indicating even OPEC executives really have no firm grasp on projecting oil prices. Nevertheless, many experts in the field have indicated the days of $100 oil are over, possibly due to better public transportation and more efficient engines, but also from the growing electric vehicle market. It will be interesting to see how consumers view electric vehicles from a cost standpoint if oil remains low. One of the key drivers in electric car popularity was higher gas prices. This can even been viewed with what types of vehicles consumers are currently purchasing. Trucks, SUVs, and larger vehicles are much more popular today than they were 5 years ago.

Future

In 2015, Tesla plans to deliver about 55,000 Model S and X vehicles, representing more than a 70 percent increase over 2014 deliveries. About 40 percent of these deliveries are planned for the first half of the year. First quarter 2015 production is expected to be about 10,000 vehicles, an increase of over 47 percent from the prior year period.

Tesla plans to achieve a 30 percent gross margin on Model S for Q4 of 2015, even with foreign currency rates at current levels. But those high margins will be offset by the Model X's negative profitability for a few quarters from supply chain and production inefficiencies that are typical of a new product introduction. Tesla plans to grow its Supercharger network by over 50 percent in 2015, as well as continue other product development programs, including the Model 3 to be released in 2017.

Several concerns for analysts include that Tesla is no longer building cars only as orders come in. This departure from the past indicates that Tesla production is not as much of a build-to-order model as it has been historically. Another concern for analysts is that Tesla's investments in its Gigafactory are slow, actually totaling only $107 million in early 2015. The Gigafactory is crucial for Tesla's bid to make batteries cheap enough for the mass-market Model 3. Also a concern for analysts is that Tesla's sales in China are declining.

For Q2 of 2015, Tesla reported revenue of $954.98 million, versus expectations of $1.17 billion. The company produced a record 12,807 vehicles during Q2, while the company's Services and other revenue was $77 million, up 85 percent from a year ago. This included about $32 million of powertrain sales to Daimler, $23 million of Service revenue, and $20 million of pre-owned Model S sales. Tesla's Model X remains on track for start of deliveries in September 2015.

Oil prices remain low, so consumers are buying bigger vehicles, hurting the sale of electric vehicles. Tesla faces stiff headwinds going forward, including competition from numerous rival firms, such as GM, Ford, Audi, BMW, Toyota, Nissan, and maybe even Apple and Google. Prepare a 3-year strategic plan for CEO Elon Musk.

Ford Motor Company, 2015

www.ford.com, F

Headquartered in Dearborn, Michigan, Ford Motor Company is the second-largest U.S. automaker behind General Motors, but only the fifth-largest in the world based on vehicle sales. The company produces many different cars and trucks ranging from entry level to luxury cars. Ford's F-150 pickup truck is the most popular truck in the world for 32 years running. Ford owns stakes in several car manufacturers around the world, including Aston Martin, Jiangling, Troller, and FPV. In the past, Ford has owned portions of Jaguar, Land Rover, and Volvo. In 2011, Ford discontinued its Mercury brand that had existed since 1938. In 2015, Ford switched the body of its famous F-150 to aluminum from steel. The extra cost was $395 per truck, but fuel economy improved with the reduced weight.

Fords have been running fast lately. For Q2 of 2015, Ford reported excellent financial results, including the following:

- Global market share grew to 7.6 percent, up one-tenth percent from a year ago.
- Twelve of 16 planned global new product launches are completed; the remainder is on track.
- Introduced SYNC® 3, the all-new communications and entertainment system.
- Continued strong profit at Ford Credit; pre-tax profit of $506 million.
- Ford Smart Mobility plan moved from research to the start of implementation.
- Ford Credit launched car-sharing pilot in 6 U.S. cities and London.
- Pre-tax profit of $2.9 billion, up $269 million or 10 percent from a year ago.
- Net income of $1.9 billion, up $574 million or 44 percent from a year ago.
- After-tax earnings per share of 47 cents, up 7 cents from a year ago.
- Best company quarterly profit since 2000.
- Wholesale volume up 2 percent, driven by North America and Europe.
- Automotive revenue is about equal, with higher net pricing and volume offset by unfavorable translation effects of the strong U.S. dollar.

Copyright by Fred David Books LLC. www.strategyclub.com (Written by Forest R. David)

History

Ford traces its roots back to 1896 when Henry Ford built and marketed his first Quadricycle, a 4-wheel vehicle with a 4-horsepower engine. It was not until 1901, however, that Ford started his own car company, named the Henry Ford Company. He started Ford Motor Company in 1902 with 12 investors and $28,000 in cash. Interestingly, two of Ford's first investors in his new company were John and Horace Dodge, who later would start their own car company, called Dodge. Ford had spent nearly the entire initial investment when his first car was sold in July 1903. It did not take Ford Motor Company long, though, to start making large profits. By October 1903, Ford had turned a profit of $37,000, indicating just how popular this new equipment was going to become. The company was incorporated in 1903.

Henry Ford is world famous for his assembly line, but for the first 10 years of the company, two to three men worked on each car, and the parts were supplied by outside firms. Ford produced the famous Model T in 1908 and sold over 15 million, until production ceased in 1927. To help maintain employee morale, Ford paid workers $5 per day in 1914, double the national average. In addition, Ford reduced the workday from 9 to 8 hours. Many of Ford's workers could even afford a car they produced with the salary they earned.

In 1922, Ford acquired Lincoln Company and even began experimenting with aircraft production. In 1925, 2 years before selling the Model A automobile in 1927, Ford closed all plants for 6 months to retool and train employees on construction. By 1931, despite the great depression, Ford sold over 5 million Model A's. Ford continued to grow over the next two decades, until its IPO in 1956, which was at the time the largest IPO in history.

In 2005, Ford, along with GM, had their corporate bonds downgraded to junk status. High health-care costs, rising gas, falling market share to foreign products, a demanding United Auto Workers (UAW) union, and lack of strategic planning all contributed to the downfall. In 2007, Ford reached an agreement with the UAW on retirement benefits and other costs. The company was able to avoid a government takeover, unlike its counterpart, General Motors. Over the last several years, Ford has rebounded and continues to produce quality automobiles worldwide, as well as more and more electric and part-electric vehicles.

Internal Issues

Organizational Structure

As revealed in Exhibit 1, Ford operates using a divisional-by-geographic region organizational structure. Alan Mulally retired as CEO of Ford Motor Company on July 1, 2014, and was replaced by the then COO Mark Fields. In December 2014, the company hired a Chief Analytics Officer.

Vision/Mission

Ford does not have a published vision statement, but does have a stated mission statement, which is based on four key components and paraphrased as follows:

One Ford: Align employee efforts toward a common definition of success and optimize their collective strengths worldwide.

One team: Work together as one team to achieve automotive leadership, which is measured by the satisfaction of our customers, employees, and essential business partners, such as our dealers, investors, suppliers, unions/councils, and communities.

One plan: Aggressively restructure to operate profitably at the current demand and changing model mix.

One goal: Create an exciting and viable company delivering profitable growth for all.

Strategy

Since 2005, Ford's warranty repairs have declined 66 percent for vehicles in the first 3 months of service with average warranty costs falling 54 percent. Ford has reduced its energy use, emissions, and waste in its factories and its vehicles. The new F-150 comes with a 2.7 liter V6 EcoBoost engine, giving it the same power as a V8, with much better fuel economy. Higher engine outputs with smaller displacements are a key initiative moving forward for Ford and greatly improve fuel economy and emissions. To improve safety, many Ford products now include Blind Spot Information Systems, lane alerts, and rear parking assistance.

In 2014, Ford launched more vehicles than ever before in a single calendar year, including a new Mustang and F-150. Ford is especially proud of offering its Mustang for the first time ever in select markets in Europe and Asia, and the F-150 moving to an aluminum body will save over 700 pounds on weight with the same material strength. Currently, Ford is engaged in its largest manufacturing expansion in over 50 years by increasing capacity in six U.S. plants and by opening two new plants in Asia and one each in South America and Europe. The U.S. plants alone are expected to enjoy $6 billion of improvements. In 2013, Ford sold over 85,000 hybrid or all-electric, plug-in automobiles, up 150 percent from 2012 as the company attempts to produce, as one executive said, a Tesla for the average person. As the average age of cars increases in the United States and abroad, Ford is aggressively launching new or significantly redesigned products. In 2014, Ford introduced 23 new vehicles, up from 11 in 2013, and plans to introduce a 150 percent new product turnover by 2018.

Marketing

Ford is unveiling a slew of new high-performance models, more than 12 new go-fast models coming to market by 2020, including a super-hot new Focus model, the RS. A new high-performance "Raptor" version of its new F-150 pickup could debut, and a new Ford sports car is coming. Fast, sexy sports cars (and trucks) make for great headlines and they help develop loyal customers. Products such as the V8-powered GT version of Ford's Mustang sell well, but higher-performance models are typically niche products. That niche is growing—Ford recently reported that sales of high-performance models have risen 70 percent in the United States since

EXHIBIT 1 Ford's Organizational Structure

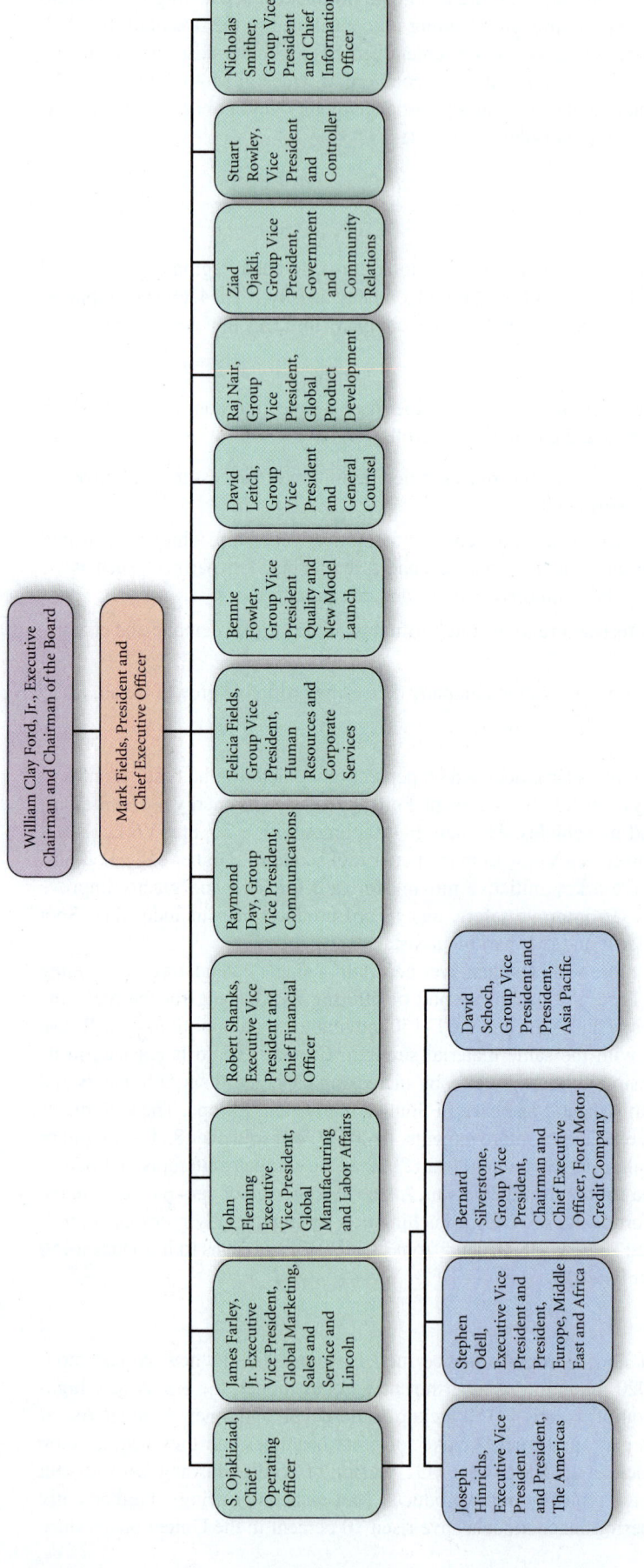

Source: Based on information in Ford's 2014 *Annual Report.*

2009, and 16 percent in Europe over the same period—but it's still small. High-performance versions of mainstream models generally make up less than 10 percent of the model's total sales. Ford reports that more than 65 percent of those who buy its "hot-hatch" Focus ST and Fiesta ST models are new to the brand, and importantly, often become loyal customers "for life."

Segments

Ford derives approximately 60 percent of its revenues from the United States, Canada, and Mexico. Virtually all the company's profits in 2014 came from these countries; the only other profitable region was Asia. Ford is in the midst of a $400 million restructuring program in Europe and anticipates Europe will become profitable sometime in 2015. South America pretax profits were slightly negative and are expected to remain so the next several years. Brazil and Argentina are the strongest markets, with Venezuela being the weakest major market.

Ford reports revenues by five regions and by process: (1) vehicle sales and (2) financial services. In 2014, Ford reported $136 billion from vehicle sales and $8.2 billion from financial services. Pretax results were just over $2.5 billion, with vehicle sales and financial services accounting for $1.8 billion. It is important to note that Ford's Pretax results were less than half the previous year for total automotive operations. See Exhibit 2.

Finance

Ford's recent income statement and balance sheet are provided in Exhibits 3 and 4, respectively. Note the decline in revenues and the dramatic decline in net income.

EXHIBIT 2 Segment Data for Ford (in millions of USD)

	2014		2013	
	Revenue	Pretax Results	Revenue	Pretax Results
North America	$82,400	$6,898	$86,500	$8,809
South America	10,800	(1,162)	8,800	(33)
Europe	29,500	(1,062)	27,300	(1,442)
Middle East & Africa	4,400	(20)	4,500	(69)
Asia Pacific	10,700	589	10,300	327
Other Automotive	NA	(755)	NA	(656)
Total Automotive minus Special Items	**135,782**	**2,548**	**139,369**	**5,368**
Financial Services	**8,295**	**1,854**	**7,548**	**1,756**

Source: Based on *2014 Quarterly and Full Year Review,* various pages.

EXHIBIT 3 Ford's Income Statement (in millions of USD)

Report Date	December 31, 2014	December 31, 2013
Revenues	$144,077	$146,917
Operating expenses	140,637	141,439
EBIT	3,440	5,478
Interest expense	797	829
Interest & other income	1,699	2,391
EBT	4,342	7,040
Tax	1,156	(135)
Noncontrolling interest	(1)	(7)
Net income	**3,187**	**7,182**

Source: Based on company documents.

EXHIBIT 4 Ford's Balance Sheet (in millions of USD)

Report Date	December 31, 2014	December 31, 2013
Assets		
Cash and equivalents	$10,757	$14,468
Marketable securities	20,393	22,100
Accounts receivable	92,819	87,309
Inventories	7,866	7,708
Total current assets	131,835	131,585
Property, plant & equipment	53,343	47,600
Long-term investments	3,357	3,679
Goodwill & intangibles	—	—
Other assets	19,992	19,315
Total assets	**208,527**	**202,179**
Liabilities		
Accounts payable	20,035	19,531
Total current liabilities	20,035	19,531
Long-term debt	119,171	114,688
Other liabilities	44,174	41,517
Total liabilities	**183,380**	**175,736**
Redeemable noncontrolling interest	342	331
Common stock	40	40
Retained earnings	24,556	23,386
Treasury stock	(848)	(505)
Pension & retirement losses and other	(20,032)	(18,231)
Paid in capital and other	21,089	21,422
Total equity	**24,805**	**26,112**
Total liabilities & equity	**208,527**	**202,179**

Source: Based on company documents.

Competitors

Competition in the automobile manufacturing business is intense among Ford, GM, Toyota, BMW, Honda, Volkswagen, Hyundai-Kia, Nissan, Mercedes, and several other firms. About 75 percent of all revenue goes to purchase raw materials, so the industry is affected substantially by prices of steel, rubber, aluminum, and other raw materials. Wages, the second-largest expense, historically have been about $70,000 per employee in the United States and account for 5 percent of total revenue expenses. Higher commodity prices and wage expenses forced GM and Chrysler into Chapter 11 bankruptcies toward the end of the economic recession. However, labor expenses were reduced after labor unions agreed to concessions.

Competition among competing models of vehicles and competing firms primarily boils down to price, fuel economy, reliability, and utility. Business customers tend to focus on utility, whether it is a construction company that needs heavy trucks or a pharmaceutical business that provides cars to its salespeople. Most consumers, however, are more focused with styling and price, but there are many exceptions and subsets of each population.

The industry is experiencing increased globalization. Firms like Ford are offering new products in existing markets and expanding into new markets. Many Japanese manufacturers are gaining market share in the United States. There are high barriers to entry, which discourages new companies from trying to enter the industry.

Exhibit 5 shows the largest automakers in the world. Other notable firms were Fiat Chrysler, BMW, Daimler, and Mazda. Although no Chinese automaker is ranked in the top 10, from 13th to

EXHIBIT 5 Top Five Automobile Manufactures based on 2014 Units Sold (10 months data, in thousands)

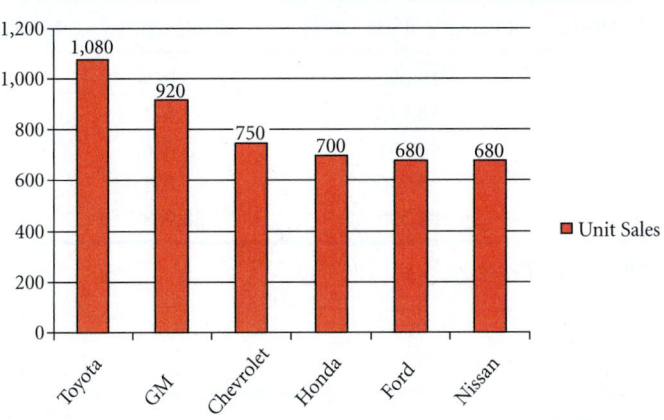

Source: Consolidated and adapted from SP Net Advantage Table.

EXHIBIT 6 Ford versus Rival Firms

	Ford	GM	Toyota
# Employees	187,000	216,000	339,000
$ Net Income	3,187 M	3,949 M	17,703 M
$ Revenue	144,007 M	155,929 M	249,472 M
$ Revenue/Employee	770,000	721,893	735,906
$ EPS Ratio	0.80	1.65	10.71
Market Cap.	63.4 B	60.8 B	213 B

Source: A variety of sources.

30th, there are 10 Chinese firms represented. Exhibit 6 provides a synopsis comparison between Ford, GM, and Toyota.

General Motors (GM) Company

Headquartered in Detroit, Michigan, GM is the largest American car manufacturing company, ranking second behind Toyota in revenues and units of vehicles sold annually. GM brands include GMC, Chevrolet, Buick, Cadillac, Opel, Wuling, Jie Fang, and Alpheon, among many others. General Motors also holds stakes in and has joint ventures with firms in Korea and China. GM is investing heavily in its electric vehicle line, which totaled 7 vehicles in 2013, and has partnered with Honda to work on hydrogen cell technologies, with a 2020 timeframe for selling vehicles.

General Motors owns OnStar, which serves 6.5 million customers across North America with an assortment of services, including alerting First Responders to your location in an accident, as well as offering driving directions. With a new application for smartphones, OnStar can reveal your tire pressure, fuel levels, and even start your car remotely.

Exhibit 7 reveals GM unit sales across world markets. Europe remains a laggard in the world vehicle market, experiencing reduced sales for both Ford and GM. South America, while enjoying an increase in industrywide sales, reported fewer unit sales of GM vehicles in 2013.

Toyota Motor Corporation

Headquartered in Aichi, Japan, with U.S. headquarters based in Torrance, California, Toyota is the largest automaker in the world in terms of revenues, and one of the largest in the U.S. market. Toyota sells vehicles in over 170 different nations and generated $214 billion in revenues over all operating segments in 2013. Popular vehicles sold in the United States include Lexus, Camry,

EXHIBIT 7 **GM Segment Data (in units sold in thousands)**

	2013		2012	
	GMC Units	Industry Wide Units	GMC Units	Industry Wide Units
North America	3,324	19,092	3,019	17,847
Europe	1,557	18,772	1,611	18,983
Asia/Pacific, Middle East, Africa	3,886	40,795	3,616	38,229
South America	1,037	5,936	1,051	5,849
World Wide	9,715	84,595	80,908	9,297

Source: Based on information in the 2013 GMC *Annual Report,* p. 3.

EXHIBIT 8 **Toyota Segment Data (in millions of USD)**

	2013		2012	
Geographic Region	Revenue	Operating Income	Revenue	Operating Income
Japan	$106,414	$4,784	$92,689	($1,718)
North America	52,161	1,842	39,441	1,547
Europe	17,290	220	16,550	148
Asia	36,399	3,121	27,674	2,131
Other	17,382	1,110	14,609	903
Intersegment elimination	(46,514)	(113)	(36,719)	(59)
Totals	183,133	10,963	154,244	2,952

Source: Based on Toyota's 2013 *Annual Report,* p. 35. (Exchange rate conversion, December 2014)

Corolla, Avalon, Rav4, 4Runner, Land Cruiser, Tacoma, Tundra, Prius, and many others, including several mini-vans.

Exhibit 8 presents the segment data for Toyota based on geographic region. It is interesting to note that revenues were up 18 percent in 2013 but operating income was up 275 percent over the same time period. In particular, operating revenues in Japan increased substantially. Toyota reported increased sales in Europe over the same time frame when both Ford and GM had losses in Europe.

Hyundai-Kia

Headquartered in Seoul, South Korea, Hyundai-Kia is the second-largest automaker in Asia and the fourth largest in the world. The firm operates the single-largest automobile manufacturing plant in the world, in Uslan, South Korea, producing over 1.5 million vehicles annually. Hyundai has become the fastest-growing automaker in the world. With extended warranties common, Hyundai has gained loyalty and significantly increased its U.S. market share. The company reported revenues in 2014 of $8.4 billion. Popular cars include the Sonata, Santa Fe, Accent, Tucson, and the Rio and Optima by Kia.

External Issues

Vehicle Variety in the USA

Exhibit 9 reveals the percent of revenue of various classes of vehicle. Cross-over utility vehicles have taken much of the demand away from SUVs, which account for only 10 percent of total U.S. market share. These vehicles look much like an SUV, but are built on car chasses and lack the towing power of an SUV. They also tend to get much better gas mileage, as automakers started applying hybrid technology to cross-overs before SUVs. Notable SUVs include the Ford Flex, Toyota Venza, and Dodge Journey. The Ford Explorer has recently been shifted to become more of a SUV style along with several other popular SUV models.

EXHIBIT 9 Breakdown on Market Share of Vehicles in the USA

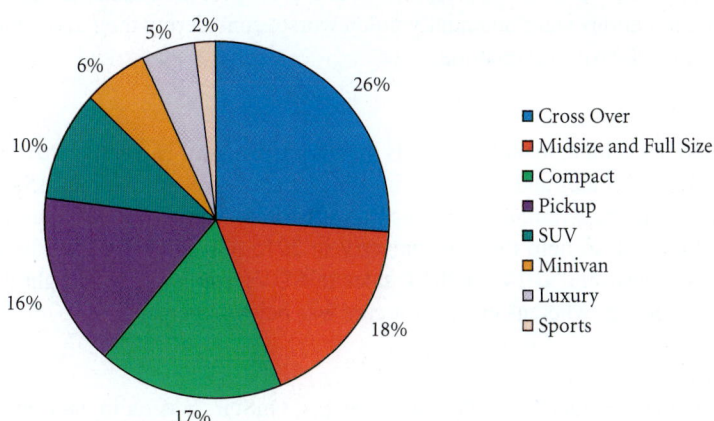

Legend:
- Cross Over
- Midsize and Full Size
- Compact
- Pickup
- SUV
- Minivan
- Luxury
- Sports

Source: Adapted and consolidated from various IBIS reports.

The next most popular style of vehicle in the United States is compact cars. Popular products in this line include the Ford Focus, Chevrolet Cruze, and the Toyota Corolla, and can start around $17,000. Smaller cars also popular include the Ford Fiesta and the Chevrolet Sonic which can start as low as $15,000. Many of these products are four-cylinders with some having the option of six cylinders. Midsize cars are also extremely popular, taking much of the market share away from larger vehicles. The Ford Fusion, Chevy Malibu, Dodge Charger, and Toyota Camry are examples of midsize vehicles. Full-size vehicles start around $30,000 with the Ford Taurus and Chevy Impala being two of the more popular options. Pickup trucks remain popular in the United States, with the F-150 the best seller in its class. Smaller size trucks such as the GMC Canyon or Chevy Colorado are not as popular as the full-size trucks. Ford's 150 and 250, GMC's Sierra, Chevy's Silverado, Toyota's Tundra, and Dodge's Ram are all popular and dominate the U.S. truck market.

Mini-vans were once super-popular because they were considered much more sporty than a station wagon; however, mini-vans and full-size vans have experienced declining sales. This line of vehicles is most popular among taxi companies and families with kids. Luxury cars account for 5 percent of the total U.S. market share; popular brands include BMW, Lexus, Cadillac, Mercedes, and several others. Sports cars account for only 2 percent of total U.S. market share; they include cars such as the Mustang, Camaro, Dodge Charger, and Corvette.

International Vehicle Market

In 2013, China became the first country to have over 20 million vehicle deliveries in a single year, with 22 million units. As of late 2014, Chinese vehicle sales were up 8 percent over the record year in 2013. In total, China enjoyed a 28 percent share as compared to the U.S. 17.5 percent share in global vehicle sales in 2013; China expects to increase its global market share lead. China will continue to put pressure on U.S., European, and Japanese automakers as new Chinese-based auto companies are formed and grow to prominence. However, it is important to note that Ford did experience a 22 percent growth in China in 2013 (partly due to its relatively small 5 percent Chinese market share) and GM and Volkswagen each have 15 percent market share in China. Therefore, the large U.S. and European players are expected be a factor for many years to come, even in China. Demand in India has been slow, with a 3 percent decline in 2014.

Europe is starting to stabilize economically, although the euro continues to decline, losing 25 percent of its value to the dollar between 2008 and 2014, putting further pressure on U.S. car manufacturers. Ford has especially experienced difficulties in Europe recently with pretax losses in both 2013 and 2012. Ford's European sales were estimated to be up 8 percent in 2014, showing improvement in the region even though Ford is expected to once again lose money in Europe in 2014. General Motors also has lost money in Europe in recent years. France remains the real laggard in western Europe with less than 2 percent vehicle sales growth. Eastern Europe exceeded a 9 percent decline and Russia nearly a 13 percent decline over 2013.

As a whole, South America experienced nearly 14 percent decline in automobile sales, with Brazil and Argentina each accounting for around a 13 percent decline in sales. Sales in other South American nations were potentially much worse, considering their economies are not nearly the size of either Brazil or Argentina.

Fuel Prices

A positive for American vehicle manufacturers is that gas prices as of November 2014 were averaging $2.92 in the United States and much less in some locales. The outlook in 2015 is for gas to remain below $3 per gallon. It remains to be seen how much further oil can fall, but the existing drop is substantial enough to help the auto industry in 2015. Oil prices fell nearly 50 percent from summer 2014 to year-end 2014. In 2014, sales of SUVs, mini-vans, and light-duty trucks increased nearly 10 percent, whereas growth for cars was below 2 percent.

High-Tech Vehicles

Many vehicles today come standard with power sockets, OnStar, XM radio, and built in Wi-Fi hotspots. These numerous extra features are all sources of profit for automakers. GM even has plans to introduce a self-driving Cadillac model in 2017, and Google claims to be in this business. Proponents of self-driving cars indicate they are safer and will save $1.3 trillion annually in the United States, along with fuel savings and fewer accidents. In addition, over $500 billion can be saved each year in productivity gains as people can work while commuting—if the driver can take his or her mind off the road completely.

Recalls and Fines

Vehicle recalls in the United States hit 22 million in 2013, a 9-year high. Hit especially hard by the recalls were Toyota, Chrysler, and Honda, accounting for 24, 21, and 13 percent of all recalls, respectively. Ford, BMW, Toyota, and several other vehicle manufacturers are recalling products containing airbags manufactured by Takata Corporation after five deaths were linked to them. As of October 2014, a class-action suit has been filed in U.S. court against Takata and several unstated automobile manufacturers. Recalls continued their upward trend in 2014 as well, resulting in billion-dollar penalties, including a $1.2 billion penalty on Toyota in 2014. Through only half of 2014, recalls were up 70 percent over the total recall amounts in all of 2013.

Access to Vehicle Loans

As of August 2014, the total balance on auto loans in the United States was $924 billion, an all-time high, and up 11 percent from the previous year. In addition, the number of delinquent auto loans has been falling, and are expected to continue to do so through 2015. Rates are slowly going up and currently are around 4.5 percent for new cars and 8.8 percent for used cars as of 2014. The lower rates and easy access to loans has been great for automakers. The average car price in 2008 was $25,000; in 2014, the average was over $33,000. Also, a strong used-car market has helped new car sells as well.

Production in North America

As wage differences around the world shrink, there is increasing attractiveness to locate manufacturing facilities back in the United States and Mexico. Factories are closer to the market, which reduces shipping costs and there is more control over operations. In 2013, GM committed to invest $16 billion in the United States over the next 3 years and Ford planned to invest $6 billion. Kia recently spent $1.5 billion in Mexico and another $10 billion is expected to be spent in Mexico from BMW, Toyota, and Daimler AG.

Future

In early 2015, Ford started production of two new engines—the 2.0-liter and 2.3-liter EcoBoost engines—for its plant in Cleveland. The 2.0-liter engine will be available in the Ford Edge. The 2.3-liter engine will be available in the Ford Mustang, Ford Explorer, and Lincoln MKC. However, for the most recent month (February 2015) available at the time this case was written, Ford reported a 1.9 percent decline in sales in the United States to 180,383 units. Ford brand's sales fell 1.7 percent to 174,219 units in the month, and Lincoln brands dropped 7.5 percent to

6,164 units. All total for the month, sales of Ford cars and utility vehicles fell 8.1 and 2.3 percent to 56,081 and 54,420 units, respectively. However, Ford's truck sales increased 4 percent, led by a 24.6 and 18.7 surge in sales of the Transit Connect and heavy trucks, respectively. Retail sales of the F-series fell 1.2 percent in February. Even Ford's two most popular two vehicles, the Focus and the Fusion, recorded a year-over-year decline in sales. The Ford Escape reported a 9.6 decline in sales for the month. A bright spot was the Ford Explorer had a 31.8 percent surge in sales in February 2015. Ford Mustang was the company's only car that reported higher sales during the month, increasing 31.9 percent to 8,454 units in February, making it the Mustang's best February sales since 2007. Since the launch of the new Mustang model, it has been the highest-selling sports car in America. But overall in February 2015, compared to the prior year period, Ford shareholders were not pleased with all the declines. Develop a 3-year strategic plan for Ford's new CEO, Mr. Mark Fields.

Harley-Davidson, Inc., 2015

www.harley-davidson.com, HOG

Headquartered in Milwaukee, Wisconsin, Harley-Davidson is an iconic brand worldwide and provides a unique customer experience few companies can match. Its ticker symbol, HOG, and its Harley Owners Group (H.O.G.) both stem from the nickname for the famous Harley motorcycle. Harley is America's largest motorcycle producer, with 2014 revenue of $6.2 billion. Harley has sales in about 90 countries, with one-third of its sales coming from outside the United States. Harley has about 1,400 independently owned dealers.

Harley-Davidson, Inc., is the parent company of Harley-Davidson Motor Company (HDMC) and Harley-Davidson Financial Services (HDFS). The former produces custom, cruiser, and touring motorcycles, and offers parts, accessories, riding gear, apparel, and general merchandise. The latter provides wholesale and retail financing and insurance to Harley-Davidson dealers and riders in the United States, Canada, and other select international markets.

Harley has not been roaring much lately. In mid-2015, the company reported earnings for their fiscal Q2 as follows:

- A 9 percent drop in consolidated revenue to $1.82 billion.
- An 11 percent decline in profits, which were just $1.44 per share.
- A 1.4 percent reduction in worldwide new motorcycle sales through its dealers.

Copyright by Fred David Books LLC. www.strategyclub.com (Written by Mark L. Frigo)

History

Harley Davidson started in a small shed in Milwaukee, Wisconsin, in 1903, where William S. Harley, age 23, and Arthur Davidson, age 22, made the first production Harley-Davidson motorcycle. In 1904, the first Harley-Davidson dealer opened in Chicago and in 1906 the first Harley factory was built in Milwaukee. Harley-Davidson Motor Co. was incorporated in 1907.

In the mid-1980s, Harley-Davidson targeted customer needs (lifestyle, freedom, adventure, community) with its unique offerings (the Harley experience) and earned price premiums (about 30 percent over competing motorcycles), while targeting a large and growing customer group at the time (baby boomers). This one-two combination of fulfilling higher-level customer needs and targeting an increasing market segment drove more than a 20-year run of excellent profitability and stock price performance.

Today, Harley remains a dominant force in the market, but faces challenges in creating products relevant to younger riders and women, as well as developing international sales in countries such as India. The company's strategic plan calls for international markets to play an increasingly significant role. For example, in 2014, international sales of new Harley-Davidson's grew at more than 5 percent and accounted for more than 36 percent of total retail Harley-Davidson motorcycle sales, up from 30 percent in 2008. For 2014, Harley's worldwide retail sales were up 2.7 percent versus the prior year.

Internal Issues

Vision/Mission

Harley publishes a statement on its website as follows: "We fulfill dreams through the experience of motorcycling, by providing to motorcyclists and to the general public an expanding line of motorcycles and branded products and services in selected market segments." Harley's vision for sustainability is "We preserve and renew the freedom to ride."

Organizational Structure

Harley's former COO, Matt Levatich, became the company's president and CEO in May 2015. Levatich had been president and Chief Operating Officer (COO) since 2009. He succeeded Chairman and CEO Keith Wandell, who retired. As illustrated in Exhibit 1, Harley's structure reflects the two business segments, as well as global vice presidents.

EXHIBIT 1 Harley-Davidson Organizational Structure

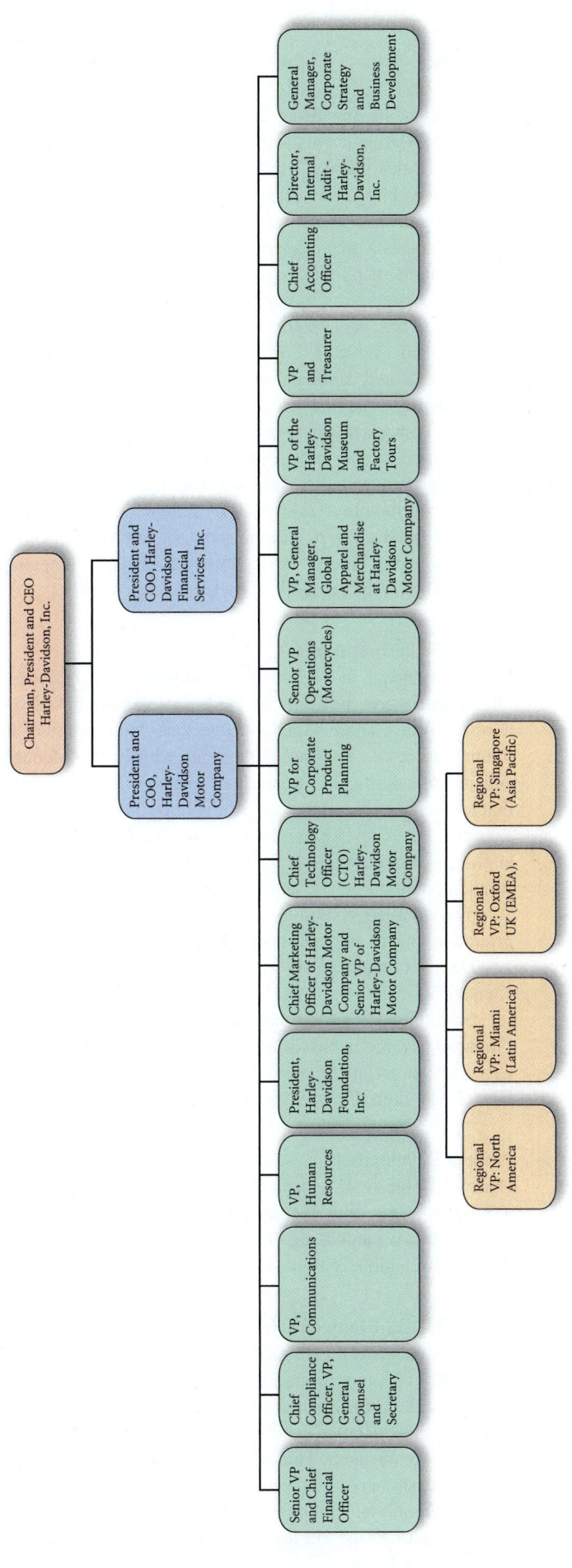

Source: Based on company documents.

Marketing

Harley's marketing strategy is designed to reach and engage customers. It spends only about 15 percent of its marketing budget on traditional media. Its marketing budget and efforts are focused on Harley events and activities, which engage and involve its customers. For example, in 2012, Harley's Chief Marketing Officer (CMO) organized an event in Rome, Italy, where Pope Francis blessed thousands of Harley riders and their motorcycles as part of the company's 110-year anniversary. Instead of outsourcing its creative advertising work to a traditional agency, Harley engages a crowd-sourcing firm and co-creates and tests its marketing ideas with its customers. Harley is pursuing efforts to lower the environmental impact of its products and operations, while promoting motorcycling and preserving the authentic Harley experience.

Harley has been trying to grow its appeal across generations, cultures, and borders. Internationally, in 2013, 35.9 percent of motorcycles were shipped to international markets. In the United States, Harley-Davidson is reaching a more diverse customer pool, and has grown among its traditional customer base. In 2013, U.S. retail sales of new Harley-Davidson motorcycles to "outreach" customers (young adults ages 18 to 34, women, African Americans, and Hispanic Americans) grew overall at more than twice the rate of sales to "core" customers—Caucasian men, ages 35 and over. From 2008 to 2013, Harley was the number-one seller of new on-road motorcycles to each of these segments. Harley also grew its market share lead and increased the share gap to the nearest competitor in each of these segments, compared to 2012. Currently, in the biggest Harley's market (United States) approximately two-thirds of the consumers fall into the category of men age 35 and older.

Supply Chain/Operations

Harley's tightly knit $1 billion-plus supply chain includes more than 300 suppliers. Key suppliers have access not only to Harley's facilities but also to its internal management system, dubbed "Ride." These suppliers have access to minutes of meetings, plans, schedules, and other internal processes, facilitating dialogue with Harley managers and employees in product design and manufacturing. In the spirit of openness, there's a detailed contract among key suppliers that spells out expectations and obligations on both sides of the company–supplier dialogue. For example, when developing the electronic fuel-injected (EFI) engine for the V-ROD bike, Harley engineers and managers collaborated with key supplier Delphi Automotive and with European firms, including Porsche and Magneti Marelli. Later, when Delphi's initial attempts to adapt an automotive-based system to a motorcycle failed, the team had to redesign the system from the ground up, which meant trusting the development of a critical component to an outsider.

Harley's manufacturing operations are located in Milwaukee, Wisconsin, for Powertrains; Kansas City, Missouri, for its Street, Sportster, Dyna, and V-Rod motorcycles; York, Pennsylvania, for its Softail and Touring motorcycles; and Bawal, India, and Manaus, Brazil. Harley-Davidson Financial Service is based in Chicago as well as Plano, Texas (wholesale finance) and Carson City, Nevada (retail finance). Regional offices are located in Miami (Latin America); Oxford, United Kingdom; Europe/Middle East/Africa (EMEA); and Singapore (Asia Pacific).

Product Development

Harley's Willie G. Davidson Product Development Center (PDC) in Wauwatosa, Wisconsin, is a 370,000-square-foot facility responsible for new product development, testing, styling, and developmental purchasing. The PDC also operates the Harley Arizona Proving Grounds and Florida Evaluation Center.

Harley Owners Group (H.O.G.)

H.O.G. is the official riding club of Harley-Davidson with over one million members and more than 1,400 chapters around the world. Today, the million-plus H.O.G. members are solidly hooked on the Harley name, sound, performance, and attire. H.O.G. enables the company to get "close to the customer" and gather invaluable feedback that can help serve Harley customers and grow the business. The owners group is invaluable in providing a means of communication between customers and the company. Many Harley customers are repeat customers who have a strong emotional attachment to the brand, which makes H.O.G. a valuable asset for the company and part of the Harley experience to its customers. It provides a significant competitive advantage for the company because no rivals to Harley come close achieving the customer loyalty of H.O.G. members.

Finance

Harley-Davidson's income statement are provided in Exhibit 2. Harley-Davidson's balance sheet are provided in Exhibit 3.

EXHIBIT 2 Harley-Davidson, Inc. Income Statement (in millions of USD)

Report Date	December 31, 2014	December 31, 2013
Revenues	$6,229	$5,900
Cost of revenue	3,788	3,752
Gross profit	2,441	2,148
Operating expenses	1,160	994
EBIT	1,281	1,154
Interest & other	2	(40)
EBT	1,283	1,114
Tax	439	380
Net income	**844**	**734**

Source: Based on Harley-Davidson's 2014 *Annual Report*, p. 51.

EXHIBIT 3 Harley-Davidson, Inc. Balance Sheet (in millions of USD)

Report Date	December 31, 2014	December 31, 2013
Assets		
Cash and equivalents	$907	$1,067
Accounts receivable	2,164	2,035
Inventories	449	425
Other current assets	428	462
Total current assets	3,948	3,989
Property, plant & equipment	883	842
Notes receivable	4,516	4,226
Goodwill & intangibles	28	30
Other assets	153	318
Total assets	**9,528**	**9,405**
Liabilities		
Accounts payable	197	240
Short-term debt	1,743	1,842
Other current liabilities	449	427
Total current liabilities	2,389	2,509
Long-term debt	3,761	3,417
Other liabilities	469	470
Total liabilities	**6,619**	**6,396**
Common stock	3	3
Retained earnings	8,459	7,853
Treasury stock	(6,303)	(5,689)
Paid in capital and other	750	842
Total equity	**2,909**	**3,009**
Total liabilities & equity	**9,528**	**9,405**

Source: Based on Harley-Davidson's 2014 *Annual Report*, p. 50.

Segments

Harley operates in two primary business segments: (1) Motorcycle & Related Products (Harley-Davidson Motor Company) and (2) Financial Services (Harley-Davidson Financial Services).

Motorcycles

Harley's motorcycle segment designs, manufactures, and sells motorcycles and a line of parts, accessories, and general merchandise and other related services. The motorcycle products are sold to retail customers through a network of independent dealers. The company manufactures six platforms of motorcycles: Touring, Dyna, Softail, Sportster, V-Rod, and Street. Harley-Davidson motorcycle engines currently range in displacement size from 494cc to 1,802cc, where Harley has been the historical market share leader in the United States for its primary market segment of engine displacements of 601+cc. Exhibit 4 reveals new Harley motorcycle retail sales worldwide increased marginally in 2014 across all regions with a 7 percent increase coming from Europe, the Middle East, and Africa (EMEA).

Harley-Davidson motorcycles feature classic styling, innovative design, distinctive sound, and superior quality with the ability to customize. The ability to customize motorcycles with special parts and accessories creates a lot of value for its customers and is highly profitable for Harley. The company operates its motorcycle segment on a global basis with sales in EMEA, Asia-Pacific, and Latin America.

Harley-Davidson's motorcycle and supporting product segment revenues by segment are provided in Exhibit 5 with revenues from financing operations excluded from the chart. The majority of segment revenues are derived from motorcycles.

Financial Services

The Financial Services business segment of the company provides wholesale and retail financing and provides insurance and insurance-related programs to dealers and their retail customers. Harley-Davidson Financial Services (HDFS) conducts business primarily in the United States and Canada. In 2014, HDFS reported $661 million in revenue from financial services up from $641 million in 2013.

External Issues

Harley-Davidson sells a vehicle that can result in injury or death. An increase in motorcycle popularity has been accompanied by increases in motorcycle-related fatalities and injuries. There were 4,957 motorcyclists killed in 2012—an increase of 7 percent from the 2011 fatality rate. According to the U.S. Department of Transportation, in terms of per vehicle mile traveled, motorcyclists were more than 26 times more likely than passenger car occupants to die in a

EXHIBIT 4 **Harley Motorcycle Retail Sales (in thousands of units)**

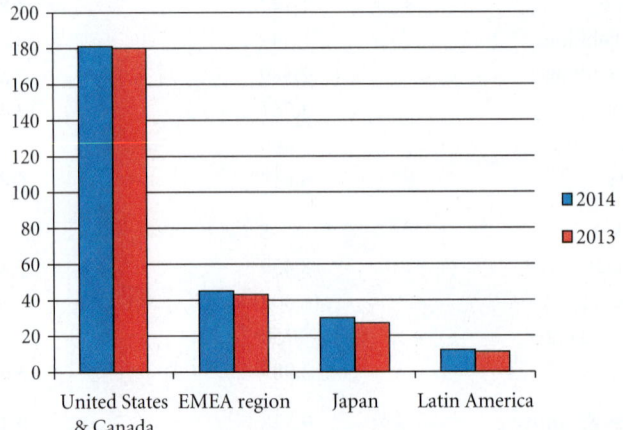

Source: Based on Harley-Davidson's 2014 *Annual Report*, p. 27.

EXHIBIT 5 Harley-Davidson's Revenue by Motorcycle Product Category (in millions of USD)

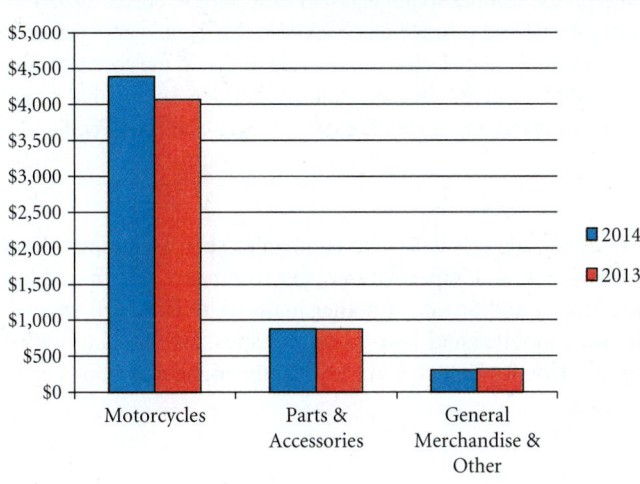

Source: Based on Harley-Davidson's 2014 *Annual Report,* p. 28.

EXHIBIT 6 Occupant Fatality Rates by Vehicle Type

	Fatality Rate	Motorcycles	Passenger Cars	Light Trucks
2012	Per 100,000 Registered Vehicles	58.63	9.66	7.92
	Per 100 Million Vehicle Miles Traveled	23.27	0.89	0.73

Source: National Highway Traffic Safety Administration and U.S. Department of Transportation. 2012 Data: Motorcycles.

traffic crash. Exhibit 6 gives related fatality data. Harley's primary market segment of motorcycles has engine displacements of 601+cc. This size vehicle falls into the category (501cc–1,000cc) that accounts for the highest number of motorcycle-related fatalities—1,756 fatalities, or 38 percent—in 2012.

The Harley Sound

The distinctive sound of a Harley-Davidson engine has been thrilling riders for decades. In the past, Harley-Davidson tried to patent the sound of its motorcycles, but after years of litigation, it withdrew its claim. The changing demographics of the company's customer base creates challenges as well as opportunities. To stay in-sync with the demands of the younger generation, Harley-Davidson initiated project "Live Wire" to design and manufacture electric motorcycles. The new design doesn't incorporate the famous Harley roaring engine sound; instead, it uses a futuristic jet-like engine sound. Noise regulations internationally as well as in the United States create a regulatory risk to Harley, as the company will work on preserving the trademark sound. Some analysts say the noise comprises noise pollution.

Electric Motorcycles

Polaris Industries declared victory in August 2015. That month, Polaris introduced its all-new, all-electric bike, named the Empulse TT, arguably the first battery-powered vehicle from a high-volume motorcycle manufacturer. The new bike costs $20,000 and can go about 110 miles per hour and travel from 60 to 80 miles before the battery is drained, depending on how aggressively it is driven and the size of the rider. Fully recharging the bike takes about 4 hours on a 240-volt outlet, or almost 9 hours on a standard 120-volt plug.

Sales of electric motorcycles are small, but the market is expected to grow tenfold by 2018. Harley's competitor, BMW, already sells a high-end electric motorcycle, and specialty manufacturers, such as Brammo (which was acquired by Polaris Industries in January 2015) and Zero, are also already in the market. Harley-Davidson is entering the emerging electric bike market in a way that will maintain or build on the distinct sound and feel of a Harley. The company in 2015 is seeing an extraordinary level of interest and positive feedback for a bike that's not even on the market. Project LiveWire is Harley-Davidson's first electric motorcycle. In 2014, the company gave more than 6,800 demo rides in the United States, with the vast majority of riders saying that it far exceeded their expectations. The demo tour is moving across Europe, Canada, and Asia-Pacific in 2015.

Competitors

Harley's primary rivals include privately held companies such as Triumph Motorcycles Limited, Ultra Motorcycle Company, and Viper Motorcycle Company. But in addition, major foreign-based rivals include Honda and Suzuki. Another major rival is Polaris Industries, although that company also sells snowmobiles and four-wheel vehicles. Exhibit 7 provides a comparison of Harley with Polaris and Honda. Note that Harley has the highest revenue per employee, which is attractive for the company.

EXHIBIT 7 A Financial Comparison of Harley-Davidson versus Rivals

	Harley-Davidson	Polaris	Honda
# Employees	6,500	7,000	204,730
$ Net Income	845 M	454 M	4,679
$ Revenue	6,228 M	4,479 M	111,137 M
$ Revenue/Employee	958,000	640,000	543,000
$ EPS Ratio	3.73	6.83	2.45
Market Cap.	12,280 M	9,880 M	61,190 M

Source: Based on company documents and a variety of other sources.

Polaris Industries (PII)

Headquartered in Minneapolis, Minnesota, Polaris Industries manufactures motorcycles, snowmobiles, and ATVs (all-terrain vehicles). Polaris motorcycles, including its Victory brand of touring and cruiser bikes, look very similar to many Harley models. Polaris Industries acquired the famous Indian Motorcycle—America's oldest bike brand—in 2011. The Indian Motorcycle is considered an iconic brand on par with Harley's brand to many motorcycle enthusiasts. The Indian Motorcycle line competes directly with Harley.

Innovation is the key to Harley and Polaris. In order for it to compete, both companies must continually update its existing product base and develop new innovative products that will attract key customer groups. Polaris's position is different from Harley-Davidson's because Polaris produces a wider variety of products other than motorcycles. On the other hand, Harley has been focused on motorcycles since its inception and is innovating its offering in that market, including electric bikes.

Polaris has been growing its business through acquisitions, alliances, and new joint ventures. For example, Polaris Industries acquired the electric motorcycle business of Brammo Inc. on January 15, 2015, which will directly compete against a Harley electric bike offering.

Honda Motor Company Ltd. (HMC)

Headquartered in Tokyo, Japan, Honda sells motorcycles as well as cars, outboard motors, generators, and various other power equipment products. For Honda's third quarter of 2015 that ended December 31, 2014, revenues in the company's motorcycle segment increased 15.8 percent to ¥463.4 billion ($3.8 billion). For that quarter, Honda's motorcycle unit sales rose 4 percent to 2.8 million motorcycles. Operating income of the motorcycle segment increased 55.2 percent to ¥53.5 billion ($444 million) on increased sales volume and model mix.

Suzuki Motor Company (SZKMY)

Headquartered in Hamamatsu, Japan, Suzuki manufactures and markets motorcycles, automobiles, outboard motors, wheelchairs, and all-terrain vehicles. Suzuki has over 57,000 employees.

Future

In early 2015, Harley-Davidson said it expects its full year company shipments to increase 4 to 6 percent to 282,000–287,000 motorcycles worldwide, and projects its operating margin for all of 2015 from the Motorcycle segment to be 18 to 19 percent. However, analysts are concerned about Harley's aging customer base, as well as its expensive products, and competition is growing more intense. Matt Levatich became Harley's President and CEO in early 2015 and needs a clear strategic plan for the company. Help Mr. Levatich with this endeavor.

Apple Inc., 2015

www.apple.com, AAPL

Apple is the world's largest corporation based on a market capitalization of about $650 billion, approximately $200 billon more than Exxon, the world's second-largest company. Apple designs, manufactures, and markets the world's single-most popular smartphone, the iPhone, even though Apple has only about 15 percent of the global market share in smartphones. Apple also produces the iPad, iPod, iCloud, Mac computers, and other accessory devices. Headquartered in Cupertino, California, Apple owns iTunes, the popular app and store where customers can download music.

New for Apple with the release of the iPhone 6 and 6 Plus is Apple Pay, where customers can pay at retail stores by scanning their phone. Apple currently operates 450 Apple stores and employs 98,000. Apple's iPhone 6 and 6+ offer larger screens to better compete with Samsung. Initial sales of the iPhone 6 and 6+ broke records, with the higher margin 6+ doing best of all. Apple's new gold smartwatch released in spring 2015 sells for $4,000 to $5,000. The aluminum model is priced at $349, and the stainless steel model at $500.

On July 21, 2015, Apple announced financial results for its fiscal 2015 third quarter that ended June 27, 2015. Specifically, the company reported quarterly revenue of $49.6 billion and quarterly net profit of $10.7 billion, compared to revenue of $37.4 billion and net profit of $7.7 billion the prior year-ago quarter. International sales accounted for 64 percent of the quarter's revenue. In that third quarter Apple's year-over-year growth rate accelerated from the first half of fiscal 2015, with revenue up 33 percent and earnings per share up 45 percent. The growth was fueled by record third quarter sales of iPhone and Mac, all-time record revenue from services, and the successful launch of Apple Watch. The company's quarterly iPhone revenue was up 59 percent over last year. Apple Music was released in July 2015 and the company plans to release iOS 9, OS X El Capitan and watchOS 2 to customers in Fall 2015.

History

Founded in 1976 by Steve Jobs and Steve Wozniak, Apple began as a personal computer company providing desktop computers for businesses and the home. The first computer, the Apple 1, was hand built by Wozniak and did not come with a keyboard or an outer case to protect the computer. The products were considered a kit, and users had to supply extra parts themselves. The Apple 1 sold for the interesting price of $666.66, or around $2,800 adjusted for inflation. Apple was incorporated in 1977 after Wozniak sold his share for $800. The Apple II was first sold in 1977 and had the first major piece of business software, VisiCalc, a spreadsheet product.

Apple went public in 1980 for $22 a share and generated more money on its IPO than any firm since Ford Motor Company 25 years earlier. Following a dispute with the Board, Steve Jobs resigned from Apple in 1985 and started a new firm. With Jobs unaffiliated with Apple for the next 15 years, Apple experimented with various other products, including CD players, digital cameras, speakers, and others. Throughout the 1990s, Apple experimented with several different product lines of personal computers, with limited success. Apple's products were generally significantly more expensive than that of competitors, not compatible with much of the leading software or with the more popular Windows machines, and also were not able to multitask as well as Windows-based machines.

By 1996, Apple was struggling immensely and the firm acquired Steve Jobs' firm, NeXT. After the Board fired the existing CEO in 1997, Jobs was back, acting as interim CEO of Apple. In the same year, Jobs identified Jonathan Ive, and the two started working to rebuild Apple's products and brand name. Ive is currently the Senior VP of Design. After several Mac upgrades and new software products such as iMovie, in 2001, Apple introduced the iPod and the firm sold 100 million units in 6 years. The year 2003 brought about the iTunes store, which synced $0.99 downloads to iPods and remains an industry leader. Apple launched the iPhone in 2008 and the iPad in 2010. In 2011, Steve Jobs passed away and current CEO Tim Cook now leads Apple.

Internal Issues

Vision/Mission

Neither at its corporate website nor in its *Form 10K* does Apple provide a written vision or mission statement labeled as such. There are statements such as the following, however, that perhaps serve as Apple's vision and/or mission:

1. "We strive to provide users of Apple products the best experience possible though innovative product designs and software."
2. "Apple designs Macs, the best personal computers in the world, along with OS X, iLife, iWork and professional software. Apple leads the digital music revolution with its iPods and iTunes online store. Apple has reinvented the mobile phone with its revolutionary iPhone and App Store, and is defining the future of mobile media and computing devices with iPad."

Organizational Structure

As indicated in Exhibit 1, Apple appears to operate from a divisional-by-process design, but absent of any presidents of divisions. However, Apple does report revenues by both region and product. Some analysts suggest that titles of Apple's executives more closely mirror how the firm reports sales, and many expect to see a COO with divisional presidents reporting to that position.

Strategy

Apple was late in producing a larger screen smartphone, but did so with the launch of the iPhone 6 and 6+ in October 2014. Apple prides itself on simplicity. Apple products are generally more user friendly than those of Windows, Android, and other operating systems, but at the sacrifice of the user being able to customize or tailor the device for their specific needs. Apple's overriding strategy always has been to produce elegant, easy-to-use products, often at a premium price point. In a November 2014 interview, CEO Cook reiterated this when asked if having just 15 percent of the global smartphone market share is a concern, by responding, "Not all market share is equal, and Apple has never been about the most; we are about being the best."

Apple also has a culture of not collecting every detail about its users. For example, Apple does not read or store iMessages or FaceTime. Even if a government were to ask for these data, Apple could not provide it, for the company simply does not keep it on file. The latest version of iOS 8 is more encrypted than ever. CEO Cook compares Apple to designing to an electronic Fort Knox.

With the release of the new iPhone 6 line, Apple introduced Apple Pay, a mobile app that enables Apple customers to use their existing Master Card, Visa, or American Express card to make mobile payments at retail stores. Apple Pay's fingerprint technology is more convenient for consumers and also more secure for credit card companies such as Visa, American Express, and MasterCard. However, competitors such as Samsung currently have a similar technology on some of their phones, and all phones will likely have a similar technology moving forward. Using Apple Pay, merchants are charged the same fee as normally charged by a credit card company, which is an average of 2 percent in the United States. Transactions in the United States annually produce more credit card fees than everywhere else in the world combined, leaving open the door for Apple to possibly transition away from credit card companies in the future. Apple could offer its own in-house credit system at much lower cost to merchants, in essence becoming a financial institution.

Keeping in line with its user-friendly products strategy, Apple must approve all third-party digital content through the iTunes Store or the App Store and iBooks store. Competitors, such as Android-based phones, tend to have less control over apps offered to their customers than does Apple. Apple prides itself on well-trained and knowledgeable salespersons with excellent customer service. Apple invests heavily in R&D, over $6 billion in 2014 alone, up nearly 100 percent from 2012. In addition, Apple is expanding its retail stores around the world.

During 2014, Apple acquired several firms, including Beats Music and Beats headphones. Apple obtained a subscription streaming music service and a headphone firm in the process. Apple's acquisitions in 2014, however, increased the firm's goodwill from $1.5 to $4.6 billion.

To keep costs low, almost all Apple hardware products are manufactured in Asia and many of these are manufactured at a single location, except for a few Macs that are manufactured in

EXHIBIT 1 Apple's Organizational Structure

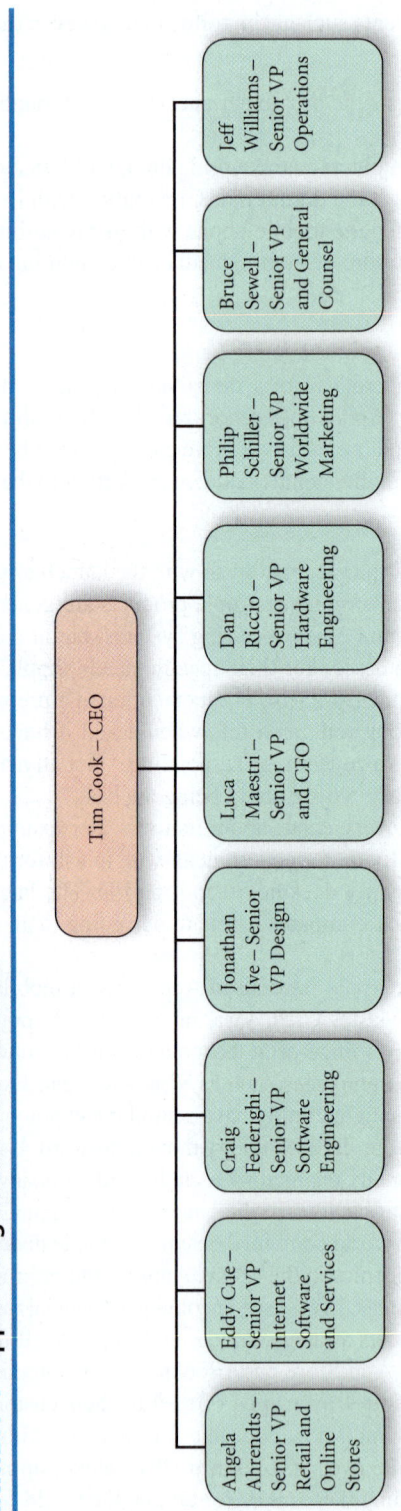

Source: Based on company documents.

EXHIBIT 2 **Apple Revenues by Region (in millions of USD)**

Revenues	2014	2013	2012
Americas	$65,232	$62,739	$57,512
Europe	40,929	37,883	36,323
China	29,846	25,417	22,533
Japan	14,982	13,462	10,571
Rest of Asia Pacific	10,344	11,181	10,741
Retail	21,462	20,228	18,828
Net Sales	182,795	170,910	156,508

Source: Based on Apple's 2014 *Annual Report*, p. 27.

the United States. While able to better maintain quality control, this does put Apple at risk over strikes, poor management, or other disruptive activities at a single location facility. To counter this problem, Apple tends to stock enough supply to cover its demand for up to 150 days, but during a new issue of an iPhone, for example, there can be supply shortages, where customers must wait weeks or even months to receive their products.

Apple has sued Samsung twice in the last couple of years for patent infringements in the hypercompetitive smartphone industry. Apple was awarded $120 million of a $2.2 billion claim for Samsung violating three patenting infringements. However, Apple was unable to prove that Samsung's action caused significant damage to its product line. To date, Samsung has been ordered to pay Apple over $1 billion in damages, and both cases have been appealed, and Apple has yet to receive any compensation. More important for Apple than the $1 billion was the desire for the legal actions to impair Samsung from being able to sell certain products. To date, this outcome does not appear likely for Apple.

Segment Data

Exhibit 2 reveals that Apple's sales increased 7 percent in 2014, following a 9 percent increase the prior year. Fiscal 2014 sales were boosted by strong iPhone 5s and 5c sales, and also account for initial sales of the iPhone 6 and iPhone 6+, released in October 2014 in the United States, one month before Apple's fiscal year ended. However, some preorder sales of iPhone 6 and 6+ are included in Apple's 2014 fiscal year. With the iPhone 6 and 6+ also comes Apple Pay, which allows customers to pay by scanning their phones at selected retail stores. As of late 2014, 83 percent of all credit card transactions in the United States were compatible with Apple Pay, with banks not offering compatible products quickly but rather coming to agreement with Apple. The company reported sales increases in all regions in fiscal 2014, except in the Rest of Asia Pacific region, which experienced a small decline. The largest percent growth came from China and Japan.

Apple's iPhone accounted for 55 percent of total 2014 revenues, up 11 percent from fiscal 2011, as indicated in Exhibit 3. Apple's iPad sales have been steady but have not increased since 2012. Apple's new iPad Air 2 hopes to reverse this trend. However, with the larger iPhone displays with the 6 and 6+ products, many customers may opt only for having one device. In a bit of a surprise for analysts, Apple's Mac sales were up 12 percent in fiscal 2014, from stronger than expected back-to-school sales on Macs. The back-to-school sales were strong enough to boost Mac revenues to $6.6 billion in Q4 of fiscal 2014, more than iPad's revenue of $5.3 billion. Mac now owns over 6 percent of the global PC market, its largest market share since 1995. Mac has gained market share on windows machines in 33 of the last 34 quarters.

iTunes, Software, and Services also continues to grow, up 12 percent from fiscal 2013. This segment includes the Apple Store, iCloud, iLife, iWork, AppleCare, and apps that many users pay to download and use on their iPhones and iPads. Apple's iPod, once the bellwether for the firm before the release of the iPhone, has been in constant decline, with sales down 61 percent from 2012 to 2014. In summer 2014, Apple discontinued making its classic iPod 160gb device on claims they could no longer get the parts. Apple's accessories segment includes headphones, Apple TV, cases, and Apple Watch. Apple Watch will be compatible only with iPhone 5 and newer products running iOS 8.0 or newer.

EXHIBIT 3 Apple Revenues by Product (in millions of USD)

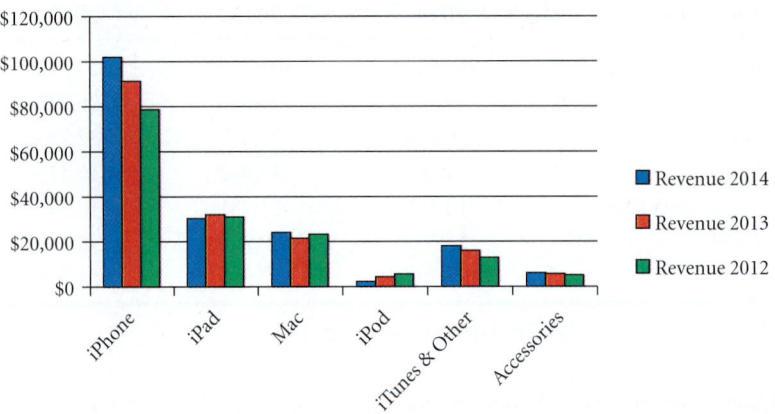

Source: Based on Apple's 2014 *Annual Report*, p. 27.

Finance

For years Apple had no long-term debt on its balance sheet. But in 2013, the firm, for the first time since 1994, used debt to finance operations, and reported $17 billion in long-term debt, and then reported $29 billion in long-term-debt in fiscal 2014, with varying maturity dates out as far as 2044. Apple is aggressively looking at financing further by debt and also for the first time with bonds backed in Euros as well. The firm reported in April 2014 that a $90 billion stock repurchase had been authorized and also raised the dividend to $0.47 per share for a 30 percent increase. Assuming $100 average stock price on the repurchases, Apple will need to purchase 900 million shares back, or around 15 percent of current shares outstanding.

Apple's current income statement and balance sheet are provided in Exhibits 4 and 5, respectively. Much of the cash on Apple's balance sheet is kept in foreign banks. In this way, Apple avoids paying U.S. corporate taxes on those earnings.

EXHIBIT 4 Income Statement (in millions of USD)

Report Date	September 27, 2014	September 28, 2013
Revenues	$182,795	$170,910
Cost of revenue	112,258	106,606
Gross profit	70,537	64,304
Operating expenses	18,034	15,305
EBIT	52,503	48,999
Interest additions	980	1,156
EBT	53,483	50,155
Tax	13,973	13,118
Net income	**39,510**	**37,037**

Source: Based on company documents.

Competitors

Apple competes in a highly competitive and rapidly changing industry that is often associated with strong customer loyalty. Apple and rival firms typically roll out new smartphones, computers, and tablets annually. Many of Apple's rivals have prices 50 to 70 percent lower on comparable products. However, in the tablet and phone market, top rival Samsung prices its top products in line with Apple prices. Competition for Apple should only increase in the future as rival firms are better able to duplicate Apple's products or even better able to persuade customers their products are just as good but significantly cheaper in price. Top competitors for Apple are Samsung and Lenovo in the smartphone, tablet, and PC markets. However, Apple faces significant competition from various other PC providers such as Dell, Sony, and Toshiba.

EXHIBIT 5 **Balance Sheet (in millions of USD)**

Report Date	September 27, 2014	September 28, 2013
Cash	$13,844	$14,259
Short-term securities	11,233	26,287
Accounts receivable	17,460	13,102
Inventories	2,111	1,764
Other current assets	23,883	17,874
Total current assets	68,531	73,286
Long-term marketable securities	130,162	106,215
Property, plant & equipment	20,624	16,597
Goodwill	4,616	1,577
Intangible assets	4,142	4,179
Other assets	3,764	5,146
Total assets	**231,839**	**207,000**
Accounts payable	30,196	22,367
Other current liabilities	33,252	21,291
Total current liabilities	63,448	43,658
Long-term debt	28,987	16,960
Deferred income taxes	20,259	16,489
Deferred revenue	3,031	2,625
Other liabilities	4,567	3,719
Total liabilities	**120,292**	**83,451**
Common stock	23,313	19,764
Retained earnings	87,152	104,256
Treasury stock	—	—
Paid in capital and other	1,082	(471)
Total equity	**111,547**	**123,549**
Total liabilities & equity	**231,839**	**207,000**

Source: Based on company documents.

EXHIBIT 6 **2014 Percent Market Share of Key Global Players**

	Apple	Android	Windows
Smart Phones	14%	81%	3%
Tablets	45%	51%	4%
Watches	0%	67%	0%

Source: Based on company documents and a variety of other sources.

Exhibit 6 provides a comparative analysis of Apple with some of its rival firms in terms of market share. Note that Apple products trail Android products substantially in market share. Apple projects to take a 35 percent market share in watches in 2015, reducing Android's share to 42 percent. In 2014, the total watch market was less than 10 million, but is expected to expand to 35 million units by year-end 2015. Exhibit 7 provides additional comparative competitive information for Apple and rival firms.

Samsung

Founded in 1938 in South Korea, Samsung specializes in semiconductors and electronic appliances. The firm did not enter the mobile communications arena until the late 1990s, but by

EXHIBIT 7 Apple versus Rival Firms

	Apple	Samsung	Lenovo
# Employees	92,000	96,900	54,000
$ Net Income	39.5 B	27.7 B	817 M
$ Revenue	182.8 B	208 B	38,707 M
$ Revenue/Employee	2 M	2 M	716,796
$ EPS Ratio	7.39	180	7.88
Market Cap.	692.7 B	—	—

Source: Based on company documents and a variety of other sources.

2010 it was producing half of its mobile phones in China. Samsung has five R&D centers in China. Samsung was 2 years behind first-mover Apple into the smartphone market with its launch in 2009 using the Bada operating system. In 2010, Samsung provided an Android-powered smartphone. In 2013, Samsung smartphones were 21 percent of the global smartphone market, making Samsung the industry leader. In addition to smartphones, Samsung also today produces tablets, televisions, Blu-rays, DVD players, cameras, refrigerators, air conditioners, washing machines, ovens, PC notebooks, printers, storage devices, and more. In addition, Samsung is engaged in providing select medical equipment such as X-rays, ultrasound, and other items.

In popular products, Samsung competes with Apple directly on the Samsung Galaxy and Note smartphones, Galaxy Tablet, TVs, watches, and laptop computers. Samsung reported revenues of over $208 billion in 2013.

Lenovo

Founded in 1984 in Beijing and headquartered in both Beijing and New York City, Lenovo acquired IBM's ThinkPad laptops and more recently IBM's lower-end servers. Lenovo did not enter the smartphone market until 2010, but its LePhone is popular in China and increasing its market share in the entry-level market space. Lenovo is also rapidly introducing the LePhone in Russia, India, Indonesia, and other neighboring Asian nations that also have developing economies. Lenovo competes with Apple primarily on PCs, since the firm has positioned itself in a lower demographic market for its smartphones.

Lenovo's 2014 revenues are expected to be in excess of $37 billion—the same as in 2013. With Lenovo's $2.9 billion acquisition of Motorola in 2014, the firm is now the world's third-largest smartphone maker, behind Samsung and Apple. Lenovo trades on the Hong Kong Stock Exchange and currently employs 54,000 people worldwide.

External Issues

In 2014, there were 234 million smartphone Internet connections in the United States. The growth rate was approximately 35 percent from 2009 to 2014, with a forecast of 313 million connections by 2019.

China

Most of the world's smartphones are manufactured in China, and the Chinese smartphone market itself increased nearly 55 percent from 2010 to 2014. Less than 1.5 million units were produced in 2003, increasing to over 500 million units in 2015. The top four smartphone manufacturers in China are Samsung, Lenovo, Apple, and HTC, accounting for over half of the total industry revenue in 2014. There is a growing fragmentation in the market as new entrants enter and now comprise 50+ percent overall market. Smartphone industry revenue will increase about 20 percent annually to around $180 billion by 2020, with over 1.5 billion units produced annually. Worldwide mobile phone shipments (all phones included) were just under 2 billion in 2014 with about 70 percent of shipped phones considered smartphones. By 2018, however, 2.2 billion mobile phones will be shipped and all but 400 million are projected to be smartphones.

Computer Manufacturing and Tablets

Computer manufacturing is a $14 billion industry in the United States alone, but sales fell over 17 percent per year between 2009 and 2014. About 62 percent of all computers manufactured in the United States are laptops, but this still leaves 38 percent of the computers manufactured being desktops. Overall projections are 5 percent declines moving forward through 2020. Tablets are projected to further make inroads into personal computers in U.S. manufacturing. However, it is important to note that at least for Apple's Q4 of 2014, Mac sales exceeded iPad sales.

Most tablets are manufactured in China, with Apple holding 27 percent of the market share, followed by Samsung and Lenovo with 12 and 8 percent, respectively, on tablets made in China. The largest players in the U.S. computer manufacturing business, which also includes servers, are HP, Dell, and IBM, with 25, 19, and 18 percent market shares, respectively. Two relative new areas that may help boost laptop sales are the new ultrabooks, extra thin laptops with no battery sacrifice, and laptops with touch glass where the user can touch the screen much like on a smartphone or tablet. Worldwide PC sales are expected to be $190 billion in 2015, tapering down to $160 billion by 2018. In 2014, PC shipments alone accounted for 56 percent of the device (PC and Tablets) shipments, but this number is expected to be reduced to 45 percent by 2018, as tablets make further inroads on PCs. (Tablets are expected to grow 9 percent a year through 2018.) Currently, Android-based phones account for just over 60 percent of smartphone operating systems, with iOS picking up much of the balance. Through 2018, the outlook is projected to remain the same.

Operating Systems

Operating systems are another large market in the United States with 2013 revenues of $45 billion expected to grow to $57 billion by 2019. Major firms by market share include Microsoft and Apple, with 62 and 20 percent of the total market. Microsoft's prominent product continues to be Windows, while Apple is the owner of iOS.

Geographic Outlook

Most smartphone markets in developed countries are expected to see growth rates subside moving forward. However, with the current culture of customers being trained to update their phones at least every 2 years, the long-term outlook for smartphone providers looks promising. The real exponential growth, though, moving forward should come from developing markets such as Brazil, India, and China. Tablet sales in the United States are projected to increase from $55 billion in 2014 to 63 billion in 2018, or a 15 percent total increase. In the Asia Pacific (not including Japan) region, tablet sales are expected to increase from $65 to $93 billion over the same time frame, or 43 percent. Sales for smartphones are expected to show similar results with respect to the major growth being in China, India, and Brazil.

During its first month in operation (July 2015), Apple Music obtained 11 million trial members, giving the App store a record-breaking month. The streaming service costs users $9.99 per month with the first 3 months free. But 2 million of those subscribers opted for the more expensive family plan costing $14.99 per month. Despite some bugs and glitches in the service, which Apple is scrambling to fix, Apple Music is a popular hit so far. If all the trial users convert to paying monthly customers, Apple will surpass most competitors. For example, 10-year-old Spotify only has 20 million paying customers, but boasts 75 million active users, Pandora has 3.3 million paid subscribers from its 79 million active user base, and Deezer has 6 million paid subscribers out of its 16 million active users. During July 2015, Apple's App store did a record-breaking $1.7 billion in transactions. Interestingly, 23 percent of the digital music market is made up of paid subscribers, who generated a collective $1.6 billion in calendar year 2014.

Future

Apple announced record financial results for 2015 fiscal first quarter that ended in December 2014. Total revenues and profits were $74.6 and $18 billion, respectively, up from $57.6 and $13.1 billion in first quarter 2014. In addition, international sales accounted for 65 percent of total revenue as the iPhone is now the most popular phone in China. International sales would have been significantly higher if not for a significant rally in the U.S. dollar against other foreign currencies over much of 2014.

Apple began shipping its Apple watch in April 2015. iPhone and Mac revenues were $51 and $7 billion, respectively, for the first quarter 2015, up 57 and 9 percent from first quarter 2014. However, iPad sales were down 22 percent over the same time frame due to people not updating their tablets as frequently, less demand than for phones, and also the new iPhone 6+ has cannibalized iPad sales.

Develop a 3-year strategic plan for CEO Tim Cook that will enable Apple to continue to compete with rivals Samsung and Lenovo. Use the template at the www.strategyclub.com website to prepare matrices and analyses. Impress Mr. Cook with your work because, according to *Financial Times,* CEO Cook was the business "Person of the Year" for 2014. In 2015, at Apple's shareholder meeting, when someone questioned the profitability of Apple's environmental initiatives, Mr. Cook responded: "We do things for other reasons than a profit motive, we do things because they are right and just. If that's a hard line for you…then you should get out of the stock."

International Business Machines (IBM) Corporation, 2015

www.ibm.com, IBM

Headquartered in Armonk, New York, IBM has over 430,000 employees worldwide that provide information technology (IT) products and services. IBM manufactures and markets computer hardware and software, and offers infrastructure, hosting, and consulting services in areas ranging from business analytics and mainframe computers to nanotechnology. IBM has more than a dozen research laboratories worldwide. For 22 consecutive years, IBM has held the record for most patents generated by a company. IBM sold its personal computer (PC) and low-end (x86) server businesses to Lenovo in 2005 and 2014 for $1.25 billion and $2.3 billion, respectively.

Disappointing Wall Street has become the trend for IBM, whose stock was the worst performer among the 30 in the Dow Jones industrial average in both 2014 and 2013—an ominous, dubious distinction for a company historically known as Big Blue. In October 2014, after 10 quarters of flat or declining sales, IBM's CEO Virginia Rometty said, "Our results this quarter are disappointing; we've got to reinvent ourselves."

In 2015, IBM paid $1.5 billion to Globalfoundries in order to divest its costly chip division. It is very unusual for any firm (in this case IBM) to pay another firm to acquire a division of your own firm. IBM is making payments to the chipmaker over three years. In the deal, privately held Globalfoundries obtained IBM's global commercial semiconductor technology business, including intellectual property and technologies related to IBM Microelectronics. Also, Globalfoundries obtained IBM's semiconductor manufacturing operations and plants in East Fishkill, New York, and in Essex Junction, Vermont, as well as access to thousands of patents and IBM's commercial microelectronics business. Globalfoundries is now IBM's exclusive server processor semiconductor technology provider for 22 nanometer (nm), 14nm, and 10nm semiconductors for the next 10 years.

In August 2015, IBM acquired Merge Healthcare, which provides medical images and clinical systems, in a $1 billion deal in order to combine that company with its Watson Health analytics unit. IBM plans to combine data and images from Merge Healthcare's medical imaging management platform with Watson's cloud-based computing platform that analyzes high volumes of data, understands complex questions posed in natural language, and proposes evidence-based answers.

A huge partner with Apple, IBM in July 2015 launched a new service that will help other corporations make the same leap from Windows to the MacBook and iPad that it has done over the last several years. The new service takes the lessons IBM just learned by installing more than 110,000 Apple devices, including iPads, MacBooks, and iPhones, across its own company, helping corporate clients make the same kind of wide-reaching tech turnover.

In June 2015, IBM acquired Compose, a database-as-a-service startup established in Birmingham, Alabama. Compose provides database services for companies so their engineers can focus on mobile and web development. Now headquartered in San Mateo, California, Compose serves about 3,600 clients and recently rebranded from MongoHQ.

Copyright by Fred David Books LLC. www.strategyclub.com (Written by Forest R. David)

History

IBM began business in the 1800s with the Tabulating Machine Company, the International Time Recording Company, and the Computing Scale Company of America, all independently operating separately as distinct corporations. In 1911, the merger of these firms was completed, creating the Computing-Tabulating-Recording Company; the name was changed to International Business Machines (IBM) in 1924. IBM has worked diligently in the last decade to shift resources and strategy away from manufacturing into service industries. For example, IBM acquired SPSS and Cognos (data analytics software) in 2009 for $1.2 billion. IBM plans to keep its high-end server business, which is less prone to commoditization by other firms' products.

In 2013, IBM acquired SoftLayer Technologies, a web hosting service, for about $2 billion. A year later, IBM initiated a partnership with Apple Inc. in enterprise mobility and also acquired the business operations of Lighthouse Security Group, LLC, a premier cloud security services provider. Financial terms were not disclosed. IBM executives accepted no bonuses in 2014 for fiscal year 2013, because the firm reported a 5 percent drop in sales and a 1 percent decline in net profit for 2013. Today, IBM is investing more than $1.2 billion, expanding its data centers and cloud-storage business and building 15 new centers, bringing the total to 40 in 2014.

The company is heavily involved in providing business consulting and business analytics services. It is investing $3 billion between 2014 and 2019 to create computer functionality to resemble how the human brain thinks. IBM says its goal is to design a neural chip that mimics the human brain, with 10 billion neurons and 100 trillion synapses, but that uses just 1 kilowatt of power.

In late 2014, IBM signed an extensive cooperative agreement with Twitter Inc. to gain access to all tweets posted now and previously to 2006, so the 10,000+ IBM consultants can help solve client problems using IBM's business analytics software. Both Twitter and IBM, as part of the agreement, are now developing data offerings for specific industries, such a banking, retail, travel, and transportation. IBM's CEO Rometty personally negotiated with Twitters' CEO Costolo to forge the partnership.

Also in late 2014, IBM introduced a new email service called IBM Verse to complement its IBM Notes software suite. With Verse, IBM hopes to address common complaints that customers have with gmail, Yahoo! email, and AOL email services, such as filter problems, spam, and weak tracking features. In early 2015, IBM announced a new product called the z13, a machine about the size of an extra-large refrigerator that reportedly is the most sophisticated computer ever built. IBM says the z13 can complete 2.5 billion transactions a day, and analysts say the product will generate $2.3 billion in revenue in 2015. Mainframe computers such as the z13 generate about 20 percent of IBM's revenues.

For the second quarter of 2015 that ended June 30, IBM's revenues fell 13 percent year-over-year to $20.8 billion, and company earnings also declined 13 percent from the year-ago period. Part of the decline was the result of IBM selling its System X server business to China's Lenovo. For Q2, IBM's sales fell 8 percent in the Americas region, but only 2 percent when backing out currency and System X effects. In IBM's Asia-Pacific segment, revenues declined 19 percent, and in the Europe/Middle East/Africa segment, revenues dropped 17 percent. In the BRIC bloc of Brazil, Russia, India, and China, IBM's revenues declined 35 percent. Even after backing out the System X and currency valuation events, IBM's organic sales to the BRIC markets fell 18 percent year-over-year.

Also in Q2, IBM's business and technology services segment revenues declined 11 percent year-over-year, while the company's software sales decreased 10 percent. The company's hardware segment revenues declined 32 percent and now comprises only 9.6 percent of Big Blue's revenues, as the company has almost totally transitioned away from hardware. On a positive note for Q2, IBM's "strategic imperatives" increased sales significantly. Specifically, the firm's cloud computing revenues rose more than 70 percent, backing out the currency and System X sale again. Similarly, business analytics revenues at IBM grew more than 20 percent, mobile services sales quadrupled, and the company's social revenues jumped 30 percent.

Values, Vision, Mission

In 2003, IBM executives and over 300,000 employees convened for the first time in 100 years to reestablish and reanalyze the company's core values and existing mission statement. Core values, according to top management at IBM, are more than ethics and legal compliance. From that 2003, 72-hour discussion, IBM decided on these three core values that all IBM employees globally are expected to live every day. Although vague, the values are:

1. Dedication to every client's success
2. Innovation that matters for our company and the world
3. Trust and personal responsibility in all relationships

At the 2003 meeting, IBM abandoned its existing more formal mission statement. As of 2015, there is still no formal mission or vision statement provided on any literature published on IBM's website. Lacking written vision and mission statements to guide strategy and direction, it is unclear whether IBM has the necessary foundation to make clear strategy decisions moving forward.

IBM is exemplary regarding workplace equality. It is no accident that IBM's CEO is a woman, Virginia Rometty. IBM provides same-sex partners of its employees with health benefits and provides an anti-discrimination clause. The Human Rights Campaign for 10 consecutive years has rated IBM 100 percent on its index of gay-friendliness. In recent years, IBM UK has ranked first in Stonewall's annual Workplace Equality Index for United Kingdom (UK) employers.

Internal Issues

Organizational Structure
Many analysts do not consider IBM's organizational structure to be exemplary. There is no chief operating officer or chief administrative office, the divisions are named in somewhat obscure ways, and the CEO is also the chairperson and president. No actual chart could be obtained, but a depiction of IBM's probable structure is given in Exhibit 1.

Strategy
Over 60 percent of IBM employees in R&D are working in fields such as "big data," cloud computing, and other key growth initiatives. This is a drastic change from 20 years ago when over 70 percent of R&D workers were focused on materials and hardware. The new IBM wants to "own the cloud," but ironically and unfortunately for IBM, the cloud will kill profit margins on mainframes, and those profit margins are still the mainstay at IBM. Michael Holland, the principal money manager of Holland & Company in New York City, says, "I am as negative on IBM as I could be. I was a long-term shareholder, and now I'm out of the stock."

IBM's 2013 *Annual Report* revealed three key "strategic imperatives" moving forward. The first of three key initiatives is to focus on the area of big data, which IBM estimates will be a $187 billion industry by year-end 2015. IBM has invested over $24 billion to date, made 30 acquisitions, and has 15,000 consultants and 400 mathematicians in this area. About two thirds of all IBM's R&D is devoted to big data. With 6,000 partners and 1,000 university partnerships, IBM is committed to evolving into a big data company.

The launch of IBM Watson Group in January 2014 promises to grow IBM revenues. Watson helps clients understand big data in a natural language, helping nontechnical people understand complex information more easily. Watson is working on recommending tailored treatments for cancer patients by scanning medical journals and patients' own DNA. Watson is a vast collection of artificial intelligence and machine-learning algorithms, sometimes called "cognitive computing." IBM has had some success with Watson-based technologies in areas such as education and health care. In 2015, IBM formed a strategic alliance with Japan's SoftBank, extending Watson's reach into that country. Until now, Watson has been operating on an English-only corpus.

IBM's second key initiative focuses on cloud computing, which IBM estimates will be a $250 billion industry by year-end 2015. Roughly 80 percent of all Fortune 500 companies today use IBM's cloud services and IBM remains a leader in this area. IBM recently acquired SoftLayer along with 14 other cloud-based firms for a total of $7 billion. Much of IBM's R&D expenses not devoted to big data are focused on the firm's cloud-computing initiative.

The third key in IBM's initiative, dubbed "systems of engagement," centers on technological social interaction products and services. IBM expects firms to double its expenses in this area by 2016. IBM's purchase of Skype and Facebook's purchase of WhatsApp are two examples of companies trying to profit off the social media revolution.

Recently, IBM announced an alliance with Apple to work in tandem to create business apps for mobile devices for IBM's corporate customers. Reeling from 8 consecutive year-over-year revenue declines, IBM is betting on Apple's popularity and simplicity to help please the IBM customer base. Roughly one third of iPad sales in 2013 were to governments or corporations. Many corporate employees use their personal Apple products at work. The new Apple IBM alliance is expected to put increasing pressure on Google and its Android platform to develop corporate partners. It remains to be seen how the difference in culture between IBM and Apple will affect the alliance. Traditionally, IBM has focused on businesses while Apple has focused on upscale personal consumers.

EXHIBIT 1 IBM's Organizational Structure

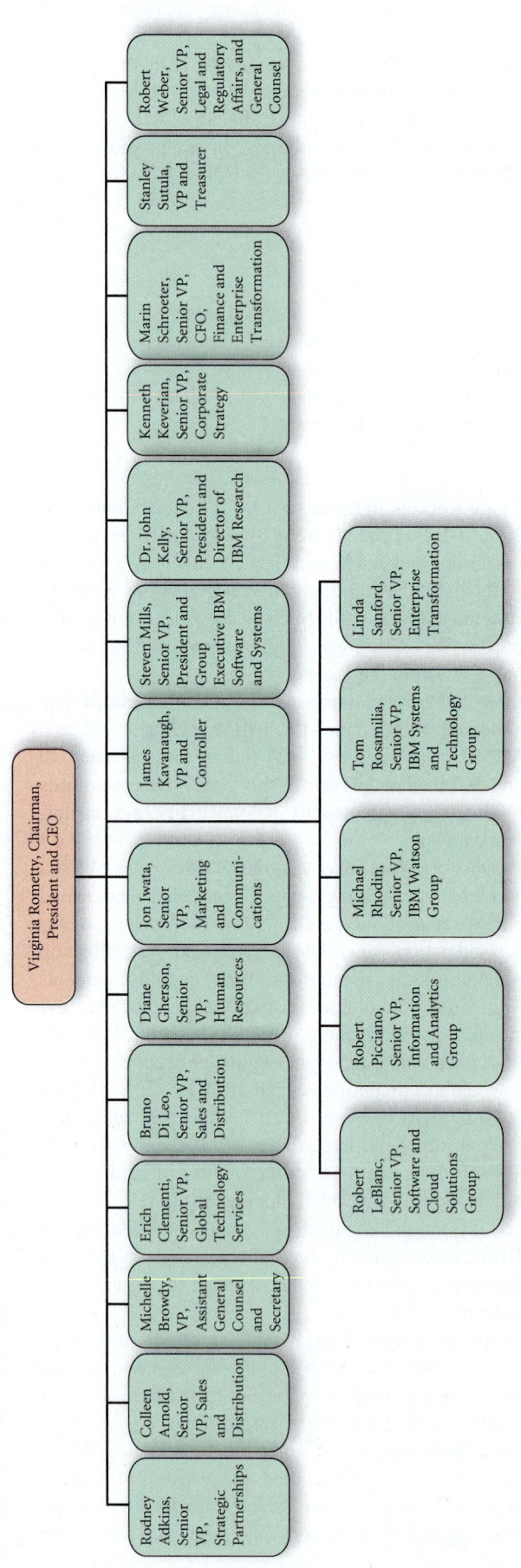

Source: Based on IBM's Company Documents.

Segment Data

IBM competes in five main business segments:

1. *Global Technology Services (GTS)* consists of delivering outsourcing services to help improve clients' existing IT infrastructures to aid in risk management, flexibility, and financial value. IBM routinely uses components from its systems technology and software segments to aid the business unit in delivering on its outsourcing services mission. GTS is IBM's largest division with respect to revenues, with the cloud-computing portion of the division being the fastest-growing and having the largest expected demand moving forward. Currently, IBM is considered the industry leader in cloud computing through heavy R&D and marketing campaigns.

2. *Global Business Services (GBS)* focuses on consulting and application management services. GBS aids businesses with new technologies—such as smarter commerce, mobile, and cloud—and provides support and maintenance for software and other products IBM offers.

3. *Software* is limited primarily to middleware and operating system software. Middleware software is designed to help clients diagnose business problems, improve efficiency, and identify new target markets. IBM provides a broad list of "capabilities" that serve more as broad category descriptions of these middleware products. They include WebSphere Software (support cloud, mobile, social), Information Management Software (data analytics software, among others), Tivoli Software (security software), Lotus Software (social networking software), and Rational Software (supports software development). Operations software is tailored and focused on improving and managing the core processes that computers use.

4. *Systems Technology* provides corporate customers with services that require large computing power. Many of IBM's clients who use products such as IBM PureSystems, IBM Smart Analytics, and IBM SmartCloud also need to purchase services from the Systems Technology segment to help run these programs. This segment offers storage systems and software, and manufactures several semiconductor products used in IBM systems and storage products. IBM is investing $3 billion between 2014 and 2019 on semiconductor research to keep IBM's hardware and software technology at the forefront.

5. *Global Finance* involves mainly leasing agreements for IBM products; this is not a major contributor to IBM's overall business portfolio, as evidenced in Exhibit 2.

Note in Exhibit 2 that IBM has declining revenues in all its segments. The 2014 numbers for GTS and Systems Technology reflect the divesture of Customer Care BPO and System x businesses.

Finance

IBM's recent income statement and balance sheet are provided in Exhibits 3 and 4, respectively. Note that IBM has financial problems.

EXHIBIT 2 **IBM's Revenues by Segment (in billion of USD)**

Business Segment	2014		2013		2012	
	Revenue	Gross Margin	Revenue	Gross Margin	Revenue	Gross Margin
GTS	$37.1	38.3%	$38.5	38.1%	$40.2	36.6%
GBS	17.8	30.8	18.4	30.9	18.6	30.0
Software	25.4	88.6	25.9	88.8	25.4	88.7
Systems Technology	10.0	39.5	14.4	35.6	17.7	39.1
Global Financing	2.0	49.4	2.0	45.6	2.0	46.5
Other	(0.5)		0.5		0.6	
Totals	92.8		99.6		104.5	

Source: Based on IBM's company documents.

EXHIBIT 3 Income Statement (in millions of USD)

Report Date	December 31, 2014	December 31, 2013
Revenues	$92,793	$98,367
Cost of revenue	46,386	49,683
Gross profit	46,407	48,684
Operating expenses	25,937	28,038
EBIT	20,470	20,646
Interest expense	484	402
EBT	19,986	20,244
Tax	4,234	3,363
Income from continuing operations	15,752	16,881
Discontinued operations	(3,730)	(398)
Net income	**12,022**	**16,483**

Source: Based on IBM's company documents.

EXHIBIT 4 Balance Sheet (in millions of USD)

Report Date	December 31, 2014	December 31, 2013
Cash	$8,476	$11,066
Accounts receivable	31,831	31,836
Inventories	2,103	2,310
Deferred taxes and prepaid expenses	7,012	6,138
Total current assets	49,422	51,350
Property, plant & equipment	10,771	13,821
Long-term receivables	11,109	12,755
Goodwill	30,556	31,184
Intangible assets	3,104	3,871
Other assets	12,570	13,242
Total assets	**117,532**	**126,223**
Taxes	5,084	4,633
Short-term debt	5,731	6,862
Accounts payable	6,864	7,461
Other current liabilities	21,921	21,198
Total current liabilities	39,600	40,154
Long-term debt	35,073	32,856
Retirement obligations	18,261	16,242
Other liabilities	12,584	14,042
Total liabilities	**105,518**	**103,294**
Common stock	52,666	51,594
Retained earnings	137,793	130,042
Treasury stock	(150,715)	(137,242)
Other	(27,730)	(21,465)
Total equity	**12,014**	**22,929**
Total liabilities & equity	**117,532**	**126,223**

Source: Based on IBM's company documents.

EXHIBIT 5 IBM versus Rival Firms

	IBM	HP	Accenture
# Employees	430,000	11,900	320,000
$ Net Income	$12,000 M	707 M	$2,941 M
$ Revenue	$92.8 B	$3.7 B	$31.8 B
$ Revenue/Employee	$215,814	$310,924	$99,375
$ EPS Ratio	$11.90	$6.72	$4.66
Market Cap.	$155 B	$7.3 B	$55.4 B

Source: Based on IBM's company documents.

Competition

Exhibit 5 provides a comparison of IBM with HP and Accenture. Note that IBM is larger than both rival firms put together.

Hewlett Packard (HP)

Based in Palo Alto, California, HP provides technologies, software, PCs, workstations, tables, calculators, and many other accessories and services to individuals as well as corporations. The company has been struggling in recent years, with both revenues and profits decreasing annually from the $127 billion and $30 billion, respectively, reported back in 2011.

Hewlett Packard prides itself on three key areas: converged cloud, big data, and security and risk management. Forrester's Wave for Private Cloud recently declared HP to be the world leader in the private cloud market, earning the highest rankings for 8 of 15 categories measured. HP prides its cloud business on providing customers with an easier installation and configuration process than traditionally cloud-based products provided. HP's new cloud technology allows users to better streamline its IT operations, design workloads in a more optimal fashion, and provide an open source design. HP's new Vertica Analytics Platform is the firm's flagship big data package that enables companies to quickly analyze large volumes of data in real time. The software provides support for both C++ and R statistical language.

In the personal systems market, HP has revenues of about $30 billion annually. Personal systems consist of notebooks, desktops, and workstations. Primarily, HP competes with Lenovo, Dell, Apple, Lenovo, and Toshiba in this segment. Printing has long been a stable for HP, competing with Canon, Lexmark, Xerox, Sieko, Epson, and others. HP's printing revenues are about $22 billion annually.

The company's Enterprise Group and Enterprise Services focus on technology infrastructure, IT services, consulting, and business outsourcing. Revenues are about $50 billion in these two segments. Top competitors in this area are IBM, Cisco, Microsoft, and Accenture. Software is a growing business worldwide, and HP competes with IBM, CA Technologies, BMC Software, and others. Software is one of the few bright spots for HP, with revenues increasing to over $4 billion in 2014.

Hewlett Packard's new Apollo 8000 system is the first super-computer to be 100 percent liquid cooled and offers direct competition to IBM's high-end server market. The Apollo 8000 is priced from $500,000 to several million dollars. In addition to being liquid cooled, the new product operates 28 percent more efficiently than any other product on the market.

Accenture

Based in Dublin, Ireland, Accenture is a management consulting and technology company. Accenture employs over 320,000 people, conducts business worldwide, and reported revenues of $32 billion in 2014, up from $27 billion in 2011. Accenture had acquisitions totaling over $800 million in 2013, most notably Acquity Group, Fjord, and AvVenta. Many of the acquisitions were focused on helping Accenture's marketing consulting businesses. Accenture recently formed a joint venture formed with GE called Taleris that enables airplanes to better anticipate aircraft maintenance issues. Accenture has seen the U.S. market grow at an annualized rate of 13 percent in revenues from 2011 to 2013, but continues to focus on emerging markets, especially Brazil.

External Audit

Industry Growth Rate

Slow information technology (IT) growth continues in 2015. IDC, a global IT data provider, estimates growth from 2012 to 2017 to be around 4.6 percent annualized, as companies are reluctant to sign long-term contracts. Moving forward, the key areas of IT growth are expected in the following areas: application management, cloud computing, business consulting, network consulting and integration, and hosted application management. The areas listed are expected to grow annualized from 2012 to 2017 at 5.2, 23.5, 7.6, 6.6, and 7.4 percent, respectively. Cloud computing clearly dominates future expectations. Some analysts in fact predict over 80 percent of all IT growth between 2012 and 2017 will be cloud related.

Areas of slower growth between 2012 and 2017 are expected to come from IT outsourcing, IT consulting, and IT hardware support at projected annualized growth rates of 1.3, 4.1, and 2.9 percent, respectively. Exhibit 6 provides detailed projections from IDC on growth yields through 2017. Note that IT outsourcing is not expected to produce any real gains during the projected period. Business consulting and outsourcing are both prime areas of interest for firms moving forward the next several years; firms without a good presence in these areas will likely look to mergers and acquisitions to provide them a quick presence in these areas.

As per IT growth by geographic region, Asia has experienced the best growth rates of late, with China up 7.7 percent, Indonesia up 6.2 percent, Vietnam up 5.0 percent, and India up 3.2 percent in 2012. Europe, still recovering from its economic debt crisis, reported the smallest growth rates, with the United Kingdom up only 0.2 percent and Germany up 0.9 percent. The United States experienced IT growth of 2.8 percent in 2012.

Computers and Servers

The desktop computer, laptop computer, and server industry has declined in the United States on average 17 percent per year from 2009 to 2014, and is expected to decline another 5 percent per

EXHIBIT 6 Projected Industry Dollar and Returns for IT (in billions of USD)

Area	2014	2015	2016	2017	2014–2017 Yields (%)
Business consulting	$92	$100	$108	$117	27%
IT consulting	33	34	36	37	12
Systems integration	121	127	132	138	14
Network consulting & integration	40	43	46	49	23
Customer application development	43	45	48	50	16
Project-based Total	**329**	**349**	**369**	**391**	**19**
Business outsourcing	177	188	198	209	32
Application management	57	60	63	65	14
Hosted application management	12	12	13	15	25
IT outsourcing	126	128	129	129	2
Network & desktop outsourcing	51	53	55	57	12
Hosting infrastructure services	39	42	44	48	21
Outsourcing Total	**461**	**482**	**503**	**524**	**14**
Hardware deployment/support	67	69	71	73	9
Software deployment/support	74	76	79	82	11
IT education/training	25	26	27	28	12
Support/training Total	**165**	**171**	**177**	**183**	**11**
Total global services spending	**955**	**1,002**	**1,049**	**1,098**	**15**

Source: Based on IDC's March 2013 forecast report.

year into 2019, despite a slight increase in demand. High standardization of products makes differentiating product lines difficult, resulting in reduced prices for manufacturers. Compounding problems, new competitors are able to enter the industry fairly easily, creating downward pressure on prices. Increases in tablet and smartphone demand also erode into PC sales, but analysts expect a sizable market for PCs to remain for quite some time.

Software

The business of data analytics, data storage, and security are growing. IBM primarily competes in the data analytics and data storage arenas, both representing around 20 percent of a $170 billion industry (in sales) in the United States alone. Smartphone apps represent about 2 percent of this industry, but further growth is expected. In total, around 3 percent growth is forecasted in the software area through 2019 in this country. But this industry requires large R&D expenses to stay current, as well as an expensive labor force, protection of patents and piracy risks, and substantial marketing.

Legal and Ethical Big Data Considerations

In the last 5 years, the general public has become especially aware and suspicious of data usage. Privacy concerns have arisen and even rights to who owns the data presents a problem moving forward for corporations in the data business. The use of data, and more specifically the information that can be derived from data, has grown faster than our legal systems can keep up. Netflix, AOL, and even the Eric Snowden incident involving release of U.S. secrets have exposed issues related to the use of big data.

Your web-browsing history, emails, texts, tweets, posts, and movements around town are now tracked. To what extent do firms need permission to obtain this personal data? Can data that an individual agreed to be collected then be sold to a third party? Should the individual be compensated for data collected from her or his actions each time the data are used? What guarantees can be made to ensure privacy so certain individuals cannot be pinpointed out of a database? The volume and nature of how data can be used is growing faster than world government legal systems can adapt to. The threat of legal issues against firms using big data is increasing daily. Complicating legal issues further, will negligence attorneys use data to prosecute corporations and governments for *not* using data to predict and foresee potential problems?

Future

In early 2015, Marriott and IBM announced a deal to move 80 percent of Marriott's old-school technology to what's known as a "hybrid" cloud built by IBM. That means Marriott will use IBM's cloud to host apps that it doesn't want to host. Marriott will keep its data centers but will update them to use the latest cloud technology. Marriott's infrastructure supports over 4,000 locations worldwide. This deal was similar to the $500 million, 6-year deal IBM signed a year ago with insurance giant The Hartford.

IBM's three initiatives focus on the cloud, big data, and systems of engagement, but the future of those industries is uncertain. In fiscal 2014, IBM divested its Customer Care BPO and System x businesses. Company revenues fell 11 percent between fiscal years 2012 and 2014; the firm's stock price fell 17 percent over the same time frame while the S&P 500 increased 60 percent. Prepare a needed, 3-year strategic plan for CEO Virginia Rometty and Big Blue.

TASER International, Inc., 2015

www.taser.com, TASR

Headquartered in Scottsdale, Arizona, TASER International develops, manufactures, and sells electrical weapons and video systems for law enforcement, military, private security, and personal defense markets. TASER's principle customer remains law enforcement officers at the federal, state, and local levels in the United States, but law enforcement personnel in over 150 countries have used TASER-brand products. Half of U.S. law enforcement officers carry a TASER product, as well as 1 in 50 officers worldwide. Products include extended range projectiles, 12-gauge pump action shotgun projectiles, handheld stun devices, video cameras, training cartridges, batteries, and other accessories. All TASER products are manufactured and assembled in Scottsdale, where the company uses six sigma methods and currently holds an ISO 9001 certification. TASER has three primary products: the stun gun, the wearable camera, and the storage cloud. About 2,000 police officers in the United States use TASER stun guns and video devices.

TASER's AXON video product is worn by first responders and law enforcement officers. The product is cloud based, providing video and audio of incidents. The firm's mission is to protect life by subduing dangerous individuals in a manner other than deadly force. With its new line of cloud-based video equipment worn by many individuals carrying TASER devices, the company reports better officer behavior and compliance by the person under questioning. In addition, law enforcement companies are able to use the recorded video to determine if excessive force was used, and protect themselves from accusations of excessive force that have become commonplace in today's society, especially after the recent Ferguson, Missouri, and New York City police killings. TASER's conducted electrical weapon (CEW) use has reduced officer and suspect injuries as well as reduced excessive force charges. TASER products may be purchased through stores, online, and through third-party retailers. The Baltimore Police Department ordered 545 of the company's X26Ps smart weapons, and the Port Authority of New York and New Jersey just ordered 50 X2s with TASER's Cam HD recorders.

As indicated at the end of this case, TASER's sales and profits continue to climb through 2015.

Copyright by Fred David Books LLC. www.strategyclub.com (Written by Forest R. David)

History

TASAR traces its history back to 1969 when NASA researcher Jack Cover began developing a powerful, yet nonlethal, device that he named Tom A. Swift's Electric Rifle after his childhood hero Tom A. Swift. However, the earliest TASER used gunpowder, forcing the product to be classified as a firearm in 1976. It was not until 1993 when Rick and Thomas Smith, along with Jack Cover, developed an electronic-controlled device did TASER take on more the function that it has today, and one in which the U.S. firearms regulators did not classily as a firearm. In 1999, the first law enforcement officers started using the TASER M26 and the firm filed for its IPO in 2001. TASER stock climbed over 9,000 percent from early 2003 to the spring of 2004, splitting three times in the process. It seemed every law enforcement agency in the United States and many abroad had to have TASERs for their officers. Also during 2004, the United Kingdom agreed to let all police forces nationwide use TASER products. In 2007, the firm introduced an extended range 12-gauge projectile and in 2009 a new 12-gauge gun. The first true handgun-shaped device was introduced in 1999, and in 2003 TASER introduced its popular and still used today TASER X26 device. Air TASER Inc. changed its name to TASER International in 2008 to reflect its growing presence in international markets. TASER's first multishot device introduced in 2009 was called the X3 and had the ability to fire three shots before being reloaded. TASER employs about 400 people and reported revenues of $165 million in 2014, up from $137 million the prior year; TASER reported 2014 net income of $19 million, up from $18 million the prior year.

Shares of TASER stock rose 5.6 percent to $24.14 on December 17, 2014, after the Los Angeles Police Department (LAPD) announced purchase of about 7,000 body-worn 860 AXON cameras in 2015. TASER shipped the cameras in the first half of 2015. The LAPD also purchased a 5-year subscription to EVIDENCE.com, offering unlimited storage for data uploading from the AXON cameras and Evidence mobile apps. TASER CEO Rick Smith said, "We collaborated closely with LAPD to create our new Officer Safety Plan to help serve agencies that want to have complete predictability of the costs of their on-officer video and TASER programs in one simple plan." The Street Ratings team rates TASER stock as a "Buy" with a ratings score of B. There is a growing demand for police body cameras, which is good news for TASER.

Internal Issues

Organization Structure

TASER removed its COO position as of January 2015 and has no plans to fill it in the near future. TASER's organizational structure is depicted in Exhibit 1.

Vision/Mission

TASER does not have a published vision statement, but on occasion CEO Rick Smith says, "Our vision is to make the bullet obsolete." Taser does have a published mission statement as published on page 5 for the company's 2013 *Annual Report*, as follows:

> Our core mission is to protect life and to protect truth through technologies that make communities safer. We are the market leader in the development, manufacture and sale of conducted electrical weapons ("CEWs") designed for use in law enforcement, military, corrections, private security and personal defense. Since our inception in 1993, we have remained committed to providing solutions to violent confrontation by developing devices with proprietary technology to incapacitate dangerous, combative, or high-risk subjects who pose a risk to law enforcement officers, innocent citizens, or themselves in a manner that is generally recognized as a safer alternative to other uses of force. More recently, to address challenges faced by law enforcement officers post-incident, we have developed a fully integrated hardware and software solution to provide our law enforcement customers the capabilities to capture, store, manage, share and analyze video and other digital evidence.

How Does a TASER Work?

TASER products are designed to provide knock-down nonlethal power protection for law enforcement personnel and other users. TASER units fire two small dart electrodes that can remain wired to the original unit or be wireless. Projectiles are powered by compressed nitrogen charges so no gun powder is used. Air cartridges must be replaced after each shot for most units, but the shocking mechanism can be re-administered, since the subject is physically connected by wires to the gun. The gun can be reloaded in seconds if needed. The actual shocking charge lasts for 5 seconds by emitting 19 charges per second, for a total of 95 individual charges, and will stop even the strongest individuals, even persons under the influence of drugs.

EXHIBIT 1 TASER's Organizational Structure

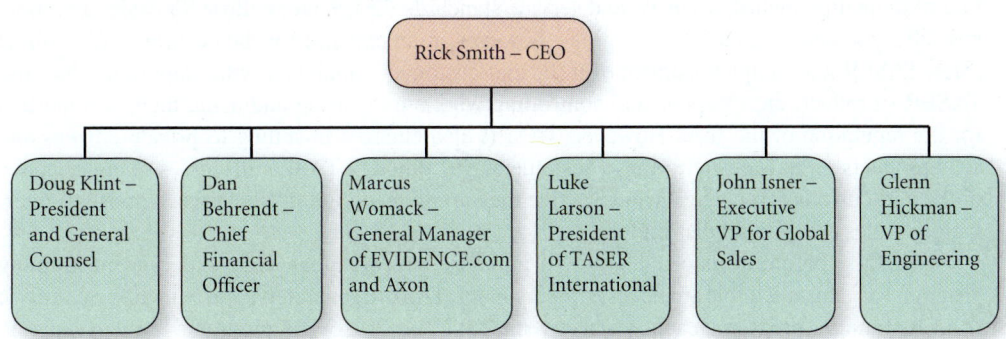

Source: Based on TASER's company documents.

Law enforcement projectiles have a maximum range of 35 feet depending on the model, and models for non-law enforcement have a maximum range of 15 feet. Current models fire electrodes that are pointed and able to penetrate heavy winter clothing. Being barbed, it is difficult to remove the electrodes while in place after the first 5-second shock is administered. During the shock, the individual generally cannot move at all as the voltage is 50,000 volts, but generally reduced to 1,800 volts by the time it makes contact with an individual. The amps are low, preventing death in almost all instances. Guns also come equipped with a confetti-like paper that shoots out with the projectiles to identify which gun was shot. Guns are also equipped with laser sights and a safety mechanism. TASERs have advantages over other nonlethal options such as batons and pepper spray that require much closer proximity, and the effects and damage of their use linger much longer than that of a TASER. Batons commonly break bones, but the shock and pain of a TASER are gone as soon as the 5-second charge completes. Pepper spray was found by police in Canada to be safer, but its effectiveness is severely compromised with some individuals. Stun guns can be purchased from Walmart and other dealers, but stun guns must hit the body and are not nearly as incapacitating as a TASER.

Markets Served

TASER primarily serves law enforcement agencies in the United States and throughout the world, although total sales outside of the United States account for only about 16 percent of total sales. In total, 17,000 law enforcement agencies in 150 different countries have purchased TASER products for either testing and or deployment. TASER also serves the U.S. military and foreign allies with devices and even employs the former head of the U.S. Military Joint Non-Lethal Weapons Directorate as its Vice President of Government and Military Programs.

One market TASER is trying to enter is the private security business. Businesses such as contract security, casinos, gas stations, and many others all have the need for a TASER device. TASER has developed several training programs and attends trade shows to help draw interest from potential private security customers. Personal protection for private citizens is another market TASER has entered with limited sales of around 3 percent. TASER is continuing to explore new markets to attract interest among people who currently carry pepper sprays or handguns for self-defense and potentially encourage persons to start caring a TASER—even persons who do not currently carry any form of protection device. TASER's new AXON and EVIDENCE.com video products are catching on quickly but still do not deliver near the sales of TASER conducted electrical weapons.

Marketing and Distribution

TASER has several programs designed to provide online education, Web and print advertisements, and physical training classes conducted globally to promote TASER products. TASER feels so strongly about its Web presence that the company offers two distinct websites, one at TASER.com and one at EVIDENCE.com.

Once TASER has an agreement to purchase, customers are able to purchase directly from TASER or they can go through a distributor. Two of the more notable distributors are one for the U.S. Military and one for the U.S. federal government. Distributors are selected based on their reputations and contact scope. TASER maintains an ongoing relationship with all distributors to ensure quality control, security, and service standards. Distributors allow for easier and more cost-effective entry into different regions, however, at an expense for the customer. With direct sales, TASER has complete control over the end-customer, which is of vital importance because TASER's products are weapons and controlling who is purchasing and using them is important for the reputation of the firm. However, TASER also engages in selling to private citizens and sells products on its website to these customers. So, although TASER discusses being selective of the end-customer, it is unclear how active they are in meeting this objective. Almost all international sales are through distributors.

Generally before a major agency will purchase new weapons, they expect a full training program to be installed to train necessary personnel. TASER generated approximately $2 million from its training programs each year between 2011 and 2013. The programs are expensive to operate, though, as TASER must pay all training personal. Law enforcement officers must pass a hands-on class after successful completion of an online curriculum. TASER offers classes for instructors, Master instructors, and several other classes specializing in various TASER-related issues.

Strategy

TASER states repeatedly that its overall mission is to protect life—both the life of the law enforcement officer and the subject. The company spends about $10 million annually on R&D and introduced the new X26P in 2013, along with the AXON body and updates to EVIDENCE.com. The company expects video technology and improvements to be a major area of potential revenue moving forward. It also is working closely with distributors overseas to identify new markets to enter, since only 1 in 50 law enforcement officers worldwide use a TASER product. TASER has a strong presence in the United Kingdom and Australia, but it is especially targeting France and Brazil currently.

Segment Data

TASER reports revenues in two segments: TASER weapons and AXON, which includes EVIDENCE.com. The TASER X26P is also one-shot conducted electrical weapon that integrates with EVIDENCE.com like the X26 but also comes with the ability to perform self-diagnostics, has an extended battery life, and has HD TASER Cam capabilities, among a few other extra features. The TASER X2 performs all the functions of the X26 and X26P but in addition allows for a second shot with dual lasers for increased accuracy and a total magazine capacity of 500 firings. TASER X26 and M26 were discontinued in 2014 and 2011, respectively, but are still in use today. In 2013, the X2, X26P, and X26 accounted for sales of $28, $28, and $34 million, respectively, leading total sales among all TASER products including accessories. TASER also produces a 12-gauge shotgun referred to as eXtended Range Electronic Projectile (XREP) that can fire a projectile upwards of 100 feet. The models just named, other than the XREP, although primarily for law enforcement and military, can also be designed for consumer markets. However, the main product for the consumer market is the TASER C2. The C2 provides the same effectiveness as the X2 and X26P but is offered at a lower price point for consumers. Maximum range of the C2 is 15 feet. Total sales of consumer products were $4 million in 2013, accounting for only 3 percent of total sales.

TASER reported over $35 million in cartridge sales in 2013 for approximately 26 percent of total sales. Sales of TASER cartridges were $33 and $25 million in 2012 and 2011, respectively, but cartridge sales accounted for 29 and 28 percent of total sales, higher than the 26 percent of total sales in 2013. Newer to the firm is its AXON and EVIDENCE.com video systems. The AXON products are video cameras that range in price from $400 to $600 for the AXON Body and AXON Flex products, respectively. TASER's main marketing strategy is emphasizing that the AXON products have a 130-degree field of view, compared to 70 degrees for many competitors, along with easily being able to mount the devices. EVIDENCE.com is available for $15 per month and allows police forces to upload video taking to the site and saves them having to manage the data themselves. Law enforcement operations that wish to maintain their own data can upload directly from AXON to their own systems.

According to TASER, excessive use of force and complaints against law enforcement are significantly reduced when officers wear AXON products. A notable law enforcement agency in California recently spent $180,000 on TASER video products, and reported an 80 percent drop in complaints and a 60 percent drop in force. In December 2014, TASER and the LAPD agreed to a new deal to outfit its police force with TASER video equipment and subscribe to EVIDENCE.com. The deal is expected to be worth "millions" over a 5-year period for TASER. With the recent Ferguson, Missouri, shooting death, President Obama has proposed funding of $263 million to outfit 50,000 police officers with cameras across the United States. This would double the number currently wearing cameras. There are currently 750,000 officers in this country. With TASER cameras, they cannot be deleted by the officer, but can be turned off. Many police forces discipline their officers for not having the cameras turned on.

As seen in Exhibit 2, TASER is struggling to turn a profit on its AXON division, reporting a net loss of $18 million in 2014, up nearly 50 percent from 2013 despite the division accounting for over a third of 2014 revenue. Exhibit 3 reveals 80 percent of companywide revenues are generated from the United States.

EXHIBIT 2 TASER's Revenues by Product Segment (in thousands of USD)

	Revenues			
	2014		2013	
	Revenues	Income	Revenues	Income
TASER Weapons	$145,613	$51,072	$127,474	$37,514
AXON	$18,912	($18,567)	$10,357	($9,566)
Total	**$164,525**	**$32,505**	**$137,831**	**$27,948**

Source: Based on TASER's Q4 2014 Report.

EXHIBIT 3 TASER's 2014 Revenue by Geographic Region

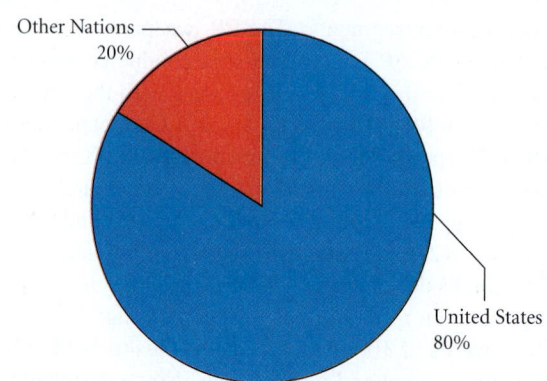

Other Nations 20%

United States 80%

Source: Based on TASER's 2014 *Annual Report* p. 53.

Finance

TASER's income statement and balance sheet are provided in Exhibits 4 and 5, respectively.

Competitors

TASER competes with many different security firms, ranging from pepper spray makers to batons to actual gun makers to video camera makers. TASER management has identified weapon accuracy, effectiveness, safety, cost, ease of use, and training provided as key drivers of success in the industry. Top competitors for TASER in the pepper spray business include MACE Security International and PepperBall Technologies, both small firms. MACE reported 2013 revenues of $8 million and no information could be found on PepperBall. Both stock prices are less than $0.10.

EXHIBIT 4 TASER's Income Statement (in thousands of USD)

Report Date	December 31, 2014	December 31, 2013
Revenues	$164,525	$137,831
Cost of revenue	62,997	51,988
Gross margin	101,548	85,843
Administrative and other expenses	54,158	48,007
R&D	14,885	9,888
EBIT	32,505	27,948
Interest & other	(194)	86
EBT	32,311	28,034
Tax	12,393	9,790
Net income	**19,918**	**18,244**

Source: Based on TASERS's 2014 *Annual Report* p. 45.

EXHIBIT 5 TASER's Balance Sheet (in thousands of USD)

Report Date	December 31, 2014	December 31, 2013
Assets		
Cash and equivalents	$48,367	$42,271
Short-term investments	32,774	9,101
Accounts receivable	30,735	22,488
Inventories	18,323	11,109
Other current assets	9,828	12,498
Total current assets	140,027	97,467
Property, plant & equipment	17,523	19,043
Deferred taxes	10,733	13,679
Goodwill & intangibles	5,321	5,552
Long-term investments	9,296	12,023
Other assets	2,468	618
Total assets	**185,368**	**148,382**
Liabilities		
Accounts payable	7,682	6,221
Other current liabilities	24,291	16,908
Total current liabilities	31,973	23,129
Deferred revenue	21,668	13,341
Other liabilities	2,621	3,565
Total liabilities	**56,262**	**40,035**
Common stock	1	1
Retained earnings	81,045	61,127
Treasury stock	(114,645)	(92,203)
Paid in capital and other	162,705	139,422
Total equity	**129,106**	**108,347**
Total liabilities & equity	**185,368**	**148,382**

Source: Based on TASERS's 2014 *Annual Report* p. 43.

To date, TASER has many smaller fringe rivals, but no major single competitor on the weapons front, other than law enforcement agencies that choose to arm officers with guns only. Several online and physical merchants produce pepper sprays and stun guns, such has Hughes Security Solutions and even Amazon and Walmart. Most of these guns require physical contact with the subject and deliver only a minor shock. To TASER's knowledge, there is no current competitor of significance in the nonlethal weapons market.

Unlike the nonlethal weapons market, the video market has many competitors and is highly fragmented. Key drivers of success include performance, size, warranty, product quality, and the ability to integrate video files into management software such as what TASER provides with its EVIDENCE.com system. TASER prides itself on the AXON Flex cameras that can be worn attached to Oakley sunglasses or other convenient places, increasing the likelihood that officers will wear the devices. The cameras can even replace a traditional car camera in certain situations. GoPro and Digital Ally are also two competing small body camera manufacturers, but, at least to date, Digital Ally has a much larger customer base with law enforcement.

Digital Ally (DGLY)

Headquartered in Lenexa, Kansas, and employing 120 people, Digital Ally produces video equipment for law enforcement, security, and other commercial applications around the world. Key products include in-car audio systems for both forward and rear views that are required for law enforcement. The firm also produces rugged video equipment for boats, motorcycles, and all-terrain vehicles, as well as a body-worn digital camera that competes with TASER's AXON Flex models. Digital Ally reported 2014 revenues of $17 million.

External Issues

Legal Issues

TASER-related deaths continue to be a concern in the United States and abroad. The U.S. Supreme Court is presently considering whether to hear a case related to a TASER death. In 2011, the Justice Department ruled using TASERs was appropriate to subdue individuals, but not to use the device multiple times. Resultant deaths in the United States from being "tasered" range from 60 by some accounts to Amnesty International's estimate of 540 deaths. The wide discrepancy in deaths stems from many TASER-related deaths being blamed on drug overdoses or heavily intoxicated individuals. Most TASER-related deaths also resulted from multiple shocks, not the single 5-second shock the device delivers. A study by the Wake Forest Baptist Medical Center of 1,000 subjects revealed 99.7 percent had no injuries or only minor scrapes or bruises after being shot with a TASER. Three "tasered" persons required hospital attention and two others died, but both deaths were not related to the TASER, according to autopsy reports. Currently, police forces allow the use of TASERs in a wide range of situations—even allowing their use on handcuffed individuals, unruly people in a public setting, and many others. With no set guidelines on TASER use, Amnesty International is campaigning to have police forces look more closely at when is proper protocol to use such a device. In Amnesty's opinion, only at times when the officer would consider using his or her firearm is the use of a TASER an option.

People with certain medical conditions, even conditions they are not aware of, can be at higher risk for death. Also, individuals on drugs or who are heavily intoxicated are at higher risk of death from a TASER. TASER claims over 2 million people have been "tasered," preventing 124,000 deaths or serious injuries when officers elected to use a TASER instead of a firearm.

TASER is currently a defendant in 16 lawsuits of wrongful death or personal injury during arrest or training. Most of the cases focus on alleged product defects. In 2009, TASER redeveloped its training programs to better insulate itself from wrongful death or injury cases. The firm will settle legal cases pre-2009, but has a policy to not settle legal cases post-2009. One notable case from pre-2009 was settled in 2013 for $2.3 million by TASER.

Regulations

TASER devices are considered weapons and subject to regulations, but most TASER products are not considered firearms by the U.S. Bureau of Alcohol, Tobacco, Firearms, and Explosives. The only product considered a firearm is the TASER XREP, since it uses a propellant instead of compressed gas for discharge. Even though not considered firearms, many states have regulations restricting the sale and use of electronic weapons, and most of these regulations apply to TASER products. Six states currently prohibit the possession of stun guns by private citizens, including the District of Columbia, Hawaii, Massachusetts, New Jersey, New York, and Rhode Island. Many of these same states also have some of the most stringent gun control laws in the country.

The U.S. government regulates the exporting of TASER products, but in most all instances the U.S. government has quickly approved of TASER sales to customers outside the United States. Sales to Canada do not require U.S. government's approval. Regulations on importing in foreign markets can be ambiguous, and TASER often works with distributors who are more familiar with local laws and restrictions. However, most nations still permit TASER products to be used by their local law enforcements, so foreign regulations are not a constraining factor as TASER expands globally.

Future

For Q2 of 2015, TASER generated revenues of $46.7 million, an increase of 25.7 percent from the second quarter of 2014. For Q2, revenues from TASER's Weapons segment increased 15.8 percent year-over-year to $37.8 million. However, the company's higher smart weapon sales were partly offset by a decrease in sales of legacy TASER X26 CEW, which was retired from production as of December 31, 2014. For Q2, the company's AXON and EVIDENCE.com revenues increased 97.5 percent to $8.9 million, due largely to a 226.1 percent increase in service revenues. TASER's Q2 profits were up 57 percent from last year, and sales of Axon on-body police cameras nearly doubled, from $4.4 billion to $8.9 million. In addition, during Q2 TASER took in $30.6 million in new orders for Axon cameras and EVIDENCE.com data storage subscriptions (revenues from storing the video generated by the Axon cameras). That last number was up 170 percent year-over-year, indicating strong growth in a high-margin business. However, a major issue facing TASER moving forward is growing costs, especially expanding into international markets. There are also many other camera options coming onto the market for police forces to choose from, and the U.S. government and other government agencies are likely to bid prices down significantly between rival firms. CEO Smith needs an effective 3-year strategic plan moving forward. Key areas of focus include improving the firm's market share in overseas markets, which accounts for less than 20 percent of total sales, keeping costs down, bargaining to gain future government contracts, and creating new markets for weapons where "less than deadly force" is a good option.

Revlon, Inc., 2015

www.revlon.com, REV

Headquartered in New York City, Revlon is a large beauty and personal care products company and is a subsidiary of MacAndrews & Forbes Holding Inc. Popular Revlon products include lipsticks, skin care products, deodorant, blush, makeup, hair and nail products, and much more, marketed under such brands as Almay, SinfulColors, Pure Ice, Revlon ColorSilk, Charlie, Jean Naté, Mitchum, Gatineau, and Ultima II. Revlon sells products worldwide through its sales force, sales representatives, and independent distributors, and licenses its trademarks to select manufacturers for complementary beauty-related products and accessories. For the quarter that ended June 30, 2015, Revlon's revenues were $482 million, up from $438 million the prior quarter, and the company's net income was $26 million, up from a negative $900,000 the prior quarter. Also during Q2 of 2015, Revlon completed its acquisition of the CBBeauty Group and exited business operations in Venezuela, moving to a distributor model in that country. Revlon's sales for Q3 of 2015 were $471.5 million, about the same as the prior year Q3, but the company's Q3 2015 net income was $6.2 million, down from $14.6 million the prior year Q3. The company's stock price declined 12 percent in 2015 through November. Thus, investors are concerned about Revlon's strategic plan and performance.

Revlon hired a new CEO in 2014, Lorenzo Delpani. He needs a clear strategic plan going forward, as rivals such as Avon, L'Oreal, Mary Kay Cosmetics, and Estee Lauder compete for market share in the industry.

Copyright by Fred David Books LLC. www.strategyclub.com (Written by Meredith E. David and Forest R. David)

History

Revlon was founded in 1932 when brothers Charles and Joseph Revson, and chemist C. R. Lachman, launched a new product—a nail enamel that came in colors other than red. Somewhat bizarre, but interestingly, the name Revlon comes from replacing the *s* in *Revson* with the L from *Lachman*. One of Charles Revson's most famous quotes to describe his business was "in the factory we make cosmetics, in the drug store we sell hope." Being the only provider of different color nail polishes, Revlon had a large leg up on competition, and within 6 years the firm was a multimillion dollar organization. By the early 1940s, Revlon had expanded its product line to include many other beauty products, including lipstick, which it remains famous for today. Revlon went public in 1955 and saw its stock price increase over 200 percent in the first two months of trading. In the 1960s, Revlon restructured into six different business units based on target customer. Throughout the next 20 years, Revlon acquired many different cosmetic-related firms to expand its product offerings, but in the 1980s, it was still losing ground to major competitors Estee Lauder, Cover Girl, Procter & Gamble, and others. Thus, in 1985, Revlon was sold to Pantry Pride and left department stores to become a mass-market beauty brand. The firm hired Claudia Schiffer, Cindy Crawford, and Christy Turlington to model its products during the 1980s. In the 1990s, Revlon introduced its Color Stay line and hired model Halle Berry to promote the products. Revlon acquired Mirage Cosmetics in 2011 and Colomer Group in 2013 and hired both Emma Stone and Olivia Wilde to promote its products. Revlon divested all of its Chinese operations in 2014.

Internal Issues

Vision/Mission

Revlon has one statement as follows on the corporate website related to vision/mission: "Revlon is a global color cosmetics, hair color, beauty tools, fragrances, skincare, anti-perspirant deodorants and beauty care products company whose vision is Glamour, Excitement and Innovation through high-quality products at affordable prices."

EXHIBIT 1 Revlon's Organizational Structure

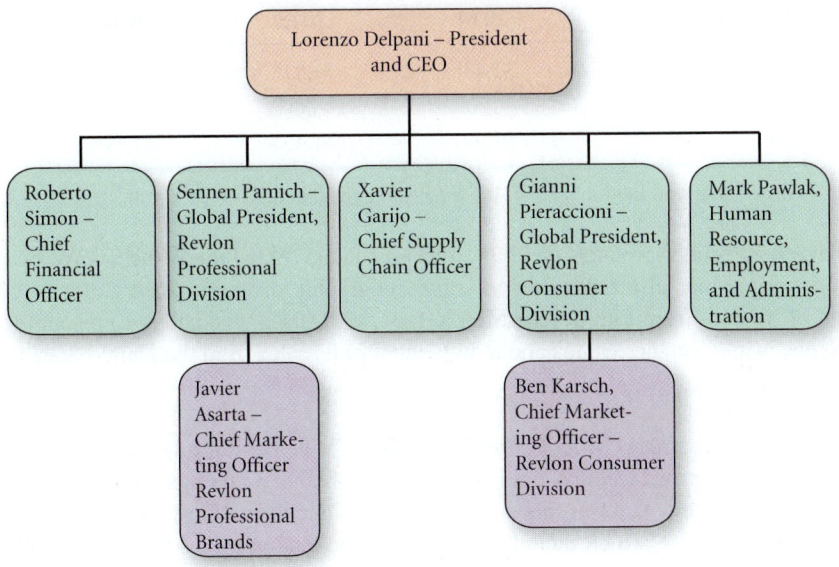

Source: Based on company documents.

Organizational Structure

Like about half of the Fortune 500 companies, Revlon does not have an executive with the title COO among its top management team. As depicted in Exhibit 1, the company has two primary divisions: Professional and Consumer. The two divisions focus on selling products to (1) beauty salons (Professional Segment) and (2) individuals (Consumer Segment), respectively. The current structure was finalized in October 2013 with the acquisition of the Colomer Group for $664 million in cash. The Colomer business comprises 100 percent of Revlon's professional segment. Let's presume that the two divisional presidents report to the CAO because sometimes that is another name for the COO position.

Marketing and R&D

Revlon uses sales representatives and independent distributors primarily in marketing. In 2013, 56 percent of all Revlon sales in the United States were derived from mass merchandisers. Revlon's largest customers in this country are Walmart, CVS, Walgreens, Boot Alliance, and Target. In November 2014, Revlon launched its "Love is On" marketing campaign in all markets globally—the firm's first global marketing campaign in over 10 years. CEO Delpani suggested the new slogan because he says love is a "universally applicable theme that has no boundaries." Audio and video of related marketing ads are played to the classic song "Addicted to Love" and feature Halle Berry, Emma Stone, and Olivia Wilde.

Revlon spent $32 million on R&D in 2014 and employs 200 people in its R&D locations in New Jersey, Florida, and California. The bulk of Revlon's products are produced at its own factories in North Carolina and in South Africa. The firm produces products for its professional segment in Florida, Spain, Italy, and Mexico, as well as through various third-party contractors.

Strategy

One of CEO Delpani's first decisions after taking over in 2014 was to divest the firm's Chinese business, which accounted for only 2 percent of total sales. Delpani also cut 15 percent, or approximately 5,000, Revlon employees. The decision to exit China came on the heels of rival Avon reporting a 67 percent decline in Chinese sales in 2013, and rival L'Oreal reporting slowing sales in China, despite the market being worth an estimated $20 billion.

Revlon's acquisition of Colomer Group bolstered the company's offerings to professional salon customers. This acquisition added the Creative Nail professional and Shellac Nail polishes to Revlon's portfolio, as well as American Crew men's hair care products. Rival cosmetics companies had recently added products and services aimed at salon customers, such as Unilever in 2011 buying Alberto-Culver for about $3.7 billion, giving it the Nexxus haircare brand. P&G, the

EXHIBIT 2 Revlon's Revenues by Customer (in millions of USD)

Revenues	2014	2013	2012
Consumer	$1,438	$1,378	$1,396
Professional	502	117	–
Total	$1,941	$1,495	$1,396

Source: Based on Revlon's 2014 *Annual Report*, p. 30 and 2014 Q4 report.

world's largest consumer-products company, recently added salon brands such as Wella Illumina hair coloring. Colomer also gave Revlon some geographic diversity since Colomer obtained about half of its sales from Europe, the Middle East, and Africa, and about 40 percent from the United States, while Revlon obtains about 56 percent of its sales from the United States.

Segments

Revlon's Consumer segment, which accounts for about 74 percent of total revenues, focuses on cosmetics products for the face, lips, eyes, and nails. Top brand names include Revlon ColorStay, which provides women with a full range of products designed for all-day use without reapplication; Revlon PhotoReady, which include products for the face and eyes that Revlon markets as able to bend and reflect light to provide women flawless airbrushed appearance in any light condition; Revlon Age Defying products that are designed for women over age 35 to mask lines and wrinkles; and Revlon Super Lustrous, the flagship wax-based lipcolor, and possibly the product the company is best known for, offered in many different colors and shades of both lipstick and lip gloss. Other products include Revlon ColorBurst, Revlon Grow Luscious, and Almay. ColorBurst focuses on lip glosses in high-shine style, opposite of the matte Super Lustrous products. Revlon's Grow Luscious and Almay are designed mostly for improving the eyelashes and hypo-allergenic products, respectively. In fact, Almay has a full line of products all centered on hypo-allergenic products. Other key products included in the consumer division include hair color products under the name ColorSilk, various beauty tools for use on the nails and eye, fragrances such as Charlie and Jean Naté, deodorants under the name Mitchum, and skin care products under brands Gatineau and Ultima II. Revlon reported profits of $347 million from its Consumer division in 2013 down from $363 million the previous year.

Revlon's Professional division accounts for about 26 percent of revenues as indicated in Exhibit 2. This division is aimed at selling products directly to professional salons rather than the consumer at mass merchant and grocery stores. Notable brands include Revlonissimo NMT, Nutri Color Crème, Sensor Perm, and Revlon Professional Equave. American Crew is another product targeting men with shampoos, conditioners, gels, and other products. Revlon's CND brand offers popular nail color and treatments to professional salons in over 80 countries. Total profits for the newly acquired professional division were $5.2 million in 2013.

Revlon's revenues by region are provided in Exhibit 3. Note that the United States contributes more than half of Revlon's revenues in 2013.

Exhibit 4 reveals Revlon's revenues by geographic region in 2014. Note that U.S. sales and international sales were both up substantially over 2013 numbers. Also note that U.S. and international revenues in Exhibit 4 do not perfectly match the data in Exhibit 3; however, total revenues for 2013 *do* match, which reflects a slight reclassification of certain revenues by Revlon.

Finance

Revlon's recent income statement and balance sheet are provided in Exhibits 5 and 6, respectively. On the balance sheet, notice the negative retained earnings because the company has been incurring losses, although for 2014 there was a positive net income of $41 million.

Competitors

The beauty products business contains over 3,000 different competitors with top companies being Procter & Gamble, Unilever, L'Oreal, Estee Lauder, Mary Kay, Avon, Helen of Troy, Coty, Ultra Salons, and Revlon. The industry is comprised of many different classes of competitors

EXHIBIT 3 Revlon's Revenues by Region for Consumer Division (in millions of USD)

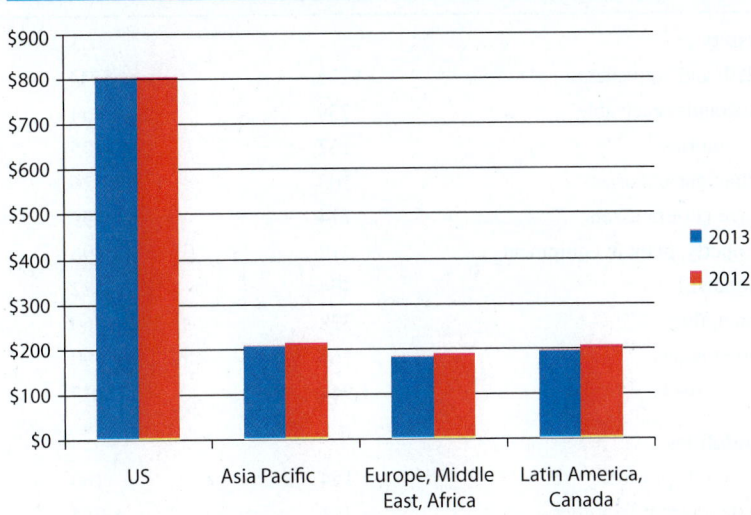

Source: Adapted from Revlon's 2013 *Annual Report*, p. 30.

EXHIBIT 4 Revlon's 2014 Revenues by Geographic Region (in millions of USD)

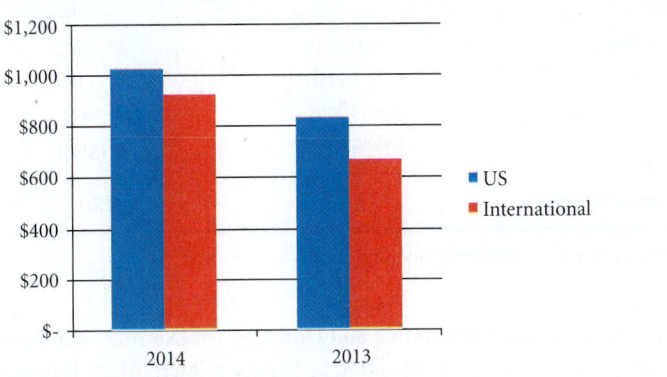

Source: Adapted from Revlon's 2014 *Annual Report.*

EXHIBIT 5 Revlon's Income Statement (in millions of USD)

Report Date	December 31, 2014	December 31, 2013
Revenues	$1,941	$1,494
Cost of revenue	668	544
Gross profit	1,273	950
Operating expenses	1,037	761
EBIT	236	189
Interest and other	118	118
EBT	118	71
Tax	78	46
EAT	40	25
Income from continuing operations	1	(30)
Net income	**41**	**(5)**

Source: Based on Revlon's company documents.

EXHIBIT 6   Revlon's Balance Sheet (in millions of USD)

Report Date	December 31, 2014	December 31, 2013
Assets		
Cash and equivalents	$275	$244
Accounts receivable	239	254
Inventories	157	175
Other current assets	103	126
Total current assets	774	799
Property, plant & equipment	212	196
Goodwill	464	472
Intangibles	328	360
Other assets	166	190
Total assets	**1,944**	**2,017**
Liabilities		
Accounts payable	154	166
Other current liabilities	311	387
Total current liabilities	465	553
Long-term debt	1,832	1,862
Other liabilities	291	198
Total liabilities	**2,588**	**2,613**
Common stock	0	0
Retained earnings	(1,411)	(1,452)
Treasury stock	(10)	(10)
Paid in capital & other	777	866
Total equity	**(644)**	**(596)**
Total liabilities & equity	**1,944**	**2,017**

Source: Based on Revlon's company documents.

with many different missions. Procter & Gamble and Unilever, for example, are the most diversified firms, selling many products not even classified as beauty related. Mary Kay and Avon both rely on direct (door-to-door) sales. Ultra Salons is fully vertically integrated, making its own products, selling them in its own stores, and even offering salons in its stores. A notable trend in the industry is less customer loyalty and increased commoditization. Many customers today are willing to mix and match and try various products based on attributes other than brand name. This bodes well for many firms, as customer spending has increased substantially as a result. However, R&D and marketing expenses are on the rise in the industry, as corporations try to attract buyers to their products by providing new and exciting selections. A comparative analysis of Revlon versus two rival firms is provided in Exhibit 7.

EXHIBIT 7   Revlon versus Avon and L'Oreal SA

	Revlon	Avon	L'Oreal SA
# Employees	6,900	36,700	77,452
$ Net Income	28 M	(124) M	3,480 M
$ Revenue	1.93 B	9.18 B	26.88 B
$ Revenue/Employee	279,710	250,136	347,053
$ EPS	0.10	(0.29)	1.16
$ Market Cap.	1.72 B	3.25 B	94.14 B

Source: A variety of sources, all based on company documents.

Avon Products, Inc. (AVP)

Headquartered in New York City and founded in 1886 "to help women become independent," Avon reported a net loss of $124 million in 2014. The company sells a wide array of beauty products, including cosmetics, fragrances, skin care, hair care, and others. The firm also sells jewelry, watches, apparel, houseware products, nutritional products, and more. Similar to rival Mary Kay, Avon competes in direct sales and provides products to over 65 countries. Most of Revlon's sales are generated in the United States, but over 85 percent of all sales of Avon are derived from foreign markets. Avon has been plagued with the stronger dollar in recent years. Approximately 30 percent of sales for Avon are derived from products other than cosmetics.

In late 2014, Avon and the U.S. government came to agreement on a fine totaling $135 million concerning bribes to Chinese officials in return for better business opportunities for Avon. One contributing factor to the fine was a letter written by an Avon executive where the person suggested that "getting a little dirty when doing business in China is not our fault," it is just how business is done in China. Rumors are that Avon is currently talking with private equity firm TPG Capital about being acquired.

Avon has not been performing well. From 2011 to 2015, the company witnessed a declining revenue trend in North America, especially in the United States, mainly due to a decrease in active representatives, partly offset by large average orders. Revenue from the United States has declined considerably from about $2,293.4 million in 2009 to nearly $1,458.2 million in 2013. Avon's revenues from the United States declined another 16 percent in the third quarter of 2014.

L'Oreal SA (LRYCY)

Headquartered outside of Paris, France, and founded in 1909, L'Oreal is known worldwide for producing quality cosmetics. It is considered the world's largest cosmetics company, selling cosmetics and hair color products in drugstores and mass merchandisers worldwide. In addition to the L'Oreal brand, other top brands include Garnier, Maybelline, Lancome, and The Body Shop. L'Oreal employs 72,000 worldwide and reported revenues in excess of $26 billion in 2013. The firm receives approximately one quarter of its sales from North America, the same percent as sales derived from Europe. The weak euro and strong dollar lately has benefited L'Oreal. To better compete against rival Estee Lauder in the United States, L'Oreal acquired Los Angeles-based NYX Cosmetics in 2014. L'Oreal's U.S. headquarters is in New York City. In June 2014, L'Oreal reached agreement with the U.S. Federal Trade Commission not to make claims about its anti-aging products, unless it had credible scientific evidence supporting the claims. The settlement followed an investigation by the commission into claims being made in relation to two products, which the commission described as "false and unsubstantiated." In 2014, L'Oréal made the commitment to ensure that none of its products is linked to deforestation, and to source 100 percent renewable raw materials by 2020. L'Oreal was recently included in the Corporate Knights "Global 100" list of the 100 most sustainable companies.

Estee Lauder Companies, Inc. (EL)

Headquartered in New York City and founded in 1946, Estee Lauder is still controlled by the Lauder family. The firm does business worldwide with over 40,000 employees. As of June 30, 2014 (the end of the fiscal year), Estee Lauder Companies had sales of more than $10.9 billion. The company is known for its skin care products, makeup, fragrances, hair care products, and many other beauty related products. Top brands include Clinique, Aveda, Bumble and Bumble, Bobbi Brown, Origins, and several others. As of 2014, the firm was aggressively expanding into the men's skin care business. In general, Estee Lauder products are considered premium and of better quality than many rivals, including Revlon, Avon, and L'Oreal. Estee Lauder typically sells its products direct to consumers or through its own stores, boutiques, specialty salons, and upscale retailers. Approximately 10 percent of Estee Lauder's total revenues are derived from Macy's.

External Issues

Lipstick Industry

The lipstick industry in the United States is valued around $1.5 billion annually and is expected to grow at an annualized rate of nearly 6 percent through 2020. Key producers are Estee Lauder, Procter & Gamble, Revlon, and L'Oreal, representing 16, 10, 5, and 3 percent of the U.S. market share, respectively. The lipstick industry has 60 manufacturers. Despite lipstick being one of the most visible cosmetic products, the industry revenue of $1.5 billion pales in comparison to the over $50 billion cosmetic product industry. The lipstick industry is much more resistant to economic downturns than many other industries, even other cosmetics products. Competitors are introducing many new styles and colors of lipstick as well, creating new sales. With the relatively cheap price of lipstick for the consumer, many women have different colors and styles for various occasions, and are willing to try new colors and products, as cost is generally not prohibitive. An area of concern for lipstick and cosmetic manufacturers generally is the increased sensitivity to possibly harsh metals, chemicals, or animal byproducts used in lipstick. The new sensitivity in the composition of lipsticks has many firms increasing their R&D and advertising budget to ensure consumers are provided the products they desire. In fact, R&D and marketing budgets now comprise 25 percent of total industry revenue. Also, there is much less brand loyalty now industrywide, and many consumers are switching from brand to brand and even using multiple different lipstick or cosmetic brands simultaneously. In addition, celebrities are increasingly posting photos of themselves without makeup and adding hashtags and other messages.

Most lipstick is categorized into either sheer or matte. Sheer lipstick products contain more oil and must be applied more often to make lips look shiny. Matte lipstick is more robust and need to be applied much less frequently. Both types of lipsticks are equally popular, accounting for 85 percent of all lipstick sold. Lip stain, lip liner, and other lip products make up the remaking 15 percent of sales.

Lipstick is sold in many different mediums, with mass merchants such as cosmetic stores, grocery stores, Walmart, and drugstores accounting for nearly half of all sales. Department stores account for another 20 percent of sales and direct to the consumer accounts for 8 percent of sales. There are several companies that deal directly to the consumer, such as Mary Kay and Avon. Interestingly, despite having great global brands in the United States, only 15 percent of total revenues are obtained from outside the states. Wholesalers account for 10 percent of total sales, but are expected to increase their share moving forward as they have better bargaining power. Imports account for $200 million of the $1.5 billion U.S. lipstick industry, with a quarter of these coming from France, likely largely contributed by French-based L'Oreal.

Hair Care, Skin Care, Cosmetics

The hair care, skin care, and cosmetic industry in the United States accounts for over $55 billion in annual sales and has enjoyed a growth rate of nearly 6 percent from 2010 through 2014. Much like the lipstick market, consumers still purchased beauty products at high rates, even during the recession. Growth is projected to continue through 2020 at a rate of nearly 4 percent. Hair care and skin care products are the two largest revenue-producing contributions to the industry as a whole, with revenues each of approximately $13 billion totaling just short of 50 percent of total revenues combined. Cosmetics, perfumes, and deodorants also contribute significantly to the industry, with total market shares of 15, 10, and 8 percent, respectively. Many of the same issues facing lipstick manufacturers are also faced in the marketing and producing of cosmetic-related products. Higher marketing and R&D expenses—along with a growing concern for reduced packaging, animal safety, and product safety—negatively impacted profits. Consumers also are quick to switch from brand to brand, and are showing less brand loyalty, presenting both threats and opportunities for producers. There is also a growing influx of imported products from around the world on all price points. Generally perceived higher-quality products are imported from Europe, whereas perceived lower-quality and lower-priced products are imported from Mexico and China. Currently, about 15 percent of revenues of U.S.-based producers are derived from overseas markets. Interestingly, overseas customers, even in Asia, tend to prefer higher-quality, more expensive products, and firms that have attempted to offer lower-quality, cheaper alternative products have not fared as well.

Hair care products, the largest segment by revenues, includes hair dye, bleaches, shampoos, conditions, hair sprays, gels, mousses, and all other products related to the hair. Shaving products are also included in this segment. Hair care products have not grown as a segment as rapidly as other products (e.g., skin care). There is growing research and marketing to suggest that expensive shampoos are not worth the money, thereby hurting this product class. In addition, many women are coloring their hair at home or going longer between visits to the salon for coloring, which hurts the industry. Also, there have been relatively few new products developed to entice buyers. This is in stark contrast to other segments such as skin care, lipsticks, perfumes, and cosmetics that often introduce new products.

Skin care products continue to grow as a percent of total industry market share as more and more people are using these products, including men. In 2014, skin care products barely trailed hair care products in industrywide sales, but are expected to be the largest revenue-producing product category moving forward. Firms promote anti-aging treatments and wrinkle-reducing creams. Even creams promoted to remove back circles from under the eyes are available. Sunscreen is also in this category. Estee Lauder's CEO recently suggested that men's skin care products may outpace companywide growth at his firm moving forward.

Other products sold making up the other 50 percent of industrywide revenue include makeup, perfumes, and other products. Makeup has been a relatively slow-growing product line for firms, but with increased demand for products that are marketed as chemical free, there is room for some moderate growth. Interestingly enough, all products contain chemicals, but this is a possible area for growth moving forward. Perfumes, especially for women, have been stagnant; however, men's colognes have grown at moderated paces and are expected to continue.

No Makeup Trends

There is a growing trend promoted by many online articles, several from the *New York Times*, and from celebrities taking photos with hashtags "no makeup" that are encouraging women to be more natural in appearance. No clear data exist yet on how popular or enduring this trend may become, but it is worth noting, and possibly a factor cosmetic firms should be aware of moving forward. The growing population of women who endorse the natural look claim that "being comfortable in your own skin and low maintenance is the true beauty; to the extent you apply layers of makeup you only become more frivolous and superficial." Various theories on why the trend is developing include attractive women wanting everyone to know just how attractive they are without the use of makeup, a new fashion trend for everyone, or possibly just laziness. Whether or not the trend will be enduring, most experts agree, it is like underdressing for the job or not brushing your hair. Therefore the impact on cosmetic firms for *now* is probably limited, but it is certainly something worth monitoring.

Future

Ronald Perelman's New York City-based MacAndrews & Forbes Inc. owns about 78 percent of Revlon. Perelman is Revlon's chairman of the board. There are rumors that Perelman may want to sell Revlon. Analysts say Revlon's EBIT margins, on average, are good at 19 percent, but the company's market capitalization to EBIT ratio of just 9.6 is substantially below the 13.3 average ratio for eight of its global peers. Some analysts report that global consumer companies would be the most likely interested in buying Revlon, such as Procter & Gamble Co. and L'Oreal. Revlon would be complementary to P&G's CoverGirl business. Unilever NV and even Coty, Inc. are among others that could be interested in Revlon. For any firm to obtain the highest acquisition price for its shareholders, a clear strategic plan is needed, showing expected increases in both revenues and profits going forward. Help CEO Delpani develop an impressive strategic plan for Revlon.

World Relief, 2015

www.worldrelief.org

MyManagementLab®

For additional assurance of learning questions which prove you understand and are able to apply the strategic concepts in this case, go to the assignment section of your MyLab.

Headquartered in Baltimore, Maryland, World Relief is a large nonprofit charity focused on helping churches and volunteers around the world serve the vulnerable and reduce human suffering. Servicing 16 countries, World Relief's 95,000 volunteers currently reach over 8.5 million people with much needed help. World Relief focuses its efforts on education health, child development, agriculture, food security, anti-trafficking, immigrant services, micro-enterprise, disaster response, and refugee resettlement.

World Relief is guided by a perspective found in the New Testament of the Bible in Matthew 25:35–40 where Jesus states that "whatever you did for one of the least of these brothers and sisters of mine, you did for me," which places the burden of caring for those in need on the shoulders of their fellow man. A recent *Annual Report* of World Relief provides photos of people in need with very personal statements regarding their needs, such as, "For I was hungry…", "I was sick…", "I was a stranger…", with personal intervention statements such as, "… and you clothed me", "… and you looked after me", and "you came to visit me…." The Christian focus on individuals helping individuals is a key factor for World Relief.

Copyright by Fred David Books LLC. www.strategyclub.com, (Written by Edward Moore, Liberty University)

World Relief currently helps refugees fleeing violence in Iraq and Syria. Over 9 million people in Syria have been forced from their homes into neighboring cities or countries and another 1.8 million displaced within the country. World Relief has provided about 7,000 people with some of what they need to survive a winter in Northern Iraq, including shelter material, clothing, and bedding.

History

Founded in 1944 as the War Relief Commission of the National Association of Evangelicals (NAE) in New York City, World Relief was created to address the humanitarian needs in post-war Europe. Through its efforts, food and clothing were shipped from the United States and distributed through a network of churches in the hardest hit communities in Europe. The War Relief Commission adopted the motto "Food for the body and food for the soul" to guide its efforts.

In 1950, the organization changed its name to World Relief and launched an aid program in Korea by establishing 140 feeding centers serving 31,000 hot meals each day. By 1956, its work in Korea had expanded to include support for orphanages, church plantings, and the establishment of a tuberculosis clinic. By 1961, the organization had 177 feeding centers in Korea and a growing network of partnerships with evangelical churches worldwide. At this same time, efforts to help the vulnerable were extended to include aid for orphans in Egypt, lepers in Taiwan, as well as aid for flood victims in Korea and earthquake survivors in China and Chile.

In 1965, as conflict spread in Southeast Asia, World Relief established projects in Vietnam, including agricultural training, a demonstration farm, and support for health programs at Vietnam's Nhatrang Christian Hospital. The organization launched a "Food for Work" program in 1968 to assist 94,000 hungry people in Chile, and a program to help Korean war refugees plant 22 million mulberry seedlings and cultivate silk worms. Both programs aimed at helping others to help themselves.

In 2004, World Relief opened its Immigration Legal Clinic in Baltimore with the goal of providing affordable legal services to immigrants, including victims of human trafficking and domestic violence. The following year, World Relief responded by providing relief and rebuilding homes in the Gulf Coast in the aftermath of Hurricane Katrina. Today, World Relief works across the globe, providing relief wherever people find themselves vulnerable as the result of natural or human-caused disasters.

Internal Issues

Vision/Mission

World Relief's vision is: "In community with the local Church, we envision the most vulnerable people transformed economically, socially, and spiritually." World Relief's mission is: "Empowering the local Church to serve the most vulnerable." World Relief says it is called to "Stand for the Vulnerable." The organization describes the why, where, what, and how that accompany the "who" it stands for. The overarching "who" (the vulnerable) is divided into specific cause areas that guide the organization's efforts, including children, women, the displaced, the devastated, and opportunity. The remaining descriptors provide the framework for and the rationale behind their efforts:

- *Why:* In response to the Christian commission to serve the vulnerable
- *Where:* Around the world in the geographic and economic gaps as well as the gap between complacence and compassion
- *How:* By leveraging skills in partnership with local churches, enabling them to better serve their communities with cultural sensitivity and technical expertise
- *What:* To empower local churches to heal individuals and communities suffering from the physical, psychological, social, and spiritual wounds of poverty.

Organizational Structure

World Relief has 23 offices in the United States and 16 countries internationally. The organization has a diverse Board of Directors, representing a wide range of public- and private-sector leaders from corporations, churches, universities, and trusts. As indicated in Exhibit 1, World Relief is structured functionally. The Director of Spiritual Formation serves as the chaplain for all World Relief offices, as well as advisor to the senior leadership team.

Ethics

World Relief has a broad list of values that guide the actions of the organization at all levels. The basis for all World Relief actions is the "example of Jesus as we serve those who are suffering from poverty and injustice, regardless of color, belief, or gender, as part of God's plan to redeem, reconcile, and restore the world. We seek to follow Jesus by living holy, humble, and honest lives individually and corporately." From this foundation, World Relief highlights the local church as the primary agent of change within communities working to integrate word and deed, and people (including staff, volunteers, clients, beneficiaries, donors, and partners) as the primary actors in making those changes happen.

Strategy

In order to empower local churches to serve the most vulnerable, World Relief's strategy leverages a combination of fund-raising, collaboration, and direct relief programs. The organization focuses its efforts on five distinct causes: (1) children, (2) women, (3) the displaced, (4) the devastated, and (5) the creation of opportunity. These causes are supported through their work in the broader areas of disaster response, child development, maternal and child health, HIV/AIDS, agricultural development, immigrant legal services, micro-financing, anti-trafficking, refugee resettlement, and many others.

World Relief trains team members to empower families, churches, and communities—all with the goal of transforming entire regions and training others through work in local churches and small groups. These local churches and small groups then impact families and communities by providing care, training, and ongoing support. These healthy families and communities are then able to exponentially influence their surrounding communities, thereby transforming entire regions of the world.

Recognizing that children are often the most vulnerable and overlooked group, World Relief provides Child Development programs in which children of all ages are placed in clubs led by trained Christian mentors, where they can learn about life, identity, health, hygiene, and safety. World Relief believes that women are the heartbeat of families and communities, and that their suffering by extension causes the entire community to suffer.

In a world filled with political violence, ethnic disputes, and economic disparities, World Relief teaches local churches in conflict areas to reconcile differences among people in order to create safe and healthy communities that can flourish. When disaster strikes, World Relief initiates Disaster Response programs that address basic needs such as food, water, and shelter. Once the initial relief efforts are underway, the organization turns its attention to rehabilitation programs with long-term solutions.

EXHIBIT 1 World Relief's Organizational Structure

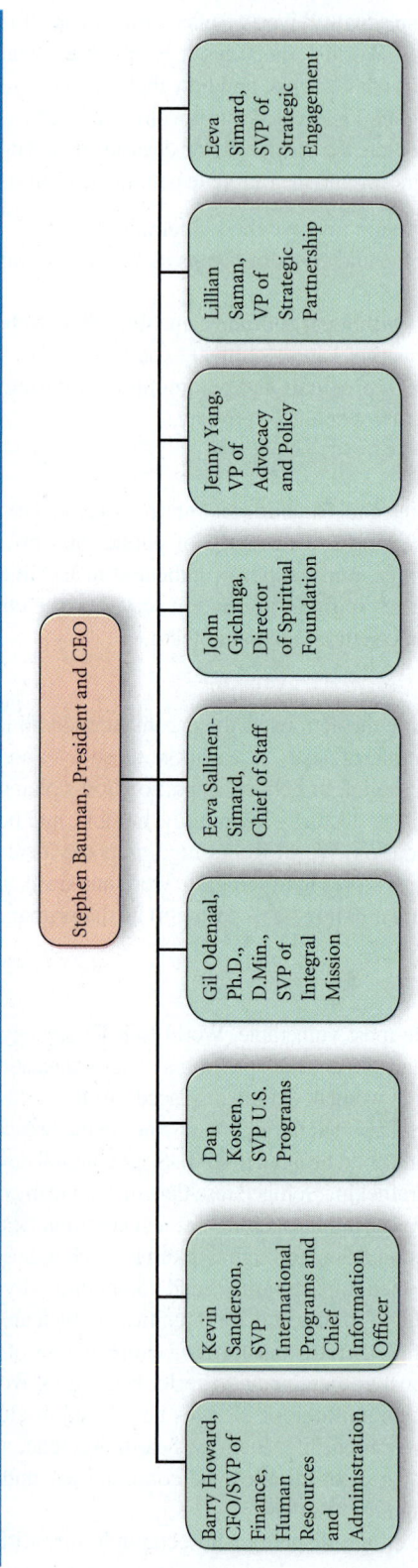

Source: Based on World Relief's organization documents.

World Relief has programs that provide financing through post-conflict and disaster micro-enterprise to equip small business owners with skills and capital to allow them to develop businesses that will improve and transform conditions in their communities. World Relief enters into partnerships with other organizations with similar goals into order to leverage their combined efforts, including the Accord Network, the Micah Network, One, Integral, Faith Alliance Against Slavery and Trafficking (FAST), CORE Group, and Live58.

Finance

World Relief generated $60 million in operating revenue in 2013 resulting from a fundraising expense of $3 million. A total of $49 million was expended by the organization in direct support of programs to help those in need while only $6 million went to general and administrative costs. The organization's 2014 Financial Statement shows similar results with a total of $61 million in operating revenue based on a fundraising expense of $3 million, with a total of $54 in program expenses and supporting expenses of $10 million. In total, the firm lost $3.5 million in 2014.

World Relief generated $61 million in revenue during 2014, up 3 percent from the previous year. Given in Exhibit 2, the organization's Statement of Activities, which is similar to the income statement of a for-profit organization, indicates that $13 million of this was in the form of

EXHIBIT 2 World Relief's Statement of Activities (in millions of USD)

Report Date	2014	2013
Operating Activities		
Support and Revenues		
Private Contributions	$13.00	$16.71
Government and Other Public Grants	41.16	36.45
MED Banking Revenue	1.92	1.73
Other Revenue	5.11	4.36
Total Revenues	61.19	59.25
Net Assets Released from Restrictions	–	–
Total Support and Revenue	**61.19**	**59.25**
Expenses		
Program Ministries		
USA Programs	33.55	31.31
Overseas Programs	17.10	13.27
Disaster Response	3.72	5.06
Total Program Ministries	**54.36**	**49.64**
Support Ministries		
General and Administrative	6.64	5.96
Fundraising	3.37	3.10
Total Support Ministries	10.01	9.06
Total Expenses	**64.37**	**58.70**
Revenues and Support Over Operating Expenses	**(3.18)**	**0.55**
Other Changes		
Gain on Minority Interest in Net Assets	0.86	0.87
Loss on Discontinued Operations	(1.17)	(1.22)
Impairment Recover of Discontinued Operations	–	1.21
Change in Net Assets	**(3.50)**	**1.41**
Net Assets at Beginning of Year	20.91	19.50
Net Assets at End of Year	**17.41**	**20.91**

Source: Based on World Relief's organization documents.

private contributions with another $41 million in government grants and other public grants. The remaining revenue came from other sources, including MED Banking revenue. Total operating expenses were $64 million, resulting in a shortfall of $3 million. World Relief's balance sheet, called a Statement of Financial Position, is provided in Exhibit 3.

For a nonprofit organization, it is important to measure the efficiency with which an organization raises funds and converts those funds into programs that support its mission. Charity Navigator (www.charitynavigator.com) is a nonprofit organization providing guidance regarding the performance of nonprofit organizations. World Relief spent $54 million on programs in support of its mission in 2014, representing 84 percent of its total revenue, as revealed earlier in Exhibit 2, under Support Ministries. Data from Charity Navigator shows that 7 out of 10 nonprofit companies spend at least 75 percent on programs, so World Relief is in the top tier for

EXHIBIT 3 World Relief's Statement of Financial Position (in millions of USD)

Report Date	2014	2013
Assets		
Current Assets		
Cash and Cash Equivalents	$7.04	$9.02
Investments, at Market	0.40	0.24
Receivables		
Grants	3.66	3.27
Contributions	0.51	2.45
Other	0.07	0.30
Total Current Assets	**11.67**	**15.28**
Non-current Assets		
Microenterprise and Agricultural Loans	4.59	3.84
Prepaid Expenses and other Assets	0.61	0.56
Minority Interest in Net Assets	6.15	5.29
Plant & Equipment – Net of Accumulated Depr.	4.21	3.49
Assets of Discontinued Operations	–	1.24
Total Non-current Assets	**15.56**	**14.42**
Total Assets	**27.23**	**29.69**
Liabilities and Net Assets		
Current Liabilities		
Accounts Payable and Accrued Liabilities	3.83	2.97
Deferred Revenue	0.36	0.28
Total Current Liabilities	**4.20**	**3.25**
Non-current Liabilities		
General	2.18	2.00
Microenterprise/Agricultural Development	2.13	2.41
Other Liabilities	1.31	1.10
Liabilities of Discontinued Operations	–	0.02
Total Non-current Liabilities	**5.62**	**5.54**
Total Liabilities	**9.82**	**8.78**
Net Assets		
Unrestricted	13.65	16.65
Temporarily Restricted	3.76	4.26
Total Net Assets	**17.41**	**20.91**
Total Liabilities and Net Assets	**27.23**	**29.69**

Source: Based on World Relief's organization documents.

EXHIBIT 4 World Relief's Total 2014 Expense Breakdown

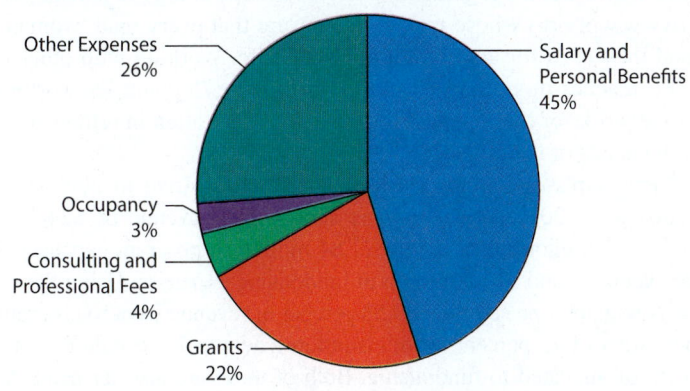

Source: Based on World Relief's 2014 financial statements.

the conversion of revenue to programs. Total administrative and fundraising expenses for 2014 were $6 million and $3 million, respectively, as shown in Exhibit 2 under Support Ministries. These two categories represent 10 and 5 percent of total expenses. The best performing nonprofit organizations, according to Charity Navigator, keep their administrative expenses below 15 percent and fundraising expenses below 10 percent. Thus, World Relief is operationally efficient in both categories when compared to industry norms. However, despite the breakdowns provided in Exhibit 2 on Program and Support Ministries, Exhibit 4 provides a consolidated total of how funds were spent. It is important to note, whether listed as Program or Support Ministries, Salary and Personal Benefits accounts for 45 percent of all expenses in 2014, followed by Grant-related expenses totaling 22 percent of total revenues. Other expenses included over 20 other expenses.

Another metric to consider is the return on fundraising expenses. According to Charity Navigator, top-performing nonprofit companies spend less than $0.10 to raise $1.00 in revenue. During 2014, the World Relief raised a total of $60 million with a fundraising expense of $3 million, placing it in the top tier with an expense of $0.0551 for each $1.00 raised.

Another important metric used by Charity Navigator is the working capital ratio, which measures how many years the organization could sustain its present program spending using only net assets, with the best-performing organizations having a ratio of greater than 1:1. With a current program expense of $54 million and total net assets of $17 million, World Relief has a ratio of 0.32, indicating its net assets can provide for less than one year of program operations. Taken together, these financial performance metrics reveal World Relief to be an efficient and effective organization in the area of fundraising and allocation to program expense while minimizing internal expenses. However, the organization needs to carefully consider its ability to meet program expense in the event of significant loss of revenue.

The Statement of Financial Positions in Exhibit 3 reveals a current ratio for 2014 for World Relief of 2.78, which is attractive, but down from 4.7 in 2013. This shows that the organization has solid liquidity necessary to meet its short-term liabilities. The debt to total assets ratio for 2014 is 0.56:1, indicating that a low percentage of total funds are provided by creditors. World Relief's long-term debt/net assets results in a leverage ratio of 0.32:1, indicating that the organization has a very low leverage reinforcing the findings from the total debt to net assets calculation. Taken together, these financial ratios show World Relief to be a financially healthy organization.

Competition

Numerous nonprofit humanitarian organizations with similar missions compete for the same revenue sources as World Relief, including United Way, American Red Cross, and the Peace Corp. Potential donors make choices about where to make contributions based on the operational efficiency of the nonprofit as well as its specific causes. Organizations similar to World Relief also include the World Food Program (USA), Cooperative for Assistance and Relief Everywhere (CARE), and OXFAM International.

World Food Program (WFP)

Founded in 1961, World Food Program (USA) (www.wfpusa.org) is part of the global World Food Program (www.wpf.org) whose vision is to ensure that every man, woman, and child has access to the food they need for an active and healthy life. Working with other United Nations agencies, the WFP reaches more than 80 million people in 75 countries worldwide each year. Over 11,000 people work for the organization globally, most often in remote areas of the world directly serving the needs of the hungry.

World Food Program's operations in the United States strive to eliminate hunger in the states. The organization's 2012 *Annual Report* shows total revenue of $24.40 million with a total expense of $24.05 million made up of $21.84 million in program expenses, $.0290 million in administrative expenses, and $1.92 million in fundraising expenses. Using the evaluative methods from Charity Navigator, one sees that 89.53 percent of revenue went to program expense, well above the top tier target of 75 percent. Administration made up 1.2 percent of total expense with another 8.0 percent of allocated to fundraising. Both of these are also far better than the top tier targets of less than 15 percent for administration and 10 percent for fundraising. In the area of fundraising efficiency, the organization spent $0.0787 for each dollar raised, which was right on target.

Cooperative for Assistance and Relief Everywhere (CARE)

Headquartered in Georgia and founded in 1945, CARE (www.care.org) has the broad goal of serving individuals and families in the poorest communities in the world in the fight to end global poverty. The organization works in 87 countries to support nearly 1,000 poverty-fighting emergency and development projects. CARE works to leverage its efforts through partnerships with other organizations, including foundations and trusts, corporations, humanitarian partners, and institutional donors.

CARE's reported 2013 total revenue of $492 million with a total expense of $510 million made up of $452 million in program expenses, $36 million in administrative expenses, and $22 million in fundraising expenses. The organization posted a deficit of $18.80 million during the year as its expenses exceeded revenue. The evaluative methods from Charity Navigator indicate that 92 percent of revenue went to program expense, well above the top tier target of 75 percent, keeping in mind that overall spending was in excess of revenue. Administration made up 7.1 percent of total expense with another 4.3 percent allocated to fundraising. Both of these are well ahead of the top tier targets. In the area of fundraising efficiency, the organization spent $0.0445 for each dollar raised, which was also above target.

OXFAM America

Founded in 1995, OXFAM America (www.oxfamamerica.org) is part of OXFAM International (www.oxfam.org), whose name comes from the Oxford Committee for Famine Relief founded in Britain in 1942. OXFAM is an international confederation of 17 organizations working with partners and local communities in more than 90 countries. The vision of the organization is to see a world without poverty. OXFAM desires to create a world where "people are valued and treated equally, enjoy their rights as full citizens, and can influence decisions affecting their lives." The organization's overarching goal is to create sustainable solutions to poverty through empowering people to create a future that is secure, just, and free from poverty. OXFAM America, as one of the 17 members of OXFAM International, is responsible for channeling funds and efforts within the United States toward the accomplishment of organizational goals.

OXFAM reported 2014 revenue of $68 million but expenses of $82 million made up of $63 million in program expenses, $6 million in administrative expenses, and $12 million in fundraising expenses. The organization posted a deficit of $14 million during the year. The evaluative methods from Charity Navigator reveal that 93 percent of revenue went to program expenses, which is well above the top tier target of 75 percent. Administration made up 7.6 percent of total expense, with another 15 percent allocated to fundraising. Although administrative expenses are below the top tier targets of less than 15 percent, the fundraising expenses are very high when compared to the 10 percent target. The organization was not very efficient in the area of fundraising, spending $0.1813 for each dollar raised.

External Issues

World Relief provides a broad perspective on the challenges facing world populations in their 2013 Case Statement. Every day about 22,000 children under the age of 5 die from preventable diseases, and as many as 49 percent of them live in Sub-Saharan Africa. To date, over 15 million women are living with HIV/AIDS, and in Kenya, women between 15 and 19 are three times more likely to become infected than males. Globally, over 21 million people are displaced from their homes due to persecution and conflict each year. Another 100 million globally are impacted by natural disasters. Economic limitations are also significant, with nearly 3 billion people around the world earning only $2.00 per day.

Hunger continues to be a significant issue for the world's growing population. World Food Program reports that 805 million people in the world do not have enough food, which is about 1 in every 9 people. Each year, hunger kills more people than AIDS, malaria, and tuberculosis combined. The issue has a regional aspect, with most of the world's hungry live in developing countries, where 13.5 percent of the population is undernourished. Asia has the largest number of hungry people in the world, and Sub-Saharan Africa has the highest prevalence of hunger as a percentage of population. World Food Program reports that poor nutrition causes 3.1 million deaths each year of children under age 5, accounting for 45 percent of the deaths in this vulnerable population. In developing countries, nearly one of every six children is underweight, representing nearly 100 million children. Globally, one in four children in the world have stunted growth, and 66 million primary school-aged children in the developing world attend classes hungry, with 23 million in Africa alone.

Fresh drinking water is another significant human challenge. The Nature Conservancy (www.nature.org) reports that half the world's major rivers are seriously polluted and/or depleted and that within 10 years most people on the planet will face water shortages. Water shortages are being exacerbated by the production of the food and materials we need, with agriculture alone accounting for 70 percent of the water taken from groundwater, rivers, and lakes. Additionally, excess fertilizer is finding its way back into rivers and lakes, causing odor and taste problems as well as health problems.

Future

World Relief has helped millions of people since the 1940s and continues to do so today. The organization focuses on helping children, women, the displaced, and the devastated. The firm has recently worked diligently to help many Syrian refugees flee war-stricken Syria, in addition to helping feed hungry people around the world, particularly in Africa, helping displaced disaster victims and much more. However, World Relief did lose $3 million in fiscal year 2014 and is possibly spread too thinly with its broad mission. Do you recommend that World Relief should continue to try to help as many people as it can in as many different regions, as people face many different issues? When disaster strikes or when a group of people are in need, how should World Relief respond? What in its current mission or strategy provides direction on how to allocate resources most effectively? Or do you believe that World Relief should just respond any way they can each time, even though it is difficult to be everything for everyone?

Perhaps World Relief's mission is too broad. How does its mission compare to the mission of other similar organizations, including American Red Cross and United Way? For example, the American Red Cross's international disaster response and preparedness programs provide relief and development assistance to millions of people annually who suffer as a result of natural and human-made disasters around the world. To respond quickly and effectively, the American Red Cross has pre-positioned emergency relief supplies in three warehouses managed by the International Federation in Dubai, Malaysia, and Panama. These supplies are used to respond to disasters such as the 2004 Indian Ocean tsunami disaster, the 2010 Haiti earthquake, ongoing crises in Africa, and hurricanes in the Caribbean and the Americas. An Emergency Response Unit (ERU) is another method with which the American Red Cross responds to international emergencies.

Perhaps perceptual mapping would enable World Relief to more effectively use its funds. The firm's mission, "Empowering the local church to serve the most vulnerable," is not clear and provides little direction for allocating resources, soliciting donations, or marketing the firm. Help CEO Bauman develop a 3-year strategic plan, including writing a new mission statement and developing some useful perceptual maps, that will help this organization operate more effectively and efficiently, without incurring another annual loss.

World Wildlife Fund for Nature (WWF) 2015

www.worldwildlife.org

Headquartered in Gland, Switzerland, the World Wildlife Fund by some measures is the world's largest independent, nonprofit conservation organization working in 100 countries, supported by over 1 million members within the United States and 5 million members globally. The organization has about 6,200 full-time staff members that manage an average of 1,300 projects at any one time. Since being founded in 1961, it has invested close to $10 billion in more than 13,000 conservation projects in over 150 countries. Within the United States, the WWF operates as a nonprofit organization and is headquartered in Washington, DC. The organization generated a total of $291.49 million in operating revenue in 2014, resulting from a fundraising expense of $28.70 million. A total of $224.46 million was expended by the organization in direct support of conservation programs. The symbol of WWF is the Giant Panda (the endangered black and white bear from China).

WWF opened a new office in Myanmar in late 2014 after partnering with the national government to achieve shared goals. Myanmar, located in southeast Asia, has a very rich natural capital, including three of the world's most pristine rivers, over 250 mammal species, and more than 1,000 bird species. The country's important biodiversity includes endangered species such as tigers, elephants, and Irrawaddy dolphins. Myanmar is determined to develop a green economy that can serve as a global model of how to improve life for a country's citizens, while protecting its natural capital.

In July 2015, the U.S. Fish and Wildlife Service began investigating the circumstances surrounding the killing that month of Cecil, a lion who is thought to have been lured out of his protected habitat in Zimbabwe and killed by Walter J. Palmer, an American dentist and hunter. The killing of Cecil raised global awareness for wildlife welfare on many fronts. Well known to anyone who ever visited Hwange National Park in western Zimbabwe, Cecil was killed and beheaded—the head intended as a trophy for the hunter.

Copyright by Fred David Books LLC. www.strategyclub.com (Written by Edward Moore, Liberty University)

History

The World Wildlife Fund was formed when the Morges Manifesto document was signed in 1961 by 16 of the world's leading conservationists, stating that although the expertise to protect the environment existed, the financial support for the goal did not. As a result, the document established the WWF as an international fundraising organization. It quickly established itself on the world conservation stage and opened its first office in Morges, Switzerland, with H.R.H. Prince Bernhard as its first president. In 1961, WWF funded the British National Appeal and the United States Appeal, the first two national organizations funded under WWF. Also that inaugural year, WWF approved five projects totaling $33,000 to begin conservation work with several endangered species, including the Bald Eagle.

By 1973, WWF hired its first staff scientist as a project administrator and had projects in countries across the globe, ranging from a $38,000 grant to study tiger populations in Nepal to purchasing 37,000 acres of land in Kenya to be set aside as a feeding ground and sanctuary for nearly 30 bird species, including one million flamingoes. WWF promoted the Convention on International Trade in Endangered Species of Wild Fauna & Flora (CITES), which to date has been signed by over 170 nations, all committed to ensuring wild plants and animals from runaway trade and exploitation.

By the early 1980s, in partnership with the United Nations Environment Program and the International Union for Conservation of Nature (IUCN), WWF established a program of debt-for-nature swaps in which the WWF converts portions of national debt into funding for conservation efforts. In 1985, WWF launched Wildlands and Human Needs, a new initiative intended to highlight how economic conditions of rural people who share land with wildlife can improve without negative impact to the natural habitats the wildlife relies on. By 1989, the WWF debt-for-nature swap initiative had grown and the organization was able to negotiate a $2.1 million swap for Madagascar.

In 2004, a wildlife census in Africa showed that WWF efforts to save rhinos were paying off with the population of black rhinos reaching 3,600 and white rhinos reaching 11,000. Otherwise, these animals would likely have gone extinct. WWF soon adopted a new and challenging 10-year goal to "measurably conserve 15 to 20 of the world's most important eco-regions and in so doing, transform markets, policies, and institutions in order to reduce threats to these places and the diversity of life on Earth."

Internal Issues

Vision/Mission/Ethics

The World Wildlife Fund's mission is to conserve nature and reduce the most pressing threats to the diversity of life on Earth. The organization's vision is "to build a future in which people live in harmony with nature." WWF's mission is to conserve nature and reduce the most pressing threats to the diversity of life on Earth. In an effort to increase organizational effectiveness, WWF has recently shifted its emphasis from a narrow focus on saving specific species and landscapes to a broad focus addressing the global forces and threats that are impacting specific species and landscapes. This shift has led the organization to focus its efforts on the six key areas of forests, marine, freshwater, wildlife, food, and climate.

The code of ethics calls for the organization to remain global, independent, multicultural, and nonparty political. Importantly, it also calls for objective examination of available information and a strong focus on concrete conservation solutions. The code also highlights the strategy of partnerships and collaboration to accomplish the mission as well as a focus on cost-effective operations.

Organizational Structure

The World Wildlife Fund is structured divisionally, as illustrated in Exhibit 1. There are five divisions reporting to COO Marcia Marsh, including the newest division, simply titled Oceans.

Strategy

The World Wildlife Fund's strategy relies on a combination of fundraising, collaboration, research, conservation projects, and government influence to accomplish the following:

- Protect and restore species and their habitats.
- Strengthen local communities' ability to conserve the natural resources they depend on.
- Transform markets and policies to reduce the impact of the production and consumption of commodities.
- Ensure that the value of nature is reflected in decisions made by individuals, communities, governments, and businesses.
- Mobilize hundreds of millions of people to support conservation.

The World Wildlife Fund's strategy is to partner with organizations to positively impact seven areas: forests, oceans, freshwater, wildlife, food, climate, and species. Its work on forests, for example, focuses on the threats created by growing agriculture use as well as illegal and unsustainable logging. The WWF website places the rate of loss of forests globally at a staggering 48 football fields per minute. To help mitigate this, the WWF has set a specific goal of "conserving the world's most important forests to sustain nature's diversity, benefit our climate, and support human well-being by 2020."

The organization's work on oceans focuses on promoting healthy marine ecosystems capable of sustaining livelihoods and economies while supporting biodiversity. The WWF website says 1 billion people rely on fish as an important part of their diet and that more than 520 million livelihoods are supported by fishing and its related activities.

The WWF's 2014 Living Planet Report reported that wildlife populations of mammals, birds, reptiles, amphibians, and fish have declined by 52 percent over the last 40 years. Success stories in this area include the recovery of Africa's black rhino and black bucks in the Himalayas.

EXHIBIT 1 WWF's Organizational Structure

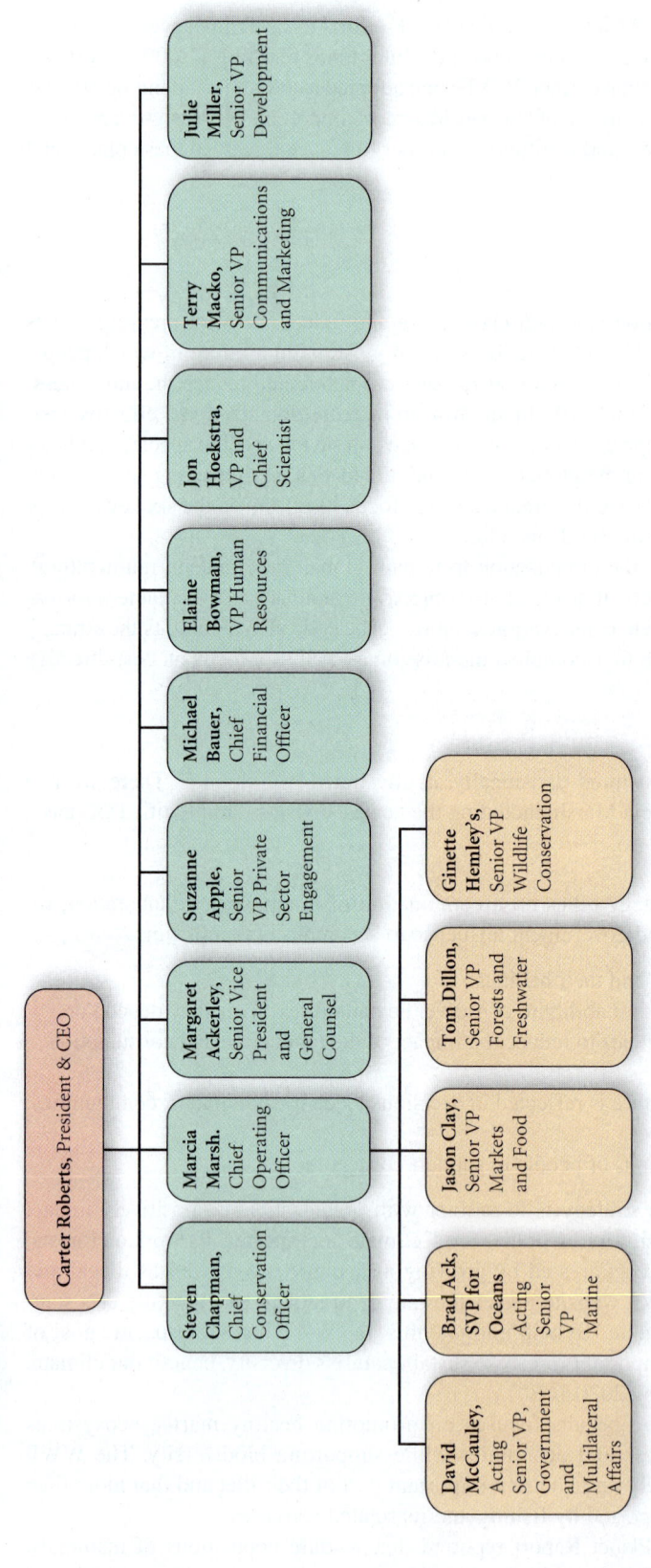

Source: Based on information from the WWF 2014 *Annual Report* as of June 30, 2014.

Current projects include efforts to conserve snow leopards in Central Asia, and ostriches and zebras in Namibia. The goal here is to "use our best science, policy influence, market based strategies, and communications to quantify and enhance the value of wildlife."

Work in the area of food focuses on the conflict created by growing demand for food and the loss of habitats and wildlife that results from that demand. WWF studies show that 7.2 billion people are currently stressing the world's ability to meet demand by consuming 1.5 times what natural resources can supply. With the world's population expected to grow to 9 billion by 2050, the demand for food is expected to double. WWF's plan is to freeze the amount of land currently allocated to food and instead focus on improving efficiency and productivity in current systems while reducing waste. WWF estimates that 1.3 billion tons of food is wasted each year—four times what is needed to feed the estimated 800 million malnourished people in the world. The overall goal is by 2050 to be able to produce enough food for everyone, using roughly the same amount of land currently in use today.

The WWF's strategy includes working with businesses to help discover new and creative ways to reduce WWF's impact on wildlife and habitats while meeting the growing global demand for goods. WWF focuses on a broad range of priority commodities, including items such as dairy, beef, timber, tuna, and many more. In a recent collaborative effort with business, the WWF established the Bioplastic Feedstock Alliance, where leading global companies have committed to the development of plastics made from plant-based material rather than fossil fuels.

Influencing Policy

Public policy has a significant impact on global conservation efforts as it can guide and control actions of individuals and organizations. The WWF actively seeks to influence governments in the United States and globally to pursue conservation actions as well as actively supporting government initiatives that align with organizational goals. In a recent policy initiative, WWF actively supported U.S. government legislation titled the Wildlife Trafficking Enforcement Act, which increased the penalties associated with wildlife trafficking. WWF went a step further and committed to working with the U.S. government to help apply those new penalties to organized crime and illegal wildlife trade to help protect a wide range of threatened species.

Partnerships

The WWF forms partnerships as a key element of its strategy. For example, Bank of America has offered a WWF Visa card since 2009 in support of global conservation. Through this program, Bank of America contributes to WWF for each new qualifying account opened and activated. Other key WWF partnerships include Avon, CARE, and Coca-Cola. Avon, with $11 billion in annual revenue, is a large producer of brochures and consumer paper products with distribution in over 120 countries. Recognizing its impact on the environment, Avon has partnered with WWF in two key areas. First, Avon is a member of WWF's Global Forest & Trade Network that focuses on sustainable pulp and paper supply chain solutions. Second, Avon has an internal customer-focused education campaign called Hello Green Tomorrow to help curb deforestation through consumer awareness.

The World Wildlife Fund's partnership with Coca-Cola was established in 2007 and was recently renewed through 2020. Through this partnership, both companies focus on efforts to improve and sustain fresh water supplies globally and specifically address Coca-Cola's value chain. The value chain enhancements within Coca-Cola include climate protection through reduced carbon content, improved social performance through renewable packaging, sustainable sourcing of agricultural resources, and improved water efficiency throughout manufacturing operations. Externally, the companies work to conserve important water sources in Asia, Africa, and the Americas, and specifically target key river basins and catchments throughout the world.

The WWF's 2014 *Annual Report* shows that individuals contributed 32 percent of total revenue, whereas corporations contributed only 4 percent, so WWF wants businesses to rally to WWF's cause more in the future.

Finance

The World Wildlife Fund generated $291 million in revenue during 2014, up 12 percent from the previous year. The Statement of Activities shown in Exhibit 2 is similar to the income statement of a for-profit organization and reveals that $136 million of the WWF revenue was in the form of direct contributions, with another $51 million in government grants and contracts. The remaining revenue came from other sources, including WWF network revenue and non-operating income. Total operating expenses were $266 million, resulting in a surplus of nearly $26 million.

As a nonprofit, it is important for WWF to measure the efficiency with which the organization raises funds and converts those funds into programs that support its mission. Charity

EXHIBIT 2 **WWF's Statement of Activities (in millions of USD)**

Report Date	2014	2013
Operating Activities		
Revenues		
Contributions	$136.58	$122.18
Government Grants and Contracts	50.82	48.22
WWF Network Revenue	17.90	16.21
Other Revenue Including Royalties	5.49	6.81
In-kind Contributions	46.96	64.30
Non-operating Income Allocated to Operations	33.75	21.73
Total Revenues	**291.49**	**279.44**
Net Assets Released from Restrictions	–	–
Net Revenues	**291.49**	**279.44**
Commercial Building Operations		
Revenues	6.10	6.68
Expenses	5.85	5.52
Net Income on Commercial Building Operations	**0.25**	**1.16**
Total Revenue and Support	**291.74**	**280.60**
Operating Expenses		
Program Services		
Conservation Field and Policy Programs	159.75	144.38
Public Education	64.71	81.74
Total Program Services	**224.46**	**226.12**
Supporting Services		
Finance and Administration	12.72	12.35
Fundraising	28.71	27.66
Total Supporting Activities	**41.43**	**40.02**
Total Operating Expenses	**265.89**	**266.13**
Revenues and Support Over Operating Expenses	**25.85**	**14.46**
Non-operating Activities		
Bequests, Endowments, and Split Income Gifts	12.19	29.21
Income on Interest Rate Swaps	0.28	5.87
Income from Investments, Net	34.47	19.42
Gain/(Loss) on Foreign Currency Exchange	0.45	(0.12)
Total Non-operating Activities	**46.94**	**54.39**
Total Allocated to Operations	(33.75)	(21.73)
Change in Net Assets from Non-Operating Activities	**13.19**	**32.66**
Change in Net Assets	39.03	47.12
Net Assets at Beginning of Year	318.82	271.69
Net Assets at End of Year	**357.85**	**318.82**

Source: Based on WWF's 2014 *Annual Report.*

Navigator (www.charitynavigator.com), a nonprofit rating organization, provides guidance when evaluating this type of performance in the form of industry norms. WWF spent $224 million on programs in support of its mission in 2014, representing 77 percent of its total revenue. Data from Charity Navigator shows that 7 out of 10 nonprofit companies spend at least 75 percent on programs, placing WWF in the top tier for the conversion of revenue to programs. Total administrative and fundraising expenses for 2014 were nearly $13 million and $29 million, respectively. These two categories represent 4.8 and 10.8 percent of total expenses. The best-performing nonprofit organizations, according to Charity Navigator, keep their administrative expenses below 15 percent and fundraising expenses below 10 percent. WWF is operationally efficient in both categories when compared to industry norms.

Another metric to consider is the return on fundraising expenses. According to Charity Navigator, top-performing nonprofit companies will spend less than $0.10 to raise $1.00 in revenue. During 2014, the WWF raised a total of $291 million with a fundraising expense of $29 million, placing them in the top tier with an expense of $0.0985 for each $1.00 raised. One final metric used by Charity Navigator is the working capital ratio that measures how many years the organization could sustain its present program spending using only net assets, with the best performing organizations having a ratio of greater than 1:1. With a current program expense of $224 million and total net assets of $358 million, the WWF has a ratio of 1.59:1, placing it again in the top tier. Taken together, these financial performance metrics reveal WWF to be an efficient and effective organization in the area of fundraising and allocation to program expense while minimizing internal expenses.

The Statement of Financial Positions in Exhibit 3 is similar to the balance sheet of a for-profit organization in that it summarizes assets and liabilities, but differs in totaling net assets rather than shareholders' equity. Despite the differences, several leading financial health metrics can be calculated. For example, the current ratio for 2014 for WWF is 2.35, up from 2.28 in 2013.

Exhibit 4 reveals 10 years (only even years data are shown) of operating revenue and program spending history. Note how the distance between the two lines becomes wider toward 2014, indicating both greater profits and efficiency. Spending decreased $2 million, and net revenues increased $12 million from 2013 to 2014.

Competitors

Donors make choices about where to make contributions based on the operational efficiency of the nonprofit organizations as well as its specific causes. The Nature Conservancy, Conservation International, and the Wildlife Conservation Society are leading wildlife and habitat conservancy nonprofit organizations and as such are competitors to WWF.

The Nature Conservancy (www.nature.org)

Headquartered in Arlington, Virginia, The Nature Conservancy was founded in 1951 with the broad goal of working around the world to protect ecologically important lands and waters for both nature and people. The organization currently has more than 1 million members and since its inception it has protected more than 119 million acres of land and thousands of miles of rivers across the globe. It has a global impact with projects in all 50 states in the United States and more than 35 countries. Its work is focused on threats to conservation, including climate change, fresh water, oceans, and land. The mission statement of the organization is similar to the WWF in that it focuses on achieving conservancy through collaborative partnerships.

The organization's 2013 total revenue was $859 million with a total expense of $752 million made up of $542 million in program expenses, $122 million in administrative expenses, and $87.88 million in fundraising expenses. Using the evaluative methods from Charity Navigator, only 63 percent of revenue went to program expense, which is below the top-tier target of 75 percent. Administration made up 16 percent of total expense, with another 11.7 percent of total expense allocated to fundraising. Both of these are also short of the top-tier targets of less than 15 percent for administration and 10 percent for fundraising. In the area of fundraising efficiency, the organization spent $0.10 for each dollar raised, which was right on target.

The Nature Conservancy also operates more than 100 marine conservation projects globally. The organization's assets totaled $6.18 billion as of 2014. The Nature Conservancy is the largest

EXHIBIT 3 WWF's Statement of Financial Position (in millions of USD)

Report Date	2014	2013
Assets		
Current Assets		
Cash and Cash Equivalents	$34.66	$32.32
Short-term Investments	35.54	25.45
Accounts Receivable	19.54	23.09
Pledges Receivable	28.96	23.13
Prepaid Assets	3.45	4.04
Other Current Assets	2.06	2.99
Total Current Assets	**124.20**	**111.00**
Non-current Assets		
Long-term Investments, Net	240.28	211.99
Pledges Receivable, Net of Current, Discount, and Allowance for Uncollectable Pledges	33.28	20.41
Long-term Trust Receivables	28.67	31.29
Bond Issuance Costs, Net of Amortization	1.14	1.24
Other Non-current Assets	4.97	14.00
Land, Building, and Equipment, Net	59.01	61.00
Total Non-current Assets	**367.35**	**339.92**
Total Assets	**491.55**	**450.93**
Liabilities and Net Assets		
Current Liabilities		
Accounts Payable and Accrued Expenses	14.86	11.73
Grants Payable	28.12	27.85
Deferred Revenue	7.78	7.14
Current Portion of Long-term Debt	2.08	2.03
Total Current Liabilities	**52.83**	**48.75**
Non-current Liabilities		
Long-term Debt, Net of Current Portion	59.51	61.60
Other Long-term Liabilities	8.02	8.14
Interest Rate Sway Liability	13.34	13.62
Total Non-current Liabilities	**80.87**	**83.36**
Total Liabilities	**133.70**	**132.11**
Commitments and Contingencies		
Net Assets		
Unrestricted	171.46	153.18
Temporarily Restricted	142.93	122.79
Permanently Restricted	43.47	42.85
Total Net Assets	**357.85**	**318.82**
Total Liabilities and Net Assets	**491.55**	**450.93**

Source: Based on WWF's 2014 *Annual Report*.

environmental nonprofit by assets and by revenue in the Americas. The Nature Conservancy echoes the concerns of the WWF surrounding drinking water. Its research shows that currently half of the world's major rivers are seriously polluted and/or depleted and that within 10 years, most people on the planet will face water shortages. While the debate surrounding climate change is ongoing, a 2014 National Oceanic and Atmospheric Administration (NOAA) report has cited that 2014 was the hottest year on record since 1880, tied with 1998 and 2010.

EXHIBIT 4 **10-Year Comparison of Revenue and Spending (in millions of USD)**

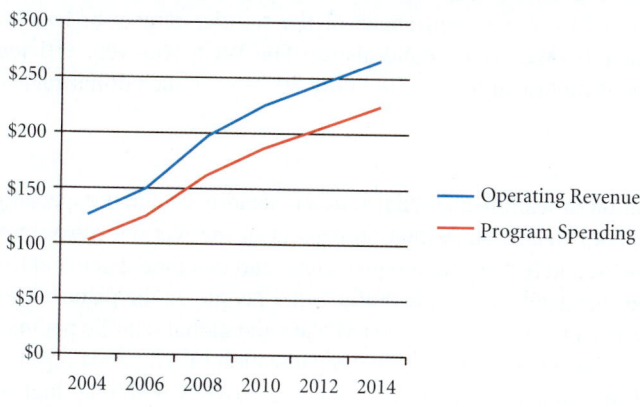

Source: Based on information on the WWF 2014 *Annual Report.*

Conservation International (www.conservation.org)

Headquartered in Arlington, Virginia, and founded in 1987, Conservation International (CI) has the broad goal of protecting nature for the benefit of everyone on our planet. The organization currently has 900 members and is working in over 30 countries. Its work is focused in three areas, including protecting our natural wealth, fostering effective governance, and promoting sustainable production. From its website, Conservation International's vision and mission statements are:

Vision: We imagine a healthy, prosperous world in which societies are forever committed to caring for and valuing nature, for the long-term benefit of people and all life on Earth.

Mission: Building upon a strong foundation of science, partnership and field demonstration, CI empowers societies to responsibly and sustainably care for nature, our global biodiversity, for the well-being of humanity.

The organization reported 2013 revenue of $96.82 million with a total expense of $144 million made up of $122 million in program expenses, $13 million in administrative expenses, and $8.7 million in fundraising expenses. The organization posted a deficit of $47 million during the year. The evaluative metrics from Charity Navigator reveal that 126 percent of CI's revenue went to program expense, well above the top tier target of 75 percent, but includes spending in excess of revenue. Administration made up 8.9 percent of total expense with another 6.1 percent of total expense allocated to fundraising. Both of these are well ahead of the top-tier targets of less than 15 percent for administration and 10 percent for fundraising. In the area of fundraising efficiency, the organization spent $0.09 for each dollar raised, which was also above target.

Wildlife Conservation Society (www.wcs.org)

Headquartered in New York City, the Wildlife Conservation Society (WCS) was founded in 1895 and has the broad goal of saving wildlife and wild places globally through a combination of science, conservation, education, and management of urban wildlife parks. The organizations flagship park is the Bronx Zoo. The WCS currently manages close to 500 conservation projects, manages more than 200 million acres of protected lands, and operates in more than 60 countries. The organization focuses its work on four issues facing wildlife and wild places, including climate change, resource exploitation, the connection between wildlife and human health, and sustainable development. The WCS website lists the mission statement for the organization as:

Mission: WCS saves wildlife and wild places worldwide through science, conservation action, education, and inspiring people to value nature.

The Wildlife Conservation Society reported 2013 revenue of $212 million with a total expense of $1.218 billion made up of $181.07 million in program expenses, $28 million in administrative expenses, and $9.52 million in fundraising expenses. The organization posted a deficit of $6.4 million. Evaluative metrics from Charity Navigator reveal that 85.41 percent of revenue went to program expense, well above the top-tier target of 75 percent. Administration made up 12.7 percent of total expense with another 4.4 percent of total expense allocated to fundraising. Both of these are well ahead of the top-tier targets of less than 15 percent for administration and 10 percent for fundraising. The WCS was very efficient and well above target in the area of fundraising, spending only $0.045 for each dollar raised.

Future

The global condition of wildlife and wild areas has steadily declined, especially in the ocean. The WWF's 2014 *Annual Report* states that 60 percent of the world's ecosystems, including water supplies, fish stocks, and fertile soil, are in decline, and that global demand for resources already requires 1.5 times the available supply. Fully 1 in 9 people on the planet suffer from hunger, yet 90 percent of the ocean's fish stocks are overfished and global wildlife populations have declined by an average of 52 percent. WWF's global organization (www.panda.org) highlights the loss of biodiversity and cites that the current extinction rate is over 1,000 times higher than what science can attribute to natural extinction losses.

The World Health Organization (www.who.int) has also weighed in on the impact of global environmental change. Its website lists leading hazards to human health as climate change, stratospheric ozone depletion, changes in ecosystems due to loss of biodiversity, changes in hydrological systems and the supply of freshwater, land degradation, and stresses on food-producing systems.

WWF reports that unsustainable agriculture practices have nearly wiped out the forest regions of Borneo and Sumatra, while all oceans are threatened by overfishing and changing sea temperatures. At the same time, expanding territory for livestock and soy production is driving deforestation in the Amazon region.

Like all organizations, WWF must establish priorities, since no firm can do all they would like to do. Develop a 3-year strategic plan that will enable WWF to best meet the challenges of the future.

Michael Kors Holdings Ltd., 2015

www.michaelkors.com, KORS

Headquartered in Hong Kong, Michael Kors Holdings is a global luxury lifestyle company with nearly 10,000 employees, specializing in the design and distribution of women's luxury accessories and clothing. The company sells its products globally, including in retail stores in London, Milan, Paris, Tokyo, and Rio de Janeiro. The company sells some men's products, but mostly it is women's fragrance products, footwear, watches, jewelry, clothing, eyewear, handbags, and small leather goods that retail from $500 to $6,000, footwear that retails from $300 to $1,200, and women's apparel which retails from $400 to $4,000. The higher-priced apparel is marketed under the more expensive Michael Kors Collection brand. But the company has a less expensive line of products marketed under the MICHAEL Michael Kors brand, with handbags from $200 to $800, and more affordable sportswear, including footwear from $70 to $500, and women's apparel from $50 to $500.

In 2014, Michael Kors announced plans to expand its men's clothing and accessories into a $1 billion business. Currently, the men's market represents less than 5 percent of company sales. The market for men's clothing and accessories is becoming increasingly saturated, as brands such as Coach and Louis Vuitton are courting men in an effort to counteract a slowdown in women's categories.

For 2015 through August 5, Michael Kors' stock has declined 47 percent compared to the S&P 500 average increase of 2.49 percent. Kors is being mentioned as a takeover target since the company's stock is depressed following disappointing earnings and revenues of late. This is in stark contrast to rival Coach, whose stock price and financial performance have been on a dramatic upswing in 2015.

Copyright by Fred David Books LLC. www.strategyclub.com (Written by Meredith E. David and Alvaro Polanco)

History

Michael Kors Holdings was founded in 1981 by aspiring fashion designer Michael Kors, who launched the Michael Kors Women's Collection, which was sold in department stores such as Bergdorf Goodman and Saks Fifth Avenue. The company had a rocky start and declared bankruptcy in 1993, but 4 years later, Kors began designing for French house Céline and launched a lower-priced line. In 2002, Kors left the French company to focus again on his own line, which was again unprofitable.

American fashion executive John D. Idol bought the Michael Kors business in 2003 for $100 million. According to Idol, "It was losing money and probably would have gone out of business had we not bought it." Idol became the company's CEO and repositioned the brand as an American jet-set lifestyle. As the Chief Creative Officer, Kors used sportswear-themed designs that garnered international acclaim. After 5 consecutive years with profitable quarters, in 2011, Michael Kors Holding Limited had one the most successful IPOs in the year, raising about $944 million after selling 47.2 million shares of stock.

In fiscal 2014, Michael Kors' retail segment reported sales of $1,593.0 million and a 26.2 percent increase in year-over-year comparable store sales. The company is progressing with its goal of expanding into large markets, especially those in Europe and Japan. However, the fashion industry is intensely competitive. In early 2015, a rival company, Coach Inc., purchased Stuart Weitzman Holdings LLC for $574 million, primarily to expand Coach's line of high-end footwear to compete with Michael Kors, Kate Spade, and other high-end fashion companies. Coach reported a decline in revenue growth in 2014, yet it still had much higher total revenue than Michael Kors.

Internal Assessment

Vision/Mission

It appears that Michael Kors Holdings has no published vision or mission statement.

Customer Base

Michael Kors continues to expand at a high rate in terms of customer base and geography. The company has begun advertising in top fashion magazines and leveraging Kors' popularity through press activities and personal appearances (e.g., on designer reality shows such as *Project Runway*). Some investors, however, are not happy with Michael Kors' ever-expanding clientele. Although the company currently offers some affordable luxury items, investors claim that providing clothing that is too affordable and attainable by larger masses might tarnish the brand's luxurious appeal. Indeed, one of the company's greatest competitive advantages stems from Michael Kors himself being globally recognized in the premium designer world and constantly receiving prestigious awards for his merits in high-end luxury fashion trends.

Organizational Structure

Michael Kors Holdings' organizational structure is shown in Exhibit 1. The six executives listed are the only persons mentioned in the company's *Form 10K*, suggesting the company is functionally (centralized) rather than divisionally (decentralized) designed. There are apparently no divisional presidents by product or by region. Note the COO is also the CFO, and the Chairman is also the CEO.

Segments

Michael Kors operates in three primary business segments: wholesale, retail, and licensing. The licensing segment generates less than 10 percent of sales. Wholesale items from both the Michael Kors Collection and the MICHAEL Michael Kors Collection are sold in nearly 2,500 department and specialty stores in North America, including Saks Fifth Avenue, Nordstrom, Neiman Marcus, and Harrods, and about 1,200 stores internationally, including nearly 550 stores in Europe.

The company's retail segment operates through nearly 300 stores in North America and about 150 stores internationally in Europe and Japan. The retail segment is divided into three retail store fronts: (1) collection stores, which sell the Michael Kors designer items; (2) lifestyle stores, which offer accessories from the MICHAEL Michael Kors sportswear line; and (3) outlet stores, which offer excess inventory and discounted items.

EXHIBIT 1 Michael Kors' Organizational Structure

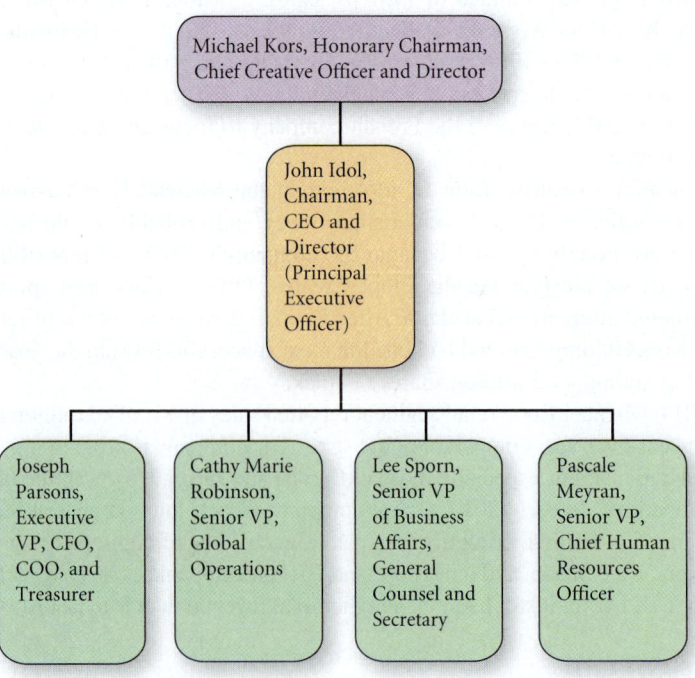

Source: Based on Michael Kors' company documents.

The company's licensing segment negotiates its trademarks on products such as cosmetics, jewelry, eyewear, watches, swimwear, and men's ties. Example licensees of Michael Kors include Fossil (for watches), Luxottica Group (for eyewear), and Estée Lauder (for fragrance). The company also licenses rights to other third parties to sell products in geographical regions, such as the Philippines, Singapore, Korea, and the Middle East.

As indicated in Exhibit 2, sales in the company's retail segment are steadily increasing in all three regions; however, it is important to note that sales in Japan only account for less than 4 percent of worldwide retail sales. Exhibit 3 reveals that the company does well selling its products through department stores, such as Saks Fifth Avenue, Nordstrom, and Macy's. Licensing is a significantly smaller segment of company sales but still managed to net $66 million in sales for fiscal 2015, an increase of 73 percent from the previous year.

As is true with most clothing companies, Michael Kors' products are made by third-party contractors in Asia, South and Central America, and Eastern Europe. The company sells products in three principal geographic markets: North America, Europe, and Japan. Exhibit 2 gives company sales and revenue by geographic location. As shown, North America continues to be Michael Kors' strongest market in terms of net retail sales. From fiscal 2013 to fiscal 2015, retail net sales in North America grew 77 percent. Note that from fiscal 2013 to fiscal 2015,

EXHIBIT 2 Fiscal Year Net Retail Sales by Segment (in millions of USD)

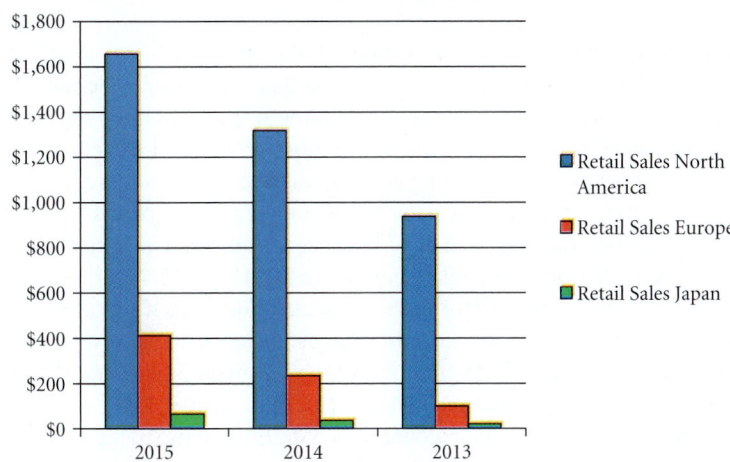

Source: Based on Michael Kors' 2015 *Annual Report*, p. 5.

EXHIBIT 3 Fiscal Year Net Wholesale Sales by Segment (in millions of USD)

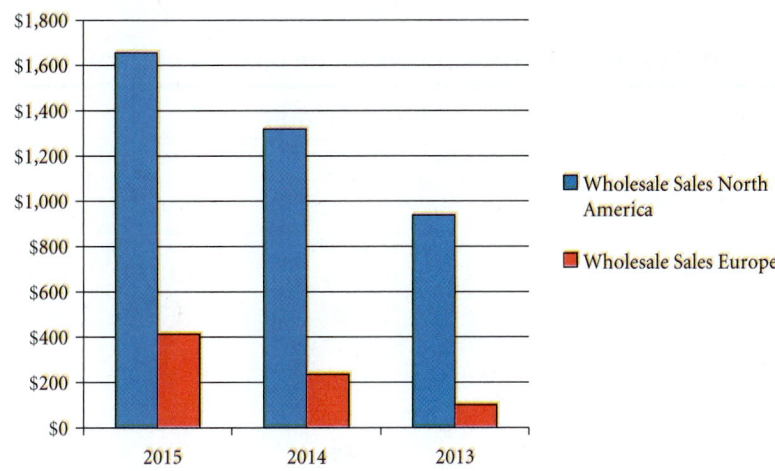

Source: Based on Michael Kors' 2015 *Annual Report*, p. 5.

retail net sales in Europe grew by over 300 percent and retail net sales in Japan grew by 200 percent. Michael Kors distribution warehouses are located in Canada, Japan, and The Netherlands, with a 500,000 sq. ft. distribution center in California.

In August 2015, shares of Michael Kors Holdings Ltd. (KORS) jumped 10 percent as the luxury lifestyle retailer reported Q2 earnings per share of 87 cents and net sales of $947.3 million. On a year-over-year basis, Q2 earnings fell 4.4 percent, but net sales grew 6.8 percent. Total Q2 revenues, including licensing revenues, were $986 million, up 7.3 percent year-over-year driven by strong demand for footwear and accessories. However, the company's comparable-store sales in Q2 decreased 9.5 percent (down 5% on constant currency), as compared to a 24.2 percent increase the prior year. For Q2, the company's Retail segment generated net sales of $523.3 million, up 9 percent year-over-year due to 107 new stores openings over the past year and higher e-commerce sales. Operating profit, however, decreased 15.3 percent to $120.9 million. For the company's Wholesale segment, Q2 revenues increased 4.2 percent to $424 million, while operating profit fell 9.6 percent to $106.3 million. The company's Licensing segment revenues rose 20.5 percent to $38.7 million while operating profit grew 30.5 percent to $21.4 million.

Regarding the company's Q2 2015 performance by region, revenues across North America grew 1.2 percent year-over-year to $727.3 million, revenues from Europe increased 16.9 percent to $216.8 million, and revenues in Japan grew 32.7 percent to $19.6 million. Michael Kors now operates about 774 stores across the globe, inclusive of licensed locations.

Finance

Michael Kors does not own any of its stores. Instead, the company leases all of its retail space, usually for a period of 10 years. For Michael Kors' Q3 that ended December 27, 2014, the company's total revenue increased 29.9 percent to $1.3 billion from $1.0 billion the prior year period. Retail net sales increased 37.0 percent to $689.4 million, driven by 114 net new store openings since the end of that third quarter. The company's wholesale net sales increased 24.4 percent to $573.8 million, while the company's licensing revenue increased 8.6 percent to $51.5 million.

Michael Kors' income statement and balance sheet are provided in Exhibits 4 and 5, respectively. Note the 32 percent growth in total revenue from 2014 to 2015. Not revealed, in Exhibit 4, revenues increased 52 percent from 2014 to 2013. Meanwhile, Coach's total revenue dropped 1 percent and net income fell 1.6 percent in 2014. However, Coach's total revenue of $1.15 billion and net income of approximately $218 million in Q1 was much higher than Michael Kors' Q1 total revenue of $641 million and net income of $125 million. It is also important to note that Michael Kors does not use a significant amount of debt to finance its strategies.

Marketing

Michael Kors spent $65.7 million in advertising in 2014, including print advertising, emails, brochures, and catalogs. The company uses its extensive customer database to target customers and mail advertising materials directly to their home. The company also owns a website in

EXHIBIT 4 Michael Kors' Income Statement (in millions of USD)

Report Date	March 29, 2015	March 29, 2014
Revenues	$4,200	$3,170
Cost of revenue and other	1,552	1,154
Gross profit	2,648	2,016
Operating expenses	1,391	1,008
EBIT	1,257	1,008
Interest & other	—	—
EBT	1,256	1,008
Tax	375	347
Net income	**881**	**661**

Source: Based on Michael Kors' 2015 *Annual Report*, p. 54.

EXHIBIT 5 Michael Kors' Balance Sheets (in millions of USD)

Report Date	March 29, 2015	March 29, 2014
Assets		
Cash and equivalents	$979	$955
Accounts receivable	363	314
Inventories	520	427
Other current assets	155	81
Total current assets	2,017	1,777
Property, plant & equipment	563	351
Goodwill	14	14
Intangible assets	62	48
Other assets	36	27
Total assets	**2,692**	**2,217**
Liabilities		
Short-term debt		—
Accounts payable	143	132
Other current liabilities	187	176
Total current liabilities	330	308
Long-term debt		—
Deferred income taxes	10	6
Other liabilities	111	97
Total liabilities	**451**	**411**
Common stock		—
Retained earnings	2,169	1,288
Treasury stock	(498)	2
Paid in capital and other	570	516
Total equity	**2,241**	**1,806**
Total liabilities & equity	**2,692**	**2,217**

Source: Based on Michael Kors' 2015 *Annual Report*, p. 53.

partnership with Neiman Marcus that buys merchandise at wholesale and sells it through the michaelkors.com website. Michael Kors Holdings expects to soon launch its own e-commerce website.

Michael Kors manages the way its products are displayed by its wholesale customers in the United States (e.g., Bergdorf Goodman, Saks Fifth Avenue, Neiman Marcus, Bloomingdale's, Nordstrom, and Macy's) and in Europe (e.g., Harvey Nichols, Selfridges, and Galeries Lafayette). In an effort to create a more personalized in-store experience, Michael Kors recently changed many of its regular department store displays into "shop-in-shops," with customized décor, flooring, and a specialized staff. This change likely assisted in increasing revenue for the wholesale segment from $1.6 billion in 2014 to $2.1 billion in 2015.

A competitive advantage of Michael Kors' is Michael Kors himself. As a world-renowned, award-winning designer, Kors leads the company's design team. The company leverages Kors' popularity through press activities and personal appearances. About 30 percent of the company's annual revenue is derived by sales from its top five wholesale customers. Nearly 15 percent of Michael Kors' total revenue in 2014 stemmed from sales by its largest wholesale customer. Thus, the loss of a wholesale customer could drastically harm the company's revenue.

Social Responsibility

With a growing concern by investors and consumers regarding corporate social responsibility, Mr. Kors is taking the initiative to help his brand be perceived as sustainable. For example, he started a "Michael Kors Month" (which takes place in July) in which hundreds of employees volunteer with the NGO "God's Love We Deliver" to help prepare meals that are distributed throughout the New York tri-state area daily. Michael Kors employees from around the globe also aid local hunger-related charities.

In 2013, in conjunction with the United Nations World Food Program (WFP) and celebrity endorser Halle Berry, Mr. Kors began the campaign "Watch Hunger Stop" to collectively help malnourished people around the globe. In this initiative, Mr. Kors designed a limited edition 100 series watch that was sold with the intent of having a percent of the earnings per watch donated to the WFP to feed the unprivileged.

As a result of marketing efforts such as these, the designer was awarded the Golden Heart Award for Lifetime Achievement. As a related marketing move, Michael Kors recently created the "Michael Kors Award for Outstanding Community Service." Recipients of the award thus far have been Hillary Rodham Clinton and Anna Wintour.

Competitors

Michael Kors faces intense competition from companies and brands such as Coach, Ralph Lauren, Kate Spade, Marc Jacobs, Calvin Klein, Burberry, Louis Vuitton, Prada, and Gucci. Competing largely on the basis of style, quality, and brand prestige, Michael Kors must constantly anticipate and ideally mold upcoming fashion trends in order to stay relevant. A comparative analysis of Kors with rival firms is provided in Exhibit 6.

Coach, Inc. (COH)

Headquartered in New York City, Coach is one of the leading designers in the United States. Founded in 1941, Coach excels in marketing women's handbags and accessories. The company also sells men's products, watches, footwear, sun wear, travel bags, and fragrances. In Coach's fiscal year 2014, women's handbags accounted for 55 percent of sales, and women's accessories accounted for 22 percent. Men's products made up 14 percent of total sales and the remaining product lines (watches, footwear, jewelry, among others) accounted for 9 percent.

Coach operates under two segments: North America and International. North America accounted for 65 percent of total sales in 2014, whereas the international segment brought 35 percent. However, the North America net sales dropped 10.9 percent to $3.10 billion, and the international segments net sales grew 5.5 percent to $1.64 billion in 2014. Interestingly, Coach's sales in China were up 20 percent in 2014 to approximately $545 million.

Similar to Michael Kors, Coach indirectly sells to department stores primarily in the United States and Canada. As of 2014, Coach directly operated 539 retail stores (332 full price and 207 factory stores) in North America, 198 in Japan, 153 in China (including Hong Kong and Macau), 97 in other Asia regions (e.g., South Korea, Taiwan, and Malaysia), and 27 in Europe. Unlike Michael Kors, Coach puts emphasis on the Asian market, whereas Kors focuses largely on the European region.

On August 4, 2015, Coach reported its fourth quarter fiscal year 2015 EPS of 31 cents, exceeding analysts' predictions by a margin of 2 cents. However, the 31 cents figure marks a fall of 28 cents from the same quarter the prior year. Also on the same date, Coach reported $1 billion in quarterly revenues, beating the consensus projection by a margin of 3.21 percent, but the company's year-over-year (YoY) revenues declined by approximately 12 percent. One

EXHIBIT 6 Michael Kors versus Rival Firms

	Michael Kors	Coach	Ralph Lauren
# Employees	9,100	10,200	14,000
$ Net Income	661 M	781 M	776 M
$ Revenue	3,310 M	4,806 M	7,450 M
$ Revenue/Employee	363,700	471,175	532,100
$ EPS Ratio	4.16	2.05	8.14
$ Market Cap.	13.9 B	11.5 B	12.1 B

Source: Based on company documents.

reason for Coach's improved performance of late has been growth at its international division. In particular, Coach's sales growth in Europe is now in double digits, and its revenues from China are growing. Also on a positive note, Coach recently successfully introduced its Stuart Vevers' designs and bought out shoemaker Stuart Weitzman.

Ralph Lauren Corporation (RL)

Headquartered in New York City, Ralph Lauren began by designing men's ties in 1967, but now is one of the top American apparel brands in the world. In addition to women's, men's, and children's clothing and accessories, the company's products also include luggage, bedding, furniture, lighting, and giftware, among other items. Ralph Lauren operates under the segments of wholesale, retail, and licensing. Its largest segment is retail, accounting for 51 percent ($3.80 billion) of net revenues in 2014. The wholesale segment followed closely behind, garnering 47 percent ($3.49 billion) of net revenues in 2014. The smallest segment, licensing, brought in 2 percent ($166 million) of net revenues.

Ralph Lauren relies heavily on department stores, with three of them accounting for nearly 50 percent of the company's wholesales. Macy's is the company's strongest wholesale customer, accounting for 25 percent of the revenue brought in by wholesaling. Ralph Lauren owns various brands, such as Polo Ralph Lauren, Ralph Lauren Purple Label, Black Label, Blue Label, Lauren Ralph Lauren, RRL, Denim & Supply Ralph Lauren, RLX Ralph Lauren, Ralph Lauren Childrenswear, Club Monaco, and Chaps. Together the company's brands cover diverse target markets. In 2013, the company had to cut its rugby brand, which resulted in the closing of 14 global retail stores.

Kate Spade & Company (KATE)

Headquartered in New York City, Kate Spade was founded in 1976 and operates under three large segments: Kate Spade, Adelington Design Group, and Juicy Couture. Inside these segments are many brands, including Kate Spade, Juicy Couture, Kate Spade Saturday, Monet, Liz Claiborne, Jack Spade, Trifari, Kensie, and Lizwear, among others that cater to customers with different backgrounds and stylistic preferences. Kate Spade mainly offers products in the women's apparel and accessory category, but it also carries men's bags and apparel, travel bags and briefcases, and home décor and bedding. The company sells its products through 118 specialty retail stores, 51 outlet stores, 42 concession stores, and 450 department stores globally. It also has e-commerce and licensing operations.

External Issues

Handbags, Luggage, and Other Accessories

The handbag and luggage industry in the United States is valued at over $10 billion annually, with an industry growth rate of 3 percent expected going forward. There are over 75,000 businesses in the market, with many being extremely small. The industry is dominated by Coach and Michael Kors, which account for 22 and 12 percent, respectively, of total industry sales volume. The industry derives nearly 30 percent of revenues from handbags alone, with costume jewelry and watches, and travel bags accounting for 18 and 15 percent, respectively. All other items account for 47 percent of total industrywide revenues. Customers between the ages of 35 and 65 account for 70 percent of total revenues.

High-Fashion Merchandise

High-end fashion clothes, shoes, and jewelry accounts for about $3 billion in sales in the United States annually, with over half the sales being derived from clothing, and another 16 percent from shoes. The industry is highly fragmented with over 50,000 companies. Michael Kors, Louis Vuitton, and Ralph Lauren account for 12 percent of total revenues in the industry, with each having about the same market share. Fashion industry sales are heavily dependent on the state of the economy, but grew less than 1 percent annually over the last 5 years.

Future

Michael Kors' strategy to market a jet-set lifestyle has proven successful among the fashion critics and customers, but its brand may lose prestige if the company continues expanding its target audience with lower-priced offerings. Overexposure of the brand could weaken its reputation in the glamorous fashion industry, which could ultimately force Michael Kors to reposition its brand. There could be a threshold where high-end fashion aficionados will turn away from the brand. By depending heavily on a select number of wholesale customers, the company faces an issue regarding the potential loss of one of these customers. For example, if Macy's decides to cut ties with Michael Kors, the company would immediately lose 25 percent of its wholesale revenue.

Kors' sales slowed in the last quarter of 2014, especially in North America, where many products were discounted in the run-up to Christmas. Investors warn of Kors' slow growth in 2015. In fact, as of October 1, 2015, Kors' stock price had fallen 42 percent for the year. The guru of uptown glamour is looking slightly fallible. Help CEO John Idol by developing a 3-year strategic plan for the company he resurrected back in 2003.

SABMiller plc, 2015

www.sabmiller.com, SAB. L

Headquartered in London, United Kingdom, SABMiller is a beer and soft-drink company that employs about 70,000 in over 80 countries. In SABMiller's fiscal year ending March 31, 2014, the company sold over 315 million hectoliters (8.3 billion gallons) of beer, generating revenues of $26.72 billion, making the firm the second-largest brewer in the world, trailing only Anheuser-Busch InBev. In total, SABMiller produces over 200 styles of beers, including famous brands Peroni from Italy, Pilsner Urquell from the Czech Republic, Miller Genuine Draft from the United States, and many more. The firm owns a 57 percent share of MillerCoors. SAB Miller also produces its own soft-drink brands, and is one of the world's largest bottlers of Coca-Cola. Shares of SABMiller can be purchased and sold on both the London and the Johannesburg stock exchanges. SABMiller distributes Coca-Cola products in Africa, Honduras, and El Salvador.

In July 2015, SABMiller reported a 1 percent decline in larger volumes for the 3 months ending June 30; the company's soft-drink volumes rose 4 percent. The company's beer volumes were down across Europe, led by a 15 percent decline in Poland. Unfavorable currency movements against the dollar also pushed SABMiller's European revenues down by 10 percent during the period. In the last year or two, the company's soft drinks sales have been up and its beer sales down. In China, SABMiller brews Snow beer through a joint venture with China Resources Enterprise, and those sales are increasing. SABMiller's biggest single market in Latin/South America is Colombia, where lager volumes rose 9 percent during the quarter, led by Aguila Light and alcohol-free Aguila Cero brands linked to sporting events. The company's overall lager volume in Latin America grew by 4 percent, and its soft-drink revenues were up by 7 percent. In Africa, the company's lager and soft-drink volumes rose 4 percent each, with the highest growth in Nigeria and Zambia. SABMiller derives about 30 percent of its profits from Africa and plans to increase its revenues in Africa by more than 10 percent over the next 3 to 5 years.

History

SABMiller traces its roots back to South Africa in 1895. The initials SAB stand for South African Breweries, with the name Miller being added to the company in 2002 to reflect the 57 percent acquisition of Miller Brewing Company. SAB first went public in 1897 in Johannesburg and was listed in London just one year later. In 1955, SAB acquired Ohlsson's and Chandlers, both rival firms in South Africa, giving SABMiller 98 percent market share in the South African beer market. SABMiller acquired Bavaria S.A. in Colombia in 2005. Bavaria was South America's second-largest brewer and producer of both Agulia and Club Colombia. SABMiller engaged in the hostile takeover of Australia-headquartered Fosters in 2009, but the acquisitions did not include European sales of Fosters, as Heineken owned rights to this market. In 2014, SABMiller divested its 39 percent stake in Tsogo Sun Holdings Limited, a casino and hotel group.

In 2014, SABMiller gained a 57 percent stake in the newly formed Coca-Cola Beverages Africa, which supplies 40 percent of all Coca-Cola beverage volumes in Africa. The two companies have combined their soft-drink bottling operations in southern and eastern Africa. As part of the deal, Coke paid $260 million to obtain world rights to SABMiller's Appletiser, a carbonated apple juice, and rights to another 19 nonalcoholic brands in Africa and Latin America. Coke benefits by having a broader spectrum of offerings away from its base of Coke, Sprite, and Fanta, while SABMiller increases its soft-drink volume to nearly 21 percent of all sales, up from 17 percent in 2009. Soft drinks grew 5 percent for SABMiller in 2014, compared to 1 percent for beer. Soft drinks are easier to produce than beer, even though margins are less.

Organizational Structure

As indicated in Exhibit 1, SABMiller appears to operate from a divisional-by-geographic region type of structure. Critics suggest that the company, however, should have more divisional presidents, and perhaps should be designed on a by-product basis. Also, note the company has no COO, so that "everyone" reports to CEO Clark at SABMiller. Except for Sue Clark, Managing Director of SABMiller Europe, all top executives are white males at the company. The company recently dissolved its Director of Group Strategy position.

Vision/Mission

It appears that SABMiller has no stated vision or mission statement.

Segments

A common beverage industry term *net producer revenue (NPR)* is defined as "group revenue less excise duties and other similar taxes including our share of associates' and joint ventures' excise duties and other similar taxes." SABMiller reports that its NPR growth in Latin America was 5 percent in fiscal 2014; however, taking into account exchange rates, the total reported NPR declined 1 percent, due to a strong U.S. dollar appreciation on many currencies worldwide, including Latin American currencies. However, the firm's lower production costs and fixed costs improved fiscal 2014 profitability. Soft drinks now make up 20.6 percent of SABMiller's total sales by volume, compared with 17.2 percent in 2009. Sales of soft drinks rose 5 percent for the company in its most recent fiscal year, compared to a 1 percent rise for beer.

Latin America

SABMiller's Latin American segment is its largest, comprising 33 percent of all earnings being generated from this region. The regional office for Lain America is in Miami, Florida. Primary strategies of the firm moving forward in Latin America include increasing light-beer sales and international brands, improving sales service, expanding bulk packaging to make beer more affordable, and improving distribution efficiencies. SABMiller is Latin America's largest brewer, operating mainly in Colombia, Ecuador, El Salvador, Honduras, Panama, and Peru. SABMiller also exports beer to Chile and Paraguay and is the third-largest brewer in Argentina.

SABMiller's beverage volumes grew across Latin America by 1 to 3 percent depending on the category, but were down slightly in both Panama and Peru due to a new excise tax increase in 2013 by these governments on beer sales. Sales in Peru of Miller Lite remain strong, though,

EXHIBIT 1 SABMiller's Organizational Structure

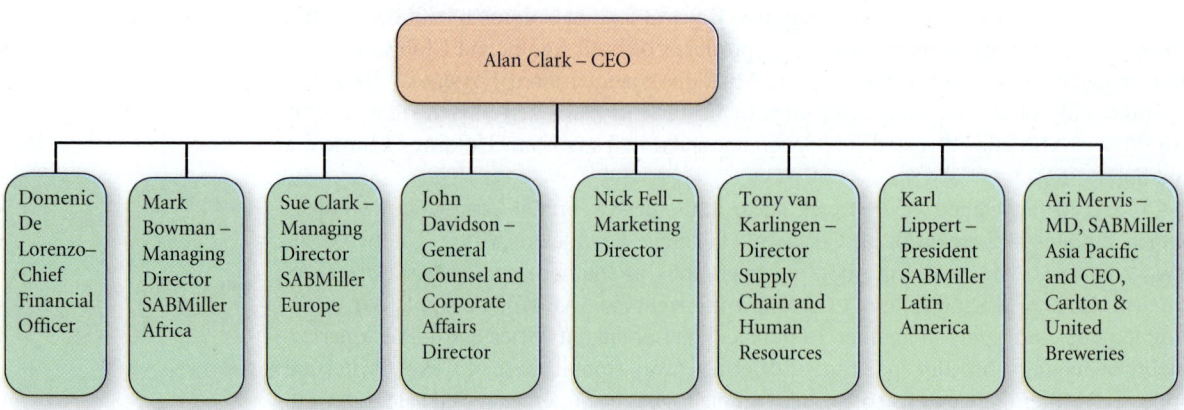

Source: Based on SABMiller's company documents.

and the beer currently accounts for 52 percent of the premium beer segment and 20 percent of the total beer segment in Peru. Soft-drink sales in Peru were up 14 percent as well. Bulk pack sales of beer, common in the United States but not in all world markets, continued to grow in Honduras, Colombia, and El Salvador. SABMiller also offers cheaper beers to customers in these regions, as many are considered low income. Light-beer sales have also been strong in this region. In Colombia, top brand Poker hit record sales volumes of 8,500,000 hectoliters, giving Poker a 41 percent market share in Colombia and the top brand for SABMiller in Latin America. SABMiller produces soft drinks across Latin America, including Coca-Cola products in both El Salvador and Honduras. As shown in Exhibit 2, soft drinks comprised 30 percent of all SABMiller hectoliters of beverages sold in 2014 in Latin America.

Europe

SABMiller's European sales accounted for only 11 percent of the company's 2014 earnings—the lowest of any region it operates. SABMiller's European headquarters are located in Zug, Switzerland. The firm's primary breweries in Europe are located in the Czech Republic, Hungry, Italy, Poland, Romania, Slovakia, Canary Islands, and the Netherlands. SABMiller is the number one or two producer of beer by market share in these primary European markets. The firm also brews products in 16 additional countries in Europe and exports heavily to seven additional European nations, with the United Kingdom and Germany being the largest.

As revealed in Exhibit 3, NPR for the company's European region increased 6 percent in 2014, partly due to the consolidation of Coca-Cola Icecek in Anadolu Efes. SABMiller bottles Coca-Cola products across Turkey and neighboring countries. Efes is a poplar Turkish beer. Also shown in Exhibit 3 is a doubling of SABMiller's soft-drink production in Europe. However, SABMiller's earnings were down 10 percent in Europe; the Czech Republic and Poland experienced 4 and 9 percent declines in lager, respectively. Italy experienced a 1 percent decline, although Peroni, an Italian beer especially popular in southern Italy, did well. Sales in the United Kingdom, Romania, and the Netherlands were up 5, 2, and 2 percent, respectively, in fiscal 2014. Turkey and Russia experienced strong soft-drink sales growth for SABMiller but lower beer sales, mostly blamed on increased regulatory measures in both countries on alcohol.

EXHIBIT 2 Segment Data for SABMiller Latin America (in millions of USD)

	2014	2013
Group Revenue	$7,812	$7,821
Group NPR	5,745	5,802
EBITA	2,192	2,112
Sales (hectoliters)		
Lager	43,586	43,007
Soft Drinks	18,514	17,866

Source: Based on SABMiller's 2014 *Annual Report*, p. 21.

EXHIBIT 3 Segment Data for SABMiller Europe (in millions of USD)

	2014	2013
Group Revenue	$6,045	$5,767
Group NPR	4,574	4,300
EBITA	703	784
Sales (hectoliters)		
Lager	43,590	45,331
Soft Drinks	14,716	7,581

Source: Based on SABMiller's 2014 *Annual Report*, p. 23.

North America

About 12 percent of SABMiller's 2014 earnings were derived from its Canada, U.S., and Mexico operations. SABMiller's North American operations are headquartered in Chicago, with a wholly owned Miller Brewing International being based in Milwaukee. SABMiller has a 57 percent share in MillerCoors, the second-largest brewer in the United States, having a 34 percent market share. One notable flavored beer is Redd's Apple Ale, the company's fastest-growing U.S. brand since 2013, which focuses mostly on 21- to 34-year-old individuals. Total North American EBITA was 8 percent higher in 2014, as indicated by Exhibit 4, despite flat revenues. Coors Light and Miller Light both experienced volume declines between 2 and 5 percent, respectively, but each gained in market share as the beer industry as a whole was relatively worse. Miller High Life and Keystone, both considered economy beers, experienced declines around 5 percent in volumes, while premium beer Miller Genuine Draft experienced a double-digit decline in sales. Coors Banquet, however, was able to enjoy volume growth of nearly 10 percent. In total, beer struggled in North America, with the most promise being in craft beers, flavored beers, and premium beers such as Coors Banquet.

Africa

SABMiller's African operations are considered "everywhere in Africa other than South Africa," which is its own segment. Regional offices are located in Johannesburg with brewing operations in 15 countries, and another 21 nations have SABMiller products through associates. In most nations in Africa where SABMiller has a brewery, it is the number-one brewery in that respective nation. The firm also has a large soft-drink presence in Africa, bottling Coca-Cola products for 21 different markets. The company's NPR and earnings growth was 4 and 12 percent, respectively, as shown in Exhibit 5. The company's top-selling beer, Castel Lite, was up 31 percent, and soft drinks were up 6 percent due in large part to gains in Ghana and Zambia.

EXHIBIT 4 Segment Data for SABMiller North America (in millions of USD)

	2014	2013
Group Revenue	$5,342	$5,355
Group NPR	4,665	4,656
EBITA	797	740
Sales (hectoliters)		
Lager (excluding contract brewing)	39,400	40,585
MillerCoors' Volumes		
Lager (excluding contract brewing)	38,051	39,268
Sales to Retailers	37,846	38,818
Contract Brewing	4,674	4,760
Soft Drinks	–	–

Source: Based on SABMiller's 2014 *Annual Report*, p. 25.

EXHIBIT 5 Segment Data for SABMiller Africa (in millions of USD)

	2014	2013
Group Revenue	$4,058	$3,853
Group NPR	3,424	3,290
EBITA	939	838
Sales (hectoliters)		
Lager	19,523	18,445
Soft Drinks	13,771	12,963
	5,829	5,726

Source: Based on SABMiller's 2014 *Annual Report*, p. 27.

EXHIBIT 6 Segment Data for SABMiller Asia Pacific (in millions of USD)

	2014	2013
Group Revenue	$5,451	$5,685
Group NPR	3,944	4,005
EBITA	845	854
Sales (hectoliters)		
Lager	71,493	67,292

Source: Based on SABMiller's 2014 *Annual Report*, p. 28.

Asia Pacific

Regional headquarters for SABMiller in Asia are in Hong Kong with brewing operations in Australia, China, India, and Vietnam. About 13 percent of the company's total EBITA is derived from the Asia Pacific region. A key initiative is building CR Snow's market leadership in China, where SABMiller enjoys a 20-year partnership with China Resource's Enterprise Limited, the largest brewer in China and producer of the most popular beer in China, Snow. SABMiller controls a 49 percent stake in Snow but Snow has a limited appeal outside of China. Total beer volume was up 6 percent in fiscal 2014, as shown in Exhibit 6, but both NPR and earnings were down for the year. In India, the company's NPR growth fell 3 percent, but in China NPR grew 17 percent, in large part to Snow's success.

South Africa

SABMiller's South African office is located in Johannesburg and is the largest producer of both beer and soft drinks in South Africa. In addition, the firm also has a 40 percent stake in Tsogo Sun Holdings, the largest casino hotel group in South Africa. About 17 percent of total earnings was derived from this region. Beer and soft-drink volumes remained the same in 2014, but the company was able to make market share gains overall. Top-performing brands are Castle Lite and Castle Milk Stout, both reporting 10 percent gains in 2014. Also, the firm introduced its first fruit-flavored beer, Flying Fish, in fiscal 2014 to the region.

Exhibit 8 shows the percent breakdown of group revenue based on geographic region.

Finance

SABMiller's income statement and balance sheet are provided in Exhibits 9 and 10, respectively.

Competitors

The global beer market is dominated by Anheuser-Busch InBev, SAB Miller, Heineken, Crown Imports, Carlsberg, Asahi, and others. In the United States alone, AB InBev, SAB Miller, Crown Imports, and Heineken account for 46, 33, 6, and 4 percent of the total market

EXHIBIT 7 Segment Data for SABMiller South Africa (in millions of USD)

	2014	2013
Group Revenue	$4,951	$5,540
Group NPR	3,997	4,475
EBITA	1,015	1,119
Sales (hectoliters)		
Lager	27,245	27,280
Soft Drinks	18,309	18,368
Other Alcohol	1,789	1,613
Hotel/Gaming Revenue	425	466

Source: Based on SABMiller's 2014 *Annual Report*, p. 31.

EXHIBIT 8 Group Revenue in 2014 by Geographic Region (as a percent)

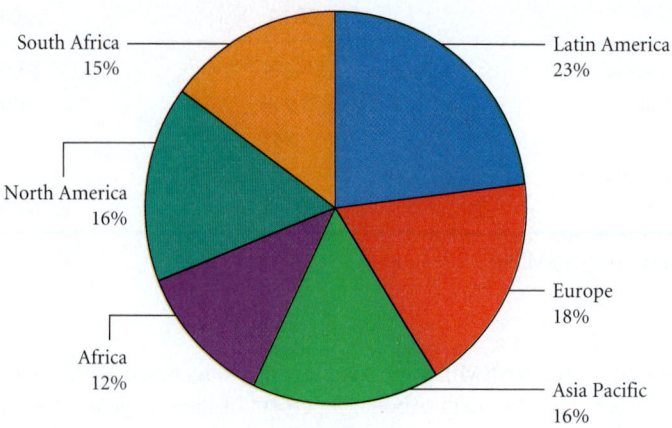

Source: Created by the author from a variety of sources.

EXHIBIT 9 SABMiller's Income Statement (in millions of USD)

Report Date	March 31, 2015	March 31, 2014
Revenues	$22,130	$22,311
Net operating expenses	(17,146)	(18,069)
EBIT	4,384	4,224
Interest & other additions	446	581
EBT	4,830	4,823
Tax	(1,273)	(1,173)
Net income	**3,557**	**3,650**

Source: Based on SABMiller's 2015 *Annual Report* documents, p. 107.

share, respectively. Other sizable brewers include Pabst, makers of Pabst Blue Ribbon, as well as Boston Beer, makers of Sam Adams, Yuengling, and Sierra Nevada, all based in the United States. Further consolidation is expected but many new micro and craft breweries are started each year. There are over 2,500 brewers in the United States, all competing on price, quality, brand, perception, distribution, and, importantly, shelf space in retail establishments. Exhibit 11 provides a comparison of SABMiller with Anheuser and Boston Beer. Note that Anheuser generates the highest revenue per employee. Boston Beer has the highest EPS, but is small compared to SABMiller.

Anheuser-Busch InBev (BUD)

AB InBev is the largest brewer in the world with a 45 percent market share in the United States and a 25 percent share globally. Headquartered in Leuven, Belgium, the firm produces more than 200 brands, including Budweiser, Stella Artois, Becks, Leffe, Michelob Ultra, Corona, and many others. Anheuser recently purchased Mexico's Grupo Modelo, but Anheuser does not have U.S. rights to Grupo Modelo products; Constellation Brands does. Anheuser has 17 brands that generate over $1 billion each. In Argentina and Brazil, the firm controls 78 and 68 percent of the beer market and 21 and 18 percent of the soft-drink market, respectively. Anheuser has long viewed advertising especially at sporting events as a key part of its strategy. The company is the only beer advertiser during the Super Bowl every year. Anheuser also has been the lead sponsor for several world cups, and most recently the Confederations Cup in Brazil. Exhibit 12 provides segment data for Anheuser. Note that Latin America North was the second-largest income-producing region, mostly thanks to Brazil, which is in this segment; however, the segment experienced declining revenues of 3.5 percent in 2013. European sales were also down, largely due to a 16 percent decrease in Russia. Sales in China were up 9 percent in 2013.

EXHIBIT 10 **SABMiller's Balance Sheet (in millions of USD)**

Report Date	March 31, 2015	March 31, 2014
Assets		
Cash and equivalents	$965	$2,081
Accounts receivable	1,711	1,821
Inventories	1,030	1,168
Other current assets	653	315
Total current assets	4,359	5,385
Property, plant & equipment	7,961	9,065
Goodwill	14,746	18,497
Intangibles	6,878	8,532
Other assets	10,967	12,272
Total assets	**44,911**	**53,751**
Liabilities		
Accounts payable	3,728	3,847
Other current liabilities	3,604	6,153
Total current liabilities	7,332	10,000
Long-term debt	10,583	12,528
Deferred tax	2,275	3,246
Other liabilities	366	495
Total liabilities	**20,556**	**26,269**
Common stock	168	167
Retained earnings	17,746	15,885
Paid in capital & other	6,441	11,430
Total equity	**24,355**	**27,482**
Total liabilities & equity	**44,911**	**53,751**

Source: Based on SABMiller's 2015 *Annual Report*, p. 109.

EXHIBIT 11 **SABMiller versus Rival Firms**

	SABMiller	Anheuser-Busch	Boston Beer
# Employees	70,000	155,000	1,200
$ Net Income	3.38 B	16 B	70 M
$ Revenue	17 B	45 B	740 M
$ Revenue/Employee	238,000	290,000	58,000
$ EPS Ratio	2.25	5.53	6.61
$ Market Cap.	54 B	188 B	3.9 B

Source: Based on various company documents.

Heineken N.V.

Headquartered in Amsterdam, Netherlands, Heineken is one of the world's largest breweries with revenues over $24 billion assuming 1 USD = 1.30 Euros. Heineken operates in over 70 nations with 190 breweries and over 200 beers. Heineken also manufactures wines, spirits, and soft drinks, but beer accounts for 85 percent of company revenues. Heineken recently purchased Asia Pacific Breweries for $4.6 billion, giving it excellent exposure in China and southeast Asia. Heineken advertises heavily during sporting events and serves as a sponsor for the U.S. Open Tennis and the Champions League soccer in Europe. Top global beer brands include Heineken, Sol, Amstel, Desperados, and Strongbow Apple Cider. Heineken's large increase in revenues in the Asia Pacific region reflects its recent acquisition of Asia Pacific Breweries.

EXHIBIT 12 **AB InBev's Financial Data (in millions of USD)**

	2013		2012	
	Revenue	EBIT	Revenue	EBIT
North America	$16,023	$5,932	$16,028	$5,911
Mexico	2,769	1,054	2,616	582
Latin America N.	10,877	5,118	11,268	5,081
Latin America S.	3,269	1,311	3,209	1,228
Western Europe	3,620	801	3,650	827
Eastern Europe	1,445	51	1,668	62
Asia Pacific	3,354	127	2,690	67
Total	43,195	14,203	42,927	13,537

Source: Based on AB InBev's 2013 *Annual Report*, pp. 56–59.

Also, like other brewers, Heineken's sales in Europe, as a whole, were down 4.5 percent in 2013. In total, other than the acquisition of Asia Pacific, sales overall were down in all regions Heineken operates.

Boston Beer (SAM)

Better known by their brand, Sam Adams, Boston Beer was founded in 1984 in Boston, Massachusetts, and is the largest craft beer producer in the United States, having 21 percent market share. The company produces 2.5 million barrels of beer annually and is famous for producing seasonal beers, wheat beers, fruit beers, and other specialty beers. The firm sells 96 percent of its beer in the United States, and reported revenues of $740 million in 2013. Boston Beer employs around 1,100 people.

Carlsberg Group

Founded in 1847 and employing 45,000 people, Carlsberg is a Danish company that controls 8 percent of the world beer market, not counting the United States. The company is focused on Europe and Asia but also sells products worldwide. The firm reported 2013 revenues of 66 billion Danish Krone, or approximately $11 billion. Carlsberg produces over 500 local beers, including Carlsberg, Tuborg, Kronebourg, Somersby Cider, Baltika, and many more. Several beers contain high alcohol content, such as Baltika #9, which is 8 percent alcohol. Baltika and many other Carlsberg beers can be purchased in the United States.

External Issues

Types of Beer

Beers are often categorized into these broad categories: premium, sub-premium, super premium, adult beverages, malt liquor, and craft beer. Premium beer is the largest and most popular category in the United States. Premium brands include Budweiser, Coors Light, Miller High Life, and others. They are sold in the United States in bulk packaging ranging from 6 to 30 packs. The category represents 42 percent of all beer sales in the states, although this category has seen declining recently in sales. Globally, in many emerging markets, customers who are used to sub-premium beers are trading up to the premium beer category. Sub-premium beers are generally more affordable than their premium counterparts and include brands such as Natural Light, Busch Light, and Keystone Light. Interestingly enough, many customers associate these beers as inferior, but in reality they are often close to the quality of premium beers. The major difference is a much lower advertising budget the premium beers have. About 17 percent of all beer sales in the United States are in the sub-premium category.

Super premium beers account for 14 percent of the total market in the United States and include brands such as Michelob Ultra and Budweiser American Ale. Sales in this category have remained relatively stable over the last 5 years. The classifications of beers are often misleading with respect to the beers' quality. Super premium beers often simply contain a higher advertising budget and status among drinkers and do not differ materially in quality. Craft beers are one of the fastest-growing segments in the beer industry. There are many different definitions of what constitutes a craft beer, with some analysts suggesting any brewery that produces less than 6 million barrels, or one that is 75 percent independently owned. Some even label craft beers based on the methods in which the beer is produced. Thus, there are no strict or set quality standards to be labeled a craft beer, but they do generally have high-quality hops, barley, and other additives. The largest craft beer producer in the United States is Boston Beer, which produces 2.5 million barrels of beer annually and controls 21 percent of the craft beer market in the country.

Adult beverages is another area growing rapidly. Apple ales, twisted teas, and hard lemonades are all examples of this category that represents 6 percent of U.S. industry revenue. Malt liquor represents 6 percent of U.S. sales and is considered any product with over the normal alcohol content for a beer, which, in the United States, is about 5.9 percent. Many customers consider malt liquor to be brands such as Ole English and Colt 45.

Global Beer Market

The outlook for beer in markets such as Africa, Latin America, and Asia should remain strong moving forward, with western Europe and the United States performing better with craft beers. In fact, there is a trading up of products worldwide. In developing markets, consumers are drinking premium beers more often, such as Miller Lite, Coors Light, and many European-based beers, whereas in developed markets, consumers are trading up to craft and specialty beers along with wine and mixed drinks. Another trend is younger drinkers no longer consider lager beer their default choice, often choosing specialty beers or other mixed drinks. Cider is increasingly popular in western Europe and Australia, as well as dark beers. However, traditional lager style beers still dominate the world beer market.

In the United States, beer sales declined just over 1 percent in 2013, after a small increase in 2012, to resume a downward trend present from 2009 through 2011. Total revenues from beer sales in the states has declined from 56 percent in 1999 to 48 percent in 2013, largely blamed on increased liquor and wine consumption. Equally troubling in the numbers is that micro-breweries such as Boston Beer and Sierra Nevada Ale have taken market share away from traditional breweries. In 2013 alone, craft beer volumes were up 17 percent in the United States. Imports are also key drivers in the U.S. market. Four of the top import brands are Mexican beers, which, as a whole, make up 50 percent of all imported beers in the United States.

One way the larger beer producers have hedged against falling beer consumption is by producing various malt beverages. Various ciders, lemonades, teas, and fruit-flavored drinks have produced good sales, but remain a relatively small percent of total revenue for such behemoths like AB InBev and SABMiller.

AB InBev Wants SABMiller

In late 2014, AB InBev was reviewing financing options to purchase SABMiller for the staggering amount of $122 billion. The risk of a hostile takeover from AB InBev remains for SABMiller, especially considering SABMiller has stronger presence in emerging markets where the real growth is present. If AB InBev were to acquire SABMiller, likely on anti-trust grounds, the 57 percent stake in MillerCoors controlled by SABMiller would have to be divested.

Exhibit 13 reveals some descriptive information about various top-selling beer brands globally.

Regulation

Regulation in the beer industry varies greatly from country to country, state to state, and city to city. Many countries, such as Turkey and Russia, have recently tightened down on alcohol sales. Also many counties in the United States are dry, not allowing beer or alcohol sales on Sundays or after certain hours at night. In some counties, there is an outright ban on all beer sales. In addition, the manner in which firms can label, advertise, and the amount of alcohol content is all heavily regulated and varies by location. Many countries have strict laws on alcohol consumption and some nations have zero tolerance laws in place regarding drinking and driving.

EXHIBIT 13 Top Beer Brands Worldwide

Rank	Brand	Owner	Home Market
1	Snow	China Resource Enterprise, SABMiller	China
2	Tsingtao	Tsingtao Brewery	China
3	Bud Light	AB InBev	USA
4	Budweiser	AB InBev	USA
5	Skol	Carlsberg, AB InBev, Unibra	Brazil
6	Yanjing	Beijing Yanjing Brewery	China
7	Heineken	Heineken	Europe
8	Harbin	AB InBev	China
9	Brahma	AB InBev	Brazil
10	Coors Light	Molson Coors	USA

Source: Based on a variety of sources, including http://www.wsj.com/articles/sabmiller-seeks-to-repeat-its-hop-on-the-global-beer-brand-wagon-1415715854?KEYWORDS=SAB Miller.

Future

Many analysts suggest that AB InBev NV could and should acquire SABMiller, the world's number-two brewer by revenue. Anheuser desires more global exposure and SABMiller already holds 57 percent of the newly created Coca-Cola Beverages Africa company (Coke owns 11.3 percent). The remaining portion is owned by Gutsche Family Investments, a major shareholder in Coke's African bottling operations. It is unclear at this point whether SABMiller's board of directors and shareholders would welcome an buyout offer from Anheuser, but it is clear that SABMiller needs a clear strategic plan going forward to assure it gets the highest offer possible if a buyout offer is to come soon. Develop a compelling 3-year strategic plan for SABMiller.

Gruma, S.A.B. de C.V., 2015

www.gruma.com, GMK

Headquartered in Monterrey, Mexico, Gruma is the largest tortilla producer in the world. Gruma uses corn flour, wheat flour and other products to produce grits, cereals, tortilla chips, taco shells, sauces, snacks, pasta, potato chips, and more. Top Gruma food brand names are Mission, Guerrero, Calidad, Maseca, and Tortimasa. The company also produces Tortec and Batitech machines that produce tortilla and tortilla chips that are sold to restaurants, supermarkets, and other food-service providers. One special feature of Gruma's machines and products is it uses a dry production method rather than using wet dough. Gruma's method yields lower costs and superior product uniformity. Over the last 10 years, Gruma has acquired several competing firms, including Albuquerque Tortilla Company, Casa de Oro Foods, and Archer Daniels Midlands stake in Azteca Milling. Gruma operates 101 manufacturing facilities serving over 113 countries and employs 18,000 people. The company's revenues for 2014 increased slightly but net income increased 33 percent. As indicated at the end of this case, Gruma continues to post outstanding financial results right on through 2015.

Copyright by Fred David Books LLC. www.strategyclub.com (Written by Forest R. David)

History

Gruma traces its roots to 1949 when Robert Gonzalez and his son Roberto Gonzalez Marrera founded Gruma in Cerralvo, Nuevo Leon, Mexico, by producing a dough that could be preserved for longer periods and used when needed. Their methods simplified the production process, saving time, labor expenses, and reduced food waste. During the 1950s, Gruma continued to prefect the quality of its products and the manufacturing process as a whole, and developed Maseca, the famous dry dough used in production. During the 1950s, a second plant was built in Nayarit, Mexico. In the 1960s, Gruma opened seven new mills and in the 1970s expanded into the United States by purchasing the Mission Foods plant in California. Gruma acquired 10 more plants in the United States in the 1980s. In 1990, it built what is today the largest tortilla plant in Los Angeles, California, allowing for greatly increased production and enough products to expand heavily throughout Central America.

Later in the 1990s, Gruma acquired Molinos Nacionales, giving the firm a presence in Venezuela. In 1994, Gruma listed its IPO on the Mexican Stock Exchange and four years later, in 1998, it became listed on the New York Stock Exchange under the ticker symbol GMK. After opening a tortilla factory in the United Kingdom in 2000, the firm later acquired tortilla factories in Holland and a corn mill in Italy. Gruma recently built a tortilla plant near Shanghai, China, and, with the purchase of Rositas, established a presence in Australia. In 2011, Gruma made acquisitions in the United States, Russia, and Turkey, and its largest acquisition to date is the $450 million purchase of Archer Daniel's stake in Azteca Milling.

Internal Issues

Vision/Mission

On their corporate website, Gruma has both a vision and mission statement, as provided here:

> **Vision Statement:** Be the absolute leader in the production, marketing and distribution of corn flour and tortillas at worldwide level, as well as one of the main producers of flatbreads, with a consolidated position within the category of basic foods worldwide.

> **Mission Statement:** Contribute to the quality of life of our customers and consumers in all operations where we participate by offering products and services of excellent quality, fitted to their lifestyles, culture and needs, generating a dynamic and profitable growth, sustainable in the long term, to create the maximum value for our stockholders by being focused mainly in our key business; corn flour, tortillas, wheat flour and flatbreads.

Organizational Structure

As indicated in Exhibit 1, Gruma operates using a divisional-by-geographic region type organizational structure. Notice the top management team is all male.

Strategy

Gruma is well positioned globally to capitalize on the growing popularity of Mexican food, but still focuses primarily on Mexico and the United States. In fact, 84 percent of all Gruma sales are derived from Mexico and the states; 7 percent of sales are derived from Europe, where flatbreads are popular, especially in the United Kingdom. Gruma is currently expanding flatbread production across Europe. Moving forward over the next three years, the company plans to expand further into U.S. retail and food-service markets where it has a presence, and to expand into new regions of the United States. Despite offering products in over 100 nations, Gruma considers the United States to offer its most profitable opportunities for expansion. Today, Mission and Guerrero tortilla brands are the top two brands in the United States, and expanding these two brands into existing U.S. as well as new U.S. markets is a top priority for Gruma.

To help facilitate further expansion into the United States and Mexico, Gruma recently acquired from Archer-Daniels-Midland 23 percent of Gruma shares that Archer Daniels owned, 45 percent of Valores Azteca SA (which owned 10 percent of Gruma), 40 percent of Molinera de Mexico (Gruma's wheat flour business in Mexico), and 100 percent of Valley Holding, which owned 20 percent of Azteca Milling, Gruma's corn flour business in the United States. The Archer Daniels transaction was the largest, totaling $450 million plus a $60 million contingency payment. Notice in Exhibit 2 that Gruma's plants are mostly in Mexico and the United States.

Segments

Gruma is a holding company that operates through various subsidiaries, as revealed in Exhibit 3. The firm is structured by geographic region with 45 percent of sales coming from the United States and 39 percent from Mexico in 2013. Central America and Europe account for 6 and 7 percent, respectively, of 2013 sales. The firm reported 49 billion pesos in revenues in 2013 and 50 billion pesos in 2014.

EXHIBIT 1 Gruma's Organizational Structure

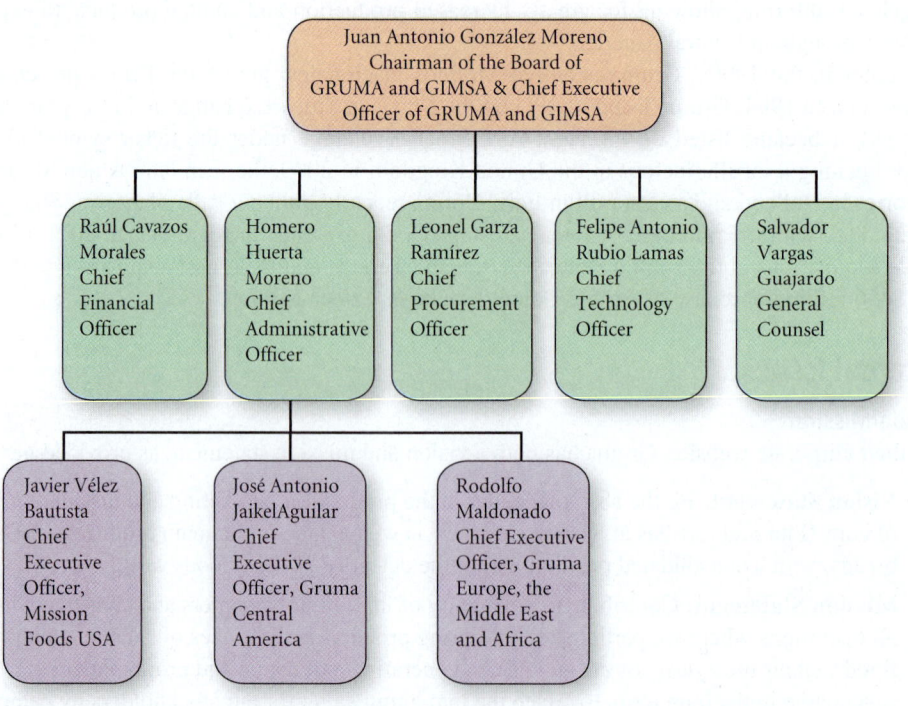

Source: Based on Gruma's company documents.

EXHIBIT 2 Gruma's Manufacturing Plants

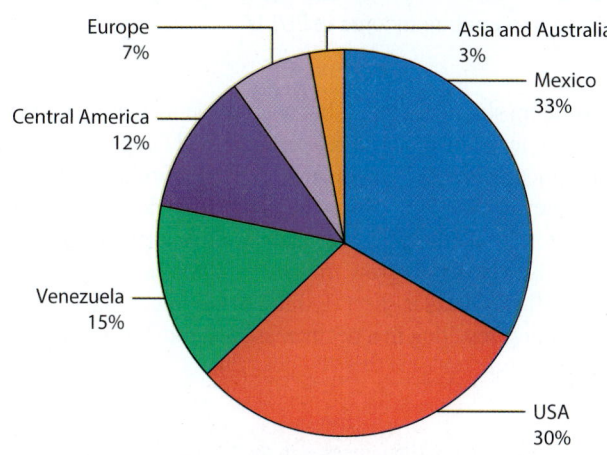

Source: Based on Gruma's company website.

EXHIBIT 3 Key 2013 Segment Data

Company	% Owned	% of 2013 Total Sales	Major Products
Mexico Operations			
Grupo Industrial Maseca, S.A.B. de C.V. ("GIMSA")	83	30	Corn flour
Molinera de México, S.A. de C.V. ("Molinera de México")	100	9	Wheat flour
USA/Europe Operations			
Gruma Corp.	100	52	Tortillas, Other tortilla-related products, Corn flour, Flatbreads, Grits, Other
Central American Operations			
Multiple	100	6	Corn flour, Tortillas, Snacks, Hearts of palm, Rice
All others	Various	3	Tortillas, Equipment manufacturing

Source: Based on two charts of the 2013 *Annual Report,* pp. 19 and 20.

Gruma operates in the United States and Europe primarily through the Mission Foods division and product line and through Azteca Milling. In 2013, 80 percent of sales volumes in the United States were derived from Mission Foods, whose products are sold to supermarkets, mass merchandisers, and independent stores along with chain restaurants, schools, hospitals, and other businesses. The Azteca Milling business currently distributes 38 percent of its corn flour to Mission Foods for use in producing tortillas and other products. Azteca also sells its products to consumers in 4-pound bags to the bulk railcar load to third-party consumers and other rival chip producers.

In Mexico, Gruma's largest subsidiary is GIMSA, responsible for the sale of corn flour used to make tortillas and other products. The firm estimates around 25 percent of all corn tortillas consumed in Mexico used corn flour produced by GIMSA through over 50 varieties of corn flour depending on the requirements of the customer. Over 75 percent of all corn flour is sold in bulk, which is considered a 20-kilo sack (44 pounds) used by restaurants and other large food producers.

Exhibit 4 provides additional segment data for Gruma, consolidated by business. Note GIMSA is operating much more efficiently than the other business units, but did experience a 300 million peso decline in operating income in 2014.

Finance

Revenues for Gruma were up slightly in 2014, but net income increased 33 percent, as indicated in Exhibit 5. Much of the gain in net income can be attributed to (1) improved corn inventory handling, (2) reduced commodity prices, and (3) focus on higher margin products. The founding family owns over 55 percent of all shares outstanding, giving the family significant voting power in determining dividends, board of directors, and other activities that require a shareholder vote. Industrywide revenue in the United States is expected to grow from $3.5 billion in 2014 to $4 billion by 2019. It is interesting to note that the firm's balance sheet (Exhibit 6) became "smaller" with reductions in both total assets and total liabilities, resulting in a net increase in equity of over 6 billion pesos.

Competitors

The tortilla industry consists of over 380 businesses in the United States alone, generating $3.5 billion in USD revenues. About half of all tortilla revenue in the states is generated by Gruma. A rival firm, Grupo Bimbo, S.A.B de C.V., also headquartered in Mexico, produces tortillas, but that company offers cakes and other snack items as well. Cargill, Inc., Grupo Minsa, S.A.B. de C.V., El Milagro, Grupo Industrial Maseca, and Reser's Fine Foods also are competitors, along with hundreds of other tortilla producers. Tyson, Hormel, General Mills, and PepsiCo's Frito Lay all produce tortillas or corn chips as well. The list of rival firms is extensive. Exhibit 7 provides a comparative analysis of Gruma with Grupo Bimbo.

EXHIBIT 4 **Additional Segment Data (in millions of Mexican pesos)**

	2014		2013	
	Sales	Operating Income	Sales	Operating Income
Gruma Corp.	$32,307	$3,212	$31,886	$2,531
GIMSA	15,074	2,129	15,944	2,448
Gruma Centroamerica	3,479	232	3,386	183
Other	(924)	450	(2,181)	(523)
Total	49,935	6,023	49,036	4,640

Source: Based on Gruma's Q4 Fiscal 2014 Report.

EXHIBIT 5 **Gruma's Income Statement (in millions of Mexican pesos)**

Report Date	December 31, 2014	December 31, 2013
Revenues	$49,935	$49,036
Cost of sales	(31,574)	(32,266)
Gross profit	18,361	16,770
Operating expenses	12,337	12,130
EBIT	6,024	4,640
Interest	1,105	988
EBT	4,919	3,652
Profit from discontinued operations	599	(147)
Tax	(1,061)	(195)
Net income	**4,457**	**3,310**
Majority net income	**4,287**	**3,163**

Source: Based on Gruma's 2014 *Annual Report*, p. 48.

EXHIBIT 6 Gruma's Balance Sheet (in millions Mexican of pesos)

Report Date	December 31, 2014	December 31, 2013
Assets		
Cash and equivalents	$1,465	$1,339
Accounts receivable	7,197	8,962
Inventories	6,557	7,644
Other current assets	250	391
Total current assets	15,469	18,336
Property, plant & equipment	17,814	17,905
Goodwill & intangibles	2,792	2,631
Other assets	4,562	3,737
Total assets	**40,637**	**42,609**
Liabilities		
Accounts payable	5,675	7,132
Other current liabilities	3,131	4,218
Total current liabilities	8,806	11,350
Long-term debt	9,324	13,096
Deferred tax	2,345	2,046
Other liabilities	2,077	1,690
Total liabilities	**22,552**	**28,182**
Common stock	5,364	5,364
Retained earnings	11,371	7,742
Other equity	1,350	1,321
Paid in capital	—	—
Total equity	**18,085**	**14,427**
Total liabilities & equity	**40,637**	**42,609**

Source: Based on Gruma's 2014 *Annual Report,* p. 47.

Grupo Bimbo, S.A.B. de C.V.

Founded in 1945 in Mexico City, Grupo Bimbo employs over 129,000 people and does business worldwide with 167 plants, but the company's principle operations are in Mexico and the United States. Top brands in Mexico include Bimbo, Marinela, Barcel, and Ricolino. Top products in Mexico include bread, chips, nuts, pastries, and other candy. In the United States, Bimbo's top brands include Sara Lee, Earth Grains, and Mrs. Bairds. Products include bread, desserts, pastries, and more. Products in Asia, Europe, and Central America closely resemble the product line offered in Mexico. The firms Tia Rosa brand is the main producer of tortillas and related products for Grupo Bimbo. The company has acquired several competitors to expand its range,

EXHIBIT 7 Grupo Bimbo's Segment Data (in millions of Mexican pesos)

	Gruma	Bimbo
# Employees	17,845	129,000
$ Net Income	4,457 M	3,513 M
$ Revenue	49,935 M	187,051 M
$ Revenue/Employee	2,798,262	1,450,000
$ EPS Ratio	9.91	0.75
Market Cap.	86 B	193 B

Source: Based on Gruma's company documents.

EXHIBIT 8 Grupo Bimbo's Segment Data (in millions of Mexican pesos)

	2014		2013	
	Revenue	Gross Profit	Revenue	Gross Profit
USA + Canada	$90,375	$45,330	$79,767	$39,981
Mexico	72,095	41,802	73,178	41,173
Latin America	21,931	9,568	20,405	8,564
Europe	6,897	2,916	5,323	2,084
Total	**187,051**	**99,098**	**174,623**	**91,376**

Source: Based on Grupo Bimbo's Q4 Fiscal 2014 Report.

including Sara Lee's North American Bakery in 2011 for $959 million USD. In 2014, the firm acquired Canada Bread Company that produces bread, buns, bagels, tortillas, and more. The acquisition of Canada Bread gave Bimbo several U.S. manufacturing and distributing facilities.

Exhibit 8 reveals Bimbo's total revenues and operating profits for each of the three key regions: the United States, Mexico, and Latin America. Note the large increase in revenues in the United States and Canada. Historically, Canada was a small fraction of total revenues, but with the 25,672 million peso acquisition of Canada Bread, Bimbo gained a significant footprint in the Canadian market. Mexican bases sales declined 1.5 percent in 2014, but Bimbo is optimistic over growth in bread, buns, and cakes in Mexico. Latin America sales were up 7.5 percent in 2014, largely from operations in Brazil and Chile. Full-year sales in Europe grew nearly 30 percent, due largely to a portion of Canada Bread's U.K. operations.

Grupo Minsa, S.A.B. de C.V.

The second-largest corn flour producer in Mexico (after Grupo Industrial Maseca), Grupo Minsa produces five different types of corn flour (or corn masa) for industrial, commercial, and home use: chip maroon green, organic blue, taco blue, tortilla con aditivo (violet), and tortilla sin aditivo under the Minsa label. Grupo Minsa's customers include food retailers, markets, distributors, and wholesalers, as well as supermarket chains and food-service companies in Mexico and the western and southwestern United States. Grupo Minsa also supplies the Mexican government with flour for its food-service operations. The company owns and operates six plants in Mexico and two in the United States.

Frito Lay

PepsiCo's Frito-Lay division is the largest salty snack provider in the United States, having brands that include Lay's, Ruffles, Doritos, Cheetos, and Fritos; Quaker Foods offers breakfast cereals (Life, Quaker Oats), rice (Rice-A-Roni), and side dishes (Near East). When it comes to snack foods, Frito-Lay has about 40 percent share of the global salty snack market. Frito-Lay dominates the U.S. snack market with a 64 percent market share in the salty snack market. The company is PepsiCo's most profitable segment, accounting for 40 percent of operating profits. However, Frito-Lay is not nearly as profitable outside the United States, primarily because of a key rival firm—Mondelez International (NASDAQ: MDLZ). Mondelez has the leading market share in every category and every region in which it competes outside the United States. Mondelez owns famous brands such as Oreo, Nabisco, Cadbury, Wheat Thins, and Trident.

Harbar

Harbar provides 2.2 percent of the U.S. tortilla market share. It serves the eastern and midwestern regions of the United States as well as a few international customers. Harbar's principle tortilla brand is Maria & Ricardo, which makes both flour and corn tortillas, along with corn chips. Harbar markets its products as organic. The firm generated $77 million in revenue in 2014.

Tyson Foods, Inc. (TSN)

Headquartered in Springdale, Arizona, Tyson Foods provides 1.7 percent of the U.S. tortilla market share. Tyson is a large U.S.-based meat and snack-producing company currently expanding into more prepared foods and snacks. Tyson's tortilla production is produced through the firm's prepared foods segment with the top brand being named Mexican Original. Tyson produces taco shells, tostadas, and corn and flour tortillas. In total, Tyson contributes $60 million in revenue to the industry in the United States.

External Issues

Geopolitical Risk

Despite being a global company and traded on the U.S. Stock Exchange, 46 percent of Gruma's assets are located in Mexico and 39 percent of sales. Another 45 percent of sales are from the United States. The Mexican peso in 2014 fell to a year-end low a total of 13 percent against the U.S. dollar. Exchange rate instability and devaluation, coupled with inflation and interest rates, are factors facing Gruma in its home market. Inflation in Mexico, for example, was 4.4, 3.8, 3.6, and 4.0 percent from 2010 through 2013, respectively. Crime rates have been higher in Mexico in recent years and several drug cartels operate in the Monterrey area, the home headquarters of Gruma. With 15 facilities in Venezuela, Gruma has a significant presence there, but the Venezuelan government continuously imposes price controls on many products, including corn and wheat. In 2013, the Venezuelan government took over control of operations at MONACA and DEMASECA, two businesses owned by Gruma, with 76 and 60 percent stakes, respectively, reduced to 24 and 40 percent after the government takeover.

Raw Materials

Gruma is heavily dependent on the price of commodities, especially corn, which accounts for almost 40 percent of total cost of sales. Wheat and wheat flour each account for 9 and 7 percent of sales, respectively, bringing the total of Gruma's three main ingredients to 56 percent of total sales. To hedge against fluctuating prices, Gruma purchases futures contracts on a regular basis. Generally, Gruma likes to assure that corn is available a full year in advance of harvest time, and guards against price 6 months ahead of time through futures. The bulk of all corn Gruma's Azteca Milling uses comes from the Texas Panhandle, adding more risk to the company, with its supply in a relative small geographic area. However, Azteca is large enough to easily access other markets for corn and does not consider securing corn supplies a significant threat moving forward.

Corn flour for Gruma's European operations comes mostly from Italy, and flour for wheat tortillas comes from various markets around the world. Wheat flour contracts are on short-term bases, unlike the longer-term contracts used to acquire corn. It is important to note that one factor hampering corn accessibility and prices is that only 15 percent of corn in the United States is used for food and beverages, with 40 percent being used for ethanol and 45 percent to feed livestock. One ingenious way firms are hedging against rising corn prices is to produce new flavor varieties of tortillas, such as sundried tomato, spinach, pepper, and others. There is good news for tortilla producers, however, in that early 2015 corn prices have fallen 50 percent from their peak in 2012. In addition, oil prices have fallen over 50 percent over the same time period.

American Tastes

The United States is becoming more and more Hispanic, and Americans increasingly want Mexican foods. Despite a carb-conscious culture, many health-minded individuals are also increasingly eating tortillas for the fiber and vitamin B3 contained in the products. Tortillas are the second-most popular bread in the United States, trailing only white bread. Helping aid the demand is a U.S. population of 17 percent Hispanic, along with growing numbers of Americans of other demographics, increasing their appetite for tortillas. Growing numbers of taco and Mexican restaurants also are driving demand.

Exhibit 9 reveals the U.S. distribution of sales based on tortilla products. Chips and other similar products are not included in the data shown in the exhibit. Over 61 percent of tortilla products are corn based with 49 percent flour based. Other products include both corn and wheat goods that are considered tortillas but not classified into the major four groups presented. About 30 percent of tortillas in the United States are sold frozen and 70 percent are sold fresh. In general, tortillas have a long shelf life so long as they are kept sealed in their bags. Corn tortillas are not only more popular but they are also healthier. The average corn tortilla contains 60 calories compared to 120 for a flour tortilla. Corn tortillas are gluten free. Most non-Hispanic Americans, however, prefer the flour tortilla that is commonly used to make burritos and tacos at restaurants.

EXHIBIT 9 U.S. Breakdown of Tortilla Revenues by Product Type

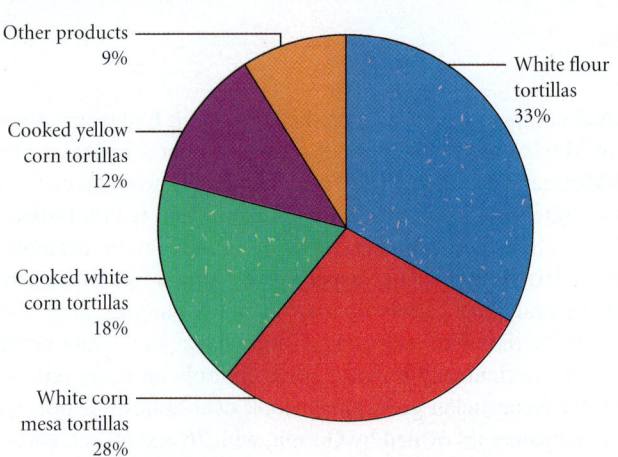

Other products 9%

Cooked yellow corn tortillas 12%

Cooked white corn tortillas 18%

White corn mesa tortillas 28%

White flour tortillas 33%

Source: A Variety of Sources

Business Culture in Mexico

Even though many Mexicans are also Americans, and about 80 percent of Mexican exports are bound for the United States, there are quite a few differences in the two countries' business culture. Mexican companies tend to be much more hierarchical (autocratic) with respect to how the firm is structured, with important decisions being made by a few key individuals in high ranks. When collaborating with management, it is suggested to match levels of seniority as closely as possible, and when dealing with subordinates, it is important to keep a human touch, much more so than in the United States. Mexican managers tend to offer detailed instructions to subordinates to aid them in performing their tasks. Meetings in Mexico often start late and run late, so be careful when scheduling multiple meetings for the same day. Business lunches tend to start later than they do in the United States and often can run 2 hours in length.

Dress is formal in Mexico, and women executives visiting are treated with respect. However, Mexico still has a glass-ceiling problem regarding women having opportunities in business. Compared to the United States, management style in Mexico is more authoritative and less participative. Mexicans, in general, work very hard for low wages, and for this reason many companies that departed Mexico 10 years ago to take advantage of lower wages in China are now returning to Mexico. If Mexico can get its drug violence under better control, the country has a very bright future for doing business globally and attracting businesses.

Future

On July 22, 2015, Gruma reported its second quarter of 2015 results. The company generated net profits of MXN (pesos) 1.156 billion while sales increased 4 percent to 960,000 metric tons. For that Q2, sales were up MXN 1.938 billion, from MXN 12.297 billion in Q2 of 2014 to a new figure of MXN 14.28 billion. The company's operating profit increased 22 percent during Q2 of 2015, due to improved performance in all its subsidiaries, particularly in the United States, as well as greater efficiencies and the positive effects of the depreciation of the Mexican peso. For Q2 of 2015, Gruma's net sales from operations outside of Mexico accounted for 73 percent of consolidated results. Also for Q2, Gruma's EBITDA experienced double-digit growth for the 13th consecutive quarter, increasing by 21 percent compared to the same period in 2014, reaching MXN 2.242 billion. Regarding its strategies during Q2 of 2015, Gruma made capital investments worth USD 33 million, most of which was spent on technology improvements, such as expanding the installed capacity of the firm's tortilla and corn flour production plants in Mexicali, and building new plants to produce tostadas in Tijuana, Mexico, and for tortilla production in Russia. Gruma is doing exceptionally well, but numerous rival firms have their eye on the company's market share and customer base. Develop a 3 year strategic plan for CEO Moreno.

Restaurant Brands International, Inc., 2015

www.rbi.com, QSR

On December 4, 2014, Burger King Worldwide (BKW) officially acquired Tim Hortons, Inc., a Canadian coffee-and-doughnut retailer, for $11.4 billion. With that deal, BKW created Restaurant Brands International (RBI), which overnight became the second-largest global quick-service restaurant in the world. The combined company, RBI, is headquartered in Oakville, outside of Toronto, Canada, although BKW was headquartered in Miami, Florida. A primary rationale for this acquisition was for BKW to save potentially millions of dollars through what is called *tax inversion*—a process where a company reduces its U.S. tax liability by relocating its headquarters to a country with lower corporate tax rates. Canada's corporate tax rate is 15 percent versus the USA's 39 percent, yielding in a potential huge annual savings in corporate taxes for BKW. As part of the deal, BKW agreed to (1) maintain employment levels at Tim Hortons' Canadian restaurants, (2) expand Tim Hortons' global presence, (3) maintain Tim Hortons' franchisee rent and royalty structure at current levels for a 5-year period, and (4) operate Tim Hortons and Burger King as separate brands, with no plans to create one unified brand.

Burger King Worldwide is the second largest global fast-food hamburger restaurant (FFHR) chain, behind McDonalds, in the quick-service restaurant (QSR) industry. Best known for the Whopper, BKW sells beef and chicken-based sandwiches along with other fast foods. Recently, BKW launched lower-calorie french fries, a gay-pride Whopper in San Francisco called "Proud Whoppers," and even brought back the *YUMBO*® sandwich.

Known internationally as "Tim Hortons Cafe and Bake Shop," Tim Hortons is Canada's largest quick-service, casual restaurant (McDonald's is #2). As of June 30, 2013, Tim Hortons has 4,304 restaurants, including 3,468 in Canada, 807 in the United States, and 29 in the Middle East. However, as of September 2014, there were fewer (3,665) Tim Hortons restaurants in Canada, but more (869) in the United States, and nearly double (56) in the Middle East (mainly on American and Canadian military bases). Tim Hortons has about 75 percent of the Canadian market for baked goods (based on the number of customers served) and about 65 percent of the Canadian coffee market (compared to Starbucks at #2 with 7 percent).

For the second quarter of 2015, Restaurant Brands International reported revenue of $1.04 billion, beating analysts' expectations of $1.01 billion. In the Burger King division, comparable store sales rose 6.7 percent in Q2, driven by product launches such as the A.1. Hearty Mozzarella Bacon Cheeseburger, Extra Long Pulled Pork Sandwich, and Chicken Fries. In the Tim Hortons division, comparable store sales increased 5.5 percent in Q2, boosted by strength in dark roast coffee and its Creamy Chocolate Chill beverage. In comparison, rival McDonald's (MCD) reported a 0.7 percent decrease in global comparable store sales during the Q2 that ended on June 30, 2015. Also during Q2, Tim Hortons added 52 net new restaurants, ending the period with 4,776 locations, while Burger King added 141 net new restaurants, ending the period with 14,528 locations. Last year, Burger King purchased Tim Hortons for $11 billion. Restaurant Brands now has over $23 billion in systemwide sales and over 19,000 restaurants in approximately 100 countries and U.S. territories.

Copyright by Fred David Books LLC. www.strategyclub.com (Written by John D. Varlaro)

History

Tim Hortons was founded in 1964 in Hamilton, Ontario, by Canadian hockey player Tim Horton and Jim Charade, after an initial venture in hamburger restaurants. In 1967, Horton partnered with investor Ron Joyce, who assumed control over operations after Horton died in 1974. Joyce expanded the chain into a multimillion business. In November 2010, Tim Hortons announced it was closing 36 stores in the northeastern United States, due to high competition with New England-based Dunkin' Brands, owner of Dunkin Donuts. In May 2014, Tim Hortons launched a new frozen drink, Frozen Green Tea, and a few months later launched a dark roast coffee blend.

Burger King Worldwide was founded in 1954 by James McLamore and David Edgerton, who opened the first location in Miami, Florida, after purchasing the trademark rights for "Insta-Burger King"—a franchise hamburger restaurant that used an insta-broiler to quickly and cheaply grill hamburgers. As franchisees of the Insta-Burger King chain, they purchased the Jacksonville, Florida-based franchise, renamed it Burger King, and successfully grew the company for the following 8 years. BKW introduced the Whopper in 1957.

In 1967, Pillsbury Company purchased Burger King and subsequently instituted several attempts to restructure the restaurant chain. After years of declining profits and poor performance, Burger King was purchased by its current parent company, 3G Capital, in 2006 for $4 billion. 3G Capital made Burger King a private company, but relisted it as a public company in 2012, while retaining approximately 70 percent ownership. 3G Capital is currently the largest shareholder of Restaurant Brands International.

Dunkin' Brands, Krispy Kreme Doughnuts, and Starbucks are rivals to Tim Hortons. McDonald's, Wendy's, Hardees, and hundreds of other hamburger chains are rivals to Burger King. Prior to the purchase, BKW had a presence in 97 countries with approximately 14,000 locations. The United States and Canada markets account for about 50 percent of these locations. Burger King Worldwide recently increased its locations in China substantially. With the creation of RBI, the international footprint of these two iconic brands now account for more than 18,000 restaurants located in 100 different countries.

Restaurant Brands International was founded on December 4, 2014.

Internal Issues

Vision/Mission/Values/Ethics

Burger King Worldwide's vision is as follows: "Our commitment to premium ingredients, signature recipes, and family-friendly dining experiences is what has defined our brand for more than 50 successful years." The company has an extensive Code of Ethics referred to as the *BKC Code* published on the website. As found in the *BKC Code*, BKW states, "Our vision is to be the most profitable QSR business, through a strong franchise system and great people, serving the best burgers in the world." The *BKC Code* further lists the following corporate values: Bold, Accountable, Empowered, Meritocratic, and Fun. The company does not have a written mission statement. The *BKC Code* is published for all franchisees, employees, and executives to follow. It specifically addresses employee culture, key business strategies, guests, and how employees can adhere to the code in all of these areas. For example, the section on employee culture addresses diversity and inclusion as well as data privacy. Safety and restaurant quality are addressed under the Guest section.

Organizational Structure

As illustrated in Exhibit 1, RBI operates using a strategic business unit type design, with there being two strategic business units (SBU): Burger King Worldwide and Tim Hortons. There are divisions by region below the two SBUs. Soon after the merger was consummated in December 2014, Daniel Schwartz was appointed CEO of Restaurant Brands International. Schwartz is leading the company's day-to-day business and is responsible for the overall business strategy. Exhibit 1 reveals other executives appointed to the RBI's leadership team.

Strategy

Restaurant Brands International is committed to fulfilling its agreed-on strategy dimensions for operating Tim Hortons. However, regarding its BKW brand, RBI is focused on (1) driving sales in the United States and Canada, (2) accelerating international development, (3) aggressively pursuing refranchising opportunities, and (4) maintaining strong focus on corporate-level cost structure. Burger King Worldwide is focused on increasing its global footprint through joint ventures and strategic partnerships. Typically, BKW provides franchisees with exclusive rights within specific regions. In return, franchisees receive minority stakes in the joint venture.

EXHIBIT 1 RBI's Organizational Structure

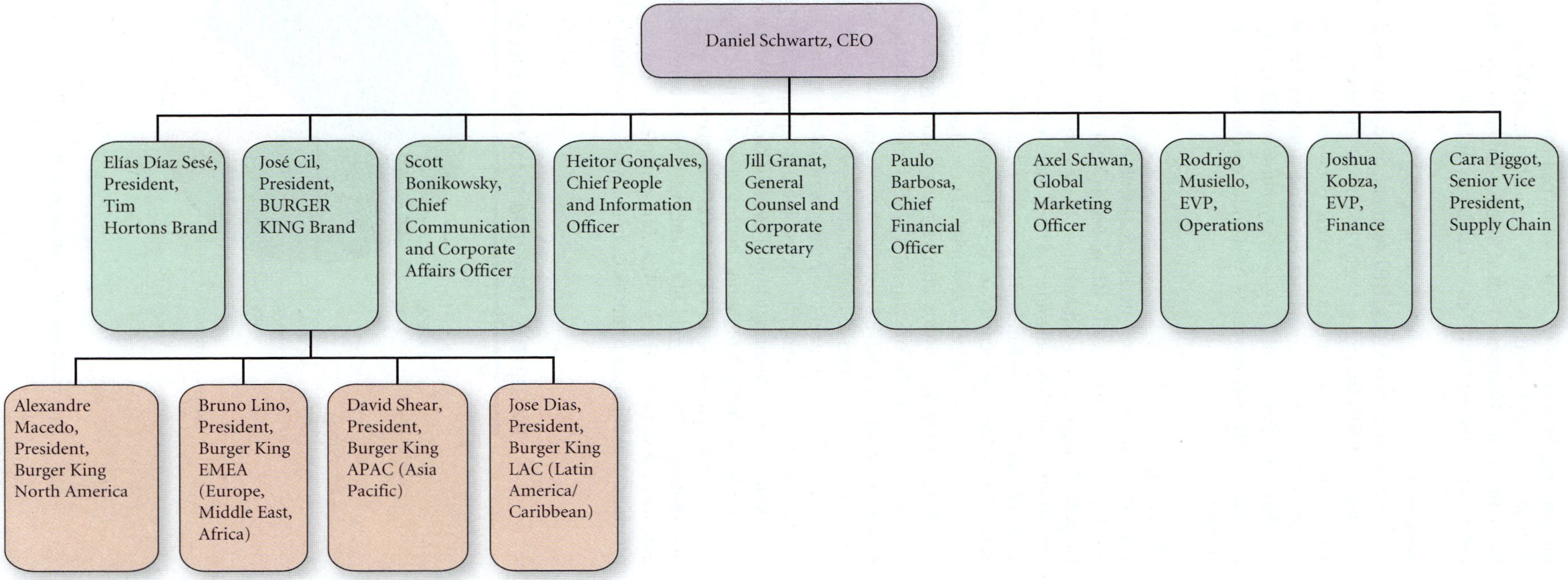

Daniel Schwartz, CEO

Elías Díaz Sesé, President, Tim Hortons Brand

José Cil, President, BURGER KING Brand

Scott Bonikowsky, Chief Communication and Corporate Affairs Officer

Heitor Gonçalves, Chief People and Information Officer

Jill Granat, General Counsel and Corporate Secretary

Paulo Barbosa, Chief Financial Officer

Axel Schwan, Global Marketing Officer

Rodrigo Musiello, EVP, Operations

Joshua Kobza, EVP, Finance

Cara Piggot, Senior Vice President, Supply Chain

Alexandre Macedo, President, Burger King North America

Bruno Lino, President, Burger King EMEA (Europe, Middle East, Africa)

David Shear, President, Burger King APAC (Asia Pacific)

Jose Dias, President, Burger King LAC (Latin America/Caribbean)

Source: Based on information provided at all three companies' websites.

Currently, BKW is focused on high growth or emerging markets. Simply stated, BKW is focused on reducing the number of corporate-owned franchises. Through these means, BKW intends to decrease costs and increase profits. In addition, BKW is focused on expanding Tim Hortons, likely first in the Northeast United States, then nationally, then globally—not necessarily in that order—but consistent with the agreed terms of the acquisition.

Segments

Reporting into its two SBUs, RBI segments its operations into five regions. Exhibit 2 details the locations of RBI's franchise-owned restaurants. Franchise-owned restaurants account for nearly 100 percent of all restaurants since RBI owned only 65 total restaurants out of over 19,000 worldwide. Note that only 24 percent of all stores are Tim Hortons.

Exhibit 3 shows RBI's segment revenues and EBITDA. Note that Tim Hortons has the poorest ratio of EBITDA/Revenues by a wide margin overall compared to the Burger King regional segments.

Marketing

The Whopper and several iterations (Double Whopper, Four Cheese Whopper, etc.) are core BKW products. Periodically BKW brings new iterations, such as the Angry Whopper and the Chipotle Whopper, for a limited time. These variations help drive new customers to BKW, while reinvigorating current customers. Other more experimental offerings have included the Pride Whopper, exclusive to San Francisco, as well as Satisfries, a healthier alternative to french fries. While BKW has significantly reduced the number of corporate-owned locations, the remaining 52 are intended to be used to test-market new products prior to wider release.

Burger King Worldwide also varies its core products globally to meet local tastes. Some examples would be the offering of a black burger in Japan, a Cheese Fondue Whopper in South Korea, and a Bacon Outback Burger in Australia. It is also only in Australia where Burger King restaurants operate under a different name—*Hungry Jack's*. This different brand further demonstrates BKW's commitment to meeting regional market needs, and helped lead to the 2.4 percent increase in global comparable sales in the third quarter of 2014.

With the new marketing slogan, *Taste is King*, BKW is focusing its marketing to put its food first. BKW has had a tumultuous history of marketing campaigns, but it has been known to be a front-runner within the FFHR and QSR markets for successful campaigns. The communication strategy integrates multiple channels to reach consumers, including social media, the BK app, and the website. The website, for example, is simple yet bold with its emphasis on food offerings. It also places promotions in the website navigation bar, again reinforcing the strategic

EXHIBIT 2 **RBI's 2014 Total Franchise Stores**

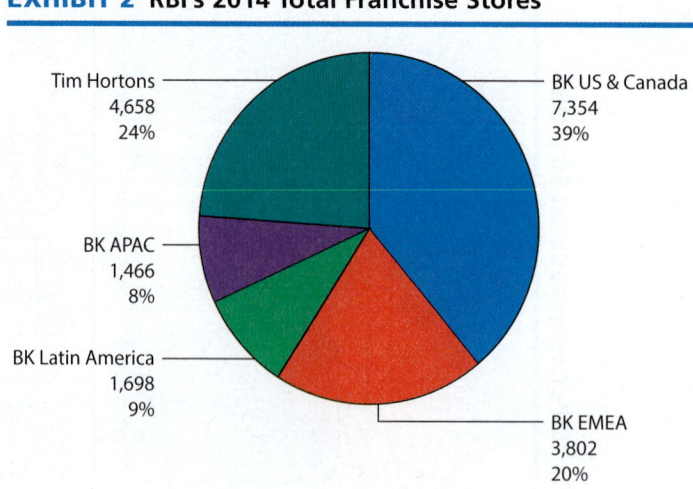

Source: Based on information in RBI's 2014 *Annual Report,* p. 6.

EXHIBIT 3 RBI's Revenues by Company-Owned versus Franchisee Restaurants (in millions of USD)

	2014		2013	
	Revenues	EBITDA	Revenues	EBITDA
BK US & Canada	640	446	655	437
BK EMEA	274	220	336	189
BK Latin America	77	69	86	67
BK APAC	64	56	58	49
Tim Hortons	142	35	—	—

Source: Based on information in RBI's 2014 *Annual Report*, pp. 120 and 121.

goal of communicating both core products and value. The Burger King app mirrors this as well, providing consumers the opportunity to find locations and receive coupons. The ability to pay by phone is also integrated into the app.

Finance

Restaurant Brands International's recent income statement and balance sheet are provided in Exhibits 4 and Exhibit 5, respectively.

Competitors

Every year, U.S. consumers spend about $75 billion in the Fast-Food Hamburger Restaurant (FFHR) category. Companies in this segment compete based on price and convenience, leading to fierce competition. For example, it is common practice within this segment to quickly expand and open new locations to leave little space for other competition. Not only is there constant price pressure, but constant marketing of deals through coupons, a common tactic to drive traffic. Yet, the products (i.e., hamburgers) may be seen as undifferentiated by consumers. Both factors necessitate competitors to manage operating expenses, while spending marketing dollars to drive foot-traffic, and while striving to create brand differentiation and loyalty. Of the $75 billion spent annually in FFHR, consumers spend about $10 billion at Burger King Worldwide Yet, BKW is only number two in this market segment, with McDonald's being number one and Wendy's close behind as number three in the market.

In addition to the real big companies such as McDonald's and Starbucks, Five Guys Enterprises, Elevation Burger, BurgerFi, and What-A-Burger compete aggressively with

EXHIBIT 4 RBI Income Statement (in millions of USD)

Report Date	December 31, 2014	December 31, 2013
Revenues	$1,197	$1,146
Operating expenses	1,015	624
EBIT	182	522
Interest and other	435	200
EBT	(253)	322
Tax expense	(24)	88
Partnership adjustments	(560)	—
Net income	**(837)**	**234**

Source: Based on RBI's 2014 *Annual Report*, p. 68.

EXHIBIT 5 RBI's Balance Sheet (in millions of USD)

Report Date	December 31, 2014	December 31, 2013
Assets		
Cash and equivalents	$1,803	$787
Accounts receivable	440	178
Inventories	194	70
Other current assets	223	39
Total current assets	2,660	1,074
Property, plant & equipment	2,540	802
Goodwill	5,851	630
Intangibles	9,441	2,796
Other assets	672	526
Total assets	**21,164**	**5,828**
Liabilities		
Accounts payable	223	31
Tim Hortons notes	1,045	—
Other current liabilities	657	315
Total current liabilities	1,925	346
Long-term debt	8,937	2,880
Other liabilities	2,681	1,086
Total liabilities	**13,543**	**4,312**
Preferred Partnership Units	3,297	—
Total stock	4,579	—
Retained earnings	—	226
Treasury stock	—	(7)
Paid in capital	—	1,240
Other	(255)	57
Total equity	**4,324**	**1,516**
Total liabilities, Preferred Partnership Units & equity	**21,164**	**5,828**

Source: Based on RBI's 2014 *Annual Report*, p. 69.

RBI. Five Guys, for example, proudly proclaims its strategy of offering healthy beef, not investing heavily in marketing and advertising, and serving all-you-can-eat peanuts and veggie burgers. Elevation Burger and BurgerFi focus on high-quality food and drinks. Elevation Burger markets its hamburgers as grass-fed, free-range, and organic—overall healthier food that is better for the environment. BurgerFi touts angus-beef burgers with craft beer and wine available for purchase. Also, there are more than a million mom-and-pop hamburger restaurants globally.

Competition for consumers is not limited to hamburger restaurants, as restaurants that sell pizza and other fast foods can compete indirectly. Yum! Brands—consisting of Kentucky Fried Chicken, Taco Bell, and Pizza Hut—represents significant indirect competition to BKW domestically and abroad. For example, there are about 4,600 KFCs and 1,000 Pizza Huts in China alone. Yum! Brands further views the Pizza Hut Casual Dining experience in China as containing untapped potential, given that two-thirds of sales are non-pizza. Yum! Brands recently began offering breakfast items, and serving breakfast even at its Taco Bell locations.

Exhibit 6 compares RBI, McDonald's (MCD), Wendy's (WEN), Starbucks Corporation (SBUX), and Dunkin' Brands (DNKN) on various metrics. Be mindful that franchised restaurants

EXHIBIT 6 Comparative Metrics for RBI and its Rival Firms

	RBI	MCD	WEN	SBUX	DNKN
$ Revenue	1.2 B	27 B	2.1 B	17 B	750 M
$ Net Income	(837) M	4.8 B	121 M	2.5 B	177 M
# Employees	4,600	420,000	32,000	191,000	1,600
$ Revenue per Employee	261 K	64,000	65,000	89,000	469,000
$ Market Capitalization	18.2 B	92 B	4 B	70 B	4.7 B
$ EPS	(2.34)	4.80	0.32	3.30	1.65

Source: Based on company documents and Yahoo! Finance.

report revenues and income on the franchisee financial statements, not the big parent company. The parent reports royalty income from franchisees (i.e., on their income statements), but the property, plant, and equipment and everything for a franchised restaurant is on the franchisee's financial statements rather than the parent company. Note that Restaurant Brands International is much smaller than McDonald's or Starbucks.

McDonald's Corporation (MCD)

Headquartered in Oakbrook, Illinois, McDonald's has about 36,000 locations in 119 countries with about 6,700 locations corporate owned. McDonald's strategy includes operating a large number of corporate-owned locations, as it is viewed integral to lead-by-example for franchisees—a very different approach from BKW's current franchise strategy. McDonald's has been struggling of late due to intense price competition in the industry.

The Wendy's Company (WEN)

Headquartered in Dublin, Ohio, Wendy's has about 6,500 restaurants, primarily in the United States and Canada. Of those 6,500 locations, about 1,100 are corporate owned. Wendy's has about 400 franchised locations outside North America, in 25 other countries.

Starbucks Corporation (SBUX)

Headquartered in Seattle, Washington, Starbucks has about 22,000 restaurants in 65 countries. Historically primarily a breakfast restaurant, Starbucks now offers dinners and alcoholic beverages, and is open longer hours per day than ever before.

Dunkin' Brands (DNKN)

Headquartered in Canton, Massachusetts, Dunkin Brands' owns, operates, and franchises quick-service restaurants under the Dunkin' Donuts and Baskin-Robbins brands worldwide. The company operates 11,500 Dunkin' Donuts restaurants and 7,600 Baskin-Robbins restaurants globally. Dunkin has avoided Canada (having only 4 locations), just as Tim Hortons has avoided the United States, obviously to avoid crossing paths very much. There are approximately 2,200 Dunkin' Donuts in the Asia Pacific region alone, with plans to dramatically increase the presence in China, with over 1,400 new locations in the next 20 years. Currently, there are 8,000 Dunkin' Brands restaurants in the United States. Like BKW, Dunkin' Donuts caters to local tastes. For example, in Korea there is the Grapefruit Coolatta, the Choco Nut Donut in Thailand, and mochi-based donuts in China.

External Issues

The Public's Concern for Health

There is an ever-growing concern regarding childhood and adult obesity. It is estimated that about one third of Americans are obese, and these figures are expected to increase. Obesity may lead to significant health issues, including diabetes and heart disease. To stave off these concerns, a number of regulations have been implemented at the local, state, and federal levels—all of which could impact RBI's operations and revenues. For example, the U.S. Food and Drug Administration (FDA) will soon be mandating all caloric values be disclosed on menus. While RBI currently provides this information on its website, it is possible that as the public's understanding of calories grows, so may the negative impact on RBI's business. Simply stated, according to the company website, the Whopper has approximately 650 calories. Since the current daily allowance recommended is 2,000 calories, the public may eventually put pressure on BKW and other restaurants to provide healthier, lower-calorie alternatives. The Satisfries is a good example of BKW attempting to meet these demands. McDonald's is trying to raise consumers' perception of the quality of its food by adding kale to the menu. McKale chips may soon be available, alongside hamburgers and fries.

Class action lawsuits have been filed against various quick-service restaurants for not appropriately notifying the public of the health risks from such foods. Various lawsuits have claimed that marketing practices have unfairly targeted children—echoing the lawsuits against tobacco in prior decades. Even if RBI is not directly affected by such lawsuits, the publicity and attention they draw can negatively impact the company. A related dietary trend is the growing number of people following specialty diets. These may range from gluten-free to vegetarian. Restaurant Brands International does offer information concerning gluten on its website, but does not necessarily offer food for those who desire these options. Yum! Brands' Pizza Hut and Domino's Pizza, however, offer gluten-free pizza as a dining option. White Castle, a fast-food hamburger restaurant famous for its beef sliders, offers veggie burgers that are prepared separately from meat-containing foods to cater to vegetarians. If more competitors begin to offer these options, it may put more pressure on BKW to deviate from its core products.

Technology and Security

As of late, retailers have been the subject of cyberattacks and breaches of security, leading to the theft of customer and employee information. One such attack against Target led to the theft of 40 million credit card numbers. Neiman Marcus also experienced an attack, where the personal information of 70 million customers was stolen. Restaurant Brands International seems exposed to such an attack since the company looks to meet the needs of the consumer through technology. For example, the BKW app allows for payment through mobile phones. Any and all information BKW is storing and transmitting through this software could be stolen. One simply can ask what happens if RBI runs a controversial marketing campaign that offends a specific individual or group? Even the company's Whopper targeted toward gays in San Francisco could make the firm vulnerable in social media. All of these threats lead to the need to invest in risk assessment and mitigation measures.

Employment Law

New minimum wage and health-care laws impact RBI. Both at the state- and federal-level minimum wage levels are being challenged. There have been open protests against the hourly wages of fast-food workers. Viewed as low-wage workers, many of these people are protesting to increase the minimum wage to $15 an hour. McDonald's as well as Burger King have been primary targets of these protests. To respond to these protests, many states have increased minimum wage. Cities have considered taking further steps, such as Seattle, where the minimum wage was increased to $15 an hour. Wal-Mart, Target, and other retailers have recently increased their minimum wage rates paid to employees.

The Patient Protection and Affordable Care Act (ACA) represents another area of increased costs for franchisees, requiring that businesses offer health care to employees meeting the hourly threshold. This is another area where franchisee costs may increase. Other changes in employment law can cause disruptions and increases in costs, such as laws related to immigration, overtime, working conditions, and family leave. These potential changes are exacerbated by BKW's global presence, as it must monitor and support franchisees across the globe.

Future

Burger King Worldwide is actively transitioning from being a USA-based, global hamburger chain, to a Canada-based diverse restaurant chain. BKW's recent Tim Hortons acquisition and the creation of Restaurant Brands International has both BKW and Tim Hortons poised to grow much faster globally—but where, when, why, and how? Some analysts assert that RBI's financial fundamentals are excellent. Same-store sales at Burger King and Tim Hortons rose 2 percent and 3 percent, respectively, in 2014, which is excellent. However, RBI operates from a desired 100 percent franchised-model, so future earnings largely rely on fixed-cost reductions and post-merger synergies. RBI shareholders are not pleased with the decline in 2014 net income, and are anxious to see growth of 5 percent-plus going forward. The new CEO of RBI, Daniel Schwartz, needs a clear strategic plan for the company. Help him develop an effective 3-year strategic plan for RBI.

Glossary

Acquisition   When a large organization purchases (acquires) a smaller firm; a merger.

Actionable responses   Meaningful in terms of having strategic implications; suggestive of potential strategies to capitalize on or compensate for.

Activity ratios   Inventory turnover and average collection period measure how effectively a firm is using its resources.

Advantage   A way to evaluate strategies; to determine if a particular strategy creates or extends a firm's competitive superiority in a selected area of activity.

Aggressive quadrant   In a SPACE matrix analysis, when the firm's directional vector points in the upper-right quadrant, the firm should pursue aggressive strategies.

Annual objectives   Short-term milestones that organizations must achieve to reach long-term objectives.

Attractiveness Scores (AS)   In a QSPM, the numerical value (rating) that indicates the relative attractiveness of each strategy given a single internal or external factor.

Auditing   The accounting process that firms undertake to have their financial statements reviewed for accuracy in order to assure compliance with the law and IRS code.

Avoidance   A method for reducing conflict through such actions as ignoring the problem in hopes that the conflict will resolve itself or physically separating the conflicting individuals (or groups).

Backward integration   A strategy seeking ownership or increased control of a firm's suppliers, such as a manufacturer acquiring its raw material source firms.

Balanced Scorecard   A framework of desired objectives; derives its name from the need of firms to "balance" quantitative (such as financial ratios and percentages) with qualitative (such as for employee morale and business ethics) objectives that are oftentimes used in strategy evaluation.

Bankruptcy   A legal document that allows a firm to avoid major debt obligations and void union contracts in order to survive and regroup as a firm. There are five major types: Chapter 7, Chapter 9, Chapter 11, Chapter 12, and Chapter 13.

Benchmarking   A management technique associated with value chain analysis, whereby a firm compares itself on a wide variety of performance-related criteria against the best firms in the industry, thus establishing standards of excellence.

Board of directors   A group of individuals above the CEO who have oversight and guidance over management and who care for shareholders' interests.

Bonus system   A form of incentive compensation whereby employees and/or managers receive a year-end or period-end reward, usually cash, based on some organizational performance criteria such as sales, profit, production efficiency, quality, and safety; used to motivate individuals to support strategy-implementation efforts.

Book value   Number of shares outstanding multiplied by stock price.

Boston Consulting Group (BCG) Matrix   A four-quadrant, strategic planning analytical tool that places an organization's various divisions as circles in a display (similar to the IE Matrix) based on two key dimensions: (1) relative market share position and (2) industry growth rate. The diagram's four quadrants (Stars, Question Marks, Cash Cows, Question Marks) each have different strategy implications.

Breakeven (BE) point   The quantity of units that a firm must sell in order for its total revenues (TR) to equal its total costs (TC).

Bribe   A gift bestowed to influence a recipient's conduct.

Bribery   Offering, giving, receiving, or soliciting of any item of value to influence the actions of an official or other person in discharge of a public or legal duty.

Business analytics   An MIS technique designed to analyze huge volumes of data to help executives make decisions; sometimes called predictive analytics or data mining.

Business ethics   Principles of behavior/conduct a firm may institute to minimize wrongdoing among employees/managers.

Business portfolio   Autonomous divisions (or profit centers or segments) of an organization as represented by circles in BCG and IE matrices.

Capacity utilization   The extent to which a manufacturing plant's output reaches its potential output; the higher the capacity utilization the better, because otherwise equipment may sit idle.

Capital budgeting   A basic function of finance; the allocation and reallocation of capital and resources to projects, products, assets, and divisions of an organization.

Cash cows   A quadrant in the BCG Matrix for divisions that have a high relative market share position but compete in a low-growth industry; they generate cash in excess of their needs, they are often milked, this is the lower-left quadrant.

Champions   Individuals most strongly identified with a firm's new idea/product/service, and whose futures are linked to its success.

Chief Information Officer (CIO)   More an external manager compared to a CTO; focuses on the firm's technical, information gathering, and social media relationship with diverse external stakeholders.

Chief Technology Officer (CTO)   More an internal manager compared to a CIO; focuses on technical issues such as data acquisition, data processing, decision-support systems, and software and hardware acquisition.

Code of business ethics   A written document specifying expected employee/manager behavior/conduct in an organization.

Collaborative machines   Robots used in manufacturing operations; these robots are flexible, capable of doing a variety of tasks.

Combination strategy   The pursuit of a combination of two or more strategies simultaneously.

Competitive advantage   Anything a firm does especially well, compared to rival firms. For example, when a firm can do something that rival firms cannot do, or owns something that rival firms desire, that can represent a competitive advantage.

Competitive intelligence (CI)   "A systematic and ethical process for gathering and analyzing information about the competition's activities and general business trends to further a business's own goals" (SCIP website).

Competitive position (CP)   One of four dimensions/axes of the SPACE Matrix; determines an organization's competitiveness, using such factors as market share, product quality, product life cycle, customer loyalty, capacity utilization, technological know-how, and control over suppliers and distributors.

Competitive Profile Matrix (CPM)   A widely used strategic planning analytical tool designed to identify a firm's major competitors and its particular strengths and weaknesses in relation to a sample firm's strategic position.

Competitive quadrant   In a SPACE Matrix analysis, when the firm's directional vector points in the lower-right quadrant it suggests that the firm should pursue competitive strategies such as horizontal integration.

Concern for employees   A component of the mission statement; are employees a valuable asset to the firm?

Concern for public image   A component of the mission statement; is the firm responsive to social, community, and environmental concerns?

Concern for survival, growth, and profitability   A component of the mission statement; does the firm strive to survive, grow, and (if for-profit) be profitable?

Conflict   A disagreement between two or more parties on one or more issues.

Confrontation   A method for reducing conflict exemplified by exchanging members of conflicting parties so that each can gain an appreciation of the other's point of view, or holding a meeting at which conflicting parties present their views and work through their differences.

Conservative quadrant   In a SPACE Matrix analysis, when the firm's directional vector points in the upper-left quadrant it suggests that the firm should pursue conservative strategies such as market penetration.

Consistency   A way to evaluate strategies; to determine if a particular strategy is supportive of overall strategies/objectives/policies of the firm.

Consonance   The need for strategists to examine sets of trends, as well as individual trends, in evaluating strategies.

Contingency plans   Alternative plans that can be put into effect if certain key events do not occur as expected.

Controlling   A basic function of management; includes all of those activities undertaken to ensure that actual operations conform to planned operations.

Convertible bonds   Notes issued by companies to raise capital through debt, but these notes/bonds can be converted into shares of stock at some point in time.

Core competence   A value chain activity that a firm performs especially well.

Cost/benefit analysis   An activity that involves assessing the costs, benefits, and risks associated with marketing decisions. Three steps are required to perform this activity: (1) compute the total costs associated with a decision, (2) estimate the total benefits from the decision, and (3) compare the total costs with the total benefits.

Cost leadership   One of Michael Porter's strategy dimensions that involves a firm producing standardized products at a very low per-unit cost for consumers who are price sensitive.

Creed statement   Another name for mission statement; a declaration of an organization's "reason for being." It answers the pivotal question, "What is our business?"

Cultural products   Include values, beliefs, rites, rituals, ceremonies, myths, stories, legends, sagas, language, metaphors, symbols, heroes, and heroines. These products are levers that strategists can use to influence and direct strategy formulation, implementation, and evaluation activities.

Culture   The set of shared values, beliefs, attitudes, customs, norms, personalities, heroes, and heroines that describe a firm. Strategists should strive to preserve, emphasize, and build on these aspects.

Customer analysis   Examination and evaluation of consumer needs, desires, and wants; involves administering customer surveys, analyzing consumer information, evaluating market positioning strategies, developing customer profiles, and determining optimal market segmentation strategies.

Customers   A component of the mission statement; individuals who purchase a firm's products/services.

Data mining   Analyzing huge volumes of information in order to determine trends and garner information to make decision making more effective.

Decision stage   Stage 3 of the strategy formulation analytical framework that involves development of the Quantitative Strategic Planning Matrix (QSPM). A QSPM uses input information from Stage 1 to objectively evaluate feasible alternative strategies identified in Stage 2. A QSPM reveals the relative attractiveness of alternative strategies and thus provides objective basis for selecting specific strategies.

Defensive quadrant   In a SPACE Matrix analysis, when the firm's directional vector goes into the lower-left quadrant it suggests that the firm should pursue defensive strategies such as retrenchment.

Defusion   A method for reducing conflict that includes playing down differences between conflicting parties while accentuating similarities and common interests, or compromising so that there is neither a clear winner nor loser, or resorting to majority rule, or appealing to a higher authority, or redesigning present positions.

De-integration   Reducing the pursuit of backward integration; instead of owning suppliers, companies negotiate with several outside suppliers.

Deliberate practice "An intense focusing on all aspects related a to subject matter or business idea"; deliberate practice goes well beyond hard work or routine practice, so much so that even the most successful entrepreneurs cannot engage in deliberate practice for more than a few hours each day. Includes examining yourself as a person, your competition, and a wide array of factors related to the entrepreneurial endeavor at hand. Several antecedents of deliberate practice include strong motivation, self-efficacy, self-discipline, delayed gratification, and self-control. Other factors are determination, strong work ethic, goal-oriented, dedication, time management, and "being on a mission." Deliberate practice entails working "hard and smart" simultaneously.

Demand void Areas in a perceptual map where there is not a cluster of ideal points indicating an unattractive group of potential customers.

Differentiation One of Michael Porter's strategy dimensions that involves a firm producing products and services considered unique industrywide and directed at consumers who are relatively price insensitive.

Directional vector In a SPACE Matrix analysis, this line begins at the origin and goes into one of four quadrants, revealing the type of strategies recommended for the organization: aggressive, competitive, defensive, or conservative.

Discount If an acquiring firm pays less for another firm than the firm's stock price multiplied by its number of shares of stock outstanding (book value or market value), then that amount minus the actual purchase price is called a discount.

Distinctive competencies A firm's strengths that cannot be easily matched or imitated by competitors.

Distribution The process of getting goods and services to market; includes warehousing, distribution channels, distribution coverage, retail site locations, sales territories, inventory levels and location, transportation carriers, wholesaling, and retailing.

Diversification strategies When a firm enters a new business/industry, either related and unrelated to its existing business/industry. Related diversification is when the old versus new business value chains possess competitively valuable cross-business strategic fits; unrelated diversification is when the old versus new business value chains are so dissimilar that no competitively valuable cross-business relationships exist.

Divestiture Selling a division or part of an organization.

Dividend decision A basic function of finance; concerns issues such as the percentage of earnings paid to stockholders, the stability of dividends paid over time, and the repurchase or issuance of stock.

Dividend recapitalizations When especially private-equity firms, but other firms also, borrow money to fund dividend payouts to themselves.

Divisional structure This type of organizational design is based on having various profit centers or segments by geographic area, by product or service, by customer, or by process. With a divisional structure, functional activities are performed both centrally and in each separate division.

Dogs A quadrant in the BCG Matrix for divisions that have a low relative market share position and compete in a low-growth industry; this is the lower-right quadrant.

Downstream activities The primary means for gaining and sustaining competitive advantages for most companies are shifting downstream. Recent research by Dawar reveals that in most industries today, *upstream activities* such as supply chain management, production, and logistics are being commoditized or outsourced by firms, whereas *downstream activities* related to consumer behavior are becoming the primary means for gaining and sustaining competitive advantage.

Educative change strategy A management technique to facilitate a firm adapting to new strategies/policies/situations by presenting to employees/managers information that reveals why the firm needs to do what is to be done; this approach can be slow but oftentimes yields high commitment.

Empirical indicators Refers to three characteristics of resources (rare, hard to imitate, not easily substitutable) that enable a firm to gain and sustain competitive advantage.

Employee stock ownership plans (ESOP) A tax-qualified, defined-contribution, employee-benefit plan whereby employees purchase stock of the company through borrowed money or cash contributions.

Empowerment The act of strengthening employees' sense of shared ownership by encouraging them to participate in decision making and rewarding them for doing so.

Environment The surroundings in which an organization operates, including air, water, land, natural resources, flora, fauna, humans, and their interrelation.

Environmental management system (EMS) When a firm or municipality operates utilizing "green" policies/practices/procedures as outlined by ISO 14001.

Environmental scanning Process of conducting research and gathering and assimilating external information; also referred to as external audit.

EPS/EBIT analysis A financial technique to determine whether debt, stock, or a combination of debt and stock is the best alternative for raising capital to implement strategies.

External audit Process of identifying and evaluating trends and events beyond the control of a single firm, in areas such as social, cultural, demographic technology, economic, political, and competition; reveals key opportunities and threats confronting an organization, so managers can better formulate strategies.

External Factor Evaluation (EFE) Matrix A widely used strategic planning analytical tool designed to summarize and evaluate economic, social, cultural, demographic, environmental, political, governmental, legal, technological, and competitive information.

External forces (1) Economic forces; (2) social, cultural, demographic, and natural environment forces; (3) political, governmental, and legal forces; (4) technological forces; and (5) competitive forces.

External opportunities Economic, social, cultural, demographic, environmental, political, legal, governmental, technological, and competitive trends/events/facts that could significantly benefit an organization in the future.

External threats Economic, social, cultural, demographic, environmental, political, legal, governmental, technological, and competitive trends/events/facts that could significantly harm an organization in the future.

Feasibility A way to evaluate strategies; to determine if a strategy is capable of being carried out within the physical, human, and financial resources of the firm.

Feng shui In China, this term refers to the practice of harnessing natural forces, which can impact how you arrange office furniture.

Financial objectives Include desired results growth in revenues, growth in earnings, higher dividends, larger profit margins, greater return on investment, higher earnings per share, a rising stock price, improved cash flow, and so on.

Financial position (FP) One of four dimensions/axes of the SPACE Matrix that determines an organization's financial strength, considering such factors as return on investment, leverage, liquidity, working capital, and cash flow.

Financial ratio analysis Quantitative calculations that reveal the financial condition of a firm and exemplify the complexity of relationships among the functional areas of business. For example, a declining return on investment or profit margin ratio could be the result of ineffective marketing, poor management policies, research and development errors, or a weak management information system. Ratios are usually compared to industry averages, or to prior time periods, or to rival firms.

Financing decision A basic function of finance; determines the best capital structure for the firm and includes examining various methods by which the firm can raise capital (for example, by issuing stock, increasing debt, selling assets, or using a combination of these approaches).

First mover advantages The benefits a firm may achieve by entering a new market or developing a new product or service before rival firms.

Fixed costs (FC) A key variable in breakeven analysis; includes costs such as plant, equipment, stores, advertising, and land.

Focus One of Michael Porter's strategy dimensions that involves a firm producing products and services that fulfill the needs of small groups of consumers.

Force change strategy A management technique to facilitate a firm adapting to new strategies/policies/situations by simply giving orders and enforcing those orders; this approach has the advantage of being fast, but it is plagued by low commitment.

Forward integration A strategy that involves gaining ownership or increased control over distributors or retailers, such as a manufacturer opening its own chain of stores.

Franchising An effective means of implementing forward integration whereby a franchisee purchases the right to own one or more stores/restaurants of a chain firm.

Friendly merger If the merger/acquisition is desired by both firms.

Functional structure A type of organizational design that groups tasks and activities by business function, such as production/operations, marketing, finance/accounting, research and development, and management information systems.

Functions of finance/accounting The basic activities performed by finance managers; consists of three decisions: the investment decision, the financing decision, and the dividend decision.

Furloughs Temporary layoffs.

Future shock High anxiety that results when the nature, types, and speed of changes overpower an individual's or organization's ability and capacity to adapt.

Gain sharing A form of incentive compensation whereby employees and/or managers receive bonuses when actual results exceed some pre-determined performance targets.

Generally accepted accounting principles (GAAP) A set of procedures or rules used by accountants, particularly in the United States, to develop financial statements.

Generally accepted auditing standards A set of accounting standards used by independent auditors to evaluate an organization's financial statements.

Generic strategies Michael Porter's strategy breakdown; consists of three strategies: cost leadership, differentiation, and focus.

Glass ceiling A term used to refer to the artificial barrier that women and minorities face in moving into upper levels of management.

Global strategy Designing, producing, and marketing products with global needs in mind, instead of solely considering individual countries.

Globalization A process of doing business worldwide, so strategic decisions are made based on global profitability of the firm rather than just domestic considerations.

Goodwill If a firm acquires another firm and pays more than the book value (market value), then the additional amount paid is called a premium and becomes goodwill, which is a line item on the assets portion of a balance sheet.

Governance The act of oversight and direction, especially in association with the duties of a board of directors.

Grand Strategy Matrix A four-quadrant, two-axis tool for formulating alternative strategies. All organizations can be positioned in one of this matrix's four strategy quadrants, based on their position on two evaluative dimensions: competitive position and market (industry) growth. Strategy suggestions ensue depending on which quadrant the firm is located.

Growth ratios Measures such as the percent increase/decrease in revenue or profit from one period to the next are important comparisons.

Guanxi In China, business behavior is based on "personal relations."

Halo error The human tendency to put too much weight on a single factor.

Horizontal consistency of objectives Objectives need to be compatible across functions; for example, if marketing wants to sell 10% more, then production must produce 10% more.

Horizontal integration Acquiring a rival firm.

Hostile takeover If the merger/acquisition is not desired by both firms.

Human resource (HR) management Also called personnel management; a basic function of management; includes activities such as recruiting, interviewing, testing, selecting, orienting, training, developing, caring for, evaluating, rewarding, disciplining, promoting, transferring, demoting, and dismissing employees, as well as managing union relations.

Industrial Organization (I/O)   An approach to competitive advantage that advocates that external (industry) factors are more important than internal factors for a firm in striving to achieve competitive advantage.

Industry analysis   Another term for external audit; conducting research to gather and assimilate external information.

Industry growth rate   The vertical axis in a BCG Matrix; the average percent increase or decrease in sales/revenues this year (versus last year) for a given industry.

Industry position (IP)   One of four dimensions/axes of the SPACE Matrix that determines how strong/weak a firm's industry is, considering such factors as growth potential, profit potential, financial stability, extent leveraged, resource utilization, ease of entry into market, productivity and capacity utilization.

Information technology (IT)   The development, maintenance, and use of computer systems, software, and networks for the processing and distribution of data.

Inhwa   A South Korean term for activities that involve concern for harmony based on respect of hierarchical relationships, including obedience to authority.

Initial public offering (IPO)   When a private firm goes public by selling its shares of stock to the public in order to raise capital.

Input stage   Stage 1 of the strategy-formulation analytical framework that summarizes the basic input information needed to formulate strategies; consists of an EFEM, CPM, and IFEM.

Integration strategies   Includes forward integration, backward integration, and horizontal integration (sometimes collectively referred to as vertical integration strategies).

Intensive strategies   Includes market development, market penetration, and product development.

Internal audit   The process of gathering and assimilating information about the firm's management, marketing, finance/accounting, production/operations, R&D, and MIS operations. The purpose is to identify/evaluate/prioritize a firm's strengths and weaknesses.

Internal-External (IE) Matrix   A nine-quadrant, strategic planning analytical tool that places an organization's various divisions as circles in a display (similar to the BCG Matrix) based on two key dimensions: (1) the segment's IFE total weighted scores on the x-axis and (2) the segment's EFE total weighted scores on the y-axis. The diagram is divided into three major regions that have different strategy implications: (1) grow and build, or (2) hold and maintain, or (3) harvest or divest.

Internal Factor Evaluation (IFE) Matrix   A strategy-formulation tool that summarizes and evaluates a firm's major strengths and weaknesses in the functional areas of a business, and provides a basis for identifying and evaluating relationships among those areas.

Internal strengths   An organization's controllable activities that are performed especially well, such as in areas that include finance, marketing, management, accounting, and MIS, across a firm's products/regions/stores/facilities.

Internal weaknesses   An organization's controllable activities that are performed especially poorly, such as in areas that include finance, marketing, management, accounting, and MIS, across a firm's products/regions/stores/facilities.

International financial reporting standards (IFRS)   A set of procedures or rules used by accountants, particularly outside the United States, to develop financial statements.

International firms   Firms that conduct business outside their own country.

Intuition   Using one's cognition without evident rational thought or analysis; based on past experience, judgment, and feelings; essential to making good strategic decisions but must not relied on heavily in lieu of objective analysis.

Inversion   A tax-avoidance tactic whereby a company acquires another firm in a country with a lower tax rate, such as Ireland, for the primary purpose of funneling revenues through that foreign country.

Investment decision   Also called capital budgeting; a basic function of finance; the allocation and reallocation of capital and resources to projects, products, assets, and divisions of an organization.

ISO 14000   A series of voluntary standards in the environmental field whereby a firm minimizes harmful effects on the environment caused by its activities and continually monitors and improves its own environmental performance.

ISO 14001   A set of standards adopted by thousands of firms worldwide to certify to their constituencies that they are conducting business in an environmentally friendly manner. These standards offer a universal technical standard for environmental compliance that more and more firms are requiring not only of themselves but also of their suppliers and distributors.

Joint venture   A strategy that occurs when two or more companies form a temporary partnership/consortium/business for the purpose of capitalizing on some opportunity.

Just-in-time (JIT)   A production approach in which parts and materials are delivered to a production site just as they are needed, rather than being stockpiled as a hedge against late deliveries.

Leverage ratios   The debt-to-equity ratio and debt-to-total assets ratio measure the extent to which a firm has been financed by debt.

Leveraged buyout (LBO)   When the outstanding shares of a corporation are bought by the company's management and other private investors using borrowed funds.

Liquidation   Selling all of a company's assets, in parts, for their tangible worth.

Liquidity ratios   The current ratio and quick ratio measure a firm's ability to meet short-term cash obligations.

Long-range planning   Deciding on future actions/objectives/policies with the aim to optimize for tomorrow the trends of today; less effective and comprehensive than strategic planning.

Long-term objectives   Specific results that an organization seeks to achieve (in more than one year) in pursuing its basic vision/mission/strategy.

Management information system (MIS)   A system that gathers, assimilates, evaluates, and converts external and internal data (facts/figures/trends) into useful information for decision making.

Market capitalization   Number of shares outstanding multiplied by stock price.

Market development   Introducing present products or services into new geographic areas.

Market penetration   Increasing market share for present products or services in present markets through greater marketing efforts.

Market segment   Areas in a perceptual map where there is a cluster of ideal points indicating an attractive group of potential customers to target.

Market value   Number of shares outstanding multiplied by stock price.

Marketing mix variables   Product, place, promotion, and price.

Marketing research   The systematic gathering, recording, and analyzing of data about problems/practices/issues related to the marketing of goods and services.

Markets   A component of the mission statement; geographic locations where a firm competes.

Matching   When an organization matches its internal strengths and weaknesses with its external opportunities and threats using, for example, the SWOT, SPACE, BCG, IE, or GRAND Matrices.

Matching stage   Stage 2 of the strategy-formulation framework that focuses on generating feasible alternative strategies by aligning internal with external factors by utilizing five matrices: BCG, IE, SWOT, GRAND, SPACE.

Matrix structure   This type of organizational design places functional activities along the top row and divisional projects/units along the left side to create a rubric where managers have two bosses—both a functional boss and a project boss—thus creating the need for extensive vertical and horizontal flows of authority and communication.

Measuring organizational performance   Activity #2 in the strategy-evaluation process; includes comparing expected results to actual results, investigating deviations from plans, evaluating individual performance, and examining progress being made toward meeting stated objectives.

Merger   When two organizations of about equal size unite to form one enterprise; an acquisition.

Mission statement   An enduring statement of purpose that distinguish one business from other similar firms; a statement that identifies the scope of a firm's operations in product and market terms and addresses the question "What is our business?" A declaration of an organization's "reason for being."

Mission statement components   (1) Customers; (2) products and services; (3) markets; (4) technology; (5) concern for survival, growth, and profitability; (6) philosophy; (7) self-concept; (8) concern for public image; and (9) concern for employees.

Motivating   A basic function of management; the process of influencing and leading people to accomplish specific objectives.

Multidimensional scaling   The same as product positioning (perceptual mapping), except encompasses three or more evaluative criteria simultaneously.

Multinational corporations   Firms that conduct business outside their own country.

Nemaswashio   U.S. managers in Japan have to be careful about this phenomenon, whereby Japanese workers expect supervisors to alert them privately of changes rather than informing them in a meeting.

Organizational culture   A pattern of behavior developed by an organization over time as it learns to cope with its problem of external adaptation and internal integration, and that has worked well enough to be considered valid and to be taught to new members as the correct way to perceive, think, and feel in the firm.

Organizing   A basic function of management; the process of arranging duties and responsibilities in a coherent manner in order to determine who does what and who reports to whom.

Outsourcing   Refers to the practice of firms using/paying other firms to perform certain activities, such as managing payroll, call centers, or even R&D.

Outstanding shares method   A method for determining the cash worth of a firm by multiplying the number of shares outstanding by the market price per share; also called book value, market value, or market capitalization.

Perceptual map   Also called product-positioning map; a two-dimensional, four-quadrant marketing tool designed to position a firm versus its rival firms in a schematic diagram in order to better determine effective marketing strategies.

Personnel management   Also called human resource management; a basic function of management; includes activities such as recruiting, interviewing, testing, selecting, orienting, training, developing, caring for, evaluating, rewarding, disciplining, promoting, transferring, demoting, and dismissing employees, as well as managing union relations.

Philosophy   A component of the mission statement; the basic beliefs, values, aspirations, and ethical priorities of the firm.

Planning   A basic function of management; the process of deciding ahead of time the strategies to be pursued and actions to be taken in the future.

Policies   The means by which annual objectives will be achieved. Policies include guidelines, rules, and procedures established to support efforts to achieve stated objectives. Policies are guides to decision making and address repetitive or recurring situations.

Porter's Five-Forces Model   A theoretical model devised by Michael Porter, who suggests that the nature of competitiveness in a given industry can be viewed as a composite of five forces: (1) rivalry among competing firms, (2) potential entry of new competitors, (3) potential development of substitute products, (4) bargaining power of suppliers, and (5) bargaining power of consumers.

Premium   If an acquiring firm pays more for another firm than that firm's stock price multiplied by its number of shares of stock outstanding (book value or market value), then the overage is called a premium.

Price-earnings ratio method   This method involves dividing the market price of the firm's common stock by the annual earnings per share and multiplying this number by the firm's average net income for the past 5 years.

Pricing   A basic function of marketing; determining the appropriate value for products and services to be charged to customers, given associated costs and competitor's prices.

Product development Increased sales by improving or modifying present products or services.

Product positioning Also called perceptual mapping; a two-dimensional, four-quadrant marketing tool designed to position a firm versus its rival firms in a schematic diagram in order to better determine effective marketing strategies.

Product and service planning A basic function of marketing; includes activities such as test marketing; product and brand positioning; devising warranties; packaging; determining product options, features, style, and quality; deleting old products; and providing for customer service.

Products or services A component of the mission statement; commodities or benefits provided by a firm.

Profit sharing A form of incentive compensation whereby some of a firm's earnings are distributed to employees/managers based on some predetermined formula; used to motivate individuals to support strategy-implementation efforts.

Profitability ratios The profit margin ratio and return on investment ratio measure the profitability of a firm's operations.

Projected financial statement analysis A financial technique that enables a firm to forecast the expected financial results of various strategies and approaches; involves developing income statements and balance sheets for future periods of time.

Protectionism When countries impose tariffs, taxes, and regulations on firms outside the country to favor their own companies and people.

Quantitative Strategic Planning Matrix (QSPM) An analytical technique designed to determine the relative attractiveness of feasible alternative actions. This technique comprises Stage 3 of the strategy-formulation analytical framework; it objectively indicates which alternative strategies are best.

Question marks A quadrant in the BCG Matrix for divisions that have a low relative market share position but compete in a high-growth industry; this is the upper-right quadrant; firms generally must decide whether to strengthen such divisions or sell them (hence a question is at hand).

Rational change strategy A management technique to facilitate a firm adapting to new strategies/policies/situations, whereby employees/managers are given incentives to be supportive while at the same time are educated as to the need to change.

Reconciliatory With regard to mission statements, the need for the statement to be sufficiently broad to "reconcile" differences effectively among diverse stakeholders; to appeal to a firm's customers, employees, shareholders, and creditors rather than alienate any group.

Reengineering Reconfiguring or redesigning work, jobs, and processes in a firm, for the purpose of improving cost, quality, service, and speed.

Related diversification When a firm acquires a new business whose value chain possesses competitively valuable cross-business strategic fits.

Relative market share position The horizontal axis in a BCG Matrix, which is the firm's particular segment's market share (or revenues or number of stores) divided by the industry leader's analogous number.

Research and development (R&D) Spending money to enhance existing products/services and/or create new and improved products.

Reshoring Refers to U.S. companies working offshore but planning to move some of their manufacturing back to the United States.

Resistance to change A natural human tendency to be wary of new policies/strategies due to potential negative consequences; if not managed then this could result in sabotaging production machines, absenteeism, filing unfounded grievances, and an unwillingness to cooperate.

Resource allocation A central strategy implementation activity that entails distributing financial, physical, human, and technological assets to allow for strategy execution.

Resource-based view (RBV) An approach that suggests internal resources to be more important for a firm than external factors in achieving and sustaining competitive advantage.

Restructuring Modifying the firm's chain of command and reporting channels to improve efficiency and effectiveness.

Retreats Formal meetings commonly held off-premises to discuss and update a firm's strategic plan; done away from the work site to encourage more creativity and candor from participants.

Retrenchment When an organization regroups through cost and asset reduction to reverse declining sales and profits.

Reviewing the underlying bases of an organization's strategy Activity #1 in the strategy-evaluation process; entails a firm developing a revised EFE Matrix and IFE Matrix to determine if corrective actions are needed.

Revised EFE Matrix Part of activity #1 in the strategy-evaluation process whereby a firm reassesses its previously determined external opportunities and threats.

Revised IFE Matrix Part of activity #1 in the strategy-evaluation process whereby a firm reassesses its previously determined internal strengths and weaknesses.

Secondary buyouts When private-equity firms buy companies from other private-equity firms.

Self-concept A component of the mission statement; the firm's distinctive competence or major competitive advantage.

Self-interest change strategy A management technique to facilitate a firm adapting to new strategies/policies/situations by attempts to convince individuals that the change is to their personal advantage. When this appeal is successful, strategy implementation can be relatively easy. However, implementation changes are seldom to everyone's advantage.

Selling A basic function of marketing; includes activities such as advertising, sales promotion, publicity, personal selling, sales force management, customer relations, and dealer relations.

Sexual harassment (and discrimination) Unwelcome sexual advances, requests for sexual favors, and other verbal or physical conduct of a sexual nature; this activity is illegal, unethical, and detrimental to any organization, and can result in expensive lawsuits, lower morale, and reduced productivity.

Six Sigma A quality-boosting process improvement technique that entails training several key persons in techniques to monitor, measure, and improve processes and eliminate defects in a firm; trained persons can earn black belts.

SO strategies Strategies that result from matching a firm's internal strengths with its external opportunities.

Social policy Guidelines and practices a firm may institute to guide its behavior toward employees, consumers, environmentalists, minorities, communities, shareholders, and other groups.

Social responsibility Actions an organization takes beyond what is legally required to protect or enhance the well-being of living things.

ST strategies Strategies that result from matching a firm's internal strengths with its external threats.

Stability position (SP) One of four dimensions/axes of the SPACE Matrix that determines how stable/unstable a firm's industry is, considering such factors as technological changes, rate of inflation, demand of variability, price range of competing products, barriers to entry into market, competitive pressure, ease of exit from market, price elasticity of demand, and risk involved in business.

Staffing Includes activities such a recruiting, interviewing, testing, selecting, orienting, training, developing, caring for, evaluating, rewarding, disciplining, promoting, transferring, demoting, and dismissing employees.

Stakeholders The individuals and groups of individuals who have a special stake or claim on the company, such as a firm's customers, employees, shareholders, and creditors.

Stars A quadrant in the BCG Matrix for divisions that have a high relative market share position and compete in a high-growth industry; this is the upper-left quadrant.

Strategic business unit (SBU) structure This type of organizational design groups similar divisions together into units; widely used when a firm has many divisions/segments in order to reduce span of control reporting to a COO.

Strategic management The art and science of formulating, implementing, and evaluating cross-functional decisions that enable an organization to achieve its objectives.

Strategic-management model A framework or illustration of the strategic-management process; a clear and practical approach for formulating, implementing, and evaluating strategies.

Strategic-management process The process of formulating, implementing, and evaluating strategies as revealed in the comprehensive model, that begins with vision/mission development and ends with strategy evaluation and feedback.

Strategic objectives Desired results such as a larger market share, quicker on-time delivery than rivals, shorter design-to-market times than rivals, lower costs than rivals, higher product quality than rivals, wider geographic coverage than rivals, achieving technological leadership, and consistently getting new or improved products to market ahead of rivals.

Strategic planning The process of formulating an organization's game plan; in a corporate setting, this term may refer to the whole strategic-management process.

Strategic Position and Action Evaluation (SPACE) Matrix Indicates whether aggressive, conservative, defensive, or competitive strategies are most appropriate for a given organization. The axes of this matrix represent two internal dimensions (financial position [FP] and competitive position [CP]) and two external dimensions (stability position [SP] and industry position [IP]). These four factors are perhaps the most important determinants of an organization's overall strategic position.

Strategies The means by which long-term objectives will be achieved. Business strategies may include geographic expansion, diversification, acquisition, product development, market penetration, retrenchment, divestiture, liquidation, and joint ventures.

Strategists The person(s) responsible for formulating and implementing a firm's strategic plan, including the CEO, president, owner of a business, head coach, governor, chancellor, and/or the top management team in a firm.

Strategy evaluation Stage 3 in the strategic-management process. The three fundamental strategy-evaluation activities are (1) review external and internal factors that are the bases for current strategies, (2) measure performance, and (3) take corrective actions; strategies need to be evaluated regularly because external and internal factors constantly change.

Strategy formulation Stage 1 in the strategic-management process; includes developing a vision/mission, identifying an organization's external opportunities/threats, determining internal strengths/weaknesses, establishing long-term objectives, generating alternative strategies, and choosing particular strategies to pursue.

Strategy-formulation analytical framework A three-stage, nine-matrix array of tools widely used for strategic planning as a guide: (stage 1: input stage; stage 2: matching stage; stage 3: decision stage).

Strategy implementation Stage 2 of the strategic-management process. Activities include establishing annual objectives, devising policies, motivating employees, allocating resources, developing a strategy-supportive culture, creating an effective organizational structure, redirecting marketing efforts, preparing budgets, developing and utilizing information systems, and linking employee compensation to organizational performance.

Strengths-Weaknesses-Opportunities-Threats (SWOT) Matrix The most widely used of all strategic-planning matrices; matches a firm's internal strengths/weaknesses with its external opportunities/threats to generate four types of strategies: SO (strengths-opportunities) Strategies, WO (weaknesses-opportunities) Strategies, ST (strengths-threats) Strategies, and WT (weaknesses-threats) Strategies.

Sum Total Attractiveness Scores (STAS) In a QSPM, this is the sum of the Total Attractiveness Scores in each strategy column; value reveals which strategy is most attractive in each set of alternatives.

Sustainability The extent that an organization's operations and actions protect, mend, and preserve, rather than harm or destroy, the natural environment.

Sustainability report A form of annual report produced by organizations to reveal their progress and activities aimed at helping, rather than harming, the natural environment.

Sustained competitive advantage Maintaining what a firm does especially well, compared to rival firms—by (1) continually adapting to changes in external trends and events and internal capabilities, competencies, and resources; and (2) effectively formulating, implementing, and evaluating strategies that capitalize upon those factors.

Synergy The $1 + 1 = 3$ effect; when everyone pulls together as a team, the results can exceed individuals working separately.

Taking corrective actions Activity #3 in the strategy-evaluation process; involves a firm making changes to competitively reposition a firm for the future.

Technology A component of the mission statement; is the firm technologically current?

Test marketing An activity to determine ahead of time whether a certain product or service or selling approach will be cost effective; also used to forecast future sales of new products.

Total Attractiveness Scores (TAS) In a QSPM, the product of multiplying the weights by the Attractiveness Scores in each row. The values indicate the relative attractiveness of each alternative strategy, considering only the impact of the adjacent external or internal critical success factor.

Treasury stock An item in the equity portion of a balance sheet that reveals the dollar amount of the firm's common stock owned by the company itself.

Tweet Posted messages of 140 characters or less on Twitter. com.

Unrelated diversification When a firm acquires a new business whose value chains are so dissimilar that no competitively valuable cross-business relationships exist.

Upstream activities The primary means for gaining and sustaining competitive advantages for most companies are shifting downstream. Recent research by Dawar reveals that in most industries today, *upstream activities* such as supply chain management, production, and logistics, are being commoditized or outsourced by firms, while *downstream activities* related to consumer behavior are becoming the primary means for gaining and sustaining competitive advantage.

Vacant niche In product/market positioning (perceptual map), this is an area in the perceptual map that reveals a customer segment not being served by the firm or rival firms.

Value chain The business of a firm, where total revenues minus total costs of all activities undertaken to develop, produce, and market a product or service yields value.

Value chain analysis (VCA) The process whereby a firm determines the costs associated with organizational activities from purchasing raw materials to manufacturing product(s) to marketing those products, and compares these costs to rival firms using benchmarking.

Variable costs (VC) A key variable in breakeven analysis; includes costs such as labor and materials.

Vertical consistency of objectives Compatibility of objectives from the CEO (corporate level) down to the presidents (divisional level) on down to the managers (functional level).

Vertical integration A combination of three strategies: backward, forward, and horizontal integration, allowing a firm to gain control over distributors, suppliers, and/or competitors respectively.

Vision statement A one-sentence statement that answers the question, "What do we want to become?"

Wa In Japan, this term stresses group harmony and social cohesion.

Whistle-blowing The act of telling authorities about some unethical or illegal activities occurring within an organization of which you are aware.

Wikis Websites that allows users to add, delete, and edit content regarding frequently asked questions and information across the firm's whole value chain of activities.

WO strategies Strategies that result from matching a firm's internal weaknesses with its external opportunities.

Workplace romance An intimate relationship between two truly consenting employees, as opposed to sexual harassment, which the EEOC defines broadly as unwelcome sexual advances, requests for sexual favors, and other verbal or physical conduct of a sexual nature.

WT strategies Strategies that result from matching a firm's internal weaknesses with its external threats.

Name Index

Subject Index